SERBIAN-EN...
SRPSKO-ENGLESKI
ENGLISH-SERBIAN
ENGLESKO-SRPSKI
DICTIONARY
REČNIK

CONCISE EDITION • SAŽETO IZDANJE

SERBIAN-ENGLISH
SRPSKO-ENGLESKI
ENGLISH-SERBIAN
ENGLESKO-SRPSKI
DICTIONARY
REČNIK

GEDDES &
GROSSET

JUGOSLOVENSKA
KNJIGA

Grupa autora

Concise Edition
SERBIAN–ENGLISH
ENGLISH–SERBIAN

DICTIONARY
REČNIK

Sažeto izdanje
SRPSKO–ENGLESKI
ENGLESKO–SRPSKI
GEDDES & GROSSET
Izdavači/Publishers

Jugoslovenska knjiga
Terazije 27, Beograd
Srbija

Geddes & Grosset
David Dale House,
New Lanark, ML119DJ
Scotland

ISBN 86-7411-065-7

List of Abbreviations
The following abbreviations are used
throughout the dictionary:

	Abbreviation	**Skraćenica**
a	adjective	pridev
adv	adverb	prilog
am(er)	American	američki
anat	anatomy	anatomija
art	article	član
astrol	astrology	astrologija
astron	astronomy	astronomija
auto	automobile	automobil
biol	biology	biologija
bot	botany	botanika
br	British	britanski
chem/hem	chemistry	hemija
com/komerc	commercial	komercijalni, trgovački
conj	conjuction	veznik
f	feminine noun	imenica ženskog roda
el	electric	električan
ekon	economy	ekonomija
fig	figurative/ly/	figurativno
fin	finance	finansije
fpl	feminine noun plural	imenica ženskog roda u množini
gradj	construction	gradjevinarstvo
gram	grammar	gramatika
geog	geography	geografija
hem	chemistry	hemija
interj	interjection	uzvik
jur	jurisprudence	pravo
kulin	culinary	kulinarski
komp	computers	informatika
lat	Latin	latinski
ling	linguistics	linvistika
m	masculine noun	imenica muškog roda
math/mat	mathematics	matematika
med	medicine	medicina
mil	military	vojni
min	mineralogy	mineralogija
mitol	mythology	mitologija

	Abbreviation	Skraćenica
mpl	masculine noun plural	imenica muškog roda u množini
mus/muz	music	muzika
n	noun/neuter	imenica/srednji rod
naut	nautical	pomorski
num	number/s	broj/evi
pl	plural	množina
pn	pronoun	zamenica
poet	poetical	pesnički
polit	policy	politika
prep	preposition	predlog
rel	religion	religija
slang/sleng	slang	sleng
sport	sport	odnosi se na sport
stom	dentistry	stomatologija
teh	technical	tehnički
theat	theatrical	pozorišni
v	verb	glagol
voj	military	vojni
zool	zoology	zoologija
žel	railway	železnički

SERBIAN–ENGLISH
SRPSKO–ENGLESKI
DICTIONARY
REČNIK

A

a *conj* but, and.
abažur *m* lampshade.
abdicirati *v* to abdicate.
ablativ *m* ablative case (*gram*).
abnormalan *a* abnormal, irregular, unusual.
abonos *m* ebony.
abortirati *v* to abort, to miscarry.
abortus *m* abortion.
abrazija *f* abrasion.
abrazivan *a* abrasive.
acetat *m* acetate (*chem*).
adaptirati *v* to adapt.
adekvatan *a* suitable, adequate.
adenoid *m* adenoids (*med*).
administracija *f* administration; office; paperwork.
admiral *m* admiral.
admiralska zastava *f* admiral's banner.
admiralski brod *m* admiralship; flagship.
adolescencija *f* adolescence.
adresa *f* address; formal petition; **na pravu ~u** (*fig*) to the right person.
adut *m* trump, trump card.
advokat *m* advocate, attorney, lawyer.
advokatska komora *f* the bar.
ađutant *m* aide-de-camp, adjutant.
aerobik *m* aerobics.
aerodrom *m* airport.
aerodromska taksa *f* airport tax.
aerosol *m* aerosol.
aerostatički *a* aerostatic.
afekt *m* strong emotion, excitement.
afera *f* scandal, affair.
afirmacija *f* recognition; affirmation.
aforizam *m* aphorism.
agencija *a* agency.
agent *m* agent; **tajni ~** secret agent.
agitator *m* agitator.
agonija *a* agony.
agregat *m* aggregate.
agresija *f* aggression.
agresivan *a* aggressive.
agresor *m* aggressor.
agronomija *f* agronomy.
ahat *m* agate.
ajkula *f* shark.

akademija *f* academy; **vojna ~** military academy; **pozorišna ~** school of drama.
akademik *m* academician.
akademski *a* academic; **~ stepen** *m* an academic degree; **~ građanin** university student.
akcenat *m* accentuation.
akcentirati *v* to accentuate, to emphasize.
akcija *f* activity, work, action; share of stock.
akcionar *m* stockholder.
akcionarsko društvo *m* joint-stock company.
ako *conj* if; **ako ne** unless.
akontacija *f* advance payment.
akord *m* chord.
aksioma *f* axiom.
akt *m* act, action; document.
akten tašna *f* briefcase.
aktiva *f* assets.
aktivirati *v* to activate.
aktivnost *f* activity.
aktuelan *a* present, up-to-date, modern, current.
akumulacija *f* accumulation.
akupunktura *f* acupuncture.
akustična viljuška *f* tuning fork.
akustika *f* acoustics.
akuzativ *m* accusative case (*gram*).
akvalung *m* aqualung.
akvarijum *m* aquarium.
alabaster *m* alabaster.
alarmni uređaj *m* burglar alarm.
ala *f* dragon.
alas *m* fisherman.
alat *m* tools, instrument.
alatka *f* tool.
album *m* album.
alegoričan *a* allegorical.
alegorija *f* allegory.
alegro *m* allegro (*mus*).
alergija *f* allergy.
alfabet *m* alphabet.
alfabetski *a* alphabetical.
alga *f* algae; seaweed.
algebarski *a* algebraic.
algebra *f* algebra.

alhemičar *m* alchemist.
alhemija *f* alchemy.
ali *conj* but, else, however.
alibi *m* alibi.
aligator *m* alligator.
alijansa *f* alliance, treaty, pact.
alimentacija *f* alimentation.
aliteracija *f* alliteration.
alka *f* door knocker, iron ring.
alkalije *fpl* alkali (*chem*).
alkalni *a* alkaline.
alkohol *m* alcohol.
alkoholičar *m* drinker, alcoholic.
alkoholni *a* alcoholic; ~a pića *npl* alcoholic drinks.
alo *interj* hello.
alternacija *f* alternation.
alternativa *f* alternative, choice, selection, option.
alternator *m* alternator.
aludirati *v* to allude.
aluminijum *m* aluminium (*br*), aluminum (*amer*).
aluzija *f* allusion.
aluzivan *a* allusive.
aljkav *a* slovenly; careless, untidy.
aljkavost *f* slovenliness.
amajlija *f* amulet, charm.
amalgam *m* amalgam.
amandman *m* amendment.
amanet *m* will, testament
amarilis *m* amaryllis (*bot*).
amater *m* amateur, non-professional.
amaterski *a* amateurish.
amazonka *f* Amazon, female warrior.
ambalaža *f* packing, wrapping material.
ambar *m* barn.
ambasada *f* embassy.
ambasador *m* ambassador.
ambasadorka *f* ambassadress.
ambicija *f* ambition.
ambiciozan *a* ambitious, eager.
ambijent *m* ambience, surroundings.
ambis *m* abyss.
amblem *m* emblem, sign, symbol, mark.
ambulanta *f* clinic for outpatients.
ambulantni bolesnik *m* outpatient.
američki *a* Amcrican.
Amerika *f* America.
ametist *m* amethyst.
amfiteatar *m* amphitheatre.

amnestija *f* amnesty.
amnestirati *v* to grant amnesty, to pardon.
amnezija *f* amnesia.
amonijak *m* ammonia.
amoralan *a* amoral.
amorfan *a* amorphous.
amortizacija *f* amortization; redemption (amortizacija zajma).
amortizer *m* buffers; shock absorber.
amper *m* amp(ere).
amplituda *f* amplitude.
amputacija *f* amputation.
amputirati *v* to amputate.
anahronizam *m* anachronism.
analgetik *m* painkiller.
anali *mpl* annals.
analitičan *a* analytical.
analitičar *m* analyst.
analiza *f* analysis, breakdwon; ~ tržišta market research.
analizirati *v* to analyse, to examine, to investigate; to explain.
analogan *a* analogous.
analogija *f* analogy.
analogni *a* analog (*amer*), analogue (*br*).
ananas *m* pineapple.
anarhičan *a* anarchic.
anarhija *f* anarchy.
anarhista *m* anarchist.
anatomija *f* anatomy.
anatomski *a* anatomical.
anđeo *m* angel.
anđeoski *a* angelic.
anegdota *f* anecdote.
aneksija *f* annexation.
anemičan *a* anaemic.
anemija *f* anaemia.
anestetik *m* anaesthetic.
anestezija *f* anesthesia; opšta (lokalna) ~ general (local) anesthesia.
angažovan *a* engaged.
angažovati *vt* to engage, to occupy, to employ.
anglicizam *m* anglicism.
anketa *f* poll, questionnaire.
anketirati *v* to poll, to canvass.
anomalija *f* anomaly.
anoniman *a* anonymous.
anonimnost *f* anonymity.
anoreksija *f* anorexia (*med*).
ansambl *m* ensemble, troupe.
antagonizam *m* antagonism.

antarktički *a* Antarctic.
antena *f* antenna, aerial.
antibiotik *m* antibiotic.
antifriz *m* antifreeze.
antihrist *m* antichrist.
antika *f* antique; classical period (Greek or Roman).
antiklimaks *m* bathos.
antikvaran *a* antiquarian.
antilop *m* antelope leather.
antilopa *f* antelope.
antimon *m* antimony (*chem*).
antipatičan *a* unpleasant, disagreeable, offensive.
antipatija *f* antipathy.
antipod *m* antipode.
antiseptički *a* antiseptic.
antitelo *m* antibody.
antiteza *f* antithesis.
antologija *f* anthology.
antracit *m* anthracite (*min*).
antropolog *m* anthropologist.
antropologija *f* anthropology.
anulirati *v* to annul.
aparat *m* apparatus, machine, device; ~ za fotokopiranje copying machine; ~ za gašenje požara fire extinguisher.
apatičan *a* apathetic.
apatija *f* apathy.
apendicit *m* appendicitis (*med*).
apetit *m* appetite.
aplaudirati *v* to applaud.
aplauz *m* applause.
apokalipsa *f* apocalypse.
apokrif *m* apocrypha.
apokrifan *a* apocryphal.
apologičan *a* apologetic.
apopleksija *f* apoplexy (*med*).
apostol *m* apostle.
apostolski *a* apostolic.
apostrof *m* apostrophe.
apoteka *f* pharmacy; drugstore.
apotekar *m* pharmacist.
apoteoza *f* apotheosis.
apozicija *f* apposition.
april *m* April.
apsida *f* apse.
apsolutan *a* absolute.
apsolutizam *m* absolutism.
apsolvent *m* advanced university student (who has satisfied all course requirements).

apsorbovati *vt* to absorb, to suck up.
apsorpcija *f* absorption.
apstraktno *adv* abstractly.
apstraktnost *f* abstraction.
arabeska *f* arabesque.
arapski *a* Arabic.
arbitar *m* arbiter, arbitrator, referee.
arbitraža *f* arbitration.
arena *f* arena; ~ za borbu s bikovima bull-ring.
argument *m* argument, reason, point, proof.
argumentacija *f* argumentation; debate.
arhaičan *a* archaic.
arhanđeo *m* archangel.
arheolog *m* archaeologist.
arheologija *f* archaeology.
arheološki *a* archaeological.
arhiđakon *m* archdeakon.
arhijerej *m* archpriest.
arhitekta *m* architect.
arhitektonski *a* architectural.
arhitektura *f* architecture.
arhiva *f* archives; files.
arhivar *m* registrar, archivist.
arija *f* aria.
aristokrat *m* aristocrat.
aristokratija *f* aristocracy.
aristokratski *a* aristocratic.
aritmetički *a* arithmetical.
aritmetika *f* arithmetic.
arkada *f* arcade.
armija *f* army, armed forces.
armiran *a* armoured; ~i beton *m* ferro-concrete.
arogancija *f* arrogance, insolence, pride.
arogantan *a* arrogant, proud, high-handed.
aroma *f* aroma.
aromaterapija *f* aromatherapy.
aromatičan *a* aromatic.
arsen *m* arsenic.
arsenal *m* armoury, arsenal.
arterija *f* artery.
arterijski *a* arterial.
arteski bunar *m* artesian well.
artičoka *f* artichoke.
artik(a)l *m* article, product; article (*gram*).
artikulacija *f* articulation.
artiljerija *f* artillery.
artiljerijska veština *f* gunnery.

artritis *m* arthritis.
asfalt *m* asphalt.
asimilacija *f* assimilation.
asketski *a* ascetic.
asonanca *f* assonance.
asortiman *m* assortment, variety, collection.
aspirant *m* candidate.
aspirin *m* Aspirin.
astma *f* asthma.
astmatičan *a* asthmatic.
astrolog *m* astrologer.
astrologija *f* astrology.
astrološki *a* astrological.
astronaut *m* astronaut, spaceman.
astronom *m* astronomer.
astronomija *f* astronomy.
astronomski *a* astronomical; big, enormous (*fig*).
asura *f* mat.
ataše *m* attache.
ateista *m* atheist.
ateizam *m* atheism.
atelje *m* atelier, studio.
atentat *m* assassination, assassination attempt.
atlas *m* atlas.
atletičar *m* athlete.
atletski *a* athletic.
atmosfera *f* atmosphere.
atmosferski *a* atmospheric; ~**i pritisak** *m* atmospheric pressure; ~**e smetnje** *fpl* atmospherics.
atom *m* atom.
atomski *a* atomic; ~**a bomba** *f* atomic bomb, nuke; ~**a energija** atomic energy, nuclear power.
atrofija *f* atrophy.
au! *excl* ouch.
auditorijum *m* auditorium; hall; spectators, audience.
aukcija *f* auction.
aura *f* aura.
autentičan *a* authentic.
autentičnost *f* authenticity.

autobus *m* bus.
autobuska stanica *f* bus stop.
autogram *m* autograph.
autokrata *m* autocrat.
autokratski *a* autocratic.
autolimar *m* auto body mechanic.
autolimarski poslovi *mpl* auto bodywork.
automat *m* automatic device, automat; ~ **za podizanje gotovine** cash dispenser, cash machine.
automatizacija *f* automation.
automatizovan *a* automated.
automatski *a* automatic.
automobil *m* car, motor car, auto; ~ **bomba** car bomb.
automobilizam *m* motoring, driving.
autonomija *f* autonomy.
autoportret *m* self-portrait.
autopsija *f* autopsy.
autoput *m* highway, freeway, speedway.
autor *m* author.
autorski honorar *m* royalty.
autorsko pravo *n* copyright.
autoritativan *a* authoritative.
autoritet *m* authority.
autorka *f* authoress.
autostoper *m* hitchhiker.
auto-škola *f* driving school.
avaj *interj* alas.
avans *m* advance payment.
avantura *f* adventure.
avanturista *m* adventurer.
avenija *f* avenue.
avet *f* phantom.
avgust, august *m* August.
avion *m* aeroplane, aircraft.
avionska pista *f* runway.
avionska pošta *f* airmail.
azbest *m* asbestos.
azbuka *f* alphabet; **Morzeova** ~ the Morse code.
azil *m* asylum.
aždaja *f* dragon.
ažurirati *v* update, speed up.

B

baba *f* old woman, grandmother.
babaroga *f* bad fairy, witch.
babica *f* midwife (*med*).
babino leto *n* Indian summer.
babura *f* green pepper.
bacač *m* thrower; ~ **diska** discus thrower; ~ **kugle** shot-putter; ~ **plamena** flame thrower.
bacanje *n* throwing.
baciti *v* to throw, to cast; to fling, to flip, to toss; to dash.
bačva *f* cask, tub, barrel.
badava *adv* gratis, gratuitously.
badem *m* almond.
bademast *a* almond-shaped; ~**e oči** *npl* almond eyes.
badminton *m* badminton.
badnjak *m* yule-log.
Badnje veče *n* Christmas Eve.
bagatela *f* thing of little value.
bagatelan *a* low (of price); ~**lne cene** *fpl* law prices.
bagrem *m* acacia (*bot*).
bahat *a* haughty, insolent, arrogant.
bajanje *n* incantation.
bajat *a* stale; ~ **hleb** stale bread.
bajka *f* fairy tale, legend.
bajonet *m* bayonet.
bajt *m* byte.
baka *f* grandma, grandmother, granny.
bakalar *m* cod, codfish.
bakalin *m* grocer.
bakalnica *f* grocer's shop.
bakaluk *m* groceries.
bakandža *f* hobnailed boot; old, worn-out shoe.
bakar *m* copper.
baklja *f* torch.
bakrorez *m* copper engraving.
baksuz *m* one who brings or has bad luck.
bakšiš *m* tip.
bal *m* ball; ~ **pod maskama** fancy-dress ball.
bala *f* bale, bundle, package.
balada *f* ballad.
balast *m* ballast.
balavac *m* slobber, greenhorn.

balaviti *v* to drool, to snivel.
balčak *m* hilt.
baldahin *m* canopy.
balega *f* dung.
balegar *m* dung beetle.
balerina *f* ballerina.
balet *m* ballet.
balistički *a* ballistic.
baliti *v* to snivel, slobber.
balkon *m* balcony.
balon *m* balloon.
balsamovati *vt* to embalm, to preserve.
balska dvorana *f* ballroom.
balustrada *f* balustrade.
bambus *m* bamboo.
banalan *a* banal; crude.
banalnost *f* commonplace.
banana *f* banana.
bančiti *v* to revel, to guzzle.
banda *f* gang.
bandit *m* bandit.
bandoglav *a* stubborn, pig-headed.
bandži skakanje *n* bungee-jumping.
bangav *a* lame, crippled, limping.
banka *f* bank.
bankar *m* banker.
bankarski činovnik *m* bank clerk.
bankarstvo *n* banking.
banket *m* banquet.
bankina *f* embankment.
banknota *f* banknote.
bankovni račun *m* bank account.
bankrot *adv* bankrupt, insolvent.
bankrotirati *v* to fail, to break, to become insolvent.
bankrotstvo *n* bankruptcy.
banja *f* spa.
bar *m* nightclub.
bar, barem *adv* at least.
bar kod *m* bar code.
bara *f* fen, marsh, pool.
baraka *f* hut, hovel.
baratati *v* to handle, to manage.
bard *m* bard.
baren *a* boiled; ~**o jaje** *n* boiled egg.
barikada *f* barricade.
bariton *m* baritone.

barjak *m* banner, flag.
barka *f* boat, bark, craft.
barmen *m* barman, bartender.
barometar *m* barometer.
baron *m* baron.
baronica *f* baroness.
baronski *a* baronial.
barut *m* gunpowder.
barža *f* barge.
bas *m* bass.
basamak *m* step.
basna *f* fable.
basnoslovan *a* fabulous.
bastion *m* bastion.
bašta *f* garden.
baštenska kuća *f* summerhouse.
baštensko crevo *n* garden hose.
baština *f* inheritance, heritage.
baštovan *m* gardener, horticulturist.
baštovanstvo *n* gardening, horticulture.
batak *m* leg of fowl.
bataljon *m* battalion.
baterija *f* battery; flash-light.
batina *f* bludgeon, cudgel, stick.
batinanje *n* beating, chastisement, caning.
batrgati se *v* to stagger, to kick.
bauk *m* bogey, bugaboo.
bauljati *v* to crawl, to creep along, to worm along.
baviti se *v* to practise, to occupy yourself, to be engaged in.
baza podataka *f* database.
bazati *v* to loiter.
bazen *m* swimming pool; pond; ~ **sa hidromasažom** whirlpool bath; ~ **za decu** paddling pool.
bazilisk *f* basilisk (*zool*).
bdenje *n* vigil.
beba *f* baby, infant.
beda *f* disaster, misery.
bedan *a* unhappy, poor, saddening, abject; ~ **prihod** *m* pittance.
bedast *a* stupid, witless.
bedem *m* bulwark, rampart.
bedro *n* hip, thigh, haunch.
begunac *m* runaway, fugitive.
behar *m* blossom.
bekstvo *n* flight, escape, elopement; ~ **od stvarnosti** escapism.
belac *m* white man.
bela rada *f* field chamomile.

belaj *m* misfortune, bad luck.
belasati se *v* to glimmer, to gleam.
beleg *m* sign, trace, mark.
beleška *f* note, remark, comment.
beleti *v* to bleach, to whiten.
beleti se *v* to be white, to show white.
beležnica *f* notebook.
beležnik *m* notary.
beli lim *m* tin plate.
beli luk *m* garlic.
beli slon *m* white elephant.
beličast *a* whitish.
belilo *n* whiting.
belina *f* whiteness.
belo *n* white colour.
belo usijan *a* white-hot.
belouška *f* grass snake.
bendžo *n* banjo.
beneficije *fpl* fringe benefits.
benzin *m* benzine, petrol.
benzinska pumpa *f* gas, filling station.
benzinski rezervoar *m* gas tank.
berba *m* gathering, harvest.
berberin *m* barber.
berbernica *f* barber's shop.
beretka *f* beret.
berza *f* stock exchange, stock market; **crna** ~ black market; ~ **rada** employment office.
berzanski mešetar *m* stockbroker.
bes *m* fury, rage.
besan *a* frantic, furious, ireful, raging, violent; ~ **pas** *m* a mad (rabid) dog.
besciljan *a* aimless, purposeless.
beseda *f* speech, oration, discourse.
beskompromisan *a* uncompromising.
beskonačan *a* endless, infinite.
beskoristan *a* useless, futile, vain.
beskraj *m* infinity.
beskrajan *a* interminable, endless, boundless.
beskrajnost *f* infinity.
beskrupulozan *a* unscrupulous.
beskrvan *a* bloodless.
beskućnik *m* homeless person; stroller, tramp, vagabond.
besmisao *m* nonsense.
besmislen *a* absurd, irrational, senseless.
besmislenost *f* absurdity, senselessness.
besmislica *f* absurdity, folly, foolishness, foolery; gibberish, humbug.

besmrtan *a* immortal, undying.
besmrtnost *f* immortality.
besneti *v* to rave, to rage, to be violent.
besnilo *n* rabies.
besplatan *a* gratuitous; ~ **uzorak** *m* free gift; sample.
besplatno *adv* gratis.
besplodan *a* sterile, futile.
bespogovorno *adv* obediently.
bespomoćan *a* helpless, dependent, feeble.
besposlen *a* idle, inactive.
besposličar *m* idler, loafer, vagabond.
besposličariti *v* to dawdle, to idle.
bespoštedan *a* merciless.
bespravan *a* rightless.
bespredmetan *a* unnecessary, superfluous.
besprekoran *a* blameless, faultless, irreproachable, spotless.
besprimeran *a* unprecedented, exceptional.
bespristrasan *a* impartial, unprejudiced, unbiased.
bespuće *n* impasse, roadless area; trackless region.
besraman *a* shameless, impudent, indecent.
besramnost *f* shamelessness.
bestemeljan *a* baseless, unfoundend.
bestraga *adv* very far; **otići** ~ *v* to disappear.
bestragija *f* ends of earth.
bestseler *m* bestseller.
besvestan *a* senseless; unconscious.
bešika *f* bladder.
beton *m* concrete.
bez *prep* without.
bez ceremonije *adv* unceremonious.
bez dna *adv* abysmal, bottomless.
bez dozvole *adv* unlicensed.
bez kičme *adv* spineless.
bez kofeina *adv* decaffeinated.
bez kostiju *adv* boneless.
bez krova nad glavom *adv* homeless.
bez majke *adv* motherless.
bez manira *adv* unmannered.
bez mirisa *adv* scentless.
bez muzičkog sluha *adv* tone-deaf.
bez obzira na *adv* despite.
bez odbrane *adv* defenceless.
bez para *adv* hard-up.
bez pomoći *adv* unaided.

bez pratnje *adv* unaccompanied.
bez premca *adv* peerless, unrivalled.
bez presedana *adv* unprecedented.
bez reči *adv* speechless.
bez sunca *adv* sunless.
bez testamenta *adv* intestate.
bez vazduha *adv* breathless.
bez vrha *adv* topless.
bez značenja *adv* meaningless.
bezakonit *a* lawless, illegal.
bezakonje *n* illegality, unlawfulness.
bezalkoholno *a* nonalcoholic; ~ **piće** soft drink.
bezazlen *a* naive, harmless.
bezbednost *f* safety, security.
bezbojan *a* colourless.
bezbol *m* baseball.
bezbolan *a* painless.
bezbožan *a* impious, godless.
bezbožnost *f* impiety, atheism.
bezbrižan *a* carefree, light-hearted, nonchalant, thoughtless, unconcerned.
bezbroj *m* umpteen, innumerability.
bezbrojan *a* countless, innumerable, overwhelming.
bezdiman *a* smokeless.
bezdušan *a* heartless.
bezdušnost *f* cruelty, heartlessness.
bezglav *a* headless, senseless.
bezglavo bežanje *n* stampede.
bezgraničan *a* boundless.
bezizlazno *adv* inextricably, hopelessly.
bezizražajan *a* expressionless, dull; ~**jno lice** *n* poker-face.
bezličan *a* impersonal.
beznačajan *a* inconsiderate, insignificant, negligible, paltry, potty.
beznadežan *a* hopeless.
bezobličan *a* shapeless.
bezobrazan *a* cheeky, impertinent.
bezobziran *a* careless, reckless.
bezobzirnost *f* indelicacy, disregard, neglect.
bezočan *a* impudent, insolent.
bezočnost *f* impudence.
bezopasan *a* inoffensive.
bezosećajan *a* insensible, insensitive.
bezub *a* toothless.
bezukusan *a* tasteless.
bezuman *a* demented, crazy, illogical, unreasonable.

bezumlje *n* absurdity, irrationality.
bezumnik *m* deranged person, madman.
bezuslovan *a* unconditional.
bezuspešan *a* inefficacious, unsuccessful.
bezvazdušan *a* airless; **~šni prostor** vacuum.
bezvoljan *a* passive, indifferent.
bezvredan *a* frivolous, worthless.
bezvrednost *f* frivolity.
bezvremen *a* timeless.
bež boja *n* beige.
beživotan *a* inanimate; lifeless.
biber *m* pepper.
biblija *f* Bible.
biblijski *a* biblical, scriptural.
bibliografija *f* bibliography.
biblioteka *f* library.
bibliotekar *m* librarian.
bicikl *m* bicycle, bike.
biciklista *m* cyclist.
bič *m* lash, whip, scourge.
biće *n* being.
bife *m* buffet, coffee house.
bifokalna stakla *f* bifocals.
biftek *m* beefsteak.
bigamija *f* bigamy.
bigamista *m* bigamist.
bik *m* bull, ox.
Bik *m* Taurus (*astrol*).
bikini *m* bikini.
bilans stanja *m* balance sheet.
bilateralan *a* bilateral.
biletarnica *f* ticket office.
bilijar *m* billiards.
bilijarski štap *m* cue.
bilion *m* billion.
bilo *n* pulse.
bilo *adv* **~ gde** wherever; **~ kada** whenever; **~ ko** anybody; **~ koji** any; **~ šta** whatever.
bilten *m* bulletin, newspaper.
biljka *f* herb, plant.
biljne gljivice *fpl* mildew.
biljni *a* vegetable; **~ sok** *m* sap.
biljožderski *a* herbivorous.
bina *f* stage.
biodiverzitet *m* biodiversity.
biograf *m* biographer.
biografija *f* biography.
biografski *a* biographical.
biohemija *f* biochemistry.

biologija *f* biology.
biološki *a* biological.
birač *m* constituent, elector, voter; **~ kanala** channel selector.
birački *a* electoral; **~ okrug** *m* constituency; **~ spiskovi** *mpl* voter registration; **~o pravo** *n* the right to vote.
birati *v* to elect, to pick.
birokrata *m* bureaucrat.
birokratija *f* bureaucracy.
birokratizam *m* red tape.
bisaga *f* saddlebag.
biser *m* pearl.
biskup *m* bishop.
biskvit *m* biscuit.
bistar *a* clever, clear, transparent, comprehensive.
bit *f* essential, gist.
bitan *a* intrinsic, substantial.
biti *v* to be; **~ nadmoćan** to predominate; **~ neposlušan** to disobey; **~ tužan** to mope; **~ u skladu** to cohere; **~ u zabludi** to be mistaken.
bitka *f* combat.
bitumen *m* bitumen.
bivak *m* encampment.
bivo *m* buffalo.
bivši *a* former, foregone.
bizaran *a* bizarre.
bizon *m* bison.
blag *a* benign, bland, clement, mild, lenient, soft-spoken, suave.
blagajna *f* box office; **~ za prodaju karata** ticket office.
blagajnik *m* bursar, cashier, paymaster, teller.
blago *n* treasure.
blago *adv* softly, gently.
blagodaran *a* grateful.
blagodet *f* boon.
blagonaklon *a* benevolent.
blagonaklonost *f* benevolence.
blagoslov *m* benediction, blessing.
blagosloviti *v* to bless.
blagost *f* clemency, gentleness, indulgence, mildness.
blagostanje *n* welfare, success, prosperousness.
Blagovesti *npl* Annunciation.
blanko ček *m* blank cheque.

blatnjav *a* sloppy.
blato *n* dirt, mud.
blatobran *m* mudguard.
blaziran *a* blase.
blažen *a* beatific, blissful.
blaženost *f* blissfulness.
blaženstvo *n* beatitude, bliss.
blebetanje *n* prattle, gossip, cackle.
bled *a* pale, wan.
bledilo *n* pallor.
blef *m* bluff.
blejanje *n* baa, bleat.
blejzer *m* sports jacket.
blesak *m* glimpse, flash, momentary glance.
blesav *a* foolish.
bleštav *a* glaring.
blic *m* flashbulb.
blistati *v* to glisten, to glitter.
blistav *a* flamboyant, garish.
blitva *f* chard, beetroot.
blizanac *m* twin.
Blizanci *mpl* Gemini (*astrol*).
blizina *f* proximity.
blizu *prep* nearly, closely.
bližnji *m* fellow men.
blok *m* bloc (*polit*); notepad.
blokada *f* blockade.
blokiranje *n* blockage.
bludnica *f* whore, strumpet.
bluza *f* blouse.
bljesak *m* flare.
bljutav *a* flavourless, insipid, unpalatable.
bljuvati *v* to vomit, to rech, to belch.
boa *f* boa (*zool*).
bob *m* bobsleigh; broad bean.
bobica *f* berry.
boca *f* bottle, carafe, phial; ~ **parfema** scent bottle.
bockati *v* to prick, to pierce, to stick; to tease (*fig*).
bockanje *n* pricking; teasing (*fig*).
bočica *f* vial.
bočni *a* lateral, sidelong; ~ **vetar** *m* sidewind; ~**a lađa crkve** *f* aisle; ~**o svetlo** *n* sidelight.
bod *m* stitch; point.
bodež *m* dagger.
bodibilding *m* body-building.
bodlja *f* thorn.
bodljikav *a* prickly.

bodriti *v* to encourage, to stimulate, to inspire.
Bog *m* God; **Hvala ~u!** Thank God!; **za ~a miloga** for God's sake.
bogaćenje *n* enrichment.
bogat *a* luxuriant, rich, wealthy; ~ **događajima** eventful; ~ **industrijalac** *m* tycoon.
bogataš *m* rich man.
bogatstvo *n* riches, richness, wealth.
boginja *f* goddess.
bogohulan *a* blasphemous.
bogohuljenje *n* blasphemy.
Bogojavljanje *n* Epiphany.
Bogorodica *f* mother of Christ.
bogoslov *m* seminarist.
bogoslovija *f* seminary.
bogosluženje *n* divine service.
boj *m* battle, combat, conflict.
boja *f* colour, paint, tint; ~ **lešnika** hazel; ~ **lica** complexion.
bojadžija *m* dyer.
bojati se *v* to fear, to be afraid.
bojazan *f* misgiving, fear, apprehension.
bojenje *n* colouring.
bojeva glava *f* warhead.
bojište *n* battlefield.
bojiti *vt* to dye, to paint.
bojkotovati *v* to boycott, to ostracize.
bojler *m* water heater.
bojni *a* fighting, war; ~ **brod** *m* battleship.
bok *m* side, flank; ~ **broda** broadside.
bokor *m* bush; cluster; stool; ~ **ruža** rosebush.
bokal *m* decanter.
boks *m* boxing.
bokser *m* boxer.
bokserske rukavice *fpl* boxing gloves.
bokserski ring *m* boxing ring.
bol *f* ache, distress, pain.
bolan *a* ailing, excruciating, painful.
bolećiv *a* compassionate.
bolesnik *m* patient; ~ **koji se leči u bolnici** in-patient; **duševni ~** mentally disturbed person.
bolest *f* ailment, disease, illness, malady, sickness.
bolestan *a* diseased, ill, invalid, sick, unhealthy, unwell; ~ **od morske bolesti** seasick.
bolešljiv *a* sickly, feeble, ailing, delicate.

bolešljivost *f* sickliness.
boleti *v* to ail, to give pain, to be painful.
bolnica *f* clinic, hospital, infirmary.
bolničar *m* attendant.
bolničarka *f* nurse, hospital nurse.
bolno *adv* smartly.
bolovanje *n* sick leave.
bolje *adv* better.
bomba *f* bomb.
bombarder *m* bombardier.
bombardovanje *n* bombardment, blitz.
bombardovati *v* to bomb.
bon *m* ticket, coupon.
bonsai *m* bonsai.
bor *m* pine.
bora *f* wrinkle, fold, plait.
borac *m* fighter; ~ **s bikovima**
  bullfighter.
borba *f* battle, struggle; ~ **s bikovima**
  bullfight; ~ **petlova** cockfight(ing);
  smrtna ~ mortal combat.
borben *a* militant, aggressive; **~a linija** *f*
  firebreak, fire line; ~ **jedinica** military
  unit; **~a pesma** marching song; **~i**
  poredak *m* battle array.
boriti se *v* to contend, to fight, to cope, to
  militate.
borovnica *f* bilberry.
bos *m* barefoot(ed).
bosiljak *m* basil.
bostan *m* melons.
bosti *v* to prod, to puncture, to prick.
bošča *f* bundle.
botaničar *m* botanist.
botanički *a* botanic(al); **~a bašta** *f*
  botanical garden.
botanika *f* botany.
božanski *a* divine, godlike; **~o**
  nadahnuće *n* divine inspiration.
božanstvo *n* deity, divinity, godhead.
Božić *m* Christmas.
božićnje drvo *f* Christmas tree.
bračni *a* conjugal, marital, matrimonial,
  nuptial; ~ **par** *m* married couple; **~a**
  zajednica *f* matrimony.
brada *f* beard, chin.
bradat *a* bearded.
bradavica *f* wart; ~ **na grudima** nipple.
brak *m* marriage, wedlock.
brakolomstvo *n* adultery.
brana *f* dam, sluice.

branik *m* rampart.
branilac *m* defender; lawyer, counsellor.
braniti *v* to guard, to defend; to prohibit.
branša *f* specialty, occupation.
branje *n* harvest.
brašno *n* flour.
brat *m* brother; ~ **po majci ili ocu** half
  brother.
brat ili sestra *m* sibling.
brati *v* to collect, to gather; ~ **cveće** to
  pick flowers.
bratoubistvo *n* fratricide.
bratski *adv* brotherly.
bratski *a* fraternal.
bratstvo *n* brotherhood, fraternity.
brava *f* lock.
bravar *m* locksmith.
brazda *f* furrow, groove, rut.
brbljanje *n* babble, gab, gossip.
brbljati *v* to blab, to gabble, to jabber.
brbljiv *a* chatty, talkative, loquacious,
  flippant.
brbljivac *m* babbler, chatterbox.
brbljivost *f* loquacity.
brdo *n* mount.
brdovit *a* mountainous; ~ **predeo** *m*
  highlands.
brektati *v* to chug, to puff, to breathe
  hard.
breme *n* weight, load.
breskva *f* peach.
brest *m* elm (*bot*).
breza *f* birch (*bot*).
brežuljak *m* knoll, hillock, hill.
brežuljkast *a* hilly.
briga *f* care, concern, solicitude.
brigada *f* brigade.
brigadni general *m* brigadier.
brijač *m* shaver, razor.
brijanje *n* shave, shaving.
brinuti se *v* to worry, to torment.
bris *m* smear.
brisač stakla *m* windscreen wiper.
brisati *v* to erase, to efface, to delete, to
  cancel, to obliterate, to wipe.
britanska funta *f* sterling.
britva *f* razor.
brižan *a* caring, anxious, concerned;
  devoted; ~ **otac** *m* a devoted father.
brkati *v* to confuse, to confound.
brkovi *mpl* moustache.

brlog *m* den, lair.
brod *m* ship, ferry; ~ **cisterna** tanker;
~ **lopatar** paddle steamer.
brodogradilište *n* dockyard, shipyard.
brodogradnja *f* shipbuilding.
brodolom *m* shipwreck.
brodolomnik *m* castaway, shipwrecked
person.
brodovlasnik *m* shipowner.
brodski dnevnik *m* logbook.
brodski ekonom *m* purser.
brodski konobar *m* steward.
broj *m* number, figure; issue; ~ **računa**
account number.
brojan *a* numerous.
brojanice *fpl* rosary.
brojilo za kilometražu *n* mileometer,
milometer.
brojiti *v* to count, to number, to score.
brojka *f* digit, cipher, figure.
brojni *a* numerical.
brokat *m* brocade.
bronhijalni *a* bronchial; ~**a astma** *f*
bronchial asthma.
bronhitis *m* bronchitis (*med*).
bronza *f* bronze.
broš *m* brooch.
broširana knjiga *f* paperback.
brošura *f* brochure.
brstiti *v* browse.
bršljan *m* ivy.
brucoš *m* fresher.
brujati *v* to hum, to sizzle, to hiss.
bruka *f* shame, disgrace, scandal.
brundati *v* to grumble, to snarl.
brusnica *f* cranberry.
brutalan *a* brutal.
brutalnost *m* brutality.
bruto *a* gross.
brvnara *f* log-cabin.
brvno *n* log, footbridge.
brz *a* quick, rapid, speedy; ~ **motorni**
čamac *m* speedboat; ~**i voz** express
train; ~**a hrana** *f* fast food.
brzina *f* rapidity, speed, speediness,
swiftness, velocity.
brzinomer *m* speedometer.
brzo *adv* apace, swiftly, quickly.
buba *f* beetle, insect, bug.
bubamara *f* ladybird.
bubanj *m* drum.

bubašvaba *f* cockroach.
bubati *vi* to cram, to swot.
bubna opna *f* eardrum.
bubnjar *m* drummer.
bubreg *m* kidney.
bubrežnjak *m* sirloin.
bubuljica *f* pimple, acne.
bucmast *a* chubby.
bučan *a* noisy, tumultuous, vociferous.
bučno *adv* noisily.
bućkalica *f* churn.
budala *f* dunce, fool, simpleton.
budan *a* awake; vigilant, watchful.
budilnik *m* alarm clock.
buditi *v* to arouse; to wake up.
budizam *m* Buddhism.
budno *adv* watchfully.
budnost *f* vigilance, wakefulness.
buduća majka *f* mother-to-be.
budući *a* future, coming, prospective.
budući da *conj* whereas, because,
considering, as, since.
budzašto *a* cheaply.
budžet *m* budget.
buđav *a* mouldy.
buđenje *n* awakening, waking.
bujan *a* lush, fertile, luxuriant.
bujati *v* to flourish, to grow, to enlarge, to
swell.
bujica *f* torrent, strong current.
buka *f* noise, fuss, hubbub, uproar.
buket *m* bouquet.
buknuti *v* to flare up, to burst up.
buktati *v* to blaze.
bukva *f* beech.
bukvalan *a* strict, literal, following to the
word.
buldog *m* bulldog.
buldožer *m* bulldozer.
buljina (sova) *f* owl.
bum *m* boom.
bumbar *m* bumblebee (*zool*).
buna *f* mutiny.
bunar *m* well.
buncati *v* to rant, to rave.
bunda *f* fur coat.
bundeva *f* pumpkin.
bungalov *m* bungalow.
bunker *m* bin, bunker.
bunovan *a* delirious, drowsy, sleepy.
buntovan *a* riotous.

buntovnički *a* seditious.
buntovnik *m* rioter.
bura *f* gale, storm, tempest.
buran *a* boisterous, gusty, stormy,
  tempestuous; **~ život** *m* tempestuous
  life; **~rno more** *n* a rough sea.
burdelj *m* brothel.
bure *n* barrel, cask.
burence *n* keg.
burgija *f* drill, borer.
burleska *f* burlesque.

burma *f* wedding ring.
burmut *m* snuff.
burmutica *f* snuffbox.
burno *adv* stormily.
buržujski *a* bourgeois.
busen *m* turf.
bušenje *n* drilling, boring, perforation.
bušilica *f* derrick, boring machine.
butina *f* thigh.
buva *f* flea.
buzdovan *m* club, cudgel.

C

car *m* czar, emperor.
carić *m* wren (*zool*).
carina *f* customs; duty; tariff.
carinik *m* customs officer.
carski *a* imperial; ~ rez *m* Caesarean section/operation (*med*).
carstvo *n* empire; životinjsko ~ fauna, animal kingdom; nebesko ~ heavenly kingdom.
cediljka *f* strainer.
cediti *v* to distil, to filter, to filtrate.
celer *m* celery.
celishodan *a* suitable, fitting.
celofan *m* cellophane.
celokupan *a* integral, complete, whole.
celokupnost *f* totality.
celuloza *f* cellulose.
cement *m* cement.
cena *f* cost, expense; ~ prevoza fare; niska (visoka) ~ low (high) price.
ceniti *v* to appraise, to value, to rate, to estimate; to appreciate.
cenovnik *m* price list.
cent *m* cent.
centar *m* centre (*br*), center (*amer*).
centralan *a* central.
centrifugalan *a* centrifugal.
cenzor *m* censor.
cenzura *f* censorship.
cenjen *a* esteemed.
cenjkati se *v* to haggle, to bargain.
ceo *a* all, whole; complete, entire; ~ iznos *m* lump sum; ~ svet everyone.
cepanica *f* clef, log.
cepidlačenje *n* pedantry.
cepidlačiti *v* to split hairs.
cepidlaka *f* hair-splitter, faultfinder.
cepiti *v* to inoculate, to vaccinate.
cepkati *v* to split, to divide.
cerekati se *v* to giggle, to chuckle, to snigger, to titter.
ceremonija, svečanost *f* ceremony.
ceremonijalni *a* ceremonial.
cerenje *n* grinning.
ceriti se *v* to grin; to laugh maliciously.
cev *f* tube.
cevovod *m* conduit, pipe, pipeline.

cicija *m* miser, skinflint.
ciča *f* intense cold; ~ zima bitter cold.
cičanje *n* squealing.
cičati *v* to squeal, to shriek.
cifarnik *m* dial.
cifra *f* cipher, figure, numeral.
Ciganin *m* Gypsy.
cigara *f* cigar.
cigareta *f* cigarette.
cigla *f* brick.
cigura *f* chicory.
cijanid *m* cyanide.
cijanovodonična kiselina *f* prussic acid (*chem*).
cika *f* out-cry, yell.
cik-cak *adv* zig-zag.
ciklon *m* cyclone.
ciklus *m* cycle, period.
ciknuti *v* to squeal.
cilindar *m* cylinder.
cilindričan *a* cylindric(al).
cilj *m* goal, mark, finishing line, winning post.
cimati *v* to tow, to pull.
cimbale *fpl* cymbals.
cimet *m* cinnamon.
ciničan *a* cynic(al), sarcastic.
cinik *m* cynic, misanthrope.
cinizam *m* cynicism.
cink *m* zinc (*chem*).
cinkovati *v* to galvanize.
cipela *f* shoe, footwear.
cirada *f* tarpaulin.
cirkulacija *f* circulation.
cirkulisati *v* to circulate.
cirkus *m* circus.
cista *f* cyst.
cisterna *f* cistern; ~ za gorivo fuel tank.
citat *m* citation.
citirati *v* cite, quote.
civilizacija *f* civilization.
civilna odbrana *f* civil defence.
civilno lice *n* civilian.
cmakanje *n* loud kissing.
cmizdrenje *n* snivelling.
coktati *v* to smack one's lips.
cokula *f* military boot.

crći *v* to die, to expire, to pass away.
crep *m* tile.
creva *npl* intestines, entrails.
crevni *a* intestinal.
crevo *n* hose; **gumeno** ~ rubber hose.
crkva *f* church.
crkveno dvorište *n* churchyard.
crkvenjak *m* sexton, verger.
crn *a* black, dark; ~ **kao ugalj** pitch black; ~ **kutija** *f* black box; ~ **lista** black list; ~ **ovca** black sheep; ~o **vino** *m* red wine; ~i **petak** *m* an unlucky day.
Crnac *m* Negro.
crnka *f* brunette.
Crnkinja *f* Negress.
crta *f* line, streak; feature, characteristic.
crtač *m* draughtsman.
crtanje *n* drawing.
crtež *m* drawing, draft.
crtica (između dve reči ili sloga) *f* hyphen.
crv *m* worm.
crven *a* red, ruddy, crimson.

crvendać *m* robin (redbreast).
crvenilo *n* redness, ruddiness.
crvenkast *a* reddish.
crvenokos *a* redheaded.
cupkati *v* to jump (up and down), to hop.
curiti *v* to leak, to run, to drip.
cura *f* maid, girl.
cvećar *m* florist.
cvećara *f* florist's (shop).
cvekla *f* beetroot.
cvet *m* flower, bloom, blossom.
cvetanje *n* efflorescence, blossoming.
cvetati *v* to bloom, to blossom, to flourish.
Cveti *fpl* Palm Sunday.
cvetna leja *f* flowerbed.
cvetni *a* floral, flowery.
cvileti *v* to whimper, to squeal, to whine.
cvokotati *v* to chatter.
cvrčak *m* cricket.
cvrčati *v* to chirp; to sizzle (mast).
cvrkutanje *n* chirping.
cvrkutati *v* to chirp, to twitter.

Č

čabar *m* tub.
čačkalica *f* toothpick.
čačkati *v* to pick; to tinker, to putter.
čađ *f* grime, soot.
čađav *a* grimy, sooty.
čaj *m* tea; ~ **sa limunom** lemon tea.
čajdžinica *f* tearoom.
čajnik *m* kettle, teapot.
čak *adv* even, but also; albeit.
čakšire *fpl* trousers.
čama *f* sadness, melancholy.
čamac *m* boat; ~ **sa ravnim dnom** punt; ~ **za spašavanje** lifeboat.
čangrizav *a* nagging, irritable, petulant.
čaplja *f* heron.
čar *m* magic, attractiveness.
čarapa *f* stocking; sock.
čarka *f* skirmish.
čaroban *a* enchanting, magical, glamorous.
čarobnjak *m* magician.
čarolija *f* witchery, sorcery, enchantment.
čaršav *m* sheet.
čaršija *f* market-place, downtown; public opinion (*fig*).
čarter let *m* charter flight.
čas *m* hour; lesson.
časna reč *f* parole.
časno *adv* honestly.
časopis *m* journal, magazine; periodical.
časovničar *m* watchmaker.
časovnik *m* clock, watch.
čast *f* honour, honesty.
častan *a* honorable.
častiti *v* to treat, to receive as a guest.
čaša *f* glass.
čašćenje *n* treat, feast.
čaura *f* capsule; cocoon.
čavka *f* jackdaw.
čavlić *m* tack.
čedan *a* chaste, innocent, pure.
čednost *f* chastity, virginity.
čedomorstvo *n* infanticide.
čega *pn* which, what.
čegrtaljka *f* rattle.
čegrtuša *f* rattlesnake (*zool*).
ček *m* cheque, money order.
čekanje *n* waiting.

čekaonica *f* waiting room.
čekati *v* to await, to wait for, to bide.
čekić *m* hammer, gavel.
čekinja *f* bristle.
čekinjast *a* bristly.
čekrk *m* winch.
čelik *m* steel.
čelni *a* frontal.
čelo *n* cello (*mus*); forehead.
čeljad *f* inmate, dweller; children.
čeljust *f* jaw.
čemer *m* bitterness.
čemeran *a* distressed; bitter.
čempres *m* cypress.
čep *m* plug, gag, bung.
čerek *m* quarter (*of meat*).
čerupati *v* to pluck; to rob, overcharge (*fig*).
čest *a* frequent.
čestar *m* thicket.
čestit *a* virtuous, honest.
čestitanje *n* congratulations.
čestitati *v* to congratulate, to felicitate.
čestitka *f* greeting(s) card; felicitation.
često *adv* repeatedly, often, frequently.
češalj *m* comb.
češati *v* to scratch.
četa *f* company; ~ **za izvršenje smaknuća streljanjem** firing squad.
četinar *m* conifer.
četinarski *a* coniferous.
četiri *num* four.
četka *f* brush; ~ **za kosu** hairbrush; ~**ica za zube** toothbrush.
četrdeset *num* forty.
četrdeseti *num a* fortieth.
četrnaest *num* fourteen.
četrnaesti *num a* fourteenth.
četvorokut *m* quadrangle.
četvoronožac *m* quadruped.
četvorostruki *a* fourfold, quadruple.
četvrt *f* quarter.
četvrtak *m* Thursday.
četvrtast *a* square.
četvrti *num a* fourth.
čeznuti *v* to hanker, to yearn, to long for.
čežnja *f* yearning, longing, aspiration.
čežnjiv *a* wistful.

čiča *m* old man.
čičak *m* thistle, bur/burr.
čiji *pn* whose.
čikati *v* to tease.
čim *adv* as soon as.
čime *pn* with what.
čin *m* action, deed; class, rank, grade; act (*theat*); ~ **kapetana** captaincy.
čini *fpl* spell, sorcery, magic.
činija *f* bowl, dish; ~ **za salatu** salad bowl.
činilac *m* factor; divisor (*math*).
činiti *v* to do, to act, to make.
činjenica *f* fact.
čioda *f* pin.
čipka *f* lace.
čir *m* abscess, sore, carbuncle, ulcer.
čist *a* clean, immaculate, pure.
čistač *m* cleaner; purifier.
čistiti *v* to clean, to purify, to expurgate.
čisto *adv* cleanly.
čistoća *f* cleanliness, purity.
čistokrvan *a* thoroughbred, pure-bloodied.
čistunac *m* purist.
čišćenje *n* cleaning, purification, sweeping.
čitak *a* legible, readable.
čitalac *m* reader.
čitanje *n* reading, perusal; ~ **sa usana** lip reading.
čitaonica *f* reading room.
čitati *v* to read, to peruse; **letimično** ~ to scan; ~ **naglas** to read out; ~ **između redova** to read between the lines.
čitav *a* unbroken, whole, integral, complete.
čitljivo *adv* legibly.
čitulja *f* death-notice, obituary.
čizma *f* boot.
član *m* member; article (*gram*).
članarina *f* membership fee.
članstvo *n* membership.
čmar *m* anus.
čmičak *m* sty(e).
čoban *m* shepherd.
čobanica *f* shepherdess.
čokolada *f* chocolate.
čorba *f* broth, soup.
čovečan *a* humane, kind-hearted, merciful.

čovečanstvo *n* humanity, mankind.
čovek *m* man, person, being; ~ **sa strane** outsider; ~ **van zakona** outlaw.
čovekolik *a* manlike.
čovekoljubiv *a* humanitarian, philanthropic.
čovekoljublje *n* philanthropy.
čovekomrzac *m* misanthrope.
čučati *v* to squat.
čudan *a* eccentric, unusual, strange, odd, queer.
čudesan *a* marvellous, wonderful, miraculous.
čuditi *v* to astonish, to amaze.
čudo *n* miracle, prodigy, wonder.
čudotvorac *m* miracle worker.
čudovište *n* monster.
čuđenje *n* astonishment, wonder, amazement.
čujan *a* audible.
čukunbaba *f* great grandmother.
čulan *a* sensual, voluptuous.
čun *m* boat, canoe.
čunak *m* tube; shuttle.
čunj *m* bowling pin; skittle.
čupav *a* tousled, dishevelled; shaggy.
čuperak *m* tuft of hair; shag.
čuti *v* to hear.
čuvar *m* caretaker, keeper; ~ **lovišta** gamekeeper; **noćni** ~ night watchman; **muzejski** ~ museum gard; ~ **reda** policeman.
čuvati *v* to take care, to keep, to conserve, to guard, to watch over.
čuvati se *v* to beware.
čuven *a* illustrious, eminent, famous.
čuvenost *f* notoriety.
čvor *m* knot, tie, hub.
čvorak *m* starling (*zool*).
čvornovat *a* gnarled, knotty.
čvoruga *f* bump.
čvrst *a* strong, hard, firm, steady, fixed; adamant, steadfast, tenacious; ~**o telo** *n* solid; ~**a volja** *f* an unyielding will; ~**a odluka** a firm decision.
čvrstina *f* sturdiness, solidity, firmness.
čvrsto *adv* tightly, firmly.

Ć

ćaknut *a* touched, crazy.
ćar *m* profit, benefit, gain.
ćarlijati *v* to blow gently.
ćaskanje *n* chitchat, small talk.
ćaskati *v* to chat, to prattle.
ćebe *n* blanket.
ćef *m* caprice, whim, fancy; desire, wish.
ćelav *a* bald, hairless.
ćelavost *f* baldness.
ćelija *f* cell; small room.
ćelijski *a* cellular.
ćerka *f* daughter.
ćevapčić *m* kebab, grilled meat.
ćilibar *m* amber.
ćilim *m* rug.
ćopav *a* hobbling, lame.
ćorak *m* blind cartridge.

ćorav *a* one-eyed.
ćorsokak *m* blind alley; deadlock; impasse.
ćošak *m* corner, bend.
ćuba *f* tuft, crest.
ćubast *a* crested.
ćud *f* temper, mood, disposition.
ćudljiv *a* whimsical, wayward.
ćufta *f* meatball; ~ **od govedine** beefburger.
ćup *m* jar, crock.
ćuprija *f* bridge.
ćurka *f* turkey; foolish woman (*slang*).
ćutanje *n* silence.
ćutati *v* to be still, to be silent.
ćutke *adv* hushed, silently.
ćutljiv *a* taciturn, silent, reserved.

D

da *conj* that; if.
da *adv* yes, yeah, ay(e).
da *part:* ~ li whether; ~ ne bi lest.
dabar *m* beaver (*zool*).
daća *f* wake (funeral repast).
dadilja *f* nanny; nurse.
dagnja *f* mussel.
dah *m* breath.
dahtati *v* to gasp, to snort.
daire *fpl* tambourine.
dakako *adv* really, indeed.
dakle *conj* well, thus, therefore.
dalek *a* faraway, distant, far, remote.
daleko *adv* afar, far away, remotely.
dalekometan *a* long-range.
dalekosežan *a* far-reaching.
dalekovidnost *f* providence, far-sightedness.
dalje, dalji *adv* farther, further, more remotely; ~ obrazovanje *n* further education; i tako ~ and so on, etc.
daljina *f* distance, remoteness.
daljinski upravljač *m* remote control.
dama *f* lady, dame; draughts (igra).
damast *m* damask.
dan *m* day, daytime; ~ isplate payday; ~ parade field day; ~ venčanja wedding day.
danak *m* tribute, offering, tax.
danas *adv* today, the present day.
današnji *a* of today; current; up-to-date; ~e novine *fpl* today's newspaper.
daninoć *m* pansy (*bot*).
dangubiti *v* to be idle, to dally.
danju *adv* by day.
dar *m* gift, present, endowment.
darežljiv *a* bountiful, generous.
darežljivost *f* bounty, generosity, largesse, munificence.
darmar *m* muddle, confusion, chaos.
darodavac *m* donor, donator.
darovati *v* to donate, to present, to bestow.
darovit *a* gifted, talented, able.
daska *f* board, plank; ~ za crtanje drawing board; ~ za igru bacanja strelica dartboard; ~ za peglanje ironing board; ~ za vožnju po talasima

surfboard; ~ koturaljka skateboard.
dašak *m* whiff, puff.
dati *v* to give, to bestow, to impart; ~ u podzakup to sublet.
datiran *a* dated.
dativ *m* dative (*gram*).
datum *m* date.
davalac *m* giver, donor, donator; ~ krvi blood donor.
daviti *v* to strangle, to suffocate.
daviti se *v* to be choked; to be drowning (u vodi).
davljenik *m* drowning person.
davnašnji, davni *a* ancient, gone by.
davno *adv* long ago, long since.
dažbina *f* duty, tax, tariff.
daždevnjak *m* salamander (*zool*).
debelo *adv* fatty.
debelo crevo *n* colon (*med*).
debelokožac *m* thick-skinned; callous person (*fig*).
debeo *a* fat, obese, adipose, plump.
debljina *f* thickness.
deca *npl* children.
decembar *m* December.
decenija *f* decade.
decimalni *a* decimal.
dečački *a* boyish.
dečak *m* boy, lad.
dečji *a* child's, children's; ~ vrtić *m* kindgergarten; ~ soba *f* nursery; ~ stolica highchair; ~ paraliza polio (*med*).
dečko *m* boyfriend.
deda *m* grandfather, grandad.
defekt *m* imperfection, defect, fault.
deficit *m* deficit.
defile *m* defilee, parade.
definicija *f* definition.
deformacija *f* deformity.
degeneracija *f* degeneration, decadence.
degradirati *v* to reduce, to inferior rank, to degrade.
degustacija *f* tasting, savouring; ~ vina wine-tasting.
dehidriran *a* dehydrated.
dejstvo *n* consequence, result; influence, effect.

dejstvovati *v* to work, perform; to act.
dekada *f* decade.
dekan *m* dean.
deklaracija *f* declaration, public announcement.
dekolte *m* decolletage, neckline, low-cut.
dekor *m* stage set, decor; scenery.
dekoracija *f* decoration.
dekorater *m* decorator.
dekret *m* decree, order, command.
delanje *n* activity, acting.
delati *v* to do, to perform, to act.
delatnost *f* activity, action, work; **neprijateljska** ~ subversive activity; **društvena** ~ social affairs.
delegirati *v* to deputize, to delegate.
delfin *m* dolphin (*zool*).
delić *m* particle, bit, molecule.
delija *m* hero, warrior.
delikatan *a* delicate, pleasant; sensitive, weak.
delikates *m* delicacy, dainty.
delilac *m* distributor; divisor (*math*).
delimičan *a* partial, incomplete, limited.
delimično *adv* partially, partly, in part; ~ se preklapati to overlap.
delirijum *m* delirium.
deliti *v* to part, to divide, to separate.
delo *n* action, work, production.
delokrug *m* scope, domain.
delovanje *n* operation.
delovati *v* to operate, to effect, to work, to perform.
deljenje *n* division, separation.
deljiv *a* divisible.
demagog *m* demagogue.
demaskirati *v* to unmask.
demobilisati *v* to demobilize.
demokrata *m* democrat.
demokratija *f* democracy.
demokratski *a* democratic.
demolirati *v* to demolish, to tear down, to smash.
demonstrator *m* demonstrator.
demontirati *v* to dismantle.
deo *m* share, part, portion; lobe.
deoba *f* partition, division.
depeša *f* telegram, cable.
depilator *m* hair remover.
deplasiran *a* out of place, unbecoming.
depo *m* store, storehouse, depot.

depozit *m* deposit.
depresija *f* depression.
derati *v* to tear, to pull apart; to skin, to peel.
derati se *v* to wear out (cepati se); to yell, to cry out, to shout.
derište, deran *n* brat, urchin.
dermatolog *m* dermatologist.
dernjava *f* yelling.
deset *num* ten.
deseti *num a* tenth.
desetkovati *v* to decimate.
desiti se *v* to happen, to chance, to occur.
desni *fpl* gums.
desni *a* right; ~ **bok broda** *m* starboard.
desno *adv* on the right.
despot *m* tyrant, oppressor.
destilacija *f* distillation.
dešifrovati *v* to decipher, to decode.
dete *n* child, kid; ~ **koje je tek prohodalo** toddler.
detektiv *m* detective.
detektor *m* detector.
detelina *f* clover.
deterdžent *m* detergent.
detinjast *a* babyish, childish, infantile.
detinjasto *adv* childishly.
detinji *a* infantile.
detinjstvo *n* childhood.
detlić *m* woodpecker (*zool*).
detonacija *f* detonation.
devalvacija *f* devaluation.
devedeset *num* ninety.
devedeseti *num a* ninetieth.
dever *m* brother-in-law.
deveruša *f* bridesmaid.
devet *num* nine.
deveti *num a* ninth.
devetnaest *num* nineteen.
devetnaesti *num a* nineteenth.
devica *f* virgin, maid.
Devica *f* Virgo (*astrol*).
deviza *f* motto, device; foreign currency.
devojački *a* girlish; ~o **prezime** maiden name.
devojčica *f* girl.
devojka *f* girlfriend, maid, maiden; ~ **sa naslovne strane** cover girl.
dezerter *m* deserter.
dezinfekciono sredstvo *n* disinfectant.

dezinfikovati *v* to disinfect.
dezinformacija *f* misinformation.
dezodorans *m* deodorant.
dezorganizacija *f* disorganization.
dezorganizovan *a* disorganized.
dezorijentisan *a* disorientated.
dežmekast *a* stocky, dumpy, heavy set.
dežurni *a* on duty.
dičan *a* glorious.
dičiti se *v* to be proud.
dići *v* to hoist.
didaktičan *a* didactic.
difrakcija *f* diffraction.
difterija *f* diphtheria.
diftong *m* diphthong.
digitalni *a* digital.
digresija *f* digression.
dijabetičar *m* diabetic.
dijadema *f* diadem.
dijafragma *f* diaphragm, midriff.
dijagnostički *a* diagnostic(al).
dijagnoza *f* diagnosis.
dijagonalan *a* diagonal.
dijagram *m* diagram.
dijalekt *m* dialect, provincialism.
dijamant *m* diamond.
dijetalan *a* dietary.
diktat *m* dictation.
diktatorski *a* dictatorial.
diktatura *f* absolute power, dictatorship.
diktirati *v* to dictate.
dilema *f* dilemma.
dim *m* smoke, fumigation.
dimenzija *f* dimension, extent; measure.
dimiti *v* to smoke.
dimljen *a* smoked; **~a haringa** smoked
  herring (kipper).
dimnjak *m* chimney, funnel.
dina *f* dune.
dinamičan *a* dynamic.
dinamit *m* dynamite.
dinastija *f* dynasty.
dinosaurus *m* dinosaur.
dinja *f* melon.
diploma *f* diploma.
diplomatija *f* diplomacy.
diplomatski *a* diplomatic; **~ kor (pasoš)**
  m diplomatic corps (passport); **~om**
  poštom by diplomatic ponch.
diplomiranje *n* graduation.
diplomirati *v* to graduate.

dirati *v* to touch; to move (uzbuđivati).
direk *m* post, beam.
direktan *a* direct; **~tna telefonska linija**
  hotline.
direktiva *f* order, instruction; **direktive**
  guidelines.
dirigent *m* conductor.
dirinčiti *v* to work hard.
dirka *f* tangent, key.
dirljiv *a* pathetic, moving, impressive,
  touching.
disanje *n* breathing, respiration.
disati *v* to breathe, to respire; **teško ~** to
  wheeze.
disciplina *f* discipline.
disekcija *f* dissection.
disertacija *f* dissertation, treatise.
disident *m* dissident.
disk *m* disc, disk.
disketa *f* diskette, floppy disk.
diskoteka *f* discotheque, disco.
diskrecija *f* discretion.
diskretan *a* prudent, discreet.
diskusija *f* discussion, debate.
diskvalifikovati *v* to disqualify.
dispanzer *m* dispensary.
dispepsija *f* dyspepsia (*med*).
distributer *m* distributor.
distrofija *f* dystrophy (*med*).
div *m* giant.
divan *a* admirable, charming, adorable,
  lovely, beautiful.
divergentan *a* divergent.
diverzant *m* saboteur, raider.
dividenda *f* dividend.
diviti se *v* to admire.
divljač *f* game, venison.
divljaštvo *n* savageness, savagery, cruelty.
divljenje *n* admiration.
divlji *a* savage, rude, wild, ferocious.
divljina *f* wilderness.
divno *a* splendid, wonderful.
divokoza *f* alpine goat.
divota *f* beauty, loveliness, marvel.
divovski *a* colossal, enormous, gigantic.
dizač tegova *m* weightlifter.
dizajn *m* design.
dizanje *n* raising, lifting.
dizati *v* to lift, to heave, to hoist.
dizel *m* diesel.
dlakav *a* hairy.

dlan *m* palm.
dleto *n* chisel.
dnevni *a* daily, diurnal; ~ **list** gazette; ~ **red** agenda; ~**a priredba** matinee; ~**a soba** living room; ~**a svetlost** daylight.
dnevnik *m* diary, chronicle, journal.
dno *n* bottom.
do *prep* until, up, to; ~ **gadosti** ad nauseam; ~ **kolena** knee-deep.
doba *n* age, era, epoch.
dobaciti *v* to hurl, to throw.
dobar *a* good, kind, obliging; ~ **dan** *m* hello; ~**ro jutro** *n* good morning; ~**ro veče** *n* good evening; ~**ra srca** *npl* kindhearted.
dobavljač *m* provider, supplier.
dobitak *m* gain, profit, produce, acquisition.
dobiti *v* to get, to receive, to win, to obtain, to procure; ~ **zube** to teethe.
dobošar *m* drummer.
dobovanje *n* drumming; ~ **kišnih kapi** patterring.
dobro *adv* well; *n* property; ~ **obavešten** knowledgeable, well informed; ~ **obučen** well-dressed; ~ **poznat** well-known; ~ **građen** well-built; ~ **vaspitan** well-bred.
dobročinstvo *n* charity, generosity.
dobroćudan *a* good-natured, meek.
dobrodošlica *f* welcome, greeting.
dobronameran *a* well-meant, kind.
dobrota *f* goodness, kindliness.
dobrotvor *m* benefactor.
dobrotvoran *a* charitable.
dobrovoljac *m* volunteer.
dobrovoljan *a* voluntary.
dobrovoljno *adv* voluntarily.
dockan *adv* late, tardily.
doček *m* reception, welcome.
doći *v* to arrive, to come, to approach.
dodatak *m* supplement, appendix, appendage, complement; additive.
dodati *v* to add, to join; to hand, to give; to add.
dodeliti *v* to allocate, to asign.
dodeljivanje *n* allocation; ~ **nagrade** to award.
dodijati *v* to trouble, to molest.
dodir *m* contact, touch.
dodirivati, dodirnuti *v* to touch, to handle.

doduše *adv* in truth.
dodvoravanje *n* adulation.
dodvoravati se *v* to ingratiate.
do đavola *interj* damn it.
događaj *m* event, occurrence, incident.
događati se *v* to happen, to befall, to chance.
dogled *m* field-glasses, telescope.
dogma *f* dogma, doctrine.
dogmatičan *a* dogmatic.
dogodine *adv* next year.
dogoreti *v* to burn down.
dogovarati se *v* to confer, to discourse.
dogovoran *a* deliberative.
dograbiti *v* to grab.
dohodak *m* income, revenue, receipts; ~ **po stanovniku** *m* per capita income.
dohvatiti *v* to grasp, to catch.
doista *adv* indeed, really.
dojaviti *v* to inform.
dojilja *f* wet-nurse.
dojiti *v* to suckle, to nurse.
dok *adv* till, until.
dokaz *m* argument, evidence, proof.
dokazati *v* to prove, to evidence, to establish.
dokaziv *a* demonstrable.
dokolica *f* leisure, time to spare.
dokon *a* idle.
dokončati *v* to end, to make an end.
dokrajčiti *v* to end, to finish.
dokučiti *v* to find out, to see through.
dokument *m* official writting, document, paper.
dokumentarni *a* documentary.
dolar *m* dollar.
dolazak *m* advent, arrival.
dolaziti *v* to arrive, to come.
dole *prep* below; downstairs; underneath.
doličan *a* fitting.
dolikovati *v* to befit, to be suitable.
dolina *f* valley, dale, glen.
dom *m* home; club, hostel.
domaći *a* domestic; home-made; ~ **zadatak** *m* homework; ~**a haljina** *f* dressing gown.
domaćica *f* hostess; housewife.
domaćin *m* host; householder.
domaćinstvo *n* household.
domalo *adv* shortly, soon.
domamiti *v* to lure, to entice.

domet *m* range, scope, reach.
domine *fpl* dominoes.
domišljat *a* ingenious, inventive.
domišljatost *f* inventiveness.
domorodac *m* native, original inhabitant.
domovina *f* homeland, fatherland.
donacija *f* donation.
doneti *v* to bring, to fetch, to convey; to bear, to yield; ~ **odluku** to make a decision; ~ **zakon** to pass a low.
donji *a* lower; ~a **strana** *f* underside; ~a **suknja** petticoat; ~e **rublje** *npl* underclothing, underwear.
dopadati se *v* to be pleased, to like, to be attracted to.
dopadljiv *a* attractive, winning.
dopis *m* letter.
dopisivati se *v* to correspond, to write letters.
dopisnica *f* postcard.
dopisnik *m* reporter; correspondent.
doplaćivati *v* to pay extra.
dopratiti *v* to accompany, to escort.
doprineti, doprinositi *v* to contribute.
doprinos *m* contribution.
dopuna *f* addition, supplement, complement.
dopunski *a* additional, complementary, supplementary, supplemental; extra.
dopust *m* leave, concession; furlough.
dopustiti *v* to allow, to permit, to concede.
dopustiv *a* admissible, permissible.
dopuštati sebi *v* to indulge.
dopuštenje *n* licence; permittance, permission.
dorastao *a* grown-up.
doručak *m* breakfast.
dosad *adv* hitherto, till now.
dosada *f* boredom, tedium.
dosadan *a* annoying, boring, tedious.
dosadašnji *a* former, previous, earlier.
dosađivati *v* to annoy, to molest, to harass, to pester.
dosegnuti *v* to reach.
doseliti se *v* to move in, to settle.
doseljenik *m* immigrant, colonist, settler.
dosetka *f* joke, pun, witticism.
dosetljiv *a* ingenious, clever, gifted.
dosije *m* dossier, file.
dosledan *a* consequent, consistent.
doslednost *f* consistency.

doslovan *a* literal, strict.
doslovno *adv* exactly, literally, verbatim.
dosta *adv* enough, sufficiently.
dostajati *v* to suffice.
dostatnost *f* sufficiency.
dostava *f* delivery, handing over.
dostaviti *v* to deliver, to transfer.
dostavnica *f* delivery note, shipping note.
dostići *v* to achieve, to catch.
dostignuće *n* achievement.
dostižan *a* attainable, conceivable.
dostojan *a* worthy, meritorious; ~ **poštovanja** venerable; ~ **poverenja** trustworthy; ~ **prezira** despicable.
dostojanstven *a* majestic, imposing, dignified, august.
dostojanstvo *n* dignity, decorum, stateliness.
dostojno *adv* fittingly.
dostupan *a* available, accessible.
došljak *m* newcomer, stranger.
dotacija *f* donation, benefaction, grant, subsidy.
doteran *a* perfected; dapper, dashing, dressy, spruce, trim.
doterivati *v* to retouch; to touch up.
dotičan *a* respective, relative, in question.
dotrajati *v* to last.
dovde *adv* so far, as far as.
doveka *adv* for ever, always.
dovesti *v* to bring, to fetch; to drive (kolima); ~ **u iskušenje** to tempt.
do viđenja *interj* goodbye, so long, see you again.
dovikivati *v* to call, to shout.
dovitljiv *a* apprehensive, creative, inventive, quick-witted.
dovoditi *v* to bring; ~ **u nepriliku** to embarrass; ~ **u zabludu** mislead.
dovoljan *a* sufficient; ~na **količina jela** bellyful.
dovoljno *adv* enough, sufficiently.
dovršiti *v* to put an end to, to finish, to terminate.
doza *f* dose.
doziranje *n* dosage.
dozivati *v* to shout, to call, to cry out.
doznaka *f* remittance, transfer.
doznati *v* to be informed, to learn, to come into knowledge.
dozvati *v* to call back, to summon.

dozvola *f* permit, permission, allowance, authorization, clearance; leave.
dozvoliti *v* to allow, to admit, to let; ~ **sebi** to afford.
dozvoljena brzina *f* speed limit.
doživeti *v* to live to see, to experience.
doživotan *a* lifelong, for life.
drač *f* weed, bramble.
drag *a* dear, endearing, darling, sweetheart.
dragi kamen *m* jewel.
dragocen *a* valuable, precious.
dragulj *m* gem, jewel.
drama *f* drama.
dramatičan *a* dramatic.
draperija *f* hangings, drapery.
drastičan *a* drastic.
draž *f* attractiveness, allure.
draženje *n* provocation.
dražiti *v* to stimulate, to excite.
drečati *v* to cry, to weep.
dremati *v* to doze, to slumber, to sleep lightly.
dremež *f* nap, snooze.
dremljiv *a* sleepy, drowsy, dormant.
dresirati *v* to train.
drevan *a* archaic, ancient, antique.
drhtanje *n* trembling, tremor, trepidation.
drhtati *v* to quake, to quiver, to shake, to tremble.
drhtav *a* shaky, tremulous.
drhtavica *f* quivering, trepidation.
driblovati *v* to dribble.
drljača *f* harrow.
drmanje *n* shaking, jerking.
drmati *v* to jolt, to jerk, to pull suddenly.
drobiti *v* to crumble, to mash, to fritter.
drolja *f* whore, prostitute.
dronjav *a* tattered, ragged.
drozd *m* thrush (*zool*).
drsko *adv* saucily, insolently.
drskost *f* effrontery, insolence, impertinence, pertness.
drška *f* handle; ~ **od metle** broomstick.
drug *m* companion, comrade, fellow, mate, playmate.
drugačiji *a* different.
drugar *m* chum, pal.
drugarstvo *n* companionship, comradeship.
drugde *adv* elsewhere.
drugi[1] *a* another, other.

drugi[2] *num a* second.
drugo *adv* secondly.
drugorazredan *a* second-class.
drukčiji *a* different, diverse.
društven *a* social, sociable, public, friendly; ~**i život** *m* social life; ~**i sektor** public sector; ~**a imovina** *f* public property.
društveno *adv* sociably.
društvenost *f* sociableness.
društvo *n* society; company, association.
druželjubivost *f* convivality.
drven *a* wooden; ~**a građa** timber; ~**a oplata** panel; ~**i konj** hobbyhorse; ~**i malj** mallet; ~**i moljac** woodworm.
drvenarija *f* woodwork.
drvo *n* tree; ~ **za ogrev** firewood.
drvored *m* alley.
drvorez *m* wood carving.
drvorezac *m* wood engraver.
drvoseča *m* lumberjack, woodcutter.
drzak *a* brash, impudent, insolent, arrogant, haughty.
držač *m* holder; ~ **koplja** shaft.
držanje *n* bearing, pose, attitude.
držati *v* to hold, to keep.
država *f* state, country, government.
državljanin *m* citizen.
državljanstvo *n* citizenship, nationality.
državni *a* state, national; ~**i udar** *m* coup d'etat; ~ **budžet** governmental budget; ~**o prvenstvo** *n* national championship.
državnik *m* statesman; ~**čka veština** statesmanship.
dubak *m* baby walker.
dubina *f* depth, profundity.
dubok *a* deep, profound, gaping; ~**a posekotina** gash; ~**a zdela** tureen.
duboko *adv* deeply, profoundly; ~ **poštovanje** reverence; ~ **poštovati** to revere; ~ **zamrzavanje** deep-freeze.
duborez u drvetu *m* woodcut, engraving.
dućan *m* shop, store.
dud *m* mulberry tree.
duet *m* duet (*mus*).
dug[1] *m* debt, debit, due (*fin*).
dug[2] *a* long, lengthy.
duga *f* rainbow.
dugačak *a* lengthy, long; ~ **korak** stride.
dugme *n* button, knob.
dugo *adv* a long time, for a long time.
dugokos *a* long-haired.

dugonog *a* long-legged.
dugoročan *a* long-term.
dugotrajan *a* lasting, long lasting.
dugovanje *n* debt, due, debit.
dugovati *v* to owe, to be indebted to.
dugovečnost *f* longevity.
dugovi *mpl* arrears.
duh *m* ghost, spirit.
duhovit *a* witty, funny, clever; ~ **odgovor** repartee; ~**a primedba** wisecrack.
duhovito *adv* wittily.
duhovni *a* spiritual, immaterial, ghostly.
duhovnički *a* clerical, ecclesiastic.
dunuti *v* to blow.
dunja *f* quince.
dupli *a* double, dual.
duplja *f* cavity, hollow.
durbin *m* field-glass, telescope.
duriti se *v* to pout, to be sullen.
duša *f* soul, spirit.
dušek *m* mattress.
duševan *a* warm, tender.
duševni *a* mental, spiritual; ~**o zdrav** sane; ~**o zdravlje** *n* sanity.
dušnik *m* throttle, windpipe.
duvaljka *f* blowpipe.
duvan *m* tobacco.
duvankesa *f* tobacco pouch.
duvati *v* to blow, to puff.
dužan *a* due, owing, indebted.
duže *adv* longer.
dužica *f* iris.
dužina *f* length, extent, longitude (*geograf*).
dužinski *a* longitudinal.

dužnik *m* debtor.
dužnost *f* duty, obligation.
dva, dve *num* two; **dve nedelje** fortnight.
dvadeset *num* twenty.
dvadeseti *num a* twentieth.
dvanaest *num* twelve.
dvanaesti *num a* twelfth.
dvaput *adv* twice.
dvesta *num* two hundred.
dvestoti *num a* the two hundreth.
dvoboj *m* duel, combat.
dvogled *m* binoculars.
dvogodišnji *a* biennial.
dvoje *n* couple, two persons.
dvojezičan *a* bilingual.
dvojka *f* deuce (u kartama); figure two.
dvojno *a* double.
dvoličan *a* two-faced, false.
dvoličnost *f* double-dealing, duplicity.
dvopek *m* biscuit cracker, rusk.
dvor *m* court.
dvorac *m* castle.
dvorana *f* hall.
dvoredan *a* double-breasted.
dvorište *n* court, courtyard, patio.
dvosed *m* two-seater.
dvosekli *a* double-edged.
dvosmislen *a* ambiguous, evasive.
dvosmislenost *f* ambiguity.
dvostih *m* couplet.
dvostruk *a* double, duplicate, dual, twofold; ~**i podbradak** *m* double chin.
dvostruko *adv* doubly.
dvoumiti se *v* to hesitate, to demur.

DŽ

džabe *adv* gratis, free; in vain.
džak *m* sack.
džakuzi *m* jacuzzi.
džamija *f* mosque.
dželat *m* executioner, hangman.
džem *m* jam.
džemper *m* sweater, sweatshirt.
džentlmen *m* gentleman.
džep *m* pocket, pouch.
džepni *a* pocket; ~ **računar** *m* calculator; **~a maramica** *f* handkerchief; **~a lampa** flashlight.
džeparac *m* pocket money.
džeparoš *m* pickpocket.

džez *m* jazz.
džezva *f* coffee-pot.
džigerica *f* liver.
džin *m* giant, colossus.
džinovski *a* colossal, gigantic.
džip *m* jeep.
džojstik *m* joystick.
džokej *m* jockey.
džombast *a* bumpy, uneven, rough, lumpy.
džuboks *m* jukebox.
džudo *m* judo.
džumbus *m* disorder, chaos, confusion.
džungla *f* jungle.

Đ

đak *m* schoolboy.
đakon *m* deacon.
đakonije *fpl* sweetmeats, delicacies.
đavo *m* devil, demon, Satan.
đavolak *m* goblin.
đavolast *a* mischievous.
đavolski *adv* devilish, diabolic,
  satanically.
đavolji *a* fiendish.
đeram *m* draw-beam of a well.

đerdan *m* necklace.
đipiti *v* to jump, to spring.
đon *m* sole.
đjubrivo *n* fertilizer.
đubretar *m* dustman.
đubrište *n* dump.
đumbir *m* ginger.
đurđevak *m* lily of the valley.
đuveč *m* stew.
đuvegija *m* bridegroom.

E

efekt *m* effect, outcome.
efektan *a* effective; convincing.
efikasan *a* efficacious, effectual, effective.
efikasnost *f* effectiveness.
egoist *m* ego(t)ist.
egzaktan *a* precise, exact, faultless.
egzistencija *f* existence, existing, being.
egzotičan *a* exotic.
eho *m* echo.
ekcem *m* eczema.
ekipa *f* team, small company; ~ **za spašavanje** rescue team.
eklektičan *a* eclectic.
ekolog *m* ecologist, environmentalist.
ekologija *f* ecology.
ekološki *a* environmental; ~ **sistem** ecosystem; ~ **turizam** ecotourism; ~**a taksa** ecotax.
ekonomičan *a* economic(al), sparing, saving.
ekonomista *m* economist.
ekonomski *a* economic(al); ~**e nauke** economics.
ekran *m* screen.
Ekselencija *f* Excellency.
ekser *m* nail.
ekskurzija *f* excursion, journey, tour.
ekspedicija *f* expedition.
ekspeditivan *a* expeditious.
ekspert *m* specialist, expert.
eksploatacija *f* exploitation.
eksplodirati *v* to detonate, to explode.
eksplozija *f* blast, explosion, detonation, blowout.
eksploziv *m* explosive.
ekspres *m* express (train); ~ **lonac** pressure cooker.
ekstaza *f* ecstasy, trance.
ekstra *a* extra, special, particular.
ekstrakt *m* extract, essence.
ekstremistički *a* extremist.
ekvator *m* equator.
ekvatorijalni *a* equatorial.
ekvivalentan *a* equivalent.
elan *m* elan, ardor, enthusiasm.
elastičan *a* springy, elastic.

elastičnost *f* springiness, elasticity.
elegantan *a* chic.
elegija *f* elegy.
elektricitet *m* electricity.
električan *a* electric(al); ~**čna centrala** *f* power station; ~**čna ograda** electric fence; ~**čna struja** electric current; ~**čno ćebe** *n* electric blanket.
električar *m* electrician.
elektrificirati *v* to electrify.
elektrokardiogram *m* electrocardiogram.
elektron *m* electron.
elektronska *a* electronic; ~ **pošta** *f.* e-mail; ~ **trgovina** e-commerce.
elektrotehnika *f* electrical engineering.
eliminisati *v* to eliminate, to exclude.
eliptičan *a* elliptic(al).
elisa *f* propeller.
emajl *m* enamel.
emancipacija *f* emancipation, enfranchisement.
embargo *m* embargo.
emigracija *f* emigration, migration; **politička** ~ enrigres.
emigrant *m* emigrant.
emigrirati *v* to emigrate, to migrate.
emisar *m* emissary, delegate.
emisija *f* broadcast; ~ **novca** putting into circulation.
emitovati *v* to broadcast, to radio.
emocija *f* feeling, emotion, excitement.
emotivan *a* emotional, emotive.
emulzija *f* emulsion.
enciklopedija *f* encyclopaedia.
endemičan *a* endemic.
energetika *f* energetics.
energičan *a* energetic, enterprising, active.
energija *f* energy, efficacy, power; **sunčana** ~ solar power.
entuzijasta *m* enthusiast.
entuzijazam *n* enthusiasm.
epidemijski *a* epidemic.
epilepsija *f* epilepsy.
epileptičan *a* epileptic.
episkop *m* bishop (orthodox).
epitet *m* epithet.

epizoda *f* episode, incident, occurrence.
epruveta *f* test tube.
era *f* era, epoch, period, age.
ergela *f* stud farm, horse farm.
erotski *a* erotic.
erupcija *f* eruption.
esej *m* essay.
eskadron *m* cavalry troop.
eskalacija *f* escalation.
eskalirati *v* to escalate.
eskont *m* discount.
esnaf *m* guild.
estetski *a* aesthetic.
ešalon *m* military train, military transport.
etapa *f* stage, phase.
eter *m* ether.
etika *f* ethics.
etički *a* ethical.
etiketa *f* label, tag.
etimologija *f* etymology.

etimološki *a* etymological.
etnički *a* ethnic.
eto *interj* there.
etos *m* ethos.
eufemizam *m* euphemism.
evakuacija *f* evacuation.
eventualan *a* possible.
evidencija *f* evidence.
evidentan *a* evident, clear, apparent.
evnuh *m* eunuch.
evo *interj* here is, here are.
evro *m* Euro.
Evropa *f* Europe.
Evropska unija *f* European Union.
Evropska zajednica *f* European Community.
Evropski parlament *m* European Parliament.
experiment *m* experiment, trial, test.
ezoteričan *a* esoteric.

F

fabrika *f* factory, mill, plant; ~ **obuće** shoe factory.
fabula *f* plot, story, theme.
fagot *m* bassoon (*mus*).
fah *m* calling, profession, vocation; **poštanski** ~ box-office, post-office, box.
fakat *m* fact, real existence, truth, reality.
faks *m* fax.
faktor *m* factor, determining element.
faktura *f* invoice.
fakultativan *a* optional.
fakultet *m* faculty.
faličan *a* false, defective.
faliti *v* to be missing.
falsifikat *m* forgery, counterfeiting.
falsifikovan *a* forged, counterfeited.
falsifikovati *v* to falsify, to forge.
fama *f* rumor, hearsay.
familija *f* family.
familijaran *a* familiar; intimate, amicable.
famozan *a* famous, famed, well-known.
fanatik *m* enthusiast, zealot, fanatic.
fanfara *f* fanfare.
fantastičan *a* fantastic.
fantazija *f* fancy, imagination.
fantazirati *v* to dream, to muse.
far *m* headlight; lighthouse.
farba *f* paint.
farma *f* farm, ranch.
farmaceutski *a* pharmaceutical.
farmerke *fpl* denims, jeans.
fasada *f* front, facade, anterior.
fascikla *f* folder.
fascinirati *v* to fascinate, to charm.
faširati *v* to grind, to chop.
fašista *m* fascist.
fatalan *a* fatal, fateful.
fatamorgana *f* mirage, Fata Morgana.
fauna *f* fauna.
faza *f* phase, stage, period.
fazan *m* pheasant.
februar *m* February.
feder *m* spring, coil.
federacija *f* federation.
fekalije *fpl* fecal, fecals, feces.
fen za kosu *m* hairdryer.

fenomen *m* phenomenon.
fenjer *m* lantern, lamp.
fer *a* fair, just, objective, honest.
feribot *m* car-ferry.
festival *m* festival.
feudalizam *m* feudalism.
feudalni *a* feudal.
fiberglas *m* fibreglass.
fićfirić *m* dandy, vain fellow.
fijaker *m* coach, carriage, fiacre.
fijuk *m* whistle, whiz.
fikcija *f* fiction, concoction.
fiksirati *v* to attach, to rivet, to cement, to fasten.
fil *m* stuffing; filling.
filantrop *m* philanthropist.
filharmonija *f* philarmonic orchestra.
filigran *m* filigree.
filijala *f* branch.
film *m* cinema, motion picture, movie.
filmski *a* film, movie; ~ **žurnal** *m* newsreel; ~**a kamera** *f* cine camera, movie camera; ~**a zvezda** film star.
filolog *m* philologist.
filologija *f* philology.
filovati *v* to fill, to stuff.
filozof *m* philosopher.
filozofija *f* philosophy.
filter *m* filter; ~ **za ulje** oil filter.
fin *a* delicate; fine; sensitive; refined.
finalan *a* final, last, terminal.
finalista *m* finalist.
finansijer *m* financier.
finansijski *a* financial, fiscal, monetary; ~**a sredstva** *fpl* financial resources.
fino *adv* finely, nicely.
finoća *f* refinement; purity.
fioka *f* drawer.
firma *f* firm, company; sign-board (natpis).
fiskultura *f* physical culture.
fišek *m* paper bag; cartridge (metak).
fitilj *m* wick.
fizičar *m* physicist.
fizički *a* physical; ~ **napor** *m* physical effort; ~**o obračunavanje** *n* physical force, fighting; ~ **radnik** laborer.

fizija *f* merger.
fiziolog *m* physiologist.
fiziologija *f* physiology.
fizioterapija *f* physiotherapy.
flanel *m* flannel.
flaster *m* plaster, sticking plaster.
flaša *f* bottle.
flauta *f* flute.
fleka *f* stain, blot.
fleksija *f* inflection.
flert *m* flirting.
flok *m* jib (*naut*).
flomaster *m* felt-tip pen, fibre-tip pen.
flor *m* crep.
flora *f* flora, plants.
flota *f* fleet; **trgovačka ~** *f* merchant fleet.
flotila *f* flotilla.
fluor *m* fluoride.
fljisnuti *v* to slap.
foaje *m* foyer, lobby.
fobija *f* phobia.
foka *f* seal (*zool*).
folklor *m* folklore.
fond *m* fund, stock, capital; **investicioni ~** investment fond.
fondacija *f* foundation.
fonetika *f* phonetics.
fonetički *a* phonetic; **~ zapis** phonetic transcription.
fontana *f* fountain.
forma *f* form, fashion, shape; condition.
formalnost *f* formality.
format *m* format, size, *pl* dimensions.
formirati *v* to form, to fashion, to shape, to mould.
formula *f* formula.
formular *m* form, application.

formulisati *v* to formulate, to word, to phrase.
forsirati *v* to force, to press, to urge.
forsirani marš *m* forced march.
forum *m* forum, gathering.
fosfor *m* phosphorus (*chem*).
fotelja *f* armchair, easy chair.
foto-aparat *m* camera.
fotograf *m* photographer.
fotografija *f* photograph, photo.
fotografski *a* photographic.
fotokopija *f* photocopy.
fragment *m* fragment, bit, part, piece.
frajer *m* idler, loafer.
frak *m* tailcoat.
franko *adv* paid, free on board.
frapantan *a* remarkable, unusual, striking.
frapirati *v* to amaze, to stun.
fraza *f* phrase, idiom.
frekvencija *f* frequency.
freska *f* fresco.
frizer *m* hairdresser.
frizura *f* hairstyle.
frižider *m* refrigerator, icebox.
frktati *v* to snarl.
frotir *m* towelling.
fudbal *m* football, soccer.
fudbaler *m* footballer.
fundamentalist *m* fundamentalist.
fundamentalizam *m* fundamentalism.
funkcija *f* function.
funkcionalan *a* functional.
funta *f* pound, pound sterling.
furgon *m* baggage car.
furnir *m* veneer.
fusnota *f* footnote.
futrola *f* case, sheathe, holster (za pištolj).

G

gacati *v* to plot, to flounder, to trudge; ~ po blatu to trudge through mud.

gačac *m* rook, crow.

gaće *fpl* drawers, trousers, pants.

gaćice *fpl* panties, underpants.

gad *m* scoundrel, cad.

gadan *a* nasty, disgusting, nauseous; evil,spiteful;bad; ~ čovek *m* an evil person; ~no vreme *n* bad weather.

gaditi se *v* to be nauseated, to be disgusted with.

gadljiv *a* nauseated, squeamish.

gadost *f* smt. repulsive; oath, curseword, dirty word.

gađati *v* to aim, to shoot.

gađenje *n* abhorrence, disgust.

gaf *m* gaffe, blunder, faux pas.

gaj *m* coppice, copse, grove.

gajba *f* crate.

gajde *fpl* bagpipe.

gajiti *v* to raise, to bring up, to rear, to graw; to cherish, to foster; ~ decu to bring up; ~ cveće to grow flowers; ~ nadu to cherish a hope.

gajtan *m* braid, cord, flex.

gakati *v* to quack, to cackle.

galaksija *f* galaxy.

galama *f* uproar, noise, clamour.

galamiti *v* to scream, to be noisy, to roar.

galantan *a* courteous, gallant, polite.

galanterijska radnja *f* haberdasher's shop.

galeb *m* seagull.

galerija *f* gallery.

galija *f* galley.

galon *m* gallon.

galop *m* gallop.

gamad *f* vermin, pests.

gangrena *f* gangrene.

gangster *m* gangster.

ganut *a* touched, moved.

ganuti *v* to move, to touch, to affect.

ganutljivo *adv* affectingly.

garancija *f* guarantee, warranty.

garav *a* swarthy, black, sooty.

garaža *f* garage.

garderoba *f* wardrobe; dressing room; clothes.

garnirati *v* to trim, to decorate.

garnitura *f* set, assortment, suite; crew, team.

garnizon *m* garrison.

garsonjera *f* bachelor flat, studio flat, one-room apartment.

gasiti *v* to quench, to extinguish; to turn off (struju).

gasiti se to disappear, to go out, to fade.

gasna svetiljka *f* gas light.

gasometar *m* gas meter.

gasovit *a* gaseous, gassy.

gastronomski *a* gastronomic.

gatara *f* fortune-teller.

gavran *m* raven.

gaza *f* gauze.

gazda *m* boss, master; landlord.

gazdarica *f* mistress, housewife.

gazdinstvo *n* economy, farm.

gazela *f* gazelle (*zool*).

gaziti *v* to walk, to step, to wade.

gde *adv* where, whereabout(s).

gegati se *v* to waddle, to sway.

gejzir *m* geyser.

gel *m* gel.

gen *m* gene.

generalni *a* general; ~ direktor *m* managing director; ~a popravka *f* general overhaul.

genetički inženjering *m* genetic engineering.

genetika *f* genetics.

genijalan *a* ingenious, imaginative, brilliant; ~ potez *m* coup.

genijalnost *f* ingenuity.

genije *m* genius, brain.

genitiv *m* genitive (*gram*).

geograf *m* geographer.

geografija *f* geography.

geografski *a* geographical; ~a širina *f* latitude.

geolog *m* geologist.

geologija *f* geology.

geološki *a* geological.

geometrija *f* geometry.

geometrijski *a* geometric(al).

gerijatrijski *a* geriatric.

gerila *f* guerrilla.
gerilski rat *m* guerrilla warfare.
geslo *n* slogan, motto.
gest *m* gesture.
gestikulirati *v* to gesticulate.
geto *m* ghetto.
gibak *a* lithe, supple, elastic, pliant, limber.
gibati *v* to swing, to sway, to rock; ~ **se** to move.
giht *m* gout.
giljotina *f* guillotine.
gimnastičar *m* gymnast.
gimnastički *a* gymnastic.
gimnazija *f* gym(nasium), secondary school, high school (*amer*).
ginekolog *m* gynaecologist.
ginuti *v* to perish, to be killed, to die, to pass away.
gipko *a* nimbly.
gipkost *f* suppleness, flexibility.
gips *m* gypsum; plaster cast (*med*).
gitara *f* guitar.
glačati *v* to polish, to shine; to iron.
glad *f* famine; hunger; desire, longing (*fig*).
gladak *a* smooth, level, sleek.
gladan *a* hungry, starved, famished.
gladijator *m* gladiator.
gladovanje *n* starvation.
glagol *m* verb.
glagolski *a* verbal; ~**o vreme** *n* tense; ~ **pridev** *m* participle.
glas *m* voice; part, voice (*mus*); vote (*polit*).
glasački *a* electoral; ~ **listić** *m* ballot paper; ~**o mesto** *n* polling place; ~**o telo** *n* electorate.
glasan *a* loud, noisy.
glasanje *n* voting.
glasina *f* hearsay, rumour.
glasnik *m* herald, messenger.
glasno *adv* aloud, loudly.
glasnogovornik *m* loudspeaker.
glasovni *a* vocal; phonetic (*ling*).
glatko *adv* smoothly.
glava *f* head; chapter; figurehead; **usijana** ~ hot head; **pametna** ~ a keen mind; **izgubiti** ~ *v* to perish.
glavni *a* main, chief, principal, major, cardinal, leading, capital; ~ **kuvar** *m*

chef; ~ **naslov** headline; ~ **zgoditak** jackpot; ~**a ličnost** *f* protagonist; ~**a linija voza** main line; ~**a ulica** main street; ~**a knjiga** ledger; ~**o sidro** *n* sheet anchor.
glavnokomandujući *a* commander-in-chief.
glavobolja *f* headache; trouble, concern (*fig*).
gle *interj* see! look!.
glečer *m* glacier.
gledalac *m* spectator, bystander, onlooker.
gledalište *n* public, audience, spectators.
gledati *v* to look, to see, to watch; ~ **kroz prste** to be indulgent; ~ **svoja posla** to mind one's own business; ~ **u karte** to tell fortunes.
gledište *n* aspect, viewpoint.
gležanj *m* ankle.
glib *f* mire, mud.
glicerin *m* glycerine.
glina *f* clay.
glista *f* worm.
globa *f* penalty, fine.
globalan *a* global, total, entire; ~**lno zagrevanje** *n* global warming.
globalizacija *f* globalization.
glodar *m* rodent.
glog *m* hawthorn.
glomazan *a* big, large, bulky.
gluma *f* acting.
glumac *m* actor.
glumica *f* actress.
glup *a* brainless, dull, silly, stupid, witless.
glupan *m* blockhead, fool.
glupost *f* stupidity, nonsense, silliness, fudge.
gluv *a* deaf.
gluvoća *f* deafness.
gluvonemi *m* deaf and dumb, deaf-mute.
gljiva *f* fungus.
gmizati *v* to crawl, to creep.
gnev *m* anger, wrath, fury, rage.
gnezdo *n* nest.
gnojiti se *v* to fester, to ulcerate.
gnojivo *n* manure, fertilizer.
gnusan *a* abhorrent, nauseous, loathesome, disgusting.
gnušanje *n* loathing.

gnušati se *v* to abhor.
gnjavator *m* bore, pest.
gnjaviti *v* to press, to crush; to annoy, to bother (dosađivati); to delay (odugovlačiti).
gnječiti *v* to press, to squeeze.
gnjida *f* nit.
gnjurac *m* diver.
go *a* naked, nude, bare; **~lo stenje** *n* barren rocks; **~la istina** *f* the bare truth.
godina *f* year; **godine između 13 i 19** teens.
godišnja renta *f* annuity.
godišnjak *m* almanac, yearbook.
godišnje, godišnji *a* annual, yearly; **~ doba** *n* season; **jednom ~** per annum.
godišnjica *f* anniversary.
goditi *v* to please.
gojaznost *f* obesity.
gojiti se *v* to gain weight, to get fat.
golem *a* huge, vast, enormous, monstrous.
golenica *f* shinbone, shank.
golf *m* golf.
golicati *v* to tickle.
golicljiv *a* ticklish.
golišav *a* naked, scantily dressed.
golman *m* goalkeeper.
golobrad *a* beardless; young.
gologlav *a* bareheaded, hatless.
goloruk *a* unarmed.
golotinja *f* bareness, nudity.
golub *m* pigeon, dove; **~ pismonoša** carrier pigeon; **~ mira** dove of peace.
golubarnik *m* dovecot(e).
golubica *f* dove.
golja *m* scantily dressed person; poor person.
gomila *f* pile, heap, agglomeration, accumulation, mass; crowd, pack; **~ ljudi** mob, crowd.
gondolijer *m* gondolier.
gong *m* gong.
gonič *m* driver; **~ stoke** cattle driver; **~ divljači** beater.
goniti *v* to chase, to pursue, to follow, to hound.
gonjenje *n* persecution, pursuit.
gora *f* mount, mountain.
gorak *a* bitter, acrid.
gorčina *f* bitterness.
gord *a* dignified, proud.

gore *adv* up, upstairs, above, upward.
gorenje *n* combustion.
goreti *v* to burn, to be on fire.
gori *a* worse.
gorila *m* gorilla.
gorivo *n* fuel.
gornji *a* upper, top.
gorostas *m* giant, colossus.
gorušica *f* heartburn; mustard (*bot*).
gospodar *m* master.
gospodariti *v* to manage, to domineer, to govern, to overrule, to prevail.
gospodin *m* gentleman; sir; Mister, Mr.
gospodski stalež *m* gentry.
gospođa *f* madam, lady, mistress; Mrs.
gospođica *f* Miss.
gost *m* guest, visitor, caller.
gostinska soba *f* guest room.
gostionica *f* inn, tavern, restaurant.
gostiti *v* to entertain, to treat.
gostoljubiv *a* hospitable.
gostoljubivo *adv* hospitably.
gostoprimstvo *n* hospitality.
gotov *a* done, finished, over, completed; **~ novac** *m* cash.
gotovo *adv* hardly, almost.
gotski *a* gothic.
goveđi *f* beef.
goveđi *a* beef; **~a supa** *f* beef broth; **~e pečenje** *n* roast beef.
govno *n* shit, muck, excrement.
govor *m* speech, talk, address, discourse.
govoriti *v* to speak, to converse, to talk, to chat; **~ nepovezano** to splutter, to sputter; **~ o moralu** to moralize.
govorljiv *a* loquatious, talkative, garrulous, glib, voluble.
govorni *a* spoken; **~ jezik** *m* spoken language; **~o znanje jezika** *n* spoken knowledge of language.
govornica *f* platform, tribune.
govornik *m* orator, speaker.
gozba *f* feast, banquet.
grabežljiv *a* rapacious, greedy, grasping.
grabežljivost *f* rapacity, rapaciousness.
grabiti *v* to seize, to grab.
grabljiv *a* grasping.
grabljivac *m* greedy person; predator (životinja); **ptica ~vica** *f* bird of prey.
grabulje *fpl* rake.
grad *m* city, town.

gradilište *n* building site.
graditelj *m* builder.
graditi *v* to build, to construct.
gradnja *f* construction.
gradonačelnica *f* mayoress.
gradonačelnik *m* mayor.
gradski *a* municipal, urban; ~ **beležnik** *m* town clerk; ~**a većnica** *f* town hall; ~**a četvrt** (town) ward; ~ **bedemi** *mpl* city ramparts.
građanin *m* citizen.
građanski *a* civic, civil; ~**o pravo** *n* civil law; ~ **rat** *m* civil war.
građenje *n* construction, building, raising.
građevinski inženjer *m* civil engineer.
grafički *a* graphic(al).
grafika *f* graphics.
grafikon *m* graph.
grafiti *mpl* graffiti.
graja *f* noise, clamour.
graktati *v* to croak, to crow.
gram *m* gram.
gramatički *a* grammatical.
gramatika *f* grammar.
gramziv *a* greedy, avaricious.
grana *f* bough, branch.
granata *f* grenade, shell.
granati se *v* to branch out, to ramify.
grančica *f* sprig, twig.
granica *f* border, boundary, frontier; limit; **prelaz preko ~e** *m* border crossing.
graničar *m* frontier gard.
graničiti *v* to limit.
graničiti se *v* to border.
granit *m* granite.
granuti *v* to come up, to rise.
grao *a* grey.
grašak *m* pea.
graviranje *n* etching.
gravitacija *f* gravitation.
gravura *f* engraving.
grb *m* coat of arms.
grba *f* hump, hunchback.
grcati *v* to sob, to cry.
grč *m* convulsion, cramp, spasm.
grčevit *a* convulsive, spasmodic.
grčiti *v* to clench, to contract, to twist.
grdan *a* huge, immense; ugly, hideous.
grditi *v* to reprimand, to scold, to upbraid.
grdnja *f* rebuke, reproach, reprimand.
grdosija *f* monster, giant.

greben *m* ridge, reef, chiff; mountain range, crest; **koralni ~** coral reef.
greda *f* beam, rafter.
greh *m* sin, transgression.
grejač *m* heater.
grejanje *n* heating.
grejati *v* to warm, to heat.
grejati se *v* to warm oneself, to bask.
grejpfrut *m* grapefruit.
grepsti *v* to scrape, to scratch.
grešan *a* sinful.
grešiti *v* to err, to make a mistake, to be wrong.
greška *f* error, mistake, fault, lapse.
grešnik *m* sinner.
grgeč *m* perch (*zool*).
grgurav *a* curly (of hair).
grickati *v* to bite, to nibble.
grimasa *f* grimace.
grimizan *a* purple.
grip *m* influenza.
gristi *v* to bite, to chew, to gnaw.
griva *f* mane.
grivna *f* bangle.
Grk *m* Greek.
grleni zvuk *a* guttural.
grlica *f* turtledove (*zool*).
grlić *m* neck (of a bottle); muzzle (of a firearm); ~ **materice** cervix.
grliti se *v* to embrace, to hug, to clasp.
grlo *n* throat; pharynx.
grmeti *v* to thunder.
grmljavina *f* rumble of thunder.
grm *m* bush, shrub.
grmovit *a* bushy.
grnčarija *fpl* earthenware, pottery; crockery.
grob *m* grave, tomb, sepulchre.
grobar *m* grave digger.
groblje *n* burial place, cemetery, graveyard.
grobnica *f* crypt, tomb.
grof *m* count, earl.
grofica *f* countess.
grofovija *f* county.
grohot *m* loud laughter.
groktati *v* to grunt.
grom *m* thunder, thunderbolt.
gromobran *m* lightning rod, lightning conductor.
gromoglasan *a* noisy, loud.

gromovnik *m* thunderer.
gromuljica *f* lump.
groteskan *a* grotesque.
grotlo *n* crater, opening.
grozan *a* atrocious, awful, dreadful, terrible, gruesome, horrendous.
grozd *m* bunch, cluster.
groznica *f* fever, shiver.
grozničav *a* feverish, hectic.
grozota *f* enormity, atrocity.
grožđe *n* grape.
grub *a* boorish, rude, impolite, coarse, crude, indelicate; ~ **glas** *m* a rough voice; ~ **štof** coarse fabric; ~**a skica** *f* a rough sketch; ~**a ocena** an approximate estimate; ~**o platno** *n* coarse linen.
grubijan *m* boor, barbarian.
grubost *f* crudeness, rudeness, roughness.
gruda *f* land, soil, country; lump.
grudi *fpl* bosom, chest, breast, bust.
grudnjača *f* breastbone.
grudnjak *m* brassiere.
grudobran *m* battlement, rampart.
grudva *f* clod; ~ **snega** snowball.
grudvica *f* blob.
grumen *m* clod, lump.
grupa *f* group, faction, clump.
gruvati *v* to roar.
guba *f* leprosy.
gubavac *m* leper.
gubitak *m* loss, wastage.
gubiti *v* to lose, to misplace; ~ **boju** to discolour, to tarnish; ~ **perje** to moult.
gubitnik *m* loser; underdog.
gucnuti *v* to drink, to sip.
gudura *f* ravine, gorge.
gugutati *v* to coo.

guja *f* adder.
guma *f* rubber; tire (*amer*), tyre (*br*).
gumica za brisanje *f* eraser.
gumno *n* threshing floor.
gunđati *v* to grumble, to mumble.
gurati *v* to push, to hustle, to jab, to jostle, to poke.
gurkati *v* to nudge.
gurman *m* gourmand, gourmet.
gurnuti *v* to shove.
gusan *m* gander.
gusar *m* pirate.
gusenica *f* caterpillar.
guska *f* goose.
guščija koža *f* goose bumps, goose flesh.
gust *a* dense, thick.
gustina *f* density.
guša *f* throat; goiter (*med*).
gušenje *n* choking, strangulation, suffocation, suppression.
gušiti se *v* to suffocate.
gušobolja *f* sore throat, angina.
gušter *m* lizard.
gutanje *n* gulping.
gutati *v* to swallow, to gulp.
gutljaj *m* gulp, drink, dram, sip.
guvernanta *f* governess.
guverner *m* governor.
guz *m* buttock.
guzica *f* arse.
gužva *f* throng, crowd, jam.
gužvati *v* to crumple, to crease.
gvozden *a* iron; ~**a ograda** *f* an iron fence; ~**o doba** *n* the iron age.
gvožđe *n* iron.
gvožđurija *f* hardware.

H

habanje *n* wearing off.
habati *v* to wear out.
hadžija *m* pilgrim.
hadžiluk *m* pilgrimage.
hajati *v* to care, to mind.
hajde *interj* come on.
hajduk *m* brigand, highwayman.
hajka *f* chase.
halapljiv, halav *a* voracious.
haljina *f* dress, gown.
hamburger *m* hamburger.
haos *m* chaos, disorder, confusion.
haotičan *a* chaotic, messy, disordered.
hapsiti *v* to arrest, to seize, to take into custody.
hapšenje *n* arrest, imprisonment.
harač *m* tax.
harčiti *v* to spend, to consume.
harfa *f* harp.
harfista *m* harpist.
haringa *f* herring.
harlekin *m* harlequin.
harmoničan *a* harmonious.
harmonika *f* accordion, mouth organ.
harpun *m* harpoon.
hartija *f* paper; **~ za pisma** writing-paper, note-paper; **~ za crtanje** drawing paper.
hauba *f* hood.
havarija *f* damage.
hazard *m* peril, risk, danger.
hazardni *a* hazardous, risky; gambling; **~e igre** *fpl* games of chance.
hej *interj* hey, hello.
heklati *v* to crochet.
heljda *f* buckwheat (*bot*).
helikopter *m* helicopter.
hemičar *m* chemist.
hemija *f* chemistry.
hemijski *a* chemical; **~o čišćenje** *n* dry-cleaning; **~a olovka** *f* ballpoint (pen); **~o.**
 oružje *n* chemical agents.
hemisfera *f* hemisphere.
hemoroidi *mpl* haemorrhoids (*med*).
hemoterapija *f* chemotherapy.
hendikep *m* handicap.

hendikepiran *a* handicapped.
hepatitis *m* hepatitis (*med*).
heraldika *f* heraldry.
hermelin *m* ermine (*zool*).
hermetičan *a* airtight, hermetic, pressurized.
heroj *m* hero.
herojski *a* epic, heoric.
heruvim *m* cherub.
heteroseksualan *a* heterosexual.
hidrant *m* hydrant.
hidrauličan *a* hydraulic.
hidroavion *m* seaplane, hydroplane.
hidroelektričan *a* hydroelectric.
hidrokrilac *m* hydrofoil.
hi-fi *m* hi-fi.
higijena *f* hygiene.
higijenski *a* hygienic; **~ uložak** *m* sanitary towel.
hijena *f* hyena.
hijerarhija *f* hierarchy.
hijeroglif *m* hieroglyph.
hijeroglifski *a* hieroglyphic; **~o pismo** *m* hieroglyphic writing.
hiljada *num* thousand.
hiljaditi *num a* thousandth.
himna *f* anthem, hymn.
hiperbola *f* hyperbole.
hipermarket *m* hypermarket.
hipnotisati *v* to hypnotise; to mesmerize.
hipohondričan *a* hypochondriac.
hipohondrija *f* hypochondria.
hipoteka *f* mortgage.
hipotetičan *a* hypothetical.
hir *m* fantasy, caprice, whim.
hiromantija *f* palmistry.
hirurg *m* surgeon, operator.
hirurgija *f* surgery.
hirurški *a* surgical; **~ nož** *m* lancet; **~a sala** *f* operating room.
histeričan *a* hysterical.
histerija *f* hysterics.
hitac *m* missile; shot, gunshot.
hitan *a* hasty, instant, urgent, pressing; **~ sastanak** *m* emergency meeting.
hitnost *f* urgency.
hitrina *f* quickness, velocity, speediness.

hlad *m* shade, umbrage.
hladan *a* chilly, cold, cool, frigid.
hladnoća *f* coldness, chilliness.
hladnokrvan *a* cold-blooded, imperturbable.
hladnokrvno *adv* calmly.
hladnokrvnost *f* placidity, coolness.
hladovina *f* shade; coolness.
hlapeti *v* to evaporate.
hleb *m* bread, loaf.
hlor *m* chlorine (*chem*).
hloroform *m* chloroform.
hmelj *m* hop.
hobi *m* hobby.
hobotnica *f* octopus (*zool*).
hod *m* gait, walk, amble.
hodati *v* to walk, to go on foot.
hodnik *m* corridor, passage.
hodočasnik *m* pilgrim.
hodočašće *n* pilgrimage.
hokej *m* hockey; ~ **na ledu** *m* ice hockey; ~ **na travi** field hockey.
hoklica *f* stool.
homeopata *m* homeopathist.
homeopatija *f* homeopathy.
homogen *a* homogeneous.
homoseksualan *a* homosexual.
honorar *m* fee.
honoraran *a* part-time; **raditi ~no** *v* to work part-time.
hor *m* choir, chorus.
horda *f* horde.
hormon *m* hormone.
horoskop *m* horoscope.
horski pevač *m* chorist, chorister.
hotel *m* hotel.
hrabar *a* brave, courageous, adventurous, bold, audacious, plucky.
hrabrost *f* courage, boldness, bravery, daring, audacity, valour, fortitude; **izgubiti ~** *v* to lose heart.
hram *m* temple; church.
hramati *v* to limp, to walk lame.
hrana *f* food, nourishment.
hranilac porodice *m* breadwinner.
hraniti *v* to feed, to nourish.
hranljiv *a* nourishing, nutritious.
hrapav *a* rough, rugged; ~ **glas** *m* hoarse voice.

hrapavost *f* roughness, coarseness.
hrast *m* oak.
hrčak *m* hamster.
hren *m* horseradish.
hrenovka *f* hot-dog.
hrid *m* cliff.
hripanje *n* wheezing.
Hrist *m* Christ.
hrišćanski *a* Christian.
hrišćanstvo *n* Christendom.
hrkati *v* to snore.
hrkanje *n* snoring.
hrliti *v* to rush, to hurry.
hrom[1] *m* chrome, chromium.
hrom[2] *a* lame, limping.
hroničan *a* chronic.
hronika *f* chronicle.
hronologija *f* chronology.
hronološki *a* chronological.
hronometar *m* chronometer.
hropac *m* death-rattle.
hrpa *f* heap, pile, accumulation.
hrskav *a* crunchy, crisp.
hrskavica *f* cartilage, gristle.
hrt *m* greyhound.
hrupiti *v* to burst into.
hrvač *m* wrestler.
htenje *n* will, volition.
hteti *v* to want, to wish, to desire.
huligan *m* punk.
huliti *v* to blaspheme.
hulja *f* scoundrel, rogue, rascal.
humanista *m* humanist.
humka *f* hillock.
humor *m* humour.
hunta *f* junta.
huškanje *n* harangue, instigation.
hvala *f* thankfulness, gratitude, gratefulness; praise.
hvalisati se *v* to boast, to brag.
hvalisav *a* boastful, vaunting.
hvalisavac *m* braggart, boaster.
hvaliti *v* to commend, to praise.
hvalospev *m* eulogy.
hvaljenje *n* praising.
hvat (=1.82m) *m* fathom.
hvatanje *n* catching, seizure, capture.
hvatati *v* to grasp, to snatch, to catch.

I

i *conj* and, too, also.
iako *adv* although, even if, even though.
ići *v* to go, to move, to walk; ~ **lagano** to amble; ~ **postrance** to sidle; ~ **do kraja** to go through.
idealan *a* perfect, ideal.
idealista *m* idealist.
ideja *f* idea, notion, thought.
identifikacija *f* identification.
identifikovati *v* to identify.
identitet *m* identity.
ideologija *f* ideology.
idiličan *a* idyllic.
idiom *m* idiom.
idiomatski *a* idiomatic.
idiot *m* idiot.
idiotski *a* idiotic.
idol *m* idol.
idolopoklonstvo *n* idolatry.
igda *adv* never, ever.
igde *adv* anywhere.
igla *f* needle; **šivaća** ~ sewing needle; **štrikaća** ~ knitting needle; ~ **za kosu** hairpin.
iglo *m* igloo.
ignorisati *v* to disregard, to ignore.
igra *f* game, play; ~ **dame** *f* draughts; ~ **karata** *f* card game.
igrač *m* player; dancer; ~ **golfa** *m* golfer.
igračka *f* toy, plaything.
igralište *n* playground; sportsfield; ~ **za golf** *n* golf course.
igrani film *m* feature film.
igrati *v* to dance; to play.
ikad *adv* ever, at some time or other; **bolje** ~ **nego nikad** better late than never.
iko *pn* anybody.
ikonografija *f* iconography.
ikra *f* spawn, roe.
ili *conj* or; ~... ~ either... or.
ilovača *f* clay.
ilustrativan *a* illustrative.
ilustrovati *v* to illustrate; to elucidate.
iluzija *f* illusion.
iluzoran *a* ilusory.
imalac *m* proprietor, owner.

imanje *n* estate, property, holding.
imati *v* to have, to own, to possess; ~ **za posledicu** to entail; ~ **zatvor** to be constipated.
ime *n* name, first name.
imela *f* mistletoe.
imenica *f* noun, substantive (*gram*).
imenilac *m* denominator.
imenovanje *n* appointment, nomination.
imenjak *m* namesake.
imetak *m* property; fortune.
imigracija *f* immigration.
imigrant *m* immigrant.
imitacija *f* imitation.
imovina *f* possession, property, belongings; **lična** ~ private property; **nepokretna** ~ real estate.
imitirati *v* to imitate, to copy.
imperativan *a* imperative, urgent.
imperator *m* emperor.
imperatorka *f* empress.
imperija *f* empire.
imperijalizam *m* imperialism.
implikacija *f* implication.
imponovati *v* to impress.
impozantan *a* imposing, impressive.
impregnirati *v* to impregnate, to imbue.
impresija *f* sensation, impression.
improvizovan *a* improvised, extempore or impromptu.
improvizovati *v* to improvise, to extemporise, ad lib.
impuls *m* impulse, impetus.
impulsivan *a* impulsive.
imućan *a* opulent, rich, well-off, well-to-do.
imun *a* immune.
inače *adv* else, otherwise.
inat *m* spite, obstinacy.
inauguracija *f* inauguration.
inauguralan *a* inaugural.
incident *m* event, incident.
inč *m* inch.
inčun *m* anchovy.
indigo *m* carbon paper, indigo.
indikacija *f* indication, symptom.
indikativan *a* indicative.

indiskrecija *f* indiscretion.
individualan *a* individual, separate.
individualnost *f* individuality, personality.
indosirati *v* to endorse.
indukcija *f* induction.
industrija *f* industry, production.
industrijalac *m* industrialist.
industrijalizacija *f* industrialization.
industrijski *a* industrial, manufacturing;
~ **poligon** *m* industrial park.
inercija *f* inertia.
infekcija *f* infection.
infektivan *a* infectious; contagious.
inferiornost *f* inferiority.
inficirati *v* to infect, to taint.
infinitiv *m* infinitive (*gram*).
inflacija *f* inflation.
informacija *f* information, intelligence.
informisati *v* to inform, to acquaint with.
infracrven *a* infra-red.
infrastruktura *f* infrastructure.
infuzija *f* infusion.
inhibicija *f* inhibition.
inhibiran *a* inhibited.
inicijalno *a* initially.
inicijativa *f* initiative; **dati ~u** *v* to
propose.
inkarnacija *f* incarnation.
inkompatibilnost *f* incompatibility.
inkontinencija *f* incontinence (*med*).
inkontinentan *a* incontinent.
inkubator *m* incubator.
inkvizicija *f* inquisition.
inscenacija *f* scenery, staging, pageant;
concoction.
inscenirati *v* to stage; ~ **književno delo**
to dramatize.
insekt *m* insect.
insekticid *m* insecticide.
insinuacija *f* insinuation.
insistirati *v* to insist, to urge.
insolventan *a* insolvent.
inspekcija *f* inspection; **tržišna** ~ market
(sanitary) inspection; **devizna** ~ foreign
exchange inspection.
inspektor *m* inspector.
instalacija *f* installation.
instinkt *m* instinct, flair.
institucija *f* institution, organized society.
instruktor *m* instructor.
instrument *m* instrument.

instrumentalan *a* instrumental.
insulin *m* insulin.
integracija *f* integration.
integrisati *v* to integrate, to merge.
intelektualan *a* intellectual.
inteligencija *f* intelligence, intelligentsia.
inteligentan *a* intelligent.
intendant *m* intendant, quartermaster.
intenzitet *m* intensity.
intenzivan *a* intensive.
interakcija *f* interaction.
interesantan *a* interesting.
interfejs *m* interface.
interfon *m* intercom.
internat *m* boarding school.
internet igraonica *m* internet cafe.
interpunkcija *f* punctuation.
interval *m* interval.
intervencija *f* intervention.
intervju *m* interview.
intimnost *f* intimacy.
intoksikacija *f* intoxication.
intonacija *f* intonation.
intravenski *a* intravenous (*med*).
intriga *f* intrigue, plot.
intrigantan *a* intriguing.
introspekcija *f* introspection.
introvertna osoba *f* introvert.
intuicija *f* intuition.
intuitivan *a* intuitive.
invalid *m* invalid; **ratni** ~ war invalid,
disabled veteran; **doživotni** ~
permanently disabled.
invalida *f* disability pension.
invalidska kolica *f* wheelchair.
invazija *f* invasion.
inventar *m* inventory, list of goods.
investicija *f* investment, investing.
investirati *v* to invest.
inženjer *m* engineer.
inženjering *m* engineering.
inje *n* hoarfrost.
injekcija *f* injection, shot (*slang*).
iole *adv* if at all.
ionako *adv* already, anyway, anyhow.
ipak *adv* yet, however.
irelevantan *a* irrelevant.
irigacija *f* irrigation, watering.
iritirati *v* to irritate.
ironičan *a* ironic(al), mocking.
ironija *f* irony, mockery.

irvas *m* reindeer.
iscediti *v* to squeeze out.
isceliti *v* to heal, to cure, to remedy.
iscepan *a* ragged, tattered, torn.
iscrpan *a* exhaustive, detailed.
iscrpljen *a* worn out, exhausted; depleted.
iscrpljenost *f* exhaustion.
iscuriti *v* to leak out.
isečak *m* cutting, section; **~ci iz novina** *mpl* clippings.
iseći *v* to cut, to cut out, to cut off; to curve.
iseliti *v* to dislodge, to turn out, to evict.
iseliti se *v* to change residence, to move.
iseljavanje *n* removal, displacement; **prinudno ~** eviction.
iseljenik *m* emigrant.
ishaban *a* worn.
ishod *m* consequence, outcome, effect, result.
ishrana *f* food, nourishment.
ishraniti *v* to nourish, to supply with food.
iskaljati *v* to foul, to dirty, to soil.
iskašljati *v* to cough out.
iskaz *m* statement, evidence.
iskićen *a* adorned, decorated.
iskidati *v* to tear apart; to blow down.
iskidati se *v* to break, to dispart.
iskipeti *v* to boil over.
iskisnuti *v* to get soaked.
iskliznuti *v* to slip out.
isključenje *n* elimination, expulsion, excommunication.
isključiti *v* to eliminate, to exclude, to expel; to cut off, to unplug.
iskobeljati se *v* to extricate oneself.
iskop *m* excavation.
iskopati *v* to dig out, to unearth; to exhume.
iskopavanje *n* excavation.
iskopavati *v* to excavate.
iskopčati *v* to disconnect; to switch off (struju).
iskoreniti *v* to uproot, to exterminate, to eradicate.
iskorenjivanje *n* eradication.
iskoristiti *v* to utilize, to make use of.
iskorišćavanje *n* exploitation.
iskovati *v* to forge, to coin.
iskra *f* sparkle, spark.

iskrasti se *v* to steal away.
iskrcati *v* to unload, to discharge.
iskrcavanje *n* disembarkation.
iskrcavati se *v* to disembark; to land.
iskrčiti *v* to clear.
iskren *a* open, sincere, straightforward; heartfelt.
iskreno *adv* sincerely, heartily.
iskrenost *f* frankness, sincerity, candour.
iskričav *a* sparkling, effervescent.
iskriviti *v* to bend, to curve, to contort.
iskrivljen *a* distorted.
iskrojiti *v* to cut out.
iskrpiti *v* to repair, to mend, to patch.
iskrvariti *v* to bleed.
iskup *m* redemption; ransom.
iskusan *a* experienced, skillful, competent; **~ lekar ili advokat** *m* practitioner.
iskustvo *n* experience.
iskušenje *n* temptation, lure.
islabiti *v* to weaken, to debilitate.
islam *m* Islam.
islamski *a* Islamic.
islednik *m* examining magistrate; coroner.
isleđenje *n* inquiry, investigation.
ismejati *v* to laugh at, to deride, to ridicule.
ismejavanje, ismevanje *n* derision, mockery, ridicule.
ispadati, ispasti *v* to fall; to turn out.
isparavanje *n* evaporation.
isparenja *fpl* fumes.
ispariti *v* to evaporate.
isparljiv *a* volatile.
ispaša *f* pasture, pasturage.
ispaštanje *n* atonement, expiation.
ispeći *v* to bake.
ispeglati *v* to iron.
ispevati *v* to compose; to sing.
ispičutura *f* hard drinker, soaker.
ispijen *a* haggard.
ispirati *v* to wash out, to rinse; to gargle.
ispit *m* examination, test.
ispitivač *m* examiner, questioner.
ispitivanje *n* examining; interrogation; probation; **~ krvi** *n* blood test; **~ tržišta** market research.
ispitivati *v* to investigate; to examine; to enquire/inquire.
isplatiti *v* to pay out, to pay down.
isplatiti se *v* to be worthwhile, to pay.

isplesti *v* to knit.
isplivati *v* to swim out; to get out of, to manage; ~ **iz dugova** to get out of debt.
ispljunuti *v* to spit out.
ispod *prep* under, beneath, underneath.
ispoljiti *v* to manifest, to show, to exhibit.
isporuka *f* consignment, delivery.
ispostaviti *v* to make out.
ispovedati se *v* to confess.
ispovednik *m* confessor.
ispraćaj *m* farewell, leave-taking.
isprati *v* to rinse, to wash away; ~ **nekome mozak** to brainwash.
ispratiti *v* to accompany, to follow.
isprava *f* document, pass, passport; ~ **o pravu vlasništva** title deed.
ispravan *a* correct, proper, serviceable.
ispraviti *v* to rectify, to revise; to straighten.
ispraviti se *v* to sit up; to correct oneself.
ispravljanje *n* rectification, correction.
isprazniti *v* to evacuate, to vacate, to empty.
ispred *prep* before, in front of, ahead of.
ispregnuti *v* to unharness.
isprekidan *a* broken, intermittent, interrupted.
ispremeštati *v* to remove to other places.
ispreturati *v* to disarrange, to throw into disorder.
ispričati *v* to narrate, to tell, to describe, to recount.
isprljati *v* to foul, to dirty, to soil.
isprljati se *v* to become dirty.
isprobati *v* to try out.
isprositi *v* to obtain by begging; to cadge; to ask in marriage.
isprsiti se *v* to throw oneself.
isprskati *v* to splash, to dash, to bespatter.
isprskati se *v* to crack, to split.
ispružen *a* prostrate.
ispružiti se *v* to stretch out, to hold out, to extend.
isprva *adv* at first, in the beginning.
ispržiti *v* to fry, to frizzle; to roast.
ispuniti *v* to fill up, to make full; ~ **molbu** *v* to comply.
ispunjenje *n* accomplishment, realization, fulfillment.
ispupčen *a* convex.
ispupčenost *f* convexity.

ispust *m* outlet, loophole.
ispustiti *v* to release, to let go, to let down.
ispuštati *v* to emit; to let down.
istaći, istaknuti *v* to bring out, to put forward; to underline, to emphasize; to hoist, to raise.
istaknut *a* prominent, eminent, distinguishing.
isterati *v* to drive out, to thrust out; to exorcise.
istezanje *n* tension, stretching, straining.
isti *a* same, identical.
isticanje *n* leak, leakage.
isticati *v* to flow out.
isticati se *v* to be prominent; to distinguish oneself (*fig*).
istina *f* truth, fact, reality.
istinit *a* factual, true.
istinitost *f* truthfulness, right.
istinoljubiv *a* truthful.
istisnuti *v* to oust, to squeeze out.
isto *adv* the same.
istočni *a* eastern, easterly.
istočno *adv* eastward(s), to the east.
istočnjački *a* oriental.
istok *m* east.
istopiti *v* to melt, to dissolve.
istoričar *m* historian.
istorija *f* history.
istorijski *a* historic(al).
istovariti *v* discharge, to unload, to disburden.
istovetan *a* equal, identical.
istovetnost *f* sameness, identity.
istovremen *a* simultaneous.
istraga *f* investigation, enquiry, inquiry, inquisition.
istrajan *a* constant, steady, persevering.
istrajati *v* to persevere, to persist.
istrajnost *f* perseverance, persistence.
istraživač *m* investigator, explorer; prospector.
istraživanje *n* investigation; exploration (terena); research.
istraživati *v* to investigate; ~ **teren** to explore.
istrebiti *v* to exterminate, to extirpate.
istrebljenje *n* extermination.
istrebljivač *m* exterminator.
istrgnuti *v* to pull out.

istrošen *a* worn out, spent.
istrošiti (se) *v* to wear out.
istup, istupanje *m* appearance; withdrawal.
istupiti *v* to appear; to perform.
isukati *v* to draw, to unsheathe; ~ **mač** to unsheathe a sword.
Isus *m* Jesus.
isušivanje *n* drainage.
isušivati *v* to drain.
išarati *v* to ornament, to decorate.
iščašenje *n* dislocation.
iščašiti *v* to dislocate, to wrench.
iščekivanje *n* expectance, expectancy.
iščeznuti *v* to disappear.
išijas *m* sciatica (*med*).
iverak *m* flounder, plaice (*zool*).
ivica *f* edge, border.
ivičnjak *m* kerb.
iz *prep* from.
iza *prep* after, following; behind.
izabrati *v* to choose, to select.
izaći *v* to go out, to come out, to step out.
izaslanik *m* deputy, envoy, messenger, emissary.
izaslanstvo *n* deputation, delegation.
izazivač *m* challenger, provoker.
izazivački *a* evocative, provocative, irritating.
izazivajući *a* defiant.
izazivanje *n* defiance, provocation.
izazivati *v* to defy, to challenge.
izazov *m* challenge.
izazvati *v* to instigate, to cause.
izbaciti *v* to eliminate, to throw out, to eject.
izbacivanje *n* ejection.
izbaviti *v* to save, to rescue, to liberate.
izbegavanje *n* evasion.
izbegavati *v* to avoid, to escape, to evade, to elude.
izbeglica *f* refugee, fugitive, runaway.
izbezumiti se *v* to go mad.
izbezumljen *a* distraught.
izbirljiv *a* fastidious.
izbiti *v* to beat.
izbledeo *a* bleached, blanched, faded.
izbliza *adv* from nearby.
izbočen *a* convex, rounding.
izbočina *f* protuberance, bulge.
izbočiti se *v* to stick out.

izbor *m* choice, option.
izbori *mpl* elections.
izborni *a* elective, electoral.
izbosti *v* to prick out, to stab, to pierce.
izbrbljati *v* to blurt out, to blab.
izbrisati *v* to efface, to wipe out, to erase.
izbrojati *v* to count, to reckon.
izbušiti *v* to bore, to drill, to perforate.
izdah *m* exhalation, expiration.
izdaja *f* betrayal, treason, treachery.
izdajnički *a* treacherous, betraying.
izdajnik *m* traitor.
izdaleka *adv* from afar, from far away.
izdanak *m* offshoot, sprout.
izdanje *n* edition, issue, publication.
izdašan *a* fertile, productive, prolific; generous.
izdati *v* to betray; to lay out (novac); to issue; to serve (ručak); to publish (knjiga).
izdavač *m* publisher.
izdavački *a* publishing.
izdavanje *n* delivery, giving.
izdavati se *v* to pretend to be.
izdisanje *n* expiration, exhalation.
izdisati *v* to exhale, to expire.
izdržati *v* to bear, to support, to withstand.
izdržavanje *n* support, maintenance, sustenance; ~ **rastavljene žene** alimony.
izdržljiv *a* durable, persisting.
izdržljivost *f* endurance, stamina; durability.
izdubiti *v* to hollow out.
izduvati *v* to clean (by blowing out).
izduvati se *v* to catch one's breath.
izdužen *a* oblong.
izdužiti *v* to elongate.
izdvajanje *n* isolation.
izdvajati, izdvojiti *v* to separate, to set aside, to single out.
izdvajati se *v* to excel, to single oneself out.
izgarati *v* to be consumed; to crave.
izgaziti *v* to trample down, to stamp.
izgladnelo *adv* hungrily.
izgladneo *a* famished, starved.
izgladneti *v* to be famished, to be starving.
izgled *m* view, prospect; appearance, outlook.
izgledati *v* to seem, to appear.

izgnanik *m* outcast.
izgnanstvo *n* exile.
izgovarati *v* to pronounce.
izgovor *m* pronunciation; pretext.
izgraditi *v* to construct, to build, to erect.
izgrditi *v* to scold, to snub.
izgrednik *m* troublemaker.
izgubiti *v* to lose.
izgubljeno-nađeno *n* lost and found.
izgužvati *v* to crumple, to rumple.
izići *v* to come out, to go out.
iziskivati *v* to need, to necessitate.
izjasniti se *v* to express one's opinion.
izjašnjenje *n* explanation.
izjava *f* declaration, statement.
izjednačiti *v* to equalize, to make even; to counterbalance.
izjuriti *v* to drive out.
izlagač *m* lecturer, speaker; exhibitor.
izlagati *v* to exhibit, to expose, to expound.
izlaz *m* exit; ~ **u slučaju nužde** emergency exit; ~ **u slučaju požara** fire escape.
izlazak sunca *m* sunrise.
izlaziti *v* to come out, to go out.
izlečiti *v* to heal, to remedy.
izlečiv *a* curable.
izlepiti *v* to paste, to cover with glue.
izlet *m* excursion, picnic; outing.
izliti *v* to pour out.
izliti se *v* to overflow; to pour out.
izliv *m* drain, sink; flow; ~ **krvi u mozak** cerebral haemorrhage; ~ **besa** outpouring of furry.
izlog *m* shop window, show window.
izložba *f* exhibition; ~ **cveća** *f* flower show.
izložbeni prostor *m* showroom.
izložen *a* exposed; ~ **promaji** *a* drafty (*amer*), draughty (*br*).
izloženost *f* exposure.
izlučenje *n* secretion.
izlučiti *v* to secrete.
izmaći *v* to move away.
izmaglica *f* haze.
izmamiti *v* to entice, to wheedle.
između *prep* among(st); between.
izmeniti *v* to alter.
izmenljivo *a* changeable.
izmeriti *v* to weigh; to measure.
izmešan *a* mixed.

izmešati *v* to mix up, to intermingle.
izmet *m* excrement.
izmicati *v* to dodge, to move away.
izmirenje *n* conciliation, propitiation, reconcilement.
izmisliti *v* to devise, to invent.
izmišljati *v* to fabricate, to imagine.
izmišljen *a* fictional, fictitious, imaginative.
izmoriti *v* to tire out, to exhaust.
izmrljan *a* stained, smudged.
izmučen *a* haggard, worn out, tired.
iznad *prep* above, over.
iznajmiti *v* to hire, to lease, to rent, to let; ~ **stan** to rent an apartment.
iznajmljivanje automobila *n* car hire.
iznebuha *adv* unexpectedly, suddenly.
iznenada *adv* suddenly, all of a sudden.
iznenadan *a* sudden; ~**na sreća** *f* godsend.
iznenađenje *n* surprise.
izneti *v* to bring out, to expose, to express.
izniman *a* exceptional.
iznos *m* amount, sum, total.
iznositi *v* to take out, to bring out.
iznova *adv* anew, newly, afresh.
iznuditi, iznuđivati *v* to extort, to defraud.
iznuđivanje *n* extortion, blackmail.
iznuren *a* exhausted, emaciated.
iznutrice *fpl* entrails, intestines.
izobilje *n* abundance, exuberance.
izobličavanje *n* distortion.
izobličen *a* disfigured, distorted.
izobličiti *v* to disfigure, to distort.
izolacija *f* isolation, loneliness; **električna** ~ insulation; ~ **zvuka** soundproofing.
izolovati *v* to isolate; to insulate.
izolaciona traka *f* insulating tape.
izopačen *a* perverse, wicked, distorted.
izopačenost *f* perversity; depravity.
izopštiti *v* to excommunicate.
izostajanje *n* absence.
izostati *v* to be absent, to miss; ~ **iz škole** to be absent from school; ~ **s posla** to miss work.
izračunati *v* to calculate, to compute.
izračunljiv *a* calculable.
izrada *f* production, workmanship.
izrađen po meri *a* tailor-made.
izrasti *v* to grow up.

izraz *m* expression; ~ **lica** countenance.

izrazit *a* emphatic, pronounced; distinct, characteristic.

izraziti *v* to express, to declare.

izražajan *a* expressive.

izražavanje *n* expression, mode of speech.

izreći *v* to say; to pass (the sentence).

izreka *f* sentence, proverb, saying; byword.

izrezati *v* to carve.

izrezbariti *v* to decorate by carving.

izričan *a* assertive, determinate, explicit, categorical.

izrod *m* misfit, degenerate person.

izroditi *v* to give birth.

izroditi se *v* to degenerate.

izručenje *n* extradition, relegation; delivery.

izručiti *v* to deliver; to pour out; ~ **zločinca** to extradite.

izučen *a* trained, qualified.

izum *m* discovery, invention, contraption.

izumeti *v* to invent.

izumiranje *n* extinction.

izuzetak *m* exception.

izuzetan *a* exceptional, exclusive.

izuzev *adv* save, except.

izuzimanje *n* exclusion.

izvan *prep* outside, out of, beyond, besides; ~ **palube** *adv* outboard.

izvanredan *a* remarkable, stupendous, superb, wonderful.

izvanredno *adv* remarkably.

izvedena reč *f* derivative.

izvesno *adv* certainly.

izvesti *v* to take out, to lead; to export; to perform; to deduct; ~ **zaključak** to deduce; to execute.

izvestiti *v* to notify.

izveštač *m* informant, informer.

izveštačen *a* affected, artificial, finicky, lackadaisical.

izveštaj *m* report, information, news, message.

izvetriti *v* to air, to ventilate.

izvidnica *f* vanguard; reconnaissance.

izviđač *m* scout.

izviđati *v* to reconnoitre.

izvijati *v* to curve.

izvijen *a* crooked.

izvikan *m* ill-famed.

izvikati se *v* to shout.

izviniti *v* to forgive, to excuse, to pardon.

izviniti se *v* to make an appology, to offer an excuse, to apologize.

izvinuti *v* to twist, to sprain.

izvinjavati *v* to forgive, to pardon.

izvinjenje *n* apology, excuse, pardon, justification.

izviriti *v* to peep out.

izvlačenje *n* extraction, drawing out.

izvod *m* abstract, excerpt; ~ **iz matične knjige rođenih** birth certificate.

izvodljiv *a* feasible, possible, practicable.

izvođač *m* performer; ~ **radova** contractor.

izvođenje *n* performance, exhibition.

izvojevati *v* to win, to gain.

izvor *m* font, fountain, spring; resource, source, root, origin; ~**ska voda** *f* spring water.

izvoran *a* genuine.

izvoz *m* export, exportation.

izvoziti *v* to export.

izvoznik *m* exporter.

izvrgnuti *v* to expose to; ~ **satiri** to satirize.

izvrstan *a* exquisite, excellent.

izvršenje *n* execution.

izvršiti *v* to execute, to accomplish; ~ **zločin** to perpetuate.

izvući *v* to extricate, to take out, to pull out.

J

ja *pn* I; myself.
jablan *m* poplar (*bot*).
jabuka *f* apple; *n* apple-tree (drvo).
jabukovača *f* cider.
jačanje *n* strengthening.
jačati *v* to strenghten, to make strong.
jačina *f* strength, intensity, force.
jad *m* sadness, sorrow; misfortune; woe.
jadan *a* miserable, deplorable, pitiable; woeful, wretched.
jadnica *f* poor creature.
jadnik *m* poor thing, poor man.
jadno *adv* miserly.
jagnje *n* lamb.
jagoda *f* strawberry.
jagodica *f* cheekbone.
jagorčevina *f* primrose (*bot*).
jaguar *m* jaguar.
jahač *m* horseman, rider, equestrian.
jahačica *f* horsewoman.
jahački *a* equestrian; ~će odelo *n* riding habit; ~ća staza *f* bridle path.
jahanje *n* riding; horsemanship.
jahta *f* yacht.
jaje *n* egg.
jajnik *m* ovary.
jak *a* strong, forceful, vigorous, intense; ~ nalet vetra *m* squall; ~a svetlost *f* glare.
jakna *f* jacket.
jalov *a* barren, unfruitful.
jama *f* pit, cavity.
jamačan *a* certain.
januar *m* January.
Japanac *m* Japanese.
jara *f* heat.
jarac *m* Capricorn (*astrol*).
jarak *m* ditch, trench; ~ ispunjen vodom moat.
jaram *m* yoke; servitude (*fig*).
jarbol *m* flagpole, mast.
jard *m* yard (mera).
jarebica *f* partridge (*zool*).
jarki *a* glaring, glittering.
jaruga *f* ravine, gully.
jasan *a* clear, bright; articulated, explicit, distinct; plain, vivid.

jasen *m* ash (*bot*).
jasika *f* aspen (*bot*).
jasle *fpl* crib, manger.
jasmin *m* jasmine.
jasno *adv* clear; obviously; distinctly; ~ kao dan clear as noon day.
jasnoća *f* clearness, clarity.
jastog *m* lobster.
jastučić za igle *m* pincushion.
jastučnica *f* pillowcase.
jastuk *m* pillow, cushion, pad.
jato *n* flock, flight; ~ riba shoal.
jaukanje *n* lamentation, wailing.
java *f* reality.
javan *a* public; ~vno mišljenje *n* public opinion; ~vno nadmetanje competitive bidding; ~vno glasanje open balloting.
javašluk *m* negligence.
javiti *v* to inform of, to notify; to let know.
javiti se *v* to salute, to greet; to report.
javnost *f* publicity.
javor *m* maple.
jaz *m* gulf, gap (*fig*).
jazavac *m* badger.
jazbina *f* den, hole; burrow, lair.
jecaj *m* sob.
ječam *m* barley.
ječanje *n* echoing, reverberation; ~ od bola groaning.
jedak *a* acrimonious, bitter; angry.
jedan *num* one.
jedanaest *num* eleven.
jedanaesti *num a* eleventh.
jedanput *adv* once.
jedar *a* firm, sound.
jedini *a* only, alone, single.
jedinica *f* unit; izborna ~ *f* electoral unit.
jedinstven *a* unique.
jedinstvo *m* unity, concord.
jediti se *v* to vex, to harass, to worry.
jednačina *f* equation (*mat*).
jednako *adv* equally.
jednakost *f* equality.
jednina *f* singular.
jednobojno *adv* monochrome, of the same colour.
jednoboštvo *n* monotheism.

jednodnevan *a* lasting for one day; **~vni izlet** *m* one-day excursion.
jednoglasan *a* unanimous.
jednoglasnost *f* unanimity.
jednogodac, jednogodišnjak *m* yearling.
jednoličan *a* monotonous, uniform.
jednom *adv* once, upon a time.
jednoobraznost *f* uniformity.
jednorog *m* unicorn.
jednosložna reč *f* monosyllable.
jednostavan *a* simple, plain.
jednostavnost *f* simplicity.
jednostruk *a* single.
jedrenjak *m* sailing boat.
jedrenje *n* sailing; gliding; **~ na dasci** windsurfing.
jedrilica *f* glider.
jedriti *v* to sail.
jedro *n* sail.
jedva *adv* barely, hardly; **~ vidljivo** *adv* imperceptibly.
jeftin *a* cheap, inexpensive.
jegulja *f* eel.
jeka *f* reverberation, echoing, echo.
jela *f* fir tree (*bot*).
jelen *m* deer, stag.
jelo *n* dish, food; **~ bez hranljivih sastojaka** junk food; **omiljeno ~** favourite dish.
jelovnik *m* menu.
jemac *m* warranter, guarantor.
jemstvo *n* guarantee, warranty; security.
jendek *m* ditch.
Jenki *m* Yankee.
jer *conj* because.
jeres *f* heresy.
jeretik *m* heretic.
jesen *f* autumn, fall.
jesenji *a* autumnal.
jesetra *f* sturgeon.
jesti *v* to eat, to take food; **~ i piti halapljivo** to guzzle; **~ malim zalogajima** *v* to nibble.
jestiv *a* eatable, edible.
jetkost *f* acrimony, anger.

jetra *f* liver.
jetrva *f* sister-in-law.
jevanđelski *a* evangelic(al).
jevanđelje *n* gospel.
Jevrejin *m* Jew, Hebrew.
jevrejski *a* Jewish.
jevtin *a* inexpensive, cheap.
jeza *f* tremor, shudder.
jezero *n* lake; loch.
jezgro *n* nucleus, core.
jezgrovit *a* substantial, concise.
jezik *m* tongue; **govorni ~** language.
jeziv *a* creepy, terrible.
jezuita *m* Jesuit.
jež *m* hedgehog.
jod *m* iodine (*chem*).
joga *f* yoga.
jogunast *a* obstinate.
jogurt *m* yoghurt.
jorgan *m* eiderdown; quilt.
jorgovan *m* lilac.
još *adv* still, yet.
jova *f* alder-tree (*bot*).
jubilej *m* jubilee.
juče *adv* yesterday.
judaizam *m* Judaism.
jug *m* south.
jugoistok *m* south-east.
juli *m* July.
junački *a* heroic, brave.
junakinja *f* heroine.
junaštvo *n* heroism, courage, bravery.
june *n* young cow or bull.
juni *m* June.
junica *f* heifer.
juriš *m* attack, assault, onset.
juriti *v* to run, to race.
juta *f* jute.
jutarnji *a* morning.
jutro *n* morning.
jutro zemlje *n* acre (160 square rods).
jutros *adv* this morning.
juvelir *m* jeweller.
juvelirnica *f* jeweller's shop.
južni *a* southerly, southern.

K

k, ka *prep* to, toward.
kabanica *f* rain-coat, cloak.
kabast *a* bulky, cumbersome.
kabina *f* cabin, booth; ~ **pilota** *f* cockpit.
kabl, kabel *m* cable.
kablovska televizija *f* cable television.
kaca *f* vat, tub.
kad(a) *conj/adv* when, whenever; ~ **tad**
   sooner or later.
kada *f* bathtub.
kadar *a* able, capable, competent.
kadet *m* cadet.
kadgod *adv* sometimes, occasionally.
kaditi *v* to fumigate; to flatter (*fig*).
kafa *f* coffee; **crna** ~ black coffee; **bela** ~
   cafe au lait.
kafana *f* cafe, coffee-house.
kafena kašičica *f* teaspoon.
kaiš *m* strap, belt.
kajanje *n* regret, repentance, penitence.
kajati se *v* to feel remorse, to repent.
kajgana *f* scrambled eggs.
kajsija *f* apricot.
kakao *m* cocoa.
kakav *pn* what, in what manner.
kako *adv* how, in what manner; ~ **da ne!**
   by all means!; **bilo** ~ any how, anyway.
kakogod *adv* however.
kaktus *m* cactus.
kakvoća *f* quality.
kalaj *m* tin.
kalauz *m* pass-key, latch-key.
kaldrma *f* cobbled road.
kalem *m* coil, reel, spool; graft (*bot*).
kalemiti *v* to inoculate, to graft.
kalendar *m* calendar.
kalibar *m* calibre.
kaligrafija *f* calligraphy.
kalkulacija *f* calculation, computation.
kalorija *f* calorie.
kaluđer *m* monk.
kaluđerica *f* nun.
kalup *m* form, shape, mould.
kaljača *f* galosh.
kaljav *a* muddy, slimy.
kaljenje *n* hardening.
kama *f* dagger.

kamatna stopa *f* interest rate.
kamčiti *v* to wheedle.
kameleon *m* chameleon.
kamen *m* stone, rock, pebble; ~
   spoticanja stumbling block; ~ **temeljac**
   cornerstone, keystone; **dragi** ~ precious
   stone.
kamenit *a* rocky, stony.
kamenovanje *n* stoning.
kamera *f* camera.
kamerman *m* cameraman.
kamfor *m* camphor.
kamila *f* camel.
kamilica *f* camomile.
kamin *m* fireplace.
kamion *m* truck, lorry.
kamiondžija *m* truck driver.
kampanja *f* campaign.
kamp *m* camp; campsite.
kamper *m* camper.
kamuflaža *f* camouflage.
kanabe *n* couch.
kanal *m* canal, channel.
kanalizacija *f* sewerage.
kancelar *m* chancellor.
kancelarija *f* office.
kancelarijski materijal *m* stationery.
kancerozan *a* cancerous, carcinogenic.
kandidat *m* applicant, candidate.
kandidovati *v* to nominate.
kandilo *n* sanctuary lamp.
kandirano voće *n* candied fruit.
kandža *f* claw, clutch.
kanibalizam *m* cannibalism.
kaniti *v* to intend.
kaniti se *v* to hesitate.
kanta za smeće *f* can, dustbin, trash can;
   ~ **za zalivanje** *f* watering-can.
kantar *m* steelyard.
kantina *f* canteen.
kanu *m* canoe.
kanjon *m* canyon.
kao *conj* like, as, for.
kap *f* drop; blood-stroke (*med*).
kapa *f* cap, bonnet.
kapak *m* lid; **očni** ~ eyelid; **prozorski** ~
   shutter.

kapalica *f* dropper, eyedropper.
kapanje *n* dripping.
kapara *f* earnest-money.
kapati *v* to drip, to trickle.
kapela *f* chapel.
kapelan *m* chaplain.
kapetan *m* captain, skipper.
kapija *f* gate, gateway.
kapilarni *a* capillary.
kapirati *v* to understand, to catch on.
kapital *m* capital, stock.
kapitalisati *v* to capitalize.
kapitalista *m* capitalist.
kapitalizam *m* capitalism.
kapitulacija *f* capitulation.
kaplar *m* corporal.
kaplja *f* drop.
kapric *m* caprice.
kapriciozan *a* capricious.
kapuljača *f* hood.
kaput *m* coat, greatcoat, overcoat.
karabatak *m* leg (of a bird).
karabin *m* carbin.
karakter *m* character.
karakterističan *a* characteristic,
  distinctive.
karamela *f* caramel, toffee.
karanfil *m* carnation, pink.
karanfilić *m* clove.
karantin *m* quarantine.
karat *m* carat.
karavan *m* caravan.
karburator *m* carburetter, carburetor.
kardinal *m* cardinal.
kardinalan *a* cardinal, basic.
karfiol *m* cauliflower.
kari *m* curry.
karijera *f* career.
karijes *m* caries (*stom*).
karika *f* link.
karikatura *f* caricature, cartoon.
karikirati *v* to caricature, to cartoon.
kariran *a* plaid; check.
karlica *f* pelvis (*anat*).
karmin *m* lipstick.
karneval *m* carnival.
karta *f* card, ticket; **~ za ulazak u avion**
  boarding card (pass).
kartanje *n* gambling.
kartel *m* cartel.
karton *m* cardboard.

kartoteka *f* card-index.
karusel *m* merry-go-round .
kas *m* trot.
kasa *f* cash-box, pay-box.
kasač *m* trotter (horse).
kasan *a* late.
kasapin *m* butcher.
kasarna *fpl* barracks.
kasati *v* to trot.
kaseta *f* cassette.
kasetofon *m* cassette player, recorder.
kasica prasica *f* piggy bank.
kasino *m* casino.
kasir *m* cashier.
kaskader *m* stuntman; **~ka** *f* stuntwoman.
kasnije *adv* later, after.
kasno *adv* late.
kasta *f* caste.
kastracija *f* castration.
kaša *f* gruel, mash.
kašalj *m* cough.
kašika *f* spoon; **~ za jelo** *f* tablespoon.
kašmir *m* cashmere.
katalizator *m* catalyst.
katalog *m* catalogue.
katanac *m* padlock.
katar *m* catarrh (*med*).
katarakt *m* cataract.
katastar *m* land-register.
katastrofa *f* catastrophe, crash, disaster.
katedrala *f* cathedral.
kategoričan *a* categorical, direct, explicit.
kategorija *f* category.
kategorisati *v* to categorize.
katkad *adv* sometimes, occasionally.
katolik *m* catholic.
katran *m* tar.
kauboj *m* cowboy, cowhand.
kaucija *f* bail.
kavez *m* cage; **~ za ptice** birdcage.
kavga *f* quarrel, dispute.
kavijar *m* caviar.
kazaljka *f* pointer, hand; **mala ~** the hour-
  hand; **velika ~** the minute-hand.
kazati *v* to tell, to say, to declare.
kazna *f* punishment, chastisement,
  retribution; **novčana ~** penalty.
kaznen *a* penal, punitive, criminal; **~o**
  popravni dom *m* house of correction;
  ~i zakon penal code; criminal
  code.

kazniti *v* to punish, to castigate.
kažiprst *m* forefinger, index finger.
kći *f* daughter.
kec *m* ace.
kecelja *f* apron, pinafore.
kečap *m* ketchup.
kečiga *f* sturgeon.
kedar *m* cedar (*bot*).
kej *m* quay, pier.
kelner *m* waiter.
kelnerica *f* barmaid.
kengur *m* kangaroo.
kepec *m* midget.
ker *m* dog.
keramički *a* ceramic.
keruša *f* bitch.
kesa *f* bag.
kesten *m* chestnut.
kestenjaste boje *a* auburn, maroon.
kevtati *v* to yelp.
kibernetika *f* cybernetics.
kicoš *m* dandy.
kičica *f* brush.
kičma *f* spine, backbone.
kičmeni *a* spinal, vertebral; ~ **pršljen** *m*
   vertebra.
kićanka *f* tassel.
kićenje *n* adorning, decoration,
   embellishing.
kidati *v* to pull apart, to tear.
kidisati *v* to attack.
kidnaper *m* kidnapper.
kidnapovati *v* to kidnap.
kifla *f* roll.
kijamet *m* bad weather.
kijati *v* to sneeze.
kika *f* tress, pigtail.
kikiriki *m* peanut.
kiks *m* blunder, faux-pas.
kila *f* hernia (*med*).
kilo *m* kilo.
kilobajt *m* kilobyte.
kilogram *m* kilogram.
kilometar *m* kilometre (*br*), kilometer
   (*amer*).
kilometraža *f* mileage.
kim *m* caraway.
kinđuriti se *v* to spruce, to prink.
kinin *m* quinine.
kinjiti *v* to torment, to harass.
kiosk *m* kiosk, newspaper stand.

kip *m* statue.
kipar *m* sculptor.
kipeti *v* to boil.
kirija *f* rent, revenue.
kiseli, kiseo *a* sour; ~ **krastavac** *m* sour
   pickles, gherkin; ~ **kupus** *m* sauerkraut;
   ~**la voda** *f* mineral water.
kiselina *f* acid, acidity.
kiseonik *m* oxygen.
kiša *f* rain; **kisela** ~ acid rain.
kišni *a* rainy; ~ **mantil** raincoat;
   waterproof, mackintosh; ~**na glista** *f*
   earthworm.
kišnica *f* rainwater.
kišobran *m* umbrella.
kit *m* whale (*zool*).
kita *f* posy, nosegay, bunch; cock (*anat*).
kititi *v* to adorn, to decorate.
kivan *a* resentful, angry.
klackalica *f* seesaw.
klada *f* log.
kladionica *f* betting shop.
klađenje *n* betting.
klanac *m* gorge, ravine.
klanica *f* butchery, slaughter-house.
klanjati se *v* to make a bow, to bow.
klasa *f* class.
klasičan *a* classic(al).
klasifikacija *f* classification.
klatiti se *v* to rock, to swing, to dangle.
klatno *n* pendulum.
klauzula *f* clause.
klavir *m* piano.
klecati *v* to totter.
klečati *v* to kneel.
kleka *f* juniper.
klepetati *v* to clatter.
klešta *fpl* tongs, pliers.
kleti *v* to curse, to damn.
kleti se *v* to swear, to make an oath.
kletva *f* curse.
kleveta *f* calumny, slander, aspersion, libel.
klevetanje *n* defamation.
klevetnički *a* libellous, slanderous.
klica *f* germ.
klicanje[1] *n* germination.
klicanje[2] *n* cheering.
klicati *v* to hail, to cheer.
kliconoša *m* carrier.
klijati *v* to germinate, to sprout.
klijent *m* client.

klika *f* clique, clan.
klima *f* climate.
klimaks *m* climax.
klimanje (glavom) *n* nodding.
klimati se *v* to dangle.
klimatizovan *a* air-conditioned.
klimav *a* shaky, rickety.
klin *m* wedge.
klip *m* piston, plunger; ~ **kukuruza** corncob.
klipan *m* lout.
klizajući *a* sliding.
klizalište *n* skating rink.
klizaljka *f* skate.
klizanje *n* skating; ~ **na ledu** ice skating.
klizav *a* slippery.
klokotati *v* to gurgle.
klompa *f* wooden shoe.
klon *m* clone.
kloniran *a* cloned.
kloniti se *v* to avoid, to elude.
klonulost *f* depression, exhaustion.
klonuo *a* drooped, exhausted.
klonuti *v* to sink; to be low-spirited (duhom).
klopka *f* trap, snare, decoy.
klozet *m* water closet, WC, lavatory.
klub *m* club.
klupa *f* bench; pew.
kljakav *a* crippled.
klješta *fpl* pincers; ~ **za orahe** *fpl* nutcrackers.
kljova *f* tusk.
ključ *m* key; clue (*fig*).
ključaonica *f* keyhole.
ključati *v* to boil, to seethe.
ključna kost *f* collarbone.
kljun *m* beak; ~ **broda** prow, bow.
kmet *m* serf.
kneževina *f* principality.
knjiga *f* book; **crna** ~ blacklist; **glavna** ~ ledger; ~ **mudrosti** book of knowledge; ~ **žalbi** complaint book.
knjigovezac *m* book-binder.
knjigovodstvo *n* book-keeping.
knjigovođa *m* book-keeper.
knjiški moljac *m* bookworm.
knjižar *m* bookseller.
knjižara *f* bookstore.
književan *a* literary.
književnost *f* literature.

ko *pn* who.
koalicija *f* coalition.
kob *f* doom, fatality.
kobac *m* sparrow-hawk.
koban *a* fatal, fateful, ominous.
kobasica *f* sausage.
kobila *f* mare.
kobilica broda *f* keel.
kocka *f* cube; ~ **za bacanje** die; ~ **šećera** lump.
kockanje *n* gambling.
kockar *m* gambler.
kockati se *v* to gamble.
kočije *fpl* carriage.
kočnica *f* brake.
kod *prep* at, by, with.
kodeks *m* code.
koeficijent *m* coefficient.
koegzistencija *f* coexistence.
kofa *f* bucket.
kofein *m* caffeine.
kofer *m* suitcase.
koga *pn* whom.
kojegde *adv* anywhere.
kojekakav *a* any, whatsoever.
kojekako *adv* somehow.
kojekud *adv* anywhere, wheresoever.
koješta *n* nonsense.
koji *pn* which, that.
kokain *m* cocaine.
koka-kola *f* Coke.
koketiranje *n* flirtation.
kokice *fpl* popcorn.
kokodakati *v* to cackle.
kokos *m* coconut.
kokošinjac *m* henhouse.
kokoška, kokoš *f* hen.
koks *m* coke.
koktel *m* cocktail, highball.
kola *f* vehicle, carriage, car; **bolnička** ~ ambulance.
kolac *m* stake, picket, pile.
kolač *m* cake, pastry, tart; ~ **začinjen đumbirom** gingerbread.
kolebanje *n* hesitancy.
kolebati se *v* to waver, to fluctuate.
kolebljiv *a* wavering.
koledž *m* college.
kolega *m* colleague; ~ **s posla** workmate; ~ **sa studija** fellow student.
kolekcionar *m* collector.

kolektivan *a* collective.
koleno *n* knee.
kolera *f* cholera.
kolevka *f* cradle.
koliba *f* cottage, hut.
kolibri *m* humming-bird.
kolica *fpl* small cart; **dečja ~** *fpl* pram.
količina *f* quantity, amount.
količinski *a* quantitative.
količnik *m* quotient.
kolika *f* colic (*med*).
koliko *adv* how much, how many.
kolikogod *adv* somewhat, no matter how much.
koliko-toliko *adv* fairly well, so-so.
kolona *f* column.
kolonijalan *a* colonial.
kolonjska voda *f* eau de Cologne.
kolos *m* colossus.
kolosek *m* track.
kolovođa *m* ringleader.
kolut *m* ring, disk; hoop; **~ sira** wheel of cheese, loaf of cheese.
koljač *m* slaughterer.
kolje *npl* paling.
koma *f* coma.
komad *m* piece, fragment.
komadić *m* bit, morsel.
komanda *f* command; **vrhovna ~** supreme command.
komandna soba control room.
komandos *m* commando.
komandovati *v* to command.
komarac *m* mosquito, gnat.
komatozan *a* comatose.
kombinezon *m* pettycoat; *mpl* overalls.
komedija *f* comedy, play.
komedijaš *m* clown.
komentar *m* comment, commentary.
komercijalan *a* commercial.
komesar *m* commissioner; superintendant.
komesarijat *m* commissariat; police station.
komešanje *n* commotion.
komešati se *v* to move, to bustle.
kometa *f* comet.
komforan *a* comfortable.
komičar *m* comedian.
komičarka *f* comedienne.
komitet *m* committee.
komora *f* chamber; **mračna ~** dark room.

komotan *a* loose, comfortable, roomy; **~ čovek** easy-going.
kompaktan *a* compact, firm.
kompas *m* compass.
kompenzacija *f* compensation.
komplikacija *f* complication, complexity.
kompliment *m* compliment.
komponenta *f* component.
kompozitor *m* composer.
kompromis *m* compromise.
komšija *m* neighbour.
komuna *f* commune.
komunikacija *f* communication.
komunista *m* communist.
komunizam *m* communism.
konac *m* thread, yarn.
konačan *a* final, definitive, terminal.
koncentracioni logor *m* concentration camp.
koncept *m* draft, rough copy, sketch.
koncert *m* concert.
koncesija *f* concession.
kondenzacija *f* condensation.
kondicija *f* condition, fitness.
kondom *m* condom.
konfederacija *f* confederacy.
konfekcija *f* ready-made clothing.
konferencija *f* conference; **~ za štampu** press conference.
konfiskacija *f* confiscation, expropriation.
konfuzan *a* mixed-up.
kongres *m* congress.
kongresmen *m* congressman.
konkavan *a* concave.
konkubina *f* concubine.
konkurencija *f* competition, rivalship.
konkurentan *a* competitive.
konopac *m* rope, string, line; **~ za udicu** fishing-line; **~ za veš** clothes-line.
konoplja *f* hemp; cannabis.
konsultant *m* consultant.
kontakt *m* contact, touch.
kontaktna sočiva *fpl* contact lenses.
kontaktni ključ *m* ignition key.
kontaminacija *f* contamination.
kontejner *m* container.
kontinuitet *m* continuity.
kontracepcija *f* contraception; **pilule za ~u** *fpl* birth-control pills.
kontraproduktivan *a* counterproductive.

kontrola f control; ~ **pasoša** passport control; ~ **rađanja** birth control.
kontrolna šipka f dipstick.
kontrolni punkt m checkpoint.
kontrolni toranj m control tower.
konvergencija f convergence.
konvertibilan a convertible.
konverzacija f conversation, discourse, speech.
konzerva f preserve.
konzervativac m conservative.
konzul m consul.
konzularan a consular.
konj m horse; ~ **za vuču** m cart-horse.
konjak m cognac.
konjica f cavalry.
konjički eskadron m squadron.
konjska snaga f horsepower.
konjska trka f horse race.
konjugacija f conjugation (*gram*).
konjunktiv m subjunctive (*gram*).
kooperativan a cooperative.
kop m coalmine.
kopač m digger.
kopati v to dig.
kopča f clasp, buckle.
kopija f duplicate, copy.
kopile n bastard.
kopito n hoof.
koplje n javelin, lance, spear.
kopnen a continental; ~**e snage** fpl land forces.
kopno n mainland.
koprena f veil.
kopriva f nettle.
kora f crust; ~ **drveta** bark; ~ **voća** peel.
koračati v to step, to stride, to walk.
korak m step, pace, footstep.
koral m coral.
koralni greben m coral reef.
korbač m whip.
korektan a correct, accurate; honest, decent; ~**na igra** f fair play.
korektor m reader, proof-reader.
korelacija f correlation.
koren m root.
korenit a radical.
korida f bullfight.
korisnik m beneficiary.
korisnost f usefulness, utility.
korist f use, utility; benefit; profit, advantage.

koristan a profitable, helpful, beneficial, useful.
koristiti v to use, to utilise.
koristoljublje n self interest.
korišćenje n use.
korito n trough.
kormilar m helmsman; leader (*fig*).
kormilo n helm, rudder.
kornjača f tortoise, turtle.
korov m weed.
korpa f basket; ~ **za rublje** f clothes basket.
korpus m corps.
kos m blackbird (*zool*).
kos a oblique, slanting, sloping.
kosa[1] f hair.
kosa[2] f scythe.
kosač m mower.
kosilica za travu f lawnmower.
kosina f slope, hillside.
kositi v to mow.
koska f bone.
kosmat a hairy.
kosmički a cosmic; ~ **brod** m spacecraft.
kosmonaut m cosmonaut.
kosmopolitski a cosmopolitan.
kost f bone.
kostur m skeleton; framework (*fig*).
koš m basket; **grudni** ~ thorax.
košarka f basketball.
koščat a bony, gaunt.
košnica f beehive, hive.
koštan a bony; ~**a srž** f marrow.
koštica f pit, stone, kernel; small bone.
košulja f shirt.
košuta f doe, roe.
kotao m boiler.
kotlet m cutlet.
kotlina f depression, low place.
kotrljanje n rolling.
kotrljati v to roll.
koturača f pulley blocks.
koturaljke fpl roller skates.
kotva f anchor.
kovač m blacksmith, forger.
kovačnica f smithy, blackmith's.
kovati v to forge, hammer.
kovčeg m chest.
koverat m envelope.
kovitlac m whirl, to spin, to swirl.
kovrdžav a curly.

koza *f* goat.
kozmetički *a* cosmetic; ~a operacija
  uklanjanja bora *f* face-lift.
koža *f* skin; leather; ~ divokoze *f* chamois
  leather; lakovana ~ patent leather .
krađa *f* theft, stealing, larceny; književna
  ~ plagiarism.
kraj¹ *m* end, extremity; ~ puta branch.
kraj² *m* region, area; neighbourhood.
kraj³ *prep* next, to, near, beside.
krajnik *m* tonsil.
krajnji *a* extreme, utmost, uttermost.
krak *m* leg.
kralj *m* king.
kraljevina *f* kingdom, realm.
kraljevski *a* royal, regal.
kraljica *f* queen.
kran *m* crane.
krasiti *v* to adorn, to decorate.
krastav *a* scabby.
krastavac *m* cucumber.
krasti *v* to steal, to poach, to purloin.
krasuljak *m* daisy.
kratak *a* brief, short; curt, laconic; ~
  boravak *m* sojourn; ~ka biografija *f*
  curriculum vitae; ~ka čarapa sock.
kratkoća *f* brevity, shortness.
kratkovid *a* near-sighted, short-sighted.
kratkovidost *f* short-sightedness.
krava *f* cow.
kravata *f* necktie, tie.
krckati *v* to crunch.
krčag *m* jug.
krčati *v* to rumble.
krčkati *v* to simmer.
krčma *f* inn, tavern.
krčmar *m* inn-keeper.
krdo *n* herd, drove.
kreč *m* lime.
krečiti *v* to whitewash.
krečnjak *m* limestone.
kreda *f* chalk.
kredenac *m* cupboard, buffet.
kreditna kartica *f* credit card.
kreditno pismo *n* letter of credit.
kreja *f* jay (*zool*).
kreket *m* croaking.
krem *m* cream; ~ od vanile custard.
krema za lice *f* face cream; ~ za brijanje
  shaving cream.
krematorijum *m* crematory.

kremen *m* flint.
krenuti *v* to move.
krepko *adv* lustily, vigorously.
kresati *v* to prune, to trim.
kresta *f* crest.
kretanje *n* motion, movement.
kreten *m* imbecile, idiot.
krevet *m* bed; ~ u kabini berth.
krhak *a* brittle, fragile.
krhkost *f* frailty.
krigla *f* mug, pitcher.
krijumčar *m* smuggler.
krijumčarenje *n* smuggling, contraband.
krik *m* cry, scream.
krilat *a* winged.
krilatica *f* catchphrase, catchword.
krilo *n* wing; lap; flank (*mil*).
kriminal *m* crime; organizovani ~
  organized crime.
kristal *m* crystal.
kristalan *a* crystalline; ~no čist crystal-
  clear.
kriška *f* slice, piece.
krišom *adv* secretly, stealthily.
kriterijum *m* criterion.
kriti *v* to conceal, to hide, to secrete.
kritičan *a* critic(al), crucial.
kritičar *m* critic, reviewer, judge.
kritika *f* criticism.
kriv *a* hooked, awry, crooked, curved;
  guilty, faulty; wrong, false.
krivac *m* culprit, offender.
krivica *f* guilt, delinquency.
krivina *f* curve, bend.
krivo *adv* crookedly, askew; wrongly; ~
  se zakleti *v* to perjure.
krivokletstvo *n* perjury.
krivonog *a* bandy-legged.
krivotvoriti *v* to forge, to falsify.
krivudati *v* to wind, to twist, to zigzag.
kriza *f* crisis.
krkljanac *m* bustle, tumult.
krma *f* stern of a ship.
krma *f* fodder, food (for cattle).
krmača *f* sow.
krmaniti *v* to steer.
krmenadla *f* pork chop.
krntija *f* wreck.
krnj *a* chipped.
krofna *f* doughnut.
krojač *m* tailor.

krojačica *f* dressmaker.
krojački *a* tailor's; ~ **lutka** *f* tailor's dummy.
krokodil *m* crocodile.
krompir *m* potato.
kros *m* cross-country.
krotkost *f* tameness, gentleness.
krov *m* roof; ~ **od slame** thatched roof.
kroz *prep* through, throughout.
krpa *f* rag; ~ **za sudove** dish cloth; ~ **za prašinu** duster.
krpiti *v* to mend, to repair, to darn.
krst *m* cross.
krsta *fpl* small of the back.
krstarenje *n* cruise.
krstarica *f* cruiser.
krstaški rat *m* crusade.
krstiti *v* to baptize, to christen.
kršan *a* robust, strapping.
kršenje *n* infraction, infringement.
kršten *a* christened.
krštenje *n* baptism, christening.
krtičnjak *m* molehill.
krug *m* circle, round.
kruna *f* coronet, crown.
krunisanje *n* coronation.
kruniti *v* to crumble.
krupan *a* large, big, great; considerable; ~**ni plan** *m* close-up.
kruška *f* pear.
krut *a* rigid, stiff.
krutost *f* rigidity.
kružan *a* circular, circled, round; ~**ni put** *m* ring road.
kružiti *v* to circulate, to move in circle.
krv *f* blood.
krvarenje *n* bleeding, haemorrhage; ~ **iz nosa** *n* nosebleed.
krvav *a* bloody, bleeding; terrific, great (*fig*).
krvavica *f* black sausage.
krvni *a* blood; ~ **pritisak** *m* blood pressure; ~ **sud** blood vessel; ~**a grupa** *f* blood group.
krvopija *f* blood sucker.
krvoproliće *n* bloodshed, massacre.
krvožedan *a* bloodthirsty.
krznen *a* furry.
krzno *n* fur.
ksilofon *m* xylophone (*mus*).
kub *m* cube.

kubni *a* cubic.
kucati *v* to knock, to rap; to beat, to pulsate (srce); to tick (sat).
kučka *f* bitch.
kuća *f* house, building; **robna ~** department store; **javna ~** bordello.
kućni *a* house; ~ **poslovi** *mpl* housework; ~ **lekar** *m* family doctor; ~ **ljubimac** pet.
kuda *adv* where.
kuditi *v* to rebuke, to blame.
kudrav *a* curly.
kuga *f* plague, pestilence.
kugla *f* globe, sphere.
kuglana *f* bowling alley, skittle-alley.
kuglanje *n* bowling.
kuglica *f* small ball; pellet.
kuhinja *f* kitchen.
kujundžija *m* silversmith, goldsmith.
kuka *f* hook, crook.
kukanje *n* lamentation, wailing.
kukast *a* hooked.
kukavica *f* coward; cuckoo (ptica).
kukavičluk *m* cowardice.
kukurikanje *n* crowing.
kukuruz *m* maize, corn.
kukuruzne pahuljice *fpl* cornflakes.
kula *f* turret, tower.
kulinarski *a* culinary.
kulinarstvo *n* cookery.
kulminacija *f* culmination.
kulminirati *v* to culminate.
kult *m* cult.
kultura *f* culture.
kulturan *a* cultural.
kum *m* godfather.
kuma *f* godmother.
kumče *n* godchild, godson.
kumica *f* goddaughter.
kuna *f* marten.
kunić *m* rabbit.
kunjati *v* to be indisposed.
kupa *f* cone (*mat*).
kupac *m* buyer, customer, purchaser.
kupač *m* bather.
kupaći *a* bathing; ~ **kostim** *m* bathing suit, swimsuit; ~**e gaće** bathing trunks.
kupanje *n* bathing.
kupast *a* conic(al).
kupati (se) *v* to bath; to take a bath; to swim.

kupatilo *n* bathroom.
kupe *m* compartment.
kupina *f* blackberry.
kupiti *v* to buy, to purchase.
kupke *fpl* baths.
kupola *f* dome.
kupon *m* coupon.
kupovina *f* shopping.
kupus *m* cabbage.
kurir *m* courier, messenger.
kurs *m* course, route; **devizni** ~ exchange rate.
kuršum *m* bullet.
kurva *f* whore, street-walker.
kurziv *m* italic.
kustos *m* curator, custodian.
kusur *m* change.
kutija *f* box, case; ~ **od kartona** carton; ~ **za alat** tool box; ~ **šibica** matchbox.
kutlača *f* ladle.

kutnjak *m* molar tooth.
kuvar *m* cook; cookbook.
kvačilo *n* clutch.
kvadrat *m* square.
kvaka *f* door knob, knob.
kvalifikacija *f* qualification; *pl* qualifications, requirements.
kvalitet *m* quality.
kvar *m* breakage, malfunction; damage.
kvaran *a* bad, rotten.
kvarc *m* quartz.
kvariti *v* to spoil, to mar; to corrupt.
kvasac *m* yeast.
kvasiti *v* to water, to wet.
kvocati *v* to cluck.
kvočka *f* brood-hen.
kvota *f* quota, quantity.
kvrga *f* knot, knob.
kvrgav *a* gnarled, knotty.

L

labav *a* loose, slack.
labavost *f* slackness.
labilan *a* unstable.
laboratorija *f* laboratory.
labud *m* swan.
lađa *f* ship, vessel, boat.
lagan *a* light.
lagano *adv* slowly; ~ **oticati** *v* to ooze; ~ **trčati** *v* to jog.
laganje *n* fib, lying.
lagati *v* to lie.
lager *m* stock; warehouse.
lagodan *a* easy, mild.
laguna *f* lagoon.
laik *m* layman.
lajanje *n* barking.
lajati *v* to bark, to yelp.
lajavac *m* barking dog; chatterbox.
lak *a* easy, not difficult.
lak *n* varnish; ~ **za kosu** *m* hairspray; ~ **za nokte** *n* nailpolish.
lakat *m* elbow.
lakirati *v* to varnish.
laknuti *v* to feel relieved.
lako *adv* easily, readily; ~ **svarljiv** *adv* digestible.
lakoća *f* easiness.
lakom *a* gluttonous, greedy.
lakomislenost *f* shallowness, levity.
lakomo *adv* avidly.
lakonski *a* short, laconic, brief.
lakorečiv *a* eloquent.
lakouman *a* frivolous, shallow.
lakoveran *a* credulous, gullible.
lakovernost *f* credulity, gullibility.
lakrdija *f* farce, humbug.
lakrdijaš *m* clown, joker.
lakrdijaški *a* farcical.
lala *f* tulip.
lampa *f* lamp.
lan *m* flax.
lanac *m* chain.
lančana reakcija *f* chain reaction.
lane[1] *adv* last year.
lane[2] *n* fawn.
lansirati *v* to launch.
lapavica *f* slush.

larmati *v* to cry out, to clamour.
laser *m* laser.
laserski štampač *m* laser printer.
lasica *f* weasel (*zool*).
laskanje *n* flattery.
laskati *v* to flatter.
laskavac *m* wheedler.
laso *m* lasso.
lasta *f* swallow.
lastiš *m* rubber-band.
latica *f* petal.
latiti se *v* to tackle, to try.
lav *m* lion.
lava *f* lava.
lavabo *m* sink, washbasin.
lavanda *f* lavender.
lavež *m* bark, barking.
lavica *f* lioness.
lavina *f* avalanche.
lavirint *m* labyrinth, maze.
lavor *m* washbowl, washbasin.
laž *f* lie, lying, untruth; ~ **iz nužde** white lie.
lažan *a* false, bogus, fallacious; ~**na uzbuna** *f* false alarm.
lažljivac *m* liar.
lebdeti *v* to float, to hover.
lečiti *v* to heal, to treat.
leći *v* to lie down.
led *m* ice.
leden *a* freezing, frosty, icy; ~**a kiša** *f* freezing rain; ~**i breg** *m* iceberg.
ledenica *f* icicle.
leđa *f* back.
legalizovati *v* to legalize.
legat *m* legate.
legendaran *a* legendary, fabulous.
legija *f* legion.
legitimacija *f* identity card.
leglo *n* breeding place; hotbed; litter.
legura *f* alloy.
lek *m* cure, medicament, drug, remedy.
lekar *m* doctor, physician.
lekcija *f* lesson.
lekovit *a* medicinal, medical, healthy.
lelek *m* moaning, lamentation.
lelujati se *v* to flutter.

lemanje *n* thrashing.
lemati *v* to thrash, to beat.
lenčariti *v* to laze.
lenger *m* anchor, ground tackle.
lenština *f* slacker, sluggard.
lenj *a* indolent, lazy, inactive.
lenjir *m* ruler.
lenjo *adv* lazily.
lenjost *f* indolence, laziness.
leopard *m* leopard.
lep *a* beautiful, fair, bonny; good-looking, handsome.
lepak *m* glue.
lepiti *v* to paste, to glue.
lepljiv *a* adhesive, sticky.
lepljivost *f* adhesiveness.
lepo *adv* beautifully, nice, nicely.
lepota *f* beauty.
lepršati *v* to flutter.
leptir *m* butterfly; ~ **mašna** *f* bow tie.
lepuškast *a* nice-looking, pretty.
leš *m* corpse.
lešina *f* carcass.
lešinar *m* vulture.
lešnik *m* hazelnut.
let *m* flight.
letak *m* flysheet, leaflet.
letargičan *a* lethargic.
letargija *f* lethargy.
leteći *a* flying; ~ **tanjir** *m* flying saucer; ~ **odred** mobile detachment.
leteti *v* to fly, to wing, to pilot.
leti *adv* in summer.
letimičan *a* cursory, hasty.
letina *f* crop, harvest.
letnji *a* summer.
letnjikovac *m* summer-house.
leto *n* summer.
letopis *m* annals.
letos *adv* this summer.
letovalište *n* summer resort.
levak *m* funnel.
levi *a* left, sinistral.
levoruk *a* left-handed.
ležaj *m* bunk, bed.
ležati *v* to lie.
ležati na jajima *v* to hatch.
ležerno *adv* nonchalantly.
ležište *n* bearing.
liberalan *a* liberal.
lice *n* face, visage, countenance; person;

front (prednja strana); facade (kuće); right side (tkanine).
licemer *m* hypocrite.
licemeran *a* hypocritical, sanctimonious.
licemerje *n* hypocrisy.
licitacija *f* public sale, auction sale.
ličan *a* personal, private; ~**ni interes** *m* self-interest; ~**ni oglasi** *mpl* personal column; ~**na svojina** *f* private property.
ličiti *v* to resemble, to be like.
ličnost *f* personality.
liferovati *v* to furnish.
lift *m* elevator, lift.
lignja *f* squid.
lihvar *m* usurer.
lik *m* face, visage; shape, form (oblik).
liker *m* liqueur.
likovanje *n* exultation.
likovati *v* to exult, to triumph.
likovna umetnost *f* fine art.
likvidacija *f* liquidation.
likvidirati *v* to liquidate.
lilihip *m* lollipop.
limfa *f* lymph (*anat*).
limun *m* lemon; lemon tree.
limunada *f* lemonade.
linčovati *v* to lynch.
lingvista *m* linguist.
lingvistički *a* linguistic.
linija *f* line.
linijski *a* linear; ~ **putnički brod ili avion** *m* liner; ~ **sudija** linesman.
linjati se *v* to molt; to fade; to peel (off).
lipa *f* lime tree, linden tree.
liposukcija *f* liposuction.
lirski *a* lyrical.
lisac *m* fox.
lisica *f* vixen, she-fox.
lisice *fpl* handcuffs, manacle(s).
list *m* leaf; ~ **hartije** *m* sheet.
lista *f* lista; ~ **adresa za slanje** *f* mailing list; ~ **čekanja** *f* waiting list.
lišaj *m* lichen.
lišće *npl* leaves, foliage.
lišiti *v* to dispossess, to deprive; ~ **nasledstva** *v* disinherit.
litar *m* litre.
liti *v* to pour.
litica *f* cliff, crag.
liturgija *f* liturgy.
livac *m* founder, moulder.

livada *f* meadow.
liven *a* cast; **~o gvožđe** *n* cast iron.
livnica *f* foundry.
livreja *f* livery.
lizati *v* to lick.
lobanja *f* skull.
logičan *a* logical.
logika *f* logic.
logor *m* camp.
logorovanje *n* camping.
logorska vatra *f* bonfire.
logotip *m* logo.
loj *m* tallow.
lojalan *a* loyal.
lojalnost *f* loyalty.
lokal *m* premises; shop.
lokalizovati *v* to localize.
lokalni *a* local; **~a anestezija** *f* local anaesthetic; **~a vlast** local government.
lokalno *adv* locally.
lokomotiva *f* engine, locomotive.
lokva *f* pool, pond.
lokvanj *m* water lily (*bot*).
lom *m* fracture; disorder (nered).
lomača *f* stake; pyre.
loman *a* fragile, weak; easily broken.
lomiti *v* to crack, to break, to fracture.
lomljiv *a* breakable.
lonac *m* pot.
lončar *m* potter.
lopata *f* shovel, spade.
lopatica *f* spatula; shoulder-blade (*anat*).
lopov *m* thief; shoplifter.
lopta *f* ball; globe, sphere.
losion *m* lotion; **~ posle brijanja** aftershave lotion.
losos *m* salmon.
loš *a* bad, evil, faulty; **~a ishrana** malnutrition; **~a probava** *f* indigestion; **~e ponašanje** *n* misbehaviour, misconduct.
lov *m* hunting, shooting.
lovac *m* hunter, huntsman.

lovački pas *m* hound.
loviti *v* to hunt, to chase.
lovočuvar *m* warden (game).
lovor *m* laurel.
lovorika *f* laurel.
lozinka *f* password, watchword.
ložač *m* stoker.
ložiti *v* to heat.
lubenica *f* watermelon.
lucidan *a* lucid.
luckast *a* foolish, silly.
lučiti *v* to secrete.
lučki *a* harbour; **~ radnik** *m* docker.
lud *a* crazy, insane, mad, demented.
ludački *a* manic, lunatic; **~a košulja** *f* straitjacket.
ludak *m* fool, madman, lunatic.
ludilo *n* insanity, lunacy, madness.
ludnica *f* lunatic asylum, madhouse.
ludo *adv* madly.
ludost *f* folly, nonsense.
luk[1] *m* bow; arch (zidani).
luk[2] *m* onion.
luka *f* port, harbour.
lukav *a* sly, cunning, canny.
lukavstvo *n* ruse, trick, slyness.
lukobran *m* breakwater.
lukovica *f* bulb.
luksuz *m* luxury.
lula *f* pipe.
lumpovanje *n* drinking bout, spree.
lumpovati *v* to revel, to carouse.
lunjati *v* to loiter, to lag.
lupa *f* magnifying glass.
lupanje *n* beating, banging.
lupati *v* to bang, to knock; to talk nonsense.
lupež *m* swindler, knave.
luster *m* chandelier.
lutalica *f* rover.
lutati *v* to roam, to rove, to wander.
lutka *f* doll; puppet.
lutrija *f* lottery.

LJ

ljaga *f* blemish, stain, tarnish.
ljigav *a* slippery, slimy.
ljigavac *m* spineless person.
ljiljan *m* lily.
ljubak *a* graceful, lovable.
ljubav *f* love, affection, regard.
ljubavni *a* love; ~o pismo *n* love letter.
ljubavnik *m* lover.
ljubazan *a* amiable, kind, considerate, gracious.
ljubazno *adv* amiably, kindly, affably.
ljubaznost *f* amiability, kindness, courtesy.
ljubičica *f* violet.
ljubimac *m* favourite.
ljubljenje *n* kissing.
ljubomora *f* jealousy.
ljubomoran *a* jealous.
ljubopitljiv *a* curious, inquisitive.

ljudožder *m* cannibal.
ljudski *a* human; *adv* humanly.
ljudstvo *n* humankind, mankind.
ljuljaška *f* swing.
ljuljati *v* to swing, to rock.
ljupko *adv* sweetly.
ljupkost *f* grace, sweetness.
ljuska *f* husk, hull; peel; ~ od jajeta eggshell.
ljuskar *m* shellfish.
ljuštiti *v* to peel; to skin; to shell.
ljut *a* angry, furious, wrathful; ~a paprika *f* hot pepper; ~a rakija strong brandy; ~ zima a severe winter.
ljutić *m* buttercup.
ljutit *a* angry, ireful.
ljutnja *f* anger, fury, annoyance.
ljutito *adv* angrily.

M

ma *conj* any; ~ **kako** anyhow; ~ **ko** anybody.
mač *m* sword.
mačak *m* tomcat.
mače *n* kitten.
mačevalac *m* swordsman.
mačiji *a* feline.
mačka *f* cat.
maćeha *f* stepmother.
mada *conj* although, though.
mađija *f* magic; spell.
mađioničar *m* conjurer, magician.
magacin *m* depot, store, storehouse, warehouse.
magarac *m* donkey, ass.
magareći *a* donkey; ~ **kašalj** *m* whooping-cough.
magistrala *f* highway, main road.
magla *f* fog, mist.
maglovit *a* foggy, hazy, misty.
magnet *m* magnet.
magnetičan *a* magnetic(al).
magnetofon *m* tape recorder.
mahati *v* to wave, to brandish; ~ **repom** to wag.
mahinalan *a* mechanical, automatic.
mahnit *a* crazy, mad; furious, frenzied.
mahovina *f* moss.
mahuna *f* pod.
maj *m* May.
majčinski *a* maternal.
majica *f* vest, undershirt; ~ **sa kratkim rukavima** tee-shirt, T-shirt.
majka *f* mother.
majmun *m* monkey, ape.
majmunisanje *a* aping.
majmunski *a* apish, monkey.
majonez *m* mayonnaise.
majstor *m* craftsman, artisan; master; **šahovski** ~ chess master.
majstorica *f* play-off.
majstorski *a* masterly, perfect.
majstorsko delo *n* masterpiece.
mak *n* poppy.
makar *adv* at least; ~ **da** *conj* although.
makaze *fpl* scissors; ~**ice za nokte** *fpl* nail scissors.

maketa *f* model, sketch.
maknuti *v* to remove, to move.
maksimalan *a* maximal, peak.
malaksati *v* to grow weak.
malarija *f* malaria.
maler *m* misfortune, calamity.
mali, malen *a* little, small; ~ **čamac** *m* dinghy; ~ **oglas** classified advertisement.
malina *f* raspberry.
malo, malko *adv* a little, a bit.
maločas *adv* a while ago.
malodušan *a* faltering, faint-hearted.
malokrvan *a* anaemic.
maloletan *a* under-age.
malopre *adv* a little while ago.
maloprodaja *f* retail trade.
maltene *adv* almost.
malter *m* mortar; **gipsani** ~ stucco.
maltretirati *v* to mistreat.
malj *m* mallet; **kovački** ~ sledgehammer.
mama *f* mummy.
mamac *m* bait, decoy.
mamipara *f* lure.
mamlaz *m* thickhead.
mamurluk *m* hangover.
mamuza *f* spur.
mana *f* blemish, fault.
manastir *m* monastery, convent.
manastirski *a* monastic.
mandarina *f* mandarin; tangerine (*bot*).
mandat *m* mandate; term; **poslanički** ~ parliamentary term.
manevar *m* manoeuvre.
mangup *m* rascal, hoodlum.
manifest *m* manifesto, declaration.
manifestacija *f* manifestation.
manijak *m* maniac.
manikir *m* manicure.
manipulacija *f* manipulation.
manipulisati *v* to manipulate, to handle.
manir *m* manner, behaviour.
manometar *m* stream gauge, manometer.
mansarda *f* garret, attic.
mantija *f* cassock.
mantil *m* overcoat, coat.
manžeta *f* cuff, wristband.

manjak *m* deficit, deficiency.
manje, manji *a* fewer; less, lesser; smaller.
manjina *f* minority.
manjkati *v* to fail, to want.
manjkav *a* deficient, imperfect.
mapa *f* map.
marama *f* kerchief; neckerchief.
maramica *f* handkerchief.
maraton *m* marathon.
margarin *m* margarine.
marihuana *f* marijuana.
marinirati *v* to marinate.
mariti *v* to like, to care.
marka *f* brand; **poštanska** ~ stamp.
marketing *m* marketing.
marljiv *a* busy, industrious, diligent.
marljivost *f* diligence.
marmelada *f* marmalade.
marš *m* march.
mart *m* March.
marva *f* cattle, live-strock.
marža *f* margin.
masa *f* mass.
masaža *f* massage.
maser *m* masseur.
maserka *f* masseuse.
masivan *a* massive, bulky.
maska *f* mask; ~ **za kiseonik** oxygen mask.
maskara *f* mascara.
maslac *m* butter.
maslačak *m* dandelion.
maslina *f* olive.
maslinovo *a* olive; ~ **ulje** *n* olive oil.
masnica *f* bruise.
masnoća *f* fat.
mason *m* freemason.
mast *f* fat, grease.
mastan *a* greasy.
mastilo *n* ink.
mašice *fpl* tongs.
mašina *f* machine, engine; ~ **za pranje rublja** washing machine; ~ **za pranje sudova** dishwasher.
mašinerija *f* machinery.
mašinovođa *m* engine driver.
mašta *f* fancy, imagination.
maštovit *a* imaginative.
matematičar *m* mathematician.
matematika *f* mathematics, maths.

materica *f* womb, uterus (*anat*).
Materice *fpl* Mother's Day.
materija *f* matter, substance; stuff, fabric (tkanina).
materijalan *a* material; ~**lna sredstva** *npl* capital assets; ~**lna davanja** financial contributions; ~**lni gubici** *mpl* losses in equipment (materiel).
materinski *a* maternal, motherly.
materinstvo *n* motherhood.
maternji *a* maternal; ~ **jezik** *m* mother tongue.
matica *f* queen-bee; main current (reka); source, home (središte).
matičar *m* registrar.
mator *a* old, aged.
maukati *v* to mew.
mauzolej *m* mausoleum.
maza *f* pet, favourite.
mazati *v* to grease, to oil; to paint (slikati).
mazga *f* mule.
maziti *v* to pamper, to coddle.
mazivo *n* lubricant, grease.
mazohista *m* masochist.
mećava *f* blizzard.
med *m* honey.
medalja *f* medal.
medaljon *m* locket, medallion.
medeni mesec *m* honeymoon.
medicina *f* medicine; medicament (lek).
meditacija *f* meditation.
mediteranski *a* Mediterranean.
meduza *f* jellyfish.
medved *m* bear.
međaš *m* boundary-stone; landmark.
među *prep* between, among.
međuigra *f* interlude.
međunarodni *a* international.
međurasni *a* interracial.
međusobno *a* mutually.
megafon *m* megaphone.
megdan *m* duel.
mehaničar *m* mechanic.
mehanizam *m* mechanism.
mehovi *mpl* bellows.
mehur *m* bubble.
mekan *a* soft, tender.
mekinje *fpl* bran.
mekoća *f* softness.
mekušac *m* mollusc (*br*), mollusk (*amer*); weakling (*fig*).

melanholija *f* melancholy.
melem *m* balm, ointment, salve.
melez *m* mongrel.
melodičan *a* melodious, musical.
melodija *f* melody, tune.
meljava *f* grinding.
membrana *f* membrane.
memla *f* mould.
memorandum *m* memo, memorandum.
mena *f* change.
menadžer *m* manager.
mene *pn* me.
menica *f* draft, bill of exchange.
menstruacija *f* menses.
mentalitet *m* mentality.
menza *f* mess-room.
menjač *m* gear lever.
menjati *v* to change, to alter.
mera *f* mera, extent.
merdevine *fpl* ladder.
merenje *n* measuring; weighing.
mermer *m* marble.
merodavan *a* competent, qualified.
mesar *m* butcher.
mesarnica *f* butcher's (shop).
mesec *m* moon; month (kalendarski).
mesečar *m* sleepwalker, nightwalker.
mesečina *f* moonlight.
mesečni *a* monthly.
mesing *m* brass.
mesingan *a* brazen.
mesiti *v* to knead.
mesnat *a* fleshy, meaty.
meso *n* meat; flesh.
mesožder *m* carnivorous animal.
mestimice *adv* here and there.
mesto *n* room, space; seat; position, place; station; ~ **boravka** domicile; ~ **rođenja** birthplace; ~ **stanovanja** home address; **radno** ~ job.
mešanac *m* mongrel.
mešati *v* to mix, to mingle.
mešati se *v* to interfere, to interpose; ~ **u tuđe poslove** *v* to meddle.
mešavina *f* mixture.
mešetar *m* broker.
mešovit *a* mixed, composite.
meta *f* target, aim.
metabolizam *m* metabolism.
metafizički *a* metaphysical.
metafora *f* metaphor.

metaforički *a* metaphoric(al).
metak *m* bullet.
metal *m* metal.
metalurgija *f* metallurgy.
metamorfoza *f* metamorphosis.
metar *m* meter (*amer*), metre (*br*).
meteorologija *f* meteorology.
meteorološki *a* meteorological.
metež *m* confusion, disorder, turmoil.
metil *m* methanol.
metla *f* broom.
metoda *f* method.
metrički *a* metric.
metvica, nana *f* mint.
mi *pn* we.
micati se *v* to move.
mig *m* wink.
migavac *m* wink.
migoljiti se *v* to wriggle.
migrena *f* migraine.
mikrob *m* microbe.
mikročip *m* microchip.
mikrofon *m* microphone, mike.
mikroskopski *a* microscopic.
mikrotalas *m* microwave.
mikser *m* food mixer, food processor.
milenijum *m* millennium.
miligram *m* milligram.
mililitar *m* millilitre.
milimetar *m* millimetre.
milion *m* million.
milionar *m* millionaire.
milioniti *num a* millionth.
milom *adv* willingly.
milosrdan *a* charitable.
milosrđe *n* charity.
milost *f* mercy, grace.
milostinja *f* alms.
milostiv *a* merciful, pitiful.
milovanje *n* caress.
milovati *v* to fondle, to caress.
milja *f* mile.
miljenik *m* favourite.
mina *f* mine.
minđuša *f* ear-ring.
mineralna voda *f* mineral water.
minijatura *f* miniature.
minimalan *a* minimal.
minirati *v* to blast; to undermine (*fig*).
ministar *m* minister.
ministarski *a* ministerial.

ministarstvo *n* ministry; ~ **mornarice** admiralty.
minolovac *m* minesweeper.
minsko polje *n* minefield.
minuli *a* last, past.
minut *m* minute.
minuti *v* to pass, to elapse.
miomiris *m* fragrance.
mir *m* peace; rest, ease; quietness, serenity; **pusti me na ~** leave me alone.
miran *a* peaceful, serene, tranquil; quiet.
miraz *m* dowry.
mirenje *n* reconciliation.
miris *m* smell, scent; odour, perfume; **prijatan ~** a pleasant odour; **čulo ~a** *n* sense of smell.
mirisan, mirišljav *a* odorous, fragrant.
miriti *v* to reconcile.
mirno *adv* calmly, quietly.
mirnodopski *a* peaceful, peacetime.
mirođija *f* dill (*bot*).
miroljubiv *a* pacific.
mirovanje *n* rest, inaction.
mirovni *a* peace; ~ **sudija** *m* justice of peace; ~ **ugovor** peace treaty.
mirta *f* myrtle.
misao *f* thought, idea, reflection.
misija *f* mission, charge, errand.
misionar *m* missionary.
mislilac *m* thinker.
misliti *v* to think, to meditate.
misterija *f* mystery.
mističan *a* mystic(al).
mistrija *f* trowel.
miš *m* mouse.
mišić *m* muscle (*anat*).
mišićav *a* muscular, musculous, sinewy.
mišljenje *n* opinion, judgment/judgement; thinking, reflection.
mišolovka *f* mousetrap.
mit *m* myth, fable, legend.
miting *m* meeting.
mito *m* bribe.
mitologija *f* mythology.
mitraljez *m* machine gun.
mlad *a* young, juvenile.
mlada *f* bride.
mladalački *a* youthful.
mladenci *mpl* the newlyweds.
mladež *m* mole; *mpl* young people.
mladić *m* young man, youngster.

mladićki *a* youthful.
mladolik *a* young-looking.
mladost *f* youth.
mladoženja *m* bridegroom.
mladunče *n* cub.
mlađi *a* younger, junior.
mlak *a* lukewarm, tepid.
mlatiti *v* to thrash, to beat.
mlaz *m* jet, stream (voda); shaft (svetlost); bhest (vazduh).
mlazni *a* jet; ~ **motor** *m* jet engine.
mlečan *a* milky, milk; **~ni proizvodi** *mpl* dairy products.
mlekara *f* dairy.
mleko *n* milk; ~ **u prahu** *n* powdered milk.
mlin *m* mill.
mlinar *m* miller.
mlitav *a* flabby, lax; loose.
mnogi *pn* many, several.
mnogo *adv* much, plenty, a lot.
mnogobrojan *a* numerous.
mnogostran *a* versatile.
mnogostruk *a* multiple.
mnoštvo *n* multitude.
množenje *n* multiplication (*mat*).
množina *f* multitude, plurality.
množiti se *v* to multiply.
mobilisati *v* to mobilize.
močvara *f* swamp, marsh, bog.
močvaran *a* marshy, swampy, boggy.
moć *f* power, force; might; ~ **navike** the force of habit.
moćan *a* mighty, potent.
moći *v* can, to be able to; may.
moda *f* fashion, vogue.
modar *a* blue; livid (od hladnoće).
modem *m* modem.
moderan *a* fashionable, up-to-date.
modifikacija *f* modification.
modiskinja *f* milliner.
modna revija *f* fashion show.
modrica *f* bruise.
modul *m* module.
modulacija *f* modulation.
modulirati *v* to modulate.
mogućan *a* possible, feasible, plausible.
mogućnost *f* possibility.
moj *pn* mine; my.
mokar *a* wet.
mokasine *fpl* loafers.

mokraća *f* urine.
mokriti *v* to urinate, to piss.
molba *f* application, request, entreaty.
molećiv *a* appealing.
molekul *m* molecule.
molilac *m* petitioner, applicant.
moliti *v* to beg, to solicit, to implore.
moliti se *v* to pray.
molitva *f* prayer.
molitvenik *m* prayer book.
moljac *m* moth.
momak *m* boy, young man; groom; bachelor.
momenat *m* moment.
monah *m* monk.
monarhija *f* monarchy.
moneta *f* currency, money.
monokl *m* monocle.
monolog *m* monologue, soliloquy.
monopol *m* monopoly.
monopolisati *v* to monopolize.
monoton *a* monotonous.
monotonija *f* monotony.
monstruozan *a* monstrous.
monsun *m* monsoon.
montaža *f* mounting, installation.
montažna traka *f* assembly line.
montiranje *n* instalment.
monumentalan *a* monumental.
moral *m* morality, morals, ethics.
moralan *a* moral.
morati *v* ought to, must, to be obliged to.
morbidan *a* morbid.
more *n* sea.
morfijum *m* morphine.
mornar *m* mariner, sailor.
mornarički *a* naval.
morski *a* sea; marine; ~ **pas** *m* shark; ~**a bolest** *f* seasickness; ~**a luka** seaport; ~**a obala** seacoast, seaside.
morž *m* walrus.
most *m* bridge.
mošti *fpl* relics.
mošus *m* musk.
motel *m* motel.
motika *f* hoe.
motka *f* pole, bar, stick.
motivisan *a* motivated.
motor *m* engine, motor.
motorcikl *m* motorbike, motorcycle.
motorni *a* motor; ~ **čamac** *m* motorboat; ~**o vozilo** *n* motor vehicle.

motriti *v* to watch.
mozaik *m* mosaic.
mozak *m* brain.
možda *adv* perchance, perhaps.
moždani *a* cerebral.
mračan *a* dark, gloomy, dusky; ~**na komora** *f* darkroom.
mrak *m* dark, gloom, bleakness.
mrav *m* ant (*zool*).
mravinjak *m* ant hill.
mravojed *m* ant-eater.
mraz *m* frost.
mrcvariti *v* to cut up; to torment.
mrešćenje *n* spawning.
mreža *f* net, network; ~ **za kosu** hairnet; **žičana** ~ screen; **paukova** ~ spider web; **železnička (električna)** ~ rail (electric) system.
mrgodan *a* morose, sullen.
mrk *a* dark.
mrkva *f* carrot.
mrlja *f* fleck, speck, smudge, spot.
mrmljati *v* to mutter.
mršav *a* slender, skinny, lank; meagre.
mršavljenje *n* slimming, losing weight.
mrštiti se *v* to frown, to pucker.
mrtav *a* dead, lifeless; ~ **pijan** dead-drunk.
mrtvačka kola *f* hearse.
mrtvački sanduk *m* coffin.
mrtvačnica *f* morgue, mortuary.
mrtvorođenče *n* stillborn.
mrva *f* crumb.
mrviti se *v* to crumble.
mrzak *a* odious, hateful, obnoxious.
mrzovoljan *a* morose, ill-humoured, sulky.
mržnja *f* hate, hatred, animosity.
mržnjenje *n* freezing.
mucati *v* to stammer, to stutter.
mučan *a* tormenting; difficult; awkward.
mučenik *m* martyr.
mučeništvo *n* martyrdom.
mučenje *n* torment, torture.
mučnina *f* nausea.
mućkati *v* to shake; to plot (*fig*).
mudar *a* wise.
mudrac *m* sage.
mudrost *f* wisdom.
mufte *adv* for nothing.
muk *m* hush.

muka *f* anguish, pain, suffering.
mukati *v* to moo, to bellow.
mukotrpan *a* hard, laborious.
mula *f* mule.
multimedijalan *a* multimedia.
mulj *m* mud, slime.
muljevit *a* slimy.
mumija *f* mummy.
mumlati *v* to mumble, to grumble.
municija *f* ammunition, munitions.
munuti *v* to push, to shove.
munja *f* lightning.
munjevit *a* swift as lightning.
murdarluk *m* negligence.
musav *a* slobbery.
musti *v* to milk.
mušica *f* midge, fly.
muškarača *f* tomboy.

muškarčina *f* he-man.
muški *a* male, masculine; ~ **toalet** *m*
gents; **~a ruka** *f* a firm hand.
mušterija *f* customer, buyer, client.
muštikla *f* cigarette holder.
mutan *a* muddy, unclear, turbid.
mutiti *v* to stir, to mix; to disturb, to
confuse.
muvati se *v* to wander about.
muzej *m* museum.
muzičar *m* musician.
muzika *f* music.
muzikalan *a* musical.
muž *m* husband, man.
muževan *a* manly, manful.
muževno *adv* manfully.
muževnost *f* manhood, manliness.

N

na *prep* on, upon; ~ **konju** horseback; ~ **obali** ashore; ~ **pola puta** halfway, midway; ~ **sreću** happily.

nabaciti *v* to propose, to suggest.

nabasati *v* to come across suddenly.

nabaviti *v* to procure, to supply, to gather.

nabavljač *m* supplier.

nabediti *v* to insinuate, to ascribe.

nabijen *a* crammed.

nabirati *v* ruffle.

nabiti *v* to ram down, to force down; ~ **na kolac** *v* to impale.

naboj *m* charge.

nabor *m* crease, fold, pleat.

nabosti *v* to prick, to stick.

nabrati *v* to pluck, to gather, to pick.

nabrojati *v* to enumerate.

nabubati *v* to cram up.

nabubriti *v* to swell.

nabusito *adv* gruffly, roughly.

nacediti *v* to squeeze.

nacepati *v* to chop, to cut.

nacija *f* nation, race.

nacionalista *m* nationalist.

nacionalizam *m* nationalism.

nacionalizovati *v* to nationalize.

nacist *m* Nazi.

nacrt *m* plan, design, scheme.

načelo *n* principle, maxim, tenet.

načičkati *v* to set thickly.

način *m* manner, way; ~ **života** lifestyle.

načitan *a* well-read, lettered.

naći *v* to find.

nad *prep* above, over.

nada *f* hope, expectation.

nadahnuće *n* inspiration.

nadahnuti *v* to inspire.

nadaleko *adv* far, widely, remotely.

nadanje *n* hoping.

nadaren *a* talented, gifted.

nadati se *v* to hope, to hope for.

nadbiskup *f* archbishop.

nadbiskupija *f* archbishopric.

nadčovečanski *a* superhuman.

nadesno *adv* to the right.

nadev *m* stuffing, filling.

nadgledati *v* to oversee, to supervise.

nadgradnja *f* superstructure.

nadgrobni *a* funeral, funerary; ~ **spomenik** *m* gravestone, tombstone; ~ **natpis** epitaph; ~**o slovo** *n* funeral sermon.

nadimak *m* nickname.

nadimanje *n* flatulence.

nadjačati *v* to overpower.

nadležan *a* competent, proper.

nadmašiti *v* to surpass.

nadmen *a* haughty.

nadmeno *adv* haughtily.

nadmetanje *n* contest.

nadmoć *f* superiority, supremacy.

nadmoćan *a* dominant, predominant, prevalent.

nadmudriti *v* to outwit, to baffle.

nadnica *f* wage, salary.

nadničar *m* day labourer.

nadobudan *a* suspicious, pretentious.

nadohvat *adv* at random, close to.

nadoknada *f* compensation.

nadoknaditi *v* to compensate; ~ **štetu** to indemnify.

nadoknadiv *a* recoverable, retrievable.

nadole *adv* downward(s).

nadomak *adv* near, at hand.

nadraživ *a* irritable; ~**žujuće sredstvo** *n* irritant.

nadrealizam *m* surrealism.

nadrilekar *m* quack, fake doctor.

nadstrešnica *f* awning.

naduvati *v* to inflate; to fill with air; to exaggerate (*fig*).

nadvisiti *v* to surmount, to surpass.

nadvladati *v* to subdue, to overcome.

nadzemni *a* overground.

nadzor *m* supervision.

nadzornik *m* overseer, superintendant, supervisor.

nadzvučni *a* supersonic.

nadživeti *v* to outlive.

nađubriti *v* to fertilize, to manure.

nafta *f* petroleum, oil.

nag *a* naked, undressed, bare.

nagađanje *n* guesswork.

nagađati *v* to guess.

nagao *a* abrupt, quick, hasty, rash.
nagib *m* slant, slope.
naginjati *v* to bend, to lean.
naglasak *m* accent, astress; emphasis.
naglavce *adv* headlong.
naglost *f* rashness, impetuousness.
nagluv *a* hard of hearing.
nagnan *a* forced, driven.
nagnut *a* sloping, inclined.
nagodba *f* agreement, mutual promise.
nagomilati *v* to agglomerate, to accumulate.
nagonski *a* instinctive, spontaneous.
nagovaranje *n* persuasion.
nagovarati *v* to persuade.
nagoveštaj *m* hint, indication.
nagovoriti *v* to persuade, to coax.
nagrabusiti *v* to get into trouble.
nagrada *f* prize, recompense, reward, retribution.
nagraditi *v* to reward.
nagrditi *v* to deface.
nagrizanje *n* corrosion.
nagurati *v* to push, to cram.
nahoče *n* foundling.
nahraniti *v* to give food, to feed.
naići *v* to come across.
naime *adv* namely, that is to say.
naimenovanje *n* nomination, designation, appointment.
naivan *a* naive, simple, unsophisticated.
naivnost *f* artlessness.
naizmeničan *a* alternate, in turn; ~**na struja** *f* alternating current.
najam *m* rent, hire.
najamnički *a* mercenary.
najaviti *v* to announce, to report.
najbliže *adv* nearest.
najbolji *adv* best.
najbrže *adv* fastest.
najdalje *adv* farthest, furthest.
najdublje *adv* inmost, innermost.
najedanput *adv* suddenly, at once.
najezda *f* invasion, raid.
najgore *adv* worst.
najkasniji *a* the latest.
najmanje *adv* least of all.
najmiti *v* to engage, to hire.
najniže *adv* lowest.
najpre *adv* first, firstly.
najstariji *a* eldest.

najveći *a* the biggest.
najviši *a* supreme, topmost, uppermost.
najzad *adv* at last, finally.
nakana *f* intention.
nakaza *f* monster, monstrosity.
nakaznost *f* deformity, monstrosity.
nakićen *a* adorned, decorated.
nakit *m* jewels, jewelry (*amer*), jewellery (*br*).
nakititi *v* to adorn, to ornament.
naklonost *f* favour.
naklonjenost *f* liking, affection.
naknada *f* reimbursement, compensation; ~ **za bolovanje** sick pay.
nakon *prep* after.
nakostrešen *a* bristling.
nakovanj *m* anvil.
nakraj *prep* at the end.
nakrcati *v* to load.
nakresan *a* boozy, tipsy, drunken.
nakrivljen *a* lop-sided, crooked.
nakupiti *v* to accumulate.
nakvasiti *v* to moisten, to wet, to water.
nalaz *m* find; **lekarski** ~ diagnosis.
nalazište *n* location, finding place.
nalepnica *f* label.
nalevo *adv* to the left, on the left.
naličje *n* reverse, other side.
nalik *a* similar, resembling.
naliti *v* to pour, to pour out.
naliv pero *m* fountain pen.
nalog *m* order, command.
naljutiti *v* to antagonize, to make angry.
nama *pn* to us.
namagarčiti *v* to make an ass of oneself.
namamiti *v* to allure, to inveigle.
namćorast *a* surly, sullen.
namena *f* destination, determination.
namera *f* intention, purpose, design.
nameravan *a* purposeful, intended.
namerno *adv* intentionally.
namestiti *v* to place, to set, to put; to arrange, to make.
namesto *adv* rather, instead, in lieu of.
nameštaj *m* furniture.
nameišten *a* furnished; affected (izveštačen).
nameštenje *n* post, position.
namet *m* duty, tax, toll.
nametljiv *n* importunate, troublesome.
nametljivac *m* intruder, busybody, meddler.

namigivati *v* to wink, to blink.
namiguša *f* flirt, coquette.
namiriti *v* to settle, to pay.
namočiti *v* to soak, to impregnate.
namrštiti se *v* to frown.
naneti *v* to deposit, to bring; to cause; ~
  bol to cause a pain.
nanišaniti *v* to aim.
nanizati *v* to string, to file.
naniže *adv* downward(s).
nanos *m* deposit.
naočari *fpl* spectacles, glasses; ~ **za**
  sunce *fpl* sunglasses.
naočit *a* presentable, impressive, striking.
naodmet *adv* unnecessary.
naoko *adv* apparently, ostensibly.
naopako *adv* inside out, topsy-turvy,
  upside-down.
naoružan *a* armed.
naoružanje *n* armament.
naoštren *a* sharpened.
napad *m* assault, attack, onset, onslaught.
napadač *m* assailant, attacker.
napadati, napasti *v* to attack, to assail.
napamet *adv* by heart.
napasnik *m* aggressor.
napet *a* strained, tight.
napetost *f* tension, tenseness.
napipati *v* to find by feeling.
napismeno *adv* in writing.
napit *a* drunk, inebriated.
napitak *m* beverage, drink.
napiti se *v* to get drunk.
naplatiti *v* to be paid in cash.
napojnica *f* tip, fee.
napokon *adv* finally, at last.
napolje *adv* out, outward.
napomena *f* notice, remark, comment.
napon *m* tension; **visoki** ~ high tension.
napor *m* effort, endeavour, strain.
naporan *a* hard, wearying, strenuous.
naporedan *a* parallel, side by side.
naprasan *a* sudden, abrupt.
naprasit *a* impetuous, hot-headed.
naprava *f* device, apparatus, gadget.
napred *adv* ahead, onward, in advance.
napredak *m* progress, improvement.
napredan *a* progressive.
napredovanje *n* advancement, progress.
napredovati *v* to make progress, to
  advance.

napregnut *a* highly strung.
naprezanje *n* exertion, strain.
naprstak *m* thimble.
napukao *a* cracked.
napuniti *v* to fill, to make full, to fill up.
napustiti *v* to abandon, to desert, to leave.
napuštanje *n* abandonment, desertion.
napušten *a* desolate.
nar *m* pomegranate (*bot*).
naramak *m* armful.
naramenica *f* suspenders.
narastao *a* grown up.
narav *f* temper, temperament, nature.
naravno *adv* certainly, indeed, surely.
narcis *m* daffodil (*bot*).
narečje *n* dialect.
naredan *a* following, next.
naredba *f* order, command, direction.
narednik *m* sergeant.
narkoman *m* drug addict.
narkomanija *f* drug addiction.
narkotičan *a* narcotic.
naročit *a* distinctive, special, particular.
naročito *adv* especially, notably.
narod *m* nation, folk; people, population.
narodni *a* national; popular, public; ~**a**
  muzika *f* folk music; ~**a biblioteka**
  public library.
naručiti *v* to order, to indent.
naručilac *m* orderer.
naručje *n* armful.
narudžbina *f* commission, order.
narugati se *v* to ridicule, to rally.
narukvica *f* bracelet.
naružiti *v* to mar, to deface; to scold.
nas *pn* us.
nasamariti *v* to dupe.
naseliti *v* to populate, to settle.
naseljavanje *n* settlement.
naseljen *a* inhabited.
naseljenik *m* settler.
nasilan *a* violent.
nasilje *n* violence.
nasip *m* dam, embankment.
naslaga *f* deposition, layer.
nasledan *a* hereditary.
naslediti *v* to inherit.
naslednica *f* heiress.
naslednik *m* heir; successor.
nasledstvo *n* heritage, inheritance, legacy.
naslepo *adv* blindly.

naslon *m* support, rest.
naslonjača *f* armchair.
naslov *m* title, heading, caption.
naslovni *a* title; **~a strana** *f* front page, title page; **~a uloga** the title role.
naslutiti *v* to feel a premonition.
nasmejan *a* laughing.
nasmešen *a* smiling.
nastaniti se *v* to settle.
nastati *v* to begin, to originate, to arise.
nastava *f* teaching; education.
nastavak *m* continuation; sequel.
nastaviti *v* to proceed, to continue.
nastavnica *f* schoolmistress.
nastavnik *m* schoolmaster, schoolteacher.
nastojanje *n* endeavour, attempt, effort.
nastradati *v* to perish, to be ruined.
nastran *a* eccentric, strange, abnormal.
nastranost *f* eccentricity.
nastranu *adv* apart, aside.
nastrešnica *f* eaves.
nastrojen *a* disposed.
nastup *m* outbreak; attack; appearance.
nasukati se *v* to be stranded.
nasumce *adv* blindly.
nasuprot *adv* opposite to, against.
naš *pn* our, ours.
našaliti se *v* to make a joke.
naškoditi *v* to damage, to harm.
natenane *adv* leisurely, slowly.
naterati *v* to compel, to force, to oblige.
natezati *v* to stretch, to tighten.
natmuren *a* frowning, sullen.
natopiti *v* to saturate, to wet.
natovaren *a* fraught, loaded.
natpis *m* inscription, writing.
natprirodan *a* supernatural.
natrag *adv* back, backwards.
natrpan *a* overcrowded.
naučni *a* scientific.
naučnik *m* scholar, scientist.
nauditi *v* to do harm to.
nauka *f* science.
naumiti *v* to intend, to mean.
nautički *a* nautical.
navići se *v* to get used to.
navika *f* habit.
naviknut *a* accustomed.
navoditi *v* to quote, to cite.
navodnici *fpl* quotation marks.
navodno *adv* allegedly.

navodnjavanje *m* watering, irrigation.
navoštiti *v* to wax.
navrat nanos *adv* hastily.
nazad *adv* back.
nazadan *a* conservative, retrograde.
nazdraviti *v* to toast, to drink a toast.
nazeb *m* cold.
naziv *m* name, title.
nazvati *v* to entitle.
nažalost *adv* unfortunately.
ne *adv* no, not.
neadekvatan *a* inadequate.
neaktivan *a* inactive.
neaktivnost *f* inactivity.
nebeski *a* celestial, heavenly.
nebitan *a* immaterial.
nebo *n* heaven, sky.
nebriga *f* negligence, carelessness.
nebrojen *a* unnumbered.
necivilizovan *a* uncivilized.
nečastan *a* dishonourable.
nečist *a* impure, unclean.
nečitak, nečitljiv *a* illegible.
nečovečan *a* inhuman.
nečovečnost *f* inhumanity.
nečujan *a* silent, inaudible.
nečuven *a* unheard-of.
nećak *m* nephew.
nećaka *f* niece.
nećkanje *n* hesitation.
nećkati se *v* to hesitate.
nedaća *f* mishap, misfortune.
nedaleko *adv* nearly, not remotely.
nedavan *a* recent, late.
nedavno *adv* recently, lately.
nedelo *n* crime, demeanour.
nedelja *f* Sunday; week.
nedeljni *a* Sunday; weekly; **~ časopis** *m* a weekly magazine; **~e novine** *fpl* Sunday newspaper.
nedeljno *adv* weekly; **jednom ~** once weekly.
nedeljiv *a* indivisible.
nedisciplinovan *a* undisciplined.
nedokučiv *a* unobtainable, unfathomable.
nedoličan *a* unbecoming, indecent.
nedopustiv *a* inadmissible.
nedosledan *a* inconsequent, inconsistent.
nedostatak *m* deficiency, lack, shortcoming, want.
nedostižan *a* inaccessible, elusive.

nedostojan *a* unbecoming, unworthy.
nedoumica *f* hesitation, indecision.
nedovoljan *a* insufficient, deficient.
nedovršen *a* unfinished.
nedozvoljen *a* forbidden.
nedruštven *a* unsociable.
nedužan *a* innocent, not guilty.
neefikasan *a* inefficient.
neefikasnost *f* inefficiency.
neformalnost *f* informality.
nega *f* care.
negde *adv* somewhere, someplace; **tu ~** *adv* hereabouts.
nego *conj* than.
negodovanje *n* indignation, resentment.
negostoljubiv *a* inhospitable, unfriendly.
negostoljubivost *f* inhospitability.
nehat *m* negligence.
nehotice *adv* involuntarily.
nehotičan *a* involuntary.
nehrišćanski *a* unchristian.
neimar *m* constructor, builder.
neiscrpan *a* inexhaustible.
neiskren *a* devious, insincere.
neiskrenost *f* insincerity.
neiskusan *a* inexperienced.
neiskustvo *f* inexperience.
neiskvaren *a* pure, unsophisticated.
neisplaćen *a* due, owing.
neispravan *a* incorrect, wrong.
neistinit *a* untrue.
neistinitost *f* falsity.
neistražen *a* unexplored.
neizbežan *a* inevitable, unavoidable.
neizbežno *adv* inevitably.
neizbrisiv *a* indelible; deep, profound (*fig*).
neizdržljiv *a* intolerable, unbearable.
neizlečiv *a* incurable.
neizlečivost *f* incurability.
neizmenljiv *a* unalterable.
neizmerno *adv* immensely.
neizreciv *a* inexpressible, unspeakable.
neizvesnost *f* suspense, uncertainty.
neizvestan *a* uncertain.
neizveštačen *a* artless, unaffected.
neizvodljiv *a* unfeasible.
nejasan *a* indistinct, vague.
nejednak *a* unequal.
nejednakost *f* inequality, diversity.
nejestiv *a* inedible.

neka *adv* let.
nekada *adv* once, once upon a time.
nekako *adv* somehow.
nekažnjen *a* unpunished.
nekažnjivost *f* impunity.
neki *pn* some, certain.
nekolicina *f* several, some.
nekontrolisan *a* uncontrollable.
nekoristan *a* ineffectual, useless.
nekrolog *m* obituary.
nekvalifikovan *a* unqualified, unskilled.
nelagodnost *f* uneasiness.
nelogičan *a* illogical.
nelojalan *a* disloyal, unfaithful.
nelojalnost *f* disloyalty.
neljubazan *a* unkind.
nem *a* dumb, mute.
nemaran *a* negligent, careless.
nemaština *f* penury, poverty.
nemilosrdan *a* merciless, ruthless, uncharitable.
nemilost *f* disgrace.
neminovan *a* inevitable, unavoidable.
nemir *m* disquiet, excitement, unrest.
nemiran *a* restless, unrestful.
nemoć *f* weakness, infirmity.
nemoćan *a* powerless, weak, impotent.
nemoguć *a* impossible; unbearable.
nemogućnost *f* impossibility.
nemoralan *a* immoral, bad, wicked.
nenadmašan *a* unparalleled, unsurpassed.
nenadoknadivo *adv* irretrievably.
nenameran *a* unintentional.
nenametljiv *a* unobtrusive, guarded.
nenaoružan *a* unarmed.
nenaseljen *a* unsettled.
nenastanjen *a* uninhabited.
nenaviknut *a* unaccustomed.
nenormalan *a* abnormal, aberrant.
neobavešten *a* uninformed.
neobavezan *a* optional, not obligatory.
neobičan *a* extraordinary, uncommon, unusual.
neobjašnjiv *a* inexplicable.
neobjavljen *a* unpublished.
neobrazovan *a* uneducated, ignorant.
neobuzdan *a* unruly, ungovernable.
neočekivan *a* unexpected.
neočekivanost *f* suddenness.
neodgovoran *a* irresponsible.
neodložan *a* urgent, pressing.

neodlučan *a* hesitant, indecisive.
neodlučnost *f* indecision.
neodobravati *v* to disapprove.
neodoljiv *a* irresistible.
neodređen *a* indefinite, indeterminate, vague; **~i član** *m* a, an (indefinite article) (*gram*).
neograničen *a* unlimited, indeterminable.
neometan *a* undisturbed.
neopažen *a* unobserved.
neophodan *a* indispensable.
neopisiv *a* indescribable.
neopoziv *a* irrevocable, irreversible.
neopravdan *a* unjustified.
neoprezan *a* inconsiderate, careless, incautious.
neopreznost *f* carelessness.
neoprostiv *a* inexcusable, unforgivable.
neorganski *a* inorganic.
neosetljiv *a* insensitive, unfeeling.
neoskrnavljen *a* unprofaned, pure.
neoslabljen *a* unimpaired.
neosnovan *a* groundless, unfounded.
neosporan *a* undeniable, unquestionable, undisputed.
neoštećen *a* undamaged.
neotesan *a* raw, unfinished.
neotporan *a* non-resistant.
neotuđiv *a* inalienable.
neovlašćen *a* unauthorized.
neozleđen *a* unharmed, unhurt, uninjured.
neoženjen *a* unmarried.
neparan *a* odd.
nepažljiv *a* inattentive, heedless.
nepažljivo *adv* inadvertently.
nepce *n* palate.
nepismen *a* illiterate.
neplaćen *a* outstanding, unpaid, owing.
neplodan *a* barren, fruitless, sterile.
nepobediv *a* invincible.
nepobitan *a* irrefutable.
nepodeljen *a* undivided.
nepodesan *a* inappropriate, ineligible, unfit.
nepodmitljiv *a* incorruptible.
nepodmitljivost *f* incorruptibility.
nepodnošljiv *a* insufferable, intolerable.
nepodudaran *a* incongruous.
nepodudarnost *f* incongruity.
nepogrešiv *a* infallible, unerring, impeccable.

nepojmljiv *a* incomprehensible, inconceivable.
nepokolebljiv *a* unfaltering, unwavering.
nepokornost *f* unruliness.
nepokretan *a* stationary, fixed.
nepomičan *a* motionless.
nepomirljiv *a* irreconcilable, implacable.
neponovljiv *a* unique, unrepeatable.
nepopravljiv *a* incorrigible.
nepopularan *a* unpopular.
nepopustljiv *a* inflexible, obstinate.
nepopustljivost *f* insistence, obstinacy.
neporeciv *a* irrefutable.
neposlušan *a* disobedient, naughty, insubordinate.
neposlušnost *f* disobedience, insubordination.
neposredan *a* direct.
neposredno *adv* directly.
nepostojan *a* changeable, inconstant.
nepostojeći *a* nonexistent.
nepošten *a* dishonest, fraudulent.
nepoštovanje *f* disrespect.
nepotizam *f* nepotism.
nepotpun *a* partial, incomplete.
nepotreban *a* needless, useless, unnecessary.
nepotvrđen *a* unconfirmed.
nepouzdan *a* unreliable, uncertain.
nepoverenje *n* disbelief, suspicion.
nepoverljiv *a* distrustful.
nepovezan *a* incoherent.
nepovezanost *f* incoherence.
nepovoljan *a* unfavourable.
nepovrediv *a* invulnerable.
nepovređen *a* intact.
nepoznat *a* unknown, unfamiliar.
nepozvan *a* uninvited.
nepoželjan *a* objectionable, undesirable.
nepraktičan *a* impractical.
nepraktičnost *f* impracticability.
nepravda *f* injustice, unfairness.
nepravedan *a* unfair, unjust.
nepravilan *a* irregular.
nepravilnost *f* irregularity.
nepravovremen *a* untimely.
neprecizan *a* imprecise.
nepredvidiv *a* unpredictable.
nepredviđen *a* unforeseen, unexpected.
neprekidan *a* ceaseless, continuous, incessant.

neprelazan *a* intransitive (*gram*); impassable.

nepremostiv *a* insurmountable.

neprestan *a* ceaseless, incessant; ~o ponavljanje *n* reiteration.

nepričljiv *a* taciturn.

neprihvatljiv *a* inadmissible.

neprijatan *a* disagreeable, unpleasant; distasteful.

neprijatelj *m* enemy, foe.

neprijateljski *a* adverse, hostile, unfriendly.

neprijateljstvo *n* enmity, hostility.

neprijatnost *f* unpleasantness, trouble.

neprikladan *a* improper, inappropriate, unbecoming, unseemly.

neprilika *f* nuisance, trouble.

neprimetan *a* imperceptible, undistinguishable.

nepripremljen *a* offhand, unprepared.

neprirodan *a* abnormal, unnatural; forced.

nepristojan *a* indecent, coarse, disreputable.

nepristojnost *f* indecency.

nepristrasan *a* impartial, unbiased, unprejudiced.

nepristrasnost *f* impartiality.

nepristupačan *a* inaccessible, unapproachable.

nepriznat *a* unacknowledged.

neprobojan *a* impenetrable; ~ za metke *a* bulletproof.

neprocenjiv *a* invaluable.

neprohodan *a* impassable.

nepromenljiv *a* changeless, invariable.

nepromišljen *a* imprudent, reckless, unthinking.

nepromišljenost *f* imprudence.

nepromočiv *a* waterproof.

neprosvećen *a* unenlightened.

neprovidan *a* non-transparent.

nepušač *m* non-smoker.

nerad *m* laziness, inaction.

neradnik *m* idler, laggard.

nerado *adv* grudgingly, unwillingly.

neraspoložen *a* depressed, indisposed.

neravan *a* rough, uneven.

nerazdvojan *a* inseparable.

nerazjašnjiv *a* inexplicable.

nerazrešiv *a* insoluble, unsolvable.

nerazuman *a* irrational, unreasonable, unwise.

nerazumljiv *a* incomprehensible, unintelligible.

nerazumno *adv* unreasonably.

nerazvijen *a* undeveloped.

nerealan *a* unrealistic, unreal, fictitious.

nered *m* disorder, confusion.

nerešen *a* unsettled, open.

nerešiv *a* insoluble.

nervirati se *v* to be nervous.

nesagoriv *a* fireproof, incombustible.

nesalomiv *a* unbreakable; unyielding.

nesanica *f* insomnia, sleeplessness.

nesavitljiv *a* inflexible, unbending.

nesavršen *a* defective, imperfect.

nesebičan *a* unselfish.

neseser *m* vanity case.

nesiguran *a* insecure, unsure, doubtful.

nesigurnost *f* insecurity.

nesklad *m* dissonance, disharmony.

nesklon *a* unwilling.

neskroman *a* immodest, shameless.

nesložan *a* discordant.

neslužben *a* unofficial.

nesmotren *a* negligent, incautious.

nesnosan *a* insupportable, sufferable.

nesporan *a* indisputable.

nesporazum *m* misunderstanding, misapprehension.

nesporno *adv* indisputably.

nesposoban *a* incapable, incompetent, inept.

nesposobnost *f* disability, inability, incompetence.

nespretan *a* clumsy, awkward.

nesrazmeran *a* disproportionate.

nesrećan *a* unfortunate, unhappy, unlucky; ~ slučaj *m* accident.

nestabilan *a* unstable.

nestabilnost *f* instability.

nestalan *a* unsteady.

nestanak *m* disappearance.

nestašan *a* playful, shallow.

nestašica *f* deficiency, lack.

nestašluk *m* escapade.

nestati *v* to vanish, to disappear.

nestrpljenje *n* impatience.

nestrpljiv *a* impatient, restless.

nestvaran *a* unreal.

nesuglasica *f* disagreement, difference, dispute.

nesumnjiv *a* undoubted, certain, sure, doubtless.
nesumnjivo *adv* indubitably.
nesvarljiv *a* indigestible.
nesvestan *a* unaware, unconscious.
nesvestica *f* fainting fit, swoon.
nesvršen *a* unfinished.
neškodljiv *a* harmless, innocuous, inoffensive.
nešto *pn* something, anything, some.
netačan *a* inaccurate, incorrect.
netačnost *f* fallibility, inaccuracy.
netaknut *a* untouched.
netolerancija *f* intolerance.
netrpeljiv *a* intolerant.
neubedljiv *a* inconclusive, unconvincing.
neučtiv *a* discourteous, impolite, disrespectful.
neučtivost *f* discourtesy, impoliteness.
neudoban *a* uncomfortable, inconvenient.
neudobno *adv* uncomfortably.
neuglađen *a* not polished; unmannerly.
neugodan *a* disagreeable, unpleasant.
neukost *f* ignorance.
neukrašen *a* unadorned.
neukrotiv *a* indomitable, untamable.
neukusan *a* unsavoury, tasteless.
neumeren *a* immoderate, intemperate.
neumesan *a* inopportune, unfit, inappropriate.
neumoljiv *a* implacable, pitiless, unrelenting.
neumoljivo *adv* implacably.
neumoran *a* indefatigable, tireless.
neuništiv *a* indestructible.
neunosan *a* unprofitable.
neuobičajen *a* unconventional.
neuporediv *a* incomparable, matchless, unequalled.
neupotrebljen *a* unused, new.
neuprljan *a* stainless, spotless.
neuravnotežen *a* unbalanced, ill-balanced.
neuredno *adv* disorderly.
neurednost *f* untidiness, disorder.
neuron *m* neurone.
neurotičan *a* neurotic.
neuroza *f* neurosis.
neuspeh *m* failure, unsuccessfulness.
neuspešan *a* ineffective, ineffectual, unsuccessful.

neustavan *a* unconstitutional.
neustrašiv *a* fearless, intrepid, undaunted.
neutešan *a* disconsolate, inconsolable.
neutralan *a* neutral.
neutralnost *f* neutrality.
neutron *m* neutron.
neutronska bomba *f* neutron bomb.
neuverljiv *a* unconvincing.
neuzdrman *a* unshaken.
nevaspitan *a* unmannerly, impolite, rude, uncivil.
nevažan *a* unimportant.
neven *m* marigold.
neveran *a* unfaithful.
nevernost *f* infidelity, unfaithfulness.
neverovatan *a* amazing, incredible, improbable, unbelievable.
nevesta *f* bride.
nevešt *a* inexpert, unskillful, awkward.
nevezan *a* unconnected, disconnected.
nevičnost *f* ineptitude.
nevidljiv *a* invisible, imperceptible.
nevidljivo *adv* invisibly.
neviđen *a* unseen.
nevin *a* guiltless, innocent.
nevinost *f* innocence.
nevolja *f* trouble.
nezaboravak *m* forget-me-not (*bot*).
nezaboravan *a* unforgettable.
nezabrinut *a* untroubled.
nezačinjen *a* unseasoned.
nezadovoljan *a* discontented, dissatisfied, displeased.
nezadovoljavajući *a* unsatisfactory.
nezadovoljstvo *n* displeasure, dissatisfaction.
nezahvalan *a* thankless, ungrateful.
nezahvalnost *f* ingratitude.
nezainteresovan *a* disinterested, uninterested, indifferent.
nezakonit *a* illicit, unlawful.
nezakonitost *f* illegality, unlawfulness.
nezamenljiv *a* irreplaceable.
nezamisliv *a* inconceivable, unimaginable, unthinkable.
nezanimljiv *a* uninteresting, tiresome.
nezaposlen *a* unemployed.
nezaposlenost *f* unemployment.
nezasit *a* insatiable, greedy, voracious.
nezaslužen *a* undeserved, undeserving.
nezaštićen *a* unprotected, defenceless.

nezauzet *a* unoccupied, vacant.
nezavidan *a* unenviable.
nezavisnost *f* independence.
nezavistan *a* independent, free.
nezgoda *f* disadvantage, accident, misadventure.
nezgodan *a* annoying, uncomfortable.
nezgrapan *a* awkward, clumsy.
nezgrapnost *f* awkwardness.
neznabožac *m* heathen, pagan.
neznalica *fm* ignoramus, dunce.
neznatan *a* insignificant, slight.
neznatno *adv* slightly.
nezreo *a* immature, premature.
nezvaničan *a* informal, unofficial.
nežan *a* fine, gentle, tender, fond.
neženstvo *n* celibacy.
neženja *m* bachelor.
nežno *adv* gently.
nežnost *f* tenderness, fondness.
ni *conj* neither; ~ ... ~ neither ... nor.
nigde *adv* nowhere.
nijansa *f* hue, shade, tint, nuance.
nikada *adv* never.
nikl *m* nickel.
niko *pn* nobody.
nilski konj *m* hippopotamus.
nipodaštavati *v* to scorn.
nipošto *adv* by no means.
nisko *adv* low.
niskost *f* meanness, baseness.
niša *f* alcove, niche.
nišan *m* mark, target, aim.
nišaniti *v* to aim.
ništa *pn* nothing, anything.
ništica *f* naught, nought.
nit *f* thread, yarn.
nitkov *m* rascal, wretch, miscreant, villain.
nivelisati *v* to level, to make equal.
niz[1] *m* range, line, series.
niz[2] *prep* down.
nizak *a* low; base, mean (podao); ~ **sto** *m* coffee table.
nizašta *adv* for nothing.
nizbrdo *adv* downhill.
noć *f* night.

noćiti *v* to spend the night.
noćna, noćni *a* night, nocturnal; ~ **mora** *f* nightmare; ~ **smena** night shift; ~ **klub** *m* nightclub.
noga *f* leg, foot (stopalo); ~ **od kreveta** bedpost.
nogari *mpl* trestle.
noj *m* ostrich.
nokat *m* nail, fingernail.
nokaut *m* knock-out.
nominalan *a* nominal, titular; ~**na vrednost** *f* face value.
normalan *a* normal, natural.
nos *m* nose.
nosač *m* bearer, porter, carrier.
nosila *fpl* stretcher.
nositi *v* to bear, to carry; to wear.
nosni *a* nasal.
nosorog *m* rhinoceros.
nostalgičan *a* homesick, nostalgic.
nostalgija *f* homesickness.
nov *a* new, novel; ~ **novcat** brand-new.
Nova godina *f* New Year.
novac *m* money, coin.
novajlija *m* beginner, novice.
novčani *a* monetary, fiscal, pecuniary; ~**a kazna** *f* fine.
novčanik *m* purse, wallet.
novembar *m* November.
novina *f* innovation, novelty.
novinar *m* journalist.
novine *fpl* newspaper.
novinska agencija *f* news agency, press agency.
novorođenče *n* newborn, babe, baby.
nozdrva *f* nostril.
nož *m* knife.
nuditi *v* to offer, to present.
nuklearan *a* nuclear; ~**na fizika** *f* nuclear physics; ~**no oružje** *npl* nuclear weapons; ~**na energija** *f* nuclear energy.
nula *f* zero, naught.
nusprodukt *m* by-product.
nužnik *m* lavatory, latrine.
nužno *adv* necessarily.
nužnost *f* necessity.

NJ

njakati *v* to bray.
njega *pn* him.
njegov *pn* his; **njegovo** its; **njena** her(s).
njihanje *n* swinging, rocking.

njihov *pn* their(s).
njuh *m* flair, smell, scent.
njušiti *v* to sniff, to smell.
njuška *f* muzzle, snout.

O

o *prep* about, relative to.
oaza *f* oasis.
oba *a* both.
obadva, obadvoje, oboje *a* both.
obala *f* coast, shore, seaside.
obalski *a* coastal; **~a straža** *f* coastguard.
obamrlost *f* lethargy, torpor.
obao *a* round.
obarač *m* trigger.
obaranje *n* felling.
obarati *v* to knock down.
obaška *adv* separately.
obaveštenje *n* notice, information, news.
obavestiti *v* to inform, to mention, to enlighten.
obaveza *f* commitment, obligation.
obavezan *a* incumbent, compulsory, obligatory.
obavezati *v* to compel, to force.
obaviti *v* to accomplish, to transact.
obazriv *a* cautious, prudent.
obazrivost *f* circumspection, prudence.
obdariti *v* to endown, to endue.
obdukcija *f* post mortem examination.
obećanje *n* promise.
obećavajući *a* promising.
obed *m* meal.
obeležiti *v* to mark.
obeležje *n* criterion, mark.
obeshrabren *a* discouraged, depressed.
obeshrabrenje *n* discouragement.
obeshrabriti *v* to discourage, to dishearten.
obesiti *v* to hang, to suspend.
obest *f* insolence.
obeštećenje *n* reparation.
obezbediti *v* to provide, to procure, to make sure.
obezglaviti *v* to decapitate; to confuse (*fig*).
obeznaniti se *v* to faint, to faint away.
obezvrediti *v* to make worthless; to underestimate.
obezvređenje *n* depreciation.
običaj *m* custom, use.
običan *a* ordinary, common, usual, plain, simple; **~ni ljudi** the common people; **~na žena** a simple woman.

obići *v* to go round, to visit.
obijač *m* burglar.
obilan *a* abundant, abounding, ample, plentiful.
obilazak *m* visit.
obilje *n* affluence, aboundance.
obim *m* perimeter, circumference; dimension.
obiman *a* voluminous.
obiti *v* to force, to break into; to rob.
objasniti *v* to explain, to make clear.
objašnjenje *n* explanation.
objava *f* proclamation, announcement.
objaviti *v* to announce, to declare.
objekat *m* object, thing; property.
objektivan *a* objective, impartial, unbiassed.
oblačan *a* cloudy.
oblačiti *v* to dress.
oblak *m* cloud.
oblakoder *m* skyscraper.
oblanda *f* wafer.
oblast *f* region, district.
obletati *v* to fly round.
oblik *m* configuration, form, shape; figure.
obliti *v* to pour over.
obližnji *a* nearby.
obljuba *f* violation, defloration.
oblutak *m* pebble.
obmana *f* delusion, deceit, illusion.
obmotati *v* to wrap round.
obnavljanje *n* restitution, renovation.
obnova *f* renovation, renewal.
obnoviti *v* to renovate, to renew.
obod *m* border, edge; brim (šešira).
obodriti *v* to encourage.
obogatiti *v* to enrich, to make rich.
oboje *num* both, the pair.
obojen *a* tinted, coloured.
oboleti *v* to sicken, to become ill.
oboriti *v* to overset, to overturn, to overthrow.
obostran *a* mutual.
obožavalac *m* admirer, fan.
obožavanje *n* adoration, worship.
obožavati *v* to adore, to idolize, to venerate.

obračun *m* settlement, reckoning.
obrada *f* management, treatment; cultivation; ~ **podataka** data processing; ~ **teksta** word processing.
obradiv *a* workable, adaptable; cultivable, cultivatable.
obrastao *a* overgrown; ~ **korovom** weedy; ~ **trskom** reedy.
obratan *a* opposite, contrary.
obrati *v* to gather, to pick.
obraz *m* face, cheek.
obrazac *m* form, pattern.
obrazlagati *v* to elucidate, to explain.
obrazovan *a* educated, cultured, literate.
obred *m* ceremony, rite.
obrezati *v* to circumcise.
obrezivanje *n* circumcision.
obrijati *v* to shave.
obris *m* contour, outline.
obrisati *v* to wipe, to rub.
obrnuti *v* to turn round, to revert, to invert.
obrok *m* meal, ration; ~ **umesto doručka i ručka** brunch.
obrt *m* turnover (promet).
obrub *m* edging, hem.
obruč *m* hoop.
obrva *f* brow, eyebrow.
obuća *f* footwear.
obućar *m* shoemaker, cobbler.
obučavanje *n* teaching, tuition, instruction.
obučavati *v* to teach, to instruct.
obučen *a* clad.
obuhvaćen *a* included, comprised.
obuka *f* training.
obustava *f* suspense, abolition, stoppage.
obuzet *a* engrossed; ~ **strahom** panic-stricken.
obveznica *f* bond, obligation.
obzir *m* consideration.
ocena *f* estimate, valuation.
oceniti *v* to esteem, to value.
ocrniti *v* to make black; to defame, to speak ill of.
ocrtati *v* to trace, to delineate.
očajan *a* desperate, agonizing.
očajanje *n* despair, hopelessness.
očajnički *adv* despairingly.
očaran *a* enthralled.
očarati *v* to enchant, to bewitch.
očaravajući *a* enthralling, fascinating.

očekivanje *n* expectation.
očekivati *v* to expect.
očešljati *v* to comb.
očetkati *v* to brush up.
očevidac *m* eyewitness.
oči *npl* eyes.
očigledan *a* evident, apparent, obvious.
očinski *adv* fatherly, paternal.
očinstvo *n* fatherhood, paternity.
očistiti *v* to clean, to cleanse.
očit *a* evident.
oční *a* eye, ophthalmic; ~**a jabučica** *f* eyeball; ~ **kapak** *m* eyelid.
očnjak *m* eyetooth.
očuh *m* stepfather.
očuvati *v* to preserve.
oćutati *v* to be silent.
od *prep* away, from, since.
odabiranje *n* selection.
odabrati *v* to select, to choose.
odaja *f* room, chamber.
odakle *adv* from where.
odan *a* affectionate, devoted.
odanost *f* devotion.
odašiljač *m* transmitter.
odaslati *v* to expedite, to send off.
odati *v* to betray, to disclose.
odavanje pošte *n* homage.
odavno *adv* long ago.
odbaciti *v* to discard, to reject.
odbijanje *n* denial, refusal, rejection, rebuff.
odbijati *v* to refuse, to deny, to decline.
odbitak *m* deduction, allowance.
odbojka *f* volleyball.
odbojnik *m* bumper.
odbor *m* committee.
odbrambeni *a* defensive.
odbrana *a* defence, plea.
odbrojavanje *n* countdown.
odeća *f* garment, clothes, attire.
odeljenje *n* division, section, department, ward (u bolnici); ~ **za intenzivnu negu** intensive care unit.
odelo *n* clothes, coat; dress, costume; suit.
odenuti *v* to dress.
odgađanje *n* adjournment, postponement.
odgajivač *m* breeder, grower.
odgovarajući *a* corresponding, adequate, appropriate.
odgovor *m* reply, answer, response.

odgovoran *a* accountable, reponsible, answerable, liable.

odgovoriti *v* to answer, to respond, to reply.

odgovornost *f* accountability, responsibility, liability.

odgristi *v* to bite off.

odista *adv* indeed, really.

odjedanput *adv* suddenly, at once.

odjeknuti *v* to resound.

odlagati *v* to defer, to delay, to postpone.

odlazak *m* departure, going away; exodus; withdrawal.

odlaziti *v* to depart.

odlediti *v* to defrost.

odličan *a* excellent.

odložiti *v* to adjourn, to postpone.

odlučan *a* decisive, determined, resolute.

odlučiti *v* to decide, to resolve.

odlučno *adv* decidedly.

odlučujući *a* crucial.

odluka *f* decision, resolution.

odmah *adv* immediately, at once, straight away.

odmaralište *n* resort, resting place.

odmazda *f* reprisal, revenge, retaliation.

odmeriti *v* to measure, to apportion.

odmetnik *m* outlaw, proscript, renegade.

odmor *m* rest, repose; break.

odmotati *v* to unroll; to disentangle.

odnos *m* relation, relationship, ratio.

odnosan *a* respective.

odnositi se *v* to concern, to pertain, to refer.

odnosno *adv* respectively.

odobravati *v* to approve, to acclaim.

odobrenje *n* approbation, approval; permission, leave.

odobriti *v* to approve (of).

odoka *adv* approximately, roughly.

odoleti *v* to resist, to stand out, to withstand.

odora *f* robe, dress.

odrastao *a* adult, grown-up.

odraz *m* reflection, image.

odraziti *v* to reflect.

odrečan *a* negative.

odreći se *v* to reject, to decline, to renounce; to refuse.

odred *m* detachment, draft, squad.

odredba *f* definition.

odredište *n* destination.

odrediti *v* to determine, to appoint, to assign; to prescribe.

određen *a* definitive, conclusive, certain, positive.

odrešiti *v* to untie, to unfasten; ~ **kesu** to disburse.

odricanje *n* negation, denial, disclaimer, renunciation; ~ **od prestola** abdication.

odronjavanje *n* landslide.

odrpanac *m* ragamuffin.

održavanje *n* maintenance, keeping; conservation.

odsada *adv* from now on, in the future.

odsečak *m* segment, snip.

odseći *v* to cut off; ~ **glavu** to behead, to decapitate.

odsek *m* department, section.

odseliti *v* to move.

odsjaj *m* reflection, gleam.

odskočiti *v* to jump, to bounce; to stand out, to distinguish (*fig*).

odskora *adv* recently.

odstojanje *n* distance, interval.

odstraniti *v* to remove; to exclude.

odstupanje *n* deviation, exception; retreat (*mil*).

odstupiti *v* to step back, to step away; to withdraw.

odsudan *a* decisive.

odsustvo *n* absence; leave.

odsutan *a* absent, missing.

odškrinuti *v* to leave ajar.

odštampati *v* to print.

odšteta *f* amends, compensation, indemnity.

odustati *v* to renounce, to drop.

oduševljen *a* elated, delighted, enthusiastic.

oduševljenje *n* exaltation, exhilaration, delight, ecstasy.

oduvati *v* to blow away.

oduzeti *v* to take away; to revoke; to deduct; ~ **nevinost** to deflower.

oduzimanje *n* deduction, subtraction (*mat*).

odvajanje *n* separation, severance.

odvažno *adv* bravely.

odvažnost *n* intrepidity, bravery, courage.

odveć *adv* too much.

odvezati *v* to untie, to unfasten.

odvijač *m* screwdriver.

odviti *v* to unroll, to unfold.
odvodna cev *f* drainpipe, waste pipe.
odvojen *a* separate, apart, asunder; detached.
odvojiti *v* to separate, to sever, to cut off.
odvratan *a* abominable, detestable, disgusting, repulsive, repugnant.
odvratiti *v* to dissuade, to divert, to avert.
odvratnost *f* abomination, disgust, aversion, revulsion, loathing.
odvrnuti *v* to unscrew, to turn off.
odžak *m* chimney.
oficir *m* officer.
ofsajd *m* offside.
oganj *m* fire, flame.
oglas *m* advertisement; placard.
oglasna tabla *f* bulletin board.
ogled *m* experiment, test.
ogledalo *n* looking glass, mirror.
ogledni *a* experimental.
oglodati *v* to gnaw.
ognjište *n* fireside, fireplace, hearth.
ogorčen *a* resentful.
ogorčenost *f* resentment, bitterness.
ogovarati *v* to gossip, to backbite.
ograda *f* fence, hedge; ~ **na stepeništu** banisters, handrail; **živa** ~ hedge.
ogradica za decu playpen.
ogranak *m* branch, section, subdivision.
ograničen *a* narrow-minded (*fig*).
ograničenje *n* limitation, restriction.
ograničiti *v* to restrict, to limit, to retrench.
ogrebotina *f* scratch.
ogrešiti se *v* to sin.
ogrlica *f* necklace.
ogrnuti *v* to put on, to drape.
ogroman *a* enormous, huge, immense.
ogrozd *m* gooseberry.
ogrtač *m* cape.
oguglati *v* to get accustomed to.
oguliti *v* to peel off.
oh *interj* ah.
ohol *a* haughty, lofty.
oholost *f* haughtiness, pride.
ohrabrenje *n* encouragement.
oj *interj* hey.
ojačati *v* to strengthen.
ojed *m* sore.
okaljati *v* to dirty.
okarakterisati *v* to characterize.
okean *m* ocean.

okeanski *a* oceanic.
okićen *a* bedecked, decorated.
okititi *v* to decorate, to adorn.
oklagija *f* rolling pin.
oklevati *v* to hesitate, to waver.
oklevetati *v* to slander, to asperse, to vilify.
oklop *m* armour.
oklopni *a* armour; ~**a kola** *f* armoured car.
okno *n* window-pane.
oko *prep* about, around.
oko *n* eye.
okolina *f* environment, environs, surroundings.
okolišanje *n* circumlocution, digression.
okolišati *v* to digress.
okolni *a* adjoining, neighbouring.
okolnost *f* circumstance.
okomit *a* perpendicular, vertical.
okomiti se *v* to be intent upon.
okončan *a* accomplished, finished, terminated.
okoreo *a* inveterate; callous, insensible.
okosnica *f* framework, outline.
okovati *v* to put in irons, to shackle.
okovratnik *m* collar.
okrečiti *v* to whitewash.
okrenuti *v* to turn, to turn over.
okrepljujući *a* invigorating, refreshing.
okretan *a* agile, lively.
okretanje *n* rotation, turn.
okretati *v* to turn, to rotate, to revolve.
okretnica *f* turn table.
okretnost *f* agility, dexterity, skillfulness.
okrilje *n* shelter, protection.
okriviti *v* to blame, to accuse.
okrpiti *v* to repair, to mend.
okrug *m* district, province.
okrugao *a* rotund, round.
okruglast *f* roundish.
okrutan *a* cruel, inhuman, hard-hearted, fierce.
okrutnost *f* cruelty, ruthlessness.
okružiti *v* to encircle, to encompass.
okružni *a* district; ~ **javni tužilac** *m* district attorney; ~ **sud** district court.
oktava *f* octave (*mus*).
oktobar *m* October.
okuka *f* bend, curve.
okupati se *v* to bathe, to wash.
okupiti *v* to assemble, to gather.
okus *m* taste.

okvir *m* frame.
olabaviti *v* to loosen, to relax, to slack(en).
olakšavajući *a* extenuating, attenuant.
olakšanje *n* alleviation, relief.
olakšati *v* to alleviate, to facilitate.
oličavati *v* to personify, to impersonate, to embody.
Olimpijske igre *fpl* Olympic Games.
ološ *m* riff raff, scum.
olovan *a* leaden.
olovka *f* pencil.
oltar *m* altar.
oluja *f* storm, tempest; ~ **sa grmljavinom** thunderstorm; ~ **sa gradom** hailstorm.
oluk *m* gutter pipe.
olupina *f* wreckage.
omaći se *v* to slide, to slip; to escape (reč).
omađijati *v* to enchant, to bewitch.
omalovažavanje *n* disregard, slight.
omalovažiti *v* to belittle, to snub, to disregard.
omamljenost *f* stupor, dazement.
omanji *a* smallish.
omaška *f* lapse, error, mistake.
omekšati *v* to soften, to mollify; to mitigate.
ometati *v* to encumber, to hinder, to inhibit.
omiljen *a* favoured.
omlet *m* omelette.
omogućiti *v* to enable, to make possible.
omot *m* cover, covering; package, casing.
omražen *a* hateful.
omršaveti *v* to grow thin.
omrznuti *v* to become hateful, to take a dislike.
on *pn* he.
ona *pn* she.
onako *adv* in that way.
onamo *adv* there, yonder.
onda *adv* then, when, now and then.
one *pn* they.
onesposobiti *v* to incapacitate, to disable.
onesvestiti se *v* to faint, to swoon.
oni *pn* they.
ono *pn* it.
opadanje *n* decadence, decline.
opak *a* vicious, venomous.
opasač *m* girdle, belt.
opasan *a* dangerous, perilous, risky, hazardous.

opaska *f* comment, note, remark.
opasnost *f* danger, peril.
opat *m* abbot.
opatica *f* abbess.
opatija *f* abbey.
opažanje *n* perception, discernment.
opaziti *v* to perceive, to see, to espy.
opeka *f* brick.
opelo *n* funeral service.
opera *f* opera; opera house (zgrada).
operativan *a* operational.
opet *adv* again, afresh, once more.
opijanje *n* inebriation, boozing (*slang*).
opipavati *v* to touch, to grope.
opipljiv *a* palpable, tangible.
opis *m* description, picture.
opisan *a* descriptive.
opisati *v* to describe, to depict; to circumscribe (krug).
opiti se *v* to get drunk, to be intoxicated.
opklada *f* bet, wager.
opkoliti *v* to encircle, to surround.
opkoračiti *v* to straddle.
oplakati *v* to lament, to mourn.
oploditi *v* to fertilize.
oplodnja *f* fertilization.
oploviti *v* to circumnavigate.
opljačkati *v* to rifle, to rob, to plunder.
opna *f* membrane, web.
opomena *f* caution, warning.
opominjući *a* cautionary.
oponašanje *n* mimicry.
opor *a* acerbic.
oporavak *m* convalescence, recovery.
oporeziv *a* taxable.
oporezivanje *n* taxation.
oportunist *m* opportunist.
oporuka *f* testament, last will.
opovrgnuti *v* to refute.
opoziv *m* recall, retraction, revocation.
opozvati *v* to countermand, to revoke.
opraštanje *n* pardon, forgiveness; adieu, farewell.
oprati *v* to wash, to cleanse.
opravdan *a* valid.
opravdanje *n* justification, excuse, plea.
opravdano *adv* justifiably.
opravdati *v* to justify, to account for.
opraviti *v* to repair, to refit.
opredeljenje *n* destination; orientation; siding.

oprema *f* equipment, outfit, kit; **devojačka**
~ *f* dowry; ~ **za novorođenče** *f* layette.
opremiti *v* to equip, to fit out.
oprez *m* wariness, care, caution.
oprezan *a* alert, careful, cautious,
guarded, wary.
oprezno *adv* warily, advisedly.
opreznost *f* prudence, caution, alertness.
oprostiti *v* to forgive, to condone.
oprostiv *a* excusable.
oproštaj *m* pardon, forgiveness,
absolution.
opruga *f* spring.
opružiti se *v* to stretch, to sprawl.
opržiti *v* to scorch, to burn.
opsada *f* siege.
opsedati *v* to besiege; ~ **misli** to be obsessed.
opsednut *a* obsessive.
opseg *m* extent, amplitude.
opservatorija *f* observatory.
opsežan *a* extended, wide, large.
opstanak *m* existence, being.
opširan *a* expansive, detailed,
circumstantial.
opšte *a* general; ~ **pravo** *n* common law.
opštenje *n* communication, intercourse.
opština *f* community, commune;
municipality.
opterećenje *n* load, burden.
optičar *m* optician.
optički *a* optic (al).
optimista *m* optimist.
optimistički *a* optimistic.
optužba *f* accusation, arraignment,
charge.
optuženi *a* accused.
optužiti *v* to accuse, to arraign, to charge,
to indict.
optužnica *f* indictment.
optužujući *a* accusatory.
opunomoćiti *v* to authorize, to delegate.
opusteli *a* deserted, empty.
opustiti se *v* to relax.
opušak *m* cigarette end, butt.
orah *m* walnut, nut.
orahova ljuska *f* nutshell.
oran *a* disposed, willing.
orao *m* eagle.
oraščić *n* nutmeg (*začin*).
orati *v* to plough, to till.
oreol *m* halo.

organ *m* organ.
organizacija *f* organization.
organizam *m* organism.
organizovati *v* to organize, to coordinate.
organizovano putovanje *n* package tour.
orgazam *m* orgasm.
orgija *f* orgy.
orguljaš *m* organist.
orhideja *f* orchid.
originalnost *f* originality.
orijentalni *a* oriental.
orkan *m* hurricane.
orkestar *m* orchestra.
orlić *m* eaglet.
orlovski *a* aquiline; ~ **nokti** *mpl*
honeysuckle.
orman *m* cabinet; closet; cupboard; ~ **za**
knjige *m* bookcase; ~ **za odela**
wardrobe; ~ **za posuđe** sideboard; ~ **za**
odlaganje spisa filing cabinet.
ornament *m* ornament.
ornitologija *f* ornithology.
oronuo *a* weak, feeble, ruined, rundown.
orositi *v* to bedew, to besprinkle.
ortak *m* partner, associate.
ortopedski *a* orthopaedic.
oruđe *n* tool, instrument, utensil.
oružar *m* gunsmith.
oružje *n* weapon, arm.
osa *f* axis; wasp (*zool*).
osakaćenje *n* mutilation.
osakatiti *v* to maim, to cripple, to mutilate.
osam *num* eight.
ošamariti *v* to slap, to spank.
osamdeset *num* eighty.
osamdeseti *num a* eightieth.
osamdesetogodišnjak *m* octogenarian.
osamiti se *v* to be secluded, to live in
seclusion.
osamnaest *num* eighteen.
osamnaesti *num a* eighteenth.
osavremeniti *v* to modernize, to bring up
to date.
osećaj *m* sensation, feeling, perception.
osećajan *a* emotional, sentimental,
responsive.
osećajno *adv* feelingly.
osećanje *n* emotion, feeling, sense,
sentiment.
osećati *v* to feel; ~ **odvratnost** to loathe.
osedlati *v* to saddle.

oseka *f* ebb, tide.
osemenjavanje *n* insemination.
osetan *a* perceptible, perceivable, appreciable.
osetljiv *a* sensitive, sensible; susceptible.
osetljivost *f* sensibility, sensitivity.
osigurač *m* safety fuse (*el*).
osiguranje *n* insurance.
osigurati se *v* to insure.
osiguravač *m* insurer.
osim *prep* save, except, barring.
osionost *f* arrogance.
osip *m* rash.
osiromašen *a* impoverished.
osiromašiti *v* to impoverish.
oskrnaviti *v* to desecrate, to profane.
oskudan *a* scarce, deficient, wanting.
oskudica *f* scantiness, scarcity.
oslabiti *v* to weaken, to give way; to debilitate, to impair.
oslobađanje *n* acquittal, exoneration, release.
oslobođen *a* exempt; ~ **poreza** tax-free; ~ **carine** duty-free.
oslobođenje *n* exemption; liberation.
osloboditi *v* to liberate, to free, to clear; ~ **optužbe** to exonerate.
oslonac *m* support.
osmatrati *v* to observe, to scan.
osmeh *m* smile.
osmi *num a* eighth.
osmougao *m* octagon.
osmuditi *v* to singe.
osnivač *m* founder, establisher.
osnivati *v* to establish, to found, to set up.
osnov *m* foundation, basis.
osnova *f* base, ground, groundworks.
osnovati *v* to establish, to found; to constitute.
osnovni *a* basic, elementary, fundamental; ~**a škola** *f* primary school; ~ **ton** *m* keytone.
osoba *f* person, body, thing.
osobenost *f* characteristic, particularity, singularity.
osoblje *n* personnel, staff.
osoran *a* gruff, rude, surly.
osornost *f* surliness.
osovina *f* axis.
ospice *fpl* measles.
osporavati *v* to dispute, to contradict; ~ **vrednost** to depreciate.

osposobljen *a* qualified.
osramotiti *v* to dishonour, to disgrace.
osrednji *a* mediocre, middling.
osrednjost *f* mediocrity.
oštar *a* sharp; harsh, keen, poignant; acrid, acute.
ostatak *m* remainder, rest, remnant.
ostati *v* to remain, to stay.
ostava *f* larder, pantry.
ostaviti *v* to abandon, to leave.
ostavka *f* resignation.
ostavljen *a* forlorn.
osteopata *m* osteopath.
ostrići *v* to shear.
ostriga *f* oyster.
ostrvljanin *m* islander.
ostrvo *n* island, isle.
ostrvski *a* insular.
ostvarenje *n* realization, fruition.
ostvarivost *f* feasibility.
osuda *f* censure, condemnation; disapproval, blaim, rebuke.
osuditi *v* to condemn, to blame.
osujetiti *v* to hinder, to obstruct.
osumnjičen *a* suspected.
osušen *a* dry; parched.
osušiti *v* to dry.
osvajač *m* conqueror, invader.
osvanuti *v* to dawn, to break.
osvestiti se *v* to recover consciousness, to revive.
osveta *f* revenge, vengeance.
osvetiti *v* to avenge, to revenge.
osvetiti se *v* to retaliate, to take revenge.
osvetliti *v* to illuminate, to lighten.
osvetljenje *n* illumination.
osvetoljubiv *a* revengeful, vindicative.
osveženje *n* refreshment.
osvežiti *v* to freshen, to refresh; to cool.
osvojiti *v* to conquer, to win.
ošamućen *a* dazed.
ošamutiti *v* to stun, to astound.
oštetiti *v* to hurt, to harm, to blemish.
oštrina *f* acuteness, sharpness.
oštro *adv* sharply; ~**g vida** *a* eagle-eyed.
otac *m* father.
otadžbina *f* native land, fatherland.
otcepiti se *v* to secede.
otcepljenje *n* secession.
otečen *a* swollen.
oteklina *f* swelling.

oteliti se *v* to calve.
oterati *v* to beat off, to drive off.
oteti *v* to snatch, to hijack, to grab.
otezati *v* to delay.
otežavanje *n* aggravation.
otići *v* to depart, to start, to go, to leave; to withdraw.
otimač *m* hijacker, robber.
otimati *v* to snatch, to grab, to abduct.
otirač *m* doormat.
otisak *m* facsimile; imprint; ~ **prsta** fingerprint.
otkačiti *v* to unhook.
otkada *adv* since when.
otkako *adv* since.
otkazati *v* to reject, to deny; to cancel.
otkazivanje *n* denial, refusal; cancellation.
otključati *v* to unlock.
otkopčati *v* to unbutton, to uncouple.
otkriće *n* discovery, revelation, disclosure, detection.
otkriti *v* to discover, to reveal, to uncover.
otkucati *v* to typewrite.
otkup *m* ransom.
otmen *a* elegant, genteel, refined.
otmenost *f* elegance.
otmica *f* abduction, kidnapping.
otpad *m* waste, junk, trash.
otpadnik *m* deserter, renegade.
otpasti *v* to fall off.
otpis *m* depreciation; write-off.
otplivati *v* to swim away.
otpor *m* resistance, opposition.
otporan *a* resisting, immune.
otpratiti *v* to accompany, to follow.
otprema *f* forwarding, dispatch, shipment.
otpremiti *v* to dispatch, to send.
otprilike *adv* about, approximately.
otpustiti *v* to dismiss.
otpuštanje *n* dismissal, discharge.
otrcan *a* shabby, worn out, ragged.
otrcano *adv* shabbily.
otresti *v* to shake down.
otrezniti *v* to sober.
otrov *m* poison, venom.
otrovan *a* poisonous, venomous.
otuđen *a* estranged, alienated.
otuđenje *n* alienation.
otuđenost *f* estrangement.
otuđiti *v* to alienate, to estrange; to dispossess.

otupeti *v* to become dull, to deaden.
otvarač *m* opener; ~ **za konzerve** can opener; ~ **za boce** bottle-opener.
otvaranje *n* opening.
otvarati *v* to open.
otvor *m* opening, aperture, orifice, hole.
otvoren *a* open; candid, forthright, frank, plain-spoken, open-minded, outspoken.
otvoreno *adv* bluntly, frankly, freely.
otvorenost *f* candour, openness.
otvrdnuti *v* to harden.
ovaj *pn* this.
Ovan *m* Aries (*astrol*).
ovan *m* ram.
ovaploćen *a* incarnate.
ovaploćenje *n* embodiment.
ovca *f* sheep, ewe.
ovčetina *f* mutton.
ovčija koža *f* sheepskin.
ovde *adv* here.
ovekovečiti *v* to eternize, to perpetuate.
ovi *pn* these.
ovisan *a* dependent.
ovlastiti *v* to authorize.
ovlaš *adv* superficially.
ovlašćenje *n* authorization, permit.
ovlažiti *v* to dampen, to moisten.
ovoliko *adv* so much, as much.
ovozemaljski *a* worldly.
ovuda *adv* this way.
ozaren *a* beaming.
ozbiljan *a* serious, demure, grave, sober, steady.
ozbiljnost *f* gravity, earnestness.
ozdraviti *v* to convalesce.
ozdravljenje *n* recovery.
ozleda *f* injury.
ozlediti *v* to harm, to wound.
ozlojeđen *a* indignant.
označiti *v* to mark, to designate.
oznaka *f* characteristic, mark, sign; ~ **čina** *f* insignia.
ozon *m* ozone.
ožalošćen *a* aggrieved.
ožedneti *v* to get thirsty.
oženiti se *v* to get married.
oženjen *a* married.
ožiljak *m* scar.
oživeti *v* to animate, to enliven; to resuscitate.
oživljavanje *n* revival, resuscitation.

P

pa *adv* and, well.
pabirčiti *v* to glean.
pacijent *m* patient.
pacov *m* rat.
pače *n* duckling.
pad *m* downfall, flop.
padati *v* to fall, to tumble; ~ u oči to strike (somebody).
padavica *f* epilepsy.
padavina *f* rainfall.
padina *f* slope, obliquity.
padobran *m* parachute.
padobranac *m* paratrooper.
paganski *a* pagan.
pahuljast *a* flaky.
pahuljica *f* flake.
pajac *m* clown.
pakao *m* hell, inferno.
paket *m* packet; parcel.
paklen *a* infernal, hellish.
pakost *f* spitefulness, malice.
pakovanje *n* packing; packaging; wrapping.
pakovati *v* to pack.
palac *m* thumb (na ruci); toe (na nozi).
palačinka *f* pancake, crepe.
palata *f* palace.
paleta *f* palette.
palica *f* stick, baton, wand.
palikuća *f* incendiary.
paliti *v* to kindle, to light.
paluba *f* deck; gornja ~ upper deck.
paljba *f* firing off, fire.
paljenje *n* ignition.
paljevina *f* burning; arson.
pamćenje *n* memory, sense, thinking, mind.
pametan *a* brainy, smart, intelligent, reasonable, wise; ~na ideja *f* brainwave.
pamtiti *v* to keep in mind; to remember.
pamuk *m* cotton.
pancir *m* armour.
paničan *a* panicky.
panika *f* panic, scare.
panorama *f* panorama, prospect, view.
pansion *m* boarding house.

pantalone *fpl* trousers.
panter *m* panther.
panj *m* block, stump.
papa *m* Pope.
papagaj *m* parrot.
papaja *f* papaw, papaya.
papak *m* hoof.
papazjanija *f* stew; mess, confusion (*fig*).
paperje *n* fluff, down.
papinski *a* papal.
papir *m* paper; ~ za pisanje writing paper.
papirna kesa *f* paper bag.
paprat *f* fern.
papren *a* piquant, sharp.
paprika *f* green pepper; crvena ~ red pepper; paprika.
paprikaš *f* stew.
papuča *f* slipper.
par *m* pair, couple, twosome.
para *f* steam, vapour; money, coin.
parabola *f* parable, parabola (*mat*).
parada *f* parade, display.
paradajz *m* tomato.
paradna uniforma *f* dress uniform.
paradni korak *m* goose step.
paradoks *m* paradox.
parafin *m* paraffin.
paragraf *m* paragraph, clause.
paraliza *f* paralysis.
paralizovan *a* paralytic.
paralizovati *v* to paralyse.
paran *a* even.
paranoičan *a* paranoid.
parastos *m* requiem, mass.
parati *v* to rip.
parazit *m* parasite, sponger (*slang*).
parcela *f* allotment, lot.
parče *n* bit, piece, morsel.
parenje *n* coupling, pairing.
parfem *m* perfume.
pariti *v* to steam.
park *m* park.
parking *m* parking lot; car park.
parkiranje *n* parking.
parlament *m* parliament.
parni *a* steam; ~a lokomotiva *f* steam engine.

parničenje *n* litigation.
parobrod *m* steamer, steamboat.
parodija *f* parody, travesty.
paroh *m* parson.
parohija *f* parish.
parter *m* gound floor, first floor; pit (u pozorištu).
particip *m* participle (*gram*).
partitura *f* score.
partizan *m* partisan.
partner *m* partner, associate.
pas *m* dog; ~ čuvar *m* watchdog; ~ tragač *m* bloodhound.
pasijans *m* solitaire.
pasirati *v* to strain.
pasji *a* dog's; ~ život *m* a dog's life.
pasmina *f* breed, race, blood.
pasoš *m* passport.
pasta *f* pasta; ~ za zube toothpaste.
pasti *v* to fall, to tumble.
pastir *m* shepherd, herdsman.
pastor *m* pastor, minister.
pastorak *m* stepson.
pastorka *f* stepdaughter.
pastrmka *f* trout.
pastuv *m* stallion, stud.
pasulj *m* beans.
pašnjak *m* pasture, grassland.
patent *m* patent; ~ zatvarač zip, zip fastener.
patiti *v* to suffer, to feel pain.
patka *f* duck.
patnja *f* suffering.
patologija *f* pathology.
patološki *a* pathological.
patrijarh *m* patriarch.
patriota *m* patriot.
patriotizam *m* patriotism.
patrola *f* patrol.
patrolna kola patrol car.
patuljak *m* dwarf, elf; gnome.
patvoren *a* forged, fake.
paučina *f* cobweb.
pauk *m* spider.
paun *m* peacock.
pauza *f* pause, break.
pavijan *m* baboon (*zool*).
paviljon *m* pavilion.
pazar *m* bazaar.
pazikuća *m* caretaker.
pazuho *n* armpit.

pažljiv *a* attentive, considerate, mindful.
pažnja *f* attention, attentiveness, consideration.
pčela *f* bee.
pčelinjak *m* beehive.
pecanje *n* angling.
peckati *v* to tease, to tingle; to provoke (*fig*).
pečat *m* stamp; seal; državni ~ privy seal.
pečatni vosak sealing wax.
pečenje *n* baking.
pečurka *f* mushroom.
peć *f* stove, furnace.
pećina *f* cave, grotto.
pedala *f* pedal.
pedantan *a* pedantic(al).
peder *m* homosexual, gay.
pedeset *num* fifty.
pedeseti *num a* fiftieth.
pedijatrija *f* paediatrics.
pedikir *m* chiropodist.
pega *f* spot, stain, patch, freckle (od sunca).
pegav *a* freckled.
peglanje *n* ironing.
pehar *m* beaker, goblet; cup.
pejsaž *m* landscape, scenery.
pekar *m* baker.
pekara *f* bakery.
pelene *fpl* nappies, swaddling-clothes.
pelikan *m* pelican.
pena *f* foam, froth.
penast *a* foamy.
penicilin *m* penicillin.
penušav *a* frothy.
penzija *f* pension.
penzionisanje *n* retirement.
penjanje *n* ascension, ascent, climbing.
penjati se *v* to ascend, to climb.
pepeljara *f* ashtray.
pepeo *m* ash, cinder.
perač *m* washer; ~ prozora window cleaner.
perad *f* poultry.
peraja *fpl* fin, flipper.
perčin *m* pigtail.
pergament *m* parchment.
periferija *f* periphery; ~ grada suburbs, outskirts.
periferno *a* peripheral.
perika *f* wig.

perina *f* eiderdown.
period *m* period, time, while.
periodičan *a* periodic(al).
perionica *f* laundry.
perjanica *f* plume.
perje *n* plumage, feathers.
perla *f* bead.
permutacija *f* permutation.
pernat *a* feathered; **~a živina** *fpl* fowl.
pernica *f* pencil case.
pero *n* feather, plume; pen (za pisanje).
peron *m* platform.
perorez *m* penknife.
personifikacija *f* personification.
perspektiva *f* perspective.
peršun *m* parsley.
pertla *f* shoelace, shoestring.
peruška *f* whisk.
perut *f* dandruff.
pesak *m* sand.
pesimist *m* pessimist.
pesma *f* song; **mornarska ~** shanty.
pesnica *f* fist.
pešačiti *v* to march, to walk, to hike.
pešačka staza *f* footpath.
pešački prelaz *m* pedestrian crossing.
pešadija *f* infantry.
pešak *m* pedestrian.
peščan *a* sandy; **~i sat** *m* hour glass; **~i sprud** a shoal.
peščara *f* sandpit.
peškir *m* towel.
pet *num* five.
peta *f* heel.
petak *m* Friday.
petao *m* cock.
peti *num* a fifth.
peti se *v* to mount.
peticija *f* petition.
petlić *m* cockerel.
petlja *f* loop, noose, knot.
petnaest *num* fifteen.
petnaesti *num* a fifteenth.
petparački *a* cheap, shabby.
petsto *num* five hundred.
pevac *m* cock.
pevač *m* singer; **operski ~** opera singer.
pevanje *n* singing.
pevati *v* to sing.
pica *f* pizza.
piće *n* beverage, liquor, drink.

pijaca *f* market.
pijan *a* drunk, drunken, groggy, plastered.
pijanica *f* drunkard.
pijanista *f* pianist.
pijanka *f* binge, orgy.
pijavica *f* leech.
pijedestal *m* pedestal.
pijuckanje *n* sipping.
pijuk *m* pickaxe.
pikantan *a* piquant, sharp, high-seasoned.
pikirati *v* to nosedive.
pilana *f* sawmill.
pile *n* chick, chicken.
pilula *f* pill.
piljar *m* greengrocer.
piljarnica *f* greengrocer's shop.
pinceta *f* tweezers.
pingvin *m* penguin.
pion *m* pawn.
pionir *m* pioneer.
pipak *m* tentacle, feeler.
pipati *v* to touch, to feel, to handle.
piramida *f* pyramid.
pirat *m* pirate.
piraterija *f* piracy.
pire *m* puree; **krompir ~** mashed potatoes.
pirinač *m* rice.
pisac *m* writer; **~ pozorišnih komada** playwright; **~ romana** novelist.
pisaća mašina *f* typewriter.
pisaći sto *m* writing desk.
pisak *m* mouthpiece.
pisanje *n* writing.
pisar *m* clerk, scribe.
pisati *v* to write.
piskav *a* shrill.
piskavost *f* shrillness.
pismen *a* literate; **~ čovek** *m* scholar; **~a izjava** *f* affidavit.
pismo *n* letter; message; character (slovo); **kreditno ~** bill of credit.
pisoar *m* urinal, public lavatory.
pišati *v* to piss (*slang*), to urinate.
pištati *v* to bleep.
pištolj *m* pistol.
pita od voća *f* pie, tart; **~ s jabukama** apple pie.
pitak *a* drinkable.
pitanje *n* query, question.
pitati *v* to ask.

piti *v* to drink.
pitom *a* tame.
piton *m* python.
pivar *m* brewer.
pivara *f* brewery.
pivo *n* ale, beer.
plac *m* parcel, piece of ground.
plač *m* weeping.
plaćanje *n* payment, paying.
plaćenik *m* hireling, mercenary.
plafon *m* ceiling, roof; limit (granica).
plagijat *m* plagiarism.
plah *a* impetuous, impulsive, rash.
plahovitost *f* impetuosity.
plakar *m* cupboard; closet, wardrobe.
plakati *v* to cry, to weep.
plamen *m* blaze, flame.
plamenac *m* flamingo.
plan *m* plan; design; program; map; ~ puta itinerary; ~ grada map; ~ rada schedule.
planer *m* planner.
planeta *f* planet.
planina *f* mountain.
planinar *m* mountaineer, alpinist.
planinarenje *n* mountaineering, alpinism.
planinski *a* alpine.
planiranje *n* planning.
planirati *v* to project, to plan.
plantaža *f* plantation.
planuti *v* to flame up, to glint.
plast *m* stack; ~ sena haystack.
plastična hirurgija *f* plastic surgery.
plastika *f* plastics.
plašiti *v* to frighten, to intimidate.
plašiti se *v* to be afraid.
plašljiv *a* cowardly.
plašt *m* cloak.
plata *f* salary, remuneration, wages.
platforma *f* platform.
platina *f* platinum.
platiti *v* to pay.
platni spisak *m* payroll.
platno *n* cloth; canvas.
plav *a* blue; blond; ~i patlidžan *m* eggplant.
plavičast *a* bluish.
plavokos *a* fair-haired.
plavook *a* blue-eyed.
plaža *f* beach, strand.
pleća *npl* shoulders.

pleme *n* tribe, clan.
plemenit *a* noble.
plemenitost *f* nobility.
plemenski *a* tribal.
plemić *m* nobleman.
plen *m* booty, loot, prey.
ples *m* dance.
plesanje *n* dancing.
plesna dvorana *f* dance hall.
plesač *m* dancer.
plesniv *a* musty, mouldy.
plesti *v* to knit.
plićak *m* shoal.
plik *m* blister.
plima *f* tide; ~ i oseka ebb and flow.
plimski *a* tidal.
plin *m* gas.
plinara *f* gasworks.
pliš *m* plush, velvet.
plišani meda teddy bear.
plitak *a* shallow.
plitkost *f* shallowness.
plivač *m* swimmer; ~čki bazen swimming pool.
plivanje *n* swimming; leđno ~ back stroke; prsno ~ breast stroke.
ploča *f* plate, slab.
pločica *f* tile.
pločnik *m* pavement.
plod *m* fruit; result (*fig*); foetus.
plodan *a* arable, fertile; fruitful, prolific.
plodnost *f* fertility, fruitfulness.
plodovi mora *mpl* seafood.
plotun *m* volley, round.
plovak *m* buoy.
plovidba *f* navigation.
ploviti *v* to navigate, to sail.
pluća *npl* lungs.
plug *m* plough.
pluta *f* cork.
plutati *v* to float.
pljačka *f* robbery, plunder.
pljačkaš *m* marauder, robber.
pljačkati *v* to loot, to plunder.
pljeskanje *n* clapping, applause.
pljeskati *v* to applaud, to clap.
pljoska *f* flask.
pljusak *m* downpour, shower.
pljuštati *v* to patter, to pour.
pljuvačka *f* drivel, spittle, spit.
pljuvanje *n* spitting.

po *prep* by, from, to; per.
pobaciti *v* to abort, to miscarry.
pobačaj *m* abortion, miscarriage.
pobeći *v* to escape, to fly, to flee, to elope.
pobeda *f* conquest, victory.
pobednički *a* triumphant.
pobednik *m* prizewinner, winner.
pobedonosan *a* victorous.
pobesneti *v* to enrage.
pobijati *v* to disprove.
pobiti *v* to slaughter, to massacre.
poboljšanje *n* amelioration, improvement.
poboljšati *v* to improve, to ameliorate.
pobožan *a* devout, pious, religious.
pobožnost *f* piety.
pobrinuti se *v* to take care, to beware.
pobuda *f* incentive, motive, inducement.
pobuditi *v* to evoke, to induce.
pobuna *f* revolt, riot.
pobuniti se *v* to mutiny, to strike, to revolt.
pobunjenički *a* rebellious.
pobunjenik *m* rebel, revolter.
pocepan *a* torn.
pocepati *v* to tear.
pocrneo *a* blackened.
pocrneti *v* to blacken.
pocrveneo *a* blushing.
pocrveneti *v* to turn red.
počasni *a* honorary; titular; **~a straža** *f* honour guard.
početak *m* beginning, commencement, start.
početi *v* to begin, to start.
početni *a* initial.
početnik *m* beginner.
pod[1] *m* floor.
pod[2] *prep* under, beneath.
podaci *mpl* data.
podao *a* ignoble, vile, base.
podatak *m* fact, information.
podbaciti *v* to put under; to be insufficient, to fail.
podbadanje *n* instigation.
podbadati *v* to incite, to instigate.
podbradak *m* double chin.
podbuniti *v* to incite, to instigate, to stir up.
podbuo *a* puffy, boated.
podela *f* division, partition.
podeliti *v* to divide, to share, to dispense.

poderan *a* ragged, torn.
poderati *v* to tear, to rip.
podesan *a* proper, suitable, pertinent.
podesiti *v* to arrange, to adjust.
podići *v* to raise, to lift.
podizanje *n* raising.
podizati *v* to elevate, to erect.
podjarmljivanje *n* subjugation.
podjednak *a* equivalent.
podjednako *adv* equally, evenly.
podlac *m* knave, villain.
podlaktica *f* forearm.
podleći *v* to succumb, to yield.
podloga *f* base, basis, foundation.
podlost *f* meanness, baseness.
podložan *a* liable, subject to.
podmazati *v* to lubricate.
podmetnuti *v* to put under; to plant, to conceal; **~ požar** to set a fire.
podmićivanje *n* bribery, corruption.
podmiriti *v* to satisfy.
podmitljiv *a* corruptible.
podmornica *f* submarine.
podmukao *a* insidious, perfidious, treacherous.
podnaslov *m* subtitle.
podne *n* midday, noon.
podneti *v* to present, to stand; **~ molbu** to plead; **~ ostavku** to resign.
podnosilac *m* petitioner, applicant.
podnositi *v* to present; to support.
podnošljiv *a* compatible, endurable, supportable, tolerable.
podoban *a* eligible.
podobnost *f* eligibility.
podozrenje *n* suspicion, doubt.
podozriv *a* suspicious.
podozrivo *adv* askance.
podrazumevati *v* to implicate, to imply.
podražajni *a* imitative.
podražavati *v* to imitate, to mimic.
podređen *a* inferior, subordinate.
podređenost *f* subordination.
podrhtavati *v* to tremble, to quake.
podrigivanje *n* belching.
podrška *f* maintenance, support.
podrugivati se *v* to laugh at.
podrugljivo *adv* sneeringly.
podrum *m* basement, cellar.
podržati *v* to sustain, to uphold.
podsekretar *m* undersecretary.

podsetiti *v* to remind.
podsetnik *m* directory.
podsmeh *m* gibe/jibe, sneer.
podsmehnuti se *v* to make fun, to gibe/jibe.
podsmešljivo *adv* jestingly.
podstaći *v* to induce, to abet.
podstanar *m* subtenant; boarder.
podstrek *m* goad, impetus, inducement.
podsvest *f* subconsciousness.
podučavanje *n* instruction, teaching.
podudaran *a* congruous, conformable.
podudarati se *v* to concur, to correspond, to tally.
podudarno *adv* concurrently.
podudarnost *f* congruity.
poduhvat *m* undertaking.
podupirač *m* support, prop, buttress.
podvala *f* fake, trick.
podvezica *f* garter.
podvig *m* feat, achievement.
podviknuti *v* to shout.
podvodni *a* underwater; **~a struja** *f* undercurrent; **~ greben** *m* reef.
podvrći se *v* to undergo.
podvući *v* to emphasize, to underline.
podzemlje *n* underground, underworld.
podzemni *a* subterranean; **~ prolaz** *m* subway.
poema *f* poem.
poezija *f* poetry.
pogađanje *n* negotiation, bargaining.
pogan *f* dirt, excrements.
pogasiti *v* to extinguish, to quench.
pogdegde *adv* here and there.
pogdekad *adv* seldom, from time to time.
pogled *m* glance.
pogledati *v* to look at, to look on.
pognut *a* bent, stooping.
pogodan *a* suitable, proper.
pogodba *f* bargain, deal.
pogoditi *v* to hit; to guess.
pogodnost *f* convenience.
pogođen *a* affected.
pogoršanje *n* deterioration, aggravation.
pogoršati *v* to deteriorate, to exacerbate.
pogotovo *adv* particularly.
pogovor *m* epilogue.
pogranični *a* border, frontier.
pogrbiti se *v* to stoop.
pogrbljen *a* bent, stooping.
pogrdan *a* abusive, insulting.

pogreb *m* funeral, burial.
pogrebni *a* funeral; **~a kola** *f* hearse (vehicle); **~a povorka** mourning train.
pogrešan *a* erroneous, wrong, mistaken.
pogrešiti *v* to make an error, to make a mistake, to err.
pogrešiv *a* fallible.
pogrešno *adv* by mistake, faultily; **~ razumeti** *v* to misunderstand; **~ tumačiti** to misinterpret; **~ uputiti** to misdirect.
poguban *a* ruinous.
pogubiti *v* to lose; to execute.
pohaban *a* threadbare, worn-out.
pohađati *v* to attend, to frequent.
pohlepa *f* avarice, greed, greediness.
pohlepan *a* avaricious, greedy.
pohlepno *adv* greedily.
pohod *m* visit, call; **ratni ~** campaign.
pohotan *a* lascivious, carnal, lustful.
pohvala *f* praise, commendation.
pohvalan *a* çomplimentary, praiseworthy.
pohvaliti *v* to commend, to praise.
pohvalno *adv* commendably.
pohvatati *v* to catch, to seize.
poimence *adv* by name.
poistovetiti *v* to identify, to regard as identical.
pojačanje *n* amplification.
pojačati *v* amplify, to reinforce, to intensify.
pojačivač *m* amplifier.
pojam *m* concept, notion, conception.
pojas *m* belt, girdle.
pojata *f* stable.
pojava *f* apparition, appearance; phenomenon; occurrence.
pojaviti se *v* to appear, to occur, to emerge.
pojedinačno *adv* individually.
pojedini *a* individual.
pojedinost *f* detail, circumstance.
pojednostaviti *v* to simplify.
pojeftiniti *v* to become cheaper, to reduce prices.
pojesti *v* to eat, to consume.
pojmiti *v* to understand, to conceive.
pojuriti *v* to rush.
pokajanje *n* remorse, repentance.
pokajati se *v* to repent.
pokajnički *a* penitent, repentant.

pokazati *v* to show, to demonstrate, to exhibit.
pokipeti *v* to boil over.
poklanjati *v* to grant, to give away.
poklapanje *n* coincidence.
poklapati se *v* to coincide.
poklon *m* gift, present; ~ **čestitka** *m* gift-voucher.
pokloniti *v* to give, to grant.
poklopac *m* cover, lid.
pokojni *a* deceased; lost.
pokolenje *n* generation.
pokolj *m* carnage, massacre, slaughter.
pokop *m* burial.
pokora *f* penance.
pokoran *a* submissive, obedient.
pokoriti se *v* to submit, to obey.
pokornost *f* submissiveness.
pokraj *prep* by, close to.
pokrajina *f* province, country.
pokrajinski *a* provincial.
pokret *m* movement, motion; ~ **rukom** gesture; ~ **za ženska prava** women's lib; ~ **zelenih** green movement.
pokretan *a* mobile, movable, portable, moving; ~**ne stepenice** *fpl* escalator.
pokretljivost *f* mobility.
pokriti *v* to cover, to deck.
pokrivač *m* blanket, rug; covering, plaid.
pokroviteljstvo *n* patronage, protection, auspices.
pokuljati *v* to gush.
pokušaj *m* trial, attempt.
pokušati *v* to attempt, to endeavour, to try.
pokvaren *a* perverse, bad, spoilt.
pokvarenost *f* corruption, depravity, immorality.
pokvariti *v* to spoil, to mar; to bungle.
pokvasiti *v* to water, to moisten.
pol *m* sex; pole (*geog*).
pola *a* half; ~ **sata** half-hour; **na ~ puta** midway.
polagano *adv* slowly.
polarni *a* arctic, polar.
polaskati *v* to flatter.
polazak *m* departure, start.
polazni *a* starting; ~**a tačka** *f* starting point.
poleđina *f* back, background.
polemički *a* argumentative.
polen *m* pollen.

polenska groznica *f* hay fever.
polet *m* impulse, impetus.
poletan *a* impulsive.
poletanje *n* takeoff.
polica *f* shelf.
policajac *m* policeman, cop.
policija *f* police.
policijski *a* police; ~**a stanica** *f* police station; ~ **čas** *m* curfew.
poliester *m* polyester.
polietilen *m* polyethelene.
poligamija *f* polygamy.
politehnički *a* polytechnic.
politi *v* to water, to sprinkle.
političar *m* politician.
politički *a* political.
politika *f* policy; politics.
politura *f* polish, lustre.
polni *a* sexual; ~ **organi** *mpl* genitals; ~ **snošaj** *m* intercourse.
polovan *a* second-hand.
polovina *f* one half.
položaj *m* situation, circumstance, condition; station; site.
položiti *v* to lay down.
polubrat *m* stepbrother.
polucilindar *m* bowler hat.
polufinale *n* semifinal.
poluga *f* lever; ~ **zlata ili srebra** bullion.
polukrug *m* semicircle.
polukružan *a* semicircular.
polumesec *m* crescent, half-moon.
poluostrvo *n* peninsula.
poluprovodnik *m* semiconductor.
polusestra *f* stepsister.
poluton *m* semitone.
poluvreme *n* half-time.
polje *n* field; **naftno ~** oilfield.
poljoprivreda *f* agriculture, husbandry.
poljoprivredni *a* agricultural.
poljubac *m* kiss.
pomagati *v* to assist, to help, to aid.
pomahnitao *a* insane, delirious, mad.
pomajka *f* foster mother.
pomalo *adv* a little.
pomama *f* madness, rage, frenzy.
pomanjkanje *n* lack, absence.
pomenuti *v* to mention, to notice.
pomeriti *v* to move, to displace.
pomešati *v* to mingle, to mix; to confound, to confuse (zbuniti se).

pomešati (se) *v* to blend.
pomfrit *m* French fries.
pomilovanje *n* amnesty, general pardon.
pomirenje *n* conciliation, reconciliation.
pomiriti *v* to reconcile.
pomirljiv *a* reconcilable.
pomisao *f* thought, idea.
pomoć *f* assistance, help, aid.
pomoći *v* to help, to aid.
pomoćni *a* ancillary, auxiliary, subsidiary.
pomoćnik *m* assistant, helper.
pomodan *a* stylish, fashionable.
pomorandža *f* orange.
pomorski *a* marine, nautical, sea; ~a
  bitka *f* sea battle; ~a **karta** nautical
  chart.
pompezan *a* ceremonious, pompous.
pomračenje *n* eclipse.
pomrčina *f* dark, darkness.
pomučiti se *v* to take pains.
ponajviše *adv* most of all.
ponaosob *adv* separately.
ponašanje *n* behaviour, conduct,
  demeanour.
ponašati se *v* to behave, to conduct
  oneself.
ponavljanje *n* repetition.
ponavljati *v* to repeat, to say again.
ponedeljak *m* Monday.
ponekad *adv* occasionally, sometimes.
poništenje *n* annihilation, annulment.
poništiti *v* to annul, to abolish, to
  invalidate, to nullify.
ponizan *a* humble, meek, submissive.
poniziti *v* to debase, to humiliate, to degrade.
poniznost *f* humbleness, meekness,
  humility.
ponižavajući *a* derogatory.
ponižavati *v* to disparage.
poniženje *n* abasement, humiliation,
  debasement.
ponoć *f* midnight.
ponor *m* chasm, precipice, abyss.
ponos *m* pride.
ponosan *a* proud.
ponovni *a* repeated; ~ **izbor** *m* re-election;
  ~o **uspostavljanje** *n* re-establishment;
  ~o **sjedinjenje** reunion.
ponovo *adv* afresh, again, repeatedly;
  ~ **otvoriti** *v* to reopen; ~ **posetiti** to
  revisit; ~ **razmatrati** to reconsider.

ponton *m* pontoon.
ponuda *f* offering.
ponuditi *v* to offer, to tender, to hold out,
  to bid.
poočim *m* foster father.
pop *m* clergyman, priest.
popeti se *v* to climb, to go up, to walk up.
popis *m* inventory, list; census
  (stanovništva).
popiti *v* to drink, to take a drink.
poplava *f* flood, flooding.
poplaviti *v* to inundate, to flood, to
  overflow.
popločati *v* to inlay.
popodne *n* afternoon.
popraviti *v* to amend, to rectify, to
  correct; to repair, to mend.
popravka *f* correction, repair.
popravljiv *a* reparable.
popreko *adv* across.
poprsje *n* bust.
poprskati *v* to spatter, to sprinkle.
popularnost *f* popularity.
popuniti *v* to fill up.
popust *m* discount; reduction.
popustiti *v* to relent, to unbend; to
  decrease, to diminish.
popustljiv *a* acquiescent, compliant;
  indulgent.
popustljivost *f* condescension,
  indulgence.
pora *f* pore.
porast *m* growing, growth.
poraz *m* defeat, debacle.
porazan *a* disastrous, crushing.
porcelan *m* chinaware, porcelain.
pored *prep* beside(s), close to.
poredak *m* order.
porediti *v* to compare with.
poređati *v* to align.
poređenje *n* comparison.
poreklo *n* origin, descent, extraction;
  parentage, ancestry.
poremećen *a* disturbed, deranged.
poremetiti *v* to distract, to disarrange, to
  upset.
poreski *a* tax; ~ **obveznik** *m* tax payer.
porez *m* tax; ~ **na dohodak** income tax.
poreznik *m* tax collector.
poricanje *n* negation.
poricati *v* to deny, to disclaim, to refute.

pornografija *f* pornography.
porobiti *v* to enslave.
poročnost *n* wickedness.
porodica *f* family.
porodični *a* family, home; ~ **posao** *m* family business.
porodilište *n* maternity hospital.
porođaj *m* childbirth, confinement.
porok *m* vice.
porota *f* jury.
porotnik *m* juror, juryman.
porozan *a* porous, pory.
portir *m* door-keeper, gate-keeper.
portret *m* portrait, likeness, picture.
porub *m* hem, seam.
poručiti *v* to order; to send a message.
poručnik *m* lieutenant.
poruga *f* scorn.
poruka *f* message.
porušiti *v* to demolish, to pull down.
posada *f* crew.
posaditi *v* to seat, to sit.
posao *m* work, labour, job; chore; dealings, doings.
posavetovati *v* to give advice.
poseban *a* especial, particular, special.
posebno *adv* specifically, separately.
poseći *v* to cut down.
posednik *m* owner, possessor, holder.
posedovanje *n* ownership, possession.
posedovati *v* to possess, to own.
posejati *v* to sow.
poseta *f* visit, call.
posetilac *m* caller, visitor.
posetiti *v* to visit.
posilni *m* orderly.
posinak *m* foster child.
poslagati *v* to stack, to pile up.
poslanica *f* epistle.
poslanik *m* delegate, representative, member of parliament.
poslanstvo *n* legation, embassy.
poslastica *f* delicacy, dessert.
poslastičar *m* confectioner.
poslastičarnica *f* confectionery.
poslati *v* to send, to send out.
posle *prep* afterwards.
posledica *f* consequence, corollary, outcome, aftermath.
poslednji *a* last, final, ultimate; ~ **rok** *m* deadline.

poslepodne *n* afternoon.
posleratni *a* post-war.
poslodavac *m* employer.
poslovan *a* businesslike; ~ **čovek** *m* businessman.
poslovica *f* proverb, saying.
poslovičan *a* proverbial.
poslušan *a* docile, dutiful, obedient, manageable.
poslušnost *f* obedience.
poslužavnik *m* tray.
poslužiti *v* to serve.
posmatrač *m* observer; ~ **ptica** bird-watcher.
posmatranje *n* observation.
posmatrati *v* to observe, to watch.
posmrtni *a* posthumous; ~ **marš** *m* dead march.
posni *a* fast.
pospan *a* sleepy, somnolent.
pospano *adv* sleepily.
pospanost *f* somnolence, drowsiness, sleepiness.
posredan *a* indirect, collateral.
posrednik *m* go-between, intermediary, mediator.
posredništvo *n* brokerage, agency.
posredovanje *n* mediation.
posredovati *v* to intercede, to mediate.
postati *v* to become, to get, to grow.
postava *f* lining.
posteljica *f* afterbirth, placenta (*anat*).
posteljina *f* bed-clothes.
postepen *a* gradual.
postići *v* to attain, to realize, to act.
postiđen *a* ashamed, abashed.
postiti *v* to fast.
postojano *adv* steadily.
postojanost *f* constancy, firmness, steadiness.
postojanje *n* existence, subsistence, being.
postojati *v* to exist, to be.
postojeći *a* existent, existing.
postrance *adv* sideways.
postupak *m* handling, procedure, proceedings, treatment.
postupan *a* progressive.
postupiti *v* to treat, to deal.
posuda *f* vessel, receptacle.
posumnjati *v* to suspect.

posvađati v to fall out with, to wrangle.
posveta f dedication, address.
posvetiti v to dedicate.
posvetiti se v to devote.
pošiljalac m sender.
poširati v to poach.
pošta f mail, post; post office (zgrada).
poštanski a postal; ~**a marka** f postage stamp; ~ **činovnik** m postmaster; ~**o sanduče** n postbox, letter box.
poštar m postman.
poštarina f postage.
pošten a honest, honourable, fair.
pošteno adv fairly, honourably.
poštenje n honesty, integrity.
pošto adv whereas, since.
poštovan a respectable, revered.
poštovanost n respectability.
poštovanje n deference, respect, veneration.
poštovati v to esteem, to venerate.
potaja f secrecy.
potajan a clandestine, secret, stealthy.
potajno adv underhand.
potamaniti v to destroy.
potapanje n submersion.
potapšati v to pat.
potceniti v to underestimate, to underrate.
potcenjivanje n indignity.
potcrtati v to underline.
potčiniti v to subjugate, to subordinate.
potčinjeni m subordinate.
poteći v to flow, to run; to spring, to emanate.
potencijal m potential.
potera f pursuit.
potez m stroke, dash.
poticati od v to derive.
potiljak m nape.
potisnuti v to repress, to repel; to drive back.
potišten a crestfallen, despondent, dispirited, downhearted.
potištenost f consternation, dejection.
potkazati v to denounce.
potkopati v to undercut, to undermine, to discredit.
potkovan a shod.
potkovica f horseshoe.
potkratiti v to curtail, to shorten.
potkresati v to undercut.
potkrovlje n loft.

potok m brook.
potomak m descendant.
potomstvo n offspring, posterity.
potop m deluge, flood.
potopiti v to sink, to soak, to submerge.
potpetica f heel.
potpis m signature.
potpomaganje n aid, assistance, help.
potpora f support.
potpredsednik m vice-chairman, vice-president.
potpun a absolute, entire, integral, full-fledged.
potpuno adv outright, utterly.
potraga f pursuit, search.
potražiti v to look for, to look about.
potražnja f demand.
potrčati v to run, to speed, to move swiftly.
potreba f need, necessity.
potreban a necessary, needy.
potrepština f requisite.
potres m concussion, shock.
potresti v convulse, to shake.
potrošač m consumer.
potrošački a consumers; ~**o društvo** n consumer society.
potrošan a expendable.
potrošiti v to spend.
potrošnja f consumption.
potvrda f confirmation, corroboration.
potvrdan a affirmative.
potvrditi v to certify, to confirm, to corroborate, to authenticate.
poučan a instructive.
poučavanje n instruction, education, teaching.
pouka f lesson, warning.
pouzdan a dependable, safe, reliable, trusted.
pouzdano adv safely.
pouzdanje n reliance, confidence, faith.
povećanje n augmentation, increase, gain, raise.
povećati v to enlarge, to raise.
povećavati v to magnify.
povećavati se v to increase.
povelja f charter.
poverenik m confidant, trustee, commissary.
poverenje n confidence, faith, trust; credit.

poveriti *v* to confide, to entrust.
poveriti se *v* to confess.
poverljiv *a* confidential.
povetarac *m* breeze, light wind.
povez *m* binding.
povezan *a* related.
povezanost *f* coherence, connection.
povijati *v* to draw down; to wrap up; to band.
povik *m* shout, scream.
povišavati *v* to heighten, to elevate.
povišica *f* rise, advance.
poviti u pelene *v* to swaddle.
povlačenje *n* recession, retreat, withdrawal.
povlađivati *v* to connive, to approve.
povlastica *f* favour, prerogative, privilige.
povod *m* cause, ground, motive.
povoditi se *v* to sway.
povodom *adv* with, regarding.
povoljan *a* advantageous, favourable, auspicious, opportune; ~ **položaj** *m* advantage point.
povorka *f* procession.
povraćaj *m* refund, relapse.
povraćati *v* to vomit.
povratak *m* return.
povratan *a* recurrent; **~tna sprega** *f* feedback.
povratiti *v* to regain, to retrieve.
povreda *f* contusion, injury.
povrediti *v* to hurt.
povremen *a* occasional, periodical, cyclic.
površan *a* superficial.
površina *f* surface.
površinska rana *f* flesh wound.
povučen *a* withdrawn, retired.
povučenost *f* reticence.
poza *f* pose.
pozadi *adv* behind, in the rear.
pozadina *f* background.
pozajmica *f* loan, lend.
pozajmiti *v* to borrow, to lend.
pozajmljivač *m* borrower.
pozdrav *m* greeting, salutation.
pozdraviti *v* to greet, to salute.
poziranje *n* sitting.
poziv *m* call, invitation; vocation.
pozlata *f* gilding, gilt.
poznanstvo *n* acquaintance.

poznat *a* familiar, well-known; ~ **po zlu** notorious.
poznavanje *n* knowledge.
pozor *m* attention.
pozorišni *a* theatrical; ~ **posetilac** *m* theatregoer; ~ **plakat** a play-bill.
pozorište *n* theatre.
pozornica *f* scene, stage.
pozvati *v* to call, to invite, to summon.
požuda *f* lust, desire.
požurivati *v* to hasten.
praćka *f* sling.
pradeda *m* great-grandfather.
prag *m* doorstep, threshold.
pragmatičan *a* pragmatic.
prah *m* dust.
praktičan *a* practical.
praktičnost *f* practicality.
pramac *m* bow.
pramen *f* lock, tuft.
pranje *n* ablution, washing; ~ **četkom** scrubbing; ~ **sudova** washing up; ~ **novca** money laundering.
prasak *m* crash.
prase *n* pig.
praskozorje *n* daybreak.
prastar *a* ancient, old.
prašak *m* powder; ~ **za pecivo** *n* baking powder.
prašina *f* dust.
prašnjav *a* dusty.
praštanje *n* forgiveness, pardoning.
praštati *v* to forgive, to pardon.
prati *v* to launder, to wash.
pratilac *m* companion, fellow; accompanist.
pratiti *v* to accompany, to follow.
pratnja *f* convoy, entourage.
praunuče *n* great-grandchild.
prav *a* straight; right (pravilan).
pravac *m* direction, route.
pravda *f* justice, equity, fairness.
pravdati *v* to justify, to account for.
pravdati se *v* to offer an excuse.
pravedan *a* righteous.
pravednost *f* righteousness.
pravi *a* true, veritable, complete.
pravičan *a* equitable, impartial, unbiassed.
pravilo *n* rule, regulation.
praviti *v* to make, to work, to form, to do.
pravni *a* legal, lawful; **~a nadležnost** *f* jurisdiction; **~o lice** *n* juristic person.

pravnik *m* lawyer, attorney, jurist.
pravo *adv* directly, direct, straight.
pravolinijski *a* rectilinear.
pravopis *m* orthography, spelling.
pravosuđe *n* judiciary, justice.
pravougaoni *a* rectangular.
pravougaonik *m* rectangle.
pravoveran *a* orthodox.
pravovremen *a* timely.
prazan *a* blank, empty, vacant, void.
praziluk *m* leek.
praznični *a* festive, holiday.
praznik *m* holiday, celebration.
praznina *f* emptiness, vacancy.
praznoruk *a* empty-handed.
praznoveran *a* superstitious.
praznoverje *n* superstition.
pražnjenje *n* discharge.
prdeti *v* to fart.
pre *prep* before, previous, prior, ago.
prebaciti *v* to throw over, to get across; to
   reproach (*fig*).
prebivalište *n* abode, domicile, dwelling,
   residence.
prebivati *v* to abide, to sojourn, to stay.
prebukirati *v* to overbook.
preceniti *v* to overestimate, to overvalue,
   to overrate.
prečaga *f* crossbar, rail.
prečica *f* shortcut.
prečistiti *v* to refine, to purify.
prečišćavanje *n* refinement, purification.
prečka *f* perch.
prečnik *m* diameter.
preći *v* to go over, to cross, to pass.
prećutan *a* tacit, unspoken, implied.
predah *m* respite.
predaja *f* surrender.
predajnik *m* transmitter.
predak *m* ancestor, forefather.
predano *adv* devotedly.
predanost *f* devotion.
predati *v* to deliver; to transmit.
predati se *v* to capitulate.
predavač *m* lecturer.
predavanje *n* lecture.
predbračni *a* premarital.
predeo *m* locality, region.
predgovor *m* foreword, preface, prologue.
predgrađe *n* suburb.
predjelo *n* hors d'oeuvre.

predlagač *m* proposer.
predlog *m* proposition, proposal.
predložiti *v* to propose, to suggest; ~
   kandidata *v* to nominate.
predmet *m* object, subject, thing, article.
prednapregnuti *a* prestressed; ~ **beton** *m*
   prestressed concrete.
prednost *f* preference, advantage,
   prerogative.
prednji *a* front, anterior, fore, frontal; ~**a**
   noga *f* foreleg; ~**a vuča** front-wheel
   drive; ~ **deo** *m* front part.
predočiti *v* to demonstrate, to show.
predodređenost *f* predestination.
predohrana *f* prevention.
predosećanje *n* anticipation, presentiment.
predostrožan *a* cautious, careful.
predračun *m* estimate.
predrasuda *f* prejudice.
predratni *a* pre-war.
predsedavajući *m* chairman.
predsedavati *v* to preside.
predsednik *m* president; ~ **vlade** premier,
   prime minister.
predsedništvo *n* presidency.
predskazanje *n* prediction; forecast.
predsoblje *n* antechamber, lobby.
predstava *f* idea, notion.
predstaviti *v* to present, to portray, to
   describe, to picture.
predstaviti sebi *v* to visualize.
predstavljanje *n* representation.
predstavljati *v* to represent, to personify.
predstavnica *f* spokeswoman.
predstavnik *m* representative, exponent,
   spokesman.
predstojeći *a* impending, approaching,
   coming.
predstraža *f* outpost, advance guard.
predubeđenje *m* preconception.
predugačak *a* lengthy.
preduhitriti *v* to anticipate, to forestall.
predumišljaj *m* premeditation,
   deliberation.
preduslov *m* precondition.
predusretljiv *a* affable, obliging.
predusretljivost *f* affability.
preduzeće *n* enterprise, business; ~ **sa**
   ograničenim jemstvom *n* incorporated
   company (inc).
preduzeti *v* to undertake, to attempt.

preduzetnik *m* entrepreneur.
preduzimljiv *a* enterprising.
predvideti *v* to anticipate, to foresee.
predviđanje *n* foresight.
predvorje *n* vestibule.
predzadnji *a* penultimate.
pređašnji *a* preceding, former, previous.
prefinjen *a* genteel, sophisticated.
prefrigan *a* cunning, crafty, sly.
pregaziti *v* to run over.
pregled *m* survey, review; check up (*med*).
pregledan *a* distinct.
pregovaranje *n* negotiation.
pregovarati *v* to negotiate.
pregrada *f* partition wall.
pregršt *f* handful.
prehlada *f* cold.
prehrambeni proizvodi *mpl* food stuffs.
preimućstvo *n* advantage.
preistorijski *a* prehistoric.
prejesti se *v* to overeat.
prek *a* irritable, touchy; ~**i sud** *m* court martial.
prekid *m* intermission, interruption, break; ~ **uzbune** all clear; ~ **vatre** cease fire.
prekidati *v* to interrupt, to break, to discontinue.
preklinjati *v* to beg, to beseech, to entreat.
preko *adv* opposite; *prep* over, from, via.
prekomeran *a* excessive.
prekomerno *adv* inordinately, unduly.
prekor *m* rebuke.
prekoračiti *v* to overstep, to pass over.
prekoračenje *n* transgression; ~ **bankovnog računa** overdraft.
prekoran *a* reproachful.
prekoriti *v* to reproach, to blame, reprehend.
prekovremeni rad *m* overtime.
prekrasan *a* splendid, magnificent, wonderful.
prekršaj *m* breach, violation.
prekršiti *v* to infringe, to violate.
prekvalifikacija *f* retraining.
prelamanje *n* refraction.
prelamati *v* to refract.
prelaz *m* transition, crossing; ~ **na reci** ford.

prelazan *a* transitional, transitive (*gram*).
prelaženje *n* passing.
preliti *v* to pour over.
preliv za salatu *m* salad dressing.
prelivanje *n* basting.
prelom *m* break; fracture (*med*); ~ **sloga** make up.
preljubnica *f* adulteress.
preljubnički *a* adulterous.
preljubnik *m* adulterer.
prema *prep* toward(s); ~ **severu** northward(s); ~ **tome** accordingly.
premalo *adv* too little, not enough; ~ **zaračunati** *v* to undercharge.
premaz *m* coating, coat.
premda *conj* although, though.
premeštaj *m* shift.
premeštati *v* to displace, to move.
premijer *m* prime minister.
premijera *f* first night, premiere.
premoren *a* tired out.
prenapet *a* overstrained.
prenaseliti *v* to overpopulate.
prenatrpani *a* overcrowded.
prenemaganje *n* affectation.
preneraziti *v* to amaze, to astound.
preneti *v* to transmit, to transfer.
prenos *m* transmission; ~ **menice** endorsement; ~ **putem radija** broadcasting.
prenositi *v* to communicate.
preobraziti *v* to transform.
preobražaj *m* transformation.
preopteretiti *v* to overwork (radom).
preosetljiv *a* touchy, sensitive.
preostao *a* residuary.
prepad *m* attack, raid, shock.
prepelica *f* quail.
prepeličar *m* spaniel.
prepirati se *v* to argue, to quarrel, to dispute, to bicker.
prepirka *f* altercation, squabble, bickering.
prepis *m* copy, transcript.
prepiska *f* correspondence, communication.
preplanuo *a* tanned, sunburnt.
prepoloviti *v* to halve.
prepona *f* obstacle, bar, barrier; crotch, groin (*med*).
preporod *m* renaissance, revival.

preporučiti *v* to recommend, to suggest; to register.
preporučena pošiljka *f* registered mail.
preporučljiv *a* advisable.
preporuka *f* recommendation, advice.
prepoznati *v* to recognize, to identify.
prepoznavanje *n* recognition.
prepraviti *v* to remake.
prepreden *a* shrewd, artful, cunning.
prepredeno *adv* archly.
prepredenost *f* craftiness, shrewdness.
prepreka *f* barrier, obstacle, hindrance, hurdle.
prepričati *v* to retell.
preprodavac *m* retailer.
prepun *a* overfull.
prepustiti *v* to give up, to abandon, to resign.
prerada *f* alteration, treatment.
preran *a* precocious.
prerasti *v* to outgrow.
prerija *f* prairie.
prerušiti *v* to disguise.
presađivanje *n* transplantion.
presaviti *v* to fold, to double over.
preseći *v* to cut; to interrupt.
presrećan *a* overjoyed, blissful.
prestanak *m* cessation.
prestati *v* to quit, to stop, to cease.
presti *v* to spin; to purr (mačka).
prestići *v* to outrun, to pass.
presto *m* throne.
prestolonaslednik *m* crown prince.
prestonički *a* metropolitan.
prestrašiti *v* to terrify, to frighten.
prestravljen *a* aghast.
prestupna godina *f* leap year.
prestupnik *m* delinquent, malefactor, transgressor.
presuda *f* judgement, verdict, sentence.
presudan *a* decisive.
presuditi *v* to judge, to pass a sentence.
presvlačiti se *v* to disguise.
preteča *f* forerunner, predecessor, precursor.
preteći *a* menacing, threatening.
pretegnuti *v* to outweigh, to outbalance.
preteran *a* excessive, exorbitant, exaggerated.
preterati *v* to overdo; to exaggerate.
prethoditi *v* to precede.

prethodni *a* previous, preliminary, preceding.
prethodnik *m* antecedent, predecessor.
pretiti *v* to threaten.
pretnja *f* menace, threat.
pretovariti *v* to overload.
pretplata *f* subscription.
pretplatiti se *v* to subscribe.
pretplatnik *m* subscriber.
pretpostaviti *f* to assume, to presume, to presuppose, to suppose.
pretpostavka *f* assumption, hypothesis, presumption, supposition.
pretpostavljeni *m* superior.
pretražiti *v* to search, to ransack.
pretresati *v* to argue, to discuss, to debate.
pretrpati *v* to cram, to stow.
preturiti *v* to overturn, to thrown down.
pretvaranje *n* transformation; conversion, simulation.
preuranjen *a* premature.
preurediti *v* to readjust.
preuveličavanje *n* exaggeration.
preuzimanje *n* takeover.
prevaga *f* preponderance.
prevagnuti *v* to overbalance.
prevara *f* deceit, deception, delusion, fraud, hoax, guile.
prevariti *v* to cheat, to swindle.
prevazići *v* to surpass, to excel.
prevesti *v* to translate.
previjati se *v* to writhe.
previše *adv* too much.
prevlast *f* domination, supremacy.
prevod *m* translation.
prevodilac *m* translator.
prevoz *m* conveyance, transport, transportation.
prevoziti *v* to transport, to convey.
prevoznik *m* carrier, hauler.
prevremen *a* abortive.
prevrnuti *v* to capsize, to turn over, to upset.
prevrtljiv *a* inconstant, changeful, variable.
prezime *n* surname.
prezimiti *v* to hibernate.
prezir *m* contempt, scorn.
prezirati *v* to despise, to disdain.
preznojiti se *v* to perspire, to sweat.
prezren *a* contemptible.

prezriv *a* contemptuous, scornful.
preživar *m* cud, ruminant.
preživati *v* to ruminate.
preživeti *v* to survive.
preživela osoba *f* survivor.
prgav *a* vehement, impetuous.
pri *prep* at, with, over, by.
prianjati *v* to adhere.
pribadača *f* safety pin.
pribeležiti *v* to make a note, to annotate.
pribežište *n* refuge, asylum.
pribirati *v* to collect, to gather.
približan *a* approximate.
približiti se *v* to approach.
pribor *m* equipment, implement, outfit; ~
  za prvu pomoć first-aid kit; ~ **za jelo**
  eating utensils; ~ **za pisanje** stationary.
pribranost *f* self-possession, composure.
priča *f* story, tale.
pričati *v* to relate, to tell, to narrate.
pričekati *v* to await, to wait for.
pričesni *a* sacramental.
pričešće *n* communion.
pričiniti se *v* to appear, to look, to seem.
pričljiv *a* loquacious, talkative.
pričvrstiti *v* to affix, to fix, to attach.
pride *adv* extra.
pridev *m* adjective (*gram*).
pridika *f* lecture, sermon.
pridošlica *f* newcomer.
prigovarati *v* to object, to deprecate, to
  remonstrate.
prigovor *m* objection, caveat.
prigradski *a* suburban.
prigušiti *v* to suffocate, to stifle, to deafen
  (zvuk).
prihod *m* income, revenue, emolument.
prihvatanje *n* acceptance.
prihvatiti *v* to accept, to take.
prihvatljiv *a* acceptable.
prihvatljivost *f* acceptability.
prijatan *a* agreeable, enjoyable, cute,
  gracious, nice, pleasant; savoury (za
  njuh); palatable (za ukus).
prijatelj *m* friend; buddy (*slang*).
prijateljski *a* amicable, friendly.
prijateljstvo *n* friendliness, friendship.
prijatno *a* cosily.
prijatnost *f* pleasure, agreeableness.
prijava *f* announcement, advice,
  notification; declaration.

prijem *m* admittance, reception;
  entertainment; party.
prijemni *a* receiving; ~ **ispit** *m* entrance
  examination; ~**o odeljenje** *n* receiving
  ward.
prikaz *m* demonstration, presentation.
prikazati *v* to present, to introduce, to
  depict.
prikazivati *v* to display, to perform.
prikladan *a* suitable, fitting.
prikladno *adv* suitably.
prikolica *f* trailer, caravan.
prikopčati *v* to buckle, to fasten.
prikovati *v* to nail up.
prikradati se *v* to prowl.
prikriti *v* to conceal, to suppress.
prikrivanje *n* cover-up, hiding.
prikupiti *v* to collect, to bring together.
prilagoditi *v* to adapt, to adjust, to
  accommodate, to conform.
prilagodljiv *a* adaptable.
prilagođavanje *n* accommodation,
  adaptation.
prilazni put *m* driveway.
prilepiti *v* to stick.
priličan *a* sufficient.
prilika *f* occasion, opportunity, chance.
prilikom *prep* on the occasion of.
priliv *m* afflux, influx.
prilog *m* contribution, addendum,
  appendix, attachment, enclosure; adverb
  (*gram*).
priloški *a* adverbial.
priložiti *v* to enclose, to attach.
primalac *m* recipient; ~ **novca** payee.
primamiti *v* to allure, to tempt, to bait.
primamljiv *a* inviting, tempting,
  attractive.
primati *v* to accept, to receive; to
  entertain (goste).
primedba *f* objection, remark.
primeniti *v* to apply.
primenljiv *a* applicable.
primenljivost *f* applicability.
primenjen *a* applied.
primer *m* example, instance.
primerak *m* copy; specimen, sample.
primeran *a* exemplary.
primetan *a* conspicuous, noticeable,
  discernible.
primetno *adv* perceptively, perceivably.

primirje *n* armistice, truce.
primiti *v* to receive; ~ **državljanstvo** to naturalize; ~ **u članstvo** to affiliate.
primorje *n* coast, shore.
primorski *a* maritime, coastal.
princ *m* prince.
princeza *f* princess.
princip *m* principle.
prineti *v* to bring to.
prinuda *f* coercion, constraint, compulsion.
prinudan *a* compulsive, compulsory, forcible; **~dno sletanje** *n* emergency landing; **~dno zadržavanje** detention.
prinuditi *v* to constrain, to enforce, to compel.
priobalni *a* coastal, inshore.
pripadati *v* to appertain, to belong.
pripajanje *n* annexation.
pripisati *v* to ascribe, to attribute.
pripit *a* tipsy.
pripitomiti *v* to domesticate, to make tame.
pripojiti *v* to adjoin, to annex.
pripovedački *a* narrative.
pripovedati *v* to narrate, to recount, to relate.
pripravan *a* prepared.
pripravnost *f* readiness.
priprema *f* preparation.
pripremiti *v* to prepare, to get ready.
pripremni *a* preliminary; ~ **rad** *m* groundwork.
priredba *f* show, spectacle.
prirez *m* additional tax.
priroda *f* nature.
prirodan *a* natural, genuine.
priručni *a* hand; **~čna blagajna** *f* petty cash.
priručnik *m* handbook, manual.
prisan *a* intimate; ~ **drug** *m* bosom friend.
priseban a collected, calm.
prisilan *a* compelling.
prisiljen *a* forced.
prisluškivati *v* to eavesdrop, to overhear.
prismotra *f* surveillance.
prisnost *f* familiarity.
prispeće *n* arrival.
pristalica *f* adherent, follower, supporter.
pristanak *m* consent, assent, acquiescence.
pristanište *n* port, wharf, harbour.

pristati *v* to agree, to acquiesce, to consent.
pristojan *a* decent, becoming, seemly, well-behaved.
pristojnost *f* decency, propriety.
pristrasan *a* prejudiced, biassed.
pristup *m* accession, admission, admittance.
pristupačan *a* accessible, approachable, user-friendly.
pristupačnost *f* accessibility, affability.
prisutnost *f* attendance, presence.
prisvajanje *n* appopriation.
prisvojiti *v* to appropriate, to arrogate.
prišipetlja *f* hanger-on.
priticati *v* to accrue.
pritisak *m* pressure, stress.
pritka *f* pole.
pritoka *f* tributary.
pritužba *f* accusation.
pritvor *m* arrest.
privatan *a* personal, private; ~ **život** *m* privacy; **~tni detektiv** private eye; **~tna praksa** *f* private practice; **~tna svojina** private property.
privezak *m* pendant; ~ **za ključeve** *m* key ring.
prividan *a* imaginary, apparent.
priviđanje *n* hallucination.
privilegija *f* privilege, favour.
privlačan *a* alluring, attractive, engaging, fetching, pretty.
privlačiti *v* to attract.
privlačnost *f* attraction.
privreda *f* public economy, business.
privremen *a* provisional, temporary.
privremeno *adv* temporarily.
privrženost *f* devotion, affection, adherence.
prizemlje *n* ground-floor.
priznanica *f* receipt, IOU (I owe you) (kod duga).
priznanje *n* confession, acknowledgement, admission.
priznati *v* to confess, to acknowledge.
prizor *m* spectacle, site.
prizvati *v* to call, to invite, to evoke.
prizvuk *m* overtone, tone.
prkositi *v* to defy.
prljav *a* dirty, filthy, grubby, scruffy, sordid, squalid; **~a i neuredna žena** *f* slut.

prljavština *f* filth(iness), squalor.
proba *f* test, trial; experiment; rehearsal (u pozorištu).
probati *v* to try, to rehearse.
probavni *a* digestive.
probijen *a* perforated.
probiti *v* to perforate, to pierce.
problem *m* problem.
probni *a* probationary, tentative; ~ **pilot** *m* test pilot.
proboj *m* break, gap, opening; breakthrough.
probuditi *v* to wake, to waken, to rouse.
procediti *v* to filtrate, to percolate.
procena *f* appraisal, assessment, estimation, valuation.
procenat *m* percentage, rate.
proceniti *v* to assess, to estimate, to evaluate, to appraise.
procep *m* crevice, fissure.
proces *m* process; action.
procvat *m* prosperity, welfare; blooming.
proći *v* to pass.
prodaja *f* sale.
prodati *v* to sell.
prodavac *m* salesman, seller, vendor; ~ **novina** *m* newsagent.
prodavačica *f* saleswoman.
prodavnica *f* shop, store; ~ **duvana** tobacconist's; ~ **galanterijske robe** haberdashery; ~ **igračaka** toyshop; ~ **obuće** shoe shop.
prodiranje *n* penetration.
prodoran *a* piercing, penetrating.
prodreti *v* to penetrate.
produbiti *v* to deepen.
produktivan *a* productive.
produktivnost *f* productivity.
produžiti *v* to prolong, to lengthen.
profesija *f* profession.
profesionalan *a* professional.
profesor *m* professor.
profitiranje *n* profiteering.
profućkati *v* to spend profusely, to squander.
proglasiti *v* to proclaim; ~ **krivim** to convict.
prognati *v* to banish, to ostracize, to exile.
prognoza *f* prognosis, forecast; ~ **vremena** weather forecast.
progoniti *v* to persecute, to pursue.

progonstvo *n* deportation.
program *m* programme, platform.
programer *m* programmer.
programiranje *n* programming.
progresivan *a* progressive.
progutati *v* to swallow.
prohujati *v* to pass by quickly.
proizvod *m* product, produce.
proizvodnja *f* manufacture, production.
proizvođač *m* producer, generator.
proizvoljan *a* optional, non-obligatory.
proizvoljnost *f* arbitrariness.
projektant *m* designer.
projektil *m* missile, projectile.
projektovati *v* to design.
proklet *a* accursed, damned.
prokleti *v* to curse, to damn.
prokletstvo *n* damnation, malediction.
proklijati *v* to germinate.
prokrijumčariti *v* to smuggle.
prokule *fpl* Brussels sprout, broccoli.
prolaz *m* gateway, passage, thoroughfare; transit.
prolazan *a* ephemeral, passable, transient.
prolaznik *m* passer-by.
proleće *n* spring, springtime.
proliv *m* diarrhoea.
promaja *f* draught.
promašaj *m* failure, faux pas.
promašiti *v* to miss.
promatrač *m* viewer.
promena *f* alteration, change.
promeniti *v* to change, to alter.
promenljiv *a* changeable, commutable, fickle, variable.
promišljeno *adv* advisedly, deliberately.
promocija *f* promotion.
promoter *m* promoter.
promrzao *a* frostbitten.
promrzlina *f* chilblain, frostbite.
promućuran *a* cunning, sly, shrewd.
promukao *a* hoarse, husky.
promuklost *f* hoarseness, huskiness.
pronaći *v* to find, to discover.
pronalazač *m* inventor.
pronalazački *a* ingenious, inventive.
pronalazak *f* discovery, invention.
pronevera *f* embezzlement.
proneveriti *v* to embezzle.
pronicljiv *a* astute, observant.
pronicljivo *adv* observantly.

pronicljivost *m* insight, acumen.
propadanje *n* declension, fall, ruin.
propaganda *f* propaganda, advertising.
propalica *f* good-for-nothing.
propao *a* gone.
propast *f* debacle, perdition, ruin.
propinjati se *v* to rear up.
propis *m* rule, regulation.
propisati *v* to enact, to prescribe.
propisno *adv* duly.
propoved *f* sermon.
propovedaonica *f* pulpit.
propovedati *v* to preach.
propust *m* omission, oversight.
propustiti *v* to omit, to neglect.
proračun *m* estimate, estimation, calculation.
prored *m* space, interval.
proricanje *n* foreboding, prediction.
proricati *v* to foretell, to predict.
proročanski *a* prophetic.
proročanstvo *n* prophecy.
prorok *m* prophet, soothsayer.
prosečan *a* average, mean.
prosejati *v* to sift, to sieve.
prositi *v* to beg.
prosjak *m* beggar.
proslava *f* celebration, commemoration; ~ **prilikom useljenja** *f* house-warming party.
proslaviti *v* to celebrate.
proslediti *v* to forward.
proso *n* millet.
prospekt *m* prospectus.
prost *a* homely, ordinary, usual, uncouth.
prostački *a* vulgar, common.
prostak *m* simpleton.
prostitucija *f* prostitution.
prostitutka *f* prostitute.
prosto *adv* commonly, simply.
prostor *m* area, space.
prostorija *f* room, premises.
prostota *f* homeliness, simplicity.
prostran *a* roomy, spacious.
prostranost *f* roominess, spaciousness.
prostranstvo *n* space, expanse.
prosuti *v* to spill, to pour out.
prosvećen *a* enlightened.
prošireni *a* broadened, widened; ~**a vena** *f* varicose vein.
proširenost *f* expansion.

proširiti *v* to broaden, to widen; ~ **vidokrug** to enlarge, to expend.
prošli *a* bygone, past.
protein *m* protein.
proterati *v* to deport, to evict; ~ **iz domovine** to expatriate.
proterivanje *n* eviction, expulsion.
protestovati *v* to protest.
protezati *v* to stretch, to extend.
proticati *v* to run out, to elapse.
protiv *prep* against, versus.
protivavionski *a* anti-aircraft.
protiviti se *v* to resist, to oppose.
protivljenje *n* opposition.
protivnik *m* adversary, opponent.
protivotrov *m* antidote.
protivpožarni alarm *m* fire alarm.
protivrečiti *v* to contradict, to disagree.
protivrečan *a* conflicting.
protivrečnost *f* contradiction, inconsistency.
protivustavan *a* unconstitutional.
protivzakonit *a* illegal.
protokol *m* protocol.
prototip *m* prototype.
protuva *f* vagabond.
proučiti *v* to study, to scrutinize.
prouzrokovati *v* to bring about, to cause.
provala *f* outbreak; housebreaking.
provalija *f* abyss.
provalna krađa *f* burglary.
provalnik *m* burglar, housebreaker.
proveravanje *n* verification, examination.
proveriti *v* to verify.
provetriti *v* to ventilate.
providan *a* transparent.
providnost *f* transparency.
provincija *f* province.
proviriti *v* to peep through.
provodadžija *m* matchmaker.
provreti *v* to boil.
proza *f* prose.
prozaičan *a* prosaic.
prozebao *a* frozen, chilled.
proziran *a* limpid, clear.
prozor *m* window; ~ **na krovu** skylight; ~ **na boku broda** porthole.
prozorski *a* window; ~**o krilo** *n* window sash; ~**o okno** window pane.
proždirati *v* to devour, to gobble.
proždrljiv *a* voracious.

proždrljivost *f* gluttony.
prsa *f* chest, breast, bosom.
prskanje *n* splash, sprinkling.
prsluče *n* brassiere, bra.
prsluk *m* bodice, vest; ~ **za spašavanje** life jacket.
prst *m* finger.
prsten *m* ring; circle.
pršljen *m* vertebra.
prštati *v* to crackle.
prtljag *m* baggage, luggage.
pruga *f* streak, line; **železnička** ~ *f* railway line.
prut *m* wand, switch.
pružiti *v* to offer, to proffer, to render.
prvenstveno *adv* before all, firstly.
prvenstvo *n* priority.
prvi *a* first, foremost, prime; **~a pomoć** *f* first aid.
prvobitan *a* original, primary; former; primeval.
prvoklasan *a* first-class.
prvorazredan *a* first-rate.
pržiti *v* to fry, to roast.
pseći *a* dog; **~a kućica** *f* kennel.
psetance *n* pup, puppy.
pseudonim *m* pseudonym, false name, alias.
psiha *f* psyche, soul.
psihijatar *m* psychiatrist.
psihijatrija *f* psychiatry.
psihijatrijski *a* psychiatric.
psihoanalist *m* psychoanalyst.
psihoanaliza *f* psychoanalysis.
psiholog *m* psychologist.
psihologija *f* psychology.
psihološki *a* psychological.
pšenica *f* wheat.
ptica *f* bird, fowl.
ptičja perspektiva *f* bird's-eye-view.
publika *f* audience.
pucanj *m* shot, explosion.
pucanje *n* firing, shooting.
puckaranje *n* crackling.
pući *v* to burst; to break.
puder *m* powder; ~ **u kamenu** compact powder; ~ **za lice** face powder.
puding *m* pudding.

puk *m* regiment; common people.
puki *a* mere, bare, pure.
pukotina *f* fissure, opening, crack, crevasse.
pukovnik *m* colonel.
pulover *m* pullover.
pult *m* stand, rostrum, podium.
pun *a* complete, full; ~ **ljubavi** loving; ~ **nade** hopeful; ~ **poverenja** trustful; ~ **puncat** brimful; **~a kašika** *f* spoonful; ~ **mesec** *m* full moon.
punačak *a* plump.
punč *m* toddy.
puniti *v* to fill; ~ **gorivom** to refuel.
punoća *f* fullness, plentitude.
punoglavac *m* tadpole.
punomoć *f* power of attorney.
pupak *m* navel.
pupčana vrpca *f* umbilical cord.
pupoljak *m* bud.
puritanac *m* puritan.
pust *a* bleak, waste, abandoned; **~a zemlja** *f* wasteland.
pustinja *f* desert.
pustinjak *m* hermit, recluse.
pustinjački život *m* hermitage.
pustiti *v* to leave, to let, to allow.
pustolov *m* adventurer, daredevil.
pustoš *f* devastation, desolation.
pustošiti *v* to devastate, to ravage.
pušač *m* smoker.
puščana vatra *f* gunfire.
puška *f* gun.
puškarnica *f* loop-hole.
put[1] *m* road, way, trek.
put[2] *f* skin.
putem *prep* by means of, by way of.
puten *a* carnal, sensual.
puter *m* butter.
putir *m* chalice.
putnik *m* passenger, traveller.
putokaz *m* sign-post, road-sign.
putovanje *n* journey, travelling, voyage, travel; ~ **autobusom** coach trip.
puzati *v* to creep, to crawl.
puzavica *f* creeper.
puž *m* snail.

R

rabat *m* discount, rebate, deduction.
rabin *m* rabbi.
racija *f* raid.
racionalan *a* rational.
račun *m* account; calculation; bill; **tekući**
~ current account.
računanje *n* calculation.
računar *m* computer.
računarstvo *m* computer science.
računati *v* to count.
računovodstvo *n* accountancy.
računovođa *m* accountant.
račvast *a* bifurcated, branching, forked.
račvati se *v* to fork, to branch.
rad[1] *m* labour, work, employment, job;
paper; ~ **na terenu** fieldwork;
intelektualni ~ (intellectual) brain-
work; **ručni** ~ manual work; **fizički** ~
manual labour work.
rad[2] *a* willing, disposed.
radan *a* active, diligent, laborious.
radi *prep* on account of, because of,
owing to.
radije *adv* preferably, rather.
radijus *m* radius.
radikalizam *m* radicalism.
radio *m* radio, wireless; ~ **u kolima** car
radio.
radioaktivan *a* radioactive.
radionica *f* workshop.
raditi *v* to do, to work, to labour; to have
a job, to be employed.
radni *a* working; ~**a snaga** *f* manpower,
workforce; ~ **dan** *m* weekday; ~**o vreme**
n office hours.
radnički *a* working, proletarian; ~**a klasa**
f working-class.
radnik *m* worker, labourer, workman.
rado *adv* readily.
radoholik *m* workaholic.
radost *f* joy, delight.
radovanje *n* rejoicing.
radovati se *v* to rejoice, to gladden.
radoznalost *f* curiosity.
radoznao *a* curious, inquisitive.
rađanje *n* birth.
raf *m* shelf, rack.

rafal *m* burst of fire.
rafinerija *f* refinery.
ragbi *m* rugby.
rahitičan *a* rickety.
rahitis *m* rickets.
raj *m* paradise.
rak *m* crab, crayfish; cancer (bolest);
Cancer (*astrol*).
raketa *f* rocket, skyrocket.
rakija *f* brandy.
ralica za sneg *f* snowplough.
rame *n* shoulder.
ran *a* early.
rana *f* sore, wound, injury.
ranac *m* backpack, haversack, knapsack,
rucksack.
randevu *m* rendezvous.
rang *m* rank, order, position.
ranije *adv* beforehand.
raniti *v* to hurt, to injure, to wound.
rano *adv* soon, early; ~ **detinjstvo** *n*
infancy.
ranjiv *a* vulnerable.
rapsodija *f* rhapsody.
rasa *f* race, breed.
rasad *m* seedlings.
rasan *a* full-blooded, thorough-bred.
rasaniti se *v* to wake up.
rascep *m* split, division.
rascvetan *a* florid; prosperous.
raseći *v* to cut, to divide by an edged tool.
rasejan *a* absent-minded, distracted.
rasejanost *f* distraction, absence of mind.
rasejeno *adv* absently.
rashladiti *v* to cool.
rashod *m* expense, charge, cost.
rasipan *a* improvident, wasteful.
rasipanje *n* dissipation.
rasipati *v* to waste, to squander.
rasipnik *m* spendthrift.
rasipništvo *n* extravagance, wastefulness.
rasistički *a* racist.
raskid *m* separation, severance,
disruption.
raskinuti *v* to disrupt, to sever, to break;
to cancel (ugovor).
rasklimatan *a* shaking, unsteady.

raskol *m* schism (*rel*).
raskolnički *a* schismatic.
raskomadati *v* to lacerate, to cut up.
raskoračen *a* astride.
raskoš *f* glamour, luxury, splendour.
raskošan *a* gorgeous, splendid, luxurious.
raskrinkavanje *n* denunciation.
raskrsnica *f* crossroad, intersection.
rasni *a* racial.
raspadati se *v* to decompose, to disintegrate.
raspakovati *v* to unpack, to unwrap.
raspaliti *v* to flare up.
raspaljiv *a* inflammatory.
raspasti se *v* to fall to pieces.
raspeće *n* crucifixion.
raspevan *a* singing, happy.
raspis *m* circular.
raspitivati se *v* to inquire.
rasplakati *v* to make cry.
raspodela *f* distribution.
raspodeliti *v* to distribute, to assign.
raspolaganje *n* disposal, disposition, management.
raspoložen *a* disposed, friendly.
raspoloženje *n* mood, temper, disposition, frame of mind.
raspoložiti se *v* to be in high spirits.
raspoloživ *a* disposable, available.
raspored *m* disposition, layout, ordering; ~ **časova** time-table.
rasporediti *v* to dispose, to arrange.
raspoznati *v* to recognize, to identify.
rasprava *f* debate, discussion, treatise.
raspravljati se *v* to dispute.
rasprodaja *f* selling-off, sale.
rasprostranjen *a* prevailing, widespread.
raspust *m* vacation, holidays.
raspustiti *v* to disband.
rastanak *m* farewell, parting.
rastaviti *v* to separate, to disintegrate, to sever.
rastavljati *v* to dismantle.
rastegljiv *a* elastic, springy.
rastegljivost *f* elasticity.
rastegnuti *v* to extend, to outstretch.
rasterati *v* to dispel, to disperse.
rastezanje *n* extension, stretching.
rastezati *v* to dilate, to extend.
rasti *v* to grow, to increase, to vegetate.
rastojanje *n* distance, extent.

rastopiti *v* to dissolve, to melt.
rastrgnuti *v* to tear to pieces, to dismember.
rastrojen *a* deranged, shattered.
rastrubiti *v* to blare, to proclaim.
rastumačiti *v* to explain, to explicate, to comment.
rastužiti *v* to make sad, to afflict, to sadden.
rastvarač *n* solvent.
rastvaranje *n* dissolution.
rastvarati *v* to dissolve.
rastvor *m* solution, mixture.
rastvorljiv *a* soluble.
rasuđivanje *n* reasoning.
rasuti *v* to disperse, to scatter.
rasveta *f* lighting.
rasvetliti *v* to elucidate.
rasčlaniti *v* to dismember.
rasčlanjen *a* disjointed, dismembered.
raštrkati se *v* to disperse.
rat *m* war, warfare.
ratifikovati *v* to ratify, to countersign.
ratni *a* war, of war; ~ **brod** *m* warship; ~a **mornarica** *f* navy; ~a **varka** stratagem.
ratnik *m* warrior.
ratoboran *a* warlike, militant.
ravan *a* even, flat, plane.
ravnati *v* to plane, to level, to equate.
ravnica *f* plain.
ravnina *f* flatness.
ravnodnevica *f* equinox.
ravnodušan *a* impassive, indifferent, listless.
ravnodušnost *f* indifference.
ravnomeran *a* regular, even, equal.
ravnomerno *adv* regularly, evenly.
ravnopravnost *f* equality.
ravnostrani *a* equilateral.
ravnoteža *f* equilibrium, balance, poise.
razabrati *v* to comprehend, to understand, to distinguish.
razapeti *v* to crucify.
razarač *m* destroyer.
razarajući *a* devastating.
razaranje *n* destruction, demolition.
razbacati *v* to scatter.
razbarušen *a* dishevelled.
razbesneti *v* to infuriate, to madden, to enrage.
razbijati *v* to smash, to batter.

razbiti *v* to break, to shatter.
razblažiti *v* to dilute.
razboj *m* loom.
razbojnik *m* robber, bandit, ruffer.
razboleti se *v* to fall sick, to become ill.
razborit *a* discerning, reasonable.
razborito *adv* reasonably.
razboritost *f* reason, mind, rationality.
razdeliti *v* to divide, to distribute.
razdor *m* difference, discord.
razdragan *a* jovial, overjoyed.
razdragati *v* to enrapture.
razdraženost *f* exasperation, irritation.
razdražiti *v* to provoke, to irritate.
razdražljiv *a* irascible, irritable, nervous, testy.
razdražljivost *f* irritability.
razdražujući *a* irritating.
razgaliti *v* to refresh, to cool off.
razglasiti *v* to give notice, to herald.
razglasni uređaj *m* public-address system.
razgledati *v* to examine, to inspect; to go sightseeing.
razgledanje *n* observation, examination, inspection; ~ znamenitosti sightseeing.
razgolititi *v* to bear, to uncover, to reveal.
razgovarati *v* converse.
razgovetan *a* articulate, distinct, clear.
razgovor *m* conversation, dialogue, talk, speech.
razgovoran *a* talkative, loquacious, voluble.
razgranati *v* to develop, to branch.
razgraničenje *n* demarcation.
razigranost *f* animation, gaiety.
razilaziti se *v* to differ, to dissent.
razilaženje *n* divergence.
razjaren *a* raging, frantic, furious.
razjasniti *v* to clarify, to explain.
razjašnjenje *n* clarification, elucidation.
razjašnjiv *a* explicable.
razjedati *v* to erode.
razlaganje *n* discourse.
različak *m* cornflower (*bot*).
različit *a* dissimilar, unlike, varied.
različitost *f* diversity, dissimilarity, discrepancy, variance.
razlika *f* difference, distinction, discrepancy.
razlikovati *v* to discern, to discriminate, to differentiate, to distinguish.

razlog *m* cause, ground, motive, reason.
razlomak *f* fraction (*mat*).
razmak *m* distance, space, interval, span.
razmatranje *n* consideration, contemplation.
razmatrati *v* to consider, to envisage.
razmaziti *v* to indulge, to spoil, to cosset, to dote.
razmena *f* interchange, exchange.
razmeniti *v* to exchange, to change.
razmera *f* dimension, proportion.
razmestiti *v* to rearrange.
razmetljiv *a* ostentatious, showy, boastful.
razmimoilaženje *n* discord.
razmisliti *v* to meditate, to ruminate, to ponder, to think about.
razmišljanje *n* thinking, speculation, deliberation.
razmišljati *v* to think, to speculate, to deliberate, to muse.
razmotriti *v* to view, to envisage.
razmrsiti *v* to unravel.
razneti *v* to deliver.
razni *adv* various.
razno *adv* miscellaneous.
raznolikost *f* variety.
raznorodan *a* heterogeneous, diverse.
raznovrstan *a* assorted, sundry.
razočaran *a* disappointed, disillusioned, disenchanted.
razočarati *v* to disappoint, to disillusion.
razočarenje *n* disappointment, disillusion.
razonoda *f* amusement, diversion.
razoran *a* destructive, ruinous.
razoriti *v* to destroy, to demolish.
razoružanje *n* disarmament.
razoružati *v* to disarm.
razotkriti *v* to disclose.
razraditi *v* to elaborate, to work out.
razrešiti *v* to disengage, to discharge.
razrok *a* cross-eyed, squint.
razum *m* reason, sense, intelligence.
razuman *a* reasonable, rational, sensible.
razumeti *v* to understand, to comprehend.
razumevanje *n* comprehension, understanding.
razumljiv *a* clear, comprehensible, intelligible, understandable.
razumno *adv* sensibly.
razuzdan *a* wanton, wild, lewd.

razveden *a* divorced.
razvedriti *v* to clear up, to brighten up.
razvesti (se) *v* to (be) divorce.
razvijati *v* to develop, to evolve.
razvitak *m* evolution, development.
razvod *m* divorce.
razvodna tabla *f* switchboard (*tech*).
razvodnica *f* usherette (npr. u pozorištu).
razvoj *m* development; process, growth.
razvrat *m* debauchery.
razvratan *a* debauched, lecherous.
razvrstati *v* to classify, to categorize.
razvučen *a* prolonged.
razvući *v* to draw out, to stretch.
raž *f* rye.
ražalostiti *v* to sadden.
ražanj *m* skewer, spit.
rđa *f* corrosion, rust.
rđav *a* bad, evil, vile, wicked.
reagovati *v* to react.
reakcija *f* reaction.
realističan *a* real, down-to-earth.
realnost *f* reality.
rebro *n* rib.
recepcija *f* lobby, desk; reception.
recept *m* recipe; prescription.
recikliran *a* recycled.
recitovanje *n* declamation, recital.
recitovati *f* to recite, to rehearse.
recka *f* notch, mark.
reč *f* word, phrase; promise.
rečenica *f* sentence, phrase, clause.
rečit *a* eloquent.
rečitost *f* eloquence.
rečni *a* riverside; **~o korito** riverbed; **~a obala** riverbank.
rečnik *m* dictionary, vocabulary; glossary.
reći *v* to say, to speak, to talk.
red *m* order, row, queue; **~ i mir** law and order.
redak *a* rare, infrequent, scarce, sparse.
redigovati *v* to edit.
redni *a* ordinal.
redom *adv* successively, in succession.
redosled *m* sequence, order; **~ događaja** sequence of events.
redov *m* private, soldier.
redovan *a* regular.
redovitost *m* regularity.
redovno *adv* regularly, invariably.
ređati *v* to range, to arrange in a row.

ređe *adv* not so often.
referat *m* report.
refleksan *a* reflex.
reflektor *m* reflector, searchlight, spotlight.
reforma *f* reform, reformation.
reformator *m* reformer.
regata *f* regatta.
regentstvo *n* regency.
registar *m* register, index, list.
registrovati *v* to register, to record.
registrovati se *v* to be married at the registry office.
regresivan *a* regressive.
regrut *m* recruit.
regrutacija *f* recruiting.
regrutovanje *n* enlistment.
regulisanje *n* regulation.
regulisati *v* to regulate.
rehabilitacija *f* rehabilitation.
rehabilitovati *v* to rehabilitate.
rejv muzika *f* rave music.
reka *f* river.
reket *m* racket.
reklama *f* advertisement.
reklamirati *v* to advertise; to complain.
reklamna tabla *f* billboard.
rekonstruisati *v* to reconstruct.
relaksacija *f* relaxation.
relevantan *a* relevant.
relikvija *f* relic.
reljef *m* relief.
remek delo *m* masterpiece.
remen *m* strap.
remetiti *v* to disturb.
remorker *m* tugboat.
ren *m* horseradish.
rende *n* plane, grater.
rendgen *m* X-ray.
renoviranje *n* renovation, restoration.
renovirati *v* to renovate, to renew, to refresh.
renta *f* income, revenue; rent.
rentabilnost *m* profitability.
reorganizacija *f* reorganization.
reorganizovati *v* to reorganize.
reosigurati *v* to reinsure.
rep *m* tail.
repa *f* turnip.
reportaža *f* coverage, footage.
represivan *a* repressive.
repriza *f* (theatre) second showing; repetition.

reprodukcija *f* reproduction.
reprodukovati *v* to reproduce.
reptil *m* reptile.
republički *a* republican.
republika *f* republic.
resor *m* department.
respirator *m* respirator, life-support system (*med*).
restoran *m* restaurant.
restriktivan *a* restrictive.
rešenost *f* resolve, determination.
rešenje *n* solution.
rešetka *f* grate, grid, grille; bars.
rešeto *n* riddle.
rešiti *v* solve, to clear, to determine; ~ arbitražom to arbitrate.
rešo *m* hotplate.
retko *adv* seldom, rarely.
retkost *f* rarity, scarcity.
retorički *a* rhetorical.
retorika *f* rhetoric.
retrospektivan *a* retrospective.
retuširati *v* to touch up.
reumatičan *a* rheumatic.
reumatizam *f* rheumatism.
revanš *m* revenge.
rever *m* lapel.
revers *m* receipt.
revija *f* review.
revizija *f* re-examination, auditing.
revizor *m* auditor.
revnost *f* eagerness, zeal, ardour.
revnostan *a* zealous.
revolt *m* revolt; revulsion, indignation.
revolucija *f* revolution.
revolucionarni *a* revolutionary.
revolver *m* revolver, gun.
revolveraš *m* gunman.
rez *m* incision, cutting.
reza *f* bolt, latch.
rezak *a* acid, stinging, sharp.
rezanci *mpl* noodles.
rezbarija *f* carving.
rezervisano *a* reserved.
rezervni *a* spare.
rezervoar *m* reservoir, tank.
rezonanca *f* resonance.
rezultat *m* result, effect, outcome.
režati *v* to growl, to snarl.
režim *m* regime.
riba *f* fish.

ribar *m* fisherman.
ribarnica *f* fishmonger's (shop).
ribizla *f* currant.
riblji *a* fish, fishy; ~a kost *f* fishbone; ~e ulje *n* cod-liver oil.
ribnjak *m* fishery.
ribolov *m* fishing.
ricinus *m* castor oil.
riđokos *a* sandy, ginger.
rika *f* roar.
rima *f* rhyme.
rimokatolik *m* Roman Catholic.
ringla *f* burner; ~ na gas gas burner.
ris *m* lynx (*zool*); ream (papir).
riskantan *a* risky.
ritam *m* rhythm.
ritati se *v* to kick.
ritmičan *a* rhythmical.
rival *m* rival, competitor.
rizičan *a* risky.
rizik *m* risk, danger, hazard.
rizničar *m* treasurer.
rob *m* slave.
roba *f* commodity, merchandise, ware, goods; ~ široke potrošnje consumer goods.
robna kuća *f* department store.
rod *m* sex; gender (*gram*); relation, kin; crop.
rodbina *f* connection, relations.
roditeljevi roditelji *mpl* grandparents.
roditelji *mpl* parents.
roditeljski *a* parental.
roditi *v* to bear, to bring to birth, to beget.
roditi se *v* to be born.
rodni *a* natal; ~o mesto *m* hometown.
rodoljubiv *a* patriotic.
rodoskrnavljenje *n* incest.
rodoskrvni *a* incestuous.
rodoslov *m* genealogy, pedigree.
rodoslovni *a* genealogical.
rođak *m* kinsman, cousin, relative.
rođen *a* born; nee (rođena – prezime sa kojim su rođene udate žene).
rođendan *m* birthday.
rog *m* horn.
rogat *a* horned.
rogonja *m* cuckold.
roj *m* swarm.
rojalista *m* royalist.
rok *m* term, time limit.

rokenrol *m* rock and roll.
rola *f* part.
roletna *f* Venetian blind.
rolšue *fpl* roller skates.
roman *m* novel.
romansa *f* romance.
romantičan *a* romantic.
romb *m* rhombus.
romboid *m* rhomboid.
rominjati *v* to drizzle.
ronilac *m* diver, plunger.
roniti *v* to dive.
ropac *m* death rattle.
ropski *a* slavish, menial.
ropstvo *n* bondage, servitude, slavery; oppression (*fig*).
rosa *f* dew.
rospija *f* brawling woman, scold, vixen.
roštilj *m* barbecue, grill.
rotkvica *f* radish.
rov *m* trench, ditch.
rovarenje *n* plotting.
rovit *a* soft, weak.
rožnat *a* horny.
rožnjača *f* cornea.
rt *m* cape (*geog*); promontory.
rub *m* brink, border, rim; seam (šav).
rubin *m* ruby.
rublje *n* underclothes, underwear.
rubni *a* marginal.
rubrika *f* section, heading.
ručak *m* dinner, lunch, luncheon.
ručati *v* to dine, to have dinner.
ručni *a* manual; ~ **rad** *m* handiwork; ~ **prtljag** hand luggage; ~ **sat** wristwatch; ~**a kočnica** *f* handbrake; ~**a kolica** wheelbarrow; ~**a torbica** handbag.
ruda *f* ore, mineral; ~ **gvožđa** *f* iron ore.
rudar *m* miner.

rudarstvo *n* mining.
rudnik *m* mine; ~ **dijamanata** diamond field; ~ **zlata** goldmine.
rugati se *v* to mock, to sneer, to jeer.
rugoba *f* ugly person.
ruho *n* clothes.
ruka *f* arm; hand (šaka); **dići ~u na sebe** to commit suicide; **dići ~e od nečega** to abandon smt.; **iz prve ~e** firsthand.
rukav *m* sleeve.
rukavica *f* glove; ~**e bez prstiju** *fpl* mittens.
rukopis *m* handwriting; manuscript.
rukovanje *n* handshake.
rukovati *v* to handle, to manipulate.
rukovodeći *a* leading.
rulet *m* roulette.
rum *m* rum.
rumen *a* rosy.
rumen(ilo) *n* blush, rosiness.
runo *n* fleece.
rupa *f* hole, cavity.
rupica *f* dimple (na obrazu); ~ **za dugme** buttonhole.
rusvaj *m* disorder, confusion.
rušiti *v* to demolish.
rutina *f* routine.
ruzmarin *m* rosemary.
ruž *m* lipstick.
ruža *f* rose.
ružan *a* ugly, plain, unsightly; ~**žno vreme** bad weather.
ružičnjak *m* rose bed.
ružin pupoljak *m* rosebud.
ružnoća *f* ugliness.
rvanje *n* wrestling.
rvati se *v* to wrestle, to grapple.
rzati *v* to neigh.

S

s, sa *prep* with.
sabajle *adv* very early.
sabesednik *m* interlocutor.
sabirati *v* to collect, to bring together.
sablast *f* ghost, phantom.
sablastan *a* spectral, ghostly.
sablja *f* sabre.
sabljarka *f* swordfish (*zool*).
sabor *m* assembly, council.
sabotaža *f* sabotage.
sabrati *v* to add; to collect.
sačekati *v* to wait for.
sačinjavati *v* to consitute, to form, to comprise, to include.
sačmara *f* shotgun.
sačuvati *v* to conserve, to preserve, to keep, to guard.
saće *n* honeycomb.
sada *adv* now, nowadays, at once, at present.
sadašnji *a* actual, present, contemporary.
sadašnjost *f* present time.
sadejstvo *n* coordination.
saditi *v* to plant.
sadržaj *m* subject, matter; *pl* contents.
sadržati *v* to contain, to include, to involve.
safir *m* sapphire.
sag *m* carpet.
sagibanje *n* stooping.
saglasan *a* concordant, in accordance, in agreement.
saglasnost *f* compliance, concord.
sagnuti se *v* to bow, to bend.
sagorevanje *n* combustion, burning, consuming.
sagraditi *v* to build, to construct, to raise.
saharin *m* saccharin.
sahrana *f* burial, internment.
sahraniti *v* to bury, to inter.
sajam *m* fair.
sakaćenje *n* mutilation.
sakatiti *v* to mutilate, to cripple.
sakristija *f* vestry.
sakriti se *v* to conceal, to hide, to secrete.
sakriven *a* covert, concealed.
saksija *f* flowerpot.

saksofon *m* saxophone.
sakupiti *v* to gather, to collect.
salama *f* salami.
salata *f* salad; zelena ~ lettuce.
saldo *n* balance.
saletati *v* to assail, to beset.
salo *n* fat, grease.
salon *m* drawing room, parlour.
salva *f* salvo.
sam *a* alone, by one's self, unaccompanied; lonely, single.
samleti *v* to grind.
samoća *f* loneliness, solitude, seclusion.
samoglasnik *m* vowel.
samohodni *a* self-propelled.
samohran *a* self-supporting.
samonikao *a* original.
samoodbrana *f* self-defence.
samoodricanje *n* self-denial.
samopoštovanje *m* self-respect.
samopouzdan *a* presumptuous, self-confident, self-reliant.
samopožrtvovan *a* self-sacrificing.
samosažaljenje *n* self-pity.
samostalan *a* independent, self-directing, autonomous.
samostan *m* monastery.
samoubilački *a* suicidal.
samoubistvo *n* suicide.
samouk *m* self-educated person.
samouslužni *a* self-service.
samouveren *a* complacent, opinionated.
samouverenost *f* complacency.
samovoljan *a* self-willed.
samozadovoljan *a* self-satisfied, smug.
samozvanac *m* impostor.
samoživ *a* ego(t)istic, self-loving.
samrtan *a* death, mortal; ~nička postelja *f* deathbed; ~nički bled *a* pallid.
samrtan *a* death, mortal.
samur *m* sable.
san *m* dream, sleep, slumber.
sanatorijum *m* convalescent home.
sandala *f* sandal.
sanduk *m* trunk, case, chest.
sanitetska kola *f* ambulance.
sanke *fpl* sledge, sleigh.

santa *f* floating ice, block of ice.
santimetar *m* centimetre.
sanjiv *a* dozy, drowsy.
saobraćaj *m* traffic, communication.
saopštenje *n* announcement.
saopštiti *v* to declare, to announce.
saosećajan *a* soft-hearted, sympathetic.
saosećanje *n* sympathy, pity.
saosećati *v* to commiserate, to sympathize.
sapun *m* soap.
sapunast *a* soapy.
sapunica *f* lather, soapsuds.
sapunski *a* soap; ~ **mehur** *m* soap bubble.
saputnik *m* fellow traveller.
saradnik *m* collaborator, colleague, contributor.
saradnja *f* collaboration, cooperation.
sarađivati *v* to collaborate, to cooperate.
sardina *f* sardines.
sarkazam *m* sarcasm.
sarkofag *m* sarcophagus.
saslušanje *n* trial, hearing, judicial examination.
sastanak *m* meeting, assignation.
sastav *m* composition, structure.
sastaviti *v* to compose, to converge, to join.
sastavljanje *n* compilation.
sastavni deo *m* ingredient, component.
sastojati se *v* to consist.
sasvim *adv* fully, quite, absolutely; ~ **budan** *a* wide-awake; ~ **gluv** stone deaf.
sašiti *v* to sew.
sat *m* hour; watch, clock; ~ **za parkiranje** parking meter.
satana *f* Satan.
satelit *m* satellite.
satelitska TV antena *f* satellite dish.
saten *m* satin.
satir *m* satyr.
satira *f* satire.
satiričan *a* satiric(al).
satiričar *m* satirist.
satkati *v* to weave.
saučesnik *m* accomplice.
saučesništvo *n* complicity.
saučešće *n* condolence, compassion, commiseration.
sav *a* all; complete; whole.
savana *f* savanna(h).
savest *f* conscience.

savestan *a* conscientious.
savet *m* advice, admonition, council.
savetnik *m* counsellor.
savetodavni *a* advisory.
savetovanje *n* consultation, advice.
savetovati *v* to admonish, to advise, to counsel, to suggest.
savetovati se *v* to confer, to consult.
savez *m* alliance, union, coalition, league.
savezni *a* allied, federal.
saveznik *m* ally.
saviti se *v* to bend, to lean.
savitljiv *a* flexible, pliable, pliant, supple.
savitljivost *f* flexibility.
savladati *v* to overcome, to overpower, to surmount.
savladati se *v* to control oneself.
savladiv *a* surmountable.
savremen *a* modern, contemporary.
savršen *a* ideal, perfect.
savršeno *adv* incomparably.
savršenstvo *n* perfection.
saziv *m* convocation, summons.
sazivati *v* to convene, to convoke.
saznanje *n* realization, knowledge.
saznati *v* to find, to hear, to be informed.
sazvežđe *n* constellation.
sažaljenje *n* compassion, pity.
sažet *a* concise, succinct; ~ **pregled** *m* synopsis.
sažeti *v* to abridge, to epitomize.
sažvakan *a* wrinkled, tired, weary (*fig*).
scenario *m* scenario, script.
se, sebe *pn* yourself, itself, herself, himself, ourselves, themselves.
sebičan *a* ego(t)istical, selfish.
sebičnost *f* ego(t)ism, selfishness.
secirati *v* to dissect.
seckalica *f* chopper.
sečivo *n* blade.
sećanje *n* recollection, reminiscence, memory.
sećati se *v* to recollect, to remember.
seći *v* to cut, to cut up, to chop, to chip.
sedalo *n* roost (u kokošinjcu).
sedam *num* seven.
sedamdeset *num* seventy.
sedamdeseti *num* a seventieth.
sedamdesetogodišnjak *m* septuagenarian.
sedamnaest *num* seventeen.
sedamnaesti *num* a seventeenth.

sedativ *m* sedative.
sedećke *adv* sitting.
sedef *m* mother-of-pearl.
sedeti *v* to sit, to have a seat.
sedište *n* seat; ~ **u loži** box-seat; ~ **za katapultiranje** ejection seat.
sedlar *m* saddler.
sedlo *n* saddle.
sedmi *num a* seventh.
sedmica *f* week.
sedmično *a* weekly.
sedmogodišnji *a* septennial.
sednica *f* session.
sef *m* safe, strongbox.
segment *m* segment.
sejati *v* to sow.
sekira *f* axe, hatchet.
sekretar/ica *f* secretary, personal assistant.
seksi *a* sexy.
sekstant *m* sextant.
sekta *f* sect.
sektaš *m* dissenter, sectarian.
sektor *m* sector.
sekunda *f* second.
sekundaran *a* secondary.
sekutić *m* incisor tooth.
seliti (se) *v* to migrate; to move.
selo *n* village.
seljačina *f* bumpkin.
seljak *m* peasant, countryman, rustic.
semafor *m* traffic light, signal; ~ **za rezultate** scoreboard.
seme *n* seed; ~ **lana** *n* linseed.
semestar *m* semester, half-year.
senat *m* senate.
senator *m* senator.
senatorski *a* senatorial.
sendvič *m* sandwich.
senica *f* titmouse (*zool*).
senica u vrtu *f* arbour.
senka *f* shade, shadow.
seno *n* hay.
senovit *a* shadowy, shady.
senovitost *f* shadiness.
sentimentalan *a* sentimental.
senzacija *f* sensation, bombshell.
senzibilan *a* sensitive.
senzualan *a* sensual, sensuous.
senzualnost *f* sensuality.
seoba *f* migration.

seoce *n* small village, hamlet.
seoski *a* countrified, pastoral, rural; ~**a devojka** *f* wench.
septembar *m* September.
serenada *f* serenade.
serum *m* serum.
servirati *v* to serve.
servis za čaj *m* tea service, tea set.
sestra *f* sister; nurse (*med*).
sestrinski *a* sisterly.
sestrinstvo *n* sisterhood.
seta *f* melancholy, pensiveness.
setiti se *v* to remember, to recall, to recollect.
setva *f* seed time.
sevanje *n* flashing.
sever *m* north.
Severna Amerika *f* North America.
severni *a* northerly, northern.
Severni pol *m* North Pole.
severoistok *m* northeast.
severozapad *m* northwest.
sezona *f* season.
sfera *f* sphere.
sholastički *a* scholastic.
shvatanje *n* comprehension, understanding, conception, opinion.
shvatiti *v* to realize, to comprehend, to understand.
sići *v* to descend, to come down, to alight.
sićušan *a* miniature, tiny.
SIDA *f* AIDS.
sidrište *n* anchorage.
sidro *n* anchor.
sifon *m* siphon.
signal *m* signal; ~ **za slučaj opasnosti** emergency cord, emergency light.
signalizirati *v* to signalize.
siguran *a* certain, sure, secure.
sigurnosni *a* safety; ~ **pojas** *m* safety belt, seat belt.
sigurnost *f* certainty, certitude, surety; safety (bezbednost).
sijalica *f* light bulb.
sijati *v* to radiate, to give light, to shine.
sila *f* force, strength, power.
silazak *m* descent, coming down.
siledžija *m* bully, oppressor, hooligan, thug.
silno *adv* mightily, vastly.
silogizam *m* syllogism.

silovatelj *m* rapist.
silovati *v* to rape.
simbol *m* symbol.
simboličan *a* symbolic(al).
simbolizovati *v* to symbolize.
simetričan *a* symmetrical.
simetrija *f* symmetry.
simfonija *f* symphony.
simpatičan *a* likeable, engaging.
simpatija *f* sympathy, kindness, liking.
simpozijum *m* symposium.
simptom *m* symptom.
simulirati *v* to feign, to simulate, to sham.
sin *m* son.
sinagoga *f* synagogue.
sindikat *m* syndicate, trade union.
sindrom *m* syndrome.
sinhronizam *m* synchronism.
sinoć *adv* last night.
sinonim *m* synonym.
sintaksa *f* syntax.
sinteza *f* synthesis.
sipa *f* cuttle-fish.
sipati *v* to pour, to pour out, to shed.
sipljiv *a* asthmatical.
sir *m* cheese.
sirće *n* vinegar.
sirena *f* siren, hooter; mermaid (morska).
siroče *n* orphan.
siromah *m* pauper.
siromašan *a* penniless, poor, impecunious.
siromaštvo *n* destitution, impoverishment, misery, poverty.
sirotinja *f* the poor.
sirotinjska četvrt *f* slum.
sirotište *n* orphanage.
sirov *a* raw, uncooked, unboiled.
sirovost *f* rawness.
sisa *f* breast, teat.
sisaljka *f* pump.
sisanče *n* suckling.
sisar *m* mammal.
sisati *v* to suck.
sistem *m* system; ~ **analizator** *m* systems analyst.
sistematičan *a* systematic; ~ **čovek** a systematic person.
sistematski *a* systematic, orderly; ~ **rad** *m* systematic work.
sit *a* sated, satiated, fed-up.

sitan *a* little, minute, tiny, inconsiderable, insignificant.
sitnica *f* pettiness, trifle.
sitničav *a* small-minded.
sitniš *m* petty cash, small change.
sito *n* sieve, colander.
situacija *f* situation, circumstance.
siv *a* grey.
sivkasto *a* greyish.
sjaj *m* brilliance, grandeur, radiance, resplendence, lustre.
sjajan *a* brilliant, luminous, magnificent, shining, splendid, glossy.
sjašiti *v* to dismount.
sjediniti *v* to merge.
Sjedinjene Države *fpl* United States (of America).
skakač *m* jumper, diver.
skakaonica *f* diving board.
skakati *v* to jump, to leap, to spring.
skakavac *m* grasshopper, locust.
skakutanje *n* skipping, hopping.
skala *f* scale.
skalp *m* scalp.
skamenjen *a* petrified.
skandal *m* scandal.
skandalozan *a* scandalous.
skapati *v* to waste away.
skeč *m* skit.
skela *f* scaffold; ferry (preko vode).
skelet *m* skeleton.
skener *m* scanner.
skepticizam *m* scepticism.
skeptičan *a* sceptic(al) (*br*) skeptical (*amer*).
skeptik *m* sceptic (*br*), skeptic (*amer*).
skica *f* sketch, drought, outline.
skidati *v* to take off.
skija *f* ski.
skijanje *n* skiing.
skijaš *m* skier.
skijaška cipela *f* ski boot.
skinuti *v* to take down, to take off.
skitnica *f* bum, tramp, prowler, vagabond.
sklad *m* harmony, accordance, unison.
skladište *n* storehouse, warehouse.
skladištenje *n* storage.
skladno *adv* harmoniously.
sklanjanje *n* removal, putting away; declension (*gram*).
sklon *a* inclined, disposed; ~ **razmišljanju** *a* meditative.

sklonište *n* retreat, haven, shelter.
skloniti *v* to remove.
sklonost *f* inclination, disposition, propensity, predilection.
sklopiti *v* to fold, to join; ~ **savez** to federate; ~ **ugovor** to contract.
sklopiv *a* folding, foldable.
skočiti *v* to leap, to jump, to spring.
skok *m* hop, jump, bound, spring.
skončati *v* to finish.
skor *a* imminent, impendent, impending.
skorašnji *a* recent, late.
skorbut *m* scurvy.
skoro *adv* recently, almost, nearly.
skorojević *m* upstart.
skot *m* beast.
skotna *a* (*f*) pregnant (of an animal).
skraćenje *n* abbreviation, abridgement, diminution.
skrama *f* scum, skin, film.
skratiti *v* to abbreviate, to abridge, to shorten, to curtail.
skrenuti *v* to swerve, to turn, to veer.
skretanje *n* deviation, turning; digression; ~ **s autoputa** turn-off.
skretničar *m* signalman, switchman.
skrhan *a* crushed.
skrivati se *v* to hide, to conceal, to keep out of sight, to skulk.
skriven *a* furtive, latent, hidden, secret, concealed.
skrnavljenje *n* desecration.
skrojen *a* cut out.
skroman *a* diffident, humble, modest, unassuming.
skromnost *f* humility, modesty.
skrovište *n* hiding place, shelter.
skrupula *f* scruple.
skrušen *a* contrite, broken.
skučen *a* narrow, limited, scant.
skulptura *f* sculpture.
skup *m* aggregation, assemblage, gathering, group.
skup *a* costly, expensive, dear.
skupa *adv* altogether, jointly.
skupiti *v* to assemble, to amass, to compile.
skupljanje *n* conglomeration, congregation, assembly.
skupljati *v* to collect, to assemble.
skupocen *a* precious, valuable, costly.
skupština *f* assembly.

skupštinski *a* parliamentary.
skuša *f* mackerel.
skut *m* lap, hem.
skuter *m* motor scooter.
skuvan *a* done.
skuvati *v* to boil.
slab *a* weak, feeble, light, small, flaccid.
slabić *m* weakling.
slabiti *v* to make weak, to wane, to languish.
slabo *adv* feebly, faintly.
slabost *f* faintness, feebleness, weakness, indisposition.
slabouman *a* imbecile.
slad *f* malt.
sladak *a* delectable, sweet; lovely; charming; flattering (reči); **~tka voda** *f* fresh water; **~tke reči** *fpl* sweet words.
sladoled *m* ice cream.
slagati *v* to pile, to heap up.
slagati *v* to speak untruth.
slagati se *v* to live in harmony; to agree.
slajd *m* slide, film strip.
slama *f* straw.
slan *a* saline.
slanik *m* salt cellar.
slanina *f* bacon.
slanje *n* sending, forwarding, despatch.
slast *f* zest.
slati *v* to send, to forward; to mail.
slatkiši *mpl* confection, sweetmeats.
slatkoća *f* sweetness, sugariness.
slava *f* fame, glory; reputation; feast; **porodična ~** feast of patron saint.
slavan *a* famed, famous, glorious, renowned.
slavina *f* tap, cock, faucet.
slaviti *v* to glorify, to celebrate.
slavljenje *n* glorification, celebration.
slavna ličnost *f* celebrity.
slavoljubiv *a* ambitious.
slavuj *m* nightingale.
sled *m* succession.
sledbenik *m* follower, disciple.
sledeći *a* next, following, subsequent.
slediti *v* to follow, to come after, to succeed; to freeze.
slegati *v* to shrug (ramenima).
sleng *m* slang.
slep *a* blind, sightless; **~ za boje** *a* colour-blind; **~a mrlja** *f* blind spot.

slepi miš *m* bat (*zool*).
slepić *m* slowworm (*zool*).
slepilo *n* blindness.
slepo *adv* blindly.
slepoočnica *f* temporal bone (*anat*).
slez *m* mallow (*bot*).
slezina *f* spleen (*anat*).
sličan *a* alike, like, similar; ~ **po značenju** *a* synonymous.
sličnost *f* similarity, likeness, resemblance.
slika *f* painting, picture, illustration; photograph, effigy.
slikanje *n* painting.
slikar *m* painter.
slikarski *a* pictorial; ~ **stalak** *m* easel.
slikati *v* to paint, to depict, to picture.
slikovit *a* figurative, picturesque.
slikovnica *f* picture book.
slina *f* snot.
slistiti *v* to lap up, to devour.
sliv *m* confluence (reka).
slivnik *m* gutter.
slizati *v* to become friendly.
sloboda *f* freedom, liberty.
slobodan *a* free, independent, natural, gratis (besplatan); ~**na volja** *f* free will; ~**ni zidar** *m* freemason; ~**no vreme** *n* time off.
slobodouman *a* broad-minded, tolerant.
slog *m* syllable; setting.
slogovni *a* syllabic.
sloj *m* stratum, layer, bed; ~ **boje** coating.
slom *m* crash, fall, breakdown; ~ **živaca** nervous breakdown.
slomiti *v* to break, to fracture.
slomljen *a* broken.
slon *m* elephant.
slonovača *f* ivory.
slonovski *a* elephantine.
slovo *n* letter, character.
složan *a* harmonious, concordant.
složen *a* complex, complicate.
složenost *f* complexity, complication.
slučaj *m* case, incident, happening, occasion, occurrence.
slučajan *a* accidental, casual, random, incidental; **sasvim ~ no** by pure chance.
slučajnost *f* chance, coincidence.
sluga *m* servant, attendant, butler, footman, lackey.

sluh *m* hearing.
slušalice *fpl* earphones.
slušati *v* to listen, to hear; to obey, to mind.
sluškinja *f* servant girl, maid.
slušni *a* auditory; ~ **aparat** *m* hearing aid.
slutiti *v* to suspect, to surmise, to bode.
sluz *f* mucus, phlegm.
sluzav *a* mucous, slimy.
sluzokoža *f* mucous membrane (*anat*).
služba *f* service, employment, occupation, vocation; office.
službeni put *m* business trip.
službenik *m* employee, official.
služiti *v* to serve; to serve up, to help; to act as, to be.
smanjenje *n* reduction, diminution, cutback.
smanjiti *v* to minimize, to reduce, to lessen.
smaragd *m* emerald.
smatrati *v* to consider, to think, to regard, to deem.
smeće *n* refuse, rubbish, thrash.
smeđ *a* brown.
smeh *m* laugh, laughter.
smekšati *v* to mollify, to soften.
smelo *adv* courageously, spiritedly.
smena *f* shift, relay.
smer *m* direction, course, route.
smeran *a* humble, submissive.
smerati *v* to trend, to intend, to purpose.
smesta *adv* immediately, instantly, at once.
smestiti *v* to place, to put, to set; to accommodate, to house.
smeša *f* mixture, admixture, alloy.
smešan *a* comic(al), funny, ludicrous, droll, ridiculous.
smešiti se *v* to smile, to smirk, to simper.
smeštaj *m* accommodation, housing, lodging.
smet *m* drift.
smetati *v* to disturb, to intrude, to impede, to interfere.
smeten *a* confused, embarrassed, nonplussed.
smeti *v* to dare, to venture.
smetnja *f* annoyance, disturbance, hindrance, impediment, drawback.
smežuran *a* crinkled, wrinkled.
smežurati se *v* to shrivel.
smicalica *f* trick, gimmick.

smiren *a* appeased, quiet.
smiriti *v* to appease, to calm, to pacify.
smiriti se *v* to calm down, to quieten down.
smirivanje *n* pacification.
smoking *m* dinner-jacket.
smokva *f* fig.
smola *f* resin.
smolast *a* resinous.
smožden *a* smashed.
smrad *m* stench, strink.
smrdljiv *a* fetid, foetid, smelly, foul.
smreka *f* juniper (*bot*).
smrkavati se *v* to get dark.
smrskati *v* to crush, to smash.
smrt *f* death, demise.
smrtan *a* mortal, deadly; **~na kazna** *f* capital punishment, death penalty; **~ni udarac** *m* deathblow; mortal blow; **~ni greh** a mortal sin.
smrtnost *f* mortality.
smrtonosan *a* deadly, lethal; **~no oružje** *n* letal weapons; **~na bolest** a fatal illness.
smrznut *a* frozen; **~a hrana** frozen food.
smrznuti se *v* to freeze.
smučar *m* skier.
smutiti *v* to perplex, to confound.
snabdeti *v* to furnish, to find, to provide, to supply, to cater (hranom).
snabdevač *m* supplier, provider.
snabdevanje *n* supply, provision.
snaga *f* power, strength, force, vigour, energy; **~ volje** willpower.
snaha, snaja *f* sister-in-law.
snajper *m* sniper.
snažan *a* powerful, robust, vigorous, able-bodied.
snažno *adv* sturdily.
snebivanje *n* diffidence, embarrassment.
snebivljiv *a* sheepish, embarrassed.
sneg *m* snow; **grudva ~a** snowball.
snek-bar *m* snack bar.
Sneško Belić *m* snowman.
snežni *a* snowy; **~ smet** snowdrift; **~ prekrivač** snow blanket; **~a pahuljica** snowflake.
snimak *m* photograph, photo; scan; survey; **~ ultrazvukom** ultrasound scan.
snishodljiv *a* condescending, lenient.
snishodljivo *adv* condescendingly, indulgently.

snob *m* snob.
snobovski *a* snobbish.
snop *m* sheaf.
snositi *v* to suffer, to bear; to defray (trošak); to take the consequences (posledice).
snošljiv *a* bearable.
snoviđenje *n* dream, vision.
snužden *a* broken-spirited, dejected, in low spirit.
so *f* salt.
soba *f* room, apartment, chamber.
sobar *m* valet.
sobarica *f* chambermaid.
socijalista *m* socialist.
socijalizam *m* socialism.
socijalni *a* social; **~ rad** *m* social work.
sociologija *f* sociology.
sočan *a* juicy, succulent.
sočivo *n* lentil; lens.
soda *f* soda; **~ bikarbona** *f* bicarbonate of soda.
sofa *f* sofa.
sofistički *a* sophistical.
sofistika *f* sophistry.
sofizam *m* sophism.
softver *m* software.
soj *m* kind, sort.
soja *f* soya bean.
sok *m* juice.
sokak *m* lane.
soko *m* falcon, hawk.
solana *f* saltworks.
solidan *a* solid, reliable; portly.
solidarnost *f* joint responsibility.
solventnost *f* solvency.
som *m* sheat-fish.
somot *m* corduroy, velvet.
sonata *f* sonata.
sonda *f* probe.
sonet *m* sonnet.
sopstven *a* own, proper.
sopstvenik *m* proprietor.
sorta *f* sort, type, brand.
sos *m* sauce; gravy.
sotona *f* fiend, devil, satan.
sova *f* owl.
spadati *v* to fall down, to belong.
spajalica *f* paperclip, staple.
spajanje *n* adhesion, cohesion, amalgamation.

spajati *v* to join, to connect.
spakovati *v* to pack, to encase.
spaliti *v* to burn up.
spaljivanje *n* cremation.
spanać *m* spinach.
sparan *a* sultry, stuffy.
spariti se *v* to copulate; to match with.
spasavanje *n* rescue, salvage.
spasenje *n* deliverance, salvation.
Spasitelj *m* Saviour.
spasiti *v* to save, to rescue.
spavač *m* sleeper.
spavaća soba *f* bedroom.
spavaonica *f* dormitory.
spavati *v* to sleep, to lie asleep; to be inactive.
specifikacija *f* specification.
specifizirati *v* to itemize, to specify.
specijalnost *f* speciality.
sperma *f* sperm.
spiker *m* announcer, newscaster (na radiju ili TV).
spiralan *a* spiral.
spiritualist *m* spiritualist.
spiritualnost *f* spirituality.
spis *m* writing, script, writ.
spisak *m* list, schedule.
splačine *fpl* swill, dishwater.
splav *m* raft.
splavarenje *n* rafting.
spletka *f* intrigue, maneouvre.
spletkaroš *m* schemer.
spljeskati *v* to flatten, to smash.
spljošten *a* flattened.
spoj *m* junction, joint.
spojiti *v* to couple, to connect, to join.
spokoj *m* peace, calm, repose.
spokojan *a* calm, placid, tranquil.
spokojno *adv* calmly.
spokojstvo *n* peace, quiet.
spolja *adv* out, outdoors, from outside.
spoljašnji *a* exterior, outer, outward.
spomenica *f* memorial.
spomenik *m* monument.
spominjati *v* to mention, to allude.
spona *f* conjunction.
spontan *a* spontaneous.
spontanost *f* spontaneity.
spor *m* dispute, contention; litigation.
sporadičan *a* sporadic(al).
sporan *a* contentious, controversial, debatable.

sporazum *m* agreement, arrangement, settlement, convention.
sporazumno *adv* by common consent.
sporedan *a* extrinsic(al), secondary, minor; ~ **put** *m* by-road; ~ **izlaz** rear exit; ~**na zgrada** *f* outhouse.
sporno *adv* arguably.
sporo *adv* slowly, tardily.
sporost *f* slowness.
sport *m* sport.
sportista *m* sportsman.
sportistkinja *f* sportswoman.
sportski *a* sporting, sport; ~**a odeća** *f* sportswear.
sposoban *a* able, capable, efficient, apt; clever, expert.
sposobnost *f* ability, capability, capacity, competence, faculty.
spoticanje *n* stumbling.
spoticati se *v* to falter, to trip.
sprat *m* storey, floor.
sprati *v* to wash off, to wash away, to scour.
sprava *f* apparatus, contrivance, gadget, device; tool (alat).
sprečavanje *f* prevention, obstruction.
sprečavati *v* to detain, to hinder, to prevent.
spreda *prep* in front of.
sprej *m* spray.
sprema *f* qualification, grounding; larder (ostava); dowry (devojačka).
spremačica *f* charwoman.
spreman *a* ready, prepared.
spremati *v* to prepare, to make ready.
spremnost *f* readiness.
spretan *a* adroit, deft, dexterous, handy.
spretnost *f* dexterity, skilfulness.
sprijateljiti se *v* to befriend, to make friends with.
sprovesti *v* to conduct, to escort, to attend; to realise.
spuštati se *v* to descend, to decline, to lower, to land (avion).
sračunati *v* to sum up, to reckon.
sraman *a* shameful, infamous, ignominious.
sramežljiv *a* shamefaced
sramota *f* dishonour, infamy, shame, ignominy.
sranje *n* shit.

srastao *a* grown together.
sraščivanje *n* interfusion.
sravniti *v* to level, to flatten.
srazmera *f* proportion.
srazmeran *a* proportionate.
srce *n* heart; spirit, courage (*fig*).
srčani *a* cardiac, heart; ~ **udar** *m* heart attack, heart failure.
srčanost *f* heartiness, bravery.
srdačan *a* cordial, genial, hearty, warm-hearted.
srdačno *adv* warmly, wholeheartedly.
srdit *a* angry, exasperated, irritated.
srdobolja *f* dysentery, diarrhoea (*med*).
srdžba *f* anger, wrath, rage.
srebrnast *a* silvery.
srebro *n* silver.
sreća *f* happiness, luck; fortune.
srećan *a* happy, lucky, joyful, fortunate; ~ **Božić** Merry Christmas; **~na Nova godina** Happy New Year.
srećno *adv* fortunately, luckily, happily.
srećom *adv* luckily.
sreda *f* Wednesday.
sredina *f* midst, middle, mid; **životna ~** environment; **zlatna ~** the golden mean.
srediti *v* to arrange, to settle.
srednje *adv* passable, tolerable.
srednjevekovni *a* medieval.
srednji *a* middle, intermediate; **~a kategorija** *f* middleweight (boks).
sredozeman *a* mediterranean.
sredstvo *n* means, method, way; funds, resources; ~ **za smirenje** tranquillizer; ~ **za jačanje** tonic; ~ **za uništavanje korova** weedkiller.
sresti (se) *v* to meet, to come across.
srna *f* roe, doe.
srndać *m* roebuck.
srnetina *f* venison.
srodan *a* related, akin, kindred, congenial; **~ni jezici** related languages; **~na duša** fellow-soul.
srodnici po bračnom drugu *mpl* in-laws.
srp *m* sickle.
srž *f* core, crux.
stabilnost *f* stability, firmness.
stablo *n* trunk.
stabljika *f* stalk, stem.
stado *n* drove, herd.
stagnacija *f* stagnation.

stagnirati *v* to stagnate.
staja, štala *f* stable.
stajaći *a* standing, stagnant.
stajanje *n* standing.
stajati *v* to stand.
staklar *m* glazier.
staklarija *f* glassware.
staklast *a* glassy.
staklenik *m* greenhouse, hothouse.
staklo *n* glass.
stalak *m* stand; ~ **za sušenje veša** clotheshorse.
stalan *a* constant, continual, permanent.
stalno *adv* continually, unceasingly.
staložen *a* level-headed, staid, sedate.
staloženost *f* sedateness.
stambena zgrada *f* apartment house.
stan *m* rooms, apartment, flat, condominium, housing; ~ **na dva sprata** *m* duplex; **u ~u** indoor.
stanar *m* inhabitant, lodger, occupant, tenant.
stanarina *f* rent.
standard *m* standard.
standardni engleski standard English.
staniol *m* tinfoil.
stanovati *v* to reside, to dwell, to inhabit.
stanovište *n* attitude, standpoint.
stanovnik *m* inhabitant, resident.
stanovništvo *n* population.
stanje *n* state, condition, circumstance, situation; ~ **bankovnog računa** bank statement.
star *a* old, aged, decripit; antique, ancient (starinski); worn-out (iznošen); used (korišćen); **~i broj časopisa** *m* back issue; **~i drug** crony.
starac *m* oldman, elder.
starački *a* senile.
staranje *n* attention, care.
staratelj *m* guardian, trustee.
starateljstvo *n* custody, guardianship.
starešinstvo *n* seniority, rank.
staromodan *a* old-fashioned, outdated, unfashionable.
starosedeoci *mpl* aborigines.
starost *f* old age, advanced age.
starudija *f* junk, bric-a-brac.
stas *m* stature.
stasit *a* tall, shapely.
statistički *a* statistical.

statistika *f* statistics.
stativa *f* goalpost.
statua *f* statue.
statut *m* statute.
stav *m* attitude, carriage, demeanour.
staviti *v* to put, to place, to set; ~ **na pogrešno mesto** to misplace; ~ **van snage** to abolish; ~ **znakove interpunkcije** to punctuate.
stavka *f* item, post.
staza *f* path, pathway, footway.
staž *m* training, period, experience.
stažista *m* intern.
steći *v* to acquire, to buy, to purchase, to gain.
steg *m* standard, banner.
stegnut *a* clenched.
stegnuti *v* to clasp, to clutch, to grasp, to clench, to compress, to tighten.
stena *f* rock, cliff.
stenica *f* bug, bedbug (*zool*).
stenograf *m* shorthand typist.
stenografija *f* shorthand.
stenjanje *n* moaning, groaning.
stepen *m* degree, grade, level; **u najvišem ~u** eminently.
stepenik *m* stair, step.
stepenište *n* staircase.
stepenovanje *n* gradation.
stereotip *m* stereotype.
sterilan *a* sterile.
sterilnost *f* sterility.
stetoskop *m* stethoscope.
stezanje *n* contraction; grasp, pressure.
stezati *v* to grasp, to constrict, to press.
steznik *m* corset.
stid *m* shame.
stidljiv *a* bashful, shy, timid, coy.
stidljivost *f* shyness, timidity.
stih *m* verse, line.
stihijski *a* spontaneous, uncontrolled, unchecked.
stil *m* style, method, manner.
stimulacija *f* stimulation.
stimulans *m* stimulus.
stimulativno sredstvo *n* stimulant.
stimulisati *v* to stimulate.
stipendija *f* scholarship.
stipendist *m* scholar.
stipsa *f* alum.
stisak *m* squeeze, pressure.
stiskati *v* to press, to squeeze, to wring.

stisnuti *v* to clinch.
stišati *v* to calm, to compose, to appease.
stjuard *m* flight attendant.
stjuardesa *f* stewardess.
sto[1] *num* hundred.
sto[2] *m* table; ~ **za bilijar** billiard-table; ~ **za kartanje** card table.
stočna hrana *f* fodder, forage.
stog *m* stack, haystack.
stoga *adv* therefore.
stogodišnjak *m* centenarian.
stogodišnjica *f* centenary.
stoički *a* stoical.
stojeća lampa *f* floor lamp.
stoka *f* cattle, livestock.
stolar *m* cabinet-maker; carpenter, joiner.
stolarska radnja *f* joinery.
stolarstvo *n* carpentry.
stolica *f* chair; ~ **na rasklapanje** folding chair; ~ **za ljuljanje** rocking chair.
stolnjak *m* tablecloth.
stomačić *m* tummy.
stoni pribor *m* cutlery.
stoni tenis *m* table tennis.
stono izdavaštvo *n* desktop publishing.
stonoga *f* centipede (*zool*).
stopa *f* rate, footprint, trace.
stopalo *n* foot.
stopiranje *n* hitchiking.
stopirati *v* to hitchike.
stoti *num a* hundredth.
stovarište *n* depot, store, stock.
stradanje *n* suffering, calamity.
stradati *v* to suffer, to be in calamity.
strah *m* dread, fright, fear, alarm; ~ **od vode** *m* hydrophobia.
strahopoštovanje *n* awe, respect.
strahota *f* horror, abomination.
strahovati *v* to be afraid of, to apprehend.
stran *a* foreign, strange, alien.
strana *f* side; page (knjiga).
stranac *m* foreigner, stranger, alien.
stranka *f* party, fraction.
strast *f* passion, ardour, desire.
strastan *a* passionate, lustful.
strašilo *n* bugbear; ~ **za ptice** *n* scarecrow
strašljiv *a* fearful, fainthearted.
strašno *adv* horribly, terribly.
strategija *f* strategy.

strateški *a* strategic.
stravičan *a* dreadful, horrible.
stražar *m* sentinel, sentry; watchman.
stražara *f* sentry box, guardroom.
stražarnica *f* watchtower.
stražnja *a* back, hinder; ~ **vrata** *f* backdoor, tailgate; ~**i čerek** *m* hindquarter.
stražnjica *f* bottom, the posterior, rump.
streha *f* eaves.
strela *f* arrow; dart.
strelac *m* archer, marksman, rifleman.
Strelac *m* Sagittarius (*astrol*).
streljaštvo *n* archery.
stremiti *v* to hurry, to rush, to aspire.
strepeti *v* to be anxious, to have apprehensions.
strepnja *f* apprehension, concern, misdoubt.
stric *m* uncle.
striktan *a* strict.
striktnost *f* strictness.
strm *a* abrupt, steep, uphill.
strmina *f* steep, slope.
strmoglavit *a* precipitate.
strmo *adv* abruptly.
strmost *m* steepness.
strnište *n* stubble.
strofa *f* strophe, stanza.
strog *a* austere, rigorous, severe, stringent; ~**o poverljiv** top-secret.
strogost *f* austerity, harshness, rigour, severity.
stroj *m* engine, machine.
strpeti se *v* to have patience.
strpljenje *n* patience.
strpljiv *a* patient.
stršljen *n* hornet.
stručan *a* technical, professional.
stručnost *f* technicality, expertise.
stručnjak *m* expert, connoisseur.
strugač *m* scraper.
strugara *f* saw mill.
strugotina *f* sawdust, *pl* scrapings.
struja *f* stream, course, flow, current.
strujanje *n* circulation, drift.
struk *m* waist, waistline.
struka *f* branch of business, line; profession.
strvina *f* carrion.
strvinar *m* scavenger.
stub *m* pillar, post.

studen *f* cold, coldness.
student *m* student.
studentski *a* student's; ~ **grad** dormitory area, campus.
studio *m* studio.
stupiti *v* to enter, to go in, to come into, to accede.
stupnjevit *a* gradual.
stvar *f* thing, object, article.
stvaralac *m* creator, maker.
stvaralački *a* creative.
stvaran *a* actual, veritable, real.
stvarati *v* to create.
stvarnost *f* reality.
stvor *m* creature, being.
stvoriti *v* to create, to make.
stvrdnuti se *v* to grow hard, to harden.
subota *f* Saturday, Sabbath.
subvencija *f* subsidy.
subvencionisati *v* to subsidize.
subverzija *f* subversion.
subverzivan *a* subversive.
sud *m* court; opinion, view, judgement; vessel, basin.
sudar *m* collision, shock, clash.
sudariti se *v* to clash, to collide.
sudbina *f* destiny, doom, fate.
sudelovati *v* to participate, to take part.
sudija *f* judge, justice.
suditi *v* to try, put on trial; to judge.
sudnica *f* courthouse, courtroom.
sudski *a* judicial, juridicial; ~ **izvršitelj** *m* bailiff; ~ **nalog** writ; ~ **poziv** subpoena, summons.
suđenje *n* lawsuit, trial, legal proceeding.
sufler *m* prompter.
sugestija *f* suggestion.
sugrađanin *m* fellow citizen.
sujeta *f* vanity, self-conceit.
sujeveran *a* surreptitious.
suknja *f* skirt.
sukob *m* conflict.
sukrivac *m* accomplice, abbetor.
sultan *m* sultan.
sultanija *f* sultana.
suma *f* sum.
sumaglica *f* fog, mist.
sumanut *a* lunatic, mad, crazy.
sumirati *v* to recapitulate, to summarize.
sumnja *f* doubt, suspicion, distrust, inkling.

sumnjičav *a* incredulous, mistrustful, doubtful.
sumnjičavost *f* incredulity.
sumnjičiti *v* to impute, to insinuate.
sumnjiv *a* doubtful, questionable, problematical.
sumoran *a* murky, sullen.
sumpor *m* sulphur.
sumporni *a* sulphurous.
sumrak *m* nightfall, twilight, dusk.
sunarodnik *m* compatriot.
sunce *n* sun.
suncobran *m* parasol, sunshade.
suncokret *m* sunflower.
sunčani *a* sunny; solar; ~ **sat** *m* sundial; ~ **zrak** sunbeam; **~e pege** *fpl* the sunspots; **~a svetlost** *f* sunlight, sunshine.
sunčanica *f* sunstroke.
sunčati se *v* to sunbathe.
sunđer *m* sponge.
sunđerast *a* spongy.
suočenje *n* confrontation.
suočiti se *v* to meet face to face.
supa *f* soup.
suparnik *m* antagonist, rival.
suparništvo *n* rivalry.
superlativ *m* superlative.
supersila *f* superpower.
suprotan *a* contrary, adverse, opposite.
suprotno *adv* contrary; ~ **od smera kazaljke na satu** anticlockwise.
suprotnost *f* contrast, reverse.
suprotstaviti se *v* to oppose, to counteract.
suprug *m* husband, spouse.
supruga *f* wife.
supstrat *m* substratum.
suptilan *a* subtle.
suptilnost *f* subtlety.
surla *f* trunk.
surogat *m* surrogate; ~ **majka** *f* surrogate mother.
surov *a* harsh, rude, cruel, inclement.
sused *m* neighbour.
susedni *a* adjacent, next; neighbouring.
susedstvo *n* neighbourhood, vicinity.
susnežica *f* sleet.
suspenzija *f* suspension.
susret *m* encounter, meeting.
sustalost *f* fatigue, exhaustion.
sustići *v* to reach, to overtake.

suša *f* drought.
sušenje *n* drying up.
sušiti *v* to dry; to smoke, to cure.
suština *f* essence.
suteren *m* basement.
suton *m* dusk.
sutra *adv* tomorrow.
suv *a* dry, dried; **~o grožđe** *n* raisin; **~e šljive** prunes; **~o zlato** pure gold.
suvenir *m* souvenir.
suverenitet *f* sovereignty.
suvišan *a* redundant, superfluous.
suviše *adv* too much.
suvišnost *f* superfluity, surplus.
suvoća *f* dryness.
suza *f* tear, drop.
suzavac *m* tear gas.
suzbijanje *n* repression.
suzbiti *v* to keep off, to ward off; to repel.
svadba *f* marriage, wedding.
svadbeni *a* wedding, bridal; ~ **poklon** *m* wedding present.
svadljiv *a* quarrelsome.
svađa *f* quarrel, dispute, feud, row, affray.
svađati se *v* to quarrel, to fall out, to wrangle.
svakakav *a* various, all kinds of.
svakako *adv* sure, at all events.
svaki *a* every, each, either; **~e noći** *adv* nightly; **~og časa** hourly.
svako *pn* everyone, everybody.
svakodnevni *a* daily, every day; **~a pojava** *f* regular occurrence.
svanuće *n* daybreak.
svastika *f* sister-in-law.
svašta *pn* all sorts of things.
svaštara *f* variety store (*amer*).
sve *a* all, everything, whole, total.
svečan *a* festive, solemn, stately.
svečanost *f* festival, festivity, gala.
sveća *f* candle.
svećica *f* spark plug (u automobilu).
svećnjak *m* candlestick.
svedočanstvo *n* certificate, testimony, report.
svedočiti *v* to testify, to attest.
svedok *m* witness.
svejedno *adv* nevertheless, all the same.
svekar *m* father-in-law.
svemir *m* universe.
svemoć *f* omnipotence.

svemoćan *a* almighty, omnipotent.
svenarodni *a* nationwide.
sveprisutan *a* ubiquitous.
sveska *f* notebook, exercise-book; volume.
svesno *adv* consciously, wittingly.
svesnost *f* awareness.
svest *f* consciousness.
svestan *a* aware, conscious.
svestran *a* all-round, universal.
sveštenica *f* priestess.
sveštenički *a* clerical, priestly.
sveštenik *m* clergyman, priest.
sveštenstvo *n* clergy, priesthood.
svet¹ *a* holy, sacred.
svet² *m* world.
Sveta trojica *f* Trinity.
sveta vodica *f* holy water.
svetac *m* saint.
svetao *a* bright, luminous, light; pale.
svetilište *n* sanctuary, shrine.
svetiljka *f* lamp.
svetionik *m* lighthouse, beacon.
svetiti se *v* to avenge, to take revenge.
svetkovina *f* fete.
svetleti *v* to glow, to shine, to emit light.
svetlo *n* light, radiance; ~ za maglu *n* fog
   light.
svetlomer *m* exposure meter.
svetlosna godina *f* light year.
svetlost *f* light; ~ sveće *f* candlelight; ~i
   pozornice *fpl* footlights.
svetlucanje *n* glimmering.
svetlucati *v* to flicker, to twinkle.
Sveto pismo *n* Scripture.
svetogrđe *n* sacrilege.
svetost *f* holiness, sacredness, sanctity.
svetovni *a* secular, lay.
svetovnost *f* worldliness.
svetski *a* world; mundane.
sveukupan *a* entire, total.

sveznalica *f* know-it-all.
svež *a* cool, fresh, bracing; ~e obojeno!
   wet paint!
svežanj *m* bundle.
svežina *f* freshness.
svila *f* silk.
svilen *a* silken, silky; ~a buba *f* silkworm.
svinja *f* pig, swine, hog, sow; divlja ~
   wild boar.
svinjac *m* pigsty.
svinjetina *f* pork.
svinjska mast *f* lard.
svirač *m* player, piper.
svirepost *f* cruelty.
svisnuti *v* to die.
svita *f* suite.
svitac *m* firefly (*zool*).
svitak *m* roll, ball, scroll; ~ pergamenta
   scroll.
svitanje *n* daybreak.
svlačenje *n* undressing, taking off.
svlačionica *f* cloakroom, dressing room.
svod *m* arch, vault; ~ stopala instep .
svodnik *m* pimp.
svojeglav *a* obstinate.
svojeglavost *f* obstinacy.
svojevoljan *a* voluntary.
svojina *f* property, possession, ownership,
   belongings.
svojstvo *n* feature, mark, trait, property.
svojta *f* kin, relationship.
svraka *f* magpie.
svrbeti *v* to itch.
svrgnuti *v* to depose, to dethrone.
svrha *f* purpose, aim.
svrstati *v* to classify.
svršavati *v* to end, to finish.
svući *v* to disrobe, to undress.
svući se *v* to divest.
svuda *adv* everywhere, throughout.

Š

šablon *m* template.
šafran *m* saffron.
šah *m* chess.
šah-mat *m* checkmate.
šahovski *a* chess; **~a figura** *f* chessman; **~a tabla** chessboard.
šaka *f* hand, palm; **koren ~e** wrist.
šakal *m* jackal.
šal *m* scarf, shawl.
šala *f* joke, jest.
šalone *fpl* shutters; blinds.
šalupa *f* sloop.
šaljiv *a* humorous, teasing, facetious.
šaljivdžija *m* jester, joker.
šaljivost *f* jocularity.
šamar *m* slap.
šampanjac *m* champagne.
šampion *m* champion.
šampionat *f* championship.
šampon *m* shampoo.
šansa *f* chance, opportunity, hazard.
šapa *f* paw.
šaputanje *n* whispering.
šaputati *v* to whisper.
šarada *f* charade.
šaren *a* motley, mottled.
šargarepa *f* carrot.
šarka *f* hinge.
šarlah *m* scarlet fever.
šarlatan *m* charlatan.
šarm *m* charm.
šarmantan *a* charming.
šator *m* tent.
šav *m* seam; suture.
šeboj *m* wallflower.
šećer *m* sugar; **~ u kockama** cube sugar; **~ u prahu** confectioner's sugar.
šećerlema *f* candyfloss.
šećerna bolest *f* diabetes.
šećerni *a* sugar, sugary; **~a repa** *f* sugar beet; **~a trska** sugar cane; **~ sirup** *m* molasses.
šegrtovanje *n* apprenticeship.
šema *f* scheme.
šepati *v* to hobble.
šepurenje *n* strutting.
šepuriti se *v* to swagger.

šeri *m* sherry.
šerif *m* sheriff.
šesnaest *num* sixteen.
šesnaesti *num a* sixteenth.
šest *num* six.
šestar *m* dividers.
šesti *num a* sixth.
šešir *m* hat.
šeširdžija *m* hatter.
šetač *m* walker.
šetalište *n* promenade, park.
šetanje *n* walking.
šetnja *f* promenade, stroll, walk.
ševa *f* lark (*zool*).
šezdeset *m* sixty.
šezdeseti *num a* sixtieth.
šiba *f* verge, switch.
šibanje *n* flogging.
šibati *v* to whip, to flog.
šibica *f* match, safety match.
šifra *f* cipher, code.
šikljati, šiknuti *v* to gush, to pour, to spout.
šilo *n* awl.
šiljak *m* peak, spike, prong.
šiljat *a* pointed.
šimpanza *f* chimpanzee.
šina *f* rail, track.
šindra *f* shingle.
šipak *m* pomegranate.
šipka *f* bar, ingot.
šiprag *m* underwood.
širenje *n* diffusion, emission, spreading.
širina *f* breadth, broadness, width.
širiti *v* to diffuse, to spread, to expand.
širok *a* broad, extensive, wide; **~e ruke** lavish.
široko *adv* broadly.
širokogrud *a* broad-minded.
širom *adv* wide; **~ otvoren** wide open.
šišanje *n* haircut.
šiške *fpl* bangs.
šiti *v* to sew.
šivaća mašina *f* sewing machine.
šivenje *n* needlework.
škembići *mpl* tripe.
škljocnuti *v* to click.

škodljiv *a* harmful, pernicious, injurious.
škoditi *v* to harm.
škola *f* school; **osnovna** ~ elementary school; **srednja** ~ secondary school; ~ **jahanja** riding school.
školice *fpl* hopscotch.
školovanje *n* schooling.
školski *a* school; ~ **raspust** *m* school vacation; ~ **drug** classmate; ~**a tabla** *f* blackboard; ~**a klupa** bench, desk.
školjka *f* clam, shell.
Škorpija *f* Scorpio (*astrol*).
škorpija *f* scorpion.
škotski viski *m* Scotch.
škrabanje *n* scribble.
škrabati *v* to doodle.
škrabotina *f* scrawl.
škrgutati zubima *v* to gnash.
škriljac *m* slate.
škripa *f* squeak.
škripac *m* scrape, difficulty, trouble.
škripav *a* creaky.
škripeti *v* to creak.
škrt *a* stingy.
škrto *adv* stingily.
škrtost *f* stinginess, cheese-paring.
škuna *f* schooner.
šlag *m* whipped cream.
šlem *m* helmet.
šljiva *f* plum; plum-tree.
šljokice *fpl* tinsels.
šljuka *f* snipe (ptica).
šljunak *m* gravel, pebbles.
šminka *f* make-up.
šmirgla *f* emery.
šmizla *f* vain, fashionable woman.
šmrkati *v* to snuffle.
šnicla *f* cutlet, shop; **bečka** ~ breaded veal cutlet.
šofer *m* chauffeur.
šolja *f* cup; ~ **za čaj** *f* teacup.
šovinista *m* chauvinist.
špageti *mpl* spaghetti.
španski *a* Hispanic.
špargla *f* asparagus.
špedicija *f* freight forwarding.
špediter *m* shipping agent.
šperploča *f* plywood.
špic *m* end, pointed part; ~ **u saobraćaju** rush hour, peak period.
špijun *m* spy.

špijunaža *f* espionage.
špiritusna lampa *f* spirit lamp.
špric *m* syringe.
šta *pn* what.
štab *m* headquarters.
štaka *f* crutch.
štampane stvari *fpl* printed matter.
štampar *m* printer.
štamparski slog *m* typeface.
štamparstvo *n* printing.
štap *m* stick, rod, bat; ~ **za pecanje** fishing rod; ~ **za šetnju** walking stick.
štapići za jelo *mpl* chopsticks.
štaviše *adv* furthermore, moreover.
štedeti *v* to economize.
štedionica *f* savings bank.
štediša *m* saver.
štedljiv *a* saving, sparing, thrifty.
štednjak *m* cooker; ~ **na gas** gas range.
štenara *f* dog kennel.
štene *n* pup, puppy.
šteta *f* damage, harm, detriment.
štetan *a* harmful, baleful, detrimental; hurtful.
štetočine *fpl* vermin.
štićenik *m* protégé.
štikla *f* heel.
štimer *m* tuner.
štimung *m* atmosphere, mood.
štipaljka za veš *f* clothes peg.
štipati *v* to pinch.
štipavica *f* gorse (*zool*).
štirak *m* starch.
štit *m* shield.
štititi *v* to defend.
štitna žlezda *f* thyroid.
štof *m* cloth.
štogod *pn* whatever, anything.
štoperica *f* stopwatch.
štrajk *m* strike, walkout; ~ **glađu** hunger strike.
štrajkač *m* striker.
štrajkbreher *m* blackleg, scab.
štrcaljka *f* squirt.
štrikati *v* to knit.
štucanje *n* hiccup.
štuka *f* pike.
štule *fpl* stilts.
šugav *a* mangy.
šuljevi *mpl* haemorrhoids.
šum *m* noise, murmur.

šuma *f* forest, wood.
šumar *f* forester, ranger.
šumarstvo *n* forestry.
šumovit *a* wooded; **~ kraj** *m* woodland.
šunka *f* ham, gammon.
šunjati se *v* to sneak, to slink.
šupalj *a* hollow.

šupljina *f* cavity.
šuškati *v* to lisp (u govoru).
šuštanje *n* rustling.
švalja *f* seamstress.
šverc *m* smuggling, black-marketing.
švrljanje *n* strolling about.

T

ta *pn* this, that.
tabak *m* sheet of paper.
tabakera *f* cigarette case.
taban *m* sole (foot).
tabela *f* table.
tabla *f* board; ~ **za igru dame** *f* chequerboard, draughtboard.
tableta *f* pill; ~ **za spavanje** *f* sleeping pill.
tabu *m* taboo.
tacna *f* saucer.
tačan *a* accurate, exact, punctual, precise.
tačka *f* dot, point; full-stop, period; ~ **ključanja** boiling point; ~ **i zapeta** *f* semicolon; ~ **smrzavanja** freezing point.
tačkast *a* dotted.
tačno *adv* exactly, precisely, punctually, right.
tačnost *f* accuracy, precision, exactitude.
tadašnji *a* of that time, of that day; then.
taft *f* taffeta.
tahometar *m* tachometer.
taj *pn* this, that; ~ **isti** selfsame.
tajan *a* clandestine, secret, underhand.
tajanstven *a* mysterious, secretive.
tajna *f* secret.
tajni *a* secret, undercover; ~ **izlaz** *m* a secret exit; **~o glasanje** *n* secret ballot; ~ **agent** *m* a secret agent; **~o se dogovoriti** *v* to conspire.
tajnost *m* secrecy.
takav *pn* such, similar; ~ **i** ~ such and such a one.
takmičar *m* contestant.
takmičenje *n* competition, contest.
takmičiti se *v* to compete, to contend.
tako *adv* so, in such a manner, in this way; thus.
takođe *adv* also, likewise.
takozvani *a* so-called.
taksa *f* duty, tax, toll.
taksi *m* cab, taxi.
taksi stanica *f* taxi rank.
taksista *m* taxi driver.
takt *m* tact.
taktika *f* tactics.

talac *m* hostage.
talas *m* wave, surge; **kratki** ~ shortwaves; ~ **vrućine** heat weave.
talasanje *n* undulation, waving.
talasast *a* wavy.
talasna dužina *f* wavelength.
talenat *m* talent, gift.
talentovan *a* talented, gifted.
talk *m* talc.
talog *m* sediment.
tama *f* darkness, dark, obscurity.
taman[1] *a* dark, dusky, obscure.
taman[2] *adv* exactly, just.
tamaniti *v* to exterminate, to destroy.
tamjan *m* incense.
tamneti *v* to become dark.
tamnica *f* prison, jail, gaol; ~ **pod zemljom** *f* dungeon.
tamničar *m* jailer.
tamnocrven *a* crimson.
tamo *adv* there, yonder; ~ **negde** *adv* thereabout(s).
tampon *m* tampon, swab.
tanak *a* thin, flimsy; slender, tenuous; ~ **papir** *m* tissue paper.
tanano *adv* subtly.
tangenta *f* tangent (*math*).
tanker *m* oil tanker.
tanjir *m* plate.
tanjirić *m* saucer.
tapaciranje *n* upholstery.
tapija *f* title-deed.
tapiserija *f* tapestry.
tapšanje *v* to tap, to clap, to applaud.
taraba *f* fence.
tarifa *f* tariff; price-list.
tartan *m* tartan.
tartuf *m* truffle.
tast *m* father-in-law.
tastatura *f* keyboard.
tašna *f* hand-bag; portfolio, case.
tašta *f* mother-in-law.
taština *f* vanity.
tata *m* dad(dy), pa.
tautologija *f* tautology.
tautološki *a* tautological.
tavan *m* attic, loft, garret.

tavanica *f* ceiling.
tavanski prozor *m* dormer window.
tavoriti *v* to live miserably, to live from hand to mouth.
taze *a* fresh; recent.
teča *m* uncle.
tečan *a* liquid; fluent (govor).
tečnost *f* liquid, liquid substance, fluid; fluency (govor).
teći *v* to flow, to pour, to run.
teg *m* weight.
tegla *f* jar.
tegliti *v* to draw, to haul, to tow.
tegoban *a* troublesome, hard to bear, onerous.
tegovi *mpl* dumbbell.
tehničar *m* technician.
tehnika *f* technique.
tehnologija *f* technology.
tehnološki *a* technological.
tekst *m* text.
tekstil *m* textile material.
tekstilna fabrika *f* cotton mill.
tekstualan *a* textual.
tekući *a* flowing, fluent, running; current, ongoing; ~a voda running water; ~ godina the current year; ~ račun the current account.
tele *n* calf.
telebank *m* telephone banking.
telefon *m* phone, telephone.
telefonski *a* telephonic; ~a govornica *f* phone box, (tele)phone booth; ~a sekretarica answering machine; ~ broj *m* (tele)phone number; ~ imenik phone book, (tele)phone directory; ~ poziv (tele)phone call.
telegraf *m* telegraph.
telegrafija *f* telegraphy.
telegrafski *a* telegraphic.
telegram *m* telegram, cable, wire.
teleks *m* telex.
telepatija *f* telepathy.
teleskop *m* telescope.
teleskopski *a* telescopic.
telesna građa *f* physique.
telesni *a* physical, bodily, corporeal.
teletina *f* veal.
televizija *f* television, telly; ~ u boji colour television.

televizijske vesti *fpl* television news.
televizor *m* television set.
telo *n* body.
telohranitelj *m* bodyguard.
tema *f* theme, topic.
temelj *m* base, basis, foundation.
temeljan *a* basic, fundamental, bottom; solid, thorough (*fig*).
temperament *m* temper, temperament, complexion.
temperatura *f* temperature.
tempiranje *n* timing.
tempirani *a* time; ~a bomba *f* time bomb; ~o gađanje time fire.
tempo *m* rate, speed.
tendencija *f* tendency.
tenis *m* tennis.
teniski reket *m* tennis racket.
tenisko igralište *n* tennis court.
teniser *m* tennis player.
tenor *m* tenor.
teolog *m* theologian.
teologija *f* theology.
teološki *a* theological.
teorema *f* theorem.
teoretičar *m* theorician.
teorija *f* theory.
teorijski *a* theoretic(al).
tepati *v* to babble, to prattle.
tepih *m* carpet, rug.
terapeut *m* therapist.
terapeutika *f* therapeutics.
terapija *f* therapy.
terasa *f* terrace.
terati *v* to urge, to press, to drive.
teren *m* terrain, land, field.
teret *m* burden, cargo, load, weight, freight.
teretni *a* freight; ~ brod *m* freighter; ~ voz freight train; ~a kola *f* cart; .
terevenka *f* revelry, spree.
terijer *m* terrier.
teritorija *f* territory.
teritorijalan *a* territorial.
termički *a* thermal.
termometar *m* thermometer.
termos boca *f* vacuum flask.
termostat *m* thermostat.
teror *m* terror.
terorisati *v* to terrorize.
terorista *m* terrorist.

teroristički *a* terroristic; ~ **napad** *m* terrorist attack.

terorizam *m* terrorism.

terpentin *m* turpentine.

tesan *a* tight; narrow, close.

tesnac *m* ravine, gorge.

testament *m* testament, last will.

testera *f* saw.

testerača *f* sawfish (*zool*).

testeraš *m* sawyer.

testisi *mpl* testicles.

testo *n* paste, dough.

teško *adv* heavily, with difficulty; ~ **disati** *v* to pant, to gasp, to wheeze; ~ **iskušenje** *n* ordeal.

teškoća *f* difficulty, obstacle, trouble, entanglement.

tetanus *m* tetanus.

tetiva *f* bowstring; sinew, tendon, ligament (telo).

tetka *f* aunt.

tetoviranje *n* tattoo.

tetreb *m* grouse (*zool*).

teturati se *v* to stagger, to totter.

teza *f* thesis, dissertation.

tezga *f* counter, desk; workbench.

težak *a* heavy, weighty, difficult, hard, trying, arduous; ~ **rad** *m* toil, drudgery.

težina *f* weight, heaviness.

težiti *v* to gravitate, to strive, to long for.

težnja *f* aspiration, longing, desire.

ti *pn* you.

ticati se *v* to concern, to relate to, to affect.

tiganj *m* frying pan, pan.

tigar *m* tiger.

tigrica *f* tigress.

tih *a* silent, calm, composed, quiet, still.

tik *adv* next to, close by.

tiket *m* coupon.

tim *m* team.

timski rad *m* teamwork.

time *adv* thereby.

tinejdžerski *a* teenage.

tinjati *v* to smoulder.

tip *m* type, model; fellow, cove (ličnost).

tipičan *a* typical.

tipograf *m* typographer.

tipografija *f* typography.

tipografski *a* typographical.

tirada *f* tirade.

tiranija *f* tyranny.

tiranin *m* tyrant, despot.

tiraž *m* impression; circulation.

tirkiz *a* turquoise.

tisa *f* larch, yew, yew-tree.

tišina *f* silence, stillness, hush.

titularni *a* titular.

tkanina *f* cloth, textile.

tkanje *n* texture; weaving.

tkati *v* to weave.

tkivo *n* fabric; tissue (*anat*).

tlačitelj *m* oppressor.

tlačiti *v* to oppress.

tlo *n* ground, soil, mould.

tmina *f* blackness, darkness, dark.

to *pn* this, it, that; ~ **jest** i.e.; ~ **isto** ditto.

toaleta *f* toilet; dress (odeća).

toaletni *a* toilet; ~ **sto** *m* dresser; ~ **papir** *m* toilet paper; ~**e potrepštine** *fpl* toiletries.

tobogan *m* toboggan, sliding board.

tobožnji *a* quasi, almost; make-believe.

točak *m* wheel.

tok *m* course, flow, stream, flux.

tokar *m* turner.

tolerancija *f* tolerance.

tolerantan *a* tolerant.

tolerisati *v* to tolerate, to indulge.

toliko *adv* so much, so many, insomuch.

tom *m* volume.

tombola *f* bingo.

ton *m* tone, sound.

tona *f* ton.

tonaža *f* tonnage.

tonuti *v* to sink, to subside, to settle.

top *m* cannon, gun, big gun.

topao *a* warm, tepid; cordial, hearty; ~ **i udoban** *a* snug; ~ **oblog** *m* poultice.

topaz *m* topaz.

topioničar *m* metallurgist, smelter.

topiti se *v* to melt.

toplota *f* warmth, heat.

toplotni *a* thermal; ~ **udar** *m* heat wave.

topljenje *n* fusion, thawing, melting.

topografija *f* topography.

topografski *a* topographic(al).

topola *f* white poplar (*bot*).

topovnjača *f* gunboat.

topovsko zrno *n* cannonball.

tor *m* corral, pen.

toranj *m* tower.

torba *f* bag, reticule, case.
torbar *m* pedlar.
torta *f* cake.
toster *m* toaster.
totalitaran *a* totalitarian.
tovar *m* consignment, freight, cargo, burden.
tovariti *v* to load, to charge, to freight, to stow.
tradicija *f* tradition.
tradicionalan *a* traditional.
trag *m* trace, track, trail; footprint.
tragati *v* to track, to chase.
tragedija *f* tragedy.
tragičan *a* tragic.
tragikomedija *f* tragicomedy.
trajan *a* everlasting, durable, permanent, continuing.
trajanje *n* duration, continuance.
trajnost *f* durability, durableness.
traka *f* band, tape, ribbon.
traktat *m* tract.
traljav *a* wretched, shabby.
trambulina *f* trampoline.
trampa *f* barter, exchange, swap.
tramvaj *m* tram.
trans *m* trance, ecstasy.
transakcija *f* transaction.
transfuzija *f* transfusion; ~ **krvi** blood transfusion.
transport *m* transportation.
trap *m* pit.
trasa *f* route, line.
trava *f* grass.
travnat *a* grassy.
travnjak *m* lawn.
tražiti *v* to search, to seek, to look for; to ask, to request.
tražnja *f* demand.
trbobolja *f* stomach-ache.
trbuh *m* belly, abdomen, paunch.
trbušast *a* potbellied.
trbušni *a* abdominal; ~**a šupljina** *f* abdomen.
trčanje *n* running, jogging.
trčati *v* to run, to race.
trebovanje *n* requisition.
trećerazredni *a* third rate.
treći *num a* third.
trem *m* porch.
trema *f* stage freight.

tren *m* instant, moment.
trend *m* trend.
trener *m* trainer.
trenerka *f* tracksuit.
trenutak *m* instant, moment, a bit.
trenutan *a* immediate, instantaneous.
trenuti *v* to wink, to take a nap.
trenje *n* friction, rubbing.
trepavica *f* eyelash.
treperenje *n* vibration, palpitation; flickering, twinkling (svetlo).
treperiti *v* to quiver, to blink.
tresak *m* bang, crash.
treset *m* peat.
tresnuti *v* to crash, to slam, to clap.
tresti *v* to shake, to agitate.
trešnja *f* cherry.
trezan *a* sober.
trezor *m* safe-deposit box, vault.
trezven *a* sedate, serious.
trezvenost *f* sobriety, abstinence.
trezvenjak *m* teetotaller.
trg *m* square, plaza.
trgnuti se *v* to be startled.
trgovac *m* trader, dealer, merchant, shopkeeper; retailer (na malo); wholesaler (na veliko); ~ **drogom** drug trafficker; ~ **galanterijskom robom** haberdasher; ~ **ribom** fishmonger.
trgovački *a* mercantile; ~ **brod** *m* merchantman; ~ **centar** shopping centre, shopping mall; ~ **naziv** trade name; ~**a roba** *f* merchandise.
trgovina *f* commerce, trading.
tri *num* three.
tribina *f* rostrum, stand, grandstand.
tricikl *m* tricycle.
tričarija *f* trinket.
trideset *num* thirty.
trideseti *num a* thirtieth.
trigonometrija *f* trigonometry.
trijumf *m* triumph.
trijumfalan *a* triumphal; ~**na kapija** *f* triumphal arc.
trik *m* trick.
triko *n* tights.
triler *m* thriller.
trinaest *num* thirteen.
trinaesti *num a* thirteenth.
triplikat *m* triplicate.
trivijalan *a* trivial.

trivijalnost *f* triviality; **~i** *fpl* trivia.
trka *f* running, race; **~ sa preponama** steeplechase.
trkač *m* runner.
trkački *a* running; **~ konj** *m* racehorse; **~a staza** *f* a running track; **~a kola** sports car.
trke *fpl* racing.
trljati *v* to rub, to massage, to chafe.
trn *m* thorn, prickle, spine; **~ u oku** *m* eyesore.
trnovit *a* thorny; laborious (*fig*).
trodimenzionalan *a* three-dimensional.
trofej *m* trophy.
trojke *fpl* triplets.
trom *a* inactive, sluggish, slack, half-hearted, languid.
trombon *m* trombone.
tromesečje *n* trimester.
tromesečni *a* three-monthly.
tromost *f* insipidness, inertness, torpor.
tropski *a* tropical.
trostruk *a* three-ply, treble.
trošak *m* expenditure, charge, outlay, cost.
trošan *a* dilapidated, perishable, ramshackle, tumbledown.
trošarina *f* excise.
trošiti *v* to spend, to squander, to expend.
trotoar *m* pavement.
trougao *m* triangle.
trougaoni *a* triangular.
trovanje *n* poisoning; **~ hranom** food poisoning; **~ krvi** blood poisoning.
trpati *v* to stow, to cram, to stuff.
trpeljiv *a* tolerant, indulgent.
trpeza *f* table.
trpezarija *f* dining room; refectory (u manastiru).
trska *f* cane, reed.
trtica *f* coccyx (*anat*).
truba *f* trumpet.
trubiti *v* to trumpet, to blow a trumpet.
trud *m* pains, effort, trouble.
trudan, trudna *a* pregnant, gravid, enceinte; **~nička haljina** *f* maternity clothes.
trudnica *f* pregnant mother, expectant mother.
trudnoća *f* pregnancy; **neželjena ~** an unwanted pregnancy.
trulež *f* rot, decay, decomposition; immorality (*fig*).
truliti *v* to decay, to rot, to decompose.

trulost *f* rottenness.
trun *m* particle, grain.
truo *a* rotten, decayed, putrid.
trup *m* trunk, torso, body; **~ broda** hulk.
trut *m* drone; idler (*fig*).
trzaj *m* jerk, twitch; spasm.
trzati se *v* to shrink, to wince.
tržni centar *m* mall (shopping).
tržnica *f* market, marketplace.
tu *adv* there, here, in this place.
tuba *f* tuba, tube.
tuberkuloza *f* tuberculosis.
tucanik *m* gravel.
tuce *n* dozen.
tuč *m* cast iron.
tuča *f* fight, brawl, beating; hail (grad).
tučnjava *f* scuffle, brawl.
tuđ *a* strange, foreign, extraneous.
tuga *f* affliction, sadness.
tugovanka *f* lament, sad story.
tumač *m* interpreter.
tumačenje *n* interpretation, explanation, annotation.
tumačiti *v* to construe, to interpret, to explain.
tumaralo *n* rambler, loafer, idler.
tumarati *v* to wander, to roam, to saunter.
tumor *m* tumour.
tuna *f* tuna.
tunel *m* tunnel.
tunika *f* tunic.
tup *a* blunt, dull; stupid, stolid; **~ udarac** *m* thud, thump.
tupost *f* bluntness, dullness.
turban *m* turban.
turbina *f* turbine.
turbulencija *f* turbulence.
turista *m* holiday-maker, tourist.
turistički *a* tourist; **~a agencija** *f* tourist office, travel agency; **~o putovanje** *n* touring.
turizam *m* tourism.
turnir *m* tournament.
turoban *a* dreary, melancholy, gloomy, sombre.
turpija *f* rasp; nail-file (za nokte).
turšija *f* pickles.
tuš *m* shower-bath; indian ink (za crtanje).
tutnjati *v* to rumble, to roar.
tužan *a* sad, sorrowful, doleful, distressing, grievous.

tužba *f* accusation, charge.
tuženik *m* defendant.
tužilac *m* accuser, plaintiff.
tužiti *v* to sue, to impeach, to indict.
tužno *adv* sadly, sorrowfully.
tvoj *pn* your(s).
tvorac *m* creator, maker, author.
tvorevina *f* creation.
tvrd *a* hard, solid, firm, callous; hard-
hearted.

tvrdica *m* miser.
tvrdina *f* hardness.
tvrditi *v* to assert, to allege, to affirm.
tvrdoglav *a* obstinate, stubborn, dogged,
wilful.
tvrdo *adv* hard.
tvrdoća *f* hardness, compactness.
tvrdoglavost *f* stubbornness, wilfulness.
tvrđava *f* fortress, fort, stronghold, citadel.
tvrđenje *n* affirmation, allegation.

U

u *prep* in, into, to, within; ~ **međuvremenu** meanwhile, in the meantime; ~ **pola cene** half price; ~ **prirodnoj veličini** life-sized; ~ **toku** during; ~ **redu** OK, okay.

ua! *interj* for shame!

ubaciti *v* to throw into, to infiltrate, to interpose.

ubediti *v* to convince.

ubedljiv *a* cogent, convincing, persuasive.

ubeđenje *n* conviction, belief.

ubica *m* assassin, killer, murdered, cut-throat.

ubijanje *n* killing, murdering.

ubilački *a* homicidal.

ubistvo *n* assassination, homicide, murder, manslaughter (iz nehata).

ubiti *v* to assassinate, to murder, to kill.

ublaženje *n* mitigation, soothing, appeasement.

ublažiti *v* to allay, to mollify, to moderate.

ubod *m* prick, puncture, thrust; stab.

ubosti *v* to prick.

ubrizgati *v* to inject.

ubrizgavanje *n* inoculation.

ubrus *m* towel.

ubrzanje *n* acceleration.

ubrzati *v* to accelerate, to speed.

ubuduće *adv* in the future, hereafter.

ucena *f* blackmail, extortion; ransom.

učen *a* learned, erudite.

učenica *f* schoolgirl.

učenik *m* pupil, schoolboy, apprentice.

učenost *f* erudition, knowledge.

učenjak *m* scientist, researcher, savant.

učenje *n* study, learning, doctrine.

učesnik *m* participant; accessory.

učestalost *f* frequency.

učestvovanje na licitaciji *n* bidding.

učešće *n* participation, partnership.

učiniti *v* to work, to make, to render.

učionica *f* classroom.

učitelj *m* teacher.

učiti *v* to learn, to teach, to instruct.

učtiv *a* polite, courteous, urbane, well-mannered.

učtivost *f* civility, courtesy, politeness.

učvrstiti *v* to consolidate, to fixate, to fasten.

učvršćivanje *n* consolidation, fixation, fastening.

ući *v* to go in, to come in, to enter.

ućutati *v* to become silent.

ud *m* limb, member.

udaljen *a* remote, distant, far-away.

udaljenost *f* remoteness.

udar *m* blow, stroke, shock; ~ **groma** thunderbolt; ~**i sudbine** whims of fate; **toplotni** ~ heatstroke.

udarac *m* impact, stroke, blow, nudge, kick, butt, stab (nožem).

udarati *v* to strike, to beat, to knock, to bash.

udaviti se *v* to drown.

udeo *m* share, part.

udica *f* fish-hook.

udisati *v* to inhale, to inspire.

udlaga *f* splint.

udoban *a* comfortable, cosy, convenient.

udobno *adv* comfortably.

udobnost *f* comfort.

udomiti *v* to shelter, to provide for; ~ **ćerku** to marry of a daughter.

udostojiti *v* to deign, to bestow.

udovac *m* widower.

udovica *f* widow.

udruženje *n* association, corporation, affiliation.

udružiti se *v* to associate, to unite, to coalesce.

udubiti se *v* to become absorbed.

udubljenje *n* recess, niche.

udvarati se *v* to woo, to court.

udžbenik *m* textbook.

udžerica *f* hut, hovel.

ugađanje *n* indulgence, pampering.

ugalj *m* charcoal, coal.

uganuće *n* sprain, dislocation.

ugao *m* angle, corner.

ugasiti *v* to extinguish, to put out.

uginuti *v* to die, to expire, to perish.

uglačan *a* polished.

uglađen *a* courtly, polite.

uglast *a* angular.

uglavnom *adv* mainly.
ugled *m* prestige, reputation, repute.
ugledna ličnost *f* personage.
ugljenik *m* carbon.
ugljenisati *v* to carbonize.
ugljenvodonik *m* carbohydrates.
ugnjaviti *v* to press, to bother.
ugnjetavanje *n* oppression.
ugodan *a* pleasant, agreeable, pleasing.
ugoditi *v* to satisfy, to please.
ugojen *a* corpulent, fat.
ugojiti *v* to fatten.
ugojiti se *v* to become fat, to grow fat.
ugovor *m* agreement, contract, treaty, pact.
ugovoren *a* agreed.
ugovoriti *v* to stipulate.
ugrabiti *v* to catch, to get hold of.
ugrejati *v* to heat, to make worm.
ugristi *v* to bite.
ugroziti *v* to danger, to imperil.
ugrožavati *v* to endanger, to imperil, to
  jeopardize.
ugurati *v* to push in, to put in, to insert.
ugušiti *v* to choke, to smother, to stifle, to
  strangle, to suppress.
uh *interj* ugh.
uhapsiti *v* to arrest, to take prisoner; to
  nab (*slang*).
uhobolja *f* earache.
uhvatiti *v* to intercept, to seize, to catch,
  to grasp.
ujak *m* uncle.
ujed *m* bite.
ujediniti *v* to incorporate, to unite, to
  unify.
ujedinjeno *adv* unitedly.
ujednačen *a* equable.
ujednačiti *v* to equalize.
ujedno *adv* simultaneously, at the same
  time.
ujesti *v* to bite, to sting (insekt).
ujna *f* aunt.
ukaz *m* edict, order, decree.
ukazati *v* to indicate, to point.
ukidati *v* to abolish, to nullify, to undo, to
  abrogate.
uklesati *v* to engrave.
uklet *a* damned, under a spell.
ukloniti *v* to dislodge.
uključiti *v* to comprise, to include, to take
  in.

uključujući *adv* including.
uknjižiti *v* to book, to register.
ukočen *a* rigid, stiff, prim.
ukočenost *f* stiffness, rigidity.
ukoliko *adv* in as much, in so far.
ukopati *v* to bury.
ukor *m* reprimand, reproach, admonition.
ukorak *adv* to keep pace with.
ukorenjen *a* ingrained, rooted, deep-
  rooted.
ukoriti *v* to chastise, to admonish.
ukosnica *f* hairpin.
ukras *m* adornment, decoration, finery.
ukrasiti *v* to decorate, to embellish, to
  trick out.
ukrasni *a* decorative, ornamental.
ukrasti *v* to steal, to purloin, to filch, to
  pilfer.
ukrašavati *v* to garnish, to decorate.
ukrašen *a* ornate, decorated.
ukratko *adv* briefly, in short.
ukrcavanje *n* embarkation.
ukrivo *adv* awry, obliquely.
ukrotitelj *m* tamer, trainer; ~ **konja**
  horse-breaker.
ukršten *a* crossbreed.
ukrutiti *v* to stiffen.
ukupan *a* total, entire, all, complete.
ukus *m* taste, flavour, savour, smack; ~
  posle jela *m* aftertaste.
ukusan *a* appetizing, delicious, palatable,
  savoury, tasteful, tasty.
ukusno *adv* mouthwatering.
ukuvati *v* to boil down.
ulagač *m* depositor, investor.
ulagati *v* to deposit, to invest.
ulagivački *a* adulatory, fawningly.
ulagivati se *v* to flatter, to paw, to kow-
  tow.
ulaz *m* entrance, gate, doorway, access,
  entry; input.
ulazna viza *f* entry visa.
ulepšati *v* to beautify, to make more
  beautiful.
ulepšavanje *n* embellishment.
ulica *f* street.
ulivanje *n* influx.
ulivati *v* to pour in, to instil.
ulizica *f* toad-eater, sycophant.
uloga *f* part, role.
uloviti *v* to catch.

ultimatum *m* ultimatum.
ultrazvuk *m* ultrasound.
uludo *adv* in vain, foolishly.
uljan *a* oily; **~a slika** *f* oil painting.
ulje *n* oil; **~ za salatu** *n* salad oil; **~ za sunčanje** *n* suntan oil.
uljez *m* interloper.
uljudan *a* courtly, polite, civil.
uljuljkivati *v* to lull.
um *m* intellect, sense, wit, reason.
umalo *adv* almost, nearly.
uman *a* sage, wise, sagacious.
umanjiti *v* to decrease, to abate, to diminish.
umaranje *n* tiring.
umarati se *v* to get tired.
umeren *a* abstemious, frugal, moderate; reasonable, proper.
umerenost *f* moderation, temperance.
umesto *adv* instead (of).
umešan *adv* crafty, clever, handy.
umešati se *v* to intervene, to interfere.
umešnost *f* artistry, craftsmanship.
umetak *m* insert.
umetnički *a* artistic, masterly; **~a galerija** *f* art gallery; **~o delo** *n* a work of art.
umetnik *m* artist.
umetnost *f* art.
umetnut *a* inlaid, inserted.
umetnuti *v* to insert.
umilan *a* dear, sweet.
umirati *v* to die; **~ od gladi** *v* to starve; **~ od dosade** to be bored to death.
umiriti *v* to calm, to pacify, to placate, to appease, to soothe.
umirući *a* dying.
umiti *v* to wash.
umnožavanje *n* reproduction, multiplying.
umnjaci *mpl* wisdom teeth.
umobolan *a* deranged, insane.
umočiti *v* to dip.
umor *m* fatigue, tiredness.
umoran *a* weary, tired.
umoriti se *v* to get tired.
umotati *v* to envelop, to wrap.
umovati *v* to think, to philosophize.
umreti *v* to die, to expire.
umrlica *f* death certificate.
umrljati *v* to stain, to blot.
unakaziti *v* to deform, disfigure.

unakrstan *a* criss-cross; **~sna vatra** *f* crossfire; **~sno ispitivanje** *n* cross examination.
unaokolo *adv* round about.
unapred *adv* beforehand, in anticipation.
unesrećen *a* afflicted, distressed; hurt.
uništenje *n* demolition, annihilation, destruction.
uništiti *v* to destroy.
univerzalan *a* universal.
univerzitet *m* university.
unosan *a* lucrative, profitable.
unuk *m* grandchild, grandson.
unuka *f* granddaughter.
unutarnji *a* inner, internal, inward.
unutra *adv* indoors, within, internally.
unutrašnji *a* interior, inner, inside; **~a guma** *f* inner tube; **~a politika** *f* the home policy; **Ministarstvo ~ih poslova** *mpl* Ministry of Internal Affairs; **organi ~ih poslova** the police, internal security forces.
unutrašnjost *f* interior, inside.
uobičajen *a* customary, habitual, usual.
uobražen *a* conceited, pretentious, supercilious, bigheaded.
uobraženost *f* conceit, vanity.
uopštavanje *n* generalization.
uopštavati *v* to generalize.
uopšte *adv* generally, in general.
upad *m* inroad, intrusion.
upadljiv *a* striking, flashy, showy.
upala pluća *f* pneumonia.
upaliti *v* to light, to kindle, to inflame.
upaljač *m* lighter.
upamtiti *v* to memorize, to remember, to keep in mind.
uparivanje *n* mating, matching.
upečatljiv *a* impressionable, impressive.
upetljanost *f* involvement.
upijač *m* blotting paper.
upijati *v* to absorb, to imbibe.
upis *m* enrollment, registration.
upisati *v* to book, to enter, to register, to inscribe.
upitni *a* interrogative.
upitnik *m* question mark (*gram*).
uplašen *a* afraid, frightened.
uplašiti *v* to frighten, to startle, to terrify.
uplata *f* payment.
uplesti *v* to twist, to twine.
upleten *a* involved.

upljuvak *m* spit.
upola *adv* halfway, partly.
uporan *a* persistent, insistent, headstrong, pig-headed.
uporedan *a* parallel, comparative.
uporediti *v* to compare, to parallel.
uporediv *a* comparable.
uporedo *adv* abreast with.
uporište *n* foothold, strongpoint, base.
uposlen *a* employed.
upotreba *f* usage, use, utilization.
upotrebljavan *a* used.
upoznat *a* acquainted with, familiar with.
upozorenje *n* caution, warning.
upozoriti *v* to warn, to forewarn, to inform, to forestall.
uprava *f* administration, management, control.
upravitelj *m* manager.
upraviteljka *f* manageress.
upraviteljski *a* managerial.
upravljanje *n* guidance, lead, management, administration.
upravljati *v* to direct, to address, to conduct; to administer, to manage, to steer; to drive.
upravni *a* administrative.
upravnik *m* administrator.
uprkos *adv* in spite of; ~ **tome** regardless.
uprljano *adv* blotchy.
uprljati *v* to soil, to defile.
upućen *a* knowing.
uputan *a* opportune, advisable.
uputiti *v* to direct, to address, to refer.
uputstvo *n* instruction.
uračunati *v* to take into account.
uraditi *v* to act, to make, to do; **uradi sam** do-it-yourself.
uragan *m* hurricane, tornado.
uredan *a* neat, orderly, tidy.
urediti *v* to arrange, to organize.
urednik *m* editor.
uredništvo *n* editorship.
urednost *f* spruceness, tidiness.
uređaj *m* appliance, apparatus.
uređenje *n* arrangement; organization; regime; **državno** ~ governmental structure.
uređivački *a* editorial; ~ **odbor** *m* editorial board.
urez *m* incision, notch, cut.

urezati *v* to incise, to indent.
urgirati *v* to urge, to push on.
urlikanje *n* howling.
urna *f* urn.
urnebes *m* bedlam.
urođen *a* congenital, inborn, inbred.
urođenički *a* aboriginal.
uroniti *v* to immerse, to plunge.
uručiti *v* to deliver, to transmit, to pass by hand.
urvina *f* cliff, abyss.
usaditi *v* to implant.
usaglasiti *v* to coordinate, to harmonize.
usaglašen *a* coherent, harmonious.
usaglašenost *f* compatibility, coordination, conformity.
usamljen *a* lonely, solitary.
usamljenost *f* solitude, seclusion, loneliness, privacy.
usavršiti *v* to improve, to perfect.
useći *v* to incise.
usedelica *f* spinster.
useknuti se *v* to blow one's nose.
useliti se *v* to move into, to settle in.
usev *m* crops.
ushićen *a* delighted, ecstatic, rejoiced, rapturous.
ushićenost *f* rapture.
ushićenje *n* elation.
usijan *a* incandescent, red hot; **~a glava** *f* hothead.
usisavanje *n* intake, suction.
usisavati *v* to aspirate, to suck in.
usisivač *m* vacuum cleaner.
usitniti *v* to break up, to granulate; to change (novac).
usklađen *a* adjusted, harmonized.
usklađivati *v* to harmonize; to adjust, to reconcile.
usklik *m* exclamation, interjection.
uskoro *adv* soon, shortly, before long, anon.
Uskrs *m* Easter.
uskrsnuće *n* resurrection.
uskršnje jaje *n* Easter egg.
usled *prep* because of, on account of.
uslediti *v* to ensue.
uslov *m* condition, proviso, stipulation.
uslovan *a* conditional.
usloviti *v* to condition.
usluga *f* service.

uslužan *a* obliging, accommodating, helpful.
usmen *a* oral.
usna *f* lip.
usnuo *a* asleep.
usoliti *v* to put into salt.
uspavanka *v* lullaby.
uspavati se *v* to oversleep.
uspavljujući *a* soporific.
uspeh *m* success.
uspešan *a* successful, lucky, effectual.
usplahiren *a* fussy, nervous.
uspomena *f* reminiscence, keepsake, souvenir, memento.
uspostaviti *v* to establish.
uspravan *a* upright, vertical, erect.
usprotiviti se *v* to oppose, object.
usred *prep* amid(st), amongst, in the middle of.
usredsrediti se *v* to concentrate.
usredsređen *a* intent.
usredsređivanje *n* concentration.
usta *f* mouth.
ustajanje *n* rising.
ustanak *m* insurrection, rebellion, uprising.
ustanik *m* insurgent, rebel.
ustanova *f* establishment, institution.
ustanoviti *v* to institute, to establish, to ascertain.
ustav *m* constitution.
ustava *f* sluice, dem.
usto *adv* in addition, moreover.
ustoličiti *v* to enthrone.
ustuknuti *v* to recede, to give up, to recoil.
ustupiti *v* to cede, to concede.
ustvari *adv* in fact, in reality.
usud *m* fate, destiny.
usuditi se *v* to dare, to venture.
usvojen *a* adopted, adoptive.
usvojenje *n* adoption.
usvojiti *v* to adopt.
ušće *n* estuary.
ušećeriti *v* to sugar, to candy; ~ **voće** to candy fruits.
ušiti *v* to sew in.
ušljiv *a* lousy.
ušteda *f* savings, spare money.
uštinuti *v* to pinch.
uštirkati *v* to starch.

uštrojiti *v* to castrate.
utaboriti se *v* to encamp.
utakmica *f* competition, contest, match.
uteći *v* to escape, to run away.
uteha *f* consolation, solace.
utešitelj *m* comforter.
utešiti *v* to comfort, to console.
uticaj *m* influence, leverage.
uticajan *a* influential.
uticati (na nešto) *v* to influence, to affect.
utisak *m* impression, effect, sensation.
utkati *v* to interweave.
utočište *n* refuge, harbour.
utoliko *adv* in so much as.
utorak *m* Tuesday.
utovariti *v* to embark, to load.
utroba *f* bowels, gut; womb (majčina).
utučen *a* depressed, down-hearted.
utučenost *f* dejection, depression, despondency.
utvrditi *v* to fortify; to affirm, to establish.
utvrđenje *n* fort, fortress.
uvažen *a* reputable, respectable.
uvek *adv* always, ever.
uveličati *v* to enhance, to enlarge.
uvenuti *v* to wilt, to wither, to fade.
uveravanje *n* assurance.
uveravati *v* to reassure, to assure.
uveren *a* confident, assured, certain.
uverenje *n* conviction; testimonial, certificate.
uveriti *v* to persuade, to assure.
uvesti *v* to introduce, to shown in.
uvežbanost *f* practice, training.
uvis *adv* up, upwardly.
uvo *n* ear.
uvod *m* introduction, prelude, preface.
uvodni *a* introductory, preparatory, incipient.
uvodnik *m* leading article.
uvojak *m* curl, ringlet, tress.
uvoz *m* importation, import.
uvoziti *v* to import.
uvoznik *m* importer.
uvreda *f* affront, offence, insult, outrage.
uvrediti *v* to insult, to humiliate.
uvredljiv *a* insulting, offensive.
uvući *v* to draw in.
uzajamni *a* mutual, reciprocal.
uzajamnost *f* reciprocity.

uzajmiti *v* to lend; to borrow.
uzak *a* narrow.
uzaludan *a* futile, vain.
uzastopni *a* consecutive, successive.
uzbuditi *v* to excite, to stir up.
uzbudljiv *a* breathtaking, exciting,
  excitable.
uzbuđen *a* excited, agitated.
uzbuđeno *adv* excitedly, agog.
uzbuđenje *n* excitement, excitability,
  thrill, agitation.
uzbuna *f* alarm.
uzburkan *a* turbulent.
uzda *f* bridle, curb, reins.
uzdah *m* sigh.
uzdati se *v* to rely, to trust.
uzdići *v* to elevate, to raise, to promote.
uzdržati se *v* to restrain, to refrain, to
  abstain.
uzdržljiv *a* self-controlled, temperate,
  continent.
uzdržljivost *f* abstinence, restraint.
uzduž *adv* along.
uzengije *fpl* stirrups.
uzeti *v* to take.
uzgajati *v* to cultivate, to breed, to grow.
uzgoj *m* cultivation.
uzica *f* lead, line, string, leash.
uzmak *m* retreat, withdrawal.
uznemiravanje *n* disturbance.
uznemiravati *v* to disturb, to harass, to
  intrude.
uznemiren *a* disturbed, troubled, uneasy,
  vexed.
uznemirenost *f* agitation, uneasiness.

uznemiriti *v* to perturb, to intrude, to
  disturb, to unsettle, to derange.
uznemirujući *a* disquieting, disturbing.
uznositi *v* to extol.
uzor *m* example, pattern, paragon, model.
uzorak *m* sample, specimen.
uzrečica *f* saying, proverb.
uzročan *a* causal, causative.
uzrok *m* cause, origin.
uzrujanost *f* excitement, flurry.
uzrujati *v* to agitate.
uzurpacija *f* encroachment, usurpation.
uzverati se *v* to clamber.
uzvičnik *m* exclamation mark.
uzvik *m* cry, exclamation, outcry.
uzviknuti *v* to cry out, to exclaim.
uzvišen *a* exalted, lofty, sublime, high.
uzvišenost *f* eminence, sublimity.
uzvišenje *n* elevation, swell.
uzvišica *f* hill.
uzvraćati *v* to reciprocate, to requite.
užar *m* rope maker.
užas *m* dismay, horror.
užasan *a* appalling, horrible.
užasavajući *a* horrific.
uže *n* cord; **~ za spasavanje** lifeline; **~ za
  tegljenje** towrope.
užina *f* collation, light repast.
uživanje *n* delight, enjoyment, pleasure.
uživati *v* to enjoy, to delight in; **~ glas** to
  be reputed.
užurban *a* bustling, hasty, hurried,
  precipitate.
užurbano *adv* hastily.

V

vabiti *v* to allure, to decoy, to lure.
vadičep *m* corkscrew.
vaditi *v* to extract, to draw out.
vaga *f* balance.
vagina *f* vagina.
vagon *m* coach, wagon, truck; ~ **restoran** dining car.
vajarstvo *n* sculpture, statue.
vajati *v* to carve, to cut; to scalp.
vakcina *f* vaccine.
vakcinacija *f* vaccination.
vakcinisati *v* to vaccinate.
vakuum *m* vacuum.
valcer *m* waltz.
valuta *f* currency.
valjak *m* roller.
valjan *a* worthy, excellent, good.
valjati se *v* to roll over.
valjda *adv* maybe, perhaps.
valjušak *m* dumpling.
vampir *m* vampire.
van *adv* outward, out of door.
vanbračan *a* extramarital, illegitimate.
vanbračnost *f* illegitimacy.
vandalizam *m* vandalism.
vangla *f* wide kitchen pan.
vanila *f* vanilla.
vanlinijski *a* off-line.
vannastavni *a* extracurricular.
vanredan *a* extraordinary; ~**no stanje** *n* emergency.
vansezonski *a* off-season.
vanškolski *a* extramural.
vapaj *m* wailing, cry.
varalica *f* rogue, swindler, impostor, con man.
varanje *n* fraudulence, imposture, forgery.
varati *v* to deceive, to swindle.
varenje *n* digestion.
varičele *fpl* chickenpox.
varijacija *f* variation.
varijete *m* variety show.
variole *fpl* smallpox, variola.
variti *v* to brew, to boil, to digest.
varjača *f* ladle.
varka *f* sham.
varljiv *a* deceptive, fallacious, false.

varnica *f* spark.
varoš *f* town, city.
varvarin *m* barbarian.
varvarizam *m* barbarism.
varvarski *a* barbarous.
varvarstvo *n* barbarity.
vasiona *f* universe, cosmos.
vaspitanje *n* education, upbringing.
vaspitati *v* to educate, to bring up.
vaš *pn* your, yours.
vašar *m* fair.
vaš(ka) *f* louse (*zool*).
vat *m* watt (*el*).
vata *f* cotton-wool.
vatra *f* fire; fever (temperatura); firing (puščana).
vatren *a* ardent, burning, fervent, fiery; ~**o oružje** *n* firearm.
vatrenost *f* ardour.
vatrogasac *m* fireman.
vatrogasni *a* fire; ~**a kola** *f* fire engine; ~**a stanica** fire station.
vatromet *m* fireworks, crackers.
vatrostalni *a* ovenproof, refractory.
vaza *f* vase.
vazal *m* retainer, vassal.
vazda *adv* always.
vazduh *m* air.
vazduhoplovni *a* air, flying; ~**a kompanija** *f* airline; ~**o pristanište** *n* air terminal.
vazdušni *a* air; ~ **balon** *m* air pump; ~ **jastuk** airbag; ~ **most** airlift; ~**a bolest** *f* airsickness.
važan *a* important, considerable, momentous; ~**na ličnost** *f* VIP (very important person).
važeći *a* effective, operative.
važnost *f* importance, consequence.
večan *a* eternal, everlasting, endless.
veče *n* evening, eve.
večera *f* supper.
večeras *adv* tonight, this evening.
večernji *a* evening; ~**a haljina** *f* evening dress; ~**a škola** finishing school, night school.
večit *a* eternal, perpetual.

večnost *f* eternity.
već *adv* already, even now.
većanje *n* counsel.
veće *n* council, board.
veći *a* bigger, greater, larger; higher, taller.
većina *f* majority, greater number.
vedar *a* clear, unclouded; serene; cheery.
vedrina *f* cheerfulness, good spirits; serenity.
vedro *n* pail.
vegetacija *f* vegetation.
vegetarijanac *m* vegetarian.
vejati *v* to winow; to snow.
vejavica *f* snow-storm.
vek *m* century, hundred years.
vekna *f* loaf of bread.
velelepnost *f* pageantry.
velemajstor *m* grand master.
veletrgovina *f* wholesale.
veličanstven *a* grandiose, majestic, imperial.
veličanstvenost *f* magnificence.
veličanstvo *n* majesty (titula).
veličina *f* bigness, greatness, magnitude; size.
veliki *a* large, big, great, gross; ~ **kašalj** *m* whooping cough; **~e boginje** *fpl* smallpox; **~o slovo** *n* capital letter.
Veliki petak *m* Good Friday.
velikodostojnik *m* dignitary.
velikodušan *a* generous, magnanimous.
velikodušnost *f* generosity, magnanimity.
vena *f* vein.
venac *m* garland, wreath; mountain range (planinski).
venčani *a* married, wedded; ~ **list** *m* marriage certificate.
venčanica *f* wedding dress.
venčanje *n* wedding.
venčati *v* to marry.
veneričan *a* venereal.
ventil *m* valve.
ventilacija *f* ventilation.
ventilator *m* ventilator.
venuti *v* to fade, to wither, to pine.
veo *m* veil.
veoma *adv* exceedingly, very, greatly, very much, highly.
vepar *m* boar.
vera *f* belief, creed, credence, faith; religion.

veran *a* faithful, true, loyal; ~ **originalu** lifelike.
veranda *f* veranda(h).
verenica *f* fiancee.
verenički prsten *m* engagement ring.
verenik *m* fiance.
veresija *f* credit.
veridba *f* betrothal.
veriti se *v* to be betrothed, to be engaged.
vermut *m* vermouth.
vernik *m* believer.
vernost *f* allegiance, faithfulness.
verodostojan *a* believable, trustworthy, credible.
verodostojnost *f* credibility.
veroloman *a* treacherous, perfidious.
verovatan *a* probable, likely, credible, possible.
verovati *v* to believe.
verovatno *adv* presumably, probably.
verovatnoća *f* probability, likelihood.
verski *a* religious.
vertikalan *a* vertical.
verzija *f* version.
veseliti se *v* to rejoice, to take delight.
veselo *adv* gaily, merrily, cheerfully.
veselje *n* exhilaration, gaiety, merriment, mirth.
veseo *a* cheerful, gay, hilarious, jocular, jolly, merry, mirthful.
veslač *m* rower.
veslati *v* to row.
veslo *n* oar.
vest *f* news, intelligence, message.
vesti *v* to embroider.
vesti *fpl* news, information.
vešala *fpl* gallows.
vešalica *f* coat hanger, hanger.
vešt *a* artful, handy, skilful, skilled, versed, capable.
veštački *a* artificial, fictitious; **~o osemenjivanje** *n* artificial insemination.
veštak *m* appraiser, valuer.
veštica *f* hag, witch.
veština *f* adroitness, artfulness, expertise, skill, mastery, proficiency.
vešto *adv* ably, finely, cleverly, artfully.
vetar *m* wind; ~ **u leđa** *m* tailwind.
veterina *f* veterinary science.
veterinar *m* veterinary surgeon, vet.
veterinarski *a* veterinary.

veto *n* veto.
vetrenjača *f* windmill.
vetrobran *m* windscreen.
vetrokaz *m* weather cock.
vetrovit *a* windy.
veverica *f* squirrel.
vez *m* embroidery.
veza *f* bond, connection, coupling, relation; **ljubavna** ~ liaison.
vezati *v* to bind, to tie, to tether.
vezen *a* embroidered.
vezivanje *n* binding.
veznik *m* conjunction.
vežba *f* exercise, training, practice.
vežbanka *f* exercise book.
vi *pn* you.
vibrirati *v* to vibrate, to swing.
vicekonzul *m* vice-consul.
vid *m* eyesight, sight, vision.
vidanje *n* healing.
video *m* video; camcorder; ~ **igra** *f* video game; ~ **traka** video tape; ~ **kaseta** video cassette.
videti *v* to see.
vidik *m* horizon, view, vista.
vidljiv *a* manifest, visible.
vidljivo *adv* visibly.
vidljivost *f* visibility.
vidovit *a* clairvoyant.
vidra *f* otter (*zool*).
vihor *m* whirlwind.
vijadukt *m* viaduct.
vijugati *v* to wind.
vijugav *a* sinuous, tortuous, winding; ~ **put** *m* serpentine.
vika *f* clamour, bawling, shouting.
vikati *v* to bellow, to shout, to yell, to exclaim.
vikend *m* weekend.
vila *f* fairy; villa, country seat.
vile *fpl* pitchfork.
vilin konjic *m* dragonfly.
viljuška *f* fork.
viljuškar *m* fork-lift truck.
vime *n* udder.
vinil *m* vinyl.
vino *n* wine.
vinograd *m* vineyard.
vinova loza *f* vine.
vinski *a* wine; ~ **podrum** *m* wine cellar; ~**a čaša** *f* wine glass.

vinuti se *v* to soar, to rise aloft; to take off.
viola *f* viola.
violina *f* fiddle, violin.
violinista *m* fiddler, violinist.
violončelo *n* violoncello, cello.
vir *m* eddy, whirlpool, vortex.
viriti *v* to peer, to peep, to peek, to protrude.
virus *m* virus.
viseći *a* pending, hanging; ~ **most** *m* suspension bridge; ~**a mreža za ležanje** *f* hammock.
visibaba *f* snowdrop.
visina *f* height, altitude, highness; pitch (ton).
viski *m* whisky.
viskozan *a* viscous.
visok *a* high, lofty, great; tall.
visoko *adv* high, aloft; ~ **ceniti** *v* to appraise.
visoravan *f* plateau.
višak *m* surplus, excess, superfluity, overspill.
više *adv* more, higher.
višegodišnji *a* perennial.
vitak *a* slim, slender.
vitamin *m* vitamin.
viteški *a* chivalrous.
viteštvo *n* chivalry.
vitez *m* knight.
vitkost *f* slenderness.
vitlo *n* swift.
vivisekcija *f* vivisection.
viza *f* visa.
vizija *f* vision.
vizir *m* visor, viewfinder.
vlada *f* government, body, ruling power.
vladanje *n* demeanour, deportment.
vladar *m* monarch, ruler.
vladati *v* to govern, to dominate, to command.
vladavina *f* reign, rule.
vlaga *f* dampness, humidity, moisture, wetness.
vlakno *n* fibre, filament.
vlas *f* hair.
vlasnik *m* proprietor, owner; ~ **obveznica** bond holder; ~ **patenta** patentee; ~ **radnje** shopkeeper; ~ **zalagaonice** pawnbroker; ~ **zemljišta** landowner.

vlasništvo *n* property, ownership, possession.
vlastelin *m* landlord.
vlastelinka *f* landlady.
vlastiti *a* own.
vlasulja *f* wig.
vlažan *a* damp, humid, moist.
vo *m* ox.
voće *n* fruit.
voćni *a* fruit; ~ **sok** *m* juice.
voćnjak *m* orchard.
vod *m* lead, line; squad, platoon (*mil*).
voda *f* water; ~ **za piće** drinking water.
vodeći *a* leading, most important.
vodeni *a* aquatic, water; ~ **znak** *m* watermark; **~a boja** *f* watercolour.
vodič *m* guide; guide book.
voditi *v* to guide, to lead, to conduct; ~ **istragu** *v* to prosecute.
vodnik *m* sergeant.
vodnjikav *a* watery.
vododelnica *f* watershed.
vododerina *f* gully.
vodoinstalater *m* plumber.
Vodolija *m* Aquarius (*astrol*).
vodomar *m* kingfisher.
vodonik *m* hydrogen.
vodopad *m* waterfall.
vodoravan *a* horizontal, level.
vodostaj *m* high water, water level.
vodovod *m* waterworks, aqueduct.
vodozemac *m* amphibian.
vođa *m* leader, head.
vođenje *n* leadership; ~ **domaćinstva** housekeeping.
vojni *a* military; ~ **obveznik** *m* conscript; **~a obaveza** *f* conscription; **~a parada** review of troops; **~a tajna** military secret.
vojnički *a* military, soldierly; **~a truba** *f* bugle(horn).
vojnik *m* soldier, combatant.
vojska *f* army.
vokativ *m* vocative (*gram*).
voki-toki *m* walkie-talkie.
volan *m* steering wheel.
volt *m* volt (*el*).
voltaža *f* voltage (*el*).
volja *f* will, determination, volition, disposition, mood.
voljan *a* willing, inclined, disposed.

voljen *m* beloved.
voljnost *f* willingness.
vosak *m* beeswax, wax.
votka *f* vodka.
voz *m* train.
vozač *m* driver.
vozačka dozvola *f* driver's licence.
vozački ispit *m* driving test.
vozilo *n* vehicle.
voziti *v* to drive.
vožnja *f* driving; ~ **čamcem** boating.
vrabac *m* sparrow.
vrač *m* wizard, conjurer, sorcerer, magician.
vračanje *n* witchcraft, sorcery.
vračara *f* sorceress.
vraćanje *n* recurrence, return, reversion; ~ **duga** *n* repayment.
vraćati se *v* to return, to recur.
vragolan *m* imp.
vrana *f* crow.
vraški *a* confoundedly, deucedly, devilish.
vrat *m* neck.
vrata *f* door.
vratar *m* doorman, usher.
vratiti *v* to remand, to requit, to replace, to revert.
vratni *a* cervical, jugular.
vratoloman *a* hazardous, risky.
vrba *f* willow.
vrbovati *v* to enlist, to recruit.
vrč *m* mug, pitcher.
vrebati *v* to lurk, to lay in ambush.
vreća *f* bag; ~ **peska** *f* sandbag; ~ **za spavanje** sleeping bag.
vrećica *f* pouch.
vredan *a* valued, worthy, diligent; ~ **pažnje** worthwhile; ~ **pohvale** laudable; ~ **spomena** memorable.
vrednost *f* price, value, worth.
vređanje *n* abuse.
vređati *v* to offend, to resent, to insult.
vreme *n* time; weather (klima); ~ **za jelo** mealtime; ~ **odlaska** checkout; ~ **posete** visiting hours; ~ **setve** sowing time; ~ **za spavanje** bedtime.
vremenski *a* time; **~a proba** *f* time trial; **~a skala** time scale; **~a zona** time zone; ~ **razmak** *m* time lag.
vrenje *n* boiling, fermentation, effervescence.

vreo *a* hot, boiling.
vres *f* heather (*bot*).
vreteno *n* spindle.
vrh *m* summit, top, apex; ~ **brda** pinnacle; ~ **prsta** fingertip.
vrhovni *a* paramount, supreme; ~**a vlast** *f* supremacy.
vrhunac *m* culmination, pinnacle, highlight.
vrisak *m* scream, screech, shriek.
vrli *a* virtuous, honest, blameless.
vrlina *f* virtue, worth, value.
vrlo *adv* very, greatly, very much; ~ **dubok** *a* profound; ~ **težak** ponderous.
vrpca *f* ribbon.
vrpoljiti se *v* to fidget.
vrsta *f* sort, kind, nature, character.
vrstan *a* competent, capable.
vršalica *f* threshing-machine.
vršiti *v* to execute, to do, to effect, to exert.

vrt *m* garden.
vrteška *f* merry-go-round.
vrtlog *m* swirl, vortex, whirlpool.
vrtoglav *a* giddy.
vrtoglavica *f* dizziness, vertigo.
vruć *a* hot, warm.
vrućina *f* heat.
vucibatina *f* vagrant, good-for-nothing.
vuča *f* traction.
vući *v* to drag, to draw, to haul, to pull, to tug.
vuk *m* wolf.
vukodlak *m* vampire, werewolf.
vulgaran *a* vulgar.
vulgarnost *f* vulgarity.
vulkan *m* volcano.
vulkanski *a* volcanic.
vuna *f* wool.
vunen *a* woolen (*br*), woollen (*amer*).
vunena roba *f* woolens.

Z

za *prep* for, pro, in favour of, on behalf of; instead.

zabaciti *v* to throw back.

zabačen *a* godforsaken, out-of-way, isolated, remote; ~ tiho mesto *n* hideaway.

zabadati *v* to stick into, to drive in.

zabadanje *n* pinning into, sticking.

zabadava *adv* gratis, gratuitously, free of cost.

zabašuriti *v* to suppress, to hush up, to cover up.

zabat *m* gable.

zabava *f* amusement, entertainment, fun, pastime.

zabavan *a* amusing, entertaining.

zabavište *n* núrsery school, playground.

zabavljač *n* entertainer.

zabavljati *v* to amuse, to entertain.

zabeleška *f* annotation, note, remark.

zabeležiti *v* to record, to note, to make a note.

zabezeknut *a* flabbergasted, stunned.

zabitan *a* remote, solitary, isolated.

zabiti *v* to pound in, to drive in, to hammer in.

zablenut *a* standing agape, open-mouthed.

zablistati *v* to glisten, to shimmer.

zabluda *f* misapprehension, error, mistake, delusion.

zaboleti *v* to suffer pain; to insult, to hurt.

zaborav *m* oblivion, forgetfulness.

zaboravan *a* forgetful, oblivious.

zaboraviti *v* to forget, to abandon; to neglect.

zaboravljen *a* forgotten.

zaboravnost *f* forgetfulness.

zabosti *v* to stick into, to drive.

zabran *m* enclosure, grove.

zabrana *f* prohibition, ban.

zabraniti *v* forbid, to prohibit, to proscribe, to inhibit.

zabranjen *a* forbidden; ~o pušenje *n* no smoking.

zabrazditi *v* to plough (*br*)/plow (*amer*), to go too far.

zabrinut *a* anxious, worried, solicitious, preoccupied, troubled, concerned.

zabrinuti se *v* to be anxious.

zabrinutost *f* anxiety, worry, solicitude.

zabrinjavajući *a* worrying.

zabuna *f* confusion, indistinctness, embarrassment; error, mistake.

zabušant *m* shirker.

zabušiti *v* to avoid, to shirk, to get off from.

zaceliti *v* to heal, to make sound.

zacelo *adv* surely.

zacrveneti se *v* to become red, to turn red.

zacvileti *v* to squeal.

začaranost *f* enchantment.

začarati *v* to bewitch, to enchant.

začas *adv* immediately, instantly, at once.

začeće *n* conception.

začelje *n* head.

začepiti *v* to close, to shut, to stop; to cork, to stopper (bocu).

začetak *m* origin, beginning.

začin *m* spice, seasoning.

začinjen *a* flavoured, seasoned, spicy.

začuditi *v* to astonish, to surprise.

začuditi se *v* to be amazed, to be astonished.

zaći *v* to go behind, to decline, to go down.

zaćutati *v* to become silent.

zadah *m* bad smell.

zadatak *m* task, duty, assignment, lesson.

zadati *v* to inflict (udarac); to promise (reč).

zadaviti *v* to strangle, to throttle.

zadesiti *v* to befall, to happen to one.

zadevati *v* to tease, to provoke.

zadići *v* to lift up.

zadihan *a* winded, gasping.

zadihati se *v* to lose one's breath.

zadimljen *a* smoky.

zadirkivanje *n* chaff, teasing, banter.

zadirkivati *v* to tease.

zadiviti *v* to amaze.

zadivljen *a* admiringly.

zadivljujući *a* astonishing.

zadnji *a* back, hind (zadnja noga); last; ~ čas last-minute; ~ sprat top floor.

zadnjica *f* buttocks, posterior.

zadobiti *v* to bring over, to gain, to sustain.
zadocniti *v* to be late.
zadovoljan *a* content, satisfied, glad, pleased.
zadovoljavajući *a* satisfactory.
zadovoljenje *n* contentment, satisfaction.
zadovoljiti *v* to satisfy, to be content.
zadovoljno *adv* contentedly.
zadovoljstvo *n* pleasure, satisfaction.
zadreti *v* to encroach, to enter.
zadrt *a* stubborn, obstinate, dogged.
zadruga *f* community.
zadržati *v* to retain, to keep back, to hold back, to suspend.
zadržavanje *n* retention, delay.
zadržavati se *v* to linger.
zadubljen *a* absorbed, engrossed, bemused.
zadugo *adv* for a long time.
zadušnice *fpl* All Soul's Day.
zadužbina *f* foundation, endowment; memorial.
zadužbinar *m* founder, endower.
zaduženje *n* indebtedness, debit; charge, commission, order; obligation, responsibility.
zagaditi *v* to pollute.
zagasit *a* dark, deep.
zagasiti *v* to extinguish.
zaglaviti *v* to wedge, to clench.
zaglavlje *n* title.
zagledati se *v* to get catch of; to fall in love with (u devojku).
zaglušiti *v* to deafen, to make deaf.
zagnojen *a* festering, suppurating.
zagnjuriti *v* to dip, to plunge.
zagonetan *a* puzzling, mysterious.
zagonetka *f* enigma, riddle, puzzle, mystery.
zagorčiti *v* to embitter, to make bitter.
zagoreo *a* burned.
zagovarati *v* to keep by talking; to speak in favour of.
zagovornik *m* protector, patron.
zagrada *f* barrier, fence; brackets (u tekstu).
zagraditi *v* to fence in; to wall in; to put in brackets (tekst).
zagrađen *a* enclosed; walled.
zagrejati *v* to warm, to make warm.

zagrižen *a* fanatical, over-jealous.
zagrliti *v* to cuddle, to embrace.
zagrljaj *m* embrace, hug, clusp, fold.
zagrobni život *m* afterlife.
zagubiti *v* to misplace, to lose, to mislay.
zagubiti se *v* to get lost.
zagubljen *a* mislaid.
zagušenje *n* asphyxia.
zagušiti *v* to asphyxiate, to suffocate, to choke.
zagušljiv *a* stifling, stuffy, suffocating, poky.
zahladneti *v* to become cold.
zahod *n* lavatory, latrine.
zahtev *m* demand, claim, want, requirement, pretension.
zahtevan *a* demanding.
zahtevati *v* to demand, to claim, to ask for, to insist on, to require.
zahuktati se *v* to rush off.
zahvalan *a* appreciative, grateful, thankful.
zahvaliti *v* to thank, to express gratitude.
zahvalnost *f* gratefulness, gratitude, thankfulness.
zahvat *m* clutch, hold, grip, grasp.
zahvatiti *v* to take hold of, to catch; to take (vodu).
zaigrati *v* to start dancing.
zainteresovati *v* to interest.
zaista *adv* indeed, truly, of course, really.
zajam *m* loan, credit.
zajamčen *a* vouched for, guaranteed, warranted.
zajapuriti se *v* to blush, to become red (in the face).
zajaukati *v* to give a piercing cry, to scream with pain.
zajecati *v* to moan, to sob.
zaječati *v* to resound.
zajedljiv *a* sarcastic, cutting, biting.
zajednica *f* community, fellowship.
zajednički *a* common, collective, corporate; ~ **život** *m* cohabitation.
zajedno *adv* together; ~ **sa** along with.
zajmodavac *m* creditor.
zakačiti *v* to hook up.
zakasneo *a* belated, overdue, late.
zakasniti *v* to come late, to be late.
zakašnjenje *n* delay.
zakazati *v* to appoint, to arrange, to fix.

zakivak *m* rivet.
zaklati *v* to slaughter, to slay, to kill.
zakleti se *v* to swear, to take an oath.
zakletva *f* oath.
zaklon *n* screen, shield, shelter.
zaklopiti *v* to shut, to cover with lid.
zaključak *m* conclusion, deduction, inference.
zaključiti *v* to conclude, to come to a conclusion, to deduce.
zaključno *adv* inclusive, inclosing.
zakočiti *v* to stop (by braking).
zakon *m* law.
zakonik *m* code, collection of laws.
zakonit *a* lawful, legal, legitimate.
zakonitost *f* legality, legitimacy.
zakonodavac *m* lawmaker, lawgiver, legislator.
zakonodavan *a* legislative.
zakonodavstvo *n* legislation, legislature.
zakopati *v* to bury, to inter.
zakopčan *a* buttoned; reserved.
zakrčiti *v* to block, to stop up, to close.
zakrpa *f* patch, repair.
zakrvavljen *a* bloodshot.
zakržljao *a* stunted, undersized.
zakucati *v* to nail; to knock, to rap (na vrata).
zakulisni *a* secret, underhand, offstage.
zakup *m* lease, rental, tenancy.
zakupac *m* renter, tenant; leaseholder (stana).
zakuska *f* snack, luncheon, light meal.
zakuvati *v* to concoct.
zalagaonica *f* pawnshop.
zalazak sunca *m* sunset.
zaleđen *a* frozen; glacial, ice-bound.
zalemiti *v* to braze, to solder.
zalepiti *v* to fix, to stick, to glue.
zalepljen *a* glued, sticking together.
zalet *m* start, run.
zaliha *f* reserve, stock, store, hoard, provision.
zalistak *m* valve.
zaliti *v* to soak, to wet.
zaliv *m* bay, gulf, creek.
zalizan *a* smooth, sleek, slick.
zalog *m* pledge, pawn.
zalogaj *m* mouthful, morsel, bite, tidbit.
založen *a* pawned.
založiti *v* to pawn, to pledge.

zalud *adv* in vain.
zaludan *a* unavailing; idle (besposlen).
zaludno *adv* idly.
zaluđen *a* infatuated.
zalupiti *v* to shut with noise, to slam.
zalutao *a* lost, astray.
zalutati *v* to go astray.
zaljubiti se *v* to enamour, to fall in love.
zaljubljen *a* amorous, in love; **~o gledati** *v* to ogle.
zamaći *v* to disappear, to move out of sight.
zamagljen *n* blurred, dimmed, fogged.
zamah *m* sway, swing.
zamak *m* castle, manor-house.
zamalo *adv* almost.
zamamljiv *a* attractive, seductive, alluring.
zamazan *a* smeared; unclean, dirty.
zamena *f* substitute, substitution; barter, exchange, interchange.
zamenica *f* pronoun (*gram*).
zamenik *m* substitue.
zameniti *v* to barter, to change, to exchange; to supersede, to stand for, to represent; to mistake for.
zameranje *n* objection; offence.
zametak *n* bud; embryo, germ, foetus.
zamisao *f* thought, idea, notion; brainchild.
zamisliti *v* to preconceive, to imagine.
zamisliv *a* imaginable.
zamišljen *a* pensive, thoughtful.
zamka *f* noose; trap, snare, pitfall.
zamočiti *v* to plunge, to dip.
zamoliti *v* to ask, to ask for, to apply for.
zamor *m* fatigue, weariness, tiredness.
zamoran *a* tiresome, tiring, fatiguing, weary, back breaking.
zamorče *n* guinea pig.
zamotati *v* to enfold, to envelop, to wrap up.
zamračiti *v* to darken, to obscure.
zamrli *a* extinct; dead; **~ grad** dead city; frozen (*fig*).
zamrsiti *v* to embroil, to entangle, to mess up.
zamršen *a* intricate, entangled; embroiled.
zamrzivač *m* freezer.
zamrznut *a* frosted, frozen.
zamrznuti *v* to freeze.
zanat *m* craft, handicraft, trade.
zanatlija *m* craftsman.

zanemariti *v* to neglect, to omit.
zanemeo *a* numb.
zanemeti *v* to become silent.
zanesen *a* fanatic, ecstatic, exalted.
zanesenjak *m* devotee, fanatic, enthusiast.
zanimanje *n* occupation, vocation, business, pursuit, calling.
zanos *m* ecstasy, fanaticism, excitation, excitement, trance.
zanosan *a* delightful, ravishing, captivating, seductive.
zao *a* bad, evil, malicious, wicked.
zaobilazak *m* bypass.
zaobilazan *a* indirect, roundabout.
zaobilazni *a* circuitous; ~ **put** *m* detour.
zaokrugljen *a* rounded, completed.
zaostajati *v* to lag behind, to be behind.
zaostao *a* retarded, backward.
zapad *m* west.
zapadno *adv* westward.
zapaliti *v* to ignite, to kindle, to light.
zapaljeno *a* aflame.
zapaljenje *n* inflammation; ~ **grla** laryngitis; ~ **krajnika** tonsillitis; ~ **plućne maramice** pleurisy.
zapaljivo *a* flammable.
zapamtiti *v* to bear in mind, to remember.
zapanjen *a* amazed, stunned, stupified, astounded.
zapanjujući *a* startling.
zapara *f* moist, heat, oppressiveness.
zapaziti *v* to behold, to find, to see.
zapažen *a* noticed; prominent, noticeable (istaknut).
zapeta *f* comma.
zapis *m* record, entry, note.
zapisničar *m* secretary, recorder.
zaplašiti *v* to appal, to daunt, to intimidate.
zaplena *f* confiscation, sequestration.
zapleniti *v* to confiscate.
zaplet *m* intricacy, complication, plot.
zaploviti *v* to set sail, to start sailing.
započeti *v* to commence, to initiate, to begin, to start.
zapomaganje *n* crying for help.
zaposesti *v* to occupy, to take possession.
zaposlenje *n* employment, occupation, vocation, business.
zaposliti *v* to employ, to occupy, to engage.

zapostaviti *v* to neglect, disregard.
zapovedati *v* to command, to order.
zapovednički *a* imperious, overbearing, authoritative.
zapravo *adv* in fact.
zaprepastiti *v* to astound, to stun, to daze, to perplex.
zaprepašćen *a* stunned, dumbfounded, dazed.
zapretiti *v* to threaten, to menace.
zaprositi *v* to propose, to ask in marriage.
zaptivač *m* gasket.
zapušač *m* stopper, cork.
zapušenje krvnih sudova *n* coronary.
zapušiti *v* to close, to shut.
zapušten *a* unlooked-for, neglected.
zapuštenost *f* dilapidation.
zaračunati *v* to include in the account, to calculate.
zaraćen *a* belligerent, engaged in war.
zarada *f* earnings, wages; income, revenue; profit, gain.
zaraditi *v* to earn, to win, to gain.
zarastao *a* cicatrized, healed up; covered (korovom).
zaravan *m* plateau.
zaraza *f* infection, contagion, epidemic.
zarazan *a* infectious, contagious, catching, communicable.
zaraziti *v* to infect, to contaminate.
zarđalost *f* rustiness.
zarđao *a* rusty, corroded.
zarez *m* comma; cut, notch, incision.
zariti *v* to bury; to plung.
zarobiti *v* to capture, to make prisoner, to seize.
zarobljenik *a* captive, prisoner.
zarobljeništvo *n* captivity.
zaroniti *v* to dive, to plunge, to dip.
zaronjenje *n* immersion.
zaručen *a* affianced, bethrothed.
zaručnica *f* fiancee, bride to be.
zaručnik *m* fiance.
zaruke *fpl* betrothal, engagement.
zasada *adv* for the moment.
zasaditi *v* to plant, to implant.
zaseban *a* separate, detached.
zaseći *v* to cut into, to scotch.
zaseda *f* ambush.
zasedanje *n* session, meeting.

zaseniti *v* to dazzle, to blind, to fascinate, to overshadow.
zasićen *a* saturated.
zasititi *v* to satiate, to sate, to saturate.
zasladiti *v* to sweeten.
zaslepiti *v* to dazzle, to make blind.
zaslepljenost *f* blindness, infatuation.
zasleplujući *a* dazzling.
zasluga *f* merit, praise, credit.
zaslužan *a* deserving, meritorious.
zaslužiti *v* to deserve, to merit, to be worthy of.
zasmejati *v* to make laugh.
zasnivati *v* to found, to establish.
zasnivati se *v* to be based.
zaspati *v* to drop asleep.
zastakliti *v* to glaze.
zastareo *a* obsolete, out-of-date, superannuated, outmoded, bygone.
zastava *f* flag, banners, colours.
zastavica *f* pennant.
zastideti *v* to make ashamed.
zastoj *m* pause, standstill, hold-up, intermission; ~ **saobraćaja** traffic jam.
zastor *m* curtain.
zastraniti *v* to diverge, to swerve, to deviate.
zastranjivanje *n* aberration.
zastrašiti *v* to frighten, to scare, to browbeat.
zastrašivanje *n* deterrent.
zastrašujući *a* frightening.
zastupati *v* to represent, to stand for; to hold (mišljenje).
zastupništvo *n* representation, agency, advocateship.
zašećeren *a* sugared, sweetened.
zaštićen *a* sheltered, protected.
zaštita *f* protection, guard, safeguard, advocacy.
zaštititi *v* to protect, to guard.
zaštitni *a* protective; ~ **šlem** *m* crash helmet; ~ **znak** trademark; ~**e naočari** *fpl* goggles.
zaštitnik *m* protector, patron.
zašto *adv* why, wherefore, what for.
zateći *v* to surprise, to catch, to find.
zatečen *a* caught.
zategnut *a* taut, tight, tense.
zategnuti *v* to stretch, to strain, to tighten.
zatim *adv* then, afterwards.

zatišje *n* lull, remission, calm, breathing spell.
zato *adv* therefore, for that reason.
zatočenik *m* captive, prisoner.
zaton *m* bay, golf.
zatražiti *v* to require, to claim, to demand.
zatreskati se *v* to fall in love.
zatrovan *a* poisoned.
zatrovati *v* to poison, to embitter.
zatucan *a* stupid; narrow-minded; bigoted.
zaturiti *v* to lose, to mislay.
zatvaranje *n* closure; ~ **u tamnicu** confinement.
zatvor *m* imprisonment, prison, capture, arrest, jail; constipation.
zatvoren *a* closed, shut; arrested.
zatvorenik *m* prisoner, jailbird.
zatvoriti *v* to close, to shut, to stop, to apprehend, to arrest.
zaustaviti *v* to stop, to halt, to check, to hinder, to suppress.
zauške *fpl* mumps.
zauvek *adv* for ever, for evermore, forever.
zauzet *a* busy, occupied.
zauzeti *v* to occupy, to hold.
zauzimanje *n* occupation, occupancy, intercession.
zavada *f* difference, quarrel, feud.
zavaditi *v* to divide, to make hostile.
zavaditi se *v* to fall out, to wrangle.
zavaliti se *v* to lounge, to loll.
zavarati *v* to mystify, to deceive.
zavariti *v* to weld.
zaveden *a* misdirected, misguided.
zavera *f* conspiracy, plot, combination, scheme.
zaverenik *m* conspirator.
zavesa *f* curtain, hangings.
zavesti *v* to entice, to seduce.
zaveštanje *n* bequest.
zaveštati *v* to bequeath.
zavet *m* vow, promise, pledge.
zavetrina *f* lee-side.
zavežljaj *m* package, bundle.
zavičaj *m* native land, homeland.
zavidan *a* enviable.
zavideti *v* to envy, to begrudge.
zavidljiv *a* envious.
zavijati *v* to howl, to yell.

zavisan *a* dependent, conditioned.
zavisiti *v* to depend.
zavisnost *f* addiction, dependency.
zavist *f* envy.
zaviti *v* to wrap up, to swathe.
zavitlati *v* to hurl.
zavod *m* institution, institute, establishment.
zavodljiv *a* seductive, tempting, alluring.
zavodnik *m* seducer, enticer, inveigler.
zavođenje *n* allurement, seduction, enticement.
zavoj *m* bandage, dressing.
zavoleti *v* to take a liking to, to become partial.
završetak *m* completion, ending, termination.
završiti *v* to finalize, to finish, to end, to terminate.
završni *a* eventual; final, last; **~ račun** *m* annual balance sheet.
zavrtanj *m* screw.
zavrteti *v* to swing, to shake, to twirl.
zaziranje *n* apprehension, dread.
zbabati se *v* to become old, to become wrinkled.
zbaciti *v* to throw off; **~ s prestola** to dethrone.
zbeg *m* refuge, shelter.
zbijanje *n* condensation, compression.
zbilja *f* reality; *adv* really.
zbir *m* sum, total; **~ bodova** score.
zbirka *f* collection.
zbirni *a* cumulative, collective.
zbog *adv* because of, on account of.
zbogom *int* goodbye, farewell, adieu.
zbor *m* meeting, assembly.
zbrka *f* confusion, mess, disarray, mix-up.
zbuniti *v* to baffle, to abash, to bewilder, to confound, to fluster.
zbunjen *a* embarrassed, flustered, bewildered.
zbunjenost *f* bewilderment.
zbunjivati *v* to delude, to disconcert.
zbunjujući *a* confusing.
zdanje *m* building.
zdela *f* dish, bowl.
zdepast *a* podgy, thickset, plump, stocky.
zdrav *a* well, healthy, wholesome, sound; lusty, salubrious; **~ razum** *m* common sense.

zdravac *m* geranium (*bot*).
zdravlje *n* health, soundness, healthfulness.
zdravo *intj* hi, hello.
zeba *f* chaffinch (*zool*).
zebra *f* zebra.
zec *m* hare; rabbit.
zečar *m* beagle (pas).
zejtin *m* oil.
zelen *a* green, verdant; young, without experience; *f* vegetables.
zelena salata *f* lettuce.
zelenaš *m* usurer.
zelenaštvo *n* usury.
zelenilo *n* greenery.
zelenkast *a* greenish.
zemaljski *a* terrestrial, earthly.
zembilj *m* string bag.
zemička *f* bun.
zemlja *f* earth, globe; country, ground, land, soil.
zemljak *m* countryman, fellow countryman.
zemljani *a* earthen, earthy.
zemljoposednik *m* land-holder, landowner.
zemljoradnik *m* farmer.
zemljoradnja *f* farming, agriculture.
zemljotres *m* earthquake.
zemljouz *m* isthmus.
zenica *f* pupil (of the eye).
zenit *m* zenith.
zet *m* son-in-law.
zevati *v* to yawn, to gape.
zgaziti *f* to trample, to crash.
zglob *m* joint; **~ prsta** knuckle.
zgoda *f* opportunity, occasion.
zgodan *a* opportune, timely; pretty, nice, charming.
zgotoviti *v* to make ready, to prepare.
zgrabiti *v* to grab, to grasp, to take hold of, to catch.
zgrada *f* building, house, edifice.
zgranuti *v* to scandalize, to shock.
zgrčen *a* cramped.
zgrušati se *v* to coagulate, to curdle.
zgusnuti *v* to thicken, to solidify.
zgužvati *v* to crease, to wrinkle, to crumple.
zid *m* wall.
zidni *a* mural; **~o slikarstvo** *n* mural

painting; **~e tapete** *fpl* wallpaper; **~e novine** wall newspaper.

zidar *a* bricklayer, mason, plasterer.

zidarski zanat *m* bricklaying.

zidarstvo *n* masonry.

zima *f* winter.

zimski *a* wintry; **~ sport** *m* winter sports; **~ san** hibernation; **~a bašta** *f* hothouse; winter garden.

zimzelen *m* evergreen.

zlatača *f* toadstool.

zlatan *a* golden, gold; **~na ribica** *f* goldfish; **~na sredina** the golden mean; **~na svadba** golden anniversary.

zlatar *m* goldsmith.

zlatnik *m* gold coin.

zlato *n* gold.

zlikovac *m* malefactor, criminal.

zlo *n* badness, evil, harm, wrong.

zloba *f* malevolence, malice, rancour, venom, hate, bitterness.

zloban *a* malevolent, malicious, spiteful.

zločin *m* crime, guilt, felony.

zločinac *m* delinquent, criminal, miscreant, culprit.

zločinački *a* criminal.

zloćudan *a* malign, malignant.

zlokoban *a* ill-fated, sinister.

zlonameran *a* malevolent, evil-minded, inimical, malicious.

zloslutan *a* ominous, foreboding.

zlosrećan *a* unfortunate.

zlostavljati *v* to maltreat, to mishandle, to abuse.

zloupotreba *f* malpractice, misusage misapplication.

zlovolja *f* moodiness, bad temper.

zlovoljan *a* moody, sulky, sullen.

zlovoljnost *f* sullenness.

zmaj *f* dragon; kite.

zmija *f* snake, serpent; **~ otrovnica** viper, adder.

zmijolik *a* snaky.

značaj *m* significance, importance, weight.

značajan *a* considerable, significant, eminent, meaningful.

značenje *n* meaning.

značiti *v* to mean, to design, to signify.

značka *f* badge, ensign.

znak *m* sign, token, mark; symbol;

gesture; symptom; **~ uzvika** exclamation mark; **vodeni ~** watermark; **hemijski ~** chemical symbol; **~ci bolesti** *mpl* symptoms of a disease.

znalac *m* connoisseur, expert.

znamenit *a* celebrated, famed, famous; **~ dan** *m* red-letter day.

znamenje *n* symbol, emblem, sign, type, omen.

znanje *n* cognizance, knowledge, know-how.

znatan *a* considerable, extensive, ample, great, large, telling.

znati *v* to know, to be aware of.

znatno *adv* considerably, extensively, greatly.

znoj *m* perspiration, sweat.

znojiti se *v* to perspire, to sweat.

zob *f* oats.

zobena kaša *f* porridge.

zodijak *m* zodiac.

zolja *f* wasp.

zona *f* zone.

zoolog *m* zoologist.

zoologija *f* zoology.

zoološki *a* zoological; **~ vrt** *m* zoo.

zora *f* dawn, daybreak, dawning.

zračiti *v* to air, to ventilate.

zrak *m* ray, beam, gleam.

zrelost *f* maturity, matureness, ripeness.

zreo *a* mature, ripe.

zreti *v* to ripen, to mature, to grow ripe.

zrnce *n* granule.

zrno *n* grain.

zub *m* tooth; **zubi** *pl* teeth; **~ očnjak** *m* eyetooth.

zubar *m* dentist.

zubarstvo *n* dentistry.

zubni *a* dental; **~ kamenac** *m* tartar; **~a proteza** *f* denture.

zubobolja *f* toothache.

zujanje *n* buzz, buzzing.

zujati *v* to hum, to buzz.

zumbul *m* hyacinth (*bot*).

zupčanik *m* cogwheel, gear wheel.

zupčast *a* jagged, cogged.

zvaničan *a* official, formal; **~no saopštenje** *n* comminique.

zvečarka *f* rattlesnake (*zool*).

zvečati *v* to clang.

zveket *m* rattle.
zveketati *v* to clink, to rattle.
zvekir *m* knocker.
zver *f* beast; bestial person, brute (*fig*).
zverka *f* wild animal; **velika ~** big gun (*fig*).
zverokradica *m* poacher.
zverski *a* brutal.
zverstvo *n* atrocity, beastiality, beastliness.
zvezda *f* star; **~ lutalica** comet; **polarna ~** North Star; **vitlajemska ~** the Star of Bethlehem; **filmska ~** film star.
zvezdan *a* starry, starred; stellar.
zvezdica *f* asterisk.

zviždati *v* to whistle, to hiss.
zvonar *m* ringer, bell-ringer.
zvončić *m* bluebell (harebell).
zvonik *m* belfry.
zvoniti *v* to ring abell, to tinkle.
zvono *n* bell; chime; **~ na vratima** doorbell.
zvonjava *f* pealing, ringing, chiming.
zvrk *m* spinning top.
zvučni *a* sonorous, sounding; **~ efekti** *mpl* sound effects; **~ signal** *m* buzzer; **~a traka** *f* soundtrack.
zvučnik *m* loudspeaker, megaphon.
zvuk *m* sound, tone.

Ž

žaba *f* frog, toad.
žabokrečina *f* frog-spawn; stagnation (*fig*).
žad *m* jade.
žagor *m* murmur; undertone.
žalba *f* complaint, grievance.
žalilac *m* appellant.
žaliti se *v* to appeal, to complain.
žalosno *adv* sadly, sorrowfully.
žalost *f* bereavement, grief, mourning, sorrow.
žalostan *a* lamentable, mournful, regretful, rueful, sorrowful; **~sna vrba** *f* weeping willow.
žalostiti se *v* to grieve.
žaljenje *n* regret.
žaoka *f* sting.
žar *f* embers; fervour.
žarač *m* poker.
žargon *m* jargon.
žarište *n* focus.
žbun *m* bush, shrub.
žbunje *n* shrubbery, undergrowth.
žderonja *m* glutton.
ždrebac *m* stallion.
ždrebe *n* colt, foal.
ždrebica *f* filly.
žedan *a* thirsty.
žeđ *m* thirst.
želatin *m* gelatin(e).
žele *m* jelly.
želeti *v* to wish, to want.
železnica *f* railway, railroad.
železnički *a* railway; **~ nasip** *m* embankment; **~a pruga** *f* railway; **~a postaja** railway-station.
želudac *m* stomach.
želudačni *a* gastric.
želja *f* desire.
željan *a* desirous, eager, wishful.
željeni *a* desirable.
željezara *f* ironworks.
žena *f* female, woman; **~ policajac** policewoman; **~ ubica** murderess.
ženiti (se) *v* to marry, to espouse.
ženomrzac *m* misogynist.
ženskast *a* womanish.

ženski *a* female, feminine; **~ manastir** *m* nunnery; **~ pokret** feminism; **~o rublje** *n* lingerie.
ženstven *a* effeminate, womanly.
ženstvenost *f* effeminacy.
žersej *m* jersey.
žestina *f* vehemence.
žestok *a* vehement.
žetelac *m* harvester, reaper.
žeti *v* to reap.
žetva *f* harvest.
žezlo *n* sceptre.
žica *f* string, wire.
žičara *f* cable car.
žig *m* brand, hallmark.
žigati *v* to twinge.
žigosati *v* to stigmatize.
žilav *a* leathery.
žilavost *f* tenacity.
žir *m* acorn.
žirafa *f* giraffe.
žitarice *fpl* corn, cereals.
žitnica *f* granary.
živ *a* alive, living, existing, alive; **~ pesak** *m* quicksand; **~i jezici** *mpl* living languages; **~o biće** *n* living person.
živa *f* mercury, quicksilver.
živac *m* nerve.
živahan *a* animated, brisk, lively, spirited, sprightly, vivacious.
živahnost *f* animation, alacricity, liveliness, sprightliness.
živeti *v* to live, to exist, to be alive; to dwell; **~ zajedno** to cohabit.
živež *m* provision, victuals.
živina *f* poultry.
živopisan *a* picturesque, graphic.
život *m* life, living.
životinja *f* animal, beast, brute.
životinjski *a* bestial, beastly, brutish.
životni *a* life, vital; **~ vek** *m* life span; lifetime; **~a snaga** *f* vitality.
žlezda *f* gland (*anat*).
žljeb *m* groove.
žongler *m* juggler.
žonglirati *v* to juggle.
žreb *m* lot.

žrtva *f* sacrifice; victim.
žrtveni *a* sacrificial; ~ **jarac** *m* scapegoat.
žrtvovati *v* to victimize.
žrvanj *m* millstone.
žuborenje *n* murmur.
žuč *f* gall, bile.
žučni *a* bilious; ~ **kamenac** *m* gallstone; ~ **mehur** gall bladder.
žućkast *a* sallow, yellowish.
žudeti *v* to crave, to aspire, to covet.
žudnja *f* craving, longing.
žulj *m* corn, callus, bunion.

žumance *n* yolk.
žur *m* party.
žuran *a* hurried.
žurba *f* haste, rush.
žuriti *v* to hurry, to bustle, to hasten.
žurnalistika *f* journalism.
žurno *adv* speedily.
žut *a* yellow.
žutica *f* jaundice.
žvakaća guma *f* bubble gum, chewing gum.
žvakati *v* to chew, to masticate, to munch.

ENGLISH–SERBIAN
ENGLESKO–SRPSKI
DICTIONARY
REČNIK

A

a *art* neodređeni član (*gram*); jedan, jedna, jedno.

a.m. *adv* pre podne (skraćenica od *ante meridien*).

aback *adv* natrag, nazad; **to be taken ~** zapanjen, preneražen.

abacus *n* računaljka.

abandon *v* ostaviti, napustiti.

abandonment *n* napuštanje, odustajanje od.

abase *v* poniziti, omalovažiti.

abasement *n* poniženje, omalovaženje.

abash *v* zbuniti, dovesti u nepriliku.

abate *v* umanjiti, utišati; oboriti, ukinuti, staviti van snage.

abatement *n* umanjenje, sniženje, ukidanje.

abbess *n* opatica, igumanija.

abbey *n* opatija, manastir.

abbot *n* opat, iguman, starešina manastira.

abbreviate *v* skratiti.

abbreviation *n* skraćenje.

abdicate *v* odreći se, dati ostavku, abdicirati.

abdication *n* odricanje od, abdikacija.

abdomen *n* trbušna šupljina .

abdominal *a* trbušni.

abduct *v* otimati, silom odvoditi.

abduction *n* otmica.

abed *adv* u ili na postelji , krevetu.

aberrant *a* nenormalan, nastran, koji odstupa.

aberration *n* zastranjivanje, skretanje sa pravog puta.

abet *v* podstaći, nagovoriti na.

abeyance *n* privremena neaktivnost, privremena obustava (zakona i sl.).

abhor *v* gnušati se, gaditi se; mrzeti.

abhorrence *n* gađenje, gnušanje.

abhorrent *a* gnusan, odvratan.

abide *v* prebivati, živeti; trpeti.

ability *n* sposobnost, veština; darovitost.

abject *a* bedan, prezren, kukavan.

abjure *v* odreći se, odustati.

ablative *n* ablativ (*gram*).

ablaze *a* u plamenu, u vatri.

able *a* sposoban, obdaren; vešt; biti u stanju.

able-bodied *a* snažan; zdrav.

ablution *n* pranje; ispiranje.

ably *adv* vešto, spretno.

abnegation *n* odricanje; odbijanje, poricanje.

abnormal *a* nenormalan; neprirodan.

abnormality *n* neprirodnost; nepravilnost.

aboard *prep* na palubi, na brodu; **to go ~** ukrcati se.

abode *n* prebivalište; stan.

abolish *v* staviti van snage, poništiti, ukinuti.

abolition *n* obustava, poništenje.

abominable *a* odvratan, gadan.

abomination *n* odvratnost, nešto što izaziva gađenje.

aboriginal *a* urođenički; iskonski.

aborigines *n* starosedeoci.

abort *v* pobaciti, roditi pre vremena; pretrpeti neuspeh.

abortion *n* pobačaj, nedonošče; neuspeh.

abortive *a* prevremen, jalov; neuspeo.

abound *v* obilovati; **~ with** vrveti nečim.

about *prep* oko, okolo; *adv* približno; **I carry no money ~ me** nemam para pri sebi; **~ ready** skoro gotov; **yesterday we were talking ~ you** juče smo govorili o vama .

above *prep* nad, iznad; ne dalje od; **~ mentioned** gore navedeno.

aboveboard *adv* iskreno, pošteno.

abrasion *n* abrazija, zguljivanje, trenje.

abrasive *n* abrazivan, koji se bruši.

abreast *adv* uporedo, u istoj liniji.

abridge *v* skratiti, ograničiti.

abridgement *n* skraćenje, ograničenje.

abritration *n* arbitraža, rasprava pred izabranim sudom.

abroad *adv* iza granice, iz inostranstva; **to go ~** otići u inostranstvo.

abrogate *v* ukinuti (zakon, običaj).

abrogation *n* ukidanje.

abrupt *a* strm, vrletan; iznenadan; žestok.

abscence *n* odsutnost, izostajanje.

abscess *n* čir, abces.

abscond *v* sakriti se, prikrivati se.

absent *a* odsutan; rasejan; *v* izostati, udaljiti se.

absentee *n* odsutni; koji ne živi kod kuće.
absently *adv* rasejano.
absent-minded *a* rasejan.
absolute *a* potpun, savršen, čist; **~ly** *adv* sasvim, potpuno.
absolution *n* oproštaj, oslobađanje od kazne.
absolve *v* osloboditi od.
absorb *v* apsorbovati; progutati.
absorbent *n* sredstvo koje upija.
absorption *n* apsorpcija; upijanje.
abstain *v* uzdržavati se; ne upotrebljavati (npr. piće).
abstemious *a* umeren, uzdržljiv; **~ly** *adv* umereno.
abstinence *n* uzdržljivost, umerenost.
abstract *n* izvod, kratak pregled; zamišljen pojam.
abstraction *n* apstraktnost; rasejanost.
abstractly *adv* apstraktno.
abstruse *a* nejasan; teško shvatljiv; dubok.
absurd *a* besmislen, apsurdan; **~ly** *adv* apsurdno, smešno.
absurdity *n* besmislenost, apsurdnost.
abundance *n* izobilje, bogatstvo.
abundant *a* obilan; **~ly** *adv* obilno.
abuse *n* vređanje, psovanje; *v* grditi, vređati, loše postupati.
abusive *a* pogrdan, uvredljiv.
abut *v* dodirivati nešto, primicati se nečemu.
abysmal *a* bez dna, nedosežan.
abyss *n* provalija, ponor, bezdan.
acacia *n* bagrem.
academic *a* akademski, univerzitetski, teoretski; *n* naučnik.
academician *n* akademik .
academy *n* akademija; viša ili visoka škola.
accede *v* stupiti, pristupiti; složiti se sa.
accelerate *v* ubrzati.
acceleration *n* ubrzanje.
accent *n* naglasak; *v* naglasiti, isticati.
accentuate *v* akcentirati, podvući.
accentuation *n* akcenat, naglašavanje.
accept *v* prihvatiti, složiti se; dopustiti.
acceptability *n* prihvatljivost.
acceptable *a* prihvatljiv; prijatan.
acceptance *n* prihvatanje, saglasnost; odobravanje.

access *n* pristupačnost; prilaz.
accessible *a* pristupačan; dostupan; popustljiv.
accession *n* pristup; stupanje (na dužnost); saglasnost.
accessory *n* učesnik; *pl* pribor.
accident *n* nesrećan slučaj, nesreća.
accidental *a* slučajan, nehotičan; sporedan; **~ly** *adv* slučajno.
acclaim *v* odobravati, burno aplaudirati.
acclamation *n* klicanje, oduševljeno pozdravljanje.
acclimatize *v* prilagoditi se novim prilikama.
accommodate *v* prilagoditi se; izgladiti (spor); staviti na raspolaganje.
accommodating *a* uslužan, ljubazan; popustljiv, pomirljiv.
accommodation *n* prilagođavanje, pogodnost; stan, smeštaj.
accompaniment *n* pratnja (*mus*); uzgredno delo.
accompanist *n* pratilac, pratilja (*mus*).
accompany *v* pratiti.
accomplice *n* saučesnik (npr. u zločinu).
accomplish *v* izvršiti, ispuniti, obaviti.
accomplished *a* okončan, završen; otmen, lepo vaspitan, usavršen.
accomplishment *n* ispunjenje, dostignuće; obrazovanje.
accord *n* saglasnost, sporazum; sklad; **of one's own ~** dobrovoljno, od svoje volje.
accordance *n* slaganje, podudaranje; **in ~ with** u saglasnosti sa, shodno.
according *adv* prema tome, saglasno; zato, na taj način.
accordion *n* harmonika.
accost *v* pozdraviti , obraćati se nekome.
account *n* račun, obračun; **on no ~** nikako, ni u kom slučaju; **on one's own ~** za svoj račun; **to call to ~** pozvati na odgovornost; **to ~ for** odgovarati.
account number *n* broj računa.
accountability *n* odgovornost.
accountable *a* odgovoran.
accountancy *n* računovodstvo, knjigovodstvo.
accountant *n* računovođa, ovlašćeni revizor.
accrue *v* priticati, narasti.

accumulate v nakupiti, narasti, akumulirati.

accumulation n nagomilavanje; zgrtanje; hrpa, gomila.

accuracy n tačnost.

accurate a tačan; uredan; brižljiv; **~ly** adv tačno, uredno.

accursed a proklet, zlosrećan.

accusation n optužba.

accusative n akuzativ (gram).

accusatory a optužujući, optužni.

accuse v optužiti, okriviti.

accused n optuženi.

accuser n tužilac, tužilja.

accustom v navići se, privići se (na nešto).

accustomed a naviknut; uobičajen.

ace n kec (na kartama); jedinica (na kockama); **within an ~ of** za dlaku, zamalo.

acerbic a opor, gorak, kiseo, jedak.

acetate n acetat, so sirćetne kiseline.

ache n bol; v boleti.

achieve v dostići.

achievement n dostignuće, ispunjenje.

acid n kiselina; a kiselo, kisela.

acid rain n kisela kiša.

acidity n kiselost.

acknowledge v priznati, dopustiti; potvrditi prijem (pisma).

acknowledgement n priznanje, potvrda; nagrada.

acme n vrhunac, najviša tačka.

acne n bubuljice, akne.

acorn n žir.

acoustics n akustika, nauka o zvuku.

acquaint v upoznati, saopštiti, izvestiti.

acquaintance n poznanstvo, poznanik.

acquiesce v pristati (na nešto), odobriti; prećutno se složiti.

acquiescence n pristanak (pasivni); odobravanje.

acquiescent a popustljiv, pokoran.

acquire v steći, dobiti.

acquisition n dobitak; tekovina.

acquit v osloboditi se (od nečega); opravdati.

acquittal n oslobađanje, pravdanje.

acre n jutro zemlje; njiva, oranica.

acrid a oštar, jedak; zajedljiv.

acrimonious a jedak; razdražljiv.

acrimony n jetkost, zajedljivost; žučnost.

across adv popreko, s one strane; prep preko, kroz.

act v uraditi, delati; glumiti, predstaviti; n radnja, delo, čin; akt, uredba; ponašanje; kratka molitva.

acting n gluma, igra; koji radi.

action n čin, delatnost, rad.

activate v aktivirati.

active a radan, vredan, aktivan.

activity n aktivnost, delovanje, preduzimanje.

actor n glumac.

actress n glumica.

actual a stvaran, pravi; savremen; **~ly** adv stvarno, zaista; u pravi čas.

actuary n pisar, beležnik; statističar osiguranja.

acumen n pronicljivost.

acupuncture n akupunktura.

acute a oštar, pronicljiv; **~ly** adv oštro; **~ angle** oštar ugao; **~ question** goruće pitanje.

acuteness n oštrina, pronicljivost; prodornost.

ad lib v improvizovati.

ad nauseam adv do gadosti (lat).

adage n izreka, poslovica.

adamant a čvrst, nepokolebljiv; n dijamant.

adapt v prilagoditi, preraditi, udesiti.

adaptability n prilagodljivost.

adaptable a prilagodljiv.

adaptation n prilagođavanje; prerada, udešavanje.

add v dodati, pridodati, dopuniti; **to ~ up** sabrati.

addendum n prilog, dopuna.

adder n guja, zmija otrovnica.

addict n narkoman, onaj ko se predaje uživanju (npr. droga).

addiction n zavisnost, sklonost ka nečemu.

addition n dodavanje, dopuna; suma.

additional a dopunski, dodatni; naknadni.

additive n dodatak (npr. u hrani).

address v uputiti; rešavati; n adresa; oslovljavanje; govor; ponašanje.

adduce v predočiti; pozvati se na.

adept a vešt, iskusan.

adequacy n srazmernost, dostatnost; podudaranje.

adequate *a* odgovarajući, prikladan; dovoljan; **~ly** *adv* srazmerno, dovoljno.

adhere *v* prianjati, pristajati.

adherence *n* privrženost, odanost, vernost.

adherent *a* lepljiv; privržen; pristalica.

adhesion *n* spajanje, lepljenje, prianjanje.

adhesive *a* lepljiv, spojni, adhezioni.

adieu *n* opraštanje; zbogom.

adipose *a* debeo, krupan.

adjacent *a* susedni, bliski; koji se graniči.

adjectival *a* pridevski.

adjective *n* pridev.

adjoin *v* pripojiti, sastaviti.

adjoining *a* okolni, susedni.

adjourn *v* odložiti, odgoditi.

adjournment *n* odgađanje; prekid (sednice).

adjudicate *v* presuditi.

adjunct *n* dopuna, dodatak; pomoćnik.

adjust *v* prilagoditi.

adjustable *a* podesiv, prilagodiv.

adjustment *n* nameštanje; sastavljanje; montiranje.

adjutant *n* pomoćnik; ađutant (*voj*).

administer *v* upravljati; obavljati; prepisati, dati lek; **to ~ an oath** zakleti nekoga.

administration *n* rukovođenje poslovima; administracija; ministarstvo, vlada.

administrative *a* upravni, administrativni; izvršni.

administrator *n* upravnik, administrator.

admirable *a* divan, izvrstan.

admirably *adv* izvrsno.

admiral *n* admiral.

admiralship *n* admiralski brod.

admiralty *n* Ministarstvo mornarice; admiralitet.

admiration *n* divljenje, predmet obožavanja.

admire *v* diviti se.

admirer *n* obožavalac, ljubitelj.

admiringly *adv* zadivljeno.

admissible *a* dopustiv, prihvatljiv.

admission *a* priznanje; dopuštanje; prilaz.

admit *v* dozvoliti, odobriti; pustiti; priznati.

admittance *n* prijem; dozvola; priznanje.

admittedly *adv* kao što je svima poznato.

admixture *n* smeša; primesa.

admonish *v* savetovati; opomenuti; napomenuti.

admonition *n* savet; primedba, ukor.

admonitory *a* ukoran; koji opominje.

adolescence *n* adolescencija, mladost.

adopt *v* usvojiti; prihvatiti; pozajmiti.

adopted *a* usvojen.

adoption *n* usvojenje; biranje; prihvatanje.

adoptive *a* usvojen, stečen posvajanjem.

adorable *a* divan.

adorably *adv* divno, s obožavanjem.

adoration *n* obožavanje.

adore *v* obožavati.

adorn *v* krasiti, ulepšavati.

adornment *n* ukras.

adrift *a* neukotvljen; nošen događajima, prepušten slučaju.

adroit *a* spretan, snalažljiv.

adroitness *n* veština, spretnost; lukavost.

adulation *n* dodvoravanje.

adulatory *a* ulagivački.

adult *a* odrastao, zreo.

adulterate *a* falsifikovan, krivotvoren; *v* dodavati mešanjem; falsifikovati.

adulteration *n* falsifikovanje; kvarenje.

adulterer *n* preljubnik, brakolomnik.

adulteress *n* preljubnica.

adulterous *a* preljubnički; bezbožnički.

adultery *n* brakolomstvo, preljuba.

advance *v* napredovati, razvijati se; platiti unapred; pozajmiti; **to make ~s** udvarati se; povisiti cenu; napredovati u službi.

advanced *a* napredan; uspešan.

advancement *n* napredovanje; povišenje; uspeh.

advantage *n* preimućstvo, prednost; **to take ~** iskoristi, imati korist.

advantageous *a* povoljan; **~ly** *adv* korisno.

advantageousness *n* korist; prednost.

advent *n* dolazak; nastup; pojava.

adventitious *a* pomoćni; sporedni, slučajni.

adventure *n* avantura, događaj, doživljaj.

adventurer *n* avanturista; probisvet.

adventurous *a* hrabar; opasan; preduzimljiv; **~ly** *adv* pustolovno.

adverb *n* prilog (*gram*).

adverbial *a* priloški; **~ly** *adv* priloški.

adversary *n* protivnik, suparnik.
adverse *a* neprijateljski; nepovoljan; štetan.
adversity *n* nepovoljna okolnost; nesreća, nedaća.
advertise *v* reklamirati, objaviti, dati oglas.
advertisement *n* reklama, oglas.
advertising *n* propaganda, reklama.
advice *n* savetovanje, konsultacija; saopštenje, obaveštenje.
advisability *n* korisnost.
advisable *a* preporučljiv; poželjan.
advise *v* savetovati; izvestiti, obavestiti.
advisedly *adv* promišljeno, svesno.
advisory *a* savetodavni.
advocacy *n* zaštita; advokatura; širenje, propagiranje.
advocate *n* advokat; zaštitnik; *v* braniti, štititi.
advocateship *n* zastupništvo.
aerial *a* vazdušni.
aerobics *n* aerobik.
aeroplane *n* avion.
aerosol *n* aerosol.
aerostatic *a* aerostatički.
aesthetic *a* estetski; istančan; **~s** *n* estetika.
afar *adv* daleko; **from ~** izdaleka.
affability *n* predusretljivost; ljubaznost.
affable *a* predusretljiv; učtiv.
affair *n* posao, stvar; predmet.
affect *v* uticati (na nešto); pretvarati se; uzbuditi; ganuti.
affectation *n* prenemaganje, afektacija.
affected *a* pogođen; oboren (bolešću); povređen; neiskren; **~ly** *adv* izveštačeno, neprirodno.
affectingly *adv* ganutljivo; osećajno.
affection *n* privrženost, ljubav; bolest; uzbuđenje.
affectionate *a* odan; nežan; **~ly** *adv* nežno; srdačno.
affidavit *n* pismena izjava (pod zakletvom).
affiliate *v* primiti u članstvo.
affiliation *n* udruženje; filijala, podružnica.
affinity *n* rodbina, srodstvo; sličnost.
affirm *v* utvrditi, potvrditi.
affirmation *n* tvrđenje, potvrđivanje.

affirmative *a* potvrdan; **~ly** *adv* potvrdno.
affix *v* pričvrstiti; zalepiti; *n* dodatak, afiks.
afflict *v* naneti bol; ožalostiti, rastužiti.
affliction *n* tuga, bol; nesreća.
affluence *n* obilje, bogatstvo.
affluent *a* obilan, bogat.
afflux *n* priliv, priticanje.
afford *v* dozvoliti sebi, pružiti mogućnost.
affray *n* svađa, tučnjava.
affront *n* uvreda; *v* uvrediti.
aflame *a, adv* zapaljeno, u vatri.
afloat *a, adv* ploveći, na vodi.
afraid *a* uplašen; **I am ~** plašim se.
afresh *adv* ponovo, iznova.
aft *a, adv* krmeni, na krmi (*naut*).
after *prep* iza; posle; kroz; *adv* pozadi; kasnije; **~ all** konačno, na kraju krajeva.
afterbirth *n* posteljica.
after-effects *npl* posledica; naknadno dejstvo.
afterlife *n* zagrobni život.
aftermath *n* posledice; ostava.
afternoon *n* poslepodne.
aftershave *n* losion posle brijanja.
aftertaste *n* ukus posle jela .
afterwards *adv* posle, kasnije.
again *adv* ponovo, opet; **~ and ~** više puta; **he's himself ~** oporavio se.
against *prep* protiv; **~ the grain** uz dlaku; nasuprot.
agate *n* ahat (poludragi kamen).
age *n* doba (života), vek, period; **under ~** maloletan; *v* stariti, ostariti.
aged *a* star, u godinama.
agency *n* agencija, posredovanje.
agenda *n* dnevni red; podsetnik.
agent *n* agent, posrednik; sredstvo.
agglomerate *v* nagomilati, nakupiti.
agglomeration *n* gomila, aglomeracija.
aggrandizement *n* povećanje.
aggravate *v* otežati, pogoršati.
aggravation *n* otežavanje, pogoršavanje.
aggregate *n* agregat; skup.
aggregation *n* skup, masa.
aggression *n* agresija, napad.
aggressive *a* agresivan, nasrtljiv.
aggressor *n* agresor, napadač.
aggrieved *a* ožalošćen, oštećen.
aghast *a* prestravljen, užasnut.

agile *a* okretan, hitar.
agility *n* okretnost, hitrina, spretnost.
agitate *v* uzrujati, potresti.
agitation *n* uznemirenost; razmatranje; agitacija.
agitator *n* agitator; podstrekač.
ago *adv* pre (koji je bio pre); **long ~** u davnoj prošlosti.
agog *a* uzbuđeno, nestrpljivo.
agonizing *a* očajan.
agony *n* agonija, mučenje, patnja.
agree *v* pristati, složiti se.
agreeable *a* prijatan, drag; odgovarajući; **~ with** slagati se sa.
agreeableness *n* prijatnost; saglasnost.
agreeably *adv* prijatno; saglasno
agreed *a* ugovoren; saglasan; Pristajem!.
agreement *n* sporazum, ugovor.
agricultural *a* poljoprivredni, zemljoradnički.
agriculture *n* poljoprivreda, zemljoradnja.
agronomy *n* agronomija.
aground *a* nasukan; koji je naseo.
ah *interj* oh.
ahead *adv* napred, spreda; **go ~** nastavi, produži.
ahoy! *interj* hoj! (*naut*).
aid *v* pomoći; **to ~ and abet** pružiti pomoć; *n* pomoć, pomoćnik.
aide-de-camp *n* ađutant (*voj*).
AIDS *n* SIDA (skraćenica od sindroma stečene imunološke deficitnosti).
ail *v* boleti, tištati; uznemiravati.
ailing *a* bolan, nezdrav.
ailment *n* bolest, slabost.
aim *v* nišaniti; težiti; ciljati; *n* meta, cilj; nišan.
aimless *a* besciljan; **~ly** *adv* besciljno.
air *n* vazduh; *v* vetriti, provetravati.
air balloon *n* vazdušni balon.
air force *n* ratno vazduhoplovstvo.
air freshener *n* osveživač vazduha.
air gauge *n* manometar.
air pump *n* vazdušna pumpa, vazdušni šmrk.
air terminal *n* vazduhoplovno pristanište, terminal.
airbag *n* vazdušni jastuk.
airborne *a* vazdušnodesantni.
air-conditioned *a* klimatizovan.

air-conditioning *n* klimatizacija, erkondišn.
aircraft *n* avion; vazduhoplovstvo.
airless *a* bezvazdušni; zagušljiv.
airlift *n* vazdušni most.
airline *n* vazduhoplovna kompanija, vazdušna linija.
airmail *n* avionska pošta; **by ~** avionom.
airport *n* aerodrom.
airport tax *n* aerodromska taksa.
airstrip *n* poletno-sletna staza.
airtight *a* hermetičan, koji ne propušta vazduh.
airy *a* vazdušast; nestvaran; providan.
aisle *n* bočna lađa crkve; prolaz između sedišta.
ajar *a* odškrinut; poluotvoren.
akimbo *adv* podbočen, sa rukama na kukovima.
akin *a* srodan; iz iste porodice.
alabaster *n* alabaster.
alacrity *n* živahnost; pripravnost.
alarm *n* uzbuna; znak za uzbunu; *v* dići uzbunu, uzbuditi.
alarm clock *n* budilnik.
alarmist *n* zloslutnik, čovek koji širi alarmantne vesti.
alas *interj* avaj!, jao!.
albeit *conj* čak i ako.
album *n* album.
alchemist *n* alhemičar.
alchemy *n* alhemija.
alcohol *n* alkohol.
alcoholic *a* alkoholni; *n* alkoholičar.
alcove *n* niša; udubljenje u zidu.
alder *n* jova, joha (*bot*).
ale *n* pivo.
alert *a* oprezan; budan; *n* znak na uzbunu.
alertness *n* opreznost, budnost; hitrost, brzina.
algae *npl* alge; morske trave.
algebra *n* algebra.
algebraic *a* algebarski.
alias *n* pseudonim; lažno ime.
alibi *n* alibi, dokaz o nepostojanju krivice.
alien *a* strani, tud, daleki; *n* stranac.
alienate *v* otuđiti, udaljiti.
alienation *n* otuđenje, udaljavanje.
alight *v* sići, izaći; *a* zapaljen; osvetljen.

align *v* poređati; postrojiti; poravnati se.
alike *a* sličan, nalik na; *adv* isto tako, na isti način.
alimentation *n* alimentacija, izdržavanje; ishrana.
alimony *n* hranjenje; izdržavanje.
alive *a* živ; živahan; koji radi; svestan.
alkali *n* alkalija; lužina.
alkaline *a* alkalni.
all *a* sav, celi; *adv* sasvim, potpuno; ~ **at once**, ~ **of a sudden** najedanput; ~ **the same** svejedno; ~ **the better** utoliko bolje; **not at** ~ nikako; **once and for** ~ zauvek; *n* sve, sav, celi.
all clear *n* prekid uzbune.
all right *adv* dobro; u redu.
allay *v* ublažiti (bol); smanjiti, suzbiti.
allegation *n* tvrđenje; navod, navođenje.
allege *v* tvrditi, izjaviti; pozivati se na nešto.
allegiance *n* vernost, odanost.
allegorical *a* alegoričan; ~**ly** *adv* alegorijski.
allegory *n* alegorija.
allegro *a adv* alegro (*mus*).
allergy *n* alergija.
alleviate *v* olakšati; ublažiti.
alleviation *n* olakšanje.
alley *n* drvored; uska ulica, prolaz.
alliance *n* savez.
allied *a* savezni; rodbinski; blizak.
alligator *n* aligator.
alliteration *n* aliteracija.
allocate *v* dodeliti, doznačiti.
allocation *n* dodeljivanje; doznaka.
allot *v* odrediti; dodeliti; razdeliti.
allow *v* dozvoliti; dopustiti; priznati; isplatiti; **to** ~ **for** uzeti u obzir.
allowance *n* dozvola, dopuštanje; džeparac; popust.
allowedly *adv* kako je poznato.
alloy *n* legura.
all-round *a* svestran.
allspice *n* piment, najgvirc (*bot*).
allude *v* spominjati, smerati.
allure *v* očarati; mamiti.
allurement *n.* zavođenje; privlačnost.
alluring *a* privlačan; primamljiv; ~**ly** *adv* primamljivo.
allusion *n* aluzija; nagoveštavanje.
allusive *a* aluzivan; ~**ly** *adv* aluzivno.

alluvial *a* nanosni.
ally *n* saveznik; *v* stupiti u savez.
almanac *n* godišnjak, almanah.
almighty *a* svemoguć; svemoćan.
almond *n* badem.
almost *adv* gotovo, skoro.
alms *n* milostinja.
aloft *prep* visoko, gore.
alone *a* sam, osamljen; *adv* samo, jedino; **to leave** ~ ostaviti na miru.
along *adv* uzduž, s kraja na kraj; ~**side** pored.
aloof *adv* daleko, udaljeno.
aloud *a* glasno; javno.
alphabet *n* alfabet, abeceda.
alphabetical *a* alfabetski, abecedni, azbučni.
alpine *a* planinski, alpski.
already *adv* već.
also *adv* takođe, isto tako.
altar *n* oltar.
altarpiece *n* oltarski kip.
alter *v* izmeniti, promeniti, preinačiti.
alteration *n* promena, izmena.
altercation *n* prepirka, svađa.
alternate *a* naizmeničan; *v* izmenjivati se; ~**ly** *adv* naizmenično.
alternating *a* naizmeničan (kod struje).
alternation *n* alternacija.
alternative *n* alternativa, izbor; *a* alternativan; ~**ly** *adv* alternativno.
alternator *n* alternator, generator naizmeničnog napona.
although *conj* premda, iako, mada.
altitude *n* visina, nadmorska visina.
altogether *adv* skupa, zajedno.
alum *n* stipsa.
aluminium *n* aluminijum.
always *adv* uvek, stalno.
amalgam *n* amalgam.
amalgamate *v* spajati, integrisati.
amalgamation *n* amalgamacija, integracija.
amanuensis *n* prepisivač.
amaryllis *n* amarilis (*bot*).
amass *v* skupiti, zgrnuti.
amateur *n* amater.
amateurish *a* amaterski, diletantski.
amatory *a* ljubavni, ljubavnički.
amaze *v* zapanjiti.
amazement *n* zapanjenost; čuđenje.

amazing *a* neverovatan; ~**ly** *adv* neverovatno.
Amazon *n* amazonka; reka Amazon.
ambassador *n* ambasador, izaslanik.
ambassadress *n* ambasadorka.
amber *n* ćilibar; *a* ćilibarski.
ambidextrous *a* sposoban da dobro upotrebljava obe ruke; spretan; dvoličan.
ambient *a* okolni, koji okružuje.
ambiguity *n* dvosmislenost.
ambiguous *a* dvosmislen, dvoznačan; ~**ly** *adv* dvosmisleno.
ambition *n* ambicija, slavoljublje, težnja.
ambitious *a* ambiciozan; častoljubiv; ~**ly** *adv* ambiciozno.
amble *v* ići lagano; ići kasom (kod konja).
ambulance *n* sanitetska kola; poljska bolnica.
ambush *n* zaseda; **to lie in** ~ biti u zasedi; *v* napasti iz zasede.
ameliorate *v* poboljšati, popraviti.
amelioration *n* poboljšanje.
amenable *a* odgovoran, nadležan; pristupačan.
amend *v* popraviti, ispraviti.
amendable *a* izmenljivo, popravljivo.
amendment *n* amandman; poboljšanje.
amends *npl* odšteta.
amenities *npl* običaji, način ponašanja; komfor.
amenity *n* prijatnost, ljubaznost.
American *a* američki; *n* Amerikanac.
amethyst *n* ametist.
amiability *n* ljubaznost; društvenost.
amiable *a* ljubazan; privlačan.
amiably *n* ljubazno.
amicable *a* prijateljski, srdačan.
amicably *adv* prijateljski, ljubazno.
amid(st) *prep* usred, sred, među.
amiss *adv/a* nije u redu; **something's** ~ nešto nije u redu; **to take** ~ uzeti za zlo.
ammonia *n* amonijak.
ammunition *n* municija.
amnesia *n* amnezija.
amnesty *n* amnestija, pomilovanje.
among(st) *prep* između, među.
amoral *a* amoralan.
amorous *a* zaljubljen; ~**ly** *adv* ljubavni.
amorphous *a* amorfan.

amount *n* iznos, suma; količina; vrednost; *v* iznositi; vredeti.
amp(ere) *n* amper (*el*).
amphibian *n* vodozemac, amfibija.
amphitheatre *n* amfiteatar.
ample *a* obilan, veliki, širok.
amplification *n* pojačanje, amplifikacija.
amplifier *n* pojačavač.
amplify *v* pojačati, proširiti.
amplitude *n* amplituda, širina, opseg.
amply *adv* obimno, opširno.
amputate *v* amputirati, odseći ud.
amputation *n* amputacija.
amulet *n* amajlija.
amuse *v* zabavljati; zanimati.
amusement *n* zabava, razonoda.
amusing *a* zabavan; ~**ly** *adv* zabavno.
an *art* neodređeni član (slabi oblik), koristi se pre reči koje počinju samoglasnikom ili nemim *h*; jedan, jedna jedno.
anachronism *n* anahronizam.
anaemia *n* anemija, malokrvnost.
anaemic *a* anemičan, malokrvan.
anaesthetic *n* anestetik.
analog *a* analogni (računar).
analogous *a* analogan, sličan.
analogy *n* analogija, sličnost, podudarnost.
analyse *v* analizirati, ispitivati; raščlaniti.
analysis *n* analiza.
analyst *n* analitičar.
analytical *a* analitičan; ~**ly** *adv* analitički.
anarchic *a* anarhičan, bez reda.
anarchist *n* anarhista.
anarchy *n* anarhija.
anatomical *á* anatomski.
anatomize *v* anatomisati.
anatomy *n* anatomija.
ancestor *n* predak.
ancestral *a* nasleđen.
ancestry *n* poreklo, preci.
anchor *n* sidro; utočište; *v* usidriti se, ukotviti se; **to cast (raise)** ~ baciti (podići) sidro.
anchorage *n* sidrište; uporište.
anchovy *n* inčun, sardela.
ancient *a* stari, prastari, antički; *n* starac.
ancillary *a* pomoćni (*gram*); službeni.
and *conj* i (sastavni veznik).

anecdote *n* anegdota, zabavna pričica.
anemone *n* sasa (*bot*).
anew *adv* iznova, nanovo.
angel *n* anđeo.
angelic *a* anđeoski.
anger *n* gnev, bes; *v* naljutiti (se).
angle *n* ugao; udica; *v* pecati ribu.
angler *n* pecaroš.
anglicism *n* anglicizam.
angling *n* pecanje.
angrily *adv* ljutito.
angry *a* ljutit, srdit, razdražen.
anguish *n* muka, bol, patnja.
angular *a* uglast, oštar.
animal *n* životinja.
animate *v* oživeti; nadahnuti; *a* živ, živahan.
animated *a* živahan.
animation *n* živahnost, veselost.
animosity *n* neprijateljstvo, mržnja, zloba.
animus *n* zlonamernost, neprijateljski odnos.
anise *n* anis (*bot*).
aniseed *n* anis (seme).
ankle *n* gležanj; ~ **bone** skočna kost.
annals *npl* letopis, anali.
annex *v* pripojiti, pridružiti; *n* dopuna, prilog.
annexation *n* aneksija, pripajanje.
annihilate *v* uništiti, poništiti, ukinuti.
annihilation *n* poništenje, uništenje, istrebljenje.
anniversary *n* godišnjica.
annotate *v* pribeležiti, praviti pribeleške.
annotation *n* tumačenje, komentar, objašnjenje.
announce *v* objaviti, saopštiti, izvestiti.
announcement *n* saopštenje, objavljivanje.
announcer *n* spiker (na radiju), objavljivač.
annoy *v* dosađivati, smetati.
annoyance *n* smetnja, dosađivanje; muka, neprijatnost.
annoying *a* dosadan.
annual *a* godišnji, jednogodišnji.
annually *adv* godišnje.
annuity *n* godišnja renta, anuitet.
annul *v* poništiti, ukinuti, anulirati.
annulment *n* poništenje.

annunciation *n* najava, objavljivanje.
anodyne *a* sredstvo za umirenje.
anoint *v* namazati, miropomazati.
anomalous *a* neprirodan, nepravilan.
anomaly *n* anomalija.
anon *adv* uskoro, odmah.
anonymity *n* anonimnost.
anonymous *a* anoniman, bezimen; ~ly *adv* anonimno.
anorexia *n* anoreksija, nemanje apetita.
another *a* drugi, još jedan; one after ~ jedan za drugim.
answer *v* odgovoriti, odazvati se; **to ~ for** odgovarati za; *n* odgovor; rešenje; replika.
answerable *a* odgovoran.
answering machine *n* telefonska sekretarica.
ant *n* mrav.
ant hill *n* mravinjak.
antagonism *n* antagonizam, neprijateljstvo.
antagonist *n* suparnik, protivnik.
antagonize *v* naljutiti.
antarctic *a* antarktički.
anteater *n* mravojed.
antecedent *n* prethodnik; prethodni član; *pl* preci.
antechamber *n* predsoblje.
antedate *v* antidatirati, staviti raniji datum.
antelope *n* antilopa.
anterior *a* prednji, prethodni.
anthem *n* himna.
anthology *n* antologija.
anthracite *n* antracit.
anthropologist *n* antropolog.
anthropology *n* antropologija.
anti-aircraft *a* protivavionski, protivvazdušni.
antibiotic *n* antibiotik.
antibody *n* antitelo.
antichrist *n* antihrist.
anticipate *v* predvideti, predosetiti, upozoriti.
anticipation *n* predosećanje, iščekivanje.
anticlockwise *adv* suprotno od smera kazaljke na satu.
antidote *n* protivotrov.
antifreeze *n* antifriz.
antimony *n* antimon (*hem*).

antipathy *n* antipatija, odvratnost.
antipode *n* antipod.
antiquarian *n* antikvaran, starinski; ljubitelj starina.
antiquated *a* staromodan, prestareo, zastareo.
antiquity *n* antika, antička umetnost; starost.
antiseptic *a* antiseptički.
antisocial *a* nedruštven.
antithesis *n* antiteza, suprotnost.
antler *n* rog sa parošcima.
anvil *n* nakovanj.
anxiety *n* zabrinutost, nemir, zebnja; želja.
anxious *a* zabrinut, uznemiren; ~ly *adv* zabrinuto; to be ~ pribojavati se; biti željan.
any *a* bilo koji, svaki, ijedan; ~body ma ko, bilo ko, svako; ~how u svakom slučaju, svakako; nikako; ~ more nikad više; ~ place ma gde; ~thing išta, bilo. bilo šta.
apace *adv* brzo.
apart *adv* odvojeno, nezavisno, po strani.
apartment *n* soba, stan.
apartment house *n* stambena zgrada.
apathetic *a* apatičan, ravnodušan.
apathy *n* apatija, ravnodušnost.
ape *n* majmun.
aperture *n* otvor.
apex *n* vrh.
aphorism *n* aforizam.
apiary *n* pčelinjak.
apiece *adv* svaki, po komadu.
aplomb *n* samopouzdanje.
apocalypse *n* apokalipsa.
apocrypha *npl* apokrifi.
apocryphal *a* apokrifan, lažni.
apologetic *a* apologičan, pomirljiv.
apologist *n* branilac; apologet.
apologize *v* izvinjavati, pravdati.
apology *n* izvinjenje, odbrana.
apoplexy *n* apopleksija, kap.
apostle *n* apostol, propovednik.
apostolic *a* apostolski.
apostrophe *n* apostrof; obraćanje.
apotheosis *n* apoteoza, obožavanje.
appal *v* zaplašiti, prestrašiti.
appalling *a* užasan.
apparatus *n* aparat, sprava, uređaj.

apparel *n* odeća, nošnja.
apparent *a* očigledan, jasan; ~ly *adv* izgleda, očevidno.
apparition *n* pojava; utvara, avet.
appeal *v* žaliti se, apelovati, moliti; *n* žalba, apelacija, proglas.
appealing *a* molećiv; privlačan.
appear *v* pojaviti se, istupiti.
appearance *n* pojava, izgled.
appease *v* umiriti, smiriti.
appellant *n* žalilac, podnosilac žalbe.
append *v* dodati, pripojiti.
appendage *n* dodatak, prilog.
appendicitis *n* apendicitis (*med*), zapaljenje slepog creva.
appendix *n* prilog, dodatak; slepo crevo (*med*).
appertain *v* pripadati, odnositi se.
appetite *n* apetit, ukus, želja.
appetizing *a* ukusan, privlačan.
applaud *v* pljeskati, pozdravljati, odobravati.
applause *n* aplauz.
apple *n* jabuka.
apple pie *n* pita s jabukama; in ~ order u potpunom redu.
apple tree *n* jabukovo drvo.
appliance *n* uređaj, sprava.
applicability *n* primenljivost.
applicable *a* primenljiv; prikladan.
applicant *n* kandidat, podnosilac molbe.
application *n* molba; predstavka; primena.
applied *a* primenjen.
apply *v* primeniti; odnositi se na.
appoint *v* odrediti; propisati; ustanoviti.
appointee *n* naimenovana osoba.
appointment *n* imenovanje; nalog; ugovoreni sastanak.
apportion *v* odmeriti, podjednako razdeliti.
apportionment *n* raspodela.
apposite *a* prikladan, prigodan.
apposition *n* apozicija (*gram*), imenski dodatak.
appraisal *n* procena, ocena.
appraise *v* proceniti, oceniti.
appreciable *a* osetan, merljiv; procenljiv.
appreciably *adv* primetno, osetno.
appreciate *v* ceniti; shvatiti; razumeti; biti zahvalan.

appreciation *n* priznanje, zahvalnost; razumevanje; povećanje vrednosti.
appreciative *a* zahvalan.
apprehend *v* zadržati, lišiti slobode; razumeti; strahovati.
apprehension *n* lišavanje slobode; moć shvatanja.
apprehensive *a* dovitljiv, oštrouman; pun predosećaja.
apprentice *n* učenik, šegrt; *v* dati na zanat.
apprenticeship *n* šegrtovanje.
apprise *v* visoko ceniti.
approach *v* približiti se; obratiti se nekom; *n* približavanje; prilaz; pristup.
approachable *a* pristupačan.
approbation *n* odobrenje, potvrda.
appropriate *v* prisvojiti; dodeliti; *a* prikladan, svojstven.
approval *n* odobrenje, pristanak.
approve (of) *v* odobriti.
approximate *v* približno odgovarati; *a* približan, sličan; ~ly *adv* slično.
approximation *n* približna vrednost.
apricot *n* kajsija.
April *n* april.
apron *n* kecelja.
apse *n* apsida, polukružni deo crkve.
apt *a* sposoban, vešt; podesan; ~ly *adv* pogodno, zgodno.
aptitude *n* sposobnost, sklonost.
aqualung *n* akvalung.
aquarium *n* akvarijum.
Aquarius *n* Vodolija (*astrol*).
aquatic *a* vodeni.
aqueduct *n* vodovod, akvadukt.
aquiline *a* orlovski.
arabesque *n* arabeska.
Arabic *a* arapski; arapski jezik.
arable *a* plodan, obradiv.
arbiter *n* arbitar, izabrani sudija, posrednik.
arbitrariness *n* proizvoljnost, arbitrarnost.
arbitrary *a* proizvoljno; samovoljno.
arbitrate *v* rešiti arbitražom.
arbitrator *n* arbitar.
arbour *n* senica u vrtu; vreteno, osovina.
arcade *n* arkada, zasvođeni hodnik.
arch *n* svod, luk; *a* lukav, prepreden.
archaeological *a* arheološki.

archaeologist *n* arheolog.
archaeology *n* arheologija.
archaic *a* arhaičan, starinski, zastareo.
archangel *n* arhanđeo.
archbishop *n* nadbiskup.
archbishopric *n* nadbiskupija.
archer *n* strelac, streličar.
archery *n* streljaštvo, streličarstvo.
architect *n* arhitekta.
architectural *a* arhitektonski.
architecture *n* arhitektura.
archives *npl* arhiva.
archivist *n* arhivista.
archly *adv* predemo, lukavo.
archway *n* nadsvođen prolaz.
arctic *a* polarni, severni.
ardent *a* vatren, strastven; ~ly *adv* strastveno.
ardour *n* vatrenost, žestina.
arduous *a* težak, naporan.
area *n* prostor, područje.
arena *n* arena, poprište borbi.
arguably *adv* sporno, koje se može osporiti.
argue *v* prepirati se; dokazati; ubediti.
argument *n* dokaz, argument; rasprava, diskusija.
argumentation *n* argumentacija.
argumentative *a* polemički.
aria *n* arija (*mus*).
arid *a* suv; neplodan; dosadan.
aridity *n* isušenost; nezanimljivost.
Aries *n* Ovan (*astrol*).
aright *adv* dobro; to set ~ ispraviti.
arise *v* naići; pojaviti se; ustati; uskrsnuti.
aristocracy *n* aristokratija, plemstvo.
aristocrat *n* aristokrat.
aristocratic *a* aristokratski.
arithmetic *n* aritmetika.
arithmetical *a* aritmetički; ~ly *adv* aritmetički.
ark *n* kovčeg.
arm *n* ruka, drška, grana; *v* naoružati (se).
armament *n* naoružanje, oružane snage.
armchair *n* naslonjača.
armed *a* naoružan; utvrđen.
armful *n* naručje, naramak, pregršt.
armhole *n* otvor za rukav.
armistice *n* primirje, prestanak neprijateljstva.
armour *n* oklop, oklopne jedinice.

armoured car *n* oklopna kola.
armoury *n* arsenal, stovarište oružja.
armpit *n* pazuho.
armrest *n* naslon za ruke.
army *n* vojska; *a* vojni.
aroma *n* aroma.
aromatherapy *n* aromaterapija.
aromatic *a* aromatičan, mirisan.
around *prep* oko, otprilike; *adv* približno, oko.
arouse *v* buditi, probuditi; izazvati.
arraign *v* optužiti, podneti tužbu; prigovarati.
arraignment *n* optužba.
arrange *v* pripremiti, prirediti, spremiti.
arrangement *n* uređenje, sređenje.
arrant *a* zao, ozloglašen.
array *n* red, stroj, poredak.
arrears *npl* dugovi; svršetak, rep.
arrest *n* hapšenje, zatvaranje; *v* hapsiti, zadržati.
arrival *n* dolazak.
arrive *v* doći, prispeti.
arrogance *n* osionost, arogancija.
arrogant *a* arogantan, osion.
arrogate *v* prisvojiti.
arrogation *n* prisvajanje (bespravno).
arrow *n* strela, strelica.
arsenal *n* arsenal, skladište oružja.
arsenic *n* arsen.
arson *n* paljevina (namerna).
art *n* umetnost; zanat; veština.
art gallery *n* umetnička galerija.
arterial *a* arterijski.
artery *n* arterija (*med*).
artesian well *n* arterski bunar.
artful *a* vešt; lukav.
artfulness *n* veština.
arthritis *n* artritis.
artichoke *n* artičoka.
article *n* predmet, artikal; članak; član.
articulate *v* razgovetan, jasan.
articulated *a* jasan, artikulisan.
articulation *n* artikulacija; zglob, zglavak.
artifice *n* lukavstvo, smicalica; veština.
artificial *a* veštačko; ~**ly** *adv* veštački.
artificial insemination *n* veštačko osemenjavanje.
artillery *n* artiljerija.

artisan *n* majstor, zanatlija.
artist *n* umetnik, slikar, glumac.
artistic *a* umetnički.
artistry *n* umešnost.
artless *a* neizveštačen, jednostavan; ~**ly** *adv* prirodno, jednostavno.
artlessness *n* naivnost, jednostavnost.
as *conj* kada; pošto, ukoliko; mada; ~ **for** što se tiče; ~ **to** u pogledu.
asbestos *n* azbest.
ascend *v* penjati se, dizati, uzleteti.
ascendancy *n* nadmoć, dominacija.
ascension *n* penjanje ; Vaznesenje.
ascent *n* penjanje; napredovanje.
ascertain *v* ustanoviti, razjasniti.
ascetic *a* asketski; *n* asketa.
ascribe *v* pripisati.
ash *n* jasen (*bot*); *pl* pepeo, prah.
Ash Wednesday *n* Čista Sreda (*rel*).
ashamed *a* postiđen.
ashore *adv* na obali, ka obali; **to go** ~ iskrcati se.
ashtray *n* pepeljara.
aside *adv* na stranu, po strani.
ask *v* pitati, tražiti; moliti; **to** ~ **after** pitati o; **to** ~ **for** zamoliti; **to** ~ **out** pozvati na izlazak.
askance *adv* podozrivo; iskosa.
askew *adv* krivo, koso.
asleep *a* usnuo, pospan; **to fall** ~ zaspati.
asparagus *n* špargla.
aspect *n* gledište, izgled, pogled.
aspen *n* jasika (*bot*).
aspersion *n* kleveta; prskanje.
asphalt *n* asfalt.
asphyxia *n* zagušenje (*med*).
asphyxiate *v* zagušiti, ugušiti.
aspirant *n* kandidat, pripravnik.
aspirate *v* usisavati (*teh*); izgovarati sa aspiracijom; *n* aspirata, suglasnik sa aspiracijom.
aspiration *n* težnja, želja, aspiracija; usisavanje (*teh*).
aspire *v* žudeti, težiti.
aspirin *n* aspirin.
ass *n* magarac, glupak; **she** ~ magarica.
assail *v* saletati; vršiti napad.
assailant *n* napadač, neprijatelj.
assassin *n* ubica (plaćeni).
assassinate *v* ubiti.
assassination *n* ubistvo.

assault *n* napad, juriš, pretnja; *v* napadati, jurišati.
assemblage *n* skup, zbor.
assemble *v* okupiti, sazvati; montirati.
assembly *n* skupština, zasedanje skupštine; montiranje.
assembly line *n* montažna traka.
assent *n* pristanak; *v* pristati, dati saglasnost.
assert *v* tvrditi, dokazivati.
assertion *n* dokazivanje, tvrđenje; zaštita svojih prava.
assertive *a* izričan, uporan.
assess *v* proceniti, odmeriti.
assessment *n* procena, oporezivanje.
assessor *n* oporezivač, sudski pomoćnik.
assets *npl* aktiva, imovina.
assiduous *a* marljiv, usrdan; **~ly** *adv* marljivo, istrajno.
assign *v* odrediti, dodeliti, nameniti.
assignation *n* sastanak (randevu), zadatak.
assignment *n* određivanje, namena, dodela.
assimilate *v* prilagoditi, asimilovati.
assimilation *n* asimilacija, pretapanje.
assist *v* pomagati, učestvovati.
assistance *n* pomoć, podrška.
assistant *n* pomoćnik , zamenik, asistent.
associate *v* udružiti se, ujediniti se; *a* spojen, povezan, udružen; *n* pomoćnik, kolega, drug.
association *n* društvo, udruženje, drugarstvo.
assonance *n* asonanca.
assorted *a* raznovrstan, sortiran.
assortment *n* asortiman, izbor.
assuage *v* umiriti, ublažiti, utoliti.
assume *v* pretpostaviti, preuzeti, predstavljati se kao.
assumption *n* pretpostavka, preuzimanje na sebe.
Assumption *n* Velika Gospojina (*rel*), Bogorodičino Vaznesenje.
assurance *n* uveravanje, obećanje, jemstvo.
assure *v* uveriti, obećati, zajamčiti.
assuredly *adv* nesumnjivo, sigurno.
asterisk *n* zvezdica, znak.
astern *a, adv* na krmi, prema krmi.
asthma *n* astma.

asthmatic *a* astmatičan.
astonish *v* začuditi, zadiviti.
astonishing *a* zadivljujući; **~ly** *adv* začuđujući.
astonishment *n* čuđenje, divljenje.
astound *v* zaprepastiti.
astray *adv* zalutao; **to go ~** zalutati; **to lead ~** dovesti u zabludu.
astride *adv* opkoračke.
astringent *a* koji steže; jedak, zajedljiv.
astrologer *n* astrolog.
astrological *a* astrološki.
astrology *n* astrologija.
astronaut *n* astronaut.
astronomer *n* astronom.
astronomical *a* astronomski.
astronomy *n* astronomija.
astute *a* pronicljiv, lukav.
asylum *n* azil, utočište.
at *prep* kod, na, u; **~ once** odmah; **~ all** uopšte; **~ all events** u svakom slučaju; **~ first** prvo; **~ last** najzad.
atheism *n* ateizam.
atheist *n* ateista.
athlete *n* atletičar, sportista.
athletic *a* atletski, sportski.
atlas *n* atlas.
atmosphere *n* atmosfera.
atmospheric *a* atmosferski.
atom *n* atom.
atom bomb *n* atomska bomba.
atomic *a* atomski.
atone *v* popraviti; okajati.
atonement *n* ispaštanje, izmirenje.
atrocious *a* grozan, loš, užasan; **~ly** *adv* užasno, strašno.
atrocity *n* zverstvo, grozota.
atrophy *n* atrofija (*med*).
attach *v* pričvrstiti, privezati, pripojiti.
attache *n* ataše.
attachment *n* prilog; pričvršćivanje; odanost, privrženost.
attack *v* napadati, jurišati; *n* napad.
attacker *n* napadač.
attain *v* postići, dobiti.
attainable *a* dostižan.
attempt *v* pokušati, preduzeti; napasti; *n* pokušaj, poduhvat; napad, atentat.
attend *v* pohađati, prisustvovati; obraćati pažnju; **to ~ to** postarati se za nešto.

attendance *n* prisutnost, posećivanje; nega.

attendant *n* sluga, čuvar.

attention *n* pažnja; briga; nega.

attentive *a* pažljiv, brižljiv, učtiv; ~ly *adv* uslužno, pažljivo.

attenuate *v* razblažiti, istanjiti.

attest *v* svedočiti, potvrditi.

attic *n* tavan, mansarda.

attire *n* odeća, nošnja.

attitude *n* stanovište, stav, odnos.

attorney *n* advokat, zastupnik.

attract *v* privlačiti, privući, mamiti.

attraction *n* privlačnost.

attractive *a* privlačan.

attribute *v* pripisati; *n* osobina, karakteristika; atribut (*gram*).

attrition *n* trenje; iscrpljivanje.

au pair *n*. osoba koja čuva decu (za stan i hranu i pritom uči jezik).

auburn *a* kestenjaste boje.

auction *n* aukcija, javna prodaja.

auctioneer *n* voditelj aukcije.

audacious *a* hrabar, drzak; ~ly *adv* odvažno, drsko.

audacity *n* hrabrost, drskost.

audible *a* čujan, razgovetan.

audibly *adv* zvučno, čujno.

audience *n* publika, slušaoci, gledaoci; audijencija, prijem.

audit *n* revizija (finansijska), poreska kontrola; *v* pregledati knjige, izvršiti reviziju.

auditor *n* revizor, kontrolor.

auditory *a* slušni.

augment *v* povećati.

augmentation *n* povećanje, augmentacija (*ling*).

August *n* avgust.

august *a* dostojanstven, veličanstven.

aunt *n* tetka, ujna, strina.

aura *n* aura.

auspices *npl* predznak, predviđenje.

auspicious *a* povoljan; ~ly *adv* srećno.

austere *a* strog, surov; asketski; ~ly *adv* strogo.

austerity *n* strogost, uzdržljivost; škrtost.

authentic *a* autentičan.

aunthentically *adv* autentično.

authenticate *v* potvrditi.

authenticity *n* autentičnost.

author *n* autor, pisac, tvorac.

authoress *n* autorka.

authoritarian *a* koji traži poslušnost.

authoritative *a* autoritativan; ~ly *adv* autoritativno.

authority *n* autoritet; stručnjak; uprava; punomoćje.

authorization *n* ovlašćenje, dozvola.

authorize *v* ovlastiti.

authorship *n* autorstvo.

autocrat *n* autokrata.

autocratic *a* autokratski.

autograph *n* autograf.

automated *a* automatizovan.

automatic *a* automatski.

automation *n* automatizacija.

autonomy *n* autonomija.

autopsy *n* autopsija.

autumn *n* jesen.

autumnal *a* jesenji.

auxiliary *a* pomoćni.

avail *v* koristiti, služiti; **to ~ oneself of** iskoristiti nešto; *adv* **to no ~** uzalud, beskorisno.

available *a* dostupan, na raspolaganju.

avalanche *n* lavina, bujica.

avarice *n* pohlepa.

avaricious *a* pohlepan, škrt.

avenge *v* svetiti se; osvetiti.

avenue *n* avenija, put, prilaz, ulica.

aver *v* tvrditi, izjaviti.

average *v* izračunati prosečan broj; *n* prosečan broj, prosek, obračun štete.

aversion *n* odvratnost, antipatija.

avert *v* odvratiti, skrenuti; sprečiti.

aviary *n* kavez za ptice.

avoid *v* izbegavati, poništiti.

avoidable *a* izbežljiv, koji se može izbeći.

await *v* čekati, očekivati.

awake *v* buditi, probuditi; *a* budan, svestan.

awakening *n* buđenje.

award *v* dodeljivanje nagrade; *n* nagrada; kazna.

aware *a* svestan.

awareness *n* svesnost.

away *adv* od , udaljeno; **far and ~** daleko.

awe *n* strahopoštovanje.

awesome, awe-inspiring *a* koji uliva strahopoštovanjem.

awful *a* strašan, užasan, grozan; veliki;
~**ly** *adv* strašno.
awhile *adv* kratko vreme, za neko vreme.
awkward *a* nezgrapan, nespretan;
nezgodan; ~**ly** *adv* nespretno, nezgodno.
awkwardness *n* nezgrapnost, nespretnost,
nezgodan položaj.
awl *n* šilo.

awning *n* nadstrešnica (od cirade).
awry *adv* kriv, izobličen; pogrešan.
axe *n* sekira; **to get the** ~biti otpušten s
posla.
axiom *n* aksioma, činjenica.
axis *n* osovina, osa.
axle *n* osovina (*teh*).
ay(e) *excl* da, jeste, potvrdan odgovor.

B

baa *n* blejanje; *v* blejati.
babble *v* brbljanje, romor, mrmor.
babbler *n* brbljivac.
babe, baby *n* novorođenče, odojče, beba;
  naivko.
baboon *n* pavijan; grub čovek.
baby carriage *n* kolica za bebe.
baby sitter *n* lice koje čuva decu.
babyish *a* detinjast.
bachelor *n* neženja; akademski stupanj,
  bakaleureat.
back *n* leđa; naslon; pozadina; *adv*
  pozadi, natrag, pre nečega; **a few years**
  ~ pre nekoliko godina; *v* podržati.
backbite *v* ogovarati.
backbiter *n* ogovarač.
backbone *n* kičma, oslonac.
back breaking *a* zamoran.
back door *n* stražnja vrata; *a* zakulisan.
backer *n* zaštitnik, podržavalac.
backgammon *n* trik trak, igra s kockama.
background *n* pozadina, zaleđe.
backlash *n* jaka reakcija; zazor, mrtvi hod
  (*teh*).
backlog *n* zalihe, rezerve; zaostatak
  (nezavršenog posla).
back number *n* stari broj časopisa.
backpack *n* ranac, ruksak.
backside *n* zadnji deo, zadnjica.
back stroke *n* leđni stil plivanja.
backward *a* obrnut unazad, suprotan;
  zaostao; ~**ly** *adv* natrag, unazad.
bacon *n* slanina, bekon.
bad *a* loš, rđav; bolestan; štetan;
  pokvaren; ~**ly** *adv* loše, pokvareno.
badge *n* značka, oznaka.
badger *n* jazavac; *v* ugnjaviti, navaliti.
badminton *n* badminton.
badness *n* zlo, pokvarenost.
baffle *v* zbuniti; pregraditi (*teh*).
bag *n* torba, tašna, kesa.
baggage *n* prtljag.
bagpipe *n* gajde.
bail *n* kaucija, jemstvo; vedro, ispolac; *v*
  jemčiti, položiti kauciju.
bailiff *n* sudski izvršitelj; upravnik
  imanja.

bait *v* primamiti, dražiti; zadirkivati; *n*
  mamac.
baize *n* gruba vunena tkanina.
bake *v* ispeći, peći.
baker *n* pekar; ~**'s dozen** 13 komada.
bakery *n* pekara.
baking *n* pečenje.
baking powder *n* prašak za pecivo.
balance *n* vaga, terazije; ravnoteža;
  bilans; **to lose one's** ~ izgubiti
  ravnotežu; *v* uravnotežiti; saldirati;
  balansirati.
balance sheet *n* bilans stanja.
balcony *n* balkon, terasa.
bald *a* ćelav.
baldness *n* ćelavost.
bale *n* bala, denjak; *v* pakovati u bale.
baleful *a* štetan; ~**ly** *adv* štetno.
ball *n* lopta, zrno; klupko.
ballad *n* balada.
ballast *n* balast, teret.
ballerina *n* balerina.
ballet *n* balet.
ballistic *a* balistički.
balloon *n* balon, aerostat.
ballot *n* glasački listić, glasačka kutija; *v*
  glasati.
ballpoint (pen) *n* hemijska olovka.
ballroom *n* balska dvorana.
balm, balsam *n* melem, balsam.
balmy *a* lekovit; mirisav; mek, nežan.
balustrade *n* balustrada.
bamboo *n* bambus.
bamboozle *v* prevariti.
ban *n* zabrana, progonstvo; *v* prognati.
banal *a* banalan.
banana *n* banana.
band *n* traka, pantljika; opseg; družina,
  banda.
bandage *n* zavoj; *v* zaviti.
bandit *n* bandit.
bandstand *n* podijum za orkestar.
bandy *v* izmenjati; raznositi.
bandy-legged *a* kriv.
bang *n* tresak, lupnjava; *v* lupiti, udariti.
bangle *n* grivna.
bangs *npl* šiške.

banish v prognati, proterati; otkloniti.
banishment n progonstvo.
banister(s) n(pl) ograda na stepeništu.
banjo n bendžo.
bank n banka; nasip; obala; grupa;
naslaga; v uložiti, poslovati s bankom;
to ~ on računati na.
bank account n bankovni račun.
bank clerk n bankarski činovnik.
banker n bankar.
banking n bankarstvo; **electronic ~**
elektronsko bankarstvo.
banknote n banknota.
bankrupt a bankrotiran; n bankrot.
bankruptcy n bankrotstvo.
bank statement n stanje bankovnog
računa.
banner n zastava, barjak.
banquet n banket.
banter n šala, zadirkivanje.
baptism n krštenje.
baptismal a kršten.
baptistery n krstionica.
baptize v krstiti.
bar n šipka, pregrada; prepreka; tabla;
advokatska komora; kafana, bar, šank; v
zatvoriti rezom; pregraditi, zabraniti.
bar code n bar kod.
barbarian n varvarin; a varvarski.
barbarism n varvarizam (ling).
barbarity n varvarstvo; okrutnost,
svirepost.
barbarous a varvarski; svirep.
barbecue n roštilj; meso pečeno na roštilju.
barber n berberin; muški frizer.
barber's shop n berbernica.
bard n bard, pevač, pesnik.
bare a nag, go; prazan; v razgoliti, otkriti.
barefaced a golobrad; bezočan, drzak.
barefoot(ed) a bos, bosonog.
bareheaded a gologlav.
barelegged a golih nogu.
barely adv jedva.
bareness n golotinja; praznoća.
bargain n pogodba, dobar posao; v
pogađati se, cenjkati; **to ~ for** očekivati.
barge n barža, dereglija.
baritone n bariton.
bark n lavež; kora od drveta; v lajati.
barley n ječam.
barmaid n kelnerica.

barman n barmen.
barn n ambar, žitnica.
barnacles npl naočare.
barometer n barometar.
baron n baron.
baroness n baronica.
baronial a baronski; veličanstven.
barracks npl kasarna, baraka.
barrage n brana; baraž (voj).
barrel n bure; cev vatrenog oružja.
barrel organ n mehaničke orgulje.
barren a neplodan, jalov; oskudan.
barricade n barikada; zapreka; v
zabarikadirati, preprečiti.
barrier n prepreka, pregrada, barijera;
brana.
barring adv osim, sem.
barrow n ručna kolica; brežuljak.
bartender n barmen.
barter v trampa, razmena; v trampiti,
razmeniti.
base n osnova, temelj; baza (hem); baza
(voj); a osnovni; nizak; pokvaren; v
zasnovati, bazirati.
baseball n bezbol, lopta za bezbol.
baseless a bestemeljan.
basement n podrum.
baseness n niskost, nedostojnost,
pokvarenost.
bash v udariti, tresnuti.
bashful a stidljiv, snebivljiv; **~ly** adv
stidljivo.
basic a osnovni, glavni; bazični; **~ally** adv
osnovno.
basil n bosiljak.
basin n sud, umivaonik, lavor; bazen.
basis n osnova, osnov, razlog.
bask v grejati se; uživati.
basket n korpa, kotarica; koš.
basketball n košarka.
bass n bas, basista.
bass drum n veliki bubanj.
bassoon n fagot.
bastard n kopile, vanbračno dete; kučkin
sin.
baste v preliti, naliti.
basting n prelivanje.
bastion n bastion (voj); bedem; hram
(fig).
bat n štap; slepi miš (zool); v jak udarac.
batch n gomila, serija, količina.

bath *n* kupanje, kada.
bathe *v* okupati se.
bathing suit *n* kupaći kostim.
bathos *n* antiklimaks, najniža tačka.
bathroom *n* kupatilo; nužnik.
baths (spa) *n* kupke.
bathtub *n* kada za kupanje.
baton *n* palica.
battalion *n* bataljon.
batter *v* udariti, tući, rušiti.
battering ram *n* ovan (*voj*).
battery *n* baterija (*voj*); baterija, akumulator; telesna povreda.
battle *n* borba, bitka, operacija; *v* boriti se.
battle array *n* borbeni poredak.
battlefield *n* bojište, bojno polje.
battlement *n* grudobran.
battleship *n* bojni brod.
bawdy *a* nepristojan, skaredan.
bawl *v* viknuti, derati se.
bay *n* zaliv; odeljenje; udubljenje; lavež; *v* lajati.
bay window *n* prozor na zatvorenom balkonu.
bayonet *n* bajonet.
bazaar *n* pijaca, bazar, čaršija.
be *v* biti, postojati; biti prisutan.
beach *n* obala, plaža.
beacon *n* svetionik; opomena.
bead *n* perla, zrnce; *pl* niska.
beagle *n* zečar.
beak *n* kljun, nos.
beaker *n* pehar.
beam *n* greda, balvan; snop, zrak, mlaz; *v* usmeriti, upraviti.
bean *n* pasulj, grah, bob; **green ~, French ~** boranija.
bear *v* nositi, snositi; roditi; podneti; držati se.
bear *n* medved; **she ~** medvedica.
bearable *a* snošljiv, podnošljiv.
beard *n* brada.
bearded *a* bradat.
bearer *n* nosač, nosilac; donosilac.
bearing *n* držanje; ležište; odnos.
beast *n* životinja, zver; **~ of burden** tovarna životinja.
beastliness *n* zverstvo, gadost.
beastly *a* životinjski, zverski; gadan; *adv* strašno, užasno.

beat *v* izbiti, istući, udariti, pobediti; **to be beaten** pretrpeti poraz; *v* lupiti; *n* udarac, otkucaj.
beatific *a* blažen.
beatify *v* proglasiti blaženim.
beating *n* tuča, bijenje, kucanje; poraz.
beatitude *n* blaženstvo.
beautiful *a* lep; **~ly** *adv* lepo.
beautify *v* ulepšati.
beauty *n* lepota, lepotica; **~ salon** frizerska radnja; **~ spot** veštački mladež.
beaver *n* dabar.
because *conj* jer, zbog.
beckon *v* dati znak, prizvati rukom.
become *v* postati, nastati; dolikovati.
becoming *a* pristojan, zgodan, privlačan.
bed *n* krevet, postelja.
bedclothes *npl* krevetsko rublje.
bedding *n* krevetsko rublje (dušek, jastuk itd.); prostirka; naslaga.
bedecked *a* okićen, ukrašen.
bedlam *n* urnebes, ludnica.
bedpost *n* noga od kreveta.
bedridden *a* prikovan za krevet.
bedroom *n* spavaća soba.
bedspread *n* krevetski pokrivač, ćebe.
bedtime *n* vreme za spavanje.
bee *n* pčela; moba.
beech *n* bukva.
beefburger *n* ćufte od govedine; hamburger.
beefsteak *n* biftek.
beehive *n* košnica.
beeline *n* najkraći put.
beer *n* pivo.
beeswax *n* vosak.
beet *n* cvekla, repa.
beetroot *n* blitva.
beetle *n* buba; drveni tučak, malj.
befall *v* zadesiti, postići.
befit *v* dolikovati.
before *adv/prep* pre, ranije, ispred; napred; već.
beforehand *adv* ranije.
befriend *v* sprijateljiti se.
beg *v* preklinjati, moliti; prosjačiti, tražiti milostinju.
beget *v* roditi, stvoriti.
beggar *n* prosjak.
begin *v* početi, započeti.
beginner *n* početnik, novajlija.

beginning n početak.
begrudge v zavideti.
behalf n korist; **on ~ of** u ime nekoga.
behave v ponašati se, vladati se, postupati.
behaviour n ponašanje, vladanje.
behead v odseći glavu.
behind prep iza, pozadi; adv zaostao, zakasnio.
behold v posmatrati, pogledati.
behove v biti potreban.
beige a bež boja.
being n biće; postojanje.
belated a zakasneo.
belch v bljuvati; podrignuti; izbaciti.
belfry n zvonik.
belie v protivrečiti, lažno predstaviti.
belief n vera, uverenje, ubeđenje.
believable a verodostojan.
believe v verovati.
believer n vernik.
belittle v omalovažiti.
bell n zvono, zvonce.
bellicose a ratoboran.
belligerent a zaraćen, ratoboran.
bellow v vikati, derati se; n rika, mukanje, urlik.
bellows npl mehovi.
belly n trbuh, stomak, utroba.
bellyful n dovoljna količina jela.
belong v pripadati.
belongings npl svojina, lične stvari, pokretni imetak.
beloved a voljen, omiljen.
below adv/prep dole, niže, ispod, pod.
belt n pojas, kaiš, remen; zona.
bemoan v oplakati.
bemused a zadubljen (u misli).
bench n klupa; mesto sudije; mesto u skupštini.
bend v saviti, poviti, pognuti, iskriviti; n krivina, okuka, luk.
beneath adv/prep ispod, pod, niže.
benediction n blagoslov.
benefactor n dobrotvor, mecena.
benefice n korist, prihod.
beneficent a dobrotvoran, blagotvoran.
beneficial a koristan, dobrotvoran.
beneficiary n korisnik.
benefit n korist, naknada; v koristiti.
benefit night n predstava u pozorištu u korist nekog glumca.

benevolence n blagonaklonost, dobročinstvo.
benevolent a blagonaklon, dobrotvoran, dobronameran.
benign a blag, dobar, blagotvoran.
bent n sklonost.
benzine n benzin.
bequeath v zaveštati.
bequest n zaveštanje, zaostavština.
bereave v lišiti, oduzeti, ucveliti.
bereavement n žalost.
beret n beretka.
berm n bankina, nasip.
berry n bobica.
berserk a lud.
berth n krevet u kabini, mesto; sidrište.
beseech v preklinjati, moliti.
beset v saletati, opsedati; nasekirati.
beside(s) prep pored; osim, sem; adv uostalom, uz to, sem toga.
besiege v opsedati, saletati.
best a najbolji; adv najbolji; n ono što je najbolje.
bestial a životinjski, zverski; **~ly** adv zversko.
bestiality n zverstvo, bestijalnost.
bestow v pokloniti, darovati, dodeliti.
bestseller n bestseler.
bet n opklada; v opkladiti se, kladiti se.
betray v izdati, odati, prevariti.
betrayal n izdaja.
betroth v veriti se, zaručiti.
betrothal n veridba.
better a/adv bolje; **so much the ~** utoliko bolje; v poboljšati, nadmašiti.
betting n klađenje.
between prep između, među.
bevel n kosina; uglomer.
beverage n piće.
bevy n jato; grupa, skup.
beware v čuvati se.
bewilder v zbuniti.
bewilderment n zbunjenost.
bewitch v začarati.
beyond prep posle, izvan, van, iznad, preko.
bias n pristrasnost, predrasuda; kosa linija.
bib n portikla.
Bible n biblija.
biblical a biblijski.
bibliography n bibliografija.

bicarbonate of soda *n* soda bikarbona.
bicker *v* prepirati se, svađati.
bicycle *n* bicikl.
bid *v* ponuditi, poželeti; narediti;
  nadmetati se; *n* ponuda; pokušaj.
bidding *n* učestvovanje na licitaciji,
  podnošenje ponuda; naredba, molba.
bide *v* čekati.
biennial *a* dvogodišnji.
bifocals *npl* bifokalna stakla.
bifurcated *a* račvast, razdvojen.
big *a* veliki, krupan, ogroman.
bigamist *n* bigamista, dvoženac.
bigamy *n* bigamija, dvoženstvo.
Big Dipper *n* Veliki medved (*astrol*).
bigheaded *a* uobražen.
bigness *n* veličina.
bigot *n* fanatik, bigot, čovek pun
  predrasuda.
bigoted *a* netrpeljiv.
bike *n* bicikl.
bikini *n* bikini.
bilberry *n* borovnica.
bile *n* žuč.
bilingual *a* dvojezičan, bilingvalan.
bilious *a* žučni.
bill *n* račun; plakat, oglas; novčanica;
  isprava.
billboard *n* reklamna tabla, bilbord.
billet *n* stan, konak; nalog za smeštaj
  (*voj*).
billiards *npl* bilijar.
billiard-table *n* sto za bilijar.
billion *n* bilion (*br*), milijarda (*am*).
bin *n* bunker; ograđeno mesto; podrumska
  prostorija; kanta za đubre.
bind *v* vezati, zaviti; obavezati.
binder *n* vezilac; knjigovezac; kapara,
  kaucija, garantni iznos.
binding *n* vezivanje, spajanje, povez, vez.
binge *n* pijanka, terevenka.
bingo *n* tombola (jedna vrsta).
binoculars *npl* dvogled, durbin.
biochemistry *n* biohemija.
biodegradable *a* koji se raspada
  bakteriološkim putem.
biographer *n* biograf.
biographical *a* biografski.
biography *n* biografija.
biological *a* biološki.
biology *n* biologija.

biped *n* dvonog.
birch *n* breza.
bird *n* ptica; devojka (*sleng*).
bird's-eye-view *n* ptičja perspektiva.
bird-watcher *n* posmatrač ptica.
birth *n* rađanje, porođaj; loza, poreklo.
birth certificate *n* izvod iz matične
  knjige rođenih, krštenica.
birth control *n* kontrola rađanja.
birthday *n* rođendan.
birthplace *n* mesto rođenja.
birthright *n* pravo prvorođenog.
biscuit *n* biskvit, dvopek, suvo pecivo.
bisect *v* račvati se, prepoloviti.
bishop *n* biskup, episkop.
bison *n* bizon.
bit *n* komadić, mala količina; novčić.
bitch *n* kuja; zla žena.
bite *v* ujesti, ugristi, grickati; **to ~ the**
  dust poginuti u boju; *n* ujed, ubod;
  zalogaj; meze.
bitter *a* gorak, ogorčen, ljut, oštar; **~ly**
  adv gorko, oštro.
bitterness *n* gorčina.
bitumen *n* bitumen.
bizarre *a* bizaran, čudan.
blab *v* brbljati, izbrbljati; nagovoriti.
black *a* crn, crne boje; *n* crna boja,
  crnina; crnac.
blackberry *n* kupina.
blackbird *n* kos.
blackboard *n* školska tabla.
black box *n* crna kutija.
blacken *v* pocrniti, ocrniti; pocrneti.
black ice *n* nevidljiva poledica.
blackjack *n* vrsta kartaške igre; ručno
  napadačko oružje.
blackleg *n* štrajkbreher, razbijač štrajka;
  lopov; crni prišt.
black list *n* crna lista.
blackmail *n* ucena; *v* uceniti.
black market *n* crna berza.
blackness *n* tmina, crnilo, mrak.
black pudding *n* krvavica.
black sheep *n* crna ovca; nevaljalac.
blacksmith *n* kovač, potkivač.
blackthorn *n* crni trn, crni glog.
bladder *n* bešika, mehur.
blade *n* sečivo, oštrica; list; mač.
blame *v* okriviti, kriviti nekoga; *n* krivica;
  odgovornost.

blameless *a* besprekoran; **~ly** *adv*
  besprekorno; bez krivice.
blanch *v* izbledeti, pobledeti.
bland *a* blag, učtiv.
blank *a* prazan, bezizrazan; tup; *n*
  praznina; obrazac.
blank cheque *n* blanko ček, neispunjen
  ček.
blanket *n* ćebe, pokrivač.
blare *v* rastrubiti, treštati.
blase *a* blaziran, zasićen.
blaspheme *v* huliti, bogohuliti.
blasphemous *a* bogohulan.
blasphemy *n* bogohuljenje.
blast *n* eksplozija, udar vetra; strujanje; *v*
  porušiti, uništiti, srušiti.
blast-off *n* lansiranje.
blatant *a* drečav; javan; očigledan.
blaze *n* plamen, požar; blesak; *v* blesnuti,
  planuti.
bleach *v* beleti, obeliti; *n* belilo.
bleached *a* izbledeo; bezbojan.
bleachers *npl* nepokrivene tribine.
bleak *a* pust; mračan, turoban.
bleakness *n* mrak, tmina, pustoća.
bleary *a* mutan; **~~eyed** krmeljivih očiju.
bleat *n* blejanje; *v* blejati.
bleed *v* krvariti, ispustiti krv.
bleeding *n* krvarenje, puštanje krvi.
bleep *v* pištati (kao signal), škripati.
blemish *v* oštetiti, pokvariti; *n* mana,
  nedostatak.
blend *v* pomešati; *n* mešavina.
bless *v* blagosloviti.
blight *v* razoriti, upropastiti.
blind *a* slep, ćorav; **~ alley** ćorsokak; *v*
  oslepeti, zaslepeti; *n* slepac; prevara;
  žaluzina; **Venetian ~** roletna.
blinders *npl* naočnjaci.
blindfold *v* povezati oči; *a* vezanih očiju.
blindly *adv* slepo.
blindness *n* slepilo.
blind side *n* slepa mrlja.
blind spot *n* slepa mrlja.
blink *v* trepnuti, treperiti, svetlucati.
blinkers *npl* trepćuće svetlo, mačje oči.
bliss *n* blaženstvo, sreća.
blissful *a* blažen, srećan; **~ly** *adv* srećno.
blissfulness *n* blaženost.
blister *n* plik, mehur; *v* izazvati plikove.
blitz *n* bombardovanje (iznenadno).

blizzard *n* mećava.
bloated *a* nadut, naduven.
blob *n* grudvica, gromuljica.
bloc *n* blok (*polit*).
block *n* panj, klada; blok; ulica; kocka;
  ~ (up) *v* preprečiti, blokirati.
blockade *n* blokada; *v* blokirati.
blockage *n* blokiranje, zapušavanje.
blockbuster *n* jaka bomba (*fig*).
blockhead *n* glupan; panj; klada.
blond *a* plav, plavokos; *n* plavokos
  muškarac, plavuša.
blood *n* krv.
blood donor *n* davalac krvi.
blood group *n* krvna grupa.
bloodhound *n* pas tragač.
bloodily *adv* krvavo, prokleto.
bloodiness *n* svirepost (*fig*).
bloodless *a* beskrvan, bez krvoprolića.
blood poisoning *n* trovanje krvi.
blood pressure *n* krvni pritisak.
bloodshed *n* krvoprolíće.
bloodshot *a* zakrvavljen.
bloodstream *n* krvotok.
bloodsucker *n* krvopija, pijavica,
  gulikoža.
blood test *n* ispitivanje krvi.
bloodthirsty *a* krvožedan.
blood transfusion *n* transfuzija krvi.
blood vessel *n* krvni sud.
bloody *a* krvav, proklet; **~ minded** *a*
  odbojan, svadljiv.
bloom *n* cvet; *v* cvetati.
blossom *n* cvet, cvetanje.
blot *v* umrljati, iskrmačiti; *n* mrlja, ljaga.
blotchy *a* uprljano.
blotting paper *n* upijač.
blouse *n* bluza.
blow *v* duvati, trubiti, zviždati; **to ~ up**
  dići u vazduh; zapaliti; *n* udarac.
blowout *n* eksplozija.
blowpipe *n* duvaljka.
blubber *n* kitova mast; *v* jecati, plakati.
bludgeon *n* batina.
blue *a* plav.
blue blood *n* plemić, plava krv.
bluecoat *n* policajac (*sleng*).
bluebell (harebell) *n* zvončić, divlji
  zumbul.
blueprint *n* shematski plan.
bluff *n* blef, obmana; blefirati.

bluish *a* plavičast.
blunder *n* velika greška; *v* pogrešiti.
blunt *a* tup; iskren, otvoren; *v* zatupiti.
bluntly *adv* otvoreno, bez uvijanja.
bluntness *n* tupost, nabusitost.
blur *n* zamagljenost; *v* zamagliti, zamutiti.
blurt out *v* izbrbljati, izvaliti.
blush *n* rumen; *v* porumeneti, pocrveneti.
blustery *a* hvalisavo.
boa *n* boa, zmija.
boar *n* vepar; **wild** ~ divlji vepar.
board *n* tabla, daska; ishrana; komisija, odbor; *v* ukrcati se; obložiti daskama; hraniti se.
boarder *n* podstanar.
boarding card (pass) *n* karta za ulazak u avion.
boarding house *n* pansion.
boarding school *n* internat.
boast *v* hvalisati se, razmetati se; *n* hvalisanje.
boastful *a* hvalisav, razmetljiv.
boat *n* čamac, brod.
boating *n* vožnja čamcem; veslanje.
bobsleigh *n* bob.
bode *v* slutiti, predosetiti.
bodice *n* prsluk, gornji deo ženske haljine.
bodily *a/adv* telesni; u potpunosti, u celini.
body *n* telo; leš; trup aviona; **any~** bilo ko; **every~** svako, svi.
body-building *n* bodibilding.
bodyguard *n* telohranitelj, telesna straža.
bodywork *n* autolimarski poslovi.
bog *n* močvara.
boggy *a* močvarno.
bogus *a* lažan.
boil *v* skuvati, prokuvati; ključati; *n* ključanje; čir.
boiled egg *n* bareno (kuvano) jaje.
boiler *n* kotao, kazan; bojler.
boiling point *n* tačka ključanja.
boisterous *a* buran, bučan; ~ **ly** *adv* žestoko, burno.
bold *a* hrabar, odvažan, samopouzdan; **~ly** *adv* smelo, odvažno.
boldness *n* hrabrost; bestidnost.
bolster *n* jastuk, podloga; *v* podupreti, učvrstiti.
bolt *n* reza, zavrtanj; *v* zatvoriti rezom; napustiti, pobeći.

bomb *n* bomba; ~ **disposal** onesposobljavanje neeksplodiranih bombi.
bombard *v* bombardovati.
bombardier *n* bombarder.
bombardment *n* bombardovanje.
bombshell *n* senzacija, iznenađenje; bomba (*fig*).
bond *n* veza, spona, ugovor; obaveza; obveznica.
bond holder *n* vlasnik obveznica.
bondage *n* ropstvo.
bone *n* kost; *v* izvaditi kosti.
boneless *a* bez kostiju.
bonfire *n* logorska vatra.
bonnet *n* ženski šešir, kapica.
bonny *a* lep, prijatan.
bonsai *n* bonsai.
bonus *n* dopunska nagrada, premija.
bony *a* koščat.
boo *v* zviždati, izviždati.
booby trap *n* mina iznenađenja, zamka.
book *n* knjiga, tekst, blok; *v* optužiti, privesti u policijsku stanicu; rezervisati.
bookbinder *n* knjigovezac.
bookcase *n* orman za knjige.
bookkeeper *n* knjigovođa.
bookkeeping *n* knjigovodstvo.
bookmaker *n* bukmejker (čovek koji prima opklade).
bookmarker *n* oznaka u knjizi.
bookseller *n* knjižar.
bookstore *n* knjižara.
bookworm *n* knjiški moljac.
boom *n* bum, uspon, brz porast; *v* gruvati, tutnjati; brzo procvetati.
boon *n* blagodet, korist.
boor *n* grubijan, neotesanko.
boorish *a* grub, neotesan.
boost *n* pomoć; guranje; porast; *v* pogurati; povećati, podići.
booster *n* pristalica, navijač.
boot *n* čizma; **to get the** ~ *v* biti otpušten.
booth *n* kabina, tezga, štand.
booty *n* plen.
booze *v* piti alkoholno piće.
border *n* granica, ivica; *v* graničiti se; oivičiti.
borderline *n* granica, demarkaciona linija.
bore *v* probušiti rupu; dosaditi; *n* bušilica; kalibar; gnjavator.

boredom *n* dosada.
boring *a* dosadan.
born *a* rođen.
borrow *v* pozajmiti.
borrower *n* pozajmljivač.
bosom *n* grudi, nedra, naručje.
bosom friend *n* prisan drug.
boss *n* gazda, šef.
botanic(al) *a* botanički.
botanist *n* botaničar.
botany *n* botanika.
botch *v* pokvariti (*sleng*).
both *a* oba, obe; obojica; *conj* i.i.
bother *v* ugnjaviti, dosaditi; pobrinuti se o nečemu; *n* briga.
bottle *n* boca, flaša; *v* razliti u boce; prikriti osećanja.
bottleneck *n* grlić boce; usko grlo (*fig*).
bottle-opener *n* otvarač za boce.
bottom *n* dno, dubina; *a* najniži.
bottomless *a* bez dna.
bough *n* grana.
boulder *n* veliki kamen.
bounce *v* odskočiti, baciti da odskoči, skočiti; *n* odskok.
bound *n* skok; *v* skočiti, jurnuti; *a* siguran.
boundary *n* granica, međa.
boundless *a* bezgraničan.
bounteous, bountiful *a* darežljiv, obilan.
bounty *n* darežljivost; premija, nagrada.
bouquet *n* buket; miris, buke.
bourgeois *a* buržujski.
bout *n* takmičenje; nastup, napad.
bovine *a* goveđi; trom, spor.
bow[1] *v* sagnuti se, pognuti, pokloniti se, pokoriti se; *n* klanjanje, naklon.
bow[2] *n* luk; gudalo.
bow tie *n* leptir mašna.
bowels *npl* utroba, creva.
bowl *n* činija, pehar, zdela; *v* kuglati se.
bowler *n* kuglaš.
bowler hat *n* polucilindar.
bowling *n* kuglanje.
bowling alley *n* kuglana.
bowstring *n* tetiva (na luku).
box *n* kutija, sadržina kutije; ~ **on the ear** šamar; *v* staviti u kutiju; ošamariti.
box office *n* blagajna.
boxer *n* bokser.
boxing *n* boks.

boxing gloves *npl* bokserske rukavice.
boxing ring *n* bokserski ring.
box-seat *n* sedište u loži.
boy *n* dečak, mladić.
boycott *v* bojkotovati; *n* bojkot.
boyfriend *n* dečko.
boyish *a* dečački.
bra *n* prsluče.
brace *n* potpora, podupirač; spona; par, dvoje.
bracelet *n* narukvica.
bracing *a* svež, okrepljujući.
bracken *n* paprat (*bot*).
bracket *n* držač, podupirač; zagrada; **to ~ with** izjednačiti.
brag *n* hvalisavac; *v* hvalisati se.
braid *n* gajtan; kika, pletenica; *v* oplesti.
brain *n* mozak, glava, pamet; *v* razbiti glavu nekome.
brainchild *n* zamisao.
brainless *a* glup, bez pameti.
brainwash *v* isprati nekome mozak.
brainwave *n* pametna ideja; moždani talas (*med*).
brainy *a* pametan.
brake *n* kočnica; *v* kočiti, ukočiti.
brake fluid *n* tečnost za kočnice.
brake lining *n* obloga kočnice.
brake shoe *n* papuča kočnice.
bramble *n* drač, kupina.
bran *n* mekinje.
branch *n* grana, ogranak; filijala; *v* račvati se, razgranati.
brand *n* marka, žig, znak; *v* žigosati.
brandish *v* mahati.
brand-new *a* nov novcat.
brandy *n* rakija, brendi.
brash *a* drzak.
brass *n* mesing; starešina; novac.
brassiere *n* prsluče.
brat *n* derište.
bravado *n* razmetanje hrabrošću.
brave *a* hrabar; *v* pružiti otpor; *n* ratnik; **~ly** *adv* hrabro.
bravery *n* hrabrost.
brawl *n* tuča, svađa; *v* svađati se.
brawn *n* mišićavost, snaga.
bray *v* njakati; *n* njakanje magarca.
braze *v* zalemiti.
brazen *a* mesingan, metalan; drzak; *v* drsko se ponašati.

breach *n* prekršaj, neispunjenje, narušavanje.

bread *n* hleb; novac (*sleng*); **brown ~** crni hleb.

breadbox (breadbin) *n* kutija za hleb.

breadcrumbs *npl* mrvice od hleba.

breadth *n* širina, prostranstvo.

breadwinner *n* hranilac porodice.

break *v* slomiti, polomiti, razbiti; prekršiti; prekinuti; raskinuti; **to ~ into** preći u; **to ~ out** pobeći, planuti; *n* prelom, prekid, odmor; **~ of day** u zoru, u svanuće.

breakage *n* kvar, lom.

breakdown *n* analiza; kvar, defekt, slom.

breakfast *n* doručak.

breaking *n* lom, lomljenje.

breakthrough *n* proboj, prodor.

breakwater *n* lukobran.

breast *n* grudi, prsa, dojka.

breastbone *n* grudnjača, sternum.

breastplate *n* grudni oklop.

breastroke *n* prsni stil.

breath *n* dah.

breathe *v* disati, udisati.

breathing *n* disanje.

breathing spell *n* zatišje, pauza.

breathless *a* bez vazduha, bez daha.

breathtaking *a* uzbudljiv, veličanstven.

breed *n* pasmina, vrsta; *v* roditi, odgajiti; vaspitati; množiti se.

breeder *n* odgajivač.

breeding *n* poreklo, loza; vaspitanje; odgoj.

breezy *a* svež, vetrovit.

brethern *n* braća (*obsol pl* od brother).

breviary *n* brevijar, trebnik.

brevity *n* kratkoća, kratkotrajnost.

brew *v* variti, skuvati; *n* piće koje se vari.

brewer *n* pivar.

brewery *n* pivara.

briar, brier *n* trn, šipak, divlja ruža.

bribe *n* mito; *v* dati mito, podmititi.

bribery *n* podmićivanje.

bric-a-rac *n* starudija, tričarije.

brick *n* cigla, opeka; sjajan momak; *v* ređati cigle.

bricklayer *n* zidar (koji zida ciglama).

bricklaying *n* zidarski zanat.

bridal *a* svadbeni, venčani.

bride *n* nevesta.

bridegroom *n* mladoženja.

bridesmaid *n* deveruša.

bridge *n* most; zubna proteza; kobilica (*mus*); **to build a ~ over** *v* izgraditi most preko.

bridle *n* uzda; *v* zauzdati, obuzdati.

brief *a* kratak; *n* kratak napis; uputstva; izvod.

briefcase *n* akten tašna.

briefly *a* ukratko, kratko.

brigade *n* brigada.

brigadier *n* brigadni general .

brigand *n* hajduk, razbojnik.

bright *a* svetao, jasan, sjajan; pametan; **~ly** *adv* svetlo.

brighten *v* razvedriti.

brightness *n* sjajnost, bistrina.

brilliance *n* sjaj, briljantnost.

brilliant *a* sjajan, briljantan; **~ly** *adv* sjajno.

brim *n* ivica, rub, obod.

brimful *a* pun puncat, pun do vrha.

bring *v* doneti, dovesti, privesti, uvesti; **to ~ about** dovesti do, izazvati; **to ~ forth** roditi, izneti; **to ~ up** othraniti, vaspitati.

brink *n* rub, ivica.

brisk *a* živahan, oštar.

brisket *n* prsa.

briskly *adv* živahno, oštro.

bristle *n* čekinja; *v* nakostrešiti se.

bristly *a* čekinjast.

brittle *a* lomljiv, krt.

broach *v* načeti, otvoriti.

broad *a* širok, prostran, opšti.

broad bean *n* bob.

broadcast *n* emisija, prenos; emitovati, prenositi.

broadcasting *n* prenos putem radija.

broaden *v* proširiti.

broadly *adv* široko.

broad-minded *a* širokogrud, slobodouman.

broadness *n* širina.

broadside *n* bok broda; bočni plotun.

brocade *n* brokat.

broccoli *n* prokule.

brochure *n* brošura.

brogue *n* provincijski izgovor engleskog jezika (uglavnom irski).

broil *v* ispeći na žaru; peći.

broken *a* slomljen; isprekidan; **~ English** iskvaren engleski.

broker *n* mešetar, trgovački posrednik.
brokerage *n* posredništvo.
bronchial *a* bronhijalni.
bronchitis *n* bronhitis.
bronze *n* bronza; *v* bronzirati.
brooch *n* broš, igla.
brood *v* izleći, ležati na jajima; razmišljati; *n* leglo, mladunci.
brood-hen *n* kvočka.
brook *n* potok.
broom *n* metla.
broomstick *n* drška od metle.
broth *n* čorba, supa.
brothel *n* burdelj, javna kuća.
brother *n* brat; fratar.
brotherhood *n* bratstvo; udruženje.
brother-in-law *n* dever; zet; pašenog; šurak.
brotherly *a* bratski.
brow *n* obrva.
browbeat *v* zastrašiti.
brown *a* smeđ, mrk; ~ **paper** *n* pakpapir; ~ **bread** *n* crni hleb; ~ **sugar** *n* žuti šećer; *n* smeđa boja.
browse *v* brstiti; prelistavati.
browser *n* onaj ko prelistava.
bruise *v* napraviti modricu; dobiti modricu; *n* modrica.
brunch *n* obrok umesto doručka i ručka.
brunette *n* crnka, crnokosa.
brunt *n* glavni udar, glavni teret.
brush *n* letka; kičica; sukob, sudar; *v* četkati.
brushwood *n* šiprag, šikara.
brusque *a* grub, osoran.
brutal *a* brutalan, svirep; **~ly** *adv* brutalno, zverski.
brutality *n* brutalnost.
brutalize *v* učiniti brutalnim, učiniti svirepim.
brute *n* životinja, zver; *a* životinjski, zverski.
brutish *a* životinjski, zverski; **~ly** *adv* životinjski.
bubble *n* mehur, klobuk; velika prevara; *v* ispuštati mehuriće, ključati.
bubblegum *n* žvakaća guma.
bucket *n* kofa, vedro.
buckle *n* kopča, spona, šnala; *v* saviti, izviti; zakopčati se.
buckshot *n* sačma.

bucolic *a* seljački.
bud *n* pupoljak, začetak; *v* napupiti.
buddhism *n* budizam.
budding *a* novajlija, koji počinje.
buddy *n* prijatelj.
budge *v* pomeriti, pokrenuti.
budget *n* budžet.
buff *n* gola koža.
buffalo *n* bivo; bufalo.
buffers *npl* amortizer, ublaživač; pufer.
buffet *n* bife; postavljen sto; *v* ošamariti; nositi.
buffoon *n* pajac, budala.
bug *n* insekt, buba; prislušni uređaj; mana, defekt.
bugbear *n* strašilo.
bugle (horn) *n* vojnička truba.
build *v* graditi, izgraditi, sazidati.
builder *n* graditelj.
building *n* zgrada, izgradnja.
bulb *n* lukovica; sijalica; loptica.
bulbous *a* loptast.
bulge *v* izbočiti se; *n* izbočina, ispupčenje.
bulk *n* obim, veličina; glavna masa; rasut; **in ~** na veliko.
bulky *a* kabast, masivan, glomazan.
bull *n* bik; snažan krupan čovek.
bulldog *n* buldog.
bulldozer *n* buldožer.
bullet *n* metak, zrno.
bulletin board *n* oglasna tabla.
bulletproof *a* neprobojan za zrna.
bullfight *n* korida, borba s bikovima.
bullfighter *n* borac s bikovima, toreador.
bullion *n* poluga zlata ili srebra.
bullock *n* june, uškopljen bik.
bull-ring *n* arena za borbu s bikovima.
bull's-eye *n* pogodak, centar mete.
bully *n* siledžija, nasilnik.
bulwark *n* bedem, bastion.
bum *n* skitnica.
bumblebee *n* bumbar.
bump *n* sudar, čvoruga, lak udarac; *v* udariti, lupiti.
bumper *n* odbojnik.
bumpkin *n* seljačina, klipan.
bumpy *a* džombast, grbav, neravan.
bun *n* zemička, kolačić.
bunch *n* grozd, veza, kita.
bundle *n* svežanj, naramak; snop; *v* zamotati.

bung *n* čep; *v* baciti.
bungalow *n* bungalov.
bungee-jumping *n* bandži skakanje.
bungle *v* pokvariti, nevešto uraditi; šeprtljati.
bunion *n* žulj.
bunk *n* ležaj.
bunker *n* bunker.
buoy *n* plovak, bova.
buoyant *a* plovan; bodar, živahan.
burden *n* teret, breme; *v* opteretiti.
bureau *n* orman, plakar; pisaći sto sa fijokama.
bureaucracy *n* birokratija.
bureaucrat *n* birokrata.
burglar *n* provalnik, obijač.
burglar alarm *n* alarmni uređaj.
burglary *n* provalna krađa.
burial *n* sahrana, pogreb.
burial place *n* groblje.
burlesque *n* burleska, farsa; *a* burleskni.
burly *a* snažan, krupan.
burn *v* spaliti, zapaliti, opeći, progoreti; *v* opekotina.
burner *n* ringla, ploča, gorionik.
burning *a* vatren, jarki, gorući.
burrow *n* jazbina, rupa; *v* kopati jamu.
bursar *n* blagajnik, stipendista.
burst *v* pući; raskinuti; prsnuti; **to ~ into tears** briznuti u plač; **to ~ out laughing** prsnuti u smeh; **to ~ into flames** planuti; *n* eksplozija, rasprskavanje.
bury *v* zakopati; sahraniti.
bus *n* autobus.
bus stop *n* autobuska stanica.
bush *n* žbun, grm, grmlje.
bushy *a* grmovit; gust.
busily *a* zauzet poslom.
business *n* zanimanje, posao, trgovina, biznis.
businesslike *a* poslovan, efikasan.
businessman *n* poslovan čovek, trgovac.
business trip *n* službeni put.
businesswoman *n* poslovna žena.
bust *n* grudi, bista.

bustle *v* žuriti se, komešati; *n* žurba, užurbanost.
bustling *a* užurban.
busy *a* zauzet, zaposlen; pun posla; prometan.
busybody *n* nametljivac, lice koje svuda zabada nos.
but *conj* a, ali, nego, već.
butcher *n* mesar, kasapin; krvnik; *v* iskasapiti.
butcher's (shop) *n* mesarnica, kasapnica.
butchery *n* klanica; pokolj.
butler *n* nadzornik posluge, majordom.
butt *n* udar glavom; nišan, meta; kundak puške; *v* bosti, udarati glavom; upadati.
butter *n* buter, maslac; *v* namazati buterom, ulagivati se.
buttercup *n* ljutić (*bot*).
butterfly *n* leptir.
buttermilk *n* mlaćenica, spremanje maslaca.
buttocks *npl* zadnjica.
button *n* dugme; *v* pritisnuti dugme.
buttonhole *n* rupica za dugme; cvet u rupici od kaputa.
buttress *n* podupirač, potpora; *v* podupreti.
buxom *a* punačka (žena).
buy *v* kupiti, nabaviti.
buyer *n* kupac, nabavljač.
buzz, buzzing *n* zujanje, brujanje; *v* zujati, žagoriti, brujati; telefonirati.
buzzard *n* mišar (*zool*).
buzzer *n* zvučni signal.
by *prep* kraj, pokraj, pored, do; **~ and ~** uskoro, ubrzo; **~ the ~** uzgred budi rečeno; **~ all means** svakako; **~ no means** nikako.
bygone *a* prošli.
by-law *n* statut, propis, zakon.
bypass *n* zaobilazak, bajpas (*med*).
by-product *n* nusprodukt, sporedni proizvod.
by-road *n* sporedan put.
bystander *n* gledalac, posmatrač.
byte *n* bajt (*komp*).
byword *n* izreka, krilatica.

C

cab *n* taksi.
cabbage *n* kupus.
cabin *n* kućica, brvnara; kabina.
cabinet *n* orman, plakar; kabinet, savet ministara.
cabinet-maker *n* solar.
cable *n* kabl, debelo uže; telegram.
cable car *n* žičara.
cable television *n* kablovska televizija.
cache *n* tajno skladište.
cackle *v* kokodakati, gakati; *n.* kokodakanje, gakanje.
cactus *n* kaktus.
cadence *n* ritam, kadenca (*mus*).
cadet *n* kadet, pitomac.
cadge *v* isprositi.
Caesarean section/operation *n* carski rez (*med*).
cafe *n* kafana, kafić.
cafeteria *n* kafeterija, ekspres restoran.
caffeine *n* kofein.
cage *n* kavez, koš; *v* staviti u kavez, zatočiti.
cagey *a* lukav, prepreden.
cajole *v* nagovoriti, pobuditi, privoleti.
cake *n* torta, kolač; komad.
calamitous *a* koban, porazan.
calamity *n* nesreća, propast, beda.
calculable *a* izračunljiv.
calculate *v* izračunati, proceniti.
calculation *n* računanje, račun, proračun.
calculator *n* džepni računar, kalkulator, digitron.
calculus *n* kamen (*med*); izračunavanje.
calendar *n* kalendar.
calf *n* tele, mladunče; nezreo čovek.
calibre *n* kalibar.
call *v* pozvati, nazvati, viknuti; telefonirati; to ~ for doći, zahtevati, predvideti; to ~ on svratiti, posetiti, pozvati; to ~ attention skrenuti pažnju; to ~ names opsovati; *n* zov, poziv; poseta; obaveza; telefonski poziv; zanimanje.
caller *n* posetilac, gost.
calligraphy *n* kaligrafija.
calling *n* poziv, zanimanje.

callisthenics *n* gimnastika.
callous *a* tvrd, žuljevit; neosetljiv.
calm *n* mir, tišina; *a* miran, tih; *v* smiriti, stišati; ~ly *adv* mirno, tiho.
calorie *n* kalorija.
calumny *n* kleveta, lažna optužba.
Calvary *n* Kalvarija; raspeće.
calve *v* oteliti (se).
camcorder *n* video.
camel *n* kamila.
cameo *n* kameja.
camera *n* kamera, foto-aparat; sudijska soba.
cameraman *n* kamerman.
camomile *n* kamilica (*bot*).
camouflage *n* kamuflaža, maskiranje.
camp *n* logor, tabor; kamp; *v* logorovati, kampovati; refugee ~ kamp za izbeglice.
campaign *n* kampanja, pohod; run-up-to-the-election ~ predizborna kampanja; *v* učestvovati u kampanji.
camper *n* kamper, karavan.
camphor *n* kamfor.
camping *n* logorovanje, kampovanje.
campsite *n* kamping, logorište.
campus *n* studentski grad.
can *v* moći, umeti; *n* konzerva, kanta.
canal *n* kanal.
cancel *v* otkazati, izbrisati, ukinuti.
cancellation *n* otkazivanje, poništenje.
cancer *n* rak (*med*); Rak (*astrol*).
cancerous *a* kancerozan.
candid *a* otvoren, iskren; ~ly *adv* iskreno.
candidate *n* kandidat.
candied *a* kandirano.
candle *n* sveća.
candlelight *n* svetlost sveće, sumrak.
candlestick *n* svećnjak.
candour *n* otvorenost, iskrenost.
candyfloss *n* šećerlema, bombone.
cane *n* trska; štap, palica.
canine *a* pas; očnjak.
canister *n* limena kanta, kanister.
cannabis *n* konoplja, kanabis.
cannibal *n* ljudožder, kanibal.
cannibalism *n* kanibalizam.

cannon n top, oruđe.
cannonball n topovsko zrno.
canny a lukav, mudar, vešt.
canoe n kanu, čamac.
canon n kanon; ~ **law** kanonsko pravo.
canonization n kanonizacija, posveta.
can opener n otvarač za konzerve.
canopy n baldahin, kupola.
cantankerous a svadljiv, mrzovoljan.
canteen n kantina, vojnička menza.
canter n laki galop.
canvas n platno, šatorsko platno,
   slikarsko platno, slika.
canvass v anketirati, ispitivati; skupljati
   glasove pred izbor.
canvasser n anketar, skupljač glasova.
canyon n kanjon, klisura.
cap n kapa, kačket; poklopac.
capability n sposobnost, moć.
capable a sposoban, kadar.
capacity n sposobnost, mogućnost,
   kapacitet; svojstvo.
cape n ogrtač, kabanica.
caper n skok; nestašluk, ludorija; v
   ludirati se.
capillary a kapilarni.
capital a glavni, odličan; n kapital,
   glavnina; glavni grad, prestonica.
capital punishment n smrtna kazna.
capitalism n kapitalizam.
capitalist n kapitalista.
capitalize v kapitalisati; **to ~ on**
   iskoristiti.
capitulate v predati se, kapitulirati.
capitulation n kapitulacija, predaja.
caprice n kapric, ćef.
capricious a kapriciozan; ~**ly** adv
   kapriciozno.
Capricorn n Jarac (astrol).
capsize v prevrnuti, preturiti.
capsule n čaura, omotač (anat);
   kapsula.
captain n kapetan, komandant; kapiten.
captaincy, captainship n čin kapetana.
captivate v očarati, zaneti.
captivation n očaravanje.
captive n zarobljenik.
captivity n zarobljeništvo.
capture n zarobljavanje, hapšenje,
   zatvaranje; v zarobiti, uhvatiti, osvojiti.
car n automobil, kola.

carafe n boca.
caramel n karamela.
carat n karat.
caravan n karavan.
caraway n kim (bot).
carbohydrates npl ugljenvodonik.
car bomb n automobil bomba, bomba
   podmetnuta u automobil. **carbon** n
   ugljenik; indigo.
carbon copy n kopija.
carbon paper n indigo.
carbonize v ugljenisati.
carburettor n karburator.
carcass n lešina (zaklane životinje).
carcinogenic a kancerozan.
card n karta, čestitka, karton; **pack of ~s**
   špil karata.
cardboard n karton.
card game n igra karata.
cardiac a srčani.
cardinal a glavni; crvene boje; n kardinal;
   crvena boja.
card table n sto za kartanje.
care n briga, zabrinutost; pažnja; zaštita;
   v brinuti se; negovati, starati se; **what
   do I ~?** Šta to mene briga? **to ~ for** v
   voleti.
career n karijera; v juriti, galopirati.
carefree n bezbrižan.
careful a oprezan, brižljiv; ~**ly** adv
   oprezno.
careless a neoprezan, nehatan; ~**ly** adv
   neoprezno, nepažljivo.
carelessness n neopreznost.
caress n milovanje; v milovati.
caretaker n čuvar, kućepazitelj.
car-ferry n feribot.
cargo n teret, tovar.
car hire n iznajmljivanje automobila,
   rent-a-kar.
caricature n karikatura; v karikirati.
caries n karijes.
caring a brižan.
carnage n pokolj.
carnal a puten, pohotan; ~**ly** adv pohotno.
carnation n karanfil.
carnival n karneval.
carnivorous a mesožderan.
carol n vesela pesma, božićna pesma.
car park n parking, parkiralište.
carpenter n stolar, drvodelja.

carpentry *n* stolarstvo, drvodeljstvo.
carpet *n* tepih, ćilim; pokrivač; *v* pokriti tepihom.
carpeting *n* tepisi.
car radio *n* radio u kolima.
carriage *n* kočije, fijaker; transport, prevoz; stav, držanje.
carrier *n* nosač; prevoznik, transportno sredstvo; prenosilac bolesti.
carrier pigeon *n* golub pismonoša.
carrion *n* strvina, lešina.
carrot *n* šargarepa, mrkva.
carry *v* nositi, voziti, preneti; usvojiti; **to ~ out** sprovesti, izvršiti; **to ~ weight** biti opterećen, imati uticaja; **to ~ on** nastaviti, obavljati.
cart *n* teretna kola, kolica; *v* odneti, odvesti.
cartel *n* kartel.
carthorse *n* konj za vuču.
cartilage *n* hrskavica.
carton *n* kutija od kartona.
cartoon *n* karikatura, crtani film.
cartridge *n* metak, čaura.
carve *v* izrezati, urezati, izrezbariti.
carving *n* rezbarija.
carving knife *n* veliki nož (za rezanje mesa).
car wash *n* uređaj za pranje automobila.
case *n* slučaj, predmet, parnica; **in ~** u slučaju.
cash card *n* kartica za podizanje gotovine iz automata.
cash dispenser, cash machine *n* automat za podizanje gotovine.
cashier *n* blagajnik.
cashmere *n* kašmir.
casing *n* omot, futrola, obloga.
casino *n* kasino.
cask *n* bure.
casket *n* kovčeg (mrtvački), kutija.
cassette *n* kaseta.
cassette player, recorder *n* kasetofon.
cassock *n* mantija.
cast *v* baciti; izliti, odliti; *n* bacanje; kalup, odliv.
cast iron *n* liveno gvožđe.
castanets *npl* kastanjete.
castaway *n* brodolomnik.
caste *n* kasta.
castigate *v* kazniti, kritikovati.

castle *n* zamak, kula.
castor oil *n* ricinus.
castrate *v* kastrirati, uškopiti.
castration *n* kastracija, škopljenje.
casual *a* slučajan, neočekivan; **~ly** *adv* slučajno.
casualty *n* ranjenik, *pl* poginuli.
cat *n* mačka.
catalogue *n* katalog.
catalyst *n* katalizator.
catapult *n* katapult, praćka.
cataract *n* katarakta, mrena (*med*).
catarrh *n* katar (*med*).
catastrophe *n* katastrofa.
catcall *n* zviždanje.
catch *v* uloviti, uhvatiti; shvatiti; zakačiti; **to ~ cold** prehladiti se; **to ~ fire** zapaliti se; *n* hvatanje; lov; zamka; prilika.
catching *a* zarazan.
catch phrase *n* krilatica.
catch word *n* krilatica.
catchy *a* privlačan; koji se lako pamti.
catechism *n* katehizam.
categorical *a* kategoričan, odlučan; **~ly** *adv* odlučno, kategorično.
categorize *v* categorisati, razvrstati.
category *n* kategorija.
cater *v* snabdeti hranom; zadovoljiti, udovoljiti.
caterer *n* onaj ko isporučuje hranu; onaj ko pruža ugostiteljske usluge.
catering *n* fabrika gotovih jela, preduzeće koje pruža usluge snabdevanja hranom.
caterpillar *n* gusenica.
cathedral *n* katedrala, saborna crkva.
catholic *a* katolik; sveobuhvatan.
cattle *n* stoka, marva.
caucus *n* sastanak članova partije.
cauliflower *n* karfiol.
cause *n* uzrok, razlog; stvar; *v* prouzrokovati, izazvati.
causeway *n* uzdignut put.
caustic *a* kaustičan; jedak, zajedljiv.
cauterize *v* podvrći kauterizaciji.
caution *n* opreznost; razboritost; upozorenje; *v* upozoriti.
cautionary *a* opominjući, koji opominje.
cautious *a* oprezan, obazriv.
cavalier *a* osion, ohol; nehatan.
cavalry *n* konjica.
cave *n* pećina, špilja.

caveat *n* prigovor, protest (*jur*).
cavern *n* velika pećina; kaverna (*med*).
cavernous *a* sličan pećini; pun pećina.
caviar *n* kavijar.
cavity *n* šupljina, duplja; karijes (*stom*).
cease *v* prekinuti, prestati.
cease-fire *n* prekid vatre, obustava vatre.
ceaseless *a* neprekidan; ~ly *adv*
  neprekidno.
cedar *n* kedar, kedrovina.
cede *v* ustupiti, priznati.
ceiling *n* tavanica, plafon; vrhunac.
celebrate *v* proslaviti, slaviti.
celebration *n* proslava, svečanost.
celebrity *n* slavna ličnost.
celery *n* celer.
celestial *a* nebeski.
celibacy *n* neženstvo, celibat.
cell *n* ćelija (*biol*); ćelija u zatvoru.
cellar *n* podrum.
cello *n* čelo, violončelo.
Cellophane™ *n* celofan.
cellular *a* ćelijski.
cellulitis *n* celulitis.
cellulose *n* celuloza (*hem*).
cement *n* cement, vezivno tkivo; *v*
  cementirati, spojiti.
cemetery *n* groblje.
cenotaph *n* spomenik u obliku grobnice,
  kenotaf.
censor *n* cenzor, kritičar.
censorious *a* kritički raspoložen.
censorship *n* cenzura.
censure *n* osuda; *v* osuditi, prigovoriti.
census *n* popis stanovništva.
cent *n* cent (stoti deo dolara).
centenarian *n* stogodišnjak.
centenary *n* stogodišnjica; *a* stogodišnji.
centigrade *n* sto stepeni Celzijusa.
centimetre *n* santimetar, centimetar.
centipede *n* stonoga.
central *a* centralan; ~ly *adv* centralno.
centralize *v* centralisati.
centre (*br*), **center** (*amer*) *n* centar,
  središte; *v* centrirati, usmeriti.
centrifugal *a* centrifugalan.
century *n* vek.
ceramic *a* keramički.
cereals *npl* jelo od prekrupe, cerealije,
  žitna kaša.
cerebral *a* moždani, cerebralan (*med*).

ceremonial *a/n* ceremonijalni,
  ceremonija.
ceremonious *a* pompezan, ceremonijalni.
ceremony *n* ceremonija, svečanost.
certain *a* siguran, uveren, pouzdan; ~ly
  adv sigurno.
certainty, certitude *n* sigurnost, sigurna
  činjenica.
certificate *n* svedočanstvo, potvrda,
  uverenje.
certified mail *n* preporučena pošiljka.
certify *v* potvrditi, overiti; proglasiti (npr.
  ludim).
cervical *a* vratni, cervikalan (*med*).
cessation *n* prestanak, prekid.
cesspool *n* nužnička jama.
chafe *v* trljati, trti; nasekirati.
chaff *n* mekinje, otpaci; podsmeh.
chaffinch *n* zeba (ptica).
chagrin *n* jad, žalost; razočaranje.
chain *n* lanac, okovi; trgovinska mreža,
  lanac.
chain reaction *n* lančana reakcija.
chain store *n* prodavnica koja pripada
  trgovinskom lancu.
chair *n* stolica; katedra; predsedništvo; *v*
  predsedavati.
chairman *n* predsedavajući; direktor
  preduzeća; šef katedre.
chalice *n* putir.
chalk *n* kreda.
challenge *n* izazov; *v* izazvati.
challenger *n* izazivač.
chamber *n* komora; odeljenje; dvorana.
chambermaid *n* sobarica.
chameleon *n* kameleon.
chamois leather *n* koža od divokoze.
champagne *n* šampanjac.
champion *n* šampion; *v* boriti se za
  nešto.
championship *n* šampionat, prvenstvo.
chance *n* slučajnost, slučaj; prilika,
  mogućnost, sreća; **by** ~ slučajno.
chancellor *n* kancelar.
chancery *n* sud časti.
chandelier *n* luster.
change *v* promeniti, izmeniti; preći;
  presvući se; smeniti; *n* promena,
  izmena; kusur; sitan novac, sitnina.
changeable *a* promenljiv.
changeless *a* nepromenljiv, stalan.

channel *n* kanal, prolaz, plovni put; *v* uputiti, kanalisati.

channel selector *n* birač kanala.

chant *n* crkvena pesma; *v* pevati, skandirati.

chaos *n* haos.

chaotic *a* haotičan.

chapel *n* kapela, crkvica; služba božja.

chaplain *n* kapelan.

chapter *n* glava, poglavlje; period u istoriji.

char *v* spremačica.

character *n* karakter, ličnost.

characteristic *a* karakterističan.

characteristically *adv* karakteristično.

characterize *v* okarakterisati.

charade *n* šarada, pretvaranje.

charcoal *n* ugalj (drveni).

chard *n* blitva (*bot*).

charge *v* obavezati; optužiti; opteretiti; jurišati; naplatiti; *n* odgovornost, briga; optužba; štićenik; trošak, cena; teret.

charge card *n* kreditna karta.

chargeable *a* naplativ, koji može da se stavi na račun.

charitable *a* milosrdan; ~ly *adv* milosrdno, dobrotvorno.

charity *n* milosrđe, milostinja, dobrotvorna ustanova.

charlatan *n* šarlatan.

charm *n* šarm, čar; privlačnost; amajlija; *v* očarati, šarmirati.

charming *a* šarmantan.

chart *n* pomorska karta; tabela, grafikon.

charter *n* povelja; pravo, povlastica; zakup, čarter; *v* zakupiti.

charter flight *n* čarter let.

chase *v* goniti, terati, juriti; *n* potera, lov.

chasm *n* ponor.

chaste *a* čedan, neporočan.

chasten *v* kazniti, popraviti.

chastise *v* ukoriti; izudarati; kazniti.

chastity *n* čednost, neporočnost.

chat *v* ćaskati; *n* ćaskanje, ćeretanje.

chatter *v* cvokotati; brbljati; *n* brbljanje; cvokot.

chatterbox *n* brbljivac.

chatty *a* brbljiv.

chauffeur *n* šofer.

chauvinist *n* šovinista.

cheap *a* jeftin, nije skup: loš; ~ly *adv* jeftino.

cheapen *v* pojeftiniti.

cheat *v* prevariti, obmanuti, podvaliti; *n* prevara, prevarant, varalica.

check *v* zaustaviti; kontrolisati, pregledati; usporiti; slagati se; *n* ograničenje; kontrola, provera.

checkerboard (**chequerboard**) (*amer*), **draughtsboard** (*br*) *n* tabla za igru dame.

checkers, chequers *vidi* **draughts**.

checkmate *n* šah-mat.

checkout *n* vreme odlaska; provera.

checkpoint *n* kontrolni punkt.

check-up *n* pregled, provera.

cheeerfulness *n* vedrina, veselost.

cheek *n* obraz; zadnjica; drskost.

cheekbone *n* jagodica.

cheeky *a* bezobrazan, drzak.

cheer *n* veselost; uzvik odobravanja, čestitanja; *v* bodriti, radosno pozdraviti.

cheerful *a* veseo, raspoložen; ~ly *adv* veselo.

cheese *n* sir.

cheese-paring *n* škrtost.

chef *n* glavni kuvar.

chemical *a* hemijski; *n* hemikalija.

chemist *n* hemičar; apotekar.

chemistry *n* hemija.

chemotherapy *n* hemoterapija.

cheque (*br*), **check** (*amer*) *n* ček.

cherish *v* gajiti, negovati.

cherry *n* trešnja; višnja; *a* boje trešnje.

cherub *n* heruvim, anđeo, nedužno dete.

chess *n* šah.

chessboard *n* šahovska tabla.

chessman *n* šahovska figura.

chest *n* grudi, prsa; sanduk, orman; ~ of drawers orman sa fijokama, komoda.

chestnut *n* kesten; kestenjasta boja.

chew *v* žvakati, sažvakati, gristi; pričati.

chewing gum *n* žvakaća guma.

chic *a* elegantan, šik.

chicanery *n* prevara, obmana.

chick *n* pile, pilence; mladunče.

chicken *n* pile, kokoš; piletina.

chickenpox *n* variček (srednje boginje).

chickpea *n* naut, leblebija.

chicory *n* cigura.

chide *n* kritikovati, izgrditi.

chief *a* glavni; ~ly *adv* glavno, najviše; *n* vođa, šef, poglavar.

chief of state *n* načelnik štaba.
chieftain *n* vođ, poglavica.
chilblain *n* promrzlina.
child *n* dete; čedo; **from a** ~ odmalena;
  with ~ trudna.
childbirth *n* porođaj.
childhood *n* detinjstvo.
childish *a* detinjast, bezazlen; **~ly** *adv*
  detinjasto.
childishness *n* detinjatost.
children *n* deca (*pl* od **child**).
chill *n* drhtavica , jeza; *v* ohladiti,
  prohladiti.
chilly *a* hladan, suv.
chime *n* zvono; *v* skladno zvoniti.
chimney *n* odžak, dimnjak.
chimpanzee *n* šimpanza.
chin *n* brada, podvaljak.
chinaware *n* porcelan.
chink *n* pukotina; zveket; sitan novac; *v*
  zveckati.
chip *v* seći, lomiti, odlomiti; *n* iver, klada;
  parče; žeton.
chiropodist *n* pedikir.
chirp *v* cvrkutati; *n* cvrkut.
chirping *n* cvrkutanje.
chisel *n* dleto; izrezati; isklesati.
chitchat *n* ćaskanje.
chivalrous *a* viteški, galantan.
chivalry *n* viteštvo.
chlorine *n* hlor (*hem*).
chloroform *n* hloroform.
chock-full *a* pun puncat.
chocolate *n* čokolada.
choice *n* izbor; *a* odabran, odličan.
choir *n* hor.
choke *v* ugušiti, zagušiti; zadaviti.
cholera *n* kolera.
choose *v* izabrati, birati; odlučiti.
chop *v* seći, odseći; faširati; *n* odrezak,
  šnicla, kotlet.
chopper *n* seckalica; helikopter (*sleng*).
chopsticks *npl* štapići za jelo (kod
  Kineza).
choral *a* horski.
chord *n* akord (*mus*); skladnost; žica.
chore *n* posao (obično kućni).
chorist, chorister *n* horski pevač.
chorus *n* hor; pripev; refren.
Christ *n* Hrist.
christen *v* krstiti.

Christendom *n* hrišćanstvo.
christening *n* krštenje.
Christian *a* hrišćanski; *n* hrišćanin.
Christmas *n* Božić.
Christmas Eve *n* Badnje veče.
chrome *n* hrom.
chronic *a* hroničan, okoreo.
chronicle *n* hronika.
chronological *a* hronološki.
chronometer *n* hronometar.
chubby *a* bucmast, debeljuškast.
chuck *v* potapšati; baciti.
chuckle *v* cerekati se; pritajeno se smejati.
chug *v* brektati, roptati.
chum *n* drugar, prisni prijatelj (*sleng*).
chunk *n* debelo parče, komad.
church *n* crkva.
churchyard *n* crkveno dvorište.
churlish *a* prostački, grub, vulgaran.
churn *n* bućkalica; *v* bućkati, mućkati.
cider *n* jabukovača, sok od jabuke.
cigar *n* cigara.
cigarette *n* cigareta.
cigarette case *n* tabakera.
cigarette end *n* opušak.
cigarette holder *n* muštikla.
cinder *n* pepeo, ugljen.
cinema *n* film; bioskop.
cinnamon *n* cimet.
cipher *n* cifra.
circle *n* krug; *v* zaokružiti, kružiti.
circuit *n* kružni put; kolo (*el*); obilazak,
  krug.
circuitous *a* zaobilazni, kružni.
circulate *v* cirkulisati, kružiti.
circulation *n* cirkulacija, kolanje, opticaj.
circumcise *v* obrezati.
circumcision *n* obrezivanje.
circumference *n* obim, periferija.
circumflex *n* cirkumfleks (*ling*) vrsta
  naglaska.
circumlocution *n* okolišanje, zaobilazan
  govor.
circumnavigate *v* oploviti.
circumscribe *v* opisati, ograničiti.
circumspect *a* oprezan, obazriv.
circumspection *n* obazrivost.
circumstance *n* okolnost, prilika; stanje
  (*fin*).
circumstantial *a* slučajan; podroban,
  opširan.

circumstantiate *v* potkrepiti dokazima.
circumvent *v* nadmudriti, obmanuti.
circumvention *n* obmana; zaobilazak.
circus *n* cirkus; raskrsnica.
cistern *n* cisterna; rezervoar.
citadel *n* tvrđava, citadela.
citation *n* citat, navođenje sudskog precedenta.
cite *v* citirati, navesti; pozvati na sud.
citizen *n* državljanin, građanin.
citizenship *n* državljanstvo, građanstvo.
city *n* grad, varoš.
civic *a* građanski.
civics *n* nauka o građanskim pravima i dužnostima .
civil *a* građanski, civilni, državni; građevinski; učtiv; **~ly** *adv* građanski, učtivo.
civil defence *n* civilna odbrana.
civil engineer *n* građevinski inženjer.
civilian *n* civilno lice, civil.
civility *n* učtivost.
civilization *n* civilizacija.
civil law *n* građansko pravo.
civil war *n* građanski rat.
clad *a* obučen, odeven.
claim *v* zahtevati, tražiti; tvrditi; *n* zahtev, potraživanje; tvrdnja.
claimant *n* tražilac.
clairvoyant *n* vidovit.
clam *n* školjka, rak (*zool*); ćutljivo.
clamber *v* uzverati se, popeti.
clammy *a* lepljiv.
clamour *n* vika, galama; *v* praviti buku.
clamp *n* spojnica, spoj; *v* učvrstiti; **to ~ down on** postati stroжiji, oštriji.
clan *n* klan.
clandestine *a* potajan, tajan.
clang *n* zvečanje, jek; *v* zvečati.
clap *v* pljeskati, aplaudirati.
clapping *n* pljeskanje, tapšanje.
claret *n* crvenkasto vino.
clarification *n* razjašnjenje.
clarify *v* razjasniti.
clarinet *n* klarinet.
clarity *n* jasnoća, bistrina.
clash *v* sudariti se, sukobiti se; *n* sudar; obračun.
clasp *n* kopča, spona; igla; *v* zakopčati, stegnuti; zagrliti.
class *n* klasa, stalež; razred; *v* klasirati.

classic(al) *a* klasičan; *n* klasičar; uzor, primer.
classification *n* klasifikacija, raspoređivanje.
classified advertisement *n* mali oglas.
classify *v* razvrstati.
classmate *n* školski drug.
classroom *n* učionica.
clatter *v* klepetati, kloparati; *n* klepet.
clause *n* rečenica, klauzula.
claw *n* kandža; *v* grepsti kandžama.
clay *n* glina, ilovača.
clean *a* čist, prazan; *v* počistiti, očistiti; oprati.
cleaning *n* čišćenje, spremanje.
cleanliness *n* čistoća.
cleanly *a* čist; *adv* čisto.
cleanse *v* očistiti.
clear *a* jasan, vedar; razumljiv; bistar; *adv* jasno; *v* očistiti, raščistitit; skloniti, spremiti; ocariniti.
clearance *n* dozvola, odobrenje.
clear-cut *a* očigledan, oštrih obrisa.
cleaver *n* mesarski nož.
clef *n* notni ključ (*mus*).
cleft *n* pukotina.
clemency *n* blagost, popustljivost.
clement *a* blag.
clenched *a* stegnut, stisnut.
clergy *n* sveštenstvo.
clergyman *n* sveštenik.
clerical *a* sveštenički.
clerk *n* pisar, referent; prodavac u radnji.
clever *a* bistar, pametan, vešt; **~ly** *adv* pametno, vešto.
click *v* škljocnuti; složiti se, zaljubiti se; imati sreće (*sleng*).
client *n* klijent.
cliff *n* litica.
climate *n* klima.
climax *n* klimaks, vrhunac.
climb *v* popeti se, penjati se.
climber *n* planinar.
climbing *n* penjanje, planinarenje.
clinch *v* stisnuti, zgrabiti.
cling *v* čvrsto se držati, pripijati se.
clinic *n* bolnica, klinika.
clink *v* zveketati; *n* zveket.
clip *v* spajati, stezati; podsecati, potkresati; *n* šišanje; spajanje; igla, stega.

clippings *npl* isečci iz novina.
clique *n* klika, grupa.
cloak *n* plašt, pokrivač; izgovor; *v* ogrnuti se plaštom.
cloakroom *n* svlačionica, garderoba.
clock *n* časovnik, sat.
clockwork *n* mehanizam časovnika, časovnik; *a* po planu.
clod *n* grumen zemlje; nezgrapan, nepokretan čovek.
clog *n* prepreka; bukagije; klompe; *v* smetati, ometati, zatrpati.
cloister *n* manastir, samostan.
clone *n* klon; *v* klonirati.
cloned *a* kloniran.
close *v* zatvoriti, završiti, skupiti; *n* kraj, završetak; *a* blizak; tesan; zbijen; usredsređen; *adv* blisko; **~ by** blizu.
closed *a* zatvoren.
closely *adv* pažljivo, temeljno; gusto.
closet *n* orman u zidu; šupa; nužnik.
close-up *n* krupni plan, detaljan snimak.
closure *n* zatvaranje.
clot *n* grudvica; ugrušak (*med*).
cloth *n* tkanina, sukno, stolnjak.
clothe *v* oblačiti, pokrivati.
clothes *npl* odelo, haljina, rublje.
clothes basket *n* korpa za rublje.
clothes peg *n* štipaljka za veš.
clotheshorse *n* stalak za sušenje veša.
clothesline *n* konopac za veš.
clothes peg *n* štipaljka za veš.
clothing *n* odelo.
cloud *n* oblak; tamna mrlja, zamućenost; pokrov; *v* naoblačiti se, smračiti, zamračiti.
cloudy *a* oblačan, maglovit, zamagljen.
clout *n* krpa; šamar.
clove *n* karanfilić; češanj (npr. belog luka).
clover *n* detelina.
clown *n* lakrdijaš, klovn.
club *n* klub, društvo, udruženje; batina, štap.
club car *n* kola prve klase (*žel*).
clue *n* ključ (za odgonetanje nečeg).
clump *n* grupa; gruda, grumen.
clumsily *adv* nespretno.
clumsiness *n* nespretnost, nesklad.
cluster *n* grozd, kita (cveća), roj (pčela); *v* tiskati se, rasti u grozdovima.

clutch *n* hvatanje, zahvat; kandža; *v* stezati, uhvatiti.
clutter *v* galamiti, stvarati paniku.
coach *n* vagon, kočija; nastavnik; trener; *v* podučavati, biti trener.
coach trip *n* putovanje autobusom.
coagulate *v* zgrušati se, koagulisati.
coal *n* ugalj, kameni ugalj.
coalesce *v* udružiti se, stvoriti koaliciju.
coalfield *n* područje sa naslagama kamenog uglja.
coalition *n* koalicija, ujedinjenje.
coalmine *n* kop, rudnik uglja.
coarse *a* grub, prost, sirov; **~ly** *adv* grubo, neotesano.
coast *n* primorje, morska obala.
coastal *a* obalski, priobalni.
coastguard *n* obalska straža.
coastline *n* obala.
coat *n* kaput, sako; krzno životinje; sloj farbe; opna; *v* oblagati.
coat hanger *n* vešalica.
coating *n* sloj boje; materijal za kaput.
coax *v* nagovoriti, pridobiti.
cob *n* klip (kukuruza).
cobbler *n* obućar.
cobbles, cobblestones *npl* kocka, kaldrma.
cobweb *n* paučina, tanak veo.
cocaine *n* kokain.
coccyx *n* trtica.
cock *n* petao; oroz; sedište pilota; *v* nakriviti, zabaciti; dići nos.
cock-a-doodle-doo *n* kukurikanje.
cockerel *n* petlić.
cockfight(ing) *n* borba petlova.
cockle *n* neravnina, nedostatak; jestiva školjka.
cockpit *n* kabina pilota; arena za borbu petlova.
cockroach *n* bubašvaba.
cocktail *n* koktel; laktaš.
cocoa *n* kakao.
coconut *n* kokos.
cocoon *n* čaura.
cod *n* bakalar.
code *n* kodeks, šifra; zbirka zakona.
cod-liver oil *n* riblje ulje.
coefficient *n* koeficijent, množitelj.
coercion *n* prinuda, nasilje.
coexistence *n* koegzistencija.

coffee *n* kafa.
coffee break *n* odmor, pauza za kafu.
coffee house *n* bife.
coffee table *n* nizak sto.
coffee-pot *n* džezva.
coffer *n* kofer, sanduk; državna blagajna.
coffin *n* mrtvački sanduk, raka.
cog *n* vršak, izbočina, zubac.
cogency *n* neospornost.
cogent *a* ubedljiv, neosporiv.
cognac *n* konjak.
cognate *a* rođak; srodni jezici.
cognition *n* poznavanje, saznanje, spoznaja.
cognizance *n* znanje, nadležnost; odlikovanje.
cogwheel *n* zupčanik.
cohabit *v* živeti zajedno, stanovati zajedno.
cohabitation *n* zajednički život.
cohere *v* biti u skladu, slagati se.
coherence *n* povezanost, spajanje; doslednost.
coherent *a* usaglašen, povezan; dosledan.
cohesion *n* spajanje, kohezija.
coil *n* kalem, kotur; *v* namotati.
coin *n* novac, moneta, pare; kovati novac; pričati izmišljotine.
coincide *v* poklapati se; dogoditi se istovremeno.
coincidence *n* poklapanje, podudaranje; slučajan sticaj okolnosti.
coke *n* koks.
Coke™ *n* koka-kola.
colander *n* sito.
cold *a* hladan, neosetljiv; **~ly** *adv* hladno; neosetljivo; *n* hladnoća, nazeb.
cold sore *n* labijalni herpes (*med*).
cold-blooded *a* hladnokrvan, neuzbudljiv.
coldness *n* hladnoća.
coleslaw *n* salata od kupusa.
colic *a* kolika (*med*).
collaborate *v* sarađivati.
collaboration *n* saradnja.
collapse *v* odroniti se, srušiti; klonuti; *n* odronjavanje, pad, propast; opadanje životne aktivnosti organizma.
collapsible *a* složiv, za sklapanje.
collar *n* okovratnik, ogrlica.
collarbone *n* ključna kost.
collate *v* uporediti, sravniti.

collateral *a* posredan, drugostepeni; *n* zalog.
collation *n* sređivanje, sravnjivanje; užina, zakuska.
colleague *n* kolega.
collect *v* skupljati, prikupljati.
collection *n* zbirka, kolekcija; skupljanje.
collective *a* kolektivan, zbirni; **~ly** *adv* kolektivno.
collector *n* kolekcionar, skupljač; kontrolor.
college *n* koledž, škola za višu nastavu; univerzitet (*amer*).
collide *v* sudariti se.
collision *n* sudar, sukob.
colloquial *a* razgovorni, uobičajeni; **~ly** *adv* kolokvijalni, uobičajeni.
colloquialism *n* narodni jezik, razgovorni izraz.
collusion *n* ugovor, tajni sporazum.
colon *n* debelo crevo (*med*); dve tačke.
colonel *n* pukovnik.
colonial *a* kolonijalan.
colonist *n* doseljenik.
colossal *a* džinovski.
colossus *n* kolos, džin.
colour *n* boja, nijansa, rumenilo; *pl* zastava; *v* obojiti, osvetleti.
colour-blind *a* slep za boje.
colourful *a* mnogobojan.
colouring *n* bojenje, obojenost; boja lica; kolorit.
colourless *a* bezbojan, bled.
colour television *n* televizija u boji.
colt *n* ždrebe; novajlija (*sleng*).
column *n* kolona; stub; stubac; rubrika.
columnist *n* novinski komentator.
coma *n* koma (*med*).
comatose *a* komatozan.
comb *n* češalj, češagija; *v* češljati.
combat *n* bitka; *v* boriti se.
combatant *n* vojnik, borac; zaštitnik.
combination *n* povezivanje, kombinacija.
combine *v* sjediniti, udružiti, povezati.
combustion *n* gorenje, izgaranje; oksidacija.
come *v* doći ; **to ~ across/upon** *v* nabasati na; **to ~ by** *v* dobiti; prolaziti mimo; **to ~ down** *v* sići; **to ~ from** *v* voditi poreklo, poticati od; **to ~ into** *v* ući; naslediti; **to ~ round/to** *v* doći k sebi, povratiti se; **to ~ up with** *v* izneti predlog.

comedian *n* pisac šaljivih komada; komičar.

comedienne *n* komičarka.

comet *n* kometa, zvezda repatica.

comfort *n* udobnost; uteha; podrška; komfor; *v* tešiti, umiriti.

comfortable *a* udoban, komforan; zadovoljan.

comfortably *adv* udobno.

comforter *n* utešitelj; krevetski pokrivač, perina.

comic(al) *a* smešan, zabavan; ~ly *adv* smešno, komično.

coming *n* prispeće, dolazak; *a* koji dolazi.

comma *n* zarez (*gram*).

command *v* komandovati, naređivati, vladati; *n* naređenje, komanda.

commandment *n* naredba, zapovest.

commando *n* komandos.

commemorate *v* proslavljati, obeležiti.

commemoration *n* proslava, svečanost; komemoracija.

commence *v* započeti, početi.

commencement *n* početak; dan dodele školskih svedočanstava.

commend *v* hvaliti, preporučiti, poveriti.

commendably *adv* pohvalno.

commensurate *a* usklađen, prilagođen, odgovarajući.

comment *n* komentar, tumačenje; *v* komentarisati, tumačiti.

commentary *n* komentar, objašnjenje.

commerce *n* trgovina, razmena.

commercial *a* komercijalan, trgovački.

commiserate *v* saosećati.

commiseration *n* saosećanje.

commissariat *n* komesarijat.

commission *n* komitet; punomoć; ovlašćenje; komisiona prodaja; *v* poručiti; dati oficirski čin.

commissioner *n* komesar; opunomoćenik.

commit *v* predati; poveriti; uputiti.

commitment *n* obaveza; izvršenje; predavanje sudu; privrženost.

committee *n* komitet, odbor, komisija.

commodity *n* roba široke potrošnje.

common *a* zajednički, opšti; običan; jednostavan, prost; **in ~** zajedničko; *n* zadružno zemljište; pustara.

commoner *n* osoba nižeg staleža.

common law *n* opšte pravo.

commonly *adv* prosto, obično.

commonplace *n* banalnost; *a* otrcan.

common sense *n* zdrav razum.

commonwealth *n* politička zajednica, federacija.

commotion *n* uzbuđenje, metež, jurnjava.

commune *v* komuna, opština.

communicable *a* zarazan, infektivan; govorljiv.

communicate *v* prenositi, saopštavati, sporazumevati se.

communication *n* saobraćaj, veza, komunikacija.

communicative *a* razgovoran, komunikativan.

communion *n* opštenje; pričest.

Communique *n* zvanično saopštenje, kominike.

communism *n* komunizam.

communist *n* komunista.

community *n* opština, zajednica; podudarnost.

community centre *n* opštinski klub.

community chest *n* opštinska ustanova za javno dobro.

commutable *a* promenljiv.

commutation ticket (*amer*) *n* sezonska vozna karta. *Vidi takođe* **season ticket**.

commute *v* menjati, trampiti; promeniti smer struje; redovno putovati.

compact *a* kompaktan, zbijen; *n* sporazum, dogovor; tvrdi puder; ~ly *adv* kompaktno, sažeto.

companion *n* drug, ortak, saputnik.

companionship *n* drugarstvo.

company *n* društvo, udruženje; gosti; trgovačko društvo.

comparable *a* uporediv.

comparative *a* uporedni stepen (*gram*), komparativ.

compare *v* uporediti, sravniti.

comparison *n* poređenje, komparacija.

compartment *n* odeljenje, kupe; pregrada.

compass *n* kompas, busola.

compassion *n* sažaljenje, bolećivost, saučešće.

compassionate *a* bolećiv, sažaljiv.

compatibility *n* usaglašenost, usklađenost.

compatible *a* podnošljiv, kompatibilan.

compatriot *n* sunarodnik.
compel *v* naterati, prinuditi.
compelling *a* prisilan.
compensate *v* nadoknaditi, kompenzovati; nagraditi.
compensation *n* kompenzacija, nadoknada; nagrada.
compete *v* takmičiti se; konkurisati.
competence *n* sposobnost, spremnost; nadležnost.
competent *a* nadležan, ovlašćen; ~**ly** *adv* kompetentno.
competition *n* takmičenje, utakmica; konkurs.
competitive *a* konkurentan.
competitive bidding *n* javno nadmetanje, licitacija.
compilation *n* sastavljanje, kompilacija.
compile *v* skupiti, prikupiti.
complacency *n* samouverenost, dobrodušnost.
complacent *a* samouveren; dobrodušan.
complain *v* žaliti se, jadikovati.
complaint *n* žalba, nezadovoljstvo.
complement *n* dopuna; objekt (*gram*).
complementary *a* dopunski.
complete *a* pun, potpun, celovit; ~**ly** *adv* puno, potpuno; *v* završiti, dovršiti.
completion *n* završetak, prestanak; komplet.
complex *a* složen.
complexion *n* boja lica; izgled; aspekt.
complexity *n* složenost.
compliance *n* saglasnost; preterana uslužnost.
compliant *a* popustljiv.
complication *n* složenost; komplikacija.
complicity *n* saučesništvo.
compliment *n* kompliment, ljubaznost; *v* pozdravljati, čestitati.
complimentary *a* pohvalan, laskav; besplatan.
comply *v* ispuniti molbu; pridržavati se (pravila).
component *a* komponenta, sastavni deo.
compose *v* sastaviti, sročiti; komponovati.
composed *a* miran, uzdržan.
composer *n* kompozitor.
composite *a* mešovit, složen.
composition *n* sastav, delo; jedinjenje.
compositor *n* slagač.

compost *n* kompost, đubrivo.
composure *n* mirnoća, staloženost.
compound *v* spojiti, sastaviti; izmešati; *a* sastavljen, složen.
comprehend *v* razumeti, shvatiti.
comprehensible *a* razumljiv, dostižan.
comprehensibly *adv* razumljivo.
comprehension *n* razumevanje, shvatanje; obuhvatanje.
comprehensive *a* bistar, koji lako shvata; svestran; ~**ly** *adv* svestrano.
compress *v* stegnuti; *n* oblog, kompres.
comprise *v* uključiti, obuhvatiti.
compromise *n* kompromis, ustupak; *v* pogoditi se.
compulsion *n* prinuda.
compulsive *a* prinudan, obavezan; ~**ly** *adv* obavezno.
compulsory *a* prinudan.
compunction *n* kajanje, griža savesti.
computation *n* obračun, izračunavanje.
compute *v* izračunati, prebrojati.
computer *n* računar, kompjuter.
computer science *n* računarstvo.
comrade *n* drug.
comradeship *n* drugarstvo.
con *v* učiti napamet; *n* bubanje.
concave *a* konkavan, udubljen.
conceal *v* kriti, prikrivati.
concealment *n* prikrivanje; sklonište.
concede *v* ustupiti; složiti se.
conceit *n* uobraženost, taština; hir, prohtev.
conceited *a* uobražen.
conceivable *a* dostižan, razumljiv.
conceive *v* naumiti, zamisliti.
concentrate *v* usredsrediti se, koncentrisati se.
concentration *n* usredsređivanje, koncentracija.
concentration camp *n* koncentracioni logor.
concentric *a* koncentričan, koji ima zajednički centar.
concept *n* pojam, opšti utisak.
conception *n* shvatanje, misao, zamisao.
concern *v* odnositi se, zanimati, interesovati; *n* interes, učešće; udeo; značaj; važnost.
concerning *prep* odnosno, u odnosu na.
concert *n* koncert.

concerto *n* solistički koncert.
concession *n* koncesija, ustupanje prava.
conciliate *v* miriti, zadobiti poverenje.
conciliation *n* pomirenje, izmirenje.
concise *a* sažet, kratak, skraćen; ~**ly** *adv* sažeto, koncizno.
conclude *v* zaključiti, odlučiti, rešiti.
conclusion *n* zaključak.
conclusive *a* zaključni, ubedljiv; ~**ly** *adv* zaključno.
concoct *v* zakuvati, kuvati, zamesiti.
concoction *n* kuvanje; izmišljotina.
concord *n* saglasnost, sporazum, konvencija.
concordant *a* saglasan, skladan, harmoničan.
concourse *n* nagomilavanje, gomilanje.
concrete *n* beton; konkretna stvar; *v* zgusnuti, konkretizovati.
concubine *n* konkubina.
concur *v* podudarati se, poklapati se.
concurrence *n* potpomaganje; sticaj okolnosti.
concurrently *a* podudarno; konkurentski.
concussion *n* potres, kontuzija.
condemn *v* osuditi, presuditi; odbaciti.
condemnation *n* osuda, presuda.
condensation *n* kondenzacija.
condense *v* zgušnjavati, kondenzovati.
condescend *v* snishodljivo se ophoditi, udostojiti.
condescending *a* snishodljiv.
condescension *n* popustljivost, snishodljivost.
condiment *n* začin.
condition *v* usloviti; *n* uslov; stanje; položaj.
conditional *a* uslovan, uslovljen; ~**ly** *adv* uslovno.
conditioned *a* uslovljen.
condolences *npl* saučešće.
condom *n* kondom, prezervativ.
condominium (*amer*) *n* stan (u vlasništvu).
condone *v* oprostiti, zaboraviti.
conducive *a* koji vodi, koji sprovodi.
conduct *n* ponašanje, rukovođenje; dirigovanje; *v* ponašati se, upravljati.
conductor *n* dirigent, šef orkestra; rukovodilac; kondukter.
conduit *n* cevovod, vodovod.
cone *n* kupa; šišarka.

confection *n* slatkiši; konfekcija.
confectioner *n* poslastičar.
confectionery *n* poslastičarnica.
confederacy *n* konfederacija; savez.
confer *v* savetovati se; prisvojiti, dodeliti.
conference *n* konferencija, savetovanje.
confess *v* poveriti se, priznati.
confession *n* priznanje; veroispovest.
confessor *n* ispovednik.
confidant *n* poverenik, opunomoćenik.
confide *v* poveriti, verovati.
confidence *n* poverenje, samopouzdanje.
confidence trick *n* prevara.
confident *a* uveren, samopouzdan.
confidential *a* poverljiv, tajni.
configuration *n* oblik, konfiguracija.
confine *v* ograničiti se, omeđiti.
confinement *n* zatvaranje u tamnicu; porođaj.
confirm *v* potvrditi, podržati.
confirmation *n* potvrda, utvrđivanje.
confiscate *v* zapleniti, konfiskovati.
confiscation *n* konfiskacija.
conflagration *n* veliki požar.
conflict *n* sukob, konflikt.
conflicting *a* protivurečan.
confluence *n* sliv reka, sastavljanje.
conform *v* prilagoditi se, držati se pravila.
conformity *n* usaglašenost.
confound *v* zbuniti, zgranuti; poremetiti planove.
confrontation *n* suočenje, konfrontacija; sravnjenje.
confuse *v* brkati, pomešati, zbuniti; praviti nered.
confusing *a* zbunjujući.
confusion *n* zbrka, zabuna, nered.
congeal *v* zamrznuti se, zgrušati se, stegnuti.
congenial *a* srodan, blizak; podesan.
congenital *a* urođen, kongenitalni.
congested *a* prepun krvi (*med*); pretrpan.
congestion *n* nagomilavanje, zakrčenost; navala krvi (*med*).
conglomerate *n* konglomerat, skup međusobno povezanih elemenata; *v* nagomilati se; *a* nagomilan.
conglomeration *n* skupljanje, konglomeracija.
congratulate *v* čestitati.
congratulations *npl* čestitanje, čestitka.

congratulatory *a* pozdravni.
congregate *v* skupljati, gomilati.
congregation *n* skupljanje; sastanak; opština; parohijani.
congress *n* kongres, skupština, zbor.
congressman *n* kongresmen , član kongresa.
congruity *n* podudarnost, kongruencija.
congruous *a* podudaran.
conic(al) *a* kupast, koji ima oblik kupe.
conifer *n* četinar.
coniferous *a* četinarski (*bot*).
conjecture *n* pretpostavka, dosetka; *v* pretpostavljati, predviđati.
conjugal *a* bračni.
conjugate *v* menjati (*gram*), konjugirati; sjediniti.
conjugation *n* konjugacija (*gram*).
conjunction *n* spona, sticaj; veza (*gram*).
conjuncture *n* sticaj (okolnosti).
conjure *v* moliti, preklinjati; vraćati, bajati.
conjurer *n* mađioničar, čarobnjak.
connect *v* spajati, povezivati.
connection *n* veza, spajanje, sastavljanje; sredstvo.
connivance *n* popustljivost, povlađivanje.
connive *v* povlađivati.
connoisseur *n* stručnjak, znalac.
conquer *v* osvojiti, pobediti.
conqueror *n* osvajač, pobednik.
conquest *n* pobeda, osvajanje.
conscience *n* savest.
conscientious *a* savestan, pošten; ~**ly** *adv* savesno.
conscientious objector *n* lice koje odbija da služi vojsku zbog religioznih ubeđenja.
conscious *a* svestan, razuman; ~**ly** *adv* svesno.
consciousness *n* svest.
conscript *n* vojni obveznik.
conscription *n* vojna obaveza, vrbovanje.
consecrate *v* posvetiti, blagosloviti.
consecration *n* posvećenje, blagoslov.
consecutive *a* uzastopan; ~**ly** *adv* uzastopno.
consensus *n* konsenzus.
consent *n* pristanak, dozvola; *v* pristati, dozvoliti.
consequence *n* posledica, rezultat, važnost.

consequent *a* dosledan, sledeći; ~**ly** *adv* dosledno.
conservation *n* održavanje, čuvanje, konzerviranje.
conservative *a* konzervativac, reakcionar.
conservatory *n* staklena bašta, topla leja.
conserve *v* čuvati, održavati.
consider *v* razmatrati, razmišljati, uzeti u obzir, nameravati.
considerable *a* značajan, važan, veliki; ~**ly** *adv* značajno.
considerate *a* pažljiv, uviđavan; ~**ly** *adv* pažljivo.
consideration *n* razmatranje, prosuđivanje.
considering *prep* računajući sa, uzimajući u obzir.
consign *v* predati, poveriti; otpremiti robu.
consignment *n* tovar, partija robe; otpremanje robe.
consist *v* sastojati se, poklapati se.
consistency *n* doslednost, postojanost.
consistent *a* dosledan, izdržljiv; ~**ly** *adv* dosledno, čvrsto.
consolable *a* utešiv.
consolation *n* uteha.
console *n* utešiti.
consolidate *v* učvrstiti, ujediniti se.
consolidation *n* učvršćivanje, konsolidacija.
consonant *a* saglasan, skladan; *n* suglasnik, konsonant (*gram*).
consort *n* suprug, supruga; saputnik.
conspicuous *a* primetan, istaknut, isturen; ~**ly** *adv* primetno.
conspiracy *n* zavera, konspiracija.
conspirator *n* zaverenik.
conspire *v* tajno se dogovoriti.
constancy *n* postojanost , vernost.
constant *a* stalan, nepromenljiv; ~**ly** *adv* stalno.
constellation *n* sazvežđe.
consternation *n* potištenost, strah.
constipated *a* imati zatvor.
constituency *n* birački okrug, kupci, klijentela.
constituent *n* birač, poverilac; sastojak; *a* izborni; sastavni.
constitute *v* osnovati, obrazovati; odrediti.

constitution *n* ustav, osnovni zakon; poredak.

constrain *v* prinuditi, naterati; zatvoriti u tamnicu.

constraint *n* prinuda, pritisak; tamnovanje.

constrict *v* stezati, sužavati.

construct *v* graditi, podizati, stvarati.

construction *n* gradnja, izgradnja; građevina, zgrada.

construe *v* tumačiti, objašnjavati; upravljati.

consul *n* konzul.

consular *a* konzularan.

consult *v* savetovati se, konsultovati, obavestiti se.

consultant *n* konsultant.

consultation *n* savetovanje, konsultacija.

consume *v* upotrebljavati, trošiti; istrošiti.

consumer *n* potrošač.

consumer goods *npl* roba široke potrošnje.

consumer society *n* potrošačko društvo.

consummate *v* usavršiti, završiti; *a* besprekoran, celovit.

consummation *n* dovršenje, završenje; cilj.

consumption *n* potrošnja; tuberkuloza pluća.

contact *n* dodir, kontakt.

contact lenses *npl* kontaktna sočiva.

contagious *a* zarazan, prenosan.

contain *v* sadržati, suzbijati; zaustaviti.

container *n* sud, rezervoar, kontejner.

contaminate *v* zaraziti, pokvariti; **~d** *a* kontaminiran, zaražen.

contamination *n* kontaminacija, zaraženost.

contemplate *v* posmatrati, razmišljati.

contemplation *n* razmatranje, razmišljanje; namera.

contemporaneous, contemporary *a* sadašnji, istovremeni.

contempt *n* prezir, omalovažavanje.

contemptible *a* prezren, dostojan prezira.

contemptibly *adv* prezreno.

contemptuous *a* preziv; **~ly** *adv* prezrivo.

contend *v* boriti se, takmičiti se; osporavati.

content *a* zadovoljan; *n* zadovoljstvo; sadržina; zapremina, obim.

contentedly *adv* zadovoljno.

contention *n* spor, prepirka, svađa.

contentious *a* sporan, prkosan; **~ly** *adv* sporno.

contentment *n* zadovoljenje, zadovoljstvo.

contest *v* prepirati se, boriti; boriti se za istinu; *n* takmičenje, megdan.

contestant *n* takmičar, kandidat.

context *n* dopuna teksta, dodatak.

contiguous *a* dodirni, granični.

continent *a* uzdržljiv, umeren, čedan; *n* kopno, kontinent.

continental *a* kopnen.

contingency *n* slučaj, nepredviđena okolnost.

contingent *n* kontingent; **~ly** *adv* slučajan, nepredviđen.

continual *a* stalan, neprekidan; **~ly** *adv* stalno, neprekidno.

continuation *n* nastavljanje, obnavljanje.

continue *v* nastavljati, služiti kao nastavak; protezati se.

continuity *n* kontinuitet.

continuous *a* neprekidan, stalan; **~ly** *adv* stalno.

contort *v* iskriviti, unakaziti.

contortion *n* iskrivljenost.

contour *n* obris, kontura.

contraband *n* krijumčarenje; *a* krijumčarski.

contraception *n* kontracepcija.

contraceptive *n* kontraceptivno sredstvo; *a* kontraceptivno.

contract *v* sklopiti ugovor, zaključiti sporazum; sklopiti poznanstvo; dobiti (bolest); *n* ugovor, pogodba, sporazum.

contraction *n* stezanje, skraćivanje.

contractor *n* izvođač radova, preduzimač.

contradict *v* osporavati, protivrečiti.

contradiction *n* protivrečnost, poricanje.

contraption *n* izum; čudna naprava.

contrary *a* suprotan, nepovoljan; *n* suprotnost; **on the ~** nasuprot.

contrast *n* suprotnost, oprečnost, kontrast; *v* suprotstaviti se, razlikovati.

contravention *n* kršenje pravila.

contribute *v* doprinositi, potpomagati.

contribution *n* doprinos, saradnja; članak.

contributor *n* saradnik, pomoćnik, pisac članaka; darodavac.

contributory *a* koji doprinosi.
contrite *a* koji se kaje.
contrition *n* kajanje, skrušenost.
contrivance *n* izum, pronalazak; izmišljotina.
contrive *v* pronaći, izumeti, uspeti.
control *n* uprava, rukovodstvo, vlast, vladanje; provera, kontrola.
control room *n* komandna soba.
control tower *n* kontrolni toranj.
controversial *a* sporan.
controversy *n* spor, diskusija.
contusion *n* povreda, kontuzija.
conundrum *n* šaljiva zagonetka.
conurbation *n* širenje gradova.
convalence *v* ozdraviti, oporaviti se.
convalescence *n* oporavak.
convalescent *a* koji se oporavlja.
convene *v* sazivati, skupljati.
convenience *n* pogodnost, udobnost; nužnik; interes.
convenient *a* udoban, prikladan, odgovarajući; ~**ly** *adv* prikladno.
convent *n* manastir, samostan.
convention *n* sporazum, ugovor, skupština.
conventional *a* uslovan, opštepriznat, utvrđen, konvencionalan.
converge *v* sastaviti se, spojiti, ujediniti.
convergence *n* konvergencija.
conversant *a* upoznat, upućen.
conversation *n* razgovor, konverzacija.
converse *v* razgovarati.
conversion *n* pretvaranje, preobraćanje.
convert *v* pretvarati se, preobratiti; *n* onaj koji je prešao u drugu partiju (veru).
convertible *a* konvertibilan; *n* kabriolet.
convex *a* ispupčen, konveksan.
convexity *n* ispupčenost, konveksnost.
convey *v* prevoziti, prenositi, otpremiti.
conveyance *n* prevoz, transport; prevozno sredstvo.
convict *v* proglasiti krivim, dokazati krivicu; *n* osuđenik, robijaš.
conviction *n* ubeđenje, uverenost; osuda, presuda.
convince *v* ubediti, uveriti.
convincing *a* ubedljiv; ~**ly** *adv* ubedljivo.
convival *a* praznićan, veseo.
conviviality *n* druželjubivost.
convoke *v* sazivati (skupštinu, kongres).

convoy *n* pratnja, konvoj.
convulse *v* potresti, zatresti; izazivati grčeve.
convulsion *n* grč, stezanje, konvulzija; kolebanje, potres.
convulsive *a* grčevit, konvulzivan; ~**ly** *adv* grčevito.
coo *v* gugutati.
cook *n* kuvar, kuvarica; *v* kuvati, skuvati; izmisliti.
cookbook *n* kuvar (knjiga).
cooker *n* štednjak, peć, šerpa; lažov.
cookery *n* kulinarstvo.
cool *a* svež, miran, priseban, hladan; *n* hladovina; *v* rashladiti se, ohladiti.
coolly *adv* hladno, mirno, prisebno.
cooperate *v* sarađivati, raditi zajedno, udružiti se.
cooperation *n* saradnja, udruživanje, kooperacija.
cooperative *a* kooperativan, zajednički.
coordinate *v* usaglasiti, uskladiti, koordinirati.
coordination *n* sadejstvo, koordinacija.
cop *n* policajac (*sleng*).
cope *v* boriti se, uhvatiti se u koštac.
copier *n* aparat za kopiranje.
copious *a* obilan, bogat, rečit; ~**ly** *adv* bogato, plodno.
copper *n* bakar, kotao; bakarni novčić.
coppice, copse *n* gaj, šikara.
copulate *v* spariti se, imati snošaj.
copy *n* primerak, rukopis, kopija; uzorak, obrazac; *v* prepisivati, umnožavati, kopirati.
copybook *n* sveska, beležnica.
copying machine *n* aparat za fotokopiranje.
copyright *n* autorsko pravo.
coral *n* koral.
coral reef *n* koralni greben.
cord *n* uže, konopac, žica.
cordial *a* srdačan, ljubazan; srčani; ~**ly** *adv* srdačno.
corduroy *n* somot, velvet.
core *n* jezgro, srž; suština, bitnost.
cork *n* pluta, zapušač; *v* zapušiti, začepiti.
corkscrew *n* vadičep.
corn *n* žitarice, kukuruz, zrno; žulj.
corncob *n* klip kukuruza.
cornea *n* rožnjača.

corned beef n usoljena govedina.
corner n ugao, ćošak, kutak.
cornerstone n kamen temeljac, ugaoni kamen.
cornet n kornet, fišek.
cornflakes npl kukuruzne pahuljice.
cornflour n kukuruzni štirak.
cornflower n različak (bot).
cornice n krovni venac, karniša.
corollary n posledica.
coronary n zapušavanje krvnih sudova (tromboza); a srčani.
coronation n krunisanje.
coroner n islednik (koji vodi istragu o nasilnoj smrti).
coronet n kruna.
corporal n kaplar.
corporate a zajednički, korporativni.
corporation n udruženje, korporacija.
corporeal a telesni.
corps n korpus (voj).
corpse n leš.
corpulent a ugojen, razvijen.
corpuscle n najsitnija čestica, atom, elektron.
corral n tor, koral.
correct v ispravljati, popravljati, praviti; a pravilan, veran, tačan; **~ly** adv pravilno.
correction n popravka, ispravljanje.
corrective a popravni, koji ispravlja; n ispravka, korektiv.
correlation n korelacija, međusobni odnos.
correlative a koji je u skladu.
correspond v podudarati se, dopisivati se, odgovarati.
correspondence n podudarnost, sličnost; prepiska.
correspondent a odgovarajući; n dopisnik.
corridor n hodnik.
corroborate v potvrditi, potkrepiti.
corroboration n potvrda.
corroborative a koji potkrepljuje.
corrode v zarđati, razjedati; izložiti se dejstvu korozije.
corrosion n rđa, korozija.
corrosive a koji nagriza, jedak.
corrugated iron n valoviti čelik.
corrupt v kvariti, podmićivati, truliti; a pokvaren, potkupljiv, izopačen.

corruptible a podmitljiv.
corruption n pokvarenost, podmitljivost, korupcija.
corset n steznik, korset.
cosily adv prijatno, udobno.
cosmetic a kozmetički; n kozmetičko sredstvo.
cosmic a kosmički.
cosmonaut n kosmonaut, astronaut.
cosmopolitan a kosmopolitski.
cosset v razmaziti.
cost n cena, vrednost; obračun; v koštati, stajati.
costly a skup.
costume n odeća, nošnja, kostim.
cosy a udoban, prijatan.
cottage n koliba, brvnara.
cotton n pamuk, konac, vata.
cotton mill n tekstilna fabrika.
cotton wool n pamuk, vata.
couch n divan, otoman, kauč.
cough n kašalj; v kašljati.
council n savet, savetovanje.
councillor n član saveta.
counsel n većanje, savetovanje; namera.
counsellor n savetnik, savetodavac.
count v računati, obračunavati, smatrati; **to ~ on** računati na nekoga; n račun, obračun.
countdown n odbrojavanje.
countenance n izraz lica; podrška, potpora.
counter n tezga; žeton.
counteract v suprotstaviti se, protiviti se.
counterbalance v izjednačiti ; n protivteža.
counterfeit v falsifikovati, podražavati, pretvarati se; a lažan, falsifikovan.
countermand v opozvati, izdati suprotno naređenje.
counterpart n kopija, prepis.
counterproductive a kontraproduktivan.
countersign v ratifikovati, overiti potpisom.
countess n grofica.
countless a bezbrojan.
countrified a seoski.
country n zemlja, predeo, domovina, teren; periferija, unutrašnjost; a seoski.
countryman n zemljak, sugrađanin; seljak.

county n grofovija; okrug.
coup n genijalan potez; ~ **d'etat** n državni prevrat.
couple n dvoje, par; v sjediniti se, povezati u parove.
couplet n dvostih.
coupon n kupon, odrezak, talon.
courage n hrabrost, odvažnost, smelost.
courageous a hrabar, odvažan, smeo; **~ly** adv hrabro.
courier n kurir.
course n kurs, tok, odvijanje; način vladanja; jelo; **of ~** naravno, svakako.
court n dvorište, igralište; sud, članovi suda; v udvarati se, izložiti se.
court martial n preki sud.
courteous a učtiv, uljudan, uglađen; **~ly** adv učtivo.
courtesan n kurtizana.
courtesy n učtivost.
courthouse n sudnica, sud.
courtly a uglađen, otmen.
courtroom n sudnica.
courtyard n dvorište.
cousin n rođak, brat/sestra od strica, tetke, ujaka, bratanac, sestričina.
cove n mali zaliv; skriveni kut; svod, luk.
covenant n sporazum, ugovor; v zaključiti sporazum.
cover n poklopac, omot, korice; skrovište; izgovor; v pokrivati, kriti, uviti, savladati.
cover girl n devojka s naslovne strane.
coverage n reportaža; visina odštete.
coveralls npl radno odelo, kombinezon.
covering n pokrivač.
covert a sakriven, tajni; **~ly** adv tajno.
cover-up n prikrivanje, zataškivanje.
covet v žudeti, maštati.
covetous a pohlepan, gramziv.
cow n krava.
coward n kukavica.
cowardice n kukavičluk, bojažljivost.
cowardly a/adv plašljiv, malodušan.
cowboy, cowhand n kauboj.
cower v naježiti se, skupiti se (od straha).
coy a stidljiv, sramežljiv; **~ly** adv stidljivo.
crab n rak; dizalica (teh).
crab apple n divlja jabuka.
crack n pukotina, napuklina, pucanje;

udarac, šamar; v pucati, napraviti pukotinu; **to ~ down on** postati strožiji.
cracker n vatromet; tanak dvopek, kreker.
crackle v prštati, praskati.
crackling n puckaranje.
cradle n kolevka, postolje; v uljuljkivati.
craft n zanat, veština.
craftiness n prepredenost, lukavstvo.
craftsman n zanatlija, stručnjak, majstor.
craftsmanship n umešnost, umetnički rad.
crafty a umešan, vešt; lukav.
crag n litica, oštar greben.
cram v napuniti, prepuniti, ugurati.
crammed a nabijen, nakljukan, pretrpan.
cramp n grč, spazam; stega; v stezati, zgrčiti, stisnuti.
crampon n penjalica, krampon.
cramped a zgrčen, stegnut, ukočen.
cranberry n brusnica (bot).
crane n kran, dizalica; ždral (ptica).
crash v tresnuti, srušiti, udariti; n lupa, tresak, slom.
crash helmet n zaštitni šlem.
crass a krajnji, potpuni; sirov, grub.
crate n sanduk, koleto.
crater n grotlo, krater.
crave v žudeti, želeti; preklinjati.
craving n žudnja, velika želja.
crawl v gmizati, mileti, puzati; plivati kraul.
crayfish n rak.
crayon n kreda u boji, olovka u boji.
craze n moda, ćud, ćef.
crazy a lud, bezuman; oduševljen nečim.
creak v škripeti.
cream n krem, krema; mileram, pavlaka; **cold ~** krema za lice.
crease n nabor, rub, brazda; gužvati se.
create v stvarati, praviti.
creation n tvorevina, proizvod, stvaranje.
creative a stvaralački, kreativan.
creator n stvaralac, autor, kreator.
creature n stvor, živo biće; kreatura; hulja.
credence n vera, poverenje.
credentials npl punomoćje, ovlašćenje; akreditivno pismo.
credibility n verodostojnost, uverljivost.
credible a verovatan, moguć; dostojan poverenja.

credit n poverenje, vera; poštenje; značaj; kredit; v verovati; pripisati; odobriti.

credit card n kreditna kartica.

creditable a pohvalan, zaslužan.

creditably adv pohvalno.

creditor n zajmodavac, kreditor.

credulity n lakovernost.

credulous a lakoveran; ~ly adv lakoverno.

creed n vera, ubeđenje.

creek n zaliv, rukavac (reke), potok.

creep v puzati, gmizati, šunjati se, mileti.

creeper n puzavica (bot).

creepy a jeziv, grozan; od koga podilaze žmarci.

cremate v sagoreti, spaliti.

cremation n spaljivanje, kremacija.

crematorium n krematorijum.

crescent n polumesec, mesečev srp; a u obliku polumeseca.

crest n kresta, ćuba; greben.

crested a ćubast.

crestfallen a potišten, klonuo.

crevasse n pukotina (na glečeru).

crevice n napuklina, rascep.

crew n posada, banda, družina.

crib n jasle, dečji krevetac.

cricket n cvrčak; kriket.

crime n zločin, prestup.

criminal a zločinački, kriminalan; n zločinac, kriminalac.

crimson a tamnocrven, rumen.

cripple v osakatiti, onesposobiti.

crisis n kriza, odlučan trenutak.

crisp a hrskav; svež.

criss-cross a unakrstan.

criterion n obeležje, mera, merilo.

critic n kritičar, strog sudija.

critic(al) a kritičan, opasan, odlučujući; ~ally adv kritično.

criticism n kritika, stroga ocena.

criticize v osuđivati, kritikovati.

croak v graktati, kreštati.

crochet v heklati; n hekleraj.

crockery n grnčarija.

crocodile n krokodil.

crony n stari drug.

crook n kuka, kukica, lopov, varalica.

crooked a izvijen, kriv; nepošten.

crop n rod, letina; v davati prinos, roditi.

cross n krst, raspeće; hibrid; v preseći, prevesti; prekrstiti se; a poprečan; suprotan; ljut.

crossbar n prečaga, poprečna greda.

crossbreed n ukrštanje, hibrid.

cross-country n kros, kros takmičenje.

cross-examine v unakrsno .

crossfire n unakrsna vatra.

crossing n ukrštanje, raskrsnica; prelaz.

cross-purpose n nesporazum; **to be at ~s** loše se razumeti, raditi jedan protiv drugoga.

cross-reference n upućivanje.

crossroad n raskrsnica.

crotch n prepona (anat); račve.

crouch v sakriti se, pritajiti se; savijati kičmu.

crow n vrana, krik; v kukureknuti; radovati se.

crowd n gomila, gužva, masa, društvo; v nagurati se, nabiti se, prepuniti.

crown n kruna, venac; v krunisati; nagraditi.

crown prince n prestolonaslednik.

crucial a odlučujući, kritičan.

crucible n sud od vatrostalnog materijala; teško iskušenje.

crucifix n raspeće.

crucify v razapeti, raspeti.

crude a grub, sirov, zelen, nedovršen; ~ly adv grubo.

cruel a okrutan, nemilosrdan; težak; ~ly adv okrutno.

cruelty n bezdušnost.

cruet set/stand n karafindl.

cruise n krstarenje, plovidba; v ploviti, krstariti.

cruiser n krstarica.

crumb n mrvica (hleba).

crumble v mrviti, osipati se, raspadati.

crumple v gužvati, gnječiti; naborati se.

crunch v krckati, zdrobiti.

crunchy a hrskav.

crusade n krstaški rat.

crush v smrskati, zgnječiti, zdrobiti; n gužva, vreva, smrtni udarac; veliki zanos (fig).

crust n kora maska, talog.

crusty a pokriven korom; svadljiv.

crutch n štaka, podrška, stalak.

crux n srž.

cry v plakati, moliti, viknuti; n plač, vapaj, krik, poklič.

crypt *n* grobnica, kripta.
cryptic *a* tajan.
crystal *n* kristal, brušeno staklo.
crystal-clear *a* kristalno čist.
crystalline *a* kristalan, providan.
crystallize *v* pretvarati se u kristale.
cub *n* mladunče, žutokljunac.
cube *n* kub, kocka.
cubic *a* kubni.
cuckoo *n* kukavica.
cucumber *n* krastavac.
cud *n* preživar; **to chew the** ~ dugo razmišljati (*fig*).
cuddle *v* zagrliti, milovati, maziti; *n* zagrljaj.
cudgel *n* batina, močuga.
cue *n* bilijarski štap, tak; replika; red.
cuff *n* manžeta; pljuska, ćuška.
culinary *a* kulinarski.
cull *v* srediti, rasporediti, odabrati.
culminate *v* kulminirati, dostići najvišu tačku.
culmination *n* kulminacija, najviša tačka.
culpable *a* kriv, zločinački.
culpably *adv* krivo, zločinački.
culprit *n* krivac, zločinac.
cult *n* kult, obožavanje.
cultivate *v* uzgajati, kultivisati, razvijati.
cultivation *n* uzgoj, kultura, razvitak.
cultural *a* kulturan, prosvećen.
culture *n* kultura.
cumbersome *a* kabast, glomazan, težak.
cumulative *a* zbirni, celokupan, zajednički.
cunning *a* lukav, prepreden; **~ly** *adv* vešto, lukavo; *n* lukavost, veština.
cup *n* šolja; pehar.
cupboard *n* kredenac.
curable *a* izlečiv.
curate *n* paroh.
curator *n* kustos, član uprave.
curb *n* uzda; suzbijanje; *v* obuzdavati, smiriti.
curd *n* kravlji sir, švapski sir.
curdle *v* zgrušavati se, skameniti se.
cure *n* lek; lečenje, kura; *v* lečiti, izlečiti.
curfew *n* policijski čas.
curiosity *n* radoznalost, znatiželja.
curious *a* radoznao, ljubopitljiv; **~ly** *adv* ljubopitljivo.

curl *n* uvojak, kovrdža, kolut, spirala; *v* uviti, ukovrdžati se.
curly *a* kovrdžast.
currant *n* ribizla; zrno suvog grožđa.
currency *n* valuta, novac; monetarni sistem; primena.
current *a* tekući, sadašnji; aktuelan; *n* struja.
current assets *n* likvidna sredstava.
curriculum vitae *n* kratka biografija (*lat*).
curry *n* kari (začin).
curse *v* prokleti, ukleti, opsovati; *n* prokletstvo, kletva.
cursor *n* kursor.
cursory *a* letimičan, površan.
curt *a* kratak, sažet; grub.
curtail *v* skratiti, smanjiti, saseći.
curtain *n* zavesa.
curtsy *n* kniks, naklon, klanjanje; *v* pokloniti se.
curvature *n* krivina, zavoj.
curve *v* izvijati, uvijati, savijati; *n* kriva linija, grafikon; krivina.
cushion *n* jastuk; umetak.
custard *n* krem od vanile.
custodian *n* kustos, tutor.
custody *n* starateljstvo, zaštita, čuvanje; hapšenje.
custom *n* običaj, navika; carina.
customary *a* uobičajen, običan.
customer *n* kupac, stalni gost.
customs *npl* carina; običaji, navike.
customs officer *n* carinik.
cut *v* seći; saseći; sniziti; kositi; krojiti; **to ~ short** prekinuti, skratiti; **to ~ one's teeth** dobiti zube; *n* posekotina, rana udarac; sniženje; **to ~ a fine figure** izgledati sjajno; **~ and dried** šablonski.
cutback *n* smanjenje, umanjenje.
cute *a* prijatan, sjajan; pametan.
cutlery *n* stoni pribor; nožarski zanat.
cutlet *n* kotlet, odrezak.
cut-rate *a/adv* po sniženoj ceni.
cut-throat *n* ubica, koljač; *a* koljaški.
cutting *n* isečak, sečenje; *a* oštar, prodoran.
cyanide *n* cijanid.
cybernetics *n* kibernetika.
cycle *n* ciklus, završen krug; bicikl; *v* voziti se biciklom; ponavljati se ciklički.

cyclist *n* biciklista.
cyclone *n* ciklon.
cygnet *n* mlad labud.
cylinder *n* cilindar, bubanj.
cylindric(al) *a* cilindričan, valjkast.
cymbals *n* cimbale, činele (*mus*).

cynic(al) *a* ciničan, bezobziran; *n* cinik.
cynicism *n* cinizam, bezobzirnost.
cypress *n* čempres.
cyst *n* cista (*med*).
czar *n* car.

D

dab *n* lak udarac; mrlja.
dabble *v* pokvasiti, poprskati; baviti se nečim amaterski.
dad(dy) *n* tata, otac.
daddy-long-legs *n* kosac (pauk).
daffodil *n* narcis.
dagger *n* bodež.
daily *a* dnevan, svakodnevan; *adv* svakodnevno; *n* dnevne novine.
daintily *adv* prefinjeno, probirljivo.
dainty *a* ukusan, prijatan, fini.
dairy *n* mlekara.
dairy maid *n* muzilja.
dairy products *n* mlečni proizvodi.
daisy *n* krasuljak, tratinčica (*bot*).
dale *n* dolina.
dally *v* dangubiti, zabavljati se; udvarati se.
dam *n* nasip, brana, ustava; *v* pregraditi.
damage *n* šteta, kvar, gubitak; vrednost (*sleng*).
damask *n* damast; *a* damaski.
dame *n* dama, gospodarica.
damn *v* kleti, preklinjati, osuđivati.
damnable *a* gnusan, koji zaslužuje prokletstvo.
damnably *adv* gnusno.
damnation *n* prokletstvo, osuda.
damned *a* proklet; *adv* vrlo, veoma (*sleng*).
damp *a* vlažan; *n* vlaga, para; potištenost; *v* ovlažiti.
dampen *v* ovlažiti, politi vodom.
dampness *n* vlaga, vlažnost.
dance *n* ples, igra, igranka; *v* plesati, igrati.
dance hall *n* plesna dvorana.
dancer *n* igrač, plesač.
dandelion *n* maslačak.
dandruff *n* perut.
dandy *a* kicoški, doteran.
danger *n* opasnost, pretnja.
dangerous *a* opasan, preteći; **~ly** *adv* opasno.
dangle *v* klatiti se, visiti; dražiti.
dank *a* mokar, vlažan.
dapper *a* doteran, uredan.

dappled *a* šaren, pegav.
dare *v* usuditi se, osmeliti se; prkositi.
daredevil *n* pustolov, usijana glava.
daring *n* hrabrost, srčanost; *a* hrabar, odvažan; **~ly** *adv* odvažno, smelo.
dark *a* taman, mračan, tužan; *n* mrak, tama; neznanje.
dark glasses *npl* naočare za sunce.
darken *v* zamračiti, potamneti.
darkness *n* tama, mrak.
darkroom *n* mračna komora.
darling *n, a* dragi, ljubljeni; miljenik.
darn *v* krpiti; psovati (*sleng*).
dart *n* strela, strelica; žaoka; nagli pokret.
dartboard *n* daska za igru bacanja strelica.
dash *v* baciti, tresnuti, uništiti, pljusnuti; *n* silovit pritisak, udarac; crtica.
dashboard *n* šoferska tabla.
dashing *a* doteran; poletan, odvažan.
dastardly *a* kukavički, podao.
data *npl* podaci, dokazi, činjenice.
data processing *n* obrada podataka.
database *n* baza podataka.
date *n* datum, period; sastanak; urma; *v* staviti datum; zabavljati se.
dated *a* datiran, zastareo.
dative *n* dativ (*gram*).
daub *v* mazati, loše slikati; malterisati.
daughter *n* ćerka; **~-in-law** snaja.
daunt *v* zaplašiti, obeshrabriti.
dawdle *v* besposličariti, dangubiti.
dawn *n* zora; *v* svanuti, razdaniti se.
day *n* dan; **by ~** danju; **~ after** iz dana u dan.
day labourer *n* nadničar.
daybreak *n* svitanje.
daylight *n* dnevna svetlost; javnost, publicitet; **~ saving time** letnje vreme (letnje računanje vremena).
daytime *n* dan, doba dana.
daze *v* zaprepastiti, zbuniti.
dazed *a* ošamućen.
dazzle *v* zaslepiti, zaseniti.
dazzling *a* zaslepljujući.
deacon *n* đakon.

dead *a* mrtav, napušten, besvestan;
~**wood** *n* suvo granje; beskoristan
materijal; ~ **silence** *n* mrtva tišina; **the ~**
npl pokojnici.
dead heat *n* mrtva trka (*sport*).
dead march *n* posmrtni marš.
dead-drunk *a* mrtav pijan.
deaden *v* otupeti, izgubiti snagu, oslabiti.
deadline *n* poslednji rok.
deadlock *n* ćorsokak, bezizlazan položaj.
deadly *a* smrtonosan, smrtan; užasan,
strašan; *adv* smrtonosno.
deaf *a* gluv.
deafen *v* prigušiti zvuk, zaglušiti.
deaf-mute *n* gluvonemi.
deafness *n* gluvoća.
deal *n* pogodba, količina, deljenje; **a
great ~** mnogo; **a good ~** dobar posao; *v*
trgovati, poslovati, podeliti; **to ~ in/with**
trgovati nečim.
dealer *n* trgovac.
dealings *npl* posao, postupak.
dean *n* dekan; doajen diplomatskog kora.
dear *a* drag, mio; skup; ~**ly** *adv* ljubazno,
milo.
dearth *n* nestašica, oskudica.
death *n* smrt, propast, kraj.
deathbed *n* samrtnička postelja.
deathblow *n* smrtni udarac.
death certificate *n* umrlica.
death penalty *n* smrtna kazna.
death sentence *n* smrtna presuda.
debacle *n* propast, rasulo.
debar *v* sprečiti, isključiti.
debase *v* poniziti, pogoršati; sniziti
vrednost.
debasement *n* poniženje, sniženje
vrednosti.
debatable *a* sporan.
debate *n* rasprava, polemika, debata; *v*
raspravljati, prosuđivati.
debauched *a* razvratan.
debauchery *n* razvrat, razuzdanost;
pijanstvo.
debilitate *v* oslabiti.
debit *n* zaduženje; *v* zadužiti, upisati u
dug.
debt *n* dug; **to get into ~** pasti u dug.
debtor *n* dužnik, debitor.
debunk *v* razgolititi, otkriti (*sleng*).
decade *n* decenija, dekada.

decadence *n* opadanje, raspadanje,
dekadencija.
decaffeinated *a* bez kofeina.
decanter *n* bokal.
decapitate *v* odseći glavu.
decay *v* truliti, raspasti se; *n* raspadanje,
trulež.
deceased *a* pokojni, umrli.
deceit *n* prevara, lukavstvo.
deceitful *a* lažljiv, lukav; ~**ly** *adv* lažljivo.
deceive *v* varati.
December *n* decembar.
decency *n* pristojnost, uljudnost.
decent *a* pristojan, skroman, ljubazan;
~**ly** *adv* pristojno.
deception *n* prevara, prepredenost.
deceptive *a* varljiv.
decibel *n* decibel.
decide *v* odlučiti, rešiti.
decided *a* odlučan, određen.
decidedly *adv* odlučno.
decidious *a* lišćarski (*bot*).
decimal *a* decimalni.
decimate *v* desetkovati.
decipher *v* dešifrovati, odgonetnuti.
decision *n* odluka, zaključak.
decisive *a* presudan, odlučujući; ~**ly** *adv*
presudno.
deck *n* poluga; špil karata.
deckchair *n* ležaljka na palubi.
declaim *v* recitovati, javno nastupati.
declamation *n* recitovanje, deklamacija.
declaration *n* izjava, deklaracija.
declare *v* objaviti, proglasiti; izjaviti.
declension *n* propadanje, odbijanje;
deklinacija (*gram*).
decline *v* spuštati se, propadati, deklinirati
(*gram*); *n* propadanje, sniženje (cena).
decode *v* dešifrovati.
decompose *v* rastaviti, analizirati;
raspadati se.
decomposition *n* razlaganje, raspadanje,
truljenje.
decor *n* dekor.
decorate *v* ukrasiti; odlikovati.
decoration *n* dekoracija, ukrašavanje;
orden.
decorative *a* ukrasni.
decorator *n* dekorater.
decorous *a* pristojan, uljudan; ~**ly** *adv*
pristojno.

decorum *n* dostojanstvo, etikecija.
decoy *n* klopka, zamka; mamac, iskušenje.
decrease *v* umanjiti, smanjiti; opadati; *n* smanjenje.
decree *n* dekret, naredba; *v* izdati dekret.
decrepit *a* star, trošan, oronuo.
decry *v* uvrediti, poniziti.
dedicate *v* posvetiti.
dedication *n* posveta, namena.
deduce *v* izvesti zaključak, utvrditi.
deduct *v* odbiti, oduzeti.
deduction *n* oduzimanje, obračunavanje.
deed *n* čin, radnja, delo, posao.
deem *v* smatrati, misliti.
deep *a* dubok, nizak; taman (boja).
deepen *v* produbiti; potamneti.
deep-freeze *n* duboko zamrzavanje, zamrzivač.
deeply *adv* duboko.
deer *n* jelen, srna.
deface *v* naružiti, unakaziti.
defamation *n* klevetanje.
default *n* nedostatak; neizvršenje obaveza; *v* ne platiti; izgubiti parnicu zbog izostanka.
defaulter *n* neplatiša.
defeat *n* poraz; *v* poraziti, pobediti.
defect *n* nedostatak, mana.
defective *a* nesavršen, defektan.
defence *n* odbrana.
defenceless *a* bez odbrane.
defend *v* štititi, braniti.
defendant *n* tuženi.
defensive *a* odbrambeni, zaštitni; ~**ly** *adv* odbrambeno.
defer *v* odlagati, odložiti; poštovati.
deference *n* poštovanje.
deferential *a* snishodljiv, pun poštovanja.
defiance *n* izazivanje, otvorena neposlušnost.
defiant *a* izazivajući.
deficiency *n* nedostatak (*med*), manjak.
deficient *a* manjkav, oskudan.
deficit *n* deficit, manjak.
defile *v* uprljati, okaljati, oskrnaviti.
definite *a* određen, tačan, jasan; ~**ly** *adv* jasno.
definition *n* odredba, opredeljenje, preciznost.

definitive *a* konačno, odlučujući; ~**ly** *adv* definitivno.
deflate *v* ispumpati, sniziti (cene).
deflect *v* uklanjati se, savijati se.
deflower *v* oduzeti nevinost, deflorisati.
deform *v* nagrditi, unakaziti.
deformity *n* nakaznost, deformacija.
defraud *v* iznuditi, proneveriti.
defray *v* snositi trošak.
defrost *v* odlediti, otapati.
defroster *n* uređaj za odleđivanje.
deft *a* spretan, umešan; ~**ly** *adv* spretno.
defunct *a* mrtav.
defuse *v* dezaktivirati.
defy *v* prkositi.
degenerate *v* izroditi se, degenerisati; *a* izrod, degenerik.
degeneration *n* degeneracija (*med*).
degradation *n* poniživanje, pad, degradacija.
degrade *v* poniziti; raščiniti.
degree *n* stepen, položaj, rang.
dehydrated *a* dehidriran.
de-ice *v* odlediti.
deign *v* udostojiti.
deity *n* božanstvo.
dejected *a* obeshrabren, bezvoljan.
dejection *n* utučenost, snuždenost.
delay *v* odlagati, zadržavati; *n* odlaganje.
delectable *a* sladak, prijatan.
delegate *v* opunomoćiti, delegirati; *n* izaslanik, delegat.
delegation *n* izaslanstvo, delegacija.
delete *v* brisati, precrtati, poništiti.
deliberate *v* razmotriti, razmišljati; *a* nameran, proračunat; ~**ly** *adv* namerno.
deliberation *n* razmišljanje, prosuđivanje.
deliberative *a* dogovoran.
delicacy *n* poslastica, delikates; finoća, prefinjenost.
delicate *a* fin, nežan, taktičan, osetljiv; ~**ly** *adv* fino.
delicious *a* ukusan, divan; ~**ly** *adv* divno.
delight *n* uživanje, zadovoljstvo; *v* diviti se, uživati.
delighted *a* ushićen.
delightful *a* zanosan, bajan; ~**ly** *adv* zanosno.
delineate *v* ocrtati, opisati, iskazati.
delinquency *n* krivica, zločin; propust.
delinquent *n* zločinac, delinkvent.

delirious *a* bunovan, pomahnitao, deliričan.

delirium *n* delirijum.

deliver *v* predati, uručiti, dostaviti; porađati (*med*).

deliverance *n* spasenje, oslobođenje.

delivery *n* dostava, predaja; držanje govora.

delude *v* zbunjivati.

deluge *n* potop, poplava.

delusion *n* prevara, zabluda; manija (*med*).

delve *v* kopati, zadubiti se u nešto.

demagogue *n* demagog.

demand *n* potražnja, molba, potreba, zahtev; *v* tražiti, pitati.

demanding *a* zahtevan.

demarcation *n* razgraničavanje.

demean *v* ponašati se, vladati se.

demeanour *n* vladanje, držanje.

demented *a* bezuman, mahnit.

demise *n* smrt, preminulost; predaja po nasledstvu.

democracy *n* demokratija.

democrat *n* demokrata.

democratic *a* demokratski.

demolish *v* rušiti, razbiti.

demolition *n* uništenje, rušenje.

demon *n* đavo, zao duh, demon.

demonstrable *a* dokaziv, koji se može dokazati.

demonstrably *adv* dokazivo.

demonstrate *v* dokazivati, prikazivati, demonstrirati.

demonstration *n* prikaz, demonstracija.

demonstrative *a* očigledan, ubedljiv; pokazni.

demonstrator *n* demonstrator.

demoralization *n* obeshrabrenje, moralni pad.

demoralize *v* podrivati disciplinu, demoralisati.

demote *v* premestiti u niže zvanje, degradirati.

demur *v* dvoumiti se, buniti se; sumnjati.

demure *a* ozbiljan, odmeren; lažno skroman; **~ly** *adv* ozbiljno.

den *n* jazbina, sklonište; sobičak.

denial *n* odricanje, otkaz, odbijanje.

denims *npl* farmerke.

denomination *n* naziv, naimenovanje; vrednost novca.

denominator *n* imenilac, imenitelj (*mat*).

denote *v* obeležavati, pokazivati.

denounce *v* optužiti, teretiti, denuncirati.

dense *a* gust, zbijen; tup, glup.

density *n* gustina.

dent *n* udubljenje, ulegnuće; *v* utiskivati.

dental *a* zubni, zubarski.

dentifrice *n* pasta za zube.

dentist *n* zubar.

dentistry *n* zubarstvo.

denture *n* zubna proteza.

denude *v* razgoliti, ogoliti.

denunciation *n* raskrinkavanje, optužba, dostava.

deny *v* poricati, odbijati.

deodorant *n* dezodorans.

depart *v* odlaziti, otputovati.

department *n* odsek, odeljenje; oblast.

department store *n* robna kuća.

departure *n* odlazak, udaljavanje; kraj, smrt.

depend *v* zavisiti, oslanjati se; **~ on/upon** zavisiti od nekoga/nečega.

dependable *a* pouzdan.

dependant *n* potčinjeni, izdržavani član porodice.

dependency *n* zavisnost, podređen položaj.

dependent *a* zavisan.

depict *v* prikazati, opisati.

depleted *a* iscrpljen, potrošen.

deplorable *a* jadan, žalostan.

deplorably *adv* jadno.

deplore *v* oplakivati, sažaljevati.

deploy *v* razviti (trupe).

depopulate *v* smanjiti broj stanovnika.

deport *v* proterati, izgoniti.

deportation *n* progonstvo, izgnanstvo.

deportment *n* vladanje, ponašanje.

deposit *v* ulagati, polagati, staviti na stranu; *n* depozit, zaloga, ulog u banci.

deposition *n* naslaga, talog; svedočenje pod zakletvom.

depositor *n* ulagač.

depot *n* stovarište, depo.

deprave *v* kvariti, podrivati.

depraved *a* izopačen.

depravity *n* izopačenost, nemoralnost.

deprecate *v* prigovarati, protestvovati.

depreciate *v* osporavati vrednost, gubiti vrednost.

depreciation *n* obezvređenje, deprecijacija.
depredation *n* pljačka, pustošenje.
depress *v* ugnjetavati, tlačiti, gušiti.
depressed *a* utučen, deprimiran, zaostao.
depression *n* depresija.
deprive *v* lišiti.
depth *n* dubina; pučina; tamna boja.
deputation *n* izaslanstvo, delegacija.
depute *v* predati punomoćje, delegirati.
deputize *v* delegirati, zamenjivati nekoga.
deputy *n* izaslanik, zamenik.
derail *v* izbaciti iz koloseka.
deranged *a* rastrojen.
derelict *a* napušten.
deride *v* ismejavati, rugati se.
derision *n* ismejavanje, ruganje.
derivation *n* poreklo, izvor; izvođenje porekla, etimologija (reči).
derivative *n* izvedena reč (*gram*), derivativ.
derive *v* poticati od, izvoditi.
dermatologist *n* dermatolog.
derogatory *a* ponižavajući.
derrick *n* bušilica, pokretna dizalica.
desalinate *v* odsoliti.
descant *n* diskant (*muz*); melodija, napev.
descend *v* spuštati se; voditi poreklo; opustititi se.
descendant *n* potomak.
descent *n* silazak, strmina; poreklo, loza.
describe *v* opisati, ocrtati.
description *n* opis, prikaz; rod.
descriptive *a* opisan, pregledan.
descry *v* razgledati, primetiti.
desecrate *v* oskrnaviti.
desecration *n* skrnavljenje.
desert[1] *n* pustinja; *a* pust, nenaseljen.
desert[2] *v* napustiti, ostaviti; **~s** *npl* zasluge.
deserter *n* dezerter.
desertion *n* napuštanje, dezerterstvo.
deserve *v* zaslužiti, biti dostojan.
deservedly *adv* prema zaslugama.
deserving *a* zaslužan.
deshabille, dishabille *n* golišavost.
desideratum *n* nešto što nedostaje .
design *v* projektovati, nacrtati, napraviti plan; *n* nacrt, plan; namera.
designate *v* odrediti, predodrediti, ukazati.
designation *n* oznaka; imenovanje.

designedly *adv* namerno, sa predumišljajem.
designer *n* projektant, konstruktor, dizajner.
desirability *n* poželjnost.
desirable *a* željeni.
desire *n* želja; molba; *v* želeti, hteti, moliti.
desirous *a* željan, koji žudi za nečim.
desist *v* prestati, stati s radom.
desk *n* pisaći sto, školska klupa; pul, stalak.
desktop publishing *n* stono izdavaštvo.
desolate *a* napušten, pust, zapušten; nesrećan.
desolation *n* pustoš, usamljenost.
despair *n* očajanje, beznadežnost; *v* očajavati.
despairingly *a* očajnički.
despatch=dispatch
desperado *n* razbojnik (na divljem zapadu).
desperate *a* očajan, beznadežan; **~ly** *adv* očajno.
desperation *n* očajanje.
despicable *a* dostojan prezira.
despise *v* prezirati, ne podnositi nekoga.
despite *prep* bez obzira na.
despoil *v* pljačkati.
despondency *n* utučenost, potištenost.
despondent *a* potišten.
despot *n* tiranin, samodržac.
despotic *a* tiranski, despotski.
dessert *n* poslastica, slatko (za jelo).
destination *n* odredište, mesto opredeljenja.
destine *v* odrediti, opredeliti.
destiny *n* sudbina.
destitute *a* oskudan, siromašan.
destitution *n* siromaštvo.
destroy *v* uništiti, porušiti.
destruction *n* razaranje, rušenje.
destructive *a* razoran, rušilački, štetan.
desultory *a* nepovezan, isprekidan.
detach *v* odvojiti, rastaviti.
detached *a* odvojen, razdvojen; ravnodušan.
detachment *n* odred (*voj*); odvajanje.
detail *n* pojedinost, detalj; **in ~** podrobno; *v* podrobno pričati; odrediti.
detain *v* sprečavati, usporavati.

detect *v* otkriti, otkrivati, obelodaniti.
detection *n* otkriće, opažanje.
detective *n* detektiv.
detector *n* detektor.
detention *n* prinudno zadržavanje, stavljanje u pritvor.
deter *v* zadržavati, odvraćati.
detergent *n* deterdžent.
deteriorate *v* pogoršati, pokvariti.
deterioration *n* pogoršanje, dotrajalost.
determination *n* određivanje, rešenje; odlučnost.
determine *v* odrediti, ustanoviti; ograničiti.
determined *a* odlučan, rešen.
deterrent *n* zastrašivanje; zastrašujuća sila.
detest *v* mrzeti, gajiti odvratnost.
detestable *a* odvratan, mrzak.
dethrone *v* svrgnuti s prestola.
detonate *v* eksplodirati, detonacija.
detonation *n* detonacija.
detour *n* zaobilazni put.
detract *v* umanjiti, omalovažiti; oklevetati.
detriment *n* šteta, gubitak.
detrimental *a* štetan, škodljiv.
deuce *n* dvojka (u kartama); izjednačenje, đus (tenis); đavo (*sleng*).
devaluation *n* devalvacija, gubitak vrednost.
devastate *v* pustošiti, razarati.
devastating *a* razarajući.
devastation *n* pustoš.
develop *v* razvijati se, usavršavati; pokazati se; razviti (sliku).
development *n* razvoj, rašćenje, usavršavanje.
deviate *v* skretati.
deviation *n* odstupanje, skretanje.
device *n* naprava, uređaj, sprava; plan.
devil *n* đavo, vrag.
devilish *a* đavolski, paklen; ~**ly** *adv* pakleno.
devious *a* neiskren, nepošten; okolišan, zaobilazan.
devise *v* izmisliti, izumeti.
devoid *a* lišen nečega, koji oskudeva.
devolve *v* predati (obaveze); preći nasledstvom.
devote *v* posvetiti se, predati se (nečemu).

devoted *a* odan, posvećen.
devotee *n* zanesenjak, ljubitelj.
devotional *a* molitven.
devour *v* proždirati, gutati.
devout *a* pobožan; iskren; ~**ly** *adv* pobožno.
dew *n* rosa, suza, kap.
dewy *a* orošen, vlažan, svež.
dexterity *n* spretnost, veština, umešnost.
dexterous *a* spretan, vešt.
diabetes *n* šećerna bolest, dijabetes (*med*).
diabetic *n* dijabetičar.
diabolic *a* đavolski, vraški, veoma zao; ~**ally** *adv* žestoko.
diadem *n* dijadema.
diagnosis *n* dijagnoza (*med*).
diagnostic *a* dijagnostički; ~**s** *n* dijagnostika.
diagonal *a* dijagonalan ; ~**ly** *n* dijagonalno.
diagram *n* dijagram, šema.
dial *n* cifarnik, brojčanik.
dialect *n* narečje, govor, dijalekt.
dialling code *n* karakterističan broj telefonske mrežne grupe.
dialogue *n* razgovor, dijalog.
diameter *n* prečnik.
diametrical *a* suprotan, dijametralni; ~**ly** *adv* suprotno.
diamond *n* dijamant, brilijant; ~**s** (suit of) *npl* karo (u kartama).
diamond field *n* rudnik dijamanata .
diaphragm *n* dijafragma, pregrada.
diarrhoea *n* proliv, dijareja (*med*).
diary *n* dnevnik, kalendar.
dice *npl* kocke (za igranje).
dictate *v* diktirati, izdiktirati; *n* diktat; propis, nalog.
dictation *n* diktat, govoriti u pero.
dictatorial *a* diktatorski.
diction *n* način izražavanja, dikcija.
dictionary *n* rečnik.
didactic *a* didaktičan.
die[1] *v* umreti, poginuti; **to ~ away** izgubiti se; **to ~ down** stišati se, jenjavati.
die[2] *n* kocka (za igru); slučaj, uspeh.
diehard *n* krajnji konzervativac; tvrdoglav čovek.
diesel *n* dizel.
diet *n* hrana, ishrana, dijeta; *v* biti na dijeti.

dietary *a* dijetalan, dijetetski.
differ *v* razilaziti se (u mišljenju), ne slagati se.
difference *n* razlika, različitost.
different *a* drukčiji, različit, razni; **~ly** *adv* drugačije.
differentiate *v* razlikovati se; odlikovati se.
difficult *a* težak.
difficulty *n* teškoća, prepreka.
diffidence *n* snebivanje.
diffident *a* skroman, plašljiv; **~ly** *adv* skromno.
diffraction *n* difrakcija.
diffuse *v* širiti, rasturati, razbacivati; *a* rasturen.
diffusion *n* širenje, difuzija.
dig *v* kopati, rovariti; bubati; *n* iskopina, iskopavanje; udarac laktom; sarkastična primedba.
digest *v* variti (hranu); sistematizovati; osvajati.
digestible *a* lako svarljiv.
digestion *n* varenje, probava.
digestive *a* probavni.
digger *n* kopač, sprava za kopanje.
digit *n* brojka, cifra.
digital *a* digitalni.
dignified *a* gord, dostojanstven.
dignitary *n* velikodostojnik, visoki zvaničnik.
dignity *n* dostojanstvo; visoko zvanje; društvena elita.
digress *v* odstupati, skretati.
digression *n* digresija, zastranjivanje.
dike, dyke *n* nasip, brana; jarak; lezbejka (*sleng*).
dilapidated *a* trošan, sklon padu.
dilapidation *n* zapuštenost, trošnost.
dilate *v* rastezati, širiti.
dilemma *n* dilema.
diligence *n* marljivost, priljeznost.
diligent *a* radan, marljiv; **~ly** *adv* radno.
dilute *v* razblažiti, razvodniti, razrediti.
dim *a* taman, mračan; mutan, nejasan; slab; *v* pomračiti, gasiti se.
dime *n* srebrni novac 10 centi (*amer*).
dimension *n* razmera, veličina, dimenzija.
diminish *v* umanjivati, smanjiti, slabiti.
diminution *n* skraćenje, umanjenje.
diminutive *n* diminutiv (*gram*).
dimmer *n* regulator svetla.

dimple *n* rupica (na obrazu); malo ulegnuće.
din *n* buka, tutnjava.
dine *v* ručati, častiti ručkom.
dinghy *n* mali čamac.
dingy *a* mutan, taman.
dinner *n* ručak.
dinner-jacket *n* smoking, svečano odelo.
dinosaur *n* dinosaurus.
dint *n* posredovanje, ulegnuće; **by ~ of** pomoću.
diocese *n* dijaceza.
dip *v* umočiti, zamočiti, potopiti; *n* potapanje.
diphtheria *n* difterija.
diphthong *n* diftong.
diploma *n* diploma.
diplomacy *n* diplomatija.
diplomatic *a* diplomatski, taktičan.
dipstick *n* kontrolna šipka.
dire *a* grozan, strašan.
direct *a* neposredan, otvoren, direktan; *v* usmeriti, upravljati, ciljati.
direction *n* pravac, smer; uprava, rukovodstvo.
directly *a* neposredno, otvoreno; smesta, bez odlaganja.
director *n* rukovodilac, direktor; režiser; dirigent.
directory *n* podsetnik, adresar.
dirt *n* blato, đubre; zemlja, tlo; prljavština; **cheap as ~** džabe, vrlo jeftin.
dirty *a* prljav; nepristojan; nizak.
disability *n* nesposobnost, nemoć.
disabled *a* nesposoban za rad, osakaćen.
disabuse *v* osloboditi nekoga zablude .
disadvantage *n* nezgoda, smetnja; nezgodan položaj.
disadvantageous *a* nezgodan, nepogodan.
disaffected *a* otuđen.
disagree *v* protivurečiti, ne slagati se, svađati se.
disagreeable *a* neprijatan.
disagreeably *adv* neprijatno.
disagreement *n* nesuglasica, nesklad.
disallow *v* odbiti, odbaciti.
disappear *v* iščeznuti, nestati, sakriti se.
disappearance *n* nestanak.
disappoint *v* razočarati, prevariti.
disappointed *a* razočaran.

disappointment *n* razočarenje, prevarena nada.
disapproval *n* osuda, neodobravanje.
disapprove *v* neodobravati, osuditi.
disarm *v* razoružati.
disarmament *n* razoružanje.
disarray *n* zbrka, zabuna, nered.
disaster *n* beda, nesreća.
disastrous *a* porazan, katastrofalan.
disband *v* raspustiti, rasformirati.
disbelief *n* nepoverenje.
disbelieve *v* neverovati.
disburse *v* odrešiti kesu, isplatiti.
disc, disk (*amer*) *n* disk.
discard *v* odbaciti, izbaciti.
discern *v* razlikovati, primećivati.
discernible *a* primetan.
discerning *a* razborit, pronicljiv.
discernment *n* razlikovanje.
discharge *v* istovariti, otpustiti; vršiti; ukinuti; isprazniti; *n* istovar; pucanj; pražnjenje; isticanje; isplata.
disciple *n* učenik, sledbenik; apostol.
discipline *n* disciplina, red; *v* kazniti.
disclaim *v* poricati, ne priznavati.
disclaimer *n* odricanje, poricanje.
disclose *v* razotkriti, raskrinkati.
disclosure *n* otkriće, obelodanjivanje.
discolour *v* gubiti boju, menjati boju.
discolouration *n* gubljenje boje.
discomfort *n* neudobnost, uznemirenost.
disconcert *v* zbunjivati, dovoditi u zabunu.
disconnect *v* razjediniti, odvojiti.
disconsolate *a* neutešan, nesrećan; **~ly** *adv* neutešno.
discontented *a* nezadovoljan.
discontinue *v* prekidati, prestajati.
discord *n* razmimoilaženje, nesklad.
discordant *a* nesložan, neskladan.
discotheque, disco *n* diskoteka.
discount *n* popust, eskont menice, računska stopa; *v* popuštati, smanjiti cenu; ne računati sa nečim.
discourage *v* obeshrabriti, odvratiti.
discouraged *a* obeshrabren.
discouragement *n* obeshrabrenje.
discourse *n* razlaganje, govor.
discourteous *a* neučtiv; **~ly** *adv* neučtivo.
discourtesy *n* neučtivost.
discover *v* otkriti, razotkriti, pronaći.

discovery *n* pronalazak, otkriće; razvoj.
discredit *v* potkopavati ugled, diskreditovati.
discreet *a* oprezan, uzdržljiv; **~ly** *adv* oprezno, razborito.
discrepancy *n* različitost, nesklad, razilaženje.
discretion *n* razboritost, opreznost, diskrecija.
discretionary *a* samovoljan, neograničen.
discriminate *v* razlikovati, raspoznavati, praviti razliku.
discursive *a* diskurzivan.
discuss *v* pretresati, diskutovati; jesti sa zadovoljstvom.
discussion *n* diskusija, pregovori.
disdain *v* prezirati, omalovažiti; *n* prezir, oholost.
disdainful *a* nadmen, prezriv; **~ly** *adv* prezrivo.
disease *n* bolest, oboljenje.
diseased *a* bolestan, oboleo.
disembark *v* iskrcavati se, silaziti.
disembarkation *n* iskrcavanje.
disenchant *v* razočarati.
disenchanted *a* razočaran.
disenchantment *n* razočarenje.
disengage *v* razrešiti, osloboditi, izbaviti se.
disentangle *v* odmotati, ispetljati se.
disfigure *v* izobličiti, unakaziti.
disgrace *n* nemilost, progonstvo, sramota; *v* sramotiti, ponižavati.
disgraceful *a* nečastan, sraman; **~ly** *adv* sramno.
disgruntled *a* nezadovoljan, razljućen.
disguise *v* presvlačiti se, prerušavati se; *n* prerušavanje, maska.
disgust *n* odvratnost; *v* izazivati odvratnost.
disgusting *a* odvratan.
dish *n* činija, tanjir, jelo; *v* ređati u činiju; prevariti; rasturiti, upropastiti; **to ~ up** deliti hranu, servirati.
dishcloth *n* kuhinjska krpa.
dishearten *v* obeshrabriti, rastužiti.
dishevelled *a* razbarušen.
dishonest *a* nepošten, nesavestan; **~ly** *adv* nesavesno.
dishonesty *n* nepoštenje.
dishonour *n* sramota, poruga; neplaćanje po menici; *v* sramotiti.

dishonourable *a* nečastan, sraman.
dishonourably *adv* nečasno.
dishtowel *n* krpa za brisanje sudova.
dishwasher *n* mašina za pranje sudova; perač sudova.
disillusion *v* razočarenje.
disillusioned *a* razočaran.
disinclination *n* neraspoloženost, nedostatak želje.
disinclined *a* nenaklonjen, nesklon.
disinfect *v* dezinfikovati.
disinfectant *n* dezinfekciono sredstvo.
disinherit *v* lišiti nasledstva.
disintegrate *v* rastaviti, usitniti.
disinterested *a* nezainteresovan, ravnodušan, apatičan; ~ly *adv* nezainteresovano.
disjointed *a* raščlanjen, nepovezan.
diskette *n* disketa.
dislike *n* neprijateljstvo, nesklonost, odvratnost; *v* osećati odvratnost.
dislocate *v* iščašiti, pomeriti, poremetiti.
dislocation *n* iščašenje, premeštanje.
dislodge *v* ukloniti, isterati, proterati.
disloyal *a* nelojalan, izdajnički; ~ly *adv* nelojalno.
disloyalty *n* nelojalnost, neverstvo.
dismal *a* mračan, čemeran, ružan.
dismantle *v* rastavljati, demontirati, razoružati.
dismay *n* užas, strah.
dismember *v* raščlaniti, razdeliti; lišiti članstva.
dismiss *v* otpustiti, raspustiti, proterati.
dismissal *n* otpuštanje, otkaz, udaljivanje, odstranjivanje; dopust.
dismount *v* sjašiti, zbaciti s konja.
disobedience *n* neposlušnost, nepokoravanje.
disobedient *a* neposlušan, nepokoran.
disobey *v* biti neposlušan, ne pokoravati se.
disorder *n* nered, neredi; bolešljivost, poremećaj.
disorderly *a* neuredan, netačan; bučan.
disorganization *n* dezorganizacija.
disorganized *a* dezorganizovan.
disorientated *a* dezorijentisan.
disown *v* odricati se, ne priznavati.
disparage *v* ponižavati, govoriti sa potcenjivanjem.

disparaging *a* omalovažavajući.
disparity *n* nejednakost, nepodudarnost.
dispassionate *a* bespristrasan.
dispatch *v* otpremiti, odaslati, poslati; *n* slanje, otpremanje, obaveštenje.
dispel *v* rasterati, razvejati.
dispensary *n* dispanzer; apoteka.
dispense *v* podeliti, izdavati (lekove); biti bez.
disperse *v* rasuti, širiti, raspršiti.
dispirited *a* potišten, utučen.
displace *v* premeštati, zameniti, ukloniti.
display *v* prikazivati, pojavljivati se, razmetati se; *n* prikaz, izložba.
displeased *a* nezadovoljan, ljutit.
displeasure *n* nezadovoljstvo, neugodnost.
disposable *a* raspoloživ, slobodan.
disposal *n* raspolaganje, raspored, razmeštaj.
dispose *v* rasporediti, raspolagati.
disposed *a* raspoložen.
disposition *v* raspored, dispozicija; naklonost.
dispossess *v* otuđiti, lišiti prava svojine.
disproportionate *a* nesrazmeran, disproporcionalan.
disprove *v* pobijati, opovrgavati.
dispute *v* raspravljati se, prepirati se, diskutovati.
disqualify *v* diskvalifikovati.
disquiet *n* nemir, uzbuđenje.
disquieting *a* uznemirujuće.
disquisition *n* istraživanje, ispitivanje, naučna rasprava.
disregard *v* ignorisati, ne obraćati pažnju.
disreputable *a* nepristojan, onaj koga bije loš glas.
disrespect *n* nepoštovanje, neučtivost.
disrespectful *a* neučtiv; ~ly *adv* neučtivo.
disrobe *v* svući, svući se.
disrupt *v* raskinuti, srušiti.
disruption *n* raskid, rascep.
dissatisfaction *n* nezadovoljstvo, nelagodnost.
dissatisfied *a* nezadovoljan.
dissect *v* rasecati, otvoriti.
dissection *n* disekcija, seciranje (*med*).
dissension *n* nesklad, svađa.
dissent *v* razilaziti se u mišljenju; *n* nesloga; sektaštvo.

dissenter n sektaš, otpadnik.
dissertation n disertacija.
dissident n disident.
dissimilar a različit.
dissimilarity n različitost.
dissimulation n disimulacija.
dissipate v rasturiti se, raspasti se; lumpovati.
dissipation n rasipanje; raskalašnost.
dissociate v razjediniti, razdvojiti.
dissolute a razuzdan.
dissolution n rastvaranje; razlaganje; raskid.
dissolve v rastvarati, razlagati, rastvoriti.
dissonance n disonanca (muz); nesklad.
dissuade v odvratiti, odgovarati od nečega.
distance n rastojanje, udaljenost, vremenski razmak; **at a ~** na odstojanju; v ostaviti daleko iza sebe.
distant a daleki, udaljen.
distaste n odvratnost.
distasteful a neprijatan, gadan.
distend v raspirivati, naduvavati.
distil v cediti, destilisati.
distillation n destilacija.
distinct a jasan, upečatljiv; različit; određen, očigledan; **~ly** adv jasno.
distinctive a naročit, karakterističan.
distinguish v razlikovati se, odlikovati se; prepoznati.
distort v izobličiti, iskriviti.
distorted a iskrivljen.
distortion n izobličavanje, izvrtanje.
distract v poremetiti, odvraćati pažnju.
distracted a rasejan, lud; **~ly** adv izbezumljeno.
distraction n rasejanost, ludilo.
distraught a izbezumljen.
distress n bol, jad, nevolja; iznurenost; v naneti bol, ožalostiti.
distressing a tužan, koji zabrinjava.
distribute v raspodeliti, širiti, razmestiti, distribuirati.
distribution n raspodela, distribucija.
distributor n distributer, delilac.
district n okrug, srez, pokrajina.
distrustful a nepoverljiv, sumnjičav.
disturb v uznemiravati, smetati, osujetiti.
disturbance n uznemiravanje, uzbuđenje.
disturbed a poremećen.

disturbing a uznemirujući.
disuse n neupotreba.
ditch n jarak, rov, šanac.
dither v uzrujavati.
ditto adv to isto, isto toliko.
ditty n pesmica.
diuretic n diuretik, sredstvo za povećanje lučenja mokraće (med).
diurnal a dnevni, svakodnevni.
dive v roniti, zagnjuriti; iznenada nestati; n ronjenje, skok u vodu.
diver n ronilac.
diverge n skretati, razilaziti se.
divergence n razilaženje.
divergent a divergentan.
diverse a drukčiji, različit; **~ly** adv drukčiji.
diversion n skretanje; diverzija; zabava, razonoda.
diversity n različitost, raznovrsnost.
divert v odvratiti, skrenuti; razonoditi.
divest v svući se, skinuti odelo.
divide v deliti, razdvojiti.
dividend n dividenda; deljenik (mat).
dividers npl šestar.
divine a božanski, božanstven.
diving n skokovi s daske.
diving board n skakaonica.
divinity n božanstvo.
divisible a deljiv.
division n deljenje (mat), deoba; pregrada; divizija; podela.
divisor n delilac (mat).
divorce n razvod, razdvajanje; v razvesti se, raskinuti brak.
divorced a razveden.
divulge v objaviti, razglasiti.
dizziness n vrtoglavica.
dizzy a koji ima vrtoglavicu.
do v raditi, obaviti, činiti.
docile a poslušan, koji lako uči.
dock n pristanište, kolosek; optuženička klupa; v uvesti brod u dok.
docker n lučki radnik.
dockyard n brodogradilište.
doctor n lekar, doktor.
doctrine n učenje, doktrina.
document n isprava, dokument.
documentary a dokumentarni.
dodge v izmicati, izbegavati.
doe n košuta, srna; **~ rabbit** zečica.

dog *n* pas, kuće.
dog kennel *n* štenara.
dogged *a* tvrdoglav, uporan; ~ly *adv* uporno.
dogmatic *a* dogmatičan, odlučan.
dogmatically *adv* dogmatično.
doings *npl* posao, rad, ponašanje.
do-it-yourself *n* uradi sam (*sleng*).
doleful *a* tužan, žalostan.
doll *n* lutka.
dollar *n* dolar.
dolphin *n* delfin (*zool*).
domain *n* imanje; područje, oblast.
dome *n* kupola, svod.
domestic *a* domaći, porodični.
domesticate *v* pripitomiti; vezati se za kuću.
domesticity *n* porodičnost.
domicile *n* mesto boravka.
dominant *a* nadmoćan.
dominate *v* vladati, gospodariti.
domination *n* prevlast, nadmoć.
domineer *v* gospodariti, zapovedati.
domineering *a* nadmen, zapovednički.
dominion *n* dominion, posed.
dominoes *npl* domine.
donate *v* darovati, pokloniti.
donation *n* donacija.
done *a* skuvan, pečen.
donkey *n* magarac.
donor *n* darodavac; donor (*med*).
doodle *v* škrabati, žvrljati.
doom *n* sudbina, usud.
door *n* vrata.
doorbell *n* zvono na vratima.
door knob *n* kvaka (na vratima).
doorman *n* vratar, portir.
doormat *n* otirač.
doorstep *n* prag.
doorway *n* ulaz u kuću.
dormant *a* dremljiv, koji spava.
dormer window *n* tavanski prozor.
dormitory *n* spavaonica, studentski dom.
dormouse *n* puh (*zool*).
dosage *n* doziranje, određena količina.
dose *n* doza, obrok; *v* davati lek u određenim količinama.
dossier *n* dosije.
dot *n* tačka, sitna stvar.
dote *v* razmaziti.
double *a* dvostruk, dvojni; *v* udvostručiti; *n* dvojnik.

double-breasted *a* dvoredan.
double chin *n* dvostruki podbradak.
double-dealing *n* dvoličnost.
double-edged *a* dvosekli; dvosmislen.
double entry *n* dvojno (knjigovodstvo).
double over *v* presaviti.
doubly *a* dvostruki, dupli.
doubt *n* sumnja; *v* sumnjati, sumnjičiti.
doubtful *a* sumnjiv, neodlučan, nesiguran.
doubtless *adv* nesumnjivo, vrlo verovatno.
dough *n* testo, gusta masa.
douse *v* politi, ukvasiti.
dove *n* golubica.
dovecot(e) *n* golubarnik.
dowdy *a* loše obučen, bez ukusa.
down *n* pahuljica, paperje; *prep* na, po, duž, niz; *adv* dole; to sit ~ sesti; upside ~ naopak.
downcast *a* oboren, spušten; potišten.
downfall *n* pad, propast; pljusak.
downhearted *a* potišten, klonuo.
downhill *adv* nizbrdo.
down payment *n* prva rata, depozit.
downpour *n* pljusak, provala oblaka.
downright *a* očigledan, potpun.
downstairs *adv* dole, niz.
down-to-earth *a* realističan.
downtown *adv* u poslovnoj četvrti grada.
downward(s) *adv* nadole, niz.
dowry *n* miraz, prirodni dar.
doze *v* dremati.
dozen *n* tuce, dvanaest.
dozy *a* sanjiv; glup.
drab *a* sivosmeđe boje; jednoličan.
draft *n* crtež, skica, nacrt; ček.
drafty *a* izložen promaji.
drag *v* vući, navući, dovući; *n* kočnica, teška obaveza.
dragnet *n* mreža; traganje.
dragon *n* zmaj, aždaja.
dragonfly *n* vilin konjic (*zool*).
drain *v* isušivati, drenirati, odvoditi vodu; *n* vodovod, kanalizaciona cev.
drainage *n* isušivanje, drenaža.
drainpipe *n* odvodna cev.
drake *n* vodeni cvet.
dram *n* gutljaj.
drama *n* drama.

dramatic *a* dramatičan; izveštačen.
dramatically *adv* dramatično.
dramatist *n* pisac drama.
dramatize *v* inscenirati književno delo.
drape *v* ogrnuti se, namestiti zavese; *n* draperija, zavesa.
drastic *a* odlučan, oštar, žestok.
draughts *npl* igra dame (u kartama).
draw *v* vući, tegliti, povlačiti; **to ~ blood** pustiti krv, dati krv.
drawback *n* smetnja, prepreka, mana.
drawer *n* crtač; ladica, fijoka.
drawing *n* crtanje, crtež.
drawing board *n* daska za crtanje.
drawing room *n* salon, soba za primanje.
drawl *v* otezati u govoru, razvlačiti reči.
dread *n* strah, strava; *v* bojati se.
dreadful *a* strašan, užasan; **~ly** *adv* strašno.
dream *n* san, spavanje; *v* sanjati, maštati.
dreary *a* turoban, dosadan.
dredge *v* kopati bagerom.
dregs *npl* ostaci, talog.
drench *v* nakvasiti, pokvasiti.
dress *v* odenuti, obući; previti ranu; *n* haljina, odelo, nošnja.
dresser *n* toaletni sto, orman.
dressing *n* pripravljanje, priređivanje; grdnja; začin.
dressing gown *n* domaća haljina.
dressing room *n* svlačionica, šminkernica.
dressmaker *n* krojačica.
dressy *a* doteran, elegantan.
dribble *v* driblovati; kapati, cureti.
dried *a* suv, sasušen.
drift *n* strujanje, skretanje; pravac, smer; *v* ploviti, ići polako; prepustiti se; zanositi se.
driftwood *n* naneto drvo.
drill *n* burgija, bušilica; vojna obuka; *v* bušiti; obučavati.
drink *v* piti, napiti se; *n* piće, napitak; čaša vina.
drinkable *a* pitak.
drinker *n* alkoholičar, koji pije.
drinking water *n* voda za piće, pijaća voda.
drip *v* kapati; *n* curenje; dosadna osoba (*sleng*).
dripping *n* kapanje.

drive *v* voziti, upravljati; terati, doterati; dovesti; ukucati; *n* vožnja; put, auto-put; pogon.
drivel *n* pljuvačka, bale; glupo brbljanje.
driver *n* vozač, vozovođa.
driver's licence *n* vozačka dozvola.
driveway *n* prilazni put, prolaz.
driving *n* vožnja, voženje.
driving school *n* auto-škola.
driving test *n* vozački ispit.
drizzle *v* rominjati, rositi.
droll *a* smešan, čudan.
drone *n* trut, lenština.
drool *v* balaviti.
droop *v* klonuti, malaksati; oklembesiti se.
drop *n* kap, kapljica; gutljaj; pad; *v* kapati, curiti; **to ~ out** ispasti, nestati.
drop-out *n* maloletnik koji je napustio školu.
dropper *n* kapalica, pipeta.
dross *n* otpaci, šljaka.
drought *n* suša.
drove *n* stado, čopor; gomila.
drown *v* udaviti se, tonuti, potopiti se.
drowsiness *n* pospanost.
drowsy *a* sanjiv, pospan.
drudgery *n* težak rad.
drug *n* lek, droga; *v* davati lek, uzimati drogu.
drug addict *n* narkoman.
drug addiction *n* narkomanija.
drug trafficker *n* trgovac drogom.
drum *n* bubanj, cilindar; *v* udarati u doboš.
drum majorette *n* mažoretkinja.
drummer *n* bubnjar.
drumstick *n* dobošarska maljica.
drunk *a* pijan, ošamućen.
drunkard *n* pijanica.
drunken *a* pijan.
dry *a* suv, presušen; dosadan; *v* osušiti.
dry-cleaning *n* hemijsko čišćenje.
dryness *n* suvoća.
dual *a* dvostruk, dupli.
dual-purpose *a* sa dve funkcije.
dubbed *a* nasinhronizovan.
dubious *a* sumnjiv, sumnjičav, nesiguran.
duck *n* patka; *v* zagnjuriti se.
duckling *n* pače.
dud *n* nesrećnik, neuspeh; neeksplodirana granata.

due *a* dužan, pravovremen; određen, nadležan; *adv* tačno, pravo; *n* dug, pozajmica.
duel *n* dvoboj.
duet *n* duet (*muz*).
dull *a* glup, tup; tmuran; *v* otupiti, oslabiti.
duly *adv* propisno, pravilno.
dumb *a* nem, bezglasan, ćutljiv; glup; ~ **ly** *adv* nemo.
dumbbell *n* tegovi.
dumbfounded *a* zaprepašćen, iznenađen.
dummy *n* krojačka lutka, maketa; budala, glupak.
dump *n* đubrište, hrpa otpadaka; *v* istovariti, prevrnuti.
dumping *n* iskrcavanje; prodaja robe na stranom tržištu po nižim cenama.
dumpling *n* valjušak, puding.
dumpy *a* dežmekast.
dunce *n* budala, tupoglavac.
dune *n* dina, peščani nanos.
dung *n* balega, gnoj.
dungarees *npl* farmerke.
dungeon *n* tamnica pod zemljom.
dupe *n* naivčina, lakoveran čovek; *v* prevariti, nasamariti.
duplex *n* stan na dva sprata, zgrada sa dva stana, dupleks.
duplicate *n* prepis, duplikat; *v* udvostručiti, napraviti prepis.
duplicity *n* dvoličnost.

durability *n* trajnost, izdržljivost.
durable *a* izdržljiv, postojan.
duration *n* trajanje, vreme.
during *prep* u toku, za vreme, dok.
dusk *n* suton.
dust *n* prašina, prah, pometnja, zbrka; *v* brisati prašinu; isprašiti; zaprašiti.
dustbin *n* kanta za smeće.
duster *n* krpa za prašinu.
dustman *n* đubretar.
dusty *a* prašnjiv, zaprašen.
Dutch treat *n* kad svako plaća za sebe.
dutiful *a* poslušan, pokoran, poštuje obaveze; ~**ly** *adv* poslušno.
duty *n* dug, obaveza, služba; dažbina.
duty-free *a* oslobođeno carine.
dwarf *n* patuljak; *v* sprečiti da raste; učiniti nešto malim.
dwell *v* živeti, obitavati, boraviti.
dwelling *n* prebivalište, kuća.
dwindle *v* smanjivati se, iščeznuti.
dye *v* bojiti, obojiti; *n* boja, nijansa.
dyer *n* bojadžija.
dying *a* umirući, smrtni; *n* umiranje; ~ **man** samrtnik.
dynamic *a* dinamičan, odlučan.
dynamite *n* dinamit.
dynasty *n* dinastija.
dysentery *n* srdobolja, dizenterija (*med*).
dyspepsia *n* dispepsija (*med*).
dystrophy *n* distrofija (*med*).

E

each *pn* svaki; ~ **other** jedan drugog, jedan drugom.
eager *a* željan, žudan; **~ly** *adv* željno.
eagerness *n* revnost, žar.
eagle *n* orao.
eagle-eyed *a* oštrog vida.
eaglet *n* orlić.
ear *n* uvo, sluh; **to play by** ~ improvizovati.
earache *n* uhobolja.
eardrum *n* bubna opna.
early *a* ran, preran, prevremen; *adv* rano, prerano.
earmark *v* obeležiti (žigom).
earn *v* zaraditi, zaslužiti.
earnest *a* ozbiljan; **~ly** *adv* ozbiljno.
earnestness *n* ozbiljnost.
earnings *npl* zarada.
earphones *npl* slušalice.
earring *n* minđuša, naušnica.
earth *n* zemlja, tlo, kopno; *v* zakopati u zemlju, zatrpati u rupu.
earthen *a* zemljan.
earthenware *n* grnčarija, zemljano posuđe.
earthquake *n* zemljotres, potres.
earthworm *n* kišna glista.
earthy *a* zemljan, ovozemaljski; grub, prost.
earwig *n* uholaža (*zool*); doušnik.
ease *n* mir, spokojstvo; lakoća; **at** ~ voljno; *v* olakšati, ublažiti; popustiti.
easel *n* slikarski stalak, nogare.
easily *adv* lako; verovatno.
easiness *n* lakoća.
east *n* istok, istočnjak.
Easter *n* Uskrs.
Easter egg *n* uskršnje jaje.
easterly *a* istočni.
eastern *a* istočni; koji živi na Istoku.
eastward(s) *adv* istočno.
easy *a* lak, miran, pristupačan; **~-going** lakomislen, bezbrižan.
easy chair *n* fotelja.
eat *v* jesti; pojesti; hraniti se.
eatable *a* jestiv; **~s** *npl* hrana.
eau de Cologne *n* kolonjska voda.

eaves *npl* streha, nadstrešnica.
eavesdrop *v* prisluškivati.
ebb *n* oseka, pad, propadanje; *v* odlivati, opadati; gasiti se.
ebony *n* abonos.
eccentric *a* čudan, nastran.
eccentricity *n* nastranost, ekscentričnost.
ecclesiastic *a* duhovni, crkveni.
echo *n* eho; *v* odjekivati, ponavljati zvuk.
eclectic *a* eklektičan.
eclipse *n* pomračenje, gubitak sjaja; *v* pomračiti.
ecologist, environmentalist *n* ekolog.
ecology *n* ekologija.
e-commerce *n* elektronska trgovina.
economic(al) *a* ekonomski, privredni.
economics *npl* ekonomske nauke, ekonomija.
economist *n* ekonomista.
economize *v* štedeti, ekonomisati.
economy *n* gazdinstvo; štednja; ušteđevina.
ecosystem *n* ekološki sistem.
ecotax *n* ekološka taksa.
ecotourism *n* ekološki turizam.
ecstasy *n* zanos, ushićenost.
ecstatic *a* ushićen, izvan sebe; **~ally** *adv* ushićeno.
eczema *n* ekcem.
eddy *n* vir, vihor; *v* kovitlati se.
edge *n* ivica, rub, porub; oštrica; planinski greben; *v* oštriti, porubiti.
edgeways, edgewise *adv* sa napred isturenom oštricom.
edging *n* obrub, traka; rub, ivica.
edgy *a* oštar, razdražen.
edible *a* jestiv, za jelo.
edict *n* ukaz, edikt.
edification *n* pouka, nauk.
edifice *n* zgrada, zdanje.
edify *v* poučiti, naučiti.
edit *v* redigovati, prirediti.
edition *n* izdanje, broj novina.
editor *n* urednik, redaktor.
editorial *a* uređivački.
educate *v* vaspitati, razvijati.
education *n* vaspitanje, obrazovanje.

eel *n* jegulja.
eerie *a* stravičan, strašan.
efface *v* brisati, izgladiti.
effect *n* ishod, dejstvo; posledica; utisak;
~s *npl* stvari, imovina; *v* činiti, stvarati,
proizvoditi.
effective *a* važeći, koji je na snazi;
stvaran; ~ly *adv* uspešno, efektno.
effectiveness *n* efikasnost, delotvornost.
effectual *a* uspešan, efektivan; ~ly *adv*
uspešno.
effeminacy *n* ženstvenost, razneženost.
effeminate *a* ženstven, sličan ženi.
effervescence *n* vrenje, kipljenje.
effete *a* istrošen, iscrpljen.
efficacy *n* uspešnost, delovanje.
efficiency *n* spremnost, gotovost;
umešnost.
efficient *a* stvaran, uspešan, spretan.
effigy *n* slika, lik, obličje.
effort *n* napor, pokušaj; dostignuće.
effortless *a* lak, bez napora.
effrontery *n* drskost, bezobrazluk.
effusive *a* plahovit, neobuzdan.
egg *n* jaje ; odličan posao; to ~ on *v*
podstrekavati.
eggcup *n* stalak za kuvano jaje.
eggplant *n* plavi patlidžan.
eggshell *n* ljuska od jajeta.
ego(t)ism *n* sebičnost, egoizam.
ego(t)ist *n* egoista.
ego(t)istical *a* sebičan.
eiderdown *n* jorgan (od paperja).
eight *num* osam.
eighteen *num* osamnaest.
eighteenth *num a* osamnaesti,
osamnaestina.
eighth *num a* osmi, osmina.
eightieth *num a* osamdeseti, osamdeseti
deo.
eighty *num* osamdeset.
either *pn* svaki, oboje, i jedan i drugi;
conj ili.
ejaculate *v* uzviknuti; ejakulirati.
ejaculation *n* usklik; lučenje.
eject *v* izbaciti, isterati.
ejection *n* izbacivanje; pražnjenje.
ejection seat *n* sedište za katapultiranje.
eke *v* popuniti, nadoknaditi.
elaborate *v* razraditi, obraditi; *a* detaljan,
podroban; ~ly *adv* detaljno.

elapse *v* proticati, prolaziti.
elastic *a* rastegljiv, elastičan.
elasticity *n* rastegljivost, elastičnost.
elated *a* oduševljen, pun poleta.
elation *n* ushićenje.
elbow *n* lakat; *v* gurati laktovima.
elbow-room *n* prostor za kretanje.
elder *n* starac, starešina; *a* stariji po
godinama.
elderly *a* postariji.
eldest *a* najstariji.
elect *v* birati, izabrati; *a* izabran.
election *n* izbori, izbor.
elective *a* izborni, izabrani.
elector *n* birač, glasač.
electoral *a* izborni.
electorate *n* glasačko telo.
electric(al) *a* električan; ~ domestic
appliances električni kući aparati.
electric blanket *n* električno ćebe.
electric current *n* električna struja.
electric fence *n* električna ograda.
electrician *n* električar, elektrotehničar.
electricity *n* elektricitet.
electrify *v* elektrificirati.
electrocardiogram *n* elektrokardiogram.
electron *n* elektron.
electronic *a* elektronski; ~s *npl*
elektronika.
elegance *n* otmenost, elegancija.
elegant *a* otmen, elegantan; ~ly *adv*
otmeno.
elegy *n* elegija.
element *n* osnovni element, sastav.
elemental *a* elementaran, stihijski.
elementary *a* osnovni, početni, elementaran.
elephant *n* slon.
elephantine *a* slonovski, glomazan.
elevate *v* podizati, povisiti, uzdići.
elevation *n* uzvišenje, visina; podizanje.
elevator *(n* lift, dizalica.
eleven *num* jedanaest.
eleventh *num a* jedanaesti; jedanaestina.
elf *n* patuljak, kepec.
elicit *v* otkriti, izazvati; izmeniti.
eligibility *n* podobnost, kvalifikovanost.
eligible *a* podoban, odgovarajući.
eliminate *v* izbaciti, isključiti, odstraniti.
elk *n* los.
elliptic(al) *a* eliptičan (*mat*).
elm *n* brest (*bot*).

elocution *n* govornička veština; dikcija.
elongate *v* izdužiti, rastezati se,
produžiti.
elope *v* pobeći (sa ljubavnikom); sakriti
se.
elopement *n* bekstvo.
eloquence *n* rečitost, govorljivost.
eloquent *a* rečit; ~ly *adv* rečito.
else *pn* još, osim, inače.
elsewhere *adv* drugde, na drugom mestu.
elucidate *v* rasvetliti, razjasniti.
elucidation *n* razjašnjenje, tumačenje.
elude *v* izbegavati, izvlačiti se.
elusive *a* nedostižan , neuhvatljiv.
emaciated *a* iznuren, iscrpljen, koji je
smršao.
e-mail *n* elektronska pošta.
emanate (from) *v* poteći iz.
emancipate *v* osloboditi, emancipovati.
emancipation *n* emancipacija.
embalm *v* balsamovati, sačuvati od
zaborava.
embankment *n* nasip, brana, ozidana
obala.
embargo *n* embargo.
embark *v* utovariti, ukrcati.
embarkation *n* ukrcavanje.
embarrass *v* dovoditi u nepriliku,
zbunjivati; opteretiti.
embarrassed *a* zbunjen; u neprilici.
embarrassment *n* zabuna, smetnja;
zamršenost; neprijatnost.
embassy *n* ambasada, poslanstvo.
embed *v* ukopavati, umetnuti; urezati.
embellish *v* ukrasiti, doterati.
embellishment *n* ulepšavanje,
doterivanje.
embers *npl* žar, pepeo.
embezzle *v* proneveriti (novac).
embezzlement *n* pronevera.
embitter *v* zatrovati, pokvariti, ogorčiti.
emblem *n* amblem, znamenje.
emblemetic *a* simbolički.
embodiment *n* ovaploćenje, oličenje;
ujedinjenje.
embody *v* oličavati, ostvariti; sastojati se,
sadržati u sebi.
embrace *v* grliti se; obuhvatati; *n* zagrljaj.
embroider *v* vesti, izvesti; ulepšati.
embroidery *n* vez, vezenje.
embroil *v* zamrsiti, zapetljati; posvađati.

embryo *n* zametak, embrion.
emendation *n* popravka, ispravka,
izmena.
emerald *n* smaragd.
emerge *v* pojaviti se, isploviti; pokazati
se.
emergency *n* vanredno stanje, neočekivan
događaj.
emergency cord *n* signal za slučaj
opasnosti.
emergency exit *n* izlaz u slučaju nužde.
emergency landing *n* prinudno sletanje.
emergency meeting *n* hitan sastanak.
emery *n* šmirgla.
emigrant *n* emigrant, iseljenik.
emigrate *v* emigrirati, iseliti se.
emigration *n* emigracija, iseljenje.
eminence *n* uzvišenost, eminencija.
eminent *a* značajan, čuven, istaknut; ~ly
adv značajno.
emission *n* širenje, zračenje, ispuštanje.
emit *v* ispuštati, širiti, lučiti.
emolument *n* prihod, zarada, dohodak.
emotion *n* osećanje, emocija,
emocionalnost.
emotional *a* osećajan, uzbuđen,
emocionalan.
emotive *a* emotivan.
emperor *n* imperator.
emphasis *n* naglasak, naglašavanje,
akcent, isticanje.
emphasize *v* podvlačiti, davati značaj,
naglašavati.
emphatic *a* izrazit, podvučen, snažan;
~ally *adv* snažno.
empire *n* imperija.
employ *v* zaposliti, koristiti.
employee *n* službenik, onaj ko je
zaposlen.
employer *n* poslodavac.
employment *n* zaposlenje, zanimanje,
služba.
emporium *n* trgovačko središte, velika
radnja.
empress *n* imperatorka.
emptiness *n* praznina, pustoš.
empty *a* prazan, šupalj; *v* isprazniti,
izručiti, prosuti.
empty-handed *a* praznoruk, praznih ruku.
emulate *v* takmičiti se, nadmetati se.
emulsion *n* emulzija.

en route *adv* na putu, usput.
enable *v* omogućiti, odobriti.
enact *v* propisati, odrediti.
enamel *n* emajl, glazura, gleđ; *v* gleđosati, išarati.
enamour *v* zaljubiti se.
encamp *v* utaboriti se.
encampment *n* bivak, privremeni logor.
encase *v* spakovati, staviti u sanduk.
enchant *v* očarati, opčiniti.
enchanting *a* čaroban.
enchantment *n* začaranost, čarolija.
encircle *v* okružiti, opkoliti.
enclose *v* priložiti, umetnuti, ubaciti.
enclosure *n* prilog; ograda.
encompass *v* okružiti, obuhvatati.
encore *adv* ponovo, na bis.
encounter *n* susret, sudar; okršaj; *v* sresti se (neočekivano); sudariti se.
encourage *v* bodriti, podsticati, huškati.
encouragement *n* ohrabrenje, podstrek; podrška.
encroach *v* posegnuti, nasrnuti.
encroachment *n* uzurpacija, povreda (tuđe svojine).
encrusted *a* pokriven korom.
encumber *v* ometati, otežavati, opteretiti.
encumbrance *n* prepreka, smetnja, teškoća; teret, breme.
encyclopaedia *n* enciklopedija.
end *n* kraj; ivica; smrt; ostatak; posledica; cilj; **to what ~**? Zbog čega?; **to no ~** nema svrhe; *v* okončati, završiti.
endanger *v* ugrožavati, izlagati opasnosti.
endear *v* omiliti, učiniti dragim.
endearing *a* drag, mio.
endearment *n* privrženost, nežnost.
endeavour *v* pokušati, nastojati, truditi se; *n* pokušaj.
endemic *a* endemičan.
ending *n* završetak, kraj.
endive *n* endivija (*bot*).
endless *a* beskonačan, beskrajan; **~ly** *adv* beskonačno.
endorse *v* indosirati, izvršiti prenos menice; potvrditi.
endorsement *n* prenos menice, potvrda, odobrenje.
endow *v* obdariti.
endowment *n* dar; doprinos, prilog.
endurable *a* podnošljiv.

endurance *n* izdržljivost, otpornost, čvrstina.
endure *v* podnositi, trpeti.
endways, endwise *adv* uspravno.
enemy *n* neprijatelj, protivnik.
energetic *a* energičan.
energy *n* snaga, moć, energija.
enervate *v* malaksati, slabiti.
enfeeble *v* iznuriti, oslabiti.
enfold *v* zamotati, pokrivati, uvijati.
enforce *v* prinuditi, prisiljavati, nametnuti; primeniti, sprovesti u život.
enforced *a* primenjen.
enfranchise *v* osloboditi; dati biračka prava.
engage *v* najmiti, iznajmiti; obavezati; dati reč; raditi, biti zauzet.
engaged *a* angažovan; veren.
engagement *n* posao, zanimanje; obaveza; veridba.
engagement ring *n* verenički prsten.
engaging *a* privlačan, primamljiv.
engender *v* produbiti, izazvati, prouzrokovati.
engine *n* motor, oruđe, mašina; parna lokomotiva.
engine driver *n* mašinovođa.
engineer *n* inženjer, mehaničar, mašinovođa.
engineering *n* inženjering, tehnika.
engrave *v* uklesati, rezati; utuviti.
engraving *n* gravura, drvorez, bakrorez.
engrossed *a* obuzet, zaokupljen, apsorbovan.
engulf *v* gutati, obuzimati; suzbijati.
enhance *v* uveličati; pojačati.
enigma *n* zagonetka, enigma.
enjoy *v* uživati, veseliti se, zadovoljiti se.
enjoyable *a* prijatan.
enjoyment *n* uživanje, zadovoljstvo; posedovanje.
enlarge *v* povećavati se, proširiti se, uveličavati.
enlargement *n* povećavanje, uveličavanje.
enlighten *v* obavestiti, posvetiti; rasipati svetlost.
enlightened *a* prosvećen, obavešten.
enlist *v* vrbovati, regrutovati; obezbediti.
enlistment *n* regrutovanje, rok službe.
enliven *v* oživeti, bodriti.
enmity *n* neprijateljstvo, mržnja.

enormity *n* grozota, podlost.
enormous *a* ogroman, golem; strašan;
~**ly** *adv* ogromno, strašno.
enough *adv* dovoljno, dosta; *n* dovoljna
količina.
enquire, inquire *v* ispitivati, istraživati;
to ~ about raspitivati se o nečemu; **to ~
into** razmotriti, istražiti.
enquiry, inquiry *n* istraga, traganje,
ispitivanje.
enrage *v* pobesneti, razbesneti.
enrapture *v* razdragati.
enrich *v* obogatiti.
enrichment *n* bogaćenje.
enrol *v* registrovati se, upisati se; stupiti u
vojsku.
enrolment *n* upis.
ensign *n* značka, znak; zastava, barjak
(*voj*).
enslave *v* porobiti, podjarmiti.
ensue *v* uslediti, proizaći.
ensure *v* obezbediti, osigurati.
entail *v* imati za posledicu, povlačiti za
sobom.
entangle *v* zamrsiti, zaplesti.
entanglement *n* teškoća, smetnja,
neprilika.
enter *v* ući, ulaziti; stupiti, upisati se;
uneti u zapisnik; **to ~ into** stupiti,
početi, začeti.
enterprise *n* preduzeće, poduhvat;
preduzimljivost.
enterprising *a* preduzimljiv, snalažljiv.
entertain *v* primati, zabavljati; voditi
računa, računati sa.
entertainer *n* zabavljač.
entertaining *a* zabavan.
entertainment *n* zabava, razonoda;
gostoprimstvo.
enthralled *a* očaran, zanet.
enthralling *a* očaravajući.
enthrone *v* ustoličiti.
enthusiasm *n* entuzijazam, polet, revnost.
enthusiast *n* entuzijasta.
enthusiastic *a* oduševljen, zanesen.
entice *v* zavesti, namamiti, privući.
entire *a* potpun, savršen, besprekoran;
čist; ~**ly** *adv* potpuno, sasvim,
isključivo.
entitle *v* nazvati, opunomoćiti.
entity *n* srž, bitnost, suština.

entourage *n* pratnja, okolina.
entrails *npl* iznutrice, creva.
entrance *n* ulaz, ulazak, pristup.
entrance examination *n* prijemni ispit.
entrance fee *n* prijavna taksa.
entrant *n* učesnik.
entrap *v* uhvatiti u klopku, prevariti.
entreat *v* preklinjati, moliti.
entreaty *n* molba, preklinjanje.
entrepreneur *n* preduzetnik.
entrust *v* poveriti.
entry *n* ulazak, pristup; upis.
entry visa *n* ulazna viza.
entwine *v* uplitati, obavijati; obuhvatati.
enumerate *v* nabrojati, prebrojati.
enunciate *v* izložiti, formulisati;
proglasiti.
enunciation *n* javna izjava, iskaz.
envelop *v* umotati, zaviti; obuhvatati.
envelope *n* koverat; omotač.
enviable *a* zavidan.
envious *a* zavidljiv; ~**ly** *adv* zavidljivo.
environment *n* okolina, sredina.
environmental *a* ekološki, središni.
environs *npl* okolina.
envisage *v* predočiti, prosuđivati.
envoy *n* izaslanik, poslanik.
envy *n* zavist; *v* zavideti, priželjkivati.
ephemeral *a* prolazan, kratkotrajan.
epic *a* herojski, epski.
epidemic *a* epidemijski; *n* epidemija,
masovna zaraza.
epilepsy *n* epilepsija, padavica.
epileptic *a* epileptičan.
epilogue *n* ishod, epilog.
Epiphany *n* Bogojavljenje.
episcopacy *n* episkopat, biskupstvo.
episode *n* epizoda, uzgredan događaj.
epistle *n* poslanica, pismo, poruka.
epithet *n* epitet.
epitome *n* sažet prikaz.
epitomize *v* sažeti.
epoch *n* doba, vremensko razdoblje,
epoha.
equable *a* ujednačen, staložen.
equably *adv* ujednačeno.
equal *a* istovetan, isti; *n* jednak, ravan; *v*
ravnati se, upravljati se.
equality *n* ravnopravnost, jednakost.
equalize *v* ujednačiti, izjednačiti,
uravnotežiti.

equally adv podjednako.
equanimity n hladnokrvnost, staloženost.
equate v ravnati, izravnati.
equation n jednačenje; jednačina (mat).
equator n ekvator.
equatorial a ekvatorijalni.
equestrian a jahački.
equilateral a ravnostrani.
equilibrium n ravnoteža.
equinox n ravnodnevica, ekvinocij.
equip v opremiti, snabdeti.
equipment n oprema, pribor.
equitable a pravičan, nepristrasan, pravedan.
equitably adv pravično.
equity n pravičnost, nepristrasnost.
equivalent a ekvivalentan.
equivocal a dvosmislen; sumnjiv; ~ly adv dvosmisleno.
equivocate v okolišati, vrdati.
equivocation n okolišanje.
era n doba, razdoblje, vek, era.
eradicate v iskoreniti.
eradication n iskorenjivanje, čupanje.
erase v brisati, čistiti, strugati.
eraser n gumica za brisanje.
erect v podizati, osnovati, graditi; a uspravan, vertikalan.
erection n uspravljanje, uzdizanje; građevina, gradnja; sklapanje, montiranje.
ermine n hermelin.
erode v razjedati, nagrizati.
erotic a erotski.
err v pogrešiti, promašiti; biti kriv.
errand n zadatak, nalog, poruka.
errata npl greška u pisanju, štamparska greška.
erratic a nedosledan, nepravilan; nesiguran, nestalan.
erroneous a pogrešan, netačan, neispravan; ~ly adv pogrešno.
error n greška, zabluda; odstupanje.
erudite a učen, načitan.
erudition n učenost, erudicija.
erupt v izbacivati; buknuti.
eruption n erupcija.
escalate v eskalirati.
escalation n eskalacija.
escalator n pokretne stepenice, eskalator.
escapade n nestašluk; ludorija; bekstvo iz tamnice.

escape v pobeći, izmaći, umaći; n bekstvo; spasavanje; gubitak; **to have a narrow** ~ jedva se izvući.
escapism n bekstvo od stvarnosti.
eschew v izbegavati, uzdržavati se.
escort n oružana pratnja, konvoj.
esoteric a ezoteričan, nejasan.
especial a poseban, naročit, osobit; ~ly adv posebno, osobito.
espionage n špijunaža.
esplanade n šetalište.
espouse v ženiti se, udavati se; podržati.
essay n pregled, opis, esej.
essence n suština, bit; postojanje; esencija; miris.
essential n bit, bitnost; neophodni predmeti; a bitan, suštinski; ~ly adv bitno, osnovno.
establish v osnivati, zasnivati; ustanoviti; urediti; dokazati.
establishment n ustanova; službenički kadar; ustanovljenje; uvođenje.
estate n imanje, imovina; položaj.
esteem v poštovati, ceniti, uvažavati; n poštovanje.
estimate v proceniti, oceniti; praviti predračun; približno izračunati; n ocena, procena.
estimation n procena; poštovanje.
estrange v odstraniti, udaljiti, otuđiti.
estranged a otuđen.
estrangement n otuđenost.
estuary n ušće (reke).
etch v gravirati po metalu.
etching n graviranje.
eternal a večit, večan; ~ly adv večito.
eternity n večnost.
ether n etar, eter.
ethical a etički, moralan.
ethics npl etika.
ethnic a etnički.
ethos n etos.
etiquette n nalepnica, etiketa; etikecija.
etymological a etimološki.
etymology n etimologija.
Eucharist n pričešće, euharistika.
eulogy n hvalospev, pohvala.
eunuch n evnuh.
euphemism n eufemizam.
euro n evro.
Europe n Evropa.

European Community *n* Evropska
zajednica.
European Parliament *n* Evropski
parlament.
European Union *n* Evropska unija.
evacuate *v* isprazniti, očistiti, evakuisati.
evacuation *n* evakuacija.
evade *v* izbegavati, izmicati, kloniti se.
evaluate *v* proceniti, oceniti.
evangelic(al) *a* jevanđelski.
evaporate *v* ispariti, hlapiti, isparavati.
evaporated milk *n* kondenzovano mleko.
evaporation *n* isparavanje, isušivanje.
evasion *n* izbegavanje, odstupanje,
skretanje.
evasive *a* dvosmislen, nejasan,
izbegavajući; **~ly** *adv* dvosmisleno.
eve *n* veče, veče uoči.
even *a* ravan, gladak; isti, jednak; paran;
adv mada, čak, štaviše; *v* izravnati,
izgladiti; **to ~ out** izjednačiti, poravnati.
even-handed *a* nepristrasan.
evening *n* veče, večernja zabava.
evening dress *n* večernja haljina, svečana
haljina.
evenly *adv* podjednako.
evenness *n* podjednakost, glatkost.
event *n* događaj, slučaj; ishod.
eventful *a* bogat događajima.
eventual *a* završni, zaključni; moguć.
eventuality *n* mogućnost, moguć događaj.
ever *adv* uvek, bilo kada; **for ~ and ~**
večito, zauvek; **~ since** od tada; **~ so
much** vrlo mnogo, veoma mnogo.
evergreen *a* zimzelen; *n* zimzelena biljka.
everlasting *a* trajan, večit.
evermore *adv* zauvek.
every *a* svako, svaki; **~where** svuda, na
svakom mestu; **~thing** sve; **~one, ~body**
svi, svaki čovek.
evict *v* proterati, iseliti; odugovlačiti (na
sudu).
eviction *n* proterivanje, iseljenje.
evidence *n* dokaz, svedočanstvo,
očiglednost; *v* dokazivati, svedočiti.
evident *a* očigledan, očevidan; **~ly** *adv*
očigledno.
evil *a* zao, zloban, pakostan; *n* zlo,
nesreća.
evil-minded *a* zlonameran.
evocative *a* izazivački.

evoke *v* pobuditi, izazvati.
evolution *n* razvitak, evolucija.
evolve *v* razvijati, odvijati; ispuštati miris.
ewe *n* ovca.
exacerbate *v* pogoršati, razdražiti,
razljutiti.
exact *a* tačan, precizan; *v* zahtevati.
exacting *a* preteran, iscrpljujući; koji
mnogo traži.
exactly *a* tačno, sasvim tako, savršeno.
exactness, exactitude *n* tačnost,
određenost, pravilnost.
exaggerate *v* preterivati, preuveličavati.
exaggeration *n* preuveličavanje.
exalt *v* uzdizati, veličati, hvaliti.
exaltation *n* oduševljenje, ushićenje, zanos.
exalted *a* uzvišen, uzdignut; ponesen,
oduševljen.
examination *n* ispit, pregled, ispitivanje.
examine *v* razmatrati, posmatrati;
proučavati; preslišavati.
examiner *n* ispitivač, inspektor, revizor.
example *n* primer, uzor.
exasperate *v* naljutiti, razdražiti;
podsticati; pojačati.
exasperation *n* razdraženost, ljutina.
excavate *v* iskopavati, kopati.
excavation *n* iskopavanje; rupa, iskop.
exceed *v* prevazilaziti, biti neumeren;
odlikovati se.
exceedingly *adv* veoma, izvanredno.
excel *v* izdvajati se, odlikovati se.
excellence *n* nadmoćnost, veština,
preimućstvo.
Excellency *n* Ekselencija (titula).
excellent *a* odličan, izvrstan, sjajan; **~ly**
adv odlično.
except *v* isključiti, prigovoriti; **~(ing)**
prep osim, izuzev.
exception *n* izuzetak.
exceptional *a* izuzetan, neobičan.
excerpt *n* izvod, odlomak.
excess *n* preterivanje, neumerenost; ispad.
excessive *a* preteran, suvišan; **~ly** *adv*
preterano.
exchange *v* razmeniti, zameniti; *n*
zamena, razmena; berza.
exchange rate *n* kurs.
excise *n* trošarina, porez na promet.
excitability *n* uzbuđenje, uzbudljivost.
excitable *a* uzbudljiv.

excite v uzbuditi, uzrujati.
excited a uzbuđen.
excitement n uzrujanost, uzbuđenje.
exciting a uzbudljiv.
exclaim v uzviknuti, uskliknuti.
exclamation n usklik, uzvik.
exclamation mark n znak uzvika.
exclamatory a uzvični.
exclude v isključiti.
exclusion n izuzimanje, izuzetak.
exclusive a izuzetan, naročit; prvoklasan; zatvoren.
excommunicate v izopštiti, izbaciti.
excommunication n isključenje, ekskomunikacija.
excrement n izmet, pogan.
excruciating a bolan, veoma bolan.
exculpate v opravdati, osloboditi krivice.
excursion n izlet, šetnja, kratko putovanje.
excusable a koji se može izviniti, opravdati.
excuse v praštati, izviniti, oprostiti, opravdati; n izvinjenje, opravdanje, izgovor; **~ me!** Izvinite!.
execute v izvršiti, ispuniti; kazniti.
execution n izvršenje, izvođenje; kazna; dejstvo.
executioner n dželat.
executive a uzvršni; n izvršna vlast, izvršni organ, rukovodilac.
executor n sudski izvršilac, izvršilac oporuke.
exemplary a primeran, uzoran.
exemplify v služiti za primer, primerom pokazati.
exempt a oslobođen (poreza).
exemption n oslobođenje, poresko oslobođenje, poreska olakšica.
exercise n vežba, treniranje; zanimanje, rad; upotreba; v vežbati; ostvariti, ispoljavati.
exercise book n vežbanka.
exert v vršiti (uticaj), naprezati.
exertion n naprezanje, trud, napor.
exhale v izdisati, osloboditi paru, dati oduška.
exhaust n ispuštanje, ispusna cev (teh); v ispustiti; istrošiti; ispumpati.
exhausted a iscrpljen, iznuren.
exhaustion n iscrpljenost, iznurenost; pražnjenje; razorenost.

exhaustive n iscrpan (npr. istraživanje).
exhibit v izlagati, prikazivati; n izloženi predmet, eksponat; stvarni dokaz.
exhibition n izložba, pokazivanje.
exhilarating a koji stimuliše, koji razveseljava.
exhilaration n veselje, raspoloženje.
exhort v nagovarati, savetovati, opominjati.
exhortation n podsticanje.
exhume v iskopati, ekshumirati.
exile n izgnanstvo, progon, egzil; v prognati, proterati.
exist v postojati, biti, živeti.
existence n postojanje, život, prisutnost.
existent a postojeći, prisutan.
existing a postojeći.
exit n izlaz, odlazak sa pozornice; v otići, izaći.
exodus n odlazak, izlazak.
exonerate v osloboditi optužbe.
exoneration n oslobađanje.
exorbitant a preteran, prekomeran.
exorcise v isterati (đavola).
exorcism n isterivanje.
exotic a egzotičan, inostrani.
expand v širiti se, povećavati, razvijati se, procvetati.
expanse n prostranstvo, širina, ekspanzija.
expansion n proširenost, ekspanzija.
expansive a opširan; koji se širi.
expatriate v proterati iz domovine.
expect v očekivati, nadati se; pretpostaviti.
expectance, expectancy n iščekivanje, verovatnoća.
expectant a koji očekuje, koji računa.
expectant mother n trudnica.
expectation n očekivanje, iščekivanje; izgledi za budućnost.
expediency n celishodnost.
expedient a koristan, umesan, pogodan; unosan; n probitačnost, korisnost; **~ly** adv korisno.
expedite v odaslati, otpremiti.
expedition n ekspedicija; brzina, žurba.
expeditious a ekspeditivan; **~ly** adv ekspeditivno.
expel v isključiti, izbaciti, proterati.
expend v trošiti, izdavati novac.

expendable *a* potrošan, za jednokratnu upotrebu.
expenditure *n* trošak, izdatak, rashodi.
expense *n* cena, koštanje, trošak.
expense account *n* račun troškova (službenih).
expensive *a* skup; ~ly *adv* skupo.
experience *n* iskustvo, slučaj; doživljaj; *v* doživeti.
experienced *a* iskusan.
experiment *n* ogled, opit, eksperiment; *v* vršiti opite, eksperimentisati.
experimental *a* ogledni, eksperimentalan; ~ly *adv* eksperimentalno.
expert *a* stručnjak, specijalista, ekspert.
expertise *n* veština, ekspertiza.
expiration *n* izdisanje, izdah; istek, kraj.
expire *v* izdisati, gasiti se; isticati.
explain *v* objasniti.
explanation *n* objašnjenje, tumačenje.
explanatory *a* koji objašnjava.
expletive *a* umetnuta reč; psovka.
explicable *a* razjašnjiv, objašnjiv.
explicit *a* jasan, tačan; iskren; ~ly *adv* jasno.
explode *v* eksplodirati, razbesneti se.
exploit *v* koristiti, iskorišćavati; eksploatisati; *n* podvig.
exploitation *n* iskorišćavanje, eksploatacija.
exploration *n* istraživanje.
exploratory *a* istraživački, izviđački.
explore *v* istraživati, ispitivati.
explorer *n* istraživač; sonda (*med*).
explosion *n* eksplozija, plamen.
explosive *a/n* eksploziv, eksplozivan; praskav (*ling*).
exponent *n* predstavnik; tumač; eksponent stepena (*mat*).
export *v* izvozi; *n* izvoz; izvozna roba.
exporter *n* izvoznik.
expose *v* izneti, otkriti, izložiti; izobličiti.
exposed *a* izložen; otkriven; osvetljen (film).
exposition *n* opis, objašnjenje, tumačenje; izložba.
expostulate *v* savetovati, nagovarati.
exposure *n* izloženost; položaj tela; prepuštanje; eksponaža.
exposure meter *n* svetlomer.
expound *v* izlagati, objašnjavati.

express *v* izneti; *a* tačan, jasan, određen; brzi, hitan, vanredni; *n* brzi voz; kurir; hitna pošiljka.
expression *n* izraz; izraz lica.
expressionless *a* bezizražajan.
expressive *a* izražajan; ~ly *adv* izražajno.
expressly *adv* naročito, posebno; tačno, jasno.
expressway *n* auto-put.
expropriate *v* konfiskovati, eksproprijatizovati.
expropriation *n* konfiskacija, eksproprijacija.
expulsion *n* proterivanje, otpuštanje.
expurgate *v* čistiti.
exquisite *a* izvrstan, odličan; snažan; ~ly *adv* izvrsno.
extant *a* postojeći, koji se sačuvao do danas.
extempore *a* improvizovan, bez pripreme.
extemporize *v* improvizovati.
extend *v* protezati, širiti se, produžiti.
extension *n* rastezanje, proširenje, širenje, produženje.
extensive *a* širok, prostran, krupan; ~ly *adv* široko.
extent *n* rastojanje, prostranstvo; stepen.
extenuate *v* smanjiti, umanjiti, olakšati.
extenuating *a* olakašavajući (*npr.* ~ **circumstances** olakšavajuće okolnosti).
exterior *a* spoljašnji, spoljni.
exterminate *v* iskoreniti, istrebiti.
extermination *n* uništenje, istrebljenje.
external *a* spoljni, spoljašnji; ~ly *adv* spolja.
extinct *a* izumrli, ugašen.
extinction *n* izumiranje, gašenje, slabljenje.
extinguish *v* ugasiti (svetlo, nadu); gušiti; uništiti.
extinguisher *n* aparat za gašenje požara.
extirpate *v* iskoreniti, istrebiti; odstraniti (*med*).
extol *v* uznositi, preterano hvaliti.
extort *v* iznuđivati, izvlačiti.
extortion *n* iznuđivanje, ucena.
extra *adv* dopunsko, vanredno; *n* dodatak, vanredno izdanje.
extraction *n* izvlačenje; poreklo; ekstrakt.
extracurricular *a* vannastavni.

extradite *v* izručiti.
extradition *n* izručenje (zločinca).
extramarital *a* vanbračni, preljubnički.
extramural *a* vanškolski, vanredni.
extraneous *a* tuđ, stran, dalek.
extraordinarily *adv* neuobičajeno,
neobično, čudno, vanredno.
extraordinary *a* neobičan, čudan, osobit.
extravagance *n* rasipništvo, preterivanje;
nastranost.
extravagant *a* nastran, neobičan;
rasipnički.
extreme *a* krajnji; izvanredan; suprotan; *n*
krajnost, najviši stepen; **~ly** *adv* veoma,
krajnje.
extremist *a* ekstremistički.
extremity *n* kraj, završetak; krajnje mere.
extricate *v* izvući, izneti; izdvajati (*hem*).
extrinsic(al) *a* sporedan, spoljašnji;
neobičan.

extrovert *a* otvoren , društven,
ekstrovertan.
exuberance *n* izobilje, bogatstvo.
exuberant *a* obilan, bogat, bujan; **~ly** *adv*
bogato.
exude *v* lučiti, izlučivati.
exult *v* likovati, slaviti.
exultation *n* likovanje, slavlje.
eye *n* oko, vid, pogled; gledište; *v*
pogledati, uprti oči.
eyeball *n* očna jabučica.
eyebrow *n* obrva.
eyelash *n* trepavica.
eyelid *n* očni kapak.
eyesight *n* vid, čulo vida.
eyesore *n* trn u oku; ruglo.
eyetooth *n* očnjak.
eyewitness *n* očevidac, svedok.
eyrie *n* kuća na visokoj steni; visoko
gnezdo.

F

fable *n* basna, bajka, laž; sadržaj, tema; mit, legenda.

fabric *n* materijal, tkanina.

fabricate *v* izmišljati, lagati; proizvoditi, graditi.

fabrication *n* gradnja; izmišljotina, laž.

fabulous *a* basnoslovan; legendaran; neverovatan; golem.

facade *n* fasada; pročelje.

face *n* lice; obraz; *v* gledati nekoga, suprotstaviti se; **to ~ up to** pogledati hrabro u oči, biti dorastao.

face cream *n* krema za lice.

face-lift *n* kozmetička operacija uklanjanja bora.

face powder *n* puder za lice.

facet *n* brušenje; vid, aspekt.

facetious *a* šaljiv; dosetljiv, vragolast; podrugljiv **~ly** *adv* šaljivo.

face value *n* nominalna vrednost.

facial *a* koji se tiče lica, lični.

facile *a* lak; lakoveran, popustljiv; okretan.

facilitate *v* olakšati, pomoći; omogućiti.

facility *n* lakoća; okretnost, veština; lakovernost.

facing *n* prednja strana, pročelje, obloga; prevlaka.

facsimile *n* otisak, snimak; prepis originala, faksimil.

fact *n* činjenica; čin, delo; istina; **in ~ u** stvari, zapravo.

faction *n* grupa, frakcija; razdor, rascep, neslaganje.

factor *n* činilac, faktor, važan momenat.

factory *n* fabrika, radionica, manufaktura.

factual *a* istinit, činjenični.

faculty *n* sposobnost, talenat; sila, moć.

fad *n* hir; omiljena zabava, modno ludilo.

fade *v* venuti; bledeti; nestajati; gubiti se.

fail *v* manjkati, nedostajati; izostati; propasti.

failing *n* nedostatak; pogreška, slabost; neuspeh.

failure *n* neuspeh, propust, izostanak, nestašica.

faint *v* onesvestiti se; umoriti se, oslabiti; iščeznuti; **~ly** *adv* klonuto.

fainthearted *a* strašljiv, malodušan.

faintness *n* slabost, nemoć, umor; plašljivost (*fig*).

fair *a* lep, ljubak; plav (kosa), svetao; ljubazan, prijatan, pošten *adv* lepo, čisto, jasno *n* sajam.

fairly *adv* pošteno, pravično, iskreno, prikladno; lepo, čisto.

fairness *n* lepota; čistoća; poštenje; iskrenost; pravednost.

fair play *n* korektna igra, pošten postupak.

fair trade *n* slobodna trgovina.

fairy *n* vila, dobar ili zao duh; čarobnica.

fairy tale *n* bajka.

faith *n* vera, religija; vernost, odanost; poverenje.

faithful *a* veran, pošten, istinit, iskren; pouzdan; dostojan, tačan **~ly** *adv* verno, istinito, iskreno.

faithfulness *n* vernost, odanost.

fake *n* podvala, falsifikat; varanje; izmišljotina; imitacija; varalica *adj* lažan *v* varati, krasti.

falcon *n* soko.

falconry *n* lov sa sokolovima, uzgoj sokolova za lov, sokolarstvo.

fall *v* pasti, padati, strmoglaviti se; **to ~ asleep** zaspati; **to ~ back** ustuknuti, povući se; ne održati obećanje; **to ~ behind** zaostati; **to ~ down** pasti, propasti; **to ~ for** zaljubiti se; nasesti; **to ~ in** upasti, postrojiti se; **to ~ short** podbaciti, zaostati; **to ~ sick** razboleti se; **to ~ in love** zaljubiti se; *n* pad; propadanje (*fig*).

fallacious *a* lažan, sumnjiv, prividan; **~ly** *adv* lažno.

fallacy *n* lažnost, prividnost; zabluda; pogrešan zaključak.

fallibility *n* netačnost, pogrešivost.

fallible *a* pogrešiv.

fallow *a* neobrađen, pust; crvenkastožut; riđast; **~ deer** jelen lopatar.

false *a* lažan, dvoličan; neispravan; nezakonit; izdajnički; izmišljen; **~ly** *adv* lažno, netačno, dvolično.

false alarm n lažna uzbuna.
falsehood, falseness n lažnost, nepoštenje, dvoličnost; izdaja.
falsify v falsifikovati; izvrnuti (činjenicu); ne održati reč.
falsity n neistinitost, dvoličnost; licemerje.
falter v spoticati se, posrtati; mucati; oklevati.
faltering a malodušan, koji okleva.
fame n slava, ugled, dobar glas; glasine, govorkanje.
famed a slavan, čuven, na glasu.
familiar a poznat, prisan, porodični; običan, svakidašnji.
familiarity n prisnost, poverljivost; upoznatost.
familiarize v upoznati, odomaćiti, naviknuti.
family n porodica, članovi porodice, ukućani; dom; rod.
family business n porodični posao.
family doctor n kućni lekar.
famine n glad, nestašica, umiranje od gladi.
famished a izgladneo.
famous a slavan, čuven; javan; ~ly adv čuveno.
fan n obožavalac, ljubitelj, navijač.
fan belt n remen na ventilatoru.
fanatic a zanesen, zaslepljen, fanatičan.
fanaticism n zanos, zanesenost, zaslepljenost, fanatizam.
fanciful a čudan, neobičan; maštovit; čudnog oblika; ~ly adv čudno.
fancy n mašta, fantazija, izmišljotina, uobraženje; moda; v maštati, zamišljati.
fancy-dress ball n bal pod maskama.
fancy-goods npl pomodna, luksuzna roba.
fanfare n fanfara, truba; trubljenje.
fang n zub očnjak, otrovni zub zmije; koren zuba; šiljak (oruđa).
fantastic a fantastičan, prividan; čudesan; maštovit; ~ally adv fantastično.
fantasy n mašta, fantazija, sanjarija.
far adv daleko, mnogo, vrlo, jako; ~ and away nesumnjivo, svakako; ~ off daleko, davno.
faraway a dalek, udaljen, odsutan (duhom), sanjarski.
farce n lakrdija, farsa; šala.

farcical a lakrdijaški, smešan; neprirodan, apsurdan.
fare n cena prevoza.
farewell n rastanak, oproštaj.
farm n farma; v obrađivati zemlju.
farmer n zemljoradnik, farmer, upravitelj imanja.
farmhand n najamni radnik, poljoprivredni radnik.
farmhouse n dom farmera.
farming n zemljoradnja.
farmland n obradiva zemlja.
farmyard n gumno.
far-reaching a dalekosežan.
fart n prdež, vetar; v prdeti.
farther adv dalje; a udaljeniji, dalji.
farthest adv najdalje; a najudaljeniji, najdalji.
fascinate v osvojiti, očarati, fascinirati.
fascinating a očaravajući, privlačan, fascinantan.
fascination n očaravanje, opsena, fascinacija.
fascism n fašizam.
fascist n fašista.
fashion n oblik, moda, kroj, običaj; **people of** ~ mondenski svet; v dati oblik, prilagoditi.
fashion show n modna revija.
fashionable a moderan, pomodan, otmen, elegantan; ~bly adv moderan.
fast v postiti, uzdržavati se od jela; n post; a čvrst, jak.
fast food n brza hrana.
fasten v učvrstiti, utvrditi; držati se; adv čvrsto.
fastener, fastening n učvršćivanje, ojačavanje, vezivanje.
fastidious a izbirljiv, hirovit, osetljiv; ~ly adv hirovito.
fat a mastan, debeo, krupan; n mast, salo, debljina.
fatal a koban, fatalan, sudbonosan; neizbežan; ~ly kobno.
fatalism n verovanje u sudbinu, fatalizam.
fatalist n fatalist.
fatality n kob, nesreća, smrt, poguban uticaj.
fate n sudbina, kob, usud.
fateful a koban, sudbonosan, zlokoban.
father n otac.

fatherhood n očinstvo.
father-in-law n tast, svekar.
fatherland n domovina, otadžbina.
fatherly a očinski.
fathom n hvat (=1.82m), sežanj, dubina (mora); v meriti dubinu.
fatigue n umor; zamor, trud; muka; v umarati se.
fatten v ugojiti, toviti; udebljati se; obogatiti se (fig).
fatty a debeo, mastan, uljast.
fatuous a blesav, glup, smešan, isprazan.
fault n greška, nedostatak; mana; uvreda.
faultfinder n cepidlaka.
faultless a besprekoran, bez greške, bez mane.
faulty a loš, nesavršen; pokvaren, neispravan.
fauna n fauna, životinjsko carstvo.
faux pas n promašaj, netaktičnost.
favour n naklonost, blagonaklonost; zaštita; usluga; v pomagati, štititi.
favourable a povoljan, pogodan, koristan, preporučiv.
favourably adv korisno.
favoured a omiljen, poštovan, privilegovan.
favourite n miljenik, ljubimac, favorit; a voljen, omiljen.
favouritism n pristrasnost, favoritizam.
fawn n mladunče, lane; v mahati repom, ulagivati se.
fawningly adv ulagivački.
fax n faks; v poslati faksom.
fear v bojati se, strepiti; n strah.
fearful a strašan, užasan, plašljiv, bojažljiv; ~ly adv plašljivo.
fearless a neustrašiv, ~ly adv neustrašivo.
fearlessness n neustrašivost.
feasibility n ostvarivost, izvodljivost, izvršivost.
feasible a izvodljiv, koristan; moguć, ostvariv.
feast n gozba, svetkovina, veselje; v slaviti.
feat n podvig, junaštvo; veština; spretnost.
feather n pero.
feather bed n ležaj od perja.
feature n crta lica, pojava, izgled; osobina, obeležje; v dati oblik, uobličiti.
feature film n igrani film.

February n februar.
federal a savezni, federalni.
federalist n federalista.
federate v sklopiti savez, udružiti, stupiti u savez.
federation n savez, federacija.
fed-up a sit.
fee n honorar, plata, nagrada; vlasništvo; školarina; ulaznica.
feeble a slab, nemoćan, malaksao; bled.
feebleness n slabost, iznemoglost.
feebly adv slabo, malaksalo, mutno.
feed v hraniti, toviti, uzgajati; jesti; **to ~ on** hraniti se nečim; n hrana, ishrana.
feedback n povratna sprega.
feel v osećati; pipati; smatrati; n osećanje.
feeler n pipak (zool); antena; izviđač.
feeling n osećanje, osećaj.
feelingly adv osećajno, nežno, milostivo.
feign v simulirati, izmisliti; pretvarati se.
feline a mačiji; prevrtljiv, neveran, lukav.
feelingly adv osećajno, nežno, milostivo.
fellow n drug, kolega, član naučnog društva.
fellow citizen n sugrađanin.
fellow countryman n zemljak.
fellow feeling n saosećanje, saučešće.
fellow men npl bližnji.
fellowship n zajednica, bratstvo; prijateljstvo.
fellow student n kolega sa studija.
fellow traveller n saputnik; simpatizer, pristalica.
felon n prestupnik, kriminalac; izdajnik.
felony n krivično delo, težak zločin.
felt n pust; filc.
felt-tip pen, fibre-tip pen n flomaster.
female n žena, devojka.
feminine a ženskog roda, ženski, koji se tiče žena.
feminism n ženski pokret, feminizam; ženski karakter, ženske osobine.
feminist n pobornik ravnopravnosti žena i muškaraca; feminist.
fen n bara, močvara, blato.
fence n ograda, plot, zid; branik; v braniti se, utvrditi.
fencing n ograđivanje; mačevanje.
fennel n mirođija.
ferment n kvasac, ferment; uzbuna, uzbuđenje (fig); v ključati.
fern n paprat.

ferocious *a* okrutan, divlji, ljut; ~**ly** *adv*
   okrutno, divlje.
ferocity *n* okrutnost, divljaštvo, surovost.
ferret *n* čvrsti kanap, *v* tražiti, pretražiti;
   to ~ out iščeprkati.
ferry *n* brod, skela, trajekt; *v* prevoziti.
fertile *a* plodan, obilan, bogat.
fertility *n* plodnost, bogatstvo, obilje.
fertilization *n* oplodnja, oplođivanje.
fertilize *v* oploditi, učiniti plodnim.
fertilizer *n* đubrivo, gnojivo.
fervent *a* vatren, užaren; ~**ly** *adv* vatreno.
fervid *a* vreo, vruć, vatren.
fervour *n* žar, žestina, vrućina.
fester *v* gnojiti se, upaliti se, truliti.
festival *n* festival, svečanost, proslava.
festive *a* svečan, praznični.
festivity *n* svečanost, veselje, svetkovina.
fetch *v* dovesti, doneti; doći do.
fetching *a* privlačan, prijatan, ljubak.
fete *n* svetkovina, svečanost, praznik.
fetid, foetid *a* smrdljiv, koji zaudara.
feud *n* svađa, neprijateljstvo, zavada;
   feud.
feudal *a* feudalni.
feudalism *n* feudalizam.
fever *n* groznica.
feverish *a* grozničav, uzbuđen, nemiran.
few *a* malo, **a ~** nekolicina; **~ and far**
   between veoma retko, nesvakidašnji.
fewer *a* manje; *adv* malo.
fewest *a* najmanje.
fexibility *n* savitljivost, gipkost,
   fleksibilnost.
fiancé *n* verenik.
fiancée *n* verenica.
fib *n* laganje, izmišljotina, neistina; *v*
   lagati.
fibre *n* vlakno, nit; grančica.
fibreglass *n* fiberglas, fiber.
fickle *a* promenljiv, nestalan; prevrtljiv.
fiction *n* maštanje, izmišljotina;
   beletristika.
fictional *a* izmišljen.
fictitious *a* izmišljen, lažan, nestvaran,
   fiktivan ~**ly** *adv* izmišljeno.
fiddle *n* violina, *v* svirati na violini.
fiddler *n* violinista.
fidelity *n* odanost, vernost, istinitost,
   poštenje.
fidget *v* vrpoljiti se, biti nemiran.

fidgety *a* nemiran, nervozan, uzvrpoljen.
field *n* polje, njiva, oranica; pašnjak;
   površina; pozadina; teren.
field day *n* dan parade, značajan dan.
fieldmouse *n* poljski miš.
fieldwork *n* rad na terenu, rov, šanac.
fiend *n* sotona, đavo, demon, čudovište.
fiendish *a* đavolji, zloban, zao, proklet.
fierce *a* okrutan, divlji, ljut, žestok; ~**ly**
   adv okrutno.
fierceness *n* zverstvo, divljaštvo,
   krvoločnost, neobuzdanost.
fiery *a* vatren, usijan; ljut; ratoboran.
fifteen *num* petnaest.
fifteenth *num a* petnaesti.
fifth *num a* peti.
fiftieth *num a* pedeseti.
fifty *num* pedeset.
fig *n* smokva .
fig tree *n* stablo smokve.
fight *v* boriti se, tući se, ratovati; *n* borba,
   bitka.
fighter *n* borac, bokser.
fighting *n* bojni, ratoboran, borben.
fig-leaf *n* list smokve .
figurative *a* slikovit, figurativan,
   simboličan, tipičan; ~**ly** *adv* slikovito.
figure *n* oblik, figura, pojava, karakter; *v*
   uobličiti; **to ~ out** izračunati, pronaći,
   oceniti.
figurehead *n* glava, lice koje se nalazi na
   čelu nečeg.
filament *n* vlakno, končic, prašnik.
filch *v* ukrasti, ugrabiti, dići.
filcher *n* lopov .
file *n* dosije, fascikla, popis; imenik; *v*
   arhivirati; **to ~ in / out** predati/povući
   dokumenta.
filing cabinet *n* ormar za odlaganje spisa.
fill *v* puniti, natočiti; zadovoljiti;
   naduvati; **to ~ in** popuniti, **to ~ up**
   natočiti.
fillet *n* povez; butina; pečenica.
fillet steak *n* meso bez kostiju, krtina.
filling station *n* benzinska pumpa.
fillip *n* pucketanje prstima, podsticaj,
   pobuda; sitnica.
filly *n* ždrebica.
film *n* opna, film; *v* prevući tankom
   opnom, snimati film.
film star *n* filmska zvezda.

film strip n slajd.

filter n filter, cedilo; cigareta s filterom (*sleng*); v filtrirati, cediti.

filter-tipped a sa filterom.

filth(iness) n prljavština; nemoral.

filthy adj prljav, nečist; nemoralan (*fig*).

fin n peraja, kormilo.

final a konačan, poslednji; ~ly adv konačno; ~ stages zaključna faza.

finale n finale.

finalist n finalista.

finalize v završiti, dati konačan oblik nečemu.

finance n nauka o finansijama, finansije.

financial a finansijski.

financier n finansijer.

find v naći, otkriti; smatrati; proglasiti (krivim, nevinim na sudu); **to ~ out** saznati; **to ~ one's self** snaći se; n nalaz, otkriće.

findings npl alat, pribor, oruđe.

fine a nežan, uglađen, jasan; n prekid, kraj; v platiti novčanu kaznu.

fine arts npl likovne umetnosti.

finely a vešto, fino, lukavo.

finery n ukras, nakit, raskoš.

finesse n nežnost, prefinjenost; lukavost.

finger n prst, kazaljka na satu; v pipati, opipati.

fingernail n nokat .

fingerprint n otisak prsta.

fingertip n vrh prsta.

finicky a izveštačen, precizan; izbirljiv.

finish v završiti, dovršiti, stići na cilj; **to ~ off** doterati; **to ~ up** dovršiti.

finishing line n cilj.

finishing school n večernja škola.

finite a krajnji, konačan, ograničen.

fir tree n jela.

fire n vatra, plamen, požar; oduševljenje (*fig*); v zapaliti, upaliti.

fire alarm n protivpožarni alarm, protivpožarna uzbuna.

firearm n vatreno oružje.

fireball n meteor.

firebreak, fire line n borbena linija, borbeni položaj.

fire engine n vatrogasna kola; vatrogasni šmrk.

fire escape n izlaz za slučaj požara.

fire extinguisher n aparat za gašenje požara.

firefly n svitac.

fire station n vatrogasna stanica.

fireman n vatrogasac.

fireplace n kamin, ognjište.

fireproof a nesagoriv, vatrostalan.

fireside n ognjište, dom.

firewater n žestoko piće.

firewood n drvo za ogrev.

fireworks npl vatromet; duhovitost (*fig*).

firing n pucanje, gađanje; loženje; vatra, gorivo.

firing squad n četa za izvršenje smaknuća streljanjem.

firm a tvrd, čvrst; nepromenljiv, stalan; n firma; ~ly adv čvrsto.

firmament n nebeski svod, nebo.

firmness n postojanost, čvrstoća, jačina.

first a prvi.

first aid n prva pomoć.

first name n ime.

first-aid kit n pribor za prvu pomoć.

first-class a prvoklasni; n prvi razred.

first-hand a neposredan.

first-rate a prvorazredan, odličan, najbolji.

fiscal a finansijski, fiskalni.

fish n riba, riblje meso; v loviti ribu.

fishbone n riblja kost.

fisherman n ribar, ribolovac, ribarska barka.

fish farm n ribnjak.

fish market n ribarnica .

fishing n ribolov.

fishing line n konopac za udicu.

fishing rod n štap za pecanje.

fishing tackle n pribor za ribolov.

fishmonger n trgovac ribom.

fishmonger's (shop) n ribarnica.

fishy a riblji, koji obiluje ribom; bezizražajan.

fissure n pukotina, naprslina, rascep.

fist n pesnica, šaka.

fit n napad, grčevi, trzavica; a u dobroj formi; v urediti, namestiti; **to ~ out** opremiti, naoružati; **to ~ in** slagati se, uklapati se.

fitness n kondicija, prikladnost, primerenost.

fitted carpet n itison, tepih koji u potpunosti pokriva pod sobe.

fitter *n* modelar, krojač.
fitting *a* prikladan, pogodan; *n*
nameštanje, montaža; ~s *pl* električni
uređaji.
five *num* pet.
fix *v* pričvrstiti, prilepiti, prikačiti; **to ~ up**
fiksirati, utvrditi datum.
fixation *n* učvršćivanje, fiksiranje;
opsesija.
fixed *a* čvrst, nepomičan, fiksiran.
fixture *n* čvrstoća, trajnost; armatura.
fizz *v* pištati; ključati; peniti se.
fizzle *v* šištati; ugasiti se, izjaloviti.
fizzy *a* uzavreo, penušav, koji ključa.
flabbergasted *a* zabezeknut.
flabby *a* mlitav, sasušen; slab, bled.
flaccid *a* slab, mlitav, labav.
flag *n* zastava, kamena ploča; *v* klonuti,
oboriti glavu.
flagpole *n* jarbol, postolje za zastavu.
flagrant *a* jasan, zloglasan, gnusan.
flagship *n* admiralski brod.
flair *n* njuh, njušenje; instinkt.
flak *n* protivavionska artiljerija,
protivavionska vatra.
flake *n* pahuljica, iskra, varnica.
flaky *a* pahuljast, ljuskav.
flamboyant *a* blistav, sjajan, preterano
nakićen.
flame *n* plamen, vatra, žar, strast.
flamingo *n* plamenac, flamingo.
flammable *a* zapaljivo.
flank *n* bok, strana, krilo; *v* napasti s boka.
flannel *n* flanel.
flap *n* lak udarac, poklopac, jezik (na
cipelama); *v* udariti; lepršati.
flare *v* bljesak, svetlosni signal; **to ~ up**
razbuktati se, rasplamsati se.
flash *n* sevanje, bljesak.
flashbulb *n* blic.
flashy *a* jeftin, drečav.
flask *n* pljoska.
flat *a* ravan, pljosnat, ispružen; jednoličan;
n ravnina; stan; ~ly *adv* ravno.
flatness *n* ravnina, jednoličnost, plitkost.
flatten *v* izravnati, spljoštiti, istegnuti.
flatter *v* laskati, umiljavati se.
flattering *a* laskav.
flattery *n* laskanje, ulagivanje, dodvoravanje.
flatulence *n* nadimanje, naduvenost (*fig*);
taština.

flaunt *v* vijoriti se; razmetati se,
paradirati.
flavour *n* miris, aroma, ukus, začin; *v*
začiniti.
flavoured *a* začinjen, ukusan, mirisan.
flavourless *a* bljutav, bezukusan, bez
mirisa.
flaw *n* pukotina, greška, mana.
flawless *a* besprekoran; bez mane, bez
mrlje.
flax *n* lan, laneno vlakno.
flea *n* buva.
flea bite *n* ujed buve; trica, malenkost.
fleck *n* mrlja, pega, mladež; mrvica.
flee *v* pobeći, bežati, izbegavati.
fleece *n* runo; *v* šišanje ovaca.
fleet *n* flota; vozni park.
fleeting *a* koji plovi, koji beži, brz,
nestalan.
flesh *n* meso (ljudsko), čovečje telo;
jezgro (voća).
flesh wound *n* površinska rana.
fleshy *a* mesnat, debeo; smrtan.
flex *n* gajtan; *v* savijati.
flexible *a* savitljiv, gibak, okretan,
fleksibilan.
flick *n* lak udarac; *v* lako udariti.
flicker *v* svetlucati, trepereti, lepršati.
flier *vidi* **flyer**.
flight *n* let, letenje, putovanje; polet.
flight attendant *n* stjuart, stjuardesa.
flight deck *n* pilotska kabina.
flimsy *a* tanak, redak, slab.
flinch *v* odustati, ustuknuti, prezati.
fling *v* baciti; skočiti; žuriti; poleteti.
flint *n* kremen.
flip *v* baciti, odapeti; pljesnuti; skočiti.
flippant *a* brbljiv, brzoplet, neuljudan.
flipper *n* peraja.
flirt *v* baciti, udariti žestoko.
flirtation *n* koketiranje, flert.
flit *v* lepršati, pobeći, pojuriti.
float *v* plutati, plivati, lebdeti; *n* plivanje,
plutanje.
flock *n* pramen, čuperak; stado; *v*
gomilati.
flog *v* udarati, tući, bičevati.
flogging *n* batinanje, šibanje, kažnjavanje.
flood *n* poplava, plima, bujica, tok; *v*
poplaviti, preplaviti.
flooding *n* poplava.

floodlight *n* svetlo reflektora, svetlo koje zaslepljuje.

floor *n* pod, tlo, parket, sprat; *v* popločati.

floorboard *n* drvo kojim se oblaže pod, parket, brodski pod.

floor lamp *n* stojeća lampa.

floor show *n* program (u baru).

flop *n* pad, udaranje, neuspeh, fijasko.

floppy *a* koji mlitavo visi, nemaran, površan.

floppy disk *n* disketa.

flora *n* flora, biljno carstvo.

floral *a* cvetni.

florescence *n* cvetanje, cvat, vreme cvetanja.

florid *a* rascvetan, cvetan, kićen.

florist *n* cvećar, trgovac cvećem, botaničar.

florist's (shop) *n* cvećara.

flotilla *n* flotila.

flounder *n* iverak, koprcanje; *v* koprcati se, komešati se.

flour *n* brašno.

flourish *v* bujati, ojačati, napredovati; *v* procvat, napredak.

flourishing *a* koji cveta.

flout *v* ismevati nekoga, rugati se.

flow *v* teći, curiti; *n* tok, struja, plima.

flow chart *n* dijagram koji pokazuje redosled radnji.

flower *n* cvet, ukras; *v* cvetati.

flowerbed *n* cvetna leja.

flowerpot *n* saksija.

flower show *n* izložba cveća.

flowery *a* cvetni, kićen.

flu *n* grip, prehlada.

fluctuate *v* kolebati se, njihati, lelujati se.

fluctuation *n* kolebanje, neodlučnost, fluktuacija.

fluency *n* lakoća, fluentnost.

fluent *a* lak, rečit, fluentan; ~**ly** *adv* lako.

fluff *n* paperje, pahuljica; ~**y** *a* paperjast; ~**ily** *adv* mekano, pahuljasto.

fluid *a* tekući; *n* fluid, sok.

fluidity *n* tečno stanje.

fluke *n* neočekivan, srećan slučaj.

fluoride *n* fluor.

flurry *n* uzrujanost, uzbuđenost, razdraženost.

flush *v* ravnati, izjednačiti; **to~ out** isprati; *n* mlaz vode, crvenilo.

flushed *a* crveno, rumeno.

fluster *v* zbuniti, opiti; uzrujati se.

flustered *a* zbunjen.

flute *n* flauta.

flutter *v* lepršati, leteti; drhtati; *n* lepršanje, nemir.

flux *n* tok, strujanje, nadolaženje plime.

fly *v* leteti, odleteti, uzleteti, juriti; **to ~ away/off** odleteti; *n* letenje, let; muva, insekt; 'šlic' na pantalonama.

flyer *n* letač.

flying *n* letenje, uzletanje; avijacija.

flying saucer *n* leteći tanjir.

flypast *n* preletanje.

flysheet *n* letak.

foal *n* ždrebe.

foam *n* pena; *v* peniti.

foam rubber *n* sunđerasta guma.

foamy *a* penast, penušav.

focus *n* žarište, središte, fokus.

fodder *n* stočna hrana.

foe *n* neprijatelj, dušmanin.

foetus *n* plod, fetus.

fog *n* magla, koprena; bujna trava, mahovina.

foggy *a* maglovit, zamagljen, oblačan.

fog light *n* svetla za maglu.

foible *n* slabost, slaba strana.

foil *v* snabdeti lisnatim ukrasom, pobrkati, izbrisati; nadjačati; *n* folija.

fold *n* nabor, bora; *v* presaviti; **to ~ up** složiti.

folder *n* fascikla, folder.

folding *a* sklopiv, preklopni.

folding chair *n* stolica na rasklapanje.

foliage *n* lišće.

folio *n* list knjige, strana knjige.

folk *n* narod, pleme, rasa.

folk music *n* narodna muzika.

folk song *n* narodna pesma.

folklore *n* folklor, narodne priče, običaji, verovanja.

follow *v* pratiti nekoga, progoniti; izvršavati; držati se nečega; **to ~ up** progoniti u stopu, dodati.

follower *n* pristalica, sledbenik; vernik, pratilac.

following *a* koji sledi, sledeći; *n* pratnja, sledbenici.

folly *n* ludost, glupost, ćudljivost.

foment *v* grejati, zagrevati, stavljati vruće obloge; pobadati, raspirivati (*fig*).

fond *a* nežan, pun ljubavi; isuviše poverljiv, nepromišljen; **~ly** *adv* nežno.
fondle *v* milovati.
fondness *n* nežnost, ljubav.
font *n* izvor, krstionica.
food *n* hrana, ishrana, prehrambeni proizvodi.
food mixer *n* mikser.
food poisoning *n* trovanje hranom.
food processor *n* mikser, mašinica za mlevenje.
food stuffs *npl* prehrambeni proizvodi.
fool *n* ludak, budala; lakrdijaš; *v* obmanjivati.
foolhardy *a* drzak, ludo hrabar.
foolish *a* blesav, luckast, nepromišljen; **~ly** *adv* luckasto, blesavo.
foolproof *a* jednostavan, razumljiv; osiguran, zaštićen, bezbedan (*teh*).
foolscap *n* kancelarijski papir.
foot *n* stopalo, noga; pešadija; fut (oko 30,5 cm); osnova, postolje; **on/by ~** pešačiti.
footage *n* reportaža.
football *n* fudbal, fudbalska lopta.
football pools *n* kladionica.
football pools coupon *n* tiket.
footballer *n* fudbaler.
footbrake *n* kočnica.
footbridge *n* brvno.
foothills *n* pobrđe.
foothold *n* uporište, oslonac; uporište, baza (*voj*).
footing *n* uporište, oslonac, temelj; zbir.
footlights *n* svetlosti pozornice, rampa.
footman *n* sluga, lakej.
footnote *n* fusnota.
footpath *n* pešačka staza.
footprint *n* otisak stopala.
footsore *a* koji ima ranjave noge.
footstep *n* korak; odjek koraka; trag (stopala).
footwear *n* obuća, čarapa.
for *prep* za, na; od, u, radi; **ask ~** raspitivati se; **what ~** zbog čega.
forage *n* stočna hrana; snabdevanje stočnom hranom.
foray *n* prepad, nalet.
forbid *v* zabraniti, nedopuštati; **God ~** Ne daj Bože!
forbidding *a* kojim se zabranjuje, odbijajući.

force *n* sila; snaga, moć; nasilje; **~s** *pl* trupe, čete; *v* prisiliti.
forced *a* prisiljen, prinuđen; neprirodan; ubrzan.
forced march *n* forsirani marš.
forceful *a* jak, ubedljiv; važeći.
forcible *a* prinudan; jak, ubedljiv.
forcibly *adv* snažno.
ford *n* prelaz na reci, gaz, plićak; *v* pregaziti (reku).
fore *n* prednji deo; pramac, kljun (broda); **to the ~** odmah tu, pod rukom.
forearm *n* podlaktica, ruka (od šake do lakta).
foreboding *n* proricanje, predznak, nagoveštaj (obično nečeg lošeg).
forecast *v* predskazivati, proricati; prognozirati; *n* prognoza.
forecourt *n* dvorište javnog objekta.
forefather *n* predak, praotac.
forefinger *n* kažiprst.
forefront *n* prednja strana, lice; istureni položaj (*voj*); središte događaja; **in the ~ of** u centru pažnje.
forego *v* predhoditi.
foregone *a* unapred odlučen; neizbežan, pristrasan.
foreground *n* prednji plan.
forehead *n* čelo.
foreign *a* stran, inostrani.
foreign exchange *n* devize, strana valuta.
foreigner *n* stranac, tuđinac.
foreleg *n* prednja noga.
foreman *n* rukovodilac gradnje, majstor; starešina porotnika.
foremost *a* najistaknutiji, osnovni, glavni; prednji, prvi.
forenoon *n* prepodne, jutro.
forensic *a* sudski, sudbeni; **~ scientist** *n* sudski veštak.
forerunner *n* preteča, prethodnik.
foresee *v* predvideti, naslutiti.
foreshadow *v* slutiti, proricati, nagoveštavati.
foresight *n* predviđanje.
forest *n* šuma.
forestall *v* upozoriti, preduprediti.
forester *n* šumar.
forestry *n* šumarstvo.
foretell *v* proricati, predskazivati.
forethought *n* promišljenost, obazrivost; staranje.

forever *adv* zauvek, za večita vremena.
forewarn *v* upozoriti, opomenuti.
foreword *n* predgovor, uvod (za knjigu).
forfeit *n* novčana kazna, globa; *v* proigrati, zapleniti.
forge *n* kovačnica; *v* kovati; falsifikovati; **to ~ ahead** probiti se na prvo mesto.
forger *n* kovač; falsifikator.
forgery *n* falsifikat, krivotvorina; lažan potpis.
forget *v* zaboraviti.
forgetful *a* zaboravan, nemaran.
forgetfulness *n* zaboravnost, nemarnost.
forget-me-not *n* nezaboravak, spomenak (*bot*).
forgive *v* oprostiti, opraštati.
forgiveness *n* praštanje, oproštaj.
fork *n* viljuška; vile; račvanje; odvajanje (puteva); *v* razdvajati se; **to ~ out** krvariti.
forked *a* račvast, razdvojen, rascepan.
fork-lift truck *n* viljuškar.
forlorn *a* ostavljen, napušten, zabačen; nesrećan; izgubljen.
form *n* oblik, forma; stas, figura (čoveka); *v* formirati, oblikovati.
formal *a* zvaničan, svečan, ustanovljen; površan; pravilan; ~ly *adv* zvanično, svečano.
formality *n* formalnost; formalni postupak.
format *n* format; *v* rasporediti.
formation *n* oblikovanje, formacija, stvaranje.
formative *a* koji stvara, koji obrazuje.
former *a* prethodni, bivši, protekli, raniji; davni; ~ly *adv* ranije, nekada.
formidable *a* grozan, strašan; znatan, veliki; naporan.
formula *n* formula; osnovne pretpostavke, dogma.
formulate *v* formulisati.
forsake *v* napustiti, ostaviti.
fort *n* utvrđenje.
forte *a* sposobnost, forte (*muz*), glasno.
forthcoming *a* koji dolazi, predstojeći, nastupajući.
forthright *a* otvoren, iskren.
forthwith *a* odmah, smesta.
fortieth *num a* četrdeseti.
fortification *n* fortifikacija; *pl* utvrđenja.

fortify *v* utvrditi; potkrepiti, ojačati (hranom).
fortitude *n* hrabrost, duhovna moć.
fortnight *n* dve nedelje; ~ly *a/adv* dvonedeljni; jednom u dve nedelje.
fortress *n* utvrđenje, tvrđava.
fortuitous *a* slučajan; ~ly *adv* slučajno, neočekivano.
fortunate *a* srećan, uspešan, povoljan; ~ly *adv* na sreću, srećno.
fortune *n* sreća, uspeh; bogatstvo.
fortune-teller *n* gatara, vračara.
forty *num* četrdeset.
forum *n* forum; sud.
forward *a* prednji, isturen; rano sazreli; ~s *adv* napred; *v* uputiti; doprinositi.
forwardness *n* spremnost, dozrelost; drskost.
fossil *a* okamenjen, fosilni.
foster *v* hraniti; bodriti; gajiti (nadu); vaspitavati.
foster child *n* posinak, posvojče.
foster father *n* poočim.
foster mother *n* pomajka, dadilja.
foul *a* neugodnog mirisa, prljav, zagađen; pokvaren; zarazan; ~ly *adv* nepravilno, nečasno; *v* ukaljati.
foul play *n* nepoštena igra, verolomstvo.
found *v* postaviti, zasnivati; stvoriti, ustanoviti.
foundation *n* temelj, utemeljivanje, osnova; fond; zadužbina.
founder *n* osnivač, utemeljivač; *v* odroniti se, popustiti.
foundling *n* nahoče, vanbračno dete.
foundry *n* livnica, livničarski zanat.
fount, fountain *n* izvor, vrelo, vodoskok, česma.
fountainhead *n* poreklo, izvor.
four *num* četiri; *n* četvorka.
fourfold *a* četvorostruki.
foursome *n* igra u četvoro.
fourteen *num* četrnaest.
fourteenth *num a* četrnaesti.
fourth *num a* četvrti; *n* četvrtina, četvrti deo.
fowl *n* pernata živina, kokoš.
fox *n* lisica; lisičije krzno.
foyer *n* foaje.
fracas *n* prasak; galama, bučna svađa.
fraction *n* deljenje; razlomak; frakcija.
fracture *n* prelom, naprslina; fraktura; *v* slomiti, smrviti.

fragile *a* lomljiv, krt, trošan; slab.
fragility *n* lomljivost, trošnost; nežnost.
fragment *n* komad, odlomak, deo.
fragmentary *a* nepotpun, krnj, nepovezan.
fragrance *n* miomiris, prijatan miris.
fragrant *a* miomirisan, prijatnog mirisa; **~ly** *adv* miomirisno.
frail *n* korpa, kotarica; *a* neotporan, slab, bolešljiv.
frailty *n* krhkost, neotpornost.
frame *n* okvir, ram; sastav; kostur; *v* umetnuti, uramiti.
frame of mind *n* raspoloženje.
framework *n* kostur, okosnica; uređenje; uramljivanje.
franchise *n* povlastica; građansko pravo; privilegija; pravo učešća na izborima.
frank *a* otvoren, iskren, neposredan.
frankly *adv* otvoreno, iskreno.
frankness *n* iskrenost, otvorenost.
frantic *a* besan, mahnit, pomaman.
fraternal *a* bratski; **~ly** *adv* bratsko.
fraternity *n* bratstvo, zajednica.
fraternize *v* pobratiti se, bratimiti se.
fratricide *n* bratoubistvo, bratoubica.
fraud *n* prevara, lopovluk, obmana.
fraudulence *n* varanje.
fraudulent *a* nepošten, lopovski; **~ly** *adv* nepošteno.
fraught *a* natovaren, pun, bremenit.
fray *n* bučna svađa, tuča.
freak *n* hir, prohtev; nakaza.
freckle *n* pega od sunca.
freckled *a* pegav.
free *a* slobodan, dobrovoljan; drzak; besplatan, javni; otvoren; *v* osloboditi; **to ~ oneself from trouble** rešiti se nevolje.
free kick *n* slobodan udarac.
freedom *n* sloboda, nezavisnost.
free-for-all *n* po svaku cenu, situacija u kojoj se ne bira sredstvo do cilja.
free gift *n* besplatan uzorak.
freehold *n* neograničeno vlasništvo.
freelance *a* plaćenik, najamnik; dobrovoljac; nezavisni novinar, pisac.
freely *adv* otvoreno, slobodno.
freemason *n* slobodni zidar, mason.
freemasonry *n* slobodno zidarstvo.
freepost *n* oslobođeno poštarine.

freethinker *n* slobodni mislilac.
freethinking *n* slobodno mišljenje.
free trade *n* slobodna trgovina.
freeway *n* auto-put.
freewheel *v* voziti na ler.
free will *n* slobodna volja.
freeze *v* smrznuti se, zamrzavati.
freeze-dried *a* smrznuta, vakumirana (hrana).
freezer *n* zamrzivač.
freezing *a* leden, hladan, koji rashlađuje.
freezing point *n* tačka smrzavanja.
freight *n* teret; prevoz tereta; vozarina.
freight train *n* teretni voz.
freighter *n* teretni brod.
French bean *n* mahune.
French fries *npl* pomfrit.
French window *n* staklena vrata.
frenzied *a* mahnit.
frenzy *n* ludilo, bes, besnilo.
frequency *n* učestalost, frekvencija.
frequent *a* čest, učestao; **~ly** *adv* često; *v* posećivati.
fresco *n* freska, zidno slikarstvo.
fresh *a* svež, nov; čist, neiskusan.
freshen *v* osvežiti, rashlađivati se.
fresher *n* brucoš.
freshly *adv* skoro, nedavno.
freshness *n* svežina, čistoća.
freshwater *a* slatka voda.
fret *v* ukrasiti; razjedati; mučiti se.
friar *n* monah, kaluđer.
friction *n* trenje, trljanje; neslaganja, sukobi.
Friday *n* petak; **Good ~** Veliki petak.
friend *n* prijatelj, drug; poznanik; saradnik.
friendless *a* koji je bez prijatelja, usamljen.
friendliness *n* prijateljstvo.
friendly *a* prijateljski, društven.
friendship *n* prijateljstvo.
frieze *n* porub.
frigate *n* jedrenjak, fregata.
fright *n* strah, bojazan; strašilo.
frighten *v* uplašiti, zaplašiti.
frightened *a* uplašen, prestrašen.
frightening *a* zastrašujući.
frightful *a* strašan; ružan; **~ly** *adv* strašno.
frigid *a* hladan, leden; ravnodušan; **~ly** *adv* hladno.

fringe *n* resica, kita; rub; šiška.
fringe benefits *n* beneficije.
frisk *v* skakati; razdragano trčati.
frisky *a* veseo, živahan, razdragan.
fritter *v* drobiti, raskomadati; **to ~ away** potrošiti na sitnice.
frivolity *n* bezvrednost; lakomislenost, površnost.
frivolous *a* bezvredan; lakomislen, površan.
frizz(le) *v* uvijati (se); pržiti (se) uz cvrčanje; malaksati od vrućine.
frizzy *a* kovrdžav.
fro *adv:* **to go to and ~** gore-dole, tamo-amo.
frog *v* žaba.
frolic *v* veseliti se, praviti nestašluke.
frolicsome *a* veseo, razigran, nestašan.
from *prep* od, iz, na, po.
front *n* prednja strana, istureni deo; fasada; *a* prednji, frontalni.
frontal *a* prednji.
front door *n* ulazna vrata.
front page *n* naslovna strana.
frontier *n* granica.
front-wheel drive *n* prednja vuča.
frost *n* mraz, hladnoća; ravnodušnost; *v* zamrzavati se.
frostbite *n* promrzlost, promrznuto mesto.
frostbitten *a* promrzao, promrznut.
frosted *a* zamrznut.
frosty *a* leden, studen, smrznut.
froth *n* pena; tričarije; *v* peniti se; trabunjati.
frothy *a* penušav.
frown *v* namrštiti se, mrko pogledati, neodobravati.
frozen *a* smrznut; bezosećajan; krut.
frugal *a* umeren, štedljiv; jevtin, skroman; **~ly** *adv* štedljivo; skromno.
fruit *n* plod, voćka, voćni proizvod.
fruit juice *n* voćni sok.
fruit salad *n* voćna salata.
fruit seller, greengrocer *n* piljar, prodavac voća.
fruit shop, greengrocer's shop *n* piljarnica, prodavnica voća.
fruit tree *n* voćka.
fruiterer *n* prodavac voća.
fruitful *a* plodan; koristan, probitačan; **~ly** *adv* plodno.

fruitfulness *n* plodnost.
fruition *n* ostvarenje (želja).
fruitless *a* neplodan; nekoristan; **~ly** *adv* neplodno.
frustrate *v* remetiti, osujetiti, uništiti.
frustrated *a* uznemiren, frustriran.
frustration *n* poremećaj (planova), rušenje (nada), frustracija.
fry *v* pržiti.
frying pan *n* tiganj.
fuchsia *n* fuksija (*bot*).
fudge *n* glupost; poslednja vest (u novinama); izmišljotina.
fuel *n* gorivo, ogrev, tečno gorivo.
fuel tank *n* cisterna za gorivo.
fugitive *a* koji je pobegao; kratkotrajan, prolazan.
fugue *n* fuga.
fulcrum *n* oslonac, središte okretanja.
fulfil *v* ispuniti, ostvariti; okončati.
fulfilment *n* ispunjenje, ostvarenje.
full *a* pun, ceo; obilan; *adv* u potpunosti, potpuno.
full-blown *a* u punom cvatu.
full-fledged *a* potpun.
full-length *a* u prirodnoj veličini.
full moon *n* pun mesec.
fullness *n* punoća; obilje.
full-scale *a* u prirodnoj veličini, potpun.
full-time *a* s punim radnim vremenom, redovni.
fully *adv* sasvim, potpuno.
fulsome *a* preteran; gadan.
fumble *v* pipati (u mraku), preturati.
fume *v* kaditi; prijatno mirisati.
fumes *npl* isparenja.
fumigate *v* kaditi.
fun *n* zabava, veselje; šala.
function *n* funkcija, dužnost, službeni posao.
functional *a* funkcionalan.
fund *n* fond, glavnica, osnovna sredstva, kapital; *v* ulagati novac u hartije; stvarati zalihe.
fundamental *a* osnovni, bitan; **~ly** *adv* osnovno.
fundamentalism *n* fundamentalizam.
fundamentalist *n* fundamentalist.
funeral *n* pogreb, sahrana.
funeral service *n* pogrebne usluge.
funereal *a* pogrebni.

fungus *n* gljiva, pečurka, plesen.
funnel *n* levak; jama od granate; dimnjak.
funny *a* smešan, zabavan; čudan, nastran.
fur *n* krzno, dlaka; koža; krznena roba.
fur coat *n* bunda; krzneni kaput.
furious *a* besan, mahnit; ~**ly** *adv* besno.
furlong *n* osmina engleske milje
   (201,167m).
furlough *n* dopust, odsustvo.
furnace *n* peć, topionica; iskušenje.
furnish *v* snabdeti, donositi; snabdeti
   nameštajem.
furnishings *npl* kućne potrepštine,
   nameštaj; oprema, uređaj.
furniture *n* nameštaj.
furrow *n* brazda; duboka bora; *v* orati;
   naborati.
furry *a* krznen, postavljen krznom.
further *a* dalji; *adv* dalje; dodatni, osim
   toga, pored toga.

further education *n* dalje obrazovanje.
furthermore *adv* štaviše, osim toga.
furthest *adv* najdalji, najudaljeniji.
furtive *a* skriven, neprimetan; ~**ly** *adv*
   kradom.
fury *n* bes, pomama; besna žena, furija.
fuse *v* rastopiti, topiti, stapati; *v* fitilj,
   topljenje.
fuse box *n* kutija sa osiguračima.
fusion *n* topljenje; legura; udruživanje;
   fuzija.
fuss *n* buka; komešanje, jurnjava;
   uzbuđenje.
fussy *a* usplahiren, užurban, uzvrpoljen.
futile *a* uzaludan, nekoristan; prazan,
   površan.
futility *n* beskorisnost, uzaludnost;
   praznina, površnost.
future *a* budući; *n* budućnost.

G

gab n brbljanje, torokanje (*sleng*).
gabble v brbljati, mrmljati; n brbljanje, blebetanje.
gable n zabat.
gadget n naprava, pribor, sprava.
gaffe n pogrešan korak, gaf.
gag n čep, zapušač; v začepiti, ućutkati nekoga.
gaiety n veselje, razdraganost.
gaily adv veselo, svetlo.
gain n povećanje, porast; dobitak, korist; v zaraditi, postići.
gait n hod, način hoda; brzina.
gala n svečanost, proslava.
galaxy n galaksija.
gale n bura, snažan vetar; razdraganost.
gall n žuč, zloba, jed.
gall bladder n žučni mehur (*anat*).
gallant a hrabar, srčan; pažljiv, učtiv.
gallery n galerija; publika, gledaoci.
galley n galija.
gallon n galon (mera zapremine).
gallop n galop; v juriti galopom; brzo čitati ili govoriti.
gallows npl vešala.
gallstone n žučni kamenac.
galore adv u izobilju.
galvanize v cinkovati, galvanizovati.
gambit n gambit, početni potez (šah).
gamble v kockati se, igrati se, špekulisati; n kockanje, opasan poduhvat.
gambler n kockar, kartaroš, špekulant.
gambling n kockanje.
game n igra, razonoda; zamisao; lukavstvo; divljač; v kockati se.
gamekeeper n čuvar lovišta.
gaming a igrajući.
gammon n šunka; prevara, podvala.
gamut n skala, gama (*muz*).
gander n gusan; budala, glupak.
gang n banda, družina; smena; brigada.
gangrene n gangrena.
gangster n gangster.
gangway n prolaz između sedišta; skela (*građ*).
gap n otvor, pukotina; rupa; izostanak.
gape v zevati, zinuti, blenuti, zuriti.

gaping a dubok, otvoren.
garage n garaža.
garbled a iskrivljen, izobličen.
garden n bašta, vrt.
gardener n baštovan, vrtlar.
garden-hose n baštensko crevo.
gardening n baštovanstvo.
gargle v ispirati (grlo).
gargoyle n ukras sa grotesknim likom.
garish a blistav, zaslepljujući.
garland n venac, ukras za glavu.
garlic n beli luk, češnjak.
garment n odeća, odelo; pojedini deo odeće.
garnish v ukrašavati, doterivati; dodavati; n ukrasi.
garret n tavan, mansarda.
garrison n garnizon, posada (*voj*); v odrediti za službu u garnizon.
garrotte, garrote v garota.
garrulous a govorljiv, brbljiv.
garter n podvezica.
gas n plin, benzin, gorivo.
gas burner n ringla na gas.
gaseous a gasovit, nalik na plin.
gash n duboka posekotina, duboka rana; v duboko zaseći.
gasket n zaptivač.
gas light n gasna svetiljka.
gas mask n gas-maska.
gas meter n gasometar.
gasp v teško disati, gušiti se; zinuti; n otežano disanje.
gas range n štednjak na gas.
gassy a gasovit, pun gasa.
gas tank n benzinski rezervoar.
gastric a želudačni, stomačni.
gastronomic a gastronomski, gurmanski.
gasworks npl plinara.
gate n ulaz, izlaz; brana; kolska vrata.
gateway n prolaz, podvožnjak.
gather v nabaviti, skupiti; brati; izvoditi zaključak.
gathering n skup, skupština, skupljanje.
gauche a nespretan, nezgrapan.
gaudy a neukusan, drečeći, kitnjast.
gauge n mera, opseg; kalibar, šablon; v meriti, proceniti.

gaunt *a* koščat, mršav, slab.
gauze *n* gaza; sumaglica.
gay *a* veseo, sjajan, šaren; lakomislen; homoseksualan (*sleng*).
gaze *v* posmatrati, napregnuto gledati; *n* prodoran pogled.
gazelle *n* gazela.
gazette *n* dnevni list, službeni list.
gazetteer *n* rečnik geografskih imena.
gear *n* pomoćni uređaji (*teh*); uređaj; brzina; oprema.
gearbox *n* menjačka kutija (*teh*).
gear lever *n* menjač (*teh*).
gear wheel *n* zupčanik (*teh*).
gel *n* gel.
gelatin(e) *n* želatin.
gem *n* dragulj, dragi kamen, nakit.
Gemini *n* Blizanci (*astrol*).
gender *n* rod (*gram*).
gene *n* gen.
genealogical *a* rodoslovni, genealoški.
genealogy *n* rodoslov, genealogija.
general *a* opšti; glavni, osnovni; običan; **in ~** u principu, uopšte; **~ly** *adv* uglavnom; *n* general, vojskovođa.
general election *n* opšti izbori.
generality *n* celokuponost; veći deo, većina.
generalization *n* uopštavanje, generalizacija.
generalize *v* uopštavati.
generate *v* stvarati, rađati; izazivati, pobuditi.
generation *n* pokolenje, naraštaj, generacija.
generator *n* proizvođač; generator (*teh*).
generic *a* srodan, svojstven; zajednički.
generosity *n* velikodušnost, darežljivost.
generous *a* velikodušan, plemenit, izdašan.
genetic engineering *n* genetički inženjering.
genetics *npl* genetika.
genial *a* srdačan, ljubazan; veseo; pun života.
genitals *npl* polni organi, genitalije.
genitive *n* genitiv (*gram*).
genius *n* genije, nadarenost.
genteel *a* prefinjen, lepo vaspitan.
gentile *n* paganin; hrišćanin.
gentle *a* nežan, dobar, srdačan; mek; poslušan.

gentleman *n* gospodin, pristojan čovek; plemić.
gentleness *n* blagost, dobrota.
gently *adv* nežno, lagano, blago.
gentry *n* gospodski stalež.
gents *n* muški toalet (*sleng*).
genuflection *n* savijanje kolena.
genuine *a* izvoran, istinski, iskren; **~ly** *adv* iskreno, pravo.
genus *n* rod, vrsta (*biol*).
geographer *n* geograf.
geographical *a* geografski.
geography *n* geografija.
geological *a* geološki.
geologist *n* geolog.
geology *n* geologija.
geometric(al) *a* geometrijski.
geometry *n* geometrija.
geranium *n* zdravac, geranijum (*bot*).
geriatric *a* gerijatrijski.
germ *n* zametak, plod, embrion (*biol*).
germinate *v* proklijati; oživljavati.
gesticulate *v* gestikulirati.
gesture *n* pokret ili znak rukom, gest.
get *v* dobiti, nabaviti; doputovati; uhvatiti; imati; biti obavezan, biti dužan da; **to ~ somewhere** imati uspeha; **to ~ through** savladati.
geyser *n* gejzir.
ghastly *a* strašan, užasan.
gherkin *n* kiseli krastavac.
ghetto *n* geto, jevrejska četvrt.
ghost *n* duh, sablast; aluzija.
ghostly *a* duhovni, avetinjski.
giant *n* div, džin.
gibberish *n* besmislica , nerazumljiv govor.
gibe *v* podsmehnuti se, rugati se; *n* podsmeh, ruganje.
giblets *npl* iznutrice, sitnež.
giddiness *n* nesvestica, vrtoglavica; lakomislenost.
giddy *a* vrtoglav, koji oseća nesvesticu; lakomislen.
gift *n* poklon, dar; nadarenost, sposobnost.
gifted *a* darovit, obdaren, sposoban.
gift voucher *n* poklon-čestitka.
gigantic *a* džinovski, ogroman.
giggle *v* cerekati se.
gild *v* kititi, ukrašavati; pozlatiti.
gilding, gilt *n* pozlata.

gill *n* podbradak, podvaljak; *pl* škrge.

gilt-edged *a* sa pozlaćenim ivicama.

gimmick *n* smicalica, trik; prevara (*sleng*).

gin *n* džin.

ginger *n* đumbir; oduševljenje; riđasta boja.

gingerbread *n* kolač začinjen đumbirom.

giraffe *n* žirafa.

girder *n* greda, nosač, stub.

girdle *n* opasač, pojas.

girl *n* devojčica, devojka; služavka; nevesta.

girlfriend *n* devojka, drugarica.

girlish *a* devojački, sličan devojčici.

giro *n* žiro (račun).

girth *n* obim, veličina, opseg.

gist *n* bit, suština.

give *v* davati, dodeliti; plaćati; uručiti; predati; donositi; posvetiti; prirediti; **to ~ away** pokloniti; izdati; **to ~ back** vraćati; osvetiti se; **to ~ in** podnositi; predati; popuštati; **to ~ off** isparavati; **to ~ out** razglasiti; nestati; **to ~ up** otkazati; odustati.

gizzard *n* guša, želudac.

glacial *a* zaleđen, hladan, ledeni.

glacier *n* glečer.

glad *a* zadovoljan, radostan; blistav, sjajan; **I am ~ to see** milo mi je da vas vidim; **~ly** *adv* rado.

gladden *v* radovati se, veseliti se.

gladiator *n* gladijator.

glamorous *a* čaroban, privlačan, zanosan.

glamour *n* raskoš, čarobnost.

glance *n* pogled; blesak; *v* pogledati; sinuti.

gland *n* žlezda; krajnici.

glare *n* jaka svetlost; lažni nakit; ukočeni pogled; *v* ukočeno gledati; zaslepljujuće sijati.

glaring *a* bleštav; upadljiv; ukočenog pogleda.

glass *n* staklo; čaša; ogledalo; **~es** *pl* naočare; *a* staklen, od stakla.

glassware *n* staklarija.

glassy *a* staklast.

glaze *v* zastakliti, glačati, polirati.

glazier *n* staklar.

gleam *n* slaba svetlost; odsjaj; tračak; *v* odražavati se; svetleti.

gleaming *a* sjajan, svetlucav.

glean *v* pabirčiti, napabirčiti.

glee *n* veselje, likovanje.

glen *n* dolina.

glib *a* govorljiv, rečit, oštar; **~ly** *adv* rečito.

glide *v* klizati, kliziti; šunjati se.

gliding *n* jedrenje.

glimmer *n* svetlucanje; tračak nade; *v* pritajeno svetleti.

glimpse *n* blesak, letimičan pogled; *v* spaziti u prolazu.

glint *v* planuti, buknuti, jako zablistati.

glisten, glitter *v* blistati, sijati.

gloat *v* radovati se, naslađivati se.

global *a* globalan.

globalization *n* globalizacija.

global warming *n* globalno zagrevanje.

globe *n* kugla, lopta; zemljina lopta.

gloom, gloominess *n* mrak, tama; snuždenost; **~ily** *adv* mračno; natmureno.

gloomy *a* mračan; potišten.

glorification *n* hvaljenje, slavljenje, uzdizanje.

glorify *v* slaviti, veličati; ukrašavati.

glorious *a* slavan, čuven; izvanredan; **~ly** *adv* slavno, divno.

glory *n* slava, pobeda; velelepnost.

gloss *n* lažan sjaj, varljiva spoljašnost; *v* učiniti sjajnim; zataškati; **to ~ over** prikriti grešku.

glossary *n* rečnik sa tumačenjima, glosar.

glossy *a* sjajan, blistav.

glove *n* rukavica.

glove compartment *n* pregradac za sitne stvari u automobilu.

glow *v* svetleti, tinjati, plamteti; *n* svetlost; zanos, vatra; živahnost.

glower *v* ljutito gledati.

glue *n* lepak, tutkalo; *v* lepiti, zalepiti.

glum *a* mračan, natmuren, zlovoljan.

glut *n* zasićenost, preterivanje, višak.

glutinous *a* lepljiv.

glutton *n* žderonja, nezasit čovek.

gluttony *n* proždrljivost.

glycerine *n* glicerin.

gnarled *a* čvornovat; nezgrapan.

gnash *v* škrgutati zubima.

gnat *n* komarac, mušica.

gnaw *v* gristi, glodati; razjedati.

gnome *n* patuljak, kepec, šumski duh.

go *v* ići, hodati, voziti se; krenuti; proći; gubiti; postupiti; **to ~ ahead** ići napred; **to ~ away** otići; **to ~ back** vratiti se; **to ~ by** prolaziti; zavisiti; **to ~ for** računati se, smatrati se; napadati nekoga; **to ~ off** odlaziti, bežati; rasprsnuti se; **to ~ on** nastaviti; približiti se; brbljati; **to ~ out** izlaziti; obustaviti; **to ~ up** dizati se; rasti.

goad *n* podstrek, podsticaj; *v* podstrekavati; naljutiti.

go-ahead *a* napred; *n* dozvola za kretanje.

goal *n* cilj, odredište; gol (*sport*).

goalkeeper *n* golman.

goalpost *n* stativa.

goatherd *n* pastir.

gobble *v* proždirati.

go-between *n* posrednik.

goblet *n* pehar, krčag.

goblin *n* đavolak, kućni duh.

God *n* Bog, božanstvo.

godchild *n* kumče.

goddaughter *n* kumica.

goddess *n* boginja.

godfather *n* kum.

godforsaken *a* zabačen, udaljen; napušten od svih.

godhead *n* božanstvo.

godless *a* bezbožan.

godlike *a* božanski.

godly *a* pobožan, božanski.

godmother *n* kuma.

godsend *n* iznenadna sreća, srećan događaj.

godson *n* kumče (muško).

goggles *npl* zaštitne naočari.

going *n* odlazak, put, kretanje; *a* tekući, aktuelan.

gold *n* zlato; bogatstvo, blago.

golden *a* zlatan, dragocen, skupocen; **~ rule** zlatno pravilo.

goldfish *n* zlatna ribica.

goldmine *n* rudnik zlata.

goldsmith *n* zlatar.

golf *n* golf.

golf ball *n* loptica za golf.

golf club *n* palica za golf; klub igrača golfa.

golf course *n* igralište za golf.

golfer *n* igrač golfa.

gondolier *n* gondolijer.

gone *a* propao, izgubljen; istekao; umrli.

gong *n* gong.

good *a* dobar, dobronameran; svež; prijatan, ljubazan; *adv* dobro; *n* dobro, korist; *npl* roba.

goodbye *n* doviđenja, zbogom.

Good Friday *n* Veliki petak.

good-looking *a* lep, zgodan, privlačan.

good-natured *a* dobroćudan.

goodness *n* dobrota; izvrsnost.

goodwill *n* raspoloženje, spremnost, dobra volja.

goose *n* guska, glupak, budala.

gooseberry *n* ogrozd.

goose bumps, goose flesh *n* guščija koža; žmarci.

goose-step *n* paradni korak.

gore *n* krv (*poet*); *v* probosti, proburaziti.

gorge *n* klanac, tesnac; progutana hrana; *v* prejesti se.

gorgeous *a* raskošan, velelepan.

gorilla *n* gorila.

gorse *n* štipavica, žutilovka (*bot*).

gory *a* okrvavljen, krvav.

goshawk *n* jastreb-kokošar.

gospel *n* jevanđelje; versko ubeđenje.

gossamer *n* leteća paučina; tanka gaza.

gossip *n* brbljanje, ćeretanje; spletka; *v* brbljati; ogovarti.

gothic *a* gotski.

gout *n* giht (*med*); kaplja.

govern *v* vladati, upravljati.

governess *n* guvernanta, vaspitačica.

government *n* vlada; uprava.

governor *n* guverner; upravnik; šef, gazda (*sleng*).

gown *n* haljina.

grab *v* zgrabiti, ščepati; prisvojiti.

grace *n* privlačnost, ljupkost; naklonost; milosrđe; **to say ~** pomoliti se za stolom; *v* ukarašavati; nagraditi.

graceful *a* ljubak, skladan, graciozan; otmen; **~ly** *adv* ljupko.

gracious *a* prijatan, popustljiv, blag; milostiv; **~ly** *adv* prijatno.

gradation *n* stepenovanje, gradacija; stupanj, stepen razvitka.

grade *n* stepen, čin, zvanje; ocena; vrsta.

gradient *n* strmina, nagib; gradijent (*fiz*).

gradual *a* postepen; **~ly** *adv* postepeno.

graduate v diplomirati; podeliti na stepene.
graduation n diplomiranje, svečanost povodom završetka školovanja.
graffiti n grafiti, škrabanje po zidovima.
graft n kalem, izdanak; presađivanje tkiva (*med*); v kalemiti; presaditi tkivo.
grain n zrno, žito; granulacija; priroda, sklonost.
gram n gram.
grammar n gramatika; uvod u nauku.
grammatical a gramatički; ~ly adv gramatički pravilno.
granary n žitnica, ambar.
grand a veliki, važan, osnovni; raskošan, sjajan.
grandad n deda.
grandchild n unuk, unuka.
granddaughter n unuka; **great ~** praunuka.
grandeur n sjaj, raskoš; otmenost; veličina.
grandfather n deda; **great ~** pradeda.
grandiose a veličanstven, grandiozan; uobražen.
grandma, grandmother n baka, stara majka.
grandparents npl roditeljevi roditelji.
grand piano n veliki klavir.
grandson n unuk; **great ~** praunuk.
grandstand n tribina.
granite n granit.
granny n baka.
grant v poklanjati, davati, darivati; dopuštati; **to take for ~ed** prihvatiti kao gotovu činjenicu; n poklon; pomoć, dotacija; dozvola.
granulate v usitniti, izdrobiti; pretvoriti u granule.
granule n zrnce, granule.
grape n grožđe; **bunch of ~s** grozd grožđa.
grapefruit n grejpfrut.
graph n grafikon.
graphic(al) a grafički; slikovit, pregledan; ~ally adv grafički.
graphics n grafika.
grapple v rvati se, dohvatiti se.
grasp v zgrabiti, razumeti; n stezanje, zagrljaj; sposobnost shvatanja.
grasping a grabljiv.

grass n trava, travnjak.
grasshopper n skakavac.
grassland n pašnjak.
grass snake n belouška.
grassy a travnat.
grate n rešetka, ograda; v strugati; škripati.
grateful a zahvalan, prijatan; ~ly adv zahvalno.
gratefulness n zahvalnost.
grater n rende.
gratification n zadovoljenje, uživanje.
gratify v zadovoljiti, pričinjavati zadovoljstvo.
grating n rešetka; a koji škripi, hrapav; oštar.
gratis adv besplatno.
gratitude n zahvalnost, blagodarnost.
gratuitous a besplatan; bezrazložan; ~ly adv besplatno.
gratuity n novčani poklon, napojnica.
grave n grob; a važan, uticajan, značajan; ~ly adv važno.
grave digger n grobar.
gravel n šljunak, pesak.
gravestone n nadgrobni spomenik, nadgrobna ploča.
graveyard n groblje.
gravitate v težiti, naginjati.
gravitation n gravitacija.
gravity n ozbiljnost, važnost; trezvenost.
gravy n sos, sos od pečenja.
graze v pasti stoku, izvesti stoku na pašu; okrznuti.
grease n salo, slanina; mazivo; v zamastiti, 'podmazati' (dati mito).
greasepaint n šminka za glumce.
greasy a mastan, zamašćen.
great a veliki, ogroman, odličan; snažan; iskusan; vešt; ~ly adv veliko, ogromno.
greatcoat n kaput, kabanica.
greatness n veličina, sjaj, slava.
greedily adv pohlepno, gramzivo.
greediness, greed n pohlepa, gramzivost, požuda.
greedy a pohlepan, lakom, škrt.
Greek n Grk, Grkinja; grčki.
green a zelen, ozeleneo; biljni, nezreo; n zelena boja, zelena farba; mladost, snaga; pl kuhinjsko zelje, zelen.
green belt n zeleni pojas.

greenery *n* zelenilo.
greengrocer *n* piljar.
greenhouse *n* staklenik, staklena bašta.
greenhouse effect *n* dejstvo staklene bašte.
greenish *a* zelenkast.
green movement *n* pokret zelenih.
greenness *n* nezrelost, naivnost, neiskustvo.
greet *v* pozdraviti; dočekati.
greeting *n* pozdrav; doček.
greeting(s) card *n* čestitka.
grenade *n* granata (*voj*).
grenadier *n* grenadir; bacač granata.
grey *a* siv, tmuran, mračan, potišten; *n* siva boja, sivo odelo.
greyish *a* sivkasto.
greyhound *n* hrt.
grid *n* rešetka, mreža.
gridiron *n* roštilj, rešetka.
grief *n* žalost, bol, nesreća, jad.
grievance *n* žalba, pritužba, razlog nezadovoljstva.
grieve *v* žalostiti se, rastužiti se.
grievous *a* tužan; mračan, bolan; ~ly *adv* tužno.
griffin *n* grifon, lav sa orlovskom glavom (*mit*).
grill *n* roštilj, rešetka; jelo na roštilju; *v* peći na roštilju; mučiti.
grille *n* rešetka.
grim *a* okrutan, strašan, grub.
grimace *n* grimasa, iskrivljeno lice.
grime *n* čađ, prljavština.
grimy *a* čađav, prljav.
grin *n* cerenje; *v* ceriti se, keziti se.
grind *v* samleti, smrviti, izdrobiti; kinjiti.
grinder *n* vodenica za mlevenje kafe; brusač.
grip *n* zahvat, stezanje ruke; moć shvatanja; putna torba; *v* zgrabiti; izazivati grčeve; ugnjetavati.
grisly *a* strašan, užasan.
gristle *n* hrskavica.
gristly *a* hrskavičav.
grit *n* sitan pesak, šljunak; upornost, izdržljivost.
groan *v* stenjati, teško uzdisati; *n* stenjanje.
grocer *n* bakalin.
grocer's shop *n* bakalnica.

groceries *npl* bakaluk, prehrambeni proizvodi.
groggy *a* pijan, nesiguran na nogama.
groin *n* prepone, slabine.
groom *n* momak, sluga, konjušar; mladoženja; *v* timariti, negovati konja.
groove *n* žljeb, udubljenje; navika.
grope *v* opipavati, pipajući tražiti put.
gross *a* veliki, golem, debeo, krupan; prost, jeftin; ~ly *adv* krupno, prosto, debelo.
grotesque *a* groteskan.
grotto *n* pećina.
ground *n* zemlja, tlo, teren; vrt; osnova; talog; tema; *v* obrazložiti; podučavati; položiti; nasukati se.
ground-floor *n* prizemlje.
grounding *n* sprema, oprema.
groundless *a* neosnovan, bezrazložan; ~ly *adv* neosnovano.
groundwork *n* pripremni rad.
group *n* grupa; skup; *v* prikupiti se, grupisati se.
grouse *n* tetreb; *v* gunđati.
grove *n* gaj, šumica.
grovel *v* puziti pred nekim, ulagivati se.
grow *v* rasti, jačati, uvećavati se; postati; uzgajati; ~ up odrasti.
grower *n* odgajivač.
growing *a* koji raste, koji se razvija.
growl *v* režati, gunđati; grmeti; *n* režanje, gunđanje.
grown-up *n* odrastao čovek.
growth *n* razvoj, rastenje; poreklo; povećanje, porast.
grub *n* larva; hrana (*sleng*).
grubby *a* prljav, zamazan, neuredan.
grudge *n* neraspoloženje, pizma; *v* žaliti se; zavideti.
grudgingly *adv* nerado, protiv volje.
gruelling *a* naporan, iscrpljujući.
gruesome *a* grozan, strašan, odvratan.
gruff *a* osoran, oštar; rapav; ~ly *adv* osorno.
gruffness *n* grubost, nabusitost, osornost.
grumble *v* gunđati, žaliti se.
grumpy *a* mrzovoljan, razdražljiv.
grunt *v* groktati, gunđati.
guarantee *n* garancija, jamstvo, zalog; *v* jamčiti.
guard *n* zaštita, straža; budnost; garda; *v* čuvati; stražariti; suzbijati.

guarded *a* oprezan.
guardian *n* staratelj, tutor; stražar.
guardianship *n* starateljstvo.
guardroom *n* stražarnica.
guerrilla *n* gerila, partizanski način
 ratovanja.
guerrilla warfare *n* gerilski rat.
guess *v* nagađati, pogoditi, pretpostaviti; *n*
 pretpostavka, nagađanje.
guesswork *n* nagađanje.
guest *n* gost, stanar.
guest room *n* gostinska soba.
guffaw *n* grohotan smeh.
guidance *n* upravljanje, rukovođenje.
guide *v* voditi, predvoditi, rukovoditi,
 upravljati; *n* vođa.
guide book *n* vodič (knjiga).
guide dog *n* pas vodič.
guidelines *npl* direktive, smernice.
guild *n* esnaf.
guile *n* prevara, izdaja, podmuklost.
guillotine *n* giljotina; *v* giljotinirati.
guilt *n* krivica.
guiltless *a* nevin.
guilty *a* kriv, pogrešan.
guinea pig *n* zamorče, morsko prase.
guise *n* pojava, izgled; maska.
guitar *n* gitara.
gulf *n* morski zaliv; ponor; vir.
gull *n* galeb; glupak.
gullet *n* grlo, ždrelo; jednjak.
gullibility *n* lakovernost.
gullible *a* lakoveran.
gully *n* vododerina, klanac, jarak.
gulp *n* gutanje, veliki gutljaj; *v* gutati;
 gušiti se.

gum *n* guma, kaučuk; desni; *v* zalepiti;
 lučiti smolu, kaučuk.
gun *n* puška, top, oruđe; pištolj, revolver.
gunboat *n* topovnjača.
gunfire *n* puščana vatra.
gunman *n* revolveraš.
gunner *n* nišandžija (*voj*).
gunnery *n* artiljerijska veština.
gunpoint *n* pod pretnjom oružja.
gunpowder *n* barut.
gunshot *n* hitac, pucanj; puškomet, domet.
gunsmith *n* oružar.
gurgle *v* klokotati, žuboriti.
guru *n* guru; stručnjak.
gush *v* pokuljati, izliti se; *n* jaka kiša,
 bujica.
gushing *a* zanesen.
gust *n* nalet vetra, pljusak; nastup gneva.
gusto *n* sklonost, naklonost, ukus.
gusty *a* buran, vetrovit.
gut *n* utroba, crevo; odlučnost, snaga;
 jaruga; *v* izvaditi utrobu; pljačkati;
 halapljivo jesti.
gutter *n* slivnik, oluk; društveni ološ.
guttural *a* grleni zvuk.
guy *n* momak, čovek, osoba.
guzzle *v* jesti i piti halapljivo; propiti (npr.
 novac).
gym(nasium) *n* gimnazija; gimnastička
 dvorana.
gymnast *n* gimnastičar.
gymnastic *a* gimnastički; ~s *npl* gimnastika.
gynaecologist *n* ginekolog.
gypsum *n* gips.
Gypsy *n* Ciganin, Ciganka.
gyrate *v* okretati se u krug.

H

haberdasher *n* trgovac galanterijskom robom.

haberdashery *n* prodavnica galanterijske robe .

habit *n* navika, običaj; telesna građa, sklop; osobina.

habitable *a* pogodan za stanovanje.

habitat *n* prebivalište, sredina.

habitual *a* uobičajen, običan; ~ly *adv* obično.

hack *n* rana, povreda; motika; raga, iznuren čovek; *v* raseći, klesati; kašljati.

hackneyed *a* otrcan, banalan.

haddock *n* bakalar.

haemorrhage *n* krvarenje, izliv krvi (*med*), hemoragija.

haemorrhoids *npl* hemoroidi (*med*).

hag *n* veštica.

haggard *a* izmučen, zbunjen, preplašen.

haggle *v* cenjkati se, prepirati se.

hail *n* tuča; grad; pozdrav; *v* padati (grad); pozdraviti, dozivati.

hailstorm *n* oluja sa gradom.

hair *n* kosa, dlaka; čekinja.

hairbrush *n* četka za kosu.

haircut *n* šišanje.

hairdresser *n* frizer.

hairdryer *n* fen za kosu, hauba za sušenje kose.

hairless *a* ćelav.

hairnet *n* mrežica za kosu.

hairpiece *n* umetak od kose , tupe.

hairpin *n* ukosnica.

hairpin bend *n* oštra krivina.

hair remover *n* depilator.

hair-splitting *n* cepidlačenje.

hairspray *n* lak za kosu.

hairstyle *n* frizura.

hairy *a* dlakav, kosmat.

hale *a* zdrav, snažan.

half *n* polovina, deo; *a* polovičan, delimičan.

half-caste *n* melez.

half-hearted *a* trom, mlitav, malodušan.

half-hour *n* pola sata, koji traje pola sata.

half-moon *n* polumesec.

half-price *a* u pola cene.

half-time *n* poluvreme.

halfway *adv/a* na pola puta.

hall *n* dvorana; predsoblje; zajednička trpezarija.

hallmark *n* žig, oznaka, obeležje.

hallow *v* posvetiti, oglasiti svetim.

hallucination *n* priviđanje, halucinacija.

halo *n* oreol, venac, svetlost.

halt *v* zaustaviti se; kolebati se, oklevati; *n* zastoj; odmor.

halve *v* prepoloviti.

ham *n* šunka.

hamburger *n* hamburger.

hamlet *n* seoce, zaselak.

hammer *n* čekić; *v* udarati čekićem, zakucavati.

hammock *n* viseća mreža za ležanje.

hamper *n* velika korpa sa poklopcem; *v* smetati, ometati.

hamstring *v* osakatiti.

hand *n* ruka, šaka; vlast; veština; rukopis; skazaljka na satu; **at ~** pri ruci; *v*. uručiti; pomoći; pridržati.

handbag *n* ručna torbica, putna torba.

handbill *n* letak.

handbook *n* priručnik, vodič.

handbrake *n* ručna kočnica.

handcuff *n* lisice.

handful *n* pregršt.

handicap *n* hendikep, smetnja, prepreka.

handicapped *a* hendikepiran.

handicraft *n* zanat, ručni rad.

handiwork *n* ručni rad, tvorevina.

handkerchief *n* džepna maramica.

handle *n* drška, ručka; povod; *v* rukovati; postupiti; trgovati.

handlebars *npl* upravljač bicikla (ili motocikla).

handling *n* postupak, manupulisanje.

handrail *n* ograda na stepeništu.

handshake *n* rukovanje, stisak ruke.

handsome *a* lep, pristojan; izdašan; ~ly *adv* lepo, pristojno.

handwriting *n* rukopis.

handy *a* vešt, umešan; koji je pri ruci.

hang *v* obesiti, visiti.

hanger *n* vešalica, kuka, privezak.

hanger-on *n* prišipetlja; prepredenjak.
hangings *npl* zavese, draperije.
hangman *n* dželat.
hangover *n* mamurluk.
hang-up *n* prepreka, inhibicija (*sleng*).
hanker *v* čeznuti, žudeti, sanjati o
   nečemu.
haphazard *a* slučajan, nasumičan.
hapless *a* nesrećan, loše sreće.
happen *v* dešavati se, dogoditi se;
   slučajno se naći.
happening *n* slučaj, događaj.
happily *adv* na sreću, srećom.
happiness *n* sreća.
happy *a* srećan, zadovoljan; koristan.
harangue *n* huškanje, haranga; *v* huškati.
harass *v* uznemiravati, mučiti.
harbinger *n* preteča, glasnik.
harbour *n* luka; utočište, sklonište; *v*
   usidriti se u luci; dati utočište.
hard *a* tvrd, otporan, jak; surov; vredan,
   radan; ~ **of hearing** tvrd na ušima, ko
   slabo čuje; ~ **by** sasvim blizu, odmah tu.
harden *v* otvrdnuti, očeličiti se; postati
   neosetljiv.
hard-headed *a* praktičan.
hard-hearted *a* okrutan, tvrda srca.
hardiness *n* hrabrost, izdržljivost.
hardly *adv* jedva, tek; sa mukom.
hardness *n* tvrdina, čvrstina.
hardship *n* oskudica, iskušenje.
hard-up *a* bez para.
hardware *n* gvožđurija.
hardwearing *a* otporan.
hardy *a* hrabar, neustrašiv, jak, otporan.
hare *n* zec.
hare-brained *a* nesmotren, lakouman.
hare-lipped *a* sa zečjom usnom.
haricot *n* paprikaš; pasulj (*kulin*).
harlequin *n* harlekin.
harm *n* šteta, nepravda, zlo; *v* oštetiti.
harmful *a* štetan, opasan.
harmless *a* neškodljiv, bezopasan.
harmonic *a* harmonijski ton (*muz*).
harmonious *a* harmoničan, skladan; ~**ly**
   adv harmonično.
harmonize *v* usklađivati, harmonizovati.
harmony *n* sklad, skladnost, harmonija.
harness *n* konjska oprema, am; *v*
   uprezati.
harp *n* harfa.

harpist *n* harfista.
harpoon *n* harpun.
harpsichord *n* klavsen, klavicimbal
   (*muz*).
harrow *n* drljača.
harry *v* uništavati, pljačkati; mučiti.
harsh *a* oštar, neprijatan; okrutan,
   bezdušan; ~**ly** *adv* oštro, okrutno.
harshness *n* strogost, surovost; hrapavost.
harvest *n* žetva; prihod, dobit; *v* skupljati
   letinu; proslaviti se.
harvester *n* žetelac.
hash *n* ragu, jelo od seckanog mesa
   (*kulin*); zbrka.
hassock *n* jastuče za klečanje.
haste *n* žurba, hitnost; **to be in** ~ žuriti
   se.
hasten *v* požurivati, ubrzavati; žuriti se.
hastily *adv* užurbano, na brzu ruku.
hasty *a* hitan, užurban, nepromišljen.
hat *n* šešir, kapa.
hatbox *n* kutija za šešir.
hatch *v* ležati na jajima, gajiti piliće;
   pripremati, smišljati; **to** ~ **a plot/
   scheme** skovati zaveru; *n* gajenje pilića;
   vratanca; leglo.
hatchet *n* sekira.
hatchway *n* otvor na palubi.
hate *n* mržnja, odvratnost; *v* mrzeti, ne
   podnositi.
hateful *a* omražen, omrznut.
hatred *n* mržnja, neprijateljstvo.
hatter *n* šeširdžija.
haughtily *adv* nadmeno, oholo.
haughtiness *n* oholost, nadmenost.
haughty *a* ohol, nadmen.
haul *v* vući, tegliti, prevoziti; *n* teglenje.
hauler *n* prevoznik.
haunch *n* bedro, but.
haunt *v* često posećivati, proganjati (u
   mislima), uporno se vraćati na isto
   mesto; *n* luka, jazbina.
have *v* imati, posedovati; znati, shvatiti.
haven *n* sklonište, utočište; luka.
haversack *n* ranac, ruksak.
havoc *n* pustošenje, razaranje,
   uništavanje.
hawk *n* soko, jastreb; otimač; *v* loviti sa
   sokolom; progoniti.
hawthorn *n* glog (*bot*).
hay *n* seno.

hay fever *n* polenska groznica.
hayloft *n* pojata, senik.
hayrick, haystack *n* plast sena.
hazard *n* šansa; opasan poduhvat; *v* staviti na kocku, usuditi se.
hazardous *a* opasan, nesmotren.
haze *n* izmaglica, para.
hazel *n* boja lešnika, leska; *a* svetlo-smeđi.
hazelnut *n* lešnik.
hazy *a* maglovit, mutan, pokriven parom.
he *pn* on.
head *n* glava, glavica (eksera); vrh; poglavlje; *v* predvoditi, upravljati; krenuti; staviti naslov; **to ~ for** ići prema.
headache *n* glavobolja.
headdress *n* šešir.
headland *n* rt.
headlight *n* prednje svetlo na vozilu.
headline *n* glavni naslov, zaglavlje.
headlong *adv* naglavce, strmoglavce, navrat-nanos.
headmaster *n* upravnik škole.
head phones *npl* naglavne slušalice.
headquarters *npl* štab, komanda.
headroom *n* slobodan prostor, među prostor.
headstrong *a* uporan, tvrdoglav.
headwaiter *n* šef sale, glavni konobar.
headway *n* napredovanje.
heady *n* nagao, nesmotren.
heal *v* lečiti, izlečiti, zalečiti.
health *n* zdravlje.
healthy *a* zdrav, koristan za zdravlje.
heap *n* hrpa, gomila, mnoštvo; *v* nagomilavati, skupljati.
hear *v* čuti, slušati; saznati.
hearing *n* sluh; saslušanje.
hearing aid *n* slušni aparat.
hearsay *n* glasina, glas.
hearse *n* mrtvačka kola.
heart *n* srce, duša; suština; srčanost; **by ~** napamet; **with all my ~** od sveg srca.
heart attack *n* srčani udar, infarkt miokarda (*med*).
heart failure *n* srčani udar.
heartbreaking *a* koji razdire dušu; nesnosan, dosadan.
heartburn *n* gorušica.
heartfelt *a* iskren.
hearth *n* ognjište, kamin, peć.

heartily *adv* iskreno, srdačno, toplo.
heartiness *n* srčanost.
heartless *a* bezdušan, bez srca.
hearty *a* srdačan, iskren, topao.
heat *n* vrućina, vrelina, usijanost; *v* ložiti, zapaliti.
heat wave *n* toplotni udar.
heater *n* grejač, grejalica.
heathen *n* neznabožac, paganin; **~ish** *a* divljački, paganski.
heather *n* vres (*bot*).
heating *n* grejanje, zagrevanje.
heave *v* dizati, izvlačiti; teško disati; *n* dizanje; povraćanje.
heaven *n* nebo, nebeski svod.
heavenly *a* nebeski; božanstven, divan.
heavily *adv* teško.
heavy *a* težak, plah, buran; nepodnošljiv; mračan.
Hebrew *n* Jevrejin.
heckle *v* dobaciti, upasti govorniku u reč.
hectic *a* grozničav, uzbuđen.
hedge *n* ograda, živica, pregrada; *v* ograditi živicom; izbegavati objašnjenja.
hedgehog *n* jež, bodljikavo prase.
heed *v* obraćati pažnju, pažljivo slušati; *n* pažnja!.
heedless *a* nepažljiv, nebrižljiv; **~ly** *adv* nepažljivo.
heel *n* peta, potpetica; podlac (*sleng*); **to take to one's ~s** uhvatiti maglu.
hefty *a* krupan, veliki, snažan.
heifer *n* junica.
height *n* visina, rast; vrh; najviša tačka.
heighten *v* povišavati, pojačavati.
heinous *a* odvratan, užasan, ogavan.
heir *n* naslednik; **~ apparent** naslednik sa pravom nasleđa.
heiress *n* naslednica.
heirloom *n* nasleđena stvar.
helicopter *n* helikopter.
hell *n* pakao.
hellish *a* pakleni.
helm *n* kormilo.
helmet *n* šlem.
help *v* pomagati, pomoći; dodavati, dati jelo; uzdržati se; **I cannot ~ it** ne mogu a da ne..; ne mogu da izdržim a da ne..; *n* pomoć, spas; služavka, pomoćnik.
helper *n* pomoćnik, pomagač.
helpful *a* koristan.

helping *n* pomoć; obrok jela.
helpless *a* bespomoćan, nemoćan; **~ly** *adv* bespomoćno.
helter-skelter *adv* neorganizovano, na vrat-na nos.
hem *n* porub, ivica; *v* kašljucati.
he-man *n* muškarčina, pravi muškarac.
hemisphere *n* hemisfera, polulopta.
hemp *n* konoplja.
hen *n* kokoška.
henceforth, henceforward *adv* odsada.
henchman *n* pristalica, sledbenik.
henhouse *n* kokošinjac.
hepatitis *n* hepatitis, zapaljenje jetre (*med*).
her *pn* nju, ju, njoj, joj, njome (zavisni padež od **she**).
herald *n* glasnik; poznavalac grbova.
heraldry *n* heraldika, poznavanje grbova.
herb *n* biljka, trava; *pl* lekovite biljke.
herbaceous *a* sličan travi.
herbivorous *a* biljožderski.
herd *n* stado; gomila, rulja.
here *adv* ovde, tu, ovamo; eto.
hereabout(s) *adv* negde tu, negde u blizini.
hereafter *adv* ubuduće.
hereby *adv* ovim, tim.
hereditary *a* nasledan, koji se prenosi s kolena na koleno.
heredity *n* naslednost.
heresy *n* jeres.
heretic *n* jeretik, krivovernik; *a* jeretičan.
herewith *adv* uz ovo (se prilaže), s ovim se (prilaže).
heritage *n* nasledstvo, nasleđe.
hermetic(al) *a* hermetički, čvrsto zatvoren; **~ally** *adv* čvrsto zatvoreno.
hermit *n* pustinjak.
hermitage *n* pustinjački život, pustinjački stan.
hernia *n* kila, hernija (*med*).
hero *n* heroj, junak.
heroic *a* junački, herojski; **~ally** *adv* herojski.
heroine *n* junakinja, heroina.
heroism *n* junaštvo, herojstvo.
heron *n* čaplja.
herring *n* haringa.
hers *pn* njena.
herself *pn* sebe, samog sebe.

hesitant *a* neodlučan, kolebljiv.
hesitation *n* kolebljivost, neodlučnost.
heterogeneous *a* raznorodan.
heterosexual *a* heteroseksualan.
hew *v* seći, cepati, tesati.
heyday *n* vrhunac, napon snage.
hi *excl* zdravo, hej.
hiatus *n* zev (*ling*); jaz, praznina.
hibernate *v* prezimiti; provesti zimu u spavanju (zimski san).
hiccup *n* štucanje; *v* štucati.
hickory *n* hikori, američki orah (*bot*).
hide *v* kriti se, sakrivati se; *n* krzno, koža.
hideaway *n* zabačeno tiho mesto.
hideous *a* odvratan, strašan, užasan; **~ly** *adv* odvratno, strašno.
hiding place *n* skrovište.
hierarchy *n* hijerarhija.
hieroglyphic *a* hijeroglifski; *n* hijeroglif.
hi-fi *n* hi-fi, radio gramofon visoke vernosti reprodukcije .
higgledy-piggledy *adv* u neredu, pobrkano.
high *a* visok, uzvišen; glavni, vrhovni; jak, oštar; skup.
highball *n* koktel (u visokoj čaši).
highchair *n* dečja stolica.
high-handed *a* arogantan.
highlands *npl* brdovit predeo.
highlight *n* vrhunac, najvažniji događaj.
highly *adv* veoma, jako; povoljno.
highly strung *a* napregnut, napet.
highness *n* visina, visok stepen; visost, visočanstvo.
high water *n* vodostaj.
highway *n* autoput.
hijack *v* oteti, kidnapovati.
hijacker *n* otimač, kidnaper.
hike *v* pešačiti.
hilarous *a* veseo, razdragan.
hill *n* uzvišica, brežuljak, breg.
hillock *n* humka.
hillside *n* kosina, padina brežuljka.
hilly *a* brežuljkast.
hilt *n* balčak, ručica.
him *pn* njega, ga, njemu, mu (zavisni padež od **he**).
himself *pn* sebe, sebe samog.
hind *a* zadnji; *n* sluga; košuta.
hinder *v* ometati, praviti prepreke.
hindmost *a* poslednji, najudaljeniji.

hindquarter *n* stražnji čerek.
hindrance *n* smetnja, prepreka.
hindsight *n* nišan; kasno uviđanje.
hinge *n* šarka, zglob.
hint *n* nagoveštaj, aluzija; *v* naslutiti,
 nagovestiti.
hip *n* bedro; šipak; utučenost.
hippopotamus *n* nilski konj.
hire *v* iznajmiti, najmiti; *n* najam, zakup.
hire purchase *n* plaćanje na rate.
his *pn* njegov.
Hispanic *a* španski; *n* osoba španskog
 porekla.
hiss *v* zviždati, izviždati, siktati.
historian *n* istoričar.
historic(al) *a* istorijski; **~ally** *adv*
 istorijski.
history *n* istorija.
histrionic *a* glumački, izveštačen.
hit *v* udariti, oboriti; **to ~ each other**
 sudariti se; *n* udarac; pogodak; uspeh.
hitch *v* vući, pritezati, zakačiti; *n* trzaj;
 čvor.
hitchhiker *n* autostoper.
hitchike *v* stopirati.
hitchiking *n* stopiranje.
hitherto *adv* dosad, do ovog časa.
hive *n* košnica, ljudski mravinjak.
hoard *n* zalihe; *v* skupljati, praviti zalihe.
hoarfrost *n* inje, slabi mraz.
hoarse *a* promukao; **~ly** *adv* promuklo.
hoarseness *n* promuklost.
hoax *n* prevara, lukavstvo, podvala; *v*
 prevariti.
hobble *v* šepati, hramati.
hobby *n* hobi, strast, omiljena zabava.
hobbyhorse *n* drveni konj (igračka); hobi.
hockey *n* hokej.
hodgepodge *n* mišmaš, smeša.
hoe *n* motika; *v* kopati.
hoist *v* dizati; *n* dizanje, uzbrdica.
hold *v* držati, izdržati; obuhvatiti;
 zaustavljati; smatrati; **to ~ on to** držati
 se za nešto; nastaviti da se radi; *n*
 držanje, posedovanje; zahvat.
holder *n* držač; držalac, vlasnik.
holding *n* imanje; držanje; fond.
hold-up *n* zastoj; pljačka.
hole *n* rupa, otvor; udubljenje.
holiday *n* praznik; **~ s** *pl* godišnji odmor,
 raspust.

holiday-maker *n* turista.
holiness *n* svetost, nepovredivost.
hollow *a* šupalj, prazan; *n* praznina;
 ulegnuće; *v* izdubiti.
holly *n* zelenika, božikovina (*bot*).
hollyhock *n* slezovača (*bot*).
holocaust *n* razaranje, uništenje,
 holokaust.
holster *n* futrola za pištolj.
holy *a* sveti, posvećen.
holy water *n* sveta vodica.
homage *n* odavanje pošte, poštovanje.
home *n* dom, kuća; domovina; ognjište;
 porodica; utočište.
home address *n* mesto stanovanja.
home shopping programme (TV) *n*
 kupovina iz fotelje.
homeless *a* bez krova nad .
homeliness *n* prostota; ružnoća.
homely *a* prost, domaći, ružan.
home-made *a* domaći, napravljen kod
 kuće.
homeopathist *n* homeopata.
homeopathy *n* homeopatija.
homesick *a* nostalgičan.
homesickness *n* nostalgija.
hometown *n* rodno mesto.
homeward *a* prema kući.
homework *n* domaći zadatak.
homicidal *a* ubilački.
homicide *n* ubistvo.
homogeneous *a* homogen, istovrstan.
homosexual *a* homoseksualan.
honest *a* pošten, iskren; istinski, pravi;
 ~ly *adv* pošteno.
honesty *n* poštenje.
honey *n* med, slast; dragi/a.
honeycomb *n* saće.
honeymoon *n* medeni mesec.
honeysuckle *n* orlovi nokti (*bot*).
honorary *a* počasni.
honour *n* čast, slava; *v* poštovati, ceniti.
honourable *a* pošten, plemenit.
honourably *adv* pošteno.
hood *n* kapuljača; poklopac; krov.
hoodlum *n* mangup, siledžija.
hoof *n* kopito.
hook *n* kuka, kopča; klopka; **by ~ or by
 crook** bilo kako bilo; na svaki način; *v*
 zakačiti; loviti.
hooked *a* kukast; odan.

hooligan *n* siledžija, huligan.
hoop *n* obruč, kolut.
hooter *n* sirena.
hop *n* hmelj (*bot*); skok, skakanje; *v* poskakivati; igrati.
hope *n* nada; *v* nadati se, iščekivati.
hopeful *a* pun nade, koji daje nade; ~ly *adv* puno nade; nadajmo se (*sleng*).
hopeless *a* beznadežan; ~ly *adv* beznadežno.
hopscotch *n* školice (dečja igra).
horde *n* horda, banda, družina.
horizon *n* vidik, horizont.
horizontal *a* vodoravan, horizontalan; ~ly *adv* vodoravno.
hormone *n* hormon.
horn *n* rog; sirena.
horned *a* rogat.
hornet *n* stršljen (*zool*).
horny *a* rožnat; žuljevit.
horoscope *n* horoskop.
horrendous *a* grozan.
horrible *a* strašan, užasan.
horribly *adv* strašno.
horrid *a* odvratan.
horrific *a* užasavajući.
horrify *v* uplašiti, zastrašiti.
horror *n* užas, strava.
hors d'oeuvre *n* predjelo.
horse *n* konj.
horseback *adv* na konju.
horse-breaker *n* ukrotitelj konja.
horse chestnut *n* divlji kesten.
horsefly *n* konjska muva.
horseman *n* jahač, konjanik.
horsemanship *n* jahanje, veština jahanja.
horsepower *n* konjska snaga.
horse racing *n* konjske trke.
horse race *n* konjska trka.
horseradish *n* hren.
horseshoe *n* potkovica.
horsewoman *n* jahačica.
horticulture *n* baštovanstvo, hortikultura.
horticulturist *n* baštovan.
hose *n* crevo.
hosiery *n* radnja sa čarapama.
hospitable *a* gostoljubiv.
hospitably *adv* gostoljubivo.
hospital *n* bolnica.
hospitality *n* gostoprimstvo.
host *n* domaćin, gazda; mnoštvo, vojska.

hostage *n* talac.
hostess *n* domaćica, gazdarica.
hostile *a* neprijateljski.
hostility *n* neprijateljstvo.
hot *a* vreo, vatren; oštar, ljut (ukus).
hotbed *n* leglo, klijalište.
hotdog *n* vruće viršle u zemički.
hotel *n* hotel.
hot-headed *a* naprasit, nepromišljen.
hothouse *n* staklenik.
hotline *n* direktna telefonska linija, 'crveni telefon'.
hotplate *n* rešo.
hound *n* lovački pas; nitkov.
hour *n* sat, čas.
hour-glass *n* peščani sat.
hourly *adv* svakog časa, često, neprekidno.
house *n* kuća, zgrada, stan; domaćinstvo; pozorište; *v* naseliti, smestiti; doseliti se.
houseboat *n* barka u kojoj se stanuje.
housebreaker *n* provalnik.
housebreaking *n* provala.
household *n* domaćinstvo.
householder *n* domaćin.
housekeeping *n* vođenje domaćinstva.
house-warming party *n* proslava useljenja .
housewife *n* domaćica.
housework *n* kućni poslovi.
housing *n* stan, stanovanje, smeštaj; utočište.
hovel *n* udžerica.
hover *v* kružiti, vrteti se.
how *adv* kako, na koji način; ~ do you do! Kako ste! Drago mi je!.
however *adv* ma kako, ma koliko.
howl *v* zavijati, urlati, stenjati; *n* zavijanje, ječanje.
hub *n* čvor, središte; muž (*sleng*).
hubbub *n* buka, graja, galama.
hubcap *n* ratkapna (*auto*).
hue *n* nijansa, boja; hajka.
huff *n* srdžba; in a ~ ljutit.
hug *v* čvrsto zagrliti; *n* zagrljaj.
huge *a* ogroman, divovski; ~ly *adv* ogromno.
hulk *n* trup broda; nezgrapan čovek.
hull *n* ljuska, mahuna; trup broda, kostur aviona.
hum *v* zujati, brujati, pevušiti.

human *a* ljudski, čovečji.
humane *a* čovečan, human; **~ly** *adv*
čovečno, humano.
humanist *n* humanista.
humanitarian *a* čovekoljubiv.
humanity *n* čovečanstvo, ljudski rod.
humanly *adv* ljudski.
humble *a* skroman, smeran; siromašan; *v*
poniziti.
humbleness *n* poniznost.
humbly *adv* smerno, skrušeno.
humbug *n* besmislica, prevara, glupost.
humdrum *a* jednoličan, dosadan.
humid *a* vlažan, mokar.
humidity *n* vlaga.
humiliate *v* uvrediti, poniziti.
humiliation *n* poniženje, uvreda.
humility *n* skromnost, poniznost.
humming *n* koji pevuši, koji zuji;
snažan.
humming-bird *n* kolibri.
humorist *n* komičar, humorista.
humorous *a* šaljiv, komičan, zabavan; **~ly**
adv šaljivo.
humour *n* humor; raspoloženje, volja; *v*
povlađivati nekome.
hump *n* grba, humka.
hunch *n* sumnja, predosećanje; debela
kriška; grba; **~backed** *a* grbav.
hundred *num* sto, stoti deo, jedna stotina.
hundredth *num* a stoti.
hundredweight *n* centa.
hunger *n* glad; *v* osećati glad.
hunger strike *n* štrajk glađu.
hungrily *adv* izgladnelo.
hungry *a* gladan.
hunt *v* loviti, progoniti; *n* lov, potera.
hunter *n* lovac.
hunting *n* lov.
huntsman *n* lovac.
hurdle *n* prepreka, prepona.
hurl *v* zavitlati, baciti.
hurricane *n* uragan.

hurried *a* žuran; **~ly** *adv* žurno, hitno, brzo.
hurry *v* žuriti, hitati, požurivati; *n* žurba.
hurt *v* povrediti, pozlediti; uvrediti; *n*
povreda, rana.
hurtful *a* štetan; **~ly** *adv* štetno.
hurtle *v* udariti o nešto, sudariti se sa nečim.
husband *n* muž, suprug.
husbandry *n* poljoprivreda, zemljoradnja.
hush *n* tišina, ćutanje; *v* ućutati se, umiriti
se.
husk *n* ljuska, mahuna, spoljni omotač.
huskiness *n* promuklost.
husky *a* promukao.
hustings *n* izborna kampanja.
hustle *v* gurati se, požurivati, tiskati se.
hut *n* koliba, baraka.
hutch *n* sanduk, škrinja; koliba.
hyacinth *n* zumbul (*bot*).
hydrant *n* hidrant.
hydraulic *a* hidrauličan; **~s** *npl*
hidraulika.
hydroelectric *a* hidroelektričan.
hydrofoil *n* hidrokrilac.
hydrogen *n* vodonik, hidrogen.
hydrophobia *n* strah od vode.
hyena *n* hijena (*zool*).
hygiene *n* higijena.
hygienic *a* higijenski.
hymn *n* himna.
hyperbole *n* hiperbola, preterivanje.
hypermarket *n* hipermarket.
hyphen *n* crtica između dve reči ili sloga
(*gram*).
hypochondria *n* hipohondrija.
hypochondriac *a* hipohondričan.
hypocrisy *n* licemerje.
hypocrite *n* licemer, hipokrita.
hypocritical *a* licemeran, hipokritski.
hypothesis *n* pretpostavka, hipoteza.
hypothetical *a* hipotetičan; **~ly** *adv*
hipotetički.
hysterical *a* histeričan.
hysterics *npl* histerija, napad histerije.

I

I *pn* ja; ~ **myself** ja lično.
i.e. *adv* to jest (Lat. id est).
ice *n* led, sladoled; *v* zamrznuti, zalediti.
ice age *n* ledeno doba.
iceberg *n* ledeni breg.
ice-bound *a* zaleđen, ukliješten u ledu.
icebox *n* frižider, lednjak.
ice cream *n* sladoled.
ice hockey *n* hokej na ledu.
ice skating *n* klizanje na ledu.
icicle *n* ledenica.
iconography *n* ikonografija.
icy *a* leden, hladan.
idea *n* misao, predstava, ideja.
ideal *a* savršen, idealan; zamišljen,
   nestvaran; ~**ly** *adv* savršeno.
idealist *n* idealista.
identical *a* istovetan, identičan.
identification *n* identifikacija.
identify *v* identifikovati.
identity *n* identitet, istovetnost.
ideology *n* ideologija.
idiom *n* idiom, narečje, dijalekt.
idiomatic *a* idiomatski, razgovorni; mesni.
idiot *n* idiot, budala.
idiotic *a* idiotski.
idle *a* besposlen, dokon; uzaludan.
idleness *n* dokonost.
idler *n* neradnik, lenština.
idly *adv* zaludno.
idol *n* idol.
idolatry *n* idolopoklonstvo.
idolize *v* obožavati.
idyllic *a* idiličan.
if *conj* ako, kad; ~ **not** ako ne.
igloo *n* iglo.
ignite *v* zapaliti, usijati.
ignition *n* paljenje (*hem*).
ignition key *n* kontakt ključ.
ignoble *a* podao, nizak, neugledan.
ignominious *a* sraman, nečastan; ~**ly** *adv*
   sramno.
ignominy *n* sramota.
ignoramus *n* neznalica.
ignorance *n* neukost, glupavost.
ignorant *a* neobrazovan, neupućen,
   glupav; ~**ly** *adv* glupavo, neupućeno.

ignore *v* ignorisati, ne uzimati u obzir.
ill *a* bolestan; loš, štetan; *n* zlo, šteta; *adv*
   loše, teško, jedva.
ill-fated *a* koban, nesrećen.
ill-advised *a* nesmotren.
illegal *a* protivzakonit, ilegalan; ~**ly** *adv*
   protivzakonito, ilegalno.
illegality *n* nezakonitost.
illegible *a* nečitak, nerazgovetan.
illegibly *adv* nečitko, nerazgovetno.
illegitimacy *n* vanbračnost.
illegitimate *a* vanbračno; ~**ly** *adv*
   vanbračno.
illicit *a* nezakonit, zabranjen.
illiterate *a* nepismen, neuk.
illness *n* bolest.
illogical *a* nelogičan.
ill-timed *a* neumestan.
ill-treat *v* loše postupati.
illuminate *v* osvetliti, rasvetliti.
illumination *n* osvetljenje, osvetljenost,
   iluminacija.
illusion *n* iluzija, varka, opsena.
illustrate *v* ilustrovati.
illustration *n* slika, ilustracija.
illustrative *a* ilustrativan.
illustrious *a* čuven, proslavljen.
ilusory *a* iluzoran.
image *n* odraz, lik, prilika; sličnost.
imagery *n* oblik, lik, prikaz.
imaginable *a* zamisliv, koji se može
   zamisliti.
imaginary *a* prividan, imaginaran.
imagination *n* mašta, uobrazilja.
imaginative *a* izmišljen, nestvaran.
imagine *v* zamišljati, pretpostaviti.
imbalance *n* neuravnoteženost.
imbecile *n* slaboumnik, imbecil, glupan; *a*
   slabouman, imbecilan.
imbibe *v* upijati, udahnuti; prisvojiti.
imbue *v* nakvasiti, natopiti.
imitate *v* podražavati, imitirati.
imitation *n* imitacija.
imitative *a* podražajni.
immaculate *a* čist, neuprljan.
immaterial *a* nebitan, nestvaran.
immature *a* nezreo, nedorastao.

immeasurable a neizmeran, ogroman.
immeasurably adv neizmerno.
immediate a trenutan, hitan, neodloživ;
~ly adv hitno, neodložno.
immense a ogroman, golem; ~ly adv
ogromno.
immensity n neizmernost.
immerse v uroniti, uvući.
immersion n zaronjenje.
immigrant n imigrant, doseljenik.
immigrate v doseljavati se, imigrirati.
immigration n imigracija, doseljavanje.
imminent a neminovan; blizak; preteći.
immobile a nepomičan, nepokretan.
immobility n nepomičnost.
immoderate a neumeren, preteran; ~ly
adv neumereno.
immodest a neskroman, nepristojan,
bezobrazan.
immoral a nemoralan, pokvaren.
immorality n pokvarenost, odsustvo
morala.
immortal a besmrtan.
immortality n besmrtnost.
immortalize v učiniti besmrtnim.
immune a imun, otporan.
immunity n otpornost, imunost.
immutable a neizmenljiv, bezuslovan.
imp n vragolan.
impact n udarac, sudar.
impair v oslabiti, oštetiti, pokvariti.
impale v nabiti na kolac.
impalpable a neopipljiv, nedostižan.
impart v dati, podeliti, razglasiti.
impartial a nepristrasan, pravedan; ~ly
adv nepristrasno.
impartiality n nepristrasnost.
impassable a neprolazan, neprohodan.
impasse n ćorsokak, bezizlazan položaj.
impassive a ravnodušan, neosetljiv, miran.
impatience n nestrpljenje.
impatient a nestrpljiv, nepodnošljiv; ~ly
adv nestrpljivo.
impeach v posumnjati, optužiti, okriviti.
impeccable a nepogrešiv, besprekoran.
impecunious a siromašan, bez novca.
impede v smetati, činiti prepreke.
impediment n smetnja, prepreka.
impel v podsticati, terati.
impending a predstojeći, blizak.
impenetrable a neprobojan, nedokučiv.

imperative a imperativan, potreban.
imperceptible a neprimetan, beznačajan.
imperceptibly adv jedva vidljivo.
imperfect a nesavršen, nepotpun;
nedovršen; ~ly adv nesavršeno; n
imperfekt (gram).
imperfection n nesavršenost, mana.
imperial a veličanstven, vladarski.
imperialism n imperijalizam.
imperious a zapovednički, uporan; ~ly
adv uporno, zapovedno.
impermeable a nepromočiv.
impersonal a bezličan, objektivan; ~ly
adv objektivno, bezlično.
impersonate v oličavati, igrati ulogu.
impertinence n drskost, bezobrazluk.
impertinent a bezobrazan, drzak; ~ly adv
bezobrazno.
imperturbable a hladnokrvan, miran.
impervious a neprohodan, nepristupačan.
impetuosity n plahovitost.
impetuous a plah, nagao; ~ly adv
plahovito, naglo.
impetus n podstrek, pobuda.
impiety n bezbožnost.
impinge (on) v povrediti, posegnuti.
impious a bezbožan, opak.
implacable a neumoljiv, nepomirljiv.
implacably adv neumoljivo.
implant v usaditi, utisnuti.
implement n pribor, oruđe, sprava.
implicate v podrazumevati; uplesti,
zaplesti, implicirati.
implication n implikacija, sudelovanje.
implicit a koji se podrazumeva,
implicitan; ~ly adv implicitno.
implore v moliti, preklinjati, nagovarati.
imply v podrazumevati, značiti.
impolite a neučtiv, neuljudan.
impoliteness n neučtivost.
import v uvoziti; značiti, podrazumevati;
n uvoz.
importance n važnost, veliki značaj.
important a važan, značajan.
importation n uvoz.
importer n uvoznik.
importunate a istrajan, sporan, nametljiv.
importune v dosađivati, saletati.
importunity n nametanje, dosađivanje.
impose v imponovati; prinuditi; staviti (u
dužnost).

imposing *a* impozantan.
imposition *n* namet, teret, nametanje.
impossibility *n* nemogućnost.
impossible *a* nemoguć.
impostor *n* samozvanac, varalica.
impotence *n* nemoć, slabost, nesposobnost.
impotent *a* nemoćan, slab; **~ly** *adv* nemoćno.
impound *v* oduzeti, konfiskovati; zatvoriti.
impoverish *v* osiromašiti, dovesti do prosjačkog štapa.
impoverished *a* osiromašen.
impoverishment *n* siromaštvo.
impracticability *n* nepraktičnost.
impractical *a* nepraktičan.
imprecation *n* prokletstvo.
imprecise *a* neprecizan.
impregnable *a* neosvojiv, nesavladiv.
impregnate *v* natopiti, napuniti; oploditi.
impregnation *n* oplođenje.
impress *v* utisnuti žig, uticati; ostaviti utisak.
impression *n* utisak, otisak; štampanje.
impressionable *a* upečatljiv.
impressive *a* impresivan.
imprint *n* otisak; *v* otisnuti, zapamtiti.
imprison *v* zatvoriti u tamnicu.
imprisonment *n* zatvor.
improbability *n* neverovatnost.
improbable *a* neverovatan.
impromptu *a* improvizovan, bez prethodne pripreme; *adv* improvizovano.
improper *a* neprikladan, nepristojan, netačan; **~ly** *adv* nepristojno.
impropriety *n* neprikladnost; kršenje pravila.
improve *v* poboljšati, usavršiti se.
improvement *n* poboljšanje.
improvident *a* rasipan; nesmotren.
improvise *v* improvizovati.
imprudence *n* nepromišljenost, nesmotrenost.
imprudent *a* nepromišljen.
impudence *n* bezočnost, drskost.
impudent *a* drzak, bezobrazan; **~ly** *adv* drsko.
impugn *v* pobijati, napadati.
impulse *n* impuls, podstrek.

impulsive *a* impulsivan, plah, nagao.
impunity *n* nekažnjivost.
impure *a* nečist, pokvaren; **~ly** *adv* pokvareno.
impurity *n* nečistoća, primesa.
in *prep* u, na; u toku, kroz.
inability *n* nesposobnost, nemogućnost.
inaccessible *a* nedostižan, nepristupačan.
inaccuracy *n* netačnost.
inaccurate *a* netačan.
inaction *n* mirovanje, neaktivnost.
inactive *a* neaktivan, nepokretan.
inactivity *n* neaktivnost.
inadequate *a* neadekvatan, neodgovarajući.
inadmissible *a* neprihvatljiv, nedopustiv.
inadvertently *adv* nepažljivo, nemarno; nehotično.
inalienable *a* neotuđiv.
inane *a* prazan, besmislen, bez sadržaja.
inanimate *a* beživotan.
inapplicable *a* neprimenljiv.
inappropriate *a* nepodesan, neodgovarajući.
inasmuch *adv* imajući u vidu, pošto.
inattentive *a* nepažljiv.
inaudible *a* nečujan, nerazgovetan.
inaugural *a* inauguralan, uvodni.
inaugurate *v* inaugurisati.
inauguration *n* inauguracija.
inauspicious *a* nepovoljan, zloslutan.
in-between *a* srednji.
inborn, inbred *a* urođen, nasledan.
incalculable *a* neprocenjiv, koji se ne može izračunati; nesiguran.
incandescent *a* usijan, užaren.
incantation *n* bajanje.
incapable *a* nesposoban.
incapacitate *v* onesposobiti.
incapacity *n* nesposobnost.
incarcerate *v* zatvoriti, utamničiti.
incarnate *a* ovaploćen, otelotvoren.
incarnation *n* inkarnacija, ovaploćenje.
incautious *a* neoprezan; **~ly** *adv* neoprezno.
incendiary *n* palikuća; buntovnik.
incense *n* tamjan; *v* kaditi; razjariti.
incentive *n* pobuda, podsticanje.
inception *n* početak.
incessant *a* neprekidan, neprestan; **~ly** *adv* neprekidno.

incest *n* rodoskrnavljenje, incest.
incestuous *a* rodoskrvni.
inch *n* inč (2,54 cm); mala količina; ~ **by**
~ stopu po stopu.
incidence *n* opseg, delokrug rada.
incident *n* slučaj, događaj, epizoda.
incidental *a* slučajan; sporedan,
svojstven; ~**ly** *adv* slučajno.
incinerator *n* peć (za spaljivanje otpadaka).
incipient *a* uvodni, početni.
incise *v* useći, zarezati; uklesati.
incision *n* urez, usek.
incisive *a* oštar, rezak; prodoran.
incisor *n* sekutić.
incite *v* podbadati, nagovarati.
inclement *a* surov, hladan.
inclination *n* sklonost, naklonost; nagib.
incline *v* sklon, naklonjen; nagnuti se.
include *v* sadržati, obuhvatiti.
including *prep* uključujući.
inclusion *n* uključivanje, obuhvatanje.
inclusive *a* zaključno; koji sadrži.
incognito *adv* inkognito, tajno.
incoherence *n* nepovezanost.
incoherent *a* nepovezan, nedosledan; ~**ly**
adv nepovezano.
income *n* dohodak, prihod, zarada.
income tax *n* porez na dohodak.
incoming *a* prispeli, koji dolazi.
incomparable *a* savršen, neuporediv.
incomparably *adv* savršeno.
incompatibility *n* inkompatibilnost,
neusaglašenost.
incompatible *a* neuskladiv,
inkompatibilan.
incompetence *n* nesposobnost,
neuračunljivost.
incompetent *a* nesposoban, nenadležan,
nekompetentan; ~**ly** *adv* nekompetentno.
incomplete *a* nepotpun, nezavršen.
incomprehensibility *n* neshvatanje,
nerazumevanje.
incomprehensible *a* nerazumljiv,
neshvatljiv.
inconceivable *a* nezamisliv, neverovatan.
inconclusive *a* neubedljiv; ~**ly** *adv*
neubedljivo.
incongruity *n* nepodudáranje, neslaganje;
neumesnost.
incongruous *a* nepodudaran, koji se ne
slaže; ~**ly** *adv* nepodudarno.

inconsequential *a* nedosledan, nelogičan.
inconsiderate *a* beznačajan, neznatan; ~**ly**
adv beznačajno.
inconsistency *n* protivurečnost,
nedoslednost.
inconsistent *a* nedosledan, nepostojan.
inconsolable *a* neutešan.
inconspicuous *a* neprimetan, koji ne pada
u oči.
incontinence *n* inkontinencija,
nezadržavanje.
incontrovertible *a* nesporan, nepobitan.
inconvenience *n* neugodnost, neudobnost;
v uznemiriti, smetati.
inconvenient *a* nepriklađan, neudoban;
nepristojan; ~**ly** *adv* neprikladno.
incorporate *v* ujediniti, spojiti, uključiti u
članstvo.
incorporated company (inc) *n* preduzeće
sa ograničenim jemstvom.
incorporation *n* udruživanje, savez.
incorrect *a* netačan, pogrešan,
neispravan; ~**ly** *adv* netačno, pogrešno.
incorrigible *a* nepopravljiv.
incorruptibility *n* nepodmitljivost.
incorruptible *a* nepodmitljiv.
increase *v* povećavati se, rasti,
umnožavati se; *n* rast, porast, povećanje.
increasing *a* sve veći; koji raste; ~**ly** *adv*
sve više.
incredible *a* neverovatan, nemoguć.
incredulity *n* sumnjičavost, neverovanje.
incredulous *a* sumnjičav.
increment *n* porast, povećanje; prirast.
incriminate *v* optužiti, okriviti, kriviti.
incrust *v* ukrasiti.
incubate *v* gajiti, ležati na jajima.
incubator *n* inkubator.
inculcate *v* utuviti, uliti u glavu.
incumbent *a* obavezan; koji je stavljen u
dužnost; *n* službenik.
incur *v* podvrgavati se, navlačiti; zapasti
(u dug).
incurability *n* neizlečivost.
incurable *a* neizlečiv.
incursion *n* napad, nalet, upad.
indebted *a* dužan, zadužen; obavezan.
indecency *n* nepristojnost.
indecent *a* nepristojan; ~**ly** *adv*
nepristojno.
indecision *n* neodlučnost.

indecisive *a* neodlučan, neodređen, nejasan.
indecorous *a* neumestan, lošeg ukusa.
indeed *adv* zaista, stvarno; zbilja.
indefatigable *a* neumoran, nepopustljiv.
indefinite *a* neodređen, neograničen; ~ly *adv* neodređeno.
indelible *a* neizbrisiv, neuništiv.
indelicacy *n* bezobzirnost, grubost, prostota.
indelicate *a* grub, prost; bezobziran.
indemnify *v* nadoknaditi štetu, osigurati.
indemnity *n* odšteta, naknada.
indent *v* urezati, zaseći; nasilno oduzeti, rekvirirati.
independence *n* nezavisnost.
independent *a* nezavisan, samostalan; ~ly *adv* nezavisno.
indescribable *a* neopisiv.
indestructible *a* neuništiv.
indeterminate *a* neodređen, nejasan; nerešen.
index *n* registar; popis; strelica.
indexed *a* unet u registar, unet u pregled sadržaja.
index finger *n* kažiprst.
indicate *v* ukazivati, navoditi; označiti; prepisati (*med*).
indication *n* uputstvo; nagoveštaj, znak; simptom.
indicative *a* indikativan (*gram*); koji nagoveštava; *n* indikativ (*gram*).
indicator *n* putokaz, indikator.
indict *v* optužiti.
indictment *n* optužnica.
indifference *n* ravnodušnost, nemarnost, nevažnost.
indifferent *a* ravnodušan, nemaran; prosečan, običan; nevažan; ~ly *adv* ravnodušno, prosečno.
indigenous *a* domorodački, domaći.
indigent *a* siromašan, oskudan.
indigestible *a* nesvarljiv.
indigestion *n* loša probava.
indignant *a* ozlojeđen, ogorčen.
indignation *n* negodovanje, ozlojeđenost.
indignity *n* potcenjivanje, nepoštovanje.
indigo *n* indigo.
indirect *a* zaobilazan, posredan; indirektan; ~ly *adv* indirektno.
indiscreet *a* nepromišljen, neskroman; indiskretan; ~ly *adv* indiskretno.

indiscretion *n* indiskrecija.
indiscriminate *a* koji ne pravi razlike, zbrkan; ~ly *adv* bez razlike; zadovoljava se malim.
indispensable *a* neophodan, obavezan.
indisposed *a* neraspoložen; indisponiran, nesklon.
indisposition *n* slabost, poboljevanje; neraspoloženje.
indisputable *a* nesporan, nesumnjiv.
indisputably *adv* nesporno, bez sumnje.
indistinct *a* nejasan, neodređen, mutan; ~ly *adv* neodređeno.
indistinguishable *a* koji se ne može razlikovati.
individual *a* pojedini, karakterističan; osoben; ~ly *adv* karakteristično; *n* osoba, pojedinac.
individuality *n* individualnost, samosvest.
indivisible *a* nedeljiv, beskrajno mali.
indivisibly *adv* nedeljivo, beskrajno malo.
indoctrinate *v* poučavati, indoktrinirati.
indoctrination *n* nastava, indoktrinacija.
indolence *n* lenjost, nemar, nehat.
indolent *a* lenj, nehatan; bezbolan (*med*).
indomitable *a* neukrotiv, nesavladiv.
indoors *adv* unutra, kod kuće.
indubitably *adv* nesumnjivo, neosporno.
induce *v* pobuditi, podsticati; inducirati (*el*).
inducement *n* podstrek, pobuda, podsticaj.
induction *n* indukcija; uvođenje.
indulge *v* dopuštati sebi; maziti, štedeti; pružati zadovoljstvo.
indulgence *n* blagost, popustljivost; povlastica; odlaganje plaćanja.
indulgent *a* snishodljiv, blag, pokroviteljski; ~ly *adv* snishodljivo.
industrial *a* industrijski, proizvodni.
industrialist *n* industrijalac.
industrialization *n* industrijalizacija.
industrialize *v* industrijalizovati.
industrial park *n* industrijski poligon.
industrious *a* marljiv, vredan.
industry *n* industrija.
inebriated *a* pijan, opijen.
inebriation *n* opijanje.
inedible *a* nejestiv, koji nije za jelo.
ineffable *a* neopisiv, neiskazan; zabranjen.

ineffective *a* neefikasan, neuspešan, uzaludan; **~ly** *adv* uzaludno, neuspešno.
ineffectual *a* neuspešan, nesposoban; **~ly** *adv* neuspešno, bez učinka.
inefficiency *n* neefikasnost, neuspešnost.
inefficient *a* neefikasan, nesposoban.
ineligible *a* nepodesan, bezvredan.
inept *a* nesposoban, neprikladan.
ineptitude *n* nevičnost, nepodesnost.
inequality *n* nejednakost, razlika.
inert *a* trom, mlitav, inertan.
inertia *n* inercija, tromost.
inescapable *a* neizbeživ.
inestimable *a* neocenjiv.
inevitable *a* neizbežan, neminovan.
inevitably *adv* neizbežno, neminovno.
inexcusable *a* neoprostiv.
inexhaustible *a* neiscrpan, neumoran.
inexorable *a* neumoljiv.
inexpedient *a* nekoristan, nesvrsishodan.
inexpensive *a* jevtin, koji nije skup.
inexperience *n* neiskustvo.
inexperienced *a* neiskusan.
inexpert *a* nevešt, neupućen.
inexplicable *a* neobjašnjiv.
inexpressible *a* neizreciv.
inextricably *adv* bezizlazno, nerazrešivo.
infallibility *n* nepogrešivost.
infallible *a* nepogrešiv.
infamous *a* sraman, ozloglašen, nedostojan; **~ly** *adv* sramno.
infamy *n* sramota, ljaga; podlost.
infancy *n* rano detinjstvo.
infant *n* malo dete, maloletnost.
infanticide *n* čedomorstvo.
infantile *a* detinji, početni.
infantry *n* pešadija.
infatuated *a* zaluđen, zaveden.
infatuation *n* zaslepljenost, zaljubljenost.
infect *v* zaraziti.
infection *n* zaraza, infekcija.
infectious *a* zarazan, infektivan.
infer *v* pretpostaviti, izvesti zaključak.
inference *n* zaključak, izvođenje.
inferior *a* podređen, loš, slabiji, niži; *n* podređeno lice.
inferiority *n* inferiornost.
infernal *a* paklen, đavolski.
inferno *n* pakao, podzemlje.
infest *v* napasti, provaliti.
infidel *n* nevernik, paganin.

infidelity *n* nevernost, izdaja.
infiltrate *v* ubaciti, infiltrirati.
infinite *a* beskonačan, bezgraničan; **~ly** *adv* beskonačno.
infinitive *n* infinitiv (*gram*).
infinity *n* beskrajnost, neograničena količina.
infirm *a* nemoćan, slab, neodlučan.
infirmary *n* bolnica.
infirmity *n* nemoć, telesni ili duhovni nedostatak.
inflame *v* upaliti, raspaliti, zapaliti.
inflammation *n* zapaljivanje, upala (*med*).
inflammatory *a* raspaljiv, zapaljiv (*med*).
inflatable *a* koji može da se naduva.
inflate *v* naduvati, naduvati cene; stvoriti inflaciju.
inflation *n* inflacija (*fin*); naduvavanje.
inflection *n* fleksija (*gram*), promena.
inflexibility *n* nesavitljivost.
inflexible *a* nesavitljiv.
inflexibly *adv* nesavitljivo.
inflict *v* zadati udarac, naneti bol.
influence *n* uticaj, delovanje; *v* delovati, uticati.
influential *a* uticajan.
influenza *n* grip.
influx *n* ulivanje, priliv.
inform *v* obavestiti, saopštiti, izvestiti; optužiti.
informal *a* nezvaničan, prirodan.
informality *n* neformalnost.
informant *n* izveštač, dopisnik; doušnik.
information *n* informacija, obaveštenje; znanje; optužba; **~ system** informacioni sistem.
infraction *n* kršenje, prelom.
infra-red *a* infracrven.
infrastructure *n* infrastruktura.
infrequent *a* redak; **~ly** *adv* retko.
infringe *v* prekršiti, narušiti zakon.
infringement *n* kršenje.
infuriate *v* razbesneti.
infuse *v* sipati, uliti; popariti.
infusion *n* infuzija, ulivanje.
ingenious *a* pronalazački, dovitljiv; **~ly** *adv* dovitljivo.
ingenuity *n* genijalnost.
ingenuous *a* otvoren, iskren; prostodušan; **~ly** *adv* otvoreno.

inglorious *a* neslavan, sraman; **~ly** *adv*
   neslavno.
ingot *n* šipka, poluga.
ingrained *a* ukorenjen, natopljen.
ingratiate *v* dodvoravati se.
ingratitude *n* nezahvalnost.
ingredient *n* sastavni deo, sastojak.
inhabit *v* stanovati, živeti, prebivati.
inhabitant *n* stanovnik.
inhabited *a* naseljen.
inhale *v* udisati, uvlačiti.
inherent *a* nerazdvojiv, prisutan.
inherit *v* naslediti.
inheritance *n* nasledstvo.
inheritor *n* naslednik.
inhibit *v* ometati, kočiti, zaustaviti.
inhibited *a* inhibiran.
inhibition *n* inhibicija, ometanje, kočenje.
inhospitable *a* negostoljubiv.
inhospitably *adv* negostoljubivo.
inhospitality, inhospitableness *n*
   negostoljubivost.
inhuman *a* nečovečan, neljudski,
   nehuman; **~ly** *adv* nehumano.
inhumanity *n* nečovečnost.
inimical *a* zlonameran, štetan, neprijateljski.
inimitable *a* neuporediv.
iniquitous *a* nepravedan, nezakonit.
iniquity *n* bezakonje, nepravda.
initial *a* početan, prvobitan; *n* inicijal.
initially *adv* inicijalno.
initiate *v* započeti, uputiti u tajnu.
initiation *n* uvođenje.
initiative *n* inicijativa, preduzimljivost.
inject *v* ubrizgati, ubaciti.
injection *n* injekcija, ubrizgavanje.
injudicious *a* nepromišljen, nerazuman.
injunction *n* naredba, sudski nalog.
injure *v* kvariti, štetiti; ozlediti, povrediti.
injury *n* ozleda , rana; nepravda.
injury time *n* vreme ozleđivanja.
injustice *n* nepravda.
ink *n* mastilo.
inkling *n* sumnja, nagoveštaj.
inkstand *n* pribor za pisanje, mastionica.
inlaid *a* umetnut, inkrustriran.
inland *a* unutarnji; *adv* unutar, sa
   unutrašnje strane.
in-laws *npl* srodnici po bračnom drugu.
inlay *v* popločati, pokriti; staviti intarziju.
inlet *n* morski rukavac, zaton.

inmate *n* stanar, ukućanin.
inmost *a* najdublji, najskrovitiji.
inn *n* krčma, svratište.
innate *a* urođen.
inner *a* unutarnji.
innermost *a* najdublji.
inner tube *n* unutrašnja guma (*auto*).
innkeeper *n* krčmar.
innocence *n* nevinost, naivnost.
innocent *a* nevin, nedužan; **~ly** *adv* nedužno.
innocuous *a* neškodljiv; **~ly** *adv*
   neškodljivo.
innovate *v* obnavljati, uvoditi novine.
innovation *n* novina, novotarija,
   inovacija.
innuendo *n* insinuacija, nagoveštaj.
innumerable *a* bezbrojan, nebrojen.
inoculate *v* kalemiti, cepiti.
inoculation *n* ubrizgavanje.
inoffensive *a* bezopasan, neškodljiv.
inopportune *a* neumesan,
   nepravovremen.
inordinately *adv* prekomerno, nesređeno.
inorganic *a* neorganski.
in-patient *n* bolesnik koji se leči u bolnici.
input *n* ulaz, input; ulaganje sredstava.
inquest *n* istraga, utvrđivanje.
inquire *v* raspitivati se, istraživati; **to ~**
   about raspitati se o nečemu; **to ~ after**
   pitati za nekoga; **to ~ into** ispitivati,
   istraživati.
inquiry *n* istraga.
inquisition *n* inkvizicija; istraga,
   istraživanje.
inquisitive *a* radoznao, željan znanja.
inroad *n* upad, prepad, navala.
insane *a* lud, umobolan.
insanity *n* ludilo.
insatiable *a* nezasit, željan.
inscribe *v* upisati, staviti natpis.
inscription *n* natpis.
inscrutable *a* nedokučiv, tajanstven.
insect *n* insekt.
insecticide *n* insekticid.
insecure *a* nesiguran, nepouzdan.
insecurity *n* nesigurnost, nepouzdanost.
insemination *n* osemenjavanje.
insensible *a* bezosećajan, neosetljiv; bez
   svesti.
insensitive *a* neosetljiv.
inseparable *a* nerazdvojan, nerazdeljiv.

insert *v* umetnuti, uvrstiti, uneti.
insertion *n* dodatak, umetanje.
inshore *a* priobalni.
inside *n* unutrašnjost, unutarnji deo,
unutarnja strana; *adv* unutra, iznutra.
inside out *adv* naopako.
insidious *a* podmukao, pritajen; ~ly *adv*
podmuklo.
insight *n* shvatanje, pronicljivost.
insignia *npl* oznake čina; znak
raspoznavanja.
insignificant *a* beznačajan, ništavan.
insincere *a* neiskren.
insincerity *n* neiskrenost.
insinuate *v* insinuirati; dodvoriti se; sejati;
prišapnuti.
insinuation *n* insinuacija.
insipid *a* bljutav; dosadan.
insipidness *n* tromost; bljutavost.
insist *v* zahtevati, insistirati.
insistence *n* nepopustljivost, zahtevanje,
insistiranje.
insistent *a* uporan, nepopustljiv.
insole *n* unutrašnji đon.
insolence *n* oholost, drskost.
insolent *a* drzak, bezobrazan; ~ly *adv* drsko.
insoluble *a* nerešiv, nerastvoriv.
insolvency *n* insolventnost, nesposobnost
plaćanja.
insolvent *a* insolventan, koji ne može da
plati.
insomnia *n* nesanica.
insomuch *conj* toliko.
inspect *v* razgledati, nadgledati; istražiti.
inspection *n* inspekcija, pregled.
inspector *n* inspektor.
inspiration *n* nadahnuće, inspiracija.
inspire *v* nadahnuti, oduševiti.
instability *n* nestabilnost, nestalnost.
install, instal *v* uvesti, postaviti,
montirati.
installation *n* instalacija, nameštanje,
montiranje.
instalment *n* montiranje, sprovođenje;
rata, obrok.
instance *n* primer, slučaj, zahtev; for ~ na
primer.
instant *a* hitan, neodložan, tekući; ~ly *adv*
hitno, ovog momenta.
instantaneous *a* trenutan, istovremen; ~ly
adv trenutno.

instead (of) *prep* umesto, namesto.
instep *n* svod stopala (*anat*).
instigate *v* izazivati, podbadati, navoditi.
instigation *n* podbadanje.
instil *v* ulivati (npr. navike); kapati (lek).
instinct *n* instinkt, prirodni nagon.
instinctive *a* nagonski, instinktivan; ~ly
adv instinktivno.
institute *v* osnovati, utemeljiti; odrediti; *n*
institut.
institution *n* ustanova, institucija;
osnivanje.
instruct *v* obučavati, poučavati; dati
uputstva.
instruction *n* uputstvo, naredba;
obučavanje.
instructive *a* poučan.
instructor *n* instruktor.
instrument *n* instrument, oruđe.
instrumental *a* instrumentalan;
pomoćni.
insubordinate *a* neposlušan,
nedisciplinovan.
insubordination *n* neposlušnost,
nepokornost.
insufferable *a* nepodnošljiv, nesnosan.
insufferably *adv* nepodnošljivo.
insufficiency *n* nedovoljnost,
insuficijencija.
insufficient *a* nedovoljan; ~ly *adv*
nedovoljno.
insular *a* ostrvski; uskogrud (*fig*).
insulate *v* izolovati.
insulating tape *n* izolaciona traka.
insulation *n* izolacija.
insulin *n* insulin.
insult *v* uvrediti, vređati.
insulting *a* uvredljiv.
insuperable *a* nepremostiv.
insurance *n* osiguranje (*komerc*).
insurance policy *n* polisa osiguranja.
insure *v* osigurati se, obezbediti.
insurgent *n* ustanik.
insurmountable *a* nepremostiv.
insurrection *n* ustanak, pobuna.
intact *a* nepovređen, nedirnut, čitav.
intake *n* usisavanje.
integral *a* potpun, ceo, integralni;
sastavni; *n* integral (*mat*).
integrate *v* integrisati, popunjavati.
integration *n* integracija.

integrity *n* poštenje; potpunost,
celovitost; integritet.
intellect *n* um, sposobnost, mišljenje, duh.
intellectual *a* intelektualan, duhovan,
pametan.
intelligence *n* inteligencija, pamet,
bistrina; obaveštenje; tajna obaveštajna
služba.
intelligent *a* inteligentan, pametan.
intelligentsia *n* inteligencija.
intelligible *a* razumljiv, shvatljiv.
intelligibly *adv* razumljivo.
intemperate *a* neumeren, neobuzdan;
oštar; **~ly** *adv* neumereno.
intend *v* nameravati, kaniti.
intendant *n* intendant.
intended *a* nameran, namenjen.
intense *a* jak, intenzivan; **~ly** *adv* jako,
intenzivno.
intensify *v* pojačavati se.
intensity *n* intenzitet, jačina.
intensive *a* intenzivan, jak.
intensive care unit *n* odeljenje za
intenzivnu negu.
intent *a* usredsređen, pažljiv; **~ly** *adv*
pažljivo, usredsređeno; *n* namera.
intention *n* namera, nakana, želja.
intentional *a* nameran, hotimičan; **~ly** *adv*
namerno.
intepreter *n* tumač, prevodilac.
inter *v* sahraniti.
interaction *n* interakcija, uzajamni uticaj.
intercede *v* posredovati, zalagati se .
intercept *v* uhvatiti, zaustaviti, zadržati.
intercession *n* zauzimanje, posredovanje.
interchange *n* razmena, zamena;
premeštanje.
intercom *n* interfon, unutrašnja veza.
intercourse *n* polni snošaj, opštenje.
interest *v* zainteresovati; *n* interesovanje;
kamata.
interesting *a* interesantan, zanimljiv.
interest rate *n* kamatna stopa.
interface *n* interfejs, međusklop.
interfere *v* smetati, ometati, mešati se.
interference *n* smetnja, prepreka,
mešanje.
interim *a* privremen; prethodan.
interior *a* unutrašnji.
interior design *n* dizajn enterijera.
interjection *n* usklik, uzvik (*gram*).

interlock *v* spojiti se, povezati se.
interlocutor *n* sabesednik.
interloper *n* uljez, nametljivac.
interlude *n* međuigra, interludij (*muz*).
intermediary *n* posrednik.
intermediate *a* srednji, koji je u sredini.
interment *n* sahrana, ukop.
interminable *a* beskrajan.
intermingle *v* izmešati, pomešati.
intermission *n* prekid; odmor između dva
čina.
intermittent *a* isprekidan, sa prekidima.
intern *n* stažista.
internal *a* unutarnji, unutrašnji; **~ally** *adv*
unutrašnji, interno.
international *a* međunarodni.
internet cafe *n* internet igraonica.
interplay *n* uzajamno dejstvo.
interpose *v* ubaciti, umetnuti; uplitati se.
interpret *v* tumačiti, objasniti; prevoditi.
interpretation *n* tumačenje, objašnjenje;
interpretacija.
interracial *a* međurasni.
interregnum *n* međuvlada, interegnum.
interrelated *a* u međusobnom odnosu.
interrogate *v* pitati, ispitati, istražiti.
interrogation *n* ispitivanje, pitanje.
interrogative *a* upitni (*gram*).
interrupt *v* prekinuti, ometati.
interruption *n* prekidanje, zaustavljanje.
intersect *v* seći, presecati, ukrštavati.
intersection *n* raskrsnica; presecanje.
intersperse *v* rasuti, posejati;
ispremeštati.
intertwine *v* ispreplesti se.
interval *n* interval (*muz*); prekid, stanka.
intervene *v* umešati se, uplitati se.
intervention *n* intervencija, mešanje.
interview *n* intervju, razgovor; *v*
intervjuisati, razgovarati.
interweave *v* utkati, protkati; ispreplesti.
intestate *a* bez testamenta.
intestinal *a* crevni, intestinalni.
intestine *n* creva, utroba.
intimacy *n* intimnost, blizina.
intimate *n* prisan prijatelj; *a* blizak,
prisan, intiman; **~ly** *adv* intimno; *v*
nagovestiti, saopštiti.
intimidate *v* plašiti, zastrašiti.
into *prep* u, na.
intolerable *a* nepodnošljiv, nesnosan.

intolerably *adv* nepodnošljivo.
intolerance *n* netolerancija, nepodnošljivost.
intolerant *a* netrpeljiv.
intonation *n* intonacija, naglašavanje.
intoxicate *v* opiti, uzbuditi.
intoxication *n* intoksikacija, opijanje, trovanje.
intractable *a* tvrdoglav, neukrotiv; koji se teško leči.
intransitive *a* neprelazan (*gram*).
intravenous *a* intravenski.
intrepid *a* neustrašiv, odvažan; ~ly *adv* neustrašivo.
intrepidity *n* odvažnost, neustrašivost.
intricacy *n* komplikovanost.
intricate *a* zamršen, nejasan; ~ly *adv* zamršeno, nejasno.
intrigue *n* intriga, spletka, smutnja; *v* spletkariti.
intriguing *a* intrigantan, zanimljiv.
intrinsic *a* bitan, svojstven; ~ally *adv* bitno, svojstveno.
introduce *v* uvesti, predstaviti nekome.
introduction *n* uvod, predstavljanje.
introductory *a* uvodni, pristupni.
introspection *n* introspekcija, samoposmatranje.
introvert *n* introvertna osoba, povučena osoba.
intrude *v* uznemiriti, nametati se, upadati.
intruder *n* nametljivac.
intrusion *n* upadanje, napadanje.
intuition *n* intuicija, pronicljivost.
intuitive *a* intuitivan.
inundate *v* plaviti, navodnjavati.
inundation *n* navodnjavanje, poplava.
inure *v* prekaliti, naviknuti na nešto.
invade *v* osvojiti, upasti.
invader *n* osvajač, napadač.
invalid *a* bolestan, nesposoban za rad; nevažeći; *n* invalid.
invalidate *v* poništiti, učiniti nevažećim.
invaluable *a* neprocenjiv.
invariable *a* nepromenljiv, stalan.
invariably *adv* redovno.
invasion *n* invazija, upad.
invective *n* grdnja, psovke.
inveigle *v* namamiti, zavesti.
invent *v* izumeti, izmisliti.

invention *n* izum, dovitljivost, inventivnost.
inventive *a* pronalazački, inventivan.
inventor *n* pronalazač.
inventory *n* popis, inventar.
inverse *a* suprotan, obrnut.
inversion *n* obrtanje, premeštanje; inverzija (*gram*).
invert *v* obrnuti, okrenuti.
invest *v* investirati, uložiti; zaodenuti, obući.
investigate *v* ispitivati, istraživati.
investigation *n* istraga, istraživanje.
investigator *n* istraživač; islednik.
investment *n* investicija.
inveterate *a* okoreo, zagrižen.
invidious *a* uvredljiv, nepodnošljiv.
invigilate *v* nadzirati đake na ispitu.
invigorating *a* okrepljujući.
invincible *a* nepobediv.
invincibly *adv* nepobedivo.
inviolable *a* nepovrediv.
invisible *a* nevidljiv.
invisibly *adv* nevidljivo.
invitation *n* poziv.
invite *v* pozvati, moliti; privlačiti.
inviting *a* primamljiv, privlačan.
invoice *n* faktura (*komerc*).
invoke *v* dozivati, obraćati se; zaklinjati.
involuntarily *adv* nehotice, nenamerno.
involuntary *a* nehotičan.
involve *v* sadržavati, uvući, obaviti.
involved *a* upleten, zapleten.
involvement *n* upetljanost, učešće.
invulnerable *a* nepovrediv.
inward *a* unutarnji, duševni, duhovni; ~s *adv* unutra.
iodine *n* jod (*hem*).
IOU (I owe you) *n* priznanica (kojom se priznaje dug).
irascible *a* razdražljiv, plahovit.
irate, ireful *a* besan, razdražen, ljut.
iris *n* dužica (*anat*); perunika (*bot*).
irksome *a* zamoran, dosadan, mučan.
iron *n* gvožđe; pegla; okovi; *a* gvozdeni; *v* peglati; zakovati.
ironic *a* ironičan, podrugljiv; ~ly *adv* ironično.
ironing *n* peglanje.
ironing board *n* daska za peglanje.

iron ore *n* ruda gvožđa.
ironworks *npl* željezara.
irony *n* ironija.
irradiate *v* svetleti, osvetljavati.
irrational *a* nerazuman; iracionalan.
irrecognizable *a* neprepoznatljiv, koji se ne može prepoznati.
irreconcilable *a* nepomirljiv, nespojiv.
irrefutable *a* nepobitan, neoboriv.
irregular *a* nepravilan, neregularan; nezakonit; ~ly neregularno.
irregularity *n* nepravilnost, neravnomernost, neregularnost.
irrelevant *a* irelevantan, sporedan, nebitan.
irreligious *a* nereligiozan, bezveran.
irreparable *a* nepopravljiv, nepovratan.
irreplaceable *a* nezamenljiv, nenadoknadiv.
irrepressible *a* neukrotiv, nezadrživ.
irreproachable *a* besprekoran, bez mane.
irresistible *a* neodoljiv.
irresolute *a* neodlučan; ~ly *adv* neodlučno.
irresponsible *a* neodgovoran.
irretrievably *adv* nenadoknadivo, nepopravljivo.
irreverence *n* nepristojnost.
irreverent *a* nepristojan, neuljudan; ~ly *adv* nepristojno.
irrigate *v* ispirati (*med*); polivati, orositi.
irrigation *n* irigacija, ispiranje (*med*); kvašenje.

irritability *n* razdražljivost, nadražljivost.
irritable *a* razdražljiv.
irritant *n* nadražujuće sredstvo (*med*).
irritate *v* iritirati, dražiti, razdražiti.
irritating *a* razdražujući.
irritation *n* razdraženost.
Islam *n* islam.
Islamic *a* islamski.
island *n* ostrvo.
islander *n* ostrvljanin.
isle *n* ostrvo (*poet*).
isolate *v* izolovati, odvojiti (*hem*); usamiti.
isolation *n* izdvajanje, samoća.
issue *n* izdavanje, izdanje, emisija; ishod; potomstvo; sporno pitanje; *v* izaći; izdati, objaviti; snabdeti, dodeliti.
isthmus *n* zemljouz, prevlaka.
it *pn* on, ona, ono; ovo; to.
italic *n* kurziv.
itch *n* svrab, šuga; *v* svrbeti.
item *n* tačka, član, pitanje; predmet; obaveštenje.
itemize *v* specificirati, navesti stavku po stavku.
itinerant *n* putnik, sezonac.
itinerary *n* plan puta.
its *pn* njegovo, njeno, svoj, svoja, svoje.
itself *pn* sam, sama, samo; sebe, sebi, sobom.
ivory *n* slonovača, slonova kost.
ivy *n* bršljan (*bot*).

J

jab *v* gurati, probadati, bosti.
jabber *v* brbljati.
jack *n* čovek, momak; mornar.
jackal *n* šakal; pomoćni radnik.
jackboots *npl* visoke čizme.
jackdaw *n* čavka.
jacket *n* jakna; omot knjige; omotač,
   ljuska.
jack-knife *v* veliki perorez.
jackpot *n* glavni zgoditak.
jacuzzi *n* džakuzi.
jade *n* žad.
jagged *a* zupčast, nazupčen.
jaguar *n* jaguar.
jail, gaol *n* tamnica, zatvor.
jailbird *n* zatvorenik, bivši zatvorenik
   (*sleng*).
jailer, jailor or **gaoler** *n* tamničar.
jam[1] *n* džem, slatko od voća (conserve)
jam[2] *n* gužva (throng, mob); zastoj
   (stoppage, standstill); smetnje; **traffic ~**
   zastoj saobraćaj.
jangle *v* larmati, galamiti.
January *n* januar.
Japanese *n* Japanac, Japanka; japanski jezik.
jar *v* svađati se, ići na živce; *n* krčag,
   tegla; neslaganje.
jargon *n* žargon.
jasmine *n* jasmin.
jaundice *n* žutica (*med*); zloba, zavist.
jaunt *n* izlet, šetnja.
jaunty *a* veseo, živahan, bezbrižan.
javelin *n* koplje.
jaw *n* čeljust, vilica; usta; klanac; klješta.
jay *n* kreja, sojka.
jazz *n* džez.
jealous *a* ljubomoran, zavidljiv.
jealousy *n* ljubomora, zavist.
jeans *npl* farmerke, džins.
jeep *n* džip.
jeer *v* ismejavati, rugati se; *n* poruga,
   ismejavanje.
jelly *n* žele, pihtije.
jellyfish *n* meduza, mekušci.
jeopardize *v* ugroziti, izlagati opasnosti.
jerk *n* trzaj, hitac, iznenadan udarac; *v*
   gurnuti, trzati.

jerky *a* isprekidan.
jersey *n* žersej, džemper.
jest *n* šala, poruga, ismejavanje.
jester *n* šaljivdžija, lakrdijaš.
jestingly *adv* podsmešljivo.
Jesuit *n* jezuita, isusovac.
Jesus *n* Isus.
jet *n* mlazni avion; mlaz; sjajna crna boja.
jet engine *n* mlazni motor.
jettison *n* bacanje tereta u more.
jetty *n* pristanište, gat, nasip.
Jew *n* Jevrejin.
jewel *n* dragi kamen; dragocenost; blag.
jeweller *n* juvelir.
jeweller's shop *n* juvelirnica.
jewellery *n* nakit, dragulj.
Jewish *a* jevrejski.
jibe *n* podsmeh.
jig *n* džig, vrsta brzog plesa; matrica,
   uzorak.
jigsaw *n* testera; **~ puzzle** slaganje slike
   na komadiće.
jilt *v* napuštati; zavoditi.
jinx *n* baksuz, nesreća.
job *n* posao, rad, zadatak.
jockey *n* džokej.
jocular *a* veseo, zabavan.
jocularity *n* šaljivost.
jog *v* lagano trčati, pretrčati; podstaći.
jogging *n* trčanje.
join *v* spojiti se, povezati se; upisati se; **to
   ~ in** pridružiti se.
joiner *n* stolar.
joinery *n* stolarska radnja.
joint *n* zglob (*anat*); spoj; komad mesa; *a*
   opšti, zajednički.
jointly *adv* skupa, zajednički.
joint-stock company *n* akcionarsko
   društvo (*komerc*).
joke *n* šala, dosetka; *v* šaliti se.
joker *n* šaljivčina; džoker.
jolly *a* veselo, radostan.
jolt *v* drmati, truckati se; *n* trzaj.
jostle *v* gurati, gurnuti.
journal *n* časopis, dnevnik.
journalism *n* žurnalistika, novinarstvo.
journalist *n* novinar.

journey *n* putovanje, vožnja, šetnja; *v* putovati.
jovial *a* razdragan, veseo, društven; **~ly** *adv* razdragano, veselo.
joy *n* radost, zadovoljstvo.
joyful, joyous *a* srećan, zadovoljan, veseo; **~ly** *adv* srećno.
joystick *n* džojstik, komandna palica.
jubilant *a* oduševljen.
jubilation *n* oduševljenje, ushićenje.
jubilee *n* jubilej.
Judaism *n* judaizam, jevrejstvo.
judge *n* sudija; *v* suditi.
judgement *n* presuda, sudska odluka.
judicial *a* sudski; **~ly** *adv* sudski.
judiciary *n* pravosuđe, sudstvo.
judicious *a* razuman, razborit, pametan.
judo *n* džudo.
jug *n* krčag; tamnica.
juggle *v* žonglirati; podvaliti.
juggler *n* žongler.
jugular *a* vratni.
juice *n* sok; suština; benzin (*sleng*).
juicy *a* sočan; vlažan.
jukebox *n* džuboks.
July *n* juli.
jumble *v* gurati se; *n* gomila, gužva.
jump *v* skakati, skočiti, preskočiti; *n* skok.
jumper *n* skakač, padobranac.

jumpy *a* razdražljiv, nervozan.
juncture *n* spajanje, sastavljanje.
June *n* juni.
jungle *n* džungla.
junior *a* mlađi (po godinama, po zvanju), junior.
juniper *n* smreka (*bot*).
junk *n* starudija; komad hleba, mesa.
junk food *n* jelo bez hranljivih sastojaka.
junta *n* hunta.
jurisdiction *n* pravna nadležnost, jurisdikcija.
jurisprudence *n* jurisprudencija, pravna nauka.
jurist *n* pravnik, jurista.
juror, juryman *n* porotnik.
jury *n* porota.
just *a* pravedan, doličan; tačan; **~ly** *adv* tačno; **~ as** kao, tek; **~ now** upravo sada.
justice *n* pravosuđe, sudija; pravednost.
justifiably *adv* opravdano.
justification *n* opravdanje, izvinjenje; potkrepljivanje.
justify *v* pravdati.
jut *v* viriti; **to ~ out** štrčati.
jute *n* juta.
juvenile *a* mladenački, mlad, juvenilan.
juxtapose *v* postaviti jedno uz drugo.
juxtaposition *n* položaj jedne stvari pored druge, jukstapozicija.

K

kaleidoscope *n* kaleidoskop.
kangaroo *n* kengur.
kebab *n* ćevapčić.
keel *n* kobilica broda.
keen *a* oštar, jak, preduzimljiv; živ.
keenness *n* oduševljenje, žudnja.
keep *v* držati, održati; čuvati, sačuvati.
keeper *n* čuvar, stražar; dežurni.
keepsake *n* uspomena, poklon za uspomenu.
keg *n* burence.
kennel *n* pseća kućica, koliba.
kerb *n* ivičnjak.
kernel *n* košćica, jezgro; suština.
ketchup *n* kečap.
kettle *n* čajnik; kazan.
kettle-drum *n* talambas, timpan.
key *n* ključ; zbirka zadataka, rešenje; ključ, tonalitet (*muz*); dirka.
key ring *n* privezak za ključeve.
keyboard *n* tastatura, klavijatura.
keyhole *n* ključaonica.
keynote *n* osnovni ton, tonalitet (*muz*).
key ring *n* privezak za ključeve.
keystone *n* kamen temeljac.
khaki *n* zemljana boja, kaki boja.
kick *v* ritati se, udarati, buniti se; *n* udarac nogom; ritanje.
kid *n* dete, detence; jare; antilop koža.
kidnap *v* kidnapovati, nasilno odvesti.
kidnapper *n* kidnaper, otimač.
kidnapping *n* otmica, kidnapovanje.
kidney *n* bubreg (*anat*).
killer *n* ubica.
killing *n* ubijanje.
kiln *n* peć za pečenje cigli.
kilo *n* kilo, kilogram.
kilobyte *n* kilobajt.
kilogram *n* kilogram.
kilometre *n* kilometar.
kilt *n* kilt (suknja koju nose Škoti).
kin *n* rodbina, rod; **next of ~** najbliži rođaci.
kind *a* ljubazan, dobar, drag; *n* rod; razred; vrsta.
kindergarten *n* dečji vrtić.
kind-hearted *a* dobar, mekog srca.

kindle *v* paliti, potpaliti, raspaliti.
kindliness *n* dobrota.
kindly *a* dobronameran, ljubazan, dobar.
kindness *n* ljubaznost, pažnja, dobrota.
kindred *a* srodan, sličan, rođački.
kinetic *a* energičan, pun života.
king *n* kralj, car.
King's English *n* standardni engleski (*sleng*).
kingdom *n* kraljevstvo, carevina.
kingfisher *n* vodomar.
kiosk *n* kiosk.
kiss *n* poljubac; *v* ljubiti se, poljubiti se.
kissing *n* ljubljenje.
kit *n* oprema; torba; alat.
kitchen *n* kuhinja.
kitchen garden *n* povrtnjak.
kitchen maid *n* mlada služavka, sudopera.
kite *n* zmaj od hartije; grabljivac; varalica; soko.
kitten *n* mače.
knack *n* veština, spretnost; način.
knapsack *n* ranac, ruksak.
knave *n* podlac, varalica; pub (u kartama).
knead *v* mesiti, gnječiti, masirati.
knee *n* koleno.
knee-deep *a* do kolena.
kneel *v* klečati, pasti na kolena.
knell *n* pogrebna zvona; loš znak.
knife *n* nož.
knight *n* vitez.
knit *v* plesti; sastaviti, spajati; **to ~ the brows** namrgoditi se, sastaviti obrve.
knitter *n* pletilja.
knitting needle *n* štrikaća igla.
knob *n* dugme, ručica; drška; kvrga.
knock *v* kucati, lupati; udarati; razbiti; oboriti; **to ~ down** oboriti udarcem; *n* udarac.
knocker *n* zvekir.
knock-kneed *a* krivonog.
knock-out *n* nokaut (u boksu).
knoll *n* brežuljak.
knot *n* čvor, mašna, kvrga; čvor (mera dužine); *v* vezati u čvor.

knotty *a* čvornovat; zapetljan.
know *v* znati, poznavati, biti upućen.
know-how *n* znanje, veština (*sleng*).
knowing *a* upućen; vešt; ~**ly** *adv* vešto, znalački.
know-it-all *n* sveznalica.

knowledge *n* znanje, saznanje, nauka.
knowledgeable *a* dobro obavešten.
knuckle *n* zglob prsta; kolenica; šarka.
kow-tow *v* ulagivati se.

L

label *n* etiketa, nalepnica.
laboratory *n* laboratorija.
laborious *a* naporan, težak; marljiv; ~ly *adv* naporno.
labour *n* rad, posao; napor; **to be in** ~ ležati u porođajnim mukama.
labourer *n* radnik (nekv.).
labyrinth *n* lavirint.
lace *n* gajtan, čipka; *v* vezati vrpcom; ukrasiti.
lacerate *v* raskomadati, rastrgati; razdirati, mučiti (osećaje).
lack *n* pomanjkanje, nestašica; *v* nemati, manjkati.
lackadaisical *a* izveštačen, koji se prenemaže; pun čežnje.
lackey *n* sluga; *v* ulagivati se, dodvorivati se.
laconic *a* kratak, sažet, lakonski.
lacquer *n* lak; *v* premazati lakom, lakirati.
lad *n* dečak, mladić, momak.
ladder *n* merdevine, lestvice; sredstvo za postizanje uspeha.
ladle *n* kutlača, varjača; *v* crpsti, vaditi; **to ~ out** sipati.
lady *n* dama, gospođa; titula; ljubljena.
ladybird *n* bubamara.
lad-killer *n* kazanova.
ladylike *a* kao gospođa.
ladyship *n* gospinstvo, **her** ~ milostiva gospođa.
lag *v* zaostajati, kasniti, vući se; uhapsiti.
lager *n* vrsta piva.
lagoon *n* laguna.
laid-back *a* opušten.
lair *n* jazbina, brlog; obor za stoku.
laity *n* laici.
lake *n* jezero.
lamb *n* jagnje; *v* jagnjiti se.
lame *a* hrom, sakat; *v* sakatiti, učiniti hromim.
lament *n* kukanje, žalopojka; *v* jadati se, oplakivati.
lamentable *a* žalostan, tužan; jadan.
lamentation *n* jadikovanje.
laminated *a* lisnat, pločast, u slojevima.
lamp *n* svetiljka, fenjer.
lampoon *n* satira, pogrdan spis ili članak.

lance *n* koplje, harpun; hirurški nožić; *v* probosti kopljem.
lancet *n* hirurški nož, lanceta.
land *n* zemlja; država; tlo; *v* iskrcati se na obalu.
land-holder *n* zemljoposednik.
landing *n* iskrcavanje na obalu.
landing strip *n* pista; pomoćni aerodrom.
landlady *n* vlastelinka; sopstvenica kuće; vlasnica pansiona i sl.
landlord *n* vlastelin, posednik, spahija; gostioničar.
landmark *n* međaš, granični znak; prekretnica.
landowner *n* vlasnik zemljišta.
landscape *n* pejsaž, okolina, krajolik.
landslide *n* odronjavanje.
lane *n* sokak, uska ulica; puteljak.
langoustine *n* jastog.
language *n* jezik, govor.
languid *a* trom, mlitav, bez života.
languish *v* slabiti; čeznuti.
lank *a* mršav, vitak.
lanky *a* visok, dugih nogu.
lantern *n* fenjer; kamera svetionika.
lap *n* skut, nabor (na haljini); nedra; *v* zaviti, složiti; isturiti se.
lapel *n* rever.
lapse *n* greška, propust; zastranjenje; *v* skrenuti sa pravog puta; pasti (moralno).
larceny *n* krađa.
larch *n* tisa, ariš (*bot*).
lard *n* mast, salo; *v* prošarati slaninom.
larder *n* ostava.
large *a* veliki, krupan; širok; velikodušan; **at** ~ na slobodi; opširno; ~ly *adv* izdašno; u velikim razmerama.
largesse *n* darežljivost; bogati darovi.
lark[1] *n* ševa (*zool*).
lark[2] *n* šala, zabava; *v* šaliti se, zabavljati se; ~ **about** *v* zbijati obesne šale, ludo se zabavljati.
larva *n* ličinka; punoglavac.
laryngitis *n* zapaljenje grla.
larynx *n* grlo, grkljan.
lascivious *a* pohotan, požudan, lascivan.
laser *n* laser.

laser printer n laserski štampač.
lash n bič; trepavica; v bičevati; privezati.
lasso n laso.
last a poslednji, krajnji; prošli; v trajati; izdržati; adv poslednji put; n kraj; **at ~** na kraju.
lastly adv na poslednjem mestu (kod nabrajanja).
last-ditch a zadnji.
lasting a dugotrajan; izdržljiv, postojan.
last-minute a zadnji čas.
latch n kvaka, reza; v zaključati se.
latch-key n ključ od patentne brave; kalauz.
late a kasan; zakasneo; umrli; adv kasno; skoro.
lately adv u poslednje vreme, nedavno.
latent a skriven, pritajen.
lateral a bočni, vodoravan; sporedan.
lathe n tokarska tezga.
lather n sapunica; konjski znoj; v nasapunjati se.
Latin America n Latinska Amerika.
Latin American n Latinoamerikanac; a latinoamerički.
latitude n geografska širina; opširnost (u izlaganju).
latrine n zahod, nužnik (u logoru ili barakama).
latter a poslednji; pozniji, noviji.
lattice n rešetka.
laudable a vredan pohvale.
laugh n smeh; v smejati se.
laughing stock n predmet ismejavanja.
laughter n smeh, smejanje.
launch[1] n porinuće broda u vodu; motorni čamac.
launch[2] v lansirati; porinuti brod u vodu.
launder v prati.
launderette n praonica.
laundry n perionica; rublje (za pranje).
laurel n lovor; v ovenčati lovorovim vencem.
lava n lava.
lavatory n nužnik, toalet.
lavender n lavandula.
lavish a široke ruke, rasipan; izdašan; v rasipati.
law n zakon, propis; pravo; **~ and order** n red i mir; **~ abiding** a poslušan zakonu.
law court n sud.
lawful a zakonit, zasnovan na zakonu; **~ly** adv zakonito.

lawless a bezakonit, protivzakonit.
lawlessness n bezakonje, anarhija.
lawmaker n zakonodavac.
lawn n travnjak; tanko laneno platno.
lawnmower n kosilica za travu.
lawsuit n suđenje, proces.
lawyer n advokat, pravnik.
lax a mlitav, slab; nemaran; rasklimatan.
laxative n laksativ.
laxity n mlitavost; rasklimatanost, olabavljenost.
lay v položiti; polagati; smestiti; **to ~ into** navaliti na.
layabout n besposličar.
layer n naslaga, sloj.
layette n oprema za novorođenče.
layman n svetovnjak, laik; nestručnjak.
layout n raspored, planiranje; stanje poslovanja.
laze v lenčariti, dangubiti.
lazily adv lenjo.
laziness n lenjost.
lazy a lenj.
lead[1] n upravljanje, inicijativa; primer; uputstva; v voditi; upravljati, biti na čelu.
lead[2] n glavna uloga; povodac (za psa)
leader n vođa, lider; vodič.
leadership n vođenje, upravljanje.
leading a vodeći, rukovodeći, čeoni; n. **~ article** vodeći članak.
leaf n list; stranica (knjige).
leaflet n letak, mala brošura; listić.
league n savez, liga; morska milja.
leak n oticanje, propuštanje tečnosti; v procuriti.
leaky a koji propušta; koji ima rupe.
lean[1] v savijati se; nasloniti se, odupreti se.
lean[2] a mršav; posan.
leap v skočiti, skakati; n skok, odskok.
leap year n prestupna godina.
learn v učiti, saznati; poučavati nekoga.
learned a učen, naučni.
learner n onaj koji uči, početnik.
learning n učenje, znanje, učenost.
lease n zakup, najam; sporazum o zakupu; v davati ili uzimati pod zakup.
leasehold n zakupljena zemlja.
leash n uzica, spreg; v držati na uzici.
least a najmanji, minimalan; **at ~** najmanje; **not in the ~** ni najmanje.
leather n koža, izrađevine od kože.

leathery *a* žilav, sličan koži.
leave *n* dozvola, dopuštenje; odlazak;
   odsustvovanje; *v* otputovati, odlaziti;
   napustiti.
leaven *n* kvasac; *v* staviti kvasac; dati
   podstreka.
leavings *n* ostaci, otpaci.
lecherous *a* razvratan.
lecture *n* predavanje; ukor, opomena; *v*
   držati predavanje; očitati lekciju.
lecturer *n* predavač; docent.
ledge *n* izbočina, ivica, rub; greben.
ledger *n* glavna knjiga, knjiga salda;
   poprečna greda.
lee *n* zavetrina; zaklon.
leech *n* pijavica.
leek *n* praziluk.
leer *v* zlobno/lukavo gledati.
lees *npl* otpaci, talog; društveni ološ.
leeward *a* prema zavetrini.
leeway *n* slobodno delovanje.
left *a* levi; **on the ~** na levo.
left-handed *a* levoruk; nespretan (*pren*).
leftovers *n* otpaci.
leg *n* noga; krak; nogavica.
legacy *n* nasledstvo, zaostavština.
legal *a* zakonit, po zakonu; pravnički; **~ly**
   adv zakonito.
legal holiday *n* (*amer*) državni praznik.
legality *n* zakonitost.
legalize *v* legalizovati, ozakoniti.
legal tender *n* zvanični kurs.
legate *n* legat, poslanik.
legatee *n* naslednik.
legation *n* izaslanstvo; strana misija.
legend *n* bajka, legenda.
legendary *a* legendaran.
legible *a* čitak, jasan.
legibly *adv* čitljivo.
legion *n* legija; vojska.
legislate *v* izdavati zakone.
legislative *a* zakonodavan.
legislaton *n* zakonodavstvo.
legislator *n* zakonodavac.
legislature *n* zakonodavstvo.
legitimacy *n* zakonitost.
legitimate *a* zakonit; opravdan; **~ly** *adv*
   zakonsko, pravovaljano; *v* ozakoniti.
leisure *n* dokolica, slobodno vreme; **~ly** *a*
   neužurban; **at ~** nezaposlen, dokon, bez
   žurbe.

lemon *n* limun.
lemonade *n* limunada.
lemon tea *n* čaj sa limunom.
lemon tree *n* limunovo drvo.
lend *v* pozajmiti; podeliti; pružiti.
length *n* dužina; veličina; trajanje; **at ~**
   konačno, napokon.
lengthen *v* produžiti (se).
lengthways, lenghtwise *adv* po dužini.
lengthy *a* predugačak, razvučen.
lenient *a* blag, obziran.
lens *n* leća, optičko staklo.
Lent *n* Veliki post.
lentil *n* sočivo, leća.
leopard *n* leopard.
leotard *n* plesni triko.
leper *n* gubavac.
leprosy *n* guba.
lesbian *n* lezbijka.
less *a* manji, neznatniji; *adv* manje, u
   manjoj meri.
lessen *v* smanjiti (se); ublažiti; oslabiti.
lesser *a* manji, neznatniji.
lesson *n* zadatak; čas; lekcija.
lest *conj* da ne bi.
let *v* dozvoliti, pustiti, dati da; prepustiti.
lethal *a* smrtonosan, smrtni.
lethargic *a* letargičan; bolesno pospan;
   trom.
lethargy *n* letargija; tromost, apatija.
letter *n* slovo; pismo.
letter box, postbox *n* poštansko sanduče.
lettering *n* tip slova; natpis.
letter of credit *n* kreditno pismo.
lettuce *n* zelena salata.
leukaemia *n* leukemija.
level *a* vodoravan, ravan; u ravnoteži; *n*
   nivo, položaj, vodoravna površina; *v*
   poravnati; nivelisati.
leve-headed *a* staložen, razborit,
   uravnotežen.
lever *n* poluga.
leverage *n* uticaj, moć; snaga poluge.
levity *n* lakomislenost.
levy *n* raspis, određivanje (poreza) i sl.;
   dobrovoljci; *v* prikupljati (vojsku);
   nametnuti; oporezovati.
lewd *a* razuzdan; nemoralan.
lexicon *n* leksikon.
liability *n* odgovornost; obaveze,
   zaduženje; teret.

liable *a* odgovoran; koji jamči; obavezan.
liaison *n* veza (ljubavna); udruženje.
liar *n* lažljivac.
libel *n* kleveta; *v* javno klevetati.
libellous *a* klevetnički.
liberal *a* liberalan; darežljiv; slobodouman; **~ly** *adv* slobodoumno, liberalno.
liberality *n* darežljivost; slobodoumnost.
liberate *v* osloboditi, pustiti na slobodu.
liberation *n* oslobođenje.
libertine *n* slobodoumnik; razvratnik, nemoralna osoba.
liberty *n* sloboda; neograničenost; svojevoljnost.
librarian *n* bibliotekar, knjižničar.
library *n* biblioteka, knjižnica.
libretto *n* libreto, operni tekst.
licence *n* dopuštenje, odobrenje, licenca, dozvola.
license (*br*), **licence** (*amer*) *v* dozvoliti, odobriti; izdati dozvolu.
licentious *a* razuzdan, razvratan.
lichen *n* lišaj.
lick *v* lizati; udarati, tući (*sleng*).
lid *n* poklopac.
lie *n* laž, neistina, varka; *v* lagati, slagati.
lie down *v* leći.
lieu *n* mesto **in ~ of** umesto, u zamenu.
lieutenant *n* poručnik; zamenik, pomoćnik.
life *n* život; življenje, vek; **for ~** za ceo život.
lifeboat *n* čamac za spašavanje.
lifeguard *n* lična straža.
life jacket *n* prsluk za spašavanje.
lifeless *a* mrtav, bez života.
lifelike *a* veran originalu.
lifeline *n* uže za spasavanje.
life sentence *n* doživotna robija.
life-sized *a* u prirodnoj veličini.
life sentence *n* doživotna robija.
life span *n* životni vek.
lifestyle *n* način života.
life-support system *n* respirator, aparat za održavanje života.
lifetime *n* trajanje života.
lift *v* dizati, podići; uzdizati se.
ligament *n* ligament; vez, povez.
light *n* svetlost, osvetljenje; vatra; sveća, sijalica; *a* svetao; jasan; lagan; *v* osvetliti (se); zapaliti (se); **~ up**

rasvetliti; obasjati, ozariti se; zapaliti (cigaretu)
light bulb *n* sijalica.
lighten *v* osvetliti; svetleti, sijati; sevnuti.
lighter *n* upaljač.
light-headed *a* lakouman, nepostojan; koji oseća vrtoglavicu.
light-hearted *a* bezbrižan, veseo.
lighthouse *n* svetionik.
lighting *n* rasveta.
lightly *adv* lagano.
lightning *n* munja, bljesak munje.
lightning-rod *n* gromobran.
lightweight *a* lagan (po težini).
light year *n* svetlosna godina.
ligneous *a* drven, napravljen od drveta.
like *a* sličan, gotovo isti, nalik, poput; *adv* tako, slično tome; *v* voleti, dopadati se.
likeable *a* simpatičan.
likelihood *n* verovatnoća, mogućnost.
likely *a* verovatan; podesan, sposoban.
liken *v* upoređivati, nalaziti sličnost.
likeness *n* sličnost; slika.
likewise *adv* takođe, isto tako.
liking *n* naklonjenost; sklonost.
lilac *n* jorgovan.
lily *n* ljiljan; **~ of the valley** đurđevak.
limb *n* ud; grana; rub nebeskog tela.
limber *a* gibak, savitljiv; hitar.
lime *n* kreč; vrsta limuna; lipa; **~ tree** lipa.
limestone *n* krečnjak.
limit *n* granica, ograničenje; kraj; *v* ograničiti.
limitation *n* ograničenje; ograničenost; krajnji rok.
limitless *a* neograničen, bez granica, beskrajan.
limousine *n* limuzina.
limp *v* hramati, šepati; *n* šepanje, hramanje; *a* gibak; mlitav, slab.
limpet *n* prilepak (školjka); čičak (nametljivac) (*fig*).
limpid *a* proziran, bistar, providan.
line *n* linija, crta; konopac; bora; *v* obeležiti linijom; obložiti, postaviti; **~ up** *v* postrojiti se u red.
lineage *n* poreklo; rod.
linear *a* linijski; uzan i dugačak.
linen *n* grubo platno, platnena roba; rublje.
liner *n* linijski putnički brod ili avion.
linesman *n* linijski sudija.

linger v zadržavati se; oklevati; kasniti; odugovlačiti.
lingerie n žensko rublje.
lingering a dugotrajan, spor; čežnjiv (pogled).
linguist n lingvista, jezikoslovac.
linguistic a lingvistički, jezični.
linguistics n jezikoslovlje, nauka o jezicima, lingvistika.
liniment n tečna mast; lekovita mast za opekotine.
lining n postava; obrub.
link n karika; okovi; veza; mera za dužinu; v spajati, vezivati.
linnet n konopljarka (ptica).
linoleum n linoleum.
linseed n seme lana.
lint n meko laneno platno za povijanje rana.
lintel n gornji prag vrata.
lion n lav; pl znamenitosti (grada).
lioness n lavica.
lip n usna; ivica, rub; drskost.
liposuction n liposukcija.
lip read v čitanje sa usana.
lipstick n ruž za usne.
liqueur n liker.
liquid a tečan, židak; proziran; nestalan; n tečnost.
liquidate v likvidirati; isplatiti (dug); obaviti stečaj.
liquidation n likvidacija; stečaj; raspuštanje.
liquidize v pretvoriti u tekućinu.
liquor n piće (amer); rastvor.
liquorice n slatki koren; vrsta slatkiša.
lisp v šuškati, nejasno izgovarati reči; tepati; n nejasan (šuškav) izgovor; tepanje.
list[1] n spisak, popis; v unositi u spisak, nabrojiti.
list[2] v nagnuti se (brod), visiti.
listen v slušati, osluškivati; poslušati.
listless a ravnodušan, nehajan; apatičan.
litany n litanija.
literal a doslovan, tačan; ~ly adv doslovno, verno originalu.
literary a književan, učen.
literate a pismen, obrazovan.
literature n književnost.
lithe a gibak, vitak; žustar.
lithograph n litografija.

lithography n litografija (veština).
litigation n parničenje.
litigious a sklon pravdanju.
litre n litar.
litter n otpaci; nosiljka; nered; v praviti đubre ili nered; prostirati slamu.
little a mali, sitan; neznatan, nizak; ~ by ~ malo-pomalo; n mala količina; malenkost.
liturgy n liturgija.
live[1] v živeti, postojati, biti živ; to ~ on živeti od nečega; v to ~ up to živeti u skladu sa nečim.
live[2] a živ, pun energije; gorući; direktan (prenos).
livelihood n sredstva za život.
liveliness n živahnost.
lively a živahan, pun života, veseo.
liven up v oživeti, živnuti, uliti život (u nekoga ili nešto).
liver n jetra.
livery n livreja; cehovska odora.
livestock n živi inventar, domaća stoka.
livid a samrtnički bled; jako zao.
living n život, življenje, način života; a živ, savremen.
living room n dnevna soba.
lizard n gušter.
load v tovariti, natovariti; obasuti (poklonima, pohvalama); n teret, tovar; teška briga.
loaded a natovaren.
loaf n hleb, pogača; glava šećera.
loafer n besposličar, danguba, skitnica.
loam n ilovača, plodna zemlja.
loan n zajam, pozajmica.
loathe v osećati odvratnost, gaditi se; ne voleti.
loathing n gnušanje, mrskost, odvratnost.
loathsome a gadan, odvratan.
lobby n predsoblje, hodnik; kuloar.
lobe n deo; resica (uha), jagodica (prsta).
lobster n jastog.
local a lokalni, domaći.
local anaesthetic n lokalna anestezija.
local government n lokalna vlast.
locality n mesto; naseobina; položaj.
localize v lokalizovati.
locally a lokalno; domaće.
locate v rasporediti; naseliti; odrediti položaj.

location *n* nalazište; položaj; mesto stanovanja.
loch *n* jezero.
lock *n* brava; uvojak; *v* zaključati (se); spojiti (se).
locker *n* ormarić s bravom.
locket *n* medaljon.
lockout *n* prekid rada poslodavca.
locksmith *n* bravar.
lockup *n* tamnica (*amer*); garaža (*br*).
locomotive *n* lokomotiva.
locust *n* skakavac.
lodge *n* kolibica, kućica; vratareva kućica; *v* stanovati; nastaniti.
lodger *n* stanar; podstanar.
loft *n* potkrovlje; golubarnik.
lofty *a* uzvišen; ohol; vrlo visok.
log *n* klada, deblo.
logbook *n* brodski dnevnik.
logic *n* logika.
logical *a* logičan; razuman.
logo *n* logotip.
loin *n* krsta; bedro, butina.
loiter *v* bazati, dangubiti.
loll *v* zavaliti se, ispružiti se; plaziti se.
lollipop *n* lilihip.
loneliness *n* samoća.
lonely *a* usamljen; napušten.
long[1] *n* dug; dugotrajan; dosadan.
long[2] *v* žudeti; čeznuti.
long-distance call *n* međugradski telefonski poziv.
longevity *n* dugovečnost, dug život.
long-haired *n* dugokos.
longing *n* žudnja.
longitude *n* dužina (*geograf*).
longitudinal *a* dužinski.
long-legged *a* dugonog.
long-playing record *n* longplej ploča.
long-range *a* dalekometan, dalekosežan.
long-term *a* dugoročan.
long-winded *a* pričljiv.
look *v* pogledati, zuriti, posmatrati; **to ~ after** paziti na nekog; **to ~ for** tražiti; očekivati; **to ~ forward to** unapred uživati u nečemu; **to ~ out for** biti na oprezu; *n* pogled, izgled.
looking glass *n* ogledalo.
lookout *n* koš jarbola; osmatračnica.
loom[1] *n* razboj;

loom[2] *v* nazirati se u daljini.
loop *n* petlja.
loophole *n* puškarnica.
loose *a* labav; slobodan; neuredan; **~ly** *adv* labavo.
loosen *v* olabaviti; otkopčati, odrešiti; visiti.
loot *v* pljačkati; *n* plen, pljačka.
lop *v* odseći, potkresati grane.
lop-sided *a* nakrivljen, naheren.
loquacious *a* brbljiv, govorljiv.
loquacity *n* brbljivost.
lord *n* lord; gospodin, gazda; kralj.
lore *n* nauka, učenost.
lose *v* izgubiti; zametnuti; propustiti; pretrpeti gubitak; **to ~ weight** oslabiti.
loss *n* gubitak, gubljenje; neuspeh; **to be at a ~** biti u teškom položaju.
lost and found office *n* biro za izgubljene stvari.
lot *n* žreb; udeo; sudbina; zemljište; **a ~** mnogo.
lotion *n* losion; tečnost za ispiranje.
lottery *n* lutrija; puki slučaj.
loud *a* glasan, bučan; upadljiv, drečav; **~ly** *adv* glasno.
loudspeaker *n* zvučnik; glasnogovornik.
lounge *n* lenčarenje, dokolica; soba za odmor.
louse *n* vaš; gnjida.
lousy *a* ušljiv, prljav; loš; šugav.
lout *n* klipan, neotesanac.
lovable *a* ljubak, dražestan, zlatan.
love *n* ljubav, zaljubljenost, drago biće; **to fall in ~** zaljubiti se; *v* voleti; želeti.
love letter *n* ljubavno pismo.
love life *n* ljubavni život.
lovely *a* divan, čaroban; ljubak.
lover *n* ljubavnik; udvarač.
lovesick *a* koji vene od ljubavi, koji čezne za ljubavlju.
loving *a* pun ljubavi, nežan, odan.
low *a* nizak; slabašan; tih; utučen; *v* mukati.
low water, low tide *n* najniži vodostaj.
lower *a* niži; *v* spustiti se; spuštati (čamac, zastavu).
lowest *a* najniži.
lowland *n* niska zemlja, nizina.
lowliness *n* niskost, primitivnost; poniznost.

lowly *a* skromna položaja, ponizan.
loyal *a* lojalan, veran, odan, privržen; ~**ly**
  adv lojalno.
loyalty *n* lojalnost, vernost; privrženost.
lozenge *n* romb; pastila; bombon.
lubricant *n* mazivo, sredstvo za
  podmazivanje.
lubricate *v* podmazati.
lucid *a* lucidan; sjajan; jasan.
luck *n* sreća; uspeh; sudbina.
luckily *adv* srećom, na sreću, sretnim
  slučajem.
luckless *a* nesretan, bez sreće.
lucky *a* sretan, koji ima sreću.
lucrative *a* unosan; koristan.
ludicrous *a* smešan; apsurdan; komičan.
lug *v* vući (se); micati se sporo i teško.
luggage *n* prtljag.
lugubrious *a* tužan, žalostan.
lukewarm *a* mlak; ravnodušan (*fig*).
lull *v* uljuljkivati; utišati; umiriti (se); *n*
  zatišje, smirivanje.
lullaby *n* uspavanka.
lumbago *n* lumbago, krstobolja.
lumberjack *n* drvoseča.
luminous *a* svetao, sjajan, blistav; jasan.
lump *n* gruda, grumen; hrpa; čvoruga; ~
  together *v* nagomilati; uzimati đuture.
lump sum *n* ceo iznos.
lunacy *n* ludilo; ludost.
lunar *a* mesečev; nalik Mesecu.
lunatic *a* lud, sumanut.
lunch, luncheon *n* ručak; lakši obrok oko
  podneva; *v* jesti, mezetiti.

lungs *n* pluća.
lurch *n* nagnutost (broda); nesiguran hod,
  teturanje; *v* nagnuti se, nakrenutise;
  teturati se
lure *n* iskušenje; mamac.
lurid *a* sablastan; grozan; samrtnički bled.
lurk *v* vrebati, biti u zasedi.
luscious *a* slastan; sočan; sladak;
  mirišljav.
lush *a* bujan, sočan.
lust *n* požuda; strast; *v* žudeti, čeznuti.
lustful *a* strastven, pohotan, bludan; ~**ly**
  adv.
lustily *adv* krepko; snažno; veselo.
lustre *n* sjaj; slava; odlikovanje.
lusty *a* zdrav, krepak; čvrst, otporan.
lute *n* lutnja (*muz*); sredstvo za
  oblepljivanje.
Lutheran *n* luteran.
luxuriance *n* raskoš, raskošnost; bujanje,
  obilje.
luxuriant *a* bogat, raskošan, plodan;
  bujan.
luxuriate *v* uživati; bujati.
luxurious *a* raskošan, luksuzan; koji voli
  raskoš, rasipnički; ~**ly** *adv* raskošno.
luxury *n* raskoš, luksuz; bujnost; užitak.
lying *n* laž, lažljivost; ležanje.
lymph *n* limfa; izvor-voda.
lynch *v* linčovati.
lynx *n* ris (*zool*).
lyrical *a* lirski.
lyrics *npl* reči (tekst) pesme; lirska pesma.

M

macaroni *n* makaroni.
macaroon *n* vrsta kolačića.
mace *n* službeni štap; žezlo; buzdovan.
macerate *v* smekšati namakanjem;
izmršaviti postom.
machination *n* mahinacija, spletkarenje.
machine *n* mašina, stroj; oruđe.
machine gun *n* mitraljez.
machinery *n* mašinerija; mehanizam,
pogon.
mackerel *n* skuša.
mad *a* lud, sulud; besan; zaluđen nečim.
madam *n* gospođa; vlasnica bordela.
madden *v* razbesneti; izludeti nekog;
naljutiti nekog.
madder *n* broć (*bot*); boja dobijena od
broća.
madhouse *n* ludnica.
madly *adv* ludo; divlje; suludo.
madman *n* ludak.
madness *n* ludilo; mahnitost; bes.
magazine *n* časopis; stovarište municije.
maggot *n* larva; ćudljivost, hir.
magic *n* magija; *a* magičan; čaroban;
~ally *adv* magično.
magician *n* čarobnjak, mađioničar.
magisterial *a* sudski; diktatorski;
ovlašćen; ~ly *adv* sudsko.
magistracy *v* suđenje.
magistrate *n* mirovni sudija.
magnanimity *n* velikodušnost.
magnanimous *a* velikodušan; ~ly *adv*
velikodušno.
magnet *n* magnet.
magnetic *a* magnetičan; privlačan.
magnetism *n* magnetizam; privlačnost
(*fig*).
magnificence *n* veličanstvenost; divota;
sjaj.
magnificent *a* sjajan, veličanstven; ~ly
adv sjajno.
magnify *v* povećavati; preuveličavati.
magnifying glass *n* lupa.
magnitude *n* veličina, značaj.
magpie *n* svraka.
mahogany *n* mahagoni.
maid *n* devojka; služavka.

maiden *n* devojka; usedelica.
maiden name *n* devojačko prezime.
mail *n* pošta; poštanska torba, kola;
oklop.
mail order *n* narudžbina kupca preko
pošte.
mail train *n* poštanski voz.
mailing list *n* lista adresa za slanje.
maim *v* osakatiti; nagrditi.
main *a* glavni; najvažniji; in the ~
uglavnom.
mainland *n* kopno, kontinent.
main line *n* glavna linija (*žel*).
mainly *adv* uglavnom.
main street *n* glavna ulica.
maintain *v* održavati; čuvati; ne odustati
od.
maintenance *n* podrška, oslonac.
maize *n* kukuruz; žuta boja.
majestic *a* veličanstven; ~ally *adv*
veličanstveno.
majesty *n* veličanstvo (titula);
veličanstvenost.
major *a* glavni, veći; važniji; *n* major.
majority *n* većina; punoletstvo.
make *v* praviti, uraditi; činiti; to ~ for
doprinositi; to ~ up sastaviti, popuniti;
to ~ up for nadoknaditi; to ~ off with
something otići; *n* rad; proizvod.
make-believe *n* tobožnji; pretvaranje.
makeshift *a* privremen.
make-up *n* šminka.
make-up remover *n* sredstvo za skidanje
šminke.
malady *n* bolest.
malaise *n* slabost.
malaria *n* malarija.
malcontent *a* nezadovoljan.
male *a* muški; *n* muškarac; samac.
malevolence *n* zloba, pakost,
zlonamernost.
malevolent *a* zloban, zlurad; ~ly *adv*
zlobno.
malfunction *n* kvar.
malice *n* zloba; zlonamernost.
malicious *a* zloban; zlonameran.
malign *a* zloćudan, štetan; *v* klevetati.

malignant *a* zloćudan; zloban, zlurad; **~ly**
  adv zloćudno, zlobno.
mall (shopping) *n* tržni centar.
malleable *a* rastegljiv; popustljiv.
mallet *n* drveni malj.
mallow *n* slez.
malnutrition *n* loša ishrana.
malpractice *n* zloupotreba dužnosti.
malt *n* slad.
maltreat *v* zlostavljati, mučiti.
mammal *n* sisavac.
mammoth *a* golem, divovski.
man *n* čovek; muškarac; ohrabriti.
manacle(s) *n* lisice, ručni okovi.
manage *v* upravljati, voditi.
manageable *a* poslušan, povodljiv.
management *n* upravljanje, rukovanje.
manager *n* upravitelj, rukovodilac,
  menadžer.
manageress *n* upraviteljka, direktorka.
managerial *a* upraviteljski, direktorski,
  menadžerski.
managing director *n* generalni direktor.
mandarin *n* mandarina; mandarin.
mandate *n* mandat; nalog; punomoć.
mandatory *a* punomoćni; prinudan,
  obavezan.
mane *n* griva.
manfully *adv* muževno, junački.
manger *n* jasle.
mangle *n* stroj za valjanje rublja; *v* seći,
  komadati; sakatiti.
mangy *a* šugav; prljav.
manhandle *v* terati ljudskom snagom.
manhood *n* muževnost, zrelost; hrabrost.
man-hour *n* radni sat.
mania *n* mania, ludilo; zaluđenost.
maniac *n* manijak, ludak.
manic *a* ludački.
manicure *n* manikiranje; manikirka.
manifest *a* vidljiv, jasan; *v* javno
  pokazivati, manifestovati.
manifestation *n* manifestacija; znak,
  pokazivanje.
manifesto *n* manifest, javni proglas.
manipulate *v* manipulisati, upravljati,
  rukovoditi; krivotvoriti.
manipulation *n* manipulacija, rukovanje,
  postupak.
mankind *n* čovečanstvo, ljudski rod.
manlike *a* čovekolik.

manliness *n* muževnost.
manly *a* muževan; muškobanjasta.
man-made *a* umetnički.
manner *n* način, stav; običaji; ponašanje;
  pl društvene prilike.
manoeuvre *n* manevar, zavaravanje;
  spletka.
manpower *n* radna snaga.
mansion *n* velika kuća, blok stambenih
  zgrada.
manslaughter *n* ubistvo (bez predumišljaja).
mantelpiece *n* kamin.
manual *a* ručni.
manufacture *n* proizvodnja; fabrikat.
manure *n* gnojivo, đubre; *v* đubriti, gnojiti.
manuscript *n* rukopis, original.
many *a* mnogi, mnogo; **~ a time** mnogo
  puta, često; **how ~ ?** koliko?; **as ~ as**
  toliko kao.
map *n* mapa, karta, plan; *v* unositi na
  mapu; **to ~ out** planirati.
maple *n* javor.
mar *v* kvariti.
marathon *n* maraton.
marauder *n* pljačkaš.
marble *n* mermer; umetničko delo u
  mermeru.
March *n* mart.
march *n* marš; brzo hodanje; pohod;
  pogranično područje; *v* marširati;
  istupati; koračati.
march past *n* paradni marš.
mare *n* kobila.
margarine *n* margarin; veštačka masnoća.
margin *n* rub, kraj; margina.
marginal *a* rubni; granični, marginalni.
marigold *n* neven.
marijuana *n* marihuana.
marinate *v* marinirati.
marine *a* morski, pomorski, nautički; *n*
  mornarica; mornar.
mariner *n* mornar, pomorac; brodar.
marital *a* bračni, supružni.
maritime *a* primorski, smešten uz more;
  nautički.
marjoram *n* majoran.
mark *n* cilj, meta; znak; trag; *v* označiti;
  ostaviti trag.
marker *n* koji beleži bodove, izostanke;
  predmet za obeležavanje mesta u
  knjizi.

market *n* tržnica; trgovina; potražnja.
marketable *a* koji ima dobru prođu, koji se može prodati.
market-garden *n* veliki povrtnjak.
marketing *n* marketing; odlaženje na pijacu, prodaja robe na pijaci.
marketplace *n* tržnica.
market research *n* analize tržnica; marketinško istraživanje.
marksman *n* strelac.
marmalade *n* marmelada.
maroon *a* kestenjaste boje.
marquee *n* veliki šator; natkriven ulaz u hotel; velika svetleća reklama.
marriage *n* brak, venčanje, ženidba, udaja.
marriage certificate *n* venčani list.
marriageable *a* sposoban za ženidbu (udaju).
married *a* oženjen, udata, venčan.
marrow *n* koštana moždina; suština, bitnost.
marry *v* ženiti (se), udavati (se); spojiti.
marsh *n* močvara, močvarno tlo.
marshal *n* maršal; šef ceremonije; šerif; šef policije.
marshy *a* močvaran.
marten *n* kuna (*zool*).
martial *a* ratnički, ratoboran; vojni; *n* ~ **law** opsadno stanje.
martyr *n* mučenik.
martyrdom *n* mučeništvo, mučenička smrt; patnje.
marvel *n* divota; čudo; *v* čuditi se; diviti se.
marvellous *a* čudesan, divan, čaroban; ~**ly** *adv* čudesno, divno.
marzipan *n* marcipan.
mascara *n* maskara.
masculine *a* muški, muževan; jak, snažan.
mash *n* kaša; topla stočna hrana od mekinja; pire krompir; izgnječiti; ~**ed potatoes** *npl* krompir pire.
mask *n* maska; *v* maskirati; kriti.
masochist *n* mazohista.
mason *n* zidar; mason.
masonry *n* zidarstvo, zidanje.
masquerade *n* maskenbal.
mass *n* masa, gomila; misa, bogosluženje.
massacre *n* pokolj, krvoproliće; *v* poklati, poubijati, masakrirati.

massage *n* masaža.
masseur *n* maser.
masseuse *n* maserka.
massive *a* masivan, čvrst, krupan, glomazan.
mass-media *npl* mas-mediji.
mast *n* jarbol, katarka.
master *n* gospodar, gazda; učitelj; majstor (umetnosti); kvalifikovani radnik; *v* zagospodariti, vladati; pokoriti; steći veliku veštinu.
masterly *a* majstorski.
mastermind *v* isplanirati; stajati iza svega.
masterpiece *n* majstorsko delo.
mastery *n* veština; savršeno vladanje nečim.
masticate *v* žvakati.
mastiff *n* rasa psa.
mat[1] *n* asura, prostirka; podmetač.
mat[2], **matt(e)** *a* taman; bez sjaja; mutan; mat.
match *n* šibica; paljenje; par; jednak po kvalitetu; utakmica; *v* slagati se; podešavati; ženiti, udavati.
matchbox *n* kutija šibica.
matchless *a* neuporediv; bez premca, jedinstven.
matchmaker *n* provodadžija.
mate *n* drug; suprug; pomoćnik; mat (u šahu); mužjak ili ženka (kod životinja); *v* spajati u par; pariti se; ženiti se; matirati.
material *a* materijalan; bitan, važan; ~**ly** *adv* bitno.
materialism *n* materijalizam.
maternal *a* materinski; po majci.
maternity clothes *npl* trudnička haljina.
maternity hospital *n* porodilište.
mathematical *a* matematički; vrlo tačan; ~**ly** *adv* matematičko; tačno.
mathematician *n* matematičar.
mathematics *npl* matematika.
maths *npl* matematika.
matinée *n* dnevna priredba.
mating *n* uparivanje.
matins *npl* jutarnja molitva.
matriculate *v* upisati se na visoku školu.
matriculation *n* upis (u visoku školu).
matrimonial *a* bračni.
matted *a* zamršen, isprepletan.

matter *n* materija, građa; stvar; suština;
  what is the ~? šta je? šta se dogodilo?;
  as a ~ of fact u stvari, zapravo; *v* biti od
  važnosti, značiti.
mattress *n* dušek, madrac; strunjača.
mature *a* zreo, dorastao; dobro
  promišljen; *v* zreti, sazreti.
maturity *n* zrelost; završenost; rok
  plaćanja po menici.
maul *v* izbiti, izmlatiti; oštro napadati.
mausoleum *n* mauzolej.
mauve *a* ružičasto-ljubičast.
maxim *n* načelo; poslovica.
maximum *n* maksimum, najveća količina.
may *aux v* moći; smeti; **~be** možda.
May *n* maj.
Mayday *n* 1. maj.
mayonnaise *n* majonez.
mayor *n* gradonačelnik.
mayoress *n* gradonačelnica.
maze *n* lavirint.
me *pn* mene, meni; ja.
meadow *n* livada.
meagre *a* mršav, slab; oskudan;
  siromašan.
meal *n* obrok, jelo, večera.
mealtime *n* vreme jela.
mean[1] *a* (o)srednji; loš, slab; škrt.
mean[2] *v* nameravati, nameniti; misliti.
mean[3] *n* sredina, srednji broj.
meander *v* krivudati, vijugati.
meaning *n* značenje; namera.
meaningful *a* značajan.
meaningless *a* bez značenja, besmislen.
meanness *n* podlost; škrtost.
meantime (in the ~), meanwhile *adv* u
  međuvremenu; dotle.
measles *npl* ospice, male boginje (*med*).
means *n* sredstva, dohodak.
measure *n* mera; merilo; veličina; *v*
  meriti, izmeriti, odmeriti.
measurement *n* merenje; veličina,
  dimenzije.
meat *n* meso; hrana, jelo.
meatball *n* ćufta.
meaty *a* mesnat; sočan.
mechanic *n* mehaničar.
mechanical *a* mehanički; strojarski,
  mašinski; **~ly** *adv* mehaničko; nesvesno.
mechanics *npl* mehanika (nauka).
mechanism *n* mehanizam, stroj.

medal *n* medalja, odlikovanje.
medallion *n* medaljon; spomen-medalja.
medallist *n* izrađivač medalja.
meddle *v* mešati se (u tuđe stvari,
  poslove).
meddler *n* nametljivac.
media *npl* sredstva komunikacije.
mediate *v* posredovati, posredovanjem
  izmiriti.
mediation *n* posredovanje; mirenje.
mediator *n* posrednik.
medical *a* medicinski.
medicate *v* lečiti.
medicated *a* lekovit.
medicinal *a* lekovit.
medicine *n* lek; medicina (nauka).
medieval *a* srednjevekovni.
mediocre *a* osrednji, mediokritetski.
mediocrity *n* osrednjost, prosečnost,
  mediokritet.
meditate *v* meditirati, razmišljati.
meditation *n* meditacija, razmišljanje.
meditative *a* sklon razmišljanju;
  zamišljen.
Mediterranean *a* mediteranski,
  sredozemni; *n* **the ~** Mediteranac.
medium *n* sredstvo, sredina; element;
  okolina; *a* srednji.
medley *n* mešavina; šareno društvo.
meek *a* dobroćudan, krotak, popustljiv,
  skroman; **~ly** *adv* ponizno, krotko.
meekness *n* poniznost.
meet *v* sresti (se), upoznati se, naići na; **to
  ~ with** naći se sa.
meeting *n* sastanak, zbor, sednica; susret.
megaphone *n* megafon.
melancholy *n* melanholija, tuga; *a* tužan,
  setan, potišten.
mellow *a* potpuno zreo, mekan (o
  plodovima); plodan (o tlu); *v* sazreti;
  smekšati(se), ublažiti (se).
mellowness *n* mekoća, blagost.
melodious *a* melodičan; skladan; **~ly** *adv*
  melodično, skladno.
melody *n* melodija, napev.
melon *n* dinja.
melt *v* topiti se, omekšati; slabiti, gubiti
  snagu.
member *n* član, pripadnik.
membership *n* članstvo; broj članova.
membrane *n* membrana, opna.

memento *n* podsetnik, predmet koji podseća na nešto; uspomena.
memo *n* memorandum.
memoir *n* uspomene, beleške, memoari.
memorable *a* vredan spomena, nezaboravan.
memorandum *n* memorandum, beleška.
memorial *n* spomenica, spomenik; molba.
memorize *v* upamtiti, naučiti napamet.
memory *n* pamćenje, sećanje, uspomena.
menace *n* pretnja, opasnost; *v* pretiti, ugrožavati.
menacing *a* preteći.
menagerie *n* menažerija.
mend *v* popraviti; zakrpiti; poboljšati (se).
mending *n* popravka.
menial *a* ropski; prost.
meningitis *n* meningitis.
menopause *n* menopauza.
menstruation *n* menstruacija.
mental *a* duševni, intelektualni, uman.
mentality *n* mentalitet; duševne sposobnosti.
mentally *adv* intelektualno, mentalno.
mention *n* napomena, nagoveštaj, spominjanje; *v* spomenuti, napomenuti.
mentor *n* mentor, mudar savetnik.
menu *n* jelovnik.
mercantile *a* trgovački.
mercenary *a* najamnički, plaćenički; koristoljubiv.
merchandise *n* trgovačka roba.
merchant *n* trgovac na veliko.
merchant marine *n* trgovačka luka.
merchantman *n* trgovački brod.
merciful *a* milostiv, milosrdan, dobra srca.
merciless *a* nemilosrdan, okrutan, bezobziran; ~**ly** *adv* nemilosrdno.
mercury *n* živa, živin preparat.
mercy *n* milost, sažaljenje, opraštanje.
mere *a* puni, potpun; pravi; ~**ly** *adv* samo, jedino.
merge *v* sjediniti (se), stopiti (se); nestati.
merger *n* fizija, udruživanje.
meridian *n* meridijan, zenit.
meringue *n* poljubac; puslica (kolač).
merit *n* zasluga, zaslužnost, vrednoća; *v* zaslužiti, biti zaslužan.
meritorious *a* zaslužan.
mermaid *n* sirena.

merrily *adv* veselo.
merriment *n* veselje, zabava.
merry *a* veseo, radostan, zabavan.
merry-go-round *n* vrteška.
mesh *n* oko (mreže), otvor; *pl* mreža.
mesmerize *v* hipnotisati.
mess *n* zbrka, nered; neprilika; zajednička trpeza (u vojsci); **to ~ up** *v* zabrljati, pokvariti nešto.
message *n* vest, poruka, obaveštenje.
messenger *n* glasnik, kurir.
metabolism *n* metabolizam.
metal *n* metal.
metallic *a* kovan, metalurški.
metallurgy *n* metalurgija.
metamorphosis *n* metamorfoza, preobražaj.
metaphor *n* metafora.
metaphoric(al) *a* metaforički.
metaphysical *a* metafizički.
metaphysics *npl* metafizika.
mete (out) *v* odmeriti, podeliti, dodeliti.
meteor *n* meteor.
meteorological *a* meteorološki.
meteorology *n* meteorologija.
meter *n* metar; brojilo; stopa.
method *n* metoda, postupak.
methodical *a* planski, promišljen, sistematski; ~**ly** *adv* plansko.
Methodist *n* metodista.
metre *n* metar, stopa; mera stiha.
metric *a* metrički.
metropolis *n* metropola, glavni grad.
metropolitan *a* prestonički; eparhijski.
mettle *n* vatrenost, odvažnost; energija; narav.
mettlesome *a* vatren, odvažan.
mew *v* zatvoriti u kavez.
mezzanine *n* međusprat.
microbe *n* mikrob.
microphone *n* mikrofon.
microscope *n* mikroskop.
microscopic *a* mikroskopski.
microwave *n* mikrotalas.
mid *a* srednji, u sredini.
midday *n* podne.
middle *a* srednji; *n* sredina, središte; struk.
middle name *n* srednje ime.
middleweight *n* srednja težina.
middling *a* osrednji; prilično zdrav.

midge *n* mušica.
midget *n* kepec, patuljak.
midi system *n* mini-linija.
midnight *n* ponoć.
midriff *n* dijafragma, trbuh, struk.
midst *n* sredina.
midsummer *n* sredina leta, letnja
ravnodnevnica.
midway *adv* na pola puta.
midwife *n* babica.
midwifery *n* posao babice.
might *n* moć, sila, snaga.
mighty *a* moćan, silan, važan, snažan.
migraine *n* migrena.
migrate *v* seliti (se), preseljavati; odleteti
(ptice).
migration *n* seoba, seljenje.
migratory *a* koji se seli, luta.
mike *n* mikrofon.
mild *a* blag, krotak, nežan; ~ly *adv* blago,
obzirno.
mildew *n* biljne gljivice.
mildness *n* blagost.
mile *n* milja , kopnena milja=1609m,
morska=1863m.
mileage *n* kilometraža.
mileometer, milometer *n* brojilo za
kilometražu.
milieu *n* milje, sredina.
militant *a* ratoboran, borben.
military *a* vojnički, vojni.
militate *v* boriti se, protiviti se.
militia *n* milicija.
milk *n* mleko; *v* musti.
milkshake *n* napitak od mleka.
milky *a* mlečan; M~ Way *n* Mlečni Put.
mill *n* mlin; fabrika; *v* mleti, valjati.
millennium *n* milenijum.
miller *n* mlinar.
millet *n* proso.
milligram *n* miligram.
millilitre *n* mililitar.
millimetre *n* milimetar.
milliner *n* modiskinja.
millinery *n* radnja ženskih šešira, ženski
šeširi (kao roba).
million *num* milion.
millionaire *n* milioner.
millionth *num a* milioniti.
millstone *n* žrvanj, mlinski kamen.
mime *n* lakrdijaš, lakrdija.

mimic *v* imitirati, oponašati.
mimicry *n* oponašanje, mimikrija.
mince *v* seckati (meso); prenemagati se,
afektirati.
mind *n* pamćenje, sećanje; mišljenje; um;
v pamtiti; brinuti se; mariti; paziti (na
nešto).
minded *a* sklon nečemu; takvih nazora.
mindful *a* pažljiv, obziran.
mindless *a* neinteligentan, slabouman.
mine[1] *pn* moj.
mine[2] *n* rudnik; mina; *v* vaditi rudu;
potkopavati; rovati (kopati).
minefield *n* minsko polje.
miner *n* rudar; miner.
mineral *a* rudni, mineralni.
mineralogy *n* nauka o rudama,
mineralogija.
mineral water *n* mineralna voda.
minesweeper *n* minolovac.
mingle *v* pomešati (se), družiti se.
miniature *n* minijatura.
minimal *a* minimalan.
minimize *v* smanjiti, umanjivati,
minimizirati.
minimum *n* minimum, najmanje.
mining *n* rudarstvo, rudarenje.
minion *n* miljenik.
minister *n* ministar, poslanik; sveštenik; *v*
pomagati, služiti.
ministerial *a* ministarski; sveštenički.
ministry *n* ministarstvo, kabinet, vlada;
sveštenstvo.
mink *n* kanadska kuna (*zool*).
minnow *n* ime za više vrsta riba (bjelica,
klen, zlatan).
minor *a* manji, manje važan; niži; *n*
maloletnik; mol, minor (*muz*).
minority *n* manjina; maloletnost.
minstrel *n* putujući pevač u srednjem
veku; pesnik, muzičar.
mint *n* metvica; kovnica novca; *v* kovati
novac.
minus *adv* manje (od); bez, lišen.
minute[1] *a* sitan; neznatan; tačan; ~ly *adv*
sitno.
minute[2] *n* minut, tren.
miracle *n* čudo; nešto izvanredno.
miraculous *a* čudesan.
mirage *n* fatamorgana, priviđenje.
mire *n* gusto blato, mulj; močvara.

mirky *a* mračan; nejasan.
mirror *n* ogledalo.
mirth *n* veselje, radost.
mirthful *a* veseo, radostan.
misadventure *n* nesreća, nesrećan slučaj.
misanthrope, misanthropist *n* mizantrop.
misapply *v* pogrešno primeniti; zloupotrebiti.
misapprehension *n* zabluda, nesporazum.
misbehave *v* ružno (nedolično) se ponašati.
misbehaviour *n* loše ponašanje.
miscalculate *v* loše (pro)računati; pogrešno oceniti.
miscarriage *n* promašaj, greška; pobačaj, abortus.
miscarry *v* ne uspeti; pobaciti, abortirati.
miscellaneous *a* mešovit, raznolik; svestran.
miscellany *n* zbirka (antologija) raznovrsnih članaka, dela.
mischief *n* šteta, kvar; povreda; inat.
mischievous *a* štetan, škodljiv; neposlušan; vragolast.
misconception *n* pogrešno shvatanje.
misconduct *n* loše ponašanje; loše upravljanje.
misconstrue *v* pogrešno tumačiti.
miscount *v* pogrešno računati.
miscreant *n* zločinac, hulja.
misdeed *n* nedelo, zlodelo, zločin.
misdemeanour *n* prekršaj.
misdirect *v* pogrešno uputiti; pogrešno upotrebiti.
miser *n* tvrdica.
miserable *a* jadan, bedan; nesrećan; siromašan.
miserly *a* jadno, bedno; škrto.
misery *n* siromaštvo, oskudica; nesreća, beda.
misfit *n* izrod; promašen čovek.
misfortune *n* nesreća, zla kob; neuspeh.
misgiving *n* bojazan, zla slutnja, zabrinutost.
misgovern *v* loše vladati.
misguided *a* zaveden na pogrešan put.
mishandle *v* zlostavljati, zloupotrebljavati; pogrešno primeniti.
mishap *n* nezgoda, nesreća.
misinform *n* pogrešno obaveštenje.

misinterpret *v* pogrešno tumačiti (shvatiti).
misjudge *v* potcenjivati nekoga; pogrešno proceniti (nešto, nekoga).
mislay *v* zaturiti, zametnuti.
mislead *v* dovoditi u zabludu; zavesti, obmanuti.
mismanage *v* loše voditi (upravljati).
mismanagement *n* loša uprava.
misnomer *n* upotreba pogrešnog naziva.
misogynist *n* ženomrzac.
misplace *v* staviti na pogrešno mesto; dati u pogrešne ruke.
misprint *v* pogrešno odštampati; *n* štamparska greška.
misrepresent *v* pogrešno (lažno) prikazati.
Miss *n* gospođica.
miss *v* promašiti; propustiti; ispustiti.
misshapen *a* izobličen, deformisan.
missile *n* projektil.
missing *a* odsutan; nestao.
mission *n* misija, poziv; izaslanstvo.
missionary *n* misionar.
misspent *a* u pogrešnu svrhu potrošen, protraćen.
mist *n* magla.
mistake *v* biti u zabludi, pogrešno razumeti; zabunom zameniti; **to be ~n** varati se, biti u zabludi; *n* greška, nesporazum.
Mister, Mr *n* gospodin.
mistletoe *n* imela.
mistress *n* gazdarica; ljubavnica.
mistrust *v* ne verovati, sumnjati; *n* nepoverenje, sumnjičavost.
mistrustful *a* sumnjičav, nepoverljiv.
misty *a* maglovit; mutan, tmuran, zamagljen.
misunderstand *v* pogrešno razumeti, krivo protumačiti.
misunderstanding *n* nesporazum, pogrešno tumačenje.
misuse *v* pogrešno upotrebiti, zloupotrebiti.
mitigate *v* omekšati; ublažiti.
mitigation *n* ublaženje.
mitre *n* mitra, biskupska kapa.
mittens *npl* rukavice bez prstiju.
mix *v* mešati, pomešati; družiti se.
mixed *a* izmešan; opijen, ošamućen.

mixed-up *a* konfuzan, zbrkan.
mixer *n* mikser.
mixture *n* mešavina; smeša; mikstura.
mix-up *n* zbrka, tučnjava.
moan *n* stenjanje, jecanje, oplakivanje; *v* stenjati; jadikovati.
moat *n* jarak ispunjen vodom.
mob *n* gomila ljudi, skup; lopovska družina.
mobile *a* pokretan; promenljiv; nestalan.
mobile phone *n* mobilni (telefon).
mobility *n* pokretnost.
mobilize *v* mobilisati.
moccasin *n* mokasine.
mock *v* rugati se, ismejavati; zadirkivati.
mockery *n* ismejavanje, ruganje; predmet ismejavanja.
mode *n* vid, metod; običaj, način.
model *n* uzor, obrazac, uzorak, model; *v* oblikovati.
modem *n* modem.
moderate *a* umeren; nizak (cena); **~ly** *adv* umereno; *v* ublažiti, smiriti, obuzdati.
moderation *n* umerenost; uzdržavanje; suzbijanje.
modern *a* savremen, moderan; nov (jezik, učenje).
modernize *v* modernizovati.
modest *a* skroman, čedan, pristojan; **~ly** *adv* skromno, čedno.
modesty *n* skromnost.
modicum *n* nešto malo, malenkost, minimum.
modification *n* modifikacija, ograničenje; preinačenje, promena.
modify *v* modificirati, preinačiti, promeniti.
modulate *v* modulirati; prilagoditi, uskladiti.
modulation *n* modulacija.
module *n* modul.
mogul *n* mogul, velika ličnost (*fig*).
mohair *n* vuna angorske koze, moher.
moist *a* vlažan, mokar; kišovit.
moisten *v* ovlažiti, pokisnuti; natopiti, pokvasiti.
moisture *n* vlaga, vlažnost.
molars *npl* kutnjaci.
molasses *npl* šećerni sirup, melasa.
mole *n* mladež.
molecule *n* molekul.

molehill *n* krtičnjak.
molest *v* dosađivati, uznemiravati; napastvovati.
mollify *a* ublažiti, umiriti.
mollusc *n* mekušac (*zool*).
mollycoddle *v* razmaziti, tetošiti; raznežiti.
molten *a* liven, izliven; rastopljen.
moment *n* momenat, tren, čas; važnost.
momentarily *adv* momentalno, trenutno.
momentary *a* momentalan, trenutačan, munjevit; prolazan.
momentous *a* važan, značajan.
momentum *n* pokretna sila, podstrek, impuls.
monarch *n* vladar, monarh, car.
monarchy *n* monarhija.
monastery *n* manastir.
monastic *a* manastirski.
Monday *n* ponedeljak.
monetary *a* novčani; monetarni.
money *n* novac.
money laundering *n* pranje novca.
money order *n* ček.
Mongol *n* Mongol, Mongolka, mongolski jezik.
mongrel *a* mešanac, nečistokrvan.
monitor *n* stariji đak koji održava red, starešina u razredu; nastavnik.
monk *n* kaluđer.
monkey *n* majmun.
monochrome *a* jednobojno.
monocle *n* monokl.
monologue *n* monolog.
monopolize *v* monopolisati, zadržati isključivo pravo.
monopoly *n* monopol.
monosyllable *n* jednosložna reč.
monotonous *a* monoton, jednoličan, dosadan.
monotony *n* monotonija, jednoličnost, dosada.
monsoon *n* monsun.
monster *n* čudovište, nakaza.
monstrosity *n* nakaznost, monstruoznost, grozota.
monstrous *a* monstruozan, nakazan, grozan; **~ly** *adv* monstruozno.
montage *n* montaža.
month *n* mesec (u kalendaru).
monthly *a* mesečni, svakog meseca; *adv* mesečno.

monument *n* spomenik.
monumental *a* monumentalan, golem.
moo *v* mukati.
mood *n* raspoloženje; volja, ćud.
moodiness *n* zlovolja; hirovitost.
moody *a* zlovoljan; hirovit.
moon *n* Mesec.
moonbeams *npl* mesečevi zraci.
moonlight *n* mesečina.
moor *v* vezivati, usidriti brod.
moorland, moor *n* močvarno tlo zaraslo trskom.
moose *n* severnoamerički los (*zool*).
mop *n* metla od lika, krpa za pranje poda; kreveljenje; *v* prati krpom pod; otrti (suze).
mope *v* biti tužan, zlovoljan, ćutljiv, duriti se.
moped *n* moped.
moral *a* moralan, poučan; **~ly** *adv* moralno.
morale *n* moralno stanje, duh.
moralist *n* moralista.
morality *n* moral, etika; pouka.
moralize *v* govoriti o moralu, moralizirati.
morals *npl* moral.
morass *n* močvara.
morbid *a* morbidan; bolestan; patološki.
more *a/adv* više, još; **never ~** nikad više; **once ~** još jednom; **~ and ~** sve više; **so much the ~** to više.
moreover *adv* osim toga, uz to, povrh toga, nadalje.
morgue *n* mrtvačnica.
morning *n* jutro; **Good ~** Dobro jutro!.
moron *n* moron, imbecil.
morose *a* mrzovoljan, mrk, namršten.
morphine *n* morfijum.
morsel *n* komadić, zalogaj.
mortal *a* smrtan, smrtonosan; **~ly** *adv* smrtno; *n* smrtnik.
mortality *n* smrtnost, mortalitet.
mortar *n* malter; minobacač.
mortgage *n* hipoteka; *v* založiti, zadužiti se na nepokretnu imovinu.
mortgage company *n* hipotekarska banka.
mortgager *n* hipotekarski dužnik.
mortification *n* suzbijanje (osećaja); poniženje, uvreda.
mortify *v* poniziti, vređati; obamreti.

mortuary *n* mrtvačnica.
mosaic *n* mozaik.
mosque *n* džamija.
mosquito *n* komarac.
moss *n* mahovina; treset.
mossy *a* pun mahovine.
most *a* najveći; *adv* najviše; **at ~** najviše, u najboljem slučaju; **~ly** *adv* većinom, ponajviše, uglavnom.
motel *n* motel.
moth *n* moljac; noćni leptir.
mothball *n* kuglica naftalina protiv moljaca.
mother *n* majka; inkubator.
motherhood *n* materinstvo, majčinstvo.
mother-in-law *n* tašta, svekrva.
motherless *a* bez majke.
motherly *a* materinski, majčinski.
mother-of-pearl *n* sedef.
mother-to-be *n* buduća majka.
mother tongue *n* maternji jezik.
motif *n* pobuda, povod, motiv.
motion *n* kretanje, pokret telom, gest; inicijativa.
motionless *a* nepomičan.
motion picture *n* film, kinematografija.
motivated *a* motivisan, inspirisan.
motive *n* povod, razlog; motiv, tema.
motley *a* šaren, raznobojan, raznolik.
motor *n* motor, stroj; motorni živac.
motorbike *n* motorcikl.
motorboat *n* motorni čamac.
motorcycle *n* motorcikl.
motor scooter *n* skuter.
motor vehicle *n* motorno vozilo.
mottled *a* šaren, prošaran.
motto *n* lozinka, geslo, moto.
mould *n* tlo, rastresita zemlja; kalup; *v* drobiti, nasipati zemlju; modelirati.
moulder *v* mrviti se, rasipati se, trunuti.
mouldy *a* buđav; zastareo.
moult *v* gubiti perje; presvlačiti se; menjati oklop.
mound *n* nasip, brežuljak, humka.
mount *n* brdo, gora; jahaći konj; nameštanje; *v* dizati se, popeti se, uzjahati; vinuti se, porasti.
mountain *n* planina, brdo.
mountaineer *n* planinar; brđanin, gorštak.
mountaineering *n* planinarenje.
mountainous *a* brdovit, planinski.

mourn *v* oplakivati, žaliti, tugovati.
mourner *n* osoba koja žali, tuguje.
mournful *a* žalostan, tužan, bolan; ~**ly**
  adv tužno, žalosno, bolno.
mourning *n* žalost, tugovanje, crnina.
mouse *n* miš.
mousse *n* mus; pena za kosu.
moustache *n* brkovi.
mouth *n* usta; gubica; otvor; grimase.
mouthful *n* zalogaj; gutljaj.
mouth organ *n* usna harmonika.
mouthpiece *n* pisak, muštikla; glasnik;
  tumač.
mouthwash *n* vodica za ispiranje usta.
mouthwatering *a* ukusno.
movable *a* pokretljiv, pomičan; pokretan
  (imovina).
move *v* micati se, premeštati se, kretati se;
  izazivati (smeh); *n* potez, pomak,
  kretanje; preseljenje; korak.
movement *n* pokret, kretanje, micanje;
  tempo, ritam; hod.
movie *n* film.
movie camera *n* filmska kamera.
moving *a* pokretan, koji se kreće; lutajući;
  dirljiv.
mow *v* kositi.
mower *n* kosač; kosilica.
much *a/adv* mnogo, vrlo; gotovo, skoro.
muck *n* đubrivo, gnoj; blato, gadost,
  podlost.
mucous *a* sluzav.
mucus *n* sluz.
mud *n* blato, mulj, glib; prljavština.
muddle *v* pokvariti, pobrkati, zamrsiti; *n*
  zbrka, nered.
muddy *a* prljav, blatnjav; zamućen,
  mutan.
mudguard *n* blatobran.
muffle *v* ogrnuti, uviti; umotati (se) radi
  topline; prigušiti (krik).
mug *n* vrč, krigla, pehar; naivčina.
muggy *a* mlak, vlažan, sparan, zagušljiv.
mulberry *n* dud; ~ **tree** dudovo drvo.
mule *n* mazga, mula; glupak, tvrdoglavac;
  hibrid.
mull *v* skuvati zaslađeno alkoholno piće.
multifarious *a* raznovrstan, raznolik.
multimedia *a* multimedijalan.
multiple *a* mnogostruk, višestruk;
  sastavljen od više delova; *n* višekratnik.

multiplication *n* množenje;
  razmnožavanje; ~ **table** tablica
  množenja.
multiply *v* množiti se; razmnožavati se.
multitude *n* množina, veliki broj; gomila.
mumble *v* mumlati, mrmljati.
mummy *n* mama; mumija.
mumps *npl* zauške.
munch *v* žvakati, mljackati.
mundane *a* svetski; zemaljski.
municipal *a* gradski, opštinski,
  komunalan; samoupravan.
municipality *n* gradska uprava.
munificence *n* darežljivost,
  velikodušnost.
munitions *npl* municija, vojne zalihe,
  oružje.
mural *n* mural.
murder *n* ubistvo, umorstvo; *v* ubiti.
murderer *n* ubica.
murderess *n* žena ubica.
murderous *a* smrtonosan, ubilački;
  krvoločan.
murky *a* sumoran, mračan, tmuran.
murmur *n* žuborenje, zujanje; šapat; *v*
  žuboriti, šuštati, zujati; šaptati;
  gunđati.
muscle *n* mišić, mišica; snaga.
muscular *a* mišićav, jak.
muse *v* razmišljati, zadubiti se u misli.
museum *n* muzej.
mushroom *n* pečurka, gljiva.
music *n* muzika.
musical *a* muzikalan, melodičan.
musician *n* muzičar.
musk *n* mošus.
muslin *n* muslin.
mussel *n* dagnja (školjka).
must *v* izražava obavezu; potrebu;
  uverenje.
mustard *n* gorušica; slačica; senf.
muster *v* skupljati (se), sakupiti (na zbor).
musty *a* plesniv, buđav, ustajao.
mute *a* nem; ćutljiv; bezglasan.
mutilate *v* osakatiti, unakaziti; pokvariti.
mutilation *n* osakaćenje.
mutiny *n* buna, ustanak; *v* pobuniti se.
mutter *v* mrmljati, gunđati, govoriti
  nerazgovetno; *n* mrmljanje, gunđanje.
mutton *n* ovčetina.
mutual *a* uzajaman, obostran; opšti,

zajednički; ~**ly** *adv* uzajamno, obostrano.

muzzle *n* njuška; ždrelo, otvor (cevi); brnjica; *v* staviti brnjicu; ućutkati.

my *pn* moj, moja, moje, moji.

myriad *n* 10.000; beskrajno veliki broj.

myrrh *n* mira (vrsta mirišljave smole).

myrtle *n* mirta.

myself *pn* ja sam, sebe, mene.

mysterious *a* tajanstven; ~**ly** *adv* tajanstveno.

mystery *n* misterija, tajna, zagonetka.

mystic(al) *a* mističan, tajanstven.

mystify *v* prikazivati tajanstvenim, dovoditi u zabludu; zaluđivati.

mystique *n* mistika, misterija.

myth *n* mit, bajka, legenda.

mythology *n* mitologija.

N

nab *v* uhapsiti, uhvatiti.

nag *n* vrsta malog konja, poni; raga; *v* prigovarati, grditi.

nagging *a* čangrizav, svadljiv.

nail *n* nokat, kandža; ekser; *v* zabijati eksere.

nailbrush *n* četka za nokte.

nailfile *n* pribor za nokte.

nail polish *n* lak za nokte.

nail scissors *npl* makazice za nokte.

naive *a* bezazlen, prirodan, naivan; neiskusan.

naked *a* go, razgolićen; ogoljen.

name *n* ime, prezime; naziv, naslov, reputacija; *v* nazvati, nadenuti ime; naznačiti.

nameless *a* nepoznat; bezimen; anoniman; neizreciv.

namely *adv* na ime, to jest.

nameplate *n* pločica sa imenom.

namesake *n* imenjak.

nanny *n* dadilja.

nap *n* dremež, kratak san; dlaka na suknu.

nape *n* potiljak, zatiljak.

napkin *n* ubrus, salveta; pelene.

nappy *n* pelena; dlakav.

narcissus *n* narcis.

narcotic *a* narkotičan, koji uspavljuje, omamljuje; *n* opojno sredstvo, narkotik.

narrate *v* pripovedati, pričati.

narrative *a* pripovedački, koji priča; *n* pripovetka, priča, pričanje.

narrow *a* uzak; tesan; ograničen; ~ly *adv* tesno; *v* sužavati se, ograničavati.

narrow-minded *a* ograničen, pun predrasuda, uskogrudan.

nasal *a* nosni, nazalni; unjkav.

nasty *a* gadan, ružan; nepristojan; prljav.

natal *a* rodni.

nation *n* narod, nacija; narodnost.

national *a* narodni, nacionalni; ~ly *adv* narodno, nacionalno.

nationalism *n* nacionalizam.

nationalist *a/n* nacionalista.

nationality *n* narod, nacionalnost.

nationalize *v* nacionalizovati.

nationwide *a* svenarodni, opštenarodni.

native *a* urođen, domaći; rođen; starosedelački; *n* urođenik, domorodac.

native language *n* maternji jezik.

natural *a* prirodan; stvaran, realan; ~ly *adv* prirodno.

natural gas *n* prirodni gas.

naturalist *n* naturalista.

naturalize *v* primiti državljanstvo; prilagoditi se.

nature *n* priroda, suština; karakter; narav.

naturopath *n* prirodno lečenje.

naught *n* nula.

naughty *a* neposlušan, nestašan; nepristojan.

nausea *n* morska bolest, muka; gađenje.

nauseate *v* gaditi se; izazivati odvratnost.

nauseous *a* odvratan.

nautical *a* nautički, pomorski.

naval *a* mornarički; brodski.

nave *n* naos.

navel *n* pupak.

navigate *v* ploviti; leteti; upravljati (brodom, avionom).

navigation *n* plovidba; navigacija.

navy *n* ratna mornarica; admiralitet.

Nazi *n* nacist.

near *prep* u blizini, pored; približno; *a* blizak; direktan; *adv* blizu, pored; tek što nije.

nearby *a* obližnji, susedni.

nearly *adv* skoro, gotovo; približno; blizu.

near-sighted *a* kratkovid.

neat *a* uredan; jednostavan, otmen; jasan; ~ly *adv* otmeno.

nebulous *a* nebulozan; nejasan, mutan.

necessarily *adv* nužno, potrebno, automatski.

necessary *a* potreban, nužan; obavezan.

necessitate *v* iziskivati potrebu, činiti neophodnim; prinuđivati.

necessity *n* nužnost, neminovnost.

neck *n* vrat; grlić (boce); vrat na violini i sl.; *v* ljubakati se.

necklace *n* ogrlica.

nectar *n* nektar.

need *n* potreba, nužda; škripac; *v* trebati, morati.

needle *n* igla, strelica; iglica.

needless *a* nepotreban, nekoristan.

needlework *n* šivenje, vez.

needy *a* potreban, oskudan, siromašan.

negation *n* poricanje; negativna veličina.

negative *a* odrečan, negativan; **~ly** *adv* negativno; *n* negativan odgovor; negativ (*foto*).

neglect *v* zanemariti, propustiti, zapustiti; *n* zanemarenost, zapušteno stanje; nebriga.

negligee *n* negliže.

negligence *n* nebriga, nerad; nemarnost; aljkavost.

negligent *a* nemaran, neradan; aljkav; **~ly** *adv* nemarno, nesavesno, ležerno.

negligible *a* beznačajan, koji se ne uzima u obzir.

negotiate *v* pregovarati, dogovarati (se).

negotiation *n* pregovori; savlađivanje teškoća.

Negress *n* crnkinja.

Negro *a* crnački; *n* crnac.

neigh *v* rzati, njištati; *n* rzanje, njištanje.

neighbour *n* sused; predmet koji se nalazi u neposrednoj blizini; *v* graničiti se, dopirati do nečeg.

neighbourhood *n* susedstvo; okolina, kraj; blizina.

neighbouring *a* susedni, granični.

neighbourly *a* susedski, prijateljski.

neither *conj* ni, niti; *pn* nijedan ni drugi.

neon *n* neon.

neon light *n* neonska svetlost.

nephew *n* nećak.

nepotism *n* nepotizam, rodbinsko protekcionaštvo.

nerve *n* živac; prisebnost, hrabrost; drskost.

nerve-racking *a* koji uzrujava.

nervous *a* razdražljiv, nervozan; koji ide na živce.

nervous breakdown *n* slom živaca.

nest *n* gnezdo; leglo životinja; prijatan kutak.

nest egg *n* ušteđevina (*fig*).

nestle *v* udobno se smestiti, kriti se.

net *n* mreža, mrežica.

netball *n* igra slična košarci.

netting *n* pletenje mreže; hvatanje mrežom.

nettle *n* kopriva.

network *n* mreža, mrežica; mreža (žel. pruge, kanali i sl.).

neurone *n* neuron.

neurosis *n* neuroza, poremećaj živčanog sistema.

neurotic *a* neurotičan.

neuter *a* srednjeg roda (*gram*).

neutral *a* neutralan, nepristrasan; neodređen (boja).

neutrality *n* neutralnost, nepristrasnost.

neutralize *v* osujetiti, onemogućiti, neutralisati.

neutron *n* neutron.

neutron bomb *n* neutronska bomba.

never *adv* nikada, nijednom; nije moguće; **~mind** nije važno.

never-ending *a* beskrajan.

nevertheless *adv* ništa manje, ipak, uprkos tome.

new *a* nov, svež; skori, nedavni; **~ly** *adv* novo, sveže, ponovo, nedavno.

New Year *n* Nova godina; **~'s Day** prvi dan Nove godine (1. januar); **~'s Eve** zadnji dan stare godine (31. decembar).

newborn *a* novorođen; preporođen.

newcomer *n* pridošlica, došljak; neznanac.

new-fangled *a* pomodarski; željan novotarija.

news *npl* vesti, novosti.

news agency *n* novinska agencija.

newsagent *n* prodavac novina.

newscaster *n* spiker na radiju ili TV.

news flash *n* najnovije vesti.

newsletter *n* bilten.

newspaper *n* novine.

newsreel *n* filmski žurnal.

next *a* sledeći; najbliži; budući; **the ~ day** sledeći dan; *adv* zatim, posle.

nib *n* pero, zašiljeni vrh pera; oštrica.

nibble *v* jesti malim zalogajima; ovlaš zagristi.

nice *a* prijatan, drag, dobar; ljubazan, pažljiv; **~ly** *adv* dobro, sjajno, ljubazno; prefinjeno.

nice-looking *a* lepuškast, privlačan.

niche *n* niša.

nick *n* beleg, zarez, oznaka; oštećeno mesto; *v* zarezati, obeležiti; pogoditi.
nickel *n* nikl, kovani novac od pet centi.
nickname *n* nadimak; *v* nadenuti nadimak.
nicotine *n* nikotin.
niece *n* nećaka.
niggling *a* sitničav.
night *n* noć, mrak; **by** ~ noću; **good** ~ Laku noć!.
nightclub *n* noćni lokal, bar.
nightfall *n* sumrak, veče.
nightingale *n* slavuj.
nightly *adv* svake noći, noću; *a* noćni.
nightmare *n* noćna mora.
night school *n* večernja škola.
night shift *n* noćna smena.
night-time *n* noć.
nihilist *n* nihilist.
nimble *a* žustar, okretan, brz; dosetljiv.
nine *num* devet.
nineteen *num* devetnaest.
nineteenth *num a* devetnaesti.
ninetieth *num a* devedeseti.
ninety *num* devedeset.
ninth *num a* deveti.
nip *v* uštinuti; zagristi; pecnuti; piti na gutljaje.
nipple *n* bradavica (na grudima); cucla; brežuljak.
nit *n* gnjida, uš.
nitrogen *n* nitrogen, dušik.
no *adv* ne; *a* nikakav, nijedan.
nobility *n* plemenitost, velikodušnost; plemstvo, plemići.
noble *a* plemenit, velikodušan; naočit; *n* plemić.
nobleman *n* plemić.
nobody *n* niko; čovek koji ne uživa ugled u društvu.
nocturnal *a* noćni.
nod *n* klimanje (glavom); dremež, dremanje; *v* klimati glavom; dremati; propustiti (nešto).
noise *n* buka, galama, dreka; zvuk.
noisily *adv* bučno; glasno.
noisiness *n* galama; bučnost.
noisy *a* bučan, glasan; drečav (boje).
nominal *a* nominalan, koji se odnosi na ime; **~ly** *adv* nominalno, neznatno, beznačajno.

nominate *v* predložiti (kandidata); imenovati, postaviti.
nomination *n* imenovanje, predlaganje (kandidata).
nominative *n* nominativ (*gram*).
nominee *n* kandidat na dužnosti ili na izborima.
nonalcoholic *a* bezalkoholno.
nonaligned *a* neangažovan; nesvrstan.
nonchalant *a* bezbrižan, nemaran; ravnodušan.
noncommittal *a* uzdržljiv.
nonconformist *n* nekonformista.
nondescript *a* teško opisiv, neodrediv, neodređen.
none *a* ni najmanje, ni u kom pogledu, nipošto.
nonentity *n* nešto što ne postoji, nepostojanje; nula (*fig*).
nonetheless *adv* ništa manje, uprkos tome, ipak.
nonexistent *a* nepostojeći.
nonplussed *a* smeten, pred zagonetkom.
nonsense *n* glupost, besmislica, budalaština; nevažne stvari.
nonsensical *a* besmislen, smušen.
nonsmoker *n* nepušač.
nonstop *a* neprekidan.
noodles *npl* rezanci, testenina; budala, tupoglavac.
noon *n* podne.
noose *n* petlja, omča, laso; zamka.
nor *conj* ni, niti.
normal *a* normalan, pravilan; redovno stanje.
north *n* sever; *a* severni, okrenut severu.
North America *n* Severna Amerika.
North Pole *n* Severni pol.
northeast *n* severoistok.
northerly, northern *a* severni.
northward(s) *adv* prema severu, na sever.
northwest *n* severozapad.
nose *n* nos, njuška; njuh.
nosebleed *n* krvarenje iz nosa.
nosedive *n* pikiranje; iznenadan napad.
nostalgia *n* nostalgija, čežnja (za domovinom).
nostril *n* nozdrva.
not *adv* ne, ni.
notable *a* koji se ističe, ugledan, znamenit, važan.

notably *adv* naročito, osobito; napadno.
notary *n* beležnik.
notch *n* zarez, usek; udubljenje, šupljina; *v* zarezati, urezati, obeležiti.
note *n* beleška, pribeleška, znak; pažnja; opaska; *v* pribeležiti; obazirati se; opaziti; primetiti.
notebook *n* beležnica, notes.
noted *a* poznat, čuven.
notepad *n* blok.
notepaper *n* hartija za pisma.
nothing *n* ništa; nula, ništica; malenkost; **good for** ~ ništarija.
notice *n* obaveštenje, saopštenje; opomena, upozorenje; *v* primetiti, obratiti pažnju; opaziti; opomenuti.
noticeable *a* primetan.
notification *n* obaveštenje; proglas.
notify *v* izvestiti, obavestiti; objaviti.
notion *n* pojam; stanovište, mišljenje; ideja.
notoriety *n* čuvenost; ozloglašenost.
notorious *a* poznat po zlu, čuven; ozloglašen; **~ly** *adv* ozloglašeno.
notwithstanding *conj* iako, premda.
nougat *n* nugat.
nought *n* ništa, ništavilo (čovek); nula.
noun *n* imenica (*gram*).
nourish *v* hraniti; gajiti (nadu).
nourishing *a* hranljiv.
nourishment *n* ishrana; hrana.
novel *n* roman; pripovetka, novela.
novelist *n* pisac romana.
novelty *n* novitet; novina; novost.
November *n* novembar.
novice *n* novajlija, početnik; iskušenik.
now *adv* sada, odmah; smesta; onda; ~ **and then** tu i tamo, ponekad.
nowadays *adv* sada, u naše doba.
nowhere *adv* nigde, nikuda.
noxious *a* štetan, ubitačan, nezdrav.
nozzle *n* ispust (na čajniku); štrcaljka; otvor; njuška.
nuance *n* postepeni prelaz, nijansa.
nuclear *a* nuklearan; ~ **power** nuklearna energija; ~ **power station** nuklearna centrala.

nucleus *n* jezgro; moždana srž; središte.
nude *a* go, obnažen; boje tela (čarape).
nudge *v* gurkati (laktom).
nudist *n* nudista.
nudity *n* golotinja.
nuisance *n* neprilika, neugodnost; neprijatan i dosadan čovek.
nuke *n* atomska bomba (*sleng*); *v* napasti atomskim oružjem.
null *a* nevažeći; koji nema zakonske snage (*jur*).
nullify *v* poništiti, ukinuti.
numb *a* zanemeo; ukočen (od hladnoće); *v* izazvati zanemelost ili ukočenost; zaprepastiti.
number *n* broj, količina; izdanje; iznos; *v* brojati, nabrajati; numerisati; obračunati se (*voj*).
numbness *n* ukočenost, mrtvilo, omamljenost.
numeral *n* broj (*gram*), brojka.
numerical *a* brojni; brojem, po broju.
numerous *a* mnogobrojan.
nun *n* kaluđerica; močvarna senica (ptica).
nunnery *n* ženski manastir.
nuptial *a* bračni, svadbeni; **~s** *npl* venčanje.
nurse *n* dadilja, dojilja; bolničarka; *v* hraniti, dojiti (dete); negovati (bolesnika).
nursery *n* dečja soba; uzgajalište; inkubator.
nursery rhyme *n* kratka pesma za malu decu.
nursery school *n* zabavište.
nursing home *n* privatna bolnica (sanatorijum).
nurture *v* odgoj, obuka; gajenje, podizanje.
nut *n* orah.
nutcrackers *npl* klješta za orahe.
nutmeg *n* oraščić (začin).
nutritious *a* hranljiv.
nutshell *n* orahova ljuska.
nylon *n* najlon; *a* najlonski.

O

oak *n* hrast; drvena hrastova građa.
oar *n* veslo; veslač.
oasis *n* oaza.
oath *n* zakletva, kletva, proklinjanje.
oatmeal *n* ovseno brašno, ovsena kaša.
oats *npl* zob u zrnu.
obedience *n* poslušnost, pokornost.
obedient *a* poslušan, pokoran; ~ly *adv*
    poslušno, pokorno.
obese *a* debeo, gojazan.
obesity *n* gojaznost.
obey *v* slušati, pokoravati se.
obituary *n* nekrolog.
object[1] *n* predmet, stvar; cilj, namera.
object[2] *v* buniti se protiv nečega,
    usprotiviti se.
objection *n* primedba, prigovor, protest;
    neodobravanje.
objectionable *a* nepoželjan, koji izaziva
    prigovore; neprijatan.
objective *a* objektivan, pravičan; stvaran,
    realan; *n* objektiv; cilj, svrha.
obligation *n* obaveza, obećanje; dužnost.
obligatory *a* obavezan; koji primorava.
oblige *v* prinuditi, primorati; učiniti
    uslugu.
obliging *a* uslužan, ljubazan.
oblique *a* kos, nakrivljen; posredan,
    prikriven; ~ly *adv* koso, nakrivljeno.
obliterate *v* brisati, precrtavati; uništiti;
    zataškati.
oblivion *n* zaborav.
oblivious *a* zaboravan; koji pruža
    zaborav.
oblong *a* izduženog oblika, duguljast.
obnoxious *a* odvratan, nepodnošljiv.
oboe *n* oboa (*muz*).
obscene *a* nepristojan, sramotan.
obscenity *n* bestidnost, nepristojnost;
    prostota.
obscure *a* taman, mračan; nejasan;
    nepoznat; ~ly *adv* nejasno, mračno; *v*
    zamračiti; potamniti.
obscurity *n* mrak, tama; nejasnoća;
    skrivenost; nepoznatost.
observance *n* pridržavanje, održavanje
    (zakona, običaja i sl.); običaj.

observant *a* pronicljiv, posmatrački;
    pažljiv; koji se pridržava zakona.
observantly *a* pronicljivo, pažljivo.
observation *n* posmatranje; pronicljivost,
    moć opažanja; primedba.
observatory *n* opservatorija;
    osmatračnica.
observe *v* posmatrati, proučavati, pratiti
    nešto.
observer *n* posmatrač; onaj koji se
    pridržava (zakona i sl.).
obsess *v* opsedati (misli); proganjati;
    obuzimati (strah).
obsessive *a* opsednut.
obsolete *a* zastareo, istrošen.
obstacle *n* prepreka, smetnja.
obstinacy *n* svojeglavost, upornost.
obstinate *a* svojeglav, uporan, tvrdoglav;
    ~ly *adv* svojeglavo, uporno, tvrdoglavo.
obstruct *v* prepreciti nekome put, zakrčiti
    saobraćaj; ometati.
obstruction *n* prepreka, začepljenje,
    smetnja; opstrukcija.
obtain *v* dobiti, postići, steći; izboriti se.
obtainable *a* koji se može dobiti.
obtrusive *a* nametljiv.
obtuse *a* nenaoštren, tup; glup.
obvious *a* očigledan, jasan; vidan; ~ly *adv*
    očigledno, jasno.
occasion *n* slučaj, prilika, mogućnost;
    okolnost; *v* dati povoda, poslužiti kao
    razlog.
occasional *a* povremen, slučajan, redak;
    prilagođen određenom trenutku; ~ly *adv*
    slučajno, povremeno.
occupant, occupier *n* stanar; privremeni
    posednik; okupator.
occupation *n* zanimanje, struka, zvanje;
    privremeno korišćenje.
occupy *v* zaposesti, zauzeti, okupirati;
    uzeti pod zakup.
occur *v* javljati se, događati se; pasti na
    pamet.
occurrence *n* slučaj, događaj, zgoda; sedište.
ocean *n* okean; mnoštvo.
oceanic *a* okeanski.
ochre *n* oker (boja).

octave *n* oktava (*muz*).
October *n* oktobar.
octopus *n* hobotnica.
odd *a* neparan; neodređen (broj); suvišan, preostao; čudan, neobičan; slučajan; **~ly** *adv* čudnovato, neobično.
oddity *n* neobičnost; nastranost; osobenjak; čudan slučaj.
oddness *n* nejednakost, neparnost; čudnovatost.
odds *npl* nejednakost, nadmoć, razlika.
odious *a* mrzak, odvratan, gadan.
odorous *a* mirišljav.
odour *n* miris, zadah; slava, ugled.
of *prep* označava pripadnost licu ili predmetu; označava: autorstvo, deo celine, materijal od koga je nešto napravljeno, razlog.
of course! *interj* naravno!.
off *a* slobodan (vreme, sati); udaljen; nerodan (letina); mrtav (sezona); bočni (strana).
offence *n* uvreda, vređanje; napad, ofanziva.
offend *v* vređati, uvrediti, ljutiti; ogrešiti se o zakon, praviti neprilike.
offender *n* uvreditelj; prekršitelj, zločinac.
offensive *a* uvredljiv; neprijatan, odvratan (miris); napadački; **~ly** *adv* uvredljivo; odvratno.
offer *v* nuditi, predlagati; pokušavati; pružiti (otpor).
offering *n* ponuda; dar; žrtva.
offhand *a* nepripremljen, improvizovan; neusiljen; *adv* nepripremljeno, improvizovano; neučtivo.
office *n* dužnost, položaj; zadatak (funkcija); usluga; ured.
office hours *npl* radno vreme.
office worker *n* kancelarijski radnik.
officer *n* oficir; činovnik.
official *a* zvaničan, državni, služben; **~ly** *adv* službeno; *n* činovnik, funkcioner.
officiate *v* vršiti dužnost; služiti misu.
officious *a* preterano uslužan, nametljiv; neobavezan; **~ly** *adv* nametljivo, preterano uslužno.
off-line *a/adv* vanlinijski, vanlinijsko.
off-season *a/adv* vansezonski, vansezonsko.
offset *v* nadoknaditi; izvršiti obračun.

offshoot *n* izdanak, mladica; grananje; bekstvo.
offshore *a* priobalni; spoljni.
offside *a* ofsajd.
offspring *n* potomstvo, potomak; plod (nečega).
offstage *adv* zakulisni, potajni; u privatnom životu.
ogle *v* zaljubljeno gledati.
oil *n* ulje; nafta, petrolej; uljane boje.
oilcan *n* kantica za podmazivanje.
oilfield *n* polje nafte.
oil filter *n* filter za ulje.
oil painting *n* uljana slika.
oil slick *n* naftna mrlja.
oil tanker *n* tanker.
oil well *n* petrolejsko vrelo.
oily *a* uljan, mastan.
ointment *n* mast (*med*).
OK, okay *a* u redu.
old *a* star; starački; dugotrajan; iznošen.
old age *n* starost.
old-fashioned *a* staromodan; starinski.
olive *n* maslina; maslinasta boja.
olive oil *n* maslinovo ulje.
Olympic Games *n* Olimpijske igre.
omelette *n* omlet.
omen *n* znamenje, slutnja, predskazanje, znak.
ominous *a* koban, zloslutan, preteći.
omission *n* propust, izostavljanje, greška.
omit *v* propustiti, izostaviti; zanemariti.
omnipotence *n* svemogućnost.
omnipotent *a* svemoguć.
on *prep* na; pored; u; posle.
once *adv* jedanput; jednom; nekada; **at ~** odjednom **all at ~** svi odjednom; **~ more** još jednom.
oncoming *a* koji pridolazi, koji se bliži.
one *a* jedan; prvi; jedini; jedinstven; **~ by ~** jedan po jedan.
one-day excursion *n* jednodnevni izlet.
one-man *a* samostalan.
onerous *a* tegoban, težak.
oneself *pn* samog sebe, sam sebe.
one-sided *a* nejednak, nesimetričan; jednostran; pristrasan.
one-to-one *a* jedno s jednim; licem u lice.
ongoing *a* tekući, u toku.
onion *n* luk, glavica luka.

on-line *a/adv* linijski; na vezi (*komerc*).
onlooker *n* gledalac; svedok; posmatrač.
only *a* jedini, jedinstven; *adv* samo, isključivo, jedino.
onset *n* početak; juriš.
onslaught *n* snažan napad; juriš .
onus *n* teret, dužnost; odgovornost.
onward *adv* koji ide napred; napredan, progresivan.
ooze *v* lagano oticati; procuriti.
opaque *a* neprovidan; tup, glup.
open *a* otvoren; iskren; javan; pristupačan; ~ **ly** *adv* iskreno; *v* otvoriti (se), započeti; **to ~ up** učiniti pristupačnim, otkriti, obelodaniti.
opening *n* otvaranje; otvor, prolaz; početak.
open-minded *a* otvoren, iskren; bez predrasuda.
openness *n* otvorenost, iskrenost.
opera *n* opera.
opera house *n* opera (zgrada).
operate *v* delovati, raditi; operisati.
operation *n* delovanje, radnja; ishod; operacija.
operational *a* operativan; spreman za akciju.
operative *a* važeći; pogonski; operativan (*med*).
operator *n* hirurg; radnik koji rukuje strojem; kinooperator; telegrafista.
ophthalmic *a* očni.
opine *v* misliti, držati.
opinion *n* mišljenje, sud; javno mnjenje.
opinionated *a* samouveren, tvrdoglav.
opponent *n* protivnik, konkurent.
opportune *a* povoljan, pravovremen.
opportunist *n* oportunist, prevrtljivac.
opportunity *n* zgoda, povoljna prilika.
oppose *v* usprotiviti se, suprotstaviti se, pobijati.
opposing *a* suprotan, protivan.
opposite *a* suprotan, oprečan; koji se nalazi sa suprotne strane; *adv* suprotno, nasuprot; *prep* nasuprot; *n* suprotnost, oprečnost.
opposition *n* protivljenje; opozicija; suprotnost; kontrast.
oppress *v* tlačiti, ugnjetavati; pritiskati.
oppression *n* ugnjetavanje, tlačenje; potištenost.

oppressive *a* koji tlači; okrutan.
oppressor *n* ugnjetač, tiranin.
optic (al) *a* optički.
optician *n* optičar.
optimist *n* optimista, čovek vedrog duha.
optimistic *a* optimistički.
optimum *a* najpovoljniji, optimalan.
option *n* izbor; pravo izbora, sloboda izbora.
optional *a* neobavezan, fakultativan.
opulent *a* imućan, bogat; raskošan, velelepan.
or *conj* ili.
oracle *n* proročanstvo; proricanje, predskazivanje.
oral *a* usmen; usni, stomatološki (*med*); ~**ly** *adv* usmeno.
orange *n* pomorandža; drvo pomorandže; narandžasta boja.
orator *n* govornik.
orbit *n* putanja; obrtaj, kruženje; očna šupljina.
orchard *n* voćnjak.
orchestra *n* orkestar; prostor za orkestar.
orchestral *a* orkestralni.
orchid *n* orhideja.
ordain *v* odrediti.
ordeal *n* teško iskušenje; božji sud.
order *n* red, doslednost; čistoća; poredak; ustav; *v* dovesti u red; narediti, propisati; poručiti.
orderly *a* uredan, čist; dobrog vladanja, učtiv; redovan.
ordinarily *adv* redovno, uobičajeno, obično.
ordinary *a* običan, uobičajen; svakidašnji; prosečan.
ordination *n* određivanje.
ordnance *n* teški topovi, artiljerija.
ore *n* kovina, ruda, metal.
organ *n* organ; oruđe; orgulje; novine.
organic *a* životni, organski.
organic farming *n* organska agrikultura.
organism *n* organizam.
organist *n* orguljaš.
organization *n* organizacija.
organize *v* urediti, prirediti, organizovati.
orgasm *n* orgazam.
orgy *n* pijanka, gozba, orgija.
oriental *a* orjentalni, istočnjački.
orifice *n* otvor; ušće; prolaz.

origin *n* poreklo; početak, izvor.
original *a* prvobitan; istinski, originalan; **~ly** *adv* poreklom; prvobitno; originalno.
originality *n* originalnost, izvornost.
originate *v* prouzrokovati, proizvesti; voditi poreklo, nastati.
ornament *n* ornament, ukras, šara; *v* ukrasiti, okititi.
ornamental *a* ukrasni, ornamentalan, dekorativan.
ornate *a* ukrašen, kićen; pun figura.
orphan *n* siroče, *a* sirotan, osirotio.
orphanage *n* sirotište.
orthodox *a* pravoveran, ortodoksan.
orthodoxy *n* pravovernost.
orthography *n* pravopis, ortografija.
orthopaedic *a* ortopedski.
Oscar *n* Oskar (filmska nagrada).
oscillate *v* oscilirati, njihati se; kolebati se.
osprey *n* vrsta orla.
ostensibly *adv* naoko, tobože.
ostentatious *a* razmetljiv, hvalisav.
osteopath *n* osteopata.
ostracize *v* prognati; bojkotovati.
ostrich *n* noj.
other *pn* drugi.
otherwise *adv* na drugi način; u drugim prilikama; ili pak, inače.
otter *n* vidra; vidrino krzno.
ouch *excl* au!.
ought *v* morati, trebati.
ounce *n* unca (mera za težinu=28,349 g); mrvica, zrnce; vrsta jaguara.
our, ours *pn* naš, naša, naše, naši.
ourselves *pn pl* mi sami, nas same, nama samima.
oust *v* istisnuti, izbaciti, izgurati.
out *adv* spolja; odsutan, izašao; procvao.
outboard *a* izvan palube, preko ivice broda; **~ motor** lagani motor pričvršćen na krmu čamca.
outbreak *n* nastup, eksplozija (gneva i sl.); izbijanje (bune).
outburst *n* nastup, provala; potok (suza).
outcast *n* izgnanik, prognanik.
outcome *n* posledica, ishod, rezultat; ispust, izlazni otvor.
outcry *n* uzvik, usklik; prigovor, protest.
outdated *a* staromodan, zastareo.

outdo *v* prevazići.
outdoor *a* koji je pod vedrim nebom; **~s** *adv* napolju, van kuće.
outer *a* spoljni, na ivici.
outer space *n* spoljni prostor.
outermost *a* krajnji spolja, ponajdalji.
outfit *n* oprema, pribor; ratna oprema.
outfitter *n* opremač; trgovac raznom opremom.
outgoing *a* koji izlazi, koji odlazi; otvoren.
outgrow *v* prerasti (nekoga, nešto); vremenom se osloboditi navika i sl.
outhouse *n* sporedna zgrada; nadgradnja, dogradnja.
outing *n* izlet van grada.
outlandish *a* prekomorski, inozeman; neobičan.
outlaw *n* čovek van zakona, begunac pred zakonom; *v* lišiti zakonske zaštite, proglasiti izvan zakona.
outlay *n* izdaci, troškovi; proračun.
outlet *n* izlaz, otvor; isticanje; trgovina.
outline *n* obris, kontura; nacrt, skica.
outlive *v* nadživeti (nekoga, nešto).
outlook *n* izgled; stanovište, gledište.
outlying *a* udaljen, dalek; spoljni.
outmoded *a* zastareo, staromodan.
outnumber *v* brojem nadmašiti.
out-of-date *a* zastareo, nesavremen.
outpatient *n* ambulantni pacijent.
outpost *n* predstraža.
output *n* proizvodnja, produkcija.
outrage *n* uvreda, pogrda; kršenje zakona ili nečijih prava; nasilje; *v* kršiti zakon; izvršiti nasilje; vređati.
outrageous *a* neobuzdan, preteran; uvredljiv, nečuven; **~ly** *adv* neobuzdano, uvredljivo, nečuveno.
outright *adv* potpuno, sasvim; jednom zauvek; otvoreno; *a* potpun, ceo.
outrun *v* prestići; pobeći od nekoga.
outset *n* polazna tačka, polazak; početak.
outshine *v* zamračiti, pomračiti; zaseniti.
outside *n* spoljna strana; spoljašnost; krajnost; *adv* spolja, napolju; *prep* izvan.
outsider *n* čovek sa strane, strano lice; nečlan; nestručna, neupućena osoba.
outsize *a* veličina manja ili veća od obične.

outskirts *npl* periferija grada, predgrađe; ivica šume.

outspoken *a* otvoren, prostodušan; izgovoren.

outstanding *a* koji se ističe; istaknut, glavni; nepodmiren (dug).

outstretch *v* rastegnuti, raširiti.

outstrip *v* prestići; nadmašiti.

outward *a* spoljašnji; vidljiv; **~ly** *adv* spolja, po spoljnom izgledu.

outweigh *v* pretegnuti, prevagnuti, biti teži.

outwit *v* nadmudriti nekog.

oval *n* jajolik oblik, oval; *a* jajolik, ovalan.

ovary *n* jajnik.

oven *n* peć.

ovenproof *a* vatrostalni.

over *prep* preko, nad, više od; **all~** sav, po celom telu, svuda; *a* gornji, viši, suvišan; **~ again** još jednom, ponovo; **~ and ~** više puta.

overall *a* opšti, sveukupni; *adv* opšte, generalno; **~s** *npl* široke radne pantalone.

overawe *v* ulivati strahopoštovanje.

overbalance *v* prevagnuti; poremetiti ravnotežu.

overbearing *a* zapovednički.

overboard *adv* preko ivice palube, u more (s broda).

overbook *v* prebukirati.

overcast *a* pokriven oblacima, oblačan.

overcharge *v* previše zaračunati; preopteretiti.

overcoat *n* kaput, ogrtač.

overcome *v* savladati, pobediti, nadjačati; obuzeti (osećanja).

overconfident *a* preterano samouveren.

overcrowded *a* prenatrpani, nagomilani.

overdo *v* preterati; preuveličavati.

overdose *n* prevelika doza (leka).

overdraft *n* prekoračenje bankovnog računa.

overdrawn *a* preterano.

overdress *v* previše se kititi (oblačiti).

overdue *a* zakasneo; kome je rok prošao.

overeat *v* prejesti se.

overestimate *v* preceniti.

overflow *v* prelivati se preko ivice, izlivati se; plaviti (reka); bujati; *n* poplava, prelivanje preko ivice.

overgrown *a* obrastao, zarastao; izrastao.

overgrowth *n* prebujan; zarastao u korov.

overhang *v* visiti nad, viriti.

overhaul *v* pažljivo pretražiti, pregledati; dostići, prestići.

overhead *adv* nad glavom, gore, odozgo.

overhear *v* prisluškivati, slučajno čuti.

overjoyed *a* presrećan, oduševljen, zanesen.

overkill *n* preteranost, prekomernost.

overland *a/adv* kopneni, preko kopna, kopnom.

overlap *v* delimično se preklapati, nalegati.

overleaf *adv* na drugoj strani (list u knjizi).

overload *v* pretovariti, preopteretiti.

overlook *v* imati (pružati) vidik na; dizati se nad; gledati odozgo; nadzirati.

overnight *adv* sinoć, noćas; *a* sinoćni, noćni.

overpass *n* preći preko; pregledati.

overpower *v* savladati, potisnuti, nadvladati.

overpowering *a* neodoljiv; tegoban.

overrate *v* preceniti.

override *v* preći preko, pregaziti (konjem); gaziti nogama.

overriding *a* glavni, najvažniji; bahat.

overrule *v* gospodariti; pobediti nekoga; odbiti (predlog).

overrun *v* preliti se; širiti se (preko granica); plaviti.

overseas *adv* preko mora; *a* prekomorski, inostrani.

oversee *v* nadgledati, nadzirati.

overseer *n* nadzornik.

overshadow *v* zaseniti, potamniti; zakloniti, zaštititi.

overshoot *v* prebaciti cilj; prevariti se u nameri.

oversight *n* propust, omaška; pregled, nadzor.

oversleep *v* uspavati se, predugo spavati.

overspill *n* višak.

overstate *v* preterivati.

overstep *v* prekoračiti.

overt *a* otvoren, javan, neskriven; **~ly** *adv* otvoreno, javno.

overtake *v* sustići, dostići; zateći, iznenaditi.

overthrow *v* oboriti, srušiti; pobediti; uništiti; *n* obaranje, pad; propast.

overtime *n* prekovremeni rad.

overtone *n* prizvuk.

overture *n* ponuda; pokušaj izmirenja; uvertira (*muz*).

overturn *v* prevrnuti (se); pasti; svrgnuti, oboriti.

overweight *a* preterano težak.

overwhelm *v* poplaviti, preplaviti, obasuti; ovladati.

overwhelming *a* bezbrojan; neodoljiv; nadmoćan.

overwork *v* preopteretiti radom, premarati se; zamarati.

owe *v* dugovati nekome; biti obavezan nekome.

owing *a* dužan, koji se još duguje; **~ to** zahvaljujući, usled, zbog.

owl *n* buljina (sova).

own *a* vlastiti; rođeni (deca, brat i sl.); **my ~** moj lični; *v* imati, posedovati; priznati (za svoje); **to ~ up** otvoreno priznati, ispovediti; odobravati.

owner *n* posednik; vlasnik.

ownership *n* posedovanje, vlasništvo.

ox *n* bik, vo, govedo; **~en** *pl* bikovi, volovi, goveda.

oxidize *v* oksidirati.

oxygen *n* kiseonik.

oxygen mask *n* maska za kiseonik.

oxygen tent *n* tanki, providni šator oko kreveta bolesnika koji mu obezbeđuje kiseonik.

oyster *n* ostriga.

ozone *n* ozon.

P

pa *n* tata, ćale.
pace *n* korak; *v* koračati, hodati.
pacific *a* miroljubiv, smiren; **P~ Ocean**
Tihi okean.
pacification *n* smirivanje, zavođenje mira.
pacify *v* umiriti, smiriti.
pack *n* paket, svežanj; *v* zaviti; pakovati.
package *n* zavežljaj; koleto; ambalaža.
package tour *n* organizovano putovanje.
packet *n* paketić, zamotuljak.
packing *n* pakovanje.
pact *n* ugovor, pakt.
pad *n* jastuk; jahaći konj; šapa.
padding *n* punjenje; postava; bujica reči.
paddle *n* kratko veslo; veslanje; *v* veslati
jednim veslom.
paddle steamer *n* brod lopatar.
paddling pool *n* bazen za decu.
paddock *n* padok; konjušnica; polje.
paddy field *n* pirinčano polje.
paediatrics *n* pedijatrija.
pagan *a* paganski, bezbožnički.
page *n* stranica knjige; paž; *v* označiti
strane brojevima.
pageant *n* inscenacija; maskarada;
parada.
pageantry *n* velelepnost, raskoš;
prividnost.
pail *n* vedro; vrh pramca.
pain *n* bol; nesreća; kazna; *v* naneti bol.
pained *a* pun bola; žalostan, uvređen.
painful *a* bolan; težak.
painkiller *n* analgetik.
painless *a* bezbolan.
painstaking *a* radan, neumoran.
paint *n* boja; šminka; *v* bojiti.
paintbrush *n* kist za bojenje.
painter *n* slikar; moler.
painting *n* slika, slikanje, slikarstvo;
bojenje.
pair *n* par, dvoje.
pal *n* drugar, prijatelj; saučesnik.
palatable *a* ukusan; tečan.
palate *n* nepce; ukus.
palatial *a* kao dvorac; veličanstven,
raskošan.
palaver *n* razgovor; brbljanje; laskanje.

pale[1] *a* bled; bez sjaja; *v* bledeti; ubledeti.
pale[2] *n* kolac; granica.
palette *n* paleta.
paling *n* kolje.
pall[1] *n* mrtvački pokrov; veo.
pall[2] *v* pokriti; zamarati.
palliative *a* koji pokriva; *n* polumera.
pallid *a* samrtnički bled; uveo.
pallor *n* bledilo.
palm[1] *n* dlan, šaka; *v* dirati; rukovati se.
palm[2] *n* palma (*bot*).
palmistry *n* hiromantija.
palpable *a* opipljiv; očigledan.
palpitation *n* treperenje.
paltry *a* beznačajan; bedan.
pamper *v* maziti.
pamphlet *n* letak; brošura.
pan *n* tiganj; šerpa.
panache *n* perjanica.
pancake *n* palačinka.
pandemonium *n* pakao.
pane *n* prozorsko staklo; umetak oplate na
prozoru.
panel *n* drvena oplata; pano; porota (*jur*).
panelling *n* panoi; oblaganje panoima.
pang *n* oštar bol; griža savesti.
panic *n* panika; strah; *v* izazvati
paniku.
panicky *a* paničan.
panic-stricken *a* obuzet strahom.
pansy *n* maćuhica (*bot*).
pant *n* teško disanje; dahtanje; *v* teško
disati; dahtati.
panther *n* panter (*zool*).
panties *n* gaćice.
pantry *n* ostava.
papacy *n* papinstvo.
papal *a* papinski.
papaw, papaya *n* papaja (*bot*).
paper *n* hartija; novine; dokumenti;
novčanice.
paperback *n* broširana knjiga.
paper bag *n* papirna kesa.
paperclip *n* spajalica.
paperweight *n* pritiskivač za hartiju.
paperwork *n* administracija; uredski
posao.

paprika *n* paprika.
par *n* jednakost; nominalna vrednost; redovna količina.
parable *n* parabola.
parachute *n* padobran; *v* spustiti se padobranom.
parade *n* parada; paradiranje; *v* ići u stroju; isticati.
paradise *n* raj.
paradox *n* paradoks.
paradoxical *a* paradoksalan, protivrečan, čudnovat.
paraffin *n* parafin.
paragliding *n* paraglajding.
paragon *n* uzor; primer (savršenstva).
paragraph *n* paragraf; kratak članak; pasus.
parallel *a* uporedan; jednak; *n* paralela; *v* učiniti paralelnim.
paralyse *v* paralizovati.
paralysis *n* paraliza.
paralytic *a* paralizovan.
paramedic *n* pomoćno medicinsko osoblje.
paramount *a* vrhovni, najviši.
paranoid *a* paranoičan.
paraphernalia *n* nakit; oprema.
parasite *n* parazit; gotovan; eksploatator.
parasol *n* suncobran.
paratrooper *n* padobranac.
parcel *n* paket; pošiljka; komad zemlje.
parch *v* sušiti; isprzžiti.
parched *a* osušen.
parchment *n* pergament.
pardon *n* izvinjenje; pomilovanje; *v* oprostiti, izviniti.
parent *n* roditelji; otac, majka.
parentage *n* poreklo; srodstvo.
parental *a* roditeljski; iskonski.
parenthesis *n* umetnuta reč; zagrade; međuvreme.
parish *n* parohija; okrug; parohljani.
parishioner *n* parohljanin.
parity *n* jednakost.
park *n* park; *v* zasađivati park.
parking *n* parkiranje.
parking meter *n* sat za parkiranje.
parking ticket *n* karta za parkiranje.
parlance *n* način govora.
parliament *n* parlament, skupština.
parliamentary *a* skupštinski, ustavni; učtiv.

parlour *n* salon; soba za razgovor.
parody *n* parodija; *v* parodirati.
parole *n* časna reč, obećanje; lozinka.
parricide *n* oceubica; izdajnik domovine.
parrot *n* papagaj.
parry *v* odbiti udarac.
parsley *n* peršun.
parsnip *n* pastrnak (*bot*).
part *n* deo; organ (*med*); deo u knjizi; uloga; *v* deliti (se), razići (se); otputovati; **to ~ with** rastati se.
partially *a* delimičan; pristrasan; *adv* delimično.
participant *n* učesnik.
participate *v* sudelovati, učestvovati.
participation *n* učešće, sudelovanje.
participle *n* particip.
particle *n* trun; partikula.
particular *a* poseban; određen; *n* pojedinost, detalj.
parting *n* rastanak; smrt; opraštanje; račvanje.
partisan *n* partizan.
partition *n* deljenje; pregrada; *v* deliti; pregrađivati.
partner *n* partner.
partnership *n* učešće, sudelovanje; zajednica.
partridge *n* jarebica.
party *n* stranka, partija; priredba.
pass *v* proći; propuštati; *n* prolaz; propusnica; **to ~ away** umreti; nestati; **to ~ by** prolaziti pored; **to ~ on** preći na nešto.
passable *a* prolazan, prohodan.
passage *n* prolaz; putovanje; hodnik.
passbook *n* štedna knjižica.
passenger *n* putnik.
passer-by *n* prolaznik.
passing *a* prelažeju.
passion *n* strast; ljubav; srdžba.
passionate *a* strastan; zaljubljen; naprasit; **~ ly** *adv* strasno.
passive *a* bezvoljan; pokoran.
passkey *n* kalauz.
Passover *n* Pasha.
passport *n* pasoš.
passport control *n* kontrola pasoša
password *n* lozinka.
past *a* prošli, protekli; bivši; *adv* mimo; *n* prošlost; *prep* preko, izvan, posle.

pasta *n* pasta.
paste *n* testo; kaša; lepak; *v* zalepiti, nalepiti.
pasteurized *a* pasterizovati.
pastime *n* zabava; razonoda.
pastor *n* pastor.
pastoral *a* seoski; pastoralan; *n* idila, pastorala.
pastry *n* poslastice, kolači.
pasture *n* pašnjak, ispaša.
pasty *a* testast; podnaduo, bled.
pat *v* ovlaš udarati; pogladiti; cupkati.
patch *n* zakrpa; flaster; krpica; *v* krpiti.
patchwork *n* pokrivač; krpež.
patent *a* patentiran; javan, povlašćen; *v* povlastiti; patentirati.
patent leather *n* lakirana koža.
patentee *n* vlasnik patenta.
paternal *a* očinski.
paternity *n* očinstvo.
path *n* staza; put; način vladanja.
pathetic *a* jadan; dirljiv; ~ally *adv* jadno; dirljivo.
pathological *a* patološki.
pathology *n* patologija.
pathway *n* staza, puteljak; mostić.
patience *n* strpljenje; istrajnost; pasijans.
patient *a* strpljiv, istrajan; *adv* strpljivo; *n* pacijent.
patio *n* dvorište.
patriarch *n* patrijarh.
patriot *n* patriota, rodoljub.
patriotic *a* rodoljubiv.
patriotism *n* patriotizam, rodoljublje.
patrol *n* patrola, izvidnica, straža; *v* patrolirati, izviđati.
patrol car *n* patrolna kola.
patrolman *n* policajac koji patrolira.
patron *n* patron, gospodar; zaštitnik; svetac.
patronage *n* pokroviteljstvo, zaštita; finansijska podrška.
patronize *v* štititi, braniti; pomagati.
patter[1] *n* dobovanje kišnih kapi; trupkanje; *v* dobovati, trupkati; brzo govoriti.
patter[2] *n* žargon, šatrovački jezik.
pattern *n* uzor; obrazac; kroj; crtež.
paunch *n* trbuh, želudac.
pauper *n* siromah, prosjak.
pause *n* pauza, prekid; oklevanje; *v* zastati; oklevati.

pave *v* patosati, popločati, asfaltirati.
pavement *n* pločnik; kolnik; kaldrma, asfalt.
pavilion *n* paviljon.
paving stone *n* kamen za popločavanje.
paw *n* šapa, ruka (*sleng*); *v* grepsti, udarati šapom.
pawn *n* pion; *v* založiti.
pawnbroker *n* vlasnik zalagaonice; lihvar.
pawnshop *n* zalagaonica.
pay *v* platiti; isplatiti; ispaštati; **to ~ back** vratiti novac; **to ~ for** platiti; okajati; **to ~ off** isplatiti; *n* plata; uplata; nagrada.
payable *a* dospeo za plaćanje.
payday *n* dan isplate.
pay envelope *n* platna koverta.
payee *n* primalac novca.
paymaster *n* blagajnik.
payment *n* uplata, plaćanje.
payphone *n* govornica.
payroll *n* platni spisak.
pea *n* grašak.
peace *n* mir, tišina.
peaceful *a* miran, tih.
peach *n* breskva.
peacock *n* paun.
peak *n* šiljak, vrh.
peak period *n* špic u saobraćaju.
peal *n* zvonjava; tutnjava; udar groma.
peanut *n* kikiriki.
pear *n* kruška.
pearl *n* biser; sedef; kap rose.
peasant *n* seljak.
peat *n* treset.
pebble *n* oblutak; vrsta gorskog kristala.
peck *n* kljucaj; *v* kljucati; probiti.
peculiar *a* neobičan, čudan, osoben; ~ly *adv* neobično, osobeno.
peculiarity *n* neobičnost, osobenost.
pedal *n* pedala; *v* okretati pedale; terati bicikl.
pedant *n* pedant; cepidlaka.
pedantic *a* pedantan.
pedestal *n* pijedestal.
pedestrian *n* pešak; *a* pešački.
pedestrian crossing *n* pešački prelaz.
pedigree *n* rodoslov; poreklo.
pedlar, peddler (*amer*) *n* torbar, prodavac; **drug peddler** trgovac drogom.

peek *v* viriti, provirivati.

peel *v* oguliti (se), oljuštiti (se); *n* ljuska, kora, koža.

peer *n* onaj koji je nekome ravan po položaju; per, lord.

peerless *a* bez premca.

peeved *a* ljut, svadljiv, razdražen.

peevish *a* zao; svadljiv, čangrizav.

peg *n* kočić; klin; kuka; *v* zabosti kočić.

pelican *n* pelikan (*zool*).

pellet *n* kuglica; tableta.

pelt[1] *n* jak udarac, pogodak; *v* gađati; pljuštati.

pelt[2] *n* krzno, koža s krznom.

pen *n* pero; pisaći pribor; tor.

penal *a* penal.

penalty *n* kazna.

penance *n* pokora.

pence/*pl* od **penny** *n* novčana jedinica.

pencil *n* olovka, pisaljka.

pencil case *n* pernica.

pendant *n* privezak.

pending *a* neodređen, nedovršen; viseći; nerešen.

pendulum *n* klatno; neodlučan čovek.

penetrate *v* prodreti, ući.

penguin *n* pingvin.

penicillin *n* penicilin.

peninsula *n* poluostrvo.

penis *n* penis.

penitence *n* kajanje, pokajanje.

penitent *a* pokajnički.

penknife *n* perorez.

pennant *n* zastavica, banderola.

penniless *a* siromašan.

penny *n* peni (novčana jedinica).

penpal *n* nepoznata osoba s kojom se dopisuje.

pension *n* penzija; *v* dodeliti penziju.

pensive *a* zamišljen, ozbiljan; ~**ly** *adv* zamišljeno.

Pentagon *n* Pentagon.

penthouse *n* nastrešnica; šupa; stan na zadnjem spratu.

pent-up *a* skriven, uzdržljiv.

penultimate *a* predzadnji.

penury *n* nemaština, oskudica.

people *n* narod, nacija; ljudi; *v* naseljavati.

pep *n* energija, polet; **to ~ up** obodriti.

pepper *n* biber; plahovitost; *v* zabiberiti.

peppermint *n* menta; bonbone od mente.

per *prep* po, preko, putem.

per annum *adv*, *a* godišnje.

perceive *v* opaziti, opažati; razumeti.

percentage *n* procenat.

perception *n* opažanje, percepcija.

perch *n* prečka.

perchance *a* možda; slučajno.

percolate *v* procediti, prečistiti.

percolator *n* cediljka, filter; aparat za filter kafu.

percussion *n* sudar, potres.

perdition *n* propast.

peremptory *a* koji ne trpi prigovor; zapovednički.

perennial *a* višegodišnji; trajan, večit.

perfect *a* završen, potpun; savršen; ~**ly** *adv* savršeno; *v* usavršiti, okončati.

perfection *n* savršenstvo; usavršavanje; vrlina.

perforate *v* probiti, probušiti.

perforated *a* probijen, probušen.

perforation *n* bušenje, probijanje.

perform *v* prikazivati, glumiti; ispuniti (obećanje).

performance *n* izvođenje; delo, čin; predstava.

performer *n* izvođač.

perfume *n* miris; parfem.

perhaps *a* možda, moguće.

peril *n* opasnost, odgovornost.

perilous *a* opasan; ~**ly** *adv* opasno.

period *n* period, razdoblje; ciklus.

periodic *a* periodičan; cikličan; ~**ally** *adv* period ično, pokatkad..

periodical *n* časopis (mesečnik).

peripheral *a* periferno; *n* periferan.

perish *v* ginuti, umirati.

perishable *a* trošan, neotporan; lako kvarljiv.

perjure *v* krivo se zakleti.

perjury *n* krivokletstvo.

perk *n* ekstra.

perky *a* veseo, živahan.

permanent *a* stalan; nepromenljiv; ~**ly** *a* stalno.

permeate *v* probiti se, prodreti; širiti se.

permissible *a* dopustiv.

permission *n* dozvola, dopuštenje.

permissive *a* popustljiv; dopušten, slobodan.

permit *v* dopustiti, dozvoliti; podnositi; *n* dozvola.

permutation *n* permutacija; zamena.
perpendicular *a* okomit, vertikalan; **~ly** *adv* okomito; *n* okomitost, lenjir, uglomer.
perpetrate *v* izvršiti (zločin), počiniti (zločin).
perpetual *a* večit, stalan; doživotan; **~ly** *adv* večno; beskonačno; doživotno.
perpetuate *v* ovekovečiti.
perplex *v* zaprepastiti, zapanjiti; uneti zabunu.
persecute *v* progoniti, dosađivati.
persecution *n* gonjenje, proganjanje.
perseverance *n* istrajnost, upornost; trpeljivost.
persevere *v* istrajati, nastojati; ne odustajati.
persist *v* istrajati; odoleti, odupreti se.
persistence *n* istrajnost, upornost; izdržljivost; doslednost.
persistent *a* uporan, istrajan; otporan; dosledan.
person *n* čovek, ličnost.
personable *a* lep, naočit.
personage *n* ugledna ličnost.
personal *a* lični; privatni; **~ly** *adv* lično; privatno.
personal assistant *n* sekretar/ica.
personal column *n* lični oglasi.
personality *n* ličnost; lično obeležje; osoba.
personification *n* personifikacija, utelovljenje.
personify *v* predstavljati, oličavati, personificirati.
personnel *n* osoblje, personal.
perspective *n* perspektiva; vidik, izgled.
perspiration *n* znoj, isparavanje, znojenje.
perspire *v* znojiti se.
persuade *v* uveriti, ubediti; nagovoriti.
persuasion *n* nagovaranje, ubeđivanje; ubedljivost; veroispovest.
persuasive *a* ubedljiv; **~ly** *adv* ubedljivo.
pert *a* drzak; otresit, preduzimljiv.
pertain *v* odnositi se; imati vezu.
pertinent *a* podesan, prikladan; **~ly** *adv* podesno.
pertness *n* drskost, smelost, preduzetnost.
perturb *v* uznemiriti, zbuniti; poremetiti.
perusal *n* čitanje; proučavanje.
peruse *v* čitati; pregledati, ispitati.

pervade *v* napuniti, natopiti, prodirati, širiti se.
perverse *a* pokvaren, izopačen, ćudljiv; **~ly** *adv* izopačeno.
pervert *v* kvariti; izopačivati, zloupotrebiti.
pessimist *n* pesimist.
pest *n* kuga, pomor; zlo, beda; gamad.
pester *v* dosađivati, uznemiravati.
pestilence *n* kuga; epidemija; otrov.
pet *n* kućni ljubimac; razmaženo dete, maza; *v* maziti, razmaziti.
petal *n* latica.
petite *a* zgodna ženica.
petition *n* peticija, zahtev; molitva; *v* moliti, zahtevati.
petrified *a* skamenjen.
petrol *n* benzin.
petroleum *n* nafta.
petticoat *n* donja suknja; žena, devojka.
pettiness *n* sitnica, malenkost; sitničavost.
petty *a* neznatan, nevažan.
petty cash *n* priručna blagajna.
petty officer *n* podoficir.
petulant *a* razdražljiv, osetljiv.
pew *n* klupa, sedište u crkvi.
pewter *n* kalaj, posuda od kalaja.
phantom *n* avet, utvara; opsena, iluzija.
pharmaceutical *a* farmaceutski.
pharmacist *n* apotekar.
pharmacy *n* apoteka.
phase *n* faza, mena.
pheasant *n* fazan.
phenomenal *a* spoljni, pojavni; izvanredan.
phenomenon *n* fenomen, neobična pojava; prirodna pojava.
phial *n* fijola, cevčica, staklena bočica.
philanthropic *a* čovekoljubiv; dobrotvoran.
philanthropist *n* filantrop, dobrotvor.
philanthropy *n* čovekoljublje, filantropija.
philologist *n* filolog.
philology *n* filologija.
philosopher *n* filozof, mislilac.
philosophic *a* filozofski; mudar, razuman; **~ally** *adv* mudro.
philosophize *v* umovati, mudrovati; razmišljati.

philosophy *n* filozofija; **natural ~** prirodna nauka.
phlegm *n* sluz; ravnodušnost, hladnokrvnost.
phlegmatic *a* sluzav; ravnodušan, hladnokrvan.
phobia *n* fobija.
phone *n* telefon; *v* telefonirati; **to ~ back** odgovoriti na poziv; **to ~ up** nazvati nekog telefonom.
phone book *n* telefonski imenik.
phone box *n* telefonska govornica.
phone call *n* telefonski poziv.
phosphorus *n* fosfor.
photocopier *n* fotokopir aparat.
photocopy *n* fotokopija.
photograph *n* fotografija; *v* fotografisati.
photographer *n* fotograf.
photographic *a* fotografski.
photography *n* fotografija; fotografisanje.
phrase *n* rečenica, izraz; stil; fraza.
phrase book *n* zbirka izraza.
physical *a* telesan, fizički; **~ly** *adv* telesno.
physical education *n* telesno vaspitanje.
physician *n* lekar.
physicist *n* fizičar.
physiologist *n* fiziolog.
physiology *n* fiziologija.
physiotherapy *n* fizioterapija.
physique *n* telesna građa, spoljašnost.
pianist *n* pijanista, klavirista.
piano *n* klavir.
piccolo *n* pikolo (*muz*).
pick[1] *v* birati, odabrati; brati; bušiti; vaditi, kopati; **to ~ out** izvaditi, vaditi; očistiti; **to ~ up** raskopati; prihvatiti, primiti; povesti.
pick[2] *n* motika, pijuk; mrlja na knjizi.
pickaxe *n* pijuk.
picket *n* kolac; drvena ograda; patrolni brod.
pickle *n* turšija; marinada; kiseli krastavci; *v* usoliti, marinirati.
pickpocket *n* džeparoš.
pick-up *n* pikap (auto).
picnic *n* izlet.
pictorial *a* slikarski; slikovit.
picture *n* slika, crtež; *v* slikati, naslikati.
picture book *n* slikovnica.
picturesque *a* slikovit.

pie *n* pita.
piece *n* komad, deo; uzorak; *v* sastaviti, vezati.
piecemeal *a* odvojen; pojedinačan; *adv* pojedinačno, postepeno.
pier *n* kamen, stub; molo, nasip.
pierce *v* probiti, prodreti, probušiti; proći.
piercing *a* prodoran, oštar.
piety *n* pobožnost, ljubav, poštovanje.
pig *n* prase, svinja.
pigeon *n* golub, **carrier** or **homing ~** golub pismonoša.
pigeonhole *n* otvor na golubarniku, pregrada u pisaćem stolu.
piggy bank *n* kasica prasica.
pigheaded *a* uporan, tvrdoglav.
pigsty *n* svinjac, prljava neuredna osoba.
pigtail *n* pletenica, perčin.
pike *n* koplje, ražanj; štuka.
pile *n* kolac, balvan; gomila; vuna; *v* gomilati, zgrtati; pretovariti.
pile-up *n* višestruki sudar automobila.
pilfer *v* ukrasti, potkradati.
pilgrim *n* hodočasnik.
pilgrimage *n* hodočašće; dugo putovanje.
pill *n* pilula; lopta.
pillage *v* pljačka, grabež.
pillar *n* stub.
pillion *n* sedište za putnika, zadnje sedište na motoru.
pillow *n* jastuk.
pillowcase *n* jastučnica.
pilot *n* kormilar, sprovodnik brodova; pilot; *v* pilotirati, upravljati.
pimp *n* svodnik.
pimple *n* bubuljica.
pin *n* čioda, ukosnica; **~s and needles** trnci; *v* pribosti, probiti.
pinafore *n* kecelja.
pinball *n* fliper.
pincers *n* klješta, pinceta.
pinch *v* štipati, uštinuti; gnječiti; *n* štipanje, stiskanje.
pincushion *n* jastučić za igle.
pine[1] *n* bor, borovina.
pine[2] *v* venuti, čeznuti; tugovati.
pineapple *n* ananas; ručna granata, bomba.
ping *n* zvižduk metka.
pink *n* karanfil; ružičasta boja.
pinnacle *n* vrh brda; mali toranj.

pinpoint *v* tačno odrediti položaj.
pint *n* pinta.
pioneer *n* pionir, prvi naseljenik.
pious *a* pobožan; nežan; ~ly *adv* pobožno.
pipe *n* cevovod, cev; frula; lula.
pipe dream *n* puka želja.
pipeline *n* cevovod.
piper *n* svirač.
piping *a* sviranje, zviždanje.
pique *n* gnev, ljutina, neraspoloženje.
piracy *n* piraterija.
pirate *n* pirat, gusar; gusarski brod.
piss *n* mokrenje.
pistol *n* pištolj.
piston *n* pokretni klip.
pit *n* jama, rupa; pećina; klopka (*fig*).
pitch[1] *n* visina (tona), nivo, stepen;
pitch[2] *v* zaliti katronom; zabosti; podići; posaditi.
pitch[3] *v* utaboriti se, smestiti se.
pitch-black *a* crn kao ugalj; taman kao u rogu.
pitcher *n* vrč, pehar.
pitchfork *n* vile.
pitfall *n* zamka, klopka.
pithy *a* jedar; jezgrovit.
pitiable *a* jadan, bedan.
pitiful *a* milostiv; jadan; ~ly *adv* jadno, beznačajno.
pittance *n* bedan prihod, skromna plata.
pity *n* milosrđe, samilost; *v* sažaljevati, žaliti.
pivot *n* klip; središte.
pizza *n* pica.
placard *n* oglas, plakat.
placate *v* umiriti, smiriti.
place *n* mesto; sedište; kuća; *v* smestiti, staviti; namestiti.
placid *a* miran, spokojan; ~ly *adv* mirno, tiho.
plagiarism *n* plagijat.
plague *n* kuga, pomor; beda; *v* zaraziti, okužiti.
plaice *n* iverak.
plaid *n* pokrivač; karirana vunena tkanina.
plain *a* jasan, očigledan; iskren; običan, jednostavan; ~ly *adv* obično, očigledno; *n* ravnica, ravan.
plaintiff *n* tužitelj, tužilac.
plait *n* bora, nabor; pletenica; *v* nabirati, plesti.

plan *n* nacrt, plan; zamisao; *v* projektovati.
plane *n* ravnica, ravan; avion; platan; *v* poravnati, strugati.
planet *n* planeta.
planetary *a* planetni; zemaljski.
plank *n* daska.
planner *n* planer.
planning *n* planiranje.
plant *n* biljka; sadnica; varka; *v* saditi.
plantation *n* plantaža.
plaque *n* kopča.
plaster *n* flaster; kreč, gips; *v* okrečiti; štukaturiti; staviti flaster.
plastered *a* pijan (*sleng*).
plasterer *n* zidar, fasader.
plastic *a* plastika.
plastic surgery *n* plastična hirurgija.
plate *n* metalna ploča; fotografska ploča; *v* prevući metalom.
plate glass *n* debelo staklo.
plateau *n* visoravan, plato.
platform *n* platforma, terasa; podijum.
platinum *n* platina.
platitude *n* plitkoća (duha).
platoon *n* vod.
platter *n* plitka zdela.
plaudit *n* pljeskanje, aplauz.
plausible *a* moguć, verovatan.
play *n* igra; pozorišni komad; šala; *v* igrati; odigrati; **to ~ down** prevariti, nasamariti.
playboy *n* plejboj.
player *n* igrač; glumac.
playful *a* nestašan, razigran, šaljiv; ~ly *adv* nestašno, šaljivo.
playground *n* igralište.
playmate *n* drug u igri .
play-off *n* majstorica, finalna utakmica.
playpen *n* ogradica (za decu).
plaything *n* igračka.
playwright *n* pisac pozorišnih komada, dramaturg.
plea *n* opravdanje, izgovor; dokaz; molba.
plead *v* podneti molbu; zastupati.
pleasant *a* prijatan, ugodan; mio, ljubak; ~ly prijatno, milo.
please *v* dopadati se; ugoditi, zadovoljiti (nekog).
pleased *a* zadovoljan, veseo.
pleasing *a* ugodan, prijatan.

pleasure *n* zadovoljstvo, uživanje.
pleat *n* nabor.
pledge *n* zalog; jamstvo; zdravica; *v* založiti; obećati; jamčiti.
plentiful *a* obilan; bogat nečim.
plenty *n* obilje, izobilje, mnoštvo.
plethora *n* punokrvnost; preobilje (*fig*).
pleurisy *n* zapaljenje plućne maramice.
pliable, pliant *a* savitljiv, mek; popustljiv.
pliers *n* mala klješta.
plight *n* loše stanje; obećanje; zaruke.
plinth *n* podnožje (osnova) stuba, ploča, stopa.
plod *v* raditi s naporom; rintati; klipsati.
plot *n* zaplet, fabula; zavera; zemljište; *v* zamišljati, intrigirati; kovati zaveru; skicirati.
plough (*br*), **plow** (*amer*) *n* plug; oranica; *v* orati; brazdati; seći; **to ~ through** s mukom se probijati.
ploy *n* manevar, varka; posao.
pluck *v* kidati, otrgnuti, brati; očistiti, operušati; *n* hrabrost; iznutrica, drob; trzanje.
plucky *a* hrabar, odvažan.
plug *n* čep, zapušač; utikač; kljuse; *v* začepiti, zapušiti; pucati.
plum *n* šljiva; suvo grožđe; tamnoljubičasta boja.
plum tree *n* šljivino drvo.
plumage *n* perje (na ptici).
plumb *n* komadić olova; libela; *adv* okomito, uspravno; *v* lemiti; staviti uspravno.
plumber *n* vodoinstalater, limar.
plume *n* pero, perjanica.
plump *a* debeo, zdepast.
plunder *v* pljačkati, harati; *n* pljačkanje; plen.
plunge *v* zamočiti (se); zagnjuriti (se), roniti; zariti; *n* poniranje; ronjenje.
plunger *n* ronilac.
pluperfect *n* pluskvamperfekt (*gram*).
plural *a* pluralni; višebrojan.
plurality *n* množina; većina.
plus *n* znak plus; *prep* više, plus, i.
plush *a* pliš.
plutonium *n* plutonijum.
ply *v* rukovati, upotrebljavati, marljivo raditi; dosađivati, nuditi, nagovarati.

plywood *n* šperploča.
pneumatic *a* ispunjen vazduhom, pneumatski.
pneumatic drill *n* pneumatska bušilica.
pneumonia *n* upala pluća.
poach *v* poširati; kradom loviti; izrovati; zagnjuriti.
poacher *n* zverokradica.
pocket *n* džep; rupa; škrinja; *v* staviti u džep; ukrasti.
pocket money *n* sitniš.
pod *n* mahuna; čaura.
podgy *a* zdepast.
poem *n* poema, pesma.
poet *n* poeta, pesnik.
poetic *a* poetika.
poetry *n* poezija.
poignant *a* oštar; jedak; gorak.
point *n* tačka; mesto; oštrica; vrh igle; granica; **~ of view** gledište, stanovište; *v* skrenuti pažnju; ukazati; pokazati pravac; **to ~ a gun** uperiti pištolj.
point-blank *a* neposredan; otvoren.
pointed *a* šiljat, oštar; **~ly** *adv* šiljato, oštro.
pointer *n* strelica, skazaljka, putokaz; nagoveštaj.
pointless *a* lišen oštrine, neduhovit; besmislen.
poise *n* ravnoteža, stabilnost.
poison *n* otrov; *v* otrovati.
poisoning *n* trovanje.
poisonous *a* otrovan, smrtonosan; škodljiv.
poke *v* gurati, turati, bosti; razgrtati.
poker *n* žarač; poker.
poker-face *n* bezizražajno lice.
poky *a* zagušljiv; tesan; neodređen; trom, spor.
polar *a* polarni.
pole *n* pol (*geog*); elektroda; magnet.
police *n* policija.
police car *n* policijska kola, marica.
policeman *n* policajac.
police station *n* policijska stanica.
policewoman *n* žena policajac.
policy *n* politika; opreznost; polisa osiguranja.
polio *n* dečja paraliza.
polish *v* glačati, gladiti; ulepšati; **to ~ off** brzo obaviti; zaključiti posao; *n* sjaj, glatkoća, politura.

polished *a* politiran; doteran; sjajan.
polite *a* uglađen, otmen, učtiv; ~**ly** *adv* otmeno, učtivo.
politeness *n* učtivost, uljudnost.
politic *a* politički; razuman; lukav.
political *a* politički, javni; narodni.
political asylum *n* politički azil.
politician *n* političar; državnik.
politics *npl* politika, upravljanje, politička ubeđenja.
polka *n* polka; ~ **dot** vrsta materijala sa uzorkom.
poll *n* glasačka lista; glasanje; spisak birača.
pollen *n* polen.
pollute *v* zagaditi; uprljati.
polo *n* polo.
polution *n* oskvrnjenje; kaljanje, prljanje.
polyester *n* poliester.
polyethelene *n* polietilen.
polygamy *n* poligamija, mnogoženstvo.
polytechnic *n* politehnički.
pomegranate *n* šipak, nar.
pomp *n* svečanost, sjaj, raskoš.
pompom *n* mitraljez; ukrasna kićanka.
pompous *a* pompezan.
pond *n* veštačko jezero; ribnjak.
ponder *v* razmisliti, pažljivo proučiti.
ponderous *a* vrlo težak, glomazan; nezgrapan.
pontiff *n* papa, arhijerej, biskup.
pontoon *n* ponton; ploveći dok; keson.
pony *n* poni; 25 funti sterlinga; čašica vina.
ponytail *n* konjski rep (frizura).
pool *n* lokva, bara; jezerce; vir; bazen; *v* izmenjati (iskustvo, obaveštenja).
poor *a* siromašan; loš; nesrećan, jadan; jeftin, ~**ly** *adv* bolešljiv, slab; *n* **the** ~ sirotinja, siromasi; ~ **me** teško meni.
pop *n* oštar zvuk; pucanj; pega; penušavo piće; **to** ~ **in/out** svratiti na čas i odmah otići.
popcorn *n* kokice.
pope *n* papa.
poplar *n* jablan, topola.
poppy *n* mak; opijum; jarko crvena boja.
populace *n* narod, svetina, rulja.
popular *a* narodni; ~**ly** *adv* narodno, popularno.
popularity *n* popularnost; raširenost.
popularize *v* popularisati.

populate *v* naseliti, nastaniti.
population *n* stanovništvo.
populous *a* gusto naseljen.
porcelain *n* porcelan, posuđe od porcelana.
porch *n* trem, predvorje; ulaz.
pore *n* pora, rupica.
pork *n* svinjetina.
pornography *n* pornografija.
porous *a* porozan.
porridge *n* zobena kaša.
port[1] *n* luka, lučki grad.
port[2] *n* porto (slatko crno vino).
portable *a* koji se može nositi.
portal *n* glavni ulaz, portal; kapija.
porter *n* nosač; vratar.
portfolio *n* kožna torba; mapa za spise.
porthole *n* prozorčić na boku broda; vratnice; puškarnica.
portico *n* trem.
portion *n* deo, delić; obrok.
portly *a* solidan, krupan; naočit.
portrait *n* porodična slika, portret; prikaz, opis.
portray *v* portretisati, podražavati.
pose *n* poza, neprirodan položaj; *v* postaviti (pitanje); zauzeti stav.
posh *a* lep, zgodan, doteran *(sleng)*.
position *n* mesto, položaj; mišljenje; *v* lokalizovati; staviti.
positive *a* određen, jasan, siguran; samouveren; uporan; ~**ly** *adv* apsolutno, sigurno.
posse *n* policijski odred; mnoštvo, gomila.
possess *v* posedovati, imati u vlasti; naterati.
possession *n* posedovanje.
possessive *a* posednički; prisvojni.
possibility *n* mogućnost, verovatnoća.
possible *a* verovatan, moguć; podnošljiv.
possibly *adv* verovatno, moguće.
post *n* stub; greda; pošta; položaj; *v* lepiti oglase, poslati poštom.
postage *n* poštarina.
postage stamp *n* poštanska marka.
postcard *n* dopisnica.
postdate *v* postradati; dolaziti posle nečega.
poster *n* oglas, plakat.
poste restante *n* post restant.
posterior *n* zadnjica, stražnjica.

posterity *n* potomstvo, budući naraštaji.
posthumous *a* posmrtan; rođen posle
  očeve smrti.
postman *n* poštar.
postmark *n* poštanski žig.
postmaster *n* poštanski činovnik.
post office *n* pošta, poštanski ured.
postpone *v* odložiti, odgoditi.
postscript *n* postskriptum, dodatak
  potpisanom pismu.
posture *n* položaj tela; stanje stvari.
post-war *a* posleratni.
posy *n* kita cveća; natpis.
pot *n* lonac, ćup; pehar (nagrada);
  napitak; marihuana; *v* staviti u ćup;
  kuvati; saditi u saksiji.
potato *n* krompir.
potbellied *a* trbušast.
potent *a* moćan, uticajan; važan;
  potentan.
potential *a* potencijal, mogućnost.
pothole *n* rupa, jama, špilja.
potion *n* napitak; travarica.
potted *a* ukuvan, konzerviran.
potter *n* lončar, grnčar.
pottery *n* grnčarija.
potty *a* beznačajan, nevažan.
pouch *n* vrećica, torba, duvankesa;
  poštanska torba.
poultice *n* topao oblog.
poultry *n* živina.
pound *n* funta (453.59 g); funta sterlinga;
  tor; *v* stucati, usitniti.
pour *v* liti, izlivati; usuti.
pout *v* duriti se, napućiti usne.
poverty *n* siromaštvo, oskudica.
powder *n* prašak, prašina; puder;
  barut.
powder compact *n* puder u kamenu.
powdered milk *n* mleko u prahu.
powder puff *n* pufna za puder.
powdery *a* kao puder, kao prah; posut
  prahom, puderom.
power *n* snaga, energija; vlast, sila; *v*
  snabdeti (elek. ili meh. energijom).
power station *n* električna centrala.
powerful *a* snažan, jak, moćan; uticajan;
  ly *adv* moćno, snažno.
powerless *a* nemoćan, slab.
practicable *a* izvodljiv, realan; prolazan,
  prohodan.

practical *a* praktičan; ostvarljiv;
  upotrebljiv; **~ly** *adv* ustvari, praktično.
practicality *n* praktičnost.
practice *n* uvežbanost, praksa; praktičan
  rad; običaj; *pl* intrige, spletkarenje.
practise *v* baviti se nečim; primeniti,
  sprovesti u delo.
practitioner *n* iskusan lekar ili advokat,
  stručnjak.
pragmatic *a* pragmatičan, koristan, poučan.
prairie *n* prerija.
praise *n* pohvala, hvaljenje; *v* hvaliti;
  slaviti, veličati.
praiseworthy *a* pohvalan, vredan hvale.
prance *v* propinjati se (konj); šepuriti se,
  razmetati se.
prank *n* šaljivi ispad, nestašluk, podvala;
  skok.
prattle *v* tepati; brbljati; *n* tepanje;
  brbljanje.
prawn *n* kozica (morska).
pray *v* moliti se; moliti, preklinjati.
prayer *n* molitva; molba.
prayer book *n* molitvenik.
preach *v* propovedati.
preacher *n* propovednik.
preamble *n* predgovor, uvodni deo.
precarious *a* koji zavisi od slučaja;
  nesiguran, opasan; neosnovan; **~ly** *adv*
  nesigurno; slučajno.
precaution *n* obazrivost, smotrenost;
  upozorenje.
precautionary *a* obazriv, smotren,
  oprezan.
precede *v* prethoditi, nalaziti se pred
  nečim; imati prednost.
precedence *n* prethođenje; prednjačenje,
  starešinstvo.
precedent *n* presedan, slučaj koji se ranije
  dogodio, primer; *a* prethodni.
precinct *n* teren; okolina; predgrađe.
precious *a* skupocen; drag, omiljen; lep.
precipice *n* ponor, provalija.
precipitate *v* strmoglaviti, sunovratiti;
  požuriti; *a* nagao; nesmotren.
precise *a* tačan, određen; uredan;
  savestan; **~ly** *adv* tačno; uredno.
precision *n* tačnost, urednost, preciznost
preclude *v* odstraniti, ukloniti; odvratiti.
precocious *a* prerano sazreo, prevremen;
  napredan.

preconceive v zamisliti, stvoriti mišljenje.
preconception n predubeđenje, predrasuda; predviđanje.
precondition n preduslov.
precursor n preteča, prethodnik.
predator n grabljivac.
predecessor n prethodnik; predak.
predestination n usud, sudbina; predodređenost.
predicament n neprijatan položaj, smetnja, teškoća.
predict v proricati.
predictable a koji se može predvideti.
prediction n proricanje, predviđanje, proročanstvo.
predilection n sklonost, naklonost.
predominant a nadmoćan.
predominate v biti nadmoćan, gospodariti.
preen v čistiti perje kljunom, mitariti.
prefab n montažna kuća.
preface n predgovor, uvodni deo; uvod.
prefer v više voleti; unaprediti.
preferable a kome se daje prednost, koji se više ceni.
preferably adv radije, više, bolje.
preference n prednost; pravo prvenstva.
preferential a koji uživa prednost; unapređenje u službi.
preferment n pretpostavljanje; prednost; unapređenje.
prefix v napisati kao uvod; dodati prefiks.
pregnancy n trudnoća; plodnost.
pregnant a trudan; bremenit, skotan.
prehistoric a preistorijski.
prejudicial a štetan, škodljiv.
prejudice n predrasuda; šteta; v unapred odrediti stav; naneti štetu.
prejudiced a pristran, obuzet predrasudom.
preliminary a pripremni, prethodni.
prelude n uvod; preludij.
premarital a predbračni.
premature a preuranjen, prenagljen; ~ly adv prerano, zrelo.
premeditation n namera, nakana.
premier n predsednik vlade.
premiere n premijera, prvo prikazivanje.
premise n pretpostavka.
premises npl napred spomenuto (jur); prostorije.

premium n nagrada, dar.
premonition n opomena; slutnja, predosećanje.
preoccupied a zabrinut, zaokupljen (mislima), zauzet (poslom).
prepaid a franko, s poštarinom plaćenom unapred.
preparation n pripremanje, priprema, spremanje.
preparatory a uvodni, pripremni.
prepare v spremati, pripremati (se).
prepared a pripravan, spreman, voljan.
preponderance n prevaga; prednost, nadmoć.
preposition n predlog.
preposterous a besmislen, naopak; promenljiv, nepostojan.
prerequisite n tražen kao preduslov .
prerogative n prednost, isključivo pravo.
prescribe v odrediti, narediti; prepisati (lek).
prescription n propis, nalog; recept.
presence n prisutnost, postojanje; držanje, izgled.
present n sadašnjost; dar, poklon; a prisutan; sadašnji; ~ly adv prisutno, sadašnje; v predstaviti, uvesti; pokazati; pokloniti; nišaniti.
presentable a naočit, pristojnog izgleda.
presentation n upoznavanje, predstavljanje.
present-day a aktuelan, sadašnji.
presentiment n predosećanje.
preservation n predohrana; očuvanost; konzerviranje.
preservative n konzervans.
preserve v čuvati, održavati; štititi; n konzerva; ukuvano voće.
preside v predsedavati.
presidency n predsedništvo.
president n predsednik, ministar, guverner.
presidential a ministarski, predsednički.
press v stezati, pritiskati; presovati; izravnati; n dnevna štampa, novinarstvo; štamparski stroj, gužva.
press agency n novinska agencija.
press conference n konferencija za štampu.
pressing a hitan, neodložan; uporan; ~ly adv hitno.

pressure n pritisak; gnječenje.
pressure cooker n ekspresni lonac.
pressurized a hermetički.
prestige n ugled, uticaj.
presumable a verovatan, predvidiv.
presumably a verovatno.
presume v pretpostaviti; usuditi se.
presumption n pretpostavka;
   samopouzdanje.
presumptuous a samopouzdan.
presuppose v pretpostaviti.
pretence n pretvaranje; izgovor; zahtev.
pretend v pretvarati se; polagati pravo.
pretender n licemer; pretendent.
pretension n zahtev, traženje; pretvaranje.
pretentious a uobražen, pretenciozan.
preterite n prošlo svršeno vreme (gram).
pretext n izgovor, pretekst; **to find a ~
   for** izgovarati se.
pretty a privlačan, divan, lepuškast; adv
   dovoljno, prilično.
prevail v gospodariti; imati prevagu;
   odoleti.
prevailing a rasprostranjen.
prevalent a nadmoćan; rasprostranjen.
prevent v odvratiti, upozoriti; smetati,
   ometati.
prevention n upozorenje, opomena.
preventive a zaštitni; preventivan.
preview n prethodno gledanje .
previous a prethodan; prevremen; **~ly**
   adv prethodno, ranije.
prewar a predratni.
prey n plen; žrtva.
price n vrednost, cena.
price list n cenovnik.
priceless a neprocenjiv.
prick v ubosti; probosti; mučiti; n ubod,
   probadanje; trn.
prickle n trn, bodlja; peckanje, svrab.
prickly a bodljikav.
pride n ponos, dika; samosvest.
priest n sveštenik.
priestess n sveštenica.
priesthood n sveštenstvo.
priestly a sveštenički.
priggish a cepidlački; uobražen.
prim a ukočen, usiljen, izveštačen.
primacy n prvenstvo; zvanje episkopa.
primarily adv prvo, prvobitno.
primary a prvi, prvobitan; glavni, osnovni.

primary school n osnovna škola.
primate n nadbiskup.
prime n najbolje doba, napon; početak,
   proleće; a najvažniji, glavni, odličan; v
   premazati osnovnom bojom; napuniti.
prime minister n premijer.
primeval a prvobitan, iskonski.
priming n raniji nadolazak plime.
primitive a prvobitan, najstariji; sirov;
   primitivan; **~ly** adv primitivno.
primrose n jagorčevina.
prince n princ; knez; knežević.
princess n princeza.
principal a glavni, osnovni, najvažniji;
   vodeći; **~ly** adv pre svega, uglavnom; n
   starešina; direktor škole.
principality n kneževina; vladavina
   princa; vlast.
principle n načelo, princip, zakon;
   prauzrok.
print v odštampati, izdati; n otisak, trag,
   štampa; novine; **out of ~** rasprodato
   izdanje.
printed matter n štampane stvari.
printer n štampar.
printing n štamparstvo; štampanje.
prior[1] a prethodni, raniji.
prior[2] n nastojnik manastira.
priority n prvenstvo, prednost.
priory n manastir, samostan.
prism n prizma.
prison n zatvor, tamnica.
prisoner n zatvorenik, zatočenik; ratni
   zarobljenik.
pristine a prastar, davan.
privacy n usamljenost, samoća; tajnost,
   poverljivost.
private a lični, privatan; usamljen;
   tajni; **~ soldier** n redov; **~ly** adv
   privatno.
private eye n privatni detektiv.
privilege n privilegija, povlastica.
prize n nagrada, premija; plata; dobitak; v
   visoko ceniti, proceniti, oceniti.
prizewinner n pobednik, dobitnik
   nagrade.
pro prep za.
probability n verovatnoća, mogućnost.
probable a verovatan, moguć;
   verodostojan.
probably adv po svoj prilici, verovatno.

probation *n* ispitivanje, proba, staž; probni rok.
probationary *a* probni.
probe *n* sonda; istraga; *v* sondirati; istraživati.
problem *n* problem; računski zadatak.
problematical *a* sumnjiv, sporan, problematičan; ~ly *adv* sumnjivo, problematično.
procedure *n* postupak, procedura; postupanje.
proceed *v* nastaviti; obnoviti; postupati; ~s *npl* prihod, dohodak.
proceedings *npl* postupak; radovi, spisi; suđenje.
process *n* razvoj, tok događaja, proces; postupak; *v* preraditi, obraditi.
procession *n* povorka, procesija.
proclaim *v* proglasiti; objavljivati; zabraniti.
proclamation *n* objava; proglas.
procrastinate *v* odlagati, odugovlačiti.
proctor *n* proktor, službenik koji se brine za red.
procure *v* obezbediti, nabaviti, pripremiti.
procurement *n* dobavljanje, nabavljanje; postizanje.
prod *v* bosti, bockati; podbadati, podstrekivati.
prodigal *a* rasipnički; darežljiv.
prodigious *a* ogroman, golem; izvanredan, neobičan; ~ly *adv* ogromno, izvanredno.
prodigy *n* darovit čovek; čudo.
produce *v* proizvesti; napisati, izdati knjigu; režirati; *n* proizvodnja, proizvod, uspeh.
producer *n* proizvođač; režiser.
product *n* proizvod; ishod, rezultat.
production *n* proizvodnja; proizvod.
production line *n* proizvodna linija.
productive *a* produktivan, koji proizvodi; plodan.
productivity *n* produktivnost.
profane *a* laički, svetovan; neprosvećen; grešan.
profess *v* javno izjaviti; priznati; pretvarati se.
profession *n* profesija, poziv.
professional *a* profesionalan, stručan; školovan.
professor *n* profesor; stručni nastavnik.
proficiency *n* veština, iskustvo, znanje.

proficient *a* iskusan, stručan.
profile *n* obris, profil.
profit *n* prihod, dobitak, zarada; *v* koristiti, donositi korist.
profitability *n* rentabilnost.
profitable *a* unosan; koristan.
profiteering *n* profitiranje.
profound *a* vrlo dubok; ~ly *adv* duboko.
profuse *a* obilan, bogat; darežljiv; ~ly *adv* darežljivo.
programme (*br*), **program** (*amer*) *n* plan, nacrt, program; *v* programirati.
programmer *n* programer.
programming *n* programiranje.
progress *n* napredak, razvitak; napredovanje.
progressive *a* progresivan; koji napreduje; ~ly *adv* progresivno, napredno.
prohibit *v* zabraniti; sprečiti.
prohibition *n* zabrana; obustava.
project *v* planirati, projektovati; sastaviti; *n* nacrt, plan.
projectile *n* projektil.
projection *n* izbočina; projekcija; plan.
projector *n* projektor.
proletarian *a* radnički, proleterski.
proletariat *n* proleterijat.
prolific *a* plodan, rodan, obilan.
prologue *n* predgovor, uvod; prolog.
prolong *v* produžiti, otegnuti.
prom *n* promenadni koncert.
promenade *n* šetnja; šetalište.
prominence *n* isticanje; izbočina; važnost.
prominent *a* istaknut; izbočen.
promiscuous *a* raznorodan, pomešan; zbrkan; slučajan.
promise *n* obećanje, nada; izgled; *v* obećati.
promising *a* obećavajući.
promontory *n* rt.
promote *v* uzdići, unaprediti; potpomagati.
promoter *n* promoter; osnivač, utemeljivač; zaštitnik.
promotion *n* unapređenje, napredovanje; potpomaganje; promocija.
prompt *a* bez odlaganja, bez oklevanja; brz; ~ly *adv* brzo, hitro; *v* navoditi, pobuđivati; suflirati.

prompter *n* sufler.
prone *a* opružen po zemlji; naklonjen, sklon.
prong *n* šiljak, zubac; vile.
pronoun *n* zamenica (*gram*).
pronounce *v* izgovarati; izjaviti, objaviti.
pronounced *a* izrazit, jasan.
pronouncement *n* izricanje; zvanična izjava.
pronunciation *n* izgovor, izgovaranje.
proof *n* dokaz; ispitivanje, proba; *a* nepromočiv; nepodmitljiv; neprobojan.
prop *v* podupirati, držati; *n* podupirač; oslonac.
propaganda *n* propaganda.
propel *v* staviti u pokret, gurnuti.
propeller *n* elisa, propeler.
propensity *n* sklonost, naklonost.
proper *a* nadležan, merodavan; pravilan; pristojan; pravi, tačan; vlastit; **~ly** *adv* pravilno, kako treba; pristojno.
property *n* vlasništvo, svojina, imovina.
prophecy *n* proročanstvo.
prophesy *v* proreći, predskazati.
prophet *n* prorok.
prophetic *a* proročanski.
proportion *n* srazmera, uzajamni odnos, veličina.
proportional *adj* proporcionalan.
proportionate *a* srazmeran, proporcionalan.
proposal *n* predlog; bračna ponuda.
propose *v* predložiti; predlagati; zaprositi.
proposition *n* predlog; tvrđenje; problem.
proprietor *n* sopstvenik, vlasnik; gazda.
propriety *n* pristojnost, uljudnost; podstrek.
prosaic *a* prozaičan; svakidašnji, dosadan.
prose *n* proza; svakidašnjica, stvarnost.
prosecute *v* voditi (poslove, istragu); proganjati sudskim putem.
prosecution *n* vođenje poslova; sudski progon; tužba.
prosecutor *n* privatni tužilac; javni tužilac.
prospect *n* predeo, vidik; perspektiva; izgledi na budućnost; *v* pregledati, ıspitati.
prospective *a* budući.
prospector *n* istraživač.
prospectus *n* prospekt.

prosper *v* napredovati, uspevati, razvijati se.
prosperity *n* procvat, blagostanje, napredovanje.
prosperous *a* rascvetan, u cvetanju.
prostitute *n* prostitutka.
prostitution *n* prostitucija.
prostrate *a* ispružen, oboren.
protagonist *n* glavna ličnost (knj. dela); glavni glumac; protagonist.
protect *v* zaštititi, sačuvati; braniti.
protection *n* zaštita, odbrana; pokroviteljstvo.
protective *a* zaštitni; preventivni; zaštitnički.
protector *n* zaštitnik; pokrovitelj; namesnik.
protégé *n* štićenik, ljubimac.
protein *n* protein (*hem*), belančevina.
protest *v* protestovati; svečano izjaviti; *n* protest, prigovor.
Protestant *n* protestant.
protester *n* protivnik; onaj koji protestuje.
protocol *n* protokol; zapisnik; prethodni dogovor.
prototype *n* prototip, prauzor, original.
protracted *a* razvučen; otegnut.
protrude *v* viriti, isticati se.
proud *a* ponosan, dostojanstven; ohol; **~ly** *adv* ponosno, plemenito.
prove *v* dokazati; isprobati; potvrditi.
proverb *n* poslovica, izreka.
proverbial *a* poslovičan; **~ly** *adv* poslovično.
provide *v* obezbediti, snabdeti; **to ~ for the needs of** zadovoljiti prirodne potrebe.
provided *conj* pod uslovom da, ako.
providence *n* dalekovidnost, smotrenost; štednja; sudbina.
province *n* pokrajina; okolina, periferija.
provincial *a* pokrajinski, provincijski; *n* provincijalac, malograđanin.
provision *n* priprema; snabdevanje; životne namirnice.
provisional *a* privremen; prethodan; **~ly** *adv* privremeno.
proviso *n* uslov, pogodba.
provocation *n* izazivanje, draženje; izazov, provokacija.

provocative *a* izazivački; koji razdražuje.
provoke *v* razdražiti, naljutiti; prouzrokovati.
prow *n* pramac, prednji deo aviona.
prowess *n* junaštvo, srčanost.
prowl *v* prikradati se, vrebati.
prowler *n* skitnica, tumaralo, vagabund.
proximity *n* blizina, susedstvo; srodstvo.
proxy *n* zamenik, zastupnik.
prudence *n* opreznost, smotrenost; razboritost, mudrost.
prudent *a* razborit, mudar; oprezan ~ly *adv* mudro, oprezno.
prudish *a* stidljiv; licemeran, izveštačen.
prune[1] *v* potkresati (suve grane); podšišati.
prune[2] *n* šljiva; tamno ljubičasta boja.
prussic acid *n* cijanovodonična kiselina.
pry *v* radoznalo posmatrati; krišom posmatrati; zavirivati.
psalm *n* psalm.
pseudonym *n* pseudonim, pozajmljeno ime.
psyche *n* psiha, duša.
psychiatric *a* psihijatrijski.
psychiatrist *n* psihijatar.
psychiatry *n* psihijatrija.
psychic *a* duhovni, duševni.
psychoanalysis *n* psihoanaliza.
psychoanalyst *n* psihoanalitičar.
psychological *a* psihološki.
psychologist *n* psiholog.
psychology *n* psihologija.
puberty *n* polna zrelost.
public *a* društven; narodni, državni; javan; ~ly *adv* narodno, javno; *n* narod, publika; javnost.
public opinion *n* javno mišljenje.
public school *n* privatna srednja škola s internatom.
public-address system *n* razglasni uređaj.
publican *n* gostioničar.
publication *n* izdanje; štampano delo, publikacija.
publicity *n* javnost, publicitet; reklama.
publicize *v* reklamirati.
publish *v* izdati; objaviti; oglasiti.
publisher *n* izdavač.
publishing *n* izdavanje; izdanje.
pucker *v* mrštiti se; nabirati se.
pudding *n* puding.

puddle *n* lokva, barica.
puerile *a* detinjast.
puff *n* dašak vetra; vazdušna struja; dim; *v* duvati u naletima; dahtati; pušiti (cigaru).
puffy *a* podbuo, natečen; silovit; razmetljiv.
pull *v* vući, tegliti; trzati; zvoniti; **to ~ down** srušiti; **to ~ in** zaustaviti; smanjiti; **to ~ off** pobediti, dobiti; svući; **to ~ out** iščupati; izvaditi; otići (voz); **to ~ through** prebroditi, preboleti; **to ~ up** zaustaviti (konja, kola); izbijati, sustići; iščupati; *n* vučenje; veslanje; gutljaj; napor.
pulley *n* kotur, točak; čekrk, dizalica.
pullover *n* pulover.
pulp *n* pulpa (zuba); voćno meso; drvna masa.
pulpit *n* propovedaonica; propovedanje.
pulsate *v* kucati, udarati, pulsirati.
pulse *n* bilo, puls; pulsiranje; ritam.
pulverize *v* samleti; raspršiti.
pumice *n* plavac (kamen).
pummel *v* mlatiti, udarati pesnicama.
pump *n* sisaljka, šmrk, pumpa; lakirana cipela; *v* napumpati; napuniti vazduhom (pluća); smestiti.
pumpkin *n* bundeva, tikva.
pun *n* dosetka, igra rečima; *v* igrati se rečima.
punch[1] *n* udarac pesnicom; snaga; *v* udariti pesnicom.
punch[2] *n* punč.
punch[3] *n* silo.
punctual *a* tačan, precizan; ~ly *adv* tačno, precizno.
punctuate *v* staviti znakove interpunkcije; izmenjivati.
punctuation *n* interpunkcija.
pundit *n* ekspert, učen čovek.
pungent *a* jedak, zajedljiv.
punish *v* kazniti; grubo postupati.
punishment *n* kažnjavanje, kazna.
punk *n* huligan; bludnica; mizerija; koještarija (*fig*).
punt *n* čamac sa ravnim dnom.
puny *a* mali, zakržljao, slabunjav.
pup *n* štene; *v* ošteniti se.
pupil *n* učenik, učenica; zenica (oka).
puppet *n* lutka, marioneta.

puppy *n* štene; detence; kicoš.
purchase *v* kupiti, zakupiti; steći; *n* kupovina; kupljena stvar; uticaj, moć.
purchaser *n* kupac.
pure *a* čist; čistokrvan; pravi; **~ly** *adv* čisto.
purée *n* pire; krem supa.
purge *v* očistiti, osloboditi; očistiti creva.
purification *n* čišćenje.
purifier *n* čistač; sredstvo za čišćenje.
purify *v* čistiti; očistiti.
purist *n* čistunac.
puritan *n* puritanac; čovek sa strogim moralnim načelima.
purity *n* čistoća, jasnoća; nevinost.
purl[1] *n* žuborenje, grgotanje.
purl[2] *n* vez zlatnom žicom, izvezen rub.
purple *a* grimizan; ljubičast; *n* grimizna boja; ljubičasta boja.
purport *v* sadržavati, značiti, pokazivati.
purpose *n* svrha, cilj, namera; uspeh; **to the ~** zgodno, korisno, u pravi čas; **to no ~** bez smisla, uzalud; **on ~** namerno.
purposeful *a* nameravan, svestan cilja.
purr *v* presti (mačka).
purse *n* novčanik, kesa, novac.
purser *n* brodski ekonom.
pursue *v* progoniti, goniti, pratiti.
pursuit *n* gonjenje, potera; posao.

purveyor *n* nabavljač, snabdevač (namirnicama).
push *v* gurati, progurati; probiti se; **to ~ aside** odgurnuti, odbiti; **to ~ off** otisnuti se (brod); otići, otputovati; **to ~ on** terati, goniti; *n* udarac, ubod; napor; pritisak; dugme.
pusher *n* laktas, prodoran čovek (*sleng*); **drug ~** *n* prodavac droge.
put *v* staviti, položiti; smestiti, baciti; izraziti; **to ~ away** skloniti, sakriti, napustiti; **to ~ down** metnuti, odložiti, suzbiti, ućutkati; **to ~ forward** izneti, predložiti; **to ~ off** odložiti, odgoditi, poći; **to ~ on** obući, navući, obuti; dodati; pretvarati se; **to ~ out** proterati; izvaditi; iščašiti; ugasiti; smetati; **to ~ up** dići, podići; izreći, ponuditi.
putrid *a* truo; smrdljiv; pokvaren.
putty *n* lepilo, kit, lem.
puzzle *n* nedoumica; zabuna; nerešiv problem; zagonetka.
puzzling *a* zagonetan, čudan, nerazumljiv.
pyjamas *npl* pižama.
pylon *n* pilon, ulaz u egipatski hram; toranj.
pyramid *n* piramida.
python *n* piton.

Q

quack[1] *v* gakati; *n* gakanje.
quack[2] *n* vrač, nadrilekar (*sleng*).
quadrangle *n* četverokut.
quadrant *n* kvadrant.
quadrilateral *a* četverostran; *n* četvorougao.
quadruped *n* četveronožac.
quadruple *a* četverostruk.
quadruplet *n* jedan od četiri; četvorka.
quagmire *n* močvara, bara.
quail *n* prepelica.
quaint *a* neobičan, čudan; zabavan.
quake *v* drhtati, tresti se.
Quaker *n* kveker.
qualification *n* svojstvo, prikladnost, kvalifikacija; ograničenje.
qualified *a* osposobljen, kvalifikovan.
qualify *v* označiti; osposobiti; ograničiti.
quality *n* kakvoća, kvalitet.
qualm *n* mučnina, mučnost; utučenost.
quandary *n* nezgodan položaj, neprilika.
quantitative *a* količinski, kvantitativan.
quantity *n* količina; velika količina.
quarantine *n* karantin, izolacija zaraznih bolesnika.
quarrel *n* svađa, prepirka, spor; *v* svađati se, prepirati se.
quarrelsome *a* svadljiv, izazivački, prgav.
quarry *n* plen, ulov; kamenolom.
quarter *n* četvrti deo nečega; ~ **of an hour** četvrt sata; *v* deliti na četiri dela.
quartermaster *n* konačar (*voj*).
quartet *n* kvartet (*muz*).
quartz *n* kvarc, kremen, belutak.
quash *v* poništiti, ukinuti; ugušiti (nešto).
quay *n* pristanište, molo, kej.
queasy *a* osetljiv, nadražen; nelagodan.
queen *n* kraljica.
queer *a* čudan, nastran; bolestan, slab.
quell *v* prigušiti, ugušiti.
quench *v* gasiti; utoliti (žeđ); ohladiti, politi hladnom vodom.
query *n* pitanje; znak pitanja; *v* pitati, obavestiti se; izraziti sumnju.

quest *n* traženje, potraga.
question *n* pitanje; ispitivanje, sumnja; istraživanje; *v* pitati; saslušavati; sumnjati.
question mark *n* upitnik.
questionable *a* sumnjiv, podozriv, nesiguran.
questioner *n* ispitivač.
questionnaire *n* upitni listić, anketa.
quibble *v* praviti dosetke; služiti se smicalicama.
quick *a* brz, hitar; okretan; snalažljiv; **~ly** *adv* hitro, brzo.
quicken *v* oživeti, oduševiti, obodriti, podstaći.
quicksand *n* živi pesak.
quicksilver *n* živa.
quick-witted *a* dovitljiv, oštrouman, snalažljiv.
quiet *a* miran, tih, ćutljiv; blag; **~ly** *adv* tiho, ćutljivo.
quietness *n* mir, tišina.
quinine *n* kinin.
quintet *n* kvintet (*muz*).
quintuple *a* peterostruk.
quintuplet *n* skup od pet.
quip *n* oštroumna dosetka, duhovito peckanje.
quirk *n* igra rečima; varka; doskočica.
quit *v* prestati sa radom; napustiti, ostaviti; *a* slobodan, oslobođen od nečeg.
quite *adv* sasvim, posve; veoma, dosta.
quits *adv* obračunati se, biti izmiren.
quiver *v* drhtati, treperiti.
quixotic *a* donkihotski.
quiz *n* šala, peckanje; šaljivdžija; proveravanje znanja; *v* šaliti se, ismejavati; proveravati znanje.
quizzical *a* šaljiv, podrugljiv; nastran.
quota *n* kvota, deo, udeo.
quotation *n* navedeno mesto, navod, citat.
quotation marks *npl* navodnici.
quote *v* navoditi, citirati; odrediti cenu.
quotient *n* količnik.

R

rabbi *n* rabin.
rabbit *n* kunić, pitomi zec.
rabbit hutch *n* kućica za kuniće.
rabble *n* gomila ljudi, rulja; ološ.
rabid *a* mahnit, besomučan; besan (pas).
rabies *n* besnilo.
race[1] *n* rasa; rod, vrsta.
race[2] n trka; *v* trkati se; juriti.
racehorse *n* trkački konj.
racial *a* rasni; etnički.
raciness *n* krepkost, jedrina.
racing *n* trke; utrkivanje.
racist *a* rasistički; *n* rasista.
rack *n* raf, polica; čiviluk; mreža za prtljag (u vagonu); *v* staviti na policu; mučiti; naprezati.
racket[1] *n* reket (za tenis).
racket[2] n buka; smicalica.
racket[3] n reket (*sleng*), ucena.
rack-rent *n* previsoka najamnina.
racy *a* jake arome; pikantan; živahan.
radiance *n* sjaj, sijanje.
radiant *a* sjajan, blistav.
radiate *v* sijati, isijavati, zračiti.
radiation *n* isijavanje, zračenje.
radiator *n* radijator (za grejanje); automobilski hladnjak.
radical *a* korenit, radikalan; **~ly** *adv* radikalno.
radicalism *n* radikalizam.
radio *n* radio; prenos; rendgenski zraci.
radioactive *a* radioaktivan; **~ fallout** *n* radioaktivno zagađenje.
radish *n* rotkvica.
radius *n* radijus; domet.
raffle *n* predmetna lutrija, tombola; *v* igrati tombolu.
raft *n* splav; *v* voziti se na splavu.
rafter *n* krovna greda; splavar.
rafting *n* splavarenje.
rag *n* krpa; rita; neslana šala.
ragamuffin *n* odrpanac.
rage *n* bes, gnev; strast, zanos; *v* besneti.
ragged *a* poderan, čupav; dronjav; nedoteran.
raging *a* besan.
ragman, rag-and-bone man *n* skupljač krpa, preprodavac stare odeće.

raid *n* prepad, upad; racija; *v* iznenada napasti.
raider *n* napadač, učesnik u prepadu.
rail[1] *n* prečaga; ograda (na stepenicama).
rail[2] n šina; železnica
rail[3] *v* zatvoriti ogradom; grditi.
railing *n* ograda.
raillery *n* zadirkivanje, podrugivanje.
railway *n* železnička pruga; *a* železnički; *v* putovati železnicom.
raiment *n* odelo, odeća (*poet*).
rain *n* kiša; *v* padati (kiša), liti.
rainbow *n* duga.
rainwater *n* kišnica.
rainy *a* kišovit, kišni (oblaci).
raise *v* podići; izazvati; povisiti (zaradu, glas); uzgajati, odgajati; skupiti (novac).
raisin *n* suvo grožđe.
rake[1] *n* grabulje; *v* grabuljati; zgrtati.
rake[2] *n* razvratnik.
rakish *a* poletan, razvratan; nagnut.
rally *v* prikupiti; ujediniti; okupiti se; oporaviti se (od bolesti).
ram *n* ovan; kljun broda; *v* udariti (pramcem); prokrčiti, probiti; zabijati.
ramble *n* šetnja, lutanje; *v* lutati; skakati s predmeta na predmet (u govoru).
rambler *n* tumaralo; puzavica (ruža) (*bot*).
ramification *n* granjanje; grane drveta.
ramify *v* razgranati (se).
ramp *n* rampa; ispad (gneva).
rampant *a* bujan; osion, neobuzdan; koji stoji na zadnjim nogama (životinje).
rampart *n* bedem; odbrana, zaštita; *v* braniti, štititi.
ramrod *n* šipka za punjenje puške (*voj*).
ramshackle *a* trošan.
ranch *n* farma.
rancid *a* užegao.
rancour *n* zloba, neprijateljstvo.
random *a* slučajan, nasumice; **at ~** nasumice.
range *n* niz; raspon; opseg; štednjak; strelište; *v* postrojiti se; klasificirati; protezati se.
ranger *n* šumar; američki komandos.

rank *a* bujan (rastinje); zarastao; užežen; *n* čin; rang; red, niz; vrsta (*voj*).
rankle *v* mučiti (uspomene i sl); gnojiti se (rana).
rankness *n* užeženost.
ransack *v* pretražiti; pljačkati.
ransom *n* otkup.
rant *v* buncati; bučno se veseliti.
rap *n* lak udarac; *v* ovlaš udariti; kuckati.
rapacious *a* grabežljiv; pohlepan; ~**ly** *adv* pohlepno, lakomo.
rapacity, rapaciousness *n* grabežljivost, pohlepnost.
rape *n* otmica; silovanje; uljana repica (*bot*); *v* oteti; silovati.
rapid *a* brz, hitar; strm; ~**ly** *adv* brzo, hitro.
rapidity *n* brzina.
rapier *n* rapir (mač).
rapist *n* silovatelj.
rapt *a* ushićen; zanesen, zaokupljen.
rapture *n* ushićenost, oduševljenje; otmica.
rapturous *a* ushićen.
rare *a* redak; izuzetan; ~**ly** *adv* retko; izuzetno, ponekad.
rarity *n* retkost; retka pojava; razređenost (vazduha i sl.).
rascal *n* nitkov; lopov; vragolan.
rash[1] *a* nagao; hitar; brzoplet; ~**ly** *adv* prenagljeno.
rash[2] *n* osip (*med*).
rashness *n* naglost, brzopletost.
rasp *n* turpija, rende; oštar zvuk; *v* strugati; zveckati.
raspberry *n* malina; ~**bush** *n* grm maline.
rat *n* pacov; begunac (*voj*).
rate *n* stopa; brzina, tempo; cena; vrsta; kurs; *v* proceniti, odrediti; smatrati.
rather *adv* radije; pre; tačnije, pravilnije; prilično.
ratification *n* potpisivanje, ratifikacija (ugovora i sl.).
ratify *v* ratifikovati.
rating *n* procena; klasa, vrsta; popularnost (emisije).
ratio *n* odnos, omer, srazmera.
ration *n* obrok, porcija; ~**s** *npl* hrana, životne namirnice; sledovanje (*voj*).
rational *a* razuman, razborit, racionalan; ~**ly** *adv* razumno.

rationality *n* razboritost, racionalnost.
rattan *n* palma trskara.
rattle *n* zveket; zvečka; brbljivac; *v* zveckati, klepetati; glasno i brzo govoriti.
rattlesnake *n* čegrtuša (zmija).
ravage *v* pustošiti, razarati; *n* pustošenje, razaranje.
rave *v* buncati; zanosno govoriti.
rave music *n* rejv muzika.
raven *n* gavran.
ravenous *a* grabežljiv; pljačkaški; pohlepan; ~**ly** *adv* grabežljivo; pohlepno.
ravine *n* tesnac; jaruga.
ravish *v* oduševiti; oteti; silovati.
ravishing *a* zanosan.
raw *a* sirov; nedokuvan, nedopečen; neobrađen; neiskusan.
rawboned *a* koščat; vrlo mršav.
rawness *n* sirovost.
ray[1] *n* zrak; zračak.
ray[2] *n* raža (riba).
raze *v* porušiti; sravniti; izbrisati (obično iz sećanja).
razor *n* britva, žilet.
reach *n* doseg; rastojanje, udaljenost; *v* pružiti; predati; dohvatiti; dopreti.
react *v* reagovati; delovati, uticati.
reaction *n* reakcija.
read *v* čitati; shvatiti; proučavati; tumačiti; glasiti.
readable *a* čitak; vredan čitanja.
reader *n* čitalac; vanredni profesor; lektor; predavač.
readily *adv* rado; lako.
readiness *n* spremnost.
reading *n* čitanje; predavanje; tumačenje.
reading room *n* čitaonica.
readjust *v* preurediti; opet prilagoditi.
ready *a* spreman; gotov; pristupačan.
real *a* stvaran, istinski, pravi; ~**ly** *adv* stvarno.
reality *n* stvarnost.
realization *n* ostvarenje; shvatanje.
realize *v* shvatiti; ostvariti; realizovati.
realm *n* kraljevina; oblast, carstvo.
ream *n* ris papira; *pl* gomila.
reap *v* žeti; ubirati plodove.
reaper *n* žetelac; žetelica (mašina).

reappear v ponovo se pojaviti.
rear[1] n zadnja strana; pozadina; leđa.
rear[2] v dizati; gajiti, uzgajati.
rearmament n ponovno naoružanje.
reason n razum; razlog; v razmišljati, prosuđivati.
reasonable a razuman; prihvatljiv, umeren.
reasonableness n razumnost.
reasonably adv razborito, opravdano; relativno.
reasoning n rasuđivanje.
reassure v uveravati, ubeđivati.
rebel n pobunjenik, ustanik; v ustati, pobuniti se.
rebellion n ustanak; buna.
rebellious a pobunjenički; neposlušan.
rebound v odbijati se.
rebuff n odbijanje; v odbiti, pružiti otpor.
rebuild v ponovo sagraditi; remontovati.
rebuke n prekor; zamerka; v zamerati.
rebut v pobiti, opovrgnuti.
recalcitrant a neposlušan, nepokoran.
recall n opoziv; podsećanje; signal za povlačenje (voj); v opozvati; setiti se.
recant v oporeći.
recantation n oporicanje.
recapitulate v sumirati.
recapitulation n zaključak, rekapitulacija.
recapture v ponovo osvojiti.
recede v ustuknuti; odustati.
receipt n priznanica; primanje; pl zarada od prodaje, pazar.
receivable a prihvatljiv; dopustiv.
receive v dobiti, primiti; prihvatiti.
recent a skorašnji, nov; savremen; ~ly adv skoro, nedavno.
receptacle n kutija; priključak (za struju).
reception n prijem, doček.
recess n udubljenje; skrovito mesto; odmor (školski) .
recession n povlačenje, odlazak; recesija (ekon).
recipe n recept (med., kulin); sredstvo.
recipient n primalac.
reciprocal a uzajaman; odgovarajući; refeleksivan (gram), povratan; ~ly adv uzajamno.
reciprocate v uzvraćati; izmenjati.
reciprocity n uzajamnost; međusobno delovanje.

recital n iscrpno pričanje; koncert (muz).
recite v recitovati; odgovarati na času; nabrajati.
reckless a nepromišljen, nemaran; ~ly adv nepromišljeno.
reckon v brojiti; sabrati; računati (na nekoga); misliti.
reckoning n račun; računanje; obračun.
reclaim v ispravljati, popraviti; tražiti povraćaj.
reclaimable a što se može tražiti natrag (učiniti boljim).
recline v nasloniti se; osloniti se; zabaciti (glavu).
recluse n pustinjak.
recognition n prepoznavanje, raspoznavanje; priznanje.
recognize v prepoznati; priznati.
recoil v ustuknuti; užasavati se (pred nečim).
recollect v sećati se.
recollection n sećanje, uspomena.
recommence v nanovo početi.
recommend v preporučiti, savetovati; poveriti nekom na čuvanje.
recommendation n preporuka, savet.
recompense n nagrada, naknada; v nagraditi, nadoknaditi.
reconcilable a pomirljiv, uskladiv.
reconcile v pomiriti; izgladiti (spor); uskladiti (mišljenja i sl.).
reconciliation n pomirenje.
recondite a nejasan, teško razumljiv.
reconnaissance n izvidnica; izviđanje (voj).
reconnoitre v izviđati (voj).
reconsider v ponovo razmatrati.
reconstruct v rekonstruisati; ponovo izgraditi.
record n zapis; registar; rekord (sport); gramofonska ploča; ~s npl arhiva; hronika; v beležiti; snimiti na traku.
recorder n zapisničar; blokflauta (muz); rekorder.
recount v pripovedati, prepričavati događaj.
recourse n traženje pomoći; utočište.
recover v dobiti natrag; nadoknaditi; oporavljati se (od bolesti).
recoverable a nadoknadiv; koji se može dobiti natrag.

recovery *n* ozdravljenje; obnavljanje; dobijanje natrag.
recreation *n* odmor, rekreacija.
recriminate *v* uzajamno se optuživati.
recrimination *n* protivoptužba, uzajamno optuživanje.
recruit *n* regrut; *v* regrutovati; pridobiti.
recruiting *n* regrutacija.
rectangle *n* pravougaonik.
rectangular *a* pravougaoni.
rectification *n* ispravljanje; prečišćavanje (*hem*).
rectify *v* ispraviti; prečistiti.
rectilinear *a* pravolinijski.
rectitude *n* iskrenost, čestitost; pravičnost.
rector *n* rektor; paroh.
recumbent *a* koji leži, naslonjen.
recur *v* vraćati se; setiti se; ponoviti se.
recurrence *n* vraćanje; ponavljanje; prisećanje.
recurrent *a* povratan, periodičan.
recycle *v* ponovo iskoristiti; reciklirati.
recycled *a* recikliran, prerađen.
red *a* crven, rumen; pocrveneo; *n* crvena boja.
red tape *n* birokratizam (*fig*).
redden *v* pocrveneti; bojiti crvenom bojom.
reddish *a* crvenkast.
redeem *v* isplatiti (dug); iskupiti; nadoknaditi.
redeemable *a* iskupljiv.
redeemer *n* iskupitelj; spasitelj.
redemption *n* iskup; otkup; spas.
redeploy *v* pregrupisati (*voj*).
red-handed *a* okrvavljenih ruku; **to catch somebody** ~ uhvatiti nekoga na samom delu.
red-hot *a* usijan; vatren.
red-letter day *n* znamenit dan.
redness *n* crvenilo, rumenilo, užarenost.
redolent *a* mirisan; koji podseća na nešto.
redouble *v* podvostručiti (se); pogoršati (se).
redress *n* ispravljanje; naknada, zadovoljenje; *v* ispraviti; dati zadovoljenje.
reduce *v* smanjiti, sniziti, skratiti.
reducible *a* svodljiv; rastavljiv; smanjiv.

reduction *n* smanjenje, sniženje (cene); redukcija.
redundancy *n* obilje; suvišnost; bujica (reči).
redundant *a* suvišan, prekomeran.
reed *n* trska; pisak, cev (orgulja).
reedy *a* obrastao trskom; piskav (glas).
reef *n* podvodni greben.
reek *n* para, dim; težak miris; *v* dimiti se; smrdeti.
reel[1] *n* kalem; rulet; kolebanje; *v* namotati; vrteti se
reel[2] *n* ples (vrsta škotske igre).
reel[3] *v* okretati se, teturati se.
re-election *n* ponovni izbor.
re-engage *v* ponovo angažovati.
re-enter *v* ponovo ući.
re-establish *v* uspostaviti, dovesti u prvobitno stanje; obnoviti.
re-establishment *n* ponovno uspostavljanje.
refectory *n* trpezarija; studentska menza.
refer *v* uputiti; odnositi se; upućivati; pozivati se (na).
referee *n* arbitar; sudija (sport).
reference *n* pozivanje na; primedba; preporuka.
refine *v* prečistiti; preraditi; usavršiti se.
refinement *n* prečišćavanje; istančanost; prepredenost; nadmudrivanje.
refinery *n* rafinerija.
refit *v* opraviti; ponovo opremiti (brod i sl.).
reflect *v* odraziti; prikazivati; razmišljati.
reflection *n* odbijanje, odsjaj; prikaz; razmišljanje.
reflector *n* reflektor; ~s *npl* mačje oči.
reflex *a* refleksivan.
reform *v* reformisati; poboljšati; *n* reforma; poboljšanje.
reformation *n* reformacija; preinačenje.
reformer *n* reformator.
reformist *n* reformista.
refract *v* prelamati (zrake).
refraction *n* prelamanje, refrakcija.
refrain *v* uzdržati se; **to ~ from something** uzdržati se od nečega.
refresh *v* osvežiti, okrepiti; obnoviti zalihe.
refreshment *n* osveženje; ~s *npl* zakuska.
refrigerator *n* frižider.

refuel *v* puniti gorivom.
refuge *n* utočište, sklonište.
refugee *n* izbeglica.
refund *n* povraćaj (novca); *v* povratiti (novac).
refurbish *v* obnoviti.
refusal *n* odbijanje.
refuse *v* odbiti; *n* smeće, otpaci.
refuse collector *n* smećar.
refute *v* poricati, pobijati.
regain *v* povratiti, ponovo steći.
regal *a* kraljevski.
regale *v* gostiti.
regalia *npl* regalije, znakovi kraljevske časti; kraljevske povlastice.
regard *v* smatrati; odnositi se; *n* obzir; poštovanje.
regarding *prep* što se tiče, s obzirom na.
regardless *adv* uprkos tome.
regatta *n* regata.
regency *n* regentstvo, namesništvo.
regenerate *a* preporođen; poboljšan; *v* preporoditi se.
regeneration *n* obnova; preporod.
regent *n* regent, namesnik.
regime *n* režim.
regiment *n* puk.
region *n* oblast, predeo; sfera.
register *n* registar; spisak; *v* zabeležiti; registrovati se; ~ed letter *n* preporučeno pismo.
registrar *n* arhivar, pisar; matičar.
registration *n* upis, prijavljivanje; registracija.
registry *n* registar; matični ured.
regressive *a* regresivan.
regret *n* žaljenje; izvinjenje; *v* žaliti.
regretful *a* žalostan.
regular *a* redovan; stalan; pravilan (*gram*); ~ly *adv* redovno, pravilno.
regularity *n* pravilnost, urednost, tačnost.
regulate *v* regulisati, srediti.
regulation *n* regulisanje; propis, odredba.
regulator *n* regulator; uređivač.
rehabilitate *v* rehabilitovati.
rehabilitation *n* rehabilitacija.
rehearsal *n* proba; ponavljanje.
rehearse *v* probati (*pozor*); ponavljati; nabrajati.
reign *n* vladavina; *v* vladati.
reimburse *v* naknaditi.

reimbursement *n* naknada.
rein *n* uzda, povodac; *v* terati konja.
reindeer *n* irvas.
reinforce *v* pojačati.
reinstate *v* ponovo postaviti.
reinsure *v* reosigurati.
reissue *v* ponovo izdati.
reiterate *v* neprestano ponavljati.
reiteration *n* neprestano ponavljanje.
reject *v* odbaciti; poreći, odbiti.
rejection *n* odbijanje, odbacivanje.
rejoice *v* radovati se.
rejoicing *n* radovanje, radost.
relapse *n* povraćaj (bolesti); *v* ponovo oboleti.
relate *v* pripovedati; odnositi se; dovesti u vezu.
related *a* povezan; srodan.
relation *n* odnos; veza; srodstvo.
relationship *n* odnos; srodstvo; povezanost.
relative *n* rođak; *a* koji se odnosi; relativan; ~ ly *adv* relativno.
relax *v* opustiti (se); odmarati se.
relaxation *n* relaksacija.
relay *n* smena (vojnika, radnika); relej; *v* preneti, poslati relejom.
release *n* oslobađanje; popuštanje; razrešenje; *v* pustiti; osloboditi.
relegate *v* prognati; lišiti čina.
relegation *n* izručenje; degradiranje.
relent *v* popustiti.
relentless *a* nemilosrdan; neumoran.
relevant *a* relevantan, bitan.
reliable *a* pouzdan.
reliance *n* pouzdanje; poverenje.
relic *n* relikvija.
relief *n* olakšanje; pomoć; oslobođenje; reljef.
relieve *v* olakšati; osloboditi; smeniti.
religion *n* vera, religija.
religious *a* pobožan, religiozan; ~ly *adv* religiozno.
relinquish *v* napustiti; odreći se.
relish *n* ukus; slast; začin; *v* uživati.
reluctance *n* nevoljnost.
reluctant *a* nerad, protiv volje.
rely *v* uzdati se, osloniti se na.
remain *v* ostati, preostati.
remainder *n* ostatak.
remains *npl* ostaci.

remand v vratiti; **to ~ in custody** vratiti u zatvor.

remark n primedba; v primetiti.

remarkable a izvanredan, izuzetan.

remarkably adv izvanredno, jako.

remarry v ponovo se oženiti, preudati se.

remedial a popravni; dopunski.

remedy n lek, pomoć; v izlečiti; popraviti.

remember v setiti se; pamtiti; pozdraviti.

remembrance n sećanje; uspomena.

remind v podsetiti.

reminiscence n uspomena, reminiscencija.

remiss a nemaran; trom.

remission n slanje; oproštenje; oslobođenje.

remit v uputiti; doznačiti (novac); ukinuti (kaznu).

remittance n doznaka, novčana pošiljka.

remnant n ostatak.

remodel v prepraviti; preudesiti.

remonstrate v prigovarati; žaliti se.

remorse n pokajanje; sažaljenje.

remorseless a nemilosrdan, okrutan, bezobziran.

remote a udaljen; dalek; **~ly** adv udaljeno.

remote control (TV) n daljinski upravljač.

remoteness n udaljenost, daljina.

removable a odstranjiv.

removal n sklanjanje; premeštaj.

remove v skloniti, ukloniti; skinuti; udaljiti; preseliti se.

remunerate v platiti, nagraditi; obeštetiti.

remuneration n plata, nagrada; obeštećenje.

render v pružiti (pomoć); učiniti; prikazivati; izvesti.

rendezvous n randevu, sastanak.

renegade n odmetnik, otpadnik.

renew v obnoviti; produžiti.

renewal n obnova; produženje.

rennet n sirište.

renounce v odreći se, odustati.

renovate v obnoviti, renovirati.

renovation n obnova.

renown n slava, renome.

renowned a slavan, čuven.

rent n kirija; zakup; v uzeti u zakup; iznajmiti.

rental n zakup; iznajmljivanje.

renunciation n odricanje, napuštanje; nepriznavanje.

reopen v ponovo otvoriti.

reorganization n reorganizacija.

reorganize v reorganizovati.

repair n popravka; v popraviti; nadoknaditi.

reparable a popravljiv, nadoknadiv.

reparation n obeštećenje.

repartee n duhovit odgovor.

repatriate v vratiti u domovinu (zarobljenike i sl.).

repay v vratiti dug; osvetiti se.

repayment n vraćanje duga; ponovno plaćanje.

repeal n opozivanje, ukidanje; v opozvati, ukinuti.

repeat v ponavljati; ponoviti se.

repeatedly adv ponovo, nekoliko puta.

repeater n ponavljač; ponovni prekršilac zakona.

repel v suzbiti, odbiti; izazivati neprijateljstvo.

repent v pokajati se; tugovati.

repentance n pokajanje, kajanje.

repentant a pokajnički.

repertory n repertoar; skladište.

repetition n ponavljanje; proba.

replace v vratiti na mesto; zamenjivati nekoga.

replant v ponovo posaditi.

replenish v napuniti.

replete a napunjen.

reply n odgovor; v odgovoriti.

report n izveštaj; raport (voj); reportaža; v podneti izveštaj; izvestiti; saopštiti.

reporter n dopisnik, reporter.

repose n odmor; v odmarati se.

repository n skladište.

repossess v ponovo uzeti u posed.

reprehend v prekoriti.

reprehensible a prekoran; vredan osude.

represent v predstavljati, zastupati; prikazati.

representation n predstavljanje, zastupanje; prikazivanje.

representative n predstavnik; a tipičan, karakterističan.

repress v potisnuti, suzbiti; ugušiti.
repression n suzbijanje; represija.
repressive a represivan.
reprieve n odlaganje izvršenja presude; predah; v odložiti izvršenje presude; dopustiti predah.
reprimand n ukor, prigovor; v prigovoriti, ukoriti.
reprint n novo izdanje; v preštampati.
reprisal n odmazda, represalija.
reproach n ukor, prekor; sramota; v ukoriti.
reproachful a prekoran, uvredljiv; sramotan; ~ly adv prekorno.
reproduce v reprodukovati; množiti se.
reproduction n reprodukcija; razmnožavanje.
reptile n reptil, gmizavac.
republic n republika.
republican a republički.
republicanism n republikanizam.
repudiate v odreći se; poricati.
repugnance n odvratnost, gađenje; nedoslednost.
repugnant a odvratan; odbojan; ~ly adv nerado, s odvratnošću.
repulse n odbijanje, otpor; v suzbiti; odbiti (napad).
repulsion n odbijanje; odvratnost.
repulsive a odvratan, odbojan.
reputable a uvažen, poštovan.
reputation n ugled, reputacija.
repute v uživati glas kao; smatrati za.
request n molba, zahtev; v zahtevati, tražiti.
request stop n zaustavljanje autobusa na molbu .
require v zahtevati; trebati.
requirement n zahtev; potreba.
requisite n potrepština; a potreban.
requisition n trebovanje, zahtev.
requite v vratiti, uzvratiti.
rescind v ukinuti.
rescue n spasavanje; v spasti.
research n istraživanje; traganje; v istraživati; tragati.
resemblance n sličnost.
resemble v ličiti (na).
resent v vređati se.
resentful a ogorčen; uvređen; ~ly adv uvređeno.
resentment n ogorčenost, srdžba.

reservation n izgovor; rezervacija.
reserve n zaliha, rezerva; v rezervisati; zadržati.
reservedly adv rezervisano, uzdržano.
reservoir n rezervoar.
reside v stanovati, prebivati, boraviti.
residence n prebivalište; stanovanje.
resident n stanovnik.
residuary a preostao; taložni; ~ legatee (jur) naslednik ostatka zaostavštine po odbitku svih troškova itd.
residue n ostatak; talog (hem).
resign v podneti ostavku; pomiriti se (s nečim).
resignation n ostavka; rezignacija.
resin n smola.
resinous a smolast.
resist v protiviti se; pružati otpor; odolevati.
resistance n otpor; otpornost.
resolute a odlučan; ~ly adv odlučno.
resolution n odluka; odlučnost.
resolve v odlučiti (se); rešiti.
resonance n rezonanca.
resonant a zvučan; rezonantan.
resort n odmaralište; utočište; v posećivati; pribeći.
resound v odjeknuti; proneti.
resource n izvor; bogatstvo.
respect n poštovanje; pogled, obzir; v poštovati; ~s npl pozdrav.
respectability n poštovanost, uvaženost.
respectable a poštovan, uvažen.
repectably adv vredno poštovanja.
respectful a pun poštovanja; učtiv; ~ly adv s poštovanjem.
respecting prep s obzirom na, što se tiče.
respective a odnosan; svoj; ~ly adv odnosno.
respirator n respirator.
respiratory a disajni.
respite n predah; odlaganje; v odgoditi (rok); dati predaha.
resplendence n sjaj, blistavost.
resplendent a sjajan, blistav.
respond v odgovoriti; reagovati.
respondent n tužena strana (u brakorazvodnoj parnici).
response n odgovor; reakcija, odziv.
responsibility n odgovornost; obaveze.
responsible a odgovoran.

responsive *a* osećajan, pun razumevanja.
rest *n* odmor; pauza (*muz*); uporište; ostatak; *v* odmoriti se; nasloniti se; nalaziti se; preostati.
restaurant *n* restoran.
resting place *n* odmaralište; grob.
restitution *n* obnavljanje; naknada.
restive *a* nestrpljiv; jogunast (konji).
restless *a* nemiran.
restoration *n* uspostavljanje; restauracija.
restorative *a* okrepljujući.
restore *v* ponovo uspostaviti; restaurirati.
restrain *v* uzdržati (se); obuzdati.
restraint *n* uzdržljivost; odmerenost.
restrict *v* ograničiti.
restriction *n* ograničenje.
restrictive *a* restriktivan, koji ograničuje.
result *n* rezultat; *v* poticati, rezultirati.
resume *v* ponovo zauzeti; nastaviti.
resurrection *n* uskrsnuće; ponovno uspostavljanje.
resuscitate *v* oživeti, vratiti snagu; vaskrsavati.
retail *n* maloprodaja; *v* prodavati na malo; prepričavati.
retain *v* zadržati; zapamtiti.
retainer *n* vazal, sluga; kapara.
retake *v* ponovo uzeti.
retaliate *v* osvetiti se; uložiti protivtužbu.
retaliation *n* odmazda, osveta.
retardation *n* zaostalost (u razvoju); usporavanje.
retarded *a* zaostao (u razvoju).
retch *v* osećati nadražaj na povraćanje.
retention *n* zadržavanje.
retentive *a* koji zadržava; dobro (pamćenje).
reticence *n* povučenost; ćutljivost.
retina *n* retina, mrežnjača (*med*).
retire *v* otići; penzionisati se; otići na spavanje.
retired *a* u penziji; povučen, u samoći.
retirement *n* penzionisanje; povučenost.
retort *n* retorta; duhovit odgovor; *v* duhovito odgovoriti.
retouch *v* doterivati, retuširati (sliku).
retrace *v* pratiti, oživeti u sećanju; vraćati se (pređenim putem).
retract *n* uvući (kandže); poreći; odgađati.
retrain *v* prekvalifikovati.

retraining *n* prekvalifikacija.
retreat *n* povlačenje, odstupanje; *v* povući se.
retribution *n* kazna, odmazda.
retrievable *a* nadoknadiv.
retrieve *v* povratiti, naći (izgubljeno); ispraviti; doneti.
retriever *n* pas aporter; retriver (vrsta psa).
retrograde *a* nazadan .
retrospect *n* osvrt, pogled unazad.
retrospection *n* retrospektiva.
retrospective *a* retrospektivan, koji se osvrće unazad.
return *n* povratak; povraćaj; prihod; *v* vratiti; ponoviti se; donositi (prihod).
reunion *n* ponovno sjedinjenje; zajednički susret.
reunite *v* ponovo sjediniti; ponovo se sastati.
rev counter *n* brzinomer.
reveal *v* otkriti; obelodaniti.
revel *v* bančiti; veseliti se.
revelation *n* otkriće; otkrovenje.
reveller *n* sudionik terevenke.
revelry *n* terevenka, lumpovanje.
revenge *n* osveta; *v* osvetiti se.
revengeful *a* osvetoljubiv.
revenue *n* prihod.
reverberate *v* odbijati; odjeknuti.
reverberation *n* odbijanje; odjek.
revere *v* duboko poštovati.
reverence *n* duboko poštovanje; *v* poštovati.
reverend *a* poštovan; častan; *n* sveštenik.
reverent *a* pun poštovanja, poštovan.
reverential *a* pun strahopoštovanja.
reversal *n* promena, preokret; ukidanje, poništenje.
reverse *n* suprotnost; naličje; *v* preokrenuti; promeniti (pravac).
reversible *a* koji se može okrenuti; sa dva lica.
reversing lights *npl* zadnji reflektori.
reversion *n* vraćanje; povratak imovine.
revert *v* vratiti se (u prvobitno stanje); vratiti ranijem vlasniku.
review *n* pregled; razmatranje; revizija; smotra (*voj*); časopis, revija; *v* pregledati; ponovo razmotriti; oceniti; izvršiti smotru.

reviewer *n* kritičar, recenzent.
revile *v* grditi, psovati.
revise *v* ispraviti; preraditi.
reviser *n* pregledač; revizor.
revision *n* ponovni pregled, revizija.
revisit *v* ponovo posetiti.
revival *n* oživljavanje, preporod; obnova.
revive *v* osvestiti se; oživeti; obnoviti (običaje i sl.).
revocation *n* opoziv.
revoke *v* opozvati.
revolt *n* pobuna, revolt; odvratnost; *v* pobuniti se; osećati odvratnost.
revolting *a* odvratan.
revolution *n* revolucija; preokret; obrtaj.
revolutionary *a* revolucionarni.
revolve *v* okretati se; smenjivati se (god.doba).
revolver *n* revolver.
revolving *a* koji se obrće.
revue *n* revija (*pozor. muz*).
revulsion *n* odvratnost; nagla promena.
reward *n* nagrada; naknada; *v* nagraditi; dati po zasluzi.
rhapsody *n* rapsodija, hvalospev.
rhetoric *n* retorika.
rhetorical *a* retorički.
rheumatic *a* reumatičan.
rheumatism *n* reumatizam.
rhinoceros *n* nosorog.
rhomboid *n* romboid.
rhombus *n* romb.
rhubarb *n* raven (*bot*).
rhyme *n* rima; *v* rimovati se.
rhythm *n* ritam; mera, metar (u stihu).
rhythmical *a* ritmičan.
rib *n* rebro; oštrica.
ribald *a* razuzdan .
ribbon *n* vrpca, traka; pramenje.
rice *n* pirinač.
rich *a* bogat; obilan; mastan; ~ly *adv* bogato, obilno.
riches *npl* bogatstvo.
richness *n* bogatstvo; obilje; sočnost.
rickets *n* rahitis (*med*).
rickety *a* rahitičan; klimav.
rid *v* osloboditi, izbaviti.
riddance *n* oslobođenje; good ~ dobro je što smo ga se otarasili!.
riddle *n* zagonetka; rešeto; *v* odgonetnuti; govoriti u zagonetkama.

ride *n* jahanje; vožnja; *v* jahati; voziti se.
rider *n* jahač; dopuna (dokumenta).
ridge *n* greben; sleme (krova); brazda; *v* praviti brazde.
ridicule *n* ismevanje; *v* ismevati.
ridiculous *a* smešan; ~ly *adv* smešno.
riding *n* jahanje.
riding habit *n* jahaće odelo.
riding school *n* škola jahanja.
rife *a* mnogobrojan; obilat; rasprostranjen.
riffraff *n* ološ, rulja; otpaci.
rifle[1] *v* opljačkati; ispreturati.
rifle[2] *n* puška.
rifleman *n* strelac.
rig[1] *n* oprema broda; brazda.
rig[2] *v* opremiti; odenuti.
rigging *n* oprema broda.
right *n* pravo; desna strana; *a* pravi; ispravan; ~! tako je!; ispravno, kako treba; desno; ~ly *adv* kako treba; pravedno.
righteous *a* pravedan; ~ly *adv* pravedno.
righteousness *n* pravednost.
rigid *a* krut; strog; ukočen; ~ly *adv* strogo, nepopustljivo.
rigidity *n* krutost, strogost; ukočenost.
rigmarole *n* besmislica.
rigorous *a* strog, rigorozan; ~ly *adv* rigorozno.
rigour *n* strogost; surovost (klime i sl.).
rim *n* rub, ivica.
rind *n* kora, ljuska.
ring[1] *n* prsten; kolut; arena; zvonjenje.
ring[2] *v* opkoliti; zvoniti; zvečati; to ~ the bell podsetiti na nešto.
ring road *n* kružni put.
ringer *n* zvonar.
ringleader *n* kolovođa.
ringlet *n* uvojak (kose).
ringworm *n* temenac (*med*).
rink (ice ~) *n* klizalište.
rinse *v* isprati.
riot *n* pobuna; razuzdanost; *v* pobuniti se; besneti.
rioter *n* buntovnik.
riotous *a* buntovan; raskalašan; ~ly *adv* buntovno; razuzdano.
rip *v* poderati; pocepati.
ripe *a* zreo, sazreo.
ripen *v* zreti, sazreti.
ripeness *n* zrelost.

rip-off *n*; **it's a ~!** To je prevara!.
ripple *n* mreškanje (vode); talasić; žubor;
 v mreškati se; žuboriti.
rise[1] *v* dići se, ustati; rasti; dizati se.
rise[2] *n* dizanje; uspon; izlazak; uzvišenje;
 porast.
rising *n* ustajanje; penjanje; izlazak
 (sunca); ustanak.
risk *n* rizik, opasnost; *v* izlagati se
 opasnosti; rizikovati.
risky *a* rizičan, riskantan.
rite *n* obred, običaj.
ritual *n* ritual, obred; *a* ritualan.
rival *n* suparnik, rival; *a* suparnički; *v*
 takmičiti se.
rivalry *n* suparništvo, rivalitet.
river *n* reka.
riverside *a* rečni, uz reku.
rivet *n* zakivak; *v* zakovati; prikovati
 (pogled i sl.).
rivulet *n* potočić.
road *n* put; ulica.
road sign *n* putokaz.
roadstead *n* (*naut*) sidrište.
roadworks *npl* radovi na putu.
roam *v* lutati, tumarati.
roan *a* crvenkastosiv.
roar *n* rika; zavijanje (vetra); tutnjava; *v*
 rikati; zavijati (vetar); tutnjati.
roast *v* pržiti; peći.
roast beef *n* goveđa pečenka.
rob *v* opljačkati; oteti.
robber *n* pljačkaš.
robbery *n* pljačka, krađa.
robe *n* odora; plašt; *v* oblačiti se.
robin (redbreast) *n* crvendać (ptica).
robust *a* snažan, robustan.
robustness *n* snažnost, krepkost, jačina.
rock *n* kamen, stena; *v* ljuljati se; uljuljkivati.
rock and roll *n* rokenrol.
rock crystal *n* kvarc.
rocket *n* raketa.
rocking chair *n* stolica za ljuljanje.
rock salt *n* kamena so.
rocky *a* kamenit; nepokolebljiv; klimav.
rod *n* štap; šipka; štap udice.
rodent *n* glodar (*zool*).
roe[1] *n* srna, košuta.
roe[2] *n* ikra, mrest.
roebuck *n* srndać.
rogue *n* varalica, lopov; vragolan.

roguish *a* lopovski; nevaljao.
roll *n* kotrljanje, valjanje; valjak; kotur;
 svitak; spisak; zemička; *v* kotrljati;
 saviti (se); zamotati.
roller *n* valjak, cilindar.
roller skates *n* koturaljke.
rolling pin *n* oklagija.
Roman Catholic *n* rimokatolik; *a*
 rimokatolički.
romance *n* romansa (*lit*); romansa (*muz*);
 romantična ljubav; romantičnost.
romantic *a* romantičan.
romp *v* bučno i razuzdano se veseliti.
roof *n* krov; vrhunac; nepce.
roofing *n* krov; krovni materijal.
rook[1] *n* vrana grakuša; varalica.
rook[2] *n* top, kula (šah).
room *n* soba; mesto; prostor.
roominess *n* prostranost.
roomy *a* prostran.
roost *n* sedalo; motka na kojoj perad
 spava; *v* sedeti na sedalu; spavati na
 motki.
root[1] *n* koren, korenaste biljke; *v*
 ukoreniti; puštati korenje; **to ~ out**
 iskoreniti.
root[2] *n* koren (*mat*).
rooted *a* ukorenjen, duboko usađen.
rope *n* konopac, uže; laso; *v* vezati
 konopcem; uhvatiti lasom.
rope maker *n* užar.
rosary *n* brojanice; ružičnjak.
rose *n* ruža.
rose bed *n* ružičnjak.
rosebud *n* ružin pupoljak.
rosemary *n* ruzmarin.
rose tree *n* ružin šib.
rosette *n* rozeta (značka); ukras u obliku
 ruže (*arh*).
rose wine *n* roze (vrsta vina).
rosewood *n* palisandrovo drvo.
rosiness *n* rumenilo, ružičasta boja.
rosy *a* rumen, ružičast.
rot *n* trulež; besmislica; neuspeh; *v*
 trunuti; kvariti.
rotate *v* okretati (se); smenjivati.
rotation *n* okretanje; smenjivanje.
rote *n* učenje napamet.
rotten *a* truo, pokvaren; neupotrebljiv;
 podao.
rottenness *n* trulost, gnjilež; pokvarenost.

rotund *a* okrugao; zvučan.

rouble *n* rublja.

rouge *n* ruž; rumenilo (za lice).

rough *a* hrapav; sirov; buran, oštar; prost; čupav; opor; *adv* grubo, oštro; **~ looking** grubog izgleda.

roughcast *n* grubo malterisanje.

roughen *v* učiniti hrapavim.

roughly *adv* grubo; približno.

roughness *n* hrapavost; neravnost; grubost; čupavost.

roulette *n* rulet.

round *n* krug; obilazak; runda; *a* okrugao; približan; **~ly** *adv* otvoreno, iskreno; potpuno; *v* zaobliti; zaokružiti; obići.

roundabout *a* zaobilazan; *n* vrteška, karusel.

roundness *n* okruglost.

rouse *v* probuditi; pobuditi; poplašiti.

rout *n* poraz; bezglavo bekstvo; *v* razbiti, naterati u bekstvo.

route *n* pravac, put, maršruta.

routine *n* rutina; *a* rutinski; ustaljen.

rove *v* lutati, tumarati.

rover *n* lutalica, skitnica.

row[1] *n* svađa, vika, tučnjava.

row[2] *n* red, niz;

row[3] *n* veslanje; *v* veslati.

rowdy *n* grubijan, siledžija.

rower *n* veslač.

royal *a* kraljevski; veličanstven; **~ly** *adv* kraljevski; sjajno.

royalist *n* rojalista .

royalties *npl* regalije, znakovi kraljevske časti; tantijeme (od autorskog prava i sl.).

royalty *n* kraljevstvo; kraljevsko dostojanstvo.

rub *n* trljanje, brisanje; teškoća; *v* trljati; ribati; izbrisati.

rubber *n* guma, kaučuk; gumica za brisanje; (*sleng*) kondom.

rubber-band *n* lastiš.

rubbish *n* smeće, otpaci; besmislica.

rubric *n* rubrika.

ruby *n* rubin.

rucksack *n* ranac, ruksak.

rudder *n* kormilo.

ruddiness *n* crvenilo, rumenilo.

ruddy *a* crven, rumen.

rude *a* grub, neobrađen; primitivan; **~ly** *adv* grubo, osorno, prostački.

rudeness *n* grubost, neučtivost.

rudiment *n* osnov, rudiment.

rue *n* ruta, rutvica (*bot*); *v* žaliti; tugovati.

rueful *a* žalostan.

ruffian *n* siledžija; *a* brutalan.

ruffle *v* nabirati; remetiti mir; buniti se.

rug *n* ćilim; pokrivač.

rugby *n* ragbi.

rugged *a* hrapav, neravan; naboran; snažan.

ruin *n* propast, slom; ruševine; *v* upropastiti; razoriti.

ruinous *a* poguban, razoran.

rule *n* pravilo; vladavina; *v* vladati, upravljati.

ruler *n* vladar; lenjir.

rum *n* rum.

rumble *v* tutnjati, grmeti.

ruminate *v* preživeti; razmišljati.

rummage *v* preturati, pretraživati.

rumour *n* glasine; *v* širiti glasine.

rump *n* stražnjica stražnji deo (*sleng*).

run *n* trčanje; tok; pravac; niz; vremenski razmak; pređeni put; *v* trčati; kretati se; teći; prolaziti; glasiti; **to ~ the risk** izlagati se opasnosti.

runaway *n* begunac.

rung *n* prečka.

runner *n* trkač; krijumčar; kurir.

running *n* trčanje; curenje; rad, kretanje; kandidovanje.

runway *n* avionska pista.

rupture *n* prelom; raskid; kila (*med*); perforacija.

rural *a* seoski, poljski.

ruse *n* lukavstvo, prevara.

rush *n* žurba; pritisak; navala; *v* požuriti; zauzeti na juriš.

rusk *n* dvopek.

russet *a* crvenosmeđ.

rust *n* rđa; snet (*bot*); *v* zarđati; oslabiti.

rustic *n* seljak; prostak; *a* seoski, priprost; grub.

rustiness *n* zarđalost.

rustle *v* šuštati; krasti stoku.

rustling *n* šuštanje.

rusty *a* zarđao; zapušten; mrzovoljan.

rut *n* brazda, kolosek; rutina; navika.

ruthless *a* nemilosrdan; **~ly** *adv* nemilosrdno, okrutno.

rye *n* raž.

S

Sabbath n subota (dan počinka i praznik Jevreja).
sable n samur; samurovina (krzno).
sabotage n sabotaža; diverzija.
sabre n sablja .
saccharin n saharin.
sachet n kesica za držanje džepne maramice; kesica sa mirišljavim prahom.
sack[1] n džak; pljačka.
sack[2] v otpustiti sa posla; opljačkati.
sacrament n krštenje, pričest; simbol; zavet.
sacramental a pričesni.
sacred a svet; duhovni (muzika); neprikosnoven.
sacredness n svetost, svetinja.
sacrifice n žrtva; prinošenje žrtve; v žrtvovati; prinositi žrtvu.
sacrificial a žrtveni.
sacrilege n svetogrđe.
sacrilegious a svetogrdan.
sad a tužan; neugodan, nemio; ~ly adv žalosno.
sadden v ražalostiti (se).
saddle n sedlo; v osedlati konja; opteretiti.
saddlebag n bisaga.
saddler n sedlar.
sadness n tuga.
safari n lovački pohod, safari.
safe n sef; a siguran, bezbedan; ~ly adv sigurno, bez opasnosti; ~ and sound zdrav i čitav.
safe-conduct n osiguran slobodan prolaz; sprovodno pismo.
safeguard n zaštita, osiguranje; v osigurati, zaštititi.
safety n bezbednost, sigurnost.
safety belt n sigurnosni pojas.
safety match n šibica.
safety pin n pribadača, zihernadla.
saffron n šafran (bot).
sage[1] n mudrac; a mudar; ~ly adv mudro; razborito.
sage[2] n žalfija (bot).
Sagittarius n Strelac (astrol).
sago n sago (palma) (bot).
sail n jedro; jedrilica; v ploviti, jedriti.

sailing n jedrenje; navigacija.
sailing boat n jedrenjak.
sailor n mornar.
saint n svetac.
sainted, saintly a sveti; svetački, pobožan.
sake n stvar, svrha; **For God's** ~ Za ime božje!.
salad n salata.
salad bowl n činija za salatu.
salad dressing n preliv za salatu.
salad oil n ulje za salatu.
salamander n daždevnjak (zool).
salary n plata, zarada.
sale n prodaja; rasprodaja; aukcija.
saleable a koji se može prodati.
salesman n prodavac.
saleswoman n prodavačica.
salient a istaknut; glavni.
saline a slan; posoljen.
saliva n pljuvačka.
sallow a žućkast (boja bolesna izgleda).
sally n pokušaj proboja; šetnja (van grada); dosetka; v izvršiti proboj; krenuti na izlet.
salmon n losos.
salmon trout n semgasta pastrmka.
saloon[1] n dvorana za primanje; kafana.
saloon[2] n zatvoreni automobil. Vidi sedan
salt n so; v posoliti.
salt cellar n slanik.
salting n soljenje; usoljavanje.
saltpetre n šalitra.
saltworks npl solana.
salubrious a zdrav, koristan po zdravlje.
salubriousness, salubrity n zdravost, lekovitost.
salutary a koristan, lekovit.
salutation n pozdrav, pozdravljanje.
salute n pozdrav; počasna paljba; pozdraviti; salutirati.
salvage n spasavanje; spašene stvari.
salvation n spasenje, spas.
salve n melem; sredstvo za umirenje.
salver n poslužavnik.
salvo n salva, plotun; burno odobravanje.
same a isti.

sameness *n* istovetnost.
sample *n* uzorak, proba; *v* probati.
sampler *n* uzimač uzoraka.
sanatorium *n* sanatorijum.
sanctify *v* osvetiti, posvetiti.
sanctimonious *a* licemeran, pritvorno pobožan.
sanction *n* dozvola; odobrenje; *v* potvrditi; odobriti.
sanctity *n* svetost, nepovredivost.
sanctuary *n* svetilište; utočište.
sand *n* pesak; *v* posuti peskom.
sandal *n* sandala.
sandbag *n* vreća peska.
sandpit *n* peščara, peskokop.
sandstone *n* peščar, peščani kamen.
sandwich *n* sendvič.
sandy *a* peščan, peskovit.
sane *a* duševno zdrav; razuman.
sanguinary *a* krvni, krvav; krvožedan.
sanguine *a* crven (kao krv); sangviničan.
sanitary towel *n* higijenski uložak.
sanity *n* duševno zdravlje, zdrav razum.
sap *n* biljni sok; prokop; *v* podrivati.
sapient *a* mudar, koji mudruje.
sapling *n* mlado stablo; mlado stvorenje.
sapper *n* pionir (*voj*).
sapphire *n* safir.
sarcasm *n* sarkazam.
sarcastic *a* zajedljiv, sarkastičan; **~ally** *adv* zajedljivo, sarkastično.
sarcophagus *n* sarkofag.
sardine *n* sardina.
sash *n* prozorski okvir; pojas, opasač.
sash window *n* prozor na dizanje i spuštanje.
Satan *n* satana, đavo.
satanic(al) *a* đavolski.
satchel *n* školska torba.
satellite *n* satelit .
satellite dish *n* satelitska TV antena.
satiate, sate *v* zasititi.
satin *n* saten; *a* satenski.
satire *n* satira.
satiric(al) *a* satiričan.
satirically *adv* satirično.
satirist *n* satiričar.
satirize *v* izvrgnuti satiri.
satisfaction *n* zadovoljstvo; zadovoljenje, satisfakcija.
satisfactorily *adv* na zadovoljstvo.

satisfactory *a* zadovoljavajući.
satisfy *v* zadovoljiti, udovoljiti; odgovarati (zahtevima).
saturate *v* zasititi; natopiti.
Saturday *n* subota.
saturnine *a* mrzovoljan; flegmatičan.
satyr *n* satir.
sauce *n* sos; drskost; *v* preliti sosom; drsko razgovarati.
saucepan *n* tiganj.
saucer *n* tanjirić, tacna.
saucily *adv* drsko, bezobrazno.
sauciness *n* drskost.
saucy *a* drzak.
saunter *v* tumarati, lunjati.
sausage *n* kobasica.
savage *a* divlji; okrutan; **~ly** *adv* divlje; okrutno.
savageness *n* divljaštvo, surovost.
savagery *n* divljaštvo; necivilizovanost.
savanna(h) *n* savana.
save *v* spasti; čuvati; štedeti; *adv* osim, osim što, ako ne; *n* uspešna odbrana (*sport*).
saveloy (sausage) *n* salfalada (kobasica).
saver *n* štediša; spasilac.
saving *a* štedljiv; *prep* osim, izuzev; *n* štedljivost; spas.
savings account *n* štedni račun.
savings bank *n* štedionica.
Saviour *n* Spasitelj (Isus).
savour *n* ukus; draž; *v* uživati (u).
savouriness *n* prijatan ukus; draženost.
savoury *a* ukusan; pikantan.
saw *n* testera; *v* testerisati.
sawdust *n* strugotina.
sawfish *n* testerača (*zool*).
sawmill *n* pilana.
sawyer *n* testeraš.
saxophone *n* saksofon.
say *v* reći; govoriti; izjaviti.
saying *n* poslovica; kazivanje.
scab *n* štrajkolomac; šuga, svrab; *v* biti kršitelj štrajka; ošugaviti.
scabbard *n* korice (za oružje).
scabby *a* krastav; šugav.
scaffold *n* skele (zidarske); gubilište.
scaffolding *n* skele.
scald *n* opekotina; *v* opariti, ožeći.
scale[1] *n* skala; ; **~s** *npl* vaga.
scale[2] *n* skala (*muz*).

scale[3] *n* krljušt, skinuti krljušt.
scale[4] *v* popeti se (na); savladati.
scallop *n* kapica (školjka); plitki tiganj; *v* izreckati; pripremiti u tiganju.
scalp *n* skalp; lobanja; *v* skalpirati.
scamp *n* nitkov .
scamper *v* trčati; pobeći.
scampi *npl* škampi.
scan *v* osmatrati; pažljivo razgledati.
scandal *n* skandal; sramota.
scandalize *v* zgranuti, skandalizovati.
scandalous *a* skandalozan; ~ly *adv* skandalozno.
scanner *n* skener, čitač.
scant, scanty *a* oskudan, nedovoljan.
scantily *adv* skučeno; nedovoljno.
scantiness *n* oskudnost.
scapegoat *n* žrtveni jarac.
scar *n* ožiljak; mrlja (sramote); *v* ostaviti ožiljak.
scarce *a* redak; deficitaran; ~ly *adv* jedva.
scarcity *n* retkost; nedovoljnost.
scare *n* panika; strah; *v* preplašiti.
scarecrow *n* strašilo za ptice.
scarf *n* šal, marama.
scarlet *n* svetlo crvena boja; *a* grimizan.
scarlet fever *n* šarlah.
scarp *n* padina, kosina.
scat *interj* čisti se!.
scatter *v* razbacati, rasuti; razdati.
scavenger *n* strvinar; ulični čistač.
scenario *n* scenarij.
scene *n* pozornica; prizor; zbivanje.
scenery *n* pejzaž; kulise (u pozorištu).
scenic *a* slikovit; pozorišni, scenski.
scent *n* miris; parfem; njuh; *v* namirisati; nanjušiti.
scent bottle *n* boca parfema.
scented *a* namirisan, parfimisan.
scentless *a* bez mirisa.
sceptic *n* skeptik.
sceptic(al) *a* skeptičan, sumnjičav.
scepticism *n* skepticizam.
sceptre *n* žezlo, skiptar.
schedule *n* spisak, popis; raspored, tabela.
scheme *n* šema; plan; spletka; *v* praviti planove; praviti spletke.
schemer *n* spletkaroš.
schism *n* raskol (*rel*).
schismatic *a* raskolnički.
scholar *n* naučnik; učenik; stipendista.

scholarship *n* učenost, obrazovanje; stipendija.
scholastic *a* sholastički; dogmatičan.
school *n* škola; učenici neke škole; *v* obrazovati; disciplinovati.
schoolboy *n* učenik.
schoolgirl *n* učenica.
schooling *n* školovanje.
schoolmaster *n* nastavnik (u srednjoj školi).
schoolmistress *n* nastavnica (u srednjoj školi).
schoolteacher *n* nastavnik, učitelj.
schooner *n* škuna (brod sa dva jarbola).
sciatica *n* išijas (*med*).
science *n* nauka .
scientific *a* naučni; ~ally *adv* naučno.
scientist *n* naučnik.
scimitar *n* kriva sablja.
scintillate *v* iskriti se, svetlucati.
scintillating *a* svetlucav.
scissors *n* makaze.
scoff *v* rugati se, podsmevati se.
scold *v* grditi, psovati; prigovarati.
scoop *n* lopatica; lopata; kutlača; *v* vaditi.
scooter (child's) *n* skuter (dečji), trotinet.
scope *n* delokrug, područje; polje rada: domet.
scorch *v* opržiti (se).
score *n* zbir bodova (*sport*); rezultat; zarez; note, partitura (*muz*); *v* pobediti; postići gol (koš, poen); zarezati.
scoreboard *n* semafor za rezultate.
scorn *n* prezir, podcenjivanje; *v* prezirati, podcenjivati.
scornful *a* preziv, podrugljiv; ~ly *adv* prezrivo, podrugljivo.
Scorpio *n* Škorpija (*astrol*).
scorpion *n* škorpija.
scotch *v* zaseći; suzbiti.
Scotch *n* škotski viski.
scoundrel *n* hulja, nitkov.
scour *v* sprati; očistiti; izribati.
scourge *n* bič; *v* bičevati.
scout *n* izviđač; skaut; izviđački avion; *v* izviđati.
scowl *n* mrk pogled; *v* mrštiti se.
scragginess *n* džombavost; mršavost.
scraggy *a* mršav, koščat; vrlo neravan (tlo).
scramble *n* gužva, jagma; *v* verati se; jagmiti se.

scrap *n* komadić; odsečak; ogrizak.
scrape *n* grebotina; struganje; *v* strugati; ogrepsti.
scraper *n* strugač; grebač.
scratch *n* ogrebotina, grebanje; svrab; *v* ogrepsti; češati se.
scrawl *n* škrabotina; *v* škrabati.
scream, screech *n* vrisak; *v* vrisnuti.
screen *n* zaklon; pregrada; sito; *v* zakloniti; ekranizovati.
screenplay *n* scenarij.
screw *n* zavrtanj, šraf; propeler; *v* zašrafiti; primorati.
screwdriver *n* odvijač, šrafciger.
scribble *n* škrabanje; *v* škrabati.
scribe *n* pisar.
scrimmage *n* tučnjava, gužva.
script *n* rukopis; tekst pozorišnog komada.
scriptural *a* biblijski.
Scripture *n* Sveto pismo, Biblija.
scroll *n* svitak pergamenta (papira).
scrounger *n* žicar.
scrub *n* pranje četkom; *v* oribati.
scrub n šipražje.
scruffy *a* prljav, zapušten.
scruple *n* skrupula, ustručavanje.
scrupulous *a* pun obzira; skrupulozan; **~ly** *adv* oprezno, obazrivo.
scrutinize *v* proučiti; pregledati.
scrutiny *n* ispitivački pogled; pažljivo proučavanje.
scuffle *n* tučnjava, gužva; *v* tući se.
scull *n* kratko veslo; lak čamac.
scullery *n* kuhinjska perionica.
sculptor *n* skulptor, vajar.
sculpture *n* skulptura; vajarstvo; *v* vajati, klesati.
scum *n* pena; društveni ološ.
scurrilous *a* grub, uvredljiv; **~ly** *adv* grubo, uvredljivo.
scurvy *n* skorbut (*med*); *a* podao.
scuttle[1] *n* posuda za ugalj.
scuttle[2] *n* žuran hod, naglo povlačenje; *v* bežati.
scuttle[3] *n* poklopac na krovu kuće, na palubi broda.
scythe *n* kosa (poljoprivredna alatka).
sea *n* more; *a* morski; **heavy ~** *n* uzburkano more.
sea breeze *n* povetarac s mora.

seacoast *n* morska obala.
sea fight *n* pomorska bitka.
seafood *n* plodovi mora.
sea front *n* lučki deo grada; niz zgrada koji gleda na more.
sea-green *a* zelen kao more.
seagull *n* galeb.
sea horse *n* morski konjić.
seal *n* pečat; žig; plomba; foka; *v* zapečatiti, zalepiti; zaplombirati.
sealing wax *n* pečatni vosak.
seam *n* šav; *v* sašiti, spojiti.
seaman *n* mornar, pomorac.
seamanship *n* veština plovidbe, pomorstvo.
seamstress *n* švalja, krojačica.
seamy *a* neprijatan, neugledan.
seaplane *n* hidroavion.
seaport *n* morska luka.
sear *v* osušiti; spržiti.
search *n* traženje; premetačina; *v* tragati; pretražiti.
searchlight *n* reflektor.
seashore *n* morska obala.
seasick *a* bolestan od morske bolesti.
seasickness *n* morska bolest.
seaside *n* morska obala.
season *n* godišnje doba; sezona; *v* dozrevati; začiniti.
season ticket *n* sezonska karta.
season ticket holder *n* vlasnik sezonske karte.
seasonable *a* odgovarajući; blagovremen.
seasonably *adv* prikladno; blagovremeno.
seasoning *n* začin.
seat *n* stolica; sedište; mesto; prebivalište; *v* posaditi, sesti; smestiti se.
seat belt *n* sigurnosni pojas.
seaward *a* okrenut moru; **~s** *adv* u pravcu mora.
seaweed *n* alge, morske trave.
seaworthy *a* pogodan za plovidbu .
secede *v* otcepiti se, izdvojiti se.
secession *n* otcepljenje, izdvajanje.
seclude *v* osamiti se; izolovati.
seclusion *n* usamljenost, izolacija.
second *n* sekunda; sekundant; drugi; *a* drugi; *v* podržati; **~ly** *adv* drugo, nadalje.
secondary *a* sekundaran, sporedan.
secondary school *n* srednja škola.

second-hand *a* polovan.
secrecy *n* tajnost.
secret *n* tajna; *a* tajni; skriven; ~ly *adv* tajno.
secretary *n* sekretar/ica; sekreter (sto).
secrete *v* izlučiti.
secretion *n* izlučenje, sekrecija.
secretive *a* tajanstven, ćutljiv.
sect *n* sekta.
sectarian *n* sektaš.
section *n* odeljenje, odsek; deo.
sector *n* sektor.
secular *a* svetovni.
secularize *v* učiniti svetovnim.
secure *a* siguran, bezbedan; *v* obezbediti; pričvrstiti; ~ly *adv* sigurno; čvrsto.
security *n* bezbednost; zalog, kaucija; garancija.
sedan *n* (*amer*) zatvor eni automobil.
sedate *a* staložen, miran; ~ly *adv* staloženo.
sedateness *n* staloženost, smirenost.
sedative *n* sedativ .
sedentary *a* koji mnogo sedi, sedeći.
sedge *n* šaš (*bot*).
sediment *n* talog.
sedition *n* poziv na ustanak, pobuna.
seditious *a* buntovnički, podrivački.
seduce *v* zavesti; nagovoriti; podmititi.
seducer *n* zavodnik.
seduction *n* zavođenje.
seductive *a* zavodljiv.
sedulous *a* marljiv, vredan; ~ly *adv* marljivo, vredno.
see *v* videti, gledati; shvatiti, razmisliti, smatrati; ispratiti.
seed *n* seme; zrno; *v* sejati; zasejati.
seedling *n* rasad.
seed time *n* setva, vreme sejanja.
seedy *a* pun semena; pohaban; iznuren.
seeing *conj* uzimajući u obzir; ~ that budući da.
seek *v* tražiti; nastojati.
seem *v* izgledati, činiti se.
seeming *a* tobožnji, prividan; *n* izgled; privid; ~ly *adv* naoko, prividno, tobože.
seemliness *n* pristojnost, prikladnost.
seemly *a* pristojan, prikladan.
seer *n* prorok, vidovit čovek.
seesaw *n* klackalica; *v* klackati se; kolebati se.

seethe *v* ključati; kipeti.
segment *n* segment.
seize *v* uhvatiti, ugrabiti; oteti.
seizure *n* osvojenje; zaplena.
seldom *adv* retko.
select *v* odabrati, izabrati; *a* odabran.
selection *n* odabiranje, selekcija.
self *n* svoje 'ja', 'ja' sam; *a* isti, bez primesa, prirodan (boja).
self-command *n* samosavlađivanje.
self-conceit *n* uobraženost, samodovoljnost.
self-confident *a* samopouzdan.
self-defence *n* samoodbrana.
self-denial *n* samoodricanje.
self-employed *a* koji radi za sebe.
self-evident *a* očigledan.
self-governing *a* nezavisan.
self-interest *n* lični interes.
selfish *a* sebičan; ~ly *adv* sebično.
selfishness *n* sebičnost.
self-medication *n* samolečenje.
self-pity *n* samosažaljenje.
self-portrait *n* autoportret.
self-possession *n* pribranost.
self-reliant *a* samopouzdan.
self-respect *n* samopoštovanje.
selfsame *a* taj isti, posve isti.
self-satisfied *a* samozadovoljan.
self-seeking *a* sebičan.
self-service *a* samouslužni.
self-styled *a* samozvani.
self-sufficient *a* nezavisan; samosvestan.
self-taught *a* samouk.
self-willed *a* samovoljan.
sell *v* prodati, prodavati; trgovati.
seller *n* prodavac.
selling-off *n* rasprodaja, rasprodavanje.
semblance *n* izgled; prividnost; sličnost.
semen *n* seme.
semester *n* semestar, polugodište.
semicircle *n* polukrug.
semicircular *a* polukružan.
semicolon *n* tačka i zapeta.
semiconductor *n* poluprovodnik.
semifinal *n* polufinale.
seminarist *n* bogoslov.
seminary *n* bogoslovija; seminar.
semitone *n* poluton (*muz*).
senate *n* senat.
senator *n* senator.

senatorial *a* senatorski.
send *v* slati, poslati, otpremiti.
sender *n* pošiljalac; adresant.
senile *a* starački, izlapeo.
senility *n* starost, izlapelost.
senior *n* stariji; učenik završnog razreda, student poslednje godine; *a* stariji.
seniority *n* starešinstvo.
senna *n* sena (*bot*).
sensation *n* osećaj; senzacija.
sense *n* osećaj, osećanje; čulo; razum; smisao, značenje.
senseless *a* besmislen; ~ly *adv* besmisleno; bezosećajno.
senselessness *n* besmislenost.
sensibility *n* osetljivost.
sensible *a* razuman, razborit.
sensibly *adv* razumno, razborito.
sensitive *a* osetljiv; senzitivan.
sensual, sensuous *a* senzualan, čulan; ~ly *adv* čulno.
sensuality *n* senzualnost; putenost.
sentence *n* rečenica (*gram*); presuda; *v* doneti presudu, osuditi.
sententious *a* poučan, mudar; ~ly *adv* poučno, mudro.
sentient *a* koji oseća.
sentiment *n* osećanje; osećajnost.
sentimental *a* osećajan, sentimentalan.
sentinel *n* stražar, straža.
sentry *n* stražar; **to stand ~** *v* strajati na straži.
sentry box *n* stražara.
separable *a* odvojiv.
separate *a* odvojen; različit; *v* odvojiti (se); razići se; ~ly *adv* posebno, odvojeno.
separation *n* odvajanje; odvojenost.
September *n* septembar.
septennial *a* sedmogodišnji.
septuagenarian *a* sedamdesetogodišnji.
sepulchre *n* grob, grobnica.
sequel *n* nastavak; naknadni događaj.
sequence *n* niz, ređanje; slaganje vremena (*gram*).
sequester *v* staviti pod zabranu (*jur*), odreći se.
sequestrate *v* zapleniti (*jur*), sekvestrirati.
sequestration *n* zaplena.
seraglio *n* sultanov dvor; harem.
seraph *n* serafim, anđeo.

serenade *n* serenada; *v* praviti (nekome) serenadu.
serene *a* miran; dostojanstven; ~ly *adv* vedro, bezbrižno.
serenity *n* mir, spokojstvo; vedrina.
serf *n* kmet, seljak; rob.
serge *n* serž (tkanina).
sergeant *n* vodnik; narednik.
serial *n* emisija, knjiga koja izlazi u nastavcima; *a* serijski, redni.
series *n* niz, ciklus; serija.
serious *a* ozbiljan, trezven; važan; ~ly *adv* ozbiljno.
sermon *n* propoved.
serous *a* serumni; koji luči serum.
serpent *n* zmija; izdajica.
serpentine *a* vijugav; *n* vijugav put; seprentina.
serrated *a* nazupčan.
serum *n* serum.
servant *n* sluga; službenik.
servant girl *n* sluškinja, kućna pomoćnica.
serve *v* poslužiti; odslužiti; učiniti uslugu; **to ~ a warrant** odslužiti kaznu.
service *n* služba, usluga, servis; servis (tenis); *v* servisirati.
serviceable *a* ispravan, upotrebljiv.
servile *a* servilan, ropski pokoran.
servitude *n* ropstvo; izdržavanje kazne.
session *n* sednica, zasedanje.
set[1] *v* staviti, položiti; primeniti; odrediti; dati; namestiti.
set[2] *n* pribor; komplet; pravac; držanje; *a* određen; postavljen; odlučan.
settee *n* mali divan.
setter *n* seter (pas).
setting *n* okolina; nameštanje; dekoracije; **~ of the sun** zalazak sunca.
settle *v* nastaniti se, smestiti se; naseliti; srediti; podmiriti; dogovarati se.
settlement *n* naseljavanje; naselje; sporazum, poravnanje; obračun.
settler *n* naseljenik.
set-to *n* tučnjava, napad.
seven *num* sedam; *n* sedmica, sedmorica.
seventeen *num* sedamnaest; *n* sedamnaestica.
seventeenth *num a* sedamnaesti; *n* sedamnaesti deo.
seventh *num a* sedmi; *n* sedmina.

seventieth *num a* sedamdeseti; *n* sedamdeseti deo.

seventy *num* sedamdeset; *n* sedamdesetica.

sever *v* odvojiti; otkinuti; prekinuti.

several *n* nekolicina, nekoliko; *a* neki, poneki.

severance *n* odvajanje; prekid.

severe *a* strog; oštar; ozbiljan; ~ly *adv* strogo; oštro.

severity *n* strogost; oštrina; ozbiljnost.

sew *v* šiti, sašiti.

sewer[1] *n* šivač, švalja.

sewer[2] *n* odvodni kanal.

sewerage *n* kanalizacija.

sewing machine *n* šivaća mašina.

sex *n* pol; seks.

sexist *n* pristaša neravnopravnosti među polovima.

sextant *n* sekstant.

sexton *n* crkvenjak.

sexual *a* polni; seksualan.

sexy *a* seksi, privlačan.

shabbily *adv* otrcano; nisko, podlo.

shabbiness *n* otrcanost, pohabanost.

shabby *a* otrcan, pohaban.

shackle *v* okovati; ~s *npl* okovi, lanci.

shade *n* senka, hlad; nijansa; *v* osenčiti; zamračiti; nijansirati.

shadiness *n* senovitost, hladovitost.

shadow *n* senka; suton.

shadowy *a* senovit.

shady *a* senovit; sumnjiv.

shaft *n* držak koplja; osovina; okno, jama.

shag[1] *n* morski gavran.

shag[2] *n* fino rezan duvan; čuperak; pliš.

shag[3] (*sleng*) *n* polni snošaj, seks.

shaggy *a* čupav, dlakav.

shake *n* drmanje; drhtanje; stisak ruke; *v* tresti; drhtati; **to ~ vigorously** snažno protresti; **to ~ hands** rukovati se.

shaking *n* tresenje, drmanje.

shaky *a* drhtav; nesiguran; nepouzdan.

shallow *a* plitak, površan.

shallowness *n* plitkost; površnost.

sham *n* varka; simulant; *v* pretvarati se; *a* lažan, prividan.

shambles *npl* zbrka.

shame *n* sramota, stid; ljaga; *v* osramotiti; stideti se.

shamefaced *a* sramežljiv, stidljiv; neodlučan.

shameful *a* sraman, ~ly *adv* sramno.

shameless *a* besraman, bestidan; ~ly *adv* besramno.

shamelessness *n* besramnost, bestidnost.

shammy (chamois) *n* koža divokoze, antilop (koža).

shampoo *n* šampon; pranje kose; *v* prati kosu.

shamrock *n* detelina.

shank *n* krak; peteljka.

shanty[1] *n* mornarska pesma.

shanty[2] *n* straćara.

shantytown *n* naselje od straćara.

shape *n* oblik; obris; stanje; *v* uobličiti.

shapeless *a* bezobličan.

shapely *a* stasit; simetričan.

share *n* udeo; deonica; *v* deliti.

sharer *n* delilac; učesnik.

shark *n* morski pas.

sharp *a* oštar; jak; grub; pronicljiv; povisilica (*muz*); ~ly *adv* oštro; odsečno; tačno.

sharpen *v* naoštriti, izoštriti.

sharpness *n* oštrina.

shatter *v* razbiti, slomiti.

shave *n* brijanje; *v* obrijati (se); okrznuti.

shaver *n* brijač; aparat za brijanje.

shaving *n* brijanje; ~s *pl* strugotine.

shaving brush *n* četkica za brijanje.

shaving cream *n* krema za brijanje.

shawl *n* šal.

she *pn* ona.

sheaf *n* snop.

shear *v* ostrići; ~s *npl* velike makaze.

sheath *n* korice (za oružje); dužica (*anat*).

shed[1] *n* nastrešnica; šupa;

shed[2] *v* proliti.

sheen *n* sjaj.

sheep *n* ovca.

sheepfold *n* ovčiji tor.

sheepish *n* snebivljiv, smeten; glup.

sheepishness *n* snebivljivost.

sheepskin *n* ovčija koža; pergament; ~jacket kožuh od ovčije kože.

sheer *a* savršen, pravi; strm; *adv* okomito.

sheet *n* čaršav; list, ploča; tabak; zateg (konop jedra) (*naut*).

sheet anchor *n* glavno sidro; glavna uzdanica.

sheeting *n* platno za čaršave; oplata.

sheet iron *n* gvozdeni lim.

sheet lightning *n* munja sevalica.
shelf *n* polica; podvodni greben; on the ~ van upotrebe.
shell *n* školjka; ljuska; omotač; granata; *v* oljuštiti; zasuti vatrom.
shellfish *n* ljuskar.
shelter *n* sklonište, zaklon; *v* prikriti; zakloniti.
shelve *v* staviti na policu; ukloniti.
shelving *n* police; stavljanje na police.
shepherd *n* čoban.
shepherdess *n* čobanica.
sherbet *n* šerbet.
sheriff *n* šerif.
sherry *n* šeri, heres vino.
shield *n* štit; *v* štititi.
shift *n* premeštaj; promena; smena; *v* premestiti; promeniti.
shinbone *n* golenica, cevanica.
shine *n* sjaj; *v* sijati.
shingle *n* šindra; šljunak.
shingles *npl* pojasni herpes (*med*).
shining *a* sjajan; blistav; *n* sijanje, blistanje.
shiny *a* sjajan.
ship *n* brod; *v* ukrcati; otpremiti.
shipbuilding *n* brodogradnja.
shipmate *n* mornar sa istog broda.
shipment *n* otprema; utovar.
shipowner *n* brodovlasnik.
shipwreck *n* brodolom.
shirt *n* košulja.
shit *excl* sranje! (*sleng*).
shiver *v* drhtati.
shoal *n* plićak.
shock *n* udar; šok; *v* potresti; uzbuditi.
shock absorber *n* amortizer.
shoddy *a* loš, jeftin, bofl.
shoe *n* cipela; potkova; *v* obući; potkovati.
shoe factory *n* fabrika obuće.
shoehorn *n* kašika za obuvanje cipela.
shoelace *n* pertla.
shoemaker *n* obućar.
shoemaking *n* obućarstvo.
shoe shop *n* prodavnica obuće.
shoestring *n* pertla.
shoot *v* gađati; ustreliti; pucati; loviti; *n* streljačko takmičenje; lov.
shooter *n* strelac.
shooting *n* pucanje; lov.
shop *n* prodavnica; radionica.

shop window *n* izlog.
shopkeeper *n* vlasnik radnje.
shoplifter *n* lopov koji krade po radnjama.
shopper *n* kupac, mušterija.
shopping *n* kupovanje.
shopping centre *n* trgovački centar (kompleks zgrada).
shopping mall *n* trgovački centar (radnje).
shore *n* obala.
short *a* kratak; nizak; nedovoljan; ~ly *adv* uskoro; ukratko.
shortcoming *n* nedostatak, mana.
shorten *v* skratiti.
shorthand typist *n* stenograf.
shortness *n* kratkoća; nestašica.
short-sighted *a* kratkovid.
short-sightedness *n* kratkovidnost.
shot *n* pucanj; metak; šut; foto snimak.
shotgun *n* sačmara.
shoulder *n* rame; rub; *v* uprtiti na rame.
shout *n* povik, uzvik; *v* vikati; zvati.
shouting *n* vikanje.
shove *v* gurnuti; *n* guranje.
shovel *n* lopata; *v* raditi lopatom.
show *n* pokazivanje; izložba; predstava; *v* pokazati; prikazati.
show business *n* šoubiznis.
shower *n* pljusak; kiša; tuš; *v* pljuštati; obasipati.
showery *a* kišovit.
showjumping *n* preskakanje prepona.
showroom *n* izložbeni prostor.
showy *a* razmetljiv.
shred *n* krpa; parče; *v* raspadati se.
shrew *n* rovka (*zool*); goropadnica.
shrewd *a* prepreden, lukav; ~ly *adv* lukavo.
shrewdness *n* prepredenost, lukavost.
shriek *n* vrisak; *v* vrisnuti.
shrill *a* piskav; prodoran.
shrillness *n* piskavost.
shrimp *n* morski račić; čovečuljak.
shrine *n* svetilište.
shrink *v* skupiti (se); izbegavati.
shrivel *v* smežurati se; zgrčiti se.
shroud *n* mrtvački pokrov; veo; *v* umotati, prekriti.
Shrove Tuesday *n* pokladni utorak.
shrub *n* žbun.
shrubbery *n* žbunje.
shrug *n* sleganje ramenima; *v* slegnuti ramenima.

shudder *n* jeza; *v* ježiti se.
shuffle *v* vući (noge); mešati.
shun *v* izbegavati.
shunt *v* skrenuti; manevrisati.
shut *v* zatvoriti.
shutter *n* kapak; zatvarač.
shuttle *n* čunak (na razboju i sl.); šatl.
shuttlecock *n* loptica za badminton.
shy *a* stidljiv; plašljiv; **~ly** *adv* stidljivo.
shyness *n* stidljivost; plašljivost.
sibling *n* brat ili sestra.
sibyl *n* sibila; proročica.
sick *a* bolestan; kome je muka.
sick leave *n* bolovanje.
sick pay *n* naknada za bolovanje.
sicken *v* oboleti.
sickle *n* srp.
sickliness *n* bolešljivost.
sickly *a* bolešljiv.
sickness *n* bolest.
side *n* strana; *a* bočni; sporedni; *v* stati na nečiju stranu.
sideboard *n* orman za posuđe.
sidelight *n* bočno svetlo; sporedan podatak.
sidelong *a* bočni.
sideways *adv* postrance, sa strane.
siding *n* opredeljenje; sporedni kolosek.
sidle *v* ići postrance.
siege *n* opsada (*voj*).
sieve *n* sito; *v* procediti, propasirati (kroz sito).
sift *v* prosejati; proveriti.
sigh *n* uzdah; *v* uzdahnuti.
sight *n* vid; prizor; **~s** *pl* znamenitosti.
sightless *a* slep.
sightly *a* naočit; privlačan.
sightseeing *n* razgledanje znamenitosti.
sign *n* znak; natpis; simptom; *v* potpisati.
signal *n* signal; znak; *a* signalni; istaknut.
signal lamp *n* signalna lampa (*žel*).
signalize *v* signalizirati.
signalman *n* skretničar (*žel*).
signature *n* potpis.
signet *n* pečat.
significance *n* značaj; važnost.
significant *a* značajan; važan.
signify *v* značiti; označiti.
signpost *n* putokaz.
silence *n* tišina; ćutanje; *v* ućutkati.
silent *a* tih; ćutljiv; **~ly** *adv* ćutke, tiho.
silex *n* kremen.

silicon chip *n* silikonski čip.
silk *n* svila.
silken *a* svilen.
silkiness *n* mekoća svile; medeni glas.
silkworm *n* svilena buba.
silky *a* svilen; nežan.
sill *n* prozorski prag, prozorska daska.
silliness *n* glupost.
silly *a* glup; *n* budala.
silver *n* srebro; *a* srebrn.
silversmith *n* kujundžija.
silvery *a* srebrnast, zvonak (glas).
similar *a* sličan; **~ly** *adv* slično.
similarity *n* sličnost.
simile *n* poređenje.
simmer *v* krčkati (se).
simony *n* simonija (trgovina crkvenim službama).
simper *n* glupo smeškanje; *v* glupo se smeškati.
simple *a* jednostavan, prost.
simpleton *n* prostak, budala.
simplicity *n* jednostavnost.
simplification *n* pojednostavljenje.
simplify *v* pojednostaviti.
simply *adv* prosto, jednostavno.
simulate *v* pretvarati se.
simulation *n* pretvaranje.
simultaneous *a* istovremen.
sin *n* greh; *v* (po)grešiti.
since *prep* od; posle; *adv* odonda; pre; *conj* otkada; otkako; jer, budući da; pošto.
sincere *a* iskren; pravi; **~ly** *adv* iskreno; **Yours ~ly** S poštovanjem (kraj pisma).
sincerity *n* iskrenost.
sinecure *n* sinekura.
sinew *n* tetiva; mišići; jačina, snaga.
sinewy *a* mišićav; snažan.
sinful *a* grešan; **~ly** *adv* grešno.
sinfulness *n* grešnost.
sing *v* pevati; otpevati; opevati, slaviti (*poet*).
singe *v* opržiti .
singer *n* pevač.
singing *n* pevanje.
single *a* jedini; usamljen; samački; *n* pojedini komad; pojedinac; samac.
singly *adv* pojedinačno.
singular *n* jednina (*gram*); *a* pojedini; poseban; **~ly** *adv* pojedinačno; posebno.

singularity *n* osobenost; neobičnost.
sinister *a* zlokoban; opak.
sink *v* potopiti; spuštati se; opadati; *n* sudopera; slivnik.
sinking fund *n* fond za isplatu dugova.
sinner *n* grešnik.
sinuosity *n* vijugavost.
sinuous *a* vijugav.
sinus *n* sinus (*anat*).
sip *n* pijuckanje; *v* pijuckati.
siphon *n* sifon.
sir *n* gospodin.
siren *n* sirena (*mit*); signalna sprava, sirena.
sirloin *n* bubrežnjak (*kulin*).
sister *n* sestra.
sisterhood *n* sestrinstvo.
sister-in-law *n* snaja; zaova; svastika.
sisterly *a* sestrinski.
sit *v* sedeti; zasedati; pozirati.
sitcom *n* komedija situacije.
site *n* položaj; gradilište.
sitting *n* poziranje; zasedanje.
sitting room *n* dnevna soba.
situated *a* smešten.
situation *n* situacija, položaj; raspored.
six *num* šest; *n* šestica.
sixteen *num* šesnaest; *n* šesnaetica.
sixteenth *num a* šesnaesti; *n* šesnaesti deo.
sixth *num a* šesti; *n* šesti deo.
sixtieth *num a* šezdeseti; *n* šezdeseti deo.
sixty *num* šezdeset; *n* šezdesetica.
size *n* veličina; broj; dimenzija.
sizeable *a* prilično velik, znatan.
skate *n* klizaljka; *v* klizati se na klizaljkama.
skateboard *n* daska-koturaljka, skejtbord.
skating *n* klizanje.
skating rink *n* klizalište.
skein *n* povesmo.
skeleton *n* skelet, kostur; okosnica.
skeleton key *n* kalauz.
sketch *n* skica; skeč; *v* skicirati.
skewer *n* ražanj; *v* nataknuti na ražanj.
ski *n* skija; *v* skijati se.
ski boot *n* skijaška cipela.
ski pants *n* skijaške pantalone.
skid *n* klizanje; zanošenje; *v* zaneti se; okliznuti se.
skier *n* skijaš.

skiing *n* skijaški sport.
skilful *a* vešt, spretan; **~ly** *adv* vešto, spretno.
skilfulness *n* veština, spretnost.
skill *n* veština; znanje, kvalifikacija.
skilled *a* vešt; kvalifikovan.
skim *v* obrati penu; letimice pročitati.
skimmed milk *n* obrano mleko.
skimmer *n* rupičasta kašika za skidanje pene.
skin *n* koža; omotač; kora; *v* odrati; svući.
skin diving *n* ronjenje s lakim ronilačkim odelom.
skinned *a* sa kožom.
skinny *a* mršav.
skip *n* skakutanje; *v* skakutati; preskakati (u čitanju).
skipper *n* kapetan (malog broda); kapetan (tima).
skirmish *n* čarka; *v* čarkati se.
skirt *n* suknja; skut; rub; *v* ići duž, graničiti se.
skirting board *n* letvica oko donjeg ruba zida .
skit *n* skeč; parodija.
skittish *a* nemiran; ćudljiv; **~ly** *adv* nemirno; ćudljivo.
skittle *n* čunj (kuglane).
skulk *v* skrivati se.
skull *n* lobanja.
skullcap *n* okrugla kapica.
sky *n* nebo.
skylight *n* prozor na krovu.
skyrocket *n* raketa.
skyscraper *n* oblakoder, neboder.
slab *n* ploča.
slack *a* labav; mlitav, opušten; nemaran.
slack(en) *v* olabaviti, popustiti; usporiti.
slacker *n* lenština; dezerter.
slackness *n* labavost.
slag *n* troska, šljaka.
slam *v* zalupiti (se).
slander *n* kleveta, spletka; *v* klevetati, ogovarati.
slanderer *n* klevetnik.
slanderous *a* klevetnički; **~ly** *adv* klevetnički.
slang *n* sleng, žargon.
slant *n* kosina; *v* nagnuti se.
slanting *a* kos, kriv.
slap *n* šamar; *adv* ravno; brzo, iznenada;

v ošamariti; tresnuti; pljeskati,
potapšati.
slash *n* udarac; posekotina; *v* saseći;
šibati.
slate *n* škriljac.
slater *n* pokrivač krovova (ploče od
škriljca).
slating *n* oštra javna kritika.
slaughter *n* pokolj; klanje (stoke); *v*
poklati, zaklati.
slaughterer *n* koljač; mesar.
slaughterhouse *n* klanica.
slave *n* rob; *v* raditi kao rob.
slaver *n* trgovac robljem; bale, pljuvačka;
v balaviti.
slavery *n* ropstvo.
slavish *a* ropski; ~ly *adv* ropski, podao.
slavishness *n* ropstvo.
slay *v* prebiti, ubiti.
slayer *n* ubica.
sleazy *a* nepostojan, slab.
sled (*amer*), **sledge, sleigh** *n* sanke.
sledgehammer *n* kovački malj.
sleek *a* gladak; uglađen; doteran.
sleep *n* san, spavanje; *v* spavati.
sleeper *n* spavač; prag; spavaća kola.
sleepily *adv* pospano.
sleepiness *n* pospanost.
sleeping bag *n* vreća za spavanje.
sleeping pill *n* tableta za spavanje.
sleepless *a* besan, bez sna.
sleepwalking *n* mesečarstvo.
sleepy *a* pospan.
sleet *n* susnežica.
sleeve *n* rukav; naglavak.
sleight *n* spretnost, veština; ~ **of hand** *n*
varka, trik.
slender *a* tanak, vitak; ~ly *adv* vitko;
mršavo.
slenderness *n* vitkost.
slice *n* kriška; deo; *v* seći na kriške.
slide *n* klizanje; klizaljka; slajd,
dijapozitiv; *v* kliziti.
sliding *a* klizajući.
slight *n* omalovažavanje; ignorisanje; *a*
tanak; lak; *v* omalovažiti.
slightly *adv* neznatno, malo.
slightness *n* neznatnost, nedovoljnost.
slim *a* vitak; neznatan.
slime *n* mulj, glib; sluz.
sliminess *n* muljevitost; sluzavost.

slimming *n* mršavljenje.
slimy *a* muljevit; sluzav.
sling *n* praćka; zavoj; kaiš; *v* baciti, izbaciti.
slink *v* šunjati se.
slip[1] *v* okliznuti se; nestati, izgubiti se.
slip[2] *n* omaška; parče, komad (papira).
slip road *n* odvojni put; izlazni put, ulazni
put (autoputa).
slipper *n* papuča.
slippery *a* klizav; nesiguran.
slipshod *a* neuredan; nemaran.
slipway *n* navoz na kojem se gradi brod.
slit *n* prorez; otvor; *v* prorezati; rasporiti.
slobber *n* balavac; *v* baliti.
sloe *n* gloginja (*bot*).
slogan *n* geslo, parola.
sloop *n* šalupa, slup (*naut*).
slop *n* prosuta tečnost; ~s *npl* bućkuriš,
splačine.
slope *n* kosina; *v* nagnuti.
sloping *a* kos, nagnut.
sloppy *a* blatnjav; aljkav.
sloth *n* lenjost.
slouch *v* držati se nemarno (pogureno),
vući se.
slovenliness *n* aljkavost; neurednost.
slovenly *a* aljkav; neuredan.
slow *a* polagan; spor; ~ly *adv* sporo,
polako.
slowness *n* sporost.
slowworm *n* slepić (*zool*).
slug *n* okruglo tane; žeton; puž golać.
sluggish *a* trom; polagan; ~ly *adv* sporo,
polagano.
sluggishness *n* tromost.
sluice *n* brana; *v* ispustiti vodu.
slum *n* sirotinjska četvrt.
slumber *n* san, dremež; *v* spavati,
dremati.
slump *n* nagli pad cena, kriza.
slur *n* nejasno izgovaranje; ljaga; *v*
nerazgovetno izgovarati; klevetati.
slush *n* lapavica.
slut *n* prljava i neuredna žena; kurva.
sly *a* lukav; ~ly *adv* lukavo.
slyness *n* lukavstvo.
smack *n* ukus; cmok; šamar; *v* osećati se;
cmoknuti; ošamariti.
small *a* malen; sitan; neznatan.
smallish *a* omanji.
smallness *n* malenost; neznatnost.

smallpox *n* velike boginje.
smart *a* pametan; žustar; elegantan; *v*
small talk *n* ćaskanje.
peckati; bolcti.
smartly *adv* bolno; žestoko; gizdavo.
smartness *n* dómišljatost; elegancija.
smash *n* razbijanje; propast; sudar; *v*
razbiti; slupati.
smattering *n* površno znanje.
smear *n* bris (*med*); *v* zamazati;
oklevetati.
smell *n* miris; *v* (po)mirisati.
smelly *a* smrdljiv.
smelt *n* snetac (riba);
smelt *v* taliti (rudu).
smelter *n* topioničar.
smile *n* osmeh; *v* osmehnuti se.
smirk *v* glupo se smeškati.
smite *v* snažno udariti; uništiti.
smith *n* kovač.
smithy *n* kovačnica.
smock *n* radnička bluza.
smoke *n* dim; *v* dimiti se; pušiti.
smoked herring (kipper) *n* dimljena
haringa.
smokeless *a* bezdiman.
smoker *n* pušač.
smoking *n* pušenje, **no –** zabranjeno
pušenje.
smoky *a* dimljiv.
smooth *a* gladak; uglađen; *v* poravnati;
izgladiti.
smoothly *adv* glatko.
smoothness *n* glatkost; uglađenost.
smother *v* ugušiti (se).
smoulder *v* tinjati.
smudge *n* mrlja; *v* zamrljati.
smug *a* samozadovoljan.
smuggle *v* prokrijumčariti.
smuggler *n* krijumčar.
smuggling *n* krijumčarenje.
smut *n* mrlja; skarednost.
smuttiness *n* prljavština; skarednost.
smutty *a* skaredan.
snack *n* zakuska, užina.
snack bar *n* snek-bar.
snag *n* teškoća, problem.
snail *n* puž.
snake *n* zmija.
snaky *a* zmijolik.
snap *n* puckanje; spona; foto snimak; *v*

pucnuti; ugrabiti; fotografisati; **to ~**
one's fingers pucketati prstima.
snapdragon *n* zevalica (*bot*).
snare *n* zamka.
snarl *v* režati; zamrsiti (se).
snatch *n* hvatanje, posezanje; *v* zgrabiti.
sneak *n* šunjalo; potkazivač; *v* šunjati se.
sneer *v* rugati se.
sneeringly *adv* podrugljivo.
sneeze *v* kijati.
sniff *v* njušiti; onjušiti.
snigger *v* cerekati se.
snip *n* odsečak; *v* odrezati.
snipe *n* šljuka (ptica); *v* pucati iz zasede.
sniper *n* snajper.
snivel *n* cmizdrenje; *v* cmizdriti.
sniveller *n* plačljivac.
snob *n* snob.
snobbish *a* snobovski.
snooze *n* dremež; *v* dremati.
snore *v* hrkati .
snorkel *n* cev za disanje (kod ronjenja),
cev za vazduh (podmornica).
snort *v* dahtati; prezirno reći.
snout *n* njuška; rilo.
snow *n* sneg; *v* padati (sneg).
snowball *n* grudva snega.
snowdrop *n* visibaba (*bot*).
snowman *n* Sneško Belić.
snowplough *n* ralica za sneg.
snowy *a* snežan; beo kao sneg; pun snega.
snub *v* izgrditi.
snub-nosed *a* koji ima prćast nos.
snuff *n* burmut.
snuffbox *n* burmutica.
snuffle *v* šmrkati.
snug *a* topao i udoban; ugodan.
so *adv* tako, na ovaj način; dakle, pa.
soak *v* potopiti; namočiti; apsorbovati.
so-and-so *n* neki, izvesni, taj i taj.
soap *n* sapun; *v* nasapunjati.
soap bubble *n* sapunski mehur.
soap opera *n* sentimentalna TV serija,
'sapunica'.
soap powder *n* sapunski prašak.
soapsuds *npl* sapunica.
soapy *a* sapunast.
soar *v* vinuti se; lebdeti visoko.
sob *n* jecaj; *v* jecati.
sober *a* trezan; trezven; **~ly** *adv* trezno;
trezveno.

sobriety *n* treznost; trezvenost.
soccer *n* fudbal.
sociability *n* društvenost, druželjubivost.
sociable *a* društven, druželjubiv.
sociably *adv* društveno, druželjubivo.
social *a* društveni, socijalni; **~ly** *adv* društveno, druželjubivo.
socialism *n* socijalizam.
socialist *n* socijalista.
social work *n* socijalni rad.
social worker *n* socijalni radnik.
society *n* društvo; udruženje.
sociologist *n* sociology.
sociology *n* sociologija.
sock *n* kratka čarapa.
socket *n* udubljenje; utičnica (*el*).
sod *n* gruda, busen.
soda *n* soda; bezalkoholno slatko piće.
sofa *n* sofa, divan.
soft *a* mekan; nežan; **~ly** *adv* tiho, polako, nežno.
soften *v* omekšati.
soft-hearted *a* saosećajan.
softness *n* mekoća.
soft-spoken *a* blag, ljubazan; koji tiho govori.
software *n* softver, kompjuterski programi.
soil *n* tlo, zemlja; mrlja; *v* uprljati se.
sojourn *n* kratak boravak; *v* kratko boraviti.
solace *n* uteha; *v* utešiti.
solar *a* sunčani (*astrol*); **~ energy** *n* sunčeva energija.
solder *n* lem, lemljenje; *v* lemiti.
soldier *n* vojnik.
soldierly *a* vojnički.
sole[1] *n* taban; đon.
sole[2] *a* jedini; isključivi.
solecism *n* kršenje gramatičkih pravila.
solemn *a* svečan; **~ly** *adv* svečano.
solemnity *n* svečanost.
solemnize *v* svečano proslaviti.
solicit *v* tražiti; saletati.
solicitation *n* traženje, zahtev.
solicitor *n* trgovački agent; advokat.
solicitous *a* zabrinut; željan; **~ly** *adv* zabrinuto; željno.
solicitude *n* zabrinutost.
solid *n* čvrsto telo; *a* tvrd; čvrst; **~ly** *adv* čvrsto.

solidify *v* zgusnuti se; očvrsnuti.
solidity *n* čvrstoća.
soliloquy *n* monolog.
solitaire *n* pasijans.
solitary *a* usamljen; *n* pustinjak; samica (u zatvoru).
solitude *n* usamljenost.
solo *n* solo (*muz*).
solstice *n* solsticij (*astron*).
soluble *a* rastvorljiv.
solution *n* rešenje; rastvor.
solve *v* rešiti.
solvency *n* solventnost, sposobnost plaćanja.
solvent *n* rastvarač; *a* solventan; koji rastvara.
some *a* neki; nekakav; bilo koji, bilo kakav; nekoliko.
somebody *n* neko; važna ličnost.
somehow *adv* nekako.
someplace *adv* negde.
something *n* nešto.
sometime *adv* nekada, pre.
sometimes *adv* ponekad, koji put.
somewhat *adv* malo, (po)nešto, donekle.
somewhere *adv* negde; nekuda.
somnambulism *n* mesečarstvo.
somnambulist *n* mesečar.
somnolence *n* pospanost.
somnolent *a* pospan.
son *n* sin.
sonata *n* sonata (*muz*).
song *n* pesma.
son-in-law *n* zet.
sonnet *n* sonet.
sonorous *a* zvučan; sonoran.
soon *adv* uskoro; **as ~ as** čim.
sooner *adv* pre, ranije.
soot *n* čađ, gar.
soothe *v* umiriti; ublažiti.
soothsayer *n* prorok, gatač.
sop *n* namočen komad hleba; mito.
sophism *n* sofizam.
sophist *n* sofista.
sophistical *a* sofistički.
sophisticate *v* učiniti prefinjenim.
sophisticated *a* prefinjen.
sophistry *n* sofistika.
soporific *a* uspavljujući; dosadan.
sorcerer *n* vrač, čarobnjak.
sorceress *n* vračara, čarobnica.

sorcery n vračanje, čarolije.
sordid a prljav; podao.
sordidness n prljavost; niskost.
sore n rana, bolesno mesto; a bolan; ~ly adv veoma jako, bolno.
sorrel n kiseljak (bot); a riđast.
sorrow n žalost, tuga.
sorrowful a žalostan; ~ly adv žalosno.
sorry a žalostan, jadan; **I am** ~ žao mi je.
sort n vrsta, sorta; v sortirati.
soul n duša.
sound[1] n zvuk; v dati zvučni znak, zvučati.
sound[2] a zdrav; ispravan; ~ly adv čvrsto, jako, zdravo.
sound[3] v sondirati.
sound effects npl zvučni efekti.
sounding board n zvučna daska, rezonator; nadstrešnica propovedaonice.
soundings npl izmeriva dubina vode (naut).
soundness n zdravlje; čvrstoća.
soundtrack n zvučna traka.
soup n supa, čorba.
sour a kiseo; mrzovoljan; ~ly adv kiselo; mrzovoljno; v zakiseliti.
source n izvor; vrelo.
sourness n kiselost; mrzovoljnost.
souse n pijanica (sleng); v usoliti; opiti.
south n jug; a južni; adv južno, prema jugu.
southerly, southern a južni.
southward(s) adv na jug.
southwester n jugozapadnjak; mornarski neprokišnjiv šešir.
souvenir n suvenir; uspomena.
sovereign a nezavisan, suveren.
sovereignty n suverenitet.
sow[1] n svinja.
sow[2] v sejati, zasejati.
sowing-time n vreme setve.
soya bean n soja.
space n prostor; kosmos; v razmaknuti.
spacecraft n kosmički brod.
spaceman n astronaut.
spacewoman n žena astronaut.
spacious a prostran; širok; ~ly adv prostrano.
spaciousness n prostranost; prostranstvo.
spade n lopata, ašov.
spaghetti n špageti.
span n razmak; raspon; v izmeriti; premostiti.

spangle n šljokica; v ukrasiti šljokicama.
spaniel n prepeličar, španijel (vrsta psa).
Spanish n Španci; španski jezik; a španski
spar[1] n greda; boks.
spar[2] v boksovati.
spare a rezervni; slobodan; oskudan; v štedeti; poštedeti; dati, odvojiti.
sparing a štedljiv; ~ly adv štedljivo.
spark n varnica, iskra.
spark plug n svećica (motor).
sparkle n iskra; blistanje; v iskriti se; blistati.
sparrow n vrabac.
sparrowhawk n kobac.
sparse a redak; oskudan; ~ly adv retko, prorеđeno.
spasm n grč.
spasmodic a grčevit.
spatter v poprskati.
spatula n lopatica, špatula.
spawn n mrest; ikra; riblja mlađ; v mrestiti se, kotiti se.
spawning n mrešćenje.
speak v govoriti, razgovarati.
speaker n govornik; zvučnik.
spear n koplje; harpun; v probosti kopljem.
special a poseban, naročit; određen; ~ly adv posebno.
speciality n specijalnost; osobenost.
species n vrsta (biol); rod, klasa.
specific n nešto specifično; pojedinost; a poseban, specifičan.
specifically adv posebno, naročito.
specification n specifikacija, detaljan opis.
specify v posebno navesti, opisati.
specimen n uzorak, primerak.
specious a varljiv; prividno dobar.
speck(le) n mrljica, tačkica; v išarati mrljicama.
spectacle n prizor; pojava; predstava.
spectacles npl naočari.
spectator n gledalac.
spectral a sablastan; spektralan; ~ **analysis** n spektralna analiza.
spectre n sablast, avet.
speculate v razmišljati; špekulisati.
speculation n razmišljanje; razmatranje; špekulacija.

speculative *a* misaon; sumnjiv.
speculum *n* spekulum (*med*); metalno ogledalo.
speech *n* govor.
speechless *a* bez reči; zanemeo.
speed *n* brzina; *v* ubrzati; žuriti.
speed limit *n* dozvoljena brzina.
speedboat *n* brz motorni čamac.
speedily *adv* žurno; brzo.
speediness *n* brzina.
speedometer *n* brzinomer.
speedway *n* autoput; trkačka staza (za automobile).
speedy *a* brz.
spell[1] *n* malo vremena, kratko vreme.
spell[2] *n* čarolija, čini.
spell[3] *v* sricati; spelovati.
spelling *n* pravopis; sricanje po slovima.
spend *v* potrošiti; provesti.
spendthrift *n* rasipnik.
spent *a* istrošen.
sperm *n* sperma.
spew *v* izbaciti, (iz)bljuvati.
sphere *n* sfera.
spherical *a* kuglast, loptast; sferni; **~ly** *adv* loptasto, sferno.
spice *n* začin; *v* začiniti.
spick-and-span *a* nov novcat; besprekoran.
spicy *a* začinjen; mirisan; nepristojan.
spider *n* pauk.
spigot *n* prsten (*teh*); slavina.
spike *n* šiljak; čavao; klas; *v* pribiti ekserima.
spill *v* prosuti; proliti.
spin *v* presti; zavrteti; *n* obrtanje.
spinach *n* spanać.
spinal *a* kičmeni (*anat*).
spindle *n* vreteno; osovina.
spine *n* kičma; bodlja.
spineless *a* bez kičme; kolebljiv, beskičmen.
spinet *n* spinet (*muz*).
spinner *n* prelac, prelja.
spinning top *n* zvrk.
spinning wheel *n* kolovrat, preslica.
spin-off *n* nusproizvod, sporedni proizvod.
spinster *n* usedelica.
spiral *a* spiralan; zavojit; **~ly** *adv* spiralno, zavojito.
spire *n* šiljak, vrh; izdanak; spirala.

spirit *n* duh, duša; raspoloženje; alkohol; *v* oduševiti; podstrekivati; **to ~ away** tajno odstraniti.
spirit lamp *n* špiritusna lampa.
spirited *a* živahan; smeo; odlučan; **~ly** *adv* sa puno duha; odvažno.
spiritless *a* bez žara, mlitav, malodušan.
spiritual *a* duhovni; produhovljen; **~ly** *adv* duhovno.
spiritualist *n* spiritualist.
spirituality *n* spiritualnost.
spit[1] *n* pljuvanje; *v* pljunuti.
spit[2] *n* ražanj.
spite *n* inat; *v* pakostiti; **in ~ of** uprkos nečemu.
spiteful *a* zloban; pakostan; **~ly** *adv* zlobno, pakosno.
spitefulness *n* pakost; zlobnost.
spittle *n* pljuvačka.
splash *n* prskanje; brčkanje; *v* poprskati; pljusnuti; brčkati se.
spleen *n* slezina (*anat*); sumornost.
splendid *a* raskošan; divan; **~ly** *adv* raskošno; divno.
splendour *n* raskoš; divota.
splice *n* upletka; *v* uplesti, splesti krajeve konopa.
splint *n* udlaga, uložak, daščica.
splinter *n* odlomak, krhotina; iver; *v* rascepiti.
split *n* rascep; pukotina; *v* rascepiti; razdeliti.
splutter, sputter *v* govoriti nepovezano .
spoil *v* pokvariti; opljačkati.
spoiled *a* pokvaren; loš.
spoke *n* spica, zubac; prečaga (na lestvama).
spokesman *n* predstavnik; port-parol.
spokesperson *n* predstavnik.
spokeswoman *n* predstavnica.
sponge *n* sunđer; brisanje; *v* obrisati sunđerom.
sponger *n* parazit, gotovan.
sponginess *n* sunđerastost; šupljikavost.
spongy *a* sunđerast; porozan.
sponsor *n* jemac; predlagač; pokrovitelj.
sponsorship *n* jemstvo; sponzorstvo.
spontaneity *n* spontanost.
spontaneous *a* spontan; **~ly** *adv* spontano.
spool *n* kalem.
spoon *n* kašika.

spoonful *n* puna kašika.
sporadic(al) *a* sporadičan, mestimičan.
sport *n* sport; šala; momak.
sports car *n* trkačka kola.
sports jacket *n* blejzer .
sportsman *n* sportista; lovac.
sportswear *n* sportska odeća.
sportswoman *n* sportistkinja.
spot *n* mrlja, pega; mesto; *v* umrljati.
spotless *a* besprekoran, neukaljan.
spotlight *n* reflektor; središte pažnje.
spotted, spotty *a* pegav; išaran.
spotty bubuljičav (lice); flekav.
spouse *n* suprug, supruga.
spout *n* odvodna cev; oluk; žleb; *v* šiknuti,
  briznuti; pričati (koješta).
sprain *n* uganuće (*med*).
sprat *n* sleđica (riba).
sprawl *v* opružiti, pasti; izvaliti se.
spray *n* sprej; prskalica; mlaz vode.
spread *n* širenje; pokrivač; opseg; *v*
  (ra)širiti; razliti se.
spree *n* terevenka; veselje.
sprig *n* grančica, izdanak.
sprightliness *n* živahnost.
sprightly *a* živahan.
spring *n* proleće; opruga; izvor; *v*
  preskočiti; skočiti.
springiness *n* elastičnost.
spring onion *n* ljutika (vrsta luka).
springtime *n* proleće.
spring water *n* izvorska voda.
springy *a* elastičan; gibak.
sprinkle *v* poprskati; sipiti.
sprinkling *n* prskanje.
sprout *n* mladica (*bot*); *v* nicati.
sprouts *npl* prokelj.
spruce *a* doteran; **~ly** *adv* doterano,
  nagizdano; *v* doterati se.
spruceness *n* urednost, doteranost.
spur *n* mamuza; podsticaj; *v* mamuznuti;
  podstaći.
spurious *a* lažan; podmetnut.
spurn *v* prezirno odbiti.
spy *n* špijun; *v* špijunirati; istraživati.
squabble *n* prepirka; *v* prepirati se.
squad *n* odred, grupa; vod (*voj*).
squadron *n* konjički eskadron; brodska
  eskadra; avionska eskadrila (*voj*).
squalid *a* prljav, zapušten; bedan.
squall *n* jak nalet vetra; dreka; *v* drečati.

squally *a* olujan; zlokoban.
squalor *n* prljavština; beda.
squander *v* rasipati; proćerdati.
square *n* kvadrat; trg; *a* četvrtast; pošten;
  v podići na kvadrat; svesti račun.
squareness *n* četvorouglost; ispravnost.
squash[1] *v* gnječiti, zgnječiti; *n* gužva.
squash[2] *n* voćni sok (razblažen od sirupa).
squash[3] *n* bundeva, tikva.
squash[4] *n* skvoš, vrsta tenisa.
squat *v* čučati; *a* zdepast.
squatter *n* čučavac; ilegalni stanar;
  bespravni naseljenik.
squeak *n* škripa; *v* škripati.
squeal *v* ciknuti, vrisnuti.
squeamish *a* pedantan; probirljiv (kod
  jela); gadljiv.
squeeze *n* stisak; ceđenje; gužva; *v*
  stisnuti; iscediti; progurati se.
squid *n* lignja.
squint *a* razrok; *v* gledati razroko;
  žmirkati; *n* razrokost; škiljenje.
squirrel *n* veverica.
squirt *n* štrcaljka; mlaz vode; *v* briznuti;
  poprskati.
stab *n* udarac bodežom; rana od uboda; *v*
  naneti udarac.
stability *n* stabilnost; nepromenljivost.
stable *n* štala; *v* smestiti u štalu; smestiti
  se; *a* postojan; stabilan.
stack *n* plast, stog; gomila; dimnjak; *v*
  sadenuti u stog; naslagati.
staff *n* osoblje; štap; notne linije (*muz*).
stag *n* jelen (mužjak); neženja.
stage *n* pozornica; etapa; faza.
stagger *v* teturati se; kolebati se.
stagnant *a* stajaći (voda); koji stagnira,
  zaostao.
stagnate *v* stagnirati, biti u zastoju.
stagnation *n* stagnacija, zastoj.
staid *a* staložen; ozbiljan.
stain *v* umrljati (se); obojiti; *n* mrlja; boja.
stainless *a* neuprljan; besprekoran; nerđajući.
stair *n* stepenik; **~s** *npl* stepenice.
staircase *n* stepenište.
stake *n* kolac; lomača; ulog; *v* obeležiti
  kocima; staviti na kocku.
stale *a* bajat; banalan; bljutav; ustajao.
staleness *n* otrcanost, starost.
stalk[1] *n* stabljika; tvornički dimnjak.
stalk[2] *v* prikradati se.

stall[1] *n* staja; pregrada; odeljak; tezga (na pijaci);
stall[2] *v* zaustaviti; zatajiti (motor).
stallion *n* ždrebac.
stalwart *n* snažna osoba; veran pristaša.
stamen *n* prašnik (*bot*).
stamina *n* izdržljivost, snaga.
stammer *v* mucati; *n* mucanje.
stamp *n* lupanje; pečat; marka; *v* lupnuti; udariti pečat; nalepiti marku.
stampede *n* bezglavo bežanje, stampedo.
stand *n* stajanje; zastoj; položaj; tezga (na ulici); tribina; *v* stajati; zaustaviti se; nalaziti se; izdržati.
standard *n* standard, norma; zastava, barjak.
standing *n* stajanje; položaj; ugled; *a* stalan; trajan; stajaći; ustaljen.
standstill *n* zastoj, prekid.
staple *n* spajalica; glavni proizvod; glavna osobina; *a* glavni; *v* spojiti spajalicom.
star *n* zvezda; filmska zvezda.
starboard *n* desni bok broda.
starch *n* štirak; *v* uštirkati.
stare *v* blenuti; **to ~ at** piljiti (u), buljiti (u); *n* piljenje.
stark *a* potpun; ukočen; *adv* potpuno.
starling *n* čvorak (ptica).
starry *a* zvezdan.
start *n* početak; start; *v* početi; staviti u pokret.
starter *n* pokretač, uzročnik; starter.
starting point *n* polazište.
startle *v* uplašiti, iznenaditi.
startling *a* zapanjujući.
starvation *n* gladovanje; smrt od gladi.
starve *v* umirati od gladi; umoriti glađu; izmučiti.
state *n* stanje; oblik; država; *v* formulisati; izneti; **the S~s** *n* Sjedinjene Američke Države.
stateliness *n* dostojanstvo; sjaj.
stately *a* svečan; veličanstven.
statement *n* izjava; finansijski izveštaj.
statesman *n* državnik.
statesmanship *n* državnička veština.
static *n* atmosferske smetnje; *a* statičan.
station *n* mesto, položaj; stanica; *v* smestiti.
stationary *a* nepokretan; stalan.
stationer *n* prodavac kancelarijskog materijala.

stationery *n* kancelarijski materijal.
statistical *a* statistički.
statistics *n* statistika.
statuary *n* vajarstvo; vajar.
statue *n* kip, statua.
stature *n* stas, rast.
statute *n* statut; zakonska odredba.
stay *n* zaustavljanje; boravak; *v* zaustaviti; ostati, boraviti; **to ~ in** ostati kod kuće; **to ~ on** ostati dalje; **to ~ up** ostati budan.
steadfast *a* čvrst, postojan; nepopustljiv; **~ly** *adv* čvrsto; postojano.
steadily *adv* postojano; uporno.
steadiness *n* postojanost; upornost.
steady *a* čvrst; pouzdan; stalan; *v* učvrstiti (se).
steak *n* komad (mesa, ribe).
steal *v* krasti; ukrasti.
stealth *n* potaja; **by ~** krišom.
stealthily *adv* krišom, potajno.
stealthy *a* potajan.
steam *n* para; *v* ispariti.
steam-engine *n* parna mašina.
steamer, steamboat *n* parobrod.
steel *n* čelik; *a* čeličan.
steelyard *n* kantar, vaga.
steep *a* strm; *v* natopiti.
steeple *n* šiljasti toranj, zvonik.
steeplechase *n* trka sa preponama.
steepness *n* strmost.
steer[1] *v* upravljati, krmaniti; ploviti.
steer[2] *n* junac.
steering *n* kormilarenje.
steering wheel *n* volan, upravljač.
stellar *a* zvezdani.
stem[1] *n* stabljika; drška; osnova (*gram*).
stem[2] *v* poticati; zaustaviti.
stench *n* smrad.
stencil *n* matrica (za umnožavanje).
stenography *n* stenografija.
step *n* korak; mera; stopa; *v* koračati.
stepbrother *n* polubrat.
stepdaughter *n* pastorka.
stepfather *n* očuh.
stepmother *n* maćeha.
stepping stone *n* kamen u vodi za prelaženje; odskočna daska (*fig*).
stepsister *n* polusestra.
stepson *n* pastorak.
stereo *n* stereo (sistem).

stereotype *n* stereotip; šablon; *v* stereotipizirati.
sterile *a* sterilan; neplodan.
sterility *n* sterilnost; neplodnost.
sterling *n* britanska funta; *a* bez primese, čist.
stern[1] *a* strog; neumoljiv; **~ly** *adv* strogo; nemilosrdno.
stern[2] *n* krma (broda).
stethoscope *n* stetoskop (*med*).
stevedore *n* obalski radnik.
stew *n* dinstano jelo; paprikaš; uzbuđenje; *v* dinstati.
steward *n* brodski konobar; stjuard (u avionu); upravitelj.
stewardess *n* stjuardesa.
stewardship *n* položaj upravnika.
stick[1] *n* štap; prut; palica.
stick[2] *v* zabosti; nalepiti; ostajati pri svome.
stickiness *n* lepljivost.
sticking plaster *n* flaster.
sticky *a* lepljiv.
stiff *a* krut; tvrd; ukočen; **~ly** *adv* kruto.
stiff neck *n* krutost vrata (*med*).
stiffen *v* ukrutiti (se).
stiffness *n* ukočenost.
stifle *v* ugušiti (se); zataškati.
stifling *a* zagušljiv.
stigma *n* ljaga, sramota.
stigmatize *v* žigosati, osramotiti.
stile *n* prelaz preko ograde.
stiletto *n* stilet, mali bodež.
still *a* miran, tih; nečujan; nepokretan; *n* tišina; destilator; *v* utišati, umiriti; destilisati; *adv* još uvek; još; međutim, ipak.
stillborn *a* mrtvorođen.
stillness *n* tišina, mir.
stilts *npl* štule.
stimulant *n* stimulativno sredstvo; podsticaj.
stimulate *v* stimulisati, bodriti.
stimulation *n* stimulacija, bodrenje.
stimulus *n* stimulans, podstrek.
sting *n* žaoka; ubod, ujed; *v* ubosti (žaokom); opaliti.
stingily *adv* škrto.
stinginess *n* škrtost.
stingy *a* škrt.
stink *n* smrad; *v* smrdeti.
stint *n* ograničenje.

stipulate *v* ugovoriti, postaviti kao uslov.
stipulation *n* uslov; ugovor; odredba.
stir *n* komešanje; gužva; *v* kretati se; mešati; uzbuditi.
stirrup *n* uzengije.
stitch *n* bod; šav; petlja, očica; *v* šiti.
stoat *n* hermelin (*zool*).
stock[1] *n* zaliha; skladište; *v* snabdevati.
stock[2] *n* akcije, osnovni kapital; stoka; deblo; poreklo.
stock exchange *n* berza.
stock market *n* berza.
stockade *n* palisada, ograda od stubova.
stockbroker *n* berzanski mešetar.
stockholder *n* akcionar.
stocking *n* čarapa (duga).
stocks[1] *npl* deonice, akcije.
stocks[2] *npl* skele brodogradilišta.
stoic *n* stoik .
stoical *a* stoički; **~ly** *adv* stoički.
stoicism *n* stoicizam.
stole *n* epitrahilj; usko krzno koje žene nose oko vrata.
stomach *n* želudac, stomak; *v* podnositi, trpeti.
stone *n* kamen; koščica (ploda); *a* kameni; *v* kamenovati.
stone deaf *a* sasvim gluv.
stoning *n* kamenovanje.
stony *a* kamenit; neosetljiv.
stool *n* hoklica; stolica (*med*).
stoop *n* sagibanje; pogrbljenost; *v* sagnuti (se).
stop *n* zaustavljanje; obustava; zadržavanje; prestanak; *v* zaustaviti; obustaviti; prestati.
stopover *n* kratak prekid puta, kratko zadržavanje.
stoppage *n* obustava; zastoj.
stopwatch *n* štoperica.
storage *n* skladištenje; skladište.
store *n* prodavnica; zaliha; skladište; *v* (u)skladištiti.
storey *n* sprat.
stork *n* roda.
storm *n* oluja, bura; *v* besneti (oluja).
stormily *adv* burno.
stormy *a* buran.
story *n* priča; istorija; radnja, zaplet.
stout *a* hrabar, odvažan; debeo, gojazan; **~ly** *adv* junački; nepokolebljivo.

stoutness n srčanost; debljina.
stove n peć.
stow v tovariti.
straggle v raštrkati se; besciljno lutati.
straggler n lutalica.
straight a prav; ravan; iskren; uspravan; adv pravo.
straightaway adv odmah.
straighten v ispraviti se; napraviti red.
straightforward a iskren.
straightforwardness n iskrenost.
strain n naprezanje, napor; uganuće; v napregnuti; zategnuti; istegnuti.
strainer n cediljka.
strait n morski tesnac; škripac.
straitjacket n ludačka košulja.
strand n obala, plaža.
strange a čudan, neobičan; nepoznat; ~ly adv čudno, neobično.
strangeness n nepoznatost; neobičnost.
stranger n stranac.
strangle v ugušiti (se).
strangulation n gušenje.
strap n kaiš; naramenica; v (tući, privezati) kaišem.
strapping a kršan, stasit.
stratagem n ratna varka, ratno lukavstvo.
strategic a strateški.
strategy n strategija.
stratum n sloj; nivo.
straw n slama; slamka.
strawberry n jagoda.
stray v zalutati; a zalutao.
streak n pruga; trag; žica; v obeležiti prugama; jurnuti.
stream n tok, struja; reka; potok; v teći; strujati.
streamer n uska traka; zastavica.
street n ulica.
strength n snaga; sila.
strengthen v ojačati.
strenuous a naporan.
stress n pritisak; opterećenje; naglasak; stres; v naglasiti.
stretch n rastezanje; pružanje; naprezanje; v rastezati; produžiti.
stretcher n nosila.
strew v rasuti; posuti.
strict a striktan; strog; precizan; ~ly adv strogo, tačno.
strictness n striktnost; strogost.

stride n dugačak korak; napredak; v koračati.
strife n razdor, nesloga.
strike n štrajk; udar; v štrajkovati; udariti.
striker n štrajkač.
striking a upadljiv, izrazit; ~ly adv izvanredno, jako.
string n žica, struna; kanap; tetiva; niz; v vezati; nategnuti; nanizati.
stringent a strog; oskudan.
stringy a vrpčast; vlaknav.
strip[1] n uska traka, pruga.
strip[2] v skinuti (se), svući; uzeti.
stripe n pruga; širit; vrsta; v išarati prugama.
strive v težiti, stremiti.
stroke n udarac; potez; kap (med); milovanje; v gladiti.
stroll n šetnja; v šetati se.
strong a jak, snažan; oštar; ~ly adv jako, uporno.
strongbox n sef.
stronghold n tvrđava, uporište.
strophe n strofa.
structure n sastav, struktura.
struggle n borba; v boriti se.
strum v prebirati (po klaviru, i sl.); loše svirati.
strut n šepurenje, razmetanje; v šepuriti se.
stub n panj; pikavac.
stubble n strnište.
stubborn a tvrdoglav, uporan; ~ly adv uporno.
stubbornness n tvrdoglavost.
stucco n gipsani malter.
stud[1] n direk; ekser; dugme.
stud[2] v pastuv; ergela.
student n student; učenik; a studentski.
studio n studio; atelje.
studio flat n garsonjera.
studious a marljiv; pažljiv; ~ly adv marljivo, pažljivo.
study n učenje; proučavanje; radna soba; studija; v učiti; proučavati; studirati.
stuff n materijal, građa; stvari; v puniti; ugurati.
stuffing n nadev.
stuffy a zagušljiv, sparan; dosadan.
stumble n spoticanje; v spotaći se.
stumbling block n kamen spoticanja.
stump n panj; ostatak; pikavac.
stun v ošamutiti.

stunner *n* izuzetna ličnost.
stunt[1] *n* majstorija, trik; prestanak
  rašćenja.
stunt[2] *v* izvoditi egzibicije; sprečiti rast.
stuntman *n* kaskader.
stuntwoman *n* kaskaderka.
stupefy *v* zapanjiti, prenerazibi.
stupendous *a* izvanredan; čudesan;
  ogroman.
stupid *a* glup; ~**ly** *adv* glupavo,
  budalasto.
stupidity *n* glupost.
stupor *n* omamljenost; ukočenost.
sturdily *adv* snažno; čvrsto; odlučno.
sturdiness *n* čvrstina, snaga.
sturdy *a* čvrst; snažan.
sturgeon *n* jesetra (riba).
stutter *v* mucati.
sty *n* svinjac.
sty(e) *n* čmičak (na oku).
style *n* stil; način; otmenost; *v* oblikovati;
  nazivati.
stylish *a* pomodan; elegantan.
suave *a* blag, ulagivački, ljubazan.
subdivide *v* dalje deliti (na manje delove).
subdivision *n* deoba na manje delove,
  podvrsta.
subdue *v* savladati, obuzdati.
subject *n* predmet; subjekt (*gram*);
  podanik; *a* podređen; podložan; *v*
  potčiniti; podvrći.
subjection *n* potčinjenost, pokoravanje.
subjugate *v* potčiniti, pokoriti.
subjugation *n* podjarmljivanje.
subjunctive *n* konjunktiv (*gram*).
sublet *v* dati u podzakup.
sublimate *v* sublimirati .
sublime *a* uzvišen; ~**ly** *adv* uzvišeno; **the**
  ~ *n* nešto uzvišeno.
sublimity *n* uzvišenost.
submachine gun *n* automat, mašinka.
submarine *n* podmornica; *a* podmorski;
  podmornički.
submerge *v* potopiti; zagnjuriti (se).
submersion *n* potapanje; zaronjenje.
submission *n* potčinjenost; predaja.
submissive *a* pokoran; ~**ly** *adv* pokorno.
submissiveness *n* pokornost.
submit *v* pokoriti se; podneti.
subordinate *a* podređen; *v* podrediti.
subordination *n* podređenost.

subpoena *n* sudski poziv; *v* pozvati na
  sud.
subscribe *v* pretplatiti se; potpisati (se).
subscriber *n* pretplatnik.
subscription *n* pretplata; potpisivanje.
subsequent *a* sledeći; ~**ly** *adv* zatim,
  posle.
subservient *a* koristan, servilan;
  podređen.
subside *v* opadati; smiriti se; sleći se (o
  tlu).
subsidence *n* sleganje; opadanje;
  stišavanje.
subsidiary *a* pomoćni.
subsidize *v* subvencionisati, dotirati.
subsidy *n* subvencija.
subsist *v* postojati; živeti; izdržavati
  nekoga.
subsistence *n* postojanje; opstanak; život.
substance *n* materija; bit, suština;
  bogatstvo.
substantial *a* bitan, suštinski; stvaran;
  bogat; ~**ly** *adv* bitno; suštinski.
substantiate *v* potvrditi, potkrepiti
  (tvrdnju).
substantive *n* imenica (*gram*).
substitute *n* zamena; zamenik; *v*
  zamenjivati.
substitution *n* zamena; supstitucija;
  zamena (igrača).
substratum *n* supstrat; podloga; niži sloj.
subterfuge *n* izgovor, izvrdavanje.
subterranean *a* podzemni.
subtitle *n* podnaslov.
subtle *a* suptilan, fin; uglađen; lukav.
subtlety *n* suptilnost, finoća; lukavost.
subtly *adv* tanano; pronicljivo.
subtract *v* oduzeti (*mat*).
suburb *n* predgrađe.
suburban *a* prigradski.
subversion *n* subverzija; rušenje,
  razaranje.
subversive *a* subverzivan; rušilački.
subvert *v* rušiti; oboriti.
succeed *v* slediti iza nečega; uspevati;
  naslediti.
success *n* uspeh.
successful *a* uspešan; ~**ly** *adv* uspešno.
succession *n* sled, niz; nasleđivanje.
successive *a* uzastopni, idući, sledeći; ~**ly**
  adv uzastopno.

successor *n* naslednik.
succinct *a* sažet; **~ly** *adv* sažeto.
succulent *a* sočan.
succumb *v* podleći, ne izdržati.
such *a* takav, onakav; **~ as** takav kakav (kao što je); **~ and ~ a one** *n* takav i takav, taj i taj, ta i ta.
suck *v* sisati.
suckle *v* dojiti.
suckling *n* sisanče, dojenče.
suction *n* usisavanje (*med*).
sudden *a* iznenadan; neočekivan; **~ly** *adv* iznenada.
suddenness *n* neočekivanost.
suds *npl* sapunica; pena.
sue *v* tužiti; povesti parnicu; tražiti.
suede *n* jelenja koža.
suet *n* salo, loj.
suffer *v* patiti; trpeti; stradati.
suffering *n* patnja.
suffice *v* dostajati, biti dosta.
sufficiency *n* dostatnost, dovoljnost.
sufficient *a* dovoljan; **~ly** *adv* dovoljno.
suffocate *v* gušiti se; ugušiti.
suffocation *n* gušenje; ugušivanje.
suffrage *n* izborno pravo, pravo glasa.
suffuse *v* obliti.
sugar *n* šećer; *v* zasladiti, pošećeriti.
sugar beet *n* šećerna repa.
sugar cane *n* šećerna trska.
sugar loaf *n* glava šećera.
sugary *a* šećerni; zaslađen.
suggest *v* predložiti; preporučiti; dopustiti; nagovestiti.
suggestion *n* sugestija; predlog.
suicidal *a* samoubilački.
suicide *n* samoubistvo; samoubica.
suit *n* odelo; kostim; parnica; proces; *v* odgovarati; prilagoditi.
suitable *a* podesan, odgovarajući.
suitably *adv* prikladno, podesno.
suitcase *n* kofer.
suite *n* svita, pratioci; apartman; svita (*muz*); garnitura.
suitor *n* molilac; udvarač.
sulkiness *n* mrzovoljnost .
sulky *a* zlovoljan.
sullen *a* sumoran, mrzovoljan; **~ly** *adv* mrzovoljno.
sullenness *n* zlovoljnost; natmurenost.
sulphur *n* sumpor (*hem*).

sulphurous *a* sumporni.
sultan *n* sultan.
sultana *n* suvo grožđe; sultanija.
sultry *a* sparan, zagušljiv.
sum *n* suma, zbir; iznos; *v* računati; **to ~ up** zbrajati; rezimirati.
summarily *adv* kratkim postupkom.
summary *a* sumaran; kratak; *n* kratak pregled, rezime.
summer *n* leto; *a* letnji.
summerhouse *n* baštenska kuća; senica.
summit *n* vrh, vrhunac; samit.
summon *v* pozvati; sazvati; sazvati zbor (*voj*).
summons *n* sudski poziv.
sumptuous *a* raskošan, divan; **~ly** *adv* raskošno, divno.
sun *n* sunce.
sunbathe *v* sunčati se.
sunburnt *a* preplanuo od sunca.
Sunday *n* nedelja; *a* nedeljni; **done/worn on ~** činiti najbolje/nositi nedeljno, praznično odelo.
Sunday driver *n* loš vozač.
sundial *n* sunčani sat.
sundry *a* raznovrstan, razni.
sunflower *n* suncokret.
sunglasses *npl* naočari za sunce.
sunless *a* bez sunca.
sunlight *n* sunčeva svetlost.
sunny *a* sunčan.
sunrise *n* izlazak sunca.
sunroof *n* klizni deo na krovu automobila koji se otvara.
sunset *n* zalazak sunca.
sunshade *n* suncobran.
sunshine *n* sunčeva svetlost; radost, veselje.
sunstroke *n* sunčanica.
suntan *n* preplanulost.
suntan oil *n* ulje za sunčanje.
super *a* sjajan, super.
superannuated *a* zastareo; vrlo star.
superannuation *n* starosna granica; penzionisanje zbog starosti.
superb *a* izvanredan, divan; **~ly** *adv* izvanredno, divno.
supercargo *n* nadzornik tereta (na brodu).
supercilious *a* uobražen, ohol; **~ly** *adv* uobraženo, oholo.

superficial *a* površan; **~ly** *adv* površno.
superfluity *n* suvišnost, nepotrebnost.
superfluous *a* suvišan.
superhuman *a* nadčovečanski.
superintendent *n* nadzornik; viši policijski činovnik.
superior *n* pretpostavljeni; *a* nadmoćan; superioran.
superiority *n* nadmoćnost; superiornost.
superlative *n* superlativ; superlativ (*gram*); *a* najviši, nenadmašan; **~ly** *adv* u najvećem stepenu; nenadmašno.
supermarket *n* velika samoposluga.
supernatural *a* natprirodan.
supernumerary *a* prekobrojan.
superpower *n* supersila.
supersede *v* zameniti; zaobići.
supersonic *a* nadzvučni.
superstition *n* praznoverje, sujeverje.
superstitious *a* praznoveran, sujeveran; **~ly** *adv* praznoverno, sujeverno.
supertanker *n* tanker velikog kapaciteta.
supervene *v* pridoći još; naići, nailaziti.
supervise *v* nadgledati, nadzirati.
supervision *n* nadzor.
supervisor *n* nadzornik.
superstructure *n* nadgradnja.
supine *a* koji leži nauznak; trom.
supper *n* večera.
supplant *v* istisnuti.
supple *a* savitljiv; poslušan.
supplement *n* dopuna.
supplementary *a* dopunski.
suppleness *n* gipkost.
suppli(c)ant *n* molilac.
supplicate *v* moliti, preklinjati.
supplication *n* molba, preklinjanje.
supplier *n* snabdevač.
supply *n* snabdevanje; zaliha; *v* snabdevati; obezbediti.
support *n* podrška, pomoć; oslonac; podupirač; *v* podržati; podupreti.
supportable *a* podnošljiv, izdržljiv.
supporter *n* pristalica.
suppose *v* pretpostaviti; dopuštati, smatrati.
supposition *n* pretpostavka.
suppress *v* ugušiti, savladati; zataškati.
suppression *n* gušenje; zataškavanje; zabrana.

supremacy *n* vrhovna vlast; prevlast; nadmoć.
supreme *a* najviši; vrhovni; **~ly** *adv* krajnje, do krajnosti.
surcharge *v* preopteretiti; previše zaračunati; *n* preopterećenje; doplata.
sure *a* siguran u sebe, uveren; pouzdan; **to be ~** zaista, svakako; **~ly** *adv* sigurno, pouzdano; *interj* svakako!.
sureness *n* sigurnost.
surety *n* jemstvo; jemac; ubeđenost.
surf *n* razbijanje talasa o obalu.
surface *n* površina; spoljašnost; *v* izbiti na površinu.
surfboard *n* daska za vožnju po talasima.
surfeit *n* neumerenost; prezasićenost.
surge *n* veliki talas; uzburkanost; *v* talasati se.
surgeon *n* hirurg.
surgery *n* hirurgija; hirurška ordinacija.
surgical *a* hirurški.
surliness *n* osornost; mrzovoljnost.
surly *a* osoran; mrzovoljan.
surmise *n* pretpostavka; *v* pretpostaviti.
surmount *v* savladati; prebroditi (poteškoće).
surmountable *a* savladljiv.
surname *n* prezime.
surpass *v* nadmašiti; prestići.
surpassing *a* koji nadmašuje; izvanredan, jedinstven.
surplus *n* višak; *a* suvišan.
surprise *n* iznenađenje; *v* iznenaditi.
surprising *a* iznenadan, neočekivan.
surrender *n* predaja, kapitulacija; *v* predati se.
surreptitious *a* potajan, skriven; **~ly** *adv* potajno.
surrogate *n* surogat, zamena; *v* zameniti.
surrogate mother *n* surogat majka.
surround *v* opkoliti.
surrounding area *n* okolina.
survey *n* pregled; geodetsko merenje; anketa; *v* pregledati; premeriti.
survive *v* preživeti; opstati.
survivor *n* preživela osoba.
susceptibility *n* osetljivost, prijemčivost.
susceptible *a* osetljiv, prijemčiv.
suspect *n* osumnjičena osoba; *v* sumnjičiti; sumnjati.
suspend *v* prikačiti; obustaviti.

suspender belt *n* pojas za čarape.
suspense *n* neizvesnost, iščekivanje.
suspension *n* suspenzija.
suspension bridge *n* viseći most.
suspicion *n* podozrenje, sumnja.
suspicious *a* podozriv; sumnjičav;
  sumnjiv; **~ly** *adv* podozrivo; sumnjivo.
suspiciousness *n* podozrivost; sumnjivost.
sustain *v* podržati; podnositi; održati.
sustenance *n* izdržavanje; ishrana;
  hranljivost; sredstva za život.
suture *n* šav (*med*), ušivanje rane.
swab *n* tampon (*med*); resasta metla za
  pranje poda.
swaddle *v* poviti u pelene.
swaddling-clothes *npl* pelene, povoji.
swagger *v* šepuriti se; razmetati se.
swallow[1] *n* gutljaj; *v* gutati.
swallow[2] *n* lastavica.
swamp *n* močvara.
swampy *a* močvaran.
swan *n* labud.
swap *n* trampa, razmena; *v* trampiti.
swarm *n* roj; jato; *v* rojiti se; nagrnuti.
swarthiness *n* garavost.
swarthy *a* crnomanjast.
swashbuckling *a* hvalisav, razmetljiv.
swathe *v* zaviti.
sway *n* zamah, njihanje; uticaj; prevlast; *v*
  ljuljati se; uticati na.
swear *v* zakleti se; psovati.
sweat *n* znoj; težak rad; *v* znojiti se;
  izmoriti se teškim radom.
sweater, sweatshirt *n* džemper, pulover.
sweep *n* čišćenje; zamah; domet; *v* očistiti
  (metlom).
sweeping *a* dalekosežan; sveobuhvatan;
  ~s *npl* pometeno smeće.
sweepstake *n* lutrija.
sweet *a* sladak; ljubazan; *adv* slatko,
  ljupko; *n* slatkoća; slatkiš.
sweetbread *n* gušterača (kod životinja);
  brizle (*kulin*).
sweeten *v* zasladiti.
sweetener *n* sredstvo za zaslađivanje.
sweetheart *n* dragi, draga.
sweetmeats *npl* slatkiši.
sweetness *n* slatkoća.
swell *n* uzvišenje; oteklina; kicoš; *v* oteći;
  naduti; *a* odličan (*col*).
swelling *n* oteklina.

swelter *v* skapavati od vrućine; kupati se
  u znoju.
swerve *v* skrenuti; zastraniti.
swift *n* vitlo; čopa (ptica); *a* brz, hitar.
swiftly *adv* brzo, hitro.
swiftness *n* brzina; okretnost.
swill *n* splačine; ispiranje; *v* lokati; ispirati.
swim *n* plivanje; *v* plivati; osećati
  vrtoglavicu.
swimming *n* plivanje.
swimming pool *n* plivački bazen.
swimsuit *n* kupaći kostim.
swindle *v* prevariti.
swindler *n* varalica.
swine *n* svinja.
swing *n* njihanje; ljuljaška; *v* njihati se;
  ljuljati se.
swinging door *n* šetajuća vrata (dvokrilna
  vrata na guranje).
switchboard *n* razvodna tabla.
swirl *n* vrtlog.
switch *n* šiba; prekidač (*el*); skretnica;
  preokret; *v* istući šibom; skrenuti;
  prebaciti; **to ~ off** ugasiti; **to ~ on** upaliti.
switchboard *n* razvodna tabla.
swivel *v* okretati se oko ose.
swoon *n* nesvestica, nesvest; *v* onesvestiti
  se.
swoop *n* prepad; *v* nasrnuti; **in one ~** u
  jednom naletu (mahu).
sword *n* mač.
swordfish *n* sabljarka (vrsta ribe).
swordsman *n* mačevalac.
sycamore *n* javor, platan (*bot*); egipatska
  smokva (*bot*).
sycophant *n* ulizica.
syllabic *a* slogovni, silabički.
syllable *n* slog.
syllabus *n* program; plan, pregled.
syllogism *n* silogizam.
sylph *n* vazdušni duh; vitka žena.
symbol *n* simbol.
symbolic(al) *a* simboličan.
symbolize *v* simbolizovati.
symmetrical *a* simetričan, skladan; **~ly**
  adv simetrično, skladno.
symmetry *n* simetrija.
sympathetic *a* saosećajan; simpatičan;
  ~ally *adv* saosećajno; simpatično.
sympathize *v* saosećati.
sympathy *n* saosećanje; simpatija.

symphony *n* simfonija.
symposium *n* simpozijum.
symptom *n* simptom, znak.
synagogue *n* sinagoga.
synchronism *n* sinhronizam, istodobnost.
syndicate *n* sindikat; udruženje.
syndrome *n* sindrom.
synod *n* sinod.
synonym *n* sinonim.
synonymous *a* sličan po značenju; **~ly**
   adv služeći se sinonimima.

synopsis *n* sažet pregled.
synoptic *a* pregledan, sažet.
syntax *n* sintaksa.
synthesis *n* sinteza.
syringe *n* špric (*med*); *v* ubrizgati.
system *n* sistem.
systematic *a* sistemski, sistematičan;
   ~ally *adv* sistemski, sistematski.
systems analyst *n* sistem analizator.

T

tab *n* jezičak (cipele); umetak; pločica; račun.

tabernacle *n* prebivalište (*rel*).

table *n* sto; tablica; tabela; *v* sastaviti tabelu; ~ **d'hôte** *n* jelovnik.

table tennis *n* stoni tenis.

tablecloth *n* stolnjak.

tablespoon *n* kašika za jelo, kutlača.

tablet *n* pločica; tableta; tabla (čokolade).

taboo *a* tabu, zabranjen; *n* tabu; *v* zabraniti.

tabular *a* tabelaran.

tachometer *n* tahometar, brzinomer.

tacit *a* prećutan; ćutljiv; tih; ~**ly** *adv* prećutno; ćutke.

taciturn *a* ćutljiv; uzdržan.

tack *n* ekser; pravac jedrenja; linija (*polit*); *v* pribiti ekserom; ravnati se prema prilikama.

tackle *n* pribor; oprema broda.

tact *n* takt.

tactician *n* taktičar.

tactics *npl* taktika.

tadpole *n* punoglavac.

taffeta *n* taft.

tag *n* etiketa; privezak; otrcana fraza; *v* staviti etiketu.

tail *n* rep; kraj (reda); pletenica; *v* slediti; pratiti; podrezati.

tailgate *n* stražnja vrata (na kamionu).

tailor *n* krojač.

tailoring *n* krojački posao.

tailor-made *a* izrađen po meri; prilagođen.

tails (tail coat) *npl* frak (*sleng*).

tailwind *n* vetar u leđa.

taint *n* mrlja; zaraženost; *v* uprljati; zaraziti.

tainted *a* pokvaren; umrljan.

take *v* uzeti; primiti; preduzeti; **to ~ apart** rasklopiti; **to ~ away** odneti; oduzeti; **to ~ back** vratiti; uzeti natrag; **to ~ down** skinuti; zabeležiti; **to ~ in** uneti; prevariti; **to ~ off** svući; izuti; poleteti; **to ~ on** latiti se; najmiti; **to ~ out** izvaditi; izvesti; **to ~ to** odati se; **to ~ up** odneti gore; sprijateljiti se; *n* uzimanje.

takeoff *n* poletanje.

takeover *n* preuzimanje; preuzimanje vlasti; ~ **bid** *n* pokušaj preuzimanja kontrole (*fin*).

takings *npl* prihodi.

talc *n* talk.

talent *n* talenat.

talented *a* talentovan.

talisman *n* talisman, amajlija.

talk *n* razgovor; govor; *v* govoriti; razgovarati; pretresati.

talkative *a* razgovorljiv, brbljiv.

talk show *n* govorni šou program.

tall *a* visok.

tally *v* podudarati se.

talon *n* kandža.

tambourine *n* daire.

tame *a* pitom; krotak, poslušan; dosadan; ~**ly** *adv* pitomo; krotko; *v* ukrotiti.

tameness *n* krotkost, pitomost.

tamper *v* mešati se (u tuđe poslove); pokvariti.

tampon *n* tampon (*med*).

tan *n* žutosmeđa boja; preplanulost; *v* preplanuti.

tang *n* oštar ukus ili miris; zveket.

tangent *n* tangenta.

tangerine *n* mandarina.

tangible *a* opipljiv; realan; primetan.

tangle *v* zamrsiti (se).

tank *n* rezervoar; tenk (*voj*).

tanker *n* brod cisterna, tanker.

tanned *a* preplanuo.

tantalizing *a* primamljiv.

tantamount *a* jednake vrednosti (značaja).

tantrum *n* provala besa.

tap[1] *n* tapšanje; čep; slavina.

tap[2] *v* potapšati; lupati; prisluškivati.

tape *n* traka, vrpca; *v* snimiti na magnetofonsku traku.

tape measure *n* krojački metar.

taper *n* tanka voštana sveća; konus.

tape recorder *n* magnetofon.

tapestry *n* tapiserija.

tar *n* katran.

target *n* meta, cilj; zadatak, plan.

tariff *n* dažbina, tarifa.
tarnish *v* gubiti boju.
tarpaulin *n* cerada.
tarragon *n* estragon (*bot*).
tart[1] *n* pita od voća; bludnica.
tart[2] *a* kiseo; opor; zajedljiv.
tartan *n* tartan, (škotska) karirana tkanina.
tartar *n* zubni kamenac.
task *n* zadatak.
tassel *n* kićanka.
taste *n* ukus; probanje; *v* probati; okusiti.
tasteful *a* ukusan; ~ly *adv* ukusno.
tasteless *a* bezukusan.
tasty *a* ukusan.
tattoo *n* tetoviranje; *v* tetovirati.
taunt *v* narugati se; *n* podsmeh.
Taurus *n* Bik (*astrol*).
taut *a* zategnut; napet.
tautological *a* tautološki.
tautology *n* tautologija.
tawdry *a* drečeći; nakinđuren.
tax *n* porez; taksa; *v* oporezovati.
taxable *a* oporeziv.
taxation *n* oporezivanje.
tax collector *n* poreznik.
tax-free *a* oslobođen poreza.
taxi *n* taksi; *v* rulati (avion).
taxi driver *n* taksista.
taxi rank *n* taksi stanica.
tax payer *n* poreski obveznik.
tax relief *n* oslobođenje od poreza.
tax return *n* poreska prijava.
tea *n* čaj.
tea service, tea set *n* servis za čaj.
teach *v* učiti, predavati; naučiti.
teacher *n* učitelj, nastavnik.
teaching *n* nastava.
teacup *n* šolja za čaj.
teak *n* tik (drvo) (*bot*).
team *n* tim, ekipa.
teamster *n* kamiondžija.
teamwork *n* timski rad.
teapot *n* čajnik.
tear *v* pocepati; poderati; cepati se; **to ~ up** pocepati, razderati; *n* suza.
tearful *a* pun suza, uplakan; ~ly *adv* sa suzama, uplakano.
tear gas *n* suzavac.
tease *v* zadirkivati.
teasing *a* šaljiv; dosadan; *n* šegačenje.
teaspoon *n* kafena kašičica.

teat *n* sisa; bradavica na sisi.
technical *a* stručni; tehnički.
technicality *n* stručnost; tehnički izraz (ili postupak).
technician *n* tehničar.
technique *n* tehnika; metod rada.
technological *a* tehnološki.
technology *n* tehnologija.
teddy (bear) *n* plišani meda.
tedious *a* dosadan; monoton; ~ly *adv* dosadno; monotono.
tedium *n* dosada; jednoličnost.
tee *n* kupica na koju se stavlja loptica u golfu; meta (u raznim igrama).
teem *v* obilovati, vrveti.
teenage *a* tinejdžerski, omladinski.
teenager *n* tinejdžer.
teens *npl* godine između 13 i 19.
tee-shirt, T-shirt *n* majica s kratkim rukavima.
teeth *npl* zubi (množina od *tooth*).
teethe *v* dobiti zube.
teetotal *a* trezvenjački.
teetotaller *n* trezvenjak.
telegram *n* telegram.
telegraph *n* telegraf.
telegraphic *a* telegrafski.
telegraphy *n* telegrafija.
telepathy *n* telepatija.
telephone *n* telefon.
telephone banking *n* telebank (niz telefona za telefoniranje većih razmera).
telephone booth *n* telefonska govornica.
telephone call *n* telefonski poziv.
telephone directory *n* telefonski imenik.
telephone number *n* telefonski broj.
telescope *n* teleskop.
telescopic *a* teleskopski.
televise *v* emitovati preko televizije.
television (TV) *n* televizija.
television news *n* televizijske vesti.
television (TV) remote *n* daljinski upravljač; birač kanala.
television set *n* televizor.
teleworker *n* radnik televizije.
teleworking *n* rad na televiziji.
telex *n* teleks; *v* slati teleksom.
tell *v* kazati, reći; pričati; razlikovati.
teller *n* blagajnik (u banci).
telling *a* znatan; efektivan.
telltale *a* izdajnički, koji odaje.

telly *n* (*sleng*) televizija.
temper *n* narav, ćud; raspoloženje; *v* ublažiti.
temperament *n* narav, temperament.
temperance *n* umerenost; trezvenost.
temperate *a* umeren.
temperature *n* temperatura.
tempest *n* oluja, bura.
tempestuous *a* buran.
template *n* šablon.
temple *n* hram.
temporarily *adv* privremeno.
temporary *a* privremen.
tempt *v* dovesti u iskušenje.
temptation *n* iskušenje.
tempting *a* primamljiv.
ten *num* deset; *n* desetica.
tenable *a* održiv, branjiv.
tenacious *a* čvrst, žilav; otporan; ~ly *adv* čvrsto, žilavo.
tenacity *n* žilavost; otpornost.
tenancy *n* zakup.
tenant *n* stanar; zakupac.
tend *v* naginjati; imati tendenciju; biti sklon.
tendency *n* tendencija; sklonost.
tender[1] *a* nežan; mek; osetljiv; ~ly *adv* nežno.
tender[2] *n* tender; ponuda; *v* ponuditi.
tenderness *n* nežnost.
tendon *n* tetiva (*anat*).
tendril *n* vitica (*bot*).
tenement *n* stan, kuća; kuća sa jeftinim stanovima.
tenet *n* načelo, princip.
tennis *n* tenis.
tennis court *n* tenisko igralište.
tennis player *n* teniser.
tennis racket *n* teniski reket.
tennis shoes *npl* sportske patike.
tenor *n* tenor (*muz*); pravac, tok.
tense[1] *n* glagolsko vreme (*gram*).
tense[2] *a* zategnut.
tension *n* napetost; zategnutost.
tent *n* šator.
tentacle *n* pipak (*zoòl*).
tentative *a* probni; privremeni; ~ly *adv* provizorno.
tenth *num a* deseti; *n* desetina.
tenuous *a* tanak; slab; neznatan.
tenure *n* posedovanje; zanimanje, položaj.
tepid *a* mlak.

term *n* rok; semestar; termin; ~s *npl* uslovi; odnosi.
terminal *a* konačan; koji umire; *n* terminal, krajnja stanica.
terminate *v* ograničiti; okončati.
termination *n* završetak; kraj roka.
terminus *n* kraj; krajnja stanica.
terrace *n* terasa.
terrain *n* teren, zemljište.
terrestrial *a* zemaljski; kopneni.
terrible *a* strašan, užasan.
terribly *adv* strašno.
terrier *n* terijer (vrsta psa).
terrific *a* strašan; izvanredan.
terrify *v* prestrašiti.
territorial *a* teritorijalan.
territory *n* teritorija.
terror *n* teror.
terrorism *n* terorizam.
terrorist *n* terorista.
terrorist attack *n* teroristički napad.
terrorize *v* terorisati.
terse *a* jezgrovit.
test *n* ispit; proba; *v* ispitati; proveriti.
testament *n* testament.
tester *n* ispitivač.
testicles *npl* testisi (*anat*).
testify *v* svedočiti.
testimonial *n* uverenje, preporuka.
testimony *n* svedočanstvo.
test pilot *n* probni pilot.
test tube *n* epruveta.
testy *a* razdražljiv, mrzovoljan.
tetanus *n* tetanus.
tether *v* vezati.
text *n* tekst.
textbook *n* udžbenik.
textiles *npl* tekstilna roba.
textual *a* tekstualan.
texture *n* tkanje; struktura.
than *conj* nego, od.
thank *v* zahvaliti (se).
thankful *a* zahvalan; ~ly *adv* sa zahvalnošću.
thankfulness *n* zahvalnost.
thankless *a* nezahvalan.
thanks *npl, interj* zahvalnost!
Thanksgiving *n* (*amer*) praznik zahvalnosti.
that *pn* koji, koja, koje; onaj, taj; *conj* da; zato da; **so** ~ tako da.

thatch *n* krov od slame; *v* pokriti krov slamom.

thaw *n* topljenje; *v* rastopiti.

the *art* određeni član (*gram*).

theatre *n* pozorište.

theatregoer *n* pozorišni posetilac.

theatrical *a* pozorišni; teatralan.

theft *n* krađa.

their *pn* njihov; **~s** *pn* njihov (predikativno).

them *pn* njima, njih.

theme *n* tema.

themselves *pn* oni sami; sebe, sebi; lično.

then *a* tadašnji, ondašnji; *adv* onda, tada; zatim; *conj* zato, dakle; **now and ~ s** vremena na vreme; povremeno.

theologian *n* teolog.

theological *a* teološki.

theology *n* teologija.

theorem *n* teorema.

theoretic(al) *a* teorijski, teoretski; **~ly** *adv* teorijski.

theorist *n* teoretičar.

theorize *v* teoretizirati.

theory *n* teorija.

therapeutics *n* terapeutika, terapija (*med*).

therapist *n* terapeut.

therapy *n* terapija.

there *adv* tu; tamo; onamo.

thereabout(s) *adv* tamo negde; blizu; otprilike toliko.

thereafter *adv* nakon toga; prema tome.

thereby *adv* time, pomoću toga; otuda.

therefore *adv* stoga, zato, radi toga, dakle, prema tome.

thermal *a* toplotni, termalni.

thermal printer *n* termički štampač.

thermometer *n* termometar, toplomer.

thermostat *n* termostat.

thesaurus *n* leksikon, rečnik sinonima.

these *pn* ovi (množina od *this*); *a* ovi.

thesis *n* teza, disertacija; naučna postavka.

they *pn* oni, one, ona.

thick *a* gust; debeo; dubok; glup.

thicken *v* zgusnuti (se); zadebljati.

thicket *n* čestar.

thickness *n* debljina; gustoća; sloj.

thickset *a* zdepast.

thick-skinned *a* debele kože; neosetljiv.

thief *n* lopov.

thigh *n* butina; butna kost.

thimble *n* naprstak.

thin *a* tanak; mršav; redak; oskudan; *v* prorediti (se).

thing *n* stvar, predmet; nešto; stvor(enje).

think *v* misliti; smatrati; nameravati; **to ~ over** promisliti; **to ~ up** izmisliti.

thinker *n* mislilac.

thinking *n* razmišljanje, mišljenje.

third *num a* treći; *n* trećina; **~ly** *adv* treće, na trećem mestu.

third rate *a* trećerazredni.

thirst *n* žeđ; *v* biti žedan.

thirsty *a* žedan.

thirteen *num* trinaest; *n* trinaestoro, trinaestica.

thirteenth *num a* trinaesti; *n* trinaesti deo.

thirtieth *num a* trideseti; *n* trideseti deo.

thirty *num* trideset; *n* tridesetoro, tridesetica.

this *a/pn* ovaj, taj; ovo, to.

thistle *n* čičak, čkalj (*bot*).

thorn *n* trn, bodlja; trnovo drvo.

thorny *a* trnovit.

thorough *a* temeljan, korenit, potpun; **~ly** *adv* temeljito, potpuno.

thoroughbred *a* čistokrvan, rasan.

thoroughfare *n* prolaz; auto put, široka ulica.

those *a/pn* oni, ti (množina od *that*).

though *conj* premda, iako, makar; čak, kad bi; *adv* doduše, ipak.

thought *n* misao.

thoughtful *a* zamišljen; brižan, pažljiv.

thoughtless *a* bezbrižan, lakomislen; nepromišljen; nepažljiv; **~ly** *adv* nepromišljeno; nesmotreno; nepažljivo.

thousand *num* hiljada; *n* hiljada; mnoštvo.

thousandth *num a* hiljaditi; *n* hiljaditi deo.

thrash *v* mlatiti, tući.

thread *n* konac, nit; loza, navoj; *v* udenuti; probiti se.

threadbare *a* pohaban, otrcan.

threat *n* pretnja.

threaten *v* pretiti.

three *num* tri; *n* trojica; troje.

three-dimensional *a* trodimenzionalan.

three-monthly *a* tromesečni.

three-ply *a* trostruk.

threshold *n* prag, ulaz.

thrifty *a* štedljiv.
thrill *n* uzbuđenje; *v* uzbuditi (se).
thriller *n* triler.
thrive *v* napredovati, uspevati; cvetati.
throat *n* grlo, vrat.
throb *v* lupati, udarati.
throne *n* presto.
throng *n* gužva; gomila; *v* gurati se,
tiskati se.
throttle *n* dušnik; regulator; *v* regulisati;
ugušiti.
through *prep* kroz; preko; pomoću; *a*
direktan; slobodan; *adv* skroz.
throughout *prep* kroz; sve vreme; *adv* do
kraja.
throw *v* baciti; zbaciti; *n* bacanje; **to ~
away** odbaciti; propustiti (priliku); **to ~
off** skinuti, zbaciti (odeću); **to ~ out**
izbaciti; **to ~ up** povratiti.
throwaway *a* za jednokratnu upotrebu.
thrush *n* drozd (vrsta ptice).
thrust *n* ubod; guranje; oslonac; potisak;
v bosti; gurnuti; izbaciti.
thud *n* tup udarac (pad); bat, topot.
thug *n* siledžija; razbojnik; ubica.
thumb *n* palac.
thump *n* tup udarac; lupa, udaranje; *v*
udariti (teškim predmetom); lupiti.
thunder *n* grom; grmljavina; *v* (za)grmeti.
thunderbolt *n* munja.
thunderclap *n* prasak groma.
thunderstorm *n* oluja s grmljavinom.
thundery *a* gromoglasan; koji
nagoveštava grmljavinu.
Thursday *n* četvrtak.
thus *adv* tako, ovako; prema tome.
thwart *v* sprečiti.
thyme *n* majčina dušica (*bot*).
thyroid *n* štitna žlezda.
tiara *n* tijara; papska kruna.
tic *n* tik (*med*).
tick[1] *n* kucanje; otkucaj; krpelj.
tick[2] *v* otkucavati; obeležiti znakom; **to ~
over** raditi minimalnom snagom
(motor).
ticket *n* karta; ulaznica; etiketa; ceduljica
(oglas).
ticket collector *n* biletar, osoba koja
pregleda ulaznice.
ticket office *n* blagajna za prodaju karata,
biletarnica.

tickle *v* golicati .
ticklish *a* golicljiv.
tidal *a* plimski.
tidal wave *n* plimski talas.
tide *n* plima i oseka; talas, struja.
tidy *a* uredan, čist; znatan.
tie *v* vezati; pričvrstiti; igrati nerešeno; **to
~ up** zavezati; povezati se; *n* veza;
kravata.
tier *n* red, niz.
tiger *n* tigar.
tight *a* tesan; zategnut; neprobojan; *adv*
čvrsto.
tighten *v* stegnuti, zategnuti.
tightfisted *a* škrt.
tightly *adv* čvrsto.
tightrope *n* nategnuto uže.
tights *npl* triko; hulahopke.
tigress *n* tigrica.
tile *n* crep; pločica; *v* pokriti (crepom).
tiled *a* pokriven (crepom, pločicama).
till[1] *n* fioka za novac.
till[2] *v* orati, obrađivati (zemlju).
tiller *n* rudo kormila.
tilt *v* nagnuti (se).
timber *n* drvena građa; greda; drveće.
time *n* vreme; doba; rok; takt, tempo (*muz*);
in ~ na vreme; **from ~ to ~** s vremena na
vreme; *v* tempirati; podesiti.
time bomb *n* tempirana bomba.
time lag *n* vremenski razmak.
timeless *a* bezvremen, večan.
timely *a* pravovremen.
time off *n* slobodno vreme.
timer *n* kontrolni sat, tajmer.
time scale *n* vremenska skala.
time trial *n* vremenska proba.
time zone *n* vremenska zona.
timid *a* stidljiv; plašljiv; **~ly** *adv*
bojažljivo.
timidity *n* stidljivost; plašljivost.
timing *n* tempiranje, podešavanje
vremena.
tin *n* kalaj; lim; limenka.
tinder *n* trud (za kresivo).
tinfoil *n* staniol.
tinge *n* trag, primesa; nijansa.
tingle *v* peckati, štipati (mraz); zujati u
ušima.
tingling *n* zujanje u ušima; štipanje
mraza.

tinker *n* kotlokrpa; ciganin.

tinkle *v* zvoniti; zvečati.

tin plate *n* beli lim.

tinsel *n* šljokice; lažan sjaj.

tint *n* boja; nijansa; *v* lako obojiti, nijansirati.

tinted *a* obojen, zasenčen.

tiny *a* sitan, majušan.

tip[1] *n* napojnica, bakšiš; *v* dati napojnicu.

tip[2] *n* obaveštenje; savet.

tip[3] *v* prevrnuti; nagnuti; istovariti; *n* smetlište.

tip-off *n* savet, informacije.

tipsy *a* pripit.

tiptop *a* prvoklasan.

tirade *n* tirada.

tire *v* umoriti (se), zamoriti (se).

tireless *a* neumoran.

tiresome *a* zamoran; dosadan.

tiring *a* zamoran.

tissue *n* tkivo; tkanje; splet.

tissue paper *n* tanak papir.

titbit *n* poslastica; zanimljiva vest.

titillate *v* golicati; prijatno uzbuditi.

title *n* naslov.

title deed *n* isprava o pravu vlasništva.

title page *n* naslovna strana.

titter *v* cerekati se, kikotati se; *n* kikot.

titular *a* titularni; naslovni.

to *prep* u; za; na; do; prema; kod; od; sa; po; da.

toad *n* žaba; odvratna osoba.

toadstool *n* zlatača (otrovna pečurka).

toast[1] *n* zdravica; *v* nazdraviti.

toast[2] *n* prepečena kriška hleba; *v* pržiti.

toaster *n* toster, naprava za prženje hleba.

tobacco *n* duvan.

tobacco pouch *n* duvankesa.

tobacconist *n* trgovac duvanom, trafikant.

tobacconist's (shop) *n* prodavnica duvana.

toboggan *n* tobogan (duge, niske saonice).

today *adv* danas.

toddler *n* dete koje je tek prohodalo.

toddy *n* punč.

toe *n* nožni prst.

together *adv* zajedno; istovremeno; neprekidno.

toil *n* težak rad; *v* teško raditi.

toilet *n* toaleta; doterivanje; WC; *a* toaletni.

toilet bag *n* torbica sa toaletnim priborom.

toilet bowl *n* WC školjka.

toilet paper *n* toaletni papir.

toiletries *npl* toaletne potrepštine, drogerijska roba.

token *n* znak, simbol; znamenje; žeton, pločica.

tolerable *a* podnošljiv; priličan.

tolerance *n* tolerancija.

tolerant *a* tolerantan.

tolerate *v* tolerisati.

toll *n* taksa; putarina; zvonjenje; *v* platiti dažbinu; zvoniti.

tomato *n* paradajz.

tomb *n* grob.

tomboy *n* muškarača, muškobanja.

tombstone *n* nadgrobni spomenik.

tomcat *n* mačak.

tomorrow *adv* sutra; *n* sutrašnjica.

ton *n* tona.

tone *n* ton, glas; duh, atmosfera; *v* uštimovati; **to ~ down** ublažiti, oslabiti.

tone-deaf *a* bez muzičkog sluha.

tongs *npl* klešta.

tongue *n* jezik; govor.

tongue-tied *a* nem; mutav; mucav.

tongue-twister *n* brzalica, fraza teška za izgovor.

tonic *n* sredstvo za jačanje (*med*).

tonight *adv* večeras, noćas; *n* ova noć.

tonnage *n* tonaža.

tonsil *n* krajnik, *pl* krajnici.

tonsillitis *n* zapaljenje krajnika.

tonsure *n* tonzura, postrig.

too *adv* previše; vrlo; takođe, isto tako.

tool *n* alatka.

tool box *n* kutija za alat.

toot *v* trubiti.

tooth *n* zub; zubac.

toothache *n* zubobolja.

toothbrush *n* četkica za zube.

toothless *a* bezub.

toothpaste *n* pasta za zube.

toothpick *n* čačkalica.

top *n* vrh; vrhunac; gornji deo; *a* gornji; najviši; *v* pokriti; stići do vrha; **to ~ off** završiti; napuniti.

top floor *n* zadnji sprat.

topaz *n* topaz (dragi kamen).

top-heavy *a* preopterećen u gornjem delu, nestabilan; glomazan.

topic *n* tema, predmet.
topical *a* aktuelan.
topless *a* bez vrha; golih grudi.
top-level *a* najviši; vrhunski.
topmost *a* najviši; najvažniji.
topographic(al) *a* topografski.
topography *n* topografija.
topple *v* oboriti, srušiti; pasti.
top-secret *a* strogo poverljiv.
topsy-turvy *adv* naopako; u krajnjem neredu.
torch *n* baklja, svetlo.
torment *n* mučenje, muka; *v* mučiti.
tornado *n* uragan.
torrent *n* bujica, potok.
torrid *a* vreo, žarki; strastven.
tortoise *n* kornjača.
tortoiseshell *a* mrkožut (sa šarama kornjačevine).
tortuous *a* vijugav.
torture *n* mučenje, tortura; *v* mučiti.
toss *v* baciti; prevrtati (se); trzati (se).
total *a* ukupan; celokupan; **~ly** *adv* ukupno.
totalitarian *a* totalitaran.
totality *n* celokupnost, celina.
totter *v* teturati se; biti nestabilan.
touch *v* dodirnuti; ganuti; okusiti; **to ~ on** dodirnuti; ovlaš spomenuti; **to ~ up** popraviti; doterati; *n* dodir; opip; veza.
touch-and-go *a* nesiguran, riskantan; opasan.
touchdown *n* spuštanje, ateriranje; postići zgoditak u ragbiju.
touched *a* ganut, dirnut.
touching *a* dirljiv.
touchstone *n* kriterijum, merilo.
touchwood *n* suvo drvo, trud.
touchy *a* preosetljiv.
tough *a* tvrd, čvrst; žilav; uporan; *n* siledžija.
toughen *v* učvrstiti, pojačati.
toupee *n* poluperika, tupe.
tour *n* putovanje; obilazak; turneja; *v* proputovati; biti na turneji.
touring *n* turističko putovanje.
tourism *n* turizam; **bicycle ~** turističko putovanje biciklom; **rural ~** seoski turizam.
tourist *n* turista.
tourist office *n* turistička agencija.

tournament *n* turnir; takmičenje.
tow *n* tegljenje (broda); tegljač; *v* vući, tegliti.
toward(s) *prep* prema, u smeru, ka; u svrhu.
towel *n* peškir.
towelling *n* frotir materijal.
towel rack *n* vešalica za peškir.
tower *n* toranj; kula.
towering *a* koji se visoko diže; ogroman.
town *n* grad.
town clerk *n* gradski beležnik.
town hall *n* gradska većnica.
towrope *n* uže za tegljenje.
toy *n* igračka.
toyshop *n* prodavnica igračaka.
trace *n* trag; crta; staza; *v* tragati; skicirati; trasirati.
track *n* trag; staza; tračnice; *v* tragati, slediti.
tracksuit *n* trenerka (*sport*).
tract[1] *n* traktat, rasprava, pamflet.
tract[2] *n* predeo, prostor; trakt, sistem (*anat*).
traction *n* vuča .
trade *n* zanat; trgovina; *v* razmeniti; trgovati.
trade fair *n* sajam.
trade name *n* trgovački naziv.
trader *n* trgovac.
tradesman *n* trgovac na malo; zanatlija.
trademark *n* zaštitni znak.
trade unionist *n* sindikalista.
trade(s) union *n* sindikat.
trading *n* trgovanje; *a* trgovački.
tradition *n* tradicija.
traditional *a* tradicionalan.
traffic *n* saobraćaj; trgovina; *v* trgovati.
traffic jam *n* zastoj saobraćaja.
trafficker *n* trgovac.
traffic lights *npl* semafor.
tragedy *n* tragedija.
tragic *a* tragičan; **~ally** *adv* tragično.
tragicomedy *n* tragikomedija.
trail *n* trag, miris; rep; staza; *v* vrebati, tražiti; vući.
trailer *n* prikolica; kratak reklamni film (za budući glavni film).
train *n* voz; skut; pratnja; *v* putovati vozom; obučiti; dresirati; trenirati; **high-speed ~** brzi, ekspresni voz.

trained *a* izučen, pripremljen; uvežban, istreniran.

trainee *n* osoba na praksi; regrut; novajlija.

trainer *n* trener; dreser.

trainers *npl* teniske patike.

training *n* obuka; trening.

trait *n* potez; crta, osobina.

traitor *n* izdajnik.

tram *n* tramvaj.

tramp *n* skitnica; 'laka' žena; *v* skitati; pešačiti; teško gaziti.

trample *v* zgaziti; gaziti.

trampoline *n* trambulina.

trance *n* trans, ekstaza; uspavanost.

tranquil *a* miran, tih.

tranquillize *v* smiriti.

tranquillizer *n* sredstvo za smirenje.

transact *v* obaviti, izvršiti.

transaction *n* transakcija; posao; izvršenje.

transatlantic *a* prekoatlantski.

transcend *v* prekoračiti granice; prevazići.

transcription *n* prepis; transkripcija.

transfer *n* prenos; premeštaj; *v* preneti; premestiti.

transform *v* preobraziti; transformisati.

transformation *n* preobražaj; transformacija.

transfusion *n* transfuzija; pretakanje.

transient *a* prolazan; privremen.

transit *n* prolaz; tranzit.

transition *n* prelaz (promena), tranzicija.

transitional *a* prelazan.

transitive *a* prelazan (*gram*).

translate *v* prevesti; protumačiti.

translation *n* prevod; tumačenje.

translator *n* prevodilac.

transmission *n* prenos, transmisija; odašiljanje.

transmit *v* preneti; otpremiti; emitovati.

transmitter *n* predajnik.

transparency *n* providnost.

transparent *a* providan.

transpire *v* ispariti; prodreti; zbiti se.

transplant *n* presađivanje; transplantacija; *v* presaditi.

transport *n* prevoz, transport; *v* prevesti, prevoziti.

transportation *n* transport, saobraćaj.

trap *n* klopka, zamka; odvodna cev; *v* uhvatiti u klopku.

trap door *n* vrata u podu ili krovu.

trapeze *n* trapez (*sport*).

trappings *npl* ukrasni odevni predmeti.

trash *n* otpaci, smeće; ološ; šund.

trash can *n* kanta za smeće.

trashy *a* loš, bezvredan.

travel *n* putovanje; *v* putovati.

travel agency *n* turistička agencija.

travel agent *n* vlasnik ili radnik turističke agencije.

traveller *n* putnik.

traveller's cheque *n* putnički ček.

travelling *n* putovanje.

travel-sickness *n* mučnina pri putovanju.

travesty *n* parodija.

trawler *n* koča (brod), lađa ribarica.

tray *n* poslužavnik.

treacherous *a* izdajnički, podmukao; nepouzdan.

treachery *n* izdaja, podmuklost.

tread *n* način hoda; stepenica; *v* koračati; stupiti.

treason *n* izdaja; **high ~** *n* veleizdaja.

treasure *n* blago, riznica; *v* gomilati; visoko ceniti.

treasurer *n* riznичar, blagajnik.

treat *v* postupiti; pretresati; častiti; *n* čašćenje; uživanje.

treatise *n* rasprava, studija.

treatment *n* postupak; lečenje.

treaty *n* ugovor, sporazum.

treble *a* trostruk; sopranski; piskav; *v* utrostručiti (se); *n* sopran (*muz*).

treble clef *n* violinski ključ (*muz*).

tree *n* drvo, stablo.

trek *n* put, pohod, ekspedicija.

trellis *n* rešetka, senica (od rešetke).

tremble *v* drhtati.

trembling *n* drhtanje; uzbuđenost.

tremendous *a* ogroman; strašan.

tremor *n* drhtanje, drhtavica.

trench *n* rov (*voj*); jama; brazda.

trend *n* trend, tendencija.

trendy *a* pomodan; savremen.

trepidation *n* drhtanje; zabrinutost; strepnja.

trespass *v* prekoračiti granice; zloupotrebiti.

tress *n* uvojak, pletenica.

trestle *n* nogari, stalak, skele.
trial *n* pokušaj, proba; sudski pretres.
triangle *n* trougao.
triangular *a* trougaoni.
tribal *a* plemenski.
tribe *n* pleme.
tribulation *n* nevolja, muka.
tribunal *n* sud.
tributary *a* podložan, vazalni.
tribute *n* danak; poštovanje, priznanje.
trice *n* trenutak.
trick *n* trik, prevara; veština; *v* prevariti;
obmanuti.
trickery *n* prevara; lukavstvo.
trickle *v* kapati, curiti; *n* kapanje, curenje.
tricky *a* lukav, prepreden.
tricycle *n* tricikl.
trifle *n* sitnica; bagatela; *v* baviti se
sitnicama; šaliti se.
trifling *a* sitan, beznačajan.
trigger *n* obarač; *v* izazvati, pokrenuti; to
~ off aktivirati.
trigonometry *n* trigonometrija.
trill *n* treperenje (zvuka); *v* podrhtavati,
treperiti.
trillion *n* trilion (*br*); bilion (*am*).
trim *a* doteran; *v* doterati; dovesti u red.
trimester *n* tromesečje.
trimmings *npl* dodaci, garnirung (uz
jelo).
Trinity *n* Sveta trojica (*rel*).
trinket *n* tričarija; jeftin nakit.
trio *n* trio (*muz*).
trip *v* hitro koračati; pogrešiti; isključiti;
to ~ up saplesti; podmetnuti nekome
nogu; *n* putovanje; lak korak; saplitanje.
tripe *n* škembići; nešto bezvredno.
triple *a* trojni; trostruk; *v* utrostručiti (se).
triplets *npl* trojke (deca).
triplicate *n* triplikat.
trite *a* otrcan, banalan.
triumph *n* trijumf; *v* trijumfovati.
triumphal *a* trijumfalan.
triumphant *a* pobednički; pobedonosan;
~ly *adv* pobednički; pobedonosno.
trivia *npl* trivijalnosti.
trivial *a* trivijalan, beznačajan; ~ly *adv*
trivijalno.
triviality *n* trivijalnost.
trolley *n* ručna kolica; vagonet; trola.
trombone *n* trombon (*muz*).

troop *n* gomila; krdo; eskadron; ~s *npl*
trupe.
trooper *n* konjički policajac; policajac
neke države (am.).
trophy *n* trofej, ratni plen.
tropical *a* tropski.
trot *n* kas; kaskanje; *v* jahati kasom.
trouble *n* nezgoda, nevolja; teškoća;
napor; *v* uznemiriti; zabrinuti; truditi se.
troubled *a* uznemiren, zabrinut.
troublemaker *n* izgrednik; agitator.
troubleshooter *n* specijalista serviser;
posebni predstavnik.
troublesome *a* neugodan; mučan;
nemiran.
trough *n* korito; jarak; udubljenje.
troupe *n* glumačka trupa.
trousers *npl* pantalone.
trout *n* pastrmka (riba).
trowel *n* mistrija.
truce *n* primirje, prekid vatre.
truck *n* kamion; otvoren teretni vagon.
truck driver *n* kamiondžija.
truculent *a* okrutan; nemilosrdan;
borben.
trudge *v* s mukom pešačiti, vući se.
true *a* istinit; stvaran; tačan; iskren.
truelove *n* dragi, draga.
truffle *n* tartuf (pečurka).
truly *adv* zaista; pravilno; stvarno.
trump *n* adut (u kartama); adut, glavno
sredstvo.
trumpet *n* truba.
trunk *n* stablo, deblo; trup, telo; putni
kovčeg.
truss *n* krovna konstrukcija; potporanj; *v*
privezati; podupreti.
trust *n* poverenje; pouzdanje; *v* verovati;
nadati se.
trusted *a* pouzdan.
trustee *n* staratelj; poverenik.
trustful *a* pun poverenja.
trustily *adv* pouzdano.
trusting *a* koji se uzda (pun poverenja).
trustworthy *a* dostojan poverenja.
trusty *a* pouzdan.
truth *n* istina; iskrenost; tačnost; in ~
uistinu.
truthful *a* istinoljubiv.
truthfulness *n* istinitost; istinoljubivost.
try *v* pokušati; probati; ispitivati; to ~ on

probati; **to ~ out** oprobati, iskušati; konkurisati; *n* pokušaj.

trying *a* težak, naporan; zamoran.

tub *n* kada; bačva.

tuba *n* tuba (*muz*).

tube *n* cev; tuba (za pakovanje).

tuberculosis *n* tuberkuloza.

tubing *n* cevi; cevovod.

tuck *n* nabor; poslastice; *v* nabrati; ugurati.

Tuesday *n* utorak.

tuft *n* pramen, čuperak.

tug *v* vući, tegliti; *n* vučenje; konopac.

tuition *n* obučavanje; školarina.

tulip *n* lala, tulipan.

tumble *v* pasti; srušiti se; nabasati; *n* pad; prevrtanje.

tumbledown *a* trošan.

tumbler[1] *n* tambler (visoka ravna čaša bez postolja).

tumbler[2] *n* akrobata, pelivan.

tummy *n* stomačić.

tumour *n* tumor.

tumultuous *a* bučan, buran; buntovan.

tuna *n* tunj (riba).

tune *n* melodija; sklad; *v* udesiti; zvučati.

tuneful *a* melodičan; blagozvučan.

tuner *n* štimer.

tunic *n* tunika.

tuning fork *n* akustična viljuška (*muz*).

tunnel *n* tunel; *v* prokopati tunel.

turban *n* turban.

turbine *n* turbina.

turbulence *n* turbulencija; gungula, metež.

turbulent *a* uzburkan; buran.

tureen *n* duboka zdela.

turf *n* busen; trkalište; *v* pokriti busenjem.

turgid *a* otečen; pompezan.

turkey *n* ćurka.

turmoil *n* metež; nemir.

turn *v* okretati (se); skrenuti; promeniti se; **to ~ around** okrenuti (se); **to ~ back** ići natrag; odbiti; **to ~ down** presaviti; odbiti; **to ~ in** predati; prijaviti; **to ~ off** ugasiti; skrenuti s puta; **to ~ on** upaliti; napasti; **to ~ out** ugasiti; **to ~ over** okrenuti; prevrnuti (se); **to ~ up** zavrnuti; pojaviti se; pojačati; *n* skretanje; promena; usluga.

turncoat *n* otpadnik, izdajnik.

turning *n* skretanje.

turnip *n* repa.

turn-off *n* skretanje s autoputa; razočarenje.

turnout *n* poseta, broj gledalaca; učešće.

turnover *n* obrt, promet.

turnstile *n* obrtni krst (automatska naplatna rampa na ulazu u podzemnu železnicu).

turntable *n* okretnica; rotaciona ploča.

turpentine *n* terpentin.

turquoise *n* tirkiz.

turret *n* kula, tornjić.

turtle *n* kornjača.

turtledove *n* grlica (ptica).

tusk *n* kljova.

tussle *n* tuča, gužva.

tutor *n* privatni učitelj; tutor; *v* podučavati, davati časove.

twang *n* zvečanje; unjkav glas.

tweezers *npl* pinceta, mala klešta.

twelfth *num a* dvanaesti; *n* dvanaesti deo.

twelve *num* dvanaest; *n* dvanaestica.

twentieth *num a* dvadeseti; *n* dvadeseti deo.

twenty *num* dvadeset; *n* dvadesetica.

twice *adv* dvaput.

twig[1] *n* grančica.

twig[2] *v* shvatiti, razumeti.

twilight *n* sumrak, suton.

twin *n* blizanac.

twine *v* uplesti; *n* kanap, uže.

twinge *v* žigati, probadati (bol); *n* žiganje.

twinkle *v* svetlucati; *n* svetlucanje.

twirl *v* okretati se, vrteti se; *n* brzo okretanje.

twist *v* uplesti; savijati; uganuti; okretati; *n* uvijanje; uganuće; preokret.

twit *n* budala, glupan (*sleng*).

twitch *v* trznuti se; povući; *n* trzanje; povlačenje.

twitter *v* cvrkutati; *n* cvrkut.

two *num* dva; *n* dvojka; dvojica.

two-door *a* koji se sastoji od dvoja vrata.

two-faced *a* sa dva lica; dvoličan.

twofold *a* dvostruk; *adv* dvostruko.

two-seater *n* dvosed.

twosome *n* par, dvoje.

tycoon *n* bogat industrijalac, tajkun.

type *n* tip, vrsta; prototip; štamparska slova; *v* otkucati; klasifikovati.

typecast *a* stereotipan; šablonski.
typeface *n* štamparski slog; dirka.
typescript *n* kucana kopija.
typewriter *n* pisaća mašina.
typewritten *a* otkucan (na mašini).
typical *a* tipičan, karakterističan.
typographer *n* tipograf.

typographical *a* tipografski, štamparski.
typography *n* tipografija, slaganje.
tyrannical *a* tiranski, silnički.
tyranny *n* tiranija.
tyrant *n* tiranin.
tyre *n* spoljna guma na točku.
tyre pressure *n* pritisak u gumi.

U

ubiquitous *a* sveprisutan.
udder *n* vime.
ugh *excl* uh! (izražava gađenje,
   užasavanje).
ugliness *n* ružnoća.
ugly *a* ružan; opasan; zloban.
ulcer *n* čir (*med*).
ulterior *a* onostran; sledeći; skriven.
ultimate *a* krajnji; konačan; ~ly *adv*
   konačno.
ultimatum *n* ultimatum.
ultramarine *n* ultramarin (modra boja); *a*
   prekomorski.
ultrasound *n* ultrazvuk.
ultrasound scan *n* snimanje ultrazvukom.
umbilical cord *n* pupčana vrpca.
umbrella *n* kišobran.
umpire *n* sudija.
umpteen *a* bezbroj.
unable *a* nesposoban.
unaccompanied *a* bez pratnje.
unaccomplished *a* neizvršen; neuglađen.
unaccountable *a* neobjašnjiv;
   neodgovoran.
unaccountably *adv* neobjašnjivo;
   neodgovorno.
unaccustomed *a* nenaviknut;
   neuobičajen.
unacknowledged *a* nepriznat; nepoznat;
   neiskusan.
unacquainted *a* neupoznat; stran; nevešt.
unadorned *a* neukrašen; jednostavan.
unadulterated *a* nerazblažen; čist.
unaffected *a* iskren, neposredan;
   nepromenjen.
unaided *a* bez pomoći, sam.
unaltered *a* nepromenjen, isti.
unambitious *a* neambiciozan, skroman.
unanimity *n* jednoglasnost.
unanimous *a* jednoglasan; ~ly *adv*
   jednoglasno.
unanswerable *a* nepobitan; neodgovoran.
unanswered *a* neuzvraćen, bez
   odgovora.
unapproachable *a* nepristupačan.
unarmed *a* nenaoružan.
unassuming *a* skroman.

unattached *a* nepričvršćen; nepridodat;
   slobodan, neoženjen.
unattainable *a* nedokučiv.
unattended *a* sam, zanemaren.
unauthorized *a* neovlašćen.
unavoidable *a* neizbežan, neophodan.
unavoidably *adv* neizbežno.
unaware *a* nesvestan.
unawares *adv* neočekivano, nenadano;
   nenamerno.
unbalanced *a* neuravnotežen.
unbearable *a* nepodnošljiv.
unbecoming *a* neprikladan, nedoličan.
unbelievable *a* neverovatan.
unbend *v* popustiti; izravnati; odvezati.
unbiased *a* nepristrasan, bez predrasuda.
unblemished *a* nezamrljan, neukaljan.
unborn *a* još nerođen.
unbreakable *a* nesalomiv, neraskidiv.
unbroken *a* čitav, nerazbijen; neprekinut;
   nenadmašen.
unbutton *v* otkopčati.
uncalled-for *a* nepoželjan, neumestan;
   nepotreban.
uncanny *a* neobjašnjiv, tajanstven;
   izvanredan.
unceasing *a* neprekidan.
unceremonious *a* bez ceremonije;
   neusiljen, prirodan.
uncertain *a* neizvestan; nesiguran;
   nestalan.
uncertainty *n* neizvesnost, nesigurnost;
   nepouzdanost.
unchangeable *a* nepromenljiv.
unchanged *a* nepromenjen.
unchanging *a* koji se ne menja.
uncharitable *a* nemilosrdan, bezobziran.
unchecked *a* nezaustavljen; neproveren.
unchristian *a* nehrišćanski; nemilosrdan;
   okoreo.
uncivil *a* neučtiv.
uncivilized *a* necivilizovan.
uncle *n* stric; ujak; teča.
uncomfortable *a* neudoban, neugodan;
   neprijatan.
uncomfortably *adv* neudobno; neugodno;
   neprijatno.

uncommon *a* neobičan, izvanredan, redak.
uncompromising *a* nepomirljiv, nepopustljiv.
unconcerned *a* bezbrižan; ravnodušan; koga se ne tiče.
unconditional *a* bezuslovan.
unconfined *a* neomeđen; slobodan.
unconfirmed *a* nepotvrđen.
unconnected *a* nevezan, nepovezan.
unconquerable *a* nepobediv, nesavladiv.
unconscious *a* nesvestan; ~ly *adv* nesvesno.
unconstrained *a* neprisiljen; dobrovoljan; neusiljen.
uncontrollable *a* nekontrolisan, neobuzdan.
unconventional *a* neuobičajen, nekonvencionalan.
unconvincing *a* neuverljiv.
uncork *v* otčepiti.
uncorrected *a* neispravljen, nepopravljen.
uncouth *a* prost, prostački.
uncover *v* otkriti; razotkriti; skinuti poklopac (kapu).
uncultivated *a* neobrađen (tlo); neobrazovan; nekulturan.
uncut *a* neisečen, neodrezan; neskraćen; nesmanjen.
undamaged *a* neoštećen, čitav.
undaunted *a* neustrašiv; neobeshrabren; nezastrašen.
undecided *a* neodlučan, neodređen, nestalan.
undefiled *a* neuprljan; neoskrnavljen; nezagađen.
undeniable *a* neosporan, jasan; odlučan.
undeniably *adv* neosporno.
under *prep* pod, ispod; podno; odozdo; prema, na osnovu; *adv* niže, dole; manje, nedovoljno, nepotpuno.
under-age *a* maloletan.
undercharge *v* premalo zaračunati.
underclothing *n* donje rublje.
undercoat *n* donji kaput; osnovni premaz (boje).
undercover *a* tajni.
undercurrent *n* podvodna struja; skrivena strujanja.
undercut *v* potkopati; podriti; konkurisati nižom cenom.

underdeveloped *a* nerazvijen.
underdog *n* gubitnik; slabiji.
underdone *a* nedopečen.
underestimate *v* potceniti.
undergo *v* podvrći se, iskusiti; podneti, pretrpeti.
undergraduate *n* nediplomirani student.
underground *n* podzemlje; podzemna železnica.
undergrowth *n* žbunje, šiblje.
underhand *adv* potajno, nepošteno; *a* potajan, nepošten.
underlie *v* ležati ispod nečega; biti u osnovi nečega.
underline *v* potcrtati; naglasiti.
undermine *v* potkopati, podriti.
underneath *adv* dole; *prep* pod, ispod.
underpaid *a* premalo plaćen.
underpants *npl* gaće.
underprivileged *a* siromašan; zapostavljen.
underrate *v* potceniti, proceniti ispod stvarne vrednosti.
undersecretary *n* podsekretar.
underside *n* donja strana, dno.
understand *v* razumeti, shvatiti; znati; saznati; podrazumevati.
understandable *a* razumljiv.
understanding *n* razumevanje; saglasnost; *a* pun razumevanja.
understatement *n* nepotpuno izražavanje (ili prikazivanje); ublažavanje; nedorečenost.
undertake *v* preduzeti; preuzeti na sebe.
undertaker *n* preduzimač; pogrebnik.
undertaking *n* poduhvat; obaveza.
undervalue *v* proceniti ispod vrednosti; potceniti.
underwater *a* podvodni; *adv* podvodno.
underwear *n* donje rublje.
underworld *n* podzemlje, pakao; kriminalni svet.
underwrite *v* osiguravati, izdavati polise za osiguranje; potpisati se.
underwriter *n* osiguravatelj; potpisnik.
undeserved *a* nezaslužen; ~ly *adv* nezasluženo.
undeserving *a* koji ne zaslužuje, bez zasluga.
undesirable *a* nepoželjan.

undetermined a neodlučan; nepoznat; neodređen.

undigested a nesvaren; neasimilovan; nesređen; nepovezan.

undiminished a nesmanjen, nesnižen.

undisciplined a nedisciplinovan; razularen.

undisguised a neprerušen; neprikriven.

undismayed a nepokoleban, neklonuo.

undisputed a neosporan, nesporan; neraspravljen.

undisturbed a neometan.

undivided a nepodeljen, čitav.

undo v otkopčati, odvezati; pokvariti; poništiti.

undoing n ukidanje; otkopčavanje; uništenje.

undoubted a nesumnjiv, neosporan; ~ly adv bez sumnje, svakako.

undress v svući (se), skinuti se.

undue a nepravovremen; nepodesan.

undulating a talasast.

unduly adv prekomerno; nepravedno; nepravilno.

undying a besmrtan, neprolazan.

unearth v iskopati; otkriti, obelodaniti.

unearthly a nadzemaljski, natprirodan; čudan; sablastan.

uneasiness n uznemirenost, zabrinutost.

uneasy a uznemiren; zabrinut; nezgodan; neudoban.

uneducated a neobrazovan; neodgojen.

unemployed a nezaposlen; ~ person n nezaposlena osoba.

unemployment n nezaposlenost.

unending a beskrajan.

unenlightened a neprosvećen; neobavešten.

unenviable a nezavidan.

unequal a nejednak; ~ly adv nepodjednako, neravnomerno.

unequalled a neuporediv.

unerring a nepogrešiv, tačan; ~ly adv nepogrešivo.

uneven a neravan; neujednačen; neparan; ~ly adv neravno; neujednačeno; promenljivo.

unexpected a neočekivan; ~ly adv neočekivano.

unexplored a neistražen.

unfailing a neiscrpan; nepogrešiv.

unfair a nepravedan; ~ly adv nepravedno.

unfaithful a neveran.

unfaithfulness n nevernost.

unfaltering a nepokolebljiv.

unfamiliar a nepoznat; neupoznat.

unfashionable a staromodan, nemoderan.

unfashionably adv staromodno.

unfasten v odvezati; otkačiti.

unfathomable a nedokučiv, neizmerljiv.

unfavourable a nepovoljan.

unfeeling a neosetljiv.

unfinished a nesvršen, nedovršen.

unfit a nepodesan, nesposoban.

unfold v odviti, razviti, otkriti.

unforeseen a nepredviđen.

unforgettable a nezaboravan.

unforgivable a neoprostiv.

unforgiving a koji ne prašta, nepomirljiv.

unfortunate a nesrećan; nepovoljan; ~ly adv nažalost.

unfounded a neosnovan.

unfriendly a neprijateljski.

unfruitful a neplodan.

unfurnished a nenamešten; nesnabdeven; neopremljen.

ungainly a nezgrapan, nespretan.

ungentlemanly a negospodski; nevaspitan.

ungovernable a neobuzdan.

ungrateful a nezahvalan; ~ly adv nezahvalno.

ungrounded a neosnovan.

unhappily adv nesrećno; neprikladno.

unhappiness n nesreća; nezadovoljstvo.

unhappy a nesrećan, tužan; neprikladan.

unharmed a neozleđen, nepovređen, bez posledica.

unhealthy a bolestan; štetan.

unheard-of a nečuven.

unheeding a nemaran, nepažljiv; nepromišljen.

unhitch v ispregnuti; otkačiti.

unhook v otkačiti.

unhoped (for) a neočekivan, nenadan.

unhurt a neozleđen; neuvređen.

unicorn n jednorog.

uniform n uniforma; a jednoobrazan, ujednačen; ~ly adv ujednačeno.

uniformity n jednoobraznost, jednolikost.

unify v ujediniti, sjediniti.

unimaginable a nezamisliv.

unimpaired *a* neoslabljen, nenarušen.
unimportant *a* nevažan.
uninformed *a* neobavešten.
uninhabitable *a* nepodesan za stanovanje.
uninhabited *a* nenastanjen.
uninjured *a* neozleđen; neoštećen.
unintelligible *a* nerazumljiv, neshvatljiv.
unintelligibly *adv* nerazumljivo; neshvatljivo.
unintentional *a* nenameran.
uninterested *a* nezainteresovan, ravnodušan.
uninteresting *a* nezanimljiv, neinteresantan.
uninterrupted *a* neprekinut.
uninvited *a* nepozvan.
union *n* savez, ujedinjenje; radnički sindikat; sloga.
unionist *n* unionist; član sindikata.
unique *a* jedinstven; unikatni.
unison *n* sklad, sloga; jednoglasje (*muz*).
unit *n* jedinica, jedinka, mera.
unitarian *n* unitarac.
unite *v* ujediniti, sjediniti; složiti se (*fig*).
United States (of America) *npl* Sjedinjene Države (Amerike).
unitedly *adv* ujedinjeno; složno.
unity *n* jedinstvo.
universal *a* univerzalan; opšti; svestran; ~ly *adv* univerzalno, opšte.
universe *n* svemir, vasiona.
university *n* univerzitet.
unjust *a* nepravedan; ~ly *adv* nepravedno.
unkempt *a* neočešljan; neuredan, zapušten.
unkind *a* neljubazan; okrutan.
unknowingly *adv* ne znajući, nesvesno.
unknown *a* nepoznat, stran.
unlawful *a* nezakonit; ~ly *adv* nezakonito.
unlawfulness *n* nezakonitost.
unleash *v* pustiti s lanca (psa); otpočeti.
unless *conj* ako ne, osim ako, osim da, ukoliko ne.
unlicensed *a* bez dozvole, divlji.
unlike, unlikely *a* različit; neverovatan.
unlikelihood *n* neverovatnost.
unlimited *a* neograničen.
unlisted *a* neunet u listu.
unload *v* istovariti; rasteretiti.
unlock *v* otključati.

unluckily *adv* na nesreću.
unlucky *a* nesrećan.
unmanageable *a* neukrotiv, neobuzdan; teško savladiv.
unmannered *a* bez manira, nevaspitan.
unmannerly *a* nevaspitan, grub.
unmarried *a* neoženjen; neudata.
unmask *v* demaskirati.
unmentionable *a* koji se ne može pomenuti.
unmerited *a* nezaslužen.
unmindful *a* nepažljiv.
unmistakable *a* nepogrešiv, očigledan.
unmistakably *adv* nepogrešivo, očigledno.
unmitigated *a* neublažen; krajnji, potpun.
unmoved *a* neganut; nepokoleban; nepokrenut.
unnatural *a* neprirodan; odvratan.
unnecessary *a* nepotreban.
unneighbourly *a* nekomšijski, nedruželjubiv.
unnoticed *a* neprimećen.
unnumbered *a* nebrojen; bezbrojan.
unobserved *a* neopažen.
unobtainable *a* čega nema, što se ne može nabaviti.
unobtrusive *a* nenametljiv.
unoccupied *a* nezauzet, slobodan.
unoffending *a* koji ne vređa; bezazlen.
unofficial *a* neslužben.
unorthodox *a* neortodoksan, nepravoveran.
unpack *v* raspakovati.
unpaid *a* neisplaćen, neplaćen; bez plate.
unpalatable *a* bljutav, neukusan; bez ukusa; neprijatan.
unparalleled *a* nenadmašan.
unpleasant *a* neprijatan; ~ly *adv* neprijatno.
unpleasantness *n* neprijatnost.
unplug *v* isključiti.
unpolished *a* neuglačan; neuglađen.
unpopular *a* nepopularan, neomiljen.
unpractised *a* nevešt, bez prakse; nepraktikovan.
unprecedented *a* bez presedana, besprimeran.
unpredictable *a* nepredvidiv.
unprejudiced *a* nepristrastan, bez predrasuda.

unprepared *a* nepripremljen.
unprofitable *a* neunosan, nekoristan.
unprotected *a* nezaštićen.
unpublished *a* neobjavljen, nepublikovan.
unpunished *a* nekažnjen.
unqualified *a* nekvalifikovan; potpun.
unquestionable *a* neosporan, nesumnjiv;
unquestionably *adv* neosporno,
  nesumnjivo.
unquestioned *a* neosporan, nesumnjiv;
  priznat.
unravel *v* razmrsiti, odgonetnuti.
unread *a* nečitan; nepročitan;
  neobrazovan.
unreal *a* nestvaran.
unrealistic *a* nerealan.
unreasonable *a* nerazuman; preteran.
unreasonably *adv* nerazumno; preterano.
unrelated *a* nepovezan, bez veze sa.
unrelenting *a* neumoljiv; nesmanjen.
unreliable *a* nepouzdan.
unremitting *a* neprestan.
unrepentant *a* nepokajnički.
unreserved *a* nerezervisan; bezrezervan,
  potpun; **~ly** *adv* bezuslovno, potpuno.
unrest *n* nemir, uzbuđenje.
unrestrained *a* neobuzdan.
unripe *a* nezreo.
unrivalled *a* bez premca.
unroll *v* odviti (se).
unruliness *n* nepokornost, neposlušnost.
unruly *a* nepokoran, neposlušan.
unsafe *a* nepouzdan; opasan; labav.
unsatisfactory *a* nezadovoljavajući.
unsavoury *a* neukusan; loš.
unscathed *a* neozleđen .
unscrew *v* odvrnuti, odviti.
unscrupulous *a* beskrupulozan,
  nesavestan.
unseasonable *a* neblagovremen;
  neumesan.
unseemly *a* nepriklada.
unseen *a* neviđen, nevidljiv.
unselfish *a* nesebičan.
unsettle *v* uznemiriti, poremetiti.
unsettled *a* nenaseljen; uznemiren;
  promenljiv; neisplaćen.
unshaken *a* neuzdrman, nepokoleban.
unshaven *a* neobrijan.
unsightly *a* ružan, neugledan.
unskilful *a* nevešt.

unskilled *a* nekvalifikovan.
unsociable *a* nedruštven.
unspeakable *a* neizreciv; neopisiv.
unstable *a* nestabilan, nesiguran.
unsteadily *adv* nepostojano, promenljivo;
  klimavo.
unsteady *a* nestalan, promenljiv; nesiguran.
unstudied *a* prirodan, neusiljen.
unsuccessful *a* neuspešan; **~ly** *adv*
  neuspešno.
unsuitable *a* neprikladan.
unsure *a* nesiguran.
unsympathetic *a* nesaosećajan, neosetljiv,
  hladan.
untamed *a* nepripitomljen; neobuzdan.
untapped *a* neiskorišćen, netaknut.
untenable *a* neodrživ, neodbranjiv.
unthinkable *a* nezamisliv; neverovatan.
unthinking *a* nepromišljen; nerazuman.
untidiness *n* neurednost.
untidy *a* neuredan.
untie *v* odvezati, razvezati.
until *prep* do; *conj* do, dok ne, sve do.
untimely *a* nepravovremen; preran.
untiring *a* neumoran.
untold *a* neispričan; neizrečen; bezbrojan.
untouched *a* netaknut.
untoward *a* nepovoljan; neugodan;
  neposlušan.
untried *a* neisproban; nesuđen.
untroubled *a* nezabrinut, spokojan,
  bezbrižan.
untrue *a* neistinit, lažan, nepravilan.
untrustworthy *a* nepouzdan.
untruth *n* laž.
unused *a* neupotrebljen; nenaviknut.
unusual *a* neobičan; **~ly** *adv* neobično,
  veoma.
unveil *v* skinuti veo; otkriti (npr.
  spomenik).
unwavering *a* nepokolebljiv.
unwelcome *a* nije dobrodošao, nemio.
unwell *a* bolestan, koji se loše oseća.
unwieldy *a* glomazan, nespretan.
unwilling *a* nesklon, nerad; **~ly** *adv*
  nerado.
unwillingness *n* nesklonost, nevoljnost.
unwind *v* odviti, odmotati (se).
unwise *a* nerazuman.
unwitting *a* nesvestan, koji ne zna.
unworkable *a* neobradiv; teško izvediv.

unworthy *a* nedostojan.
unwrap *v* raspakovati; razmotati (se).
unwritten *a* nezapisan, nepisan.
up *adv* gore, naviše, uvis; povrh, na; *prep* uz, na, povrh, po, preko, u.
upbraid *v* grditi, koriti.
upbringing *n* vaspitanje, odgoj.
update *v* ažurirati, osavremeniti.
upheaval *n* pomeranje; preokret; prevrat.
uphill *a* strm; težak; *adv* uzbrdo.
uphold *v* podržavati; podupirati.
upholstery *n* tapaciranje.
upkeep *n* održavanje.
uplift *v* podići, uspraviti.
upon *prep* na.
upper *a* gornji.
upper-class *a* viša klasa.
upper-hand *n* prevlast, prednost.
uppermost *a* najviši, najgornji; nadmoćan; **to be ~** biti prvi, imati nadmoć (ili prevlast).
upright *a* uspravan; pošten, iskren.
uprising *n* ustanak.
uproar *n* galama, buka, nered.
uproot *v* iskoreniti, iščupati.
upset *v* prevrnuti (se); zbuniti (se); uznemiriti (se); *n* prevrtanje; uzrujavanje; *a* prevrnut; uznemiren.
upshot *n* posledica, rezultat, ishod.
upside-down *a, adv* naopako, naglavce.
upstairs *adv* gore.
upstart *n* skorojević.
uptight *a* napet, nervozan.
up-to-date *a* moderan, savremen.
upturn *n* skretanje naviše; poboljšanje.
upward *a* gore, koji se kreće nagore; **~s** *adv* nagore, iznad, više.
urban *a* gradski.
urbane *a* učtiv, ljubazan, otmen.

urchin *n* derište.
urge *v* terati; nagovarati; *n* nagon, težnja.
urgency *n* hitnost.
urgent *a* hitan; vrlo potreban.
urinal *n* pisoar.
urinate *v* mokriti.
urine *n* mokraća.
urn *n* urna.
us *pn* nas, nam, nama.
usage *n* upotreba; običaj; postupak.
use *n* korišćenje, upotreba; korist; običaj; *v* upotrebljavati, koristiti; imati običaj.
used *a* upotrebljavan, polovan.
useful *a* koristan; **~ly** *adv* korisno.
usefulness *n* korisnost.
useless *a* beskoristan, uzaludan; promašen; **~ly** *adv* beskorisno, uzaludno.
uselessness *n* beskorisnost; uzaludnost.
user-friendly *a* pristupačan, prilagođen nestručnjaku.
usher *n* vratar; razvodnik.
usherette *n* razvodnica (u bioskopu, pozorištu).
usual *a* uobičajen; običan; **~ly** *adv* obično.
usurer *n* zelenaš, lihvar.
usurp *v* uzurpirati, prisvojiti.
usury *n* zelenaštvo, lihvarstvo.
utensil *n* pribor, oprema.
uterus *n* materica.
utility *n* korist, prednost.
utilize *v* iskoristiti.
utmost *a* najdalji; krajnji; najviši.
utter *a* potpun, apsolutan; *v* izgovoriti; izjaviti.
utterance *n* izražavanje; izgovor; izjava.
utterly *adv* potpuno, sasvim.

V

vacancy *n* praznina, prazno mesto.
vacant *a* prazan, slobodan; nenastanjen.
vacant lot *n* prazno gradilište.
vacate *v* isprazniti; napustiti; poništiti.
vacation *n* raspust, odmor; napuštanje.
vaccinate *v* vakcinisati.
vaccination *n* vakcinacija.
vaccine *n* vakcina.
vacuous *a* prazan; isprazan.
vacuum *n* vakum.
vacuum flask *n* termos boca.
vagina *n* vagina.
vagrant *n* skitnica.
vague *a* nejasan, neodređen; ~ly *adv*
    nejasno, neodređeno.
vain *a* uzaludan, besplodan; prazan;
    sujetan.
valet *n* sobar, sluga.
valiant *a* hrabar.
valid *a* opravdan; važeći.
valley *n* dolina.
valour *n* hrabrost.
valuable *a* dragocen, vredan; koristan; ~s
    npl dragocenosti.
valuation *n* procena.
value *n* vrednost; cena; *v* ceniti.
valued *a* vredan, cenjen.
valve *n* zalistak (srčani); ventil.
vampire *n* vampir.
van *n* kamion, kombi.
vandal *n* vandal.
vandalism *n* vandalizam.
vandalize *v* izvršiti vandalizam.
vanguard *n* prethodnica; avangarda.
vanilla *n* vanila.
vanish *v* nestati, izgubiti se.
vanity *n* taština, sujeta.
vanity case *n* neseser.
vanquish *v* savladati, pobediti.
vantage point *n* povoljan položaj.
vapour *n* para.
variable *a* promenljiv.
variance *n* različitost; odstupanje od;
    neslaganje.
variation *n* varijacija.
varicose vein *n* proširena vena.

varied *a* različit; raznolik.
variety *n* raznolikost; mnoštvo.
variety show *n* varijete.
various *a* razni, različit, raznolik.
varnish *n* lak, glazura; *v* lakirati.
vary *v* menjati (se); razlikovati se;
    varirati.
vase *n* vazna.
vast *a* ogroman, prostran.
vat *n* kaca, bačva.
vault[1] *n* svod; luk; *v* zasvoditi.
vault[2] skok; *v* skočiti.
veal *n* teleće meso, teletina.
veer *v* skrenuti; popuštati konop (*naut*).
vegetable *a* biljni; *n* biljka; ~s *npl* povrće.
vegetable garden *n* farma povrća.
vegetarian *n* vegetarijanac.
vegetate *v* rasti (biljke); životariti.
vegetation *n* vegetacija, bilje.
vehemence *n* žestina, silina.
vehement *a* žestok; ~ly *adv* žestoko.
vehicle *n* vozilo; all-terrain ~ *n* terensko
    vozilo za sve puteve.
veil *n* veo, zavesa; *v* pokriti velom.
vein *n* vena (*anat*); žila; sklonost.
velocity *n* brzina.
velvet *n* somot.
vending machine *n* automat (za prodaju).
vendor *n* prodavac.
veneer *n* furnir; površinski sloj.
venerable *a* dostojan poštovanja;
    prečasni, velečasni.
venerate *v* poštovati.
veneration *n* poštovanje.
venereal *a* veneričan.
vengeance *n* osveta.
venial *a* oprostiv.
venison *n* srnetina.
venom *n* otrov; zloba.
venomous *a* otrovan; zloban; ~ly *adv*
    otrovno; zlobno.
vent *n* otvor; izlaz; *v* provetriti.
ventilate *v* provetriti.
ventilation *n* ventilacija, provetravanje.
ventilator *n* ventilator.
ventriloquist *n* trbuhozborac.

venture *n* rizičan poduhvat; *v* izložiti opasnosti.
venue *n* mesto zločina (ili gde se vodi parnica); sastajalište.
veranda(h) *n* veranda.
verb *n* glagol (*gram*).
verbal *a* glagolski; usmeni; doslovan; **~ly** *adv* usmeno.
verbatim *adv* doslovno.
verbose *a* razvučen (stil); govorljiv.
verdant *a* zelen; nezreo.
verdict *n* presuda, osuda.
verification *n* proveravanje, potvrda.
verify *v* proveriti, potvrditi.
veritable *a* pravi, istinski.
vermicelli *npl* rezanci.
vermin *n* štetočine; ološ.
vermouth *n* vermut.
versatile *a* mnogostran, svestran.
verse *n* stih.
versed *a* vešt; upućen, verziran.
version *n* verzija, prikaz; prevod.
versus *prep* protiv.
vertebra *n* kičmeni pršljen.
vertebral *a* kičmeni.
vertebrate *a* kičmenjačk.
vertex *n* vrhunac, najviša tačka.
vertical *a* vertikalan; **~ly** *adv* vertikalno.
vertigo *n* vrtoglavica.
verve *n* polet, stvaralačka energija.
very *a* pravi, istinit; taj, onaj isti; *adv* jako, veoma, vrlo.
vessel *n* sud (za tečnost); brod; sud (*anat*).
vest *n* potkošulja; prsluk (*amer*).
vestibule *n* predvorje; komora (*anat*).
vestige *n* trag, ostatak.
vestment *n* odelo; odora.
vestry *n* sakristija; parohijska uprava.
veteran *n* veteran, bivši ratnik; *a* ostario, islužen.
veterinary *a* veterinarski.
veterinary science *n* veterina.
veterinary surgeon, vet *n* veterinar.
veto *n* veto, zabrana; *v* staviti veto.
vex *v* ljutiti; uznemiravati.
vexed *a* uznemiren; sporan.
via *prep* preko.
viaduct *n* vijadukt.
vial *n* bočica.
vibrate *v* treperiti.

vibration *n* treperenje, vibriranje.
vicarious *a* koji zastupa (zamenjuje); indirektan.
vice *n* porok; mana; prostitucija.
vice versa *adv* obrnuto, obratno.
vice-chairman *n* potpredsednik.
vice-chancellor (of a university) *n* prorektor.
vice-chancellorship *n* čast ili služba prorektora.
vicinity *n* susedstvo; okolina; blizina; **immediate ~** *n* neposredna okolina, blizina.
vicious *a* nemoralan; pogrešan; zloban; **~ly** *adv* nemoralno; pogrešno; zlobno.
victim *n* žrtva.
victimize *v* žrtvovati.
victor *n* pobednik.
victorious *a* pobedonosan.
victory *n* pobeda.
video *n* video.
video camera *n* video kamera.
video cassette *n* video kaseta.
video game *n* video igra.
video tape *n* video traka.
vie *v* takmičiti se.
view *n* vidik; mišljenje, gledište; *v* razgledati, gledati.
viewer *n* posmatrač.
viewfinder *n* vizir (na fotografskom aparatu).
viewpoint *n* gledište.
vigil *n* bdenje.
vigilance *n* budnost.
vigilant *a* budan.
vigorous *a* snažan; energičan; **~ly** *adv* snažno; energično.
vigour *n* snaga; energija.
vile *a* rđav, loš; podao.
vilify *v* oklevetati.
villa *n* letnjikovac; vila.
village *n* selo.
villager *n* stanovnik sela.
villain *n* nitkov, hulja.
vindicate *v* osloboditi (optužbe); odbraniti; osvetiti.
vindication *n* oslobođenje (optužbe); opravdanje.
vindictive *a* osvetoljubiv, osvetnički.
vine *n* vinova loza.
vinegar *n* sirće.

vineyard *n* vinograd.
vintage *n* berba grožđa; rod grožđa; vino.
vinyl *n* vinil.
viola *n* viola.
violate *v* prekršiti; silovati; povrediti.
violation *n* prekršaj; nasilje; povreda.
violence *n* nasilje; silovitost.
violent *a* nasilan, silovit; **~ly** *adv* silno, jako.
violet *n* ljubičica (*bot*).
violin *n* violina.
violinist *n* violinista.
violoncello, cello *n* violončelo.
VIP *n* važna ličnost (skraćenica od: *Very Important Person*).
viper *n* zmija otrovnica, guja.
virgin *n* devica; *a* devičanski, čedan; netaknut.
virginity *n* čednost.
Virgo *n* Devica (*astrol*).
virile *a* snažan, muževan.
virility *n* muževnost.
virtual *a* pravi, stvarni; **~ly** *adv* praktično, zapravo.
virtue *n* vrlina; predanost.
virtuous *a* čestit, moralan.
virulent *a* otrovan, pakostan; zarazan.
virus *n* virus.
visa *n* viza.
vis-a-vis *prep* nasuprot.
viscous *a* viskozan, lepljiv.
visibility *n* vidljivost.
visible *a* vidljiv.
visibly *adv* vidljivo, primetno; očigledno.
vision *n* vid; vizija.
visit *v* posetiti; obići; *n* poseta; vizita.
visitation *n* obilaženje; inspekcija.
visiting hours *npl* vreme posete.
visitor *n* posetilac; gost.
visor *n* vizir; štit (na kapi).
vista *n* vidik; prizor; perspektiva.
visual *a* vidni; optički.
visual aid *n* vizuelno nastavno sredstvo.
visualize *v* predstaviti sebi.
vital *a* životni, vitalan; bitan; **~ly** *adv* bitno; vitalno; **~s** *npl* vitalni organi.
vital statistics *npl* statistika rađanja, umiranja i brakova; dimenzije ženske figure.
vitality *n* životna snaga.

vitamin *n* vitamin.
vitiate *v* kvariti, upropastiti; poništiti.
vivacious *a* živahan, veseo.
vivid *a* jasan; živ; živopisan; **~ly** *adv* jasno; živo.
vivisection *n* vivisekcija.
vixen *n* lisica; svađalica.
vocabulary *n* leksikon, rečnik.
vocal *a* glasovni; usmen, govorni, glasan.
vocation *n* zanimanje, struka; sklonost; **~al** *a* stručni.
vocative *n* vokativ (*gram*).
vociferous *a* bučan, glasan.
vodka *n* votka.
vogue *n* moda.
voice *n* glas; glasanje; glagolski vid, stanje (*gram*); *v* izraziti.
void *a* prazan; nevažeći; *n* praznina.
volatile *a* isparljiv; nestalan.
volcanic *a* vulkanski.
volcano *n* vulkan.
volition *n* htenje; volja; odlučivanje.
volley *n* plotun; bujica; volej (*sport*).
volleyball *n* odbojka.
volt *n* volt (*el*).
voltage *n* voltaža, napon.
voluble *a* govorljiv.
volume *n* sveska, knjiga, tom; zapremina.
voluntarily *adv* dobrovoljno.
voluntary *a* dobrovoljan.
volunteer *n* dobrovoljac; *v* prijaviti se dobrovoljno.
voluptuous *a* čulan, pohotan.
vomit *v* povratiti; *n* povraćanje.
voracious *a* proždrljiv, halapljiv; **~ly** *adv* halapljivo.
vortex *n* vrtlog, vir.
vote *n* glasanje; glas (na izborima); *v* glasati.
voter *n* birač, glasač.
voting *n* glasanje.
voucher *n* jemac; jemstvo; potvrda uplate.
vow *n* zavet, zakletva; *v* dati zavet, obećati.
vowel *n* samoglasnik, vokal (*gram*).
voyage *n* putovanje.
vulgar *a* vulgaran; prost.
vulgarity *n* vulgarnost.
vulnerable *a* ranjiv; podložan.
vulture *n* lešinar (*zool*); grabljivac.

W

waddle *v* gegati se.
wade *v* gaziti; pregaziti; preći.
wafer *n* oblanda; hostija (*rel*).
waffle *n* blebetanje; vafla (vrsta poslastice).
waft *v* nositi u vazduhu; lebdeti.
wag *v* mahati; klatiti se.
wage *n* nadnica, plata; naknada.
wage earner *n* radnik, osoba koja radi za nadnicu.
wager *n* opklada; *v* opkladiti se.
wages *npl* nadnica, plata.
waggish *a* šaljiv.
waggle *v* mahati ili tresti nečim.
wagon *n* otvoreni teretni vagon; vagonet; kola.
wail *n* jaukanje; cviljenje; zavijanje; *v* jaukati; cvileti; zavijati.
waist *n* struk.
waistline *n* struk.
wait *v* čekati, iščekivati; pričekati; *n* čekanje, iščekivanje.
waiter *n* kelner; poslužavnik.
waiting list *n* lista čekanja.
waiting room *n* čekaonica.
waive *v* odreći se (prava); odustati (od).
wake[1] *v* probuditi se; buditi; *n* buđenje.
wake[2] *n* bdenje; čuvanje mrtvaca.
wake[3] *n* vodena pruga, brazda iza broda; trag.
wakefulness *n* budnost; opreznost.
waken *v* probuditi (se).
walk *v* ići, hodati; šetati; *n* hod; šetnja.
walker *n* šetač, pešak.
walkie-talkie *n* voki-toki, prenosni radio-telefon.
walking *n* šetanje; hodanje (*sport*).
walking stick *n* štap za šetnju.
walkout *n* štrajk; demonstrativno napuštanje.
walkover *n* laka pobeda (*sleng*).
walkway *n* staza, pločnik.
wall *n* zid; bedem.
walled *a* ograđen zidom; utvrđen.
wallet *n* novčanik.
wallflower *n* šeboj.
wallow *v* valjati se; srljati.

wallpaper *n* zidne tapete.
walnut *n* orah.
walrus *n* morž.
waltz *n* valcer.
wan *a* bled, iznuren, slab.
wand *n* prut, šiba; dirigentska palica.
wander *v* lutati, skitati.
wane *v* slabiti, opadati; bledeti.
want *v* hteti, želeti; oskudevati; *n* nedostatak; oskudica; nužda; potreba.
wanting *a* oskudan; nedovoljan.
wanton *a* nestašan, razuzdan; razmažen; okrutan.
war *n* rat; ratovanje.
ward *n* odeljenje (u bolnici, zatvoru); starateljstvo; štićenik.
warden (game) *n* lovočuvar; šumar.
wardrobe *n* orman za odela; garderoba.
warehouse *n* skladište.
warfare *n* rat, ratovanje.
warhead *n* bojeva glava.
warily *adv* oprezno.
wariness *n* oprez, opreznost.
warm *a* topao; zagrejan; srdačan; *v* grejati, zagrejati; **to ~ up** zagrejati (se).
warm-hearted *a* srdačan.
warmly *adv* srdačno.
warmth *n* toplota.
warn *v* upozoriti, opomenuti.
warning *n* upozorenje, opomena.
warning light *n* signalno svetlo.
warp *v* iskriviti (se), saviti (se).
warrant *n* punomoć, ovlašćenje; jemstvo; nalog.
warranty *n* jemstvo, garancija; punomoć.
warren *n* uzgajalište zečeva.
warrior *n* ratnik.
warship *n* ratni brod.
wart *n* bradavica.
wary *a* oprezan.
wash *v* prati, oprati; umiti se; *n* pranje; veš; umivanje.
wash out *n* neuspeh (*sleng*).
washable *a* koji se može prati.
washbowl, washbasin *n* lavor, umivaonik.
washer *n* perač; mašina za pranje; zaptivač.

washing *n* pranje.
washing machine *n* mašina za pranje rublja.
washing-up *n* pranje sudova.
wasp *n* osa.
wastage *n* gubitak, rasipanje.
waste *v* rasipati; proćerdati; slabiti; *n* rasipanje; otpaci; gubitak.
wasteful *a* rasipan, rasipnički; **~ly** *adv* rasipno, rasipnički.
wasteland *n* pusta zemlja, pustoš.
waste paper *n* otpaci papira, stari papir.
waste pipe *n* odvodna cev.
watch *n* sat; straža; budnost; promatranje; *v* posmatrati; gledati; paziti; stražariti.
watchdog *n* pas čuvar.
watchful *a* budan, oprezan; **~ly** *adv* budno, oprezno.
watchmaker *n* časovničar.
watchman *n* stražar.
watchtower *n* stražarnica, osmatračnica.
watchword *n* lozinka; parola.
water *n* voda; *v* zaliti; nakvasiti; razblažiti.
water closet *n* klozet.
watercolour *n* vodena boja, akvarel.
waterfall *n* vodopad.
water heater *n* bojler.
watering can *n* kanta za zalivanje.
water level *n* vodostaj.
water lily *n* lokvanj.
water line *n* vodena linija; obalna linija.
water main *n* glavna vodovodna cev.
water melon *n* lubenica.
waterlogged *a* ispunjen vodom.
watermark *n* vodeni znak (na papiru).
watershed *n* vododelnica; sliv (rečni).
watertight *a* nepromočiv, vodootporan.
waterworks *n* vodovod.
watery *a* vodnjikav; vlažan.
watt *n* vat (*el*).
wave *n* talas; valovitost; *v* lepršati se; mahati.
wavelength *n* talasna dužina.
waver *v* kolebati se; podrhtavati; vrludati.
wavering *a* koleblјiv; koji podrhtava; vrludav.
wavy *a* talasast; buran (more).
wax *n* vosak; *v* navoštiti; polirati; depilirati.
wax paper *n* voštan papir.

waxworks *n* muzej ili zbirka voštanih figura.
way *n* put, staza; način; pravac; **to give ~** zaveslati; srušiti se; ustupiti.
waylay *v* napasti iz zasede.
wayward *a* ćudljiv, svojeglav.
we *pn* mi.
weak *a* slab; neodlučan; **~ly** *adv* slabašno, slabo.
weaken *v* oslabiti.
weakling *n* slabić.
weakness *n* slabost; slaba strana.
weal, wheal *n* blagostanje; masnica, modrica.
wealth *n* bogatstvo; izobilje.
wealthy *a* bogat, imućan.
wean *v* odbiti dete od sise; odučiti, odviknuti.
weapon *n* oružje.
wear *v* nositi, biti obučen; **to ~ away** izlizati (se); istrošiti (se); **to ~ down** pohabati (se); iscrpsti; **to ~ off** nestati; istrošiti se; **to ~ out** pohabati; poderati; istrošiti; *n* nošenje, oblačenje; odelo; trošenje.
weariness *n* zamor, premorenost; dosada.
wearisome *a* zamoran; dosadan.
weary *a* umoran; dosadan.
weasel *n* lasica (*zool*); licemer.
weather *n* vreme; *v* vetriti; izložiti vremenu; prebroditi.
weather-beaten *a* istrošen vremenom.
weather cock *n* vetrokaz.
weather forecast *n* prognoza vremena.
weave *v* tkati; isplesti; izmišljati.
weaving *n* tkanje; tkivo.
web *n* tkanina, tkanje; opna; paučina; mreža.
wed *v* venčati; oženiti se; udati se.
wedding *n* venčanje.
wedding day *n* dan venčanja.
wedding dress *n* venčanica.
wedding present *n* svadbeni poklon.
wedding ring *n* burma.
wedge *n* klin; *v* pričvrstiti klinom.
wedlock *n* brak.
Wednesday *n* sreda.
wee *a* malen, sićušan.
weed *n* korov; raga; cigara; *v* pleviti; eliminisati.

weedkiller *n* sredstvo za uništavanje korova.

weedy *a* obrastao korovom; mršav.

week *n* sedmica, nedelja (dana); tomorrow ~ sutra za osam dana; yesterday ~ juče bilo osam dana.

weekday *n* radni dan.

weekend *n* vikend.

weekly *a* sedmični, nedeljni; *adv* jedanput nedeljno; svake sedmice.

weep *v* plakati; oplakivati.

weeping willow *n* žalosna vrba (*bot*).

weigh *v* izmeriti; vagati.

weight *n* težina; teret; teg.

weightily *adv* važno; značajno.

weightlifter *n* dizač tegova.

weighty *a* težak; važan.

welcome *a* dobrodošao; *inter* Dobro došao!; *v* pozdraviti dobrodošlicom.

weld *n* zavareni šav.

welfare *n* blagostanje; socijalna pomoć.

welfare state *n* socijalna država (sa socijalnim i zdravstvenim osiguranjem i sl.).

well *n* bunar; izvor;

well *a* zdrav; u dobrom stanju; *adv* dobro; kako treba; temeljito; vrlo; as ~ as kao i, baš tako kao; ~! *interj* pa!, e pa sad!.

well-behaved *a* pristojan; korektan.

wellbeing *n* blagostanje.

well-bred *a* dobro vaspitan; čistokrvan.

well-built *a* dobro sagrađen.

well-deserved *a* s pravom zaslužen.

well-dressed *a* dobro obučen.

well-known *a* dobro poznat.

well-mannered *a* učtiv, lepih manira.

well-meaning *a* dobronameran.

well-off *a* imućan, bogat.

well-to-do *a* imućan.

well-wisher *n* onaj koji želi dobro.

wench *n* seoska devojka (*sleng*).

west *n* zapad; *a* zapadni; *adv* zapadno, prema zapadu.

westerly, western *adv* prema zapadu, na zapad.

westward *adv* zapadno, na zapad.

wet *a* mokar; vlažan; vlažnost; pokvasiti; pomokriti.

wet-nurse *n* dojilja.

wet suit *n* gumeno podvodno odelo.

whack *v* udariti; *n* udarac.

whale *n* kit (*zool*).

wharf *n* pristanište.

what *pn* šta; ono što; *a* koji; kakav; *excl* šta!.

whatever *pn* bilo šta, što god, ma šta; koliko god.

wheat *n* pšenica.

wheedle *v* laskati, namamiti, izmamiti.

wheedler *n* laskavac.

wheel *n* točak; volan; kolo; *v* okretati; kotrljati.

wheelbarrow *n* ručna kolica.

wheelchair *n* invalidska kolica.

wheel clamp *n* stega točka (volana).

wheeze *v* disati teško, šištati.

when *adv* kada; otkad; za vreme, dok; *conj* kada.

whenever *adv* bilo kada, kad god.

where *adv* gde; kuda; tamo gde; any~ igde, ma gde; every~ svuda; *conj* gde; kuda.

whereabout(s) *adv* gde.

whereas *conj* pošto, s obzirom na to, dok, budući da.

whereby *adv* pomoću čega, čime.

whereupon *adv* posle čega, zatim, posle toga.

wherever *adv* bilo gde, bilo kuda, ma gde bilo.

wherewithal *n* potreban novac (sredstva).

whet *v* naoštriti; podstaći.

whether *conj* da li; bilo da.

which *pn* koji; *a* koji.

whiff *n* dašak, strujanje.

while *n* period, neko vreme; *conj* za vreme, do, sve dok; bez obzira na, dok.

whim *n* hir, mušica.

whimper *v* cvileti, cmizdreti.

whimsical *a* ćudljiv, hirovit.

whine *v* cvileti, cmizdreti; *n* cviljenje, cmizdrenje.

whinny *v* njištati, rzati.

whip *n* bič; ulupani krem; *v* bičevati, išibati; ulupati.

whipped cream *n* šlag.

whirl *v* okrenuti (se), obrnuti (se); kovitlati.

whirlpool *n* vrtlog, vir.

whirlpool bath *n* bazen sa hidromasažom.

whirlwind *n* vihor, uragan.

whisky *n* viski.
whisper *v* šaputati.
whispering *n* šaputanje.
whistle *v* zviždati; *n* zviždanje, zvižduk.
white *a* beli; bled; *n* belina, bela boja.
white elephant *n* beli slon; neuspeo poduhvat.
white lie *n* laž iz nužde.
white-hot *a* belo usijan; besan (*fig*).
whiten *v* beliti; pobeliti.
whiteness *n* belina; bledilo.
whitewash *n* kreč; *v* okrečiti.
whiting[1] *n* belilo;
whiting[2] *n* pišmolj (riba).
whitish *a* belkast.
who *pn* ko; koji.
whoever *pn* ma ko, bilo ko, koji god, ko mu drago.
whole *a* ceo, čitav; pun; *n* celina.
wholehearted *a* srdačan, iskren.
wholemeal *a* od neprosejanog brašna.
wholesale *n* veletrgovina.
wholesome *a* zdrav, koristan.
wholly *adv* sasvim, potpuno.
whom *pn* koga, kome.
whooping cough *n* veliki kašalj (*med*).
whore *n* kurva.
why *n* razlog; *conj* zašto; *excl* Pa! Dakle! Zaista!.
wick *n* fitilj; tampon od gaze (*med*).
wicked *a* nemoralan, rđav, zao; razvratan; ~ly *adv* nemoralno.
wickedness *n* poročnost, pokvarenost.
wicker *n* vrbov prut za pletenje, pleter; *a* ispleten od pruća.
wide *a* širok; prostran; širom otvoren; ~ly *adv* široko; vrlo mnogo; **far and** ~ nadaleko i naširoko.
wide-open *a* širom otvoren.
wide-awake *a* sasvim budan.
widen *v* proširiti, raširiti.
widespread *a* rasprostranjen.
widow *n* udovica.
widower *n* udovac.
width *n* širina.
wield *v* rukovati; imati.
wife *n* supruga, žena.
wig *n* perika.
wiggle *v* klimati, mrdati; koprcati se, migoljiti se.

wild *a* divlji; neobuzdan; razvratan; neobrađen.
wildlife *n* divlje životinje.
wilderness *n* divljina, pustoš.
wildly *adv* divlje.
wilful *a* tvrdoglav; nameran.
wilfulness *n* tvrdoglavost; namernost.
wiliness *n* lukavost, prepredenost.
will[1] *n* volja; testament.
will[2] *v* hteti; zaveštati.
willing *a* voljan; spreman; ~ly *adv* rado, spremno.
willingness *n* voljnost, spremnost.
willow *n* vrba (*bot*).
willpower *n* snaga volje.
wilt *v* uvenuti; klonuti.
wily *a* lukav, prepreden.
win *v* dobiti; osvojiti, pobediti; pridobiti.
wince *v* trgnuti se.
winch *n* čekrk, dizalica; poluga.
wind[1] *n* vetar; dah; vijuganje; namotaj.
wind[2] *v* zadihati se; namotati; vijugati (se).
windfall *n* opalo voće; neočekivana sreća.
wind farm *n* grupa elektroenergetskih vetro-turbina.
winding *a* vijugav, spiralan.
wind turbine *n* vazdušna elektroenergetska turbina.
windmill *n* vetrenjača.
window *n* prozor; šalter; izlog.
window box *n* prozorska kutija za cveće.
window cleaner *n* perač prozora.
window ledge *n* prozorška klupica, solbank.
windowpane *n* prozorsko okno.
windowsill *n* prozorska klupica, solbank.
windpipe *n* dušnik.
windscreen *n* vetrobran.
windscreen washer *n* perač vetrobrana.
windscreen wiper *n* brisač stakla.
windsurfer *n* osoba koja jedri na dasci.
windsurfing *n* jedrenje na dasci.
windy *a* vetrovit.
wine *n* vino.
wine cellar *n* vinski podrum.
wine glass *n* vinska čaša.
wine list *n* vinska karta.
wine merchant *n* trgovac vinom.
wine-testing *n* degustacija vina.
wing *n* krilo (ptice, aviona); krilo zgrade; krilo (*voj*); krilo (*sport*).

winged *a* krilat, na krilima.
winger *n* krilni igrač, krilo (*sport*).
wink *v* namigivati, migati; treptati, žmirkati; *n* namigivanje; treptanje.
winner *n* pobednik, dobitnik.
winning post *n* cilj (*sport*).
winter *n* zima.
winter sports *npl* zimski sport.
wintry *a* zimski; hladan.
wipe *v* obrisati.
wire *n* žica; telegram; *v* spojiti žicom; poslati telegram.
wiring *n* stavljanje el. žice, mreže (*el*).
wiry *a* koji liči na žicu; žilav, izdržljiv.
wisdom *n* mudrost; razboritost.
wisdom teeth *npl* umnjaci (zubi).
wise *a* mudar; razborit.
wisecrack *n* duhovita primedba.
wish *v* želeti, poželeti, hteti; *n* želja.
wishful *a* željan; pun želja; nerealan.
wisp *n* snopić; pramen; svežanj slame.
wistful *a* čežnjiv, tužan.
wit *n* um, razum, pamet; duhovitost.
witch *n* veštica; čarobnica.
witchcraft *n* vračanje, čarolije.
with *prep* s, sa; kod; zbog; od.
withdraw *v* otići, povući (se); ispisati (se); oteti.
withdrawal *n* odlazak; povlačenje; opozivanje.
withdrawn *a* povučen.
wither *v* venuti, uvenuti; slabiti.
withhold *v* zadržati.
within *prep* u, unutra; u roku, u toku; *adv* unutra, unutar.
without *prep* bez; a da ne; van, izvan.
withstand *v* izdržati, odupreti se.
witless *a* glup, nerazuman.
witness *n* svedok; svedočanstvo, dokaz; *v* biti svedokom; (po)svedočiti; služiti kao dokaz.
witness box *n* mesto za svedoka na sudu.
witticism *n* dosetka.
wittily *adv* duhovito.
wittingly *adv* svesno; namerno.
witty *a* duhovit.
wizard *n* vrač, čarobnjak.
wobble *v* klimati se; kolebati se.
woe *n* jad, nesreća, muka.
woeful *a* jadan, tužan; ~ly *adv* očajno.

wolf *n* vuk; pohlepan čovek; ženskaroš; she ~ *n* vučica.
woman *n* žena; ženstvenost.
womanish *a* ženskast (muškarac); ženstven.
womanly *a* ženstven.
womb *n* materica (*anat*); utroba.
women's lib *n* pokret za ženska prava.
wonder *n* čuđenje, iznenađenje; čudo; *v* čuditi se; pitati se.
wonderful *a* izvanredan, diva, čudesan; ~ly *adv* divno, čudesno.
wondrous *a* čudan, čudesan.
wont *n* navika, običaj.
won't *abbrev* skraćenica od *will not*.
woo *v* udvarati se.
wood *n* šuma; drvo.
wood alcohol *n* metil alkohol.
wood carving *n* drvorez.
woodcut *n* duborez u drvetu.
woodcutter *n* drvoseča; duborezac.
wooded *a* šumovit.
wooden *a* drven.
wood engraver *n* drvorezac.
woodland *n* šumovit kraj.
woodlouse *n* babura (*zool*).
woodman *n* drvoseča; šumar.
woodpecker *n* detlić (ptica).
woodwind *n* drveni duvački instrument.
woodwork *n* drvenarija.
woodworm *n* drveni moljac.
wool *n* vuna.
woollen *a* vunen.
woollens *npl* vunena roba.
wooly *a* vunast; dlakav; nejasan; smušen.
word *n* reč; govor, razgovor; obećanje; *v* izraziti rečima; formulisati.
word processing *n* obrada teksta.
word processor *n* procesor za obradu reči.
wordiness *n* opširnost u govoru; frazerstvo.
wording *n* način izražavanja, formulisanje.
wordy *a* opširan u govoru, razvučen, frazerski.
work *v* raditi; delovati; činiti; upravljati; napraviti; **to ~ out** izraditi; rešiti; trenirati; završiti se (dobro); *n* rad, posao; postupak; delo.
workaholic *n* radoholik.

worker *n* radnik.

workforce *n* radna snaga.

working-class *a* radnička klasa.

workman *n* radnik.

workmanship *n* stručnost, veština; obrada, izrada.

workmate *n* kolega s posla.

workshop *n* radionica; seminar.

world *n* svet; društvo; *a* zemaljski, svetovan.

worldliness *n* svetovnost; sklonost uživanjima ovoga sveta.

worldly *a* ovozemaljski, svetovan; koji voli život; belosvetski.

worldwide *a* svetski poznat, rasprostranjen širom sveta.

worm *n* crv; glista; spiralna cev (*teh*).

worn-out *a* pohaban, iznošen, pocepan; iznuren.

worried *a* zabrinut.

worry *v* brinuti (se), zabrinuti (se); uznemiravati; *n* briga; zabrinutost.

worrying *a* zabrinjavajući.

worse *a/adv* gori, gore; lošiji, lošije; ~ **and** ~ sve gore; *n* gore stanje; nešto gore.

worship *n* obožavanje; bogosluženje; predmet obožavanja; **your** ~ Vaša milost (kao titula).

worst *a* najgori; *adv* najgore; *n* najgore.

worth *n* vrednost.

worthily *adv* dostojno.

worthless *a* bezvredan.

worthwhile *a* vredan pažnje, koji se isplati.

worthy *a* dostojan, vredan poštovanja.

would-be *a* tobožnji; takozvani; budući.

wound *n* rana, povreda; uvreda; *v* raniti, povrediti.

wrangle *v* svađati se, prepirati se; bučno diskutovati; *n* prepirka, svađa.

wrap *v* zaviti, uviti, umotati, prekriti.

wrath *n* gnev, bes.

wreath *n* venac; kolut dima.

wreck *n* brodolom; olupina broda; krntija; propast; *v* prouzrokovati brodolom; porušiti.

wreckage *n* olupina; ruševine; uništenje.

wren *n* carić (ptica).

wrench *v* iščašiti; istrgnuti; *n* iščašenje; trzaj; ključ (*teh*).

wrest *v* istrgnuti, oteti; uzurpirati.

wrestle *v* rvati se.

wrestling *n* rvanje.

wretched *a* jadan, bedan.

wriggle *v* vijugati; probijati se.

wring *v* stiskati; iscediti; iznuditi.

wrinkle *n* bora, nabor; *v* naborati (se); izgužvati.

wrist *n* ručni zglob.

wristband *n* manžeta.

wristwatch *n* ručni sat.

writ *n* sudski nalog, pismena naredba; pisanje.

write *v* pisati; napisati; **to ~ down** zapisati; **to ~ off** otpisati; **to ~ up** opisati do sitnica.

write-off *n* otpis (*fin*).

writer *n* pisac; pisar.

writhe *v* previjati se (od bolova); mučiti se.

writing *n* pisanje; književni rad; rukopis; isprava.

writing desk *n* pisaći sto.

writing paper *n* papir za pisanje.

wrong *n* nepravda; zlo; *a* pogrešan, nepravedan; *adv* pogrešno; *v* naneti nepravdu.

wrongful *a* nepravedan; nezakonit.

wrongly *adv* krivo, naopako, pogrešno.

wry *a* iskrivljen, kos; ironičan.

X Y Z

xenophobia *n* ksenofobija, strah pred (ili mržnja prema) strancima.

Xmas *n* Božić, skraćeno od *Christmas*.

X-ray *n* rendgen, rendgenski snimak; rendgenski zrak.

xylographer *n* drvorezac.

xylophone *n* ksilofon (*muz*).

yacht *n* jahta; jedrilica.

yachting *n* jedrenje, jedriličarstvo.

Yankee *n* Jenki, Amerikanac; stanovnik severoistoka SAD.

yard[1] *n* jard (mera 0,914 m).

yard[2] *n* dvorište; stovarište.

yardstick *n* štap dugačak jedan jard (za merenje).

yarn *v* pripovedati; *n* pređa; priča, pripovedanje.

yawn *v* zevati; zjapiti; *n* zev, zevanje.

yawning *a* koji zjapi.

yeah *adv* (*inf*) da.

year *n* godina.

yearbook *n* godišnjak (knjiga).

yearling *n* jednogodac (životinja).

yearly *a* godišnji; *adv* svake godine.

yearn *v* čeznuti, žudeti.

yearning *n* čežnja.

yeast *n* kvasac.

yell *v* vikati; *n* vika.

yellow *a* žut; *n* žuta boja.

yellowish *a* žućkast.

yelp *v* kevtati; cvileti, zavijati; *n* kevtanje; cviljenje, zavijanje.

yes *adv* da; *n* da, potvrdan odgovor.

yesterday *adv* juče; *n* jučerašnji dan.

yet *conj* ipak, pa ipak, uprkos tome; *adv* još; već; ipak.

yew *n* tisa (*bot*).

yield *v* doneti (plod); ustupiti; predati; *n* rod; proizvod; prinos; dobitak.

yoga *n* joga (tehnika meditacije).

yoghurt *n* jogurt.

yoke *n* jaram; spona (*teh*); ropstvo.

yolk *n* žumance.

yonder *adv* tamo, eto tamo (u daljini).

you *pn* ti; vi.

young *a* mlad; neiskusan; ~er *a* mlađi.

youngster *n* mladić, dečak; dete.

your(s) *pn* tvoj; vaš.

yourself *pn* se, sebe, sebi, sobom; sam, sami.

yourselves *pn pl* množina od *yourself*.

youth *n* mladost; mladić; omladina.

youthful *a* mladalački, mlad.

youthfulness *n* mladolikost.

yuppie *a* uspešan i u trendu.

zany *a* smešan; komičan.

zap *v* pogoditi; ubiti; bombardovati, tući.

zeal *n* revnost.

zealous *a* revnostan.

zebra *n* zebra (*zool*).

zenith *n* zenit; vrhunac.

zero *n* nula.

zest *n* slast, užitak; pikantnost; polet.

zigzag *n* krivudanje, cik-cak; *a* krivudav; *v* krivudati, ići u cik-cak liniji.

zinc *n* cink.

zip, zip fastener *n* patent zatvarač, rajsferšlus.

zodiac *n* zodijak (*astrol*).

zone *n* zona; pojas.

zoo *n* zoološki vrt.

zoological *a* zoološki.

zoologist *n* zoolog.

zoology *n* zoologija.

zoom *v* zujati; popeti se brzo (avion); približavati ili udaljavati (teleobjektivom).

zoom lens *n* pokretni teleobjektiv, zum (film i TV).

JUGOSLOVENSKA KNJIGA
Terazije 27/II, Beograd
Srbija
E-mail:juknjiga@eunet.yu

Sastavljanje i prevod
odrednica na srpskom jeziku
Redakcija Jugoslovenske knjige

Za izdavača
Zoran Nikodijević

Tiraž: 10.000
Štampa i povez u Poljskoj

CIP – Каталогизација у публикацији Народна библиотека
Србије, Београд
811.163.41'374=111(038)
811.111'374=163.41(038)

SERBIAN–English, English–Serbian
Dictionary = Srpsko–Engleski,
englesko–srpski rečnik / [grupa autora; sastavljanje i prevod
odrednica na srpskom jeziku Redakcija Jugoslovenske knjige]. –
Concise ed. = Sažeto izd. – Beograd: Jugoslovenska knjiga; New
Lanark: Geddes & Grosset, 2004 (Štampano u Poljskoj). – 382 str.;
20 cm

Tiraž 10.000.

ISBN 86-7411-065-7 (JK)
1. Југословенска књига (Београд).
Редакција
а) Српско-енглески речници
б) Енглеско-српски речници

THE PRESENT POSITION

OF

CATHOLICS IN ENGLAND

THE WORKS OF
CARDINAL JOHN HENRY NEWMAN
BIRMINGHAM ORATORY
MILLENNIUM EDITION
VOLUME 1

SERIES EDITOR

JAMES TOLHURST DD

LECTURES

PRESENT POSITION OF
CATHOLICS IN ENGLAND

Addressed to the Brothers of the Oratory

IN THE SUMMER OF 1851

BY

JOHN HENRY NEWMAN, D.D.
PRIEST OF THE ORATORY OF ST. PHILIP NERI

Tempus tacendi, et tempus loquendi

with an Introduction and Notes by

ANDREW NASH

Gracewing.

NOTRE DAME

First published in 1851
Published in the Birmingham Millennium Oratory Edition in 2000
jointly by

Gracewing   University of Notre Dame Press
2 Southern Avenue,   310 Flanner Hall
Leominster   Notre Dame
Herefordshire HR6 0QF   IN 46556 USA

Library of Congress Cataloging-in-Publication Data
Newman, John Henry, 1801-1890.
    Lectures on the present position of Catholics in England: addressed to
    the brothers of the Oratory in the summer of 1851/by John Henry
    Newman; with an introduction and notes by Andrew Nash.
       p. cm. — (The Birmingham Oratory millennium edition; vol. 1)
    Includes bibliographical references.
    ISBN 0-268-01323-3 (cloth)
    1. Catholic Church–England. 2. Catholic Church–Apologetic works.
    I. Nash, Andrew (Andrew J.) II. Title. III. Series.

BX1493 .N5 2000
282'.42'09034–dc21   00-021529

UK ISBN 0 85244 443 5
US ISBN 0-268-01323-3

Additional typesetting by Action Publishing Technology Ltd,
Gloucester, GL1 1SP
Printed in England by MPG Books Ltd, Bodmin, PL31 1EG

CONTENTS

ACKNOWLEDGEMENTS

The Introduction, Textual Appendix and Editor's Notes to this edition are based on work submitted for an Open University research degree through the Maryvale Institute, Birmingham. I am grateful to my tutors, Fr. Ian Ker and Dr. Tom Woodman, for their guidance and support.

The Fathers of the Birmingham Oratory kindly gave me access to their Newman archive, and I am especially indebted to the Archivist, Gerard Tracey, for his invaluable assistance.

I am most grateful to the Newman Centre Trust for its generous financial assistance to me in my studies.

A.J.N.

INTRODUCTION

In an age in which the Pope has taken tea with the
Queen in Buckingham Palace, it is hard for us to
realise that the average nineteenth century
Englishman was an anti-Catholic bigot. The nation
which had invented the Industrial Revolution, which
prided itself as being the mother of parliamentary
democracy and saw itself as in the vanguard of social
progress, was pervasively anti-Catholic. Families
listened to sermons in their parish churches in which
their highly educated and cultured ministers
denounced the Catholic Church as the Whore of
Babylon and the Pope himself as Antichrist; Catholic
priests, particularly Jesuits, were seen as cunning
agents of a foreign power, trained in methods of
deception, constantly seeking to overthrow the cherished freedoms of the British way of life; monks and
nuns were fanatics who carried out punishments of
unspeakable cruelty on recalcitrant members of their
communities; converts to Catholicism were 'perverts'
who forfeited the right to normal relations with their
families or indeed with society. The nation as a whole

subscribed to a religious McCarthyism, in which to be
a Roman Catholic was to be un-British. It was an
ideology which was, as D.G.Paz puts it, 'an integral
part of what it meant to be a Victorian'.[1]

Newman's *Lectures on the Present Position of Catholics
in England* are an analysis of this ideology, satirising it,
demonstrating the false traditions on which it was
based and advising Catholics how they should respond
to it. They were the first thing of their kind in English
literature. They appeared at a time of national uproar,
the 'Papal Aggression' crisis of 1850–1, and they
landed Newman in court for libel. Aimed at a popular
audience, they are supremely readable, at times shocking and certainly the most humorous of any of
Newman's writings. Yet they are less well known
today than his graver work and until now have only
intermittently been available in popular editions. The
leading Newman authority, Ian Ker, sees them as a
neglected satirical masterpiece,[2] and it is the hope of
this present edition that they will gain wider recognition as much for their literary value as for their place
in religious controversy and apologetics.

I. THE HISTORICAL CONTEXT

'Papal Aggression'
Because of the gap between Newman's age and our
own, appreciating the Lectures' historical context is

---

[1] Paz, D.G., *Popular Anti-Catholicism in Mid-Victorian England* (Stanford, 1992), p. 299.

[2] Cf. Ker, I., 'Newman the Satirist', in Ker, I. & Hill, A.G. (ed.), *Newman after a Hundred Years*, (Oxford, 1990), p. 20.

particularly important. Anti–Catholicism had of course been central to British culture since the sixteenth century Protestant Reformation. For two centuries after Henry VIII's break with Rome and establishment of a Church of England of which the Crown was the Head, those who adhered to the old faith were subject to persecution. We look back with horror to those ages of barbaric religious intolerance: the hanging, drawing and quartering of Catholics under Elizabeth I and James I, and the burnings of Protestants under Mary I. The policy of a state church to which all must belong of course produced persecution of the non–conformist denominations, too; every American boy or girl knows about the Mayflower. The 'Glorious Revolution' of 1688 then ushered in the new age of tolerance for all denominations in England—except Catholicism; and what is often not realised is just how profoundly intolerant of Catholics British society was to remain right through to the age of Queen Victoria. Fortunately, in recent years anti-Catholicism in nineteenth century Britain has been the subject of a number of detailed studies.[3] We now have a much more informed picture of the context which enables us to judge how true Newman's picture is of the anti-Catholic prejudice which he confronted in his *Present Position* lectures.

This is important, because for some writers on Newman, these Lectures are the least attractive and

---

[3] Major studies include: Wolffe, J., *The Protestant Crusade in Great Britain* (Oxford, 1991); Paz, D.G., op.cit.; Wallis, F.H., *Popular Anti-Catholicism in Mid-Victorian Britain* (Lewiston, NY, 1993). These, together with virtually all other modern studies, are indebted to E.R. Norman's groundbreaking *Anti-Catholicism in Victorian England* (London, 1968).

indeed least good of Newman's writings. The Anglican historian Owen Chadwick, for instance, sees the subject matter of the lectures as a distraction for Newman, a turning aside from the major theological issues which up to then had been his main concern. He argues that in the years immediately after Newman's conversion in 1845 he distrusted his own abilities as a serious theological writer and instead, with the misplaced zeal of a convert, descended to a subject matter that was not worthy of him. Chadwick therefore summarises the Lectures as 'a refined mind bothering itself with trash'; so that when Newman painstakingly refutes such Protestant propaganda as the Maria Monk allegations, the reader 'is sad to see so delicate an instrument taking its time to prove false what no instructed person could believe true.'[4] Chadwick's implication is that educated Victorians had risen above the Protestant bigotry of the masses, so that Newman's refutation of it was unnecessary.

The particular events to which the Lectures were a response give a rather different picture. On 29th September 1850 it was announced from Rome that Catholics in England, who since Reformation times had been organised under missionary-style arrangements, were once again to have their own hierarchy of territorial bishops. In place of the Vicars Apostolic, each of whom had an area of the country to administer, new episcopal sees were created, and Cardinal Nicholas Wiseman was to be the first Archbishop of Westminster. Wiseman, though English, had lived most of his life abroad, spending twelve years in Rome as Rector of the English College (where

[4] Chadwick, O., *Newman*, (Oxford, 1983), p. 15.

English Catholics were sent to be trained for the priesthood). He was a great admirer of all things Roman, and on 7th October he announced the Pope's restoration of the Catholic hierarchy in England in a flamboyant pastoral letter 'From out of the Flaminian Gate':

> Catholic England has been restored to its orbit in the ecclesiastical firmament, from which its light had long vanished, and begins anew its course of regularly adjusted action round the centre of unity, the source of jurisdiction, of light and vigour.

Describing his own role as Archbishop of Westminster, he proclaimed that:

> We govern, and shall continue to govern, the counties of Middlesex, Hertford and Essex, as ordinary thereof, and those of Surrey, Sussex, Kent, Berkshire, and Hampshire, with the islands annexed, as administrator with ordinary jurisdiction.[5]

It seems clear that he had no idea that this triumphalist declaration would have the impact that it did. What he was announcing was, after all, merely a change in the way that English Catholics were to be organised, from administrative districts to dioceses. However, he had chosen to interpret this as being of enormous symbolic significance, and the British press took him at his word. Led by *The Times* and *Punch*, the papers

[5] See *English Historical Documents*, vol.XII (I), 1833–1874, ed. G.M. Young and W.D. Handcock, p. 366.

saw this as an outrageous attempt by the papacy to claim jurisdiction over England. It was quickly dubbed the 'Papal Aggression' and was greeted with furious denunciations as an infringement of Britain's Protestant freedom.

Then came one of the most extraordinary features of this outbreak of anti-Catholicism. The campaign was dramatically boosted by the support of no less a person than the Prime Minister himself, Lord John Russell. In a public letter to the Bishop of Durham he denounced this 'attempt to impose a foreign yoke upon our minds and consciences'.[6] Russell's motives were partly those of political opportunism. As *Punch* put it, making fun of this hijacking of a campaign in which it was playing a leading role:

> Little Jack Russell
> Got in a bustle,
> At hearing the general cry;
> A letter wrote he
> In the popular key,
> And said 'What a good boy am I!'[7]

However, Russell's deliberate stirring up of anti-Catholicism from the very pinnacle of political power is itself an indication of just how socially respectable such an ideology was.

The outcry was now national, with public meetings up and down the country in which speakers attacked the setting up of the new Catholic hierarchy with extraordinary vehemence. Petitions to the Queen

[6] Norman, op.cit. p. 160.
[7] *Punch*, 1850, Vol. 19, p. 251.

protesting against this Catholic usurpation of her prerogatives were signed by hundreds of thousands. The 'No Popery' uproar spilled over into violence with Catholic priests being pelted in the streets and Catholic churches being attacked. Yet the campaign had effectively been blessed by the government; and the public meetings and petitions were organised by the middle classes, often by the Anglican clergy themselves, with local notables and clergymen presiding over meetings and drawing up addresses. The Papal Aggression campaign thus had a most socially respectable leadership; indeed, Paz points out the part that civic pride played in the holding of such meetings, quoting the promoter of one in Southampton who wanted the town to have an anti-Catholic meeting because 'so many *Inferior* places have set us the example'.[8] Anti-Catholicism was evidently the way to become genteel.

Newman at first counselled that Catholics should not respond to this furore but should keep their heads down and wait for it to pass. Wiseman, alarmed at what he had stirred up, had already published in November a conciliatory *Appeal to the Reason and Good Feeling of the English People on the subject of the Catholic Hierarchy*. In this he explained that his language had been misunderstood, and that he was only claiming jurisdiction over his Catholic flock, many of whom were among the very poor. His reasonable tone had some effect, but the agitation continued. Papal Aggression meetings had not been everywhere equally successful, however, since Dissenters were wary of allying themselves too closely to the Church of England when it came to

[8] Paz, op.cit., p. 24.

forbidding the new Catholic bishops' titles. That amounted to support for a state church and was thus anathema to the principles of 'voluntaryism', i.e. dissenting denominations as opposed to an established church. Dissent was particularly strong in Birmingham, and there the great No Popery meeting in the Town Hall in December failed to adopt the anti-Catholic resolutions proposed by its leaders. This meeting marked the turning of the tide and may perhaps have influenced Newman in his advice about concentrating on Catholics' *local* reputation which he was to give in his final *Present Position* lecture.

However, Lord Russell's stance had forced him into taking some tangible political measures. His government committed itself to passing new anti-Catholic legislation, outlawing the use of territorial titles by the new Catholic bishops and proposing restrictions on religious orders. The Ecclesiastical Titles Bill eventually became law, but only in a watered-down version and not before it had helped to cause the government's fall. Russell formed a new administration, but the anti-Catholic rigor had proved a difficult one to ride. As the campaign continued, Catholics became more confident and entered the field to put the Church's case. Congratulating the layman John Capes on the committee he was organising for public lectures in February 1851, Newman urged that Catholics should 'make the excuse of this persecution for getting up a great organization, going round the towns giving lectures, or making speeches.'[9] Typically, Newman was very keen for

[9] *The Letters and Diaries of John Henry Newman*, Vol.XIV (London, 1963), p. 214.

laymen to be in the forefront of such public apologetics, and he worried away at Capes about the status of the committee. Capes himself started a series of lectures, and when he had to give them up through ill-health, Newman urgently asked him:

> How many good Lecturers and speakers could you collect up and down the country? ... The thing would be to keep it from becoming ecclesiastical (in which case it would fall under the priests of the place, who, if dull, would ruin the whole) ...[10]

Yet, at the end of the day, Newman himself decided to lecture. Perhaps he came to feel that Capes's committee was inadequate in its efforts—his letter to Capes certainly has a tone of frustration. His first biographer, Wilfred Ward, comments: "'If you want a thing done, you should do it yourself' says the proverb—and shortly after writing this letter Newman determined to make his own contribution to the enterprise he had suggested, though he was a priest, not a layman.'[11] Newman now took the initiative and booked the Birmingham Corn Exchange for a series of public lectures. They were to be popular in style and to be available for sale in cheap off-prints at the door. And so in these heady circumstances were his *Lectures on the Present Position of Catholics in England* born. They were delivered weekly, beginning on 30th June and finishing on 1st September 1851.

[10] Ibid, p.218.
[11] Ward, W., *The Life of John Henry Newman* (London, 1912), Vol. I, p. 263.

Anti-Catholicism

With their content, style and reception I will deal
below. At the outset, however, it can be confidently
stated that, no less than Newman's other works, they
were getting to grips with a real problem. Owen
Chadwick characterises the Papal Aggression
campaign in terms of working-class violence, racially
and economically motivated: 'The mobs of Britain
were out against Catholics. They were afraid of cheap
Irish labour, and therefore they knew nothing and
believed everything.'[12] However, this not only
ignores the upper- and middle-class nature of the
agitation's leadership but also takes no account of the
role played by the various anti-Catholic societies such
as the British Reformation Society, the Protestant
Association and the Evangelical Alliance. Chadwick's
detailed treatment of the Papal Aggression crisis in his
major study of Victorian Christianity makes scant
mention of these societies,[13] yet they were frequently
the organisers of the public meetings and petitions of
1850-1, as Paz demonstrates.[14] Further, such activity
and organisation cannot be understood except against
the background of the growth of the anti-Catholic
societies in the 1830s and 1840s and the part they
played in religious and social life. The social profile of
the membership of the two biggest of these societies
has been analysed by Wolffe: about a fifth were clergy,
and 'the backbone of membership clearly came from
the minor gentry and professions'.[15] These were the

12 Chadwick, loc. cit.
13 Chadwick, O., *The Victorian Church*, (3rd edn., London, 1987), pp.
   271-309.
14 Paz, op. cit., pp. 124-127.
15 Wolffe, op. cit., pp. 163-5

agitators and speechmakers and the publishers of the pamphlets and periodicals from which Newman culls his examples of anti-Catholicism in the *Present Position* lectures. So it now seems clear that the violent mobs of 1850-1 were not spontaneous working-class outbursts but were the results of organised anti-Catholic agitation led and funded by the middle classes and clergy.

Anti-Catholicism was fuelled by the perception that Catholics were a growing force in the land. The first attempt to grant Catholics some degree of freedom had been the Catholic Relief Act of 1778. This relatively modest measure had provoked the Gordon Riots, when the London mob, stirred up by the half crazy Lord George Gordon, reduced London to anarchy for several days (vividly described by Dickens in *Barnaby Rudge*). Order was only reimposed by the use of troops. It was fifty years before Catholics finally won their political rights in the Catholic Emancipation Act of 1829, pushed through Parliament by the arch-conservative Duke of Wellington as Prime Minister not from any pro-Catholic sympathy but as a means of dealing with Irish unrest. Such pragmatism outraged Protestant feeling and prompted increased activity by the anti-Catholic societies. Another crisis came in 1845 over the Maynooth question—the annual giving of a grant by the British government to Maynooth College which trained most of Ireland's Catholic priests. This was seen as a betrayal of Protestantism, and in this year was the occasion of meetings and petitions to Parliament, opposing the grant. The grant was in fact increased, again largely as a measure to placate the Irish Catholic

Church and thus to secure its co-operation against Irish insurrection. However, it had produced the biggest coming-together yet of the various anti-Catholic organisations in a massive Anti-Maynooth Conference, attended by representatives of all the Protestant denominations. The Papal Aggression crisis five years later was therefore a part of the pattern of organised anti-Catholic agitation which played such a prominent part in Victorian life.

The Victorian Englishman feared Catholicism because he saw it as breaking out of the confines of penal days. He saw its political emancipation and observed the building of its churches. The Catholic population of England, which had been declining in the seventeenth and eighteenth centuries, was now growing fast. The figures are subject to much debate, but according to John Bossy the Catholic population of England increased nearly tenfold between 1770 when there were about 80,000 Catholics and 1850 when there were about 750,000.[16] Bossy argues that this was only partly due to Irish immigration and mostly to the self-regeneration of the Catholic community, assisted by the gradual relaxation of the penal legislation against it. At the first synod of the restored Catholic hierarchy held at Oscott, Newman preached his celebrated sermon 'The Second Spring' in which he dramatically pictured the sudden, miraculous re-birth of the Catholic Church in England. Historians now dispute Newman's historiography,[17] but what is important is that this is both how

---

[16] Bossy, J., *The English Catholic Community 1570-1850*, (London, 1975), p. 298.

[17] e.g. Bossy, op. cit, p. 299.

Catholics themselves perceived their current strength and how Protestants too viewed, with alarm, the growth of 'popery' in their midst. The really disturbing factor for the Protestant, of course, was the Oxford Movement. Here were Oxford educated Anglican divines claiming that the Church of England was not as Protestant as everyone thought but that it was Catholic in its belief and worship, and then some of them even becoming Roman Catholics themselves. The Oxford Movement as a whole had not followed Newman into the Catholic Church in 1845. Led by Edward Pusey it now constituted a permanent party in the Anglican church. It is significant that Lord John Russell in his Durham Letter reserved his fiercest condemnation for these

> Clergyman of the Church of England, who have subscribed the Thirty-Nine Articles and acknowledged in explicit terms the Queen's supremacy, [but who] have been most forward in leading their flocks 'step by step to the very verge of the precipice'.

In the sermons and pamphlets of the Papal aggression crisis, the 'Puseyites' came in for quite as much vilification as the Catholics themselves; they were the enemy within. Numerically, conversions due to the Oxford Movement were not that significant in the overall growth of Catholicism; but their power to frighten Protestant opinion was out of all proportion to their numbers, perhaps because they came from the same classes as the leaders of anti-Catholic activity. It was the fear of the Protestant fathers of England that they would return from a 'No Popery' meeting to find that their own sons or daughters had become 'perverts' to the detested Romish faith.

So the growth of organised anti-Catholicism in the first half of the nineteenth century was a conscious reaction to a perceived threat to the professional classes by an aggressively growing Catholic Church in England. Indeed, John Wolffe argues that one of the impetuses towards the formation of the anti-Catholic societies was the decline in traditional popular anti-Catholic manifestations, such as Guy Fawkes celebrations, when the Pope was burned in effigy and it was wise for Catholics to keep indoors. These traditions were dying out, and it was felt that more organised activity had to be undertaken to revive the traditional English hostility to popery.[18] Anti-Catholicism, therefore, was essentially reactionary in nature. It drew upon the centuries-long traditional prejudice, but it was a conscious counter-attack and as such highly organised. Yet, paradoxically, it saw itself as progressive, since Catholicism was seen as a hang-over from less enlightened times. The Evangelicals, for instance, had a strong sense of their mission to transform society and rid it of its evils, and their greatest success was of course the battle against slavery. But these same reformers bracketed 'popery' with slavery as one of the other great evils to be fought against.

The evidence is now overwhelming that when Newman confronted and satirised anti-Catholicism in his 1851 Lectures he was engaging with a serious force, with powerful ideas in which 'instructed people' did

[18] op. cit., pp. 145-6.

indeed believe. John Wolffe assesses the Lectures as:

> an interesting treatment of the problem of anti-Catholicism from an observer whose partisan commitment did not cause him to slide into mere polemic and who had the advantage of viewing the religious battlefield from both sides of the tortured no man's land of Littlemore.[19]

And J.R. Griffin concludes that the value of the Lectures is precisely as history: they give a picture of the intense Protestant prejudice of the Victorian age and deserve greater study by historians of the period for that reason.[20]

The Achilli affair

'It is unfortunate' says Wolffe, 'that Newman's *Lectures on the Present Position of Catholics in England* have been remembered more for the libel action to which they gave occasion than for their actual content.'[21] Indeed, it is the interest in them as the cause of one of the more sensational episodes in Newman's life, the Achilli trial, that has perhaps eclipsed consideration of their literary qualities. Nevertheless, the reader who is not familiar with the events will want to know what happened.

One of the features of anti-Catholic campaigns was the holding of public meetings addressed by ex-Catholics, sometimes priests, who denounced their former popish errors and gave lurid accounts of the

[19] op.cit., p. 3.
[20] Griffin, John R., *A Historical Commentary on the Major Catholic Works of Cardinal Newman*, (New York, 1993). p. 66.
[21] Wolffe, op.cit., p. 3.

horrors of Catholic life. They were sometimes imposters whose motives were financial. One pair, Chylinski and Teodor (whom Newman mentions, p. 208) even sold "Wafer Gods", i.e. consecrated Communion hosts, at the door for a penny each. Others were backed by the anti-Catholic organisations who arranged meetings for them to address. One such was Giacinto Achilli, a former Dominican friar, who had been imprisoned (in a monastery) by the Inquisition for heresy, he claimed, but actually for a series of sexual offences, some against under-age young women. He had been 'rescued' from the Inquisition, however, by a group of English ultra-Protestants and brought to England as a hero six months before the Papal Aggression crisis broke. He was received by the Foreign Secretary, Lord Palmerston, greeted at a public meeting at Exeter Hall with a specially written hymn, 'Hail Roman prisoner, Hail!' and given a chapel in London. His *Dealings with the Inquisition* was a best seller. In his public lectures, sponsored by the Evangelical Alliance, he professed to have seen through the errors of Catholicism and to be a sincere Protestant, and his exciting account of the cruelties of the Inquisition made him a credible and popular anti-Catholic speaker; his meetings were very well-attended, despite his having to speak through an interpreter.

The truth about him was not long in being discovered: he had left behind him in Italy a string of seductions, and he had continued his conduct even after he had briefly been accepted as a professor at the Protestant College in Malta. Cardinal Wiseman printed a devastating exposé of him in *The Dublin*

Review as early as July 1850, giving all the offences in detail, but Achilli had not sued for libel, and this was what gave Newman the confidence to repeat the facts in the fifth of his Lectures, taking legal advice before doing so to check that he would be all right. However, within a month he heard that Achilli was going to sue him. If Achilli had not dared to bring his life under the scrutiny of a court before, why did he now? It seems that he was pushed into it by the Protestant Alliance. Newman's stature and the consequent widespread circulation of the Lectures was the main reason—he simply could not be allowed to destroy this anti-Catholic hero. Achilli had also known that if he sued *The Dublin Review* the case would be heard in Ireland where the jury would be likely to be largely made up of Catholics; whereas in Protestant Birmingham, at the height of the Papal Aggression campaign he was much more likely to find a jury who wanted to believe in him. The libel charge was officially laid against Newman in November.

Under English law, Newman had to be able to prove every one of the charges he had made—just proving some of them would not be enough. He sent to Wiseman at once for the documents on which the *Dublin Review* article had been based. Incredibly, Wiseman failed to take the matter seriously and had in fact mislaid them! He found them eventually but too late to prevent a trial. Newman and his defence committee now had to find the relevant witnesses in Italy and persuade them to come to England and give their testimony. As may be imagined, it was a massive undertaking, but various of Achilli's victims were found and agreed to come. One of Newman's lay women friends, Maria Giberne, went off to take charge of the Italian ladies and escort them from Italy. She ended having to spend months with them in Paris, since Achilli, hearing that witnesses were on their way, had managed to get the trial delayed. The suspense of waiting for the trial put Newman under a terrible strain. During this time he had also been invited to become the founding Rector of the proposed Catholic University in Dublin and was composing and delivering there the first five of the series of discourses which were to become part of *The Idea of a University*. In the dedication to this volume he later referred to 'the stress of a great anxiety' under which they had been composed. The trial finally began on 21st June 1852. It lasted three days and concluded with a strongly biased summing-up by the judge Lord Campbell. The verdict from the jury of 'pot-house fellows' (in Newman's phrase) was inevitable. Despite all the evidence of the victims and witnesses, Achilli simply denied that any of it had happened, and the jury believed him and found Newman guilty of criminal libel.

But the injustice of the verdict was widely recognised. Even *The Times*, which was strongly anti-Catholic, criticised Campbell's obvious bias and commented:

> a great blow has been given to the administration of justice in this country, and Roman Catholics will have henceforth only too good reason for asserting that there is no justice for them in matters tending to rouse the Protestant feelings of judges and juries.[22]

[22] Quoted in *Letters and Diaries*, Vol. XV, p. 108.

Newman's lawyers pressed for a new trial; though this was not granted, by now there was general agreement that the verdict had been unjust. Sentencing had been postponed, and when it came Newman did not get the prison sentence that he and everyone else was expecting: instead he only got a fine of £100 and a long lecture from Judge Coleridge about his 'moral deterioration' since he had become a Catholic. (Extraordinarily, the evidence is that Coleridge believed Newman was telling the truth about Achilli. He later wrote to Keble 'It is a very painful matter for us who must hail his libel as false, believing it is in great part true—or at least that it may be.'[23]) The fine was paid on the spot by Newman's supporters. His final legal bills were enormous but were all paid out of a fund organised by his defence committee to which Catholics both at home and abroad contributed; indeed there was £2,000 over which was used towards the building of the new University Church in Dublin and the cottage and Oratorian cemetery at Rednal.

Achilli, though he had won the case, was a discredited figure. He continued his seductions and ended up in America. Newman had to remove the 'libellous' sections of Lecture V in subsequent editions (they are reprinted in an Appendix in this edition), replacing them initially with the inscription 'De illis quae sequebantur / posteorum judicium sit '—About those things which followed / let posterity be the judge.

[23] Ms letter to Keble (Nov.8, 1852), Taylor Collection, Bodleian, quoted in Griffin, op. cit., p. 63.

II. THE TEXT

Composition

As is the case with most of Newman's writings, no manuscript of the *Lectures on the Present Position of Catholics in England* has survived, except for twelve pages of Lecture I, from the beginning to page 6, line 28 '... say for itself' (Document D.5.5 in the Birmingham Oratory Archives). There is also some preparatory material (D.5.16) containing a number of pamphlets, letters and notes which Newman made use of; I have referred to these in their relevant places in the Editor's Notes. With them are also two sheets of notes in Newman's handwriting which are of some interest since they show the stages of his working. The first sheet appears to be a second page of Newman's original planning for the Lectures. It gives brief notes for Lectures numbered 5, 6, 7 and 8, though these do not bear much relation to the final form of these Lectures, surrounded by phrases and sometimes whole sentences. There then follows a numbered list of lectures which is closer to his final arrangement, and finally a reference to a Lecture 14. It is fascinating to see these first fragmentary jottings, most of them in almost indecipherable minute handwriting, which show Newman gathering his thoughts. The second sheet appears to be an intermediate stage of more detailed planning for individual Lectures. It has been folded vertically: one half consists of references to Blackstone for the Russian Count's speech in Lecture I, a number of them ticked, presumably as each was used; the other half is headed 'June 27. for Lecture 4' and has

thirteen numbered points which outline the structure which this lecture was indeed to have. We do
not know, of course, whether Newman went
straight from this stage to a first draft. The MS of
Lecture I may be a first draft: it is neatly written but
has some corrections in ink which look as if they
have been done as he writes and further revisions in
pencil obviously added later.

These preparatory notes, together with the other
material, suggest a meticulous process of composition
by Newman, yet he was certainly writing under
great pressure of time. The first reference to the
Lectures in the Letters and Diaries comes on 19th
May when he writes to a friend for help in finding
two books he wants to refer to in Lectures I and III.
On 17th June he writes to Capes: 'I am just
commencing a set of Public Lectures at the Corn
Exchange and going to Press with them'. On the
22nd he writes to Lady Olivia Acheson, 'I am
getting into the dreadful whirlpool of those Lectures
—three months! I dread it very much.' He consulted
the London Oratorian Fr. Dalgairns on 29th June
about Lecture I, arranging for the printer to send
him both the proofs and the 'revise' which Dalgairns
was to return directly to the printer, and was writing
to him again on 4th July about Lecture II which was
to be given only three days later. On 11th July he
was writing to James Hope for an answer 'if possible, by return of post' about whether he can
comment on Spooner's absurd allegations in the
House of Commons about the new Oratory house
(see p.118ff.) without being in contempt of
Parliament. Newman says he is going to mention it

'in a public Lecture on Monday' and explains that
'The proof has come down this morning, and some
of us are rather nervous.' On the 19th he writes to
Elizabeth Bowden that he is 'quite overpowered
with work' and although he urgently wants to start
dealing with the new Catholic University he 'physically *cannot* till these Lectures are done; and I cannot
hurry the lectures—It would be like attempting to
run 50 miles an hour on the narrow gauge.' In the
same letter he mentions that he is thinking of stopping the Lectures for a week, as he indeed did,
which may indicate the pressure he felt under. On
28th August, two days before the final Lecture, he
writes to her, 'I am glad to say I am sending up my
last bit of MS to the press tonight (except the Preface
etc)'. The maximum time he could have spent, from
first notes to final drafts, is thus about three and a
half months, during which time he was extremely
busy with other matters, not least the building of the
new Oratory House in Edgbaston.

Publication

The Lectures were published individually by Burns
and Lambert as they appeared; they cost one shilling
and three pence each (a price which Cardinal
Wiseman thought excessive). The complete First
Edition was published in due course, together with a
cheap edition which omitted the title page, dedication
and preface. Newman himself had also had the individual Lectures printed for sale at tuppence each just
to those who attended at the Corn Exchange, and he
later had these bound together to make a cheap
edition. The Lectures also appeared in summarised

form in the popular Catholic magazine, *The Lamp.*
There was a second printing of Burns' edition which
bears the date 1851 but contains the asterisks and
inscription in place of the 'libellous' Achilli passage
and the date '*In fest. Nativ. S. Joan. Bapt.* 1852' so it
presumably in fact appeared in that year. The Lectures
evidently sold well since a Second Edition appeared,
identical to this. A Third Edition was published in
1857 by the Dublin publisher James Duffy who also
took over stocks of others of Newman's works from
Burns. This edition is now rare, and I have been
unable to locate a copy. Since it appeared while
Newman was busy setting up the Catholic University,
it seems unlikely that he made any revisions at this
time; there are no references to his doing so in the
Letters of this period.

There were no further printings until the Fourth
Edition which appeared in 1872 as part of the uniform
edition of all his works which Newman was now
producing. For this he revised the whole text; the
Fifth and Sixth Editions which appeared in 1880 and
1889 made only a very few further changes, all of
them minor. As the Appendix of Textual Variants
indicates, Newman's revision of the text was a
detailed one. By the Sixth Edition, 306 of the
Lectures' 416 pages contain amendments. This
demonstrates with what minute care Newman under-
took this task and suggests how much he still valued
the Lectures years after their composition. If they had
indeed been the work of an over-zealous convert who
was later embarrassed by them, one would expect any
revision to be in the direction of toning down or soft-
ening their force, but this is not the case. Almost none

of the amendments is significant as far as the argument
is concerned; they are purely stylistic. Sentences or
phrases have their word order changed, or occasionally he finds that he has been inconsistent in his use of
tense or number and corrects accordingly. This feels
like a text which was written in a hurry now being
made smoother at leisure. Even in the First Edition he
had inserted an Erratum to correct what he termed 'an
error of composition' by which he had accidentally
said the opposite of what he intended, using 'deny'
when the sentence required 'assert' (see p. 135).

About a quarter of his changes consist of additions,
a word or phrase being inserted with a clarifying or
formalising effect; he has a tendency to intensify by
the addition of a word such as 'even'. Where he
changes words rather than adding them, there is also a
slight tendency towards more formal vocabulary, e.g.
'led' becomes 'induced' (p. 53), 'still he simply relies'
becomes 'notwithstanding, he is content to rely'
(p. 99), 'in many places at once' becomes 'ubiquitous'
(p. 131), 'go among' becomes 'hold friendly intercourse with' (p. 342), 'evidence' becomes 'antecedent
proof' (p. 354, showing the influence of the *Grammar
of Assent,* perhaps). Such alterations do not amount to
a wholesale stylistic change, but they do make the
tone of the lectures slightly less immediate and more
considered. He cuts out a number of his more colloquial touches, in a way one might regret, such as the
reference to 'the boy in the story, who went and told
of his playmate, who was before him in stealing the
gooseberry pie' (p.193), 'to use a vulgar but expressive
proverb, that what is sauce for the goose is sauce for
the gander' (p.220) and 'the Englishman in Sicily,

who, when he could not get his mules by the appliance of all the Italian he could command, fair or rough, at last effected his purpose by shouting out at the pitch of his voice to his host, who had never heard a word of English in his life, "Northumberland, Cumberland, Westmoreland, and Durham."' (p. 331)

In a number of cases, his changes sharpen the argument up. For instance, he twice introduces the word 'infallible' to describe, ironically, the Protestant position (p. 76 and p. 109), perhaps in the light of the controversies following the 1870 definition of Papal Infallibility. Lecture VIII is the most heavily amended, especially the sections on Indulgences where Newman seems at pains to make his expression as precise as possible in an area which Protestants saw as vulnerable to attack. He introduces a particularly effective addition when illustrating the need to understand theological language—in this case about indulgences—in its correct context: 'So again, innkeepers paint up, "Entertainment for man and horse;" they do not add the important words, "to those who can pay for it." Every other private house in our streets has "Ring the bell" upon its door; that is, "if you have business within"' (p. 346). He had thought of this parallel with indulgences as early as October 1851 when he gave it in a letter to the wife of his friend William Froude who claimed to have seen at Marseilles lists of indulgences without any conditions attached. Lecture IV also has a large number of amendments in the section dealing with Blanco White, reflecting the controversies this had sparked off in newspapers on the subject of the number of 'infidel' priests in Spain and the complex question of intention and the validity of sacraments celebrated by an unbelieving priest. These amendments are slightly defensive in tone, as is another amendment in Lecture VI where he is clearly reacting to criticism: '... I cannot help it if, in exposing the prejudice of my countrymen, I incur the imputation of using satire against them; I do wish to do so' (p. 236).

From the Fourth Edition onwards each Lecture was also divided into numbered sections. Such divisions would, of course, have been irrelevant to the original listeners, and they give the work a treatise-like appearance which is perhaps inappropriate to the Lectures' original form. The 'libellous' passage naturally had to remain omitted from all editions printed after the court case (and continued to be omitted even in editions published after both Newman and Achilli had died). Interestingly, just before he died, Newman authorised the Catholic Truth Society to publish an edition omitting Lecture V, and this version duly appeared as *Eight Lectures on the Present Position of Catholics in England* in 1890. It is unclear why he requested the omission. One is tempted to speculate that this was a misunderstanding about not printing the Achilli passage. There certainly does not seem to be a case for regarding this version as representing a revision of the text on Newman's part. When his own publishers reprinted further editions after his death they continued to reproduce the 1889 Sixth Edition's complete text. This text, Newman's final version, is the edition reproduced here.

III. THE SATIRE

John Bull, the Protestant Englishman

In his Preface, Newman reminds his readers that these Lectures were given to the 'Brothers of the Oratory', an association of laymen attached to the Birmingham Oratory, and that the Lectures' purpose was to suggest to them 'how best to master their own position and to perform their duties in a Protestant country.' And in the first Lecture he explains that his subject is

> to inquire why it is, that, in this intelligent nation, and in this rational nineteenth century, we Catholics are so despised and hated by our own countrymen (p. 1)

So ostensibly these lectures are a sort of training for the Brothers which will take the form of an inquiry into the reasons for Protestant anti-Catholic prejudice. Throughout he does indeed address his audience as 'Brothers', and in the final Lecture he gives his advice about how they should conduct themselves.

But Newman was well aware that he had another audience: the Protestant world outside. He was, after all, a nationally known figure, the most famous of the Oxford Movement converts, and he knew that anything he said in the present excited conditions would be reported and reacted to by the Protestant world. This indirect approach by Newman to his real audience has been analysed by Carl Frandsen in his unpublished thesis on the rhetoric of these

lectures.[24] He argues that it was a well thought out
rhetorical strategy: by making a seemingly dispassionate historical analysis into the origins of anti-Catholic
prejudice, Newman could end by destroying the prejudice of the unsuspecting Protestant reader through
the very act of analysing it. Frandsen compares
Newman's strategy here to Pope's in the *Epistle to Dr.
Arbuthnot* where there is the same pose of an injured
innocent speaking to a friendly audience. Newman's
stance of a Catholic speaking to Catholics forces the
Protestant reader into the role of a bystander who is
listening in on the demolition of the absurdities of his
own Protestant bigotry. It is important to remember
that there were some Protestants actually in
Newman's audience in the Corn Exchange, as he
makes us aware at the very end of the Lectures when
he 'thank[s] those also, who, though not of our
communion, have honoured me with their attendance' (p. 402). He goes on to ask them to 'think over
what I have said even if they have not been altogether
pleased with my manner of saying it'. On the face of
it, this looks like an apology for either his lack of skill
or for being too satirical (for which his more hostile
readers did criticise him). However, more impor-
tantly, it implies that there can be no objection to the
matter of his arguments, only their manner. He knows
that any open-minded non-Catholic listeners will
actually have enjoyed his satire and will be sympathetic to 'one who has spoken boldly on an unpopular
subject in a difficult time' (p. 403).

[24] Frandsen, Carl F., *A Rhetorical Analysis of John Henry Newman's*
Lectures on the Present Position of Catholics in England, Diss., The
City University of New York, Ph.D., 1975.

Newman's strategy is all the more effective because of his use of humour which is directed at vividly realised examples of prejudiced people. Throughout the Lectures ideas or viewpoints (mostly, but not only, those of prejudice) are put into the mouths of characters whom Newman presents with great vividness. The most entertaining of these is the Russian Count in Lecture I who is a brilliant caricature of a speaker at a 'No Popery' meeting (pp. 25–41). The Notes in this edition trace the various features of an anti-Catholic speaker which Newman has given him; and modern readers can appreciate the humour better, the more we realise just how close the Count's absurdities are to the arguments used by anti-Catholic polemicists. Newman has caught their techniques perfectly—their jumbling of fact and fiction, their frantic misunderstandings of the language of Catholic theology—and makes wicked fun of them. This passage surely deserves to be in any anthology of satirical writing.

However, the episode, superbly sustained as it is, is not really typical of the rest of the book, since it works by analogy—the Count is not a realistic Russian as such. The characteristic figure in the Lectures is one who is not only realistic but very recognisable: he is the Protestant Englishman in the domestic setting of Victorian anti-Catholicism. As such, he is the unifying figure of these Lectures and gives them their satirical life. He first appears in Lecture II. He is 'John Bull' (p. 45) whose old furniture has all been replaced in the new nineteenth century except for his 'old family picture of the Man and the Lion'—his view of Catholicism. Newman makes him recognisable as a middle class English gentleman in the references to his upbringing which has provided him with his opinions 'in the nursery, in the school-room, in the lecture-class, from the pulpit, in the newspaper, in society'. He has the tone of the bluff, complacent Englishman who knows that Catholics are rogues because

> "I recollect, what a noise, when I was young, the Catholic Relief Bill made: because my father and the old clergyman said so, and Lord Eldon, and George the Third; and there was Mr. Pitt obliged to give up office, and Lord George Gordon, long before that, made a riot, and the Catholic Chapels were burned down all over the country." (p. 45)

A whole world is briefly evoked here in the mixture of home life and events read of in newspapers. The repeated use of "and" catches the tone of someone listing things which he associates in his mind, and the very heterogeneity of the items thus yoked together gives a slightly naïve quality to the sentence, whose length and simple structure are childlike. The tone of slightly defensive bluster is thus caught, with the Englishman sounding already just a little ridiculous.

The technique is intensified a few pages later. Newman again has the man speaking so that we hear his typical tone. The speaker is given a series of statements, each one longer and more defensive than the last, as if he is becoming more and more heated in an argument. Asked why he believes that Catholicism is so odious,

> he would say something of this sort: "I am *sure* it is;" he will look significant, and say, "You will find

it a hard job to make me think otherwise;" or he will look wise, and say, "I can make a pretty good guess how things go on among you;" or he will be angry, and cry out, "Those fellows, the priests, I would not believe them, though they swore themselves black in the face;" or he will speak loudly, and overbear and drown all remonstrance: "It is too notorious for proof; every one knows it; every book says it; it has been so ruled long ago. It is rather too much in the nineteenth century to be told to begin history again, and to have to reverse our elementary facts." (pp. 49–50)

The techniques being used here are those of the novelist. The man's facial expressions are conveyed with highly effective economy: 'look significant', 'look wise'—we get an impression of smugness. The colloquialisms express the same thing, while also making us feel the speaker's rising exasperation: "'pretty good guess ... Those fellows ... too notorious ... rather too much'". And there is the complacency of "'in the nineteenth century'"—a phrase which Newman nearly always uses with some degree of irony.

Of course the whole passage is ironic, for everything which the speaker says exemplifies the very problem which Newman is addressing in these lectures: Protestant prejudice. The speaker has no first-hand evidence and yet he is, at the outset, "'*sure*'". On the basis of his ignorance the speaker can make "'a pretty good guess'" about Catholic practices—but in the Lectures we are going to see just how wildly wrong such Protestant guesses are. The fact that '"every book says it"' is part of the evidence of the Protestant propaganda which Newman is going to reveal as having formed English culture since the Reformation. And the speaker's reaction to the idea of having '"to reverse our elementary facts"' reveals him as ridiculously hidebound. The man's outrage makes him a comic figure, especially as he has to 'speak loudly, and overbear and drown all remonstrance'. There is the suggestion that all this bluster perhaps conceals unease, that he protests too much. The whole passage also gains in comic effect by our hearing only one side of what is evidently a dialogue. The very silence of the other, Catholic, participant in this dialogue gives the effect of his being the calm, quiet one, patiently pursuing his questions while the Protestant becomes more and more cross. This technique isolates the character both from the narrator and from us the readers: we observe his performance with a detached amusement. In this way, Newman makes his Protestant gentleman seem a rather ridiculous figure whom we observe as a specimen of his type. His protestations are presented to us as an interesting, and entertaining, performance but certainly not serious arguments with which we have to engage.

It is not necessary for direct dialogue to be used to achieve these effects. When we next meet the Protestant gentleman a little later in Lecture II (pp. 78–80), he has been presented with a Catholic denial of the Protestant allegations of corruption. Newman starts by describing the man's reaction:

> he will laugh in your face at your simplicity, or lift up hands and eyes at your unparalleled effrontery.

But this soon changes into indirect speech which becomes increasingly colloquial and vivid:

> To tell him at his time of life, that Catholics do not rate sin at a fixed price, that they may not get absolution for a sin in prospect, ... that Catholics would not burn Protestants if they could! Why, all this is as perfectly clear to him, as the sun at noonday; he is ready to leave the matter to the first person he happens to meet; every one will tell us just the same; only let us try; he never knew there was any doubt at all about it: he *is* surprised, he thought we granted it. When he was young, he has heard it said again and again; to his certain knowledge it has uniformly been said the last forty, fifty, sixty years, and no one has ever denied it; it is so in all the books he ever looked into; what is the world coming to? What is true, if this is not? So Catholics are to be whitewashed! What next?

The characteristic phrases of the complacent gentleman—'to tell him at his time of life', 'as perfectly clear ... as the sun at noonday', 'only let us try', 'forty, fifty, sixty years' and the inevitable 'what is the world coming to?'—are the familiar tones of Letters to the Editor and speeches by backbench M.P.s. It is with this distinctive voice in our ears that we go on to read the quotations from real life anti-Catholic writings which Newman now gives (pp. 79–80). The verbatim quotations are footnoted by Newman to their real-life sources so that we know he is not exaggerating the kind of accusations that Protestants make. But the quotations appear comic because we are hearing them

in the ridiculous tone of voice which Newman has
given to the imaginary Protestant speaker. What were
intended by their authors as serious anti-Catholic allegations, now appear as absurd. Newman is making
brilliant use of the technique of ironic impersonation,
with a script partly of his own creating and partly
drawn from documentary sources.

Prejudice and fables
He does the same thing when he recounts the incidents surrounding the building of the Oratory house
at Edgbaston. He is demonstrating how Protestant
fables about Catholic behaviour lead otherwise sensible people into absurdity. In a much quoted passage
Newman describes how Protestant onlookers become
suspicious of the cellars being constructed for the
house:

> They go round the building, they peep into the
> underground brickwork, and are curious about the
> drains; they moralize about Popery and its spread;
> at length they trespass upon the inclosure, they dive
> into the half-finished shell, and they take their fill
> of seeing what is to be seen, and imagining what is
> not. (pp. 119–120)

Already here the snoopers seem slightly ridiculous:
'curious about the drains', 'take their fill', 'imagining
what is not'. Newman's tone as narrator is detached
and amused. Soon this moves into indirect speech,
and we hear the snoopers' muttered suspicions
growing:

Doubtless, there was much in the very idea of an Oratory perplexing to the Protestant intellect, and inconsistent with Protestant notions of comfort and utility. Why should so large a room be here? why so small a room there? why a passage so long and wide? and why so long a wall without a window?

The questions catch the tone of the person who is rather pleased with himself for having spotted what he is sure is a significant detail, like an amateur detective who is convinced he has found a clue.

Newman mixes narrative and indirect speech as the passage moves to its comic climax:

There was much to suggest matter of suspicion, and to predispose the trespasser to doubt whether he had yet got to the bottom of the subject. At length one question flashed upon his mind: what can such a house have to do with cellars? cellars and monks, what can be their mutual relation? monks—to what possible use can they put pits—and holes, and corners, and outhouses, and sheds? A sensation was created; it brought other visitors; it spread; it became an impression, a belief; the truth lay bare; a tradition was born; a fact was elicited which henceforth had many witnesses. *Those cellars were cells.* How obvious when once stated! and every one who entered the building, every one who passed by, became, I say, in some sort, ocular vouchers for what had often been read of in books, but for many generations had happily been unknown to England, for the incarcerations, the torturings, the starvings, the immurings, the murderings proper to a monastic establishment. (pp. 120–121)

The comedy is generated by the continual juxtaposition of Newman's detached narrative tone and the increasingly fevered colloquialism of the visitors. Thus 'the trespasser' (an economical reminder by Newman that the snoopers were actually intruding on private property) is 'predisposed ... to doubt', and then suddenly a question 'flashed upon his mind'. We hear the intruder's thoughts leaping ahead: 'what can ...? ...what can ...? ... to what possible ...?' The effect here is almost that of stream of consciousness. And then the illogic and speed of the false deduction is mirrored in the spread of the news: 'A sensation ... an impression, a belief; the truth ...; a tradition ...; a fact ... *Those cellars were cells.*' The narrated events and the reported news merge here as the ironic climax is reached: 'How obvious when once stated!' This climactic sentence functions both as the words of the onlookers and as Newman's authorial ironic comment on how false assumptions lead to completely false 'obvious' conclusions. The long sentence which concludes the passage similarly moves between Newman's voice and the voices of the Protestant onlookers. We hear Newman's ironic description of them as 'ocular vouchers' which gives them pompously exaggerated seriousness; and then we hear the excited Protestant chatter of 'often been read of in books, but for many generations happily been unknown in England'. This is followed by a list of horrors which could come from a Protestant preacher's rhetoric; 'incarcerations ... torturings ... starvings ... immurings ... murderings' which are then comically undercut by Newman's ironical use of 'proper to' a monastic establishment— as if he is accepting that this is all just as it should be! In this one sentence, then, Newman is able to move in and out of the voices he has created in the foregoing scenes. The whole passage is a dramatisation of great comic effectiveness.

In this case, of course, Newman was making use of the real incident in which the M.P. for Warwickshire, Mr. R. Spooner, made a speech in the House of Commons about the Edgbaston 'cells'. Newman now goes on to quote the speech, and Spooner's language shows that Newman's Protestant 'voices' are no exaggeration. He is helped, incidentally, by the way that reports of parliamentary debates were always couched in indirect speech:

"It was not usual for a coroner to hold an *inquest*, unless where a rumour had got abroad that there was a *necessity* for one; and how was a rumour to come *from the underground cells of the convents*? Yes, he repeated, underground cells: and he would tell them something about such places. At this moment, in the parish of Edgbaston, within the borough of Birmingham, there was a large convent, of some kind or other, being erected, and the whole of the underground was fitted up with cells; *and what were those cells for*?" (pp. 121–2)

Newman goes on to dissect the full absurdity of the accusation, particularly making fun of the fact that the alleged Catholic murderers are people such as himself, English gentlemen of exactly the same background as their accusers and indeed personally known to them, and yet they are now cast in the role of torturers because of the anti-Catholic fables of the Protestant Tradition.

Prejudice and converts

As the Lectures progress, the voice of the outraged Protestant speaker has a cumulative effect, because each time we meet the speaker we recognise his tones and anticipate the fool he is going to make of himself. In Lecture V he appears in a family setting, as the Protestant father dissuading his son who is on the point of becoming a Catholic (p. 185). The father begins affectionately:

> "My dear John or James," the father says, calling him by his Christian name, "you know how tenderly I love you, and how indulgent I have ever been to you. I have given you the best of educations and I have been proud of you."

There is a hint of self-satisfaction, and even more of emotional blackmail in this parental remonstrance. The father appears to recognise that the son has exercised his right of private judgement in converting to Catholicism, but then he says that he himself has

> "sacred duties, which are the unavoidable result of your conduct. I have duties to your brothers and sisters;—never see my face again; my door is closed to you. It wounds me to come to this decision, but what can I do?"

After the conventional beginning, the sudden "never see my face again" comes as a shock, and in the completely different religious atmosphere of today we may find this passage incredible; but Newman says that such parental reactions are so uniform that he has hesitated to describe it in case he appears to be being personal. This is a slightly disingenuous remark since he is nevertheless using it, but this is part of his rhetorical strategy, in this case to embarrass the Protestant reader who sees his fellows (or even himself) cast in a cruel light.

In a further passage (pp. 186–7), we hear the outraged parent venting his anger at what has happened. Newman perceptively identifies the reason for the animus that lies behind such anger:

> Nature pleads; and therefore, to fortify the mind, the various reasons for such severity must be distinctly passed before it, and impressed upon it, and passion must be roused to overcome affection.

The diatribe that follows, for all the seriousness of the situation, has a certain comedy:

> "Such a base, grovelling, demoralizing religion, unworthy of a man of sense, unworthy of a man! I could have borne his turning Drummondite, Plymouth-Brother, or Mormonite. He might almost have joined the Agapemone."

The list gets increasingly exotic, particularly with the Mormonites' and the Agapemone's reputations for polygamy and promiscuity (see the Notes). The father actually prefers religions of apparent sexual licence to Catholicism (perhaps because of the celibacy of the Catholic clergy, a constant source of suspicion to the contemporary Protestant mind; it may be hinted at also in 'unworthy of a man'). But the father continues:

> "I would rather see him an unbeliever; yes, I say it deliberately, Popery is worse than Paganism. I had rather see him dead. I could have borne to see him in his coffin. I cannot see him the slave of a priest."

The rising extremism of his comments is expressed through the rapidity with which he moves from "'an unbeliever'" to "'dead'". The father drives the point home to himself with the morbid detail of "'see him in his coffin'". Newman has caught the extreme language which hurt anger produces.

After this climax, Newman allows himself more humour in the second half of the passage where there are variants given to suit whatever the Catholic son has said or not said, done or not done:

> "And then the way in which he took the step: he never let me know, and had been received before I had had a hint about it;" or, "he told me what he meant to do, and then did it in spite of me;" or, "he was so weak and silly," or "so headstrong," or "so long and obstinately set upon it." "He had nothing to say for himself," or "he was always arguing." "He was inveigled into it by others,' or "he ought to have consulted others, he had no right to have an opinion. Any how he is preferring strangers to his true friends; he has shown an utter disregard of

the feelings of his parents and relations; he has been
ungrateful to his father."

The comedy here comes from the mutually contradictory responses. Each of the criticisms sounds
plausible until it is put against its opposite, so that the
reader realises that whatever the son had done, his
father would have found it wrong. Newman's juxtaposition of these different criticisms makes us realise
that none of them is the real cause of the father's
anger. They are really all just rationalisations of his
antipathy towards Catholicism. In this respect, the
passage is a psychological exploration of a parent of a
kind we are more used to finding in a novel. Newman
had already shown such an ability in his own novel
Loss and Gain, published in 1848. Readers might like
to compare the above with the equivalent passage in
the novel when the hero, Charles Reding, makes his
final visit to his mother before leaving home to
become a Catholic.[25] The writing has a different
emotional colouring because it is a mother rather than
a father speaking, but the arguments are similar.
Newman was continuing to use his novelistic skills in
the *Present Position* Lectures.

The Prejudiced Man

The most sustained depiction of the Protestant gentleman occurs in the Prejudiced Man sections of Lecture
VI (p. 236ff.). Newman invents this title himself to
'personify that ungenerous spirit which energizes and
operates so widely and so unweariedly in the

---

[25] *Loss and Gain: the Story of a Convert* (1876 edn.), pp. 345-347.

Protestant community'. Newman's technique is again the depiction of his characteristic 'voice' through indirect speech. There is also the same process, though drawn out longer, of the man gradually becoming more and more extreme as he reacts to Catholicism. First, he hears an allegation against Catholics:

> he knew all about it beforehand; it is just what he has always said; it is the old tale over again a hundred times.

Then the allegation is refuted by Catholics on unimpeachable authority. First the Prejudiced Man simply ignores this, or if he cannot:

> he draws himself up, looks sternly at the objector, and then says the very same thing as before, only with a louder voice and more confident manner. He becomes more intensely and enthusiastically positive by way of making up for the interruption, of braving the confutation, and of showing the world that nothing whatever in the universe will ever make him think one hair-breadth more favourably of Popery than he does think, than he has ever thought, and than his family ever thought before him, since the time of the fine old English gentleman.

The scene has become dramatised, with Newman moving in and out of the man's own words. Thus 'one hairbreadth' and 'his family ... before him' are the man speaking, while the last phrase is Newman placing him in the long English tradition of Protestant prejudice. When next he is asked if he has ever met any Catholics,

> he blesses himself that he knows nothing of them at all, and he never will; nay, if they fall in his way, he will take himself out of it; and if unawares he shall ever be pleased with a Catholic without knowing who it is, he wishes by anticipation to retract such feeling of pleasure.

This shows Newman's characteristic technique, the man's protestations becoming more complex, less likely—one might even say, by the last one, more paranoid. And again, 'blesses himself' and 'nay' have the colloquial ring, while 'by anticipation to retract such feeling of pleasure' is Newman's deliberately wordy re-statement, which makes the man's angry bigotry seem ludicrous by dressing it up in portentous language.

And when finally the anti-Catholic allegation has actually been acknowledged by everyone as having no evidence for it at all,

> this only makes him the more violent. For it *ought*, he thinks to be true, and it is mere special pleading to lay much stress on its not having all the evidence which it might have; for if it be not true, yet half a hundred like stories are.

What is effective here is the psychological accuracy of the depiction: the man, absurdly, thinks that an untruth 'ought' to be true. He won't admit that there is no evidence for its being true but only of its 'not having all the evidence it might have'. This is the way people re-interpret unpalatable facts to accord with their prejudices.

We get a further fully realised presentation of the Prejudiced Man 'in a specially candid humour' when some one explains, at length and in detail, some major misconception he has about Catholicism:

> He is silent for a moment, then he begins with a sentiment. "What clever fellows these Catholics are!" he says, "I defy you to catch them tripping; they have a way out of every thing. I thought we had you, but I own I am fairly beaten. This is how the Jesuits got on; always educated, subtle, well up in their books; a Protestant has no chance with them." (p. 241)

The man's initial silent pause is a deliberate piece of comic timing by Newman. We wonder how the man is going to react, so that it is all the more infuriating when we realise that no impression has been made on his prejudice at all. Comedy also comes from the way that he sounds so pleased with himself on his change of tactics. This is impenetrable smugness raised to an art form. Newman turns the knife by saying that this 'is the Prejudiced Man at best advantage' and goes on to give his more 'grave and suspicious' response:

> "I confess," he will say "I do *not* like these very complete explanations; they are too like a made up case. ... I always suspect something behind, when everything is so very easy and clear." (p. 242)

The tone reinforces the impression of the personality. The stress on "*not*" and the use of "'I always ...'" give the air of someone who is pleased with his acuteness.

This presentation of the Prejudiced Man culminates in the longest section so far in which we are taken through his changing reactions to news of converts to Catholicism (pp. 243-5). Newman numbers each stage which gives the impression that this is a standard procedure, and the brisk way he runs through them gives us the picture of the speaker falling back each time on a fresh justification of his own position, like a forced withdrawal. Much of the humour comes from the very definite way the Prejudiced Man announces his explanation at each stage; once again, indirect speech is used. The tone of each comment varies. Sometimes it is snobbishly dismissive:

> They are lack-a-daisical women, or conceited young parsons, or silly squires, or the very dregs of our large towns, who have nothing to lose, and no means of knowing one thing from another.

Sometimes it is peremptory:

> if they had clerical charges in the Protestant Church, they ought to have flung them up at once, even at the risk of afterwards finding they had made a commotion for nothing.

Or contradictory of the previous argument:

> on the other hand, what, forsooth, must these men

do when a doubt came on their minds, but at once abandon all their clerical duty and go home.

Or blustering:

as for him, it does not affect him at all; he means to die just where he is; indeed, these conversions are a positive argument in favour of Protestantism: he thinks still worse of Popery in consequence of these men going over, than he did before.

And lastly, sanctimonious:

the Prejudiced Man spreads the news about [*of a convert's reported loss of faith*] right and left in a tone of great concern and distress; he considers it very awful.

Newman runs through these differing tones in what becomes a kind of dramatic monologue, albeit one interrupted by his own authorial comments. To read these sections aloud requires frequent change of expression, the voice in quick succession hectoring, scoffing, lugubrious. Newman's public delivery of such passages must have required considerable skill.

There are earlier versions of some of this in *Loss and Gain*. Here is how the Protestant Sheffield reacts to Charles Reding telling him that their friend Willis has become a Catholic:

"Poor Willis!" [Charles] added; "one must respect a man who acts according to his conscience."

"What can he know of conscience?" said

Sheffield; "the idea of his swallowing, of his own free will, the heap of rubbish which every Catholic has to believe! in cold blood tying a collar round his neck, and politely putting the chain into the hands of a priest! ... And then the Confessional! 'Tis marvellous!" and he began to break the coals with the poker. "It's very well," he continued, "if a man is born a Catholic; I don't suppose they really believe what they are obliged to profess; but how an Englishman, a gentleman, a man here at Oxford, with all his advantages, can so eat dirt, scraping and picking up all the dead lies of the dark ages—it's a miracle!"[26]

This has all the characteristics of the Prejudiced Man: the dismissal of "'conscience'"; the recourse to standard Protestant rhetoric, "'... collar round his neck ... chain into the hands of a priest'"; and the snobbery, "'an Englishman, a gentleman, a man here at Oxford'". Later in the novel, the pompous clergyman Mr. Vincent claims that Willis after his conversion was disgusted by what he saw of Catholicism on the Continent:

"Well, Willis saw all this; and I have it on good authority," he said mysteriously, "that he is thoroughly disgusted with the whole affair, and is coming back to us."

"Is he in England now?" asked Reding.

"He is said to be with his mother in Devonshire, who, perhaps you know, is a widow; and he has

[26] Ibid., pp. 117-8.

been too much for her. Poor silly fellow, who would not take the advice of older heads! A friend of mine once sent him to me; I could make nothing of him. I couldn't understand his arguments, nor he mine. It was no good; he would make trial himself, and he has caught it."[27]

The rumour of Willis's return to Anglicanism turns out to be completely untrue. Vincent's confident assertion of it and his dismissive attitude towards the 'poor, silly fellow' make him another early version of the Prejudiced Man. The connection can be further seen in the account Vincent has just given of 'abroad':

"... there you see the Church of Rome as it really is. I have been abroad, and should know it. Such heaps of beggars in the streets of Rome and Naples; so much squalidness and misery; no cleanliness; an utter want of comfort; and such superstition; and such an absence of all true and evangelical serious-ness. They push and fight while Mass is going on; they jabber their prayers at railroad speed; they worship the Virgin as a goddess; and they see mira-cles at the corner of every street. Their images are awful, and their ignorance prodigious."[28]

In the *Present Position* Newman depicts the Prejudiced Man as a youth travelling in Catholic countries, ascribing anything he disapproves of to the malign

[27] Ibid., p. 176.
[28] Ibid.

influence of Catholicism and completely misunderstanding what he sees in churches and ceremonies because of his Protestant preconceptions. It could be *Loss and Gain*'s Mr.Vincent in his youth. The young tourist

> gets up at an English hour, has his breakfast at his leisure, and then saunters into some of the churches of the place. ... He walks about and looks at the monuments, what is this? the figure of a woman: who can it be? His Protestant cicerone at his elbow ... whispers that it is Pope Joan, and he notes it down in his pocket-book accordingly. (p. 250)

Here Newman is playing something of a trick: we have been assuming that this is another of his fictional characters, but the account turns out to be a real life one about someone Newman knew: a 'most excellent person, for whom I had and have a great esteem' who 'was positive he had seen Pope Joan in Rome'. Since in this case satirical fiction has turned out to be true, we wonder whether all the earlier satirical incidents might not also have their counterpart in reality.

Similarly, a few pages later on Newman gives a sketch of the Prejudiced Man who enters a Catholic chapel and looks with 'wonder, expectation, and disgust' at everything he sees (p. 253ff.). This too is going to turn out to be a real incident which he proceeds to quote at length, thus demonstrating that 'the plain truth is the keenest of satires'. This real-life figure was the 'Protestant Scripture Reader' who had observed the service of Benediction of the Blessed Sacrament at the Oratory Fathers' chapel in London and then published an account of his visit in the journal of the British Reformation Society in February 1850. It is the perfect illustration of the Protestant who is sure that

> He knows, and has known from a child, that Popery is a system of imposture, nay, such brazen imposture, that it is a marvel, or rather a miracle, that anyone can be caught by it.

Newman takes us through the man's account in some detail, and the full extent of his misunderstandings is gradually unfolded. The humour comes from the way that the man is trying to describe something that he does not understand and as a result makes a fool of himself. As he watches the blessing being given with the monstrance which contains the Blessed Sacrament (the whole of which he thinks is a "'star'" which the congregation are worshipping), he hears a bell rung (in fact rung by an altar server whom he doesn't notice) and immediately concludes that the whole thing is a fake miracle, worked by the priest to trick the congregation:

> "As Gordon [*the priest*] raised the Star, with his back turned to all the lighted candles on the altar, he clearly showed the Popish deceit; for in the candle-stick [*actually the monstrance*] there is a bell, that rung three times of its own accord, to deceive the blind fools more; and the light through the shawl [*part of the priest's vestments*] showed so many colours, as Father Gordon moved his body; the bell ringing they could not see, for the candlestick was covered

with part of this magic shawl, and Gordon's finger at work underneath."

The language is standard anti-Catholic rhetoric: "'Popish deceit'", "'the blind fools'", "'magic'". He ends up proclaiming confidently:

"I should be glad to see this published, that I might take it to Father Gordon, to see if he could contradict a word of it."

The irony of this could not been have been bettered by anything Newman could have invented for his fictional versions of the Prejudiced Man. We can see why Newman positioned this where he did. After the picture of the Prejudiced Man which has been built up in the preceding pages, this real-life example comes as the comic highlight of the Lecture. We may note that the extensive quotations from the Scripture Reader's own words gave Newman a chance for us to hear this 'voice' in all its absurdity. Reading them out must almost have been like doing a comic turn at a Victorian party.

Prejudice and First Principles
After presenting the Prejudiced Man in his most extreme form, it is significant that Newman's next version of the Protestant gentleman, in Lecture VII, is a more moderate, almost sympathetic, version. We now meet someone who tries not to be prejudiced, who wishes to think well of all men, including Catholics, and who decides to look dispassionately at Catholic books. This is a classic case of Newman's

indirect speaking to his real audience, for the sympathetic Protestant here is typical of one of his former Oxford Movement associates such as J.R. Bloxham, Manuel Johnson or perhaps even Pusey. Indeed, in his *Eirenicon* Pusey was later to do something like this gentleman now does: examine Catholic books of devotion in an attempt to find common ground but then criticise them for what he saw as their excesses. The sympathetic Protestant is offended by what he reads; and even after a second attempt, says Newman, such people sadly conclude:

> No: it is impossible; it is melancholy to say it, but it is no use disguising the truth from themselves; they cannot get over this or that doctrine or practice.... They are disappointed, but they never can believe, they never can even approve.(p. 272)

Newman does not follow this passage with an immediate explanation of why such Protestants are so disgusted by Catholic ideas, and we might wonder what Newman is up to here. It indeed marks a subtle strategic shift in the Lectures.

Hitherto Newman has been trying to embarrass such an intelligent Protestant by showing him the ignorance and bigotry which lies behind the 'No Popery' mindset. Hence his lengthy treatment of the Maria Monk story (pp. 161–174). He is deliberately shocking his more intelligent Protestant readership by showing them what depths anti-Catholic prejudice leads to. But of course the 'dispassionate thinker' will be sure that *he* has no such prejudices, and indeed he genuinely wanted to be fair to

Catholicism; and now Newman appears to be sympathetic to this disappointed enquirer. The satire is suspended, but this is only to allow Newman to introduce a far more comprehensive account of the origins of Protestant prejudice and to make a more direct challenge to such disappointed enquirers to re-think their experiences.

Newman starts with a lengthy account of how all our judgements are based on our antecedent reasoning which produces our First Principles. This subject fascinated Newman all his life, finally being fully explored in his *Essay in Aid of a Grammar of Assent* (1870). He saw it as a key to understanding what brings people to belief or keeps them from it. In his discussion here he is simultaneously instructing his Catholic audience about the psychology of Protestantism for them to use in their own apologet-ics and explaining to such of his indirect Protestant audience as are willing to listen exactly why they find Catholicism so distasteful. What he demonstrates is that 'so candid a man' is making the mistake of using his own first principles to judge Catholicism:

> He is a theorist, using his theory against our prac-tice, as if our practice might not have its own theory also. (p. 291)

And so even the man who thinks he is being dispas-sionate in fact 'runs into bigotry':

> Not even the intellectual, not even the candid-minded among them [Protestants], are free from inconsistency here. They begin by setting up prin-

ciples of thought and action for themselves; then,
not content with applying them to their own
thoughts and actions, they make them the rule for
criticizing and condemning our thoughts and
actions too: this, I repeat, is Bigotry, Bigotry is the
infliction of our own unproved First Principles on
others, and the treating others with scorn or hatred
for not accepting them. (p. 292)

A few pages later he is thus able to quote examples of
Protestant criticism of Catholic practices and show
that they depend on first principles which Catholics
do not accept:

It is not enough to look into our churches, and cry
"It is all a form, *because* divine favour cannot
depend on external observances;" or, "It is all a
bondage, *because* there is no such thing as sin;" or "a
blasphemy, *because* the Supreme Being cannot be
present in ceremonies;" ... I say here is endless
assumption, unmitigated hypothesis, reckless assertion: prove your, "because," "because," "because."
prove your First Principles, and if you cannot, learn
philosophic moderation. (p. 294)

The insular Englishman

Newman is aware this has been rather a 'dry' subject
matter and so he now translates this 'dispassionate
thinker' who has turned out to be a bigot into a
secular equivalent—and the satire comes back with a
vengeance:

What is all this but the very state of mind which we

ridicule, and call narrowness, in the case of those who have never travelled? We call them, and rightly, men of contracted ideas, who cannot fancy things going on differently from what they have themselves witnessed at home, and laugh at everything because it is strange. They themselves are the pattern-men; their height, their dress, their manners, their food, their language, are all founded in the nature of things; and every thing else is good or bad, just in that very degree in which it partakes, or does not partake, of them. All men ought to get up at half-past eight, breakfast between nine and ten, read the newspapers, lunch, take a ride or drive, dine. Here is the great principle of the day— dine; no one is a man who does not dine; yes, dine, and at the right hour; and it must *be* a dinner, with a certain time after dinner, and then in due time to bed. Tea and toast, port wine, roast beef; mince-pies at Christmas, lamb at Easter, goose at Michaelmas, these are their great principles. They suspect any one who does otherwise. Figs and macaroni for the day's fare, or Burgundy and grapes for breakfast!—they are aghast at the atrocity of the notion. (pp. 295-6)

As Ian Ker has said,[29] Newman is here identifying the English Protestant religious narrowness as only one aspect of an aggressive, insular culture. Ker sees this passage as a remarkable anticipation of Dickens's satirical portrait of the insular Mr. Podsnap in *Our Mutual Friend* (1865). The similarities are indeed close:

[29] Ker, I., *The Achievement of John Henry Newman,* (London, 1990), p. 177

Mr. Podsnap's world was not a very large world, morally; no, nor even geographically: ... he considered other countries ... a mistake, and of their manners and customs would conclusively observe, 'Not English!' when, PRESTO! with a flourish of the arm, and a flush of the face, they were swept away. Elsewise, the world got up at eight, shaved close at a quarter past, breakfasted at nine, went to the City at ten, came home at half-past five, and dined at seven. ... Nothing else To Be—anywhere![30]

There are further parallels with Podsnap. Newman follows the 'pattern-men' passage with the comment:

Here was a man of one idea; there are many men of one idea in the world; ... Such again are those benevolent persons who, with right intentions, but yet, I think, narrow views, wish to introduce the British constitution and British ideas into every nation and tribe upon earth; differing how much! from the wise man in the Greek epic, whose characteristic was that he was "versatile," for he had known "the cities and the *mind* of many men." (pp. 296–7)

And here is Podsnap in conversation with a Frenchman:

'It merely referred,' Mr. Podsnap explained, with a sense of meritorious proprietorship, 'to Our Constitution, Sir. We Englishmen are Very Proud

[30] Dickens, C., *Our Mutual Friend,* (World's Classics edn., 1989), p. 128.

of our Constitution, Sir. It Was Bestowed Upon Us By Providence. No Other Country is so Favoured as This Country.'...

'And *other* countries,' said the foreign gentlemen, 'They do how?'

'They do, Sir,' returned Mr. Podsnap, gravely shaking his head; 'they do—I am sorry to be obliged to say it—*as* they do.'[31]

Podsnap's style is immediately recognisable to those who know the various Protestant gentlemen of the *Present Position*.

Where Dickens works by his characteristic repetition (which he pushes to extreme—there are three repetitions of the 'eight ... nine ... ten ...' list), Newman uses more subtle sentence rhythms. The sentence beginning 'All men ought to get up...' is a series of rising phrases, ending '... eight ... ten ... newspapers ... lunch ... drive' and then coming down for the strongly emphasised 'dine'. Then this emphasis is picked up and rhythmically repeated (I italicise to demonstrate):

Here is the great principle of the day—*dine*; yes, *dine*, and at the *right hour*; and it must *be* [Newman's italics] a dinner, with a certain time *after* dinner, and then in due time *bed*.

The next sentence is also carefully structured. There is first a series of three short phrases, then three longer ones, and finally the longest phrase as the punchline:

[31] Dickens, op. cit., p. 133.

```
  /          /
Tea and toast,
  /    /
port wine,
  /    /
roast beef;
  /        (/)         /
mince-pies at Christmas,
  /              /
lamb at Easter,
  /              /
goose at Michaelmas,
    /                   /    /
these are their great principles.
```

The staccato rhythm lightly punches out the humour. These are homely foods, all with associations of the family dinner table and good cheer; but their being so rigorously tied to the seasons of the year suggests a dogged clinging to harmless but arbitrary traditions. The absurdity of their being 'great principles' is superbly brought home by the slight rhythmical delay before the last two words.

A sentence later, there is not only a patterning of stresses, but also a subtle use of alliteration:

```
  /                /                   /
Figs and maccaroni for the day's fare,
       /               /          /
or Burgundy and grapes for breakfast!
             /              /                /
- they are aghast at the atrocity of the notion.
```

Newman's choice of vocabulary here shows his acute

awareness of the words' connotations. *Figs* are not only quintessentially foreign to Englishmen, they are also rather trivial food (one doesn't 'care a fig' for something) and are thus clearly quite inadequate *fare* for a hard day's work. And drinking alcohol at *breakfast* is shocking enough to English middle-class respectability, but to drink *Burgundy* at such a time— such a respectable dinner-table drink—is virtually lèse-majesté. Both the alliteration and the stresses link the words in order to make ironic contrasts between them—or rather between the associations that the words have for the speaker who is himself the subject of Newman's irony. 'Aghast' and 'atrocity' are of course far too serious words for the context. They should express shock and horror: the long second syllable of 'agh*ast*' suggests sharply expelled breath, and the strongly fricative second syllable in 'a*tro*city' expresses the vehemence of outrage. These are expressions which should be reserved for strong moral condemnation, yet here the outrageous notion being condemned is merely the foreigner's breakfast. Newman thus subtly implies that these trivial matters of diet have become the Englishman's substitute for morality.

The passage is concluded with the 'good country gentleman' who was warned that he would have to expect 'privations and mortifications' on his Continental tour. (Note here the use of 'mortifications', a word of religious meaning for Catholics signifying sufferings voluntarily undertaken as penance for sin. Newman is again suggesting that real penitential suffering has, for the modern English Protestant, been replaced by dietary discomfort—as if his food has become his religion). The gentleman replies that:

> he had made up his mind to it, and thought himself
> prepared for anything abroad, provided he could
> but bargain for a clean table-cloth, and a good
> rump-steak every day.

This is not only showing the insularity of the
Englishman who thinks he is being a hardened traveller while in fact insisting on his English food; it is
also making fun of the English ritual of eating, in
which the spreading of the clean tablecloth has a
moral significance and the rump-steak (that thump-
ingly solid, reliable-sounding food) is 'good' in a more
than culinary sense.

Newman finds this funny, but its absurdity also cuts
the pompous Englishman down to size. Part of the
purpose of these Lectures was to put heart into his
Catholic audience in the face of Protestant hostility.
Irrespective of the exact argument Newman is pursuing here, these satirical passages make the powerful
Protestantism of his day seem ridiculous rather than
threatening. The satire is also designed to appeal to the
same readership who would laugh with Dickens,
Thackeray and George Eliot at English pomposity and
snobbishness.

Prejudice disarmed

As the Protestant English gentleman makes his final
appearances in these Lectures, he is becoming a spent
force. In Lecture IX Newman goes over some of his
arguments of the previous lectures, for instance that
Protestant criticisms of Catholic doctrines are based

on different principles from those of Catholicism which make Protestants incapable of understanding the Catholic position. He lists propositions that they have been

> taught to get by heart, without any sort of proof, as a kind of alphabet or spelling lesson [such as] "miracles have ceased long ago;" "all truth is in the Bible;" "any one can understand the Bible;" "all penance is absurd;" (p. 369)

This makes them sound like children, reciting by rote statements which they assume to be unquestionable truths. As he reminds us, Newman dealt with this question of how the Protestant 'takes the whole question for granted' in his seventh lecture; he has thus, as it were, inoculated us against them, so that these objecting Protestant voices now seem irrelevant, even tiresome.

He is now ready to replace them with a final Protestant voice, one which shows the beginnings of a change in attitude towards Catholics. For after going over his previous arguments, Newman turns in this last lecture to the strategy that he recommends Catholics to adopt in the face of Protestant hostility. It is to cultivate local sympathy as an antidote to the anti-Catholic propaganda that issues at national level from the press and other influential metropolitan organs. Every Birmingham Catholic should try to 'approve himself in his own neighbourhood' so that his Protestant neighbours will gain a good opinion of him, and say to themselves:

"Catholics are, doubtless, an infamous sect, and not to be trusted, for the *Times* says so, and Exeter Hall, and the Prime Minister, and the Bishops of the Establishment; and such good authorities cannot be wrong, but somehow an exception must certainly be made for the Catholics of Birmingham. They are not like the rest; they are indeed a shocking set at Manchester, Preston, Blackburn, and Liverpool; but, however you account for it, they are respectable men here. Priests in general are perfect monsters; but here they are certainly unblemished in their lives and take great pains with their people. Bishops are tyrants, and, as Maria Monk says, cutthroats, always excepting the Bishop of Birmingham, who affects no state or pomp, is simple and unassuming, and always in his work." And in like manner, the Manchester people will say, "O, certainly, Popery is horrible, and must be kept down. Still, let us give the devil his due, they are a remarkably excellent body of men here, and we will take care no one does them any harm. It is very different at Birmingham; there they have a Bishop, and that makes all the difference; he is a Wolsey all over; and the priests, too, in Birmingham are at least one in twelve infidels. We do not recollect who ascertained this, but it was some most respectable man, who was far too conscientious and too charitable to slander any one." (pp. 387–8)

This passage works on several fronts at once. First, the voice here is not that of the crusty old gentleman but of 'the people' of the two cities. These are the new force

in the nineteenth century whom Catholics are to wean
from their traditional Protestant prejudices. And they
are given an attractive good nature: they pay full
tribute both to Catholic people and priests and want to
protect them from harm, that is from the 'brickbats,
bludgeons, and lighted brands' of the anti-Catholic
mobs which Newman has mentioned a few lines earlier
(and which had been much in evidence during the 'No
Popery' agitations of that year). And they have a pleasant local loyalty. But they are also revealed as naïve, still
taken in by the myths of Maria Monk; they still assume
that 'some respectable man' must have proof of the
anti-Catholic accusations they have heard, and that
such a man is conscientious and charitable. After all
that we have heard in these Lectures, we know the
reality of an anti-Catholic agitator like Achilli and the
origins of the Maria Monk fictions. So the Protestant
people of Birmingham and Manchester (and by extension of all the cities) now seem pitifully ignorant, with
their basic good nature being frustrated by the malign
influence of anti-Catholic propaganda. As more
knowledgeable readers we feel sorry for them and
laugh at them at the same time. Yet crucially, from the
Catholic viewpoint they are already being rendered
harmless. The aggressively confident Protestant voices
of the earlier Lectures have been reduced to this; and
although Newman ends with a warning to his Catholic
audience that they may yet have to face martyr-like
trials, we are left in little doubt that the villain of the
piece is on his way out.

The Achilli 'confession'
There was, of course, a real-life individual villain who

featured prominently in the Lectures: Achilli. And it is interesting that when Newman came to his accusations against Achilli, he put them in the form of an ironically boasting 'confession'. It is worth reading the whole passage (including the 'libellous' section in the Appendix) not just to see what Achilli had actually done but to get its full rhetorical force. It works by accumulation: the offences get worse and worse, with the final circumlocutory '"offences which the authorities cannot get themselves to describe"' being, of course, the most effective of all, as the listener's imagination runs riot. As it goes on, the 'Achilli' voice becomes relentless as it lists what he has done. Any one of the offences would be enough to discredit him, but the sheer number, and their increasing unpleasantness, becomes overwhelming. Achilli becomes a monster, bragging of his debaucheries. This is a voice which, in its confession of moral enormities, is of course unlike any of the other anti-Catholic voices in the Lectures. But it is also unmistakably in the anti-Catholic tradition, with its Exeter Hall rhetoric: '"Mothers of England"', '"a confessor against Popery"', '"the barbarity and profligacy of the Inquisitors of Rome"'. And Newman's audience knew that Achilli was being fêted by the Protestant world as an anti-Catholic hero, a victim of the Inquisition, whose stories of horror exactly fulfilled the traditional Protestant view of Roman persecution and cruelty. So the Achilli voice which Newman has created is sufficiently like, and at the same time radically different from, his other Protestant voices to have a powerfully disturbing effect. It is, in effect, a sort of nightmare Protestant voice, speaking the right language yet admitting to the wrongest possible actions. No wonder Achilli was stung to sue—or rather that his Protestant backers pressured him to do so. For if Newman's accusations were not refuted, it was not just Achilli who would fall; the whole tradition of anti-Catholic accusations and rhetoric would be besmirched. As Newman says:

> For how, Brothers of the Oratory, can we possibly believe a man like this, in what he says about persons, and facts, and conversations, and events, when he is of the stamp of Maria Monk, of Jeffreys, and of Teodore *[see Notes]*, and of others who have had their hour, and then been dropped by the indignation or the shame of mankind? (p. 208)

And this was in fact what happened. For despite Newman's defeat in the subsequent trial, the end result was the embarrassed dropping of Achilli by his erstwhile backers. The Achilli 'voice' is, then, part of Newman's satiric strategy. But whereas the other Protestant voices in the Lectures all provoke humour to a greater or lesser degree, this one is deadly serious.

In these lectures, Newman is in effect presenting the position of Catholics in England in a kind of drama. A succession of Protestant opponents confronts Catholicism and is exposed as ignorant, prejudiced and even malicious. As a cast of villains they are (apart from Achilli) more fools than knaves, and so the whole work is good humoured, though the humour is all at their expense. Newman has made his point with devastating effectiveness, and in doing so he surely earns his place in the English satirical tradition.

IV. RECEPTION AND CRITICISM

Contemporary reactions

The audience in the Corn Exchange enjoyed the Lectures enormously. Maria Giberne heard the shouts of laughter as she paced up and down outside, ladies not being admitted. (When she came to paint her picture of Newman delivering the Lectures—reproduced on the cover of this edition—she included a laughing female figure among the audience behind the platform.) Wider reactions fell, predictably, into the Catholic and Protestant camps. Newman's exposé of Maria Monk provoked Anglican clergymen to write to the papers in defence of that book, demonstrating that such 'instructed persons' did believe in it. The Birmingham paper, *Aris's Gazette*, had lengthy correspondences on that and on Newman's analysis of Blanco White's book and the question of what proportion of priests White had claimed were secretly unbelievers like himself. Newman's fellow Oratorian Fr.John Gordon took up the correspondence on Newman's behalf. The element which attracted the greatest hostility, however, was Newman's profession of his belief in miracles in Lecture VII. This was one of the Lectures' many outrages against reason, science and common sense, according to the Bishop of Norwich, Dr. Hinds. The subsequent lengthy and courteous (and rather dull) correspondence between him and Newman was appended to the Lectures as a

Note in later editions (see pp. 408–416). Most of the Protestant reviewers were not so courteous, one paper reprinting the passage about miracles in the lives of saints (pp. 312–3) under the headline 'Melancholy Case of Mental Aberration'.

Perhaps the most substantial of the Protestant responses to the Lectures came from Archdeacon Julius Hare in *The Contest with Rome*. Hare took issue with Newman on a large number of historical points, and was particularly outraged at the way that Newman argued (Lecture V) that Protestants and unbelievers have persecuted far more than the Catholic Church has ever done. This, he says, showed that Newman 'is determined to say whatever he chooses, in despite of facts and of reason'. However, he rather spoils his case by going on to defend Protestant persecution on the grounds that 'if torrents of blood were the necessary price of the Reformation, even at that price it would not have been dearly purchast.'[32] Hare was a man of great scholarship, and some of his criticisms of Newman on matters of historical fact may have weight. But he writes from the stance of Establishment superiority, criticising Newman's tone for being 'overbearing quite to a pitch of insolence against Protestants'.[33] Catholics must evidently know their place. He also chose to organise his criticisms in the form of a series of lengthy Notes appended to his much shorter main text and indulges in lengthy Latin footnotes without translation. The contrast with Newman's clarity and fluency is striking.

---

[32] Hare, J.C., *The Contest with Rome*, (London, 1852), p. 296.
[33] Ibid, p. 266.

The Catholic commentators were of course enthusiastic. The Lectures were reviewed in *The Rambler* (founded a few years earlier by John Capes) which saw them as a kind of training manual for Catholics in how to deal with Protestants, picking out Newman's analysis of the importance of First Principles in Lecture VII as 'furnishing a key to the whole mystery of anti-Catholic hostility, and as shewing the special point of attack upon which our controversial energies should be concentrated.'[34] The reviewer (Capes himself) was alive to the Lectures' literary merit, praising Newman's 'felicity of statement' and defended his humour against those Protestant critics who are 'unable to conceive how a man can be really serious who in religious matters intermingles food for laughter with food for tears'.[35] Capes's own sense of humour seems to have been somewhat lacking, since he found the imaginary Russian Count's speech at the end of Lecture I to be 'the only weak passage of any length in the volume.'[36] He did, however, quote the whole of the 'pattern men' passage as 'the lecturer's own way of illustrating the principle ... that *in a certain sense* ridicule is the test of truth.'[37]

The other leading Catholic journal, Wiseman's *Dublin Review*, reviewed the Lectures in the following spring. It recognised the real wider Protestant audience which Newman was addressing, contrasting them to his earlier *Lectures on Certain Difficulties felt by Anglicans in submitting to the Catholic Church*, which had

---

[34] *The Rambler*, Vol. VIII, November 1851, Part XLVII, p. 387.

[35] Ibid., p. 378.

[36] Ibid., p. 379.

[37] Ibid., p. 387.

been aimed at his former fellow-Anglicans in the Oxford Movement; and it praised Newman for undertaking such a topical controversial subject when he could instead 'with the utmost ease obtain for himself a position ... among the greatest theologians the Church has ever seen.'[38] The review gave detailed coverage of Newman's 'profound psycological [sic]' analysis of prejudice in Lecture VI and, like *The Rambler*, paid particular attention to the First Principles argument of Lecture VII. Although the reviewer is clearly interested in the Lectures primarily from the apologetic point of view, he shows some awareness of their literary merit, concluding that 'our exclusive attention to the *substance* of the work, has prevented us from doing detailed justice to the inimitable excellence of its style and manner.'[39]

Interestingly, the German Catholic scholar, Dollinger, so admired the Lectures that he translated them into German,[40] providing a Foreword in which he described Newman as 'a sensitive observer and a person whose knowledge of mankind enables him to penetrate to the essence of things'. He praises Newman's ability to trace back the origins of prejudice to its first principles, praising Lecture VII as 'a masterpiece of its kind'.[41] The literary qualities of the Lectures were thus recognised early. One otherwise

---

[38] *The Dublin Review*, No.XXIII, March 1852, p. 225.

[39] Ibid., p. 257.

[40] *Borträge über die gegenwärtige Stellung der Katholiken in England.* Bon Johann Heinrich Newman, Doctor der Theologie, Priester der Congregation des heiligen Philipp Neri. Uns dem Englischen. Mit einem Vorworte ven J. Döllinger (Regensburg, 1853).

[41] Ibid., p.vi. [I am indebted to my colleague Tony Tinkel for providing me with a translation of this Foreword.]

hostile Protestant review compared Newman to
Pascal, saying that the Lectures had 'a felicity of wit
such as has rarely been witnessed in polemical divinity
since the days of the "Provincial Letters".'[42] Hare paid
a rather sour compliment to Newman's pictures of
Protestant parents as 'laughable enough, and shew his
eminent talent for buffoonery'.[43] The judgement of
the novelist George Eliot is of greater significance.
She found the Lectures 'full of clever satire';[44] she
longed to meet Newman but never did.

Critical assessments

Full appreciation of their worth had to await an age of
less heated religious controversy. Soon after
Newman's death, Richard Hutton (1891) and
Augustine Birrell (1892) included praise of the
Lectures' satirical humour in their discussions of
Newman's writings; Hutton picked out the 'bells'
passage in Lecture II (pp. 76-77)[45] and Birrell the
Russian Count's speech.[46] Newman's first biographer,
Wilfred Ward (1918), betrays perhaps a certain
embarrassment in his comment that in the Lectures,

> We have the very curious spectacle of a grave reli-
> gious apologist giving rein for the first time at the
> age of fifty to a sense of rollicking fun and gifts of
> humorous writing, which if expended on other

---

[42] Unattributed press cutting in Newman's scrapbook in the
Birmingham Oratory archives.

[43] Hare, op. cit., p. 269.[44]

[44] George Eliot, *Letters*, I, 372.

[45] Hutton, Richard H., *Cardinal Newman*, (London, 1891), pp. 214-215.

[46] Birrell, Augustine, *Res Judicatae*, (London, 1892), p. 150.

subjects would naturally have adorned the pages of Thackeray's *Punch*.[47]

He has forgotten Newman's earlier satire, for instance in parts of *The Tamworth Reading Room* and much of *Loss and Gain*. Choosing the Russian Count as the best example of satire in the Lectures, he admits that it 'certainly shows a power of sustained and, one must admit, very broad burlesque which would win distinction as a humourist *[sic]* for a mere man of letters.'[48]

Joseph Reilly (1925) felt no need to be so defensive; he also highlighted the Russian Count's speech, commenting on 'How deftly even the most minute parallelisms are insinuated and their cumulative force made to tell.'[49] He compared Newman's irony to Swift's, identifying

a certain insinuating quality in Newman's irony as if he were taking you by the arm and with laughing eyes which belied his serious face were going to tell you a rich joke, a clever repartee or an amusing blunder. You feel you are being let in, as it were, as a kind of privileged character, whose appreciation of the ridiculous has been tried and proved.[50]

Interestingly, some of the most perceptive criticism of the Lectures in the first half of the twentieth century came from France. Fernande Tardival in 1937 gave

---

[47] Ward, Wilfred, *Last Lectures*, (London, 1918), p. 113.

[48] Ibid., p. 117.

[49] Reilly, Hoseph J., *Newman as a Man of Letters*, (New York, 1925), p. 197.

[50] Ibid., p. 210.

extended consideration to them as 'le chef-d'oeuvre de la satire newmanienne.'[51] She, too, finds Newman's irony like that of Swift; and she too quotes the 'bells' passage (which, unlike other extracts, she does not attempt to translate into French) and again the Russian Count. Newman's satirical art, she says,

> shows itself at times in little incisive phrases which have a very delicate manner, made more spiritual so as to speak the truth. Then his irony tends to take an agile and supple form, in the spirit which we have come to recognise as Voltaire's. It has an unruffled style, pricking one's understanding by an unexpected bringing together of words or ideas, always attentively alert to strike with elegance, to reveal error with ease and dexterity, with a detached air, and playful tone which scarcely allows one to suspect the hostility of his intentions. He will say with an almost worldly gracefulness that the Church of England 'agrees to differ', that it is strange that Catholicism 'has been killed so often.'[52]

Among the extracts she selects for praise is the 'pattern-men' passage:

> Newman reached the perfection of his method in his sketch of the standard type of Anglican: the man of a single idea, of one set cast of mind, on whom ancestral prejudices have engraved clear and concise lines, which the artist traces in a way which you

[51] Tardival, Fernande, *La Personnalité Littéraire de Newman*, (Paris, 1937), p. 289.
[52] Ibid., p. 296.

would believe was intended for a page in *Punch*.[53]

The American critic Charles Harrold (1945, revised 1966) also hailed this passage as 'a classic in satire and parody', but it is

> only one of a number of unforgettably vivid or droll or burlesque-filled passages which attest to Newman's astonishing range of literary power. Never before or after did he use that power to its limit.[54]

More modern critics have included John Holloway (1953) who used many examples from the Lectures when analysing Newman's various techniques of argument. He sees the Russian Count's speech as an example of the *argumentum ad hominem* which Newman was to use so frequently.[55] George Tillotson (1965) described the lectures as 'Newman's one-man Exhibition of 1851.'[56] He reviews the anti-Catholic flavour of many of the novels of that time, and comments that Dickens's *A Child's History of England* in which the Pope is the villain throughout exemplifies what Newman says in the Lectures about the Protestant view of history. David Delaura (1967) notes that Matthew Arnold had certainly appreciated the Lectures; he quotes Arnold referring to

[53] Ibid., p. 393.
[54] Harrold, Charles F., *John Henry Newman. An Expository and Critical Study of His Mind, Thought and Art*, (Connecticut, 1966, 1945).
[55] Holloway, John, *The Victorian Sage*, (London, 1953), p. 172.
[56] Tillotson, G., 'Newman the Writer' in Tillotson, G. & K., *Mid-Victorian Studies*, (London, 1965), p. 322.

'all that *lion and unicorn* business which is too plentiful in our Prayer Book, on which Dr. Newman has showed such exquisite raillery, and of which only the Philistine element in our race prevents our seeing the ridiculousness.'[57]

Thomas Vargish, when dealing with the *Apologia Pro Vita Sua* in 1970, interestingly points out that:

In a sense Newman years before had created the Kingsley—surely the worst of possible Kingsleys—who figured in the controversy. 'Mr. Kingsley has read me from beginning to end in the fashion in which the hypothetical Russian read Blackstone; not I repeat from malice, but because of his intellectual build' [*Apologia*, p. 301]. The hypothetical Russian we recognise as Newman's own creation in *Lectures on the Present Position of Catholics in England* who is a parody of English anti-Roman sentiment.[58]

Frandsen's 1975 unpublished thesis analysing the rhetoric of the lectures (see above, p.XXXIV) is a systematic analysis, identifying the various rhetorical devices Newman uses, and amounts to the most detailed commentary on the Lectures yet done. Frandsen sees them as illustrating Newman's 'subtle indirect approach to controversy' in which 'he uses techniques that catch the reader unawares'. Among these are:

[57] Delaura, David J., *Hebrew and Hellene in Victorian England*, (London, 1969), p. 129.

[58] Vargish, Thomas, *Newman. The Contemplation of Mind*, (Oxford, 1970).

stating a principle with which the reader is eager to agree, but which leads logically to an outcome favorable to Newman's case; … under cover of presenting a story, [leading] the reader through irony, metaphor, and allusion, to draw conclusions … so strong that they might antagonize the reader if stated openly; … drawing on examples from history to imply guilt by association; … [suggesting] special meanings for certain words to work in conjunction with the placing of words in proximity to each other to imply the desired conclusion.

Using 'the power of subjective feeling' Newman, he says:

can build up his poetical vision of the Catholic Church step-by-step until he gains assent by having the reader fully re-experience the vision in his own mind, as well as experiencing the vision of its Protestant detractors as prejudiced and evil men.[59]

Frandsen is following Holloway here, who saw *The Idea of a University* as using these techniques.[60] Both implicitly accuse Newman of being dishonest in his method of arguing. One can perhaps agree with some of the analysis without accepting the conclusions. Despite his hostility, Frandsen's thesis is certainly worth any serious student consulting on microfilm.

Many recent critics mention *Present Position* as part of their overall interpretation of Newman's thought

[59] Frandsen, op. cit., pp. 256–261.
[60] Op.cit., pp. 168–201.

or style. However, in recent years there have been some signs that the Lectures themselves are again regaining critical attention in their own right. Ian Ker has raised the profile of Newman's satire, as indicated above.[61] In his biography of Newman he gives a helpful critical account of the Lectures, noting Newman's use of imagery which has a 'savage, Swiftian flavour' or can be 'grotesque in the Dickens manner'.[62] John Griffin's assessment of the Lectures' value as historical evidence has already been referred to above. He also sees them as representing a new attitude to the Reformation; they are 'the first major challenge to a Protestant historiography of three hundred years duration.'[63] As well as Ker's own essay on 'Newman the Satirist' in the volume marking the centenary of Newman's death which he co-edited, there is also a very helpful essay by A.O.J. Cockshut.[64] He gives a full account of the background to the Lectures and poses the question, 'Did Newman exaggerate?' to which he concludes:

> Anyone who immerses himself for a week in the relevant books, pamphlets, sermons, leading articles, and episcopal charges may well reply, 'No, he understated.' Things he omitted were often more wild and poisonous than what he included.[65]

---

[61] See also Ker, I., *The Achievement of John Henry Newman* (London, 1990).

[62] Ker, I., *John Henry Newman* (Oxford, 1990), p. 366.

[63] Griffin, op. cit., p. 57.

[64] Cockshut, A.O.J., 'The Literary and Historical Significance of the *Present Position of Catholics*', in Ker, I. & Hill, A.G. (ed.), *Newman after a Hundred Years*, (Oxford, 1990), pp. 111-128.

[65] Ibid., pp. 114-5.

and quotes from numerous anti–Catholic writings in illustration. He notes Newman's use in the Lectures of the *tu quoque* argument (replying to an accusation against the Catholic Church by finding a similar or worse example among Protestants), the Russian Count passage being the most brilliant example of this where he is able to 'turn the *tu quoque* into glorious farce.'[66] And he notes that 'the book is unusual for [Newman] too in being organised around visual images, which are not merely metaphors but symbols of clusters of ideas, events and arguments'[67] and quotes the 'bells' passage as the best example of this. He also makes the interesting observation that

As a work of literature, the book is unusual in combining so many different genres. It is fiery and tender, analytical and rhetorical, bitter, comic and solemn. At different times it is as calmly reasonable as Hume, as fiercely contemptuous as Swift, as funny as Dickens. It contains history, philosophy, psychology, persuasive argument, ridicule, and unbridled fantasy. Yet it has a single theme, a continuous thread of argument, and a strict policy of excluding the irrelevant.[68]

In the light of some of these comments, it is all the more remarkable that Newman himself said that the Lectures 'put me to less trouble than any I ever wrote.'[69] Unlike *The Idea of a University*, where he had

[66] Ibid., p. 124.
[67] Ibid., p. 125.
[68] Ibid., p. 122.
[69] *Letters and Diaries*, Vol.XXV, p. 226.

continually to redraft, or the *Apologia*, parts of which he wrote weeping, he was writing here with ease and enjoyment.

The polemical battle which Newman was fighting is, one would hope, long over. The Papal Aggression crisis turned out to be the last mass expression of 'No Popery' bigotry in England; the last anti-Catholic riots were local ones in the 1860s, although on the fringes of Protestantism the old anti-Catholic myths and rhetoric lingered on. (Incredibly, the mid-1990s saw the republication of *Maria Monk* in the United States, and Catholic controversialists had to dust down the old weapons to refute it yet again.) Mainstream non-Catholic Christians have of course left behind the bigotry of the past, and certainly at the academic level anti-Catholicism is now well-recognised and studied as a phenomenon in its own right. In one sense, therefore, the apologetic and polemical value of the *Present Position* lectures is past. In a wider sense, however, the *Present Position* lectures have a continuing relevance. British (and U.S.) culture may be post-Protestant, indeed post-Christian, but it has its own stereotypes of Catholicism whether in soap operas, with their sexually frustrated priests needing to be liberated from celibacy, or in grave newspaper and magazine articles criticising the 'oppressive' policies of the Vatican. Newman's analysis of the prejudices of his own time may well have resonances as a counter-cultural critique today.

Satire necessarily arises from particular historical circumstances, but the best satire continues to work long after those circumstances have passed. The

Lectures on the Present Position of Catholics in England surely pass that test. All those who have a good sense of humour will discover in these Lectures an English satirist of considerable skill and effectiveness; while those who usually read Newman for theological or spiritual guidance will find here a Newman who makes them laugh. They may well come to agree with Newman's own judgement that this is indeed his 'best written book.'[70]

Andrew Nash
FitzAlan House
The Oratory School

[70] Ibid., Vol.XXVI, p. 115.

TO THE

MOST REVEREND PAUL,

LORD ARCHBISHOP OF ARMAGH,

AND

PRIMATE OF ALL IRELAND.

~~~~~~~~~

MY DEAR LORD PRIMATE,

IT is the infelicity of the moment at which I write, that it is not allowed me to place the following pages under the patronage of the successor of St. Patrick, with the ceremony and observance due to so great a name, without appearing to show disrespect to an Act of Parliament.

Such appearance a Catholic is bound to avoid, whenever it is possible   The authority of the civil power is based on sanctions so solemn and august, and the temporal blessings which all classes derive from its protection are so many, that both on Christian principles and from motives of expedience it is ever a duty, unless religious considerations interfere, to profess a simple deference to its enunciations, and a hearty concurrence in its very suggestions; but how can I deny of your Grace what may almost be called a dogmatic fact, that you are what the Catholic Church has made you?

Evil, however, is never without its alleviation; and I think I shall have your Grace's concurrence, if in the present instance I recognise the operation, already commenced, of that unfailing law of Divine Providence, by which all events, prosperous or adverse, are made to tend, in one way or other, to the triumph of our Religion. The violence of our enemies has thrown us back upon ourselves and upon each other; and though it needed no adventitious cause to lead me to aspire to the honour of associating my name with that of your Grace, whose kindness I had already experienced so abundantly when I was at Rome in 1847, yet the present circumstances furnish a motive of their own, for my turning my eyes in devotion and affection to the Primate of that ancient and glorious and much enduring Church, the Church of Ireland, who, from her own past history, can teach her restored English Sister how to persevere in the best of causes, and can interchange with her, amid trials common to both, the tenderness of Catholic sympathy and the power of Catholic intercession.

Begging of your Grace for me and mine the fulness of St. Patrick's benediction,

I am, my dear Lord Primate,

Your Grace's faithful and affectionate Servant,

JOHN H. NEWMAN,

Of the Oratory.

THE ORATORY,

Sept. **1851.**

PREFACE.

It may be necessary to state, that by "Brothers of the Oratory" are meant the members of an Association or Confraternity of seculars attached, but external, to the Ecclesiastical Congregation, to which the Author belongs. These are the persons to whom the following Lectures are addressed, with a view of suggesting to them, how best, as Catholics, to master their own position and to perform their duties in a Protestant country.

The Author repeats here, what he has several times observed in the course of the Volume itself, that his object has not been to prove the divine origin of Catholicism, but to remove some of the moral and intellectual impediments which prevent Protestants from acknowledging it. Protestants cannot be expected to do justice to a religion whose professors they hate and scorn. It has been objected to the Author, as regards both this and other of his works, that he succeeds better in demolition than in construction ; and he has been challenged to draw out a proof of the truth of the Catholic Faith. Persons who so speak, should consider the state of the case more accurately :—that he has not attempted the task to which they invite him, does not arise from any misgiving whatever in his mind about the strength of his cause, but about the disposition of his audience. He has a most profound misgiving about their fairness as judges, founded on his sense of the misconceptions concerning Catholicism which generally pre-occupy the English mind. Irresistible as the proof seems to him to be, so as even to master and carry away the intellect as soon as it is stated, so that Catholicism is almost its own evidence, yet it requires, as the great philosopher of antiquity reminds us, as being a moral proof, a rightly-disposed recipient. While a community is overrun with prejudices, it is as premature to attempt to prove that doctrine to be true which is the object of them, as it would be to think of building in the aboriginal forest till its trees had been felled.

The controversy with our opponents is not simple, but various and manifold ; when a Catholic is doing one thing he cannot be doing another ; yet the common answer made to his proof of this point is, that it is no proof of that. Thus men shift about, silenced in nothing, because they have not yet been answered in everything. Let them admit what we have already proved, and they will have a claim on us for proof of more. One thing at a time is the general rule given for getting through business well, and it applies to the case before us. In a large and complicated question it is much to settle portions of it ; yet this is so little understood, that a course of Lectures might profitably confine itself simply to the consideration of the canons to be observed in disputation. Catholics would have cause to congratulate themselves, though they were able to proceed no further than to persuade Protestants to argue out one point before going on to another. It would be much even to get them to give up what they could not defend, and to promise that they would not return to it. It would be much to succeed in hindering them from making a great deal of an objection till it is refuted, and then suddenly considering it so small that it is not worth withdrawing. It would be much to hinder them from eluding a defeat on one point by digressing upon three or four others, and then presently running back to the first, and then to and fro, to second, third and fourth, and treating each in turn as if quite a fresh subject on which not a word had yet been said. In all controversy it is surely right to mark down and record what has been proved, as well as what has not ; and this is what the Author claims of the reader as regards the following Volume.

He claims, and surely with justice, that it should not be urged against his proof that Protestant views of Catholics are wrong, that he has not thereby proved that Catholicism is right. He wishes his proof taken for what it is. He certainly has not proved what he did not set about proving; and neither he nor any one else has any encouragement to go on to prove something more, until what he actually has accomplished is distinctly acknowledged. The obligations of a controversialist lie with Protestants equally as with us.

As regards his Catholic readers, he would ask leave to express a hope that he may not be supposed in his concluding Lecture to recommend to the Laity the cultivation of a controversial temper, or a forwardness and rashness and unseasonableness in disputing upon religion. No one apprehends so clearly the difficulty of arguing on religious topics, consistently with their sacredness and delicacy, as he who has taken pains to do so well. No one shrinks so sensitively from its responsibility, when it is not a duty, as he who has learned by experience his own unavoidable inaccuracies in statement and in reasoning. It is no easy accomplishment in a Catholic to know his religion so perfectly, as to be able to volunteer a defence of it.

The Author has, besides, to apologize to them for having perhaps made some quotations of Scripture from the Protestant version. If anywhere he has been led to do so, it has been in cases where, points of faith not being involved, it was necessary for the argumentative or rhetorical force of the passages in which they occur.

And lastly, he earnestly begs their prayers that he may be prospered and blest in whatever he attempts, however poorly, for God's glory and the edification of His Church.

In Fest. Nativ. B. M. V., 1851.

LECTURE I.

THERE is a well-known fable, of which it is to my purpose to remind you, my Brothers of the Oratory, by way of introducing to you the subject of the Lectures which I am proposing to deliver. I am going to inquire why it is, that, in this intelligent nation, and in this rational nineteenth century, we Catholics are so despised and hated by our own countrymen, with whom we have lived all our lives, that they are prompt to believe any story, however extravagant, that is told to our disadvantage ; as if beyond a doubt we were, every one of us, either brutishly deluded or preternaturally hypocritical, and they themselves, on the contrary were in comparison of us absolute specimens of sagacity, wisdom, uprightness, manly virtue, and enlightened Christianity. I am not inquiring why they are not Catholics themselves, but why they are so angry with those who are. Protestants differ amongst themselves, without calling each other fools and knaves. Nor, again, am I proposing to prove to you, or to myself, that knaves and fools we are not, not idolaters, not blasphemers, not men of blood, not profligates not steeped in sin and seared in conscience ;

B

for we know each other and ourselves. No, my
Catholic friends whom I am addressing, I am neither
attacking another's belief just now, nor defending myself: I am not engaging in controversy, though controversy is good in its place: I do but propose to
investigate how Catholics come to be so trodden under
foot, and spurned by a people which is endowed by
nature with many great qualities, moral and intellectual; how it is that we are cried out against by the
very stones, and bricks, and tiles, and chimney-pots
of a populous busy place, such as this town which we
inhabit. The clearer sense we have of our own honesty,
of the singleness of our motives, and the purity of our
aims—of the truth, the beauty, the power of our religion, its exhaustless fund of consolation for the weary,
and its especial correspondence to the needs of the
weak—so much the greater may well be our perplexity
to find that its advocates for the most part do not
even gain a hearing in this country; that facts, and
logic, and justice, and good sense, and right, and virtue, are all supposed to lie in the opposite scale; and
that it is bid be thankful and contented, if it is allowed
to exist, if it is barely tolerated, in a free people.
Such a state of things is not only a trial to flesh and
blood, but a discomfort to the reason and imagination:
it is a riddle which frets the mind from the difficulty
of solving it.

I.

Now then for my fable, which is not the worse because it is old. The Man once invited the Lion to be
his guest, and received him with princely hospitality.
The Lion had the run of a magnificent palace, in

which there were a vast many things to admire. There were large saloons and long corridors, richly furnished and decorated, and filled with a profusion of fine specimens of sculpture and painting, the works of the first masters in either art. The subjects represented were various ; but the most prominent of them had an especial interest for the noble animal who stalked by them. It was that of the Lion himself; and as the owner of the mansion led him from one apartment into another, he did not fail to direct his attention to the indirect homage which these various groups and tableaux paid to the importance of the lion tribe.

There was, however, one remarkable feature in all of them, to which the host, silent as he was from politeness, seemed not at all insensible ; that diverse as were these representations, in one point they all agreed, that the man was always victorious, and the lion was always overcome. The man had it all his own way, and the lion was but a fool, and served to make him sport. There were exquisite works in marble, of Samson rending the lion like a kid, and young David taking the lion by the beard and choking him. There was the man who ran his arm down the lion's throat, and held him fast by the tongue ; and there was that other who, when carried off in his teeth, contrived to pull a penknife from his pocket, and lodge it in the monster's heart. Then there was a lion hunt, or what had been such, for the brute was rolling round in the agonies of death, and his conqueror on his bleeding horse was surveying these from a distance. There was a gladiator from the Roman amphitheatre in mortal struggle with his tawny foe, and it was plain who was getting the mastery. There was a lion in a net; a lion in a trap; four lions, yoked in harness, were drawing the car of a Roman emperor; and elsewhere stood Hercules, clad in the lion's skin, and with the club which demolished him.

Nor was this all: the lion was not only triumphed over, mocked, spurned; but he was tortured into extravagant forms, as if he were not only the slave and creature, but the very creation of man. He became an artistic decoration, and an heraldic emblazonment. The feet of alabaster tables fell away into lions' paws. Lions' faces grinned on each side the shining mantelpiece; and lions' mouths held tight the handles of the doors. There were sphinxes, too, half lion half woman; there were lions rampant holding flags, lions couchant, lions passant, lions regardant; lions and unicorns; there were lions white, black and red: in short, there was no misconception or excess of indignity which was thought too great for the lord of the forest and the king of brutes. After he had gone over the mansion, his entertainer asked him what he thought of the splendours it contained; and he in reply did full justice to the riches of its owner and the skill of its decorators, but he added, "Lions would have fared better, had lions been the artists."

You see the application, Brothers of the Oratory, before I make it. There are two sides to everything; there is a Catholic side of the argument, and there is a Protestant. There is a story of two knights who met together on opposite sides of a monument: one of them praised the gold on the shield of the warrior sculptured upon it, and the other answered that it was not gold, but silver. On this issue they fought; and in the course of the combat they changed places, and were flung, dismounted and wounded, each upon the ground occupied originally by his foe. Then they discovered that the shield was gold on one side, silver on the other, and that both of them were right, and both were wrong. Now, Catholic and Protestant are not both right and both wrong ; there is but one truth, not two truths ; and that one truth, we know, is in the Catholic Religion. However, without going on just now to the question where the truth lies (which is a further question not to my present purpose), still it is certain, though truth is one, that arguments are many, and there are always two sides in every dispute—I do not say both of them supported by arguments equally cogent and convincing, of course not ; still, there *is* a Protestant side, and there *is* a Catholic side—and if you have heard but one of them, you will think nothing at all can be said on the other. If, then, a person listens only to Protestantism, and does not give fair play to the Catholic reply to it, of course he thinks Protestantism very rational and straightforward, and Catholics very absurd ; because he takes for granted the Protestant facts, which are commonly fictions, and opens his mind to Protestant arguments, which are always fallacies. A case may be made out for any one or any thing ; the veriest villain at the bar of justice is an injured man, a victim, a hero, in the defence made for him by his counsel. There are writers who dress up vice till it looks like virtue : Goethe, I believe, has invested adultery with a sentimental grace ; and Schiller's drama of the " Robbers " is said to have sent the young Germans of his day upon the high-way. The same has been reported of Gay's " Beggar's

Opera;" and in our own time a celebrated poet has thrown an interest over Cain, the first murderer. Anything **w**ill become plausible, if you read all that can be said in its favour, and exclude all that can be said against it.

Thus it comes to pass that, in a measure, every one (as I may say) has his own sphere of ideas and method of thought, in which he lives, and as to which he differs from every one else; and, unless he be a philosopher, he will be apt to consider his own view of things, his own principles, his own tastes, to be just and right, and to despise others altogether. He despises other men, and other modes of opinion and action, simply because he does not understand them. He is fixed in his own centre, refers everything to it, and never throws himself, perhaps cannot throw himself, into the minds of strangers, or into a state of things not familiar to him. So it is especially between country and country: the Englishman thinks his beef and pudding worth all the resources of the French *cuisine ;* and the Frenchman thoughts for certain, until the peace, that he had gained the battle of Trafalgar. Taking men as they are commonly found, one man is not equal to the task of appreciating the circle of ideas and the atmosphere of thought which is the life of another; and yet he will commonly be forward in criticising and condemning it; condemning it, not as having heard what it has to say for itself, but simply and precisely for the very opposite reason, because he has not.

You know it is a favourite device with writers of fiction to introduce into their composition personages of very different characters taking their respective views of one and the same transaction, or describing and criticising each other ; the interest which such an exhibition creates in the reader lying in this, that each of the persons in question is living in his own world, and cannot enter into the world of another, and therefore paints that other in his own way, and presents us with a caricature instead of a likeness, though he does not intend it. I recollect an amusing passage of this kind, out of many which might be cited, in one of Sir Walter Scott's tales,[1] which I hope it is not unbecoming to quote, since it is so much to the purpose.

A middle-aged country gentleman and his wife for a while have the care of a very young lady. The host is very matter-of-fact, and his youthful guest, on the other hand, is very romantic ; and the humour of the narrative lies in the very opposite judgments passed respectively on the guest by the host, and on the host by the guest. The elderly man, with whom the shadows and illusions of human existence are over, and who estimates things not by their appearance, but by their weight, writing to the father of his young charge with a good deal of kind feeling towards her, and some good-humoured contempt of her flightiness, tells him that she " has much of a romantic turn " in her disposition, with a "little of the love of admiration ;" that " she has a quick and lively imagination, and keen feelings, which are apt to exaggerate both the good and evil they find in life ;" that "she is generous and romantic, and writes six sheets a week to a female correspondent." " You know," he says, " how I have jested with her about her soft melancholy, and lonely walks at morning before any one is

---

[1] Guy Mannering.

up, and in the moonlight, when all should be gone to bed, or set down to cards, which is the same thing." And he ends by speaking with some apprehension and dislike of a place of amusement near his grounds, which is "the resort of walking gentlemen of all descriptions, poets, players, painters, musicians, who come to rave and recite, and madden about this picturesque land of ours. It is paying some penalty for its beauties," he adds, "if they are the means of drawing this swarm of coxcombs together."

On the other hand, the young lady, writing to a school acquaintance of her own age, says, "If India be the land of magic, this is the country of romance. The scenery is such as nature brings together in her sublimest moods ; all the wildness of Salvator here, and there the fairy scenes of Claude. I am at present the inmate of an old friend of my father. He is a different, quite a different being from my father, yet he amuses and endures me. He is fat and good-natured, gifted with strong, shrewd sense, and some powers of humour ; and having been handsome, I suppose, in his youth, has still some pretension to be a *beau garçon*, as well as an enthusiastic agriculturist. I delight to make him scramble to the top of eminences, and to the foot of waterfalls ; and am obliged in turn to admire his turnips, his lucerne, and his timothy-grass. He thinks me, I fancy, a simple, romantic miss ; so he rallies, hands, and hobbles (for the dear creature has got the gout too), and tells old stories of high life, of which he has seen a good deal ; and I listen, and smile, and look as pleasant and as simple as I can, and we do very well."

This is but a sample of what meets us in life on

every hand ; the young have their own view of things, the old have theirs ; high and low, trader and farmer, each has his own, by which he measures everything else, and which is proved to be but a view, and not a reality, because there are so many other views just as good as it is. What is true of individuals is true of nations ; however plausible, however distinct, however complete the national view of this or that matter may be, it does not follow that it is not a mere illusion, if it has not been duly measured with other views of the same matter. No conclusion is trustworthy which has not been tried by enemy as well as friend ; no traditions have a claim upon us which shrink from criticism, and dare not look a rival in the face. Now this is precisely the weak point of Protestantism in this country. It is jealous of being questioned ; it resents argument ; it flies to State protection ; it is afraid of the sun ; it forbids competition. How can you detect the sham, but by comparing it with the true ? Your artificial flowers have the softness and brilliancy of nature, till you bring in the living article, fresh from the garden ; you detect the counterfeit coin by ringing it with the genuine. So is it in religion. Protestantism is at best but a fine piece of wax-work, which does not look dead, only because it is not confronted by that Church which really breathes and lives. The living Church is the test and the confutation of all false churches ; therefore get rid of her at all hazards ; tread her down, gag her, dress her like a felon, starve her, bruise her features, if you would keep up your mumbo-jumbo in its place of pride. By no manner of means give her fair play: you dare not. The dazzling brightness of her glance, the sanctity beaming from her countenance, the melody of her voice, the grace of her movements, will be too much for you. Blacken her; make her Cinderella in the ashes; do not hear a word she says. Do not look on her, but daub her in your own way; keep up the good old sign-post representation of her. Let her be a lion rampant, a griffin, a wivern, or a salamander. She shall be red or black; she shall be always absurd, always imbecile, always malicious, always tyrannical. The lion shall not draw the lion, but the man shall draw him. She shall be always worsted in the warfare with Protestantism; ever unhorsed and disarmed, ever running away, ever prostrated, ever smashed and pounded, ever dying, ever dead; and the only wonder is that she has to be killed so often, and the life so often to be trodden out of her, and her priests and doctors to be so often put down, and her monks and nuns to be exposed so often, and such vast sums to be subscribed by Protestants, and such great societies to be kept up, and such millions of tracts to be written, and such persecuting Acts to be passed in Parliament, in order thoroughly, and once for all, and for the very last time, and for ever and ever, to annihilate her once more. However, so it shall be; it is, forsooth, our received policy, as Englishmen, our traditionary view of things, to paint up the Pope and Papists in a certain style. We have a school of painting all our own. Every character or personage has its own familiar emblem; Justice has her balance, Hope her anchor, Britannia her trident. Again, history has its conventional properties; Richard the First was the lion-hearted, and Richard the Third was the crook-back;

William the First was the Conqueror, and William the Third "the pious, glorious, and immortal." These are our first principles ; they are unalterable ; like the pillars of heaven, touch them, and you bring our firmament down. True or false is not the question ; there they are. So it is with the view we take of Popery ; its costume is fixed, like the wigs of our judges, or the mace of our mayors. Have not freeborn Britons a right to think as they please ? We rule Popery to be what we say it is, not by history, but by Act of Parliament ; not by sight or hearing, but by the national will. It is the will of the Legislature, it is the voice of the people, which gives facts their complexion, and logic its course, and ideas their definition.

2.

Now I repeat, in order to obviate misconception, I am neither assuming, nor intending to prove, that the Catholic Church comes from above (though, of course, I should not have become, or be, one of her children, unless I firmly held and hold her to be the direct work of the Almighty) ; but here I am only investigating how it is she comes to be so despised and hated among us ; since a Religion need not incur scorn and animosity simply because it is not recognized as true. And, I say, the reason is this, that reasons of State, political and national, prevent her from being heard in her defence. She is considered too absurd to be inquired into, and too corrupt to be defended, and too dangerous to be treated with equity and fair dealing. She is the victim of a prejudice which perpetuates itself, and gives birth to what it feeds upon.

I will adduce two or three instances of what I mean. It happens every now and then that a Protestant, sometimes an Englishman, more commonly a foreigner, thinks it worth while to look into the matter himself, and his examination ends, not necessarily in his conversion (though this sometimes happens too), but, at least, in his confessing the absurdity of the outcry raised against the Catholic Church, and the beauty or the excellence, on the other hand, of those very facts and doctrines which are the alleged ground of it. What I propose to do, then, is simply to remind you of the popular feeling concerning two or three of the characteristics of her history and her teaching, and then to set against them the testimony of candid Protestants who have examined into them. This will be no proof that those candid Protestants are right, and the popular feeling wrong (though certainly it is more likely that they should be right who have impartially studied the matter, than those who have nothing whatever to say for their belief but that they have ever been taught it), but, at least, it will make it undeniable, that those who do not know there *are* two sides of the question (that is, the bulk of the English nation), are violent because they are ignorant, and that Catholics are treated with scorn and injustice simply because, though they have a good deal to say in their defence, they have never patiently been heard.

1. For instance, the simple notion of most people is, that Christianity was very pure in its beginning, was very corrupt in the middle age, and is very pure

in England now, though still corrupt everywhere else : that in the middle age, a tyrannical institution, called the Church, arose and swallowed up Christianity ; and that that Church is alive still, and has not yet disgorged its prey, except, as aforesaid, in our own favoured country ; but in the middle age, there was no Christianity anywhere at all, but all was dark and horrible, as bad as paganism, or rather much worse. No one knew anything about God, or whether there was a God or no, nor about Christ or His atonement ; for the Blessed Virgin, and Saints, and the Pope, and images, were worshipped instead ; and thus, so far from religion benefiting the generations of mankind who lived in that dreary time, it did them indefinitely more harm than good. Thus, the Homilies of the Church of England say, that " in the pit of damnable idolatry all the world, as it were, drowned, continued until our age" (that is, the Reformation), "by the space of above 800 years . . . so that laity and clergy, learned and unlearned, all ages, sects, and degrees of men, women, and children, of whole Christendom (an horrible and most dreadful thing to think), have been at once drowned in abominable idolatry, of all other vices most detested of God, and most damnable to man." Accordingly, it is usual to identify this period with that time of apostasy which is predicted in Scripture, the Pope being the man of sin, and the Church being the mother of abominations, mentioned in the Apocalypse. Thus Bishop Newton says, " In the same proportion as the power of the [Roman] empire decreased, the authority of the Church increased, the latter at the expense and ruin of the former ; till at length the Pope grew up above all, and 'the wicked one' was fully manifested and 'revealed,' or the 'lawless one,' as he may be called ; for the Pope is declared again and again not to be bound by any law of God or man." " The tyrannical power, thus described by Daniel and St. Paul, and afterwards by St. John, is, both by ancients and moderns, generally denominated Antichrist, and the name is proper and expressive enough, as it may signify both the enemy of Christ, and the vicar of Christ." [2] " The mind of Europe was prostrated at the feet of a priest," says a dissenting writer. " The stoutest hearts quailed at his frown. Seated on the throne of blasphemy, he 'spake great words against the Most High,' and 'thought to change times and laws.' Many hated him, but all stood in awe of his power. Like Simon Magus he 'bewitched the people.' Like Nebuchadnezzar, 'whom he would he slew.'" I need not give you the trouble of listening to more of such language, which you may buy by the yard at the first publisher's shop you fall in with. Thus it is the Man paints the Lion. Go into the first Protestant church or chapel or public meeting which comes in your way, you will hear it from the pulpit or the platform. The Church (who can doubt it ?) is a sorceress, intoxicating the nations with a goblet of blood.

However, all are not satisfied to learn by rote what they are to affirm on matters so important, and to feed all their life long on the traditions of the nursery. They examine for themselves, and then forthwith we have another side of the question in dispute. For instance, I say, hear what that eminent Protestant

[2] Dissert. 22.

historian, M. Guizot, who was lately Prime Minister of France, says of the Church in that period, in which she is reported by our popular writers to have been most darkened and corrupted. You will observe (what makes his remarks the stronger) that, being a Protestant, he does not believe the Church really to have been set up by Christ himself, as a Catholic does, but to have taken her present form in the middle age; and he contrasts, in the extract I am about to read, the pure Christianity of primitive times, with that later Christianity, as he considers it, which took an ecclesiastical shape.

"If the Church had not existed," he observes, "I know not what would have occurred during the decline of the Roman Empire. I confine myself to purely human considerations, I cast aside every element foreign to the natural consequence of natural facts, and I say that, if Christianity had only continued, as it was in the early ages,—a belief, a sentiment, an individual conviction,—it is probable it would have fallen amidst the dissolution of the empire, during the invasion of the barbarians. . . . I do not think I say too much when I affirm, that, at the close of the fourth and the commencement of the fifth century, *the Christian Church was the salvation of Christianity.*" [3]

In like manner, Dr. Waddington, the present Protestant Dean of Durham, in his Ecclesiastical History,[4] observes to the same purport: " At this crisis," viz., when the Western Empire was overthrown, and occupied by unbelieving barbarians, "at this crisis it is not too much to assert, that *the Church was the*

---

[3] Europ. Civ., p. 56, Beckwith.   [4] Ch. xiii.

*instrument of Heaven for the preservation of the Re-
ligion.* Christianity itself, unless miraculously sustained, would have been swept away from the surface
of the West, had it not been rescued by an established
body of ministers, or had that body been less zealous
or less influential." And then he goes on to mention six special benefits which the Church of the
middle ages conferred on the world ; viz., first, she
provided for the exercise of charity ; secondly, she
inculcated the moral duties by means of her penitential discipline ; thirdly, she performed the office of
legislation in an admirable way ; fourthly, she unceasingly strove to correct the vices of the existing social system, setting herself especially against
the abomination of slavery ; fifthly, she laboured
anxiously in the prevention of crime and of war ;
and lastly, she has preserved to these ages the literature of the ancient world.

Now, without entering into the controversy about
idolatry, sorcery, and blasphemy, which concerns
matters of *opinion*, are these Protestant testimonies,
which relate to matters of *fact*, compatible with such
imputations ? Can blasphemy and idolatry be the
salvation of Christianity ? Can sorcery be the promoter of charity, morality, and social improvement ?
Yet, in spite of the fact of these contrary views of
the subject,—in spite of the nursery and schoolroom
authors being against us, and the manly and original
thinkers being in our favour,—you will hear it commonly spoken of as *notorious*, that the Church in the
middle ages was a witch, a liar, a profligate, a seducer,
and a bloodthirsty tyrant ; and we, who are her
faithful children, are superstitious and slavish, because

we entertain some love and reverence for her, who, as a certain number of her opponents confess, was then, as she is now, the mother of peace, and humanity and order.

2. So much for the middle ages ; next I will take an instance of modern times. If there be any set of men in the whole world who are railed against as the pattern of all that is evil, it is the Jesuit body. It is vain to ask their slanderers what they know of them ; did they ever see a Jesuit ? can they say whether there are many or few ? what do they know of their teaching ? "Oh ! it is quite *notorious*," they reply : "you might as well deny the sun in heaven ; it is notorious that the Jesuits are a crafty, intriguing, unscrupulous, desperate, murderous, and exceedingly able body of men ; a secret society, ever plotting against liberty, and government, and progress, and thought, and the prosperity of England. Nay, it is awful ; they disguise themselves in a thousand shapes, as men of fashion, farmers, soldiers, labourers, butchers, and ped-lars ; they prowl about with handsome stocks, and stylish waistcoats, and gold chains about their persons, or in fustian jackets, as the case may be ; and they do not hesitate to shed the blood of any one whatever, prince or peasant, who stands in their way." Who can fathom the inanity of such statements ?—which are made and therefore, I suppose, believed, not merely by the ignorant, but by educated men, who ought to know better, and will have to answer for their false witness. But all this is persisted in ; and it is affirmed that they were found to be too bad even for Catholic countries, the governments of

which, it seems, in the course of the last century, forcibly obliged the Pope to put them down.

Now I conceive that just one good witness, one person who has the means of knowing how things really stand, is worth a tribe of these pamphleteers, and journalists, and novelists, and preachers, and orators. So I will turn to a most impartial witness, and a very competent one ; one who was born of Catholic parents, was educated a Catholic, lived in a Catholic country, was ordained a Catholic priest, and then, renouncing the Catholic religion, and coming to England, became the friend and *protégé* of the most distinguished Protestant Prelates of the present day, and the most bitter enemy of the faith which he had once professed —I mean the late Rev. Joseph Blanco White. Now hear what he says about the Jesuits in Spain, his native country, at the time of their suppression.

" The Jesuits," [5] he says, " till the abolition of that order, had an almost unrivalled influence over the better classes of Spaniards. They had nearly monopolised the instruction of the Spanish youth, at which they toiled without pecuniary reward, and were equally zealous in promoting devotional feelings both among their pupils and the people at large. . . . . . Wherever, as in France and Italy, literature was in high estimation, the Jesuits spared no trouble to raise among themselves men of eminence in that depart-

---

[5] I have omitted some clauses and sentences which either expressed the *opinions* of the author, as distinct from his testimony, or which at least are irrelevant to the matter in hand ; which is simply to show, not what a Protestant can speak *against* (which no one can doubt), but what he can say in *favour* of, this calumniated body : however, to prevent misrepresentation, the entire passage shall be given at the end of the Volume.

ment. In Spain their chief aim was to provide their houses with popular preachers, and zealous, yet prudent and gentle confessors. Pascal, and the Jansenist party, of which he was the organ, accused them of systematic laxity in their moral doctrines; but the charge, I believe, though plausible in theory, was perfectly groundless in practice. . . . . . The influence of the Jesuits on Spanish morals, from everything I have learned, was undoubtedly favourable. Their kindness attracted the youth from their schools to their Company; and . . . . they greatly contributed to the preservation of virtue in that slippery age, both by the ties of affection, and the gentle check of example. Their churches were crowded every Sunday with regular attendants, who came to confess and receive the sacrament. . . . . Their conduct was correct and their manners refined. They kept up a dignified intercourse with the middle and higher classes, and were always ready to help and instruct the poor, without descending to their level. . . . . . Whatever we may think of the political delinquencies of their leaders, their bitterest enemies have never ventured to charge the Order of Jesuits with moral irregularities." Does this answer to the popular notion of a Jesuit? Will Exeter Hall be content with the testimony of one who does not speak from hereditary prejudice, but from actual knowledge? Certainly not; and in consequence it ignores all statements of the kind; they are to be uttered, and they are to be lost; and the received slander is to keep its place as part and parcel of the old stock in trade, and in the number of the heirlooms of Protestantism, the properties of its stage, the family pictures of its old mansion, in the great controversy between the Lion of the tribe of Judah and the children of men.

3. Now I will go back to primitive times, which shall furnish me with a third instance of the subject I am illustrating. Protestants take it for granted, that the history of the monks is a sore point with us ; that it is simply one of our difficulties ; that it at once puts us on the defensive, and is, in consequence, a brilliant and effective weapon in controversy. They fancy that Catholics can do nothing when monks are mentioned, but evade, explain away, excuse, deny urge difference of times, and at the utmost make them out not quite so bad as they are reported. They think monks are the very types and emblems of laziness, uselessness, ignorance, stupidity, fanaticism, and profligacy. They think it a paradox to say a word in their favour, and they have converted their name into a title of reproach. As a Jesuit means a knave, so a monk means a bigot. Here, again, things would show very differently, if Catholics had the painting ; but I will be content with a Protestant artist, the very learned, and thoughtful, and celebrated German historian, who is lately dead, Dr. Neander. No one can accuse him of any tendencies towards Catholicism ; nor does he set about to compose a panegyric. He is a deep-read student, a man of facts, as a German should be ; and as a narrator of facts, in his Life of St. Chrysostom, he writes thus :—

" It was by no means intended that the monks should lead a life of listless contemplation ; on the contrary, manual labour was enjoined on them as a duty by their rational adherents, by Chrysostom, as well as Augustine, although many fanatical mystics, and advocates of an inactive life" (who, by the way, were not Catholics, but heretics) " rejected, under the cloak of sanctity, all connexion of a laborious with a contemplative life. Cassian relates, that not only the monasteries of Egypt, but that the districts of Libya, when suffering from famine, and also the unfortunate men who languished in the prisons of cities, were supported by the labour of the monks. Augustine relates that the monks of Syria and Egypt were enabled, by their labour and savings, to send ships laden with provisions to distressed districts. The monks of the East were remarkable for their hospitality, although their cells and cloisters were infinitely poorer than those of their more recent brethren of the West. The most rigid monks, who lived only on salt and bread, placed before their guests other food, and at times consented to lay aside their accustomed severity, in order to persuade them to partake of the refreshments which were set before them. A monk on the Euphrates collected together many blind beggars, built dwellings for them, taught them to sing Christian hymns with him, and induced a multitude of men, who sought him from all classes, to contribute to their support.

" Besides the promotion of love and charity, there was another object which induced the lawgivers of monachism to enjoin labour as an especial duty. They wished to keep the passions in subjection, and to maintain a due balance between the spiritual and physical powers of human nature, because the latter, if unemployed and under no control, easily exercise a destructive influence over the former.

"Among the rules of Basil, we find the following decision respecting the trades which formed the occupation of the monks. Those should be preferred, which did not interfere with a peaceable and tranquil life; which occasioned but little trouble in the provision of proper materials for the work, and in the sale of it when completed; which required not much useless or injurious intercourse with men, and did not gratify irrational desires and luxury; while those who followed the trades of weavers and shoemakers were permitted to labour so far as was required by the necessities, but by no means to administer to the vanities of life. Agriculture, the art of building, the trades of a carpenter and a smith, were in themselves good, and not to be rejected; but it was to be feared that they might lead to a loss of repose, and cause the monks to be much separated from each other. Otherwise, agricultural occupation was particularly to be recommended; and it was by agriculture that the monks, at a later period, so much contributed to the civilization of the rude nations of the West.

"The most venerated of the monks were visited by men of every class. A weighty word, one of those pithy sentiments, uttered by some great monk, of which so many have been handed down to us, proceeding from the mouth of a man universally respected, and supported by the impression which his holy life and venerable appearance had created, when spoken at a right moment, oftentimes effected more than the long and repeated harangues of other men. The children were sent to the monks from the cities to receive their blessings; and on these occasions their minds were strewed with the seeds of Christian truth, which took deep root. Thus, Theodoret says of the Monk Peter : ' He often placed me on his knees and fed me with bread and grapes ; for my mother, having had experience of his spiritual grace, sent me to him once every week to receive his blessing.'

" The duties of education were particularly recommended to the monks by Basil. They were enjoined to take upon themselves voluntarily the education of orphans ; the education of other youths when entrusted to them by their parents. It was by no means necessary that these children should become monks ; they were, if fitted for it, early instructed in some trade or art ; and were afterwards at liberty to make a free choice of their vocation. The greatest care was bestowed on their religious and moral acquirements. Particular houses were appointed, in which they were to be brought up under the superintendence of one of the oldest and most experienced monks, known for his patience and benignity, that their faults might be corrected with paternal mildness and circumspect wisdom. Instead of the mythical tales, passages out of the Holy Scriptures, the history of the divine miracles, and maxims out of Solomon's Proverbs, were given them to learn by heart, that they might be taught in a manner at the same time instructive and entertaining.

" The monks of the East greatly contributed to the conversion of the heathen, both by their plain, sincere discourse, and by the veneration which their lives inspired : and their simple mode of living rendered it easy for them to establish themselves in any place."

Now, the enemies of monks may call this an *ex parte* statement if they will,—though as coming from a Protestant, one does not see with what justice it can undergo such an imputation. But this is not the point. I am not imposing this view of the Monastic Institute on any one ; men may call Neander's representation *ex parte ;* they may doubt it, if they will ; I only say there *are* evidently two sides to the question, and therefore that the Protestant public, which is quite ignorant of more sides than one, and fancies none but a knave or a fool can doubt the received Protestant tradition on the subject of monks, is, for the very reason of its ignorance, first furiously positive that it is right, and next singularly likely to be wrong.

Audi alteram partem, hear both sides, is generally an Englishman's maxim ; but there is one subject on which he has intractable prejudices, and resolutely repudiates any view but that which is familiar to him from his childhood. Rome is his Nazareth ; " Can any good name out of Nazareth ? " settles the question with him ; happy, rather, if he could be brought to imitate the earnest inquirer in the Gospel, who, after urging this objection, went on nevertheless to obey the invitation which it elicited, " Come and see ! "

3.

And here I might conclude my subject, which has proposed to itself nothing more than to suggest, to those whom it concerns, that they would have more reason to be confident in their view of the Catholic religion, if it ever had struck them that it needed some proof, if there ever had occurred to their minds at least the possibility of truth being maligned, and Christ being called Beelzebub ; but I am tempted, before concluding, to go on to try whether something of a monster indictment, similarly frightful and similarly fantastical to that which is got up against Catholicism, might not be framed against some other institution or power, of parallel greatness and excellence, in its degree and place, to the communion of Rome. For this purpose I will take the British Constitution, which is so specially the possession, and so deservedly the glory, of our own people ; and in taking it I need hardly say, I take it for the very reason that it is so rightfully the object of our wonder and veneration. I should be but a fool for my pains, if I laboured to prove it otherwise ; it is one of the greatest of human works, as admirable in its own line, to take the productions of genius in very various departments, as the Pyramids, as the wall of China, as the paintings of Raffaelle, as the Apollo Belvidere, as the plays of Shakespeare, as the Newtonian theory, and as the exploits of Napoleon. It soars, in its majesty, far above the opinions of men, and will be a marvel, almost a portent, to the end of time ; but for that very reason it is more to my purpose, when I would show you how even it, the British Constitution, would fare, when submitted to the intellect of Exeter Hall, and handled by practitioners, whose highest effort at dissection is to chop and to mangle.

I will suppose, then, a speaker, and an audience too, who never saw England, never saw a member of parliament, a policeman, a queen, or a London mob ;

who never read the English history, nor studied any
one of our philosophers, jurists, moralists, or poets ;
but who has dipped into Blackstone and several English writers, and has picked up facts at third or fourth
hand, and has got together a crude farrago of ideas,
words, and instances, a little truth, a deal of falsehood,
a deal of misrepresentation, a deal of nonsense, and a
deal of invention.   And most fortunately for my purpose, here is an account transmitted express by the
private correspondent of a morning paper, of a great
meeting held about a fortnight since at Moscow, under
sanction of the Czar, on occasion of an attempt made
by one or two Russian noblemen to spread British
ideas in his capital.   It seems the emperor thought
it best, in the present state of men's minds, when secret societies are so rife, to put down the movement
by argument rather than by a military force ; and so
he instructed the governor of Moscow to connive at
the project of a great public meeting which should be
opened to the small faction of Anglo-maniacs, or
John Bullists, as they are popularly termed, as well
as to the mass of the population.   As many as ten
thousand men, as far as the writer could calculate,
were gathered together in one of the largest *places*
of the city ; a number of spirited and impressive
speeches were made, in all of which, however, was
illustrated the fable of the " Lion and the Man," the
man being the Russ, and the lion our old friend the
British ; but the most successful of all is said to have
been the final harangue, by a member of a junior
branch of the Potemkin family, once one of the imperial aides-de-camp, who has spent the last thirty years
in the wars of the Caucasus.   This distinguished

veteran, who has acquired the title of Blood-sucker, from his extraordinary gallantry in combat with the Circassian tribes, spoke at great length ; and the express contains a portion of his highly inflammatory address, of which, and of certain consequences which followed it, the British minister is said already to have asked an explanation of the cabinet of St. Petersburg : I transcribe it as it may be supposed to stand in the morning print :

The Count began by observing that the events of every day, as it came, called on his countrymen more and more importunately to choose their side, and to make a firm stand against a perfidious power, which arrogantly proclaims that there is nothing like the British Constitution in the whole world, and that no country can prosper without it ; which is yearly aggrandizing itself in East, West, and South, which is engaged in one enormous conspiracy against all States, and which was even aiming at modifying the old institutions of the North, and at dressing up the army, navy, legislature, and executive of his own country in the livery of Queen Victoria. " Insular in situation," he exclaimed, " and at the back gate of the world, what has John Bull to do with continental matters, or with the political traditions of our holy Russia ? " And yet there were men in that very city who were so far the dupes of insidious propagandists and insolent traitors to their emperor, as to maintain that England had been a civilized country longer than Russia. On the contrary, he maintained, and he would shed the last drop of his blood in maintaining, that, as for its boasted Constitution, it was a crazy, old-fashioned piece of furniture, and an eyesore in the nineteenth century, and would not last a dozen years. He had the best information for saying so. He could understand those who had never crossed out of their island, listening to the songs about " Rule Britannia," and " *Rosbif*," and " Poor Jack," and the " Old English Gentleman ; " he understood and he pitied them ; but that Russians, that the conquerors of Napoleon, that the heirs of a paternal government, should bow the knee, and kiss the hand, and walk backwards, and perform other antics before the face of a limited monarch, this was the incomprehensible foolery which certain Russians had viewed with so much tenderness. He repeated, there were in that city educated men, who had openly professed a reverence for the atheistical tenets and fiendish maxims of John-Bullism.

Here the speaker was interrupted by one or two murmurs of dissent, and a foreigner, supposed to be a partner in a Scotch firm, was observed in the extremity of the square, making earnest attempts to obtain a hearing. He was put down, however, amid enthusiastic cheering, and the Count proceeded with a warmth of feeling which increased the effect of the terrible invective which followed. He said he had used the words " atheistical " and " fiendish " most advisedly, and he would give his reasons for doing so. What was to be said to any political power which claimed the attribute of Divinity ? Was any term too strong for such a usurpation ? Now, no one would deny Antichrist would be such a power ; an Antichrist was contemplated, was predicted in Scripture, it was to come in the last times. it was to grow slowly, it was to manifest itself warily and craftily, and then to have a mouth speaking great things against the Divinity and against His attributes. This prediction was most literally and exactly fulfilled in the British Constitution. Antichrist was not only to usurp, but to profess to usurp the arms of heaven—he was to arrogate its titles. This was the special mark of the beast, and where was it fulfilled but in John-Bullism? " I hold in my hand," continued the speaker, " a book which I have obtained under very remarkable circumstances. It is not known to the British people, it is circulated only among the lawyers, merchants, and aristocracy, and its restrictive use is secured only by the most solemn oaths, the most fearful penalties, and the utmost vigilance of the police. I procured it after many years of anxious search by the activity of an agent, and the co-operation of an English bookseller, and it cost me an enormous sum to make it my own. It is called ' Blackstone's Commentaries on the Laws of England,' and I am happy to make known to the universe its odious and shocking mysteries, known to few Britons, and certainly not known to the deluded persons whose vagaries have been the occasion of this meeting. I am sanguine in thinking that when they come to know the real tenets of John Bull, they will at once disown his doctrines with horror, and break off all connexion with his adherents.

" Now, I should say, gentlemen, that this book, while it is confined to certain classes, is of those classes, on the other hand, of judges, and lawyers, and privy councillors, and justices of the peace, and police magistrates, and clergy, and country gentlemen, the guide, and I may say, the gospel. I open the book, gentlemen, and what are the first words which meet my eyes? '*The King can do no wrong.*' I beg you to attend, gentlemen, to this most significant assertion; one was accustomed to think that no child of man had the gift of impeccability; one had imagined that, simply speaking, impeccability was a divine attribute; but this British Bible, as I may call it, distinctly ascribes an absolute sinlessness to the King of Great Britain and Ireland. Observe, I am using no words of my own, I am still but quoting what meets my eyes in this remarkable document. The words run thus: 'It is an axiom of the law of the land that the *King himself can do no wrong.*' Was I wrong, then, in speaking of the atheistical maxims of John Bullism? But this is far from all: the writer goes on actually to ascribe to the Sovereign (I tremble while I pronounce the words) *absolute perfection;* for he speaks thus: 'The law ascribes to the King in his political capacity ABSOLUTE PER-FECTION; the *King can do no wrong!*'—(groans). One had thought that no human power could thus be described; but the British legislature, judicature, and jurisprudence, have had the unspeakable effron-tery to impute to their crowned and sceptred idol, to their doll,"—here cries of "shame, shame," from the same individual who had distinguished himself in an earlier part of the speech—"to this doll, this puppet whom they have dressed up with a lion and a unicorn, the attribute of ABSOLUTE PERFECTION!" Here the individual who had several times interrupted the speaker sprung up, in spite of the efforts of persons about him to keep him down, and cried out, as far as his words could be collected, "You cowardly liar, our dear good little Queen," when he was immediately saluted with a cry of "Turn him out," and soon made his exit from the meeting.

Order being restored, the Count continued: "Gentlemen, I could wish you would have suffered this emissary of a foreign potentate (immense cheering), who is insidiously aiming at forming a political party among us, to have heard to the end that black catalogue of charges against his Sovereign, which as yet I have barely commenced. Gentlemen, I was saying that the Queen of England challenges the divine attribute of ABSOLUTE PERFECTION! but, as if this were not enough this Blackstone continues, 'The King, moreover, is not only incapable of *doing* wrong, but even of *thinking* wrong!! *he can never do an improper thing; in him is no* FOLLY *or* WEAKNESS!!!'" (Shudders and cheers from the vast assemblage, which lasted alternately some minutes.) At the same time a respectably dressed gentleman below the platform begged permission to look at the book; it was immediately handed to him; after looking at the passages, he was observed to inspect carefully the title-page and binding; he then returned it without a word.

The Count, in resuming his speech, observed that he courted and challenged investigation, he should be happy to answer any question, and he hoped soon to publish, by subscription, a translation of the work, from which he had been quoting. Then, resuming the subject where he had left it, he made some most forcible and impressive reflections on the miserable state of those multitudes, who, in spite of their skill in the mechanical arts, and their political energy, were in the leading-strings of so foul a superstition. The passage he had quoted was the first and mildest of a series of blasphemies so prodigious, that he really feared to proceed, not only from disgust at the necessity of uttering them, but lest he should be taxing the faith of his hearers beyond what appeared reasonable limits. Next, then, he drew attention to the point that the English Sovereign distinctly claimed, according to the same infamous work, to be the "*fount* of justice;" and, that there might be no mistake in the matter, the author declared, "that she *is never bound in justice to do anything.*" What, then, is her method of acting? Unwilling as he was to defile his lips with so profane a statement, he must tell them that this abominable writer coolly declared that the Queen, a woman, only did acts of reparation and restitution as a matter of *grace !* He was not a theologian, he had spent his life in the field, but he knew enough of his religion to be able to say that grace was a word especially proper to the appointment and decrees of Divine Sovereignty. All his hearers knew perfectly well that nature was one thing, grace another; and yet here was a poor child of clay claiming to be the fount, not only of justice, but of grace. She was making herself a first cause of not merely natural, but spiritual excellence, and doing nothing more or less than simply emancipating herself from her Maker. The Queen, it seemed, never obeyed the law on compulsion, according to Blackstone; that is, her Maker could not compel her. This was no mere deduction of his own, as directly would be seen. Let it be observed, the Apostle called the predicted Antichrist "the wicked one," or, as it might be more correctly translated, "the lawless," because he was to be the proud despiser of all law; now, wonderful to say, this was the very assumption of the British Parliament. "The Power of Parliament," said Sir Edward Coke, "is so transcendent and absolute, that it cannot be *confined* within any bounds!! It has sovereign and uncontrollable authority!!" Moreover, the Judges had declared that "it is so high and mighty in its nature, that it *may make law*, and THAT WHICH IS LAW IT MAY MAKE NO LAW!" Here verily was the mouth speaking great things; but there was more behind, which, but for the atrocious sentiments he had already admitted into his mouth, he really should not have the courage, the endurance to utter. It was sickening to the soul, and intellect, and feelings of a Russ, to form the words on his tongue, and the ideas in his imagination. He would say what must be said as quickly as he could, and without comment. The gallant speaker then delivered the following passage from Blackstone's volume, in a very distinct and articulate whisper: "Some have not scrupled to call its power—the OMNIPOTENCE of Parliament!" No one can conceive the thrilling effect of these words; they were heard all over the immense assemblage; every man turned pale; a dead silence followed; one might have heard a pin drop. A pause of some minutes followed.

The speaker continued, evidently labouring under intense emotion:—" Have you not heard enough, my dear compatriots, of this hideous system of John-Bullism? was I wrong in using the words fiendish

D

and atheistical when I entered upon this subject?
and need I proceed further with blasphemous details,
which cannot really add to ¹the monstrous bearing of
the passages I have already read to you? If the
Queen 'cannot do wrong,' if she 'cannot even think
wrong,' if she is 'absolute perfection,' if she has 'no
folly, no weakness,' if she is the 'fount of justice,' if
she is 'the fount of grace,' if she is simply 'above
law,' if she is 'omnipotent,' what wonder that the
lawyers of John-Bullism should also call her 'sacred!'
what wonder that they should speak of her as 'majesty!' what wonder that they should speak of her
as a 'superior being!' Here again I am using the
words of the book I hold in my hand. 'The people'
(my blood runs cold while I repeat them) 'are led to
consider their Sovereign *in the light of a* SUPERIOR
BEING.' 'Every one is under him,' says Bracton,
'and he is under no one.' Accordingly, the law-
books call him 'Vicarius Dei in terrâ,' 'the Vicar of
God on earth;' a most astonishing fulfilment, you
observe, of the prophecy, for Antichrist is a Greek
word, which means 'Vicar of Christ.' What wonder,
under these circumstances, that Queen Elizabeth,
assuming the attribute of the Creator, once said to
one of her Bishops: 'Proud Prelate, *I made you, and
I can unmake you!*' What wonder that James the
First had the brazen assurance to say, that 'As it is
atheism and blasphemy in a creature to dispute the
Deity, so it is presumption and sedition in a subject
to dispute a King in the height of his power!'
Moreover, his subjects called him the 'breath of their
nostrils;' and my Lord Clarendon, the present Lord
Lieutenant of Ireland, in his celebrated History of

the Rebellion, declares that the same haughty monarch actually on one occasion called himself 'a god;' and in his great legal digest, commonly called the 'Constitutions of Clarendon,' he gives us the whole account of the King's banishing the Archbishop, St. Thomas of Canterbury, for refusing to do him homage. Lord Bacon, too, went nearly as far when he called him ' Deaster quidam,' ' some sort of little god.' Alexander Pope, too, calls Queen Anne a goddess: and Addison, with a servility only equalled by his profaneness, cries out, " Thee goddess, thee Britannia's isle adores.' Nay, even at this very time, when public attention has been drawn to the subject, Queen Victoria causes herself to be represented on her coins as the goddess of the seas, with a pagan trident in her hand.

"Gentlemen, can it surprise you to be told, after such an exposition of the blasphemies of England, that, astonishing to say, Queen Victoria is distinctly pointed out in the Book of Revelation as having the number of the beast! You may recollect that number is 666 ; now, she came to the throne in the year thirty-seven, at which date she was eighteen years old. Multiply then 37 by 18, and you have the very number 666, which is the mystical emblem of the lawless King ! ! !

" No wonder then, with such monstrous pretensions, and such awful auguries, that John-Bullism is, in act and deed, as savage and profligate, as in profession it is saintly and innocent. Its annals are marked with blood and corruption. The historian Hallam, though one of the ultra-bullist party, in his Constitutional History, admits that the English tribunals are ' disgraced by the brutal manners and iniquitous partiality of the bench.' ' The general behaviour of the bench,' he says elsewhere, ' has covered it with infamy.'   Soon after, he tells us that the dominant faction inflicted on the High Church Clergy ' the disgrace and remorse of perjury.'   The English Kings have been the curse and shame of human nature.   Richard the First boasted that the evil spirit was the father of his family ; of Henry the Second St. Bernard said, ' From the devil he came, and to the devil he will go ; ' William the Second was killed by the enemy of man, to whom he had sold himself, while hunting in one of his forests ; Henry the First died of eating lampreys ; John died of eating peaches ; Clarence, a king's brother, was drowned in a butt of malmsey wine ; Richard the Third put to death his Sovereign, his Sovereign's son, his two brothers, his wife, two nephews, and half-a-dozen friends.   Henry the Eighth successively married and murdered no less than six hundred women.   I quote the words of the ' Edinburgh Review,' that, according to Hollinshed, no less than 70,000 persons died under the hand of the executioner in his reign.   Sir John Fortescue tells us that in his day there were more persons executed for robbery in England in one year, than in France in seven. Four hundred persons a year were executed in the reign of Queen Elizabeth.   Even so late as the last century, in spite of the continued protests of foreign nations, in the course of seven years there were 428 capital convictions in London alone.   Burning of children, too, is a favourite punishment with John Bull, as may be seen in this same Blackstone, who notices the burning of a girl of thirteen given by Sir

Matthew Hale. The valets always assassinate their masters ; lovers uniformly strangle their sweethearts ; the farmers and the farmers' wives universally beat their apprentices to death ; and their lawyers in the inns of court strip and starve their servants, as has appeared from remarkable investigations in the law courts during the last year. Husbands sell their wives by public auction with a rope round their necks. An intelligent Frenchman, M. Pellet, who visited London in 1815, deposes that he saw a number of sculls on each side of the river Thames, and he was told they were found especially thick at the landing-places among the watermen. But why multiply instances, when the names of those two-legged tigers, Rush, Thistlewood, Thurtell, the Mannings, Colonel Kirk, Claverhouse, Simon de Monteforte, Strafford, the Duke of Cumberland, Warren Hastings, and Judge Jeffreys, are household words all over the earth ? John-Bullism, through a space of 800 years, is *semper idem*, unchangeable in evil. One hundred and sixty offences are punishable with death. It is death to live with gipsies for a month ; and Lord Hale mentions thirteen persons as having, in his day, suffered death thereon at one assize. It is death to steal a sheep, death to rob a warren, death to steal a letter, death to steal a handkerchief, death to cut down a cherry-tree. And, after all, the excesses of John-Bullism at home are mere child's play to the oceans of blood it has shed abroad. It has been the origin of all the wars which have desolated Europe ; it has fomented national jealousy, and the antipathy of castes in every part of the world ; it has plunged flourishing states into the abyss of revolution.

The Crusades, the Sicilian Vespers, the wars of the
Reformation, the Thirty Years' War, the War of Succession, the Seven Years' War, the American War, the
French Revolution, all are simply owing to John-Bull
ideas ; and, to take one definite instance, in the course
of the last war, the deaths of two millions of the
human race lie at his door ; for the Whigs themselves,
from first to last, and down to this day, admit and
proclaim, without any hesitation or limitation, that
that war was simply and entirely the work of John-
Bullism, and needed not, and would not have been,
but for its influence, and its alone.

" Such is that 'absolute perfection, without folly
and without weakness,' which, revelling in the blood
of man, is still seeking out her victims, and scenting
blood all over the earth.   It is that woman Jezebel,
who fulfils the prophetic vision, and incurs the prophetic denunciation.   And, strange to say, a prophet
of her own has not scrupled to apply to her that very
appellation.   Dead to good and evil, the children of
Jezebel glory in the name ; and ten years have not
passed since, by a sort of infatuation, one of the very
highest Tories in the land, a minister, too, of the
established religion, hailed the blood-stained Monarchy
under the very title of the mystical sorceress.   Jezebel
surely is her name, and Jezebel is her nature ; for
drunk with the spiritual wine-cup of wrath, and given
over to believe a lie, at length she has ascended to
heights which savour rather of madness than of
pride ; she babbles absurdities, and she thirsts for
impossibilities.   Gentlemen, I am speaking the words
of sober seriousness ; I can prove what I say to the
letter ; the extravagance is not in me but in the

object of my denunciation. Once more I appeal to the awful volume I hold in my hands. I appeal to it, I open it, I cast it from me. Listen, then, once again; it is a fact; Jezebel has declared her own *omnipresence.* 'A consequence of the royal prerogatives,' says the antichristian author, 'is the legal UBIQUITY of the King!' 'His Majesty is *always present* in all his courts: his judges are the *mirror* by which the King's image is reflected;' and further, 'From this *ubiquity*' (you see he is far from shrinking from the word), 'from this *ubiquity* it follows that the Sovereign can never be NONSUIT!!' Gentlemen, the sun would set before I told you one hundredth part of the enormity of this child of Moloch and Belial. Inebriated with the cup of insanity, and flung upon the stream of recklessness, she dashes down the cataract of nonsense, and whirls amid the pools of confusion. Like the Roman emperor, she actually has declared herself immortal! she has declared her eternity! Again, I am obliged to say it, these are no words of mine; the tremendous sentiment confronts me in black and crimson characters in this diabolical book. 'In the law,' says Blackstone, 'the Sovereign is said *never to die!*' Again, with still more hideous expressiveness, 'The law ascribes to the Sovereign an ABSOLUTE IMMORTALITY. THE KING NEVER DIES.'

" And now, gentlemen, your destiny is in your own hands. If you are willing to succumb to a power which has never been contented with what she was, but has been for centuries extending her conquests in both hemispheres, then the humble individual who has addressed you will submit to the necessary con-

sequence ; will resume his military dress, and return
to the Caucasus ; but if, on the other hand, as I believe, you are resolved to resist unflinchingly this
flood of satanical imposture and foul ambition, and
force it back into the ocean ; if, not from hatred to
the English—far from it—from *love* to them (for a
distinction must ever be drawn between the nation
and its dominant John-Bullism) ; if, I say, from love
to them as brothers, from a generous determination
to fight their battles, from an intimate consciousness
that they are in their secret hearts *Russians*, that they
are champing the bit of their iron lot, and are longing
for you as their deliverers ; if, from these lofty notions
as well as from a burning patriotism, you will form
the high resolve to annihilate this dishonour of humanity ; if you loathe its sophisms, ' De minimis non
curat lex,' and ' Malitia supplet ætatem,' and ' Tres
faciunt collegium,' and ' Impotentia excusat legem,'
and ' Possession is nine parts of the law,' and ' The
greater the truth, the greater the libel '—principles
which sap the very foundations of morals ; if you wage
war to the knife with its blighting superstitions of
primogeniture, gavelkind, mortmain, and contingent
remainders ; if you detest, abhor, and abjure the tortuous maxims and perfidious provisions of its *habeas
corpus*, *quare impedit*, and *qui tam* (hear, hear) ; if you
scorn the mummeries of its wigs, and bands, and
coifs, and ermine (vehement cheering) ; if you trample
and spit upon its accursed fee simple and fee tail,
villanage, and free soccage, fiefs, heriots, seizins,
feuds (a burst of cheers, the whole meeting in commotion) ; its shares, its premiums, its post-obits, its
percentages, its tariffs, its broad and narrow gauge "
—Here the cheers became frantic, and drowned the

speaker's voice, and a most extraordinary scene of enthusiasm followed. One half of the meeting was seen embracing the other half; till, as if by the force of a sudden resolution, they all poured out of the square, and proceeded to break the windows of all the British residents. They then formed into procession, and directing their course to the great square before the Kremlin, they dragged through the mud, and then solemnly burnt, an effigy of John Bull which had been provided beforehand by the managing committee, a lion and unicorn, and a Queen Victoria. These being fully consumed, they dispersed quietly; and by ten o'clock at night the streets were profoundly still, and the silver moon looked down in untroubled lustre on the city of the Czars.

Now, my Brothers of the Oratory, I protest to you my full conviction that I have not caricatured this parallel at all. Were I, indeed, skilled in legal matters, I could have made it far more natural, plausible, and complete; but, as for its extravagance, I say deliberately, and have means of knowing what I say, having once been a Protestant, and being now a Catholic—knowing what is said and thought of Catholics, on the one hand, and, on the other, knowing what they really *are*—I deliberately assert that no absurdities contained in the above sketch can equal—nay, that no conceivable absurdities can surpass—the absurdities which are firmly believed of Catholics by sensible, kind-hearted, well-intentioned Protestants. Such is the consequence of having looked at things all on one side, and shutting the eyes to the other.

LECTURE II.

CONSIDERING, what is as undeniable a fact as that there is a country called France, or an ocean called the Atlantic, the actual extent, the renown, and the manifold influence of the Catholic Religion—considering that it surpasses in territory and in population any other Christian communion, nay, surpasses all others put together,—considering that it is the religion of two hundred millions of souls, that it is found in every quarter of the globe, that it penetrates into all classes of the social body, that it is received by entire nations, that it is so multiform in its institutions, and so exuberant in its developments, and so fresh in its resources, as any tolerable knowledge of it will be sure to bring home to our minds,—that it has been the creed of intellects the most profound and the most refined, and the source of works the most beneficial, the most arduous, and the most beautiful, —and, moreover, considering that, thus ubiquitous, thus commanding, thus philosophical, thus energetic, thus efficient, it has remained one and the same for centuries,—considering that all this must be owned by its most virulent enemies, explain it how they will;

surely it is a phenomenon the most astounding, that
a nation like our own should so manage to hide this
fact from their minds, to intercept their own vision of
it, as habitually to scorn, and ridicule, and abhor the
professors of that Religion, as being, from the nature
of the case, ignorant, unreasoning, superstitious, base,
and grovelling. It is familiar to an Englishman to
wonder at and to pity the recluse and the devotee
who surround themselves with a high enclosure, and
shut out what is on the other side of it ; but was there
ever such an instance of self-sufficient, dense, and
ridiculous bigotry, as that which rises up and walls
in the minds of our fellow-countrymen from all knowledge of one of the most remarkable phenomena
which the history of the world has seen ? This broad
fact of Catholicism—as real as the continent of
America, or the Milky Way—which Englishmen cannot deny, they will not entertain ; they shut their
eyes, they thrust their heads into the sand, and try
to get rid of a great vision, a great reality, under the
name of Popery. They drop a thousand years from
the world's chronicle, and having steeped them
thoroughly in sin and idolatry would fain drown
them in oblivion. Whether for philosophic remark
or for historical research, they will not recognise
what infidels recognise as well as Catholics—the vastness, the grandeur, the splendour, the loveliness of
the manifestations of this time-honoured ecclesiastical confederation. Catholicism is for fifteen hundred
years as much a fact, and as great a one (to put it on
the lowest ground) as is the imperial sway of Great
Britain for a hundred ; how can it then be actually
imbecile or extravagant to believe in it and to join

it, even granting it were an error ?   But this island, as far as religion is concerned, really must be called, one large convent, or rather workhouse ; the old pictures hang on the walls ; the world-wide Church is chalked up on every side as a wivern or a griffin ; no pure gleam of light finds its way in from without ; the thick atmosphere refracts and distorts such straggling rays as gain admittance.   Why, it is not even a *camera obscura ;* cut off from Christendom though it be, at least it might have a true picture of that Christendom cast in miniature upon its floor ; but in this inquisitive age, when the Alps are crested, and seas fathomed, and mines ransacked, and sands sifted, and rocks cracked into specimens, and beasts caught and catalogued, as little is known by Englishmen of the religious sentiments, the religious usages, the religious motives, the religious ideas of two hundred millions of Christians poured to and fro, among them and around them, as if, I will not say, they were Tartars or Patagonians, but as if they inhabited the moon.   Verily, were the Catholic Church in the moon, England would gaze on her with more patience, and delineate her with more accuracy, than England does now.

This phenomenon is what I in part brought before you in my last Lecture : I said we were thought dupes and rogues, because we were not known : because our countrymen would not be at the pains, or could not stand the shock of realizing that there are two sides to every question, and that in this particular question, perhaps, they had taken the false side. And this evening I am proceeding to the inquiry *how* in a century of light, where we have re-written our grammars and revolutionized our chronology, all this can possibly come to pass; how it is that the old family picture of the Man and the Lion keeps its place, though all the rest of John Bull's furniture has been condemned and has been replaced. Alas! that he should be inspecting the silks and the china, and the jewellery of East and West, but refuse to bestow a like impartial examination on the various forms of Christianity!

I.

Now, if I must give the main and proximate cause of this remarkable state of mind, I must simply say that Englishmen go by that very mode of information in its worst shape, which they are so fond of imputing against Catholics; they go by *tradition*, immemorial, unauthenticated *tradition*. I have no wish to make a rhetorical point, or to dress up a polemical argument. I wish you to investigate the matter philosophically, and to come to results which, not you only, Brothers of the Oratory, who are Catholics, but all sensible men, will perceive to be just and true. I say, then, Englishmen entertain their present monstrous notions of us, mainly because those notions are received on information not authenticated, but immemorial. This it is that makes them entertain those notions; they talk much of free inquiry; but towards us they do not dream of practising it; they have been taught what they hold in the nursery, in the school-room, in the lecture-class, from the pulpit, from the newspaper, in society. Each man teaches the other: "How do *you* know it?" "Because *he* told me." "And how does *he* know it?" "Because *I* told *him*;" or, at very best advantage, "We both know it, because it was so said when we were young ; because no one ever said the contrary ; because I recollect what a noise, when I was young, the Catholic Relief Bill made ; because my father and the old clergyman said so, and Lord Eldon, and George the Third ; and there was Mr. Pitt obliged to give up office, and Lord George Gordon, long before that, made a riot, and the Catholic Chapels were burnt down all over the country." Well, these are your grounds for knowing it ; and how did these energetic Protestants whom you have mentioned know it themselves ? Why, they were told by others before them, and those others by others again a great time back ; and there the telling and teaching is lost in fog ; and this is mainly what has to be said for the anti-Catholic notions in question. Now this is to believe on *tradition.*

Take notice, my Brothers, I am not reprobating the proper use of tradition ; it has its legitimate place and its true service. By tradition is meant, what has ever been held, as far as we know, though we do not know how it came to be held, and for that very reason think it true, because else it would not be held. Now, tradition is of great and legitimate use as an *initial* means of gaining notions about historical and other facts ; it is the way in which things first come to us ; it is natural and necessary to trust it ; it is an informant we make use of daily. Life is not long enough for proving everything ; we are obliged to take a great many things upon the credit of others. Moreover, tradition is really a ground in reason, an argument for believing, to a certain point ; but then observe, we do not commonly think it right and safe, on the score of mere vague testimony, to keep our eyes and ears so very closely shut against every other evidence, every other means of proof, and to be so furiously certain and so energetically positive that we know all about the matter in question. No ; we open our senses wide to what may be said on the other side. We make use of tradition, but we are not content with it ; it is enough to begin with, not enough to finish upon.

Tradition, then, being information, not authenticated, but immemorial, is a *prima-facie* evidence of the facts which it witnesses. It is sufficient to make us take a thing for granted, in default of real proof ; it is sufficient for our having an *opinion* about it ; it is sufficient often to make us feel it to be *safest* to act in a certain way under circumstances ; it is *not* sufficient in reason to make us *sure*, much less to make us angry with those who take a different view of the matter. It is not sufficient to warrant us to dispense with proof the other way, if it be offered to us.   Supposing, for instance, there was a general belief or impression in England, running up beyond the memory of man, though unsupported by any distinct evidence, that the composer Tallis was the author of the Protestant Hundredth Psalm tune, or that Charles the Second was poisoned, or that Bishop Butler of Durham died a Catholic, I consider we certainly should have acquiesced in the tradition, taken it for granted, and made it our own, as long as it was our only means of forming an opinion on the respective points in question.   We should have thought the fact to be such, while there was nothing to set against it.   Nor would any other course have been reasonable. But, supposing in contravention of these traditions, a manuscript of the Psalm tune in question was found in some German library, in the handwriting of Luther; or supposing a statement existed purporting to be drawn up by Charles's medical attendants, accounting for his death, and attributing it, with all appearance of truth, to some natural complaint; or, again, supposing his death was imputed to a very unlikely person, Bishop Ken, or Mr. Evelyn; or supposing Butler's chaplain had left an account of Butler's last hours, from which it was demonstrable that up to the last day of his life he was a Protestant; should we passionately reject, or superciliously make light of this separate evidence, because we were content with our tradition? or, if we were tempted to do so, could we possibly defend our conduct in reason, or recommend it to another? Surely, it would be as extravagant to refuse the presumptions or the evidence offered us in the second place, as to refuse the tradition in the first. Thus, a tradition being an anonymous informant, is of force only under the proviso that it cannot be plausibly disputed.

I am speaking of a single or solitary tradition; for if there be two or three distinct traditions, all saying the same thing, then it is a very different matter; then, as in the case of two or three independent witnesses in a judicial proceeding, there is at once a cumulation of evidence, and its joint effect is very great. Thus, supposing, besides the current belief in England, there was a local tradition, in some out of the way district in Ireland, to the effect that a certain family had gained its estates in reward for the share which its ancestor had in the assassination of Charles the Second, we should certainly consider it at least a singular coincidence ; for it would be a second tradition, and if proved to be distinct and independent, would quite alter the influence of the first upon our minds, just as two witnesses at a trial produce an effect on judge and jury simply different from what either of them would produce by himself. And in this way a multiplication of traditions may make a wonderfully strong proof, strong enough even for a person to die for, rather than consent to deny the fact attested ; and, therefore, strong enough in reason for him to be very positive upon, very much excited, very angry, and very determined. But when such strong feeling and pertinacity of purpose are created by a mere single and solitary tradition, I cannot call that state of mind conviction, but prejudice.

Yet this, I must maintain, is the sort of ground on which Protestants are so certain that the Catholic Church is a simple monster of iniquity. If you asked the first person you met why he believed that our religion was so baneful and odious, he would not say, " I have had good proofs of it ; " or, " I *know Catholics* too well to doubt it ; " or, " I am *well read in history*, and I can vouch for it ; " or, " I have lived such a long time in *Catholic countries*, I ought to know ; "—(of course, I do not mean that no one would make such a reply, but I mean that it would not be the reply of the mass of men ; far from it). No ; single out a man from the multitude, and he would say something of this sort: " I am *sure* it is ; " he will look significant, and say, " You will find it a hard job to make me think otherwise ; " or he will look wise

E

and say, " I can make a pretty good guess how things
go on among you ; " or he will be angry, and cry out,
" Those fellows, the priests, I would not believe them,
though they swore themselves black in the face ; " or he
will speak loudly, and overbear and drown all remonstrance : " It is too notorious for proof ; every one
knows it ; every book says it ; it has been so ruled
long ago. It is rather too much in the nineteenth
century to be told to begin history again, and to have
to reverse our elementary facts." That is, in other
words, the multitude of men hate Catholicism mainly
on tradition, there being few, indeed, who have made
fact and argument the primary or the supplemental
grounds of their aversion to it. And observe, they
hate it on a single, isolated tradition, not a complex,
conclusive tradition—not the united tradition of many
places. It is true, indeed, that Holland, and Geneva,
and Prussia, each has its own tradition against the
Catholic Church ; but our countrymen do in no sense
believe, from any judgment they form on those
united British and foreign traditions, but from the
tradition of their own nation alone ; which, though
certainly it comprises millions of souls, nevertheless,
is so intimately one by the continual intercourse and
mutual communication of part with part, that it cannot with any fairness be considered to contain a
number of separate testimonies, but only one. Yet
this meagre evidence, I say, suffices to produce in the
men of this generation an enthusiastic, undoubting
and energetic persuasion that we torture heretics,
immure nuns, sell licences to sin, and are plotting
against kings and governments ; all, I say, because
this was said of Catholics when they were boys. It

is the old heirloom, the family picture, which is at once their informant and their proof.

Nor is this phenomenon, remarkable as it is, without its parallel in former passages of the world's history. We have a notable instance in Holy Writ ; to which I hope I may allude without risking a theological discussion. We read there of certain parties animated with extreme religious bitterness, simply on the incentive, and for the defence, of traditions which were absolutely worthless. The popular party in Judea, at the Christian era, were the dupes of a teaching, professing, indeed, the authority of their forefathers, or what they called " the tradition of the ancients ; " but, in reality, nothing more or less than the " commandment and tradition of men ; " of fallible men, nay, not only deceivable, but actually deceived men. This was the fatal flaw in their argument ; the tradition might have been kept ever so accurately and religiously, it might with full certainty have been derived from the foregoing generation, and have existed beyond the furthest memory ; but this proved nothing while it was traceable up to *man*, not to a divine informant, as its ultimate resolution or first origin. The stream cannot rise higher than its source ; if the wellspring of the tradition be human, not divine, what profits its fidelity ? Such as is the primary authority, so will be the continuous, the latest derivation. And this, accordingly, was the judgment pronounced in the instance to which I have alluded, on both the doctrine and its upholders. " In vain do they worship Me, teaching doctrines and commandments of *men*." As is the origin, so is the tradition ; when the origin is true, the tradition will be true ;

when the origin is false, the tradition will be false. There can most surely be true traditions, that is, traditions from true sources; but such traditions, though they really be true, do not profess to prove themselves; they come accompanied by other arguments; the true traditions of Divine Revelation are proved to be true by miracle, by prophecy, by the test of cumulative and collateral evidences, which directly warrant and verify them. Such were not the traditions of the Pharisee—they professed to speak for themselves, they bore witness to themselves, they were their own evidence; and, as might have been expected, they were not trustworthy—they were mere frauds; they came, indeed, down the stream of time, but that was no recommendation, it only put the fraud up higher; it might make it venerable, it could not make it true.

Yet it is remarkable, I say, how positive and fanatical the Jewish people was in its maintenance of these lies. It was irritated, nay maddened, at hearing them denounced; rose up fiercely against their denouncers; and thought they did God service in putting them to death. It is plain, then, that a popular feeling is not necessarily logical because it is strong.

Now, of course, a great number of persons will not easily allow the fact, that the English animosity against Catholicism is founded on nothing more argumentative than tradition; but, whether I shall succeed in proving this point or not, I think I have at least shown already that tradition is, in itself, quite a *sufficient* explanation of the feeling. I am not assigning a trifling and inadequate cause to so great

an effect. If the Jews could be induced to put
to death the Founder of our Religion and His
disciples on tradition, there is nothing ridiculous
in saying that the British scorn and hatred of
Catholicism may be created by tradition also.
The great question is, the matter of fact, *is*
tradition the cause? I say it is, and in saying
so, observe, I am speaking of the multitude,
not dwelling on exceptions, however numerous in
themselves ; for doubtless there is a certain number
of men, men of thought and reading, who oppose
Catholicism, not merely on tradition, but on better
arguments ; but, I repeat, I am speaking of the
great mass of Protestants. Again, bear in mind, I
am speaking of what really *is* the fact, not of what
the mass of Protestants will *confess*. Of course, no
man will admit, if he can help it, even to himself, that
he is taking his views of the Catholic Church from
Bishop Newton, or buckling on his sword against her
preachers, merely because Lord George Gordon did
the like ; on the contrary, he will perhaps sharply
retort, " I never heard of Bishop Newton or of Lord
George Gordon—I don't know their names ; " but the
simple question which we have to determine is the
real matter of fact, and not whether the persons who
are the subjects of our investigation will themselves
admit it. To this point then, viz., the matter of fact
—*Do* Protestants go by tradition ? on which I have
said something already, I shall now proceed to direct
your attention.

How, then, stands the matter of fact ? Do the
people of this country receive their notion of the
Catholic Church in the way of argument and ex-

amination, as they would decide in favour of rail
roads over other modes of conveyance, or on plans
of parish relief, or police regulations, and the like?
or does it come to them mainly as a tradition which
they have inherited, and which they will not question,
though they have in their hands abundant reasons
for questioning it? I answer, without a doubt, it
comes to them as a tradition; the fact is patent and
palpable: the tradition is before our eyes, unmistakable; it is huge, vast, various, engrossing; it has
a monopoly of the English mind, it brooks no rival,
and it takes summary measures with rebellion.

2.

When King Henry began a new religion, when
Elizabeth brought it into shape, when her successors
completed and confirmed it, they were all of them too
wise, and too much in earnest, not to clench their
work. They provided for its continuance after them.
They, or at least the influences which ruled them
knew well enough that Protestantism, left to itself,
could not stand. It had not that internal consistency in its make, which would support it against
outward foes, or secure it against internal disorders.
And the event has justified their foresight; whether
you look at Lutheranism or Calvinism, you find
neither of those forms of religion has been able to
resist the action of thought and reason upon it during a course of years; both have changed and come
to nought. Luther began his religion in Germany,
Calvin in Geneva; Calvinism is now all but extinct
in Geneva, and Lutheranism in Germany. It could not
be otherwise; such an issue was predicted by Catho-

lics as well as instinctively felt by the Reformers, at the time that Protestantism started. Give it rope enough, and any one could prophesy its end, so its patrons determined that rope it should not have, but that private judgment should come to a close with their own use of it. There was enough of private judgment in the world, they thought, when they had done with it themselves. So they forcibly shut-to the door which they had opened, and imposed on the populations they had reformed an artificial tradition of their own, instead of the liberty of inquiry and disputation. They worked their own particular persuasion into the political framework of things, and made it a constitutional or national principle ; in other words, they established it.

Now, you may say that Catholicism has often been established also. True, but Catholicism does not *depend* on its establishment for its existence, nor does its tradition live upon its establishment ; it can do without establishment, and often dispenses with it to an advantage. A Catholic nation, as a matter of course, establishes Catholicism because it *is* a Catholic nation ; but in such a case Catholicism and its tradition come first, and establishment comes second ; the establishment is the spontaneous act of the people ; it is a national movement, the Catholic people does it, and not the Catholic Church. It is but the accident of a particular state of things, the result of the fervour of the people ; it is the will of the masses ; but, I repeat, it is not necessary for Catholicism. Not necessary, I maintain, and Ireland is my proof of it ; there Catholicism has been, not only not established ; it has been persecuted for three hundred years, and at this moment it is more vigorous than ever; whereas, I defy you to bring any instance of a nation remaining Lutheran or Calvinist for even a hundred years, under similarly unpromising circumstances. Where is the country in the whole world, where Protestantism has thriven under persecutions, as Catholicism has thriven in Ireland? You might, indeed, allege in explanation of the fact, that persecution binds a body together; but I do not think that even persecution would, for any course of years, bind Protestants together in one body; for the very principle of private judgment is a principle of disunion, and that principle goes on acting in weal and in woe, in triumph and in disappointment, and its history gives instances of this. But I am speaking, not of what is supposable under certain circumstances, but of what has been the fact; and I say, looking at the subject historically, Protestantism cannot last without an establishment, though Catholicism can; and next, I say, that that establishment of Protestantism is not the work of the people, is not a development of their faith, is not carried by acclamation, but is an act of calculating heads, of State policy, of kingcraft; the work of certain princes, statesmen, bishops, in order, if possible to make that national which as yet is not national, and which, without that patronage, never would be national; and, therefore, in the case of Protestantism, it is not a matter of the greater or less expediency, sometimes advisable, sometimes not, but is always necessary, always imperative, if Protestantism is to be kept alive. Establishmentism is the very life of Protestantism; or, in other words, Protestantism comes in upon the nation, Protestantism is maintained not in the way of reason and truth, not by appeals to facts, but by tradition, and by a compulsory tradition ; and this, in other words, is an establishment.

Now, this establishment of Protestantism was comparatively an easy undertaking in England, without the population knowing much what Protestantism meant, and I will tell you why : there are certain peculiarities of the English character, which were singularly favourable to the royal purpose. As I have just said, the legitimate instruments for deciding on the truth of a religion are these two, fact and reason, or in other words, the way of history and the way of science ; and to both the one and the other of these, the English mind is naturally indisposed. Theologians proceed in the way of reasoning ; they view Catholic truth as a whole, as one great system of which part grows out of part, and doctrine corresponds to doctrine. This system they carry out into its fulness, and define in its details, by patient processes of reason ; and they learn to prove and defend it by means of frequent disputations and logical developments. Now, all such abstract investigations and controversial exercises are distasteful to an Englishman ; they suit the Germans, and still more the French, the Italians, and the Spaniards ; but as to ourselves, we break away from them as dry, uncertain, theoretical, and unreal. The other means of attaining religious truth is the way of history ; when, namely, from the review of past times and foreign countries, the student determines what was really taught by the Apostles in the beginning. Now, an Englishman, as is notorious, takes comparatively little interest in the manners, customs, opinions, or

doings of foreign countries.   Surrounded by the sea,
he is occupied with himself; his attention is concentrated on himself; and he looks abroad only with
reference to himself.   We are a home people; we like
a house to ourselves, and we call it our castle; we
look at what is immediately before us; we are eminently practical; we care little for the past; we resign ourselves to existing circumstances; we are
neither eclectics nor antiquarians; we live in the
present.   Foreign politics excite us very little; the
Minister of Foreign Affairs may order about our
fleets, or sign protocols, at his good pleasure, provided he does nothing to cripple trade, or to raise
the price of wheat or cotton.   Much less do we care
to know how they worship, or what they believe, in
Germany or in Spain; rather, we are apt to despise
their whole apparatus of religion, whatever it is, as
odd and outlandish; and as to past times, English
divines have attempted as little for ecclesiastical
history as they have attempted for theological science.
    Now you see how admirably this temper of Eng-
lishmen fits in with the exigencies of Protestantism;
for two of the very characteristics of Protestantism
are, its want of past history, and its want of fixed
teaching.   I do not say that no Protestants have
investigated or argued; that no Protestants have
made appeals to primitive Christianity; such an assertion would be absurd; it was a rule of the game,
as it may be called, that they should do so; they
were obliged to say what it was that they held, and
to prove it they were obliged to recur to ecclesiastical
history; certainly; but they have done so because
they could not help it; they did so for the moment;

they did so for a purpose ; they did so as an *argumentum ad hominem ;* but they did so as little as they could, and they soon left off doing so. Now especially the Latitudinarian party professes to ignore doctrine, and the Evangelical to ignore history. In truth, philosophy and history do not come natural to Protestantism ; it cannot bear either ; it does not reason out any point ; it does not survey steadily any course of facts. It dips into reason, it dips into history ; but it breathes more freely when it emerges again. Observe, then ;—the very exercises of the intellect, by which religious truth is attained, are just those which the Englishman is too impatient, and Protestantism too shallow, to abide ; the natural disposition of the one most happily jumps with the needs of the other. And this was the first singular advantage of Protestantism in England : Catholics reasoned profoundly upon doctrine, Catholics investigated rigidly the religious state of other times and places : in vain,—they had not found the way to gain the Englishman ; whereas their antagonists had found a weapon of their own, far more to the purpose of the contest than argument or fact.

That weapon is, what is so characteristic of our people, loyalty to the Sovereign. If there is one passion more than another which advantageously distinguishes the Englishman, it is that of personal attachment. He lives in the present, in contrast to the absent and the past. He ignores foreigners at a distance ! but when they come to him, if they come recommended by their antecedents, and make an appeal to his eyes and his ears, he almost worships them. We all recollect with what enthusiasm the populace received Marshal Soult on his visit to London a few years ago ; it was a warm and hearty feeling, elicited by the sight of a brave enemy and a skilful commander, and it took his own countrymen altogether by surprise. The reception given to Louis Philippe, who was far from popular among us, was of a similarly hospitable character ; nay, Napoleon himself, who had been the object of our bitterest hatred, on his appearance as a prisoner off the British coast, was visited by numbers with an interest, respect, and almost sympathy, which I consider (*mutatis mutandis*) would not all have been shown towards Wellington or Blucher, had they been prisoners in France. Again, I suppose the political principles of the Emperor Nicholas are as cordially hated in England as his religious principles are in disrepute in Rome ; yet even he, on his successive visits to the two places, encountered a far less flattering reception from the Roman populace than from the people of England. Who so unpopular, thirty years ago, as that remarkable man, Lord Londonderry ? yet, when he appeared at George the Fourth's coronation, the sight of his noble figure and bearing drew shouts of applause from the multitude, who had thought they hated him. George himself, worthless as he seems to have been, for how many years had he been an object of popular admiration ! till his wife, a more urgent candidate for the eye of pity and sympathy, supplanted him. Charles the Second, the most profligate of monarchs, lived in the hearts of his people till the day of his death. It is the way with Englishmen. A saint in rags would be despised ; in broadcloth, or in silk, he would be thought something more than ordinary.

St. Francis of Assisi, bareheaded and barefooted, would be hooted ; St. Francis Xavier, dressed up like a mandarin, with an umbrella over his head, would inspire wonder and delight. A Turk, a Parsee, a Chinese, a Bonze—nay, I will say, a chimpanzee, a hippopotamus—has only to show himself in order to be the cynosure of innumerable eyes, and the idol of his hour. Nay, even more,—I will say a bold thing, —but I am not at all sure, that, except at seasons of excitement like the present, the Pope himself, however he may be abused behind his back, would not be received with cheers, and run after by admiring crowds, if he visited this country, independent of the shadow of Peter which attends him, winning favour and attracting hearts, when he showed himself in real flesh and blood, by the majesty of his presence and the prestige of his name. Such, I say, is the Englishman ; with a heart for many objects, with an innate veneration for merit, talents, rank, wealth, science, not in the abstract, however, but as embodied in a visible form ; and it is the consciousness of this characteristic which renders statesmen at this moment, of whatever cast of politics, so afraid of the appearance of cardinals and a hierarchy in the midst of the people they have to govern.

3.

These antagonist peculiarities of the English character which I have been describing, lay clear and distinct before the sagacious intellects which were the ruling spirits of the English Reformation. They had to deal with a people who would be sure to revolt from the unnatural speculations of Calvin, and

who would see nothing attractive in the dreamy and
sensual doctrines of Luther. The emptiness of a
ceremonial, and the affectation of a priesthood, were
no bribe to its business-like habits and its ingrained
love of the tangible. Definite dogma, intelligible
articles of faith, formularies which would construe,
a consistent ritual, an historical ancestry, would have
been thrown away on those who were not sensitive
of the connexion of faith and reason. Another way
was to be pursued with our countrymen to make
Protestantism live ; and that was to embody it in
the person of its Sovereign. English Protestantism
is the religion of the throne : it is represented,
realised, taught, transmitted in the succession of
monarchs and an hereditary aristocracy. It is religion grafted upon loyalty ; and its strength is not in
argument, not in fact, not in the unanswerable controversialist, not in an apostolical succession, not in
sanction of Scripture—but in a royal road to faith, in
backing up a King whom men see, against a Pope
whom they do not see. The devolution of its crown
is the tradition of its creed ; and to doubt its truth
is to be disloyal towards its Sovereign. Kings are
an Englishman's saints and doctors ; he likes somebody or something at which he can cry " huzzah,"
and throw up his hat. Bluff King Hal, glorious Bess,
the Royal Martyr, the Merry Monarch, the pious
and immortal William, the good King George, royal
personages very different from each other,—nevertheless, as being royal, none of them comes amiss, but
they are all of them the objects of his devotion, and
the resolution of his Christianity.

It was plain, then, what had to be done in order

to perpetuate Protestantism in a country such as this. Convoke the legislature, pass some sweeping ecclesiastical enactments, exalt the Crown above the Law and the Gospel, down with Cross and up with the lion and the dog, toss all priests out of the country as traitors ; let Protestantism be the passport to office and authority, force the King to be a Protestant, make his Court Protestant, bind Houses of Parliament to be Protestant, clap a Protestant oath upon judges, barristers-at-law, officers in army and navy, members of the universities, national clergy ; establish this stringent Tradition in every function and department of the State, surround it with the lustre of rank, wealth, station, name, and talent ; and this people, so impatient of inquiry, so careless of abstract truth, so apathetic to historical fact, so contemptuous of foreign ideas, will *ex animo* swear to the truth of a religion which indulges their natural turn of mind, and involves no severe thought or tedious application. The Sovereign is the source and the centre, as of civil, so of ecclesiastical arrangements ; truth shall be synonymous with order and good government ;—what can be simpler than such a teaching ? Puritans may struggle against it, and temporarily prevail ; sceptics may ridicule it, object, expose and refute ; readers of the Fathers may try to soften and embellish it with the colours of antiquity ; but strong in the constitution of the law, and congenial to the heart of the people, the royal tradition will be a match for all its rivals, and in the long run will extinguish the very hope of competition.

So counselled the Achitophels of the day ; it was devised, it was done. Then was the inauguration of the great picture of the Lion and the Man. The Virgin Queen rose in her strength ; she held her court, she showed herself to her people ; she gathered round her peer and squire, alderman and burgess, army and navy, lawyer and divine, student and artisan. She made an appeal to the chivalrous and the loyal, and forthwith all that was noble, powerful, dignified, splendid, and intellectual, touched the hilt of their swords, and spread their garments in the way for her to tread upon. And first of all she addressed herself to the Law ; and that not only because it was the proper foundation of a national structure, but also inasmuch as, from the nature of the case, it was her surest and most faithful ally. The Law is a science, and therefore takes for granted afterwards whatever it has once determined ; hence it followed, that once Protestant, it would be always Protestant ; it could be depended on ; let Protestantism be recognised as a principle of the Constitution, and every decision, to the end of time, would but illustrate Protestant doctrines and consolidate Protestant interests. In the eye of the Law precedent is the measure of truth, and order the proof of reasonableness, and acceptableness the test of orthodoxy. It moves foward by a majestic tradition, faithful to its principles, regardless of theory and speculation, and therefore eminently fitted to be the vehicle of English Protestantism such as we have described it, and to co-operate with the monarchical principle in its establishment. Moreover, a number of delicate questions which had been contested in previous centuries, and had hitherto been involved in contradictory precedents, now received once for all a Protestant solution. There had been prolonged disputes between the Pontificate and the Regale, the dispute about Investitures, of Rufus with St. Anselm, of Henry the Second with St. Thomas, of Henry of Winchester with St. Edmund ; and the eighth Harry had settled it in his own way, when, on Cardinal Fisher's refusing to acknowledge his spiritual power, he had, without hesitation, proceeded to cut off his head ; but the Law, with its Protestant bias, could now give dignity and form to what, up to this time, to say the least, were *ex parte* proceedings. It was decided, once for all, what was the rule and what the exception ; the courts gave judgment that the saints were to be all in the wrong, the kings were to be all in the right ; whatever the Crown had claimed was to be its due, whatever the Pope claimed was to be a usurpation. What could be more simple and conclusive ? the most sacred power in the order of nature, " whose voice is the harmony of the world," to whom " all things in earth do homage," the hereditary wisdom and the collective intelligence of a mighty nation in Parliament assembled, the venerable Judges of the land were retained in the interests of a party, their ripe experience, their profound thought, their subtle penetration, their well regulated prudence, were committed for good and all to the politics of a crisis.

So much for the Law ; but this was only one of those great functions of the nation which became the instrument of the Protestant Tradition. Elizabeth had an influence on her side, over and above, and even greater than the authority of the Law. She was the queen of fashion and of opinion. The principles of Protestantism rapidly became the standard generally, to which genius, taste, philosophy, learning, and investigation were constrained and bribed to submit.   They are her legacy to the nation, and have been taken for granted ever since as starting-points in all discussion and all undertakings.   In every circle, and in every rank of the community, in the court, in public meetings, in private society, in literary assemblages, in the family party, it is always assumed that Catholicism is absurd.   No one can take part in the business of the great world, no one can speak and debate, no one can present himself before his constituents, no one can write a book, without the necessity of professing that Protestant ideas are self-evident, and that the religion of Alfred, St. Edward, Stephen Langton, and Friar Bacon, is a bygone dream.   No one can be a Catholic without apologising for it.   And what is in vogue in the upper classes is ever, as we know, ambitiously aped in the inferior.   The religious observances of the court become a reigning fashion throughout the social fabric, as certainly as its language or its mode of dress ; and, as an aspirant for distinction advances from a lower grade of society to an upper, he necessarily abandons his vulgar sect, whatever it is, for the national Protestantism.   All other ways of thought are as frightful as the fashions of last year ; the present is the true and the divine ; the past is dark because its sun has set, and ignorant because it is dumb, and living dogs are worth more than dead lions.   As to Catholicism, the utmost liberality which can be extended towards it, is to call it pretty poetry, bearable in a tragedy, intolerable in fact ; the utmost charity towards its professors is to confess that they may be better than their creed,—perhaps believe it, and are only dupes,—perhaps doubt it, and are only cowards. Protestantism sets the tone in all things ; and to have the patronage of the wealthy, the esteem of the cultivated, and the applause of the many, Catholics must get its phrases by heart.

It is the profession of a gentleman ; Catholicism, of underbred persons, of the vulgar-minded, the uncouth, and the ill-connected. We all can understand how the man of fashion, the profligate, the spendthrift, have their own circles, to which none but men of their own stamp and their own opinions are admitted ; how to hate religion and religious men, to scoff at principle, and to laugh at heaven and hell, and to do all this with decorum and good breeding, are the necessary title for admittance ; and how, in consequence, men at length begin to believe what they so incessantly hear said, and what they so incessantly say by rote themselves,—begin to suspect that, after all, virtue, as it is called, is nothing else than hypocrisy grafted on licentiousness ; and that purity and simplicity and earnestness and probity are but the dreams of the young and the theoretical :—it is by a similar policy, and by a similar process, that the fathers and patrons of the English Reformation have given a substance, a momentum, and a permanence to their tradition, and have fastened on us Catholics, first the imputation, then the repute of ignorance, bigotry, and superstition.

And now I will mention a distinct vehicle of the Protestant tradition in England, which was an instance of good fortune, greater than its originators could possibly have anticipated or contrived. Protestantism became, not only the tradition of law and of good society, but the tradition of literature also. There is no English literature before the age of Elizabeth; but with the latter years of her reign begins that succession of great authors which continues to flow on down to this day.   So it was, that about the commencement of the sixteenth century learning revived; on the taking of Constantinople by the Turks, the men of letters of the imperial city, and, what was of more consequence, its libraries, became the property of the West.   Schools were opened for the cultivation of studies which had made Greece as renowned among the nations in the gifts of intellect as Judea has been in the gifts of grace.   The various perfections of the Greek language, the treasures of Greek thought, the life and taste of Greek art, after the sleep of ages, burst upon the European mind.   It was like the warmth, the cheerfulness, and the hues of spring succeeding to the pure and sublime, but fantastic forms of winter frost-work.   The barbarism, the sternness, the untowardness of the high and noble medieval school, eyed with astonishment the radiance, and melted beneath the glow of a genius unrivalled in the intellectual firmament.   A world of ideas, transcendent in beauty and endless in fertility, flooded the imagination of the scholar and the poet.   The fine arts underwent a classical development, and the vernacular tongues caught the refinement and the elegance of the age of Pericles and Alexander.   The revival began in Catholic Italy; it advanced into Catholic France; at length it showed itself in Protestant England.   A voice came forth from the grave of the old world, as articulate and keen as that of a living teacher; and it thrilled into the heart of the people to whom it came, and it taught them to respond to it in their own tongue,—and that teaching was coincident in this country with the first preaching of Protestantism. It was surely a most lucky accident for the young religion, that, while the English 'language was coming to the birth with its special attributes of nerve, simplicity, and vigour, at its very first breathings Protestantism was at hand to form it upon its own theological *patois*, and to educate it as the mouth-piece of its own tradition. So, however, it was to be ; and soon,

> As in this bad world below
> Noblest things find vilest using,"

the new religion employed the new language for its purposes, in a great undertaking, the translation of its own Bible ; a work which, by the purity of its diction, and the strength and harmony of its style, has deservedly become the very model of good English, and the standard of the language to all future times. The same age, which saw this great literary achievement, gave birth to some of the greatest masters of thought and composition in distinct departments of authorship. Shakespeare, Spenser, Sidney, Raleigh, Bacon, and Hooker are its own ; and they were, withal, more or less the panegyrists of Elizabeth and her Religion, and moreover, at least the majority of them, adherents of her creed, because already clients of her throne. The Mother of the Reformation is, in the verses of Shakespeare, " a fair vestal throned by the west ;" in the poem of Spenser she is the Faery Queen, Gloriana, and the fair huntress, Belphebe, while the militant Christian is rescued from the seductions of Popery, Duessa, by Una, the True Church, or Protestant Religion. The works of these

celebrated men have been but the beginning of a
long series of creations of the highest order of literary
merit, of which Protestantism is the intellectual basis,
and Protestant institutions the informing object.
What was wanting to lead the national mind a willing
captive to the pretensions of Protestantism, beyond
the fascination of genius so manifold and so various ?
What need of controversy to refute the claims of
Catholicism, what need of closeness of reasoning, or
research into facts, when under a Queen's smile this
vast and continuous Tradition had been unrolled
before the eyes of men, luminous with the most
dazzling colours, and musical with the most sub-
duing strains ?   Certainly the lion's artists, even had
they had the fairest play, could have set up no rival
exhibition as original and as brilliant as this.

Nor was it court poets alone, as time went on, who
swelled the torrent of the Protestant Tradition.
Milton from the middle class, and Bunyan from
among the populace, exerted an influence superior to
Shakespeare himself, whose great mind did not con
descend to the direct inculcation of a private or a
sectarian creed.   Their phrases, their sentiments, are
the household words of the nation, they have become
its interpreters of Scripture, and, I may say, its
prophets,—such is the magical eloquence of their
compositions ; so much so, that I really shall not be
far from the mark in saying of them, and this is true
of Shakespeare also, that the ordinary run of men
find it very difficult to determine, in respect to the
proverbs, instances, maxims, and half sentences, which
are in the nation's mouth, which, and how much, is
from the Bible, and how much from the authors I

have mentioned. There is a saying, " Give me the framing of a nation's proverbs, and others may frame its laws ; " and its proverbs are the produce of its literature. What, indeed, could possibly stand against the rush of vehemence of such a Tradition, which has grown fuller and fuller, and more and more impetuous, with every successive quarter of a century ! Clarendon and the statesmen, Locke and the philosophers, Addison and the essayists, Hume, Robertson, and the historians, Cowper and the minor poets, the reviews and magazines of the present century, all proceed upon the hypothesis, which they think too self-evident for proof, that Protestantism is synonymous with good sense, and Catholicism with weakness of mind, fanaticism, or some unaccountable persuasion or fancy. Verse and prose, grave and gay, the scientific and the practical, history and fable, all is animated spontaneously, or imperiously subdued, by the spirit of Henry and Elizabeth. I say, " imperiously subdued," because the Tradition of Protestantism is strong enough, not only to recommend, but to force its reception on each successive generation of authors. It compels when it cannot persuade. There is Alexander Pope, a Catholic, and who would discover it from the run of his poems ? There is Samuel Johnson, born a Protestant, yearning for the Catholic Church, and bursting out into fitful defences of portions of her doctrine and discipline, yet professing to the last that very Protestantism which could neither command his affections, nor cure his infirmities. And, in our own time, there was Walter Scott, ashamed of his own Catholic tendencies and cowering before the jealous frown of the tyrant

Tradition. There was Wordsworth, obliged to do penance for Catholic sonnets by anti-Catholic complements to them. Scott, forsooth, must plead anti-quarianism in extenuation of his prevarication ; Wordsworth must plead Pantheism ; and Burke again, must plead political necessity. Liberalism, scepticism, infidelity, these must be the venial errors, under plea of which a writer escapes reprobation for the enormity of feeling tenderly towards the Religion of his fathers, and of his neighbours around him. That Religion labours under a proscription of three centuries, and it is outlawed by immemorial custom.

No wonder, then, that Protestantism, being the religion of our literature, has become the Tradition of civil intercourse and political life ; no wonder that its assumptions are among the elements of knowledge, unchangeable as the moods of logic, or the idioms of language, or the injunctions of good taste, or the proprieties of good manners. Elizabeth's reign is "golden," Mary is "bloody," the Church of England is "pure and apostolical," the Reformers are "judicious," the Prayer Book is "incomparable," or "beautiful," the Thirty-nine Articles are "moderate." "Pope" and "pagan" go together, and "the Pope, the Devil, and the Pretender." The anti-Catholic rancour is carried into your marts of commerce ; London is burned down, and forthwith your greatest architect is instructed to set up a tall pillar to perpetuate the lie, that the Papists were the incendiaries. Take your controversy with you when you sit down to cards and let the taunting name of Pope Joan be the title of your game. Run a horse the coming year, and among your Sorcerers, Lamplighters, Malibrans, and Priams, you will find Crucifix a striking, perhaps a lucky name for your beast ; it is but the emblem of an extinct superstition. Dress up for some fancy ball, or morris-dance, and let the Grand Turk jump about on one side of you, and the Pope with cross, and beads, and triple crown, upon the other. Go to the stage of the Mountebank, and teach him, when he displays his sleight-of-hand, to give effect to his tricks by the most sacred words of the Catholic ritual. Into your very vocabulary let Protestantism enter ; let priest, and mass, and mass-priest, and mass-house have an offensive savour on your palate ; let monk be a word of reproach ; let Jesuitism and Jesuitical, in their first intention, stand for what is dishonourable and vile. What chance has a Catholic against so multitudinous, so elementary a Tradition. Here is the Tradition of the Court, and of the Law, and of Society, and of Literature, strong in themselves, and acting on each other, and acting on a willing people, and the willing people acting on them, till the whole edifice stands self-supported, reminding one of some vast arch (as at times may be seen), from which the supports have crumbled away by age, but which endures still, and supports the huge mass of brickwork which lies above it, by the simple cohesion of parts which that same age has effected. My Brothers of the Oratory, you see what I meant when I spoke of the Tradition of the Pharisees, and said that it might be powerful in influence, though it was argumentatively weak ; you see why it is that the fair form of Catholicism, as it exists in the east, west, and south, never crosses the retina of a Protestant's imagination :—it is the in-

cubus of this Tradition, which cumbers the land, and
opposes an impregnable barrier between us and each
individual Protestant whom we happen to address.
Whoever he is, he thinks he knows all about our
religion before speaking to us,—nay, perhaps much
better than we know it ourselves. And now, if I
said no more, I have said abundantly sufficient for
the point I have had in view ; and yet there is one
portion of the subject still behind, which is almost
more to my purpose than anything which I have
hitherto mentioned.

4.

Protestantism is also the Tradition of the Anglican
Clergy ; and in speaking of them with reference to it,
as I am going to speak, Brothers of the Oratory, do
not suppose me to be forgetful either of their private
worth or their social uses. As the other functions of
the Constitution subserve the temporal welfare of the
community, so does the established clergy minister to
it with a special fidelity. But here I am all along
speaking of Kings, Lords, Commons, Law, Literature,
and so also of the Clergy, not simply as parts of the
body politic, but as organs of Protestantism ; and, as
I have pointed out the office which other political
ranks and departments fulfil in its propagation, so
am I now to speak of the duties of the Religious
Establishment. I say, then, that its especial duty as
a religious body, is not to inculcate any particular
theological system, but to watch over the anti-Catholic
Tradition, to preserve it from rust and decay, to
keep it bright and keen, and ready for action on any
emergency or peril. It is the way with human na-

ture to start with vigour, and then to flag; years tell upon the toughest frames; time introduces changes; prejudices are worn away; asperities are softened; views opened; errors are corrected; opponents are better understood; the mind wearies of warfare. The Protestant Tradition, left to itself, would in the course of time languish and decline; laws would become obsolete, the etiquette and usages of society would alter, literature would be enlivened with new views, and the old Truth might return with the freshness of novelty. It is almost the mission of the established clergy, by word and writing, to guard against this tendency of the public mind. In this specially consists its teaching; I repeat, not in the shreds of Catholic doctrine which it professes, not in proofs of the divinity of any creed whatever, not in separating opinion from faith, not in instructing in the details of morals, but mainly in furbishing up the old-fashioned weapons of centuries back; in cataloguing and classing the texts which are to batter us, and the objections which are to explode among us, and the insinuations and the slanders which are to mow us down. The Establishment is the keeper in ordinary of those national types and blocks from which Popery is ever to be printed off,—of the traditional view of every Catholic doctrine, the traditional account of every ecclesiastical event, the traditional lives of popes and bishops, abbots and monks, saints and confessors,—the traditional fictions, sophisms, calumnies, mockeries, sarcasms, and invectives with which Catholics are to be assailed.

This, I say, is the special charge laid upon the Establishment. Unitarians, Sabellians Utilitarians,

Wesleyans, Calvinists, Swedenborgians, Irvingites, Freethinkers, all these it can tolerate in its very bosom ; no form of opinion comes amiss ; but Rome it cannot abide. It agrees to differ with its own children on a thousand points, one is sacred—that her Majesty the Queen is "The Mother and Mistress of all Churches ; " on one dogma it is infallible, on one it may securely insist without fear of being unseasonable or excessive—that "the Bishop of Rome hath no jurisdiction in this realm." Here is sunshine amid the darkness, sense amid confusion, an intelligible strain amid a Babel of sounds ; whatever befalls, here is sure footing ; it is, "No peace with Rome," "Down with the Pope," and "The Church in danger." Never has the Establishment failed in the use of these important and effective watchwords ; many are its shortcomings, but it is without reproach in the execution of this its special charge. Heresy, and scepticism, and infidelity, and fanaticism, may challenge it in vain ; but fling upon the gale the faintest whisper of Catholicism, and it recognises by instinct the presence of its connatural foe. Forthwith, as during the last year, the atmosphere is tremulous with agitation, and discharges its vibrations far and wide. A movement is in birth which has no natural crisis or resolution. Spontaneously the bells of the steeples begin to sound. Not by an act of volition, but by a sort of mechanical impulse, bishop and dean, archdeacon and canon, rector and curate, one after another, each on his high tower, off they set, swinging and booming, tolling and chiming, with nervous intenseness, and thickening emotion, and deepening volume, the old ding-dong which

has scared town and country this weary time ; tolling
and chiming away, jingling and clamouring and ringing the changes on their poor half-dozen notes, all
about "the Popish aggression," "insolent and insidious," "insidious and insolent," "insolent and atrocious," "atrocious and insolent," "atrocious, insolent,
and ungrateful," "ungrateful, insolent, and atrocious,"
"foul and offensive," "pestilent and horrid," "subtle
and unholy," "audacious and revolting," "contemptible and shameless," "malignant," "frightful,"
"mad," "meretricious,"—bobs (I think the ringers
call them), bobs, and bobs-royal, and triple-bob-
majors, and grandsires,—to the extent of their compass and the full ring of their metal, in honour of
Queen Bess, and to the confusion of the Holy Father
and the Princes of the Church.[1]

So it is now ; so it was twenty years ago ; nay, so
it has been in all years as they came, even the
least controversial. If there was no call for a contest,
at least there was the opportunity of a triumph. Who
could want matter for a sermon, if ever his thoughts
would not flow, whether for convenient digression, or
effective peroration ? Did a preacher wish for an
illustration of heathen superstition or Jewish bigotry,
or an instance of hypocrisy, ignorance, or spiritual
pride ? the Catholics were at hand. The deliverance
from Egypt, the golden calf, the fall of Dagon, the
sin of Solomon, the cruelties of Jezebel, the worship
of Baal, the destruction of the brazen serpent, the
finding of the Law, the captivity in Babylon, Nebucho-

[1] The foregoing lecture in 1851 was, by an accidental coincidence,
written simultaneously with an able pamphlet by Serjeant Bellasis, *apropos*
of the conduct of the Anglican clergy of the day

donosor's image, Pharisees, Sadducees, Herodians, and
Zealots, mint, anise, and cummin, brazen pots and
vessels, all in their respective places and ways, would
give opportunity to a few grave words of allusion to
the "monstrous errors," or the "childish absurdities"
of the "Romish faith." Does any one wish an example
of pride? there stands Wolsey; of barbarity? there
is the Duke of Alva; of rebellion? there is Becket;
of ambition? there is Hildebrand; of profligacy? there
is Cæsar Borgia; of superstition? there is Louis the
Eleventh; of fanaticism? there are the Crusaders.
Saints and sinners, monks and laymen, the devout
and the worldly, provided they be but Catholics, are
heaped together in one indiscriminate mass, to be
drawn forth for inspection and exposure according
to the need.

The consequence is natural;—tell a person of
ordinary intelligence, Churchman or Dissenter, that
the vulgar allegations against us are but slanders,—
simple lies, or exaggerations, or misrepresentations;
or, as far as they are true, admitting of defence or
justification, and not to the point; and he will laugh
in your face at your simplicity, or lift up hands
and eyes at your unparalleled effrontery. The utmost
concession he will make is to allow the possibility of
incidental and immaterial error in the accusations
which are brought against us; but the substance of
the traditional view he believes, as firmly as he does
the Gospel, and, if you reject it and protest against it,
he will say it is just what is to be expected of a
Catholic, to lie and to circumvent. To tell him, at
his time of life, that Catholics do not rate sin at a
fixed price, that they may not get absolution for a sin

in prospect, that priests can live in purity, that nuns do not murder each other, that the laity do not make images their God, that Catholics would not burn Protestants if they could! Why, all this is as perfectly clear to him as the sun at noonday; he is ready to leave the matter to the first person he happens to meet; every one will tell us just the same; only let us try; he never knew there was any doubt at all about it; he *is* surprised, for he thought we granted it. When he was young, he has heard it said again and again; to his certain knowledge it has uniformly been said the last forty, fifty, sixty years, and no one ever denied it; it is so in all the books he ever looked into; what is the world coming to? What is true, if this is not? So, Catholics are to be whitewashed! What next?

And so he proceeds in detail; — the Papists not worship the Virgin Mary! why, they call her " Deipara," which means " equal to God."

The Pope not the man of sin! why, it is a fact that the Romanists distinctly maintain that "the Pope is God, and God is the Pope."

The Pope's teaching not a doctrine of devils! here is a plain proof of it; Cardinal Bellarmine expressly " maintains that, if the Pope commanded us to practise vice or shun virtue, we are obliged to do so, under pain of eternal damnation."

Not a Pope Joan! why, she was " John the Eighth, her real name was Gilberta, she took the name of John English, delivered public lectures at Rome, and was at length unanimously elected Pope."

What! Councils infallible! open your eyes, my brother, and judge for yourself: " fifteen hundred public women followed the train of the Fathers of Constance."

Jesuits! here are at least twenty thousand in England ; and, horrible to say, a number of them in each of the Protestant Universities, and doubtless a great many at Oscott.

Beauty and sanctity of the Popish festivals! do you not know that the Purification "is the very feast that was celebrated by the ancient Pagan Romans in honour of the goddess Proserpina ? "

The Papists not corrupters of the Scriptures! look into their Bibles, and you will find they read the prophecy in Genesis, " *She* shall crush thy head, and thou shalt lie in wait for *her* heel."

Popery preach Christ! no; " Popery," as has been well said, " is the religion of priestcraft ; from the beginning to the end it is nothing but priest, priest, priest." [1]

I shall both weary and offend you, my Brothers, if I proceed. Even absurdity becomes tiresome after a time, and slanders cast on holy things and persons, when dwelt on, are too painful for a Catholic's ears ; yet it was necessary for my subject to give instances of the popular views of us and of our creed, as they are formed under the operation of the Tradition of Elizabeth.

Here I am reminded of another sort of Tradition, started by a very different monarch, which in the event was handled very differently. It is often told how Charles the Second once sent a grave message to the Royal Society. That scientific body was founded in

[1] *Vide* Stephen's Spirit of the Church of Rome ; Edgar's Variations ; Cramp's Text-Book of Popery, &c. ; the books I happen to have at hand.

his 'reign, and the witty king, as became his well-known character, could not help practising a jest upon it. He proposed a question for its deliberation ; he asked it, as I daresay you have often heard, to tell him how it was that a live fish weighed less heavily in water than after it was dead. The Society, as it was in duty bound, applied itself to solve the phenomenon, and various were the theories to which it gave occasion. At last it occurred to its members to determine the fact, before deciding on any of them ; when, on making the experiment, to their astonishment they found that the hypothesis was a mere invention of their royal master's, because the dead fish was not heavier in water than the living.

Well would it be if Englishmen in like manner, instead of taking their knowledge of us at (what may be called) royal hand, would judge about us for themselves, before they hunted for our likeness in the book of Daniel, St. Paul's Epistles, and the Apocalypse. They then would be the first to smile at their own extravagances ; but, alas ! as yet, there are no such signs of such ordinary prudence. Sensible in other matters, they lose all self-command when the name of Catholicism is sounded in their ears. They trust the voice of Henry or Elizabeth, with its thousand echoes, more than their own eyes, and their own experience ; and they are zealous in echoing it themselves to the generation which is to follow them. Each in his turn, as his reason opens, is indoctrinated in the popular misconception. At this very time, in consequence of the clamour which has been raised against us, children in the streets, of four and five years old, are learning and using against us terms of abuse, which will be *their* tradition all through their lives, till they are grey-headed, and have, in turn, to teach it to their grandchildren. They totter out, and lift their tiny hands, and raise their thin voices, in protest against those whom they are just able to understand are very wicked and very dangerous ; and they run away in terror when they catch our eye. Nor will the growth of reason set them right ; the longer they live, and the more they converse with men, the more will they hate us. The Maker of all, and only He, can shiver in pieces this vast enchanted palace in which our lot is cast ; may He do it in His time !

LECTURE III.

It was my aim, Brothers of the Oratory, in my preceding Lecture, to investigate, as far as time and place
allowed, how it was that the one-sided view of the
great religious controversy, which commenced between
Rome and England three centuries since, has been so
successfully maintained in this country. Many things
have changed among us during that long period ; but
the hatred and the jealousy entertained by the
population towards the Catholic Faith, and the scorn
and pity which are felt at the sight of its adherents,
have not passed away, have not been mitigated. In
that long period, society has undergone various
alterations ; public opinion has received a development new in the history of the world, and many remarkable revolutions in national principle have
followed. The received views on the causes and the
punishment of crime, on the end of government, on
the mutual relations of town and country, on international interests, and on many other great political
questions, have sustained, to say the least, great
modifications ; sciences, unknown before, bearing upon
the economy of social life, have come into being ;
medicine has been the subject of new doctrines, which

have had their influence on various civil and municipal arrangements ; how is it, then, that the feeling against Catholicism has remained substantially what it was in the days of Charles the Second or of George the Third ? How is it that Protestantism has retained its ascendency, and that Catholic arguments and Catholic principles are at once misconstrued and ignored ? And what increases the wonder is, that externally to our own island it has happened otherwise ; there is scarcely a country besides ours where Catholicism is not at least respected, even if it is not studied ; and what is more observable still, scarcely a country besides ours, originally Protestant, in which Protestantism even exists at present,—if by Protestantism is understood the religion of Luther and Calvin. The phenomenon, great in itself, becomes greater by its thus seeming to be all but peculiar to the British population.

And this latter consideration is important also, as it anticipates a solution of the difficulty which the Protestant, were he able, would eagerly adopt. He would be eager to reply, if he could, that the Protestant spirit has survived in the land amid so many changes in political and social science, because certain political theories were false, but Protestantism is true ; but if this is the case, why has it not kept its ground and made its way in other countries also ? What cause can be assigned for its decay and almost extinction in those other countries, in Germany, Holland, Switzerland and New England, diverse from each other in situation, in government, in language, and in character, where once it flourished ? Evidently it must be a cause peculiar to England ; those foreign countries must have something in common with each other which they have not in common with us. Now what is peculiar to our country is an established Tradition of Protestantism ; what those other countries have in common with each other is the absence of such Tradition. Fact and argument have had fair play in other countries ; they have not had fair play here ; the religious establishment has forbidden them fair play. But fact and argument are the tests of truth and error ; Protestantism, then, has had an adventitious advantage in this country, in consequence of which it has not been tried,—as, in the course of years, otherwise it would have been tried, and as it has been tried elsewhere—on its own merits. Instead, then, of concluding that it is true, because it has remained here during three centuries substantially the same, I should rather conclude that it is false because it has not been able during that period to remain the same abroad. To the standing, compulsory Tradition existing here, I ascribe its continuance here ; to fact and reason operating freely elsewhere, I ascribe its disappearance elsewhere.

This view of the subject is confirmed to us, when we consider, on the one hand, the character of our countrymen, and on the other, the character of those instruments and methods by which the Tradition of Protestantism is perpetuated among them. It has been perpetuated, directly or indirectly, by the sanction of an oath, imposed on all those several sources of authority and influence, from which principles, doctrines, and opinions are accustomed to flow. There is an established Tradition of law, and of the clergy, and of the court, and of the universities, and of literature, and of good society ; and all these act upon a people peculiarly susceptible of the claims of personal merit, of embodied authority, of constituted order, of rank, and of reputation in the world, and little sensitive in comparison of abstract argument, logical sequence, moral fitness, historical results, or foreign transactions.

This was the point at which I stopped last week ; now I shall continue my investigation, and I shall introduce what I have to say by means of an objection.

I.

It may be objected, then, to the conclusions at which I have arrived, that I on my part have simply ignored the fact of the innumerable multitude of independent testimonies which every one of the divines, the scholars, the lawyers, the men of letters, the statesmen, the men of the world, who have made the last three centuries glorious in Britain, has borne in his turn, in favour of Protestantism and to the disadvantage of the Catholic religion.

Bacon and Hooker, Taylor and Chillingworth, Hampden, Clarendon, and Falkland, Russell, Somers and Walpole, Hobbes and Locke, Swift and Addison, Hume and Robertson, Warburton and Horsley, Pitt and Fox, Walter Scott and Hallam, and a multitude of other illustrious names, nay, the whole host of educated men, are all separate authorities ; each speaks for himself ; they do not copy, the one from the other : there are among them men of extensive reading, profound philosophy, intimate knowledge of the world ; they are all men of intelligence, and at least able to give an opinion. It is absurd to say otherwise. This simple consideration, it may be said, overthrows from its very foundation the argument drawn out in my last week's Lecture, about the traditional character of Protestantism in England. Indeed, my argument turns against myself; for I incidentally allowed on that occasion that a number of distinct testimonies, conspiring together into one view or representation, was a real and sound reason, nay, among the strongest of conceivable reasons, in its behalf; now, this is just the state of the case as regards the argument for Protestantism, as drawn from the common consent of the English court, clergy, bar, literature, and general society.

This is what will be said; and I reply as follows:—
I do not deny that there are great names on the side of Protestantism, which require to be considered by themselves;—minds, which certainly are superior to the influences of party, the prejudices of education, the suggestions of self-interest, the seductions of place and position, and the tyranny of public opinion. And again, there are Protestant arguments, clear and broad, which remain, whether Protestantism is received, or whether it is not. I allow all this: but now I am considering, not the Protestantism of the few, but of the many: those great men, and those philosophical arguments, whatever be their weight, have no influence with the many. Crowds do not assemble in Exeter Hall, mobs do not burn the Pope, from reverence for Lord Bacon, Locke, or Butler, or for anything those gifted men have recorded. ·I am treating of the unpopularity of Catholicism, now and here, as it exists in the year 1851, and in London, or in Edinburgh, or in Birmingham, or in Bristol, or in Manchester, or in Glasgow; among the gentlemen and yeomen of Yorkshire, Devonshire, and Kent; in the Inns of Court, and in the schools and colleges of the land; and I say

this Tradition does not flow from the mouth of the
half-dozen wise, or philosophic, or learned men who
can be summoned in its support, but is a tradition of
nursery stories, school stories, public-house stories,
club-house stories, drawing-room stories, platform
stories, pulpit stories ;—a tradition of newspapers,
magazines, reviews, pamphlets, romances, novels,
poems, and light literature of all kind, literature of the
day ;—a tradition of selections from the English
classics, bits of poetry, passages of history, sermons,
chance essays, extracts from books of travel, anonymous anecdotes, lectures on prophecy, statements and
arguments of polemical writers, made up into small
octavos for class-books, and into pretty miniatures for
presents ;—a tradition floating in the air ; which we
found in being when we first came to years of reason ;
which has been borne in upon us by all we saw, heard,
or read, in high life, in parliament, in law courts, in
general society ; which our fathers told us had ever
been in their day ; a tradition, therefore, truly universal and immemorial, and good as far as a tradition
can be good, but after all, not more than a tradition
is worth : I mean, requiring some ultimate authority
to make it trustworthy. Trace up, then, the tradition
to its very first startings, its roots and its sources, if
you are to form a judgment whether it is more than a
tradition. It may be a good tradition, and yet after
all good for nothing. What profit, though ninety-
nine links of a chain be sound, if the topmost is
broken? Now I do not hesitate to assert, that this
Protestant Tradition, on which English faith hangs, is
wanting just in the first link. Fierce as are its advocates, and high as is its sanction, yet, whenever we can

pursue it through the mist of immemorial reception in which it commonly vanishes, and can arrive at its beginnings, forthwith we find a flaw in the argument. Either facts are not forthcoming, or they are not sufficient for the purpose : sometimes they turn out to be imaginations or inventions, sometimes exaggerations, sometimes misconceptions ; something or other comes to light which blunts their efficiency, and throws suspicion on the rest. Testimonies which were quoted as independent turn out to be the same, or to be contradictory of each other, or to be too improbable to be true, or to have no good authority at all : so that our enemies find they cannot do better, after all, than fall back on the general reception of the Tradition itself, as a reason for receiving the Tradition ; and they find it prudent to convict us of all manner of crimes, on the simple ground of our being notoriously accused of them.

Hard measure, scanty justice ! It is a principle of English law, that no one should bring a charge against another without being under the obligation of supporting it. Where should we be, any one of us—who would be safe—if any person who chose might, at any moment he would, impute to us what he pleased, bring us into court, call no witnesses, and obtain our conviction on his simple assertion ? Why, at very least, an accuser is bound to make oath of the truth of what he says ; and that is but the first step of an investigation, not the termination of the process. And he must swear to a fact, not to an opinion, not to a surmise, not to what he has heard others say, but to what he has witnessed or knows. Nay, even though there be reasons for being sure of the guilt of the accused, it is

a maxim of our law not to make him criminate himself, but to aim at convicting him by other means and
by other men.   It seems a plain dictate of common
equity, that an accuser should have something to
say for himself, before he can put the accused on his
defence.

This righteous rule is simply set aside in the treatment of Catholics and their religion.   Instead of the
onus probandi, as it is called, the burden of proof, lying
with the accuser, it is simply thrown upon the accused.
Any one may get up of a sudden, and may say what
he will to our prejudice, without producing any warrant
at all for the truth of his charge.   He is not called
upon to establish his respectability, or to state his
opportunities or methods of knowing ; he need not
give presumptive proof of his allegation ; he need not
give his authorities ; he need only accuse ; and upon
this the Protestant public turns round to the poor
Catholic, and asks what he has to say in his defence,
as if he had yet anything to defend.   There is a saying, that "a fool can ask more questions than a hundred wise men can answer ;" and a bigot or a fanatic
may be quite as successful.   If a man presented himself this moment and said to me, "You robbed a person in the street of his pocket-book some ten years
ago," what could I possibly say, except simply, "I
did not"?   How could I prove it was false, even if I
took on myself to do so till I was informed of the
town, or the year, or the occasion, or the person on
whom the pretended offence was committed ?   Well,
supposing my accuser went on to particulars, and said
that I committed the crime in Birmingham, in the
month of June, in the year 1840, and in the instance

of a person of the name of Smith. This, of course
would be something, but no one would say even then
that it was enough ; that is, supposing I had to reply
to him on the spot. At the very moment I might not
be able to say where I was on the specified day, and
so I could only repeat as emphatically as I was able,
that the charge was utterly untrue.

Next, supposing me to ask his reasons for ad-
vancing it ;—how he knew it was I ? did he see me ?
or was he told by an eye-witness ? and supposing he
were to decline to give me any information whatever,
but contented himself with saying " that I was
shuffling and evasive, for the thing was quite notorious." And next, supposing I suddenly recollected that, up to the year 1845, I had never once
been in Birmingham in the course of my life ; yet, on
my stating this, the accuser were to cry out that I
should not escape, in spite of my attempt to throw
dust in his eyes ; for he had a score of witnesses to
prove the fact, and that, as to the exact year it was
a mere point of detail, on which any one might be
mistaken. And supposing, on this unsupported allegation, a magistrate, without witness brought, or oath
administered, or plausibility in the narrative, in spite
of the accuser's character, which was none of the best,
in spite of the vagueness of his testimony, were to
send me to prison,—I conceive public opinion would
say I was shamefully treated.

But further, supposing when I was safely lodged in
prison, some anonymous writer, in some third-rate
newspaper, were boldly to assert that all priests were
in the practice of stealing pocket-books from passengers in the streets ; and in proof thereof were to

appeal first to the notorious case of a priest in Birmingham who had been convicted of the offence, and then to the case of a second priest which was given in detail in some manuscript or other, contained somewhere or other in the royal library of Munich, and occurring some time or other between the seventh and the seventeenth centuries ; and, supposing upon this anonymous article or letter, petitions were got up and signed numerously, and despatched to the Imperial Parliament, with the object of sending all priests to the treadmill for a period not exceeding six months, as reputed thieves, whenever they were found walking in the public thoroughfares ;—would this answer an Englishman's ideas of fairness or of humanity?

Now I put it to the experience—I put it to the conscience of the Protestant world,—whether such is not the justice which it deals out to Catholics as a matter of course. No evidence against us is too little ; no infliction too great. Statement without proof, though inadmissible in every other case, is all fair when we are concerned. A Protestant is at liberty to bring a charge against us, and challenge us to refute, not any proof he brings, for he brings none, but his simple assumption or assertion. And perhaps we accept his challenge, and then we find we have to deal with matters so vague or so minute, so general or so particular, that we are at our wit's end to know how to grapple with them. For instance, " Every twentieth man you meet is a Jesuit in disguise ; " or, " Nunneries are, for the most part, prisons." How is it possible to meet such sweeping charges? The utmost we can do, in the nature of things, is to show that this particular man, or that, is not a Jesuit ; or that this or that particular nunnery is not a prison ; but who said he was?—who said it was? What our Protestant accuser asserted was, that every *twentieth* man was a Jesuit, and *most* nunneries were prisons. How is this refuted by clearing this or that person or nunnery of the charge ? Thus, if the accuser is not to be called on to give proofs of what he says, we are simply helpless, and must sit down meekly under the imputation.

At another time, however, a definite fact is stated, and we are referred to the authority on which it is put forward. What is the authority? Albertus Magnus, perhaps, or Gerson, or Baronius, with a silence about volume and page : their works consisting of five, ten, fifteen, twenty, or thirty folios, printed in double columns. How are we possibly to find the needle in this stack of hay? Or, by a refinement of unfairness, perhaps a wrong volume or page is carelessly given ; and when we cannot find there the statement which our opponent has made, we are left in an pleasant doubt whether our ill success is to be ascribed to our eyes or to his pen.

Sometimes, again, the crime charged on us is brought out with such startling vividness and circumstantial finish as to seem to carry its own evidence with it, and to dispense, in the eyes of the public, with the references which in fairness should attend it. The scene is laid in some fortress of the savage Apennine, or in secluded Languedoc, or in remote Poland, or the high table-land of Mexico ; or it is a legend about some priest of a small village of Calabria, called Buonavalle, in the fourteenth century ; or about a monk of the monastery of S. Spirito, in S. Fillippo d'Argiro, in the time of Charlemagne. Or the story runs, that Don Felix Malatesta de Guadalope, a Benedictine monk of Andalusia, and father confessor to the Prince of the Asturias, who died in 1821, left behind him his confessions in manuscript, which were carried off by the French, with other valuable documents, from his convent, which they pillaged in their retreat from the field of Salamanca ; and that, in these confessions, he frankly avows that he had killed three of his monastic brothers of whom he was jealous, had poisoned half-a-dozen women, and sent off in boxes and hampers to Cadiz and Barcelona thirty-five infants ; moreover, that he felt no misgivings about these abominable deeds, because, as he observes with great *naïveté*, he had every day, for many years, burnt a candle to the Blessed Virgin ; had cursed periodically all heretics, especially the royal family of England ; had burnt a student of Coimbra for asserting the earth went round the sun ; had worn about him, day and night, a relic of St. Diego ; and had provided that five hundred masses should be said for the repose of his soul within eight days after his decease.

Tales such as this, the like of which it is very easy to point out in print, are suitably contrived to answer the purpose which brings them into being. A Catholic who, in default of testimony offered in their behalf, volunteers to refute them on their internal evidence, and sets about (so to say) cross-examining them, finds himself at once in an untold labyrinth of embarrassments. First he inquires, *is* there a village in Calabria of the name of Buonavalle ? *is* there a convent of S. Spirito in the Sicilian town specified ? did it *exist* in the time of Charlemagne ? who were the successive confessors of the Prince of the Asturias during the first twenty years of this century? what has Andalusia to do with Salamanca? when was the last *Auto da fé* in Spain? did the French pillage any convent whatever in the neighbourhood of Salamanca about the year 1812?—questions sufficient for a school examination. He goes to his maps, gazetteers, guide-books, travels, histories;—soon a perplexity arises about the dates : are his editions *recent* enough for his purpose? do their historical notices go *far enough back?* Well, after a great deal of trouble, after writing about to friends, consulting libraries, and comparing state-ments, let us suppose him to prove most conclusively the utter absurdity of the slanderous story, and to bring out a lucid, powerful, and unanswerable reply ; who cares for it by that time? who cares for the story itself? it has done its work ; time stops for no man ; it has created or deepened the impression in the minds of its hearers that a monk commits murder or adul-tery as readily as he eats his dinner. Men forget the process by which they receive it, but there it is, clear and indelible. Or supposing they recollect the par-ticular slander ever so well, still they have no taste or stomach for entering into a long controversy about it ; their mind is already made up ; they have formed their views ; the author they have trusted may, in-deed, have been inaccurate in some of his details ; it can be nothing more. Who can fairly impose on them the perplexity and whirl of going through a bout of controversy, where " one says," and "the other says," and " *he* says that *he* says that *he* does not say or ought not to say what he does say or ought to say?" It demands an effort and strain of attention which they have no sort of purpose of bestowing. The Catholic cannot get a fair hearing; his book remains awhile in the shop windows, and then is taken down again. So true is this, from the nature of the human mind, that even though my present audience is well disposed, not hostile, to Catholicism, I should scarcely venture, in these Lectures, to enter into any minute investigation of this or that popular calumny, from my conviction that I should be detailing matters which, except in the case of the very few, would engross without interesting, and weary without making an impression.

Yet I think I may be able still, or at least I will try, without taxing your patience to the utmost, to bring before you two or three actual specimens of the mode in which the accusation against Catholics is conducted; which may serve tc give you some insight into the value of the Tradition which king, lords and commons, are so zealous in upholding. The mighty Tradition flows on, replenished and refreshed continually by rivulets which, issuing from new fountainheads, make their way, in faithful and unfailing succession, into the main stream. I am going to put my finger on three of these small fountain-heads of the Tradition,—which, as I have already complained, are not commonly accessible;—they shall not be springs of a vulgar quality, but they shall represent the intelligence, the respectability, and the strong sense of English society. The first shall be a specimen of the Tradition of Literature, the second of the Tradition of Wealth, and the third of the Tradition of Gentlemen.

2.

1. The first, which has to do with names well known in the aristocracy of talent and learning, will be somewhat tedious, do what I will; and I shall introduce it with a story. It is related by the learned Dr. Bentley, in his controversy with Boyle, about a century and a half ago, on some point of historical criticism. In the course of that controversy, his opponent happened to spell wrongly the name of a Greek town; and when he was set right, he made answer that it was the custom of our English writers so to spell it, and he proceeded to quote as many as five of them in proof of his assertion. On this Bentley observes, " An admirable reason, and worthy to be his own; as if the most palpable error, that shall happen to obtain and meet with reception, must therefore never be mended." After this, the " slashing " critic goes on to allude to the instance of an unlearned English priest, truly or not I know not, " who for thirty years together " (perhaps it was on taking the first ablution in the Mass) " had always said, ' Quod ore mumpsimus,' instead of ' Quod ore sumpsimus,' " and when, says Bentley, " a learned man told him of his blunder, ' I'll not change,' says he, ' my old Mumpsimus for your new Sumpsimus.' " Now, this happily applies to the subject which I am going to illustrate, as you will presently see.

I need not remind you how much is said among Protestants of the gross ignorance and superstition of the middle age: indeed, we Catholics of the present date are considered its legitimate and veritable heirs. On this subject, one of the best read, most dispassionate and deservedly esteemed writers of the present day, who, if any one, might be supposed in historical matters an original authority, in his "View of the State of Europe during the Middle Ages," writes as follows :—

" In the very best view that can be taken of monasteries," he says, after allowing that many might be above reproach, " their existence is deeply injurious to the general morals of a nation. They withdraw men of pure conduct and conscientious principle from the exercise of social duties, and leave the common mass of human vice more unmixed. Such men are always inclined to form schemes of ascetic perfection, which can only be fulfilled in retirement ; but, in the strict rules of monastic life, and under the influence of a grovelling superstition, their virtue lost all its usefulness. They fell implicitly into the snares of crafty priests, who made submission to the Church, not only the condition, but the measure of all praise." Now comes the passage to which I am directing your attention. Observe, he is going on to his *proof* of what he has asserted. " He is a good Christian, says Eligius, a saint of the seventh century, who comes frequently to church, who presents an oblation that it may be offered to God on the altar ; who does not taste the fruits of his land till he has consecrated a part of them to God ; who can repeat the Creed or the Lord's Prayer. Redeem your souls from punishment, while it is in your power ; offer presents and tithes to churches, light candles in holy places, as much as you can afford, come more frequently to church, implore the protection of the saints ; for, if you observe these things, you may come with security at the day of judgment to say, 'Give unto us, O Lord, for we have given unto Thee!'" The author then continues, "With such *a definition of the Christian character*, it is not surprising that any *fraud and injustice* became honourable, when it contributed to the riches of the clergy and the glory of their order."[1]

Now, observe first, he quotes St. Eligius, or Eloi, in order to show that Catholics were at that time taught that true Christianity consisted, not in the absence of fraud and injustice, or again, of immorality, hatred, or strife—but in merely coming to church, paying tithes, burning candles, and praying to the saints. But, observe next, he does not quote from St. Eligius' own work, or refer to it on his own authority, but, well-read man as he is, notwithstanding, he is content to rely on the authority of two other writers, and (what many well-read men would have omitted to do) he candidly confesses it. He refers to Dr. Robertson, the Scotch historian, and the celebrated German historian and critic, Mosheim. I do not see, then, that much blame attaches to this writer for publishing what you will see presently is a most slanderous representation, beyond, indeed, his taking for granted the Protestant Tradition, his exercising faith in it as true, his not doubting the fidelity of the two authors in question, and, therefore, in a word, his saying " Mumpsimus " and passing it on.

Next we come to Dr. Robertson, the historian of Scotland, Charles the Fifth, and America, the friend of Hume, Adam Smith, Gibbon, and a host of literati of the latter part of last century. In his history of the reign of the Emperor Charles the Fifth, who lived at

[1] Hallam's Middle Ages, vol. iii. p. 353.

the time of the Reformation, after observing that
"the Christian religion degenerated, during those
ages of darkness, into an illiberal superstition;" that
"the barbarous nations, instead of aspiring to *sanctity
and virtue*, imagined that they satisfied every obligation of duty by a scrupulous *observance of external
ceremonies*,"—Dr. Robertson annotates as follows:—
"*All the religious maxims and practices* of the dark
ages are a proof of this. I shall produce *one remarkable testimony* in confirmation of it, from an author
canonised by the Church of Rome, St. Eloy, or
Eligius." And then he proceeds to quote, nearly in
the same words as Mr. Hallam, though omitting
some clauses and adding others, a translation from
the passage which Mosheim sets down in his history,
as if the original text of the saint's. And then he
adds the remark of Dr. Maclaine, Mosheim's English
translator, whom he is pleased to call "learned and
judicious," and whose remark he calls a "very proper
reflection." This remark is as follows:—"We see
here," says Maclaine, "a large and ample description
of the character of a good Christian, in which there
is not *the least* mention of the love of God, resignation
to His will, obedience to His laws, or of justice, benevolence, and charity towards men." Here, then, we
trace our "Mumpsimus" a step higher, from Hallam,
to Robertson, from Robertson to the "learned and
judicious" Maclaine.

Robertson and Maclaine were Scotchmen; but the
Tradition was not idle the while in the south either.
There was a certain learned Mr. White, well known,
somewhat later than Robertson, in the University of
Oxford. He was Professor of Arabic in that seat of

learning, and happened one year to preach a set of lectures, which added most considerably to his reputation. I should not have noticed the circumstances attending them, did they not throw light on the measure of authority due to the divines, scholars, historians, statesmen, lawyers, and polite writers, who are the doctors of the Protestant Tradition. The lectures in question, which are delivered at Oxford yearly, on some theological subject, are in the appointment of the governors of the place; who, feeling the responsibility attached to this exercise of patronage, anxiously look about for the safest, or the most brilliant, or the most rising, or the most distinguished of their members, to whom to commit the guardianship of Protestantism, and the fair fame of the University. Some such person Mr. White was considered; and, on his appointment, he selected for his lectures a subject of great interest—the rise and genius of Mahomet and his religion. Of learning he had enough; eloquence, perhaps, he wanted; yet what must have surprised his audience, when the time came for his exhibition, was the special elegance, splendour, and vivacity, which showed themselves in his style. His periods, far from savouring of the austereness of an oriental linguist, displayed the imagery, the antithesis, the flow and the harmony of a finished rhetorician. The historian Gibbon, no mean judge of composition, goes out of his way, to speak of his lectures as " a volume of controversy " more " elegant and ingenious " than any Mohammedan pulpit was likely to have produced, had Oxford become Mohammedan, instead of Protestant; and is pleased to observe that the writer " sustains the part of a lively and eloquent advocate " while he " sometimes rises to the merit of an historian and a philosopher." Such were the lectures delivered, and such was the reputation in consequence obtained by the Arabic Professor: however, after a time, it came to light that a great portion of the volume, at least many of its finest passages, were the writing of another. Indeed he was obliged to confess that he employed in the work, and actually paid for it, a country curate in Devonshire (who, I think, had once been a dissenting preacher), whom he supplied with the raw material of thought, and who returned it back to him in a dress suitable to the audience to whom it was to be presented. This was the man, who was getting credit for what was not his own, who, in treating of Mahomet, must make a diversion from his course—which never comes amiss in a Protestant volume—in order to bring a charge of incapability and pretence against the Catholic Church ; and what should he unluckily choose for the instrument of his attack but the identical passage of St. Eligius, and on that same authority of Mosheim, which we have already been used by Hallam, Robertson, and Maclaine. Mr. White writes thus :—

" *No representation can convey stronger ideas of the melancholy state of religion* in the seventh century, than the description of the character of a good Christian, as drawn at that period by St. Eligius, or Eloi, Bishop of Noyon." And then he quotes the extract already cited, from the pages of Mosheim.

And now we are approaching the fountain-head of the Tradition, but first I must just allude to one other author of name, who bears the same testimony to " Mumpsimus," and simply on the same authority.

This is an elegant writer, a divine and an Archdeacon of the Established Church, Jortin, who in the year 1773, published " Remarks on Ecclesiastical History." In the table of contents prefixed to the third volume, we are referred to " Eligius' *system* of Religion : " and turning to the page set against that descriptive title, we are told, " In this seventh century, . . monkery flourished prodigiously, and the monks and Popes were in the firmest union. As to true religion, here is the *sum and substance* of it, as it is *drawn up* for us by Eligius, one of the principal saints of that age." And then follows the cut and dried passage as given by Mosheim.

Now, at last, let us proceed to the first father of Mumpsimus, the Lutheran Mosheim himself. His words run thus in his Ecclesiastical History : " During this century (the seventh) true religion lay buried under a senseless mass of superstitions, and was unable to raise her head. The earlier Christians . . taught that Christ had made expiation for the sins of men by His death and His blood ; the latter " (those of the seventh century) " seemed to inculcate that the gates of heaven would be closed against none who should enrich the clergy or the Church with their donations. The former were studious to maintain a holy simplicity, and to follow a pure and chaste piety, the latter place the *substance* of religion *in external rites and bodily exercises.*" And then, in order to illustrate this contrast, which he has drawn out, between the spirituality of the first Christians and the formality of the Papists, he quotes the famous passage which has been the matter of our investigation.

Brothers of the Oratory, take your last look at

the Protestant Tradition, ere it melts away into thin air from before your eyes. It carries with it a goodly succession of names, Mosheim, Jortin, Maclaine, Robertson, White, and Hallam. It extends from 1755 to the year 1833. But in this latter year, when it was now seventy-eight years old, it met with an accident, attended with fatal consequences. Some one for the first time, instead of blindly following the traditional statement, thought it worth while first to consult St. Eligius himself. His work is in every good library ; but to no one had it occurred to take it down from the shelf, till the present Protestant Dean of Durham, Dr. Waddington, who was engaged in publishing an Ecclesiastical History at the date I have named. At first, indeed, he relied on his Protestant masters ; and taking Mosheim for his guide, and quoting St. Eligius from Mosheim's volume, he observes that, as a saint was " a person of influence in his day, we may venture to record what, in his opinion, was the *sum and substance* of true religion." Then follows the old extract. This is at the 153rd page of Dr. Waddington's work ; but, by the time he got to page 298, he had turned to the original, and the truth came out. He found that the received Protestant extract was only a small portion, nay, only sentences picked out here and there, of a very long sermon,—other sentences, of which, close by, and in the very midst of those actually quoted, contained all those very matters, the supposed absence of which was the very charge brought against St. Eligius, by Mosheim, Maclaine, Robertson, Jortin, White, and Hallam. They, forsooth, pure Protestants, had been so shocked and scandalized, that there was nothing of moral virtue in the saint's idea of a Christian, nothing of love of God or of man ; nothing of justice, of truth, of knowledge, of honesty ; whereas, in matter of fact, there turned out to be an abundance of these good things, drawn out in sentences of their own, though certainly not in the other sentences which those authors had extracted. I will quote what Dr. Waddington says, on his discovery of his mistake :—

He says that " the sense, and even the words " of the passage which he had cited, " had been previously retailed both by Robertson and Jortin, and the original quoted by Mosheim ;" but that he had since " been led to look more particularly into the life of Eligius, as it is published in the ' Spicilegium Dacherii ? ' " Then he continues, " he "—that is himself, the Author—" was pleased to discover many excellent precepts and pious exhortations scattered among the strange matter "—so he speaks as a Protestant— " with which it abounds. But at the same time it was with great sorrow and some shame, that he ascertained the *treachery* of his historical conductor," that is, Mosheim. " The expressions cited by Mosheim," he continues, " and cited, too, with a direct reference to the ' Spicilegium, ' " in which the Sermon is contained, " were forcibly brought together *by a very unpardonable mutilation* of his authority. They are to be found, indeed, in a Sermon preached by the Bishop, but found in the *society of so many good and Christian maxims*, that it had been charitable entirely to overlook them, as it was certainly unfair to weed them out and heap them together, without notice of the rich harvest that surrounds them."

He then proceeds to quote some of those exhortations of the Saint to which he alludes, and which Mosheim had omitted. For instance :—" Wherefore, my brethren, love your friends *in* God, and love your enemies *for* God, for he who loveth his neighbour hath fulfilled the law. . . . He is a good Christian who believes not in charms or inventions of the devil, but places the whole of his hope in Christ alone ; who receives the stranger with joy, as though he were receiving Christ himself, . . . who gives alms to the poor in proportion to his possessions, . . . who has no deceitful balances or deceitful measures, . . . who both lives chastely himself, and teaches his neighbours and his children to live chastely, and in the fear of God. . . . Behold, ye have heard, my brethren, what sort of people good Christians are . . . to the end that ye be true Christians, always ponder the precepts of Christ in your mind, and also fulfil them in your practice. . . . Keep peace and charity, recall the contentious to concord, avoid lies, tremble at perjury, bear no false witness, commit no theft, observe the Lord's day, . . . do as you would be done by, . . . visit the infirm, . . . seek out those who are in prison." So the holy Bishop proceeds ; and *then* he adds, " If you observe *these things*, you may appear boldly at God's tribunal in the day of judgment, and say, Give, Lord, as we have given." Scattered about in the midst of these exhortations, are the few sentences, excellent also, in spite of Dr. Waddington, though they are not the whole of Christianity, which the Protestant writers have actually quoted.

Such is the Sermon upon which Dr. Maclaine

makes this (as Dr. Robertson thinks) "very proper
reflection:" "We see here a large and ample description of the character of a good Christian, in
which there is not *the least* mention of the love of
God, resignation to His will, obedience to His laws,
or justice, benevolence, or charity towards men."
But as Mosheim and his followers have their opinion
of St. Eligius, so, in turn, has Dr. Waddington his
opinion of Mosheim. " The impression," he says,
" which " Mosheim, by " stringing together " certain
sentences " without any notice of the context, conveys to his readers, is *wholly false* ; and the *calumny*
thus indirectly cast upon his author is not the less
reprehensible, because it falls on one of the obscurest
saints in the Roman calendar. If the very essence
of history be truth, and if any deliberate violation
of that be sinful in the profane annalist, still less can
it deserve pardon ɔr mercy in the historian of the
Church of Christ."

This, as I have said, took place in 1833 : two years
later the exposure was repeated, in a brilliant paper
inserted by Dr. Maitland in an Ecclesiastical Magazine ; the Editor, moreover, drawing the special
attention of his readers to his correspondent's remarks.[2]

However, after all—after surveying the whole
course of the exposure—I could not help expressing
to myself my intense misgivings that the efforts of
Dr. Waddington and Dr. Maitland to do justice to
the saint would be in vain. I knew enough of the
Protestant mind, to be aware how little the falsehood
of any one of its traditions is an effectual reason for

[2] I do not add Dr. Lingard, as being a Catholic authority.

its relinquishing it; and I find too truly that I was not mistaken in my anticipation. Mumpsimus still reigns. In a new edition of Mosheim's history, published in 1841, the editor, a recent successor of Mr. White in the Oxford lectures, reprints those precious legacies, the text of Mosheim, the "very proper reflection" of Maclaine, and the garbled quotation from St. Eligius, for the benefit of the rising generation of divines, without a word of remark, or anything whatever to show that a falsehood had been recklessly uttered, a falsehood blindly perpetuated, a falsehood luminously exposed.

3.

2. I have given you, my Brothers, a specimen of the Tradition of Literature; now I proceed to the Tradition of Wealth, Respectability, Virtue, and Enlightened Religion ; for all these, in a country like ours, are supposed to go together, the Tradition of our merchants, traders, and men of business, and of all who have anything to lose, and are, therefore, conscientiously attached to the Constitution. And I shall select, as the organ of their Tradition, a writer whom they will at once acknowledge to be an unexceptionable representative of their ideas. If there be a periodical of the day which lays claim to knowledge of this globe, and of all that is in it, which is catholic in its range of subjects, its minute curiosity, and its world-wide correspondence, which has dealings with all the religions of the earth, and ought to have the largeness and liberality of view which such manifold intercourse is calculated to create,

it is the *Times* newspaper. No men avow so
steady a devotion to the great moral precepts embodied in the Decalogue, as its conductors, or profess
so fine a sense of honour and duty, or are so deeply
conscious of their own influence on the community,
and of the responsibilities which it involves, or are so
alive to the truth of the maxim, that, in the general
run of things, honesty is the best policy. What
noble, manly, disinterested sentiments do they utter!
what upright intention, strong sense, and sturdy
resolution, are the staple of their compositions! what
indignation do they manifest at the sight of vice or
baseness! what detestation of trickery! what solemn
resolve to uphold the oppressed! what generous sympathy with innocence calumniated! what rising of
heart against tyranny! what gravity of reprobation!
how, when Catholic and Protestant are in fierce
political antagonism, they can mourn over breaches of
charity in which they protest the while they had
no share! with what lively sensibility and withering
scorn do they encounter the accusation, made against
them by rivals every half-dozen years, of venality or
tergiversation! If anywhere is to be found the sternness of those who are severe because they are pure—
who may securely cast stones, for none can cast at
them—who, like the Cherub in the poem, are "faithful
found among the faithless"—you would say that
here at length you had found the incorruptible and
infallible, the guides in a bad world, who, amid the
illusions of reason and the sophistries of passion, see
the path of duty on all questions whatever, with a
luminousness, a keenness, and a certainty special to
themselves. When, then, I would illustrate the value

of the Anti-Catholic Tradition, as existing among the money-making classes of the community, I cannot fix upon a more suitable sample than the statements of these accomplished writers. Accordingly I refer to their columns; and towards the end of a leading article, in the course of the last month or six weeks, I find the following sentence:—" It is the practice, as our readers are aware, in Roman Catholic countries, for the clergy to post up a list of *all the crimes* to which human frailty can be tempted, placing opposite to them the *exact sum* of money for which their perpetration will be indulged." [3] And what makes this statement the more emphatic, is the circumstance that, within two or three sentences afterwards,—ever mindful, as I have said, of the Tables of the Law,—the writer takes occasion to refer to the divine prohibition, " Thou shalt not bear false witness against thy neighbour."

Such is a specimen of the Tradition, marvellous to say, as it exists among the classes who are well-to-do in the world. You see, they are so clear on the point, that, for all their mercantile sense of the value of character, their disgust at false intelligence, their severity with fraud, and their sensitiveness at libel, they have no hesitation in handing down to the next generation this atrocious imputation, that the Catholic Church proclaims that she is commissioned by the Moral Governor of the world to bestow on her children permission to perpetrate any sin whatever, for which they have a fancy, on condition of their paying her a price in money for that perpetration, in proportion to the heinousness of the offence.

[3] June, 1851.

Now this accusation is not only so grave in itself, but, miserable to say, is so industriously circulated, that, before using it for the purpose for which I have introduced it, in order to remove all suspicion against us, I am induced to go out of my way to enunciate, as briefly and as clearly as I can, what the Catholic Church really does teach upon the subject.[4] The charge in question then rests on a confusion between the *forgiveness of sins* and *admission to Church communion*, two ideas perfectly distinct from each other, both in themselves and in Catholic theology. Every scandalous sin contains in it, as we consider, two separate offences, the offence against God, and the offence against the Church ; just as Protestants would allow that murder is at once a sin against God and our neighbour, a sin in the eyes of God, and a crime in the eyes of the law. And, as human society has the arbitrary power of assigning punishments to offences against itself, heavy or light, or of overlooking the offence altogether, or of remitting the penalty when imposed, so has the Church. And as the magistrate often inflicts a fine, under sanction of the law, instead of committing to prison, so does the Church allow of the commutation of her own punishments, which are called censures, into alms to the poor, into offerings for some religious object, or even into the mere paying the expenses of the process, that is, the costs of the suit. And as the connivance or free pardon of the magistrate is no pardon in the sight of Heaven of the adulterer or the burglar, nor is

---

[4] The subject of indulgences does not enter into the charge as contained in the extract from the *Times;* but I purpose to add a word about it before the end of the Volume.

supposed to be such, so neither does the offender receive, nor is he promised, any forgiveness of his sin, either by the Church's taking off the censure (whether in consequence of an almsgiving or otherwise), or by her forbearing, which is the common case, to inflict censure altogether. It is true, the Church has the power of forgiving sins also, which I shall speak of directly ; but this is by a different instrument, and by a totally different process, as every Catholic knows.

I repeat, the Catholic who perpetrates any great and public sin offends his Maker, and offends his ecclesiastical Society ; the injury against his Maker is punished by an *ipso facto* separation from His favour ; the injury against his Society, when it is visited at all, is visited by excommunication or other spiritual infliction. The successor of St. Peter has the power committed to him of pardoning both offences, the offence against God and the offence against the Church ; he is the ultimate source of all jurisdiction whether external or internal, but he commonly restores such a sinner to the visible society of Christians, by an act of his own or of the metropolitan or ordinary, and he reconciles him to God by the agency of the priesthood. Repentance is required on the part of the offender for both restorations ; but the *sin* is forgiven, and its punishment remitted only in one of them,—viz., in the Sacrament of *Penance ;* and in this Sacrament, in which is the only real pardon, no money is, or ever can be paid. The Sacrament cannot be bought ; such an act would be a horrible crime ; you know this, my Brothers, as I know it myself ; we witness to each other that such is the received teaching among us.   It is utterly false then to assert that it has ever been held in the Catholic Church that "the perpetration of crime could be indulged" for any sum of money.   Neither for sins committed, nor sins to come, has money ever been taken as an equivalent, for one no more than for the other.   On the other hand, it is quite true that the injury done to the Church, when it happens to have been visited with a censure (which is not a common case), has certainly sometimes been compensated by the performance of some good work and in the number of such works, almsdeeds and religious offerings are included.   I repeat, the Church as little dreams of forgiving the sinner by removing the censure and readmitting him to public communion, as the magistrate by letting a culprit out of prison.

And in matter of fact, the two acts, the external reconciliation and the inward absolution, are not necessarily connected together.   The Church is composed of bad as well as good, according to the Parable, which prophesied that the net should gather of every kind ; a man then may be readmitted to visible fellowship on a general profession of repentance, yet when he proceeds to the Sacrament of Penance, may be unable to satisfy the priest that his repentance is sincere, and thus may fail of absolution.   Then he would be in a case, alas! so commonly found in the Church, and ever to be found—viz., allowed to attend mass, to hear sermons, to take part in rites, offices, and processions, and regarded as a Christian, yet debarred from the use of the Sacraments, deprived of Penance and of Holy Eucharist, getting no benefit from In-

I

dulgences, meriting nothing for his salvation, but on the contrary being separate from his God, and lying under His wrath, and a dead branch, though he has offered his alms, and is visibly connected with the trunk. On the other hand, it is quite conceivable in idea, that the spiritual reconciliation, that is, the forgiveness of sin, might be bestowed without the external or ecclesiastical restoration. Something like this took place, I think, in the case of the Emperor Napoleon, who up to the time of his death, lay under the censures of the Church, and was excommunicate, yet in his last days expressed a desire to be reconciled to God. To the ecclesiastical society whom he had offended, he was not publicly reconciled ; but it is never too late to be saved ; he confessed, he received the priest's reconciliation to the Church and to God ; and if his repentance was true, he departed with an absolute certainty of Heaven, though he had not received that pontifical restoration to the visible body to which offerings and alms have sometimes been attached.[5]

However, in spite of the clear and broad distinction I have been laying down, it is the Tradition of Protestantism, immutable and precise, as expressed in the words of its eminent Teacher and Doctor I have quoted, that the Catholic Church professes to forgive sins past and to come, on the payment of a price. So it has come down to us, so it will flow on ; and the mighty flood of falsehood is continually fed and

---

[5] I think I recollect an *absolutio post mortem*, when La Belle Poule was sent out for his remains. I do not forget the passage in the Council, *Pie admodum, ne hac ipsâ occasione quis pereat*, &c. Sess. 14, de Pœn. c. 7. *Vide* Ferrari's Biblioth. v. Absol. art. i 55—57.

kept to the full by fresh and fresh testimonies, separate
and independent, till scepticism is overcome and
opposition is hopeless. And now I am going to give
you an account of one of these original authorities,
as they are considered, who has lately presented himself to the world in the person of a zealous Protestant
clergyman, who once visited Belgium, and on occasion
of the late outcry about "Popish Aggression" was
moved to give his brethren the benefit of his ocular
testimony in behalf of one of the most flagrant
abuses and abominations of "that corrupt Church."

His account, given at a public meeting, was to the
following effect:—That in the year 1835, when on a
visit to Brussels, he was led to inspect the door of
the Cathedral, St. Gudule's ; and that there he saw
fastened up a catalogue of sins, with a specification
of the prices of which remission of each might severally
be obtained. No circumstance, it would appear,
called for his giving this information to the world for
the long space of sixteen years ; and it is a pity, for
the Protestant cause, that another sixteen did not
pass before circumstances suggested his doing so.
Why did he not consign it to some safe volume of
controversy, weighty enough for England, too heavy
for the Channel, instead of committing it to the wings
of the wind and the mercy of reporters ? Then
tranquilly and leisurely would the solemn tale have
ventured out upon platforms and into pulpits, when
contemporaries were gone, and would have taken
its place beside my own Don Felix of Andalusia and
similar worthies of Exeter Hall. But the fates willed
otherwise ; the accessory was to join the main stream
at once, and to its surprise to be tumbled violently

into its bed. The noise drew attention ; curiosity was excited ; the windings of the infant rill were prematurely tracked to its source ; so we can now put our finger on the first welling of its waters, and we can ascertain the composition of a Protestant tradition.

On the news of this portentous statement getting to Brussels, it excited a commotion which it could not rouse among the Catholics of England. We are familiarised to calumny, and have learned resignation ; the good Belgians were surprised and indignant at what they had thought no sane man would have ventured to advance. Forthwith a declaration was put forth by the persons especially interested in the Cathedral, categorically denying the charge. It is signed by the Dean of Brussels, who is also curé of the Cathedral, by his four assistant clergymen, by the churchwardens, by the judge of the high court of justice, and two other judges, and by others. They observe that they had privately asked the accuser to withdraw his statement, and on his refusal they made the following terse Declaration :—

" The undersigned look upon it as a duty to come forward and protest against the allegations of the " clergyman in question. " They declare, upon their honour, that such a notice as the one spoken of by the said clergyman has never disgraced the entrance, either of the church of St. Gudule, or of any other church of Brussels, or of the whole country. They further declare, that they have never even suspected for one instant that permission to sin could, for any possible motive, be granted, nor that any one could ever obtain remission of his sins for money. Such a doctrine they repudiate with indignation, as it is, and always has been, repudiated by the whole of the Catholic Church." This declaration is dated, " Brussels, April 2, 1851."

One thing alone was wanting to complete the refutation of the slander ; and that was, to account how its author was betrayed into so extraordinary a misrepresentation. No one will accuse a respectable person of wilful and deliberate falsehood ; did his eyes or his memory deceive him ? or did he really see something on the door, which he wrongly translated and interpreted by his prejudices ? That the latter is the true explanation of the phenomenon, is probable from a piece of information with which a Brussels journal supplies us. I dare say you know that in cathedrals and large churches abroad chairs are used for worship instead of benches ; and they are generally farmed by the beadles or others attached to the church, who let them out to all comers at the price of a small copper coin every time they are used. Now, it so happens that on the right-hand door of the transept of this church of St. Gudule there really is affixed a black board, on which there is a catalogue in the French language of the price to be paid, not for sins, but for the use of these chairs. The inscription translated runs as follows :—" A chair without cushion, one cent (about a farthing) ; a chair with cushions, two cents. On great festival days ; a chair without cushion, two cents ; a chair with cushion, four cents." This board, it may be supposed, our anti-Catholic witness mistook for that abominable sin-table, the description of which so deservedly shocked the zealous Protestants of Faversham.

Such is the ultimate resolution, as detected in a particular instance, of that uniform and incontestable Protestant Tradition, that we sell sin for money.   The exposure happened in March and April ; but Protestantism is infallible, and the judgment of its doctors irreversible ; accordingly, in the following June, the newspaper I have mentioned thought it necessary to show that the Tradition was not injured by the blow ; so out came the Tradition again, "though brayed in a mortar," not at all the worse for the accident, in that emphatic statement which I quoted when I opened the subject, and which I now quote again that I am closing it.   "It is the practice," the writer pronounces *ex cathedrâ*, "*as our readers are aware*, in Roman Catholic countries to post up a list of all the crimes to which human frailty can be tempted, placing opposite to them the exact sum of money for which their perpetration will be indulged."

4.

3. Two of my instances are despatched, and now I come to my third.   There is something so tiresome in passing abruptly from one subject to another, that I need your indulgence, my Brothers, in making this third beginning ; yet it has been difficult to avoid it, when my very object is to show what extensive subject-matters and what different classes of the community are acted on by the Protestant Tradition.   Now I am proceeding to the Legislature of the Nation, and will give an instance of its operation in a respectable political party.

In this case, its fountain springs up, as it were, under our very feet, and we shall have no difficulty at all in judging of its quality.   Its history is as follows :—

Coaches, omnibuses, carriages, and cars, day after day drive up and down the Hagley Road ; passengers lounge to and fro on the foot-path ; and close alongside of it are discovered one day the nascent foundations and rudiments of a considerable building. On inquiring, it is found to be intended for a Catholic, nay, even for a monastic establishment. This leads to a good deal of talk, especially when the bricks begin to show above the surface. Meantime the unsuspecting architect is taking his measurements, and ascertains that the ground is far from lying level ; and then, since there is a prejudice among Catholics in favour of horizontal floors, he comes to the conclusion that the bricks of the basement must rise above the surface higher at one end of the building than at the other ; in fact, that whether he will or no, there must be some construction of the nature of a vault or cellar at the extremity in question, a circumstance not at all inconvenient, considering it also happens to be the kitchen end of the building. Accordingly, he turns his necessity into a gain, and by the excavation of a few feet of earth, he forms a number of chambers convenient for various purposes, partly beneath, partly above the line of the ground. While he is thus intent on his work, loungers, gossipers, alarmists are busy at theirs too. They go round the building, they peep into the underground brickwork, and are curious about the drains ;[6] they moralise

[6] It is undeniable, though the gentleman who has brought the matter before the public has accidentally omitted to mention it, that the Protestant feeling has also been excited by the breadth of the drain, which is considered excessive, and moreover *crosses the road.* There exists some nervousness on the subject in the neighbourhood, as I have been seriously given to understand. There is a remarkable passage, too, in

about Popery and its spread ; at length they trespass upon the enclosure, they dive into the half-finished shell, and they take their fill of seeing what is to be seen, and imagining what is not. Every house is built on an idea ; you do not build a mansion like a public office, or a palace like a prison, or a factory like a shooting box, or a church like a barn. Religious houses, in like manner, have their own idea ; they have certain indispensable peculiarities of form and internal arrangement. Doubtless, there was much in the very idea of an Oratory perplexing to the Protestant intellect, and inconsistent with Protestant notions of comfort and utility. Why should so large a room be here ? why so small a room there ? why a passage so long and wide ? and why so long a wall without a window ? the very size of the house needs explanation. Judgments which had employed themselves on the high subject of a Catholic hierarchy and its need, found no difficulty in dogmatising on bedrooms and closets. There was much to suggest matter of suspicion, and to predispose the trespasser to doubt whether he had yet got to the bottom of the subject. At length one question flashed upon his

---

the scientific report, which our accuser brings forward, and which has never been answered or perhaps construed : "One of the compartments was larger than the rest, and *was evidently to be covered in without the building over it.*" This is not the first time a dwelling of mine has been the object of a mysterious interest. When our cottages at Littlemore were in course of preparation, they were visited on horseback and on foot by many of the most distinguished residents of the University of Oxford. Heads of houses and canons did not scruple to investigate the building within and without, and some of them went so far as to inspect and theorise upon the most retired portions of the premises. Perhaps some thirty years hence, in some " History of my own Times," speculations may be found on the subject, in aid of the Protestant Tradition.

mind : what can such a house have to do with cellars ? cellars and monks, what can be their mutual relation ? monks—to what possible use can they put pits, and holes, and corners, and outhouses, and sheds ? A sensation was created ; it brought other visitors ; it spread ; it became an impression, a belief ; the truth lay bare ; a tradition was born ; a fact was elicited which henceforth had many witnesses. *Those cellars were cells.* How obvious when once stated ! and every one who entered the building, every one who passed by, became, I say, in some sort, ocular vouchers for what had often been read of in books, but for many generations had happily been unknown to England, for the incarcerations, the torturings, the starvings, the immurings, the murderings proper to a monastic establishment.

Now I am tempted to stop for a while in order to *improve* (as the evangelical pulpits call it) this most memorable discovery. I will therefore briefly consider it under the heads of—1. THE ACCUSATION ; 2. ITS GROUNDS ; 3. THE ACCUSERS ; and, 4. THE ACCUSED.

First.—THE ACCUSATION.—It is this,—that the Catholics, building the house in question, were in the practice of committing *murder.* This was so strictly the charge, that, had the platform selected for making it been other than we know it to have been, I suppose the speaker might have been indicted for libel. His words were these :—" It was not usual for a coroner to hold an *inquest,* unless where a rumour had got abroad that there was a *necessity* for one ; and how was a rumour to come *from the underground cells of the convents ?* Yes, he repeated, underground cells : and he would tell them something about such places.

At this moment, in the parish of Edgbaston, within the borough of Birmingham, there was a large convent, of some kind or other, being erected, and the whole of the underground was fitted up with cells ; *and what were those cells for ?*"

Secondly.—THE GROUNDS OF THE ACCUSATION. —they are simple ; behold them : 1. That the house is built level ; 2. and that the plot of earth on which it is built is higher at one end than at the other.

Thirdly.—THE ACCUSERS.—This, too, throws light upon the character of Protestant traditions. Not weak and ignorant people only, not people at a distance—but educated men, gentlemen well connected, high in position, men of business, men of character, members of the legislature, men familiar with the locality, men who know the accused by name,— such are the men who deliberately, reiteratedly, in spite of being set right, charge certain persons with pitiless, savage practices ; with beating and imprisoning, with starving, with murdering their dependents.

Fourthly.—THE ACCUSED.—I feel ashamed, my Brothers, of bringing my own matters before you, when far better persons have suffered worse imputations ; but bear with me. *I* then am the accused. A gentleman of blameless character, a county member, with whose near relatives I have been on terms of almost fraternal intimacy for a quarter of a century, who knows me by repute far more familiarly (I suppose) than anyone in this room knows me, putting aside my personal friends ; he it is who charges me, and others like me, with delighting in blood, with enjoying the shrieks and groans of agony and despair, with presiding at a banquet of dislocated limbs, quivering muscles, and wild countenances. Oh, what a world is this! Could he look into our eyes and say it? Would he have the heart to say it, if he recollected of whom he said it? For who are we? Have we lived in a corner? have we come to light suddenly out of the earth? We have been nourished, for the greater part of our lives, in the bosom of the great schools and universities of Protestant England: we have been the foster sons of the Edwards and Henries, the Wykehams and Wolseys, of whom Englishmen are wont to make much; we have grown up amid hundreds of contemporaries, scattered at present all over the country, in those special ranks of society which are the very walk of a member of the legislature. Our names are better known to the educated classes of the country than those of any others who are not public men. Moreover, if there be men in the whole world who may be said to live *in publico*, it is the members of a College at one of our Universities; living, not in private houses, not in families, but in one or two apartments which are open to all the world, at all hours, with nothing, I may say, their own; with college servants, a common table,—nay, their chairs and their bedding, and their cups and saucers, down to their coal-scuttle and their carpet brooms,—a sort of common property, and the right of their neighbours. Such is that manner of life,—in which nothing, I may say, can be hid; where no trait of character or peculiarity of conduct but comes to broad day—such is the life I myself led for above a quarter of a century, under the eyes of numbers who are familiarly known to my accusers; such is almost the life which we all have led ever since we have been

in Birmingham, with our house open to all comers,
and ourselves accessible, I may almost say at any
hour ; and this being so, considering the *charge*, and
the *evidence*, and the *accuser*, and the *accused*, could
we Catholics desire a more apposite illustration of the
formation and the value of a Protestant Tradition ?

I set it down for the benefit of time to come ;
"though for no other cause," as a great author says,
"yet for this : that posterity may know we have not
loosely, through silence, permitted things to pass away
as in a dream, there shall be for men's information
extant thus much." One commonly forgets such
things, from the trouble and inconvenience of having
to remember them ; let one specimen last, of many
which have been suffered to perish, of the birth of an
anti-Catholic tradition. The nascent fable has indeed
failed, as the tale about the Belgian sin-table has
failed, but it might have thriven : it has been lost by
bad nursing ; it ought to have been cherished awhile
in those underground receptacles where first it drew
breath, till it could comfortably bear the light; till
its limbs were grown, and its voice was strong, and
we on whom it bore had run our course, and gone to
our account ; and then it might have raised its head
without fear and without reproach, and might have
magisterially asserted what there was none to deny.
But men are all the creatures of circumstances ; they
are hurried on to a ruin which they may see, but
cannot evade : so has it been with the Edgbaston
Tradition. It was spoken on the house-tops when it
should have been whispered in closets, and it expired
in the effort. Yet it might have been allotted, let us
never forget, a happier destiny. It might have smoul-

dered and spread through a portion of our Birmingham population ; it might have rested obscurely on their memories, and now and then risen upon their tongues ; there might have been flitting notions, misgivings, rumours, voices, that the horrors of the Inquisition were from time to time renewed in our subterranean chambers ; and fifty years hence, if some sudden frenzy of the hour roused the Anti-Catholic jealousy still lingering in the town, a mob might have swarmed about our innocent dwelling, to rescue certain legs of mutton and pats of butter from imprisonment, and to hold an inquest over a dozen packing-cases, some old hampers, a knife-board, and a range of empty blacking bottles.

Thus I close my third instance of the sort of evidence commonly adducible for the great Protestant Tradition ; not the least significant circumstance about them all being this, that though in the case of all three that evidence is utterly disproved, yet in not one of the three is the charge founded on it withdrawn.   In spite of Dr. Waddington, Dr. Maitland, and Mr. Rose, the editors of Mosheim still print and publish his slander on St. Eligius ; in defiance of the Brussels protest, and the chair tariff of St. Gudule, the Kent clergyman and the *Times* still bravely maintain our traffic in sins ; in violence to the common sense of mankind, the rack and the pulley are still affirmed to be busy in the dungeons of Edgbaston ;—for Protestantism must be maintained as the Religion of Englishmen, and part and parcel of the Law of the land.

And now, in conclusion, I will but state my conviction, which I am sure to have confirmed by every intelligent person who takes the trouble to examine the subject, that such slanders as I have instanced are the real foundation on which the anti-Catholic feeling mainly rests in England, and without which it could not long be maintained. Doubtless there are arguments of a different calibre, whatever their worth, which weigh against Catholics with half-a-dozen members of a University, with the speculative Church-restorer, with the dilettante divine, with the fastidious scholar, and with some others of a higher character of mind; whether St. Justin Martyr said this or that; whether images should be dressed in muslin, or hewn out of stone; what is the result of criticism on passages in the prophets;—questions such as these, and others of a more serious cast, may be conclusive for or against the Church in the study or in the lecture-room, but they have no influence with the many. As to those charges which do weigh with the people at large, the more they can be examined, the more, I am convinced, will they be found to be untrue. It is by wholesale, retail, systematic, unscrupulous lying, for I can use no gentler term, that the many rivulets are made to flow for the feeding the great Protestant Tradition,—the Tradition of the Court, the Tradition of the Law, the Tradition of the Legislature, the Tradition of the Establishment, the Tradition of Literature, the Tradition of Domestic Circles, the Tradition of the Populace.

LECTURE IV.

TRUE TESTIMONY INSUFFICIENT FOR THE PROTESTANT VIEW.

I.

I CAN fancy, my Brothers, that some of you may have been startled at a statement ı made at the close of my Lecture of last week. I then said, that the more fully the imputations which were cast upon us were examined, the more unfounded they would turn out to be ; so that the great Tradition on which we are perse- cuted is little short of one vast pretence or fiction. On this you may be led to ask me whether I mean to deny all and everything which can be advanced to the disadvantage of the Catholic Church, and whether I recommend you to do the same ? but this was not my meaning. Some things which are charged against us are doubtless true, and we see no harm in them, though Protestants do ; other charges are true, yet, as we think, only go to form ingenious objections ; others again are true, and relate to what is really sinful and detestable, as we allow as fully as Protestants can urge : but all these real facts, whatever their worth taken altogether, do not go any way towards proving true the Protestant Traditionary View of us ; they are vague and unsatisfactory, and, to apply a common phrase, they beat about the bush. If you would have some direct downright proof that Catholicism is what Protestants make it to be, something which will come up to the mark, you must lie ; else you will not get beyond feeble suspicions, which may be right, but may be wrong. Hence Protestants are obliged to cut their ninth commandment out of their Decalogue. " Thou shalt not bear false witness against thy neighbour " must go, must disappear ; their position requires the sacrifice. The substance, the force, the edge of their Tradition is slander. As soon as ever they disabuse their minds of what is false, and grasp only what is true,—I do not say they at once become Catholics ; I do not say they lose their dislike to our religion, or their misgivings about its working ;—but I say this, either they become tolerant towards us, and cease to hate us personally,—or, at least, supposing they cannot shake off old associations, and are prejudiced and hostile as before, still they find they have not the means of communicating their own feelings to others. To Protestantism False Witness is the principle of propagation. There are indeed able men who can make a striking case out of anything or nothing, as great painters give a meaning and a unity to the commonest bush, and pond, and paling and stile: genius can do without facts, as well as create them ; but few possess the gift. Taking things as they are, and judging of them by the long run, one may securely say, that the anti-Catholic Tradition could not be kept alive, would die of exhaustion, without a continual supply of fable.

I repeat, not everything which is said to our disadvantage is without foundation in fact ; but it is not

the true that tells against us in the controversy, but
the false. The Tradition requires bold painting; its
prominent outline, its glaring colouring, needs to be a
falsehood. So was it at the time of the Reformation;
the multitude would never have been converted by
exact reasoning and by facts which could be proved;
so its upholders were clever enough to call the Pope
Antichrist, and they let the startling accusation sink
into men's minds. Nothing else would have suc-
ceeded; and they pursue the same tactics now. No
inferior charge, I say, would have gained for them the
battle; else, why should they have had recourse to it?
Few persons tell atrocious falsehoods for the sake of
telling them. If truth had been sufficient to put down
Catholicism, the Reformers would not have had recourse to fiction. Errors indeed creep in by chance,
whatever be the point of inquiry or dispute; but I
am not accusing Protestants merely of incidental or of
attendant error, but I mean that falsehood is the very
staple of the views which they have been taught to
entertain of us.

I allow there are true charges which can be brought
against us; certainly, not only do I not deny it, but I
hardly could deny it without heresy. I say distinctly,
did I take upon me to deny everything which could be
said against us, I should be proving too much, I should
startle the Catholic theologian as well as Protestants;
for what would it be but implying that the Church
contains none within her pale but the just and holy?
This was the heresy of the Novatians and Donatists of
old time; it was the heresy of our Lollards, and others,
such as Luther, who maintained that bad men are not
members of the Church, that none but the predestinate

K

are her members. But this no Catholic asserts, every Catholic denies. Every Catholic has ever denied it, back to the very time of the Apostles and their Divine Master ; and He and they deny it. Christ denies it, St. Paul denies it, the Catholic Church denies it ; our Lord expressly said that the Church was to be like a net, which gathered of every kind, not only of the good, but of the bad too. Such was *His* Church ; it does not prove then that we are *not* His Church, because we are *like* His Church ; rather our being *like* the Primitive Christian body, is a reason for concluding that we are *one* with it. We cannot make His Church better than He made her ; we must be content with her as He made her, or not pretend to follow Him. He said, " Many are called, few are chosen ; " men come into the Church, and then they fall. They are not indeed sinning at the very time when they are brought into His family, at the time they are new born ; but as children grow up, and converts live on, the time too frequently comes, when they fall under the power of one kind of temptation or other, and fall from grace, either for a while or for good. Thus, not indeed by the divine wish and intention, but by the divine permission, and man's perverseness, there is a vast load of moral evil existing in the Church ; an enemy has sown weeds there, and those weeds remain among the wheat till the harvest. And this evil in the Church is not found only in the laity, but among the clergy too ; there have been bad priests, bad bishops, bad monks, bad nuns, and bad Popes. If this, then, is the charge made against us, that we do not all live up to our calling, but that there are Catholics, lay and clerical, who may be proved to be worldly, revengeful, licentious, slothful, cruel, nay, may be unbelievers, we grant it at once. We not only grant it, but we zealously maintain it. " In a great house," says St. Paul, " there are not only vessels of gold and silver, but also of wood and of earth ; and some indeed unto honour, but some unto dishonour." There are, alas, plenty of children of the Church, who by their bad lives insult and disgrace their Mother.

The Church, it is true, has been promised many great things, but she has not been promised the souls of all her children. She is promised truth in religious teaching ; she is promised duration to the end of the world ; she is made the means of grace ; she is unchangeable in Creed and in constitution ; she will ever cover the earth ; but her children are not infallible separately, any more than they are immortal ; not indefectible, any more than they are ubiquitous. Therefore, if Protestants wish to form arguments which really would tell against us, they must show, not that individuals are immoral or profane, but that the Church teaches, or enjoins, or recommends, what is immoral or profane ; rewards, encourages, or at least does not warn and discountenance, the sinner ; or promulgates rules, and enforces practices, which directly lead to sin ;—and this indeed they try to do, but they find the task not near so pleasant as the short and easy method of adopting strong, round, thorough-going statements, which are not true.

We do not then feel as a difficulty, on the contrary we teach as a doctrine, that there are scandals in the Church. " It must needs be, that scandals come ; nevertheless, woe to that man by whom the scandal cometh." There are, to all appearance, multitudes of Catholics who have passed out of the world unre-

pentant, and are lost ; there are multitudes living in
sin, and out of grace ; priests may and do fall, in this
or that country, at this or that time, though they are
exceptions to the rule ; or there may be parties or knots
of ecclesiastics, who take a low view of their duty, or
adopt dangerous doctrines; or they may be covetous, or
unfeeling, as other men, and use their power tyrannically,
or for selfish, secular ends.   There may be a declension
and deterioration of the priesthood of a whole country.
There may be secret unbelievers, both among clergy
and laity ; or individuals who are tending in their
imaginations and their reasonings to grievous error or
heresy.   There may be great disorders in some particular monastery or nunnery ; or a love of ease and slothful
habits, and a mere formality in devotion, in particular
orders of Religious, at particular seasons.   There may
be self-indulgence, pride, ambition, political profligacy,
in certain bishops in particular states of society, as
for instance, when the Church has been long established and abounds in wealth.   And there may have
been Popes before now, who to the letter have fulfilled
the awful description of the unfaithful servant and
steward, who began to " strike the men servants and
maid servants, and to eat and drink and be drunken."
All this may be granted ; but before the admission can
avail as an argument against the Catholic Church,
one thing has to be examined, whether on the whole
her influence and her action is on the side of what is
wrong, or rather (as is the case) simply powerful on
the side of good ; one thing has to be proved, that the
scandals within her pale have been caused by her principles, her teaching, her injunctions, or, which pretty
nearly comes to the same thing, that they do not also

exist, and as grievously (Catholics would say, they exist far more grievously), external to her.

2.

Now here is the flaw in the argument. For instance, it is plausibly objected that disorders not only sometimes do, but must occur, where priests are bound to celibacy. Even the candid Protestant will be apt to urge against us, " You must not argue from the case of the few, from persons of high principle and high education ; but taking the run of men, you must allow that the vow will not be kept by numbers of those who have got themselves to take it." Now I will not reply, as I might well do, by pointing out the caution which the Church observes in the selection of her priests ; how it is her rule to train them carefully for many years beforehand with this one thought in view, that priests they are to be ; how she tries them during their training ; how she takes one and rejects another, not with any reflection on those who are rejected, but simply because she finds they are not called to this particular state of life ; how, when she has selected a man, a hundred provisions and checks in detail are thrown around his person, which are to be his safeguard in his arduous calling ; lastly, how, when he is once called to his high ministry, he has, unless he be wonderfully wanting to himself, the power of divine grace abundantly poured upon him, without which all human means are useless, but which can do, and constantly does, miracles, as the experience, not of priest merely, but of every one who has been converted from a life of sin, will abundantly testify ;—I might enlarge on considerations such as these, but I put them aside, because I wish to address myself to the question of fact.

When, then, we come to the matter of fact, whether celibacy *has been* and *is*, in comparison of the marriage vow, so dangerous to a clerical body, I answer that I am very sceptical indeed that in matter of fact a married clergy *is* adorned, in any special and singular way, with the grace of purity; and this is just the very thing which Protestants take for granted. What is the use of speaking against our discipline, till they have proved their own to be better? Now I deny that they succeed with their rule of matrimony, better than we do with our rule of celibacy; and I deny it on no private grounds, or secret means of information, or knowledge of past years. I have lived in one place all my days, and know very few married clergymen, and those of such excellence and consistency of life, that I should feel it to be as absurd to suspect any of them of the slightest impropriety in their conduct, as to suspect the Catholic priests with whom I am well acquainted; and this is saying a great deal. When I speak of a married ministry, I speak of it, not from any knowledge I possess more than another: but I must avow that the public prints and the conversation of the world, by means of many shocking instances, which of course are only specimens of many others, heavier or lighter, which do *not* come before the world, bring home to me the fact, that a Protestant rector or a dissenting preacher is not necessarily kept from the sins I am speaking of, because he happens to be married: and when he offends, whether in a grave way or less seriously, still in all cases he has by matrimony but exchanged a bad sin for a worse, and has become an adulterer instead of being a seducer. Matrimony only does this for him, that his purity is at once less protected and less suspected. I am very sceptical, then, of the universal correctness of Protestant ministers, whether in the Establishment or in Dissent. I repeat, I know perfectly well, that there are a great number of high-minded men among the married Anglican clergy who would as soon think of murder, as of trespassing by the faintest act of indecorum upon the reverence which is due from them to others ; nor am I denying, what, though of course I cannot assert it on any knowledge of mine, yet I wish to assert with all my heart, that the majority of Wesleyan and dissenting ministers lead lives beyond all reproach ; but still allowing all this, the terrible instances of human frailty of which one reads and hears in the Protestant clergy, are quite enough to show that the married state is no sort of testimonial for moral correctness, no safeguard whether against scandalous offences, or (much less) against minor forms of the same general sin. Purity is not a virtue which comes merely as a matter of course to the married any more than to the single, though of course there is a great difference between man and man ; and though it is impossible to bring the matter fairly to an issue, yet for that very reason I have as much right to my opinion as another to his, when I state my deliberate conviction that there are, to say the least, as many offences against the marriage vow among Protestant ministers, as there are against the vow of celibacy among Catholic priests. I may go very much further than this in my own view of the matter, and think, as I do, that the priest's vow is generally the occasion of virtues which a married clergy does not contemplate even in idea ; but I am on the defensive, and only insist on so much as is necessary for my purpose.

But if matrimony does not prevent cases of immorality among Protestant ministers, it is not celibacy which causes them among Catholic priests. It is not what the Catholic Church imposes, but what human nature prompts, which leads any portion of her ecclesiastics into sin. Human nature will break out, like some wild and raging element, under any system ; it bursts out under the Protestant system ; it bursts out under the Catholic ; passion will carry away the married clergyman as well as the unmarried priest. On the other hand, there are numbers to whom there would be, not greater, but less, trial in the vow of celibacy than in the vow of marriage, as so many persons prefer Teetotalism to the engagement to observe Temperance.

Till, then, you can prove that celibacy causes what matrimony certainly does not prevent, you do nothing at all. This is the language of common sense. It is the world, the flesh, and the devil, not celibacy, which is the ruin of those who fall. Slothful priests, why, where was there any religion whatever, established and endowed, in which bishops, canons, and wealthy rectors were not exposed to the temptation of pride and sensuality ? The wealth is in fault, not the rules of the Church. Preachers have denounced the evil, and ecclesiastical authorities have repressed it, far more vigorously within the Catholic pale, than in the English Establishment, or the Wesleyan Connexion. Covetous priests ! shame on them ! but has covetousness been more rife in cardinals or abbots

than in the Protestant Bench, English or Irish?
Party spirit, and political faction! has not party, religious and political, burnt as fiercely in high-church
rectors and radical preachers, as in Catholic ecclesiastics? And so again, to take an extreme case,—be
there a few infidels among the multitudes of the
Catholic clergy: yet among the Anglican are there
really none, are there few, who disbelieve their own
Baptismal Service, repudiate their own Absolution of
the Sick, and condemn the very form of words under
which they themselves were ordained? Again, are
there not numbers who doubt about every part of
their system, about their Church, its authority, its truth,
its articles, its creeds ; deny its Protestantism, yet without being sure of its Catholicity, and therefore never
dare commit themselves to a plain assertion, as not
knowing whither it will carry them? Once more,
are there not in the Establishment those who hold
that all systems of doctrine whatever are founded in
a mistake, and who deny, or are fast denying, that there
is any revealed truth in the world at all? Yet none of
these parties, whatever they doubt, or deny, or disbelieve, see their way to leave the position in which
they find themselves at present, or to sacrifice their
wealth or credit to their opinions. Why, then, do you
throw in my teeth that Wolsey was proud, or Torquemada cruel, or Bonner trimming, or this abbot
sensual, or that convent in disorder ; that this priest
ought never to have been a priest, and that nun was
forced into religion by her father ; as if there were
none of these evils in Protestant England, as if there
were no pride in the House of Lords now, no time-
serving in the House of Commons, no servility in

fashionable preachers, no selfishness in the old, no profligacy in the young, no tyranny or cajolery in matchmaking, no cruelty in Union workhouses, no immorality in factories? If grievous sin is found in holy places, the Church cannot hinder it, while man is man: prove that she encourages it, prove that she does not repress it, prove that her action, be it greater or less, is not, as far as it goes, beneficial:— then, and not till then, will you have established a point against her.

For myself, my Brothers of the Oratory, I never should have been surprised, if, in the course of the last nine months of persecution some scandal in this or that part of our English Church had been brought to light and circulated through the country to our great prejudice. Not that I speak from any knowledge or suspicion of my own, but merely judging antecedently and on the chance of things. And, had such a case in fact been producible, it would, in the judgment of dispassionate minds, have gone for nothing at all, unless there is to be no covetous Judas, no heretical Nicolas, no ambitious Diotrephes, no world-loving Demas, in the Church of these latter days. Fraud in a priest, disorder in a convent, would have proved, not more, perhaps less, against Catholicism, than corruption in Parliament, peculation in the public offices, or bribery at elections tells against the British Constitution. Providentially no such calamity has occurred: but oh, what would not our enemies have paid for only one real and live sin in holy places to mock us withal! O light to the eyes, and joy to the heart, and music to the ear! O sweet tidings to writers of pamphlets, newspapers,

and magazines; to preachers and declaimers, who
have now a weary while been longing, and panting,
and praying for some good fat scandal, one, only
just one, well-supported instance of tyranny, or barbarity, or fraud, or immorality, to batten upon and
revel in! What price would they have thought too
great for so dear a fact, as that of one of our bishops
or one of our religious houses had been guilty of
some covetous aim, or some unworthy manœuvre!
Their fierce and unblushing effort to fix such charges
where they were impossible, shows how many eyes
were fastened on us all over the country, and how
deep and fervent was the aspiration that at least
some among us might turn out to be a brute or a
villain. To and fro the Spirit of false witness sped.
She dropped upon the floor of the Parliament House
in the form of a gentleman of Warwickshire, and told
how a nun had escaped thereabouts from a convent
window, which in consequence had ever since been
crossed with iron bars: but it turned out that the
window had been attempted by thieves, and the
bars had been put up to protect the Blessed Sacrament from them. Then she flitted to Nottingham,
and, in the guise of a town newspaper's correspondent,
repeated the tale with the concordant witness, as she
gave out, of a whole neighbourhood, who had seen
the poor captive atop of the wall, and then wander-
ing about the fields like a mad thing: but the Editor
in London discovered the untruth, and unsaid in his
own paper the slander he had incautiously admitted.
Next she forced her way into a nunnery near London,
and she assured the Protestant world that then and
there an infant had suddenly appeared among the

sisterhood ; but the two newspapers who were the
organs of her malice had to retract the calumny in
open court, and to ask pardon to escape a prosecution.

Tales, I say, such as these showed the *animus* of
the fabricators : but what, after all, would they have
really gained had their imputations been ever so true ?
Though one bad priest be found here or there, or
one convent be in disorder, or there be this or that
abuse of spiritual power, or a school of ecclesiastics
give birth to a heresy, or a diocese be neglected, nay,
though a whole hierarchy be in declension or decay,
this would not suffice for the argument of Protestantism.   And Protestantism itself plainly confesses it.
Yes, the Protestant Tradition must be fed with facts
more wholesale, more stimulating, than any I have
enumerated, if it is to keep its hold on the multitude.
Isolated instances of crime, or widespread tepidity, or
imperfections in administration, or antiquated legislation, such imputations are but milk-and-water in-
gredients in a theme so thrilling as that of Holy
Church being a sorceress and the child of perdition.
Facts that are only possible, and that only sometimes occur, do but irritate, by suggesting suspicions
which they are not sufficient to substantiate.   Even
falsehood, that is decent and respectable, is unequal
to the occasion.   Mosheim and Robertson, Jortin and
White, raise hopes to disappoint them.   The popular
demand is for the prodigious, the enormous, the
abominable, the diabolical, the impossible.   It must
be shown that all priests are monsters of hypocrisy,
that all nunneries are dens of infamy, that all bishops
are the embodied plenitude of savageness and per-

fidy. Or at least we must have a cornucopia of mummery, blasphemy, and licentiousness,—of knives, and ropes, and faggots, and fetters, and pulleys and racks,—if the great Protestant Tradition is to be kept alive in the hearts of the population. The great point in view is to burn into their imagination, by a keen and peremptory process, a sentiment of undying hostility to Catholicism ; and nothing will suffice for this enterprise but imposture, in its purest derivation from him whom Scripture emphatically calls the father of lies, and whose ordinary names, when translated, are the accuser and the slanderer.

This I shall prove as well as assert ; and I shall do so in the following way. You know, my Brothers of the Oratory, that from time to time persons come before the Protestant public, with pretensions of all others the most favourable for proving its charges against us, as having once belonged to our Communion, and having left it from conviction. If, then, Protestants would know what sort of men we really are whom they are reprobating, if they wish to determine our internal state, and build their argument on a true foundation, and accommodate their judgment of us to facts, here is the best of opportunities for their purpose. The single point to ascertain is, the trustworthiness of the informants ; that being proved, the testimony they give is definite ; but if it is disproved, the evidence is worthless.

Now I am going to mention to you the names of two persons, utterly unlike each other in all things except in their both coming forward as converts from Catholicism ; both putting on paper their personal experience of the religion they had left ; both addressing themselves especially to the exposure of the rule of celibacy, whether in the priesthood or in convents ; and, moreover, both on their first appearance meeting with great encouragement from Protestants, and obtaining an extensive patronage for the statements they respectively put forward.   One was a man, the other a woman ; the one a gentleman, a person of very superior education and great abilities, who lived among us, and might be interrogated and cross-examined at any time ; the woman, on the other hand, had no education, no character, no principle, and, as the event made manifest, deserved no credit whatever.   Whatever the one said was true, as often as he spoke to facts he had witnessed, and was not putting out opinions or generalising on evidence; whatever the other said was, or was likely to be, false.   Thus the two were contrasted : yet the truth spoken against us by the man of character is forgotten, and the falsehood spoken against us by the unworthy woman lives.   If this can be shown, do you need a clearer proof that falsehood, not truth, is the essence of the Protestant Tradition.

3.

The Rev. Joseph Blanco White, who is one of the two persons I speak of, was a man of great talent, various erudition, and many most attractive points of character.   Twenty-five years ago, when he was about my present age, I became acquainted with him at Oxford, and I lived for some years on terms of familiarity with him.   I admired him for the simplicity and openness of his character, the warmth of his affections, the range of his information, his power of conversation, and an intellect refined, elegant, and accomplished. I loved him from witnessing the constant sufferings, bodily and mental, of which he was the prey, and for his expatriation on account of his religion. At that time, not having the slightest doubt that Catholicism was an error, I found in his relinquishment of great ecclesiastical preferment in his native country for the sake of principle, simply a claim on my admiration and sympathy. He was certainly most bitter-minded and prejudiced against everything in and connected with the Catholic Church ; it was nearly the only subject on which he could not brook opposition ; but this did not interfere with the confidence I placed in his honour and truth ; for though he might give expression to a host of opinions in which it was impossible to acquiesce, and was most precipitate and unfair in his inferences and inductions, and might be credulous in the case of alleged facts for which others were the authority, yet, as to his personal testimony, viewed as distinct from his judgments and suspicions, it never for an instant came into my mind to doubt it. He had become an infidel before he left Spain. While at Oxford he was a believer in Christianity : after leaving it he fell into infidelity again ; and he died, I may say, without any fixed belief at all, either in a God or in the soul's immortality.

About the period of my acquaintance with him, he wrote various works against the Catholic Church, which in a great measure are repetitions of each other, throwing the same mass of testimonies, such as they are, into different shapes, according to the occasion.

And since his death, many years after the time I speak of, his Life has been published, repeating what is substantially the same evidence.   Among these publications one was written for the lower classes ; it was entitled, " The Poor Man's Preservative Against Popery ; " and, if I mistake not, was put upon the catalogue of Books and Tracts of the great Church of England Society, the Society for Promoting Christian Knowledge.   No work could be sent into the world with greater advantages ; published under the patronage of all the dignitaries of the Establishment, put into the hands of the whole body of the clergy for distribution, at a low price, written in an animated style, addressed to the traditionary hatred of the Catholic Church existing among us, which is an introduction to any book, whatever its intrinsic value ; and laden with a freight of accusation against her, which, as far as their matter was concerned, and the writer's testimony extended, were true as well as grave.

When I began collecting materials for this Lecture, not being able to lay my hand upon the publication at home, I sent for a copy to the Christian Knowledge depôt in this town, and to my surprise, I was told it was no longer in print.   I repeated the application at the Society's office in London, and received the same reply.   Now certainly there are reasons why a Society connected with the National Church should wish to withdraw the work of a writer, who ended, not only with hating the Papacy, but with despising the Establishment ; yet considering its facts were so trustworthy, and its evidence so important, the Society hardly would have withdrawn it, if there had been any good reason for continuing it in print.   Such a reason certainly *would* have been its popularity; I cannot conceive how persons, with the strong feelings against the Catholic religion entertained by the members of that Society, having given their solemn approbation, not only to the principle of a certain attack upon it, but to the attack itself, and being confident that the facts related were true, could allow themselves in conscience to withdraw it, on account of subsequent religious changes in the writer, supposing it actually to enjoy a sufficient ϸopularity, and to be doing good service against Catholicism ; and therefore I conclude, since it *was* withdrawn, that in spite of the forced circulation which the Society gave it, it had *not* made any great impression on the mass of men, or even interested the Established clergy in its favour. But anyhow, it never at any time was known, in matter of fact, as far as I can make out, to the population at large,—for instance, to the masses of a town such as this,—whatever consideration it may have enjoyed in the circles of the Establishment. Here, then, is a solemn testimony delivered against Catholics of which the basis of facts is true, which nevertheless has no popularity to show, is sustained at first by a forced sale, and then is abandoned by its very patrons ; and now let us consider the character of the facts of which it consists.

They are such as the writer himself was very far from thinking a light imputation on the Church he had abandoned. He considered he had inflicted on Catholicism a most formidable blow, in giving his simple evidence against it ; and it must be allowed that some of his facts are of a very grave nature. He was the subject and the witness of a most melancholy

L

phenomenon, an Apostasy from the Catholic Faith. About a hundred and fifty years ago a school of infidelity arose in Protestant England ; the notorious Voltaire came over here from France, and on his return took back with him its arguments, and propagated them among his own countrymen. The evil spread ; at length it attacked the French Catholic clergy, and during the last century there was a portion of them, I do not say a large portion, but an influential, who fraternised with the infidel, still holding their places and preferments in the Church. At the end of the century, about the time of the first sanguinary French Revolution, the pestilence spread into Spain ; a knot of the Spanish clergy became infidels, and as a consequence, abandoned themselves to a licentious life. Blanco White was one of these, and amid the political troubles in his country during the first years of this century, he managed to escape to England, where he died in the year 1841.

Now there was one circumstance which gave a particularly shocking character to the infidelity of these Spanish ecclesiastics, while it made it more intense. In France the infidel party was not afraid to profess itself infidel ; and such members of the clerical body as were abandoned enough to join it, did so openly ; frequented its brilliant meetings and lived shamelessly, like men of fashion and votaries of sin. It was otherwise in Spain ; the people would not have borne this ; public opinion was all on the side of the Catholic religion ; such as doubted or disbelieved were obliged to keep it to themselves, and thus if they were ecclesiastics, to become the most awful of hypocrites. There *can* be hypocrites in the Church, as there may be hypocrites in any religion ; but here you see *what* a hypocrite is in the Catholic Church, as seen in fact ; not a person who takes up a religious profession in order to gratify some bad end, but, for the most part, one who has learned to disbelieve what he professes, after he has begun to profess it.[1] However, such a person is, on any explanation, an object of horror ; and in Spain it was increased by the impatience, irritation, and fever of mind, which the constraint they lay under occasioned to these unhappy men. Their feelings, shut up within their breasts, became fierce and sullen ; oppressed by the weight of the popular sentiment, they turned round in revenge upon its object, and they hated Catholicism the more, because their countrymen were Catholics.[2] They became a sort of secret society, spoke to each other only in private, held intercourse by signs, and plunged into licentiousness, even as a relief to the miserable conflicts which raged within them.

Earth could not show, imagination could not picture, Satan could not create, a more horrible spectacle. You will say, how was it possible ? how could men who had, I will not merely say given themselves to God, but who had tasted the joy and the reward of such devotion, how could they have the heart thus to change ? Why, the perpetrators of the most heinous

---

[1] *E.g.*, Mr. Blanco White says of one of the Spanish ecclesiastics whom he introduces, " He was . . . one of those, who, having *originally* taken their posts in the foremost ranks of asceticism, *with the most sincere desire of improvement for himself and others*, are afterwards involved in guilt by strong temptation, and reduced to secret moral degradation, *by want of courage to throw off the mask of sanctity.*" Life, vol. i. p. 121.

[2] I think I have heard him say that he had lost his knowledge of the Spanish tongue, not having the heart to keep it up.

crimes, men who have sold themselves to the world, and have gained their full price from it, even they look back with tears to those days of innocence and peace which once were theirs, and which are irrecoverably gone. Napoleon said that the day of his first communion was the happiest day of his life. Such men, too, actually part company with the presence of religion ; they go forward on their own course, and leave it behind them in the distance. Their regret is directed to what not merely is past, but is away. But these priests were in the very bosom of the Church ; they served her altars, they were in the centre of her blessings ; how could they forget Jerusalem who dwelt within her ? how could they be so thankless towards her sweetness and her brightness, and so cruel towards themselves ? how could one who had realised that the Strong and Mighty, that the Gracious, was present on the Altar, who had worshipped there that Saviour's tender Heart, and rejoiced in the assurance of His love, how could he go on year after year (horrible !) performing the same rites, holding his Lord in his hands, dispensing Him to His people, yet thinking it all an idle empty show, a vain superstition, a detestable idolatry, a blasphemous fraud, and cursing the while the necessity which compelled his taking part in it ? Why, in the case of one who ever had known the power of religion, it is incomprehensible ; but, as regards the melancholy instance we are contemplating, it would really seem if you may take his own recollection of his early self in evidence of the fact, that he never had discovered what religion was. Most children are open to religious feelings, Catholic children of course more than others ; some indeed, might complain that, as they advance to boyhood, religion becomes irksome and wearisome to them, but I doubt whether this is true of Catholic youth, till they begin to sin. True, alas, it is, that the nearer and more urgent excitement of guilty thoughts does render the satisfactions and consolations of Paradise insipid and uninviting; but even then their reason tells them that the fault is with themselves, not with religion; and that after all heaven is not only better, but pleasanter, sweeter, more glorious, more satisfying than anything on earth. Yet, from some strange, mysterious cause, this common law was not fulfilled in this hapless Spanish boy; he never found comfort in religion, not in childhood more than in manhood, or in old age. In his very first years, as in his last, it was a yoke and nothing more; a task without a recompense.

Thus he tells us, he " entertains a most painful recollection " of the " perpetual round of devotional practices " in which he was compelled to live. He " absolutely dreaded the approach of Sunday. Early on the morning of that formidable day, when he was only eight years old, he was made to go with his father to the Dominican convent," [3] always for Mass, and every other week for confession. He did not get his breakfast for two hours, then he had to stand or kneel in the Cathedral, I suppose at High Mass, for two hours longer. Well, the second two hours probably was, as he says, a considerable trial for him. Again, from three to five he was in another church, I suppose for Vespers and Benediction. Then his father and he took a walk, and in the evening his father visited the sick in an hospital, and took his son with him. Per-

[3] P. 11.

haps his father's treatment of him, if we are to trust his recollection and impression of it, might be injudicious ; he was lively, curious, and clever, and his father, who was a truly good, pious man, it may be, did not recollect that the habits of the old are not suitable in all respects to children. Mr. Blanco White complains, moreover, that he had no companions to play with, and no books to read ; still, it is very strange indeed, that he never took pleasure in Mass and Benediction ; he calls his Sunday employments a " cruel discipline ;" [4] he describes his hearing Mass as " looking on while the priest went through it ; " [5] speaking of a season of recreation granted to him, he mentions his religious duties as the drawbacks " on the accession of daily pleasures " he had obtained. However, " Mass, though a nuisance, was over in half an hour ; confession, a more serious annoyance, was only a weekly task ; " [6] and, as if to prove what I alluded to above, that no fascination of sin had at this time thrown religion into the shade, he adds, " My life was too happy in innocent amusement to be exposed to anything that might be the subject of painful accusation." No ; it was some radical defect of mind. In like manner, saying office was to him never anything else than a " most burdensome practice." [7] " Another devotional task, scarcely less burdensome," was—what, my Brothers, do you think ? " Mental Prayer," or " Meditation ; " of which he gives a detailed and true description. He adds, " Soon after I was ordained a priest . . . . I myself was several times the leader of this mystical farce." [8] In his boyhood and youth he had to read half an hour, and to meditate on his knees another half. This for

[4] P. 12.   [5] P. 26.   [6] P. 32.   [7] P. 27.   [8] P. 29.

such a boy, might be excessive; but hear how he comments upon it: "To feel indignant, at this distance of time, may be absurd ; but it is with difficulty that I can check myself when I remember what I have suffered in the cause of religion. Alas ! my sufferings from that source are still more bitter in my old age." [9]

That a person, then who never knew what Catholicism had to give, should abandon it, does not seem very surprising ; the only wonder is how he ever came to be a priest. If we take his own account of himself it is evident he had no vocation at all : he explains the matter, however, very simply, as far as his own share in it is concerned, by telling us that he chose the ecclesiastical state in order to avoid what he felt to be more irksome, a counting-house. " I had proposed to be sent to the navy, because at that time the Spanish midshipman received a scientific education. I could not indeed endure the idea of being doomed to a life of ignorance. This was easily perceived, and (probably with the approbation of the divines consulted on this subject) no alternative was left me. I was told I must return to the odious counting-house, from which I had taken refuge in the Church. I yielded, and in yielding mistook the happiness of drying up my mother's tears for a reviving taste for the clerical profession." [1]

4

No wonder, under such circumstances, that Mr. Blanco White became an unbeliever ; no wonder that

[9] P. 29. He goes on to say that he prefers to the vague word "religion" the use of "true Christianity," but this he gave up at last.

[1] P. 52.

his friends and associates became unbelievers too, if their history resembled his. It was the case of active inquisitive minds, unfurnished with that clear view of divine things which divine grace imparts and prayer obtains. The only question which concerns us here is, Were there many such ecclesiastics in the Spanish Church? If so, it certainly would be a very grave fact; if not so, it is most melancholy certainly, but not an argument, as I can see, against Catholicism, for there are bad men in every place and every system. Now it is just here that his testimony fails; there is nothing that I can find in his works to prove that the dreadful disease which he describes had spread even so widely as in France. In the first place, he only witnesses to a small part of Spain. He seems to have only been in three Spanish cities in his life: Seville, Madrid, and Cadiz; [2] and of these, while Seville is the only one of which he had a right to speak, the metropolis and a seaport are just two of the places, where, if there was laxity, you would expect it to be found. Again, Spain is not, like England, the seat of one people, an open country, with easy communication from sea to sea. On the contrary, you have populations so different, that you may call them foreign to each other; separated, moreover, not only morally, but by the mountain barriers which intersect the country in every direction; one part does not know another, one part is not like another, and therefore Mr. Blanco White's evidence is only good as far as it extends. You cannot infer the state of the northern dioceses from a southern; of Valentia, by what you

[2] On one occasion he ran down to Salamanca from Madrid, apparently for a day or two.

are told of Seville. Inspect then his narrative itself, and see what it results in. It amounts to this—that in the first years of this century there were a few priests at Seville who had studied Jansenistic theology, and largely imported French philosophy, and that they ended in becoming infidels, and some of them unblushing hypocrites. I cannot find mention of any except at Seville : and how many there? You may count them. First, " I became acquainted with a member of the upper clergy, a man of great reading, and secretly a most decided disbeliever in all religion." Secondly, " Through him I was introduced to another dignitary, a man much older than either of us, who had for many years held an office of great influence in the diocese, but who now lived in a very retired way. He was also a violent anti-Christian, as I subsequently found." [3] Thirdly, an intimate friend of his own, who was promoted from Seville to a canonry of Cordova, and who had been chaplain to the Archbishop of Seville. [4] Fourthly, himself. I am not able to number more, as given on his own personal knowledge, [5] though he certainly thought many others existed ; [6] but this is

[3] P. 114.

[4] P. 17. I consider this to be the person mentioned in the " Evidences," p. 132, whom accordingly I have not set down as a separate instance.

[5] On his visit to Salamanca, he saw Melendez, a Deist (p. 128), who had been one of the judges of the Supreme Court at Madrid ; a poet, too ; whether an Ecclesiastic does not appear.

[6] Life, p. 117. " *Many other* members of the clergy." If he had a definite *knowledge* of others, or more than suspicion, I cannot understand his not giving us the number, or the rank, or the diocese, in short, something categorical, instead of an indirect allusion. The question, then, simply is, what his suspicions are worth. "Among my numerous acquaintance in the Spanish clergy, I have never met with any one, *possessed of bold talents*, who has not, sooner or later, changed from the

ever the case with men who do wrong ; they quiet the
voice within them by the imagination that all others
are pretty much what they are themselves. I do not
then trust his inferences.

And so again, as he fell into immoral practices
himself, so did he impute the same to the mass of the
Spanish clergy, whom he considered as "falling and
rising, struggling and falling again,"[7] in a continual
course ; but here too, from the nature of the case, he
could not speak of many on his personal knowledge.
Nor was it to be supposed that a priest, who was

---

most sincere piety to a state of unbelief." (Doblado's Letters, v.) I
observe—1. He had experience only of one diocese. 2. He evidently,
by the very form of his words, does not speak of what he *knew*, when
he says, "who *has* not *sooner or later*." 3. Observe, "possessed of *bold
talents*." In like manner, he would, I think, have said, that when he
was at Oxford, every one, "of bold talents," agreed with Archbishop
Whately, then resident in the University (and my friend as well as his) ;
but every one knows how small Dr. Whately's party was. I do not
notice a passage in the "Poor Man's Preservative" (Dial. i. pp. 32, 33),
for he is speaking of laity, and what he says of the clergy is very vague.
After all, though I have a right to ask for proof, it is not necessary for
my *argument* to deny, that the infidel party might have been as large in
Spain even as in France; though in fact it seems to have been no larger
than the small band of Apostates boasted of by the "Priests' Protection
Society" in Dublin.

[7] Evid. p. 132. Again he says, "hundreds *might* be found" who
live "a life of systematic vice" (p. 135). How very vague is "hundreds !" and "hundreds" out of 60,000 seculars, and 125,000 ecclesiastics in all, as I shall mention presently in the text. (Ibid. p. 133).
He speaks vaguely of the "crowd" of priests ; and he says the best' of
them, and he knew the best from confession, "mingled vice and superstition, grossness of feeling, and pride of office, in their character." I
suspect that coarseness with him was one great evidence of vice ; he
despised uneducated persons. "I am surprised," he says of Tavora,
Bishop of the Canary Islands (p. 129), "that a man of his *taste and information* accepted the Bishopric of a *semi-barbarous* portion of the Spanish
dominions :" and this, though he attributes it "to his desire of im-
proving the moral and intellectual state of those islands."

both disbelieving what he professed, and was breaking what he had vowed, should possess friends very different from himself. He formed the eighth of a group of ecclesiastics whom he much admired. One of these, as we have seen, was an infidel, but apparently only one ; none of them, however, were blameless in their moral conduct. Besides these friends of his, he mentions a priest of a religious congregation, who had been his own confessor, in which capacity "he had no fault to find with him, nor could he discover the least indication of his not acting up to the principles he professed," [8] who, however (as he was *told* by a young atheist merchant who knew the priest's "secret courses" well, and, "as he had afterwards sufficient

---

[8] This conscientiousness in his *duty* is remarkable in this priest, even if his account of him ought to be believed (for it stands on different grounds from those cases which he *knew*). Of himself, too, he says, his resolution was to do his *duty* to his charge, though an unbeliever. "I will not put myself forward in the Church. I will not affect zeal : whatever trust is put in me, as a confessor, I will conscientiously prove myself worthy of. I will urge people to observe every moral duty. I will give them the best advice in their difficulties, and comfort them in their distress. Such were the resolutions I made, and which, indeed, I *always* (sic) kept, in regard to the confidence reposed in my priestly office. In that respect I may positively and confidently assert, that I never availed myself of the privileges of my priesthood for anything immoral" (Life, vol. i. p. 112). This being the case, his *intention* in consecrating and administering the sacraments was valid, even though he was an unbeliever. I think my memory cannot play me false in saying, that in answer to a question once put to him, he declared emphatically that the bad priests never made use of the confessional for immoral purposes : he said, "They daren't. It would raise the people." Moreover, as time went on, he himself *withdrew altogether* from clerical duty. He speaks of another of the party, who having "for many years held an office of great influence in the diocese, now lived *in a very retired way*" (p. 114). I say all this in order to show what little bearing the unbelief of this small knot of priests had upon the Catholic population among whom they lived.

ground to be convinced," if such a vague statement is a sufficient testimony to the fact), "sinned and did penance by rotation." [9]   Another, too, is mentioned laden with similar guilt, with whom he had been intimate, but whom he describes as deficient in mere natural principle : this man got involved in money matters and died of vexation.[1]

Ten, or, if it were, twenty bad ecclesiastics form a most melancholy catalogue certainly, but are not more, after all, than Protestants have scraped together and made apostates of, out of the zealous Catholic clergy of Ireland ; and, as no one dreams of taking such melancholy cases as specimens of the Irish Church, neither are Mr. Blanco White's friends specimens of the Spanish.   He says, indeed, "hundreds might be found," still not on his personal knowledge ; and I for one cannot receive his second-hand information. However, in any case you must recollect first, that it was a time apparently of great religious declension, when Spain had imitated France, and a judgment was on the point of coming down upon the country   The Jesuits, the flower of the priesthood, whom as he says himself, "their bitterest enemies have never ventured to charge with moral irregularities," had been barbarously expelled by the government.   The Congregation of St. Philip Neri took their place, but though

---

[9]   Life, p. 121.

[1]   Life, p. 104.   He speaks (Evidences, p. 135) of two priests who died of *love*.   "Love, long resisted, seized them, at length, like madness.   Two I knew who died insane."   Even granting it, I suppose it was love of *particular objects*.   May not Protestants fall in love with persons who will not have them, or who are married ?   Dying for love is certainly an *idea* quite known in England, still more so, perhaps, in the South.

they did a great deal, they had not strength, single-handed, to stem the flood of corruption. Moreover you must consider the full number of clergy in a given place or neighbourhood, before you form a judgment upon their state as a whole. The whole number of clergy of Spain at this time amounted to 125,000 persons ; of these the seculars were as many as 60,000. In the Cathedral of Seville alone 500 Masses were said daily ; and the city was divided into twenty-six parishes, and contained besides between forty and fifty ecclesiastical establishments in addition to the monasteries.[a] The real question before us simply is, whether the proportion of bad priests at that time in the city and diocese of Seville was greater than the proportion of bad married clergy in England in the reign, we will say, of George the Second. It is to be remembered, too, that Catholic priests know each other far more intimately than is possible in the case of a married clergy ; in a large city bad priests herd together : married clergymen, in respectable station, would sin each by himself, and no one of them can turn king's evidence against the rest.

This being the extent of Mr. Blanco White's evidence about the secular priests, about monks and friars he frankly tells us he knows next to nothing, though he thinks them "gross and vulgar." But here, as in the case of the secular clergy, he suspects and believes much evil which he does not know, and which those only will receive who have implicit reliance on his judgment. As to nuns, he speaks of those of them whom he knew, as being for the most part ladies of

[a] Laborde, vol. ii.

high character and unimpeachable purity ;[3] though some were otherwise, at least to some extent. He seems to allow that reluctant nuns were comparatively few ; though he says that many were tormented by scruples, and all would have been much happier had

[3] He has a most intense *notion* that they are "prisoners;" but that does not hinder his admitting that they are *willing* prisoners. He thinks the majority live in "*a dull monotony*" (Life, p. 67). It is not wonderful that he should take the formal Parliamentary view of nuns, considering that from his youth, as I have said, he, though a Catholic, had apparently as little sense of the Real Presence (*the true and sufficient Paraclete of a Nunnery*) as the House of Commons has. The following expressions sketch his idea of a nunnery ; let it be observed, *vice* (except as an accident) is absent :—" The minute and anxious narrative of a *nervous recluse*" (p. 66). "A *sensible woman* confined for life " (Ibid.) "A soul troubled with all the fears of a *morbid conscience*" (p. 67) "The word Nunnery is a byword for *weakness of intellect, fretfulness, childishness.* In short, nun is the *superlative of old woman*" (p. 69). "Some of them were *women of superior good sense, and models of that fortitude* which," &c. (Ibid.)   "One of *those excellent persons*" (Ibid.) "The *greater part* of the nuns whom I have known, were *beings of a much higher description, females whose purity* owed nothing to the strong gates and high walls of the cloister" (Evid. p. 135).   "Some there are, I confess, among the nuns, who *never seem to long for freedom;* but the happiness boasted of in convents is generally the effect of an *honourable pride of* purpose, supported by a sense of utter *hopelessness*" (Ibid. p. 136). "*Suppose* but *one* nun in *ten thousand* wished vehemently for that liberty " (p. 137).   "The *reluctant* nuns, you say, are *few ;*—vain, unfeeling sophistry " (p. 139).   "The *most sensitive, innocent, and ardent minds*" (Ibid. p. 141).   "Crime *makes its way into*" (observe, not is congenial to) "those recesses " (Ibid. p. 135).   "It is a *notorious fact*, that the nunneries in *Estremadura and Portugal* " (*not*, that are in Seville and Andalusia) "are *frequently* infected *with vice of the grossest kind*" (Ibid. p. 135).   "*Souls* more polluted than those of *some* never fell within my observation, &c." (Life, vol. i. p. 70).   Observe, "souls ;" —to the soul he limits the sin, and he puts the word in italics, to show that this really is his meaning, and he adds "some." When it comes to the soul, the evidence is very vague ; and this, out of 500, in Seville alone !   Such on the whole is his evidence against convents : how little of fact, how much of suspicion, contempt, and hatred ! how much, again, of involuntary admission in favour of their religious condition !

they married. But this is his opinion, as distinct from his testimony; and in like manner he has other strong opinions on the miseries inflicted on men and women by celibacy;[4] but I have no reliance on his judgment—nor had any one, I think, who knew him, he had so much prejudice, and so little patience—while I have the fullest confidence in his word, when he witnesses to facts, and facts which he knew.

Such is this remarkable evidence, remarkable in the witness, and in the things witnessed, remarkable as coming from a person who had special means of knowing a Catholic country, and whose honour you may depend upon; unlike such men as Ciocci and Achilli, and others, who also have left the Church and borne witness against her, whom no sensible man credits. Here is a man you can trust; and you see how little he has to say to the purpose of Protestantism after all. He makes the most indeed of his little, but he gives us the means of judging for ourselves. Here is no conspiracy of evil, no deep-laid treachery, no disguised agents prowling about, no horrible oaths, no secret passages, trapdoors, dungeons, axes, racks, and thumbscrews; no blood and fire, no screams of despair, no wailing of children, no spectres born of feverish guilt, and flitting before the mental eye. Here is little more than what happens

---

[4] The simple question is, whether *more* nuns are eaten up with scruples—*more* are restless and discontented—*more* are old women or old maids—*more* sin grossly, than unmarried women in a Protestant country. Here, as before, I am allowing for argument's sake, the worst side of things; and nothing of all this, be it observed, even if granted, disproves—(1.) the religiousness of the great majority; (2.) the angelical saintliness of many; (3.) the excellence and utility of the institution itself, after all drawbacks; which are the points a Catholic maintains.

every day in England; for I suppose that here in Protestant England there are secret unbelievers, and men who are fair and smooth, but inwardly corrupt, and many a single female wasted by weariness and sadness, and many a married woman cursing the day she ever took her vow; for these things must be, though they ought not to be, while the nature of man is the same. And moreover, as I have said, the popular voice seems to bear me out in the view I am taking; for this testimony, given under such favourable circumstances against the Church, has been let drop out of print; for it was after all tame; it did not do its work; it did not go far enough; it was not equal to the demand; it was not in keeping with the great Protestant Tradition.

5.

No, it must contain something huge, enormous, prodigious, because the people love story books, and do not like dry matter of fact. How dull is history, or biography, or controversy, compared with a good romance, the Lives of highwaymen, a collection of ghost stories, a melodrama, a wild-beast-show, or an execution! What would a Sunday newspaper be without trials, accidents, and offences? Therefore the poor Catholic is dressed up like a scarecrow to gratify, on a large scale, the passions of curiosity, fright, and hatred. Something or other men must fear, men must loathe, men must suspect, even if it be to turn away their minds from their own inward miseries. Hence it is, if a stranger comes to a small town, that he furnishes so inexhaustible a supply of gossip to his neighbours, about who he is, what he was, whom he knows, why he comes, and when he will go. If a house is empty for a while, it is sure to be haunted. When learning began to revive, your student was the object of curious horror; and Dr. Faustus, the printer and (as the nursery rhyme goes) schoolmaster, was made a magician, and is still drawn as such in poems and romances. When, then, a Catholic Church is opened in a place, or a monastic body takes up its abode there, its novelty and strangeness are a call for fiction on those who have a talent for invention; and the world would be seriously disappointed, if all sorts of superstition were not detected in the Church's rites, and all sorts of wickedness in her priests and nuns.

The popular appetite does not clamour long in vain. It asks, and it is answered. Look at that poor degraded creature, strolling about from village to village, from settlement to farmhouse, among a primitive and simple population. She has received an injury in her head when young; and this has taken away, in part, her responsibility, while it has filled her brain with wild ideas, and given it a morbid creative power. Ere she is grown up she leaves her home, and flits here and there, the prey of any one who meets with her. Catholics are all round about her; as a child she has been in a Catholic school, and perhaps she has from time to time wandered into Catholic churches. She enters, she peers about; still and demure, yet with wild curious eyes, and her own wanton thoughts. She sees, at first glance, the sanctity and gravity of the ceremonial: she is struck with the appearance of modesty, whether in the sacred ministers or in the nuns; but her evil heart instantly sug-

M

gests that what shows so well is nothing but a show, and that close under the surface lies corruption. She contemplates the whole scene, she cannot forget it; but she asks herself, *What if* it be but a solemn mockery cloaking bad deeds? The words, the actions, so calm, so gentle, the words of peace, the sacramental actions, she carries them off with an accurate memory; those verses and responses, those sweet voices, those blessings, and crossings, and sprinklings, and genuflections. But what if they all be a cloak? And when the priest went out, or when he spoke to any one, what was it all about? And when he was in his confessional, and first one penitent, and then another came to him, what could they be saying? Ah, what indeed! what if it all be but a cloak for sin? There is the point. What if it be but a jest? Oh, the pleasant mischief! the stirring, merry fancy! to think that men can look so grave, yet love sin; that women, too, who pretend so much, need not be better than she is herself; that that meek face, or those holy hands, belong to a smooth hypocrite, who acts the angel and lives the devil! She looks closer and closer, measuring the limbs, scanning the gestures, and drinking in the words of those who unconsciously go about their duties in her presence; and imputing meanings to the most harmless and indifferent actions. It really is as she suspected, and the truth breaks upon her more and more. Her impure imagination acts upon her bodily vision, and she begins to see the image of her own suspicions in the objects she is gazing on. A sort of mirage spreads through the sacred building, or religious house, and horrors of all kind float across her brain.

She goes away, but they pursue her ;—what may not have taken place amid those holy rites, or within those consecrated walls ? The germ of a romance is already fermenting in her brain, and day after day it becomes more developed in its parts, and more consistent in its form.

Poor sinful being ! She finds herself in a Penitentiary ! no, sure, it is a religious house ; so she will consider it, so will she henceforth speak of it ; everything she sees there speaks to her of her feverish dream ; the penitents become nuns ; the very rooms, windows, passages, and stairs, she recognizes them as conventual, the very convent which her fancy has been framing. Things utterly separate from each other are confused together in her bewildered mind ; and when she comes into the world again, she thinks herself a nun escaped from confinement, and she now begins to recollect scenes of indescribable horror, which gradually become clearer and clearer. Now, Protestant public, the hour is come ; you have craved after lies, and you shall have your fill ; you have demanded, and here is the supply. She opens her mouth ; she lifts her voice ; your oracle, your prophet, your idol, O Protestant public, is about to speak ; she begins her " Awful Disclosures." Who is this hapless creature, very wicked, very mischievous, yet much to be pitied ? It is Maria Monk.

My Brothers, in what I have been saying, I have but given substance in my own way to the facts recorded of her ; but those facts are simply as I have stated them. The history of the wretched impostor was traced out and given to the world immediately on the publication of her romance. It was deposed

by divers witnesses that she was born of parents who
had lived at Montreal in Canada, about the year
1816. When about seven years old, she broke a
slate pencil on her head, and had been strange ever
since ; at the age of eight she frequented a convent
school; when about fourteen or fifteen she left her
mother's roof ; and is found successively in the
service of several persons, an hotel-keeper, a farmer,
a tradesman, and others, and then for a time was dependent on charity. From one of her mistresses she
absconded with a quantity of wearing-linen ; she was
discharged by two others for her bad conduct, and
was generally looked upon as a person of at least
doubtful character. Then she made her appearance
at Montreal itself, declaring she was daughter to Dr.
Robertson, a magistrate of the city, who had kept her
chained in a cellar for four years. This attempt failing, she next went off to the United States, appeared
at New York, and then began a second and more
successful tale against one of the convents of the city
she had left, from which she said she had escaped.
She was taken up by a party of New York Protestants, who thoroughly believed her, and reduced her
story to writing. Who was the author is not
quite certain ; two names have been mentioned, one
of them a person connected with this town. In this
book, whoever wrote it, she gives a minute description
of her imaginary convent in Montreal, and of some of
the nuns and others she professed to have known
there. On the slander making its way to Montreal,
Protestants carefully went over the calumniated convent ; and they reported, after minute inspection, that
it in no respect answered to her account of it ; indeed,

it was certain she had never been within it. It was proved, on the other hand, that her description did distinctly answer to a Penitentiary of which she had lately been an inmate, and whence she was dismissed for bad conduct ; and further, that the account she gave of her nuns in the convent answered to some of her fellow-penitents. Moreover, there is something about the book more remarkable still, not indeed as it concerns her, but as it concerns the argument I have in several of these Lectures been pursuing. I have insisted much on the traditional character of the fable, of which Catholics are the victims. It is the old lie, brought up again and again. Now this is most singularly exemplified in the infamous work I am speaking of. On its appearance the newspapers of the day asserted, without contradiction, that it was in great measure a mere republication of a work printed in the year 1731, under the title of "The Gates of Hell opened, or a Development of the Secrets of Nunneries." "Maria Monk's Pamphlet," says a Liverpool paper, "is a *verbatim* copy of that work, the only difference being a change of names." The editor of a Boston paper "pledged himself that this was the fact ; " and the editor of another "was ready to make *affidavit* that the original work was in his possession a few months previously, when it had been lent to the publishers of Maria Monk's Disclosures." To show this he copied out passages from both works, which were the same word for word.[5]

Here, then, you have a witness who is prepared to

[5] For these facts, *vide* "A complete Refutation of Maria Monk's atrocious Plot," &c., by the Rev. R. W. Wilson (now Bishop of Hobart Town), Nottingham, 1837.

go any lengths in support of the Protestant Tradition, however truth or principle may lie in her way; and offensive as it will be to you to listen, and painful to me to read, you must, for the sake of the contrast between her and Mr. Blanco White, submit to one or two of those passages from her romance, which I am able without impropriety to quote.

Now, I will give you the key to the whole book considered as a composition, and its burden, and (what may be called) its moral, as addressed to the Protestant world. It is an idea, which, as I have already said, was naturally suggested to an impure mind, and forcibly addressed itself to a curious reader. Mankind necessarily proceeds upon the notion that what is within discloses itself by what is without; that the soul prompts the tongue, inspires the eye, and rules the demeanour; and such is the doctrine of Holy Writ, when it tells us that "out of the abundance of the heart the mouth speaketh." Hence, when strangers visit a nunnery, and see the order, cheerfulness, and quiet which reigns through it, they naturally take all this as the indication of that inward peace and joy which ought to be the portion of its inmates. And again, when strangers attend Mass, and observe the venerable and awful character of the rite, they naturally are led to think that the priest is "holding up pure hands," and is as undefiled in heart as he is grave in aspect. Now it is the object of this Narrative to reverse this natural association, to establish the contrary principle, and to impress upon the mind that what is within is always what the outward appearance is not, and that the more of saintliness is in the exterior, the more certainly is there depravity and guilt in the heart. Of course it must be confessed, there have been cases where what looked fair and beautiful was but a whited sepulchre, "full within of dead men's bones and of all filthiness;" such cases have been and may be, but they are unnatural surely, not natural; the exception, not the rule. To consider this as the rule of things, you must destroy all trust in the senses; when a man laughs, you must say he is sad; when he cries, you must say he is merry; when he is overbearing in words, you must call him gentle; and when he says foolish things, you must call him wise; all because sad hearts sometimes wear cheerful countenances, and divine wisdom sometimes has condescended to look like folly. It is reported to have been said by an able diplomatist, that the use of words is to disguise men's thoughts; but the very wit of the remark lies in the preposterous principle it ironically implies. Yet still to the run of readers there is something attractive in this perverted and morbid notion, both from a sort of malevolence and love of scandal, which possesses the minds of the vulgar, and from the wish to prove that others, who seems religious, are even worse than themselves; and besides, from the desire of mystery and marvel, which prompts them, as I have said before, to have recourse to some monstrous tale of priestcraft for excitement, as they would betake themselves to a romance or a ghost story.

Thus she says in one place, or rather the writers, whoever they may be:—" I have often reflected how grievously I had been deceived in my opinions of a nun's condition—all the holiness of their lives, I now found, was merely pretended. The appearance of sanctity and heavenly-mindedness which they had shown among us novices, I found was only a disguise, to conceal such practices as would not be tolerated in any decent society in the world ; and, as for joy and peace like that of heaven, which I had expected to find among them, I learned too well that they did not exist there." [6]

Again, speaking of a picture of the infernal pit, at which the nuns were looking, she introduces a nun saying something so dreadful, that the reader hardly knows whether to laugh or to cry at it. "I remember she named the wretch who was biting at the bars of hell, with a serpent gnawing his head, with chains and padlocks on, Father Dufresne ; and she would say, Does he not look like him, when he come in to catechism with his long solemn face, and begins his speeches with, ' My children, my hope is that you have lived very devout lives ? ' " [7]

In such passages, the object of the writer is to familiarise the reader's imagination to the notion that hypocrisy is the natural and ordinary state of things, and to create in him a permanent association between any serious act whatever and inward corruption. She makes the appearance of religion to be the presumption, not of reality, but of hollowness, and the very extravagance of her statements is their plausibility. The reader says, "It is so shocking, it must be true ; no one could have invented it."

It is with a view to increase this unnatural plausibility that the writer or writers dwell minutely on various details which happen, or might easily happen, in Catholic churches and convents. For instance,

[6] P. 116.   [7] P. 82.

they say, " The old priest . . . when going to admi
nister (the Blessed Sacrament) in any country place,
used to ride with a man before him, who rang a bell
as a signal. When the Canadians heard it, whose
habitations he passed, they would come and prostrate
themselves to the earth, worshipping it as God." Of
course ; it is so ; Catholics do worship the Blessed
Sacrament, because they believe It to be our Lord
Himself. Therefore we will say so in our book, for
we wish to lie naturally, we wish to root our imposture in a foundation of truth.

Again ; " The bell rang at half-past six to awaken
us. The old nun who was acting as night-watch
immediately spoke aloud, ' Behold the Lord cometh ! '
The nuns all responded, ' Let us go and meet Him.'
Presently, we then knelt and kissed the floor." [8]

Now observe the effect of all this. When a person,
who never was in a Catholic church or convent, reads
such particulars ; when he reads, moreover, of the
lattice-work of the confessional, of the stoup of holy
water, and the custom of dipping the finger into it, of
silence during dinner, and of recreation after it ; of a
priest saying Mass with his hands first joined together, and then spread, and his face to the altar ; of
his being addressed by the title of " my father,"
and speaking of his " children," and many other
similar particulars ; and then afterwards actually sees
some Catholic establishment, he says to himself,
" This is just what the book said ; " " here is quite the
very thing of which it gave me the picture ; " and I
repeat he has, in consequence of his reliance on it, so
associated the acts of the ceremonial, the joined

[8] P. 39.

hands or the downcast eyes, with what his book went on slanderously to connect them, with horrible sin, that he cannot disconnect them in his imagination; and he thinks the Catholic priest already convicted of hypocrisy, because he observes those usages which all the world knows that he does observe, which he is obliged to observe, and which the Church has ever observed. Thus you see the very things, which are naturally so touching and so beautiful in the old Catholic forms of devotion, become by this artifice the means of infusing suspicion into the mind of the beholder.

Yes; all this outward promise of good is but a beautiful veil, hiding behind it untold horrors. Let us lift it, so far as we may do so without sharing in the writer's sin. Our heroine has passed through her noviciate, and proceeds to take the vows. Then she learns suddenly the horrors of her situation; she was, in fact, in a house of evil spirits; she represents herself, as was very natural, supposing she had been a religious person, overcome by distress, and unable to resign herself to her lot; and she was told by the Mother Superior, "that such feelings were very common at first, and that many other nuns had expressed themselves as I did, who had long since changed their minds. She even said, on her entrance into the nunnery she had felt like me. Doubts, she declared, were among our greatest enemies. They would lead us to question every path of duty, and induce us to waver at every step. They arose only from remaining imperfections, and were always evidences of sin; our only way was to dismiss them immediately, to repent, to confess them. They were deadly sins, and would condemn us to hell if we should die without confessing them. Priests, she insisted, could not sin. It was a thing impossible. Everything they did and wished was of course right." [9]

Now, my Brothers, you know there is a divine law written on the heart by nature, and that the Catholic Church is built on that law, and cannot undo it. No Priest, no Bishop, no Council can make that right which is base and shameful. In this passage the false witness would make the Protestant world believe that nuns are obliged to obey their confessors in commands strictly sinful, and horrible, and blasphemous. How different from the true witness, Mr. Blanco White! He said all he could against convents; he never hinted that religious women were taught by the priests that priests could not possibly sin, could not possibly issue a sinful command, could not possibly have a sinful wish; and therefore must be obeyed whatever they ask; he never hinted, from any experience of his, that in matter of fact they did make any sinful suggestions. His quarrel with the Catholic religion was that it was too strict, not that it was too lax; that it gave rise to nervousness, scruples, and melancholy. His utmost accusation (except as regards the unbelieving few) was that he knew some persons, and he believed there were others, who sinned, knew their sin, came and confessed it, and sinned again. There was no calling evil good, and good evil. Let her continue her revelations :—

"She also gave me another piece of information, which excited other feelings in me scarcely less dreadful. Infants were sometimes born in the convent, but they were always baptised, and immediately strangled. This secured their everlasting happiness ; for the baptism purified them from all sinfulness, and being sent out of the world before they had time to do anything wrong, they were at once admitted into heaven. How happy, she exclaimed, are those who secure immortal happiness for such little beings ! Their little souls would thank those who killed their bodies, if they had it in their power.[1]

" So far as I know, there were no pains taken to preserve secrecy on this subject. . . . I believe I learned through the nuns that at least eighteen or twenty infants were smothered, and secretly buried in the cellar, while I was a nun." [2]

The nuns, according to her account, underwent the same fate, if they would not resign themselves to the mode of life in all its details, for which alone, as it would seem, the nunnery was set up. She gives an account of the murder of one of them ; and after quoting this, I consider I may fairly be excused from quoting any more.

" I entered the door," she says, " my companions standing behind me, as the place was so small as hardly to hold five persons at a time. The young nun was standing alone, near the middle of the room ; she was probably about twenty, with light hair, blue eyes, and a very fair complexion " [3] The poor victim is brought to the Bishop, who, the writer says, " it was easy to perceive, considered her fate to be sealed, and was determined she should not escape. In reply to some of the questions put to her she was silent ; to others I heard her voice reply that she did not repent of

[1] P. 35.   [2] P. 120.   [3] P. 75.

words she had uttered, though they had been reported
by some of the nuns who had heard them ; that she
had firmly resolved to resist any attempt to compel
her to the commission of crimes which she detested.
She added that she would rather die than cause the
murder of harmless babes. 'That is enough, finish
her !' said the Bishop.   Two nuns instantly fell upon
the woman ; and in obedience to directions given by
the Superior, prepared to execute her sentence.   She
still maintained all the calmness and submission of a
lamb."   Then they gag her and throw her on a bed.
" In an instant," the narrative proceeds, " another bed
was thrown upon her.   One of the priests sprung like
a fury upon it with all his force.   He was speedily
followed by the nuns, until there were as many upon
the bed as could find room, and all did what they
could, not only to smother, but to bruise her. . . .
After the lapse of fifteen or twenty minutes, and when
it was presumed that the sufferer had been smothered
and crushed to death, (the priest) and the nuns ceased
to trample upon her, and stepped from the bed.   All
was motionless and silent beneath it.   They then
began to laugh," &c.

But I surely need not continue trash such as this,
which is as stupid as it is atrocious.   In like manner
she tells us the number of nuns killed, the number
who killed themselves, the various penances and
tortures which were common, gags, hot irons, glass
chewing, and the " cap ; " the cells, and everything
which is proper furniture of such an abode.   She
concludes the book with a solemn reflection, how hard
it is to think aright after thinking wrong.   " The
Scriptures," she is made to say, " always affect me

powerfully when I read them ; but I feel that I have but just begun to learn the great truths, in which I ought to have been early instructed. . . . The first passage of Scripture that made any serious impression on my mind, was the text on which the chaplain preached on the Sabbath after my introduction into the house, ' Search the Scriptures : ' "—and so the book ends.

I have now described, first, the character of the writer, next, the character of her book ; one point alone remains, its reception by the public. The calumny first appeared in 1836, it still thrives and flourishes in 1851. I have made inquiries, and I am told I may safely say that in the course of the fifteen years that it has lasted, from 200,000 to 250,000 copies have been put into circulation in America and England. The edition I have used is printed at Nottingham in the *present* year. A vast number of copies has been sold at a cheap rate, and given away by persons who ought to have known it was a mere blasphemous fiction. At this very time the book is found, I believe, in some of the parochial lending libraries of this place, and I hear rumours concerning some of the distributors, which, from the respect I wish to entertain towards their names, I do not know how to credit. Nor have these various efforts been without visible fruit, at least in America. A nunnery was burned down at Charlestown ; and at New York fifty houses, inhabited by Catholics, were also destroyed by fire, which extended to the Cathedral.

6.

And thus I have completed, my Brothers, the contrast I proposed to set before you. A writer of name, of character, of honour, of gentleman-like feeling, who has the *entrée* of the first and most intellectual circles of the metropolis, and is the friend of the first Protestant ecclesiastics of his day, records his testimony against Catholicism; it is in the main true, and it fails:—a worthless stroller gets her own testimony put into writing; it is a heap of fables, and it triumphantly succeeds. Let, then, the Protestant public be itself the judge:—its preference of Maria Monk to Blanco White reveals a great fact ;—truth is not equal to the exigencies of the Protestant cause; falsehood is its best friend.

Nor let it be imagined, my Brothers, that I have unfairly selected my examples, in order to serve a purpose. Inhabitants of Birmingham ought, more than others, to acquit me of this. Only two years have I been here, and each of these two has been signalised by accusations against Catholics, similar, in the disreputableness of their authors, and in the enormity of their falsehood, and in the brilliancy of their success, to the calumnies of Maria Monk. Two years ago it was Jeffreys; last year it was Teodore. You recollect how Jeffreys acted his part, how he wept, and prayed, and harangued, and raised a whole population against an innocent company of monks; and how he was convicted of fraud, and confessed his guilt, and was sent to prison. You also recollect how an impostor, called Teodore, declaimed such shocking things, and wrote such indecent pamphlets against us, that they cannot have been intended for any other purpose than to afford merriment to the haunts of profligacy and vice; yet he was followed for a time, was admitted into Protestant places of worship, and honoured as a truth-telling oracle, till at length he was plainly detected to be what every one from the first would have seen he really was, were it usual to do the same common justice to Catholics which every Protestant considers his due ;—for falsehood is the basis of the Protestant Tradition.

On the other hand, I might give you other instances similar to that of Mr. Blanco White. I might point to Mr. Steimnitz, who, within the last ten years, began his noviciate among the Jesuits, left them, turned Protestant, and published an account of the community he had quitted. He wrote to expose them, and abounded in bitterness and invective ; but as to his facts, so little had he to produce from his own personal knowledge to the disadvantage of the Institution he was attacking, and so severely did he disappoint the Protestants for whom he wrote, that they considered his work what they called a Jesuitical trick, and said that he was pretending to attack the good fathers in order really to set them off to advantage ; for truth does but prejudice the Protestant Tradition.

Falsehood succeeds for a generation, or for a period ; but there it has its full course and comes to an end. Truth is eternal ; it is great, and will prevail. The end is the proof of things. Brothers of the Oratory, surely we shall succeed, because " they say all manner of evil against us falsely for His Name's sake."

LECTURE V.

A CONSIDERATION was incidentally introduced into the argument which engaged our attention last week, Brothers of the Oratory, which deserves insisting on, in the general view which I am taking of the present position of the Catholic Religion in England. I then said that, even putting aside the special merits and recommendations of the Catholic rule of celibacy, as enjoined upon the Priesthood and as involved in Monachism, (with which I was not concerned,) and looking at the question in the simple view of it, to which Protestants confine themselves, and keeping ourselves strictly on the defensive, still, when instances of bad priests and bad religious are brought against us, we might fairly fall back upon what may be called the previous question. I mean, it is incumbent on our opponents to show, that there are fewer cases of scandal among the married clergy than among unmarried; fewer cases of mental conflict, of restlessness, of despondency, of desolation, of immorality, and again of cruel slavery and hopeless suffering, among Protestant women, whether unmarried or wives than among Catholic nuns. It must be shown that

N

in such instances of guilt or sorrow which can be adduced, the priests accused have fallen into sin, the nuns compassionated have passed from happiness to misery, distinctly *by virtue* of the vow which binds them to a single life :—for till this is proved nothing is proved.   Protestants, however, for the most part find it very pleasant to attack others, very irksome and annoying to defend themselves ; they judge us by one rule, themselves by another ; and they convict us of every sin under heaven for doing sometimes what they do every day.

This one-sidedness, as it may be called, is one of the very marks or notes of a Protestant ; and bear in mind, when I use the word Protestant, I do not mean thereby all who are not Catholics, but distinctly the disciples of the Elizabethan Tradition.   Such an one cannot afford to be fair ; he cannot be fair if he tries.   He is ignorant, and he goes on to be unjust. He has always viewed things in one light, and he cannot adapt himself to any other ; he cannot throw himself into the ideas of other men, fix upon the principles on which those ideas depend, and then set himself to ascertain how those principles differ, or whether they differ at all, from those which he acts upon himself ; and, like a man who has been for a long while in one position, he is cramped and dis-abled, and has a difficulty and pain, more than we can well conceive, in stretching his limbs, straighten-ing them, and moving them freely.

I.

This narrow and one-sided condition of the Pro-testant intellect might be illustrated in various ways.

(1.) For instance, as regards the subject of Education.
It has lately been forcibly shown that the point
which the Catholic Church is maintaining against the
British Government in Ireland, as respects the Queen's
Colleges for the education of the middle and upper
classes, is precisely that which Protestantism maintains, and successfully maintains, against that same
Government in England—viz., that secular instruction
should not be separated from religious.[1]   The
Catholics of Ireland are asserting the very same principle as the Protestants of England ; however, the
Minister does not feel the logical force of the fact ;
and the same persons who think it so tolerable to
indulge Protestantism in the one country, are irritated
and incensed at a Catholic people for asking to be
similarly indulged in the other.   But how is it that
intelligent men, who can ascend in their minds from
the fall of an apple to the revolution of a comet, who
can apply their economical and political inductions
from English affairs to the amelioration of Italy and
Spain—how is it that, when they come to a question of
religion, they are suddenly incapable of understanding
that what is reasonable and defensible in one country,
is not utterly preposterous and paradoxical in another ?   What is true under one degree of longitude,
is true under another.   You have a right indeed
to say that Catholicism itself is not true ; but you
have no right, for it is bad logic, to be surprised that
those who think it true act consistently with that
supposition ; you do not well to be angry with those
who resist a policy in Ireland which your own friends

and supporters cordially detest and triumphantly withstand in England.

(2.) Take again a very different subject. A Protestant blames Catholics for showing honour to images; yet he does it himself. And first, he sees no difficulty in a mode of treating them, quite as repugnant to his own ideas of what is rational, as the practice he abominates; and that is, the offering insult and mockery to them. Where is the good sense of showing dishonour, if it be stupid and brutish to show honour? Approbation and criticism, praise and blame go together. I do not mean, of course, that you dishonour what you honour; but that the two ideas of honour and dishonour so go together, that where you *can* apply—(rightly or wrongly, but still) —where it is *possible* to apply the one, it is possible to apply the other. Tell me, then, what is meant by burning Bishops, or Cardinals, or Popes in *effigy?* has it no meaning? is it not plainly intended for an insult? Would any one who was burned in effigy feel it no insult? Well, then, how is it *not* absurd to feel pain at being dishonoured in effigy, *yet* absurd to feel pleasure at being honoured in effigy? How is it childish to honour an image, if it is not childish to dishonour it? This only can a Protestant say in defence of the act which he allows and practises, that he is used to it, whereas to the other he is not used. Honour is a new idea, it comes strange to him; and, wonderful to say, he does not see that he has admitted it in principle already, in admitting dishonour, and after preaching against the Catholic who crowns an image of the Madonna, he complacently goes his way, and sets light to a straw effigy of Guy Fawkes.

But this is not all ; Protestants actually set up images to represent their heroes, and they show them honour without any misgiving. The very flower and cream of Protestantism used to glory in the statue of King William on College Green, Dublin ; and, though I cannot make any reference in print, I recollect well what a shriek they raised some years ago, when the figure was unhorsed. Some profane person one night applied gunpowder, and blew the king right out of his saddle ; and he was found by those who took interest in him, like Dagon, on the ground. You might have thought the poor senseless block had life, to see the way people took on about it, and how they spoke of his face, and his arms, and his legs ; yet those same Protestants, I say, would at the same time be horrified, had I used "he" and "him" of a crucifix, and would call me one of the monsters described in the Apocalypse, did I but honour my living Lord as they their dead king.

(3.) Another instance :—When James the Second went out, and the aforesaid William came in, there were persons who refused to swear fidelity to William, because they had already sworn fidelity to James ; and who was to dispense them from their oath ? yet these scrupulous men were the few. The many virtually decided that the oath had been conditional, depending on their old king's good behaviour, though there was nothing to show it in the words in which it ran : and that accordingly they had no need to keep it any longer than they liked. And so, in a similar way, supposing a Catholic priest, who has embraced the Protestant persuasion, to come over to this country and marry a wife, who among his new co-religionists would dream of being shocked at it? Every one would think it both natural and becoming, and reasonable too, as a protest against Romish superstition; yet the man has taken the vow, and the man has broken it. "Oh! but he had no business to make such a vow; he did it in ignorance, it was antichristian, it was unlawful." There are then, it seems, after all, such things as unlawful oaths, and unlawful oaths are not to be kept, and there are cases which require a dispensation; yet let a Catholic say this, and he says nothing more—(rather he says much less than the Protestant; for he strictly defines the limits of what is lawful and what is unlawful! he takes a scientific view of the matter, and he forbids a man to be judge in his own case),—let a Catholic, I say, *assert* what the Protestant *practises*, and he has furnished matter for half-a-dozen platform speeches, and a whole set of Reformation Tracts.

These are some of the instances, which might be enlarged upon, of the blindness of our opponents to those very same acts or principles in themselves, which they impute as enormities to us; but I leave them for your consideration, my Brothers, and proceed to an instance of a different character.

2.

What is a more fruitful theme of declamation against us than the charge of persecution? The Catholic Church is a persecuting power; and every one of us is a persecutor; and, if we are not by nature persecutors, yet we are forced to be persecutors by the necessity we lie under of obeying a persecuting Church. Now let us direct a careful attention to this Protestant land, which has so virtuous a horror of persecution, and so noble a loathing of persecutors, and so tender a compassion for the persecuted, and let us consider whether the multitude of men are not, to say the least, in the same boat with us; whether there is anything which we are said to do which they do not do also, anything which we are said to have done which they have not done, and therefore, whether, with this theoretical indignation of persecution on the one hand, and this practical sanction of it on the other, they are not in the very position of that great king, in his evil hour, who sentenced a transgressor, when he himself was "the man."

Now I suppose, when men speak of persecution, and say that Catholics persecute, they mean that Catholics, on the score of religious opinions, inflict punishment on persons, property, privileges, or reputation; that we hate, calumniate, mock, mob and distress those who differ from us; that we pursue them with tests, disabilities, civil penalties, imprisonment, banishment, slavery, torture and death; that we are inflexible in our tempers, relentless in our measures, perfidious in our dealings, and remorseless in our inflictions. Something of this kind will be said, with a good deal of exaggeration even at very first sight; but still, as even a candid man may perhaps fancy, with some truth at the bottom. Well, see what I propose to do. I shall not discuss any point of doctrine or principle; such a task would not fall within the scope of these Lectures; I am not going to assume that savage cruelty, ruthless animosity, frantic passion, that the love of tormenting and delight in death are right, nor am I going to assume that they are wrong; I am not entering upon any question of the moral law;—moreover I will not discuss how far Catholics fairly fall in fact under the charge of barbarity, mercilessness, and fanaticism, and for this reason, because it is not my concern; for I mean to maintain, that the acts imputed to Catholics, whatever be their character, so very closely resemble in principle what is done by Protestants themselves, and in a Protestant's judgment is natural, explicable, and becoming, that Protestants are just the very last persons in the world who can with safety or consistency call Catholics persecutors, for the simple reason, that they should not throw stones who live in glass houses.

I am maintaining no paradox in saying this; it is a truth which is maintained by intelligent Protestants themselves. There is Dr. Whately, the present Protestant Archbishop of Dublin, one of the first writers of the day, and a most violent opponent of Catholicism; listen how he speaks, at the very time he is inveighing against our Holy Religion. "The Romish Church," he says, "which has so long and so loudly been stigmatized as a persecuting Church, is, indeed, deeply stained with this guilt, but cannot with any reason be reckoned the originating cause of it. . . . This, as well as the other Romish errors, has its root in the evil heart of the unrenewed man. Like the rest, it neither began with Romanism, nor can reasonably be expected to end with it." [2]

Now, what I shall do is, to take the Protestant in his house, his family, and his circle of friends, in his occupation, and his civil and political position, as a

[2] Whately on Romanism, p. 225.

good kind father, as a liberal master, as a useful member of society ; and to consider, as regards this matter of persecution, whether, could he see himself in a looking-glass, he would not mistake himself for a Catholic.

For instance, what is the first and natural act on the part of a Protestant father of a family, when he receives the intelligence that his son or daughter, grown up to man's or woman's estate, nay, long since come of age, has become, or is on the point of becoming a Catholic ? Of course there are exceptions ; but in most cases his conduct is so uniform, so suggestive of a general law, to which particular cases belong, that I almost fear to describe it, lest, what is farthest from my wish, I seem to be personal, and to be indulging in satire, when I am but pursuing an argument. " My dear John or James," the father says, calling him by his Christian name, " you know how tenderly I love you, and how indulgent I have ever been to you. I have given you the best of educations, and I have been proud of you. There is just one thing I cannot stand, and that is Popery ; and this is the very thing you have gone and taken up. You have exercised your right of private judgment ; I do not quarrel with you for this ; you are old enough to judge for yourself ; but I too have sacred duties, which are the unavoidable result of your conduct. I have duties to your brothers and sisters ;—never see my face again ; my door is closed to you. It wounds me to come to this decision, but what can I do ? My affection for you is as strong as ever it was, but you have placed yourself under influences hostile to your father's roof and your own home, and you must take the consequences."

No one can look round him, who has much to do with conversions and converts, without seeing this fulfilled often to the letter, and *mutatis mutandis*, in a variety of parallel cases. Protestants have felt it right, just, and necessary, to break the holiest of earthly ties, and to inflict the acutest temporal suffering on those who have exercised their private judgment in the choice of a religion. They have so acted, and they so act daily. A sense of duty to religious opinions, and of the supposed religious interests of those intrusted to them, has triumphed over the feelings of nature. Years have passed, perhaps death has come, without any signs of recognition passing from the father to the son. Sometimes the severance and its consequences may be sterner still : the wife may be sent away, her children taken from her, because she felt a call in conscience to join the Catholic Church. The son has been cut off (as they say) to a shilling. The daughter has been locked up, her books burned, the rites of her religion forbidden her. The malediction has been continued to the third generation ; the grandchildren, the child unborn, has not been tolerated by the head of the family, because the parents were converts to the faith of their forefathers.

Nature pleads ; and therefore, to fortify the mind the various reasons for such severity must be distinctly passed before it, and impressed upon it, and passion must be roused to overcome affection. " Such a base, grovelling, demoralising religion, unworthy of a man of sense, unworthy of a man ! I could have borne his turning Drummondite, Plymouth-Brother, or Mormonite. He might almost have joined the

Agapemone. I would rather see him an unbeliever ; yes, I say it deliberately, Popery is worse than Paganism. I had rather see him dead. I could have borne to see him in his coffin. I cannot see him the slave of a priest. And then the way in which he took the step : he never let me know, and had been received before I had had a hint about it ; " or " he told me what he meant to do, and then did it in spite of me ; " or, " he was so weak and silly," or " so head-strong," or " so long and obstinately set upon it." " He had nothing to say for himself," or " he was always arguing." " He was inveigled into it by others," or " he ought to have consulted others, he had no right to have an opinion. Anyhow he is pre-ferring strangers to his true friends ; he has shown an utter disregard of the feelings of his parents and relations ; he has been ungrateful to his father."

These are a few out of the many thoughts which pass through the Protestant's mind under the circum-stances I have supposed, and which impel him to inflict a severe penalty on a child for a change of religion. And if there be Protestant fathers who demur to the correctness of this representation (and I am using the word Protestant in its proper sense, as I have noticed several times before), I beg to ask such parents whether, in fact, they have themselves suffered the affliction I have supposed,—I mean, that of their children becoming Catholics ; and, if they have not, I entreat them to fancy such an affliction for a moment, and how they would feel and act if it really took place. Rather they will not be able to get themselves to fancy it ; I am sure that most of them will revolt from the thought in indignation ; the very supposition irritates them. " I should like to see any son or daughter of mine turning Papist ! " is the thought which spontaneously rises to their mind.

I have been speaking of the upper and middle classes : in the lower the feeling is the same, only more uncourteously expressed, and acted on more summarily. The daughter, on her return home, tells the mother that she has been attending, and means to attend, the Catholic chapel ; whereupon the mother instantly knocks the daughter down, and takes away from her her bonnet and shawl, and the rest of her clothes to keep her in-doors : or if it is the case of a wife, the husband falls to cursing, protests he will kill her if she goes near the Catholics, and that if the priest comes here, he will pitch him out of window. Such are specimens of what Dr. Whately truly calls, ' the evil heart of the unrenewed man."

Perhaps, however, the one party or the other gives way ; milder counsels prevail with the persecutor, or the persecuted is menaced into submission. A poor child is teased and worried, till, to escape black looks, sharp speeches, petty mortifications, and the unsympathizing chill of the domestic atmosphere, she consents to go to Protestant worship ; and is forced to sit, stand, and kneel, in outward deference to a ceremonial, which she utterly disbelieves, and perhaps hates. At length, doing violence to her conscience, she loses her sense of the reality of Catholicism, grows indifferent to all religion, sceptical of the truth of everything, and utterly desponding and sick at heart and miserable. Her friends suspect her state, but it is better than Popery ; their detestation of the

Catholic religion is so intense, that, provided their child is saved from its influence, for them she may believe anything or nothing ; and as to her distress of mind, time will overcome it—they will get her married. Such is a Protestant's practical notion of freedom of opinion, religious liberty, private judgment, and those other fine principles which he preaches up with such unction in public meetings, and toasts so enthusiastically at public dinners.

Perhaps, however, there is a compromise. Terms are made, conditions extracted ; the parties who have made the mistake of thinking they might judge for themselves, are taken into favour again,—are received under the paternal roof on the rigid stipulation that no sign of Catholicism is to escape them ; their mouths are to be sealed ; their devotional manuals to be hid ; their beads must never escape from their pocket ; their crucifix must lie in a drawer ; Opinion is to be simply put down in the family.

As to domestic servants whose crime it is to be Catholics, far more summary measures are taken with them, not less cruel in effect, though more plausible in representation. They are the first to suffer from a popular cry against the Catholic religion. Perhaps some reverend person, high in station, draws public attention to this defenceless portion of the community, —not to protect them from those moral dangers which benevolent statesmen are striving to mitigate, —but to make them the objects of suspicion, and to set their masters and mistresses against them. Suddenly a vast number of young persons are thrown out of their situations, simply because they are Catholics—because, forsooth, they are supposed to be emissaries of the Jesuits, spies upon the family, and secret preachers of Popery. Whither are they to go? home they have none; trial and perils they have without number, which ought to excite remorse in the breasts of those who, at the gain of a smart argument in controversy, or a telling paragraph in a speech or a charge, are the cause of their misfortunes. They look about in vain for a fresh place; and their only chance of success is by accepting any wages, however poor, which are offered them, and going into any service, however hard, however low, however disadvantageous. Well, but let us suppose the best that can befall them: they shall be tolerated in a household and not discharged; but what is the price they pay for this indulgence! They are to give up their religious duties; never to go to confession; only once or twice a year to mass; or an arrangement is made, as a great favour, to allow them to go monthly. Moreover, they are had up into the parlour or drawing-room for family prayers, or to hear tracts and treatises, abusive of their religion, or to endure the presence of some solemn Protestant curate, who is expressly summoned to scare and browbeat, if he cannot persuade, a safe victim, whom her hard circumstances have made dependent on the tyranny of others.

Now, I would have every Protestant, to whom my words may come, put his hand on his heart and say, first, whether scenes such as I have been describing, whether in high life or in low, are not very much what he would call persecution in Catholics, and next, whether they can, by any the utmost ingenuity, be referred, in the cases supposed, to any Catholic influence as their cause. On the contrary, they come

out of the very depths and innermost shrine of the
Protestant heart: it is undeniable, the very staunchest
Protestants are the actors in them : nay, the stauncher
they are, the more faithfully do they sustain their
part : and yet, I repeat, if a similar occurrence were
reported of some Catholic family in Italy or Spain,
these very persons whose conduct I have been describing would listen with great satisfaction to the
invectives of any itinerant declaimer, who should
work up the sternness of the father, the fury of the
mother, the beggary of children and grandchildren,
the blows struck, the imprecations uttered, the imprisonment, the over-persuasion, or the compulsory
compromise, into a demonstration that Popery was
nothing else than a persecuting power, which was
impatient of light, and afraid of inquiry, and which
imposed upon fathers, mothers, and husbands, under
pain of reprobation, the duty of tormenting their
children, and discharging their servants at an hour's
warning.

Let us walk abroad with those children or servants,
who, by the spirit of Protestantism, have been sent
about their business for being Catholics, and we shall
see fresh manifestations of its intolerance. Go into
the workshops and manufactories, you will find it in
full operation. The convert to Catholicism is dismissed by his employer ; the tradesman loses his
custom ; the practitioner his patients ; the lawyer
has no longer the confidence of his clients ; pecuniary
aid is reclaimed, or its promise recalled ; business is
crippled, the shop cannot be opened ; the old is left
without provision, the young without his outfit—he
must look about for himself ; his friends fight shy of

him ; gradually they drop him, if they do not disown him at once. There used to be pleasant houses open to him, and a circle of acquaintance. People were glad to see him, and he felt himself, though solitary, not lonely ; he was by himself, indeed, but he had always a refuge from himself, without having recourse to public amusements which he disliked. It is now all at an end ; he gets no more invitations ; he is not a welcome guest. He at length finds himself in *Coventry ;* and where his presence once was found, now it is replaced by malicious and monstrous tales about him, distorted shadows of himself, freely circulated, and readily believed. What is his crime ?—he is a Catholic among Protestants.

3.

If such is the conduct of Protestant society towards individuals, what is it not against the Priest ? what against the Catholic Name itself ? Do you think it is with the good will of Establishment, Wesleyan Connection, and various other denominations of religion, that Catholics are in Birmingham at all ? do we worship—have we a place of worship,—with or against the will of the bodies in question ? Would they not close all our churches and chapels to-morrow, would they not cut the ground from under us, if they could ? what hinders them from turning us all out of the place, except that they can't ? Attend to this, my Brothers, and observe its bearing. You know what an outcry is raised, because the Roman Government does not sell or give ground to Protestants to build a Protestant Church in the centre of Rome ; that government hinders them there, because it is able : Protestants do not hinder us here, because they are not able. Can they, in the face of day, deny this?—they cannot. Why, then, do they find fault with others who do, because they can, what they themselves would do if they could ? Do not tell me, then, that they are in earnest when they speak of the "intolerance of Catholics" abroad ; they ought to come into Court with clean hands. They do just the same themselves, as far as they can ; only, since they cannot do it to their mind's content, they are determined it shall form an article of impeachment against us ; and they eagerly throw a stone that comes to hand, though it is only by an accident that it does not fall back on themselves.

It has lately been reported in the papers that the Catholics of Italy are going to build a church in London for their poor countrymen, who in great numbers are found there. Let them go to the Board of Woods and Forests (and less equitable bodies might be found), and try to negotiate a purchase of ground for a site ; would Government for a moment entertain the proposal ? would it not laugh at their impudence in asking ? would 'the people suffer the Government, even if it were disposed ? would there not be petitions sent up to the two Houses, enough to break the tables on which they were ranged,—petitions to the Queen, enough to block up the Home Office ? would not the whole press, both daily and weekly, in town and in country, groan and tremble under the portentous agitation such a project would occasion ? Happily for Catholics, other ground is to be had. But would not Court and Ministry, Establishment, Wesleyans, almost every political party, almost all the denominations of

O

London, the Court of Aldermen, the Common Council, the City Companies, the great landlords, the
Inns of Court, and the Vestries, hinder any Catholic
Church if they could? Yet these are the parties to
cry out against a line of conduct in Rome which
they do their best to imitate in London.

But this is not all: in spite of their manifesting,
every day of their lives, an intense desire to do us all
the harm in their power, wonderful to say, they go
on to reproach us with ingratitude. We evince no
gratitude, say the Protestant Bishops, for the favours
which have been shown us. Gratitude for what?
What favours have we received? the Frenchman's
good fortune, and nothing else. When he boasted the
king had spoken to him, he was naturally asked
what the king had said: and he answered that his
Majesty had most graciously cried out to him,
"Fellow, stand out of the way." Statesmen would
ignore us if they could; they recognise us in order
to coerce; they cannot coerce without recognising,
therefore at last they condescend to recognise.
When there was a proposal, several years ago, for an
interchange of ministers between England and the
Pope, then they would not have his name mentioned;
he was not to be called by any title of his own, but
by a new-fangled name, framed for the occasion. He
was to be known as "Sovereign of the Roman
States;" a title which pretty well provided, should
occasion occur, for treating with some other sovereign
power in his States who should not be he. Now
that they wish to do him an injury, forthwith they
wake up to the fact of his existence. Our statesmen
affect to know nothing of the greatest power on

earth, the most ancient dynasty in history, till it comes right across their path, and then they can recognise as foes, what before they could not recognise as gentlemen.

Indeed, if the truth must be told, so one-sided is this Protestantism, that its supporters have not yet admitted the notion into their minds, that the Catholic Church has as much right to make converts in England as any other denomination. It is a new idea to them; they had thought she ought to be content with vegetating, as a sickly plant, in some back-yard or garret window; but to attempt to spread her faith abroad—this is the real insidiousness, and the veritable insult. I say this advisedly. Some public men, indeed, have even confessed it; they have been candid enough to admit distinctly, that the Penal Bill is intended to throw a damper on our energies; and others imply it who dare not say it. There are words, for instance, imputed to the Prime Minister, with reference to a publication of my own, which put the matter in a very clear point of view. I have to acknowledge his civility to myself personally; and I am sure, though I have an aversion to his party and his politics, of twenty, nay thirty years' standing, yet I bear nothing but goodwill to himself, except as the representative of the one and of the other. But now consider what he said. It appears he had laid it down, that his only object in his Parliamentary measure was to resist any temporal pretensions of the Pope; and in proof, observe, that such pretensions were made, what does he do but quote some words which I used in a sermon preached at Chad's last October, on occasion of the Establishment of the Hierarchy. Now what was that sermon about? was there a word in it about Catholics exercising or gaining temporal power in England, which was the point on which he was insisting?—not a syllable. I may confidently say, for I know my own feelings on the subject, that the notion of any civil or political aggrandisement of Catholicism never came into my head. From the beginning to the end of the sermon, I spoke simply and purely of conversions—of conversions of individuals, of the spread of the Church by means of individual conversions, by the exercise of private judgment, by the communication of mind with mind by the conflict of opinion, by the zeal of converts, and in the midst of persecution; not by any general plan of operation, or by political movement, or by external influence bearing upon the country. Such a growth of Catholicism, intellectual, gradual, moral, peaceable, and stable, I certainly predicted and predict, and such only: yet this, though the fruit of free opinion and disputation, is adduced by the Premier as an intelligible, as a sufficient, reason for introducing a measure of coercion.

An intellectual movement must be met by Act of Parliament. Can a clearer proof be required, that not our political intrigues—for we are guilty of none —but our moral and argumentative power, is the real object of apprehension and attack? they wish to coerce us because we are zealous, and they venture to coerce us because we are few. They coerce us for the crime of being few and wishing to be many. They coerce us while they can, lest they should not dare to coerce when another twenty years has passed over our heads. "Hit him, he's down!" this is the cry of the Ministry, the country gentlemen, the Establishment, and Exeter Hall. *Therefore* are we ultramontanes; *therefore* are we aggressive; *this* is our conspiracy, that we have hearts to desire what we believe to be for the religious wellbeing of others, and heads to compass it. Two centuries ago, all England, you know, was in terror about some vast and mysterious Popish plot, which was to swallow up the whole population, without any one knowing how. What does the historian Hume—no Catholic, certainly,— say on the subject? "Such zeal of proselytism," he observes, "actuates that sect (meaning us) that its missionaries have penetrated into every nation of the globe; and in one sense there is a Popish plot perpetually carrying on against all states, Protestant, Pagan, and Mahometan."[3] The simple truth! this is the unvarnished account of the matter: we do surpass in zeal every other Religion, and have done so from the first. But this, surely, ought to be no offence, but a praise: that Religion which inspires the most enthusiasm has a right to succeed. If to cherish zeal, if to deal the blows of reason and argument, if this be political, if this be disloyal, certainly we deserve worse punishment than the deportation suggested by one member of Parliament, and the £500 penalty proposed by another.

Had indeed the ruling powers of the country, when coercion was in their power, refrained from coercion, and turned a host of controversialists in upon us instead; had a gracious answer come from the Throne

[3] Charles the Second, ch. 67.

in return for the loyal address of the Protestant Bishops, commanding them to refute us, and never to enter the royal closet again without a tail of twenty converts apiece; had a Parliamentary Committee been appointed to inquire into the best means of denying our facts, and unravelling our arguments; had a reward of some £1000 been offered for our scientific demolition, in Bridgewater Treatise or Warburton Lecture, we should have felt gratitude towards those who had rather fail in their end than be ungenerous in their measures. But for years and years the case has been just the reverse; they have ever done us all the harm that they could, they have not done only what they could not. They have only made concessions under the influence of fear. Small thanks for scanty favours; such thanks as Lazarus's for the rich man's crumbs which could not help falling from the table: it is no virtue to grant what you cannot deny. Now, what is the state of the case; Protestant sects quarrel among themselves, they scramble for power, they inflict injuries on each other; then at length they come to think it would be well to bear and forbear. They establish the great principle of toleration, not at all for our sakes, simply for the sake of each other, one and all devoutly wishing that they could tolerate each other without tolerating us. We, born Britons and members of the body politic as much as they, accidentally come under the shadow of a toleration which was meant for others. When they find that common sense and fairness are too strong for them, and that they cannot keep us out, and, moreover, that it is dangerous to do so, they make a merit of letting us in, and they wish us to be grateful for a privilege which is our birthright as much as it is theirs.

I know well there is a rising feeling, there are emergent parties in this country, far more generous and equitable, far more sensible, than to deserve these imputations; but I am speaking all along of the dominant faction, and of the children of the Tradition. As for the latter, it will be long before they realise the fact that we are on a social equality with themselves, and that what is allowable in them is allowable in us. At present, it is a matter of surprise to them that we dare to speak a word in our defence, and that we are not content with the liberty of breathing, eating, moving about, and dying in a Protestant soil. That we should have an opinion, that we should take a line of our own, that we should dare to convince people, that we should move on the offensive, is intolerable presumption, and takes away their breath. They think themselves martyrs of patience if they can keep quiet in our presence, and condescending in the heroic degree, if they offer us any lofty civility. So was it the other day, when the late agitation began; the hangers-on of Government said to us, "Cling tight to our coat-tails; we are your best friends; we shall let you off easy; we shall only spit upon you; but beware of those rabid Conservatives;" and they marvelled that we did not feel it to be the highest preferment for the Catholic Church to wait in the ante-chambers of a political party. So it is with your Protestant controversialist, even when he shows to best advantage; his great principle of disputation is that he is up, and the Catholic is down; and his great duty is to show it.

He is intensely conscious that he is in a very eligible situation, and his opponent in the gutter; and he lectures down upon him, as if out of a drawing-room window. It is against his nature to be courteous to those for whom he feels so cordial a disdain, and he cannot forgive himself for stooping to annihilate them. He mistakes sharpness for keenness, and haughtiness for strength; and never shows so high and mighty in manner as when he means to be unutterably conclusive. It is a standing rule with him to accuse his opponent of evasion and misstatement; and, when in fault of an argument, he always can impugn his motives, or question the honesty of his professions.

Such is the style of that writer to whom Cardinal Wiseman alludes in his late Appeal to the English people. The person I speak of is a gentleman and a scholar, nay, one of the most distinguished Protestant theologians of the day; but that did not hinder him, on the occasion alluded to by the Cardinal, from strutting about with indignation that a Catholic should intrude himself into the quarrels of the Establishment, and from fancying that rudeness would be an indication of superiority. In his title-page he describes his pamphlet as "A letter to N. Wiseman, D.D., *calling himself* Bishop of Melipotamus;" then he addresses him, not "Rev. Sir," but "Sir," and talks of it being reported that he has "received the form of episcopal consecration at Rome," and tells him this is no excuse for his "acting in opposition to his legitimate diocesan, the [Protestant] Bishop of Worcester." He proceeds to speak of Dr. Wiseman's "characteristic sagacity," and of the "leaders of his

party;" reminds him that "in the eyes of his superiors the end sanctifies the means," and says that a
mistake of fact, of which he accuses him, "appears to
be not quite unintentional." He is ever upon stilts, and,
as the pamphlet proceeds, there is an ever-thickening
recurrence of such rhetoric as "Excuse me, Sir," and
"Now, Sir," and "Such, Sir," and "But, Sir," and
"Yes, Sir," and "No, Sir." I should not notice this
pamphlet, which is of some years' standing, did I
think the writer at all repented of its tone, and might
not any day publish just such another. After all, it
is but an instance in detail of the Protestant Tradition; for such has been the received style of the
Church of England ever since the days of such considerable men as Laud, Taylor, Stillingfleet, and
Ussher. Moreover, it is emphatically the gentleman-
like manner of conducting the controversy with us, in
contrast to that of the pulpit or the platform, where
the speaker considers himself a sort of theological
Van Amberg, scares us with his eye, and hits up to
and fro with his cudgel.

4.

Now for another department of this petty persecution. That able writer, Dr. Whately, whom I have
already quoted in this Lecture, and whom, for the
love I bear him, from all memories, in spite of our
religious differences, I take pleasure in quoting, whenever I can do so with any momentary or partial
agreement with him—the Protestant Archbishop of
Dublin, I say, writing on the subject of persecution, is
led to speak of insult and abuse, calumny, ridicule,
and blasphemy, as directed by the professors of one

religion against those of another; and he uses the following remarkable words:—" Undoubtedly," he says, " they ought to enjoy this protection, not only of their persons and property, but of their comfort and feelings also. The State is both authorised and bound to prohibit and to guard against, by her own appropriate penalties, not only everything that may tend to a breach of the peace, but also everything that unnecessarily interferes with the comfort, and molests the feelings of any one. I say, unnecessarily, because it may be painful indeed to a man's feelings to have his opinions controverted, and to be obliged to encounter opponents; but then free discussion is necessary for the attainment and maintenance of truth. *Not so with ridicule and insult ;* to forbid these can be no violation of religious liberty, since no man can be bound in conscience to employ such weapons: they have manifestly no tendency to advance the cause of truth **;** they are, therefore, analogous to the slaughter of women and children, and other non-belligerents, which is regarded by all civilized nations as a violation of the laws of war; these being un-necessary cruelties, since they have no direct tendency to bring the war to a conclusion." And then he goes on to say, " It is evident that all this reasoning applies with equal force to the case of persons of *every religious persuasion*, whether Christians of various sects, or Jews, or Mahometans. All of these, though they must be prepared indeed to encounter fair argument, should be protected, not only from persecution, but from *insult, libel, and mockery*, as occasioning a useless interruption of public or of domestic peace and comfort ; and this being an offence against society, may justly be prohibited and punished by human laws." [4]

Here, you will observe, a writer, setting down his thoughts on persecution twenty-five years ago, when the present state of the controversy was as yet in the womb of the future, distinctly tells us that insult, abuse, and mockery, are inconsistent with religious liberty, and that they should be prohibited by law, even as directed against Mahometans. Now I accept the sentiment, though I will not adopt it without an explanation. I consider then, that in applying it to the existing state of things, we must distinguish between religious objects and rites, and the persons who acknowledge them. I cannot reprobate, in a free country like this, the ridicule of individuals, whoever they are ; and I think it would be a very evil day when it was forbidden. From the Lord Chancellor and Prime Minister, to the ephemeral charlatan or quack, who astonishes the world with his impudence and absurdity, it is desirable that all should be exposed to the ridicule of any who choose to make them the objects of it. In no other way are various abuses, or encroachments, or nuisances, or follies, so easily and gently got rid of ; it is a most healthy expression of public opinion ; it is a safety-valve for feelings, which if not allowed so harmless an escape, might end in a serious explosion. Moreover, it is our boast among the nations, that, while elsewhere it is dangerous, with us it is positively healthy. In France or in Italy, I suppose, no Government could stand against public ridicule ; the Anglo-Saxon is good-natured in his

---

[4] Letters on the Church, p. 53. I am told (1872) the Archbishop never owned the authorship of this able volume.

satire ; and he likes his rulers not at all the worse, or rather the better, that he can distort them into attitudes, and dress them up in masquerade.   And this permission must be suffered to extend to the case of persons who bear a religious profession, as well as that of others ; though in this case the line will sometimes be difficult to draw.   It will be painful, indeed, to those who look up to them, to see one whom they revere, or who is associated with what is sacred in their minds, made the subject of insult and buffoonery, as it may be annoying to the private circle and painful to the relatives of a statesman or public man, who undergoes a similar ordeal ; but, as matters go in this country, there is no sufficient ground for prohibiting, nor much wisdom in complaining.   But the case is very different when the religious rite is insulted, and the individual for the sake of the rite.   For example, were England a Catholic country, I can fancy a caricature of a fat monk or a fanatical pilgrim being quite unobjectionable ; it would argue no disrespect to the Religion itself, but would be merely a blow at an abuse of religion, in the instance of certain individuals who were no ornament to it ; on the other hand, in a Protestant land, it would or would not be an insult to Catholicism, according to the temper of the moment, and the colouring and details of the satire.   However, my business is not to draw the line between what is allowable and what is unfair as regards ridicule in matters of religion, but merely to direct your attention to this point, that I have no wish, when it can be helped, to shelter the persons of religious men under the sacredness of the Religion itself.

With this explanation, then, in favour of ridicule, I

accept Dr. Whately's doctrine as reasonable and true ; but consider, my Brothers, its application to ourselves. What a remarkable light does it cast on the relative position of Protestants and Catholics in England during the current year ! Our author tells us that insult and mockery, in religious controversy, is as cowardly and cruel as the slaughter of women and children in war, and he presses on us the duty of the State to prohibit by penalties such interference with the comforts and feelings of individuals ; now, I repeat, what a remarkable illustration have Protestants supplied to this doctrine of a Protestant divine since Michaelmas last ! The special champions of toleration, the jealous foes of persecution, how studiously and conscientiously, during nine long months, have they practised what they preached ! What a bright example have they set to that religious communion which they hold in such abhorrence on the ground of its persecuting spirit ! Oh, the one-sided intellect of Protestantism ! I appeal in evidence of it to a great banquet, where, amid great applause, the first judge of the land spoke of trampling Cardinal Wiseman's hat under his feet. I appeal to the last fifth of November, when jeers against the Blessed Sacrament and its rites were chalked up in the Metropolis with impunity, under the very shadow of the Court, and before the eyes of the Home Office and the Police. I appeal to the mock processions to ridicule, and bonfires to burn, what we hold most venerable and sacred, not only Pope, and Cardinal and Priest, but the very Mother of our Lord, and the Crucifix itself. I appeal to those ever-growing files of newspapers, whose daily task, in the tedious succession of months has been to cater for the gross palate of their readers all varieties of disgusting gossip, and of bitter reproach, and of extravagant slander, and of affronting, taunting, sneering, irritating invective against us. I appeal to the buckram nuns of Warwickshire, Nottingham, and Clapham, to the dungeons of Edgbaston, and the sin-table of St. Gudule's. I appeal to the outrageous language perpetrated in a place I must not name, where one speaker went the length of saying, what the reporters suppressed for fear of consequences, that a dear friend and brother of mine, for whose purity and honour I would die, mentioning him by name, went about the country, as the words came to the ears of those present, seducing young women. I appeal to the weekly caricatures, not of persons only and their doings, but of all that is held sacred in our doctrines and observances, of our rites and ceremonies, our saints and our relics, our sacred vestments and our rosaries. I appeal to the popular publication, which witty and amusing in its place, thought it well to leave its "sweetness" and its "fatness," to change make-believe for earnest, to become solemn and sour in its jests, and awkwardly to try its hand at divinity, because Catholics were the game. I appeal to the cowardly issue of a cowardly agitation, to the blows dealt in the streets of this very town upon the persons of the innocent, the tender, and the helpless ;—not to any insult or affliction which has come upon our-selves, for it is our portion, and we have no thought of complaining,—but to the ladies and the school-girls, who, at various times, up to the day I am record-ing it, because they are Catholics, have been the

victims of these newspaper sarcasms, and these platform blasphemies. I appeal to the stones striking
sharply upon the one, and the teeth knocked out of
the mouths of the other. Dr. Whately's words have
been almost prophetic ; mockery and insult have
literally terminated in the bodily injury of those non-
belligerents, who are sacred by the laws of all civilised
warfare. Such are some of the phenomena of a Religion which makes it its special boast to be the Prophet of Toleration.

5.

And in the midst of outrages such as these, my
Brothers of the Oratory, wiping its mouth, and clasp-
ing its hands, and turning up its eyes, it trudges to
the Town Hall to hear Dr. Achilli expose the Inquisition. Ah! Dr. Achilli, I might have spoken of
him last week, had time admitted of it. The Protestant world flocks to hear him, because he has
something to tell of the Catholic Church. He *has* a
something to tell, it is true ; he *has* a scandal to
reveal, he *has* an argument to exhibit. It is a simple
one, and a powerful one, as far as it goes—and it is
one. That one argument is himself ; it is his presence
which is the triumph of Protestants ; it is the sight of
him which is a Catholic's confusion. It is indeed our
great confusion, that our Holy Mother could have
had a priest like him. [5] He feels the force of the
argument, and he shows himself to the multitude
that is gazing on him. "Mothers of families," he
seems to say, "gentle maidens, innocent children,
look at me, for I am worth looking at. You do not

---

[5] *Vide Dublin Review* for July, 1850, and "Authentic Brief Sketch of
the Life of Dr. Giacinto Achilli." Richardsons.

see such a sight every day. Can any Church live over the imputation of such a birth as I am?"[6]

*   *   *   *   *   *

Yes, you are an incontrovertible proof that priests may fall and friars break their vows. You are your own witness; but while you *need* not go out of yourself for your argument, neither are you *able*. With you the argument begins; with you too it ends: the beginning and the ending you are both, When you have shown yourself, you have done your worst and your all; you are your best argument and your sole. Your witness against others is utterly invalidated by your witness against yourself You leave your sting in the wound; you cannot lay the golden eggs, for you are already dead.

For how, Brothers of the Oratory, can we possibly believe a man like this in what he says about persons, and facts, and conversations, and events, when he is of the stamp of Maria Monk, of Jeffreys, and of Teodore, and of others who have had their hour, and then been dropped by the indignation or the shame of mankind? What call is there on Catholics to answer what has not yet been proved? what need to answer the evidence of one who has not replied to the Police reports of Viterbo, Naples, and Corfu? He tells me that a Father Inquisitor said to him, "Another time," that you are "shut up in the Inquisition," "you" will not "get away so easily."[7] I do not believe it was said to him. He reports that a Cardinal said of him, "We must either make him a Bishop, or shut him up

---

[6] The paragraphs omitted are those which were decided by jury to constitute a libel, June 24, 1852.

[7] Dealings with the Inquisition, p. 2.

in the Inquisition." [8]   I do not believe it.   He bears witness, that "the General of the Dominicans, the oldest of the Inquisitors, exclaimed against him before the council, 'This heretic, we had better burn him alive.'" [9]   I don't believe a word of it.   "Give up the present Archbishop of Canterbury," says he, "amiable and pious as he is, to one of these rabid Inquisitors; he must either deny his faith, or be burned alive.   Is my statement false?   Am I doting?" [1] Not doting, but untrustworthy.   "Suppose I were to be handed over to the tender mercy of this Cardinal [Wiseman], and he had full power to dispose of me as he chose, without losing his character in the eyes of the nation, ... should I not have to undergo some death more terrible than ordinary?"   Dr. Achilli does not dote; they dote who trust him.

Why do I so confidently assert that he is not to be believed?—first, because his life for twenty years past creates no prepossession in favour of his veracity; secondly, because during a part of that period, according to his own confession, he spoke and argued against doctrines, which at the very time he confessed to be maintained by the communion to which he belonged; thirdly, because he has ventured to deny in the general, what official documents prove against him in the particular; fourthly, because he is not simple and clear enough in his narrative of facts to inspire any confidence in him; fifthly, because he abounds in misstatements and romance, as any one will see who knows anything of the matters he is writing about; sixthly, because he runs counter to facts known and confessed by all.

[8] Ibid. p. 27.   [9] Ibid. p. 46.   [1] Ibid. p. 75.

6.

Indeed, I should not finish my Lecture to-night, my Brothers, if I went through the series of historical facts which might be detailed in contradiction of the statements which this author advances, and in proof of the utterly false view which Protestants take of the Inquisition, and of the Holy See in connection with it. I will set down a few. A recent Catholic controversialist, a Spanish writer of great name, Dr. Balmez, goes so far as to say "that the Roman Inquisition has never been known to pronounce the execution of capital punishment, although the Apostolic See has been occupied, during that time, by Popes of extreme rigour and severity in all that relates to the civil administration."[2]—"We find," he continues, "in all parts of Europe scaffolds prepared to punish crimes against religion; scenes which sadden the soul were everywhere witnessed. Rome is an exception to the rule;—Rome, which it has been attempted to represent as a monster of intolerance and cruelty. . . . The Popes, armed with a tribunal of intolerance, have not spilt a drop of blood; Protestants and philosophers have shed torrents." Moreover, the Spanish Inquisition, against which, and not the Roman, it is more common to inveigh, though Dr. Achilli writes about the Roman, the Spanish Inquisition, which really was bloody, is confessed by great Protestant authorities, such as Ranke, and Guizot, to have been a political, not an ecclesiastical institution; its officials, though ecclesiastics, were

[2] Balmez' Protestantism, transl., p. 166.—I am rather surprised that this is stated so unrestrictedly, *vide* Life of St. Philip Neri, vol. i. ; however, the fact is substantially as stated, even though there were some exceptions to the rule.

" appointed by the crown, responsible to the crown, and removable at its pleasure." [3]   It had, indeed, been originally authorised by the Pope, who, at the instance of the civil power, granted it a bull of establishment ; but as soon as it began to act, its measures so deeply shocked him, that he immediately commenced a series of grave remonstrances against its proceedings, and bitterly complained that he had been deceived by the Spanish Government.   The Protestant Ranke distinctly maintains that it was even set up *against* the Pope and the Church.   " As the jurisdiction of the Court," he says, " rested on the Royal Supremacy, so its exercise was made available for the maintenance of the Royal authority.   It is one of those *spoliations* of the ecclesiastical power, by which this government rose into strength ; . . . in its nature and its object, it was a purely political institute." Moreover, the Pope, anxious and displeased at what was going on, appointed a new functionary to reside on the spot, with the office of Judge of Appeals from the Inquisition, in favour of the condemned : and when this expedient was evaded, he appointed special judges for particular cases ; and lastly, when the cruelty of the Spanish Government and its officials, lay and ecclesiastical, defeated this second attempt to ameliorate the evil, then he encouraged the sufferers to flee to Rome, where he took them under his protection. [4]   In this way it is recorded, that in one

[3] *Vide* an able article in the Dublin Review, June, 1850,—which is my authority for this and other facts.

[4] Gieseler says that " the Popes at first tried *to draw some advantage* from the new Institution by selling [ecclesiastical] absolution for the crime of apostasy."—Vol. iii. p. 335.   It is easy to throw out such insinuations as to objects and motives.

year he rescued 230 persons, and 200 in another. Sometimes he directly interfered in Spain itself; in the beginning of one year he liberated fifty heretics; and fifty more a month or two later; three further interpositions of mercy are recorded within the year. Sometimes he set aside and annulled the judgments passed: sometimes he managed to rescue the condemned from the infamy and civil consequences of the sentence; sometimes he actually summoned, censured, and excommunicated the Inquisitor; and often he took the part of the children of those whose property was forfeited to the crown. Moreover he refused to allow the Spanish Government to introduce their Inquisition into Naples, or the Milanese, which then belonged to Spain, from his disapprobation of its rigour.

Such conduct as this is but in accordance with the historical character of the Holy See, in all times and in all countries. Doubtless in the long course of eighteen hundred years, there are events which need explanation, and which Catholics themselves might wish otherwise; but the general tenor and tendency of the traditions of the Papacy have been mercy and humanity. It has ever been less fierce than the nations, and in advance of the age: it has ever moderated, not only the ferocity of barbarians, but the fanaticism of Catholic populations. Let the accusations which can be made against it be put in form; let the formal charges be proved: let the proved offences be counted up; and then Protestants themselves will be able to determine what judgment is to be passed on the language in which they indulge themselves against it. "An actual hell," says their present oracle, Dr. Achilli, "seems to be

at the command of this Church, and it may be known
by the name of the Inquisition. . . . The Inquisition
is truly a hell, invented by priests. . . . Christianity
suffers more now than in former times under this harsh
slavery." [5]   The Inquisition, it seems, is a hell ; then
there are many other hells in the world present and
past, and worse hells, though this is the only one of
which Dr. Achilli has had experience.   He, indeed,
may be excused for not knowing that, in his reprobation of the Inquisition, he is in fact virtually reflecting upon the nation, at whose good opinion he is
aiming ; but Protestants, had they the caution of
ordinary disputants, would have known better than
to accept a field of controversy, far less dangerous to
their enemy than to themselves. Judgment and
justice, like charity, begin at home : and before they
commiserate culprits two thousand miles away, they
would do well to feel some shame at victims of their
own making.   They are shocked, forsooth, at religious ascendancy and religious coercion at Rome ; as
if the ideas and the things were foreign to a British
soil and a British policy.   The *name* alone of the Inquisition, says Dr. Achilli, " is sufficient to incite in
the minds of all rational beings a sentiment of horror
and repugnance, little inferior to what Christians experience with respect to hell itself." [6]   A true word !
what is the Inquisition *but* a name ?   What is the Court
of Queen's Bench but a name ? why should not, in
this matter, the names be interchanged ? what has the
Inquisition done at Rome, which the Royal name and
authority has not done in England ?   The question
is, not what a tribunal is called, but what has been its

[5] Inquisition, pp. 5, 11.   [6] Ibid. p. 5.

work. Dr. Achilli, it seems, has been imprisoned by
the Inquisition, for preaching in Rome against the
religion of Rome: and has no one ever been put in
prison, or fined, or transported, or doomed to death
in England, for preaching against the religion of
England? Those adversaries, indeed, of Catholicism
pleaded that Catholicism was rebellion: and has Dr.
Achilli had nothing to do with a party not only dangerous, but actually and contemporaneously subversive of the Pontifical Government? It seems never
to occur to a Protestant, that he must not do in his
own case what he blames in another; and should he
at any time leave off a practice, he is surprised that
every one else has not left it off at the same moment,
and he has no mercy on any that has not ;—like converted prodigals, who are sternly unforgiving towards the vices they have only just abandoned themselves.

7.

It is in my own memory, that a popular writer was
convicted in the King's Bench, and sentenced to fine
and imprisonment, for parodying passages of the Anglican Prayer Book. It is within my own memory,
that an unbeliever in Christianity incurred a similar
sentence, for exposing and selling his publications in
a shop in Fleet Street. Why is Christianity to be
protected by law, if Catholicism is not? What has
the Inquisition done to Dr. Achilli, which the King's
Bench did not do, and more, to Hone and Carlyle?
Why is that so shocking to-day, which came so
natural to you thirty years ago? Not many years
have passed since Unitarian worship was a legal
offence: the Unitarian creed was felony, and Uni-

tarian congregations incurred the penalty of transportation. "If the civil magistrate," says Dr.
Whately, "have no rightful jurisdiction whatever in
religious concerns, it is quite as much an act of injustice, though of far less cruelty, to fine a Socinian,
as to burn him."[7] Nor, indeed, was burning absent;
five men were burnt in Elizabeth's reign for denying
the Holy Trinity, of whom the Protestant Bishop of
Norwich burnt three. In the next reign, the Protestant Bishop of London burnt one, and the Protestant
Bishop of Lichfield another. A third was sentenced,
but the compassion of the people saved him. Catholics have fared even worse; they have not, indeed,
been burned, but they have been tortured, hung, cut
down alive, cut open alive, quartered, and boiled.
Nay, it is only quite lately, that heavy penal inflictions have been taken off the daily acts of our religion.
Many of us, my Brothers, as you know well, wear
about us crosses, pictures, medals, beads, and the like,
blessed by the Pope; they are still illegal; an *Agnus
Dei* is still illegal. Nay, five years have not fully
passed, since the bringing them into the kingdom,
and the giving them away, and the receiving and
wearing them was punishable, by outlawry, forfeiture of all goods and chattels to the Queen, and
imprisonment for life. Yet British Law is the wonder
of the world, and Rome is Antichrist!

Nor has this prohibition been at all times an
empty menace, as it is to-day: time was, when it
was followed out into its extreme consequences. The
possession of an *Agnus Dei* was the foremost charge
in the indictment brought against the first of our

[7] Letters on the Church, p. 42.

Martyrs among the Missionary Priests in the reign of bloody Elizabeth. "As soon as the Sheriff came into the chamber," say the Acts of the martyrdom of Cuthbert Maine, "he took Mr. Maine by the bosom, and said to him, What art thou? he answered, I am a man. Whereat the Sheriff, being very hot, asked if he had a coat of mail under his doublet; and so unbuttoned it, and found an *Agnus Dei* case about his neck, which he took from him, and called him traitor and rebel, with many other opprobrious names." [8] Maine was hanged, cut down alive, falling from a great height, and then quartered. He was the first-fruit of a sanguinary persecution, which lasted a hundred years. John Wilson, while they tore out his heart said, "I forgive the Queen, and all that are the cause of my death." Edward Campion was cruelly torn and rent upon the rack divers times. "Before he went to the rack, he used to fall down at the rack-house door, upon both knees, to commend himself to God's mercy; and upon the rack he called continually upon God, repeating often the holy name of Jesus. His keeper asked him the next day, how he felt his hands and feet, he answered, 'Not ill, because not at all.' He was hanged and embowelled at Tyburn." Ralph Sherwin came next; the hangman, taking hold of him with his bloody hands, which had been busy with the bowels of the martyred priest who preceded him, said to him, thinking to terrify him, "Come, Sherwin, take thou also thy wages." But the holy man, nothing dismayed, embraced him with a cheerful countenance, and reverently kissed the blood that stuck to his hands; at

---

[8] Challoner's Missionary Priests.

which the people were much moved. He had been twice racked, and now he was dealt with as his brother before him. Thomas Sherwood, after six months' imprisonment in a dark and filthy hole, was hanged, cut down alive, dismembered, bowelled, and quartered. Alexander Brian had needles thrust under his nails, was torn upon the rack, hanged, and beheaded. George Haydock was suffered to hang but a very little while, when the Sheriff ordered the rope to be cut, and the whole butchery to be performed upon him while he was alive, and perfectly sensible. John Finch was dragged through the streets, his head beating all the way upon the stones; was then thrust into a dark and fetid dungeon, with no bed but the damp floor; was fed sparingly, and on nothing but oxen's liver. Here he was left first for weeks, then for months; till at length he was hanged, and his quarters sent to the four chief towns of Lancashire. Richard White, being cut down alive, pronounced the sacred name of Jesus twice, while the hangman had his hands in his bowels. James Claxton was first put into *little ease*, that is, a place, where he could neither stand, lie, nor sit; there he was for three days, fed on bread and water. Then he was put into the mill to grind; then he was hanged up by the hands, till the blood sprang forth at his fingers' ends: at length he was hanged, dying at the age of twenty-one years. These are the acts, these are the scenes, which Protestants, stopping their ears, and raising their voices, and casting dust into the air, will not let us inflict upon them. No, it is pleasanter to declaim against persecution, and to call the Inquisition a hell, than to consider their own devices, and the work of their own hands. The catalogue reaches to some hundred names. One was killed in this manner in 1577, two in 1578, four in 1581, eleven in 1582, thirteen in 1583 and 1584, nineteen in 1585 and 1586, thirty-nine in 1587 and 1588, and so on at intervals to the end of the seventeenth century ; besides the imprisonments and transportations, which can hardly be numbered. What will the Protestants bring against the Holy See comparable to atrocities such as these ? not, surely, with any fairness, the burnings in Queen Mary's reign, the acts, as they were, of an English party, inflamed with revenge against their enemies, and opposed by Cardinal Pole, the Pope's Legate, as well as by the ecclesiastics of Spain.

8.

My time is run out, Brothers of the Oratory, before my subject is exhausted. One remark I will make in conclusion. The horrors I have been describing are no anomaly in the history of Protestantism. Whatever theoretical differences it has had on the subject with the Catholic Religion, it has, in matter of fact, ever shown itself a persecuting power. It has persecuted in England, in Scotland, in Ireland, in Holland, in France, in Germany, in Geneva. Calvin burnt a Socinian, Cranmer an Anabaptist, Luther advised the wholesale murder of the fanatical peasants, and Knox was party to bloody enactments and bloody deeds. You would think that with scandals such as these at their door, Protestants would find it safest to let history alone, and not meddle with the question of persecution at all, from a lively consciousness of deeds identical with those

which they impute to the Catholic Church. Not a
bit of it. What then is their view of the matter?
Strange to say, they make it their plea of exculpation,
and the actual difference between Catholics and
them, that they condemn persecution on principle;
in other words, they bring their own inconsistency
as the excuse for their crime. Now I grant them, I
am far from disputing it, that a man who holds a
right principle, and occasionally, nay often, offends
against it, is better than he who holds the opposite
wrong principle, and acts consistently upon it; but
that is not the present case. The case before us is
that of persons who never once have acted on the
principle they profess—never once; for they cannot produce their instance, when Protestants, of
whatever denomination, were in possession of national
power for any sufficient time, without persecuting
some or other of their polemical antagonists. So it
has been, so it is now. Three centuries ago Protestantism in England set off on its course with murdering Catholic priests; only a few months have passed
since a clergyman of the Establishment gave out to
his congregation that transportation was too good
for us, and he thought we all ought to be put to
death. So far from the Protestant party feeling any
real shock at this avowal, a little while after, a second
clergyman, as influential in Manchester as the first
mentioned is in Liverpool, repeated the sentiment;
and still no shock or sensation in the Protestant
public was the result. Doubtless they gave their
reasons for wishing it, sufficient in their own judgment, and so too did the Protestant Elizabeth, so
too did Gardiner and the other advisers of the

Catholic Mary; but still such was the upshot of their reasons, death to every Catholic priest. The present case then is not of an individual, or a ruler, or a body politic laying down a good principle, and not being able at times and under circumstances, through passion or policy, to act up to it; no, it is the case of a religion saying one thing, and on every actual and possible occasion doing another. Can such a religion extenuate its acts on the ground of its professions? Yet this is the excuse, nay, this is the boast, the glory, of the Protestant party:—"We always do one thing, and we always say another; we always preach peace, but we always make war; we have the face of a lamb, and the claws of a dragon. And we have another boast; to be sure, we persecute, but then, as a set off, you see, we always denounce in others what we are in the practice of doing ourselves; this is our second great virtue. Observe, we, persecutors, protest against persecution,—virtue one; next, we, persecutors, blacken and curse the Papists for persecuting,—virtue two; and now for a third virtue —why, we are so superlatively one-sided, that we do not even see our own utter inconsistency in this matter, and we deny, that what is a stigma in their case is even a scandal in ours. We think that profession and denunciation make up a good Christian, and that we may persecute freely, if we do but largely quote Scripture against it."

And now I might leave Protestants to explain this matter if they can, and to unravel the mystery how it is that, after all their solemn words against persecution, they have persecuted, as I have shown, whenever, wherever, and however they could, from Elizabeth down to Victoria, from the domestic circle up to the Legislature, from black looks to the extremity of the gibbet and the stake; I might leave them, but I am tempted to make them one parting suggestion. I observe, then, it is no accident that they unite in their history this abjuration with this practice of religious coercion; the two go together I say it boldly and decidedly, and do not flinch from the avowal—Protestants attempt too much, and they end in doing nothing. They go too far; they attempt what is against nature, and therefore impossible. I am not proving this; it is a separate subject; it would require a treatise. I am only telling the Protestant world why it is they ever persecute, in spite of their professions. It is because their doctrine of private judgment, as they hold it, is extreme and unreal, and necessarily leads to excesses in the opposite direction. They are attempting to reverse nature, with no warrant for doing so; and nature has its ample revenge upon them. They altogether ignore a principle which the Creator has put into our breasts, the duty of maintaining the truth; and, in consequence, they deprive themselves of the opportunity of controlling, restraining and directing it. So was it with the actors in the first French Revolution: never were there such extravagant praises of the rights of reason; never so signal, so horrible a profanation of them. They cried, " Liberty, Equality, Fraternity," and then proceeded to massacre the priests, and to hurry the laity by thousands to the scaffold or the river-side.

Far other is the conduct of the Church. Not to put the matter on higher and doctrinal grounds, it is plain, if only to prevent the occurrence of injustice and cruelty, she must—to use a phrase of the day—

direct impulses, which it is impossible from the nature of man to destroy. And in the course of eighteen hundred years, though her children have been guilty of various excesses, though she herself is responsible for isolated acts of most solemn import, yet for one deed of severity with which she can be charged, there have been a hundred of her acts, repressive of the persecutor and protective of his victims. She has been a never-failing fount of humanity, equity, forbearance, and compassion, in consequence of her very recognition of natural ideas and instincts, which Protestants would vainly ignore and contradict: and this is the solution of the paradox stated by the distinguished author I just now quoted, to the effect that the Religion which forbids private judgment in matters of Revelation, is historically more tolerant than the Religions which uphold it. His words will bear repetition: "We find, in all parts of Europe, scaffolds prepared to punish crimes against religion; scenes which sadden the soul were everywhere witnessed. Rome is one exception to the rule; Rome, which it has been attempted to represent a monster of intolerance and cruelty. It is true, that the Popes have not preached, like the Protestants, universal toleration; but the facts show the difference between the Protestants and the Popes. The Popes armed with a tribunal of intolerance, have scarce spilt a drop of blood; Protestants and philosophers have shed it in torrents." [9]

---

[9] Since this Lecture has been in type, I have been shown De Maistre's Letters on the Inquisition, and am pleased to see that in some places I have followed so great a writer.

LECTURE VI.

PREJUDICE THE LIFE OF THE PROTESTANT VIEW.

In attributing the extreme aversion and contempt in which we Catholics are held by this great Protestant country, to the influence of falsehood and misrepresentation, energetic in its operation and unbounded in its extent, I believe in my heart I have referred it to a cause, which will be acknowledged to be both real and necessary by the majority of thoughtful and honest minds, Catholics or not, who set themselves to examine the state of the case. Take an educated man, who has seen the world, and interested himself in the religious bodies, disputes, and events of the day, let him be ever so ill-disposed towards the Catholic Church, yet I think, if he will but throw his mind upon the subject, and then candidly speak out, he will confess that the arguments which lead him to his present state of feeling about her, whatever they are, would not be sufficient for the multitude of men. The multitude, if it is to be arrested and moved, requires altogether a different polemic from that which is at the command of the man of letters, of thought, of feeling, and of honour. His proofs against Catholicism, though he considers them sufficient himself, and considers that they ought to be sufficient for the multitude, have a sobriety, a delicacy, an exactness, a nice adjustment of parts, a width and breadth, a philosophical cumulativeness, an indirectness and circuitousness, which will be lost on the generality of men. The problem is, how to make an impression on those who have never learned to exercise their minds, to compare thought with thought, to analyse an argument, or to balance probabilities. Catholicism appeals to the imagination, as a great fact, wherever she comes; she strikes it; Protestants must find some idea equally vivid as the Church, something fascinating, something capable of possessing, engrossing, and overwhelming, if they are to battle with her hopefully; their cause is lost, unless they can do this. It was then a thought of genius, and, as I think, preternatural genius, to pitch upon the expedient which has been used against the Church from Christ's age to our own; to call her, as in the first century, Beelzebub, so in the sixteenth, Anti-Christ, it was a bold, politic, and successful move. It startled men who heard; and whereas Anti-Christ, by the very notion of his character, will counterfeit Christ, he will therefore be, so far, necessarily like Him; and if Anti-Christ is like Christ, then Christ, I suppose, must be like Anti-Christ; thus there was, even at first starting, a felicitous plausibility about the very charge, which went far towards securing belief, while it commanded attention.

This, however, though much, was not enough; the charge that Christ is Anti-Christ must not only be made, but must be sustained; and sustained it could not possibly be, in the vastness and enormity of its idea, as I have described it, by means of truth. Falsehood then has ever been the indispensable condition of the impeachment which Protestants have made ; and the impeachment they make is the indispensable weapon wherewith to encounter the antagonist whom they combat. Thus you see that calumny and obloquy of every kind is, from the nature of the case, the portion of the Church, while she has enemies, that is, in other words, while she is militant,—her portion, that is, if she is to be argued with at all ; and argued with she must be, because man, from his very moral constitution, cannot content himself, in his warfare of whatever kind, with the mere use of brute force. The lion rends his prey, and gives no reason for doing so ; but man cannot persecute without assigning to himself a reason for his act : he must settle it with his conscience ; he must have sufficient reasons, and if good reasons are not forthcoming, there is no help for it ; he must put up with bad. How to conflict with the moral influence of the Church, being taken as the problem to be solved, nothing is left for him but to misstate and defame ; there is no alternative. Tame facts, elaborate inductions, subtle presumptions, will not avail with the many ; something which will cut a dash, something gaudy and staring, something inflammatory, is the rhetoric in request ; he must make up his mind then to resign the populace to the action of the Catholic Church, or he must slander her to her greater confusion. This, I maintain, *is* the case ; this I consider, *must* be the case ;—bad logic, false facts ; and I really do think that candid men, of whatever persuasion, though they will not express themselves exactly in the words I have used, will agree with me in substance ; will allow, that, putting aside the question whether Protestantism can be supported by any other method than controversy, for instance, by simple establishment, or by depriving Catholics of education, or by any other violent expedient, still, if popular controversy *is* to be used, then fable, not truth, calumny, not justice, will be its staple. Strip it of its fallacies and its fiction, and where are you ? It is no accident then that we are the victims of slander.

So much in corroboration of what I have said in former Lectures ; but I have not yet stated the full influence in the controversy, or (as it may be called) the full virtue, of this system of misrepresentation. The question may have occurred to you, my Brothers, as a philosophical difficulty, how it is that able, cultivated, enlarged minds should not only be the organs of the grossest slanders about us, but should refuse to retract them, when they have been absolutely sllenced and answered. The very courtesy of civilized life demands from them a retraction ; it is the rule among gentlemen that, even when an accuser adheres in his heart to what he has advanced against another, yet on that other's denying it, he accepts the denial and withdraws his words. It is otherwise in the contest with Catholics ; when we deny what is charged against our character or conduct, and deny it with irresistible arguments, we not only have reason to desiderate that outward consideration which the laws of society enforce, but probably are bluntly told that we lie, and there we are left, and the matter too. Doubtless this phenomenon is traceable in part to that characteristic of the human kind, noticed by philosophers, to crouch to what is in the ascendant, and to insult what is down in the world; but it partly arises from a cause to which I have not yet referred, and which I mean to make the subject of this Lecture. This cause is so obvious, that you may wonder I am so circuitous in introducing it, and why I have not treated of it before; but it properly comes in this place. I allude to the power of *Prejudice*, which is to be reckoned a principal reason why our most triumphant refutations of the facts and arguments urged against us by our enemies avail us so little; for in reality, those facts and arguments have already done their work, before their demolition arrives and in spite of their subsequent demolition, by impressing the minds of the persons who have heard and have used them with a *prejudice* against us.

I.

Now, first I must explain what Prejudice is, and how it is produced, before I go on to consider its operation. Prejudice, you know, means properly a pre-judgment, or judgment by anticipation; a judgment which is formed prior to the particular question submitted to us, yet is made to bear upon it. Thus, if a man is accused of theft, and I already believe him to be an habitual thief, I am naturally led to think that this particular charge is well-founded before going into the evidence which is actually adducible for it. In this way, previous good or bad name has so much to do with the decisions in courts of justice; slight evidence will be enough to convict a reputed thief; on the other hand, a person under accusation, in order to repel it, brings witnesses to his character. When we have this previous knowledge of persons, we say, —when their actions or they themselves come under consideration,—on the one hand, that we cannot help being " prejudiced" *against* one, and on the other, "prejudiced " or " prepossessed " *in favour* of another. Now there is nothing unfair in all this ; what is past naturally bears on the future ; from what has been, we conjecture what will be ; it is reasonable and rational to do so ; and hence, persons who have all their lives long heard nothing but what is bad of Catholics, naturally and fairly entertain a bad opinion of them ; and when a new charge is made against them, are disposed to credit it without stopping to consider the evidence.   And it matters not, whether the previous judgment, which influences their belief, be a judgment of their own forming, or be inherited ; let it be the tradition of their country ; still there is nothing strange, there is nothing wrong, in their being influenced by it.

But then observe this ;—after all, a previous judg-ment, conclusion, or belief such as this, in which consists their *prejudice*, is but vague and general ; it is not more than an opinion or inference, of greater or less strength, as the case may be, and varying with the trustworthiness of the reasons or testimony which has created it.   It cannot reasonably, and must not, be taken as infallible ;—did the persons in ques-tion so simply rest upon it, that they would not hear what could be said on the other side, as if they were quite sure nothing could be said to the purpose, they would cease to act rationally, they would be simply obstinate.   And this is Prejudice in its bad and culpable sense, the sense in which the word is commonly used, and in which I am using it here, and am imputing it to Protestants. I accuse them of making too much of the Tradition which has come down to them ; they not only take it at first sight as true, and act upon it as true (a proceeding against which nothing can fairly be said), but they put such implicit confidence in it, that they cannot bring themselves to hear what can be said on the other side. They make the Tradition practically infallible, as if it had settled the view they are to take of the subject of it once for all and for ever.

How can any one, you will say, act so absurdly, who has any pretensions to good sense and good feeling? yet it may happen in a measure to any one of us, and in the following way. Now I hope I shall not be taxing your attention, my Brothers, more than I have a right to do on an occasion such as this, in what I am going to say in explanation. Prejudice then is something more than an act of judgment ; it is not a mere act, it is a habit or state of mind. I must refer to a peculiarity, not of the English character, but of our mental constitution generally. When, then, we hear a thing said again and again, it makes what may be called an impression upon us. We not only hold it in our mind as an opinion or belief, as separate from us, as depending on the information or grounds on which we have received it, and as admitting of being thrown off the next minute at our will, should we have reasons for discarding it, but it has acted upon our mind itself, it has sunk into it, it has impressed it. No longer at our disposal as before, to keep or throw away, it becomes one of our habitual and invariable modes of judging and believing, something like the ideas we have of good and evil, and of religious duty. The idea, for instance, that justice is a virtue, or that there is a Divine Providence, is imprinted in our minds ; it is congenial to our nature, and it is true, and that, because it is found in all times and places, with exceptions too rare or inconsiderable to be worth noticing. Such an idea, I say, is true ; still there may also be impressions, similar in permanence, which yet are false and are uncongenial to our nature, and they are characterized, first, in *not* being common to all ; next, in *not* being found in the mind from the first (if I may so speak), in *not* coming thither no one knows how, that is, from heaven itself, but formed in us by the accidental occurrence of things which we have seen or heard, and another has not. These impressions are commonly created in the mind by the repetition of something striking it from without. A fact or argument is not stronger in its own nature by being repeated ; but the effect on any mind, which is passive under the infliction, *is* stronger and stronger every time it is repeated. In this way almost any idea whatever may be impressed on the mind ; a man will begin at length to think himself a fool or a knave, if every one tells him so.

This then is what comes of the perpetual talk against Catholics. It does not become truer because it is incessant ; but it continually deepens the impression in the minds of those who hear it, that Catholicism is an imposture. I say, there is no increase of logical cogency ; a lie is a lie just as much the tenth time it is told as the first ; or rather more, it is ten lies

instead of one ; but it gains in rhetorical influence.
Let it be repeated again and again ; it matters not ;
the utterer has only to go on steadily proclaiming it,
and first one, then another, will begin to believe it,
and at length it will assume the shape of a very
respectable fact or opinion, which is held by a considerable number of well-informed persons. This is
what is meant by the proverb, " Fling dirt enough and
some will stick." And if even one pertinacious
slanderer has the prospect of such success in his
slander, from this peculiarity of our nature, what
must be the effect when vast multitudes of men are
incessantly crying out to each other, with unwearied
and sleepless energy, fables and fallacies against the
Catholic Religion ? Why, each is convincing the
other, and deepening the hostile impression in his mind
with a keenness and precision which it is appalling
to contemplate ; and thus the meetings and preachings
which are ever going on against us on all sides,
though they may have no argumentative force whatever, are still immense factories for the creation of
prejudice,—an article, by means of these exertions,
more carefully elaborated, and more lasting in its
texture, than any specimens of hardware, or other
material productions, which are the boast of a town
such as this is.

Now the peculiarity of these mental impressions
is, that they do not depend afterwards upon the facts
or reasonings by which they were produced, any more
than a blow, when once given, has any continued
connexion with the stone or the stick which gave it.
To burn the stick will not salve the sore : and to
demolish the argument, as I have already said, does

not obliterate the prejudice. Suppose I have been told that my neighbour is a thief; suppose the idea has rested on my mind, and I have accustomed myself to it; and suppose I hear what it was that made my informant assert it, and examine into this, and find it to be utterly untrue; why I *may* indeed cast off my feeling against my neighbour at once and altogether, but I *may* have a great difficulty in doing so. The idea may still cling to me, and I may find it impossible, except by degrees, to overcome the associations with which he is connected in my mind, and the repugnance I feel to him; there is something I have to struggle against. And thus, even though a slander be perfectly cleared up, even though it be brought into a court of justice, and formally disconnected from the person who has been the victim of it, he is not what he was. It was a saying of the greatest of the Romans, "that Cæsar's wife should not be suspected." The slander has, as it were, stained the minds of the hearers, and only time, if even time, can wipe it out. This, then, is properly a prejudice,—not an opinion which is at our own disposal, and dependent for its presence or its dismissal on our will, but an impression, which reason indeed can act upon, and the will can subdue, but only by degrees and with trouble. It sank into the mind by the repetition of untrue representations, it must be effaced by an opposite process, by a succession of thoughts and deeds antagonistic to it. We must make it up to the injured party by acts of kindness, by friendly services, by good words, by praising him, by the desire and attempt to please and honour him, and thus gradually we shall lose all recollection of our former hard thoughts of him. On the other hand, it is quite possible to shut ourselves up in ourselves; to keep at a distance from him, and to cherish coldness or ill-will; and then, in spite of the calumnies having been triumphantly refuted, and of our nominal acquiescence, we shall be as suspicious or jealous as ever. We shall say that we are not, after all, satisfied; that we cannot, indeed, give our grounds, but that things have a suspicious appearance; and we shall look about diligently for some fresh ground of accusation against him, to justify us in such thoughts and such conduct.

Now you may recollect, Brothers of the Oratory, that, in speaking of prejudice in its first and most simple sense, as a mere anticipation or previous opinion in disparagement of another, I said there was no harm in it. It is a mere judgment, formed on previous grounds, like any judgment, which the owner puts away at once, as soon as its unsoundness is detected. But prejudice, in its second and ordinary sense, in which I have now for some time been using it—viz., as an impression or stain on the mind is not at all innocent or excusable, just the reverse. This may surprise you; you may say, How can a man help his impressions? he is passive under them; they come of themselves; he is as little answerable for what is actually stamped upon his mind, as for a wound which is inflicted on his body; but this is very far from the case, as a little consideration will show. The will goes with a prejudice; there is no compulsion or necessity; those who have prejudices are unwilling to give them up; there is no prejudice without the will; we are prejudiced, I say, because we will;

and therefore, if we did not will, we should not be prejudiced.   I do not say we could get rid of the prejudice in a day by wishing to do so ; but we should, in that case, be tending to get rid of it. Scripture speaks of those who " loved darkness rather than the light ; " and it is impossible for us to deny, from what we see on all sides, that as regards the Protestant view of Catholics, men love to be left to their own dark thoughts of us ; they desire to be able with a good reason and a good conscience to hate us ; they do not wish to be disabused, they are loth that so pleasant an error should be torn from them. First, then, I say, that prejudice depends on the will ; now, secondly, if it does depend on the will, it is not, cannot be, innocent, because it is directed, not against things, but against persons, against God's rational creatures, against our fellows, towards all of whom we owe the duties of humanity and charity.   There is a natural law, binding us to think as well as we can of every one ; we ought to be glad when imputations are removed and scandals cleared up.   And this law is observed by every generous mind : such a mind is pained to believe that bad things can be said of others with any plausibility, and will rejoice to be able to deny them, will hope they are not true, and will give the subject of them the benefit of its doubts.   Every hour, then, as it passes, bears with it protests against prejudice, when there is generosity, from the natural striving of the heart the other way. Jealousy, suspicion, dislike, thinking ill, are feelings so painful to the rightly disposed, that there is a constant reclamation going on within them, an uneasiness that they should be obliged to entertain them, and an effort to get rid of them. Nay, there are persons of such kind and tender hearts, that they would believe there is no evil at all in the world, if they could : and it is a relief to them whenever they can knock off, so to say, any part of the score of accusations which the multitude of men bring against each other. On the other hand, to close the ears to an explanation, and to show a desire that the worst may be true,— unless indeed the innocence of the individual who at present lies under a cloud involves the guilt of a vast many others instead, so that one has to strike a balance of crimes,—I say, to resolve that rumours or suspicions, for which no distinct grounds are alleged, shall be true, is simple malevolence, deplorable, shocking, inexcusable.

I do not know how any one can deny the justice of these remarks ; but observe what a melancholy comment they form on the treatment which Catholics receive in this Protestant country. Where are the tender hearts, the kind feelings, the upright under-standings of our countrymen and countrywomen ? where is the generosity of the Briton, of which from one's youth up one has been so proud ? where is his love of fair play, and his compassion for the weak, and his indignation at the oppressor, when we are concerned ? The most sensible people on the earth, the most sensitive of moral inconsistency, the most ambitious of propriety and good taste, would rather commit themselves in the eyes of the whole world, would rather involve themselves in the most patent incongruities and absurdities, would rather make sport, as they do by their conduct, for their enemies in the four quarters of the earth, than be betrayed into any portion—I will not say of justice, I will not say of humanity and mercy, but of simple reasonableness and common sense, in their behaviour to the professors of the Catholic Religion ; so much so, that to state even drily and accurately what they do daily is to risk being blamed for ridicule and satire, which, if anywhere, would be simply gratuitous and officious in this matter, where truth most assuredly, " when unadorned," is " adorned the most."   This risk, as far as I am incurring it myself in these Lectures, I cannot help ; I cannot help if, in exposing the prejudice of my countrymen, I incur the imputation of using satire against them ; I do not wish to do so ; and, observe, that nothing I have said, or shall say, is levelled at the matter or the rites of Protestant worship.   I am concerned with Protestants themselves ; moreover not with Protestants quiescent and peaceable, but with Protestants malevolent, belligerent, busy, and zealous in an aggression upon our character and conduct.   *We* do not treat *them* with suspicion, contempt, and aversion : this is their treatment of *us ;* our only vengeance, surely it is not a great one, is to make a careful analysis of that treatment.

2.

The Prejudiced man, then—for thus I shall personify that narrow, ungenerous spirit which energizes and operates so widely and so unweariedly in the Protestant community—the Prejudiced man takes it for granted, or feels an undoubting persuasion,—not only that he himself is in possession of divine truth, for this is a matter of opinion, and he has a right to his own,— but that we, who differ from him, are universally

impostors, tyrants, hypocrites, cowards, and slaves.
This is a first principle with him ; it is like divine
faith in the Catholic, nothing can shake it. If he
meets with any story against Catholics, on any or no
authority, which does but fall in with this notion of
them, he eagerly catches at it. Authority goes for
nothing ; likelihood, as he considers it, does instead
of testimony ; what he is now told is just what he
expected. Perhaps it is a random report, put into
circulation merely because it has a chance of succeeding, or thrown like a straw to the wind : perhaps it is
a mere publisher's speculation, who thinks that a
narrative of horrors will pay well for the printing : it
matters not, he is perfectly convinced of its truth ;
he knew all about it beforehand ; it is just what he
always has said ; it is the old tale over again a
hundred times. Accordingly he buys it by the
thousand, and sends it about with all speed in every
direction, to his circle of friends and acquaintance, to
the newspapers, to the great speakers at public meetings ; he fills the Sunday and week-day schools with it ;
loads the pedlars' baskets, perhaps introduces it into
the family spiritual reading on Sunday evenings,
consoled and comforted with the reflection that he
has got something fresh and strong and undeniable,
in evidence of the utter odiousness of the Catholic
Religion.

Next comes an absolute, explicit, total denial or
refutation of the precious calumny, whatever it may
be, on unimpeachable authority. The Prejudiced
Man simply discredits this denial, and puts it aside,
not receiving any impression from it at all, or paying
it the slightest attention. This, if he can : if he

cannot, if it is urged upon him by some friend, or brought up against him by some opponent, he draws himself up, looks sternly at the objector, and then says the very same thing as before, only with a louder voice and more confident manner. He becomes more intensely and enthusiastically positive, by way of making up for the interruption, of braving the confutation, and of showing the world that nothing whatever in the universe will ever make him think one hair-breadth more favourably of Popery than he does think, than he ever has thought, and than his family ever thought before him, since the time of the fine old English gentleman.

If a person ventures to ask the Prejudiced Man what he knows of Catholics personally—what he knows of individuals, of their ways, of their books, or of their worship, he blesses himself that he knows nothing of them at all, and he never will; nay, if they fall in his way, he will take himself out of it; and if unawares he shall ever be pleased with a Catholic without knowing who it is, he wishes by anticipation to retract such feeling of pleasure. About our state of mind, our views of things, our ends and objects, our doctrines, our defence of them, our judgment on his objections to them, our thoughts about him, he absolutely refuses to be enlightened: and he is as sore if expostulated with on so evident an infirmity of mind, as if it were some painful wound upon him, or local inflammation, which must not be handled ever so tenderly. He shrinks from the infliction.

However, one cannot always make the whole world take one's own way of thinking; so let us suppose the famous story, to which the Prejudiced Man has pledged his veracity, utterly discredited and scattered to the winds by the common consent of mankind :— this only makes him the more violent. For it *ought*, he thinks, to be true, and it is mere special pleading to lay much stress on its not having all the evidence which it might have ? for if it be not true, yet half a hundred like stories are. It is only impertinent to ask for evidence, when the fact has so often been established. What is the good of laboriously vindicating St. Eligius, or exposing a leading article in a newspaper, or a speaker at a meeting, or a popular publication, when the thing is notorious ; and to deny it is nothing else than a vexatious demand upon his time, and an insult to his common sense. He feels the same sort of indignation which the Philistine champion, Goliath, might have felt when David went out to fight with him. " Am I a dog, that thou comest to me with a staff ? and the Philistine cursed him by his gods." And, as the huge giant, had he first been hit, not in the brain, but in the foot or the shoulder, would have yelled, not with pain, but with fury at the insult, and would not have been frightened at all or put upon the defensive, so our Prejudiced Man is but enraged so much the more, and almost put beside himself, by the presumption of those who, with their doubts or their objections, interfere with the great Protestant Tradition about the Catholic Church. To bring proof against us is, he thinks, but a matter of time ; and we know in affairs of every-day, how annoyed and impatient we are likely to become, when obstacles are put in our way in any such case. We are angered at delays when they are but accidental, and the issue is certain ; we are not angered, but we are sobered, we become careful and attentive to impediments, when there is a doubt about the issue. The very same difficulties put us on our mettle in the one case, and do but irritate us in the other. If, for instance, a person cannot open a door, or get a key into a lock, which he has done a hundred times before, you know how apt he is to shake, and to rattle, and to force it, as if some great insult was offered him by its resistance : you know how surprised a wasp, or other large insect is, that he cannot get through a window-pane ; such is the feeling of the Prejudiced Man, when we urge our objections—not softened by them at all, but exasperated the more ; for what is the use of even incontrovertible arguments against a conclusion which he already considers to be infallible ?

This, you see, is the reason why the most overwhelming refutations of the calumnies brought against us do us no good at all with the Protestant community. We were tempted, perhaps, to say to ourselves, "What *will* they have to say in answer to this ? now at last the falsehood is put down for ever, it will never show its face again ?" Vain hope ! just the reverse : like Milton's day-star, after sinking into the ocean, it soon "repairs its drooping head,"

"And tricks its beams, and with new-spangled ore
Flames in the forehead of the morning sky."

Certainly ; for it is rooted in the mind itself ; it has no uncertain holding upon things external ; it does not depend on the accident of time, or place, or testimony, or sense, or possibility, or fact ; it depends on the will alone. Therefore, "unhurt amid the war of elements," it "smiles" at injury, and "defies" defeat ? for it is safe and secure, while it has the man's own will on its side. Such is the virtue of prejudice—it is ever reproductive ; in vain is Jeffreys exposed ; he rises again in Teodore ; Teodore is put down ; in vain, for future story-tellers and wonder-mongers, as yet unknown to fame, are below the horizon, and will come to view, and will unfold their tale of horror, each in his day, in long succession ; for these whispers, and voices, and echoes, and re-verberations, are but the response, and, as it were, the expression of that profound inward persuasion, and that intense illusion, which wraps the soul and steeps the imagination of the Prejudiced Man.

However, we will suppose him in a specially good humour, when you set about undeceiving him on some point on which he misstates the Catholic faith. He is determined to be candour and fairness itself, and to do full justice to your argument. So you begin your explanation ;—you assure him he mis-conceives your doctrines ; he has got a wrong view of facts. You appeal to original authorities, and show him how shamefully they have been misquoted ; you appeal to history and prove it has been garbled. Nothing is wanted to your representation ; it is triumphant. He is silent for a moment, then he begins with a sentiment. " What clever fellows these Catholics are ! " he says, " I defy you to catch them tripping ; they have a way out of everything. I thought we had you, but I fairly own I am beaten. This is how the Jesuits got on ; always educated, subtle, well up in their books ; a Protestant has no chance with them." You see, my Brothers, you have not advanced a step in convincing him.

R

Such is the Prejudiced Man at best advantage ; but commonly under the same circumstances he will be grave and suspicious. " I confess," he will say, " I do *not* like these very complete explanations ; they are too like a made-up case.   I can easily believe there was exaggeration in the charge ; perhaps money was only sometimes taken for the permission to sin, or only before the Reformation, but our friend professes to prove it never was taken ; this is proving too much.   I always suspect something behind, when everything is so very easy and clear."   Or again, " We see before our eyes a tremendous growth of Popery; *how* does it grow ?   You tell me you are poor, your priests few, your friends without influence ; then how does it *grow* ?   It could not grow without means ! it is bad enough if you can assign a cause ; it is worse if you cannot.   Cause there must be somewhere, for effects imply causes.   How did it get into Oxford ? tell me that.   How has it got among the Protestant clergy ?   I like all things above board ; I hate concealment, I detest plots.   There is evidently something to be accounted for ; and the more cogently you prove that it is not referable to anything which we see, the graver suspicions do you awaken, that it is traceable to something which is hidden."   Thus our Prejudiced Man simply ignores the possible existence of that special cause to which Catholics of course refer the growth of Catholicism, and which surely, if admitted, is sufficient to account for it—viz., that it is true   He will not admit the power of truth among the assignable conjectural causes.   He would rather, I am sure, assign it to the agency of evil spirits, than suspect the possibility of a religion being true which he wills should be a falsehood.

3.

One word here as to the growth of Catholicism, of conversions and converts ;—the Prejudiced Man has his own view of it all. First, he denies that there are any conversions or converts at all. This is a bold game, and will not succeed in England, though I have been told that in Ireland it has been strenuously maintained. However, let him grant the fact, that converts there are, and he has a second ground to fall back upon : the converts are weak and foolish persons,—notoriously so ; all their friends think so ; there is not a man of any strength of character or force of intellect among them. They have either been dreaming over their folios, or have been caught with the tinsel embellishments of Popish worship. They are lack-a-daisical women, or conceited young parsons, or silly squires, or the very dregs of our large towns, who have nothing to lose, and no means of knowing one thing from another. Thirdly, in corroboration :—they went over, he says, on such exceedingly wrong motives ; not any one of them but you may trace his conversion to something distinctly wrong ; it was love of notoriety, it was restlessness, it was resentment, it was lightness of mind, it was self-will. There was trickery in his mode of taking the step or inconsiderateness towards the feelings of others. They went too soon, or they ought to have gone sooner. They ought to have told every one their doubts as soon as ever they felt them, and before they knew whether or not they should overcome them or no : if they had clerical charges in the

Protestant Church, they ought to have flung them up
at once, even at the risk of afterwards finding they
had made a commotion for nothing. Or, on the
other hand, what, forsooth, must these men do when
a doubt came on their mind, but at once abandon all
their clerical duty and go to Rome, as if it were
possible anywhere to be absolutely certain ?   In short,
they did not become Catholics at the right moment ;
so that, however numerous they may be, no weight
whatever attaches to their conversion. As for him,
it does not affect him at all ; he means to die just
where he is ; indeed these conversions are a positive
argument in favour of Protestantism ; he thinks still
worse of Popery, in consequence of these men going
over, than he did before. His fourth remark is of
this sort : they are sure to come back. He prophe-
sies that by this time next year, not one of them will
be a Catholic. His fifth is as bold as the first ;—they
have come back. This argument, however, of the
Prejudiced Man admits at times of being shown to
great advantage, should it so happen that the subjects
of his remarks have, for some reason or other, gone
abroad, for then there is nothing to restrain his
imagination. Hence, directly a new Catholic is safely
lodged two or three thousand miles away, out comes
the confident news that he has returned to Protestantism ; when no friend has the means to refute it.
When this argument fails, as fail it must, by the time
a letter can be answered, our Prejudiced Man falls
back on his sixth common-place, which is to the effect
that the converts are very unhappy. He knows this
on the first authority ; he has seen letters declaring
or showing it. They are quite altered men, very

much disappointed with Catholicism, restless, and desirous to come back except from false shame. Seventhly, they are altogether deteriorated in character; they have become harsh, or overbearing, or conceited, or vulgar. They speak with extreme bitterness against Protestantism, have cast off their late friends, or seem to forget that they ever were Protestants themselves. Eighthly, they have become infidels;—alas! heedless of false witness, the Prejudiced Man spreads the news about, right and left, in a tone of great concern and distress; he considers it very awful.

Lastly, when every resource has failed, and in spite of all that can be said, and surmised, and expressed, and hoped, about the persons in question, Catholics they have become, and Catholics they remain, the Prejudiced Man has a last resource, he simply forgets that Protestants they ever were. They cease to have antecedents; they cease to have any character, any history to which they may appeal: they merge in the great fog, in which to his eyes everything Catholic is enveloped: they are dwellers in the land of romance and fable; and, if he dimly contemplates them plunging and floundering amid the gloom, it is as griffins, wiverns, salamanders, the spawn of Popery, such as are said to sport in the depths of the sea, or to range amid the central sands of Africa. He forgets he ever heard of them; he has no duties to their names, he is released from all anxiety about them; they die to him.

Now, my Brothers, unless I should be obliged to allude to myself, I could, without bringing in other instances, show you, from my own experience, that there is no exaggeration in what I have been saying.

I will go so far as to mention four facts about me, as they have been commonly reported. First, when I became a Catholic, grave persons, Protestant clergymen, attested (what they said was well known to others besides themselves) that either I was mad, or was in the most imminent danger of madness. They put it into the newspapers, and people were sometimes quite afraid to come and see me. Next, they put about, what they had prophesied beforehand as certain to be, that I had already the gravest differences with one from whom I had received nothing but kindness, and whom I regarded, and still regard, with no other feelings than those of gratitude and affection, Cardinal Wiseman. They had predicted it, and therefore so it must be, whether there was evidence of it or not. I will quote to you the words of an eminent pulpit and platform clergyman, one of those two eloquent defenders of Protestantism, who lately gave out that every Catholic Priest ought to be hanged. "He believed," said the *Manchester Courier*, reporting his speech, "that already some of those reverend gentlemen, who had betaken themselves to Rome, under the idea that they were going to a scene of beauty and piety, had found that dark was the place behind the scenes that they had painted as so beautiful. So he believed it was with Mr. Newman. (Hear, hear.) He (the speaker) was told that Mr. Newman had a most sovereign contempt for Dr. Wiseman; and he was told that Dr. Wiseman had the utmost hatred for Mr. Newman. And he believed that result was brought about from Mr. Newman having seen Dr. Wiseman more closely, and Dr. Wiseman having found out that Mr. Newman saw through the mask, and discerned him as he was." You see "the wish was father to the thought." Thirdly, when I went to Rome, then at once a long succession of reports went about, to the effect that I had quarrelled with the ecclesiastical authorities there, and had refused to be ordained on their conditions ; moreover, that I was on the point of turning Protestant, and that my friends about me had done so already. The list of good stories had not run out by the time I came back ; they were too precious to be lost, any one of them ; so it was circulated, when I came here to Birmingham, that I was suspended by the present Bishop of the diocese, and not allowed to preach. Fourthly and lastly, it has lately been put into the papers, under the sanction of respectable names, that I am not a believer in the Catholic doctrines ; and broader still in private letters, that I have given up Revealed Religion altogether. I mention these instances, not for their own sake, but to illustrate the power of prejudice. Men are determined they will *not* believe that an educated Protestant can find peace and satisfaction in the Catholic Church ; and they invent catastrophes for the occasion, which they think too certain to need testimony or proof. In the reports I have been setting down, there was not even a rag or a shred of evidence to give plausibility to them.

I have been setting forth as yet the resources of the Prejudiced Man, when he has no facts whatever on his side, but all against him ; but now let us suppose he has something or other to show ; in that case it is plain that he finds it very much easier to maintain his position. If he could do so much with no materials at all, to what will he be unequal when he has really something or other, external and objective, to bring forward in his justification? "Trifles light as air," says the poet,

> " Are to the jealous confirmation strong
> As proofs of Holy Writ."

You may be sure he makes the most of them. A vast number of matters, we easily may understand, are of daily occurrence, which admit of an interpretation this way or that, and which are, in fact, interpreted by every one according to his own existing opinions. Rival philosophers seize on new discoveries, each as being in favour of his own hypothesis; it is not indeed, many instances which are critical and decisive. Are we told of some strange appearance at night in some solitary place? Those who are fond of the marvellous, think it an apparition; those who live in the rational and tangible, decide that it has been some gleam of the moonbeam, or some wayfarer or beggar, or some trick intended to frighten the passer-by. Thus history also reads in one way to one, in another to another. There are those who think the French at the bottom of all the mischief which happens in England and Ireland; others lay it to the Russians. Our Prejudiced Man of course sees Catholics and Jesuits in everything, in every failure of the potato crop, every strike of the operatives, and every mercantile stoppage. His one idea of the Catholic Church haunts him incessantly, and he sees whole Popery, living and embodied, in every one of its professors, nay, in every word, gesture and motion of each. A Catholic Priest cannot be grave or gay, silent or talkative, without giving matter of offence or suspicion. There is peril in his frown, there is greater peril in his smile. His half sentences are filled up; his isolated acts are misdirected; nay, whether he eats or sleeps, in every mouthful and every nod he ever has in view one and one only object, the aggrandizement of the unwearied, relentless foe of freedom and of progress, the Catholic Church. The Prejudiced Man applauds himself for his sagacity, in seeing evidences of a plot at every turn; he groans to think that so many sensible men should doubt its extension all through Europe, though he begins to entertain the hope that the fact is breaking on the apprehension of the Government.

4

The Prejudiced Man travels, and then everything he sees in Catholic countries only serves to make him more thankful that his notions are so true; and the more he sees of Popery, the more abominable he feels it to be. If there is any sin, any evil in a foreign population, though it be found among Protestants also, still Popery is clearly the cause of it. If great cities are the schools of vice, it is owing to Popery. If Sunday is profaned, if there is a Carnival, it is the fault of the Catholic Church. Then, there are no private homes, as in England, families live on staircases; see what it is to belong to a Popish country. Why do the Roman labourers wheel their barrows so slow on the Forum? why do the Lazzaroni of Naples lie so listlessly on the beach? why, but because they are under the *malaria* of a false religion. Rage, as is well-known, is in the Roman like a falling sickness, almost as if his will had no part in it, and he had no responsibility; see what it is to be a Papist. Bloodletting is as frequent and as much a matter of course in the South, as hair-cutting in England ; it is a trick borrowed from the convents, when they wish to tame down refractory spirits.

The Prejudiced man gets up at an English hour, has his breakfast at his leisure, and then saunters into some of the churches of the place ; he is scandalized to have proof of what he has so often heard, the infrequency of communions among Catholics. Again and again, in the course of his tour, has he entered them, and never by any chance did he see a solitary communicant :— hundreds, perhaps, having communicated in those very churches, according to their custom, before he was out of his bedroom. But what scandalizes him most, is that even bishops and priests, nay, the Pope himself, does not communicate at the great festivals of the Church. He was at a great ceremonial, a High Mass, on Lady Day, at the Minerva ; not one Cardinal communicated ; Pope and Cardinals, and every Priest present but the celebrant, having communicated, of course, each in his own Mass, and in his own chapel or church early in the morning. Then the churches are so dirty ; faded splendour, tawdriness, squalidness are the fashion of the day ;—thanks to the Protestants and Infidels, who, in almost every country where Catholicism is found, have stolen the revenues by which they were kept decent. He walks about and looks at the monuments, what is this ? the figure of a woman : who can it be ? His Protestant cicerone at his elbow, who perhaps has been chosen by his good father or guardian to protect him on his travels from a Catholic taint, whispers that it is Pope Joan, and he notes it down in his pocket-book accordingly. I am alluding to an accident, which in its substance befell a most excellent person, for whom I had and have a great esteem, whom I am sure I would not willingly offend, and who will not be hurt at this cursory mention of an unintentional mistake. He was positive he had seen Pope Joan in Rome,—I think, in St. Peter's; nay, he saw the inscription on the monument, beginning with the words, " Joannæ Papissæ." It was so remarkable a fact, and formed so plausible an argument against the inviolateness of the chair of St. Peter, that it was thought worth inquiring into. I do not remember who it was that the female, thus elevated by his imagination, turned into in the process of investigation, whether into the Countess Matilda, or Queen Christina, or the figure of Religion in the vestibule of St. Peter's; but certainly into no lady who had any claim on the occupation of the Ecumenical See.

This puts me in mind of another occurrence, of which the publications of the day have recently been full. A lady of high literary reputation deposed that Denon and other French savans had given her the information that, in the days of the Republic or Consulate, they had examined St. Peter's chair in the Vatican Basilica, and had found that it unquestionably had come from the East, long after the age of the Apostle, for it had inscribed upon it the celebrated confession of Islamism, " There is one God, and Mahomet is his prophet." Her prejudices sharpened her memory, and she was positive in her testimony. Inquiry was made, and it turned out that the chair of which she had spoken was at Venice, not at Rome; that it had been brought thither by the Crusaders from the East, and therefore might well bear upon it the

Mahometan inscription ; and that tradition gave it the reputation of being, by no means the Roman, but the Antiochene Chair of the Apostle.   In this, as in other mistakes, there was no deliberate intention to deceive ; it was an ordinary result of an ordinary degree of prejudice.   The voucher of the story was so firmly convinced, I suppose, of the " childish absurdity and falsehood of all the traditions of the Romish Church," that she thought it unnecessary to take pains to be very accurate, whether in her hearing or her memory.

Our Prejudiced Man might travel half his life up and down Catholic Europe, and only be confirmed in his contempt and hatred of its religion.   In every place there are many worlds, quite distinct from each other : there are good men and bad, and the good form one body, the bad another.   Two young men, as is well known, may pass through their course at a Protestant University, and come away with opposite reports of the state of the place : the one will have seen all the bad, the other all the good ; one will say it is a sober, well-conducted place, the other will maintain that it is the home of every vice.   The Prejudiced Man takes care to mix only in such society as will confirm his views ; he courts the society of Protestants and unbelievers, and of bad Catholics, who shelter their own vice under the imputations they cast on others, and whose lives are a disgrace to the Church prior to their testimony.   His servants, couriers, *laquais de place*, and acquaintance, are all of his own way of thinking, and find it for their interest to flatter and confirm it. He carries England with him abroad ; and, though he has ascended mountains and traversed cities, knows scarcely more of Europe than when he set out.

But perhaps he does not leave England at all ; he never has been abroad ; it is all the same ; he can scrape together quite as good evidence against Catholicism at home. One day he pays a visit to some Catholic chapel, or he casually finds the door open, and walks in. He enters and gazes about him, with a mixed feeling of wonder, expectation and disgust ; and according to circumstances, this or that feeling predominates, and shows itself in his bearing and his countenance. In one man it is curiosity ; in another, scorn ; in another, conscious superiority ; in another, abhorrence ; over all of their faces, however, there is a sort of uncomfortable feeling, as if they were in the cave of Trophonius or in a Mesmerist's lecture-room. One and all seem to believe that something strange and dreadful may happen any moment ; and they crowd up together, if some great ceremony is going on, tiptoeing and staring, and making strange faces, like the gargoyles or screen ornaments of the church itself. Every sound of the bell, every movement of the candles, every change in the grouping of the sacred ministers and the assistants, puts their hands and limbs in motion, to see what is coming next ; our own poor alleviation, in thinking of them, lying in this,—that they are really ignorant of what is going on, and miss, even with their bodily eyes, the distinctive parts of the rite. What is our ground of comfort, however, will be their ground of accusation against us ; for they are sure to go away and report that our worship consists of crossings, bowing, genuflections, incensings, locomotions, and revolvings, all about nothing.

5.

In this matter, my Brothers, as I have already said, the plain truth is the keenest of satires; and therefore, instead of using any words of my own, I shall put before you a Protestant's account of a Benediction of the Blessed Sacrament, which he went to see in the Chapel of the Fathers the Oratory in London. I quote his words from a publication of an important body, the British Reformation Society, established in the year 1827, and supported, I believe, by a number of eminent persons, noblemen, gentlemen, and ministers of various denominations. The periodical I speak of is called "*The British Protestant, or Journal of the Religious Principles of the Reformation.*" It would seem to be one of the Society's accredited publications, as it has its device upon the title-page. In the 62nd Number of this work, being the Number for February, 1850, we are presented with "Extracts from the Journal of a Protestant Scripture Reader." This gentleman, among his missionary visits to various parts of London, dropt in, it seems, on Tuesday, January 8th, to the Roman Catholic Chapel in King William Street; which, he commences his narrative by telling us, for "the large roses of every colour, and laurel," "was more like the flower-shops in the grand row of Covent Garden than a place of worship." Well, he had a right to his opinion here as much as another; and I do not mean to molest him in it. Nor shall I say anything of his account of the Sermon, which was upon one of the January Saints, and which he blames for not having in it the name of Jesus, or one word of Scripture from beginning to end; not dreaming that a Rite was to follow, in which we not only bow before the Name, but worship the real and substantial Presence of our exalted Lord.

I need hardly observe to you, my Brothers, that the Benediction of the Blessed Sacrament is one of the simplest rites of the Church. The priests enter and kneel down; one of them unlocks the Tabernacle, takes out the Blessed Sacrament, inserts it upright in a Monstrance of precious metal, and sets it in a conspicuous place above the altar, in the midst of lights, for all to see. The people then begin to sing; meanwhile the Priest twice offers incense to the King of heaven, before whom he is kneeling. Then he takes the Monstrance in his hands, and turning to the people, blesses them with the Most Holy, in the form of a cross, while the bell is sounded by one of the attendants to call attention to the ceremony. It is our Lord's solemn benediction of His people, as when He lifted up His hands over the children, or when He blessed His chosen ones when He ascended up from Mount Olivet. As sons might come before a parent before going to bed at night, so, once or twice a week the great Catholic family comes before the Eternal Father, after the bustle or toil of the day, and He smiles upon them, and sheds upon them the light of His countenance. It is a full accomplishment of what the Priest invoked upon the Israelites, "The Lord bless thee and keep thee; the Lord show His face to thee and have mercy on thee; the Lord turn His countenance to thee and give thee peace." Can there be a more touching rite, even in the judgment of those who do not believe in it? How many a man, not a Catholic, is moved, on seeing it, to say "Oh, that I did but believe it!" when he sees the Priest take up the Fount of Mercy, and the people bent low in adoration! It is one of the most beautiful, natural, and soothing actions of the Church—not so, however, in the judgment of our young Protestant Scripture Reader, to whom I now return.

This Protestant Scripture Reader then, as he calls himself, enters the chapel, thinking, of course, he knows all about everything. He is the measure of everything, or at least of everything Popish. Popery he knows perfectly well, in substance, in spirit, in drift, in results; and he can interpret all the details when they come before him at once, by this previous, or what a theologian might term "infused," knowledge. He knows, and has known from a child, that Popery is a system of imposture, nay, such brazen imposture, that it is a marvel, or rather miracle, that any one can be caught by it—a miracle, that is, of Satan: for without an evil influence it is quite impossible any single soul could believe what the Protestant Scripture Reader would call so "transparent a fraud." As a Scripture Reader he knows well the text, Second of Thessalonians, chapter two, verse eleven, "He shall send them strong delusion that they should believe a lie," and he applies it to the scene before him. He knows that it is the one business of the Priest to take in the people, and he knows that the people are so inconceivably brutish that nothing is too gross or absurd a trick to take them in withal. If the Priest were to put up a scarecrow, they, like the silly birds, would run away as if it were a man; and he has only to handle his balls or cards, and flourish them about, and they take him for a god. Indeed, we all know, he gives out he *is* a god, and can do what he pleases, for it is sin to doubt it. It is most wonderful, certainly, as to this Popery, that in spite of the Parliament all in a bustle, passing laws, as if against typhus or cholera, yet there it is, and spread it will; however, Satan is the father of lies; that is sufficient. With this great principle, I say, clearly impressed upon his mind, he walks into the chapel, knowing well he shall find some juggling there; accordingly, he is not at all surprised at the scene which passes before him. He looks on at his ease, and draws up his own account of it, all the time that the Catholic people are bowing and singing, and the Priest incensing; and his account runs thus:—

After the sermon, he tells us (I am quoting the very words of his Journal), "another young priest came in with a long wand in his hand, and an extinguisher on the top of it, and a small candle, and he began to light others." "*Another* young priest:" he thinks we are born priests; "priest" is a sort of race, or animal, or production, as oxen or sheep may be, and there are young priests and old priests, and black priests and white priests, and perhaps men priests and women priests; and so in came this "other young priest" with a wand. "With a wand:" he evidently thinks there is something religious about this lighter and extinguisher; it is a conjuror's wand; you will, I think, see presently I am borne out in saying this. He proceeds: "The next part of the play was four priests coming to the altar" (it is as I said; everything is a priest), "four priests and

S

Gordon in the middle:" this is a mistake, and an
unwarrantable and rude use of the name of one of
the Fathers of the London Oratory, my dear brother
and friend, the Reverend Philip Gordon—for it was
not he, and he was not a priest; accordingly, I should
leave the name out, except that it adds a good deal
to the effect of the whole. "One of them," he proceeds, "took from a small cupboard on the altar,"
that is, from the tabernacle, "a gold star;" this is the
head of the Monstrance, in which is placed the
Blessed Sacrament, "and screwed it on to a candlestick," that is, the *foot* of the Monstrance, "and placed
it on the top of the altar, under the form of a beehive,
supported by four pillars," that is, under the canopy.
He calls the head of the Monstrance a star, because
it consists of a circle surrounded by rays; and he
seems to think it in some way connected with the
season of the year, the Epiphany, when the Star
appeared to the Wise Men.

"The Star," he proceeds, "glittered like diamonds,
for it had a round lamp in the middle of it;" I suppose he means the glass covering the Blessed Sacrament, which reflected the light, and you will see
clearly, as he goes on, that he actually thinks the
whole congregation was worshipping this star and
lamp. "This Star glittered like diamonds, for it had
a round lamp in the middle of it; when placed under
the beehive, the four priests began to burn incense,
waving a large thing like a lanthorn" (the thurible)
"towards the Star, and bowing themselves to kiss
the foot of the altar before the Star." Now observe,
my Brothers, I repeat, I am not blaming this person
for not knowing a Catholic rite, which he had no

means of knowing, but for thinking he knows it, when he does not know it, for coming into the chapel, with this most coxcombical idea in his head, that Popery is a piece of mummery, which any intelligent Protestant can see through, and therefore being not at all surprised, but thinking it very natural, when he finds four priests, a young priest with a wand, and a whole congregation, worshipping a gold star glittering like diamonds with a lamp in it. This is what I mean by *prejudice.*

Now you may really have a difficulty in believing that I have interpreted him rightly ; so let me proceed. "The next piece acted was, one of them went to bring down the Star, and put it on the altar, while another put something like a white shawl round Gordon's shoulders." True ; he means the veil which is put upon the Priest, before he turns round with the Blessed Sacrament in his hand. "Gordon next takes the Star, and, turning his face to the people, to raise up the Star, with part of the shawl round the candlestick, the other two priests, one on each side of him, drawing the shawl, it showed a real piece of magic art." Now what makes this so amusing to the Catholic is, that, as far as the priest's actions go, it is really so accurately described. It is the description of one who has his eyes about him, and makes the best of them, but who, as he goes on, is ever putting his own absurd comment on everything which occurs in succession. Now, observe, he spoke of "magic ;" let us see what the magic is, and what becomes of the Star, the lamp, and the candlestick with the shawl round it.

"As Gordon raised the Star, with his back to all

the lighted candles on the altar, he clearly showed the Popish deceit, for *in the candlestick there is a bell.*" Here is his first great failure of fact; he could not be looking at two places at once; he heard the bell, which the attendant was ringing at one side; he did not see it; where could it be? his ready genius, that is, the genius of his wonderful prejudice about us, told him at once where it was. It was a piece of priestcraft, and the bell was concealed inside the foot of the candlestick;—listen. "As Gordon raised the Star, with his back turned to all the lighted candles on the altar, he clearly showed the Popish deceit; for in the candlestick there is a bell, that rung three times of its own accord, to deceive the blind fools more; and the light through the shawl showed so many colours, as Father Gordon moved his body; the bell ringing they could not see, for the candlestick was covered with part of this magic shawl, and Gordon's finger at work underneath."

Such is his account of the rite of Benediction; he is so densely ignorant of us, and so supremely confident of his knowledge, that he ventures to put in print something like the following rubrical direction for its celebration :—

☞ *First, a young priest setteth up a golden, diamond-like star, with a lamp in it, sticking it on to the top of a candlestick, then he lighteth fifty candles by means of a wand with an extinguisher and wax candle upon it; then four priests bow, burn incense, and wave a lanthorn before the star; then one of the priests, hiding what he is at, by means of a great shawl about his hands and the foot of the candlestick, taketh up said candlestick, with the lamp and gold star glittering like diamonds, and beginneth secretly to tinkle with his finger a bell hid in its foot ; whereupon the whole congregation marvelleth much, and worshippeth star, lamp and candlestick incontinently.*

He ends with the following peroration :—" This is the power of priests ; they are the best play actors in this town. I should be glad to see this published, that I might take it to Father Gordon, to see if he could contradict a word of it." Rather, such is the power of prejudice, by good luck expressed in writing, and given to the world, as a specimen of what goes on, without being recorded, in so many hundred thousands of minds. The very confidence with which he appeals to the accuracy of his testimony. only shows how prejudice can create or colour, where facts are harmless or natural. It is superior to facts, and lives in a world of its own.

Nor would it be at all to the purpose to object, that, had he known what the rite really meant, he would quite as much, or even more, have called it idolatry. The point is not what *he* would think of our rites, if he understood them exactly, for I am not supposing his judgment to be worth anything at all, or that we are not as likely to be right as an individual Scripture Reader ; the question is not, what he would judge, but what he did think, and how he came to think it. His prejudice interpreted our actions.

6.

Alas, my Brothers, though we have laughed at the extravagance which shows itself in such instances of prejudice, it is in truth no matter for a jest. If I laugh, it is to hide the deep feelings of various kinds which it necessarily excites in the mind. I laugh at what is laughable in the displays of this wretched root of evil, in order to turn away my thoughts from its nature and effects, which are not laughable, but hateful and dangerous—dangerous to the Catholic, hateful to the Supreme Judge. When you see a beast of prey in his cage, you are led to laugh at its impotent fury, at its fretful motions and its sullen air and its grotesque expressions of impatience, disappointment, and malice, if it is baulked of its revenge. And, as to this Prejudice, Brothers of the Oratory, really in itself it is one of the direst, most piteous, most awful phenomena in the whole country; to see a noble, generous people the victims of a moral infirmity, which is now a fever, now an ague, now a falling sickness, now a frenzy, and now a St. Vitus's dance! Oh, if we could see as the angels see, thus should we speak of it, and in language far more solemn. I told you why in an earlier part of this Lecture;—not simply because the evil comes from beneath, as I believe it does; not only because it so falls upon the soul, and occupies it, that it is like a bad dream or nightmare, which is so hard to shake off;—but chiefly because it is one of the worst sins of which our poor nature is capable. Perhaps it is wrong to compare sin with sin, but I declare to you, the more I think of it, the more intimately does this prejudice seem to me to corrupt the soul, even beyond those sins which are commonly called most deadly, as the various forms of impurity or pride. And why? because, I repeat it, it argues so aston-

ishing a want of mere natural charity or love of our
kind. It is piercing enough to think what little faith
there is in the country ; but it is quite heartrending
to witness so utter a deficiency in a mere natural
virtue. Oh, is it possible, that so many, many men,
and women too, good and kind otherwise, should
take such delight in being quite sure that millions of
men have the sign and seal of the Evil One upon
them ! Oh, is it conceivable that they can be considerate in all matters of this life, friendly in social
intercourse, indulgent to the wayward, charitable to
the poor and outcast, merciful towards criminals,
nay, kind towards the inferior creation, towards their
cows, and horses, and swine ; yet, as regards us, who
bear the same form, speak the same tongue, breathe
the same air, and walk the same streets, ruthless, relentless, believing ill of us, and wishing to believe it !
I repeat it, they wish us to be what they believe us
to be ; what a portentous fact ! They delight to look
at us, and to believe that we are the veriest reptiles
and vermin which belied the human form divine.
It is a dear thought, which they cannot bear to lose.
True, it may have been taught them from their
youth, they never may have had means to unlearn
it,—that is not the point ; they have never *wished*
better things of us, they have never *hoped* better
things. They are tenacious of what they believe, they
are impatient of being argued with, they are angry at
being contradicted, they are disappointed when a
point is cleared up ; they had rather that *we* should
be guilty than *they* mistaken ; they have no wish at
all we should not be blaspheming hypocrites, stupid
idolaters, loathsome profligates, unprincipled rogues

and bloodthirsty demons. They are kinder even to their dogs and their cats than to us. Is it not true? can it be denied? is it not portentous? does it not argue an incompleteness or hiatus in the very structure of their moral nature? has not something, in their case, dropped out of the list of natural qualities proper to man?

And hence it is, that, calm as may be the sky, and gentle the breeze, we cannot trust the morning: at any moment a furious tempest may be raised against us, and scatter calamity through our quiet homes, as long as the Prince of the power of the air retains this sovereignty. There is ever a predisposition in the political and social atmosphere to lour and thicken. We never are secure against the access of madness in that people, whose name and blood we share. Some accident,—a papal bull, worded as papal documents have been since the beginning of time, a sudden scandal among our priests or in our convents, or some bold and reckless falsehood, may raise all England against us. Such also was our condition in the first age of the Church: the chance of the hour brought the Pagan Romans upon us. A rash Christian tore down an Imperial manifesto from its place ; the horrible Dioclesian persecution was the consequence. A crop failed, a foe appeared, it was all through the poor Christians. So speaks the Early Christian Apologist, the celebrated Tertullian, in his defence of us, about a hundred years after St. John's time. " They think the Christians," he says, "to be the cause of every public calamity, of every national ill. If the Tiber cometh up to the walls, if the Nile cometh not up to the fields, if the rain hath not fallen, if the earth hath been moved, if there be any famine, if any pestilence, *Christianos ad leonem*—to the lion with the Christians—is forthwith the cry." No limit could be put to the brutishness of the notions then entertained of us by the heathen. They believed we fed on children; they charged us with the most revolting forms of incest; they gave out that we worshipped beasts or monsters. "Now a new report of our God hath been lately set forth in this city," says the same Tertullian, "since a certain wretch put forth a picture with some such title as this,—The god of the Christians conceived of an ass. This was a creature with ass's ears, with a hoof on one foot, carrying a book and wearing a gown. We smiled both at the name and the figure." Not indeed the same, but parallel, are the tales told of us now. Scottish absurdities are gravely appropriated as precious truths. Our very persons, not merely our professions, are held in abhorrence; we are spit at by the malevolent, we are passed with a shudder of contemptuous pity by the better-natured; we are supposed to be defiled by some secret rites of blood by the ignorant. There is a mysterious pollution and repulsion about us, which makes those who feel its influence curious or anxious to investigate what it can be. We are regarded as something unclean, which a man would not touch, if he could help it; and our advances are met as would be those of some hideous baboon, or sloth, or rattle-snake, or toad, which strove to make itself agreeable.

7.

Is it wonderful, with this spirit of delusion on the faculties of the many, that charges against us are believed as soon as made? So was it two centuries ago; one or two abandoned men, Titus Oates, whom the Protestant Hume calls " the most infamous of mankind," William Bedloe, who, the same writer says, was, "if possible, more infamous than Oates," and some others, aided by the lucky accident of the assassination of a London magistrate, whose murderers were never discovered, were sufficient, by a bold catalogue of calumnies, to put the whole kingdom into a paroxysm of terror and suspicion. The fit had been some time coming on, when "the cry of a plot," says Hume, " all on a sudden, struck their ears. They were awakened from their slumber, and, like men affrighted in the dark, took every figure for a spectre. The terror of each man became a source of terror to another; and a universal panic being diffused, reason and argument, and common sense, and common humanity, lost all influence over them."

Oates and Bedloe came forward to swear against us the most atrocious and impossible falsehoods. The Pope and Propaganda had claimed possession of England; and he had nominated the Jesuits to be his representatives here, and to hold the supreme power for him. All the offices of government had been filled up under the seal of this Society, and all the dignities of the Protestant Church given away, in great measure, to Spaniards and other foreigners. The king had been condemned to death as a heretic. There had been a meeting of fifty Jesuits in London during the foregoing May, when the king's death was determined on. He was to be shot or to be poisoned. The confessor of the French king had sent to London

£10,000 as a reward for any one who would assassinate him; a Spanish ecclesiastic had offered £10,000 more; and the Prior of the Benedictines £6,000. The Queen's physician had been offered £10,000, and had asked £15,000 for the job, and had received an instalment of £5,000. Four Irish ruffians had been hired by the Jesuits at twenty guineas a-piece, to shoot the king at Windsor. Two others were also engaged, one at £1,500; the other, being a pious man, preferred to take out the money in masses, of which he was to receive 30,000. Another had been promised canonization and £500, if he was successful in the enterprise. There was a subscription going on among the Catholics all through England, to collect sums for the same purpose. The Jesuits had determined to set fire to London, Southwark, and all the chief cities of the country. They were planning to set fire to all the shipping in the Thames. Twenty thousand Catholics were to rise in London in twenty-four hours' time, who, it was estimated, might cut the throats of 100,000 Protestants. The most eminent divines of the Establishment were especially marked for assassination. Ten thousand men were to be landed from abroad in the North, and were to seize Hull; and 20,000 or 30,000 religious men and pilgrims from Spain were to land in Wales.

Is all this grave history?—it is. Do not think I have added aught of my own; it is unnecessary. Invention cannot run with prejudice. Prejudice wins. Do not my true stories of Protestantism beat the fables against Catholicism of Achilli and Maria Monk? they are a romance, true and terrible.

What came of these wild allegations, preferred by men of infamous character, and favoured by the accident of Sir Edmonsbury Godfrey's murder, by unknown assassins? "Without further reasoning," says Hume, "the cry rose that he had been assassinated by the Papists, on account of his taking Oates's evidence. The clamour was quickly propagated, and met with universal belief. Each hour teemed with new rumours and surmises. To deny the reality of the plot was to be an accomplice; to hesitate was criminal. Royalist, republican, churchman, sectary, courtier, patriot, all parties concurred in the illusion. The city prepared for its defence, as if the enemy were at its gates; the chains and posts were put up. . . . The dead body of Godfrey was carried into the city, attended by vast multitudes. . . . Seventy-two clergymen marched before; above a thousand persons of distinction followed after; and, at the funeral sermon, two able-bodied divines mounted the pulpit, and stood on each side of the preacher, lest, in paying the last duties to this unhappy magistrate, he should, before the whole people, be murdered by the Papists."

A recent historian adds to the picture:[1] "Everywhere," he says, "justices were busied in searching houses and seizing papers. All the gaols were filled with Papists. London had the aspect of a city in a state of siege. The trainbands were under arms all night. Preparations were made for barricading the great thoroughfares. Patrols marched up and down the streets. Cannon were placed round Whitehall.

---

[1] Macaulay, History, vol. i. p. 235.

No citizen thought himself safe, unless he carried under his coat a small flail loaded with lead to brain the Popish assassins."

The Parliament kept pace with the people, a solemn fast was voted, and a form of prayer drawn up; five Catholic peers were committed to the Tower on charge of high treason; a member of the Commons, who in private society spoke strongly against the defenders of the plot, was expelled the House; and both Houses, Lords and Commons, voted, almost in the form of a dogmatic decree, "that there is, and hath been, a damnable and hellish plot, contrived and carried on by the Popish recusants, for assassinating the King, for subverting the Government, and for rooting-out and destroying the Protestant succession." Titus Oates was called the Saviour of his country; was lodged in Whitehall, protected by guards, and rewarded with a pension of £1,200 a year.

I will not pursue the history of this remarkable frenzy into its deeds of blood, into the hangings, and embowellings, and the other horrors of which innocent Catholics were in due course the victims. Well had it been had the pretended plot ended with the worldly promotion of its wretched fabricators, whom at this day all the world gives up to reprobation and infamy. Oates and Bedloe were the Maria Monk, the Jeffreys, the Teodore, the Achilli of their hour, on a larger field; they spoke then as Protestant champions speak now, to the prejudices of the people: they equalled our own slanderers in falsehood and assurance,—in success they surpassed them.

We live in a happier age than our forefathers; at least, let us trust that the habits of society and the self-interest of classes and of sects will render it impossible that blind prejudice and brute passion should ever make innocence and helplessness their sport and their prey, as they did in the seventeenth century.

LECTURE VII.

*ASSUMED PRINCIPLES THE INTELLECTUAL GROUND
OF THE PROTESTANT VIEW.*

I.

THERE is a great and a growing class in the community, who wish to be fair to us, who see how cruelly we
are dealt with, who are indignant at the clamour, and
see through the calumnies, and despise the prejudice,
which are directed against us, who feel themselves to
be superior to the multitude in their feelings and their
judgments, who aim at thinking well of all men, all
persuasions, all schools of thought, and of Catholics
in the number, and to like each for what is good in
it, though they may not follow it themselves. Being
thus candid, and, in a certain sense, unbiassed, they
readily acknowledge the grandeur of the Catholic
Religion, both in history and in philosophy ; they wish
to be good friends with it ; they delight to contemplate its great heroes ; they recognise, perhaps, with
almost enthusiastic admiration, the genius and other
gifts of the intellect, which in every age have been so
profusely found among its adherents. They know
and they like individual Catholics ; they have every

desire to like us in all respects; they set their minds towards liking us, our principles, our doctrines, our worship and our ways. As far as can be said of men, they really have no prejudice. In this interesting and excellent state of mind, they take up one of our books, sincerely wishing to get on with it; alas, they are flung back at once; they see so much which they cannot abide at all, do what they will. They are annoyed at themselves, and at us; but there is no help for it; they discover, they feel that between them and us there is a gulf. So they turn from the subject in disgust, and for a time perhaps are in bad humour with religion altogether, and have a strong temptation to believe nothing at all. Time passes; they get over the annoyance, and perhaps make a second attempt to adjust their own feelings with our doctrines, but with no better success. They had hoped to have found some middle term, some mode of reconciliation; they did not expect agreement, but at least peace; not coincidence, but at least a sort of good understanding and concurrence:—whereas they find antagonism. Nor it is impossible; it is melancholy to say it, but it is no use disguising the truth from themselves; they cannot get over this or that doctrine or practice; nay, to be honest, there is no part they can acquiesce in; each separate portion is part of a whole. They are disappointed, but they never can believe, they never can even approve; if the Catholic system be true, faith in it must be a gift, for reason does not bear it out.

What are the things which so offend the candid and kindly-disposed persons in question? So many, that they do not know where to begin, nor where to end.

It is the whole system of Catholicism; our miracles, and our relics, and our legends of saints; and then our doctrine of indulgences, and our purgatory; and our views of sin, and of the virtue of penances; and our strange formalities in worship; in a word, all is extravagant, strained, unnatural, where it is not directly offensive, or substantially impossible. They never could receive any part of it, they are sure; they would find it as hard to receive one part as the whole. They must lose their moral identity, and wake up with a new stock of thoughts, principles, and argumentative methods, ere they could ever endure it.

If such is the feeling of even candid and kind men, what will be the impression produced by Catholicism on the prejudiced? You see it is a cause of shrinking from us quite independent of prejudice, for it exists among those who are not prejudiced; but it may be joined with prejudice, and then the aversion and abhorrence entertained towards us will be intense indeed. In that case, reason (that is, what the person in question takes to be such)—reason and passion will go together.

Further, consider that it is not individuals merely, here and there, but vast multitudes who are affected precisely in the same way at hearing our doctrines; millions, whole nations. Each member of them bears witness to the rest; there is the consent, intimate, minute, exact, absolute, of all classes, all ranks, all ages, all dispositions. All this is a fact; we see it before us: do we require anything more to account for the position we hold in a Protestant country? So strong does the persuasion become, that Catholicism is indefensible, that our opponents become aggressive;

T

they not only spurn our creed and our worship themselves, but they are (as they think) in a condition to maintain that we too in our hearts despise both the one and the other as really as they. They will not believe that educated men can sincerely accept either ; *they* do not hold them, therefore no one else can hold them. They conclude, therefore, that we *disbelieve* what we teach and practise ; and in consequence, that we are *hypocrites*, as professing one thing, and thinking another. Next they come to a third conclusion, that since no one acts without motives, we must have a motive in professing without believing, and it must be a *bad motive ;* for instance, gain or power : accordingly we are, first, unbelievers ; secondly, liars ; thirdly, cheats and robbers. And thus you have full-blown Priestcraft ; here you have Popery simply detected and uncloaked : and observe the course of the argument ;—Catholic Priests are infidels, are hypocrites, are rogues, why ? simply, because Protestants think Catholic doctrine and Catholic worship irrational.

2.

Here then, Brothers of the Oratory, you see I have pointed out to your notice a cause of the feeling which is cherished towards us and our religion, altogether distinct from any other I have hitherto mentioned ; and perhaps the most important of all. I say the most important, because it influences not only the multitude of men, but the men of thought, of education, of candour, those who are conscious they do wish to do us justice. The instinctive rising of the mind, of the intellect, of the reason (so they would say themselves, though, of course, and, as you will

see, I am not going to allow it), opposes itself to the
Catholic system. Is not our cause hopeless? how can
we ever overcome so overwhelmingly formidable a fact?

I acknowledge its force is very great; this is the
argument to which men mean to point, when they
talk of education, light, progress, and so on, being
the certain destruction of Catholicism. They think
our creed is so irrational that it will fall to pieces of
itself, when the sun of reason is directed in upon the
places which at present it is enveloping. And I
repeat (without of course allowing for an instant that
this spontaneous feeling, if so it may be called, is
synonymous with reason), I acknowledge that it is a
most tremendous obstacle in the way of our being
fairly dealt with. And our enemies, I say again, are
in great triumph about it; they say, " Let in education upon them; leave them to reason; set the schoolmaster upon them." Well, I allow this " reason " (to
use for the moment their own designation of it), *is* a
serious inconvenience to us: it is a hindrance in our
path; but I do not think it so invincible a weapon
as they consider it; and on this simple ground,—because, if it were so ready, so safe, and so complete a
method as they would have it, I consider they would
have been slower to take *other* methods; for instance,
slower to hang, to disembowel, to quarter, to imprison,
to banish. If this " reason " would do their work for
them so well, I do not think they would have established their " reason," instead of leaving it to fight its
own battles; I do not think we should have had so
many laws passed in favour of " Reason," and against
us the Irrational. If this " Reason," as they choose to
call it, made such short work with Catholicism, they

would not have been so frightened at what they call " Popish Aggression," or have directed a stringent Act of Parliament against a poor twentieth part of the population of England. If this innate common sense, as they desire to consider it, were so crushing, so annihilating to our claims, to our existence, why the thousands of fables, fictions, falsehoods, fallacies, put out against us? why Maria Monk, and Jeffreys, and Teodore, and Achilli? Allowing, then, as I do, the importance of the phenomenon which I have been mentioning, feeling most fully that it requires careful consideration, granting that we may be fairly asked what we have to say to it, and that we ought to account for its existence,—nevertheless, I do not think it is so decisive an argument as its own upholders would make it, else it ought to have altogether superseded all others.

In truth, the spontaneous feeling against our doctrines and worship, of which I have been speaking, has far greater influence with educated men than with the many; it is to the educated class what absurd fiction and false-witness are to the multitude : the multitude is credulous, the educated classes are speculative ; the multitude is sensitive of facts, true or false, the educated classes of theories, sound or unsound ; though I do not deny that the educated classes are credulous too, and the multitude theorists. This, then, is pretty much the state of the case ; and as in former Lectures I have directed your attention, my Brothers, to the fables and falsehoods circulated against us, as one special cause of the odium which attaches to the Catholic Name, so this evening I propose to give you some description of those views theories, principles, or whatever they are to be called, which imbue the educated and active intellect, and lead it, as it were, instinctively and spontaneously, first to pronounce the creed and worship of Catholicism absurd, and next by inference to pronounce its professors hypocritical.

I fear I have got upon a dry subject; I must make some demand on your attention, yet I cannot help it. All subjects are not equally amusing, equally easy; still it is too important a subject to omit. Did I do so, I should be said to be evading the most difficult part of the whole controversy. It is, indeed, the most important of all I have to treat; so important, that I cannot do justice to it in one Lecture, which is all I mean to give to it. So I have a double difficulty about it; one lies in my writing, the other in your attending; but I must do my best.

3

You may recollect, that, in my Lecture last week, in speaking of prejudice, I alluded to opinions and conclusions, which often went by the name of prejudices, yet should more properly be called Prejudgments or Presumptions; for this reason, because they rest on argumentative grounds, and are abandoned by their upholders when those grounds fail them, whereas a Prejudice is held tenaciously against reason. Thus a man may hold as a general fact, that Blacks are inferior to Whites in the gifts of intellect, and might thereby be led to expect that a certain Black, whom he met, would be unequal to play his part in English society; but he might yield at once when evidence was brought in proof of the ability of the particular individual in question; or again, he might yield to argument directed against his view altogether. Here would be a presumption without a prejudice. On the other hand, if he still persisted that the particular Black was weak-minded and incapable, against fact, or if he refused to reconsider his grounds, when there was reason for his doing so, then certainly he would be justly called prejudiced.

There is no difficulty so far; but, observe, there are opinions and beliefs which do not depend on previous grounds, which are not drawn from facts for which no reasons can be given, or no sufficient reasons, which proceed immediately from the mind, and which the holder considers to be, as it were, part of himself. If another person doubts them, the holder has nothing to show for their truth except that he is sure that they *are* true: he cannot say, " I will reconsider my reasons," for he has no reasons to consider. What, then, is to make him abandon them? what is to touch them? He holds them, and continues to hold them, whatever is urged against him to the contrary; and thus these opinions and beliefs look like prejudices, though they are not. They are not prejudices, because prejudices are opinions formed upon grounds, which grounds the prejudiced person refuses to examine; whereas these opinions which I am speaking of have from the first no grounds at all, but are simple persuasions or sentiments, which came to the holder he cannot tell how, and which apparently he cannot help holding, and they are in consequence commonly called First Principles. For instance, that all Blacks are unintellectual would be a prejudice, if obstinately held against facts; whereas the obstinate belief that God cannot punish in hell is rather a first principle than a prejudice, because (putting aside the authority of Revelation) it can hardly be said to come within the reach of facts at all. From what I have said, it is plain that First Principles may be false or true; indeed, this is my very point, as you will presently see. Certainly they are not necessarily true; and again, certainly there *are* ways of unlearning them when they are false: moreover, as regards moral and religious First Principles which are false, of course a Catholic considers that no one holds them except by some fault of his own; but these are further points, and some of them beyond my present subject, which is not theological; however, I mention them to prevent misconception.

Now that there must be such things as First Principles—that is, opinions which are held without proof as if self-evident,—and, moreover, that every one must have some or other, who thinks at all, is evident from the nature of the case. If you trace back your reasons for holding an opinion, you must stop somewhere; the process cannot go on for ever; you must come at last to something you cannot prove; else, life would be spent in inquiring and reasoning, our minds would be ever tossing to and fro, and there would be nothing to guide us. No man alive, but has some First Principles or other. Even if he declares that nothing can be known for certain, then that is his First Principle. He has got his place in philosophy ready marked out for him; he is of the sect called Academics or Pyrrhonists, as the case may be, and his dogma is either " Nothing can be known in itself," or " Nothing can be known even for practical purposes." Any one may convince himself of the truth of what I am saying, who examines his own sentiments; for instance, supposing, on meeting a particular person, you said you would have nothing to do with him politically, and gave as your reason, *because* he belonged to a certain political party. And, supposing, on being asked why you disliked that party, you answered, *because* their very principle was to stand upon their own rights; and then supposing you were asked why it was wrong to stand on one's own rights, and you answered again, *because* it was selfish and proud; and being asked once more, why selfishness and pride were wrong, supposing you answered that selfishness and pride were bad feelings, *because* they were the feelings of the bad angels, who stood upon their supposed rights against their Maker; or, to sum up the whole in Dr. Johnson's famous saying, because "the devil was the first Whig,"—why, in that case, you see, you would have come to a First Principle, beyond which you could not get. I am not saying whether your reasoning, or your First Principle, was true or false; that is quite another matter; I am but illustrating what is meant by a First Principle, and how it is that all reasoning ultimately rests upon such. It would be your First Principle, in the case supposed, a principle for which no reason could be given, that the bad angels are to be avoided; *thence* it would follow that what is like them is to be avoided; and *from that* again, it followed that pride and selfishness are to be avoided; and *from that* again, that the particular political party in question is to be avoided. This, I repeat, is what is called a First Principle, and you see what a bearing it has both upon thought and upon action.

It is a First Principle that man is a social being;

a First Principle that he may defend himself ; a First Principle that he is responsible ; a First Principle that he is frail and imperfect ; a First Principle that reason must rule passion.

I will set down one or two other instances of First Principles by way of further illustration.

The celebrated Roman patriot Cato stabbed himself when besieged at Utica, rather than fall into the hands of Cæsar. He thought this a very great action, and so have many others besides. In like manner Saul, in Scripture, fell on his sword when defeated in battle ; and there have been those who have reproached Napoleon for not having blown out his brains on the field of Waterloo. Now, if these advocates of suicide had been asked why they thought such conduct, under such circumstances, noble, perhaps they would have returned the querist no answer, as if it were too plain to talk about, or from contempt of him, as if he were a person without any sense of honour, any feeling of what becomes a gentleman, of what a soldier, a hero, owes to himself. That is, they would not bring out their First Principle from the very circumstance that they felt its power so intensely ; that First Principle being, that there is no evil so great in the whole universe, visible and invisible, in time and eternity, as humiliation.

Again, supposing a medical man were to say to his patient that he could not possibly get well unless he gave up his present occupation, which was too much for his health ; supposing him to say, " As to the *way* of your doing this—how you are to make your livelihood if you give it up ; or again, how you are to become a proficient in your present trade, or art, or intellectual pursuit ; or again, how, if you take that step, you can keep up your religious connections ; all these questions I have nothing to do with ; I am only speaking to you *as* a medical man ; "—nothing could be kinder or more sensible than such language ; he does not make his own medical enunciations First Principles ; he delivers his opinion, and leaves it to the patient to strike the balance of advantages. But it is just possible, to take an extreme case, that he might take another line. He might be so carried away by his love for his own science (as happens commonly to men in any department of knowledge), as to think that everything ought to give way to it. He might actually ridicule religious scruples as absurd, and prescribe something which would be simply unlawful to a religious man ; and he might give as a reason for such advice, that nature required it, and there was an end of the matter. In such case he would be going so far as to make the principles of his own science First Principles of conduct ; and he would pronounce it impossible that moral duty ought in any case to interfere with or supersede the claims of animal nature.

I will take a third instance :—I believe that some time ago various benevolent persons exerted themselves in favour of the brute creation, who endure so much wanton suffering at the hands of barbarous owners. Various speculations were set afloat in consequence, and various measures advocated. I think I have heard that one doctrine was to the effect that it was wrong to eat veal, lamb, and other young meat, inasmuch as you killed creatures which would have enjoyed a longer life, and answered the purpose of food better, had you let them live to be beef and mutton. Again, shrimp sauce, it was said, ought to give way to lobster ; for in the latter case you took one life away, in the former a hundred. ˙ Now the world laughed at all this, and would not condescend to reason ; perhaps could not, though it had the best of the question ; that is, perhaps it had not put its ideas sufficiently in order to be able to reason. However, it *had* reasons, and these reasons will be found traceable up to, this First Principle, which expresses the common theory of all mankind in their conduct towards the inferior animals—viz., that the Creator has placed them absolutely in our hands, that we have no duties to them, and that there is as little sin except accidentally, and in the particular case, in taking away a brute's life, as in plucking a flower or eating an orange. This being taken for granted, all questions are in their substance solved, and only accidental difficulties remain.

I have said enough to show you what important, what formidable matters First Principles are. They are the means of proof, and are not themselves proved ; they rule and are not ruled ; they are sovereign on the one hand, irresponsible on the other : they are absolute monarchs, and if they are true, they act like the best and wisest of fathers to us : but, if they are false, they are the most cruel and baneful of tyrants. Yet, from the nature of our being, there they are, as I have said ; there they must ever be. They are our guides and standards in speculating, reasoning, judging, deliberating, deciding, and acting ; they are to the mind what the circulation of the blood and the various functions of our animal organs are to the

body. They are the conditions of our mental life ;
by them we form our view of events, of deeds, of
persons, of lines of conduct, of aims, of moral qualities, of religions. They constitute the difference between man and man ; they characterize him. As determined by his First Principles, such is his religion,
his creed, his worship, his political party, his character,
except as far as adventitious circumstances interfere
with their due and accurate development; they are,
in short, the man.

One additional remark must be made, quite as important as the foregoing. I just now said that these
First Principles, being a man's elementary points of
thinking, and the ideas which he has prior to other
ideas, might be considered as almost part of his
mind or moral being itself. But for this very reason,
because they are so close to him, if I may so speak,
he is very likely not to be aware of them. What is
far off, your bodily eyes see ; what is close up to you
is no object for your vision at all. You cannot see
yourself ; and, in somewhat the same way, the chance
in that you are not aware of those principles or ideas
which have the chief rule over your mind. They
are hidden for the very reason they are so sovereign and so engrossing. They have sunk into you ;
they spread through you ; you do not so much appeal to them as act from them. And this in great
measure is meant by saying that self-knowledge is
so difficult ; that is, in other words, men commonly
do not know their First Principles.

Now to show you that they have this subtle and
recondite character. For instance, two persons begin
to converse ; they come upon some point on which

they do not agree : they fall to dispute. They go on arguing and arguing perhaps for hours ; neither makes way with the other, but each becomes more certain his own opinion is right. Why is this ? How is it to be explained ? They cannot tell. It surprises them, for the point is so very clear ; as far as this they are agreed, but no further ; for then comes the difference, that where one says yes, the other says no, and each wonders that the other is not on his side. How comes each to be so positive when each contradicts the other ? The real reason is, that each starts from some principle or opinion which he takes for granted, which he does not observe he is assuming, and which, even if he did, he would think too plain to speak about or attempt to prove. Each starts with a First Principle, and they differ from each other in first principles.

For instance, supposing two persons to dispute whether Milton was or was not a poet ; it might so happen, that they both took for granted that every one knew what a poet was. If so, they might go on arguing to the end of time and never agree, because they had not adjusted with each other the principles with which they started.

Now, here the mistake is very obvious ; it might, however, very easily be a First Principle which did not come so prominently forward in the discussion. It might come in by the by, neither party might see it come in at all, or even recognise it to himself as a proposition which he held in the affirmative or negative, and yet it might simply turn the decision this way or that.

Thus again it happens, to take an instance of

another kind, that we cannot tell why we like some persons and dislike others, though there are reasons, if we could reach them ; according to the lines,—

> "I do not like thee, Dr. Fell;
> The reason why I cannot tell."

Or a person says, "I do not know how it is that this or that writer so comes home to me, and so inspires me; I so perfectly agree with him," or "I can so easily follow his thoughts." Both feelings may be accounted for, at least in many cases, by a difference or agreement in First Principles between the speaker and the person spoken of, which shows itself in the words, or writings, or deeds, or life of the latter, when submitted to the criticism of the former.

Sometimes two friends live together for years, and appear to entertain the same religious views; at the end of the time they take different courses; one becomes an unbeliever, the other a Catholic. How is this? Some latent and hitherto dormant First Principle, different in each, comes into play, and carries off one to the East, the other to the West. For instance, suppose the one holds that there is such a thing as sin; the other denies it,—denies it, that is, really and in his heart, though at first he would shrink from saying so, even to himself, and is not aware he denies it. At a certain crisis, either from the pressure of controversy or other reason, each finds he must give up the form of religion in which he has been educated; and then this question, the nature of sin, what it is, whether it exists, comes forward as a turning-point between them; he who does not believe in it becomes an unbeliever; he who does, becomes a Catholic.

Such, then, are First Principles ; sovereign, irresponsible, and secret ;—what an awful form of government the human mind is under from its very constitution !

4

There are many of these First Principles, as I have called them, which are common to the great mass of mankind, and are therefore true, as having been imprinted on the human mind by its Maker. Such are the great truths of the moral law, the duties, for instance, of justice, truth, and temperance. Others are peculiar to individuals, and are in consequence of no authority ; as, for instance, to take a case which cannot often occur, the opinion that there is no difference between virtue and vice. Other principles are common to extended localities ; men catch them from each other, by education, by daily intercourse, by reading the same books, or by being members of the same political community. Hence nations have very frequently one and the same set of First Principles, of the truth of which each individual is still more sure, because it is not only his own opinion, but the opinion of nearly every one else about him. Thus, for instance, it was the opinion of the ancient pagan Romans, that every one should follow the religion of his own country, and this was the reason why they persecuted the first Christians. They thought it exceedingly hard that the Christians would take up a religion of their own, and that, an upstart religion, lately imported from Palestine. They said, " Why cannot you be contented to be as your ancestors ? we are most liberal on the point of religion ; we let a Jew follow Jewish rites, and an Egyptian the rites of Egypt, and a Carthaginian the Punic; but you are ungrateful and rebellious, because, not content with this ample toleration, you *will* be introducing into your respective countries a foreign religion." They thought all this exceedingly sensible, and, in fact, unanswerable; statesmen of all parties and all the enlightened men and great thinkers of the Empire gave in their adhesion to it; and on this First Principle they proceeded to throw our poor forefathers to the beasts, to the flame, and to the deep, after first putting them to the most varied and horrible tortures. Such was the power of an imperial idea, and a popular dogma; such is the consequence of a First Principle being held in common by many at once; it ceases to be an opinion; it is at once taken for truth; it is looked upon as plain common sense; the opposite opinions are thought impossible; they are absurdities and nonentities, and have no rights whatever.

In the instance I have mentioned, the folly and the offence, in the eyes of the Romans, was *proselytising;* but let us fancy this got over, would the Christian system itself have pleased the countrymen of Cato at all better? On the contrary, they would have started with his First Principle, that humiliation was immoral, as an axiom; they would not have attempted to prove it; they would have considered it as much a fact as the sun in heaven; they would not have even enunciated it, they would have merely implied it. Fancy a really candid philosopher, who had been struck with the heroic deaths of the Martyrs, turning with a feeling of good will to consider the Christian ethics; what repugnance would he not feel towards them on rising up from the study! to crouch, to turn the cheek, not to resist, to love to be lowest! Who ever heard of such a teaching? It was the religion of slaves, it was unworthy of a man; much more of a Roman; yet that odious religion in the event became the creed of countless millions. What philosophers so spontaneously and instinctively condemned has been professed by the profoundest and the noblest of men, through eighteen centuries;—so possible is it for our First Principles to be but the opinions of a multitude, not truths.

Now be quite sure, my Brothers, that I make clear to you the point on which I am animadverting in these instances. I am not blaming Cato and his countrymen for using their First Principles, whatever they were, while they believed them: every one must use such opinions as he has; there is nothing else to be done. What I should blame in them would be their utterly despising another system with which they did not sympathize, and being so sure that they were right; their forgetting that the Christians might have First Principles as well as they, and opposite ones; their forgetting that it was a *question* of First Principles; that the contest was not ended—that it had not begun. They viewed Christianity with disgust, at first sight. They were repelled, thrown back, they revolted from the Religion, and they took that mere feeling of theirs as an evidence that the Religion really was wrong and immoral. No, it only showed that *either* the Religion *or* they were wrong, which of the two had still to be determined. Christians had their First Principles also; "blessed are the meek," "blessed are the persecuted," "blessed are the pure-

U

hearted." These First Principles the Pagans had no right to ignore. They chose to apply their own First Principles, as decisive tests, to the examination of the precepts and practice of the Church, and by means of them they condemned her; but if they had applied Christian principles as the measure of her precepts and her practice, they would, on the contrary, have been forced to praise her. All depends on which set of principles you begin by assuming.

The same thing takes place now. A dispassionate thinker is struck with the beauty and the eloquence of the rites and ceremonies of the Catholic Church; he likes to be present at them, but he says they are addressed of course only to the imagination, not to the reason. They are indefensible in the eye of reason. What does he mean? Why this, when he explains himself:—he says he cannot understand how the Divine Being needs propitiating—is He not good? what can be the use of these ceremonies? why, too, such continual prayer? why try to get others to pray for you too, and for your object, whatever it is? what the use of *novenas?* why betake yourselves to saints? what can they do for you? So he might go on, speaking against the whole system of deprecatory and intercessory prayer, and we might be grieved and perplexed at such a line of thought in so candid a man, and we should ask ourselves how it came to be. Now if it turned out at length that the said critic disbelieved the virtue of prayer altogether, or that the Divine Being was really moved by it, or that it was of any good whatever beyond the peace and serene-ness which the exercise poured over the soul, I think you would consider that this fact quite explained those criticisms of his which distressed you; you would feel that it was nugatory to argue points of *detail* with one, who, however candid, differed from you in *principle ;* and, while you would not quarrel with him for having his own First Principles (seriously as you thought of them theologically), your immediate charge against him would be that he had forgotten that a Catholic has First Principles too, and forgotten also that we have as much right to have our theory of prayer as he to have his own. His surprise and offence constitute no proof even to himself that we are wrong; they only show, that, as we have our First Principles, which we consider true, but which are not capable of proof, so has he his. The previous question remains—Which set of principles is true? He is a theorist, using his theory against our practice, as if our practice might not have its own theory also. But, in fact, he does not dream that we have any intellectual principles whatever as the basis of what we do; he thinks *he* is the only intellectual man; he has mind on his side, it never came into our heads to have it; *we* do not know what mind is. Thus he imagines and determines, knowing nothing whatever of our acute, profound, subtle philosophers, except by name, and ridding himself of the trouble of reading their works by nicknaming them schoolmen or monks.

5.

Now I have come to the point at which the maintenance of private opinion runs into bigotry. As Prejudice is the rejection of reason altogether, so Bigotry is the imposition of private reason,—that is, of our own views and theories of our own First Principles, as if they were the absolute truth, and the standard of all argument, investigation, and judgment. If there are any men in the world who ought to abstain from bigotry, it is Protestants. They, whose very badge is the right of private judgment, should give as well as take, should allow others what they claim themselves; but I am sorry to say, as I have had occasion to say again and again, there is very little of the spirit of reciprocity among them; they monopolize a liberty which, when they set out, they professed was to be for the benefit of all parties. Not even the intellectual, not even the candid-minded among them, are free from inconsistency here. They begin by setting up principles of thought and action for themselves; then, not content with applying them to their own thoughts and actions, they make them the rule for criticizing and condemning our thoughts and actions too; this, I repeat, is Bigotry. Bigotry is the infliction of our own unproved First Principles on others, and the treating others with scorn or hatred for not accepting them. There are principles, indeed, as I have already said, such as the First Principles of morals, not peculiar or proper to the individual, but the rule of the world, because they come from the Author of our being, and from no private factory of man. It is not bigotry to despise intemperance; it is not bigotry to hate injustice or cruelty; but whatever is local, or national, or sectional, or personal, or novel, and nothing more, to make that the standard of judging all existing opinions, without an attempt at proving it to be of authority, is mere ridiculous bigotry. "*In necessariis unitas, in dubiis libertas*," is ever the rule of a true philosopher. And though I know in many cases it is very difficult to draw the line, and to decide what principles are, and what are not, independent of individuals, times and places, eternal and divine, yet so far we may safely assert,—that when the very persons who hold certain views, confess, nay, boast, nay, are jealously careful, that those views come of their own private judgment, they at least should be as jealous and as careful to keep them to their own place, and not to use them as if they came distinctly from heaven, or from the nature of things, or from the nature of man. Those persons, surely, are precluded, if they would be consistent, from using their principles as authoritative, who proclaim that they made them for themselves. Protestants, then, if any men alive, are, on their own showing, bigots, if they set up their First Principles as oracles and as standards of all truth.

This being considered, have we not, my Brothers, a curious sight before us? This is what we call an enlightened age: we are to have large views of things ; everything is to be put on a philosophical basis ; reason is to rule: the world is to begin again ; a new and transporting set of views is about to be exhibited to the great human family. Well and good ; have them, preach them, enjoy them, but deign to recollect the while, that there have been views in the world before you: that the world has not been going on up to this day without any principles whatever ; that the Old Religion was based on principles, and that it is not enough to flourish about your "new lamps," if you would make us give up our "old" ones. Catholicism, I say, had its First Prin-

ciples before you were born: you say they are false;
very well, prove them to be so: they are false, indeed,
if yours are true; but not false merely because yours
are yours. While yours are yours it is self-evident,
indeed, to you, that ours are false; but it is not the
common way of carrying on business in the world,
to value English goods by French measures, or to
pay a debt in paper which was contracted in gold.
Catholicism has its First Principles, overthrow them, if
you can; endure them, if you cannot. It is not
enough to call them effete because they are old, or
antiquated because they are ancient. It is not
enough to look into our churches, and cry, "It is all
a form, *because* divine favour cannot depend on external observances;" or, "It is all a bondage, *because*
there is no such thing as sin;" or, "a blasphemy,
because the Supreme Being cannot be •present in
ceremonies;" or, "a mummery, *because* prayer cannot
move Him;" or, "a tyranny, *because* vows are unnatural;" or, "hypocrisy, *because* no rational man can
credit it at all." I say here is endless assumption,
unmitigated hypothesis, reckless assertion; prove
your "because," "because," "because;" prove your
First Principles, and if you cannot, learn philosophic
moderation. Why may not my First Principles contest the prize with yours? they have been longer in
the world; they have lasted longer, they have done
harder work, they have seen rougher service. You
sit in your easy-chairs, you dogmatize in your
lecture-rooms, you wield your pens: it all looks
well on paper: you write exceedingly well: there
never was an age in which there was better writing;
logical, nervous, eloquent, and pure,—go and carry

it all out in the world. Take your First Principles,
of which you are so proud, into the crowded streets
of our cities, into the formidable classes which make
up the bulk of our population ; try to work society
by them. You think you can ; I say you cannot
—at least you have not as yet ; it is yet to be seen
if you can. "Let not him that putteth on his
armour boast as he who taketh it off." Do not
take it for granted that that is certain which
is waiting the test of reason and experiment. Be
modest until you are victorious. My principles, which
I believe to be eternal, have at least lasted eighteen
hundred years ; let yours live as many months. That
man can sin, that he has duties, that the Divine Being
hears prayer, that He gives His favours through
visible ordinances, that He is really present in the
midst of them, these principles have been the life of
nations ; they have shown they could be carried out ;
let any single nation carry out yours, and you will
have better claim to speak contemptuously of Catholic rites, of Catholic devotions, of Catholic belief.

What is all this but the very state of mind which we
ridicule, and call narrowness, in the case of those who
have never travelled ? We call them, and rightly, men
of contracted ideas, who cannot fancy things going
on differently from what they have themselves witnessed at home, and laugh at everything because it
is strange. They themselves are the pattern men ;
their height, their dress, their manners, their food,
their language, are all founded in the nature of things ;
and everything else is good or bad, just in that very
degree in which it partakes, or does not partake, of
them. All men ought to get up at half-past eight,

breakfast between nine and ten, read the newspapers, lunch, take a ride or drive, dine. Here is the great principle of the day—dine; no one is a man who does not dine; yes, dine, and at the right hour; and it must *be* a dinner, with a certain time after dinner, and then, in due time, to bed. Tea and toast, port wine, roast beef, mince-pies at Christmas, lamb at Easter, goose at Michaelmas, these are their great principles. They suspect any one who does otherwise. Figs and maccaroni for the day's fare, or Burgundy and grapes for breakfast!—they are aghast at the atrocity of the notion. And hence you read of some good country gentleman, who, on undertaking a Continental tour, was warned of the privations and mortifications that lay before him from the difference between foreign habits and his own, stretching his imagination to a point of enlargement answerable to the occasion, and making reply that he knew it, that he had dwelt upon the idea, that he had made up his mind to it, and thought himself prepared for anything abroad, provided he could but bargain for a clean table-cloth and a good beef-steak every day.

Here was a man of one idea; there are many men of one idea in the world: your unintellectual machine, who eats, drinks, and sleeps, is a man of one idea. Such, too, is your man of genius, who strikes out some new, or revives some old view in science or in art, and would apply it as a sort of specific or as a key to all possible subjects; and who will not let the world alone, but loads it with bad names if it will not run after him and his darling fancy, if it will not cure all its complaints by chemistry or galvanism, by little doses or great, if it will not adopt the peaked shoes of Edward III., or the steeple hats of the Puritans. Such again are those benevolent persons who, with right intentions, but yet, I think, narrow views, wish to introduce the British constitution and British ideas into every nation and tribe upon earth ; differing, how much ! from the wise man in the Greek epic, whose characteristic was that he was "versatile," [1] for he had known "the cities and the *mind* of many men." History and travel expand our views of man and of society ; they teach us that distinct principles rule in different countries and in distinct periods ; and, though they do *not* teach us that all principles are equally true, or, which is the same thing, that none are either true or false, yet they do teach us, that all are to be regarded with attention and examined with patience, which' have prevailed to any great extent among mankind. Such is the temper of a man of the world, of a philosopher. He may hold principles to be false and dangerous, but he will try to enter into them, to enter into the minds of those who hold them ; he will consider in what their strength lies, and what can be said for them ; he will do his best to analyze and dissect them ; he will compare them with others ; and he will apply himself to the task of exposing and disproving them. He will not ignore them ;—now, what I desiderate at the present day in so many even candid men, and of course much more in the multitude which is uncandid, is a recognition that Catholics *have* principles of their own ; I desiderate a study of those principles, a fair representation, a refutation. It is not enough,

[1] Πολύτροπος.

that this age has its principles too; this does not prove them true; it has no right to put ours on one side, and proceed to make its own the immediate touchstones and the sufficient tribunals of our creed, our worship, our ecclesiastical proceedings, and our moral teaching.

6.

To show in how very many instances these remarks apply to the criticisms and judgments passed by Protestants upon the details of Catholic teaching and belief, is simply impossible, on such an occasion as this.—It would be to write a book. I will take one instance, but even to that I cannot hope to do full justice; but it will be something to have drawn your attention to what seems to me an important line of thought, and to the mode of using it in the controversy in which we are engaged.

I will take, then, one of those subjects, of which I spoke in the opening of this Lecture as offensive to Protestants—viz., our belief in the miracles wrought by the relics and the prayers of the saints, which has given both occasion and scope to so many reports and narratives to their honour, true, doubtful, or unfounded, in the Catholic Church. I suppose there is nothing which prejudices us more in the minds of Protestants of all classes than this belief. They inspect our churches, or they attend to our devotions, or they hear our sermons, or they open our books, or they read paragraphs in the newspapers; and it is one and the same story—relics and miracles. Such a belief, such a claim, they consider a self-evident absurdity; they are too indignant even to laugh; they toss the book from them in the fulness of anger and contempt, and they think it superfluous to make one remark in order to convict us of audacious imposture, and to fix upon us the brand of indelible shame. I shall show, then, that this strong feeling arises simply from their assumption of a First Principle, which ought to be proved, if they would be honest reasoners, before it is used to our disadvantage.

You observe, my Brothers, we are now upon a certain question of controversy, in which the argument is *not* directly about *fact.* This is what I noticed in the opening of this Lecture. We accuse our enemies of untruth in most cases; we do not accuse them, on the whole, of untruth here. I know it is very difficult for prejudice such as theirs to open its mouth at all without some mis-statement or exaggeration; still, on the whole, they do bear true, not false witness in the matter of miracles. We do certainly abound, we are exuberant, we overflow with stories which cause our enemies, from no fault of ours, the keenest irritation, and kindle in them the most lively resentment against us. Certainly the Catholic Church, from east to west, from north to south, is, according to our conceptions, hung with miracles. The store of relics is inexhaustible; they are multiplied through all lands, and each particle of each has in it at least a dormant, perhaps an energetic virtue of supernatural operation. At Rome there is the True Cross, the Crib of Bethlehem, and the Chair of St. Peter; portions of the Crown of Thorns are kept at Paris; the Holy Coat is shown at Trèves; the Winding-Sheet at Turin; at Monza, the iron crown is formed out of a Nail of the Cross; and another Nail is claimed for the Duomo of Milan ; and pieces of our Lady's Habit are to be seen in the Escurial. The Agnus Dei, blessed medals, the scapular, the cord of St. Francis, all are the medium of divine manifestations and graces. Crucifixes have bowed the head to the suppliant, and Madonnas have bent their eyes upon assembled crowds St. Januarius's blood liquefies periodically at Naples, and St. Winifred's well is the scene of wonders even in an unbelieving country. Women are marked with the sacred stigmata ; blood has flowed on Fridays from their five wounds, and their heads are crowned with a circle of lacerations. Relics are ever touching the sick, the diseased, the wounded, sometimes with no result at all, at other times with marked and undeniable efficacy. Who has not heard of the abundant favours gained by the intercession of the Blessed Virgin, and of the marvellous consequences which have attended the invocation of St. Antony of Padua ? These phenomena are sometimes reported of Saints in their life-time, as well as after death, especially if they were evangelists or martyrs. The wild beasts crouched before their victims in the Roman amphitheatre ; the axe-man was unable to sever St. Cecilia's head from her body, and St. Peter elicited a spring of water for his jailor's baptism in the Mamertine. St. Francis Xavier turned salt water into fresh for five hundred travellers ; St. Raymond was transported over the sea on his cloak ; St. Andrew shone brightly in the dark ; St. Scholastica gained by her prayers a pouring rain ; St. Paul was fed by ravens ; and St. Frances saw her guardian Angel. I need not continue the catalogue ; here what one party urges, the other admits ; they join issue over a fact ; that fact is the claim of miracles on the part of the Catholic Church ; it is the Protestants' charge, and it is our glory.

Observe then, we affirm that the Supreme Being has wrought miracles on earth ever since the time of the Apostles : Protestants deny it. Why do we affirm, why do they deny ? we affirm it on a First Principle, they deny it on a First Principle ; and on either side the First Principle is made to be decisive of the question. Our First Principle is contradictory of theirs ; if theirs be true, we are mistaken ; if ours be true, they are mistaken. They take for granted that their First Principle is true ; we take for granted that our First Principle is true. Till ours is disproved, we have as much right to consider it true as they to consider theirs true ; till theirs is proved, they have as little ground for saying that we go against reason, as for boasting that they go according to it. For our First Principle is our reason, in the same sense in which theirs is their reason, and it is quite as good a reason. Both they and we start with the miracles of the Apostles ;[2] and then their First Principle or presumption, against our miracles, is this, " What God did once, He is *not* likely to do again ; " while our First Principle or presumption, for our miracles, is this, " What God did once, He *is* likely to do again." They say, It cannot be supposed He will work *many* miracles ; we, It cannot be supposed He will work *few.*

I am not aiming at any mere sharp or clever stroke

[2] I am arguing with Protestants ; if unbelievers are supposed, then they use virtually Hume's celebrated argument, which still is a Presumption or First Principle—viz., it is impossible to fancy the order of nature interrupted.

against them ; I wish to be serious and to investigate the real state of the case, and I feel what I am saying very strongly. Protestants say, miracles are *not* likely to occur often ; we say they *are* likely to occur often. The two parties, you see, start with contradictory principles, and they determine the particular miracles, which are the subject of dispute, by their respective principles, without looking to such testimony as may be brought in their favour. They do not say, " St. Francis, or St. Antony, or St. Philip Neri did no miracles, for the *evidence* for them is worth nothing," or " because what *looked* like a miracle was not a miracle ; " no, but they say, " It is *impossible* they should have wrought miracles." Bring before the Protestant the largest mass of evidence and testimony in proof of the miraculous liquefaction of St. Januarius's blood at Naples, let him be urged by witnesses of the highest character, chemists of the first fame, circumstances the most favourable for the detection of imposture, coincidences, and confirmations the most close and minute and indirect, he will not believe it ; his First Principle *blocks* belief. On the other hand, diminish the evidence ever so much, provided you leave some, and reduce the number of witnesses and circumstantial proof ; yet you would not altogether wean the Catholic's mind from belief in it ; for his First Principle *encourages* such belief. Would any amount of evidence convince the Protestant of the miraculous motion of a Madonna's eyes ? is it not to him in itself, prior to proof, simply incredible ? would he even listen to the proof ? His First Principle settles the matter ; no wonder then that the whole history of Catholicism finds so little response in his intellect or sympathy in his heart. It is as impossible that the notion of the miracle should gain admittance into his imagination, as for a lighted candle to remain burning, when dipped into a vessel of water. The water puts it out.

7.

The Protestant, I say, laughs at the very idea of miracles or supernatural acts as occurring at this day; his First Principle is rooted in him; he repels from him the idea of miracles; he laughs at the notion of evidence for them; one is just as likely as another; they are all false. Why? Because of his First Principle: there are no miracles since the Apostles. Here, indeed, is a short and easy way of getting rid of the whole subject, not by reason, but by a First Principle which he calls reason. Yes, it *is* reason, granting his First Principle is true; it is *not* reason, supposing his First Principle is false. It is reason, if the private judgment of an individual, or of a sect, or of a philosophy, or of a nation, be synonymous with reason; it is not reason, if reason is something not local, nor temporal, but universal. Before he advances a step in his argument, he ought to prove his First Principle true; he does not attempt to do so, he takes it for granted; and he proceeds to apply it, gratuitous, personal, peculiar as it is, to all our accounts of miracles taken together, and thereupon and thereby triumphantly rejects them all. This, forsooth, is his spontaneous judgment, his instinctive feeling, his common sense,—a mere private opinion of his own, a Protestant opinion; a lecture-room opinion; not a world-wide opinion, not an instinct ranging through time and space, but an assumption and presumption, which, by education and habit, he has got to think as certain, as much of an axiom, as that two and two make four; and he looks down upon us, and bids us consider ourselves beaten, all because the savour of our statements and narratives and reports and legends is inconsistent with his delicate Protestant sense,— all because our conclusions are different, not from our principles and premisses, but from his.

And now for the structure he proceeds to raise on this foundation of sand. If, he argues, in matter of fact, there be a host of stories about relics and miracles circulated in the Catholic Church, which, as a matter of First Principle, cannot be true; to what must we attribute them? indubitably to enormous stupidity on the one hand, and enormous roguery on the other. This, observe, is an immediate and close inference :— clever men must see through the superstition; those who do not see through it must be dolts. Further, since religion is the subject-matter of the alleged fictions, they must be what are called pious frauds, for the sake of gain and power. Observe, my Brothers, there is in the Church a vast tradition and testimony about miracles : how is it to be accounted for? If miracles *can* take place, then the *truth* of the miracle will be a natural explanation of the *report*, just as the *fact* of a man dying satisfactorily accounts for the *news* that he is dead; but the Protestant cannot so explain it, because he thinks miracles cannot take place; so he is necessarily driven, by way of accounting for the report of them, to impute that report to fraud. He cannot help himself. I repeat it; the whole mass of accusations which Protestants bring against us under this head, Catholic credulity, imposture, pious frauds, hypocrisy, priestcraft, this vast and varied superstructure of imputation, you see, all rests on an assumption, on an opinion of theirs, for which they offer no kind of proof. What then, in fact, do they say more than this, *If* Protestantism be true, you Catholics are a most awful set of knaves ?— Here, at least, is a most intelligible and undeniable position.

Now, on the other hand, let me take our own side of the question, and consider how we ourselves stand relatively to the charge made against us. Catholics, then, hold the mystery of the Incarnation ; and the Incarnation is the most stupendous event which ever can take place on earth ; and after it and henceforth, I do not see how we can scruple at any miracle on the mere ground of its being unlikely to happen. No miracle can be so great as that which took place in the Holy House of Nazareth ; it is indefinitely more difficult to believe than all the miracles of the Breviary, of the Martyrology, of Saints' lives, of legends, of local traditions, put together ; and there is the grossest inconsistency on the very face of the matter, for any one so to strain out the gnat and to swallow the camel, as to profess what is inconceivable, yet to protest against what is surely within the limits of intelligible hypothesis. If, through divine grace, we once are able to accept the solemn truth that the Supreme Being was born of a mortal woman, what is there to be imagined which can offend us on the ground of its marvellousness ? Thus, you see, it happens that, though First Principles are commonly assumed, not proved, ours in this case admits, if not of proof, yet of recommendation, by means of that fundamental truth which Protestants profess as well as we. When we start with assuming that miracles are not unlikely, we are putting forth a position which lies imbedded, as it were, and involved, in the great revealed fact of the Incarnation.

So much is plain on starting ; but more is plain too. Miracles are not only not unlikely, they are positively likely ; and for this simple reason, because, for the most part, when God begins He goes on. We conceive that when He first did a miracle, He began a series ; what He commenced, He continued : what has been, will be. Surely this is good and clear reasoning. To my own mind, certainly, it is incomparably more difficult to believe that the Divine Being should do one miracle and no more, than that He should do a thousand ; that He should do one great miracle only, than that He should do a multitude of less besides. This beautiful world of nature, His own work, He broke its harmony ; He broke through His own laws which He had imposed on It ; He worked out His purposes, not simply through it, but in violation of it. If He did this only in the lifetime of the Apostles, if He did it but once, eighteen hundred years ago and more, that isolated infringement looks as the mere infringement of a rule : if Divine Wisdom would not leave an infringement, an anomaly, a solecism on His work, He might be expected to introduce a series of miracles, and turn the apparent exception into an additional law of His providence. If the Divine Being does a thing once, He is, judging by human reason, likely to do it again. This surely is common sense. If a beggar gets food at a gentleman's house once, does he not send others thither after him? If you are attacked by thieves once, do you forthwith leave your windows open at night? If an acquaintance were convicted of a fraud, would you let that be the signal for reposing confidence in him, as a man who could not possibly deceive you? Nay, suppose you yourselves were once to see a miracle, would you not feel that experience to be like passing a line? should you, in consequence of it, declare, "I never will believe another if I hear of one?" would it not, on the contrary, predispose you to listen to a new report? would you scoff at it and call it priestcraft for the reason that you had actually seen one with your own eyes? I think you would not ; then I ask what is the difference of the argument, whether you have seen one or believe one? You believe the Apostolic miracles, therefore be inclined beforehand to believe later ones. Thus you see, our First Principle, that miracles are not unlikely now, is not at all a strange one in the mouths of those who believe that the Supreme Being came miraculously into this world, miraculously united Himself to man's nature, passed a life of miracles, and then gave His Apostles a greater gift of miracles than He exercised Himself. So far on the principle itself ; and now, in the next place, see what comes of it.

This comes of it,—that there are two systems going on in the world, one of nature, and one above nature ; and two histories, one of common events, and one of miracles ; and each system and each history has its own order. When I hear of the miracle of a Saint, my first feeling would be of the same kind as if it were a report of any natural exploit or event. Supposing, for instance, I heard a report of the death of some public man ; it would not startle me, even if I did not at once credit it, for all men must die. Did I read of any great feat of valour, I should believe it, if imputed to Alexander or Cœur de Lion. Did I hear of any act of baseness, I should disbelieve it, if imputed to a friend whom I knew and loved. And so, in like manner, were a miracle reported to me as wrought by a member of Parliament, or a Bishop of the Establishment, or a Wesleyan preacher, I should repudiate the notion : were it referred to a saint, or the relic of a saint, or the intercession of a saint, I should not be startled at it, though I might not at once believe it. And I certainly should be right in this conduct, supposing my First Principle be true. Miracles to the Catholic are facts of history and biography, and nothing else ; and they are to be regarded and dealt with as other facts ; and as natural facts, under circumstances, do not startle Protestants, so supernatural, under circumstances, do not startle the Catholic.[3] They may or may not have taken place in particular cases ; he may be unable to determine which ; he may have no distinct evidence ; he may suspend his judgment, but he will say, " It is very possible ; " he never will say, " I cannot believe it."

[3] Douglas, succeeding Middleton, lays down the sceptical and Protestant First Principle thus : " The history of miracles (to make use of the words of an author, whose authority you will think of some weight) is of a kind totally *different* from that of common events ; the one to be *suspected always of course*, without the *strongest* evidence to *confirm* it ; the other to be *admitted of course*, without *as strong* reason to *suspect* it," &c.—*Criterion*, p. 26.

Take the history of Alfred: you know his wise, mild, beneficent, yet daring character, and his romantic vicissitudes of fortune. This great king has a number of stories, or, as you may call them, legends, told of him. Do you believe them all? no. Do you, on the other hand, think them incredible? no. Do you call a man a dupe or a blockhead for believing them? no. Do you call an author a knave and a cheat who records them? no. You go into neither extreme, whether of implicit faith or of violent reprobation. You are not so extravagant; you see that they suit his character, they *may* have been; yet this is so romantic, that has so little evidence, a third is so confused in dates or in geography, that you are in matter of fact indisposed towards them. Others are probably true, others certainly. Nor do you force every one to take your own view of particular stories; you and your neighbours think differently about this or that in detail and agree to differ. There is in the Museum at Oxford, a jewel or trinket said to be Alfred's; it is shown to all comers: I never heard the keeper of the Museum accused of hypocrisy or fraud for showing, with Alfred's name appended, what he might or might not himself believe to have belonged to that great king: nor did I ever see any party of strangers, who were looking at it with awe, regarded by any self-complacent bystander with scornful compassion. Yet the relic is not to a certainty Alfred's. The world pays civil honour to it on the probability; we pay religious honour to relics, if so be, on the probability. Is the Tower of London shut against sightseers, because the coats of mail or pikes there may have half legendary tales connected with them?

why then may not the country people come up in joyous companies, singing and piping, to see the Holy Coat at Trèves? There is our Queen again, who is so truly and justly popular; she roves about in the midst of tradition and romance; she scatters myths and legends from her as she goes along; she is a being of poetry, and you might fairly be sceptical whether she had any personal existence. She is always at some beautiful, noble, bounteous work or other, if you trust the papers. She is doing alms-deeds in the Highlands; she meets beggars in her rides at Windsor; she writes verses in albums, or draws sketches, or is mistaken for the housekeeper by some blind old woman, or she runs up a hill, as if she were a child. Who finds fault with these things? he would be a cynic, he would be white-livered, and would have gall for blood, who was not struck with this graceful, touching evidence of the love which her subjects bear her. Who could have the head, even if he had the heart, who could be so cross and peevish, who could be so solemn and perverse, as to say that some of the stories *may* be simple lies, and all of them might have stronger evidence than they carry with them? Do you think she is displeased at them? Why, then, should He, the Great Father, who once walked the earth, look sternly on the unavoidable mistakes of His own subjects and children in their devotion to Him and His? Even granting they mistake some cases in particular, from the infirmity of human nature, and the contingencies of evidence, and fancy there is or has been a miracle here or there when there is not;—though a tradition, attached to a picture, or to a shrine, or to a well, be very doubtful; —though one relic be sometimes mistaken for another, and St. Theodore stands for St. Eugenius, or St. Agathocles ;—still, once take into account our First Principle, that He is likely to continue miracles among us, which is as good as the Protestant's, and I do not see why He should feel much displeasure with us on account of this error, or should cease to work wonders in our behalf. In the Protestant's view, indeed, who assumes that miracles never are, our thaumatology is one great falsehood ; but that is *his* First Principle, as I have said so often, which he does not prove but assume. If *he*, indeed, upheld *our* system, or *we* held *his* principle, in either case he or we should be impostors ; but though we should be partners to a fraud, if we thought like Protestants, we surely are not, because we think like Catholics.

8.

Such, then, is the answer which I make to those who would urge against us the multitude of miracles recorded in our Saints' Lives and devotional works, for many of which there is little evidence, and for some none to none. We think them true in the sense in which Protestants think the details of English history true. When they say that, they do not mean to say there are no mistakes in it, but no mistakes of consequence, none which alter the general course of history. Nor do they mean they are equally sure of every part ; for evidence is fuller and better for some things than for others. They do not stake their credit on the truth of Froissart or Sully, they do not pledge themselves for the accuracy of Doddington or Walpole, they do not embrace as an Evangelist, Hume, Sharon Turner, or Macaulay. And yet they do not think it necessary, on the other hand, to com-

mence a religious war against all our historical cate-
chisms, and abstracts, and dictionaries, and tales and
biographies, through the country ; they have no call
on them to amend and expurgate books of archeology,
antiquities, heraldry, architecture, geography, and
statistics, to rewrite our inscriptions, and to establish
a censorship on all new publications for the time to
come.   And so as regards the miracles of the Catholic
Church ; if, indeed, miracles never can occur, then,
indeed, impute the narratives to fraud ; but till you
prove they are not likely, we shall consider the histories which have come down to us true on the whole,
though in particular cases they may be exaggerated
or unfounded.   Where, indeed, they can certainly be
proved to be false, there we shall be bound to do our
best to get rid of them ; but till that is clear, we shall
be liberal enough to allow others to use their private
judgment in their favour, as we use ours in their
disparagement.   For myself, lest I appear in any
way to be shrinking from a determinate judgment
on the claims of some of those miracles and relics,
which Protestants are so startled at, and to be hiding
particular questions in what is vague and general, I
will avow distinctly, that, putting out of the question
the hypothesis of unknown laws of nature (that is, of
the professed miracle being not miraculous), I think
it impossible to withstand the evidence which is
brought for the liquefaction of the blood of St. Januarius at Naples, and for the motion of the eyes of
the pictures of the Madonna in the Roman States.
I see no reason to doubt the material of the Lombard
crown at Monza ; and I do not see why the Holy
Coat at Trèves may not have been what it professes
to be.   I firmly believe that portions of the True

Cross are at Rome and elsewhere, that the Crib of
Bethlehem is at Rome, and the bodies of St. Peter and
St. Paul also. I believe that at Rome too lies St.
Stephen, that St. Matthew lies at Salerno, and St.
Andrew at Amalfi. I firmly believe that the relics
of the saints are doing innumerable miracles and
graces daily, and that it needs only for a Catholic to
show devotion to any saint in order to receive special
benefits from his intercession. I firmly believe that
saints in their life-time have before now raised the
dead to life, crossed the sea without vessels, multiplied
grain and bread, cured incurable diseases, and superseded the operation of the laws of the universe in a
multitude of ways. Many men, when they hear an
educated man so speak, will at once impute the
avowal to insanity, or to an idiosyncrasy, or to imbecility of mind, or to decrepitude of powers, or to
fanaticism, or to hypocrisy. They have a right to
say so, if they will ; and we have a right to ask them
why they do not say it of those who bow down before the Mystery of mysteries, the Divine Incarnation.
If they do not believe this, they are not yet Protestants ; if they do, let them grant that He who has
done the greater may do the less. [4]

9.

And now, Brothers of the Oratory, I have come to
the end of a somewhat uninteresting, but a necessary
discussion. Your lot is cast in the world ; you are
not gathered together, as we are, into the home and
under the shadow of St. Philip ; you mix with men
of all opinions. Where you see prejudice, there, indeed, it is no use to argue ; prejudice thinks its first

[4] *Vide* Note 2 at the end of the volume.

principles self-evident. It can tell falsehoods to our dishonour by the score, yet suddenly it is so jealous of truth, as to be shocked at legends in honour of the saints. With prejudiced persons then, you will make no way; they will not look the question in the face; if they condescend to listen for a moment to your arguments it is in order to pick holes in them, not to ascertain their drift or to estimate their weight. But there are others of a different stamp of whom I spoke in the opening of this Lecture, candid, amiable minds, who wish to think well of our doctrines and devotions, but stumble at them. When you meet with such, ask them whether they are not taking their own principles and opinions for granted, and whether all they have to say against us is not contained in the proposition with which they start. Entreat them to consider how they know their existing opinions to be true; whether they are innate and necessary; whether they are not local, national, or temporary; whether they have ever spread over the earth, ever held nations together; whether they have ever or often done a great thing. If they say that penances are absurd, or images superstitious, or infallibility impossible, or sacraments mere charms, or a priesthood priestcraft, get them to put their ideas into shape and to tell you their reasons for them. Trace up their philosophy for them, as you have traced up their tradition; the fault lies in the root; every step of it is easy but the first. Perhaps you will make them Catholics by this process; at least you will make them perceive what they believe and what they do not, and will teach them to be more tolerant of a Religion which unhappily they do not see their way to embrace.

LECTURE VIII.

*IGNORANCE CONCERNING CATHOLICS THE PROTEC-
TION OF THE PROTESTANT VIEW.*

I.

You may have asked yourselves, Brothers of the
Oratory, why it was that, in exposing, as I did last
week, the shallowness of the philosophy on which our
opponents erect their structure of argument against
us, I did not take, as my illustration, an instance far
more simple and ready to my hand than that to which
I actually directed your attention. It was my object,
on that occasion, to show that Protestants virtually
assume the point in debate between them and us, in
any particular controversy, in the very principles with
which they set out; that those first principles, for
which they offer no proof, involve their conclusions;
so that, if we are betrayed into the inadvertence of
passing them over without remark, we are forthwith
defeated and routed, even before we have begun to
move forward to the attack, as might happen to
cavalry who manœuvred on a swamp, or to a guerilla
force which ventured on the open plain. Protestants
and Catholics each have their own ground, and can-

not engage on any other ; the question in dispute between them is more elementary than men commonly suppose ; it relates to the ground itself, on which the battle is legitimately and rightfully to be fought ; the first principles assumed in the starting of the controversy determine the issue. Protestants in fact do but say that we are superstitious, because it is superstitious to do as we do ; that we are deluded, because it is a delusion to believe what we believe ; that we are knaves, because it must be knavery to teach what we teach. A short and pleasant argument, easier even and safer than that extempore and im-provisatore mode of fabricating and fabling against us, of which I have said so much in former Lectures : easier and safer, inasmuch as, according to the proverb, " great wits ought to have long memories," when they deal with facts. In arguments about facts, there must be consistency, and speciousness, and proof, and circumstantial evidence ; private judgment in short becomes subject to sundry and serious liabilities when it deals with history and testimony, from which it is comparatively free when it expatiates in opinions and views. Now of this high *à priori* mode of deciding the question, the specimen I actually took was the Protestant argument against relics and miracles ; and I selected this instance for its own sake, because I wished to bring out what I thought an important truth as regarded them ; but a more obvious instance certainly would have been the surprising obtuseness, for I can use no other word, with which the Protestant Rule of Faith, which Catholics disown, is so often obtruded on us, as a necessary basis of discussion, which it is thought absurd and self-destructive not to accept, in any controversy about doctrine.

All the world knows that Catholics hold that the Apostles made over the Divine Revelation to the generation after them, not only in writing, but by word of mouth, and in the ritual of the Church. We consider that the New Testament is not the whole of what they left us ; that they left us a number of doctrines, not in writing at all, but living in the minds and mouths of the faithful ; Protestants deny this. They have a right to deny it ; but they have no right to assume their denial to be true without proof, and to use it as self-evident, and to triumph over us as beaten, merely because we will not admit it. Yet this they actually do ; can anything be more preposterous ? however, they do this as innocently and naturally as if it were the most logical of processes, and the fairest and most unexceptionable of proceedings. For instance there was a country gentleman in this neighbourhood in the course of last year, who, having made some essays in theology among his tenantry in his walks over his estate, challenged me to prove some point, I am not clear what, but I think it was the infallibility of the Holy See, or of the Church. Were my time my own, I should never shrink from any controversy, having the experience of twenty years, that the more Catholicism and its doctrines are sifted, the more distinct and luminous will its truth ever come out into view ; and in the instance in question I did not decline the invitation. However, it soon turned out that it was a new idea to the gentleman in question, that I was not bound to prove the point in debate simply by Scripture ; he considered that Scripture was to be the sole basis of the discussion. This was quite another thing. For myself, I firmly believe that in Scripture, the Catholic doctrine on the subject *is* contained; but had I accepted this gratuitous and officious proposition, you see I should have been simply recognising a Protestant principle, which I disown. He would not controvert with me at all, unless I subscribed to a doctrine which I believe to be, not only a dangerous, but an absurd error; and, because I would not allow him to assume what it was his business to prove, before he brought it forward, and because I challenged him to prove that Scripture was, as he assumed, the Rule of Faith, he turned away as happy and self-satisfied as if he had gained a victory. That all truth is contained in Scripture was his first principle; he thought none but an idiot could doubt it; none but a Jesuit could deny it; he thought it axiomatic; he thought that to offer proof was even a profanation of so self-evident a point, and that to demand it was a *reductio ad absurdum* of the person demanding;—but this, I repeat, was no extraordinary instance of Protestant argumentation; it occurs every other day.

The instance in controversy, to which I have been alluding, leads by no very difficult nor circuitous transition to the subject to which I mean to devote the present Lecture. Let it be observed, that the fallacy involved in the Protestant Rule of Faith is this,—that its upholders fancy, most unnaturally, that the accidental and occasional writings of an Apostle convey to them of necessity his whole mind. It does not occur to them to ask themselves, whether, as he has in part committed his teaching to writing so possibly he may not have expressed it in part through other channels also. Very different this from their mode of acting in matters of this world, in which nothing are they more distrustful of, or discontented with, than mere letter-writing, when they would arrive at the real state of a case in which they are interested. When a government, or the proprietors of a newspaper, would gain accurate information on any subject, they send some one to the spot, to see with his eyes. When a man of business would bring a negotiation to a safe and satisfactory conclusion, he exclaims that letters are endless, and forthwith despatches a confidential person to transact the matter with the parties with whom he is treating. We know how unwilling heads of families are to take servants by written characters, considering that writing is not minute and real enough for their purpose. Writing, of course, has special advantages, but it has its defects ; and other methods of information compensate for them. It must be recollected, too, as regards the New Testament, that it is not a technical document, like an act of Parliament, or a legal instrument, but is made up of various portions, exhibiting, more or less, the free and flowing course of thought of their respective writers. It is not worded with the scientific precision of a formal treatise, a creed, or a last will and testament. Now, works written in this natural style are especially liable to receive an interpretation, and to make an impression, not in correspondence with the writer's intention, but according to the private principles and feelings of the reader. The imagination draws the unknown or absent author in lineaments altogether different from the original. Did we suddenly see St. Peter or St.

Paul, and hear him converse, most of us would not recognise, or even suspect him to be the Apostle. How surprised we sometimes are by the sight of those of whom we have often heard speak, or whose writings we have often read! We cannot believe we have the living author before us. Hence it is common to hear it said in favour of intemperate partisans by their friends, " If you knew him, you really would like him ; he is so different from his mode of writing or speaking " ; others, on the other hand, meet with a person whom they have long admired through the medium of his works, and are quite mortified and annoyed that they like his conversation and his manners so little.

Unless my memory fails me of what I read years ago, a well-known authoress, lately deceased, supplies in her tales one or two instances in point. I recollect the description of an old-fashioned, straightforward East Indian, who had for years corresponded with the widow of a friend in England, and from her letters had conceived a high opinion of her good sense and propriety of feeling. Then, as the story goes on to tell, he comes back to England, becomes acquainted with her, and, to his disappointment, is gradually made aware that she is nothing else than a worldly, heartless, and manœuvring woman. The same writer draws elsewhere a very young lady, who, in a spirit of romance, has carried on a correspondence with another female whom she never saw ; on the strength of which, from a conviction of the sympathy which must exist between them, she runs from home to join her, with the view of retiring with her for life to some secluded valley in Wales ; but is shocked to find, on meeting her, that after all she is vulgar, unattractive, and middle-aged. Were it necessary, numberless instances might be given to the purpose; of mistakes, too, of every kind; of persons, when seen, turning out different from their writings, for the better as well as for the worse, or neither for the better nor the worse, but still so different as to surprise us and make us muse; different in opinion, or in principle, or in conduct, or in impression and effect. And thus Scripture, in like manner, though written under a supernatural guidance, is, from the nature of the case, from the defect of human language, and the infirmity of the recipient, unable by itself to convey the real mind of its writers to all who read it. Instead of its forcing its meaning upon the reader, the reader forces his own meaning upon it, colours it with his own thoughts and distorts it to his own purposes; so that something is evidently needed besides it, such as the teaching of the Church, to protect it from the false private judgment of the individual. And if this be true when the New Testament, as a whole, is contemplated, how much more certainly will it take place when Protestants contract their reading professedly to only a part of it, as to St. Paul's Epistles; and then again out of St. Paul, select the two Epistles to the Romans and Galatians; and still further, as is so common, confine themselves to one or two sentences, which constitute practically the whole of the Protestant written word! Why, of course, it is very easy to put what sense they please on one or two verses; and thus the Religion of the Apostles may come in the event to mean anything or nothing.

2.

Here, then, we are arrived at the subject on which I mean to remark this evening. Protestants judge of the Apostles' doctrine by "texts," as they are commonly called, taken from Scripture, and nothing more ; and they judge of our doctrine too by " texts " taken from our writings, and nothing more. Picked verses, bits torn from the context, half sentences, are the warrant of the Protestant Idea, of what is Apostolic truth, on the one hand, and, on the other, of what is Catholic falsehood. As they have their chips and fragments of St. Paul and St. John, so have they their chips and fragments of Suarez and Bellarmine ; and out of the former they make to themselves their own Christian religion, and out of the latter our Antichristian superstition. They do not ask themselves sincerely, as a matter of fact and history, *What* did the Apostles teach then ? nor do they ask sincerely, and as a matter of fact, *What* do Catholics teach now ? they judge of the Apostles and they judge of us by scraps, and on these scraps they exercise their private judgment,—that is, their Prejudice, as I described two Lectures back, and their Assumed Principles, as I described in my foregoing Lecture ; and the process ends in their bringing forth, out of their scraps from the Apostles, what they call "Scriptural Religion," and out of their scraps from our theologians, what they call Popery.

The first Christians were a living body ; they were thousands of zealous, energetic men, who preached, disputed, catechized, and conversed from year's end to year's end. They spoke by innumerable tongues, with

one heart and one soul, all saying the same thing ; all
this multitudinous testimony about the truths of
Revelation, Protestants narrow down into one or two
meagre sentences, which at their own will and pleasure they select from St. Paul, and at their own will
and pleasure they explain, and call the Gospel. They
do just the same thing with us ; Catholics, at least,
have a lively illustration and evidence of the absurdity of Protestant private judgment as exercised on
the Apostolic writings, in the visible fact of its absurdity as exercised on themselves. They, as their
forefathers, the first Christians, are a living body ;
they, too, preach, dispute, catechize, converse with
innumerable tongues, saying the same thing as our
adversaries confess, all over the earth. Well, then,
you would think the obvious way was, if they would
know what we really teach, to come and ask us, to
talk with us, to try to enter into our views, and to
attend to our teaching. Not at all ; they do not
dream of doing so ; they take their " texts ; " they
have got their cut-and-dried specimens from our
divines, which the Protestant Tradition hands down
from generation to generation ; and, as by the aid of
their verses from Scripture, they think they understand the Gospel better than the first Christians, so,
by the help of these choice extracts from our works,
they think they understand our doctrine better than
we do ourselves. They will not allow us to explain
our own books. So sure are they of their knowledge,
and so superior to us, that they have no difficulty in
setting us right, and in accounting for our contradict-
ing them. Sometimes Catholics are " evasive and
shuffling," which, of course, will explain everything ;

sometimes they simply " have never been told what their creed really is ; " the priest keeps it from them, and cheats them ; as yet, too, perhaps they are " recent converts," and do not know the actual state of things, though they will know in time. Thus Protestants judge us by their " texts ; " and by " texts " I do not mean only passages from our writers, but all those samples of whatever kind, historical, ecclesiastical, biographical, or political, carefully prepared, improved, and finished off by successive artists for the occasion, which they think so much more worthy of credit and reliance as to facts, than us and our word, who are in the very communion to which those texts relate. Some good personal knowledge of us, and intercourse with us, not in the way of controversy or criticism, but what is prior—viz., in the way of sincere inquiry, in order to ascertain how things really lie, such knowledge and intercourse would be worth all the conclusions, however elaborate and subtle, from rumours, false witnessings, suspicions, romantic scenes, morsels of history, morsels of theology, morsels of our miraculous legends, morsels of our devotional writers, morsels from our individual members, whether unlearned or intemperate, which are the " text " of the traditional Protestant view against us. This, then, is the last of the causes, which in the course of these Lectures I shall assign, and on which this evening I shall insist, by way of accounting for the hatred and contempt shown towards the Catholics of England by their fellow-countrymen— viz., that the Catholics of England, as a body, are not personally known.

3.

I have already observed, that in matters of this world, when a man would really get information on a subject, he eschews reports, and mistrusts understandings, and betakes himself to head-quarters. The best letters and travels about a foreign people are tame and dead compared with the view he gains by residence among them ; and when that has continued for a sufficient time, he perceives how unreal were even those first impressions, which, on his arriving, were made upon him by the successive accidents of the hour. Knowledge thus obtained cannot be communicated to others ; it is imbibed and appropriated by the mind as a personal possession ; an idea of the people among whom he lives is set up within him ; he may like them or not, but his perception is real, and, if any one questions it, he need but appeal to the circumstance of his long residence in the country, and say he has a right to an opinion, which, nevertheless, he can perhaps but poorly and partially defend. He can but give his testimony, and must be believed on his reputation. And surely, if he has a fair name for powers of observation and good sense, he may be believed without proof. He has witnessed what others argue about. He has contemplated the national character in life and in action, as it is brought out in its opinions, aims, sentiments, and dispositions in the course of the day and the year ; he has heard the words, seen the deeds, watched the manners, breathed the atmosphere, and so caught the true idea of the people ;—in other words, he has mastered their Tradition. This is what Catholics mean by Tradition,

and why they go so much by it. It does not *prove*
our doctrines to the man in question, but it will tell
him, in a way no other informant can tell him, *what*
our doctrines are. It has a substance and a reality
peculiar to itself; for it is not a sample or specimen of us merely, but it is we, our thinking, speaking, acting self; our principles, our judgments, our
proceedings. What we hold, what we do not hold,
what we like, what we hate, cannot all be written
down, whether by us or by others; you can have no
daguerreotype of intellect, affection, and will; at best
you have but a few bold strokes recorded for the benefit of others, according to the skill of the individual
artist. Those who write books about a people or a
school of men are hardly more than extempore
sketchers; or they paint from memory; if you would
have the real thing, what the men are, what they
think, what they do, close your books, take a ticket
by the first train, cross the Channel, plunge in among
them, drink them in. This is what is called painting
from the life, and what is here called life the Catholic calls Tradition, which eclipses and supersedes, when
and where it can be had, the amplest collection of
"texts" and extracts about our doctrine and polity
which was ever put together by the ablest of compilers.

Now let me quote some words of my own on this
subject, when I was a Protestant. As they are
written in controversy with Catholics, they are so
much more to my present purpose; especially as I
did not when I wrote them, see their bearing on the
point I am now insisting on. The passage is long,
but its appositeness may excuse it.

"We hear it said," I then observed, "that they [the

Catholics] go by Tradition ; and we fancy in consequence that there are a *certain definite number of statements ready framed and compiled*, which they profess to
have received from the Apostles. One may hear the
question sometimes asked, for instance, *where* their
professed Traditions are to be found, whether there is
any *collection* of them, and whether they are printed and
published. Now, though they would allow that the
Traditions of the Church are, in fact, contained in the
writings of her Doctors, still this question proceeds on
somewhat of a misconception of their real theory,which
seems to be as follows :—By tradition they mean the
whole system of faith and ordinances, which they have
received from the generation before them, and that
generation again from the generation before itself.
And in this sense undoubtedly we all go by Tradition
in matters of this world. Where is the corporation,
society,or fraternity of any kind,but has certain received
rules and understood practices, which are nowhere put
down in writing ? How often do we hear it said,
that this or that person has 'acted unusually ;' that
so and so ' was never done before ;' that it is 'against
rule,' and the like ; and then, perhaps, to avoid the
inconvenience of such irregularity in future, what was
before a tacit engagement is turned into a formal and
explicit order or principle. The need of a regulation
must be discovered before it is supplied ; and the virtual
transgression of it goes before its imposition. At this
very time, great part of the law of the land is administered under the sanction of such a Tradition : it is not
contained in any formal or authoritative code, it
depends on custom or precedent. There is no explicit
written law, for instance, simply declaring murder to

be a capital offence, unless, indeed, we have recourse to
the divine command in the ninth chapter of the book
of Genesis. Murderers are hanged by *custom*. Such
as this is the Tradition of the Church ; Tradition is
uniform custom. . It is silent, but it lives. It is
silent like the rapids of a river, before the rocks intercept it. It is the Church's . . habit of opinion and
feeling, which she reflects upon, masters and expresses,
according to the emergency. We see, then, the mistake
of asking for a complete collection of the Roman traditions ; as well might we ask for a collection of a man's
tastes and opinions on a given subject. Tradition in
its fulness is necessarily unwritten ; it is the mode in
which a society has felt or acted, during a certain
period, and it cannot be circumscribed, any more than
a man's countenance and manner can be conveyed to
strangers in any set of propositions." [1]

I see nothing to alter in these remarks, written many
years before I became a Catholic ; and you see with what
force they tell against the system of judging any body
of men by extracts, passages, specimens, and sayings—
nay, even by their documents, if these are taken by us
to be sufficient informants, instead of our studying the
living body itself. For instance, there has been lately
a good deal of surprise expressed in some quarters,
though it is not likely to have attracted your attention,
that the infallibility of the Church has never been
decreed, whether in General Council or by other ecclesiastical authority, to be a Catholic doctrine. This has
been put about as a discovery, and an important one :
and Catholics have been triumphantly asked, how it is
that the tenet which is at the bottom of their whole

[1] Prophetical Office, Lecture I. pp. 38—41.

system is nowhere set down in writing and propounded
for belief. But, in truth, there is neither novelty nor
importance in the remark : on the one hand, it has
been made again and again ;[2] and on the other, whenever it has been urged against us, it has been simply
urged from ignorance, as I have already shown you, of
the real state of the case. Is nothing true but what
has been written down? on the contrary, the whole
Catholic truth has ever lived, and only lived, in the
hearts and on the tongues of the Catholic people ; and,
while it is one mistake in the objectors in question, to
think that they know the Catholic faith, it is a second,
to think that they can teach it to Catholics. Which
party is more likely to be in possession of whatCatholics
believe, they or we? There is a maxim commonly
accepted, that " Every one is to be trusted in his own
art ; " from which it would follow, that, as Frenchmen
are the best masters of French, and pilots the best
steersmen on the river, Catholics ought to know Catholicism better than other men. Military men do not show
particular respect for the criticisms of civilians. As
for amateur physicians, I suppose most of us would
rather be doctored by the village nurse, who blindly
goes by tradition and teaching, than by a clever person,
who, among other things, has dabbled in family vade-
mecums and materia-medicas, abounds in theories and
views, and has a taste for experiments. Again, I have
heard able men, who were not lawyers, impugn the
institution of Trial by Jury ; and the answer to them
has been, " You are not learned in the law, it works

[2] *E.g.* By myself, though not in objection, in the work above quoted,
Lecture X. p. 293. By Cressy, in Dr. Hammond's Works, vol. ii. p. 635,
two centuries ago.

well." In like manner, a great statesman says of
Protestant Clergymen, that they "understand least
and take the worst measure of human affairs, of all
mankind that can write and read." Yet any one is
thought qualified to attack or to instruct a Catholic in
matters of his religion ; a country gentleman, a navy
captain, a half-pay officer, with time on his hands,
never having seen a Catholic, or a Catholic ceremonial,
or a Catholic treatise, in his life, is competent, by
means of one or two periodicals and tracts, and a set of
Protestant extracts against Popery, to teach the Pope
in his own religion, and refute a Council.

4

Suarez, Vasquez, de Lugo, Lambertini, St. Thomas,
St. Buonaventura, a goodly succession of folios on our
shelves ! You would think the doctrine would take
some time to master, which has occupied the lives and
elicited the genius of some of the greatest masters of
thought whom the world has known. Our Protestant,
however, is sure there must be very little in such works,
because they are so voluminous. He has not studied
our doctrines, he has not learned our terms ; he calls
our theological language jargon, and he thinks the
whole matter lies in a nutshell. He is ever mistaking
one thing for another, and thinks it does not signify.
Ignorance in his case is the mother, not certainly of
devotion, but of inconceivable conceit and preternatural
injustice. If he is to attack or reply, up he takes the
first specimen or sample of our doctrine, which the
Reformation Society has provided, some dreadful sentiment of the Jesuit Bellarmine, or the Schoolman Scotus.
He has never turned to the passage in the original

work, never verified it, never consulted the context, never construed its wording ; he blindly puts his own sense upon it, or the " authorized version " given to it by the Society in question, and boldly presents it to the British public, which is forthwith just as much shocked at it as he is. Now, anything is startling and grotesque, if taken out of its place, and surveyed without reference to the whole to which it belongs. The perfection of the parts lies in their subserviency to a whole ; and they often have no meaning except in their bearing upon each other. How can you tell whether a thing is good or bad, unless you know what it is intended for ? Protestants, however, separate our statements from their occasions and their objects, and then ask what in the world can be their meaning or their use. This is evident to any one whose intellect is not fettered to his particular party, and who does but take the trouble to consider Catholic doctrines, not as they stand in Reformation Tracts, torn up by the roots or planted head-downwards, but as they are found in our own gardens. I am tempted to quote a passage on the subject from a recent Review, which is as far as possible from showing any leaning to Catholicism. You will see how fully an impartial writer, neither Catholic nor Protestant, bears me out in what I have said :—

" A true British Protestant," he says, " whose notions of ' Popery ' are limited to what he hears from an Evangelical curate, or has seen at the opening of a Jesuit church, looks on the whole system as an obsolete mummery, and no more believes that men of sense can seriously adopt it, than that they will be converted to the practice of eating their dinner with a Chinaman's chopsticks instead of the knife and fork. . . . . Few even of educated Englishmen have any suspicion of the depth and solidity of the Catholic dogma, its wide and various adaptation to wants ineffaceable from the human heart, its wonderful fusion of the supernatural into the natural life, its vast resources for a powerful hold upon the conscience. . . . . Into this interior view, however, the popular polemics neither give, nor have the slightest insight. . . . . It is not among the ignorant and vulgar, but among the intellectual and imaginative ; not by appeals to the senses in worship, but by consistency and subtlety of thought, that in our days converts will be made to the ancient Church. . . . . When a thoughtful man, accustomed to defer to historical authority, and competent to estimate moral theories as a whole, is led to penetrate beneath the surface, he is unprepared for the sight of so much speculative grandeur ; and if he has been a mere Anglican or Lutheran, is perhaps astonished into the conclusion that the elder system has the advantage in philosophy and antiquity alike." [3]

You see how entirely this able writer, with no sort of belief in Catholicism, justifies what I have been saying. Fragments, extracts, specimens, convey no idea to the world of what we are ; he who wishes to know us must condescend to study us. The Catholic doctrine is after all too great to be comfortably accommodated in a Protestant nutshell ; it cannot be surveyed at a glance, or refuted by a syllogism :—and what this author says of Catholic doctrine applies to Catholic devotion also. Last week I made some observations on our miracles; and I then said that they would be scorned and rejected, or not, according as this or that

[3] Westminster Review, Jan. 1851.

First Principle concerning them **was** taken for granted ; but now I **am** going to advance **a** step further.   I really think then, that, even putting aside First Principles, no one **can** read the lives of certain of our Saints, as St. Francis Xavier, or St. Philip Neri, with seriousness and attention, without rising up from the perusal,—I do not say converted to Catholicism (that is a distinct matter, which I have kept apart throughout these Lectures),— but indisposed to renew the ridicule and scorn in which he has indulged previously.   One isolated miracle looks strange, but many interpret each other : this or that, separated from the system of which they are a part, may be perfectly incredible ; but when they are viewed as portions of a whole, they press upon the inquirer a feeling, I do not say absolutely of conviction, but at least of wonder, of perplexity, and almost of awe. When you consider the vast number which are recorded, for instance, in the Life of St. Philip, their variety, their exuberance in a short space of time, the circumstantial exactness with which they are recorded, the diversity and multitude of witnesses and attestations which occur in the course of the narrative, the thought will possess you, even though you are not yet able to receive them, that after all fraud or credulity is no sufficient account of them.   No skill could invent so many, so rapidly, so consistently, and so naturally ; and you are sensible, **and** you confess, that, whatever be the truth of the matter, you have not got to the bottom of it.   You have ceased to contemn, you have learned to respect.

5.

And so again I would say of any book which lets **you** into the private life of personages who have had any great deal to do with the government of the Church ; which brings you, so to say behind the scenes, where all pretence is impossible, and where men appear what they are : it is simply impossible, or at least it would be as good as a miracle, for any one to study such works,and still consider that the Pope was the man of sin, and the Mother of Saints a Jezebel. You see that Popes and Cardinals and Prelates are not griffins and wiverns, but men ; good men, or bad men, or neither one nor the other, as the case may be ; bold men, or weak men, worldly men or unworldly, but still men. They have human feelings, human affections, human virtues, human anxieties, human hopes and joys, whatever higher than mere human excellence a Catholic of course would ascribe to them. They are no longer, as before, the wild beasts, or the frogs, or the locusts, or the plagues of the Apocalypse ; such a notion, if you have ever entertained it, is gone for ever. You feel it to have been a ridiculous illusion, and you laugh at it. For instance, I would take such a book as Cardinal Pacca's Memoirs of Pope Pius the VIIth's captivity. Here is a book of facts : here is a narrative, simple and natural. It does not give you the history of an absolute hero or of a saint ; but of a good, religious, holy man, who would have rather died any moment than offend God ; who had an overpowering sense of his responsibility, and a diffidence in his own judgment which made him sometimes err in his line of conduct. Here, too, is vividly brought out before you what we mean by Papal infallibility, or rather what we do not mean by it : you see how the Pope was open to any mistake, as others may be, in his own person, true as it is, that whenever he spoke *ex cathedrâ* on subjects of revealed truth, he spoke as its divinely-ordained expounder. It is difficult to bring this home to you by any mere extracts from such a work ; and I shall be perhaps falling into the very fault I am exposing if I attempt to do so ; yet I cannot refrain asking you candidly, whether passages such as the following can be said to fit in with the received Protestant Tradition of the Pope, as a sort of diabolical automaton, spouting out sin and wickedness by the necessity of his nature.

When Pope Pius and Cardinal Pacca were carried off by the French from Rome, as they sat in the carriage, " The Pope," says the Cardinal, " a few minutes afterwards, asked me whether I had with me any money : to which I replied, ' Your holiness saw that I was arrested in your own apartments, so that I have had no opportunity of providing myself.' We then both of us drew forth our purses, and, notwithstanding the state of affliction we were in at being thus torn away from Rome, and all that was dear to us, we could hardly compose our countenances on finding the contents of each purse to consist, in that of the Pope of one papetto (about 10*d*.), and in mine three grossi (7½*d*.). Thus the Sovereign of Rome and his Prime Minister set forth upon their journey, literally, without figure of speech or metaphor, in true Apostolic style, conformable with the precept of our Saviour addressed to His disciples. ' Take nothing for your journey, neither staves, nor scrip, neither bread, neither money ; neither have two coats apiece.' We were without eatables, and we had no clothes except those we wore, not even a shirt ; and the habits, such as they were, were most inconvenient for travelling. . . . . With regard to money, we had precisely thirty-five baiocchi (halfpence) between us. The Pope, extending his hand, showed his papetto to General Radet, saying at the same time, 'Look here ; this is all I possess, all that remains of my principality.' " [4]

Or take again the account of the Pontiff's conduct after having been betrayed into signing the unhappy Concordat with Napoleon. " The Pope, so long as the Emperor remained at Fontainebleau, manifested no outward appearance of the feelings that agitated his heart with regard to what had happened ; but so soon as Napoleon was gone, he fell into a state of profound despondency, and was attacked by fever. Conversing with the Cardinals . . . and discussing the subject of the articles to which he had just affixed his signature, he at once saw, by the undisguised expression of their countenances, the fatal consequences likely to be the fruit of that ill-advised deed, and became so horror-struck and afflicted in consequence, that for several days he abstained from the celebration of the holy sacrifice, under the impression that he had acted unworthily. . . . . Perceiving the general disapprobation, and, as it were, shudder of the public mind among all religious, well-conducted persons, he fell into that hopeless state of deep 'melancholy, which I before attempted to describe, on the occasion of my arrival at Fontainebleau." [5] " At first sight of the Holy Father, I was thoroughly shocked and astonished to see how pale and emaciated he had become, how his body was bent, how his eyes were fixed and sunk in his head, and how he looked at me

[4] Head's Pacca, vol. i. p. 157.   [5] Ibid. vol. ii. p. 143.

with, as it were, the glare of a man grown stupid. . . . .
The solitude and silence of the place, the expression
of sadness that appeared on every countenance, added
to the recent spectacle of profound grief I had witnessed in the person of the Pope, and, above all, the
unexpectedly cold reception I had experienced from
his Holiness, occasioned me a degree of surprise, and
a sorrowful compression of heart, that it is far more
easy for an indifferent person to imagine than for
myself to describe. . . He was . . overwhelmed by a
depression of spirits the most profound, so much so,
that in the course of speaking to me of what had happened, he frequently broke forth in the most plaintive
ejaculations, saying, among many other similarly in-
terjectional expressions, that the thought of what had
been done tormented him continually, that he could
not get it out of his mind, that he could neither rest
by day nor sleep by night; that he could not eat
more than barely sufficient to sustain life." [6]

Then observe the difference after he had retracted
the deed which distressed him so much, though at the
very time he was anticipating the utmost fury of
Napoleon in consequence, whose prisoner he was.
" There suddenly appeared in his person and countenance an unexpected alteration.   Previously, the
profound grief in which, as I have before stated, he
was continually immersed, was consuming him day
by day, and was deeply imprinted on his features,
which now, on the contrary, became all at once
serene, and, as he gradually recovered his usual gaiety
of spirits, were occasionally animated by a smile.
Neither did he any longer complain of loss of appe-

[6] Head's Pacca, vol. i. p. 406.

tite, or of the inquietude and agitation that every
night, for a considerable time before, had interrupted
his repose."[7]

These passages put one in mind of the beautiful
legend contained in the Breviary of a far greater fault,
the fault of Pope Marcellinus. "In the monstrous
Diocletian persecution," says the Lesson, "Marcellinus, overcome with terror, sacrificed to the idols of
the gods; for which sin he soon conceived so great repentance, that he came in sackcloth to Sinuessa, to a
full council of Bishops, where, with abundant tears,
he openly confessed his crime. Whom, however,
none dare condemn, but all with one voice cried out,
'Thy own mouth, not our judgment, be thy judge, for
the first See is judged by none. Peter, too, by a like
infirmity of mind, failed, and by like tears obtained
pardon from God.' Then he returned to Rome, went to
the Emperor, severely reproached him for tempting him
to that impiety, and with three others was beheaded."

Popes, then, though they are infallible in their office,
as Prophets and Vicars of the Most High, and though
they have generally been men of holy life, and many
of them actually saints, have the trials, and incur the
risks of other men. Our doctrine of infallibility means
something very different from what Protestants think
it means. And so again, all the inconsistencies which
they think they find in what we teach of the sanctity of
the Priesthood compared with the actual conduct of a
portion of the members of it, would vanish, if they
understood that a priest, in a Catholic sense, as in St.
Paul's sense, is one "who can have compassion on the
ignorant, and on them that err, *for that he himself also*

[7] Head's Pacca, vol. ii. p. 187.

is encompassed with infirmity." Yet, strange to say, so little are they aware of our real doctrine on the subject, that even since these Lectures began, it has been said to me in reference to them in print, " A vulgar error in your Church is, that the Priests are so divinely protected that one of them can hardly err, can hardly sin. This notion is now at an end, as far as you are concerned." Most marvellous! This writer's idea, and the idea of most Protestants is, that we profess that all Priests are angels, but that really they are all devils. No, neither the one nor the other ; if these Protestants came to us and asked, they would find that we taught a far different doctrine—viz., that Priests were mortal men, who were intrusted with high gifts for the good of the people, that they might err as other men, that they would fall if they were not watchful, that in various times and places large numbers had fallen, so much so, that the Priesthood of whole countries had before now apostatized, as happened in great measure in England three centuries ago, and that at all times there was a certain remnant scattered about of priests who did not live up to their faith and their profession ; still that, on the whole, they had been, as a body, the salt of the earth and the light of the world, through the power of divine grace, and that thus, in spite of the frailty of human nature, they had fulfilled the blessed purposes of their institution.

But not in one or two points merely, but in everything we think and say and do, as Catholics, were we but known, what a reformation would there not at once follow in the national mind in respect to us! British fair dealing and good sense would then recover their supremacy; and Maria Monks and Teodores would find their occupation gone. We should hear no more of the laity being led blindfold, of their being forced to digest impossibilities under menace of perdition, of their struggles to get loose continually overmastered by their superstition, and of their heart having no part in their profession. The spectres of tyranny, hypocrisy, and fraud would flit away with the morning light. There would be no more dread of being burned alive by Papists, or of the gutters overflowing with Protestant blood. Dungeons, racks, pulleys, and quick-lime would be like the leavings of a yesterday's revel. Nor would the political aims and plots and intrigues, so readily imputed to us, seem more substantial; and though I suppose, there is lying, and littleness, and overreaching, and rivalry, to be found among us as among other sons of Adam, yet the notion that we monopolized these vile qualities, or had more than our share of them, would be an exploded superstition. This indeed would be a short and easy way, not of making Protestants Catholics, but of reversing their ridiculous dreams about us,—I mean, if they actually saw what they so interminably argue about. But it is not to be:—first comes in the way that very love of arguing and of having an opinion, to which my last words have alluded. Men would be sorry indeed that the controversy should be taken from the region of argument and transferred to that of fact. They like to think as they please; and as they would by no means welcome St. Paul, did he come from heaven to instruct them in the actual meaning of his "texts" in Romans iii. or Galatians ii., so they would think it a hardship to be told that they must not go on maintaining and proving, that we were really what their eyes then would testify we were not. And then, too, dear scandal and romancing put in their claim ; how would the world go on, and whence would come its staple food and its cheap luxuries, if Catholicism were taken from the market ? Why it would be like the cotton crop failing, or a new tax put upon tea. And then, too, comes prejudice, " like the horseleech, crying, Give, give : " how is prejudice to exist without Catholic iniquities and enormities? prejudice, which could not fast for a day, which would be in torment inexpressible, and call it Popish persecution, to be kept on this sort of meagre for a Lent, and would shake down Queen and Parliament with the violence of its convulsions, rather than it should never suck a Catholic's sweet bones and drink his blood any more.

Prejudice and hatred, political party, animosities of race and country, love of gossip and scandal, private judgments, resentments, sensitive jealousies, these, and a number of bad principles besides, extending through the country, present an almost insuperable obstacle to our obtaining a fair hearing and receiving a careful examination. There are other feelings, too, not wrong, as I would trust, in which before now I have participated myself, but equally drawing a *cordon* between Catholics and the rest of the population. One, for instance, is the motive frequently influencing those who really feel a great drawing towards the Catholic Church, though they are unable to accept her doctrines ; and who, wishing to act, not by affection or liking or fancy, but by reason, are led to dread lest the impulses of love, gratitude, admiration, and devotion which they feel within them, should overcome in their hearts the claims of truth and justice, and decide the matter peremptorily for them, if they subjected themselves to an intercourse with Catholics. And another consideration weighs with such Protestants as are in a responsible situation in their own communion, or are its ministers and functionaries. These persons feel that while they hold office in a body which is at war with Catholics, they are as little at liberty to hold friendly intercourse with them, even with the open avowal of their differing from them in serious matters, as an English officer or a member of Parliament may lawfully correspond with the French Government during a time of hostilities. These various motives, and others besides, better and worse, are, I repeat, almost an insuperable barrier in the way of any real and familiar intercourse between Protestants and ourselves : and they act, in consequence, as the means of perpetuating what may be considered the chief negative cause, and the simplest explanation of the absurdities so commonly entertained about us by all classes of society. Personal intercourse, then, being practically just as much out of the question with us, as with the Apostles themselves or the Jewish prophets, Protestantism has nothing left for it, when it would argue about us, but to have recourse, as in the case of Scripture, to its "texts," its chips, shavings, brickbats, potsherds, and other odds and ends of the Heavenly City, which form the authenticated and ticketed specimens of what the Catholic Religion is in its great national Museum.

6.

I am complaining of nothing which I do not myself wish to avoid in dealing with my opponents. I wish them to be judged by their traditions ; and in these Lectures I have steadily kept in view the Elizabethan Tradition, and wished to consider it the centre and the life of all they say and do. If I select their words or their acts, I wish to throw myself into them, and determine what they mean by the light of this informing principle. And I have means of doing so which many others have not, having been a Protestant myself. I have stood on their ground ; and would always aim at handling their arguments, not as so many dead words, but as the words of a speaker in a particular state of mind, which must be experienced, or witnessed, or explored, if it is to be understood. Calvin, for instance, somewhere calls his own doctrine, that souls are lost without their own free will by the necessity of divine predestination, horrible ; at least, so he is said to do, for I do not know his writings myself. Now I conceive he never can really say this ; I conceive he uses the Latin word in the sense of fearful or awful, and that to make him say "horrible" is the mere unfairness of some Lutheran adversary, who will not enter into his meaning. This is to go by the letter, not by the spirit ; by the text, not by the tradition. The lawyers, again, as I noticed in my first Lecture, speak of the "Omnipotence of Parliament ;" I never will be so unjust to them as to take them literally. I am perfectly sure that it never entered into the head of any Speaker, or Prime Minister, or Serjeant-at-arms, to claim any superhuman prerogative for the Two Houses. Those officials all feel intensely, I am sure, that they are but feeble and fallible creatures, and would laugh at any one who shuddered at their use of a phrase which has a parliamentary sense as well as a theological. Now I only claim to be heard in turn with the same candour which I exemplify so fully, when I speak myself of the omnipotence of the Blessed Virgin. When such an expression is used by a Catholic, he would be as indignant as a member of Parliament to find it perverted by an enemy from the innocent sense in which he used it. Parliament is omnipotent, as having the power to do what it will, not in France, or in Germany, or in Russia, much less all over the earth, much less in heaven, but within the United Kingdom ; and in like manner the Blessed Virgin is called omnipotent, as being able to gain from God what she desires by the medium of prayer. Prayer is regarded as omnipotent in Scripture, and she in consequence, as being the chief intercessor among creatures, is considered omnipotent too. And the same remark applies to a great number of other words in Catholic theology. When the Church is called " holy," it is not meant that her authorities are always good men, though nothing is more common with Protestants than so to suppose. " Worship," again, is another term which is commonly misunderstood ; " indulgence " is another ; " merit," " intention," " scandal," " religion," " obedience," all have their own senses, which our opponents must learn from Catholics, and cannot well find out for themselves.

I have a good old woman in my eye, who, to the great amusement of all hearers, goes about saying that her priest has given her " absolution for a week ;" what a horrid story for Exeter Hall ! Here is a poor creature, with one foot in the grave, who is actually assured by her confessor, doubtless for some due pecuniary consideration, that for a week to come she may commit any sort of enormity to which she is inclined with impunity. Absolution for a week ! then it seems, she has discounted, if I may so speak, her prospective confessions, and may lie, thieve, drink, and swear for a whole seven days with a clear conscience! But now what does she really mean? I defy a Protestant to get the meaning out of the words, even if he wished to be fair ; he must come to us for it. She means, then, that she has leave to communicate for a week to come, on her usual days of communion, whatever be their number, without coming to confession before each day. But how can her words have this meaning ? in this way, as you know, my Brothers, well. Catholics are not bound to come to confession before communion, unless they have committed some greater sin ; nor are they commonly advised by their priests to come every time, though they often do so. When, then, she said she had got absolution for a week, she meant to express, that the priest had told her that her once going to confession would be often enough, for all her days of communion, during a week to come, supposing (which was not to be expected in so pious a woman) she fell into no great sin. You see how many words it takes duly to unfold the meaning of one familiar expression.

This instance of Popish profligacy has not yet got into the Protestant prints ; but there are others, not unlike it, which before now have made a great noise in the world. I will give you an instance of a mistake, not, indeed, as to a colloquialism, but as to the force of a technical phrase. When forms are often repeated, at length they are shortened ; every schoolboy knows this in learning geometry, where at first every word of the process of proof is supplied with formal exactness, and then, as the treatise advances, the modes of expressions are abbreviated. Many of our familiar words are abbreviations of this sort ; such is an "omnibus ;" again, a "stage," in the sense of a stage-coach ; we talk of the "rail," when we mean the "rail-road ;" we speak of "laying the table" for dinner, when we mean "laying the cloth on the table ;" and a king's levy properly means his "rising in the morning," but is taken to mean his showing himself to his nobles and others who come to pay him their respects. So again, innkeepers paint up, "Entertainment for man and horse ;" they do not add the important words, "to those who can pay for it." Every other private house in our streets has "Ring the bell" upon its door ; that is, "if you have business within." And so, again, in Catholicism the word "penance," which properly means repentance, often stands for the punishment annexed to the repentance, as when we talk of the imposition of "penances." Now, in like manner, as to Indulgences, "to absolve from sin" sometimes means one of two things quite distinct from real absolution. First, it may mean nothing else but to remit the *punishment* of sin ; and next, it may mean to absolve *externally* or to *reconcile* to the Church, in the sense in which I explained the phrase in a previous Lecture.[8] Here, however, I am going to speak of the phrase in the former of these two senses—viz., as the remission of the *punishment* remaining *after* pardon of the sin. This is an indulgence ; indulgence never is *absolution* or pardon itself. At the same time it is quite certain that, as far as words go, Indulgences have sometimes been drawn up in such a form as conveys to a Protestant reader the idea of real absolution, which they always presuppose and never convey. To a person who is not pardoned

[8] In Lecture III. This sense, however, is unusual ; *vide* Ferraris, Biblioth., art. Indul., App. § 6.

(and pardoned he cannot be without repentance), an Indulgence does no good whatever; an Indulgence supposes the person receiving it to be already absolved and in a state of grace, and then it remits to him the punishment which remains due to his past sins, whatever they are; but that this is really the meaning, a Protestant will as little gather from the form of words in which it has been sometimes drawn up, as he would gather from the good old soul's words cited just now, that "absolution" means "leave to go to communion." If Protestants will not take their information from Catholics on points such as this, but are determined to judge for themselves and to insist on the letter, there is no help for it.

And the same remark in a measure applies to another expression to be found in Indulgences. In Tetzel's famous form at the beginning of the Reformation, we read as follows:—"Shouldest thou not presently die, let this grace remain in full force, and avail thee at the point of death." On this Dr. Waddington, ordinarily a cautious as well as candid writer, observes, "[It cannot] be disputed that it conferred an entire absolution, not only from all past, but also from all future sins. It is impossible with any shadow of *reason* to affix any other meaning to the conclud-ing paragraph,"[9]—which is the one I have quoted. Reason; how can reason help you here? could you have found out that "absolution" meant "leave for communion" by reason? Some things are determined by reason, others by sense, and others by testimony. We go to dictionaries for information of one kind, and to gazetteers for information of another

<hr />

[9] Reformation, vol. i. p. 27.

kind. No one discovers the price of stocks, ministerial measures, or the fashions of the new year, by reason. Whatever is spontaneous, accidental, variable, self-dependent, whatever is objective, we must go out of ourselves to determine. And such, among other instances, is the force of language, such the use of formulas, such the value of theological terms. You learn pure English by reading classical authors and mixing in good society. Go then to those with whom such terms are familiar, who are masters of the science of them, and they will read the above sentence for you, not by reason, but by the usage of the Church; and they will read it thus:—
"If thou diest not now, but time hence, this Indulgence will then avail thee, in the hour of death, that is, provided thou art then in a state of *grace*."

There is no prospective pardon in these words so explained; an Indulgence has nothing to do with pardon; it presupposes pardon; it is an additional remission upon and after pardon, being the remission of the arrears of suffering due from those who are already pardoned. If on receipt of this Indulgence the recipient rushed into sin, the benefit of the Indulgence would be at least suspended, till he repented, went to confession, gained a new spirit, and was restored to God's favour. If he was found in this state of pardon and grace at the point of death, then it would avail him at the point of death. Then, that pardon which his true repentance would gain him in the sacrament of penance, would be crowned by the further remission of punishment through the Indulgence, certainly not otherwise. If, however, a controversialist says that an ordinary Catholic cannot possibly understand all this, that is a question of fact, not of reason ; it does not stand to reason that he cannot : reason does not come in here. I do not say that an ordinary layman *will* express himself with theological accuracy, but he knows perfectly well that an Indulgence is no pardon for prospective sin, that it is no standing pardon for a state of sin. If you think he does not, come and see. That is my key-note from first to last ; come and see, instead of remaining afar off, and judging by reason.

7.

There are Protestant books explaining difficult pas-sages of the Old Testament by means of present manners and customs among the Orientals ; a very sensible proceeding, and well deserving of imitation by Protestants in the case before us : let *our* obscure words and forms be interpreted by the understand-ings and habits of the Catholic people. On the other hand, in Dean Swift's well-known tale, you have an account of certain philosophers of Laputa, who car-ried their head under their arm. These sagacious persons seldom made direct use of their senses, but acted by reason ; a tailor for instance, who has to measure for a suit of clothes, I think, is described, not as taking out his measures, but his instruments, quadrant, telescope, and the like. He measured a man as he would measure a mountain or a bog ; and he ascertained his build and his carriage as he might determine the right ascension of Sirius or the revolu-tion of a comet. It is but a vulgar way to handle and turn about the living subject who was before him ; so our Laputan retreated, pulled out his theodolite in-

stead of his slips of parchment, and made an observation from a distance. It was a grand idea to make
a coat by private judgment and a theodolite; and
depend upon it, when it came home it did not fit.
Our Protestants wield the theodolite too; they keep
at a convenient distance from us, take the angles, calculate the sines and cosines, and work out an algebraic process, when common sense would bid them
ask us a few questions. They observe latitude and
longitude, the dip of the needle, the state of the
atmosphere; our path is an orbit, and our locus is
expressed by an equation. They communicate with
us by gestures, as you talk to the deaf and dumb; and
they are more proud of doing something, right or
wrong, by a ceremony of this kind which is their
own doing, than of having the learning of the Benedictines or the Bollandists, if they are to go to school
for it.

Open their tracts or pamphlets at random, and you
will not have long to look for instances;—a priest is
told one afternoon that a parishioner wishes to go to
confession. He breaks off what he is doing, disappointed, perhaps, at the interruption, rushes into
church, takes up his stole, and turns his ear towards
his penitent. It is altogether a matter of routine
work with him, with a lifting up indeed of the heart
to his Maker and Lord, but still a matter too familiar to make any great impression on him, beyond that
of his knowing he is called to a serious duty, which he
must discharge to the best of his ability. A Scripture reader, or some such personage, opens the door,
and peeps in; he perceives what is going on, and
stands gazing. What is his comment? I wish I had

kept the paragraph, as I read it; but it was to this effect,— " I saw a priest with a poor wretch at his feet —how like a god he looked!" Can anything, my Brothers, be more unreal, more fantastic? Yet all this comes of standing gazing at the door.

How many are the souls, in distress, anxiety or loneliness, whose one need is to find a being to whom they can pour out their feelings unheard by the world? Tell them out they must; they cannot tell them out to those whom they see every hour. They want to tell them and not to tell them; and they want to tell them out, yet be as if they be not told; they wish to tell them to one who is strong enough to bear them, yet not too strong to despise them; they wish to tell them to one who can at once advise and can sympathize with them; they wish to relieve themselves of a load, to gain a solace, to receive the assurance that there is one who thinks of them, and one to whom in thought they can recur, to whom they can betake themselves, if necessary, from time to time, while they are in the world. How many a Protestant's heart would leap at the news of such a benefit, putting aside all distinct ideas of a sacramental ordinance, or of a grant of pardon and the conveyance of grace! If there is a heavenly idea in the Catholic Church, looking at it simply as an idea, surely, next after the Blessed Sacrament, Confession is such. And such is it ever found in fact,—the very act of kneeling, the low and contrite voice, the sign of the cross hanging, so to say, over the head bowed low, and the words of peace and blessing. Oh what a soothing charm is there, which the world can neither give nor take away! Oh what piercing, heart-subduing tranquillity, provoking tears of joy, is poured, almost substantially and physically upon the soul, the oil of gladness, as Scripture calls it, when the penitent at length rises, his God reconciled to him, his sins rolled away for ever! This is confession as it is in fact; as those bear witness to it who know it by experience; what is it in the language of the Protestant? His language is, I may say, maniacal; listen to his ravings, as far as I dare quote them, about what he knows just as much of as the blind know of colours: " If I could follow my heart wherever it would go," he cries about the priest, " I would go into his dark and damnable confessional, where my poor Roman Catholic countrymen intrust their wives and daughters to him, under the awful delusion of false religion; and, while the tyrant is pressing his . . infernal investigation, putting the heart and feeling of the helpless creature on the moral rack, till she sink enslaved and powerless at his feet, I would drag the victim forth in triumph from his grasp, and ring in the monster's ear, No Popery!"

These are the words of a fanatic; but grave, sober men can in their own way say things quite as absurd, quite as opprobrious. There is a gentleman,[1] who, since these Lectures began, has opened a public correspondence with me; I quoted from him just now.[2] One of his principal points, to which he gave his confident adhesion, was this, that at least one in twelve of our Priests in large towns doubts or disbelieves. How did he prove it? A conscientious person does

[1] Mr. Seely, the reputed author of several able works. The wider his name and his charge against us are circulated, the better for the cause of truth. Neither the one nor the other should be hushed up.

[2] P. 339.

not advance grave charges against others, much less the gravest possible, without the best of reasons. Even to think ill of others, without sufficient cause, is in a Catholic's estimation, an offence: but to speak out to the world a proposition such as this, distinctly to accuse his neighbour of the worst of crimes, is either a great duty or a great sin. The proof, too, should be proportionate to the imputation. And that the more, because ne went further than I have yet said: he actually singled out a place; he named Birmingham, and he insinuated that such infidels or sceptics were found among the priests of this very town. Well, then, we must suppose he speaks on the best authority; he has come to Birmingham, he knows the priests, he has some distinct evidence. He accuses us of a sin which includes blasphemy, sacrilege, hypocrisy, fraud, and virtually immorality, besides its own proper heinousness, which is of the first order, and he must have, of course, reason for what he says. What then is his method of proof? simply the Laputan. He brandishes his theodolite, he proves us to be proud rebels against our God, and odious impostors toward men, by mathematics; he draws out a rule of three sum on paper, and leaves us to settle with it as we may. He argues, that, because France had a body of infidel priests in last century, who did *not* disguise themselves, because Spain had a knot of infidels who, for *fear* of the Inquisition, did, therefore now in England, where nothing is heard of infidelity, and where there is nothing to frighten it into *silence*, it exists in every large town. Moreover, because there were infidel priests in the special 18th century, therefore there are infidel priests in the 19th.

A a

Further, because there were in France fifty or sixty or a hundred infidels among 380,000 ecclesiastics, and a sprinkling in Spain among 125,000, that there are in England infidels now in the proportion of one to twelve. To this antecedent proof he added a few cases true or false, at home or abroad, which it was impossible to examine or refute, of a professedly recent date ; and on these grounds he ventured forth with his definite assertion, simply satisfied of its truth, its equity, and its charitableness.

And now for something, if not more wonderful, at least more observable still. After thus speaking, he was surprised I should consider it a "*charge*," and a charge against the priests of Birmingham. He complains, that is, that I have given a *personal* turn to his assertion. Ah, true, I ought to have remembered that Catholic priests, in the judgment of a good Protestant, are not persons at all. I had forgotten what I have already said in the First of these Lectures ; we are not men, we have not characters to lose, we have not feelings to be wounded, we have not friends, we have not penitents, we have not congregations ; we have nothing personal about us, we are not the fellow-creatures of our accusers, we are not gentlemen, we are not Christians, we are abstractions, we are shadows, we are heraldic emblazonments, we are the griffins and wiverns of the old family picture, we are stage characters with a mask and a dagger, we are mummies from Egypt or antediluvian ornithorhynchi, we are unresisting ninepins, to be set up and knocked down by every mischievous boy ; we are the John Doe and Richard Roe of the lawyers, the Titius and Bertha of the canonists, who come forth for every occasion, and

are to endure any amount of abuse or misfortune.
Did the figures come down from some old piece
of tapestry, or were a lion rampant from an inn door
suddenly to walk the streets, a Protestant would
not be more surprised than at the notion that we
have nerves, that we have hearts, that we have sensi-
bilities. For we are but the frogs in the fable ; " What
is your sport," they said to the truant who was
pelting them, " is our destruction ; " yes, it is our portion from the beginning, it is our birthright, though
not quite our destruction, to be the helots of the pride
of the world.

8.

But more remains to be said. It often may happen
in matters of research, not indeed when the rule of
charity comes in, but in philosophical subjects and the
like, that men are obliged to make use of indirect
reasonings, in default of testimony and fact. That
was not so here. There was evidence, to a considerable
extent, the other way. Now observe this, my Brothers.
You know how anxious the Protestant world is to get
hold of any priest who has left the Catholic body.
Why ? because he would tell them *facts* about it ;
certainly Protestants are not always indifferent about
facts : that is, when they hope they will tell against us.
Well, they go to this priest or that monk, who has
transferred himself to Protestantism, in order to get
all the information about us they can. Now are Protestantizing priests and monks the only evidence of
the kind which they could obtain on the subject ?
Frenchmen who come from France are evidence about
France ; but are not Englishmen who go to France
evidence too ? If some persons come from Rome, have

none gone to Rome? and have not they too something to offer in the way of evidence? Yes, surely, they have much to say about Catholic priests. It was offered by myself to the gentleman of whom I have been speaking; it was offered, and it was not accepted. He who could argue by wholesale from some mere instance of a Catholic priest who had become a Protestant, would learn nothing from the direct avowals of a Protestant who had become a Catholic Priest. The one was the pregnant germ of an arbitrary deduction, the other was no credible testimony to a matter of fact.

Now, my Brothers, I should not insist on all this, if it merely related to any personal matter of mine; but you see, it affords a very observable illustration of the point on which I am insisting—viz., that to know Catholics is the best refutation of what is said against them. You are aware, then, that a number of highly educated Protestants have of late years joined the Catholic Church. If their former co-religionists desired to have some real and good information what Catholics are like, they could not have better than that which these persons had to offer. They had belonged to a system which allowed of the largest private judgment, and they had made use of their liberty. They had made use of it first to reject the Protestantism of the day, and to recur back to another form of Protestantism which was in some repute two hundred years ago. Further, they used their liberty to attack the See of Rome, so firmly were they persuaded that the Popedom was not a divine institution. No one can say they did not enter into the feelings of suspicion and jealousy which Protestants entertain towards Rome. For myself, though I never, as I believe, spoke against individuals, I felt and expressed this deep suspicion about the system ; and it would be well indeed for Catholicism in this country, if every Protestant but studied it with a tenth part of the care which I have bestowed on the examination and expression of Protestant arguments and views. Well, the private judgment of these men went on acting, for a Protestant can have no guide but it ; and to their surprise, as time proceeded, they found it bringing them nearer to the Catholic Church, and at length it fairly brought them into it. What did Protestants say then? Why, they said that the same private judgment which had led them into the Catholic Church, would, in course of time, lead them out of it. They said, too, that these new Catholics, when they came to see what Catholics were like, would be unable to stop among them. Mind, they put it to this test ; this was their issue ; they left the decision of the question to the event ; they knew that the persons of whom they spoke were honest men ; they knew that they had given up a great deal to become Catholics ; they were sure that they would not take part in an imposition · and therefore they said, " Let them go, they will soon come back ; let them go to Rome itself, they are sure to be disgusted ; they will meet at Rome, and in France, and in England, and everywhere, infidel priests by the bushel, and will tire of their new religion. And besides, they will soon begin to doubt about it themselves ; their private judgment will not submit to all they will have to believe, and they will go out of Catholicism as they came into it."

You observe, then, my Brothers, that our testimony is not a common one, it has a claim to be heard ; it has been appealed to by anticipation, let it then be heard after the event.   There is no doubt that the whole Protestant world would have made a great deal of our dropping off from the Catholic body ; why, then, ought it not to be struck by the fact of our continuing in it, being dutiful and loyal to it, and finding our rest in it ?   You know perfectly well Protestants would have listened greedily, if we had left and borne witness against it ; why, then, ought they not in consistency to listen seriously when we glory in it, and bear witness for it ?   Who in the whole world are likely to be more trustworthy witnesses of the fact, whether or not one in twelve of our town priests disbelieves or doubts, than these converts, men of education, of intelligence, of independent minds, who have their eyes about them, who are scattered to and fro through all the country, who are, some of them, priests themselves ?   Is there anyone who knows us personally who will dare to say we are not to be believed, not to be trusted ? no : only those who know us not.   But so it is to be ; our evidence is to be put aside, and the Laputan method to carry the day.   Catholics are to be surveyed from without, not inspected from within : texts and formulas are to prevail over broad and luminous facts.   There is a story of a logician at some place of learning, who, as he was walking one evening past the public library, was hailed by an unfortunate person from one of its windows, who told him he had been locked in by mistake when it closed, and begged him to send to his relief the official who kept the keys. Our logician is said to have looked at him attentively, pronounced the following syllogism, and walked away : " No man can be in the library after 4 o'clock P.M. You are a man : therefore you are not in the library."

And thus Catholic priests are left duly locked up by Barbara or Celarent, because, forsooth, one grain of Protestant logic is to weigh more than cartloads of Catholic testimony.

9.

No, if our opponents would decide the matter by testimony, if they would submit their assertions to the ordeal of facts, their cause is lost ; so they prefer much to go by prejudices, arbitrary principles, and texts. Evidence they can have to satisfy for the asking ; but what boots it to pipe and sing to the deaf, or to convince the self-satisfied heart against its will ?   One there was who left the Protestant religion under circumstances different from any to which I have hitherto alluded. He never joined in the religious movement which has brought so many to the Church ; nay, he wrote against that movement ; he wrote, not in bitterness and contempt, as many have done, and do, but as a gentleman and a man of serious principle ; he wrote against myself. But, though he started from so different a point, he, too, came near the Church, he, too, entered it. He did so at a great sacrifice ; he had devoted a great part of his fortune to the building of a Protestant church. It was all but finished when the call came ; he rose and obeyed it, and had to leave his means of subsistence behind him, turned into stone. He came into the Catholic Church, and he remains a layman in it. See, then, here is a witness altogether different : ought not this to content our enemies ? or are the boys in the market-place still to cry to them, " We have piped to you, and you have not danced ; we have lamented, and you have not mourned " ? Are they suspicious of those who belonged to a certain movement before they became Catholics ? here is one who opposed it : are they suspicious of a convert priest ? here is a convert layman. Now, he happens, some years after his conversion, to have written an account of his experience of the Catholic Religion ; how many of our enemies have had the grace—I can use no lighter term—have had the grace to look into it ? Yet what possible reason can they give for having neglected to study and to profit by it ? It is the grave testimony of one, in whom, as in that illustrious witness of old in the heathen country, " no cause nor suspicion " can be found, " unless concerning the law of his God."

" I came," he says, and he shall conclude this Lecture for me, " forced by my convictions, and almost against my will, into this mighty community whose embrace I had all my life dreaded as something paralyzing, enslaving, and torturing. No sooner, however, could I look around me, and mark what presented itself to my eyes, than I saw that I was in a world where all was as satisfying as it was new. For the first time I met with a body of men and women who could talk and act as Christians, without cant, without restraint, without formality, without hypocrisy. After years and years of disappointment, in which the more deeply I saw into the hearts and lives of Protestants of every class, the more clearly I perceived that the religion they professed had *not* become their second nature, but was a thing put on, which did not fit them, which confined their movements, and gave them an outward look, while it was not wrought into the depth of their being,—after years and years of this disappointment, in which the contrast between the Bible, which they praised, and the spirit of their own lives, and the doctrines they preached, struck me more bitterly each succeeding day, at length I found myself in the midst of a race, with whom Christianity was not a rule, but a principle ; not a restraint, but a second nature ; not a bondage, but a freedom ; in which it had precisely that effect which it claims to produce upon man ; in which not a few hours, or an occasional day, was set apart for religion, but in which *life* was religious ; in which men spoke at all hours, and in all occupations, of religious things, naturally, as men speak of secular things in which they are deeply interested ; in which religious thoughts and short prayers were found not incompatible with the necessary duties and pleasures which fill up the road of existence ; and in which, the more deeply I was enabled to penetrate below the surface, the more genuine was the goodness which I found, and the more inexhaustible I perceived to be those treasures of grace, which Divine Goodness places at the disposal (so to say) of every soul that seeks them within this favoured communion.

" And now, when so long a period has elapsed since my first submission to the Church, that everything like a sense of novelty has long passed away, and I have tested experimentally the value of all that she has to offer ; now that I can employ her means of grace, and take a part in the working of her system, with all that ease and readiness which long practice alone can bestow ; the more profound is my sense of her divine origin, of the divine power which resides in her, and of the boundless variety and perfection of the blessings she has to bestow. The more I know her, the more complete do I perceive to be her correspondence to what she professes to be. She is exactly what the one Church of Christ is proclaimed to be in Scripture, and nothing less, and nothing more. . . . . Truly can I say with the patriarch, 'The Lord is in this place, and I knew it not. This is no other than the house of God, and the gate of heaven.' The Catholic Church *can* be nothing less than the spiritual body of Jesus Christ. Nothing less than that adorable Presence, before which the Angels veil their faces, can make her what she is to those who are within her fold. Argument is needed no longer. The scoffings of the infidel, the objections of the Protestant, the sneers of the man of the world, pass over their heads, as clouds over a mountain peak, and leave them calm and undisturbed, with their feet resting upon the Rock of ages. They *know* in whom they have believed. They have passed from speculation to action, and found that all is real, genuine, life-giving, and enduring. . . . . I know only one fear—the fear that my heart may be faithless to Him who has bestowed on me this unspeakable blessing ; I know only one mystery, which the more I think upon it, the more incomprehensible does it appear,—the mystery of that calling which brought *me* into this house of rest, while millions and millions are still driven to and fro in the turbulent ocean of the world, without rudder, and without compass, without helmsman and without anchor, to drift before the gale upon the fatal shore." [3]

[3] Capes's "Four Years' Experience of the Catholic Religion : Burns, London, 1849," pp. 92-95. Mr. Capes returned to the Anglican Church in 1870, on occasion, I believe, of the definition by the Vatican Council of the Pope's Infallibility, but that change does not invalidate his testimony to matters of fact [Ed. 1872].

LECTURE IX.[4]

DUTIES OF CATHOLICS TOWARDS THE PROTESTANT
VIEW.

In this concluding Lecture, my Brothers of the Oratory, I shall attempt, in as few words as possible, to sum up what I have been showing in those which preceded it, and to set before you what I have proposed to myself in the investigation.

You know, then, that at this time we are all in considerable anxiety, and some risk, as regards the future prospects of Catholicism in England. Open threats in the most influential quarters are put forward, as if we might even lose the rights of British subjects, and be deprived of the free exercise of our religion. There has been an attempt to put our convents, in the eye of the law, on a level with madhouses ; and one of the Anglican Prelates in Parliament has constituted himself judge whether the dimensions of our churches were sufficient or too large for the " accommodation," to use the Protestant word, of our people. A bill, too, has been passed, about which all of us know enough, without my having the trouble to give it any designation.

The duty of the Catholic Church is to preach to the

---

[4] Written in 1851 apropos of the events of that year.

world ; and her promise and prerogative is success in preaching ; but this is a subject which has not come into the scope of our discussions in this place. What I have been saying has no direct reference to any such end. I have not urged it on you, as I well might, in the case of those who, like you, love their religion so well that they wish others to enjoy the benefit of it with them. What I have said, however, does not presuppose this ; it has not sprung out of any duty that we have of extending the limits of the Catholic pale ; it would not have been superseded, if we had no such duty. I have not been aiming at the conversion of any persons, who are not Catholics, who have heard me : I have not been defending Catholic, or attacking Protestant doctrines, except indirectly and incidentally. The condition or hypothesis with which I have been entering into the discussion has been the present anti-Catholic agitation ; and my object has been that of self-defence with reference to it. In the present state of things Catholics must, from the mere instinct of self-preservation, look about them ; they are assailed by a very formidable party, or power, as I should rather call it, in this country, by its Protestantism. In the Protestantism of the country I do not include, of course, all who are not Catholics. By Protestants I mean the heirs of the Traditions of Elizabeth ; I mean the country gentlemen, the Whig political party, the Church Establishment, and the Wesleyan Conference. I cannot over-estimate their power : they and their principles are established : yet I should be unjust, on the other hand, to all classes in the community if I made this Elizabethan Protestantism synonymous with the mind and the philosophy of the whole country. However, it is a tremendous power, and we are menaced by it ; this is the condition of things ; what must we do ? put ourselves on the defensive ; this, then, has been my scope. I have not been aggressive, but on the defensive ; and what is the first step of those who are getting ready for their defence against a foe ? to reconnoitre him. It is simply this that I have been engaged upon in these Lectures.

This, I say, has been my object, a reconnoitring or survey of a strong and furious enemy, undertaken with a view to self-defence. And I report as follows :—

I.

I find he is in a very strong position, but that he takes a very incorrect view of us, and that this is his strength and our danger. Different from the case of actual warfare, in which ignorance is weakness, here ignorance is power ; and in truth he does know as little about us as well can be conceived. He has got old pictures and old maps made years and years ago, which have come down to him from his fathers ; and instead of deigning to look at us, and learn anything about us, he adheres to them as if it were a point of faith to do so. This was the subject of my first Lecture ; I showed that the English Elizabethan Protestant had a view of our monks, Jesuits, and Church, quite his own, unlike that of his more learned brethren abroad : and moreover, that he was apparently ignorant of the existence of any view besides it, or that it was possible for any sane man to doubt it, or any honest man to deny it. Next came the cause of this phenomenon, and it was this :—Protestantism is established in the widest sense of the word; its doctrine, religious, political, ecclesiastical, moral, is placed in exclusive possession of all the high places of the land. It is forced upon all persons in station and office, or almost all, under sanction of an oath ; it is endowed with the amplest estates, and with revenues supplied by Government and by chartered and other bodies. It has innumerable fine churches, planted up and down in every town, and village, and hamlet in the land. In consequence, everyone speaks Protestantism, even those who do not in their hearts love it ; it is the current coin of the realm. As English is the natural tongue, so Protestantism is the intellectual and moral language of the body politic. The Queen *ex officio* speaks Protestantism ; so does the court, so do her ministers. All but a small portion of the two Houses of Parliament; and those who do not are forced to apologize for not speaking it, and to speak as much of it as they conscientiously can. The Law speaks Protestantism, and the Lawyers ; and the State Bishops and clergy of course. All the great authors of the nation, the multitudinous literature of the day, the public press, speak Protestantism. Protestantism the Universities ; Protestantism the schools, high, and low, and middle. Thus there is an incessant, unwearied circulation of Protestantism all over the whole country, for 365 days in the year from morning till night ; and this, for nearly three centuries, has been almost one of the functions of national life. As the pulse, the lungs, the absorbents, the nerves, the pores of the animal body, are ever at their work, as that motion is its life, so in the political structure of the country there is an action of the life of Protestantism, constant and regular. It is a vocal life ; and in this consists its perpetuation, its reproduction. What it utters, it teaches, it propagates by uttering ; it is ever impressing itself, diffusing itself all around ; it is ever transmitting itself to the rising generation ; it is ever keeping itself fresh, and young, and vigorous, by the process of a restless agitation. This, then, is the elementary cause of the view which Englishmen are accustomed to take of Catholicism and its professors. They survey us in the light of their Tradition ; and this was the subject of my second Lecture.

Well, but you will ask, Have Catholics nothing to say for themselves ? yes, a great deal, but we have no opportunity of saying it. The public will not recognize us ; it interrupts and puts us down. Men close their ears and throw up dust in the air when we begin to speak : they close their eyes when we come forward, and begin pelting us at randon. Far less will they come near us, and ask us questions, and listen to our answers. This was the subject of my foregoing or eighth Lecture, in which I had not time to say nearly as much as I had intended. I could have shown you, how first, Protestants got rid of Catholicism from the kingdom as a worship ; how next the Catholics who remained they put under crushing laws ; how every priest who said mass or exercised any function on English ground was liable to perpetual imprisonment, and any foreign priest, who was subject to the crown of England, coming into England, was guilty of high treason, and all who harboured him, of felony. I could have told you how that converting or being converted to Catholicism was high treason ; how no Catholic was allowed to inherit or purchase land ; no Catholic could hear mass without fine and imprisonment ; no Catholic might keep school under pain of imprisonment for life ; nor might, in default of schools at home, send a child abroad for education, without forfeiting all his estates, goods, and chattels, and incurring a civil out-lawry ; moreover, how, if a Catholic did not attend the established worship, he was not allowed to come within ten miles of London, nor could travel five miles from home, or bring any action at law ; and how he might not be married or buried, or have his children baptized, by any but ministers of the Established Church. I am not quoting these laws with a view to expose their wholesale cruelty and tyranny, though I might well do so ; but in order to show you how impossible it was for Catholics to defend themselves, when they were denied even to speak. You see, the Protestant Tradition had it all its own way ; Elizabeth, and her great men, and her preachers, killed and drove away all the Catholics they could ; knocked down the remainder, and then at their leisure proved unanswerably and triumphantly the absurdity of Popery, and the heavenly beauty and perfection of Protestantism. Never did we undergo so utter and complete a refutation ; we had not one word to utter in our defence. When she had thus beaten the breath out of us, and made us simply ridiculous, she put us on our feet again, thrust us into a chair, hoisted us up aloft, and carried us about as a sort of Guy Faux, to show to all the boys and riff-raff of the towns what a Papist was like. Then, as if this were not enough, lest anyone should come and ask us any-thing about our religion, she and her preachers put it about that we had the plague, so that, for fear of a moral infection, scarce a soul had the courage to look at us, or breathe the same air with us.

This was a fair beginning for the Protestantizing

of the people, and everything else that was needed followed in due time, as a matter of course. Protestantism being taught everywhere, Protestant principles were taught with it, which are necessarily the very reverse of Catholic principles. The consequence was plain—viz.,that even before the people heard a Catholic open his mouth, they were forearmed against what he would say, for they had been taught this or that as if a precious truth, belief in which was *ipso facto* the disbelief and condemnation of some Catholic doctrine or other. When a person goes to a fever ward, he takes some essence with him to prevent his catching the disorder ; and of this kind are the anti-Catholic principles in which Protestants are instructed from the cradle. For instance, they are taught to get by heart without any sort of proof, as a kind of alphabet or spelling lesson, such propositions as these :—" miracles have ceased long ago ; " " all truth is in the Bible ; " " any one can understand the Bible ; " " all penance is absurd ; " " a priesthood is pagan, not Christian," and a multitude of others. These are universally taught and accepted, as if equally true and equally important, just as are the principles " it is wrong to murder or thieve," or " there is a judgment to come." When then a person sets out in life with these maxims as a sort of stock in trade in all religious speculations, and encounters Catholics, whose opinions hitherto he had known nothing at all about, you see he has been made quite proof against them, and unsusceptible of their doctrines, their worship, and their reasoning, by the preparation to which he has been subjected. He feels an instinctive repugnance to everything Catholic, by reason of these arbitrary principles, which he has been taught to hold, and which he thinks identical with reason. "What? you have priests in your religion," he says; "but do you not know, are you so behind the world as not to know, that priests are pagan, not Christian?" And sometimes he thinks that, directly he has uttered some such great maxim, the Catholic will turn Protestant at once, or, at least, ought to do so, and if he does not, is either dull or hypocritical. And so again, "You hold saints are to be invoked, but the practice is not in the Bible, and nothing is true that is not there." And again, "They say that in Ireland and elsewhere the priests impose heavy penances; but this is against common sense, for all penances are absurd." Thus the Protestant takes the whole question for granted on starting;—and this was the subject of my seventh Lecture.

This fault of mind I called Assumption or Theorizing; and another quite as great, and far more odious, is Prejudice; and this came into discussion in the sixth Lecture. The perpetual talk against Catholicism, which goes on everywhere, in the higher classes in literary circles, in the public press, and in the Protestant Church and its various dependencies, makes an impression, or fixes a stain, which it is continually deepening, on the minds which are exposed to its influence; and thus, quite independent of any distinct reasons and facts for thinking so, the multitude of men are quite certain that something very horrible is going on among Catholics. They are convinced that we are all but fiends, so that there is no doubt at all, even before going into the matter, that all that is said against us is true, and all that is said for us is false.

These, then, are the two special daughters, as they

may be called, of the Protestant Tradition, Theory or Assumption on the one hand, and Prejudice on the other,—Theory which scorns us, and Prejudice which hates us; yet, though coming of one stock, they are very different in their constitution, for Theory is of so ethereal a nature, that it needs nothing to feed upon; it lives on its own thoughts, and in a world of its own, whereas Prejudice is ever craving for food, victuals are in constant request for its consumption every day; and accordingly they are served up in unceasing succession, Titus Oates, Maria Monk, and Jeffreys, being the purveyors, and platform and pulpit speakers being the cooks. And this formed the subject of the third, fourth, and fifth Lectures.

Such, then, is Popular Protestantism, considered in its opposition to Catholics. Its truth is Establishment by law; its philosophy is Theory; its faith is Prejudice; its facts are Fictions; its reasonings Fallacies; and its security is Ignorance about those whom it is opposing. The Law says that white is black; Ignorance says, why not? Theory says it ought to be, Fallacy says it must be, Fiction says it is, and Prejudice says it shall be.

2.

And now, what are our duties at this moment towards this enemy of ours? How are we to bear ourselves towards it? what are we to do with it? what is to come of the survey we have taken of it? with what practical remark and seasonable advice am I to conclude this attempt to determine our relation to it? The lesson we gain is obvious and simple, but as difficult, you will say, as it is simple; for the means and the end are almost identical, and in executing the one we have already reached the other. Protestantism is fierce, because it does not know you; ignorance is its strength; error is its life. Therefore bring yourselves before it, press yourselves upon it, force yourselves into notice against its will. Oblige men to know you; persuade them, importune them, shame them into knowing you. Make it so clear what you are, that they cannot affect not to see you, nor refuse to justify you. Do not even let them off with silence, but give them no escape from confessing that you are not what they have thought you were. They will look down, they will look aside, they will look in the air, they will shut their eyes, they will keep them shut. They will do all in their power not to see you; the nearer you come, they will close their eyelids all the tighter; they will be very angry and frightened, and give the alarm as if you were going to murder them. They will do anything but look at you They are, many of them, half conscious they have been wrong, but fear the consequences of becoming sure of it; they will think it best to let things alone, and to persist in injustice for good and all, since they have been for so long a time committed to it; they will be too proud to confess themselves mistaken; they prefer a safe cruelty to an inconvenient candour. I know it is a most grave problem how to touch so intense an obstinacy, but, observe, if you once touch it, you have done your work. There is but one step between you and success. It is a steep step, but it is one. It is a great thing to know your aim, to be saved from wasting your energies in wrong quarters, to be able to concentrate them on a point. You have but to aim at making men look steadily at you;

when they do this, I do not say they will become Catholics, but they will cease to have the means of making you a by-word and a reproach, of inflicting on you the cross of unpopularity. Wherever Catholicism is known, it is respected, or at least endured, by the people. Politicians and philosophers, and the established clergy, would be against you, but not the people, if it knew you. A religion which comes from God approves itself to the conscience of the people, wherever it is really known.

I am not advocating, as you will see presently, anything rude in your bearing, or turbulent, or offensive; but first I would impress upon you the *end* you have to aim at. Your one and almost sole object, I say, must be, to make yourselves known. This is what will do everything for you: it is what your enemies will try by might and main to hinder. They begin to have a suspicion that Catholicism, known to be what it really is, will be their overthrow. They have hitherto cherished a most monstrous idea about you. They have thought, not only that you were the vilest and basest of men, but that you were fully conscious of it yourselves, and conscious, too, that they knew it. They have fancied that you, or at least your priests, indulged in the lowest sensuality, and practised the most impudent hypocrisy, and were parties to the most stupid and brutish of frauds; and that they dared not look a Protestant in the face. Accordingly, they have considered, and have thought us quite aware ourselves, that we were in the country only on sufferance; that we were like reputed thieves and other bad characters, who, for one reason or another, are not molested in their dens of wickedness, and enjoy a contemptuous toleration, if they keep within bounds. And so, in like manner, they have thought that there was evidence enough at any moment to convict us, if they were provoked to it. What would be their astonishment, if one of the infamous persons I have supposed stood upon his rights, or obtruded himself into the haunts of fashion and good breeding? Fancy, then, how great has been their indignation, that we Catholics should pretend to be Britons; should affect to be their equals; should dare to preach, nay, to controvert; should actually make converts, nay, worse and worse, not only should point out their mistakes, but, prodigious insolence! should absolutely laugh at the absurdity of their assertions, and the imbecility of their arguments. They are at first unable to believe their ears, when they are made sensible that we, who know so well our own worthlessness, and know that they know it, who deserve at the least the hulks or transportation, talk as loudly as we do, refuse to be still, and say that the more we are known, the more we shall be esteemed. We, who ought to go sneaking about, to crouch at their feet, and to keep our eyes on the ground, from the consciousness of their hold upon us,—is it madness, is it plot, what is it, which inspires us with such unutterable presumption? They have the might and the right on their side. They could confiscate our property, they could pack us all out of the kingdom, they could bombard Rome, they could fire St. Peter's, they could batter down the Coliseum, they could abolish the Papacy, if they pleased. Passion succeeds, and then a sort of fear, such as a brutal master might feel, who breaks into fury at the first signs of spirit in the apprentice he has long illtreated, and then quails before him as he gets older.

And then how white becomes their wrath, when men of their own rank, men of intelligence, men of good connexions, their relations or their friends, leave them to join the despised and dishonoured company! And when, as time goes on, more and more such instances occur, and others are unsettled, and the old landmarks are removed, and all is in confusion, and new questions and parties appear in the distance, and a new world is coming in,—when what they in their ignorance thought to be nothing turns out to be something, they know not what, and the theodolite of Laputa has utterly failed, they quake with apprehension at so mysterious a visitation, and they are mad with themselves for having ever qualified their habitual contempt with some haughty generosity towards us. A proud jealousy, a wild hate, and a perplexed dismay, almost choke them with emotion.

All this because they have not taken the trouble to know us as we are in fact:—however, you would think that they had at last gained an opening for information, when those whom they have known become the witnesses of what we are. Never so little; the friends who have left them are an embarrassment to them, not an illumination; an embarrassment, because they do but interfere with their received rule and practice of dealing with us. It is an easy thing to slander those who come of the old Catholic stock, because such persons are unknown to the world. They have lived all their days in tranquil fidelity to the creed of their forefathers, in their secluded estate, or their obscure mission, or their happy convent; they have cultivated no relations with the affairs or the interests of the day, and have never entered into the public throng of men to gain a character. They are known, in their simplicity and innocence and purity of heart, and in their conscientiousness of life, to their God, to their neighbour and to themselves, not to the world at large. If any one would defame them, he may do it with impunity; their name is not known till it is slandered, and they have no antecedents to serve as a matter for an appeal. Here, then, is the fit work for those prudent slanderers, who would secure themselves from exposure, while they deal a blow in defence of the old Protestant Tradition. Were a recent convert, whose name is before the world, accused of some definite act of tyranny or baseness, he knows how to write and act in his defence, and he has a known reputation to protect him; therefore, ye Protestant champions, if there be an urgent need at the moment for some instance of Catholic duplicity or meanness, be sure to shoot your game sitting; keep yourselves under cover, choose some one who can be struck without striking, whom it is easy to overbear, with whom it is safe to play the bully. Let it be a prelate of advanced age and of retired habits, or some gentle nun, whose profession and habits are pledges that she cannot retaliate. Triumph over the old man and the woman. Open your wide mouth, and collect your rumbling epithets, and round your pretentious sentences, and discharge your concentrated malignity, on the defenceless. Let it come down heavily on them to their confusion; and a host of writers, in print and by the post, will follow up the outrage you have commenced. But beware of the converts, for they are known; and to them you will not be safe in imputing more than the ordinary infirmities of humanity. With them you must deal in the contrary way. Men of rank, men of station, men of ability, in short, men of name, what are we to do with them! Cover them up, bury them; never mention them in print, unless a chance hint can be dropped to their disadvantage. Shake your heads, whisper about in society, and detail in private letters the great change which has come over them. They are not the same persons; they have lost their fine sense of honour, and so suddenly, too; they are under the dominion of new and bad masters. Drop their acquaintance; meet them and pass them by, and tell your friends you were so pained you could not speak to them; be sure you do nothing whatever to learn from them anything about the Catholic faith; know nothing at all about their movements, their objects, or their life. Read none of their books; let no one read them who is under your influence; however, you may usefully insert in your newspapers half sentences from their writings, or any passing report, which can be improved to their disadvantage. Not a word more; let not even their works be advertised. Ignore those who never can be ignored, never can be forgotten; and all for this,—that by the violation of every natural feeling, and every sacred tie, you may keep up that profound ignorance of the Catholic Religion which the ascendency of Protestantism requires.

3.

These are but snatches and glimpses, my Brothers of the Oratory, of the actual state of the case; of the intense determination of Protestants to have nothing to do with us, and nothing true to say of us; and of the extreme arduousness of that task to which I think we should all direct our exertions. The post must be carried ; in it lies the fortune of the day. Our opponents are secretly conscious of it too ; else why should they so strenuously contest it ? They must be made to know us as we are ; they must be made to know our religion as it is, not as they fancy it ; they must be made to look at us, and they are overcome. This is the work which lies before you in your place and in your measure, and I would advise you about it thus :—

Bear in mind, then, that, as far as defamation and railing go, your enemies have done their worst. There is nothing which they have not said, which they do not daily say, against your religion, your priests, and yourselves. They have exhausted all their weapons and you have nothing to fear, for you have nothing to lose. They call your priests distinctly liars : they can but cry the old fables over and over again, though they are sadly worse for wear. They have put you beyond the pale of civilized society ; they have made you the outlaws of public opinion ; they treat you, in the way of reproach and slander, worse than they treat the convict or the savage. You cannot in any way move them by smiles, or by tears, or by remonstrance. You can show them no attention ; you can give them no scandal. Court them, they are not milder ; be rude to them, they cannot be more violent. You cannot make them think better of you, or worse. They hold no terms with you ; you have not even the temptation to concede to them. You have not the temptation to give and take ; you have not the temptation to disguise or to palter. You have the strength of desperation, and desperation does great things. They have made you turn to bay. Whatever occurs, if there be a change at all, it must be a change for the better: you cannot be disadvantaged by the most atrocious charges, for you are sure to be the objects of such, whatever you do. You are set loose from the fear of man: it is of no use to say to yourselves, "What will people say?" No, the Supreme Being must be your only Fear, as He is your only Reward.

Next, look at the matter more closely; it is not so bad as it seems. Who are these who obstinately refuse to know you? When I say, "They have done their worst," what is their "worst," and who are "they?" This is an all-important question; perhaps I shall have some difficulty in bringing out what I mean, but when you once get into my idea, there will be no degrees in your understanding it. Consider, then, that "they" means, in the main, certain centres of influence in the metropolis; first, a great proportion of members of both Houses of Parliament; next, the press; thirdly, the Societies whose haunt or home is Exeter Hall; fourthly, the pulpits of the Establishment, and of a good part of the Dissenters. These are our accusers; these spread abroad their calumnies; these are meant by "they." Next, what is their "worst?" whom do they influence? They influence the population of the whole of Great Britain, and the British Empire, so far as it is British and not Catholic; and they influence it so as to make it believe that Catholicism and all Catholics are professed and habitual violators of the moral law, of the precepts of truth, honesty, purity and humanity. If this be so, you may ask me what I can mean by saying that the "worst" is not so bad as it looks? but after all, things might be much worse.

Think a moment: what is it to me what people think of me a hundred miles off, compared with what they think of me at home? It is nothing to me what the four ends of the world think of me; I care nought for the British Empire more than for the Celestial in this matter, provided I can be sure what Birmingham thinks of me. The question, I say, is, What does Birmingham think of me? and if I have a satisfactory answer to that, I can bear to be without a satisfactory answer about any other town or district in England. This is a great principle to keep in view.

And now I am coming to a second. I grant the whole power of the Metropolis is against us, and I grant it is quite out of the question to attempt to gain it over on our side. It is true, there are various individual members of Parliament who are our coreligionists or our friends, but they are few among many; there are newspapers which act generously towards us, but they form a small minority; there are a few Protestant clergy who would be not quite carried away by the stream, if left to themselves. Granted: but still, I am forced to allow that the great metropolitan intellect cannot be reached by us, and for this simple reason, because you cannot confront it, you cannot make it know you. I said your victory was to be in forcing upon others a personal knowledge of you, by your standing before your enemies face to face. But what face has a metropolitan journal? How are you to get at it? how are you to look into it? whom are you to look at? who is to look at you? No one is known in London; it is the realm of the incognito and the anonymous; it is not a place, it is a region or a state. There is no such thing as local opinion in the metropolis ; mutual personal knowledge, there is none ; neighbourhood, good fame, bad repute, there is none ; no house knows the next door. You cannot make an impression on such an ocean of units ; it has no disposition, no connexion of parts. The great instrument of propagating moral truth is personal knowledge. A man finds himself in a definite place ; he grows up in it and into it ; he draws persons around him ; they know him, he knows them ; thus it is that ideas are born which are to live, that works begin which are to last.[5] It is this personal knowledge of each other which is true public opinion ; local opinion is real public opinion ; but there is not, there cannot be, such in London. How is a man to show what he is, when he is but a grain of sand out of a mass, without relations to others, without a place, without antecedents, without individuality ? Crowds pour along the streets, and though each has his own character written on high, they are one and all the same to men below. And this impersonality, as it may be called, pervades the whole metropolitan system. A man, not known, writes a leading article against what ?—things ? no ; but ideas. He writes against Catholicism : what is Catholicism ? can you touch it ? point at it ? no ; it is an idea before his mind. He clothes it with certain attributes, and forthwith it goes all over the country that a certain idea or vision, called Catholicism, has certain other ideas, bad ones, connected with it. You see, it is all a matter of ideas, and abstractions, and

[5] *Vide* the author's Oxford University Sermons, No. V.

conceptions. Well, this leading article goes on to speak of certain individual Catholic priests; still, does it see them? point at them? no, it does but give their names; it is a matter, not of persons, but of names; and those names, sure enough, go over the whole country and empire as the names of rogues, or of liars, or of tyrants, as the case may be; while they themselves, the owners of them, in their own persons are not at all the worse for it, but eat, sleep, pray, and do their work, as freely and as easily as before. London cannot touch them, for words hurt no one; words cannot hurt us till—till when? till they are taken up, believed, in the very place where we individually dwell. Ah! this is a very different kind of public opinion; it is local opinion; I spoke of it just now, and it concerns us very nearly.

I say, it is quite another thing when the statements which a metropolitan paper makes about me, and the empire believes, are actually taken up in the place where I live. It is a very different thing, and a very serious matter; but, observe the great principle we have arrived at; it is this :—that popular opinion only acts through local opinion. The opinion of London can only act on an individual through the opinion of his own place; metropolitan opinion can only act on me through Birmingham opinion. London abuses Catholics. "Catholic" is a word; where is the thing? in Liverpool, in Manchester, in Birmingham, in Leeds, in Sheffield, in Nottingham. Did all the London papers prove that all Catholics were traitors, where must this opinion be carried out? Not in the air, not in leading articles, not in an editor's room; but in Liverpool, in Manchester, in Birmingham, in Leeds, in Sheffield, in Nottingham. So, in order to carry out your London manifesto, you must get the people of Birmingham, Manchester, and the rest, to write their names after it ; else, nothing comes of its being a metropolitan opinion, or an imperial opinion, or its being any other great idea whatever :—you must get Birmingham to believe it of Birmingham Catholics, and Manchester to believe it of Manchester Catholics. So, you see, these great London leading articles have only done half their work, or rather, have not begun it, by proving to the world that all Catholics are traitors, till they come out of their abstractions and generalities, and for the " world," are able to substitute Birmingham, Manchester, and Liverpool ; and for " all Catholics," to substitute Catholics of Birmingham, Manchester, and Liverpool ; and to get each place in particular to accept what the great Metropolis says, and the Empire believes, in the general.

And now comes another important consideration : it is not at all easy to get a particular place, at the word of London, to accept about its own neighbourhood in particular what London says of all places in the general.   Did London profess to tell us about the price of iron generally, if it gained its information from Birmingham, and other iron markets in particular, well and good ; but if it came forward with great general views of its own, I suspect that Birmingham would think it had a prior voice in the question, and would not give up its views at the bidding of any metropolitan journal.   And the case is the same as regards Catholicism ;   London may declaim about Catholics in general, but Birmingham will put in a claim to judge of them in particular ; and when Birmingham becomes the judge, London falls into the mere office of accuser, and the accused may be heard in his defence. Thus, a Catholic of Birmingham can act on Birmingham, though he cannot act on London, and this is the important practical point to which I have been coming all along. I wish you to turn your eyes upon that local opinion, which is so much more healthy, English, and Christian than popular or metropolitan opinion; for it is an opinion, not of ideas, but of things; not of words, but of facts; not of names, but of persons; it is perspicuous, real and sure. It is little to me, as far as my personal well-being is concerned, what is thought of Catholicism through the empire, or what is thought of me by the metropolis, if I know what is thought of me in Birmingham. London cannot act on me except through Birmingham, and Birmingham indeed can act on me, but I can act on Birmingham. Birmingham can look on me, and I can look on Birmingham. This is a place of persons, and a place of facts; there is far more fairness in a place like this than in a metropolis, or at least fairness is uppermost. Newspapers are from the nature of the case, and almost in spite of themselves, conducted here on a system more open and fairer than the metropolitan system. A Member of Parliament in London might say that I had two heads, and refuse to retract it, though I solemnly denied it; it would not be believed in Birmingham. All the world might believe it; it might be the theme of country meetings; the Prime Minister might introduce it into the Queen's speech; it might be the subject of most eloquent debates, and most exciting divisions; it might be formally communicated to all the European courts; the stocks might fall, a stream of visitors set in from Russia, Egypt, and the United

States, at the news; it would not be believed in Birmingham; local opinion would carry it hollow against popular opinion.

You see, then, Brothers of the Oratory, where your success lies, and how you are to secure it. Never mind the London press; never mind Exeter Hall; never mind perambulating orators or solemn meetings: let them alone, they do not affect local opinion. They are a blaze amid the stubble; they glare, and they expire. Do not dream of converting the public opinion of London; you cannot, and you need not. Look at home, there lies your work; what you have to do, and what you can do, are one and the same. Prove to the people of Birmingham, as you can prove to them, that your priests and yourselves are not without conscience, or honour, or morality; prove it to them, and it matters not though every man, woman, and child, within the London bills of mortality were of a different opinion. That metropolitan opinion would in that case be powerless, when it attempted to bear upon Birmingham; it would not work; there would be a hitch and a block; you would be a match where you were seen, for a whole world where you were not seen. I do not undervalue the influence of London; many things its press can do; some things it cannot do; it is imprudent when it impinges on facts. If, then, a battle is coming on, stand on your own ground, not on that of others; take care of yourselves; be found where you are known; make yourselves and your religion known more and more, for in that knowledge is your victory. Truth will out; truth is mighty and will prevail. We have an instance of it before our eyes; why is it that some persons here have the hardihood to be maintaining Maria Monk's calumnies? because those calumnies bear upon a place over the ocean; why did they give up Jeffreys? because he spoke of a place close at hand. You cannot go to Montreal; you can go to Whitwick; therefore, as regards Whitwick, the father of lies eats his words and gives up Jeffreys, to get some credit for candour, when he can get nothing else. Who can doubt, that, if that same personage went over to Canada, he would give up Maria Monk as false and take up Jeffreys as true? Yes, depend on it, when he next ships off to New York, he will take the veritable account of the persecuted Jeffreys in his pocket, with an interesting engraving of his face as a frontispiece. So certain, so necessary is all this, my Brothers, that I do not mind giving you this advice in public. An enemy might say in his heart, " Here is a priest fool enough to show his game! " I have no game; I have nothing to conceal; I do not mind who knows what I mark out for you, for nothing can frustrate it. I have an intense feeling in me as to the power and victoriousness of truth. It has a blessing from God upon it. Satan himself can but retard its ascendancy, he cannot prevent it.

4.

This, I would say, Brothers of the Oratory, not only to you, but, if I had a right to do so, to the Catholics of England generally. Let each stand on his own ground; let each approve himself in his own neighbourhood; if each portion is defended, the whole is secured. Take care of the pence, and the pounds will take care of themselves. Let the London press

alone ; do not appeal to it ; do not expostulate with
it, do not flatter it ; care not for popular opinion,
cultivate local. And then if troubled times come on,
and the enemy rages, and his many voices go forth
from one centre all through England, threatening
and reviling us, and muttering, in his cowardly way,
about brickbats, bludgeons, and lighted brands, why
in that case the Birmingham people will say, " Catholics are, doubtless, an infamous set, and not to be
trusted, for the *Times* says so, and Exeter Hall, and
the Prime Minister, and the Bishops of the Establishment ; and such good authorities cannot be wrong ;
but somehow an exception must certainly be made
for the Catholics of Birmingham. They are not like
the rest : they are indeed a shocking set at Manchester, Preston, Blackburn, and Liverpool ; but, however you account for it, they are respectable men here.
Priests in general are perfect monsters ; but here they
are certainly unblemished in their lives, and take
great pains with their people. Bishops are tyrants,
and, as Maria Monk says, cut-throats, always excepting the Bishop of Birmingham, who affects no state
or pomp, is simple and unassuming, and always in
his work." And in like manner, the Manchester
people will say, " Oh, certainly, Popery is horrible,
and must be kept down. Still, let us give the devil
his due, they are a remarkably excellent body of men
here, and we will take care no one does them any
harm. It is very different at Birmingham ; there
they have a Bishop, and that makes all the difference ;
he is a Wolsey all over ; and the priests, too, in Birmingham are at least one in twelve infidels. We do
not recollect who ascertained this, but it was some

most respectable man, who was far too conscientious and too charitable to slander any one." And thus, my Brothers, the charges against Catholics will become a sort of Hunt-the-slipper, everywhere and nowhere, and will end in " sound and fury, signifying nothing."

Such is that defensive system, which I think is especially the duty of Catholics at this moment. You are attacked on many sides; do not look about for friends on the right hand or on the left. Trust neither Assyria nor Egypt; trust no body of men. Fall back on yourselves, and trust none but yourselves. I do not mean you must not be grateful to individuals who are generous to you, but beware of parties; all parties are your enemies; beware of alliances. You are your own best, and sure, and sufficient friends; no one can really hurt you but yourselves; no one can succour you but yourselves. Be content to have your conscience clear, and your God on your side.

Your strength lies in your God and your conscience; therefore it lies not in your number. It lies not in your number any more than in intrigue, or combination, or worldly wisdom. God saves whether by many or by few; you are to aim at showing forth His light, at diffusing "the sweet odour of His knowledge in every place:" numbers would not secure this. On the contrary, the more you grew, the more you might be thrown back into yourselves, by the increased animosity and jealousy of your enemies. You are enabled in some measure to mix with them while you are few; you might be thrown back upon yourselves, when you became many. The line of demarcation might be more strictly observed ; there might be less intercourse and less knowledge. It would be a terrible state of things to be growing in material power, and growing too in a compulsory exclusiveness. Grow you must ; I know it ; you cannot help it ; it is your destiny ; it is the necessity of the Catholic name, it is the prerogative of the Apostolic heritage ; but a material extension without a corresponding moral manifestation, it is almost awful to anticipate ; awful, if there should be the sun of justice within you, with so little power to cast the illumination of its rays upon the multitudes without. On the other hand, even if you did not grow, you might be able to dispense on all sides of you the royal light of Truth, and exert an august moral influence upon the world. This is what I want ; I do not want growth, except of course for the sake of the souls of those who are the increment ; but I want you to rouse yourselves to understand where you are, to know yourselves. I would aim primarily at organization, edification, cultivation of mind, growth of the reason. It is a moral force, not a material, which will vindicate your profession, and will secure your triumph. It is not giants who do most. How small was the Holy Land ! yet it subdued the world. How poor a spot was Attica ! yet it has formed the intellect. Moses was one, Elias was one, David was one, Paul was one, Athanasius was one, Leo was one. Grace ever works by few ; it is the keen vision, the intense conviction, the indomitable resolve of the few, it is the blood of the martyr, it is the prayer of the saint, it is the heroic deed, it is the momentary crisis, it is the concentrated energy of a word or a look, which is the instrument of heaven. Fear not, little flock, for He is mighty who is in the midst of you, and will do for you great things.

As troubles and trials circle round you, He will give you what you want at present—" a mouth, and wisdom, which all your adversaries shall not be able to resist and gainsay."   " There is a time for silence, and a time to speak ; " the time for speaking is come. What I desiderate in Catholics is the gift of bringing out what their religion is ; it is one of those " better gifts," of which the Apostle bids you be " zealous."   You must not hide your talent in a napkin, or your light under a bushel. I want a laity, not arrogant, not rash in speech, not disputatious, but men who know their religion, who enter into it, who know just where they stand, who know what they hold, and what they do not, who know their creed so well, that they can give an account of it, who know so much of history that they can defend it. I want an intelligent, well-instructed laity ; I am not denying you are such already : but I mean to be severe, and, as some would say, exorbitant in my demands, I wish you to enlarge your knowledge, to cultivate your reason, to get an insight into the relation of truth to truth, to learn to view things as they are, to understand how faith and reason stand to each other, what are the bases and principles of Catholicism, and where lie the main inconsistences and absurdities of the Protestant theory.   I have no apprehension you will be the worse Catholics for familiarity with these subjects, provided you cherish a vivid sense of God above, and keep in mind that you have souls to be judged and to be saved. In all times the laity have been the measure of the Catholic spirit ; they saved the Irish Church three centuries ago, and they betrayed the

Church in England. Our rulers were true, our people were cowards. You ought to be able to bring out what you feel and what you mean, as well as to feel and mean it ; to expose to the comprehension of others the fictions and fallacies of your opponents ; and to explain the charges brought against the Church, to the satisfaction, not, indeed, of bigots, but of men of sense, of whatever cast of opinion. And one immediate effect of your being able to do all this will be your gaining that proper confidence in self which is so necessary for you. You will then not even have the temptation to rely on others, to court political parties or particular men ; they will rather have to court you. You will no longer be dispirited or irritated (if such is at present the case), at finding difficulties in your way, in being called names, in not being believed, in being treated with injustice. You will fall back upon yourselves ; you will be calm, you will be patient. Ignorance is the root of all littleness ; he who can realise the law of moral conflicts, and the incoherence of falsehood, and the issue of perplexities, and the end of all things, and the Presence of the Judge, becomes, from the very necessity of the case, philosophical, long-suffering, and magnanimous.

5.

Cultivation of mind, I know well, is not the same thing as religious principle, but it contributes much to remove from our path the temptation to many lesser forms of moral obliquity. Human nature, left to itself, is susceptible of innumerable feelings, more or less unbecoming, indecorous, petty, and miserable. It is, in no long time, clad and covered by a host of little vices and disgraceful infirmities, jealousies, slynesses, cowardices, frettings, resentments, obstinacies, crookedness in viewing things, vulgar conceit, impertinence, and selfishness. Mental cultivation, though it does not of itself touch the greater wounds of human nature, does a good deal for these lesser defects. In proportion as our intellectual horizon recedes, and we mount up in the knowledge of men and things, so do we make progress in those qualities and that character of mind which we denote by the word "gentleman;" and, if this applies in its measure to the case of all men, whatever their religious principles, much more is it true of a Catholic. Your opponents, my Brothers, are too often emphatically *not* gentlemen: but it will be for you, in spite of whatever provocations you may meet with, to be manly and noble in your bearing towards them; to be straightforward in your dealings with them; to show candour, generosity, honourable feeling, good sense, and forbearance, in spite of provocation; to refrain from taking unfair or small advantages over them; to meet them half way, if they show relentings; not to fret at insults, to bear imputations, and to interpret the actions of all in the best sense you possibly can. It is not only more religious, not only more becoming, not only happier, to have these excellent dispositions of mind, but it is far the most likely way, in the long run, to persuade and succeed. You see I am speaking to you almost in a worldly way; I do not speak to you of Christian charity, lest I should adopt a tone too high for the occasion.

When men see this, they may attempt other weapons; and the more serious you are, they may make the greater efforts to pour contempt and ridicule upon you. But ridicule will not hurt you, as it hurts other religious bodies; they hate and fear Catholicism— they cannot really laugh at it. They may laugh at individuals or at details connected with it, but not at Catholicism itself. Indeed, I am disposed, in one sense, to allow the maxim of the unbeliever, which has before now given rise to so much discussion—viz., that ridicule is the test of truth. Methodism is ridiculous, so is Puritanism; it is not so with the Catholic Religion; it may be, and is, maligned and defamed; ridiculed it cannot be. It is too real, too earnest, too vigorous, to have aught to fear from the most brilliant efforts of the satirist or the wit.

You will not be able to silence your opponents; do not be surprised at it; that will not show that they do not secretly respect you. Men move in parties; what shows on the surface is no index of what is felt within. When they have made assertions, they cannot withdraw them, the shame is so great; so they go on blustering, and wishing themselves out of the awkward position in which they stand. Truth is great: a blow is struck within them: they are unnerved by the secret consciousness of failure; they are angry with themselves; and, though they do not like you at all the better for it, they will be more cautious another time. They speak less confidently henceforth; or, even if they harden themselves, and are as bold as before, others do not go with them; public opinion does not respond to them; and a calumny, which at first was formidable, falls on closed hearts and unwilling ears, and takes no root in the community at large.

This is what I think probable; I will not anticipate it can be otherwise; but still, supposing there is that prejudice existing, which, like a deep soil is able to receive any amount of false witness, of scurrility, of buffoonery, of sophistry, when directed against the Catholic Religion, and that the contempt and hatred at present felt against its adherents is kindled, by their increasing strength and intelligence, into a fiercer, prouder feeling,—what then? *noli æmulari*, be not jealous, fret not. You are not as others; you have that in you which others have not. You have in you an unearthly gift; the gift, not only of contending boldly, but of suffering well. It will not happen, it must not be expected; and yet I confess I have not that confidence on the subject which I had a year since, when I said that Catholics never could be persecuted again in England. It will not be so: yet late events have shown, that though I have never underrated the intense prejudice which prevails against us, I did overrate that Anglo-Saxon love of justice and fair dealing which I thought would be its match. Alas! that I should have to say so, but it is no matter to the Catholic, though much matter to the Englishman. It is no matter to us, because, as I have said, "Greater is He that is in you than he that is in the world." I do not, cannot think a time of serious trial is at hand: I would not willingly use big words, or provoke what is so dreadful, or seem to accomplish it by suggesting it. And for myself, I confess I have no love of suffering at all; nor am I at a time of life when a man commonly loves to risk it. To be quiet and to be undisturbed, to be at peace with all, to live in the sight of my Brethren, to meditate on the future, and to die,—such is the prospect, which is rather suitable to such as me. Yet, my Brothers, I have no doubt at all, either about myself or about Catholics generally, if trial came. I doubt not we should suffer any trial well, not from nature, but from grace ; not from what we are in ourselves, but from the wonder-working power which is amongst us, and which fills us as vessels, according to our various dimensions.

6.

Not every age is the age of Saints, but no age is not the age of Martyrs. Look into the history of the Church ; you find many instances of men trained up by laborious courses of discipline through a long life, or a period of many years. Slowly, silently, perse-veringly, often opposed by their own people, for a while looked on with suspicion even by good Catholics, lest they should be extravagant or intemperate, or self-willed (for time is necessary, as the proof of things), setting about heroic works, acting, suffering with superhuman faith, with superhuman patience, with superhuman love, and then at length dying, not by violence, but in peace,—these are what I have called by pre-eminence Saints, being the great specimens of their kind as contrasted with Martyrs. They are the produce, generally speaking, of the prosperous times of the Church, I mean when the Church is in favour of the world, and is in possession of riches, learning, power, and name. The first in history of these great creations of God, is that glorious name, St. Athanasius ; then they follow so thick, that I cannot enumerate them : St. Chrysostom, almost a martyr too, St. Basil, St. Gregory of Nazianzus, St. Augustin, St. Ambrose, St. Jerome ; in very distinct spheres of religious duty, but all of them heroes. Such, too, was St. Benedict, such St. Leo, such St. Gregory the First, St. Romuald,

St. Gregory the Seventh, St. Bernard, St. Francis, St. Thomas of Aquinum, St. Ignatius, St. Vincent of Paul. As far as human eyes can see, we have none such on earth at present ; nor again, is our age like their age. Ours is not an age of temporal glory, of dutiful princes, of loyal governments, of large possessions, of ample leisure, of famous schools, of learned foundations, of well-stored libraries, of honoured sanctuaries. Rather, it is like the first age of the Church, when there was little of station, of nobility, of learning, of wealth, in the holy heritage ; when Christians were chiefly of the lower orders ; when we were poor and ignorant, when we were despised and hated by the great and philosophical as a low rabble, or a stupid and obstinate association, or a foul and unprincipled conspiracy. It is like that first age, in which no saint is recorded in history who fills the mind as a great idea, as St. Thomas Aquinas or St. Ignatius fills it, and when the ablest of so-called Christian writers belonged to heretical schools. We certainly have little to show for ourselves ; and the words of the Psalm are fulfilled in us,—" They have set fire to Thy sanctuary ; they have defiled the dwelling-place of Thy name on the earth. Our signs we have not seen ; there is no Prophet, and He will know us no more. How long shall the enemy reproach ? is the adversary to provoke Thy name for ever ? " So was it in the first age too : they were scorned and hated as we are ; they were without the effulgence and the celebrity of later times. Yet had they nothing at all to show ? were they without their glory ? it was emphatically the age of Martyrs. The most horrible tortures which imagination can fancy, the most appalling kinds of death, were the lot, the

accepted portion, the boast and joy, of those abject
multitudes. Not a few merely, but by thousands,
and of every condition of life, men, women, boys, girls,
children, slaves, domestics, they willingly offered their
life's blood, their limbs, their senses, their nerves, to
the persecutor, rather than soil their faith and their
profession with the slightest act which implied the
denial of their Lord.

Such was the prowess of the Mother of Saints in her
valley of humiliation, when she seemed to have hardly
any great thought to show, or spirit, or intellect, or
cultivation of mind. And who were these her children
who made this sacrifice of blood so freely? what had
been their previous lives? how had they been trained?
were they special men of fasting, of prayer, and of
self-control? No, I repeat it, no; they were for the
most part common men; it was not they who did the
deed, it was not what was matured in them, it was
that unfathomable ocean of faith and sanctity which
flowed into, and through, and out of them, unto those
tremendous manifestations of divine power. It was
the narrow-minded slave, the untaught boy, the gentle
maid, as well as the Bishop or the Evangelist, who
took on them their cross, and smiled as they entered
on their bloody way. It was the soldier of the ranks,
it was the jailer or hangman suddenly converted, it
was the spectator of a previous martyrdom, nay, it
was even the unbaptized heathen, who with a joyful
song rose up and washed their robes, and made them
white in the blood of the Lamb. Nay, strange to say,
in the case of such of them as had been Christians
before the persecution, good and religious as they
were, yet still we read of disorder and extravagance,

and other lesser offences, even while in prison and in expectation of their doom, clearly showing that all of them had not that subdued and disciplined spirit which has distinguished those great lights of after times of whom I was just now speaking. Or take particular instances of martyrdom, or what resembles it, from the first age to the present time ;—what was St. Justin ? a philosopher, with great secular accomplishments, but assuredly not better grounded in Christian truth than the bulk of our own laity. What was our own St. Alban, again, but a Roman officer, who did a generous action, sheltered a priest, was converted by him, made confession of his faith, and went out to die ? And then again, St. Hermenegild, several centuries later ; a brave youth, who, by his glorious death, not only gained the crown of martyrdom, but wiped out some rash acts which history imputes to him in the course of the trial which led to it. Who was our own St. Thomas ? one who with a true heart had served his Lord and led an ascetic life even when he lived in the world, but who, before his elevation to the Primacy, had indulged in a pomp and magnificence unsuitable to the condition, not only of a priest, which he then was not, but of the inferior orders of the sacred ministry. And so, again in recent times, contemplate the heroic deaths of the martyr-priests of France during the excess of the first bloody Revolution ; yet they, although men of clear conscience and good life before, seem to have had no special notes of sanctity on their characters and histories. And so again, the most recent martyr, as he may be called, of the French Church, the late Archbishop of Paris ; he, indeed, had in every way adorned and sustained his high dignity,

by holiness of conversation and a reputation beyond
reproach ; and the last glorious act of his life was but
in keeping with all which had gone before it. True ;
but it is to my point to observe that this bright example
of self-devotion, and paternal tenderness for his flock,
is commonly said to have shrunk in anticipation, by
reason of the very gentleness and sweetness of his
natural disposition, from such rough contests as that
to which he was ultimately called ; yet, when his
Lord's word came, he calmly went forth into the ranks
of his infuriated people, stood between the mortal combatants, with the hope of separating them, and received
the wound which suddenly took him off to his eternal
reward. This, then, may be said, as a general rule, of
the individual members of the " white-robed army ; "
they have been, for the most part, men of noble zeal
and chivalrous prowess, who startled the world, startled
their friends, startled themselves by what the grace
that is in the Church enabled them to do. They shot
up at once to their high stature, and " being perfected
in a short space," as the Wise man says, " they fulfilled a long time." Thus they shone forth, and " ran
to and fro like sparks among the reeds," like those
keen and sudden fires which dart forth from some
electric mass, on due provocation, and intimate to us
the power and intensity of the awful elements which
lie concealed within it.

The Church of God cannot change ; what she was
that she is. What our forefathers were, such are we ;
we look like other men, but we have that in us which
none others have,—the latent element of an indomitable fortitude. This may not be the age of Saints, but
all times are the age of Martyrs. The arrow is on the

string, and the arm is drawn back, and, " if the Lord give the word," great will be the multitude of His champions. O my Brothers, it is difficult for you and me to realize this ; it is difficult for us to believe that we have it in us, being what we are,—but we have. And it is difficult for us to believe that this can be a time for testing it, nor do I say it is ; I think it cannot be ; I only say, that if it were to be a time for calling out the Martyr's spirit, you and I, through God's grace, have it in us. I only mean that it is profitable, in such lesser trials as may easily come upon us, to be reminded that we may humbly trust we have that in us which can sustain the greatest. And it would be profitable also for our opponents, high and low, if they too would lay this to heart. It would be well for them to recollect, that there is a certain principle, which we call zeal, and they call fanaticism. Let them beware of awaking what they would, in scoffing, call the fanatical spirit of the Catholic. For years and years the Catholics of England have borne personal slander, and insult, and injustice. In their own persons, and not merely in their religious profession, have they been treated as the adherents of no other creed have been treated, with scorn, hatred, and cruelty. Men have shrunk from coming near them, and have almost discarded from their society those who did ; as if inflicting on them the greater excommunication, as upon those who were the extremest reprobates and blasphemers on the face of the earth. They have borne, and they bear, an ill-usage, which, in its mildest and most amiable form, has never risen higher than pity and condescension. They have borne, and they bear, to be " the heathen's jest," waiting till the morning breaks, and a happier day begins.

So has it been with us up to this hour ; but let our enemies remember that, while they have their point of honour, we have ours. They have stripped us of power, wealth, name, and station ; they have left us nothing but our Apostolical inheritance. And now they wish to take from us the "little ewe-lamb," which is our only treasure. There was a saying of old, "Let alone Camarina, for 'tis best let alone." Let them, as sensible men,—I do not say, accept Catholicism as true, but admit it into their imagination as a fact. A story goes about of a sagacious states-man and monarch of our own time, who, when urged by some of his advisers to come to an open rupture with the Holy See, made answer, "If you can put your finger upon the page of history, and point out any one instance in which any civil power quarrelled with Rome with honour and success in the event, I will accede to your wishes." And it has lately been given to the world, how that sagacious politician, apostate priest as he was, Prince Talleyrand, noted it as one of Napoleon's three great political mistakes, that he quarrelled with the Pope. There is only one way of success over us, possible even in idea,—a whole-sale massacre. Let them exterminate us, as they have done before, kill the priests, decimate the laity ; and they have for a while defeated the Pope. They have no other way ; they may gain a material victory, never a moral one.

7.

These are thoughts to comfort and sustain us, what-ever trial lies before us. I might pursue them farther, but it is enough to have suggested them. Nothing more remains for me to do, but, in commending myself to your good thoughts, my Brothers, to thank those also, who, though not of our communion, have honoured me with their attendance. If I might take the liberty of addressing them directly, I would anxiously entreat them to think over what I have said, even though they have not been altogether pleased at my manner of saying it. Minds, and judgments, and tastes, are so very different, that I cannot hope to have approved myself to all, even though they be well disposed towards me, nay, to any one at all so fully, but that he may have thought that some things might have been said better, and some things were better omitted altogether. Yet I entreat them to believe that I have uttered nothing at random, but have had reasons, both for what I said and my manner of saying it. It is easy to fancy a best way of doing things, but very difficult to find it : and often what is called the best way is, in the very nature of things, not positively good, but only better than other ways. And really in the present state of things, it is difficult to say anything in behalf of Catholicism, if it is to make any impression, without incurring grave criticism of one kind or another ; and quite impossible so to say it, as not grievously to offend those whom one is opposing. But, after all, in spite of all imperfections, which are incident to the doings of every mortal man, and in spite of the differences of judgments, which will make those imperfections greater than they are, I do trust there is a substance of truth in what I have said, which will last, and produce its effect somewhere or other. Good is never done except at the expense of those who do it : truth is never enforced except at the sacrifice of its propounders. At least they expose their inherent imperfections, if they incur no other penalty ; for nothing would be done at all, if a man waited till he could do it so well that no one could find fault with it.

Under these circumstances, then, what can I desire and pray for but this ?—that what I have said well may be blest to those who have heard it, and that what I might have said better, may be blest to me by increasing my dissatisfaction with myself : that I may cheerfully resign myself to such trouble or anxiety as necessarily befalls anyone who has spoken boldly on an unpopular subject in a difficult time, with the confidence that no trouble or anxiety but will bring some real good with it in the event, to those who have acted in sincerity, and by no unworthy methods, and with no selfish aim.

NOTES.

NOTE I. (*p.* 18.)

THE following is the passage as it stands in Mr. Blanco White's work, a portion of which is extracted in Lecture I.:—

"The Jesuits, till the abolition of that order, had an almost unrivalled influence over the better classes of Spaniards. They had nearly monopolized the instruction of the Spanish youth, at which they toiled without pecuniary reward ; and were equally zealous in promoting devotional feelings both among their pupils and the people at large. It is well known that the most accurate division of labour was observed in the allotment of their various employments. Their candidates, who, by a refinement of ecclesiastical policy, after an unusually long probation, were bound by vows which, depriving them of liberty, yet left a discretionary power of ejection in the Order, were incessantly watched by the penetrating eye of the Master of Novices ; a minute description of their character and peculiar turn was forwarded to the superiors, and at the end of the noviciate they were employed to the advantage of the community, without ever thwarting the natural bent of the individual, or diverting his natural powers by a multiplicity of employments. Wherever, as in France and Italy, literature was in high estimation, the Jesuits spared no trouble to raise among themselves men of eminence in that department. In Spain their chief aim was to provide their houses with popular preachers, and zealous, yet prudent and gentle, confessors. Pascal and the Jansenist party, of which he was the organ, accused them of systematic laxity in their moral doctrines ; but the charge, I believe, though plausible in theory, was perfectly groundless in practice. If, indeed, ascetic virtue could ever be divested of its connatural evil tendency—if a system of moral perfection, that has for its basis, however disavowed and disguised, the Manichæan doctrine of the two principles, could be applied with any partial advantage as a rule of conduct, it was so in the hands of the

Jesuits. The strict, unbending maxims of the Jansenists, by urging persons of all characters and tempers on to an imaginary goal of perfection, bring quickly their whole system to the decision of experience. They are like those enthusiasts who, venturing upon the practice of some Gospel sayings in the literal sense, have made the absurdity of that interpretation as clear as noonday light. A greater knowledge of mankind made the Jesuits more cautious in the culture of devotional feelings. They well knew that but few can prudently engage in open hostility with what, in ascetic language, is called the world. They now and then trained up a sturdy champion, who, like their founder Loyola, might provoke the enemy to single combat with honour to his leaders; but the crowd of mystic combatants were made to stand upon a kind of jealous truce, which, in spite of all care, often produced some jovial meetings of the advanced parties on both sides. The good fathers came forward, rebuked their soldiers back into the camp, and filled up the place of deserters by their indefatigable industry in engaging recruits.

"The influence of the Jesuits on Spanish morals, from everything I have learned, was undoubtedly favourable. Their kindness attracted the youth from their schools to their Company; and though it must be acknowledged that many arts were practised to decoy the cleverest and the wealthiest into the order, they also greatly contributed to the preservation of virtue in that slippery age, both by ties of affection and the gentle check of example. Their churches were crowded every Sunday with regular attendants, who came to confess and receive the sacrament. The practice of choosing a certain priest, not only to be the occasional confessor but *director of the conscience*, was greatly encouraged by the Jesuits. The ultimate effects of this surrender of the judgment are indeed dangerous and degrading; but in a country where the darkest superstition is constantly impelling the mind into the opposite extremes of religious melancholy and profligacy, weak persons are sometimes preserved from either by the friendly assistance of a prudent *director*, and the Jesuits were generally well qualified for that office. Their conduct was correct, and their manners refined. They kept up a dignified intercourse with the middling and higher classes, and were always ready to help and instruct the poor, without descending to their level. Since the expulsion of the Jesuits, the better classes for the most part avoid the company of monks and friars, except in an official capacity; while the lower ranks, from which these professional saints are generally taken, and where they reappear raised, indeed, into comparative importance, but grown bolder in grossness and vice, suffer more from their influence than they would by being left without any religious ministers."

He adds this note :—

"The profligacy now prevalent among the friars, contrasted with the conduct of the Jesuits, as described by the most credible living witnesses,

is excessively striking. Whatever we may think of the political delinquencies of their leaders, their bitterest enemies have never ventured to
charge the order of Jesuits with moral irregularities. The internal policy
of that body precluded the possibility of gross misconduct. No Jesuit
could step out of doors without calling on the superior for leave and a
companion, in the choice of whom great care was taken to vary the
couples. Never were they allowed to pass a single night out of the convent, except when attending a dying person; and even then they were
under the strictest injunctions to return at whatever hour the soul departed."—*Doblado's Letters in the New Monthly Magazine,* 1821, vol. ii.
pp. 157, 158.

An objection has been taken to the validity of the argument in the latter part of the same Lecture, in which it is
attempted to expose the polemic which Protestants commonly use against the Catholic Church, by comparing it to a
supposed tirade of some Russian against England; and that,
upon the ground that the maxims of the English Constitution
(*e.g.*, the king can do no wrong) are confessedly fictions,
whereas the Church's infallibility is a dogma expressing a
truth. In this particular respect, certainly, the cases are not
parallel; but they need not be parallel for the argument. The
point urged against the Protestant is this—That, whereas
every science, polity, institution, religion, uses the words
and phrases which it employs in *a sense of its own,* or *a technical sense, Englishmen, allowing and exemplifying this very*
principle in the case of their own Constitution, will not allow
it to the divines of the Catholic Church. *E.g.,* the " Omnipotence of Parliament " is a phrase of English law, in which
the word *omnipotence* is taken otherwise than when it is ascribed to Almighty God; and so, too, when used by Catholic
divines of the Blessed Virgin. If any one exclaims against
its adoption, in the latter case, by Catholics, let him also protest against its adoption, in the former case, by English lawyers; if he rejects explanations, distinctions, limitations, in
the latter case, and calls them lame, subtle, evasive, &c., let
him do so in the former case also; whereas Protestants denounce such explanations as offered by Catholics, and take a

pride in them as laid down by English lawyers. In like manner, "the king can do no wrong" has *a* sense in constitutional law, though not the sense which the words would suggest to a foreigner who heard them for the first time; and "the Pope is infallible" has its own sense in theology, but not that which the words suggest to a Protestant, who takes the words in their ordinary meaning. And, as it is the way with Protestants to maintain that the Pope's infallibility is intended by us as a guarantee of his private and personal exemption from theological error, nay, even from moral fault of every kind; so a foreigner, who knew nothing of England, were he equally impatient, prejudiced, and indocile, might at first hearing confound the maxim, "the king can do no wrong," with the dogma of some Oriental despotism or theocracy.

For a fuller explanation of the argument, *vid.* Lecture VIII.

I may add that I have been informed since I published Lecture III., that Mr. Hallam, in a later edition than my own of his Middle Ages, has explained his severe remarks upon St. Eligius. Nothing less could be expected from a person of his great reputation.

Note II.

The question of Ecclesiastical Miracles is treated in Lecture VII. solely with reference to their general verisimilitude, or the antecedent probability or improbability of their occurrence; that is, to the pre-judgment, favourable or otherwise, which spontaneously arises in our minds, upon hearing reports or reading statements of particular miraculous occurrences. This antecedent probability depends on two conditions—viz., first of all, whether there is an existing cause adequate to the production of such phenomena; and next, since there certainly is such—viz., the Creator—whether in the particular case, the alleged miracle sufficiently resembles

His known works in character and object to admit of being ascribed to Him. Two questions remain to be determined, which do not come into discussion in the Lecture; first, whether the fact under consideration *is* really miraculous—that is, such as not to be referable to the operation of ordinary processes of nature or of art; and, secondly, whether it comes to us with such evidence, either from sight or from testimony, as warrants us in accepting it as having really taken place.

Thus the liquefaction of St. Januarius' Blood at Naples, in order to its reception as miraculous—(1) must be possible; (2) must be parallel to God's known works in nature or in revelation, or suitable to Him; (3) must be clearly beyond the operation of chemical or other scientific means, or jugglery of man or evil spirit; and (4) must be wrought publicly.

The antecedent probability of such miracles is, I repeat, all that concerned me in Lecture VII.; but I went on, at the end of it, to avow my own personal belief in some of them as facts, lest I should be suspected of making a sham defence of what I did not in my heart myself accept. Here I subjoin, from the columns of the *Morning Chronicle*, a correspondence on this subject, which took place in 1851, between the late Dr. Hinds and myself, soon after the delivery of the Lecture :—

No. 1.

DR. NEWMAN TO THE BISHOP OF NORWICH.

"THURLES, IRELAND, *October* 2.

"MY DEAR LORD,—A slip of a Norwich paper has been sent me, which purports to give a speech of the 'Bishop of the diocese,' delivered in St. Andrew's Hall, at a meeting of the British and Foreign Bible Society. Though the name of the diocese is not stated, I cannot be mistaken, under the circumstances, in ascribing the speech to your lordship. Yet I know not how to credit that certain words contained in it, which evidently refer to me, should have been uttered by one who is so liberal, so fair, and temperate in his general judgments as your lordship.

"The words are these :—' My friends, I have heard—and I am sure all of you who have heard of it will share with me in the disgust as well as the surprise with which I have heard of it—that there is a publication circulated through this land, the stronghold of Bible Christianity—a publication issuing from that Church against which we are protesting, and which is, on the other hand, the stronghold of human authority—a publication issuing from one of the most learned of its members, a man who, by his zeal as a convert, and by his position and acceptance with that Church, speaks with the authority of the Church itself, and represents its doctrines and feelings—a publication, as I have heard with dismay, read, admired, circulated, which maintains that the legendary stories of those puerile miracles, which I believe until now few Protestants thought that the Roman Catholics themselves believed; that these legends *have* a *claim to belief equally* with that Word of God which relates the miracles of our God, as recorded in the Gospel, and that *the authority of the one is as the authority of the other, the credibility of the one based on a foundation no less sure than the credibility of the other.*'

"The statements here animadverted on are as contrary to the teaching of the Catholic Church as they can be repugnant to your own views of Christian truth.

"Should I be right in supposing that you did not really impute them to me, I beg to apologise to you for putting you to the trouble of disavowing the newspaper account; but if, contrary to my expectation, you ackowledge them to be yours, I take the liberty of begging your lordship to refer me to the place in any work of mine in which they are contained.

"You will not, I am sure, be surprised if, at a moment like the present, when so many misrepresentations are made of Catholicism and its defenders, I should propose, as I do, to give the same publicity to any answer you shall favour me with, as has been given to the speech the report of which has occasioned my question.

"I am, my dear Lord, yours very faithfully,

"JOHN H. NEWMAN."

No. 2.

THE BISHOP OF NORWICH TO DR. NEWMAN.

"LONDON, *October* 8.

"My DEAR NEWMAN,—As I have already replied to an inquiry, the same as that which you make, in a letter to the Rev. W. Cobb, Roman Catholic priest in Norwich, I enclose a copy of that letter.

"If I have misrepresented you, you will, I hope, believe me when I say that it has been from misunderstanding you. Permit me to add, that what has misled me is likely, you may be sure, to mislead others. I shall rejoice, therefore, at any public statement from you which may disabuse your readers of false impressions. When you are found to be maintaining (as you appear to do) that the miracles of the apostolic age were only the beginning of a like miraculous development, to be manifested and accredited through succeeding times, and professing your belief in the facts of this further miraculous development, in terms as solemn as those of a creed, it is very difficult to avoid the impression that the scriptural narratives are to be regarded as the beginning only of a series of the like histories, partaking of their credibility and authority, although the one may be called Scripture and the other legend.

"Time and circumstances have so long divided us, that I ought to apologize for the familiar mode in which I have addressed you ; but your handwriting has brought back on my mind other days, and some dear friends, who were then friends and associates of both of us ; and I would still desire you to believe me very truly yours,

"S. NORWICH."

No. 3 (enclosed in No. 2).
THE BISHOP OF NORWICH TO MR. COBB.

"ATHENÆUM, LONDON, *October* 6.

"REVEREND SIR,—My absence from home when your letter was delivered, and my not having Dr. Newman's publications by me when I received it here, have caused a delay in my making reply to your inquiry. The work to which I alluded, when I stated, in St. Andrew's Hall, that he asserted for certain legendary accounts of miracles the same credibility which is claimed for the Scriptural narratives and statements of miracles, is his 'Lectures on Catholicism in England,' more particularly Lecture VII., p. 298. In this passage, after discriminating between some legends and others, as we discriminate between genuine Scripture and that which is either spurious or doubtful, he professes his faith in those the authority of which he pronounces to be unquestionable in terms such as these :—

"'I think it impossible to withstand the evidence which is brought for the liquefaction of the blood of St. Januarius at Naples, and for the motion of the eyes of the pictures of the Madonna in the Roman States. I firmly believe that saints, in their lifetime, have before now raised the dead to life, crossed the sea without vessels, multiplied grain and bread, cured incurable diseases, and stopped the operation of the laws of the universe in a multitude of ways. Many men, when they hear an educated man so speak, will at once impute the avowal to insanity, or to an idiosyncrasy, or to imbecility of mind, or to decrepitude of powers, or to fanaticism, or to hypocrisy. They have a right to say so if they will ; *and we have a right to ask them why they do not say it of those who bow down before the mystery of mysteries, the Divine Incarnation.*'

" He pursues the same view in his volume of ' Discourses for Mixed Congregations,' setting aside, as a thing of nought, the essential difference between the claim which Scripture has on our belief in miracles related there, and that of human legends for the like statements, and recognizing no difference but that of the marvellousness of the things related in the one or the other.

" ' They (speaking of Protestants) have not in them the principle of faith, and, I repeat it, it is nothing to the purpose to urge that at least they firmly believe Scripture to be the Word of God. In truth, it is much to be feared that their acceptance of Scripture itself is nothing better than a prejudice or inveterate feeling impressed on them when they were children. A proof of this is this—that while they profess to be so shocked at Catholic miracles, and are not slow to call them " lying wonders," *they have no difficulty at all about Scripture narratives, which are quite as difficult to the reason as any miracles recorded in the history of the saints.* I have heard, on the contrary, of Catholics, who have been startled at first reading in Scripture the narrative of the ark in the deluge, of the Tower of Babel, of Balaam and Balak, of the Israelites' flight from Egypt and entrance into the promised land, and of Esau's and of Saul's rejection, which the bulk of Protestants receive without any effort of mind.'—Page 217.

" In his speech at the Birmingham meeting, he propounded the same view, in reference to God's revelation through nature, as he has, in the preceding passages, in reference to God's written word. He said on that occasion, if his words are rightly reported—' We have no higher proof of the doctrines of natural religion—such as the being of a God, a rule of right and wrong, and the like—than we have of the Romish system,' including, I must presume, all those legendary statements which he so strongly represents as part of that system.

" It would be very satisfactory to me to have any authoritative disclaimer of these publications as exponents of your Church's views ; for they alarm me, from their tendency to bring into discredit that faith which, notwithstanding the serious differences that unhappily divide us, we still, God be thanked, hold in common, and cherish in common.

" I ought to add that, in giving those last words which you have quoted from the newspapers, the reporters must have heard me imperfectly, or have misapprehended me. I did not say that Dr. Newman asserted, for the miracles related in the Romish legends, a credibility based upon the foundation of divine revelation no less than those of Scripture. What I said was, that he claimed for the miracles related in the legends, the authorship of which was human, the same amount of credibility as for the miracles and divine revelations recorded in Scripture, the authorship of which was divine; thus leading his readers either to raise the authority of the legends to that of Scripture, or to bring down the authority of Scripture to that of the legends, the latter of which appeared to me to be the more likely result.

"I am, rev. sir, your faithful servant,

"S. NORWICH."

No. 4.

DR. NEWMAN TO THE BISHOP OF NORWICH.

"ORATORY, BIRMINGHAM, *October* 11.

"MY DEAR LORD,—I thank you for the kind tone of your letter, which it was very pleasant to me to find so like that of former times, and for the copy you enclose of your answer to Mr. Cobb.

"Your lordship's words, as reported in the Norwich paper, were to the effect that I believed the ecclesiastical miracles to have 'a claim to belief *equally* with that Word of God which relates the miracles of our God as recorded in the gospels;' that I made 'the authority of the one as the authority of the other,' and 'the credibility of the one as based on a foundation no less sure than the credibility of the other.'

"You explain this in a letter to Mr. Cobb thus :—'I did not say that Dr. Newman asserted, for the miracles related in the Romish legends, a credibility based upon the foundation of divine revelation no less than those of Scripture. What I said was, that he claimed for the miracles related in the legends, the authorship of which was human, the same amount of *credibility* as for the miracles and divine revelations recorded in Scripture, the authorship of which was divine.'

"Will you allow me to ask you the meaning of your word 'credibility'? for it seems to me a fallacy is involved in it. Archbishop Whately says that controversies are often verbal. I cannot help being quite sure that your lordship's difficulty is of this nature.

"When you speak of a miracle being *credible* you must mean one of two things—either that it is 'antecedently probable,' or *verisimile ;* or that it is 'furnished with sufficient evidence,' or *proveable.* In which of these senses do you use the word ? If you describe me as saying that the ecclesiastical miracles come to us on the same *evidence* as those of Scripture, you attribute to me what I have never dreamed of asserting ; if you understand me to say that the ecclesiastical miracles are on the same level of *antecedent probability* with those of Scripture, you do justice to my meaning, but I do not conceive it is of a nature to raise 'disgust.'

"I am not inventing a distinction for the occasion ; it is found in Archbishop Whately's works ; and I have pursued it at great length in my 'University Sermons,' and in my 'Essay on Miracles,' published in

1843, which has never been answered as far as I know, and a copy of which I shall beg to present to your lordship.

" 1. First, let us suppose you to mean by 'credible' antecedently probable, or *likely (verisimile)*, and you will then accuse me of saying that the ecclesiastical miracles are as *likely* as those of Scripture. What is there extreme or disgusting in such a statement, whether you agree with it or not ? I certainly *do* think that the ecclesiastical miracles *are* as credible (in this sense) as the Scripture miracles; nay, more so, because they come after Scripture, and Scripture breaks (as it were) the ice. The miracles of Scripture begin a new law; they innovate on an established order. There is less to surprise in a second miracle than in a first. I do not see how it can be denied that ecclesiastical miracles, as coming *after* Scripture miracles, have not to bear the brunt of that antecedent improbability which attaches, as Hume objects, to the idea of a violation of nature. Ecclesiastical miracles are *probable*, because Scripture miracles are *true.* This is all I have said or implied in the two passages you have quoted from me, as is evident from both text and context.

" As to the former passage of the two, I there say, that if Protestants are surprised at my having no *difficulty* in believing ecclesiastical miracles, I have a right to ask them why they have no difficulty in believing the Incarnation. Protestants find a difficulty in even listening to evidence adduced for ecclesiastical miracles. I have none. Why? Because the admitted fact of the Scripture miracles has taken away whatever *prima facie* unlikelihood attaches to them as a violation of the laws of nature. My whole Lecture is on the one idea of 'Assumed Principles,' or antecedent judgments or theories; it has nothing to do with proof or evidence. And so of the second passage. I have but said that Protestants 'have no *difficulty*' at all about Scripture miracles, which are quite as difficult to the *reason* as any miracle recorded in the history of the saints.' Now, I really cannot conceive a thoughtful person denying that the history of the ark at the deluge is as difficult to reason as a saint floating on his cloak. As to the third passage you quote as mine, about 'revelation through nature,' and 'legendary statements,' I know nothing about it. I cannot even guess of what words of mine it is the distortion. Tell me the when and where, and I will try to make out what I really said. If it professes to come from my recent lectures, all I can say is that what I spoke I read from a printed copy, and what I printed I published, and what is not in the printed volume I did not say.

" 2. But now for the second sense of the word 'credible.' Do you understand me to say that the ecclesiastical miracles come to us on as good *proof* or *grounds* as those of Scripture? If so, I answer distinctly, I have said no such thing anywhere. The Scripture miracles are credible, *i.e.*, proveable, on a ground peculiar to themselves on the authority of God's Word. Observe my expressions· I think it '*impossible to withstand the evidence* which is brought for the liquefaction of the blood of St. Januarius.' Should I thus speak of the resurrection of Lazarus? should I say, 'I think it impossible to *withstand the evidence* for his resurrection?' I cannot tell how Protestants would speak, but a Catholic would say, 'I believe it with a certainty beyond all other certainty, *for* God has spoken.' Moreover, I believe with a like certainty every one of the Scripture miracles, not only that apostles and prophets 'in their lifetime have *before now* raised the dead to life,' &c., but that Elias did this, and St. Peter did that, and just as related, and so all through the whole catalogue of their miracles. On the other hand, ecclesiastical miracles may be believed, one more than another, and more or less by different persons. This I have expressed in words which occur in the passage from which you quote, for, after saying of one, 'I think it *impossible to withstand the evidence* for' it, I say of another extraordinary fact no more than, 'I see *no reason to doubt*' it; and of a third, still less, '*I do not see why it may not*' be; whereas, whatever God has said is to be believed absolutely and by all. This applies to the account of the ark; I believe it, though *more* difficult to the reason, with a firmness quite different from that with which I believe the account of a saint's crossing the sea on his cloak, though *less* difficult to the reason; for the one comes to me on the Word of God, the other on the word of man.

"The whole of what I have said in my recent Lecture comes to this; that Protestants are most inconsistent and one-sided, in *refusing to go into the evidence* for ecclesiastical miracles, which, on the first blush of the matter, are not stranger than those miracles of Scripture which ·they happily profess to admit. How is this the same as saying that *when* the grounds for believing those ecclesiastical miracles *are* entered on, God's Word through His Church, on which the Catholic rests the miracles of the Law and the Gospel, is not a firmer evidence than man's word, on which rest the miracles of ecclesiastical history?

"So very clear is this distinction between verisimilitude and evidence, and so very clearly (as I consider) is my own line of argument founded on it, that I should really for my own satisfaction like your lordship's assurance that you had carefully read, not merely dipped into, my Lecture, before you delivered your speech. Certain it is, that most people, though they are not the fit parallels of a person of your dispassionate and candid mind, do judge of my meaning by bits of sentences, mine or not mine, inserted in letters in the newspapers.

"Under these circumstances, I entertain the most lively confidence that your lordship will find yourself able to reconsider the word 'disgust,' as unsuitable to be applied to statements which, if you do not approve, at least you cannot very readily refute. I am, my dear lord,

"With every kind feeling personally to your lordship,

"Very truly yours,

"JOHN H. NEWMAN."

No. 5.

" NORWICH, *October* 17.

" MY DEAR NEWMAN,—One of the secretaries of the Bible Society has asked my permission to reprint what I said as Chairman of the meeting at Norwich. I will most readily avail myself of this reprint to withdraw the expression 'disgust,' as it appears to be offensive. I will also, as is due to you, have a note appended, referring to the passages in your writings to which my observations were more particularly directed, and stating that you disavow the construction which I put on them.

" At the same time I am unable still to come to any other conclusion than that of the dangerous tendency which I have represented them to have. If you maintain, as you distinctly do, not only the *antecedent probability* (*credulity* in that sense) of the legendary miracles, but your firm belief in certain of them, specifically stated as *facts proved*, and if you further contend that these miracles are only a continuation of those recorded in Scripture, the impression appears to me inevitable, that the legendary channel through which God must have appointed them to be attested and preserved has a purpose and authority the same with Scripture. What I should fear is, not indeed that the generality of your readers will exalt legends into Scripture ; but that, seeing grounds for discrediting the legends, they will look on all narratives of miracles, scriptural and legendary, as alike doubtful, and more than doubtful. In short, your view, as I see it, tends to a scepticism and infidelity of which I fully acquit you.

" The report of your speech at Birmingham I read in the *Times*, but the quotation which I sent to Mr. Cobb, I took from a letter in the *Spectator* of Sept. 27, the writer's quotation, according with my impression of your speech as reported, containing words to that effect

" The kind present which you propose for me will, I assure you, be valued, if for no more, as a token that we are still friends, notwithstanding a wide severance in matters of faith, and that we may still believe all things and hope all things for one another.

" My dear Newman, yours truly,

"S. NORWICH.'

No. 6.

"ORATORY, BIRMINGHAM, *October* 19.

" MY DEAR LORD,—I thank your lordship with all my heart for your very kind and friendly letter just received, and for your most frank and ready compliance with the request which I felt it my duty to make to you.

"It is a great satisfaction to me to have been able to remove a misapprehension of my meaning from your mind. There still remains, I confess, what is no misapprehension, though I grieve it should be a cause of uneasiness to you—my avowal, first, that the miraculous gift has never left the Church since the time of the Apostles, though displaying itself under different circumstances, and next that certain reputed miracles are real instances of its exhibition. The former of these two points I hold in common with all Catholics; the latter on my own private judgment, which I impose on no one.

'If I keep to my intention of making our correspondence public it is, I assure you, not only as wishing to clear myself of the imputation which has in various quarters been cast upon my Lecture, but also in no slight measure, because I am able to present to the world the specimen of an anti-Catholic disputant, as fair and honourable in his treatment of an opponent, and as mindful of old recollections, as he is firm and distinct in the enunciation of his own theological view.

"That the Eternal Mercy may ever watch over you and guide you, and fill you with all knowledge and with all peace, is, my dear lord, the sincere prayer of

"Yours most truly,

"JOHN H. NEWMAN."

THE END.

PRINTED IN GREAT BRITAIN BY
THE UNIVERSITY PRESS, ABERDEEN

APPENDIX: TEXTUAL VARIANTS

The following list contains all the variants of the First Edition to be found in the Sixth. The reading to the left of the square bracket belongs to the Sixth Edition. Where a Sixth Edition reading stands unaccompanied by any variant to the right (and without a square bracket), this means that it is an addition to the First Edition. Trivial variations in capitalising, punctuation and spelling have been ignored.

Page	Line	
vi	14–15	The Oratory, 1851
ix	15	Protestants] They
xi	2–3	already
	14	even
	23	to second third and fourth] to the first, second and third
xii	19	apprehends] knows
xiii	1	The Author] He
	3–4	If anywhere he has been led to do so, it has been in cases] He has been led to do so in cases
	13	ORATORY, BIRMINGHAM,
xv	6	INSUFFICIENT FOR] unequal to
	10	THE INTELLECTUAL GROUND OF] the Intellectual Instrument of
	12	IGNORANCE CONCERNING] Want of Intercourse with
3	31	these] them
4	18	misconception] variety of misconception
5	32	the young] all the young
6	6–7	in a measure, everyone (as I may say)] everyone (as I may say), in a measure
	9	be] is
	11	to be

Page	Line	
	23	one man is] they are
	25	he] they
	29	he has] they have
7	9	tales,[1]] tales
		[1]Guy Mannering
9	1	own
	11	matter
11	19	or be
	26	from
	33	was
	33	is
13	4	and
15	28–29	History[4]] History
		[4]Ch.xiii.
17	2	certain
	32	even
19	18	middle] middling
	30	be lost] die
24	12	is] are
	13	its] their
	14	it is] they are
	25	which it elicited] made to him in consequence of it
25	8–9	of parallel greatness and excellence, in its degree and in its degree and place, of parallel greatness and excellence
	28	practitioners] the instruments of those
26	4	writers] histories
	31	once
31	14	Blackstone] writer
32	15	a statement] an indecency
34	2	blasphemous] impure
42	15	intellects] men
	19	philosophical] intellectual
43	8	at
	10	shut out] ignore
	17	Englishmen] they
	18	they] Englishmen
44	5	pure
	23	England] they
	25	England does] they do
46	22	held] said
	23	held] said
47	2	closely shut against] close to

Page	Line	
	Page	*Line*
50	4	in the face
	7–8	has been so ruled long ago] is a foregone conclusion
	19	countrymen] population
	22	their own] one
	27	only one] one only
	29	men of this generation] the national mind
51	11	at] at the date of
	13	ancients] elders
	22	up] back
	31	doctrines and commandments] for doctrines the commandments
52	9	warrant and verify] avouch and warrant
	30	this] my
	31	is in itself] though not an argumentative, is, at least,
53	1	induced] led
	10	is a certain] are a
	17	even to himself] nor, if he can help it, own even to himself
	27	viz
54	24	find] will find
55	7	in the world
	8	had done with it themselves] themselves had done with it
	18–19	nor does its tradition live upon its establishment
	23–24	and its tradition
56	8	indeed, allege in explanation of the fact] say, indeed, that such an occurrence is at least conceivable, for this reason
	25–27	if possible, to make that national which as yet is not national, and which, without that patronage,] to make, if possible, that national which was not national before it, and without it
	27–28	in the case of Protestantism
59	5	Evangelical] Evangelicals
	19	the religious state of
	22	their] its
	26–27	advantageous distinguishes] distinguishes the manly and generous heart of
60	10	by numbers
	12	all] at all
	20–21	remarkable] magnanimous
	24	had
62	6	of faith
	21	whom
63	26	try] strive

Page	Line	
64	11–12	acceptableness] reception
	29	establishment] consolidation
65	8	but
	30	on her side, over and above,] with her, other
66	21	its
67	2	in all things] to everything
	18	begin
	27	superstition.] superstition. Let the Protestant paint up Popery, and the profligate will take it for virtue.
68	10	which has made] and pursuits which make
	14	life] genius
69	2	in this country
	21	distinct] the most various
70	12	luminous] illuminate
	16	brilliant] exuberant
	28	and this is true] nay
71	2–4	others may frame its laws;" and its proverbs are the produce of its literature.] I shall have my own way with it:" This has been strikingly fulfilled in the Protestantism of England.
	5	of] and
	8–9	the philosophers] philosophy
	11	century] era
72	3	forsooth
	6	must plead
	11	That Religion] It
	14	has] is
74	5	much] he knows it much
	16	social uses] civil importance
75	4	opened] open
	11	almost the] the special
	14	specially] mainly
76	1	Wesleyans] Methodists
	4	own
	7	is infallible, on one it may securely insist without fear of being unseasonable or excessive,] may rest without any mistake
	18	special
77	15	Holy Father] Pope

[1]The foregoing Lecture in 1851 was, by an accidental coincidence, written simultaneously with an able pamphlet by Serjeant Bellasis, *apropos* of the conduct of the Anglican clergy of the day.] [1]Vide an amusing and cogent

Page	*Line*	
		argument, entitled 'The Anglican Bishops versus the Catholic Hierarchy.' Toovey, 1851.
	21	if ever] when
	22	whether
78	15	inspection and
	29	reject it and protest against] refuse to admit
	31	circumvent] deceive
80	25	under] by
81	16–17	(what may be called)
83	10	are] is
84	8–9	externally to our own island it has happened otherwise] it has happened otherwise externally to our own island
	10–11	is not at least] at least is not
	12	ours
	13	originally] once
86	19	Swift] Burnet
87	2	incidentally
89	15	the Tradition] it
	16	us] Catholics
90	27–28	even if I took on myself to do so, till I was] when I had not been
	29	occasion] date
91	8–9	advancing] saying
	27	prison] the house of correction
92	3	then to the case of a second priest] moreover to the case of another
93	25	its own evidence with it] their own evidence with them
95	27	inaccurate] misinformed
	28	fairly
96	7	scarcely venture, in these Lectures,] think it imprudent
99	15–16	notwithstanding, he is content to rely] still he simply relies
102	21–2	we have already seen used] had already been adopted
103	2	Jortin
104	13	who] while he
107	1	as Dr. Robertson thinks] what Robertson calls
	26–30	after surveying the whole course of the exposure – I could not help expressing to myself my intense misgivings that the efforts of Dr. Waddington and Dr. Maitland to do justice to the saint would be in vain.] after all, I could not help expressing to myself, after surveying the whole course of their exposure, my intense misgivings that their efforts would be in vain.
108	11	recklessly … blindly] … traditionally

Page	Line	
	12	luminously] emphatically
109	1	men avow] one avows
	3	as its conductors
	4	are] is
	5	their] his
	9	they] he
	11	their] his
	12	do they] does he
	18	they] he
	19	they protest … they had] he protests … he has
	21	do they] does he
	22	them] him
	28–29	and infallible, the guides] the guide
	30	see] sees
	33	themselves] himself
110	4	these accomplished writers] this accomplished writer
	5	their] his
	16	the writer] he
	29	proclaims] gives out
111	12	scandalous] great
112	11–12	great and public] serious
	22	such a sinner] a man
	28	only in one of them, – viz.
	29	in this Sacrament, in] here
113	32–3	deprived of Penance and of Holy Eucharist,] from Penance, Holy Eucharist, and Extreme Unction,
114	6	in idea
	8–9	Something like
	14	whom he had offended, he was not publicly reconciled] perhaps he could not be fully reconciled without sending to Rome
	16	he received the priest's reconciliation to the Church and to God] and was admitted to communion
	18	pontifical] external
115	10	testimony] witness
117	3	dated] signed
118	9	came the Tradition] it came
119	25	loungers, gossipers] gossipers, loungers
		[6]It is undeniable] [6]It is true
120		[6]… the scientific report, which our accuser brings forward, and] [6] … his builders'
	16	needs]needed
121	26	we know it] it is said

Page	Line	
	27–8	Torquemada] Ximenes
138	25	not more, perhaps less] just as much and just as little
	26	than] as
140	23	only ... only
	25	Even
141	20	then] these
	20–21	sort of men we really are] the persons really are like
	22	wish to] would
	27	proved] attained
	28	definite] definitive
142	5	meeting] having met
	6	obtaining] obtained
143	9	simply
	20	for which others were the authority] on the authority of others
144	1–2	the time I speak of
	30	its] his
	31	its] his
145	7	were] are
	33	subject] partner
146	1	an Apostasy from the Catholic Faith.
147	16	private] secret places
	24	joy ... reward]joys ... rewards
		[2] ... his] [2] ... the
148	7	too
	7	the presence] the very presence
	8	on their own course] their own way
	9	behind them
149	33	an] a
150	4	it may be] probably
	18	alluded to] observed
	19	fascination of sin] sinful excitement
152	7	would be] is
	15	to] of
	31	infer] argue
		[2] On one occasion he][2] He
153	21–22	he certainly thought] rightly or wrongly, he thought
		[6] ... number ... diocese][6] ... numbers ... dioceses
		[6] ... by the very form of his words,
		[6] ... (and my friend as well as his)
		[6] ... Dr. Whately's party] that number
		[6] ... though in fact it seems to have been no larger than the small band of Apostates, boasted of by the "Priests'

Page	*Line*	
		Protection Society" in Dublin.
154	4	then
	9	from the nature of the case
		[7] ... presently
155		[8] ... ought][8] ... is
		[8] ... This being the case, his *intention* in consecrating and administrating the sacraments was valid, even though he was an unbeliever.
		[8] ... I say all this in order to show what little bearing the unbelief of this small knot of priests had upon the Catholic population among whom they lived.
156	9–15	but are not more, after all, than Protestants have scraped together and made apostates of, out of the zealous Catholic clergy of Ireland; and, as no one dreams of taking such melancholy cases as specimens of the Irish Church, neither are Mr. Blanco White's friends specimens of the Spanish. He]Mr. Blanco White.
	16	still] though
	16–17	and I for one cannot receive his second-hand information. However, in any case,] but then
157	1	they
	2	stem] resist
	14	diocese of Seville] arch-diocese
	20	would
158		[3] ... has
		[3] ... the soul][3] ... which
		[3] ... to show that this really is his meaning, and he adds]
		[3] ... and
		[4] ... allowing, for argument's sake,][4] ... taking
		[4] ... even if granted
160	2	Protestant
	16	contain] have
	26–28	men ... men ... men ... their ... their] we ... we ... we ... our ... our
161	12–13	sorts ... sorts] manner ... manner
162	12	was] is
	13	penitent
163	9	so will she henceforth speak of it
164	4	on] in
	26	town] very place
167	1	Of course] And
	20	morbid] unhealthy

Page	Line	
	23	that ... are] ... to be
168	21	the natural and ordinary] natural, and the ordinary
	23–24	She makes ... to be] They make
	25	the very extravagance of her statements] their very extravagance
	29	writer or
171	19–21	he never hinted from any experience of his, that in matter of fact they did make any sinful suggestions.
	25	as regards] in the case of
175	8–9	Protestant public] people
	9–10	its preference of Maria Monk to Blanco White] their award
	15	Inhabitants] Men
	18	similar] the same
	21	to the calumnies] as this
176	21	does but prejudice] is no aid to
	22	a period] an era
	23	there] therein
180	6	a mode of treating] an observance in relation to
181	9	applied gunpowder, and
183	19	distress] disquiet
184	3	in fact
	8–9	and ... is] and is
185	16	John or James] son
186	31	could] would
	33	almost
188	3	to] in
191	15	which was
	16–17	which imposed] forcing upon
193	14	themselves.] themselves, like the boy in the story, who went and told of his playmate, who was before him in stealing the gooseberry pie.
	24	sent up
194	5	line of conduct] proceeding
	23	proposal ... for] talk ... of
195	10	had
	27	of
	24	party] party[3]
		... [3] The μισητος στασις of Mr. Froude: vid. Lyra Apostolica, 133.
197	6	to be for
	27	proposed by] of
199	7	of

Page	Line	
	10	themselves ... them] them ... themselves
	30	it is] is it
200	15	Such is the style of] So it is with
	20	from
	23	from
201	18	where] when
203	10	the] this
	17	Lord Chancellor] Queen

[4] ... Church, p. 53. I am told (1872) the Archbishop never owned the authorship of this able volume.][4] ... Church, p. 53.

204	11-12	annoying to the private circle and painful to the relatives] painful to the private circle and the living relations.
	26	and ... and] in ... and
206	9	must] will
	29-30	ourselves] us
208	2	birth] production
	2	am?" [6] am?"

[6] The paragraphs omitted are those which were decided by jury to constitute a libel, June 24, 1852.

3 * * * * * *] I have been a Catholic and an infidel; I have been a Roman priest and a hypocrite; I have been a profligate under a cowl. I am that Father Achilli, who, as early as 1826, was deprived of my faculty to lecture, for an offence which my superiors did their best to conceal; and who in 1827 had already earned the reputation of a scandalous friar. I am that Achilli, who in the diocese of Viterbo in February, 1831, robbed of her honour a young woman of eighteen; who in September, 1833, was found guilty of a second such crime, in the case of a person of twenty eight; and who perpetrated a third in July, 1834, in the case of another aged twenty-four. I am he, who afterwards was found guilty of sins, similar or worse, in other towns of the neighbourhood. I am that son of St. Dominic who is known to have repeated the offence at Capua, in 1834 or 1835; and at Naples again, in 1840, in the case of a child of fiteen. I am he who chose the sacristy of the church for one of these crimes, and Good Friday for another. Look on me, ye mothers of England, a confessor against Popery, for ye 'ne'er may look upon my like again.' I am that veritable priest, who, after all this, began to speak against, not only the Catholic faith, but the moral law, and perverted others by my teaching. I am the Cavaliere Achilli,

who then went to Corfu, made the wife of a tailor faithless to her husband, and lived publicly and travelled about with the wife of a chorus-singer. I am that Professor of the Protestant College at Malta, who with two others was dismissed from my post for offences which the authorities cannot get themselves to describe. And now attend to me, such as I am, and you shall see what you shall see about the barbarity and profligacy of the Inquisitors of Rome."

You speak truly, O Achilli, and we cannot answer you a word. You are a Priest; you have been a Friar; you are, it is undeniable, the scandal of Catholicism, and the palmary argument of Protestants, by your extraordinary depravity. You have been, it is true, a profligate, an unbeliever, and a hypocrite. Not many years passed of your conventual life, and you were never in choir, always in private houses, so that the laity observed you. You were deprived of your professorship, we own it; you were prohibited from preaching and hearing confessions; you were obliged to give hush-money to the father of one of your victims, as we learn from the official report of the Police of Viterbo. You are reported in an official document of the Neapolitan Police to be "known for habitual incontinency;" your name came before the civil tribunal at Corfu for your crime of adultery. You have put the crown on your offences, by, as long as you could, denying them all; you have professed to seek after truth, when you were ravening after sin.

290   10   Not doting, but untrustworthy.] He is not doting, but he is false.

16   trust] listen to

212   20   and which Catholics themselves] or which the world

213   10   in fact virtually] secretly

214   1   it seems

13   that

17–18   themselves

21–22   Anglican] Protestant

25   Christianity] Protestantism

215   6   absent] away

24–5   outlawry, forfeiture] outlawry, in civil matters, forfeiture

26   British Law] the British Constitution

216   14–15   they tore out his heart] his heart was being torn out

218   8   numbered.] numbered.[6]

Page   Line

⁶ "If you talk to me of the intolerance of Rome, or the horrors of the Inquisition," says Mr. Moore, M.P. for Mayo, in a late letter to the "Times" about Ireland, "I can submit to your inspection the original of *an Act of Parliament, passed unanimously by a whole Protestant Legislature, bishops and all,* which subjected the whole priest-hood of a whole people to obscene and horrible mutilation."

Page	Line	
219	5	on] in
	21	only] but
220	3	not of] not that of
	24	deny, that what is a stigma in their case is even a scandal in ours.] deny, to use a vulgar but expressive proverb, that what is sauce for the goose is sauce for the gander.
221	21	the duty of maintaining the truth
	29	river-side] stream
	30	conduct] wisdom
	30–31	Not to put the matter on higher and doctrinal grounds,
	32–33	injustice and cruelty] persecution
222	1–2	direct impulses, which it is impossible from the nature of man to destroy.] head a movement, which it is impossible to suppress.
	11	ideas] impulses
	12	ignore] deny
224	10	Catholicism] The Catholic Church
	12	vivid as the Church] captivating as she is
	17	preternatural] superhuman
	24	so far
	31–32	not only be made, but must
225	3	impeachment] accusation
	4	made] prefer
	4	impeachment they make] accusation they prefer
	22	for him
	26	something inflammatory
226	9	fiction] fictions
	15	the full
	20	have been] are
227	10	reckoned] considered
	14–15	and in spite of their subsequent demolition] which work their demolition has no tendency to undo
228	3	when] should
229	15	yet
	30	should] if

Page	Line	
Page	*Line*	
230	5	Providence] Being
	6	and it is true] and true
	27–28	comes of the perpetual talk against Catholics. It] the perpetual talk against Catholicism is doing in England. The clatter
231	13	incessantly] ever
	30–31	has any continued connexion with] depends on
232	5	this] it
	6	to be] is
	6	indeed
234	2	the] a
	22	mind] person
	26	its] his
235	27	moral
	29	commit themselves in the eyes of the whole world, would rather involve themselves in the most patent incongruities and absurdities, would rather make sport, as they do by their conduct, for their enemies in the four quarters of the earth] commit any weakness and incongruity, would rather make fun, as they do, for the whole world by their conduct,
236	6	beng blamed for] the blame of
	9–14	This` risk, as far as I am incurring it myself in these Lectures, I cannot help; I cannot help if, in exposing the prejudice of my countrymen, I incur the imputation of using satire against them; I do not wish to do so; and] This I cannot help; but
	15	matter] objects
	25	narrow, ungenerous spirit] supcrincumbent quality
237	31	and puts] and simply puts
	32	receiving] taking
238	1	by some friend
	2	by some opponent
	3–4	then says] goes on saying
	4	only
	5–6	He becomes more intensely and enthusiastically positive
	9	in the universe
	22	feeling of pleasure] satisfaction
	29	upon him
239	5	thinks] says
	29	To bring
	29	he thinks] as he thinks
240	15	even

Page	Line	
	30	upon] of
241	14	good] candid
	17	candour and
	30	got] get
242	8	or only before the Reformation
	26	hidden] hid
	27	the possible existence of
243	3	the] this
	5	denies that] denies the fact that
244	6	to Rome] home
	21	great
245	29	they die to him] he dies to them
249	29	on] upon
250	8	has so often] so often has
	12	communicated] been
251	8	Joannæ] Joanni
	12–13	by his imagination
	15–16	or the figure of religion in the vestibule of St. Peter's
	17	claim] claims
252	5	it was] it was but
	20	bad … good] good … bad
	27	are a disgrace to] tell against
	10	In one man] One time
	10–11	in … in … in] at … at … at
254	6	the Oratory] our Congregation
	31–32	one of the January Saints] St. Paul the first hermit
	32	for] as
256	33	handle] lift
257	17–18	(I am quoting the very words of his journal)
258	10	is placed] was
	16–19	and he seems to think it in some way connected with the season of the year, the Epiphany, when the Star appeared to the Wise Men.
259	2	know it
260	23	something like
	25–27	☛ *First a young priest setteth up a golden, diamond-like star, with a lamp in it, sticking it on the top of a candlestick; then he lighteth*] first, a young priest lighteth
	30	*the star*] a gold, diamond-like star, with a lamp in it, stuck on the top of a candlestick
261	24–25	at all
264	29	us] them
265	7	that

Page	Line	
	5–6	As determined by ... such is] According to ... is
	14	which
	18	he is very likely not to be] it is very likely he is not
	20	at all
	27	from] upon
285	6	as this
	16–17	from each other
	26	a First Principle] one
286	12	which shows] showing
288	3–4	not content ... you *will*] you will not be content ... but will
288–9	33–1	on rising up from the study
292	4	are] were
	11–12	which, when they set out they professed] which they professed, when they set out
	23–5	said, such as the First principles of morals, not peculiar or proper to the individual, but the rule of the world, because] said, not peculiar or proper to the individual, but the rule of the world, such as the First principles of Morals, because
293	8	those views] they
	9	to] in
	17–28	standards] judges
294	6	the common way of carrying] the way to carry
295	32	or does not partake
296	6	to
	21	abroad
	22	beef-steak] rump-steak
	28	revives] revises
	30	key] interpretation
	30	who
297	1	by little doses or great, if] or
	12	distinct] distant
300	32–33	here what one party urges, the other admits; they] it is agreed to on both sides: the two parties
302	8	such] the
	12	or "because what looked like a miracle was not a miracle;"
	27	such
303	7	acts] powers
	10	for them
305	8	intelligible] sensible
	30	is there to be imagined which can] remains to

Page	Line	
306	2	means of
	8	they] but they
307	9	that experience] the occurrence
	32	miracle of a Saint] report of a miracle
308	17–18	facts of history and biography] historical facts
309	17	own
	28	relic] curiosity
310	32	to a well] a well
311	4	Protestant's] Protestant
	6	error
	20	the sense] the same sense
	23	in it
312	25–26	(that is, of course the professed miracle being not miraculous)] (which is an evasion from the force of any proof)
313	12-13	superseded] stopped
	24	less[4]

[4] *Vide* Note 2 at the end of the volume.

Page	Line	
314	26	their] the
316	2	between them
	3	relates to] is about
	17	arguments about facts] cases
317	4–5	the Divine Revelation to the generation after them] to the next generation the divine revelation
	13	to
	16	they] men
	21	among his tenantry
	23	it was
318	3	the Catholic doctrine on the subject] it
	17	he thought that to offer] and that
	18–19	and that to demand it was a *reductio ad absurdam* of the person demanding
	31	whether] whether possibly
	33	possibly … in part
319	3	are they] men are
	4	letter-writing] writing
	22	portions, exhibiting,] compositions, containing,
	27–30	to receive an interpretation, and to make an impression, not in correspondence with the writer's intention, but according to the private principles and feelings of the reader.] to make an impression on him, not corrresponding to the writer's intentions, but to his own principles and feelings.

Page	Line	
320	3	surprised ... by] disappointed ... at
	4	speak
	7–8	in favour·... by their friends
321	17	own purposes] purposes
322	8	warrant] vouchers
	8	of what is Apostolic truth, on the one hand, and on the other, of what is] on the one hand, of Apostolic truth, and, on the other, of
323	32–33	"evasive and shuffling"] evasive and shuffling
324	1–2	"have never been told what their creed really is;"] have never been told what their creed really is
	4	"recent converts"] recent converts
	7	only passages from our writers] passages from our writers merely
325	9	those] the
	16	need] can
	20	testimony] witness
326	2	the man in question] an observer
	25	which was
327	26	need] want
	28	imposition] adoption
328	23	our
329	9	only lived] lived only
	11	in the objectors in question, to think that they know the Catholic faith, it is a second, to think that they can teach it to Catholics.] to think written documents sufficient, it is a second, as in this instance, to think Tradition too much. It is one mistake in the persons to whom I allude, to think they know the Catholic faith; a second to think they can teach it to us
330	10	and tracts
	20	they are so voluminous] there is so much of them
331	6	is. Now, anything] is. By means of a few words he does wonders; like the Englishman in Sicily, who, when he could not get his mules by the appliance of all the Italian he could command, fair or rough, at last effected his purpose by shouting out at the pitch of his voice to his host, who had never heard a word of English in his life, "Northumberland, Cumberland, Westmoreland, and Durham." Anything
	13	however
	15	what in the world] the world what
	17	his] their

Page	*Line*	
	19	stand in Reformation tracts] are
332	31	devotion] devotions
333	2	advance a step further] say more than this
	3	then, that, even] that
	4	can] could
	4	certain] a number
	6	without rising] but would rise
	10	has] had
	15–16	absolutely of conviction, but at least] of conviction simply, but
	20	diversity] variety
	24	after all
334	14	excellence] excellences
	23–24	an absolute hero] a hero
	25	holy
	27	and] yet
335	3	mere
	3–4	such a work] a work like this
	5–6	cannot refrain asking you candidly] can hardly refrain to ask
336	5	legend] story
	27	teach] say
339	4	in reference to them in print] about them
	10	No
	12	far
	20	certain] small
	25	that thus
	26	they
	30	not
340	29	instruct them in the actual meaning of his "texts" … , so] tell them what his "text" … actually did mean, so
	31–32	go on maintaining and proving, that we were really] continue to maintain and to prove that we were
	33	testify] tell them
341	10–11	this sort of
	21	wrong] so bad
	22	in which before now I have participated myself] for before now I have participated in them myself
342	6	hold friendly intercourse with] go among
	22	as in the case of Scripture
	26	the Catholic religion is] Catholics are
	27–28	myself wish] wish myself
343	26	superhuman] blasphemous

Page	Line	
	28	fallible] imperfect
344	9–10	gain from God what she desires by the medium of prayer] gain any thing she desires by prayer
	10	regarded as] called
	12	considered] called
345	13	so] come
	16–17	for all her days of communion] in spite of her many communions
346	7–12	So again, innkeepers paint up, "Entertainment for man and horse;" they do not add the important words, "to those who can pay for it." Every other private house in our streets has "Ring the bell" upon its door; that is, "if you have business within."
	12	again
	15	as when we talk of the imposition of "penances."
	16–17	Now, in like manner, as to Indulgences, "to absolve from sin"] And in like manner "to absolve from sin" is a phrase which
	18	First it may mean] Sometimes it means
	19–20	next, it may mean] sometimes it means
	22–26	Lecture.[8] Here, however, I am going to speak of the phrase in the former of these two senses—viz., as the remission of the *punishment* remaining *after* pardon of the sin. This is an indulgence; indulgence never is *absolution* or pardon itself.] Lecture. Now you know an Indulgence does one of these two things; it is either an *outward* reconciliation, or the remission of the *punishment* remaining after pardon of the sin; but it never is *absolution* or pardon itself.
		[8] In Lecture III. This sense, however, is unusual; *vide* Ferraris, Biblioth., art. Indulg., App. § 6.
30		absolution, which they always presuppose] *pardon*, which they always presuppose or precede
347	2	Indulgence does] Indulgence[8] does
		[8] *i.e.* Indulgence in the *second* of the two senses, which is the common one, of a remission of punishment. In the former sense, which is unusual (vid. Ferraris, Biblioth., art Indulg., App. § 6.), it has been considered in Lecture III.
	3	already
	6	whatever they are] of whatever kind
348	1	kind
	2	new
	6	among other instances] for instance

Page	*Line*	
	15–16	thee, in the hour of death, that is, provided] thee, that is, in that case in which alone an Indelgence ever can avail, i.e. *provided* that
	17	these] the
	19	it presupposes pardon
	24	be at least] simply be
	25–26	confession, gained a new spirit, and was restored to God's favour.] confession, and gained a new spirit
	32	certainly
349	4	that an ordinary layman] he
	6–7	that it is
	29	is] was
350	1	parchment] paper
	15–16	which is their own doing
351	9	out ... out
	12	be] had
	17	that
	23–24	a grant] the grant
	27	Confession is such.] such is Confession.
352	10	know
	26	now.[2]
		[2] P.339.
353	28	who, for *fear* of the Inquisition, did] who did, for *fear* of the Inquisition
354	5	antecedent proof] evidence
355	16	men] we
356	3–4	by myself
	4	have been] am
	6	some mere] the
	7	who had become a Protestant] doubting of Catholicism
	8	avowals] *word*
	11	matter of
357	6–7	the private judgement of these men] their private judgement
358	7	Protestants] it
359	16–17	that movement] it
362	28–31	[3] ... Mr. Capes returned to the Anglican Church in 1870, on occasion, I believe, of the definition by the Vatican Council of the Pope's Infallibility, but that change does not invalidate his testimony to matters of fact [Ed. 1872].
363		TITLE LECTURE IX.[4]
		[4] Written in 1851 apropos of the events of that year.

Page	Line	
364	5–6	in the case of those who, like you] as knowing you to be of their numbers who
	8	however
	9	that
	16	with] on
	19	with reference to it.
	31–32	this Elizabethan Protestantism] Protestantism, thus explained,
	33–	However, it is a tremendous power, and we are menaced by it,] Well I say we are
365	1	menaced by this tremendous power
	7	engaged upon] doing
	23	Elizabethan
367	18	the subject of] my subject in
368	1	might
	11	tyranny] injustice
	30–31	for fear of a moral infection
369	8	this or that as if] something as
	22	if
	23	just as are the principles] as such principles as
	28	has been made] is
370	17–18	Theorizing] Theory
	29	are convinced] become convinced, as they say,
371	19	about] of
372	21	becoming sure of] learning
	23	have been] are
373	11–14	I am not advocating, as you will see presently, anything rude in your bearing, or turbulent, or offensive; but first I would impress upon you the *end* you have to aim at.
	14	I say, must] then will
	29	us ... ourselves] them ... themselves
	30	we ... we] they ... they
374	5	one of
	6	his ... himself] their ... themselves
	11	should] to
	12–13	should absolutely] absolutely to
375	1	wrath] emotion
	16	perplexed] cold
	20	had at last] at last had
	31	cultivated
	33	into] to
376	15	need] call
378	21	treat] serve

Page	Line	
	22	they treat
379	4	objecs of such] marks for them
	10	obstinately] so obstinately
	28	so as to make it] to
380	27	be] lie
381	12–13	are born] arise
	13	last.[5]] last.[1]
		[5] *Vide* the author's Oxford University Sermons, No. V.]
		[1] Vide the University Sermons of the Author, No.IV
	19	antecedents … individuality] history … distinctiveness
382	6	or of … or of] or as … or as
	7–8	the owners of them
	17	makes about me] says
	31	an editor's room] editor's studies
383	4	its being
	11–12	are able to
	13	to
	14	to
	27	any] the
384	5	upon] on
	25–26	solemnly denied it] denied it upon my word
385	20	`in that case
	24	seen
	33	some] a few
386	22	as to] about
388	18	yourselves. Be] yourselves. Be true to yourselves, and success is in your hands. Be
	??	any
389	7	Apostolic] Apostolical
	13	be able to
	18	understand where] what
390	8–9	what their] what they are, what their
	17–18	so much … that they can] enough … to
	19	already
	30	keep in mind
	30	souls … a soul
	32	the Catholic spirit] Catholicism
	33	the Church] it
391	1	rulers] rulers here
	3	to
	6	the Church] us
392	27	to persuade and succeed] of persuasions and success
	31	When men see this, they] men, when they see this

Page	Line	
	32	they may] will make
393	22	by] with
394	1	is able to] will
	16	have never] never have
	28	nor am I at] I am not of
	29	when a man] which
395	7	Not every age is] Every age is not
	27	that
396	4	their age] theirs
	11	Christians] we
	18	fills it
	19	of
397	9	prowess] fruit
	11	to show
	20	unto] into
	31	such] those
398	13	of his faith
	23	then
	30–31	most recent] latest
400	12	be reminded that we may humbly trust] reflect that we may trust
	33	be "the heathen's jest,"] "Sit in the gate, and be the heathen's jest. / Silent and self-possessed,"
401	21	sagacious] profound
	28	and
402	15	were
	18–19	a best way ... it] betters ways ... them
	20	what is called
	21	only] what happens to be
	22	with ... may] others
403	8 9	desire and pray for ... that] do ... hope that
	12–13	that I may cheerfully] by leading me to
	13	anxiety] such anxiety
	15–16	with the confidence that no ... but will] and feel a sure confidence that such ... must
405	24	He adds this note: –] NOTE *on the Extract.*
406–	12–	An objection ... *vid.* Lecture VII] NOTE *on p.* 107. The
407	16	notice promised here, Lecture III., p. 107, on the doctrine of Indulgences, in connection with Absolution, has been anticipated in Lecture VIII., pp. 330–333.
407–	22–	NOTE II. The question ... ... JOHN H. NEWMAN."
416	23	

EDITOR'S NOTES

(Scripture references are to the Douay-Rheims translation which Newman mostly uses though he sometimes quotes the Authorised Version or a slightly inaccurate version of either. Where the name of a book is different in the Douay from that used today, the latter is also given in brackets.)

p. iii. *Tempus tacendi, et tempus loquendi*: 'A time to keep silence, and a time to speak' (Ecclesiastes 3:7). In the circumstances of the anti-Catholic agitation of 1850-1, Newman feels that the time has come to break silence and speak out about the true position of Catholics in English society (see p. 390).

p. lxxxvii. *The Most Reverend Paul Bishop of Armagh*: Paul Cullen (1803-78) was Archbishop of Armagh from 1849 to 1852, after which he became Archbishop of Dublin. Newman had just been asked by Cullen to help with the setting up of the new Catholic University of Dublin and was later to become its founding Rector.

p. lxxxvii. *without appearing to show disrespect to an Act of Parliament*: the Ecclesiastical Titles Act had just been rushed through Parliament in response to the setting up of the new Catholic Hierarchy. It made it illegal for anyone to assume the title of any 'pretended', i.e. Catholic, episcopal see, so Cullen was technically breaking the law if he called himself Archbishop of Armagh, and Newman is being deliberately defiant in so addressing him. No-one was ever prosecuted under this anti-Catholic legislation which was repealed in 1870.

p. lxxxviii. *whose kindness ... at Rome in 1847*: Newman had got to know Cullen while he was preparing for ordination in Rome, and Cullen had acted as censor of Newman's thesis there. Although the relationship between the two men became more difficult during Newman's period as Rector of the Dublin University, Cullen later came to Newman's help in

1867 when he vouched for Newman's orthodoxy when asked by the authorities in Rome.

p. xci. *Brothers of the Oratory*: a group of laymen ('seculars') aiming to carry out an apostolate in the world inspired by the spirit of the Oratory and under the guidance of the Oratorian priests.

p. 2. *my fable ... is old*: the story is one of Aesop's fables.

p. 3. *Samson*: see Judges 14:5-6.

p. 3. *David*: see 1 Kings (1 Samuel) 17:34-35.

p. 4. *a story of two knights*: a mediaeval allegory. In the original version a third knight arrives who tells the two disputants the truth about the shield. Newman slightly adapts the story to put the emphasis on each antagonist seeing things from his opponent's point of view.

p. 5. *Goethe*: Wolfgang von Goethe (1749–1842), the great German romantic; the reference is to his novel *Eine Leiden des jungen Werthers* (1774).

p. 5. *Schiller's drama*: *Die Räuber* by Johann von Schiller (1759–1805), the German dramatist and poet, was at one period banned for its romantic view of robbery.

p. 5. *Gay*: *The Beggar's Opera* by John Gay (1684–1732) is a play featuring low-life criminals.

p. 6. *a celebrated poet*: the verse-drama *Cain: A Mystery* by Lord Byron (1788–1824) defended both murder and incest by its eponymous biblical hero and provoked much controversy.

p. 8. *coxcombs*: foolish and vain young men.

p. 8. *Salvator*: Salvator Rosa (1615-1673), Italian painter of dramatic landscapes.

p. 8. *the fairy scenes of Claude*: Claude Lorraine (Gelée) (1600-82), French landscape painter.

p. 8. *beau garçon*: gallant and fashionable young man.

p. 10. *griffin*: a mythological monster with the legs, breast and head of an eagle and the body of a lion.

p. 10. *wivern*: a mythological winged dragon with an eagle's feet and a serpent's tail.

p. 10. *salamander*: a mythological lizard-like monster which could live in fire.

p. 10. *great societies*: the anti-Catholic organisations (see Introduction p.xvi).

p. 13. *the Homilies of the Church of England*: twenty one sermons, prescribed to be read out in churches of the Church of England, promulgated in 1542; frequently appealed to as an alternative source of authority and an important counterweight to the more Protestant Thirty-Nine Articles.

p. 13. *Bishop Newton*: Thomas Newton (1704-82), Church of England Bishop of Bristol; author of *Observations upon the Prophecies of David and the Apocalypse* in which the Antichrist was identified with the Pope. As a young man Newman had read and been greatly influenced by Newton's work, and he recorded that 'my imagination was stained by the effects of this doctrine up to the year 1843; it had been obliterated from my reason and judgment at an earlier date' (*Apologia Pro Vita Sua* (1864), Fontana Edn.1959, p. 100). He had discussed this work, which he described as the main source for the English Protestant tradition of Antichrist, in an article in the *British Critic* magazine in October 1840 ('The Protestant Idea of Antichrist', *Essays Critical and Historical*, Vol.II, Longmans, 1890, pp. 112-185). In this article Newman makes a witty critique of Newton's somewhat worldly and careerist character and life.

p. 15. *Dr. Waddington*: George Waddington (1793-1869), Dean of Durham and a traveller and noted church historian.

p. 18. *Joseph Blanco White*: (1775-1841) had been a priest in Spain but had gradually lost his faith. He came to England and was ordained a Church of England clergyman, later became a Unitarian minister and ultimately seems to have had no religious faith at all. Newman had known him well while they were both Fellows of Oriel College. The extract Newman quotes is from *Doblado's Letters* in *The New Monthly Magazine*, Vol.II, 1821, pp. 157-88; he had asked his friend David Lewis to track down this extract for him (see *The Letters and Diaries of John Henry Newman*, ed. C.S. Dessain & V.F. Blehl, Vol.XIV (London, 1963), p. 285). He gives a full account of White and quotes extensively from another of his works in Lecture IV (see pp. 142-160).

p. 19. *Pascal*: Blaise Pascal (1623-62), French mathematician, physicist and moralist.

p. 19. *the Jansenist party*: followers of Cornelius Jansen (1585-1638) who held rigorist moral views. Jansenism became a powerful movement among French Catholics; it was opposed by the Jesuits and ultimately condemned as heretical by the Church.

p. 19. *Exeter Hall*: a building in the Strand in London used by Evangelical groups for public meetings, including anti-Catholic ones. Newman uses it as shorthand for the bigoted low church Protestantism, and therefore anti-Catholicism, of his day.

p. 20. *Dr. Neander*: Johann Augustus Wilhelm Neander (1789-1850), church historian; professor at Heidelberg.

p. 20. *St.Chrysostom*: St. John Chrysostom (347-407), Archbishop of Constantinople, one of the four great Greek Doctors of the Church. He had been a hermit for some years before joining the clergy, and his sermons and letters contain advice and exhortations to the religious life. He also wrote extensive and penetrating commentaries on the Gospels and Epistles which were a major influence in the development of Christian theology.

p. 20. *Augustine*: St. Augustine of Hippo (354-430), Bishop and Doctor of the Church. His vast written output, which was one of the greatest influences on the development of Christian thought, included a Rule which was adopted by numerous religious orders, notably the canons regular and Augustinian friars.

p. 20. *Cassian*: St. John Cassian (c.360-c.435), founder of monasteries and author of two very influential works on the monastic life, the *Institutes* and the *Conferences*.

p. 20. *the Euphrates*: a river, flowing through modern day Iraq.

p. 20. *monachism*: the monastic life.

p. 22. *Basil*: St. Basil the Great (c.330-379), Bishop and Doctor of the Church. A monk in the early part of his life, he is considered the father of Eastern monasticism.

p. 23. *Theodoret*: (c.393-c.466), bishop of Cyrrhus, played a prominent role in the Eutychian controversy. For Newman's view of him, see *Historical*

Sketches, vol. ii., pp. 307-62.

p. 23. *Solomon's Proverbs*: the Book of Proverbs in the Bible, ascribed to Solomon though in fact a compilation of traditional wisdom.

p. 24. *an* ex parte *statement*: a statement made by, or in the interests of, one side only in a dispute; a one-sided view.

p. 24. *"Can any good come out of Nazareth?"*: John 1:46a; Nathanael's first reaction to hearing about Jesus, Nazareth being considered a remote and backward place.

p. 24. *"Come and see!"*: John 1:46b. Philip's reply to Nathanael who is then praised by Jesus for being 'without guile' and becomes one of the Apostles.

p. 25. *Christ being called Beelzebub*: see Mark 3:22; the scribes accuse Jesus of being able to cast out devils through the power of the prince of devils. The classic example of good being ascribed to evil.

p. 25. *Raffaelle*: the 19th century English spelling of Raphael (1483-1520), the Italian Renaissance artist.

p. 25. *the Apollo Belvidere* [sic]: normal spelling Belvedere; celebrated statue of the god Apollo, now in the Vatican gallery.

p. 26. *Blackstone*: Sir William Blackstone's (1723-80) *Commentaries on the Laws of England*, the much quoted standard authority on English law. The mis use of this by Newman's imaginary anti-British Russian speaker in what follows is a satire on the similar way that Protestant polemicists selectively quoted from and misunderstood equivalent Catholic texts such as conciliar and papal decrees and other ecclesiastical legislation.

p. 26. *farrago*: an absurdly mixed up collection.

p. 26. *an account ... a morning paper*: the account is, of course, fictional. Newman accurately imitates the newspaper style of his day.

p. 26. *Moscow*: Russia was an autocracy, and British ideas would therefore have been seen as dangerously democratic and subversive by the Czarist government. By choosing Russian ignorance of the real nature of the British legal and political system as a parallel to the Protestant attitude to Catholicism, Newman is able to ridicule Protestantism as similarly uninformed and bigoted. In the passages that follow, 'John-Bullism' is thus

Catholicism, and the anti-British Count is a typical anti-Catholic lecturer or preacher.

p. 26. *places*: public squares.

p. 26. *the Potemkin family*: descended from the famous Russian statesman, Gregori Potemkin (1739-91), lover and powerful adviser of Catherine the Great.

p. 26. *wars of the Caucasus*: wars to put down rebellious peoples on the outskirts of the Russian empire.

p. 27. *his extraordinary gallantry*: ironic; Newman implies he was extremely bloodthirsty.

p. 27. *the British minister*: the British Ambassador to Russia.

p. 27. *I transcribe it …*: the Count's speech closely resembles in style the many anti-Catholic speeches made at the time of the Papal Aggression crisis (see Introduction) and particularly one published in pamphlet form, *A Lecture Delivered at the Guildhall, Bath, On Monday, Dec.2, 1850, on the recent Papal Aggression by the Rev. M. Herbert Seymour*, of which there is a copy among the various documents Newman used in the preparation of these Lectures (under a front paper headed in Newman's handwriting '1851 Position of Catholics in England Preparatory Work'; documents D5 16 in the Archives of the Birmingham Oratory).

p. 28. *"Rule Britannia" … the "Old English Gentleman"*: traditional British songs, though the Count is mixing the genuinely patriotic and the light-hearted.

p. 28. *walk backwards*: part of the ceremony of the Opening of Parliament.

p. 28. *a Scotch firm*: a number of Scottish companies were working in Russia, often on engineering projects.

p. 28. *Antichrist … predicted in Scripture*: e.g. 1 John 2:18.

p. 29. *a book*: an anti-Catholic parallel to this would be the use made by Protestant polemicists of Canon Law, for instance in *A Lecture on Popery delivered by the Rev. Dr. Cooke at Belfast on Tuesday, Dec.3rd, 1850*, another of the pamphlets to be found among Newman's batch of *Present Position* papers.

p. 30. 'The King can do no wrong': this and the other apparently outrageous quotations from Blackstone are of course statements of the role of the Crown in jurisprudence and not, as the Count thinks, claims to moral perfection on the part of the individual monarch. Newman is drawing an implicit analogy with the Pope's infallibility when defining matters of faith or morals, frequently misunderstood by Protestants as a claim to personal impeccability. See Newman's Note I, pp. 406-7.

p. 33. *Sir Edward Coke*: (1552-1634) Lord Chief Justice, author of the *Institutes* and champion of the Common Law and the power of Parliament against the Crown; much admired in the 19th century.

p. 33. *the OMNIPOTENCE of Parliament*: in the legal sense – there is no appeal from Parliament as the highest court in the land (or was until the United Kingdom came under the jurisdiction of the European Court of Justice which would perhaps now similarly be legally regarded as 'omnipotent'.) Again, the analogy is with Rome as the Catholic Church's final court of appeal.

p. 34. *Bracton*: Henry de Bracton (d.1258), author of *De Legibus et Consuetudinibus Angliae*, the foremost medieval English jurist. The use by the Count of a single sentence from a medieval writer as evidence of the outrageous claims of 'John Bullism' parallels the use of similar quotations by anti-Catholic writers on the papacy such as Rev. Cooke quoted below.

p. 34. *'the Vicar of God on earth'*: the Rev.Cooke had been similarly shocked to find statements which seemed to claim divinity for the Pope:

> And now I charge the Romish system as being Anti-Christ because the Pope takes the very name of God ...In the extravagances of John the 22nd, he is styled "*Dominum Deum nostrum*" – "our Lord god the Pope." Then, another bishop is said and believed to have called him "another God on earth," ... Now, we are certain that the following words are used in the decretals of Pope Innocent II, 'That the Pope holds on earth the place of God almighty, or in other words that he is a God." ... Then there is another statement in the works of a very learned jurisconsult, an authority of great celebrity in the Romish Church, Philip Decius, who says, "All the acts of the Pope must be considered as the acts of God;" and again, "What is done by the Pope is considered as done by God, because he (the Pope) bears on earth the rank not of a sinless man, but of a God;" and lastly, "The Pope can do all things that God can do." Is not that a substitution of the name of the Pope for the name of God? Is not that the Pope standing in the place of God? (op.cit. p. 30).

p. 34. *my Lord Clarendon*: George Villiers, fourth Earl of Clarendon

(1800-70). The Count is confusing him with Edward Hyde, the first Earl of Clarendon (1609-74), author of *The True Historical Narrative of the Rebellion and Civil Wars in England*.

p. 35. *the 'Constitutions of Clarendon'*: nothing to do with the Earl of Clarendon! A series of laws enacted at a council summoned in 1164 by Henry II to check the power of the clergy as part of his dispute with Thomas à Beckett.

p. 35. *Lord Bacon*: Francis Bacon (1561-1626), first Baron Verulam and Viscount of St.Albans, politician, writer and philosopher. Among his professional works is a treatise on *Maxims of the Law*.

p. 35. *Alexander Pope*: (1688-1744), poet and satirist. In *The Rape of the Lock* the heroine, Belinda, is referred to, in mock-heroic style, as a 'Goddess' (Canto I, 1.7; IV, 1.79). Pope later published, pseudonymously, a *Key to the Lock* which claimed that the whole poem was a covert satire on Queen Anne.

p. 35. *Addison*: Joseph Addison (1672-1719), poet, dramatist and essayist. The phrase is from his poem *A Letter from Italy, to The Right Honourable Charles Lord Halifax*, 1.127. The 'goddess' being addressed is not Queen Anne but 'Liberty' personified.

p. 35. *represented on her coins*: the picture of Britannia on the old British penny (and the modern 50p piece) was not, of course, a representation of Victoria.

p. 35. *666, which is the mystical emblem of the lawless king!!!*: ridiculously ingenious as Newman's numerology is here, it is no more so than the numerology to be found in the *Penny Protestant Operative*, published by the Protestant Association **in the** 1840s, which had a regular page devoted to showing that the various names and titles of popes all add up to the number 666 (see D.G. Paz, *Popular Anti-Catholicism in Mid-Victorian England*, Stanford 1992, p.111).

p. 35. *Hallam*: Henry Hallam (1777-1859), historian, author of *A View of the State of Europe during the Middle Ages* which Newman quotes later (p.98).

p. 36. *the bench*: the Count puts together quotations about 'the bench' of the magistracy and 'the bench' of the Church of England bishops.

p. 36. *'the disgrace and remorse of perjury'*: Hallam is in fact referring to the crisis of the 'nonjurors', those clergy who refused in 1689 to take the oath of allegiance to William and Mary on the grounds that they had previously sworn allegiance to the now deposed James II.

p. 36. *six hundred women*: this wonderfully confused reference to Henry VIII's six wives makes a fitting climax to the garbled list of English monarchs' crimes and misfortunes. This indiscriminate mixing of fact, triviality and downright error imitates the similar lists of alleged Papal crimes to be found in anti-Catholic pamphlets.

p. 36. *the 'Edinburgh Review'*: a magazine published from 1802 onwards; it was Whig in its political outlook.

p. 36. *Hollinshed*: Raphael Holinshed (d.1580), translator and historian. His *Historie of England* was much used by Shakespeare for his History plays. There does not appear to be an article on this subject in *The Edinburgh Review*.

p. 36. *Sir John Fortescue*: (1394-1476), a principal judge in the reign of Henry VI and the first English constitutional lawyer; author of several treatises on English law.

p. 37. *Sir Matthew Hale*: (1609-76), Lord Chief Justice and author of *A History of the Common Law of England*.

p. 37. *valets ... death*: these are incidents drawn from melodramas and popular fiction.

p. 37. *Husbands sell their wives*: the novelist Thomas Hardy (1840-1928) was to make use of such a story (though without the rope round the neck) in *The Mayor of Casterbridge*, and when challenged as to its likelihood said that he had found three accounts of wife-sales in newspapers from 1826-1879 The Russian Count gives the impression that they are a regular occurrence; Newman is parodying the way that anti-Catholic polemicists quoted similarly scandalous stories as if they were typical occurrences.

p. 37. *sculls*: these are of course rowing *sculls*, not anatomical *skulls*.

p. 37. *Rush ... Jeffreys*: an extremely heterogeneous list of 'two-legged tigers', i.e. men of fierceness and cruelty. A number of them appear in the novels of Sir Walter Scott.

Rush: James Rush (d.1849) murderer of the inheritor of the estate where he was a tenant.

Thistlewood: Arthur Thistlewood (1770-1820), one of the Cato Street conspirators who planned to assassinate Cabinet ministers while they were dining at Lord Harrowby's house in Grosvenor Square, London, in 1820. He was convicted of high treason and hanged.

Thurtell: John Thurtell (1794-1824), hanged for murder.

the Mannings: Frederick George Manning (d.1849), a publican, and his wife Marie Manning (1821-1849), both hanged for murder.

Colonel Kirk: Piercy Kirke (1682-91), soldier; notorious for his cruelty towards the rebels at the Battle of Sedgmoor (1685),

Claverhouse: John Graham of Claverhouse, first Viscount Dundee (1649-89), was a powerful and oppressive figure in Scotland during the reigns of Charles II and James II; he appears in Scott's novel *Old Mortality*.

Simon de Monteforte: (1208-1265), earl of Leicester; powerful baron who opposed Henry III; accused of oppression and violence but acquitted. Later he forced the king to call a Parliament; died at the battle of Evesham.

Strafford: Sir Thomas Wentforth, 1st Earl of Strafford (1593-1641), was chief minister to Charles I. He commanded the English army which defeated the invading Scots; he was hated by Parliament which forced Charles to agree to his execution.

the Duke of Cumberland: William Augustus, Duke of Cumberland (1726-65), second son of George II; nicknamed 'the Butcher' after his defeat of the Scots at Culloden and subsequent oppression in Scotland. He appears in Scott's novel *Waverley*.

Warren Hastings: (1732-1818), first Governor-General of India. He was tried for corruption and cruelty in a celebrated case but eventually acquitted.

Judge Jeffreys: George Jeffreys (1644-89), a judge with a brutal reputation, mainly due to the 'Bloody Assizes' in which he condemned to death many followers of the Monmouth rebellion.

p. 37. semper idem: 'always the same'.

p. 37. *punishable with death*: these offences did indeed carry the death penalty at the time Blackstone wrote, but this was no longer the case in 1851, nor were the crimes which follow now capital offences.

p. 38. *The Crusades … the French Revolution*: British involvement in these events ranged from major to non-existent. Newman is again satirising the list of crimes and wars for which Protestant polemicists held the Catholic Church responsible. The Russian Count's knowledge of history shows the same kind of confused mixing of fact and fiction as that found in popular anti-Catholic tracts.

The Crusades: the various (ultimately unsuccessful) military expeditions undertaken by European armies in mediaeval times to liberate the Holy Places in Palestine from Muslim control. There were seven principal crusades between 1096 and 1270; the third was jointly led by King Richard I (the Lionheart) of England. To describe English involvement in any of the Crusades as example of 'John Bullism' is of course an anachronism.

the Sicilian Vespers: a massacre of the Normans in Sicily in 1282, the signal for which was the ringing of the church bells for Vespers. England had no involvement whatsoever.

the wars of the Reformation: these Catholic–Protestant conflicts in the 16th century were confined to continental Europe and had no direct English involvement.

the Thirty Years War: further Catholic–Protestant conflicts in the German states and beyond, lasting from 1618 to 1648, again without English involvement.

the War of Succession: this refers either to: (i) the War of Spanish Succession (1701-13) in which Britain was in alliance with the Habsburgs of Austria against France in the struggle for the Spanish throne, the Battle of Blenheim being a notable British victory under the generalship of John Churchill; or (ii) the War of Austrian Succession (1740-48) in which Britain supported Maria Theresa of Austria against Prussian aggression; this saw the last appearance on the battlefield of a reigning British monarch, George II at Dettingen in 1743.

the seven years' war: this was a renewal of the above conflict between Austria and Prussia, from 1756 to 1763, in which Britain this time entered into a military alliance with Prussia in order to keep the French occupied in Europe while Britain furthered the building of her empire in India and North America. This could indeed be seen as 'John-Bullism', Britain's involvement in the war being part of her policy of imperialist expansion.

the American war: of Independence (1776-83).

the French Revolution: the overthrow of the French monarchy and *ancien régime* and the establishment of the Republic which took place in the years following 1789. Although Britain was at war with the young republic and later with Napoleon, it is historical nonsense to claim that the Revolution itself was caused by 'John-Bull ideas'.

p. 38. *the last war*: the Napoleonic Wars which ended with the French defeat by Britain and Prussia at Waterloo in 1815. Two million is a reasonable estimate of the total number of deaths, though this would include Napoleon's disastrous invasion of Russia 1811-1812.

p. 38. *the Whigs*: the Whig Party in Parliament, under the leadership of Charles Fox, did indeed criticise some aspects of the Tory government's conduct of war against Napoleon. Whigs, especially in the earlier stages, were ambivalent towards the French Revolution. The claim that the Whigs 'down to this day' blame Britain entirely for the Napoleonic Wars is an absurdity. However, the Count could also be making a confused reference to *The History of John Bull*, a series of pamphlets by John Arbuthnot (1667-1735) which advocated the ending of Britain's war against France in the War of Spanish Succession (see above). In these the character of John Bull first appears, invented by Arbuthnot as an allegorical figure for England. Arbuthnot, however, was not a Whig but a Tory.

p. 38. *Jezebel ... the prophetic vision*: in the Bible Jezebel was the pagan wife of King Ahab. She promoted the worship of Baal and was denounced by the prophet Elijah (see 3 Kings (1 Kings) 16:31-21:25). The name also appears in the Book of Revelation, referring to a prophetess in the Church of Thyatira who is denounced by the writer for leading its members astray (Rev 2:20). Since the time of the Reformation the name had been used by Protestant controversialists as a term of abuse for the Catholic Church.

p. 38. *a prophet of her own ... the mystical sunceress*: in 1839 the Rev. Hugh McNeile, a leading figure in anti-Catholic agitation, gave a speech in which he exclaimed, 'What peace so long as that woman Jezebel lives?' He meant this as a reference to the Papacy but was widely misunderstood to have meant Queen Victoria and was thus accused of inciting his audience to assassinate the Queen (see Wolffe, *op.cit.*, p.166).

p. 39. *the awful volume which I hold in my hands*: Blackstone's *Commentaries on the Laws of England* (see above). The 'ubiquity' and 'immortality' of the Crown are, again, legal conventions which the Russian Count reads as literal statements. The parallel in the Catholic Church would be with the role of the Pope in matters such as the Holy See's universal jurisdiction.

p. 40. *sophisms*: statements of superficially clever but false reasoning. The sayings which follow are in fact legal tags of no sinister significance whatever. On the face on it, they may appear to state startling or even immoral principles. Their real meaning, however, is apparent to someone who knows their legal context and application. Similarly, statements found in Catholic manuals of ethics were frequently given sinister interpretations by Protestant polemicists. This is to be an important element in Newman's analysis of anti-Catholic prejudice when he discusses Protestant misunderstanding of Catholic theological statements in Lecture VIII.

'De minimis non curat lex': lit.'The law does not concern itself with the smallest things'; for instance, a dispute may be deemed to be over such a trivial matter that the law declines to be involved in it.

'Malitia supplet ætatem': lit. 'Malice supplies the age' i.e. of criminal responsibility. Children below the age of 10 cannot be guilty of an offence; but those between the ages of 10 and 14 may be held to be so capable if there is evidence of 'mischievous discretion' or guilty knowledge that they were doing wrong. Thus their malice supplies their 'age' of responsibility.

'Tres faciunt collegium': lit. 'Three make a company.' The eminent Roman jurist Neratius Priscus laid it down that three is the minimum number of people who can constitute a 'collegium' or company.

'Impotentia excusat legem': lit. 'Impotency excuses law'. Impossibility of performance is a valid reason for failing to fulfil an obligation imposed by law.

'Possession is nine parts of the law': possession (of e.g. land) is good against all the world except the true owner. However, possession can ripen into ownership by the passage of time; for example, 'adverse possession of land' (i.e. without the owner's agreement) for twelve years destroys the title of the owner and vests it in the possessor. Also, the holder of a negotiable instrument (such as a cheque), a factor, or a seller in an open market can give a better title than he actually has, provided the buyer takes in goods faith and for value (i.e. he pays money in the belief that the seller owns them). The true owner cannot then dispute the buyer's title to the goods (unless the thief has been convicted) and so the seller's possession of the goods (and later the buyer's possession) has been decisive. Hence the maxim.

'The greater the truth, the greater the libel': just because a statement is true, that does not necessarily stop it also being judged libellous; the person who published the true statement also has to prove that it was fair comment in

the public interest as well. If it is not fair comment, then it may be judged that the statement, even though true, should not have been published; and further that since it *is* true, the damage to the libelled person is all the greater because something true has been published about him which should not have been published, and so he has been damaged even more than if the published statement were false.

p. 40. *blighting superstitions*: what follow are further legal technical terms, without, of course, any sinister significance:

primogeniture: the law of inheritance by the eldest son

gavelkind: a law of inheritance in which the property of a man who died intestate was divided equally among all his sons.

mortmain: in mediaeval times, land which was held by the Church or other bodies (sometimes given to the Church as a means of feudal tax avoidance).

contingent remainders: part of an estate, left over from the principal inheritance, which will only be passed on in the event of some particular circumstances coming into force.

habeas corpus: lit., 'You are to produce the body'. The famous legal principle by which nobody may be imprisoned indefinitely without trial; first enshrined in Magna Carta, it has always been regarded as one of the cornerstones of English liberty.

quare impedit: lit., 'wherefore he hinders'. A writ issued on behalf of the lay patron of a benefice in the Church of England if the bishop refused to institute as parish priest the person whom the patron had appointed.

qui tam: lit., who as well', an action brought by an informer under a penal statute to recover a penalty of which the whole or part went to him. Thus he sued 'on behalf of our Lord the King as well as for himself.'

p. 40. *mummeries*: originally mediaeval popular dramas; this later became the standard Protestant term of abuse for the ceremonies of the Catholic liturgy. (At the time of the Reformation, government-funded 'mummers' were sent round England to perform mockeries of Catholic ritual as anti-Catholic propaganda.)

p. 40. *wigs, and bands, coifs and ermine*: variously worn by barristers and judges in English courts. (A *coif* was a medieval legal headdress worn by

Serjeants-at-Law, an order of senior advocates, later abolished. Newman's close friend Edward Bellasis was a Serjeant-at-Law and may have been the source of some of the legal knowledge displayed here).

p. 40. *fee simple ... feuds*: more legal terms, many of them obsolete:

fee simple: an estate free from any conditions restricting its inheritance.

fee tail: an estate which can only be inherited by a particular person and his legal heirs.

villanage: in feudal times, the holding of land by villeins who had to perform menial tasks for their feudal lord as a condition of their tenure.

free soccage: similar to the above, the tenure of land dependent on the performance of certain duties.

fiefs: in feudal times, fief was the tenure of land on the condition of military service. (Like *heriot*, *seizin* and *feuds*, this word usually only occurs in the singular; the Russian Count's use of the plural shows that he does not understand these terms.)

heriots: in feudal times, the right of the lord of a manor to the best parts of the property of certain of his tenants on their death.

seizins: the freehold possession of property.

feuds: estate or land held on condition of feudal service.

p. 40. *shares ... narrow gauge*, a confusion of terms drawn from business, finance and the railways industry, none of which the Count evidently understands:

premiums: the profits paid out by a Limited Company on the *shares* it has sold in its business.

post-obits: loans made on the expectations which the borrower has of inheriting money or property on the death of his parents or other benefactor.

broad and narrow gauge: for some time there was a 'battle of the gauges' between the narrow railway gauge originally used by George Stephenson and the broad gauge used by I.K. Brunel on the Great Western Railway. The narrow gauge was ultimately victorious and is the one used in Britain today.

This climactic peroration to the Count's speech is close in style to Seymour's lecture (see above) which also has the reaction of the audience in parentheses *(Hear!)* and *(Tremendous applause)*, as was the standard practice of the time in accounts of public meetings (and is still used in *Hansard*, the report of proceedings in Parliament). Newman's juxtaposition of these enthusiastic reactions and the absurd misunderstandings in the Count's speech effectively satirises the excited atmosphere of anti-Catholic meetings.

p. 41. *an effigy of John Bull ... and a Queen Victoria*: effigies of the Pope and of Cardinal Wiseman were frequently burned during the anti-Catholic demonstrations of 1850-1

p. 43. *professors*: those who profess, believe it (not academic Professors).

p. 43. *the recluse and the devotee*: monks and nuns, especially of 'enclosed' orders who had no contact with the outside world.

p. 43. *They drop a thousand years from the world's chronicle*: according to the commonly received Protestant version of history, Christianity had become corrupted by 'Romish' ideas by about the year 500 and was only returned to its original purity by the Reformation of the 16th century.

p. 44. *a camera obscura*: a device which throws an image of external objects onto a white screen in a darkened room; a popular novelty in Victorian times.

p. 44. *Tartars or Patagonians*: the inhabitants respectively of Central Asia and the southernmost part of South America (thus distant savages, as far as Newman's audience were concerned).

p. 45. *he should be inspecting ... of East and West*; 1851 was the year of the Great Exhibition held in the Crystal Palace in Hyde Park, London. It was designed to show off the finest produce of the British Empire.

p. 46. *the Catholic Relief Bill*: the Roman Catholic Relief Act of 1792 removed some of the legal restrictions on Catholics.

p. 46. *Lord Eldon*: John Scott (1751-1838), first earl of Eldon, statesman; Lord Chancellor under Pitt and Portland.

p. 46. *George the Third; and there was Mr. Pitt obliged to give up office*: King George III (1760-1820) was horrified at the proposal of his Prime Minister, William Pitt, that the Catholics of Ireland should be granted religious toleration as part of his plan to unite Ireland with England in the Act of Union. The King claimed that it would violate his coronation oath to uphold the Protestant religion. Pitt had committed himself to Catholic emancipation to placate Irish popular opinion, and now faced with the King's implacable opposition he felt obliged to resign in 1801.

p. 46. *Lord George Gordon*: the Roman Catholic Relief Act of 1778 was the first step in the repeal of the penal laws and gave some legal rights to Catholics on condition that they took an oath of loyalty to the Crown. However, it provoked a violent anti-Catholic reaction, led by the Protestant demagogue Lord George Gordon. This culminated in the bloody Gordon Riots in London in 1780 which were only put down by the use of the military and resulted in many deaths.

p. 47. prima-facie: at first view.

p. 47. *Tallis*: Thomas Tallis (c.1505-85), composer. The author of the 'Protestant Hundredth Psalm tune' (best known to English congregations as 'All people that on earth do dwell') is unknown; most hymn books give its source as the Genevan Psalter, c.1551.

p. 47. *Bishop Butler of Durham*: Joseph Butler (1692-1752). His *Analogy of Religion*, which defends revealed religion against the Deists, was an important influence on Newman (see *Apologia*, pp.102-3).

p.48. *Bishop Ken*: Thomas Ken, bishop and religious writer and poet (author of the hymn 'Glory to Thee, my God, this night'.).

p. 48 *Mr,Evelyn*: John Evelyn (1620-1706), writer and diarist.

p. 51. *"In vain ... of men."*: Matthew 15.9 (quoting Is 29.13).

p. 58. *protocols*: diplomatic agreements with other nations.

p. 59. *the Latitudinarian party*: theological liberals.

p. 60. *Marshal Soult*: Nicholas Soult (1769-1851) one of Napoleon's favourite and most capable generals and Wellington's opponent in the Peninsular War.

p. 60. *Louis Philippe*: (1773-1850), the 'Citizen King' of France.

p. 60. mutatis mutandis: with due alteration of details (in comparing cases).

p. 60. *Wellington*: Arthur Wellesley, first Duke of Wellington (1769-1852), soldier and statesman; the victor of Waterloo, later Prime Minister.

p. 60. *Blucher*: Field-Marshall Gebhard von Blucher (1742-1819), commander of the Prussian army at Waterloo.

p. 60. *the Emperor Nicholas*: Tsar Nicholas I of Russia (1796-1855), champion of autocracy, Orthodoxy and Russian nationalism.

p. 60. *Lord Londonderry*: Robert Stewart (1769-1822), second marquis of Londonderry, better known as Viscount Castlereagh, statesman. He became unpopular because of the Six Acts, 1819, and later the measures against Queen Caroline (see below); latterly he became mentally ill through overwork and committed suicide.

p. 60. *his wife*: Caroline of Brunswick (1768-1821) became estranged from the King immediately after their marriage in 1795. Despite her extraordinary coarseness, vulgarity and scandalously immoral personal life, she was wildly popular, especially with the London mob. Newman's father was a supporter of Caroline, while John Henry strongly disagreed. His brother Frank later recorded a violent argument between father and son on the subject.

p. 61. *St. Francis of Assisi ... would be hooted*: Newman may also have in mind the experience of Dominic Barberi (1792-1849), the Italian Passionist priest who came to England and travelled the country barefoot in his monk's habit preaching. He attracted derision for this and later adopted a more English style of dress. Newman much admired his missionary spirit and personal sanctity, however, and it was he who received Newman into the Catholic Church at Littlemore in 1845. He was beatified in 1963.

p. 61. *dressed up like a mandarin*: St. Francis Xavier (1506-1552), the great Jesuit missionary, adopted Eastern dress to assist his evangelisation of the East Indies and Japan.

p. 61. *a Parsee*: member of a Zoroastrian sect of Persian descent found in India.

p. 61. *a Bonze*: European term for a Buddhist priest.

p. 61. *cynosure*: literally a guiding star, something which attracts attention.

p. 62. *Bluff King Hal*: Henry V (1387-1422), so called in Shakespeare's play.

p. 62. *glorious Bess*: Elizabeth I (1533-1603).

p. 62. *the Royal Martyr*: Charles I (1600-49).

p. 62. *the Merry Monarch*: Charles II (1630-85).

p. 62. *the pious and immortal William*: William III (1650-1702), 'pious' in the Protestant tradition because in the 'Glorious Revolution' of 1688 he replaced the ousted Catholic James II. Since that time no Catholic can succeed to the throne.

p. 62. *the good King George*: George III (1738-1820).

p. 63. *the lion and the dog*: the heraldic supporters on the royal arms of Henry VIII. (Since 1603 the dog, a greyhound, has been replaced by a unicorn.)

p. 63. ex animo: from the heart.

p. 63. *the Achitophels of the day*: in the Bible, Achitophel was the treacherous adviser of King David. He deserted the king for David's son Absalom, who was leading a revolt, but later committed suicide (see 4 Kings (2 Kings) 25). So, in general, Achitophels are royal counsellors whose advice should not be trusted. Dryden had made this use of the name famous through his political satire *Absalom and Achitophel*.

p. 64. *The Virgin Queen*: Elizabeth I, as depicted in royal propaganda.

p. 64. *alderman*: a senior civic dignitary. 'A magistrate in English and Irish cities and boroughs, next in dignity to the Mayor; properly, as in London, the chief officer of a ward.' (O.E.D.)

p. 64. *burgess*: citizen (of a city borough).

p. 65. *disputes between the Pontificate and the Regale, the dispute about Investitures*: the arguments in the 11th and 12th centuries between the rights of the Papacy and the rights of the Crown to the appointment of Bishops to vacant Sees.

p. 65. *Rufus*: William II (1056-1100).

p. 65. *St. Anselm*: (c.1033-1109) as Archbishop of Canterbury he had a prolonged dispute with both William II and Henry I in which he defended the right of the Church to elect bishops without interference from the Crown.

p. 65. *St. Thomas*: Thomas à Beckett (1118-1170), Archbishop of Canterbury. His dispute with Henry II over the respective jurisdictions of Church and State led to his martyrdom in Canterbury Cathedral.

p. 65. *Henry of Winchester*: Henry III (1207-1272).

p. 65. *St.Edmund*: Edmund of Abingdon (c.1170-1240), Archbishop of Canterbury. He had a dispute with Henry III over the differences between church law and English common law.

p. 65. *Cardinal Fisher*: St. John Fisher (1469-1535), martyred for refusing to recognise Henry VIII's claim to be Head of the Church in England.

p. 66. *Alfred*: Alfred the Great (849-99), heroic King of Wessex, law-giver and encourager of scholarship.

p. 66. *St. Edward*: King Edward the Confessor (c.1004-1066), saintly Anglo-Saxon ruler; buried in Westminster Abbey.

p. 66. *Stephen Langton*: (1151-1228) Archbishop of Canterbury; one of the main influences in bringing about the signing of Magna Carta by King John.

p. 66. *Friar Bacon*: Roger Bacon (1214-94), Franciscan friar; founder of experimental science.

p. 68. *no English literature before the age of Elizabeth*: Newman ignores Chaucer and the other mediaeval writers. The nineteenth century revival of interest in Middle English literature was only just beginning.

p. 68. *Pericles*: (c.490-429 B.C.) Athenian statesman, general and orator at the time of Athens' greatest success and influence.

p. 68. *Alexander*: Alexander the Great (356-323 B.C.), King of Macedon and conqueror of an immense empire.

p. 69. patois: specialised language, dialect.

p. 69. *"As in ... vilest using"*: from 'The Children in the Temple' by John Keble (1792-1866), in *The Christian Year*. This collection of poems, published in 1827, was enormously influential. Newman said that in it Keble (who was to become his close friend and a leading figure in the Oxford Movement) 'struck an original note and woke up, in the hearts of thousands a new music, the music of a school, long unknown in England'

(*Apologia*, p. 108). 'The Children in the Temple' is an appeal to poets to use their gift for God's glory, in contrast to the more earthly concerns of writers, such as Byron and Shelley, who 'in idol-hymns profane/The sacred soul-enthralling strain'. It is significant that the Catholic Newman now re-applies it in the context of writers having mis-used nascent English literature to promote Protestantism.

p. 69. *Spenser*: Edmund Spenser (1552-99), poet; his most famous work is *The Faerie Queen*.

p. 69. *Sidney*: Sir Philip Sidney (1554-86), poet and soldier; his *Apologie for Poetrie* is one of the earliest pieces of literary criticism.

p. 69. *Raleigh*: Sir Walter Raleigh (1552-1618), the celebrated sea adventurer and writer.

p.69. *Hooker*: Richard Hooker (1554-1600), Church of England divine and scholar; author of *The Laws of Ecclesiastical Politie*.

p. 69. *"a fair vestal throned by the west"*: Shakespeare, *A Midsummer Night's Dream*, Act II, Scene ii, line 158.

p. 70. *Milton*: John Milton (1608-74), poet, author of the Biblical epic poem *Paradise Lost*.

p. 70. *Bunyan*: John Bunyan (1628-88), author of *The Pilgrim's Progress*.

p. 71. *Locke*: John Locke (1632-1704), philosopher, author of *An Essay concerning Human Understanding*.

p. 71. *Hume*: David Hume (1711-76), philosopher, historian and political writer, author of *A Treatise of Human Nature, History of Great Britain*.

p. 71. *Robertson*: William Robertson (1721-93), Presbyterian minister and historian, author of *A History of Scotland during the reigns of Queen Mary and James VI* and *A History of Charles V*. Newman later quotes from the latter (p. 100).

p. 71. *Cowper*: William Cowper (1731-1800), poet.

p. 71. *Samuel Johnson*: (1709-84), the great lexicographer and writer.

p. 72. *Wordsworth*: William Wordsworth (1770-1850), poet. Newman is referring to his *Ecclesiastical Sonnets* published in 1822.

p. 72. *Burke*: Edmund Burke (1729-97), political philosopher; amongst the causes that Burke championed was Catholic emancipation.

p. 72. *the Prayer Book*: the Book of Common Prayer, the Church of England's liturgical texts, written largely by Archbishop Thomas Cranmer and given its final form in 1662.

p. 72. *the Thirty-nine Articles*: the thirty-nine statements approved by Parliament in 1557 to which Anglican ministers had to subscribe. They were said to be 'moderate' in that they were designed to reject both Catholic and extreme Protestant doctrines.

p. 72. *the Pretender*: the exiled Stuart (and Catholic) claimant to the throne. There were two: the Old Pretender, James, the son of James II; and his son, the Young Pretender, Charles.

p. 72. *London is burned ... the incendiaries*: the Monument to the Great Fire of London bore an inscription claiming that the fire had been started by 'ye treachery and malice of ye popish factiö, in order to ye carrying on their horrid plott for extirpating the Protestant religion and old English liberty, and the introducing popery and slavery.' It had only been removed in 1831.

p. 72. *Pope Joan*: a supposed female pope said to have reigned between Leo IV and Benedict III in the 9th century. This myth, which dated back to the middle ages, had been debunked as early as 1640 and by a Protestant writer, but it was long commonly believed to be an historical fact by Protestants, as Newman later mentions (p. 79). It was used as the name of a popular card game which was played with the eight of diamonds, called the 'Pope Joan', removed from the pack.

p. 73. *the Mountebank*: a seller of quack medicines at fairs who drew the crowds with juggling feats and other tricks, performed on a raised platform ('bank').

p. 73. *the most sacred words of the Catholic ritual*: Newman is probably referring to the sham-Latin formula 'Hocus-pocus' which has been thought to be a corruption of the words of Consecration at Mass, 'Hoc est corpus' ('This is my body').

p. 73. *Jesuitical ... dishonourable and vile*: e.g. the Oxford English Dictionary defines 'Jesuitical' as 'deceitful, dissembling'.

p. 74. *incubus*: something which lies oppressively on the mind, a nightmare; originally, an evil spirit believed in mediaeval times to assault women sexually as they slept.

p. 75. *Unitarians*: a religious body which rejects the doctrine of the Trinity, denying that the Son and the Holy Spirit are Divine Persons. The Unitarians were descended from the liberal Presbyterians of the 17th century. The first Unitarian church opened in London in 1774. Newman was much disturbed at the way that people such as Blanco White (see above note on p.18) and his own brother Francis abandoned orthodox Christianity and ended up with Unitarian beliefs.

p. 75. *Sabellians*: Sabellianism was a heresy dating back to the early centuries of Christianity. It took various forms but latterly consisted of the view that the Son and the Holy Spirit were not divine Persons but different manifestations or 'masks' of God the Father, thus denying the Incarnation.

p. 75. *Utilitarians*: followers of the philosopher Jeremy Bentham (1748-1832). Utilitarianism rejected any standard for judging right or wrong apart from that which would bring about 'the greatest happiness of the greatest number'.

p.76. *Wesleyans*: followers of John Wesley (1703-91), Methodists.

p. 76. *Calvinists*: followers of the Protestant Reformer John Calvin (1509-64). His doctrines, notably predestination, influenced a number of Protestant bodies, especially Scottish Presbyterianism.

p. 76. *Swedenborgians*: followers of Emanuel Swedenborg (1688-1772), the Swedish philosopher, scientist and mystic who developed an esoteric religious system following a series of visions he experienced. The poet William Blake was among those influenced by him.

p. 76. *Irvingites*: followers of Edward Irving (1792-1834), a former minister of the Church of Scotland. They called themselves 'The Catholic Apostolic Church' and were satirised by Newman in his novel *Loss and Gain*.

p. 76. *Freethinkers*: those who refuse to submit their reason to the control of authority in matters of religious belief; a designation claimed especially by the deistic and other rejecters of Christianity at the beginning of the 18th century (O.E.D.).

p. 76. *"The Mother and Mistress of all Churches"*: in reality the title of St. John Lateran, the Cathedral Church of Rome and therefore the mother church of the Catholic world. Newman here satirically suggests that the Church of England applies this title to the British monarch as head of the Church of England.

p. 76. *"the Bishop of Rome hath no jurisdiction in this land"*: Article XXXVIII of the Thirty-Nine Articles.

p. 77. n.1. *an able pamphlet by Serjeant Bellasis*: Bellasis's open letter, *The Anglican Bishops, versus the Catholic Hierarchy: A Demurrer to further Proceedings* (London, 1841) contains a list of 'expressions extracted from the addresses, replies, and speeches of Anglican Bishops since October last, as reported in *The Times* newspaper' Listing a hundred and eighty-one vituperative epithets used by the bishops to describe the setting up of the restored Catholic hierarchy (e.g. 'blasphemous, unclean, apostate, arrogant, profane, pestilent, satanic' etc.), Bellasis makes the point that the Church of England cannot consistently claim that it is being 'temperate and charitable' in its reaction. Newman asked his friend Richard Stanton to get him a copy of it after it had been quoted by the Catholic M.P. John Reynolds in the House of Commons during the second debate on the Ecclesiastical Titles Bill (see *Letters and Diaries*, Vol.XIV, p. 297-8). It was later suggested to Newman that his own 'bells' passage here was based on Bellasis's pamphlet. He pointed out that 'Neither the words nor the idea occur in the [Serjeant's] pamphlet, and I am sure that I did not take it from him. *My* idea is the *monotonous* repetition in *changed* order of a *few* words, 'atrocious', 'insidious,' etc., and I got these words not from him, but from episcopal charges, as he did.' (*Letters & Diaries*, Vol.XXX, p. 136). Newman was keen, however, to make a reference to Bellasis's 'forcible pamphlet'; he even thought of reprinting it in its entirety as an appendix to a new edition of *Present Position* but decided eventually on the present footnote.

p. 78. *mint, anise, and cummin, brazen pots and vessels*: see Jesus's denunciation of the Pharisees' hypocrisy: 'You tithe mint and anise and cummin, and have neglected the weightier matters of the law, justice and mercy and faith' (Matthew 23:23). Among the Pharisees' many traditions are 'the washing of cups and brazen pots and vessels' (Mark 7:4).

p. 78. *Wolsey*: Cardinal Thomas Wolsey (1473-1530), Chancellor under Henry VIII until he fell from favour for being unable to obtain papal sanction for the king's divorce from Catherine of Aragon. He was famous for his worldliness and pomp but died a humiliated and broken man.

p. 78. *the Duke of Alva*: (1508-82), general to King Philip II of Spain; he put down the Protestant revolt of the Spanish Netherlands with great severity.

p. 78. *Hildebrand*: Pope Gregory VII (1020-85), a reforming and intransigent pope who had a prolonged conflict with the Emperor Henry IV which culminated in the latter's doing three days of public penance, kneeling in the snow at Canossa.

p. 78. *Cæsar Borgia*: (1476-1507), the ruthless son of Pope Alexander VI, who murdered his way to power.

p. 78. *Louis the Eleventh*: King Louis XI of France (d. 1483) centralised power in the hands of the Crown. In his old age he shut himself up in a stronghold for fear of assassins, dismissing his personal servants, and ruled through intrigue.

p. 79. *"Deipara" which means "equal to God."*: a classic example of Protestant misunderstanding. In classical Latin *par* does mean 'an equal', but *Deipara* is a late Latin coinage meaning 'parent (or mother) of God'.

p. 79. *"John the Eighth ... elected Pope."*: as late as February 1850, the *North British Review* (Vol.12, pp.354-370) had contained an article seriously citing such 'historical' evidence about Pope Joan, complete with details about a statue of her and her child in Rome and a portrait in Sienna Cathedral. (See also below p.251.)

p. 84. *its decay and almost extinction*: Newman had recently been reading a pamphlet *Religion, Life and Property in Danger. Extracts from Mr. Hamilton's Account of the Alarming Spread of Infidelity and Vice through Christendom* which recounted how Lutheranism was turning into scepticism in Germany. It is to be found among his *Present Position* preparatory work papers (see above).

p. 85. *an oath*: the Oath of Allegiance, acknowledging the King or Queen as Supreme Head of the Church in England and repudiating the power of the Pope, dating from Henry VIII's Act of Supremacy in 1534. There had been a new one under Elizabeth I which all clergy, judges, officials, university graduates, indeed anyone in a position of authority, had to take, acknowledging the Queen as Supreme Governor 'in all spiritual or ecclesiastical things as well as temporal.' Under James I the oath was further strengthened so that it declared that the Pope's claim to excommunicate or depose a ruler was 'damnable' and obliged the swearer to report any 'traitorous conspiracies.' It was considerably relaxed under Cromwell, when only political, not religious, loyalty was required to the government, but was restored under Charles II when a new Test Act was passed also which forced all holders of public office to receive the Anglican sacrament and added to the oath a new declaration against transubstantiation. New Acts of allegiance and supremacy, with an accompanying oath, were passed in 1699 following the 'Glorious Revolution'. This remained in force until the Catholic Relief Act of 1778 introduced a new oath which only required allegiance to George III, a declaration that it was unlawful to depose or murder a ruler, that the Pope had no civil jurisdiction in England and that no-one had the power to release the swearer from his oath. Catholics felt that they could take this oath. However, they were still allowed neither to vote nor to sit in either House of Parliament, and full political rights for Catholics only came with Catholic Emancipation in 1829. Even this Act required an oath 'not to disturb or weaken the Protestant religion' and to deny that the Pope had any political rights in England.

p. 86. *Taylor*: Jeremy Taylor (1613-67), Anglican divine, chaplain to Archbishop Laud and Charles I and later Bishop of Dromore; author of various influential controversial and spiritual works, notably *Holy Living* and *The Golden Grove*.

p. 86. *Chillingworth*: William Chillingworth (1602-44), Anglican divine and controversialist; he briefly became a Catholic but returned to the Church of England. From these experiences came his most famous book *The Religion of Protestants a safe way to Salvation*. He was latitudinarian and rationalist in his belief.

p. 86. *Hampden*: John Hampden (1594-1643), statesman; leading Parliamentarian opponent of Charles I.

p. 86. *Clarendon*: see note on p.34.

p. 86. *Falkland*: Lucius Cary, Viscount Falkland (d.1643). His house, Great Tew, in Oxfordshire became a centre for Anglican scholars and theologians. He became Secretary of State under Charles I and died fighting for the royalist cause.

p. 86. *Russell*: William Lord Russell (1639-1683), statesman; convicted of high treason and executed for complicity in the Rye House plot, a fictitious plot to assassinate Charles II fabricated by informers to implicate Whig politicians who had been discussing ways of excluding the future James II from the throne.

p. 86. *Somers*: John Baron Somers (1651-1716), lawyer and statesman; Lord Chancellor under William and Mary.

p. 86. *Walpole*: Sir Robert Walpole (1676-1745), first earl of Oxford;

Prime Minister and Chancellor of the Exchequer under George I and II.

p. 86. *Hobbes*: Thomas Hobbes (1588-1679), philosopher, best known for his work of political philosophy, *Leviathan*.

p. 86. *Swift*: Jonathan Swift (1667-1745), satirist, best known as the author of *Gulliver's Travels*.

p. 86. *Warburton*: William Warburton (1698-1779), Anglican divine and controversialist; he also produced an edition of Shakespeare.

p. 86. *Horsley*: Samuel Horsley (1733-1806), Anglican Bishop of St. Asaph; writer of mathematical and theological works.

p. 86. *Hallam*: Henry Hallam (1777-1859), historian; his best-known work is his *Constitutional History of England*.

p. 88. *small octavos*: books measuring 6 inches by $9\frac{1}{2}$ inches, the size of a school textbook as opposed to a larger volume for private use.

p. 93. *Albertus Magnus*: St. Albert the Great (1206-1280), Dominican friar and scholastic philosopher, known as the 'Universal Doctor'.

p. 93. *Gerson*: Jean Gerson (1363-1428), French theologian; Chancellor of the University of Paris.

p. 93. *Baronius*: Cesare Barone (1538-1607), church historian, author of the *Annales Ecclesiastici*; disciple of St.Philip Neri (1515-1595) and one of the first Oratorians; later a Cardinal.

p. 97. *Dr. Bentley, in his controversy with Boyle*: Richard Bentley (1662-1742) was a classical scholar and Master of Trinity College, Cambridge. Charles Boyle (1676-1731), fourth Earl of Orrery, had edited some 'Epistles of Phalaris' (a tyrant in Sicily in the 6th century B.C.) which Bentley proved to be spurious.

p. 97. *the first ablution in the Mass ... 'Quod ore sumpsimus'*: while consuming the water which had been used to cleanse his fingers and the chalice after Communion, the priest said 'Grant, O Lord, that *what we have taken with our mouth*, we may receive with a pure mind' etc.

p. 99. *Mosheim*: Johann Lorenz von Mosheim (1694-1755), church historian.

p. 99. *Adam Smith*: (1723-90), philosopher and economist, author of *An Enquiry into the Nature and Causes of the Wealth of Nations*.

p. 99. *Gibbon*: Edward Gibbon (1737-94), historian, author of the monumental *History of the Decline and Fall of the Roman Empire*.

p. 99. *literati*: men of letters, writers.

p. 100. *Dr.Maclaine*: Archibald Maclaine (1722-1804), divine, translator of Mosheim.

p. 100. *a certain learned Mr. White*: Dr.Joseph White (1745-1814), orientalist and theologian; he gave the Bampton Lectures in 1784 on Christianity and Mahometanism.

p. 102. *a country curate in Devonshire*: he was Samuel Badcock (d.1788). 'After his death, Dr. Gabriel, whose curate he had been, showed that Badcock had given Dr. White considerable assistance, and had written one whole lecture. Samuel Parr came to the defence of White, but only by claiming to be responsible himself for a fifth part of the lectures' (*Letters & Diaries*, Vol.XIV, p.287, n.2).

p. 103. *Jortin*: John Jortin (1698-1770), church historian.

p. 112. ipso facto: proved by the fact itself.

p. 112. *the metropolitan or ordinary*: archbishop or bishop.

p. 113. *a censure*: a spiritual penalty, such as excommunication.

p. 113. *the Parable ... of every kind*: see Matthew 13·47

p. 114. n.5. *an absolutio ... for his remains*: the absolution prayer said normally after a Requiem Mass to accompany the blessing of the coffin. According to a work which had just recently been published, at Napoleon's funeral this absolution 'was performed by the Cardinal Archbishop, assisted by more than two hundred priests' (Montholon, General Count, *History of the Captivity of Napoleon at St. Helena*, Vol. IV, London, 1847).

p. 114. n.5. *the passage in the Council*: The Council of Trent's decree on the Sacrament of Penance, ch.7, speaking of the reservation to the Pope of the absolution of more serious cases of sins, makes the exception: 'However, this same Church of God has always devoutly upheld that there is no reservation at the hour of death, lest this reservation be the occasion of anyone's damnation; and therefore any priest can absolve any penitent from all sins and censures' (see Clarkson, Edwards, Kelly & Welch, *The Church Teaches. Documents of the Church in English Translation*, St.Louis & London, 1955, p. 312.).

p. 118. *"though brayed in a mortar"*: see Proverbs 27:22: 'Though thou shouldst bray a fool in the mortar, as when a pestle striketh upon sodden barley, his folly would not be taken from him.' 'Bray' here means 'crush'.

p. 118. *the Legislature of the Nation*: in the House of Commons, during the second reading of the Religious Houses Bill (an unsuccessful attempt to prohibit priests from living together in communities), Mr. Richard Spooner, M.P. for North Warwickshire, had made the absurd allegation about the new Oratory house which Newman now quotes (pp. 121-2).

p. 121. *had the platform ... indicted for libel*: Newman avoids making an explicit reference to the House of Commons, where statements which might otherwise be actionable for libel are protected by privilege, in case he might be held to be in contempt of the House. He omitted Spooner's name for the same reason (see *Letters & Diaries*, Vol.XIV, p.309).

p. 122. *... and what were those cells for?"*: Newman had already replied to Spooner's accusation in a letter to *The Morning Chronicle*. He quotes the extract reproduced here and then goes on:

> The underground cells, to which Mr. Spooner refers, have been devised in order to economize space for offices commonly attached to a large house. I think they are five in number, but cannot be certain. They run under the kitchen and its neighbourhood. One is to be a larder, another is to be a coal-hole; beer, perhaps wine, may occupy a third. As to the rest, Mr. Spooner ought to know that we have had ideas of baking and brewing; but I cannot pledge myself to him, that such will be their ultimate destination. (*Letters & Diaries*, Vol.XIV, p. 283).

Newman's irony seems to have been lost on Spooner who solemnly read this reply out in the House of Commons as further evidence of popish duplicity, to the jeers of other M.P.s present who evidently had a better sense of humour. Nothing daunted, Spooner went on to claim that Oratorian priests were disguising themselves as workmen so that they could build their underground cells themselves. Newman replied to this through the press, too.

p. 122. *A gentleman ... a quarter of a century*: Spooner was the maternal uncle of Henry Wilberforce, Newman's close friend since they had been at Oxford together.

p. 123. *foster sons ... and Wolseys*: founders of the various Public Schools and Oxford colleges of which the Oxford Movement converts had been members.

p. 125. *Mr. Rose*: Henry John Rose (1800–1873), church historian.

p. 126. *St. Justin Martyr*: (c.100–c.165), lay apologist and martyr; his works are important sources for the belief and practice of the Church in the second century.

p. 129. *Novatians and Donatists*: heretical sects of the 3rd and 4th centuries respectively who held that some sins were too serious to be forgiven and that such offenders should be permanently excluded from the Church. Thus the Church, in their view, consisted only of the pure.

p. 129. *Lollards*: followers of the English mediaeval heretic William Wycliffe (c.1324–84).

p. 130. *"many are called, few are chosen;"*: Matthew 22:14.

p. 130. *an enemy ... the harvest*: cf.Matthew 13:24–30.

p. 131. *"In a great house ... unto dishonour"*: 2 Timothy 2:20.

p. 131. *indefectible*: not liable to defect; faultless.

p. 131. *"it must needs ... the scandal cometh"*: Matthew 18:7.

P. 132. *"strike the men   he drunken."*: a slightly inaccurate version of Matthew 24:49.

p.134. *public prints*: newspapers.

p. 136. *Teetotalism ... Temperance*: the former is the renunciation of all alcohol; Newman uses the latter in its original meaning of moderation in the drinking of alcohol (though by his time Temperance in fact more usually meant total abstinence).

p. 137. *disbelieve their own ... were ordained?*: Evangelicals rejected the doctrine of baptismal regeneration. Liberals such as Thomas Arnold and Archbishop Whateley rejected the interpretation of the formula in the Visitation of the

Sick as an absolution and denied the priestly nature of Ordination. In the recent Gorham case, an Anglican clergyman who had publicly stated that he did not believe in baptismal regeneration (which the Baptism Service seemed to imply) had been permitted to retain his position.

p. 137. *doubt about every part … carry them?*: these are the Anglo-Catholics. Newman's harshness towards the inconsistencies of this his own former position is also to be found in his *Lectures on Certain Difficulties felt by Anglicans in Submitting to the Catholic Church* (1850).

p. 137. *who hold that … world at all?*: these are the Liberals.

p. 137. *Torquemada*: Tomás de Torquemada (1420-98), chief officer of the Spanish Inquisition, renowned for his ruthlessness.

p. 137. *Bonner*: Edmund Bonner (c.1500-1569), Bishop of London.

p. 138. *matchmaking*: persuading two young people to marry each other.

p. 138. *Union workhouses*: institutions in which the destitute were housed at public expense but forced to work, usually in conditions of considerable harshness.

p. 138. *Nicolas*: one of the seven deacons appointed to assist the apostles in Acts 6:5. He was, erroneously, thought to be the founder of the heretical Nicolaitans condemned in the Book of Revelation 2:15.

p. 138. *Diotrephes*: a church leader criticised in 3 John 9-10 because he 'loveth to have the pre-eminence'.

p. 138. *Demas*: companion of St.Paul who accused him in 2 Timothy 4·9 of having abandoned him, 'loving this world'.

p. 139. *a gentleman of Warwickshire*: Mr.Spooner again.

p. 140. animus: hostile spirit.

p. 146. *Voltaire*: (1694-1778), French philosopher, man of letters and wit; famous for his freethinking and anti-clericalism. His real name was François Marie Arouet.

p. 148. *forget Jerusalem*: a reference to the cry of the psalmist exiled in Babylon, 'If I forget thee, O Jerusalem, let my right hand be forgotten' (Ps 136:5).

p. 159. *Ciocci*: Raffaele Ciocci, former monk turned anti-Catholic polemicist; author of *A Narrative of Iniquities and Barbarities practised at Rome in the nineteenth century* (1843) and *Disclosures of Jesuitism in Brighton* (1852). While Newman was living at Santa Croce in Rome in 1847 he wrote to his sister Jemima:

> I don't know whether you ever heard of a man called Ciocci or the like – a poor man who was a Cistercian novice and turned Protestant – I have only just heard of him – but he has been made much of in the speeches at Exeter Hall, and has written a book, which (I believe) has gone through many editions, in which he tells all manner of stories of Sta Croce, which was his monastery, and poor St. Eusebio, the Jesuit Retreat House, which lies before us, which it makes me laugh to think of, when I see the monks here or grope up the staircase in the dark. They attempted to murder him here, he says, and St Eusebio is full of trap doors in the bed rooms. I don't know which are the most incongruous agents in such fee-fam-fum doings, the humdrum Cistercians with whom we live, or the plodding, methodical, unromantic Jesuits. (*Letters and Diaries*, Vol.XIII, p. 103)

p. 159. *Achilli*: see Introduction pp. xxi-xxv.

p. 163. *penitentiary*: a refuge for former prostitutes who wish to reform their life.

p. 163. *Maria Monk*: *The Awful Disclosures of Maria Monk*, first published in New York in 1836 and republished in England in 1851.

p. 166. *those passages ... to quote*: a number of scenes in the work are pornographic. Wolffe (op.cit.) comments: "Maria Monk represented a cultural milieu which, in the area of sexuality, had some points of contact with evangelicalism but had a fundamentally different focus, owing more to pornography and a popular fascination with mystery and violent crime than to religion.' (pp. 125-6)

p. 167. *"full within ... all filthiness"*: Matthew 23:27.

p. 167. *an able diplomatist ... disguise men's thoughts*: Newman is mistaken; the saying actually comes from Voltaire: 'Ils ne se servent de la pensée que pour autoriser leurs injustices, et n'emploient les paroles que pour déguiser leurs pensées' [Men use thought only to justify their wrong-doings, and words only to disguise their thoughts] in his *Dialogue XIV, Le Chapon et de la Poularde* (1673).

p. 175. *Jeffreys*: William Thomas Jeffrey claimed in 1849 that he had been held against his will in Mount St. Bernard's Cistercian Monastery in Leicestershire. His story was published in *The Protestant Watchman of the Midland District* and as a pamphlet. The Cistercians denied the truth of Jeffrey's story but were not believed, and local colliers threatened to blow up the monastery and burn down a local Catholic school. Meanwhile, the editor of the *Watchman*, the Birmingham anti-Catholic activist Thomas Ragg, had become suspicious of Jeffreys' veracity and on further investigation concluded that he was a fraud. Ragg led a party to accompany Jeffreys to the monastery where, despite the presence of a large and excited anti-Catholic crowd, his ignorance of the building was soon evident, and he broke down. He ended up serving three months in Stafford prison. See D.G. Paz, op. cit, pp. 122-3, who refers to *A Full Report of a most Extraordinary Investigation which took place on Tuesday, June 26, 1849, at Mount St.Bernard Monastery, Leicestershire,* 6th ed. (Birmingham, 1849).

p. 175. *Teodore*: 'John Victor Teodor, a former priest, and his colleagues Chylinski and Dobrogost claimed to be Polish nationalists hounded into England by Russian, Prussian, and Austrian forces; they found that they could make a living by pandering to the Evangelicals, lecturing, and performing, "in all its pomp, the Romish Mass" to paying customers ("Wafer Gods" sold at the door for 1*d.* each).' (Paz, op.cit., p. 26, who adds in a footnote that they may have been confidence men.)

p. 176. *Mr.Steimnitz*: [sic] Andrew Steinmetz (1816-1877); during a varied career he spent a year in the Jesuit novitiate at Stonyhurst from 1838-9. The book based on his experiences which Newman refers to was *The Novitiate, or A Year among the English Jesuits, A Personal Narrative* (1846, 3rd edn.1850); he also wrote a *History of the Jesuits* (1848). Later works included *The Romance of Duelling in All Times and Countries* (1868) and *The Gaming Table, Its Votaries and Victims in All Times and Countries* (1870).

p. 176. *"they say ... Name's sake."*: see Matthew 5:11.

p. 179. *the Queen's Colleges*: There was no university in Ireland open to Irish Catholics, since Trinity College, Dublin, was, like Oxford and Cambridge, only open to Protestants. In 1845 the government of Sir Robert Peel had decided to establish a non-denominational Queen's University with colleges in various parts of Ireland, thus attempting to side-step the religious question by providing only secular university education for Irish Catholics. The majority of the Irish bishops opposed the plan, as did the Pope who suggested instead the founding of a Catholic university, the project in which Newman was to become involved as Rector.

p. 181. *one night*: 8th April 1836.

p. 181. *Dagon*: in the Bible, the image of the god Dagon who was worshipped by the Philistines was found broken in pieces on the ground after the captured Ark of the Covenant had been placed in his temple. See Judges 16:23 and 1 Samuel 5:2ff.

p. 181. *how they spoke ... and his legs*: Newman is quoting from the account in the *Dublin Annals* which a friend had copied out for him (documents D5 16 in the Archives of the Birmingham Oratory).

p 181. *monsters described in the Apocalypse*: see Revelation 13. The identification of the two beasts with various Popes or other prominent Catholics was common in anti-Catholic polemic.

p. 181. *persons who refused ... fidelity to James*: the non-jurors, the nine Anglican bishops and four hundred clergy who refused to swear the Oath of Allegiance to William and Mary after the 'Glorious Revolution' and were ejected from their livings as a result.

p. 182. *matter for ... Reformation tracts*: one of the standard Protestant charges against Catholicism was that it countenanced the breaking of oaths, especially by means of convoluted casuistry.

p. 186. *Drummondite*: another name for the Irvingites (see above note on p. 76), after Henry Drummond (1786-1860), banker and member of Parliament, who was a founder member of this sect with Irving. He was a noted anti-Catholic and used his parliamentary privilege to slander Catholic clergy (see below p. 206).

p. 186. *Plymouth-Brother*: the Plymouth Brethren were founded in 1827 by John Darby, a former Church of Ireland minister, and Edward Cronin, a former Catholic. Believing that all the existing Christian churches were corrupt, the Brethren lived in small, exclusive communities. Newman's brother Francis was a member for a while.

p. 186. *Mormonite*: the Mormons were founded in America in 1836 by Joseph Smith. By 1851 they had made their great trek to Utah and founded Salt Lake City. They were best known for their practice of polygamy.

p. 187. *the Agapemone*: 'Proper name of an association of men and women established at Spaxton in Somerset by the Rev Henry James Prince; a similar establishment conducted by his successor, the Rev. John Hugh

Smyth-Pigott, at Clapton, London. Also *gen.* establishment of this kind, an abode-of-love; esp. with unfavourable implication' (O.E.D). The implication was that the members of this sect practised sexual promiscuity among themselves.

p. 187. *I would rather see ... the slave of a priest*: this passage echoes an anti-Catholic speech of which Newman kept a newspaper cutting (in scrapbook B2.1 in the Birmingham Oratory archives). Rev. Mr. Greig speaking at a meeting of the masters of Orange lodges was reported as saying that:

> The papists ought not to have the same privileges as other religious sects. Even Infidels and Atheists were better than the papists, as they could do no harm, whilst the Roman Catholics surrendered their brains to the priests, and they were not fit subjects for liberty.

p. 189. *As to domestic servants ... against them*: Ragg's *Protestant Watchman* claimed that 'Catholic servants repeat family secrets in the confessional and sprinkle holy water on children when their employers' backs are turned' (Paz, op.cit. p.122, quoting the *Protestant Watchmen*, No.3 (May 1849), p. 38 and No.8 (Oct.1849), pp. 95-96.)

p. 192. *He at length ... in* Coventry: a saying taken from the dislike of the citizens of Coventry for soldiers and the taboo they consequently placed upon women seen associating with them. Thus when someone is 'sent to Coventry' no notice is taken of him; he is made to feel that he is in disgrace by no-one having any dealings with him.

p. 192. *malicious and monstrous tales ... readily believed*: this (like much of this paragraph) was Newman's own experience; he repeatedly had to deny rumours that he had left the priesthood, got married, lost his faith etc.

p. 193. *petitions*: petitions to Parliament were a much used tactic by the anti-Catholic organisations. 'Parliament in 1851 received 1,686 petitions with 264,864 signatures protesting Roman Catholic encroachments, 28 petitions with 5,225 signatures praying for the passage of the Ecclesiastical Titles Bill, and 2,541 petitions with 756,578 signatures praying that the penalties for violation of the Ecclesiastical Titles Bill be made more stringent.' (Paz, op. cit. p. 42.)

p. 194. *The Court of Aldermen ... the Vestries*: all these bodies either owned land in London or controlled its use:

The Court of Aldermen: the assembly of senior councillors of the City of London (see above note on p. 64).

the Common Council: the administrative body of the City of London.

the City Companies: the corporations, originally representing mediaeval trade guilds, now of senior London businessmen.

the Inns of Court: the legal societies, based in London, which have the right to admit people to practise as barristers.

the Vestries: parish councils.

p. 194. *the Frenchman's good fortune* i.e. bad fortune (similar to 'French leave' - leave taken without permission).

p. 194. *a proposal … and the Pope*: an Act to establish official diplomatic relations with the Pope was passed by Parliament in 1848 but it contained the proviso that the papal ambassador could not be a priest. This was unacceptable to Rome, and so the plan failed.

p. 195. *the Penal Bill*: the Ecclesiastical Titles Bill (see above note on p.xiv).

p. 195. *a sermon preached at St.Chad's last October*: 'Christ Upon the Waters', later published in *Sermons Preached on Various Occasions* (Longmans, 1881) pp. 121-62. No such reference by Russell to the sermon appears in any of his speeches in the House of Commons recorded in *Hansard*. The phrases 'imputed to …' and 'It appears that …' suggest some uncertainty on Newman's part. The sermon was widely attacked. *The Times* misrepresented Newman as having compared the newly installed Bishop Ullathorne (at whose enthronement the sermon was preached) to Christ risen from the tomb, and Dean Tait of Carlisle accused Newman of blasphemy. Even when Newman got him to admit that the *Times* version was false, Tait refused to withdraw the charge.

p. 197. *ultramontanes*: supporters of an extreme interpretation of the powers of the Papacy. The word comes from the French term for those who looked 'beyond the mountains' (i.e. the Alps) to Italy for control of the church by Rome. Those who favoured more power being exercised by the local church were in contrast termed 'Cisalpine'. In England before Catholic Emancipation the Cisalpine Club of laymen had favoured compromise with the government and had been involved in fierce controversies with the opposing party led by Bishop Milner. It is significant that Newman here assumes that 'ultramontane' is a derogatory term.

p. 197. *Popish plot*: the alleged Catholic plot against the government invented by Titus Oates (1649-1705) which was the occasion of much anti-Catholic agitation. Oates was later revealed as a fraud and his entire plot as a fiction.

p. 197. *the deportation suggested by one member of Parliament and the £500 penalty proposed by another:* during a debate in the House of Commons on the Ecclesiastical Titles Bill Mr. W. Miles, M.P., put forward an amendment that the penalty for a Catholic bishop who used a territorial title should be deportation from the United Kingdom. Sir George Grey, M.P., criticised this as being ineffective since the offender could re-enter the country again immediately, and he proposed that transportation (i.e. to Australia) was the only effective penalty. Colonel Sibthorpe M.P. proposed an amendment that the £100 fine proposed in the Bill be raised to £500. In the same speech Sibthorpe had also proposed that, after the payment of the fine, an offender 'should be banished from the United Kingdom during the period of his natural life.' These amendments were all rejected; no fines were ever paid since no-one was ever prosecuted under the Act.

p. 198. *Bridgewater Treatise:* Francis Henry Egerton (1756-1828), 8th Earl of Bridgewater, left £8,000 to be paid to the authors of the best treatises on the power and wisdom of God as manifested in creation. There were eight such treatises published, 1833-40.

p. 198. *Warburton Lecture:* annual lectures named after William Warburton (1698-1779), Anglican Bishop of Gloucester, founded 'to prove the truth of Revealed Religion in general, and of the Christian in particular, from the completion of the prophecies in the Old and New Testaments, which relate to the Christian Church, especially to the apostasy of Papal Rome' (quoted by Newman in 'The Protestant Idea of Antichrist', (see above note on p.13) p.130. Newman went on to comment, 'It is only surprising that such a foundation has not done more in behalf of its object. In matter of fact, after three lectures had passed in succession, a fourth could not be found, and for some time there was a suspension of the lecture. Mr. Davison *[an earlier Warbuton lecturer]* has but one discourse on the subject, and an able and respected writer, whose Lectures have just appeared *[Archdeacon Lyall]*, does not bestow upon us even one.').

p. 198. *Lazarus's for the rich man's crumbs:* see Luke 16: 19-31.

p. 200. *a drawing-room window:* the drawing-room was usually on the first floor of a house.

p. 200. *Cardinal Wiseman ... in his late Appeal to the English people: An Appeal to the Reason and Good Feeling of the English People on the subject of the*

Catholic Hierarchy, London, 1850 (see Introduction p. xiii).

p. 200. *one of the most distinguished Protestant theologians of the day*: William Palmer (1803-85) of Worcester College, Oxford; his pamphlets, *Letters to N. Wiseman, D.D., calling himself Bishop of Melipotamos*, had been published in 1841-2.

p. 201. *Laud*: William Laud (1573-1645), Archbishop of Canterbury under Charles I; he attempted to impose a 'high church' uniformity on the Church of England but was opposed by the Puritans in Parliament and executed on the charge of treason.

p. 201. *Stillingfleet*: Edward Stillingfleet (1635-99), Anglican Bishop of Worcester and popular preacher and writer.

p. 201. *Ussher*: James Ussher (1581-1656), Anglican Archbishop of Armagh and author of numerous theological and historical works.

p. 201. *Van Amberg*: Isaac Van Amburgh (or Van Amberg) (c.1805-65), American circus animal trainer. He visited Europe with his menagerie, performing at Drury Lane in 1838-9 where Queen Victoria went to see him six times in January and February 1839.

p. 205. *Michaelmas last*: 29th September, Feast of St.Michael the Archangel, 1850, the date on which the restoration of the Catholic Hierarchy had been announced (see Introduction, pp. x-xiii).

p. 205. *the first judge of the land ... Cardinal Wiseman's hat*: Lord Chancellor Cottenham, who in a speech at a Mansion House dinner on 9th November 1850 declared his intention of crushing Wiseman's red cardinal's hat underfoot.

p. 206. *the buckram nuns of Warwickshre, Nottingham and Clapham*: buckram is a coarse linen stiffened with paste, but its meaning here is the proverbial one of 'non-existent' as in Falstaff's claim that he was attacked by 'four rogues in buckram' in Henry IV Part I, Act II, sc.iv. Newman is referring to the false accusation by Charles Newdegate M.P. in a speech on the Ecclesiastical Titles Bill in March 1851 who claimed that some years ago a nun escaped from the convent near his own house at Arbury in Warwickshire and that 'within a week afterwards 15 cwt, of iron stanchions were put to barricade the windows and convert the place into a perfect prison.' This accusation was refuted by John Hardman in a letter to *Aris's Gazette* in May:

Having instituted a minute enquiry, I am able to assert positively that there *never* was any escape of any inmate from the convent at Atherstone, to which, no doubt, Mr. Newdegate alludes, nor *any attempted* escape. With respect to the barring of the windows, the following are the facts: - In the year 1840, two robberies were effected at the Convent Chapel within a few months of each other, and on the last occasion the Tabernacle, containing the Blessed Sacrament, was carried away. After these robberies, one or two bars were put up to each of five or six lower windows, and the doors were made more secure to prevent a repetition of the burglaries. (Press cutting in scrapbook B2.1 at the Birmingham Oratory)

The nuns at Atherstone were Dominicans. There were Sisters of Mercy at Nottingham and the Order of Notre Dame at Clapham, against whom similar false accusations had presumably been made.

p.206. *the dungeons of Edgbaston*: see above, note on p.122.

p.206. *the sin-table of St.Gudule's*: see above pp.115-118.

p.206. *the outrageous language ... seducing young women*: Henry Drummond, M.P. (see above, note on p.186), in the course of a speech in the House of Commons on 7th February 1851, said, referring to Fr. Frederick Faber, the superior of the London Oratory, 'that fellow Faber went about the country seducing young women'. Faber could not sue for slander because parliamentary privilege protected Drummond. Newman had advised Faber that he would have to ignore it for this reason (see *Letters and Diaries*, Vol.XIV, p.210). However, the words were omitted from *Hansard*, the official publication of Parliament's proceedings and from newspaper reports of the speech for fear of libel. Hence Newman's qualifying phrase, 'as the words came to the ears of those present'. Newman refers to the House of Commons as 'a place I must not name' in case his quotation of Drummond's remark might lay him open to a charge of contempt of parliamentary privilege.

p.206 *the popular publication*: the magazine *Punch*, which played a leading rôle in the 'Papal Aggression' press campaign.

p.208. n.6. *The paragraphs omitted ...* : for these paragraphs, see Appendix, pp.427-8.

p.210. *Dr.Balmez*: Jaime Luciano Balmez (1810-48), Spanish philosopher, author of *El Protestantismo comparado con el Catolicismo*, 4 vols, 1842-4.

p. 210. *Ranke*: Leopold von Ranke (1795-1886), German Lutheran ecclesiastical historian, Professor at Berlin, best known for his History of the Popes.

p. 210. *Guizot*: François Pierre Guillaume Guizot (1787-1874), French historian; became Prime Minister of France in 1847.

p. 211. n.4. *Gieseler*: Johann Karl Ludwig Giesler (1792-1854), German Protestant ecclesiastical historian; the quotation is from his *Lehrbuch der Kirchengeschichte*, translated into English by S. Davidson and J.W. Hull as *A Compendium of English History* (5 volumes, 1846-55) which became a standard work.

p. 213. *the Court of Queen's Bench*: a Division of the High Court of Justice, the supreme court of judicature of England; it hears Common Law cases.

p. 214. *Hone*: William Hone (1780-1842), bookseller and publisher of political lampoons for one of which he was unsuccessfully prosecuted.

p. 214. *Carlyle*: *[sic]* Richard Carlisle (1790-1843), freethinker, repeatedly imprisoned for publishing anti-religious and seditious literature; he became celebrated by libertarians as a martyr for the liberty of the press.

p. 215. *Socinian*: someone who holds the views of Faustus Socinus and his brother, 16th century Italian theologians, who denied the divinity of Christ.

p. 215. *an* Agnus Dei: a circular wax tablet on which is stamped the figure of a lamb, representing Christ, made from the remains of the Paschal candles and solemnly blessed by the Pope on the Thursday after Easter. The wearing of these was a popular mediaeval devotion, and in penal times this became an expression of Catholic loyalty.

p. 215. *five years … imprisonment for life*: a number of anti-Catholic laws, carrying such penalties, were finally repealed in 1844, though they had long been a dead letter.

p. 216. n.8. *Challoner's Missionary Priests*: Bishop Richard Challoner (1691-1781), Vicar Apostolic of the London District, the outstanding leader of English Catholicism in the 18th century. Among his many works was *Memoirs of the Missionary Priests* (2 volumes, 1741-2).

p. 218. *Anabaptist*: member of the sect founded in 1521 in Germany which denied the efficacy of infant baptism and therefore rebaptised adults.

p. 219. *a clergyman of the Establishment ... put to death*: On 8th December 1850 the Rev. Hugh McNeile, Canon of Chester and incumbent of St.Paul's, Liverpool, (see above, note on p. 38) preached a sermon in which he attacked the Catholic practice of Confession. Discussing the case of Catholic priests who would refuse to give information about a murder which they had received under the seal of the confessional, he went on to demand the death penalty for all such priests:

> I would make it a capital offence to administer the confession in this country. Transportation would not satisfy me, for that would merely transfer the evil from one part of the world to the other. Capital punishment alone would satisfy me. Death alone would prevent the evil. That is my solemn conviction. (Press cutting in Newman's scrapbook B2.1 at the Birmingham Oratory)

Following a complaint by a member of the congregation, McNeile withdrew 'the atrocious sentiment which I uttered this morning' at evening service later that same day. However, he subsequently wrote a lengthy exculpatory letter to the papers on the subject, in which he continued to argue that a priest who heard the confession of a murderer and refused to divulge it deserved capital punishment. In a lecture in Kendall a few days later, the Rev. Hugh Stowell of Manchester supported McNeile. A newspaper account of his speech reported that:

> In speaking of the Confessional he described the Priest sitting as God in his chair, and hearing the darkest secrets, which he did not reveal to any mortal man, for they were entrusted to him as to God. Even if a murder was confessed, the Priest would refuse to make it known. The Scripture says, 'Thou shalt do no murder,' and he (Mr.Stowell) unhesitatingly declared that the man who could listen to the confession and not make it known was an accessory after the fact; *and he did not think that his dear brother, Dr. M'Neile, went too far, when he declared his opinion that such a man ought to be hanged!* [italics in the original report] (Press cutting in scrapbook B2.1 at the Birmingham Oratory)

Newman was attacked by a Congregationalist minister, Brewin Grant, in one of his pamphlets *Orations to the Oratorians*, for failing to indicate that McNeile only wanted capital punishment for priests who had heard a murderer's, or intended murderer's, confession, not for all priests. Although this was a fair criticism, it remains true that McNeile and Stowell, who were prominent Anglican clergymen, had publicly called for the death penalty for the exercise of a Catholic sacramental practice. As Newman says, 'doubtless they had their *reasons*', but their views were hardly consistent with the claim that Protestants were opposed to all religious persecution.

p. 219. *Gardiner*: Stephen Gardiner (c.1490-1555), Bishop of Winchester.

p. 222. n.9 *De Maistre*: Joseph De Maistre (1753-1821), French ecclesiastical writer; he wrote on the relationship between the Church and secular authorities, notably in *Du pape* (1819).

p. 232. *the greatest of the Romans ... not be suspected*": Julius Caesar (c.102-44 B.C.), recorded in Plutarch's *Lives*, Julius Caesar, x, 6; more usually quoted as 'Caesar's wife must be above suspicion.'

p. 234. *"loved darkness rather than the light"*: John 3:19.

p. 236. *"when unadorned," is "adorned the most."*: James Thompson (1700-48): "For loveliness / Needs not the foreign aid of ornament, / But is when unadorned adorned the most", *Autumn*, l.204. Thompson is best known as the author of 'Rule Britannia.'

p. 239. *the Philistine champion ... by his gods."*: 1 Kings (1 Samuel) 17:43.

p. 240. *Milton's day-star ... of the morning sky."*: *Lycidas*, l.169-171. Milton's text reads 'repairs *his* head' and 'tricks *his* beams'. Newman has either misremembered or adapted the lines to his context.

p. 240. *"unhurt amid the war ..." "defies" defeat*: Joseph Addison, *The Campaign*, V, l.28.

p. 246. *one of those two eloquent defenders of Protestantism who lately gave out that every Catholic priest ought to be hanged*: see above note on p. 219.

p. 248. *"Trifles light as air ... of Holy Writ"*: Shakespeare, *Othello*, III, iii, 326-8. Newman had made use of this quotation in the same context in his sermon 'Faith and Reason Contrasted as Habits of Mind' (*Fifteen Sermons Preached before the University of Oxford* (1843, revised edition 1872):

> ... it is scarcely necessary to point out how much our inclinations have to do with our belief. It is almost a proverb, that persons believe what they wish to be true. ... The case is the same as regards preconceived opinions. Men readily believe reports unfavourable to persons they dislike, or confirmations of theories of their own. "Trifles light as air" are all that the predisposed mind requires for belief and action. (p.189)

The ideas in this sermon underlie Newman's approach both in this Lecture and in Lecture VII.

p. 248. *operatives*: factory workers

p. 249. *Lazzaroni*: idlers

p. 249. *falling sickness*: epilepsy

p. 250. *Lady Day*: the Feast of the Annunciation, 25th March.

p. 250. *the Minerva*: the church of the Dominican house in Rome.

p. 250. *cicerone*: a guide who is expert in showing the tourist the sights of a foreign town.

p. 251. *the Countess Matilda*: (1046-1115), Countess of Tuscany, supporter of the reforming Pope Gregory VII.

p. 251. *Queen Christina*: (1626-89) of Sweden; she converted to Catholicism and was buried in Rome.

p. 251. *a lady of high literary reputation*: Lady Morgan (1783-1859) who wrote under the name Sydney Owenson; her most celebrated novel was *The Wild Irish Girl*. Newman's information on her confusion over St.Peter's chair came from a press cutting now to be found in scrapbook B2.1 at the Birmingham Oratory.

p. 251. *Denon*: Dominique Vivant Denon (1747-1825), painter; Director-General of Museums under Napoleon whom he accompanied, together with other eminent scholars, on his expedition to Egypt.

p. 251. *savans*: savants, men of learning

p. 251. *the Republic or Consulate*: the first French Republic, 1792-9, was followed by the Consulate established by Napoleon in 1799 which lasted until he declared himself Emperor in 1804.

p. 252. *the Antiochene Chair*: according to tradition, St.Peter established his See at Antioch before transferring it to Rome.

p. 252. laquais de place: hired groom

p. 253. *the cave of Trophonius*: Trophonius, together with his brother Agamedes, built a treasury for the King of Elis, leaving a secret entrance by which they could later rob it. When they did so, Agamedes was caught in a trap, so Trophonius cut his brother's head off to avoid detection himself. Later Trophonius was himself swallowed up into an underground chamber where he lived on to be consulted as an oracle. Those who visited him in his cave always emerged looking very gloomy, so it became a saying that depressed people had been visiting the cave of Trophonius.

p. 253. *Mesmerist*: a hypnotist, after Friedrich Mesmer (1733-1815), German doctor and founder of 'animal magnetism'.

p. 255. *"The Lord bless thee ... give thee peace"*: Numbers 6:24-6.

p. 262. *St. Vitus's dance*; a disease, chorea, in which the limbs, body and face undergo uncontrollable spasms.

p. 264. *Tertullian*: Quintus Tertullian (c.150-230); the quotation is from his *Apologeticus*.

p. 265. *Scottish absurdities*: anti-Catholic societies had recently grown in force in Scotland and had considerable influence on English anti-Catholic bodies (see Wolffe, *op.cit.*, pp. 159ff, 196).

p. 266. *Titus Oates*: (1649-1705) inventor of the fictitious 'Popish Plot'. For a full account of this episode see Kenyon, J.P., *The Popish Plot* (London, 1972).

p. 266. *Hume*: see above note on p. 71. The quotation is from his *History of Great Britain* (1754-61).

p. 266. *William Bedloe*: Titus Oates's accomplice.

p. 266. *Propaganda*: the Sacred Congregation for the Propagation of the Faith, the Roman department in charge of foreign missions; Great Britain was classed as mission territory.

p. 268. n.1. *Macaulay*: Thomas Babington Macaulay (1800-59); the first volume of his *History of England from the Accession of James II* had been published in 1849.

p. 276. *a stringent Act of Parliament*: the Ecclesiastical Titles Act (see note on p. lxxxvii).

p. 279. *Academics or Pyrrhonists*: sceptics in philosophy. The original Academy was founded by Plato (c.427-348 B.C.) who was not a sceptic but did hold that the objects of our sense-perception are not the objects of true knowledge; Arcesilaus (315-241 B.C.), founder of the Second

Academy said that he was certain of nothing, not even of the fact that he was certain of nothing; Carneades of Cyrene (214-129 B.C.), founder of the Third Academy, taught that knowledge is impossible and that there is no criterion of truth. Pyrrho of Elis (c.360-c.270 B.C.) taught that we can only know how things appear to us, not their inner substance.

p. 280. *Dr.Johnson ... the first Whig,"*: See Boswell's *Life of Samuel Johnson* (Everyman Edn., London, 1963), Vol.II, p.232.

p. 281. *Cato*: Marcus Porcius Cato (d.46 B.C.), Roman statesman, follower of the Stoic philosophy, opponent of Julius Caesar.

p. 281. *Saul, in Scripture, fell on his sword*: see 1 Paralipomenon (1 Chronicles) 10:4.

p. 286. *"I do not like thee, Dr.Fell..."*: the original version is 'I do not love you, Dr.Fell; / But why I cannot tell; / But this I know full well, / I do not love you, Dr.Fell' an adaptation by Thomas Brown (1663-1704) of an epigram by the Roman writer Martial (40-104). Brown was attacking Dr.John Fell (1625-86) who was Dean of his college, Christ Church, Oxford.

p. 292. "In necessarius unitas, in dubiis libertas,": 'unanimity in essential matters, freedom of opinion in doubtful matters'.

p. 295. *"let not him that putteth on his armour boast as he who taketh it off"*: cf.3 Kings (1 Kings) 20:11.

p. 296. *galvanism*: the production of electricity by chemical means.

p. 297. *the wise man in the Greek epic*: Odysseus; see Homer, *The Odyssey*, i.I.

p. 299-300. *At Rome ... the Escurial*: the list of relics which follows contains some which would not necessarily be accepted today as authentic but which were usually believed to be so by Catholics in Newman's time.

the True Cross: what is believed to be a beam of Christ's cross is kept in the church of Sancta Croce in Gerusalemme in Rome; the cross had been discovered in the Holy Land in the fourth century. Newman lived at Sancta Croce in the spring of 1847 while he was making his noviciate as an Oratorian.

the Crib of Bethlehem: five pieces of wood, known as the 'sancta culla', are kept in the basilica of Sancta Maria Maggiore in Rome. Their authenticity as part of the infant Christ's manger is highly unlikely; they are thought to be the remains of a 'Christmas crib' set up there.

the Chair of St. Peter: this is kept behind the high altar in St. Peter's Basilica.

portions of the Crown of Thorns: in the church of Saint Chapelle. The relic was actually destroyed in the French Revolution.

the Holy Coat: this relic, kept in Trèves Cathedral, Germany, is said to be Christ's tunic.

the Winding-Sheet: the celebrated Turin Shroud, which has been the subject of intense scientific investigation in recent years, including a carbon-dating test which apparently indicated that the cloth is of mediaeval origin. The debate about its authenticity, however, continues.

the iron crown ... formed out of a Nail of the Cross: this is the 'Iron Crown of Lombardy', kept in Monza Cathedral, N.Italy.

the Escurial: the monastery and royal palace of Philip II of Spain, near Madrid.

p. 300. *the scapular*: a devotional article worn under ordinary clothes by some Catholics; originally a small cloak, it was later abbreviated to two small pieces of cloth, usually bearing an image, e.g. of Our Lady, attached by two cords which run over the shoulders. The most common scapular is that associated with the Carmelite order. There was a legend that the Virgin Mary gave the scapular to St.Simon Stock and promised salvation to those who died wearing it.

p.300, *the cord of St Francis*: another devotional article, worn around the waist in imitation of the cord of the Franciscan habit.

p. 300. *St. Januarius ... St. Frances*: Newman's citing of the miraculous events associated with these saints and his avowal of his belief in the truth of them (below, pp. 312-3) attracted much opprobrium from non-Catholics. His attitude should be seen in the context of his argument about First Principles which follows.

St. Januarius's blood: in the Caraffa Chapel in Naples Cathedral there is kept a crystal vial containing a black substance which liquefies and looks like fresh blood on the feast day of St. Januarius and certain other days when it is exposed to the veneration of the people. Januarius, a bishop, was martyred in 305, but the existence of the relic is not recorded until 1389. There are a number of similar liquefactions in the Naples area. In recent years it has been suggested that the substance may be a naturally occurring one (i.e. the liquefaction is in fact due to one of the then 'unknown laws of nature' which Newman mentions later on p. 312).

St. Winifred's Well: according to late mediaeval legend, St. Winifred was a niece of St. Beuno, an abbot; when she refused the attentions of one Caradoc he cut off her head but was immediately himself swallowed up into the earth. St. Beuno restored her head and she lived the rest of her life as a nun. A spring appeared where her head had fallen. This spring at Holywell in north Wales was a centre of miraculous healing, pilgrimages to the site having continued even after the Reformation and down to today.

stigmata: apparent wounds on the body in the places where Christ was pierced during his crucifixion; first recorded of St. Francis of Assisi.

St. Anthony of Padua: (1195-1231), a Franciscan friar and noted preacher. Devotion to him was very strong in the nineteenth century; he is popularly invoked to help find lost objects.

St. Cecilia: a legendary martyr; the somewhat grisly story of the various attempts made to kill her occurs in a sixth century Passion of St. Cecilia which is now thought to be fictitious.

St. Peter elicited a spring of water: although not mentioned in the New Testament, St. Peter's martyrdom at Rome, c.64, is historically certain. The Mamertine Prison on the Capitoline Hill was the place where condemned criminals were imprisoned, and tradition makes this the place of St. Peter's imprisonment. The legend about the spring perhaps owes something to the story about St. Paul baptising his gaoler in Acts 16:25-34.

St. Raymond: Nonnatus (d.1240), so called because he was said not to have been born normally but to have been taken from his mother's womb after her death in labour. As a co-founder with St. Peter Nolasco of the Order of Our Lady of Ransom he is said to have sold himself into slavery to the Moors to ransom captives and later to have become a Cardinal.

St. Andrew: the apostle.

St. Scholastica: (c.480-543), sister of St. Benedict; the shower of rain was to keep her brother from leaving her when she wanted to continue discussing divine matters with him.

St. Paul: the apostle.

St. Frances: of Rome (1384-1440), laywoman and later foundress of a religious community.

p. 305. *the Breviary*: the book of liturgical 'hours' of prayers recited daily by priests and members of religious orders. An account of each saint's life was affixed to the Office for his or her feastday, usually emphasising the miraculous elements in the saints' lives. (The modern equivalent, produced after the Second Vatican Council, has removed almost all such miraculous references).

p. 305. *the Martyrology*: the official list of martyrs and other saints. The modern writer on hagiology, Donald Attwater, described the Roman Martyrology, which had been promulgated in 1584 and was still in use in Newman's day and later, as having 'long been in need of drastic historical revision and correction' (*A Dictionary of Saints* (1965), p. 25).)

p. 308. *Alexander or Coeur de Lion*: Alexander the Great (356-323 B.C.) and King Richard I (1157-99), both celebrated for their military exploits.

p. 308. n.3. *Douglas*: John Douglas (1721-1807), Anglican bishop and controversialist.

p. 308. n.3. *Middleton*: Conyers Middleton (1683-1750), Anglican divine and theological controversialist. His views on miracles were expressed in *An Introductory Discourse to a larger work ... concerning the Miraculous Powers which are supposed to have subsisted in the Christian Church from the earliest ages ...* (1747) and *A Free Enquiry into the Miraculous Powers* etc. (1749). Newman had originally followed Douglas's and Middleton's principles in his essay on scriptural miracles for the Encyclopedia Metropolitana in 1826 when he was 'drifting in the direction of liberalism' (see *Apologia*, p. 105). As he did in his subsequent 1843 essay on ecclesiastical miracles, Newman is thus here making a critique of his former views.

p. 308. n.3. Crieron: *[sic]* 'Criterion', a journal kept by Douglas while abroad in 1748-9, subsequently published in his *Miscellaneous Works* (1820).

p. 311. *St. Theodore stands for St. Eugenius, or St. Agathocles*: since these three martyrs all come from the same period, the Diocletian persecution, and their lives are obscure, it is not surprising that they should be easily confused. Newman had a detailed knowledge of this period, as many sections of the *Essay on the Development of Christian Doctrine* and the last chapter of *An Essay in Aid of a Grammar of Assent* show.

St. Theodore Tyro of Euchaita was said to be a soldier and to have died at Amasea c.306; he was venerated as one of the three great 'warrior saints' of the East, along with St.George and St. Demetrius. Newman mentions him as one of the 'Knights without reproach or fear' in his poem 'Valentine to a Little Girl' in *Verses on Various Occasions* (1890 edn), p. 291.

St. Eugenius: died c.302 together with St. Canisius and their companions.

St. Agathocles: was one of a group of fifteen who were put to death in Pamphylia in 304.

p. 311. *thaumatology*: the description or discussion of the miraculous.

p. 311. *Froissart*: Jean Froissart (1337-1410), French chronicler. His 'Chroniques' have been described as 'the work of a literary artist rather than a trustworthy historian, but [they] give a faithful picture of the broad features of his period' (*Concise Oxford Dictionary of English Literature*, 2nd Edition, 1970, p. 208).

p. 311. *Sully*: Maximillian Béthune, Duke of Sully, chief minister of Henry IV of France; his memoirs, *Les Oeconomies Royales de Sully*, are notably partisan in their presentation of his own and his royal master's merits.

p. 311. *Doddington*: George Bubb Doddington (1691-1762), M.P. for Bridgewater and later Baron Melcombe; he constantly switched his political allegiance, and his posthumously published Diary shows his egotism.

p. 311. *Walpole*: Horace Walpole (1717-97), fourth Earl of Oxford, man of letters. He is best known for his own letters which are of great social and anecdotal interest; but Newman may also have in mind his historical work *Historic Doubts on the Life and Reign of Richard III* of which it has been said that 'he had a good subject, but was too languid to undertake proper research' (Sampson, G., *The Concise Cambridge History of English Literature*, 3rd Edition, 1972, p. 449).

p. 311. *Sharon Turner*: (1768-1847), author of a *History of the Anglo-Saxons from the Earliest Period to the Norman Conquest*, *The History of England from the Norman Conquest to 1500* and other volumes. He has been described as an antiquarian rather than a historian.

p. 317. *a country gentleman in this neighbourhood*: Sir Francis Goodricke (see *Letters and Diaries* Vol.XVIII, p. 430).

p. 320. *a well-known authoress, lately deceased*: Letitia Elizabeth Landon (1802-38). The references are to her novel *Romance and Reality*, published in 1831.

p. 322. *Suarez*: Francisco Suarez (1548-1617), Spanish Jesuit philosopher and theologian.

p. 322. *Bellarmine*: St. Robert Bellarmine (1532-1621), influential theologian and controversialist of the Counter-Reformation period. He was not canonised until 1930, when he was also declared a Doctor of the Church.

p. 328. *there has been lately a great deal of surprise expressed in some quarters*: a reference to Rev. G.S. Faber's pamphlet *Papal Infallibility, a Letter to a Dignitary of the Church of Rome* (London 1851). G.S. Faber was the uncle of Newman's fellow Oratorian Frederick William Faber (see above), and had challenged his nephew in October 1849 on the question of the Church's infallibility never having been defined. F.W. Faber had consulted Newman about it (see *Letters and Diaries*, Vol.XIII, p. 274).

p. 329. *family vade-mecums*: popular manuals (literally, for carrying in one's pocket) of general useful information, including basic medical advice.

p. 329. *materia-medicas*: scientific books about medicines.

p. 330. *a great statesman*: this quotation has not proved traceable. The style and sentiments would fit George Canning (1770-1827), Tory politician and eventually Prime Minister; he was a supporter of Catholic Emancipation.

p. 330. *Vasquez*: Gabriel Vasquez (1549-1604), Spanish Jesuit theologian.

p. 330. *de Lugo*: Cardinal John de Lugo (d 1660), Spanish theologian.

p. 330. *Lambertini*: Prospero Lorenzo Lambertini (1675-1759), antiquarian of renowned erudition, elected Pope in 1740 as Benedict XIV; he was an outstanding administrator and a great patron of historical and other studies. He is best remembered for his classic work *De Servorum Dei Beatificatione et Beatorum Canonizatione* which continued to have a predominant influence over the procedure for saints' causes even into the late 20th century.

p. 330. *St. Thomas*: Aquinas (1225-1274), theologian, the greatest of the mediaeval Doctors of the Church. His *Summa Theologica* is the classic exposition of scholastic theology.

p. 330. *St. Buonaventura*: (1221-1274) bishop and theologian; a Doctor of the Church.

p. 330. *the Schoolman Scotus*: John Duns Scotus (1270-1308), one of the leading scholastic theologians and philosophers, known as the 'doctor subtilis.'

p. 332. *this able writer*: James Martineau (1805-1900), Unitarian minister and man of letters; he was a leading contributor to the *Westminster Review.*

p. 334. *the plagues of the Apocalypse*: see Revelation 15:5-16:21.

p. 334. *Pope Pius VIIth's captivity*: following the annexation of the Papal States in 1809, the Pope excommunicated Napoleon who retaliated by having him arrested and forcibly deported to France where he remained until Napoleon's abdication in 1814.

p. 335. *'Take nothing ... coats apiece.'*: see Luke 9:3.

p. 336. *the unhappy Concordat with Napoleon*: the church-state agreement signed in 1801 by which the position of the Church in France was regulated after the upheavals of the French Revolution. Its terms were quite radical in the concessions it made to the role of the state, but it was made even more so by an extra set of articles added by Napoleon by which the exercise of the papal power in France was limited, along the lines advocated by the 'Gallican' theologians. The papal legate, Cardinal Caprara, was tricked into consenting to these articles, but they were subsequently rejected by the Pope.

p. 338. *Pope Marcellinus*. reigned 296-304.

pp. 338-9. *"who can have compassion ... with infirmity"*: see the Letter to the Hebrews 5:2. (Modern biblical scholarship no longer considers St. Paul to be the author of this letter.)

p. 339. *it has been said to me, in reference to them in print*: by Robert Seeley (1798-1886), publisher and religious controversialist, of pronounced Evangelical and anti-Catholic views. Seeley had a public correspondence with Newman in the *Morning Herald* in August 1851 (see *Letters and Diaries*, Vol.XIV, pp. 322-9). Newman names him below on p. 352.

p. 340. *"texts" in Romans iii. or Galatians ii.*: references to 'justification by faith', regarded by Protestant controversialists as disproving Catholic doctrine.

p. 341. *"like the horseleech, crying, Give, give:"*: see Proverbs 30:15: 'The horseleech hath two daughters, crying Give, give' - an image of insatiable greed.

p. 343. *Speaker*: the 'chairman' of the House of Commons.

p. 343. *Serjeant-at-arms*: an officer of the House of Commons whose original function was to assist the Speaker to keep order among the Members of Parliament. By Newman's time it had become largely a ceremonial post, though M.P.s could (and still can) incur his censure for behaviour which breached the traditions of the House.

p. 345. ... *though they often do so*: this practice died out during the twentieth century, especially after the Second Vatican Council.

p. 347. *Dr. Waddington*: see above note on p.15; the quotation is from his *History of the Reformation on the Continent* (1841).

p. 349. *Dean Swift's well-known tale*: *Gulliver's Travels*, Part III.

p. 350. *Benedictines*: monks of the order St. Benedict (480-547), associated throughout its history with scholarship.

p. 350. *Bollandists*: the Jesuit editors of the Lives of the Saints, a multi-volume work begun in the 17th century and continuing, despite interruption by the French Revolution, right into modern times; the first volume of a new series had been published in 1845. The name came from the Jesuit John Bolland (1596-1665), the first editor of this massive scholarly project.

p. 351. *How many are the souls ... the conveyance of grace!*: a striking echo of a passage from Charlotte Brontë's *Villette* published in 1850. The overall tenor of the novel is strongly anti-Catholic, but at one point the Protestant heroine is moved by an impulse to go to Confession, at which she feels that

the mere relief of communication in an ear which was human and sentient, yet consecrated – the mere pouring out of some portion of long accumulating, long pent-up pain into a vessel whence it could not be again diffused – had done me good. I was already solaced. (Worlds Classics edn, London, 1906, p. 184).

p. 352. n.1. *Mr.Seely*: [*sic*] Robert Seeley (see note on p. 339 above).

p. 354. *ornithorhynchi*: duck-billed platypuses. These animals, found only in Australia, are regarded as curiosities because they are aquatic furry mammals with duck like beaks and lay eggs like birds.

p. 354. *the John Doe and Richard Roe of the lawyers*: fictitious names for the plaintiff and the defendant in hypothetical legal cases, used by convention (until the law was changed in 1852).

p. 354. *the Titius and Bertha of the canonists*: parallel fictional names used by moral theologians.

p. 355. *the frogs in the fable*: one of Aesop's fables about a boy stoning frogs for his amusement.

p. 355. *helots*: slaves in ancient Sparta.

p. 356. *it was offered by myself to the gentleman*: in his letter to Seeley of 5th August 1851 in the *Morning Herald* Newman challenged Seeley's implication that there were unbelieving Catholic priests in Birmingham by affirming the faith of himself and his Oratorian companions and all the other priests in the city at that time whom he listed by name.

p. 356. *a number of highly educated Protestants … two hundred years ago*: members of the Oxford Movement, such as Newman himself; he identifies the Tractarian position held by them as that of the 'high church' Anglican divines of the 17th century.

p. 359. *a Barbara*: 'a syllogism in *Barbara* is one of which both the major and minor premises, and the conclusion, are universal affirmatives: thus, all animals are mortal, all men are animals, ∴ all men are mortal' (O.E.D.). In Seeley's case: 'one in twelve of all Catholic priests are secret unbelievers; Birmingham contains more than twelve Catholic priests; ∴ one in twelve of the Catholic priests in Birmingham are unbelievers.'

p. 359. *Celarent*: a syllogism in which 'the major premiss and the conclusion are universal negatives, and the minor premiss a universal affirmative' (O.E.D.). In Seeley's case: 'No group of Catholic priests consists entirely of true believers in the faith; you are a group of Catholic priests in Birmingham; ∴ you do not all truly believe in the faith.'

p. 359. *One there was*: John Moore Capes (1812–89). Originally an opponent of the Oxford Movement, he was received into the Catholic Church in 1845. During the Papal Aggression crisis he was the chairman of a committee of Catholic laymen set up to campaign in defence of the

Church and gave some lectures himself (see Introduction pp.xiv–xv). His later relations with Newman were not always easy: he founded the *Rambler* magazine whose liberal tone caused Newman problems; he sent his son to the Oratory School but disagreed with Newman's handling of the 1861 crisis over the first headmaster. When he left the Church in 1870 over the definition of Papal Infallibility, he claimed that Newman did not believe it either, an accusation which Newman publicly refuted.

p. 362. *the patriarch*: Jacob; see Genesis 28:17.

p. 363. *to put our convents … on a level with madhouses*: a Bill put forward in the House of Commons in 1851 proposed that convents be inspected along the lines of the regular inspection of lunatic asylums.

p. 363. *a bill, too, has been passed*: the Ecclesiastical Titles Act (see above note on p.lxxv).

p. 366. ex officio: by virtue of her office

p. 369. ipso facto: proved by the fact itself

p. 374. *the hulks*: prison ships

p. 374. *they could bombard Rome*: not the scaremongering by Newman it might seem: at the height of the 'Papal Aggression' crisis, the government was actually urged to declare war on the Papal States by Lord Winchilsea (Public Record Office 30/22/8F: Fortescue to Russell, 11 November 1850; quoted in Chadwick, O., *The Victorian Church*, London 1971, p. 295).

p. 391. n.5. *the author's Oxford University Sermons, No.V*. 'Personal Influence the Means of Propagating the Truth', preached on 22nd January 1832; a relevant passage reads:

Men persuade themselves, with little difficulty, to scoff at principles, to ridicule books, to make sport of the names of good men; but they cannot bear their presence: it is holiness embodied in personal form, which they cannot steadily confront and bear down: so that the silent conduct of a conscientious man secures for him beholders of a feeling different in kind from any which is created by the mere versatile and garrulous Reason. (*Fifteen Sermons Preached before the University of Oxford*, 3rd edn., 1871, p. 92.)

p. 388. *Hunt-the-slipper*: a traditional parlour game.

p. 388. *"sound and fury, signifying nothing"*: see *Macbeth* Act V, Scene v, l.27-8.

p. 388. *Trust neither Assyria nor Egypt*: the powerful states to the north and south of Israel respectively; in the Old Testament the Prophets continually warned the Israelites against putting their trust in military alliances with them. By analogy, therefore, Newman means any powerful elements in contemporary Britain, possibly even referring directly to the two political parties, the Whigs and the Conservatives.

p. 388. *diffusing "the sweet odour of His knowledge in every place:"*: a slight misquotation of II Corinthians 2:14: 'Now thanks be to God, who always maketh us to triumph in Christ Jesus and manifesteth the odour of his knowledge by us in every place.'

p. 389. *Attica*: the region of ancient Greece which contained the city of Athens, where Plato, Aristotle and other philosophers taught.

p. 389. *Elias*: Elijah (see 3 Kings (1 Kings) 17-4 Kings (2 Kings) 2). Newman uses the Latin version of the name used in the Catholic Douay Bible.

p. 389. *Athanasius*: St. Athanasius (296-373), bishop and Doctor of the Church, champion of Catholic orthodoxy against the Arian heresy; his extraordinary life and career feature in Newman's first published work, *The Arians of the Fourth Century* (1832). Newman had a deep admiration for him, ranking him with St. Augustine and St. Thomas Aquinas as great minds who had formed Catholic theology (cf. *Apologia*, p. 285).

p. 389. *Leo*: Pope St. Leo the Great (d.461), champion of Catholic orthodoxy against the Eutychian heresy; his 'tome' on the nature and person of Christ was the basis of the doctrine proclaimed by the Council of Chalcedon. Newman had described these dramatic events in his *Essay on the Development of Christian Doctrine* (1845, revised edn.1878), Ch.6, Section 3.

p. 390. *Fear not, little* flock: see Jesus' words of encouragement to his disciples, Luke 12:32.

p. 390. *for he who is mighty ... great things*: a paraphrase of part of the Magnificat (Luke 1:49); Newman's Catholic audience are thus paralleled with the Blessed Virgin Mary.

p. 390. *"a mouth, and wisdom ... to resist and gainsay"*: see Luke 21:15.

p. 390. *"There is a time for silence, and a time to speak"*: see above note on p.iii.

p. 390. *"better gifts"*: see I Corinthians 12:31.

p. 390. *a napkin*: in the Parable of the Talents, the man who did nothing with the talent given to him by his master kept it 'laid up in a napkin'; see Luke 19:20.

p. 390. *your light under a bushel*: see Matthew 5:15.

p. 390. *they saved the Irish Church three centuries ago ... our people were cowards*: a reference to events in England under Elizabeth I when the Catholic bishops appointed under Mary were imprisoned while there was no widespread popular opposition to the re-imposition of Protestantism. In Ireland, however, the people remained fiercely loyal to the Catholic faith in the face of English domination. This critical reference to the English Catholic laity may seem surprising, given Newman's celebrated championing of the role of the laity (for instance in his 1859 article *On Consulting the Faithful in Matters of Doctrine*). However, it perhaps reflects some frustration on his part at the limited scale of an organised response by Catholic laymen to the Papal Aggression crisis (see Introduction, p.xiv–xv). The whole passage has often been read as a plea for education to be opened up to the Catholic laity and not reserved for clerics. However, Newman is in fact making a severe exhortation of the laity themselves. His implication is that they must not betray the Church by their inaction as they did at the time of the Reformation, and his comment that 'in all times the laity have been the measure of the Catholic spirit' is thus double-edged.

p. 391–2. *Cultivation of mind ...true of a Catholic*: this passage strikingly anticipates a central argument of 'Discourses on the Nature and Scope of a University Education' which Newman was to compose as his inaugural lectures as Rector of the Catholic University in Dublin (later the first part of *The Idea of a University*).

p. 393. *Methodism is ridiculous, so is Puritanism*: Newman perhaps has in mind the excesses of 'enthusiasm' associated with early Methodism and the severe dress code and censorious attitudes associated with the Puritans. Both were the subject of satirical attack by writers such as Henry Fielding.

p. 394. noli aemulari: see Proverbs 3.31: 'Envy not the unjust man.'

p. 394. *a year since, when I said ...*: cf. *Lectures on Certain Difficulties felt by Anglicans in Catholic Teaching*, Vol.I, pp. 29-30:

> As to the Catholic Church herself, no vicissitude of circumstances can hurt her which allows her fair play. If, indeed, from the ultimate resolution of all heresies and errors into some one form of infidelity or scepticism, the nation was strong enough to turn upon her in persecution, then indeed she might be expelled before now. Then persecution would do its work, as it did three centuries ago. But this is an extreme case, which is not to be anticipated.

p. 394. *"Greater is He that is in you than he that is in the world."*: see 1 John 4:4.

p. 395. *St. Gregory Nazianzus*: (329-390) bishop and Doctor of the Church; known as 'The Theologian'.

p. 395. *St. Ambrose*: (334-397), bishop and Doctor of the Church; a Roman governor who was elected Bishop of Milan, his sermons greatly influenced St. Augustine (see above, p.20).

p. 395. *St. Jerome*: (342-420), Doctor of the Church; responsible for the 'Vulgate' Latin translation of the Bible.

p. 395. *St. Gregory the First*: Pope St. Gregory the Great (540-604), Doctor of the Church; reforming Pope who, amongst other things, sent St. Augustine to convert the English.

p. 395. *St. Romuald*: (950-1027), abbot; monastic reformer

p. 396. *St. Bernard*: of Clairvaux (1090-1153), abbot, Doctor of the Church; monastic reformer, founder of the Cistercian order.

p. 396. *St. Francis*: of Assisi (1181-1226).

p. 396. *St. Ignatius*: Loyola (1491-1556), founder of the Jesuits.

p. 396. *St. Vincent of Paul*: (1580-1660), founder of the Congregation of the Mission (Vincentians) and the Sisters of Charity.

p. 396. *the words of the Psalm*: Psalm 73:7-10.

p. 397. *washed their robes ... in the blood of the Lamb*: cf. Revelation 7:14.

p. 398. *St. Justin*: see above note p.126.

p. 398. *St. Alban*: (d.209), protomartyr of Britain; the city of St. Albans grew up around the monastery which housed his shrine.

p. 398. *St. Hermenegild*: (d.585) son of the king of Spain, was brought up an Arian but converted to Catholicism. His 'rash acts' occurred in his subsequent war against his Arian father who, after a temporary reconciliation, eventually had him executed.

p. 398. *our own St. Thomas*: Thomas à Becket (see above note on p. 65).

p. 398. *the late Archbishop of Paris*: Mgr. Denis-August Affre (1793-1848). Originally very agitated by the revolutionary events of the 'June Days', he achieved a sudden serenity after a night spent in prayer and went out into the streets on Sunday 25th June to mediate between the workers and the military. He successfully negotiated a truce which lasted about an hour, but shooting broke out again following a misunderstanding and he was hit by a shot from the soldiers behind him. He died the following day.

p. 399. *as the Wise man says*: the quotation is from Wisdom 4:13.

p. 399. *"ran to and fro like sparks among the reeds"*: Wisdom 3:7.

p. 400. *"the heathen's jest"*: from Newman's own poem 'The Patient Church'. The opening stanza reads: 'Bide thou thy time! / Watch with meek eyes the race of pride and crime, / Sit in the gate, and be the heathen's jest, / Smiling and self-possest. / O thou, to whom is pledged a victor's sway, / Bide thou the victor's day!' (*Verses on Various Occasions*, 1890 edn., p. 92); in the first edition Newman had made the source of his phrase more obvious by quoting the whole of lines 3 and 4. As with his quotation of Keble, above p.69, it is significant that Newman now re-applies to Catholicism lines which originally had an Anglican context.

p. 401. *"the little ewe lamb*: see 2 Kings (2 Samuel) 12:3. When King David acquired the wife of Uriah the Hittite by getting him killed in battle, the prophet Samuel brought home to the King his crime by telling him a parable about a poor man who 'had nothing at all but one little ewe lamb' which was then taken from him by a rich man. David was angry with this imaginary rich thief, and then Samuel told him 'You are the man'. David saw the parallel with his own actions and repented. The parallel Newman is suggesting is therefore with the anti-Catholic government who, like David, are treating Catholics unjustly, in this case by trying to deprive them of the one thing that Catholics have, the apostolic succession in the persons of the newly restored hierarchy. The use of the 'ewe lamb' as a pathetic image of a poor person's sole remaining possession had became a literary commonplace.

p. 401. *"Let alone Camarina, for 'tis best let alone."*: a warning by the Delphic oracle to the people of Camarina in Sicily who had asked if they should drain the pestiferous marshes, also called Camarina, around their town; they ignored the warning, with disastrous results. The saying became a proverb against interfering with something which is bad in case you make it worse. It therefore means 'let sleeping dogs lie.'

p. 401. *Prince Talleyrand*: Charles Maurice de Talleyrand-Périgord (1754-1838), French politician and diplomat, formerly a bishop.